ANNALS OF OPERA

ANNALS OF OPERA

1597–1940

COMPILED FROM THE

ORIGINAL SOURCES

BY

ALFRED LOEWENBERG

WITH AN INTRODUCTION

BY

EDWARD J. DENT

Second edition, revised and corrected

ROWMAN AND LITTLEFIELD

NEW YORK

1970

To the Memory of

OSCAR GEORGE THEODORE SONNECK

1873-1928

PREFACE

THE bulk of the present work was finished before the war broke out. For various reasons publication was delayed till now. In the meanwhile the manuscript has undergone considerable alterations and additions, and while the annals nominally close with the year 1940, references to still more recent revivals and publications have been included when of sufficient importance.

The book is intended to be a skeleton history of opera, in dates and other facts. It is therefore arranged chronologically, but by means of the copious indexes it can also be used as a dictionary of operas. There are no descriptions of plots, no musical analyses, no personal critical comments. The facts are to speak for themselves, and every care has been taken to verify them so that they may serve as a safe ground on which to build a real history of opera, yet to be written. The selection of some three or four thousand operas out of a total number of— I dare not offer a guess, was also chiefly guided by objective historical principles. Of older operas, preferably such have been chosen as are still extant in one form or another; of more recent works, those have been selected that have obtained success or attracted attention outside their countries of origin. Even so, the number of entries could easily have been doubled; but the book had to be kept within reasonable limits.

The term 'opera' is used here in its widest possible sense, covering both 'grand opera' (as it is sometimes called), that is, opera with recitatives, and opera with spoken dialogue. Confining it to the former would result in omitting works like *The Magic Flute* and *Carmen*. Moreover, there are included examples of offshoots like the Italian intermezzo, the English ballad opera, the French vaudeville, the German 'melodrama'; the pasticcio in its various types; border cases like Dassoucy's *Andromède*, Weber's *Preciosa* and Stravinsky's *Histoire du Soldat*; the modern operetta in different countries. Not included are plays with incidental music even by famous composers (such as *Egmont* or *Peer Gynt*), nor oratorios, cantatas, etc., unless they were at a later date presented in operatic form, such as Liszt's *St. Elizabeth* and Debussy's *L'Enfant Prodigue*.

It is stated on the titlepage that the book was 'compiled from the original sources.' That is to say, I did not rely upon second or third hand information. Whenever possible the dates and other particulars were collected from the original scores and librettos, from play-bills, contemporary newspapers and periodicals; next there came memoirs, letters and diaries, and the various bibliographical works, catalogues, and theatrical chronologies. For the more recent years, and for countries newspapers of which are not easily available, official publications of the opera-houses, and lists provided for the purpose by the authorities proved a great help. Here a certain inequality was unavoidable;

while I received from some towns, as for instance, Zagreb or Helsinki, all the information I required, it was in other cases impossible even to get an answer, as for instance from Bucharest.

A few explanations of the methods employed in the arrangement of the book may find their appropriate place here. The entries are given in the chronological order of their first performances. This implies that only such operas are recorded as were actually produced on the (public or private) stage, a rule which has been broken once or twice in exceptional cases (see for instance col. 297). The year of performance is always repeated at the top of the page, in order to simplify the task of finding a particular opera. Whenever possible, the exact day and month of the first performance are given. Where the day could not be established, the month or the season is indicated. Operas of which only the year of production is known are placed in the middle of that year. Of all the operas mentioned in these annals, John Blow's *Venus and Adonis* appears to be the only one of which even the year is uncertain; it has been tentatively inserted under 1684 for reasons which are explained in the entry. Dates in [] brackets are approximate, in most cases taken from dedications or licences in the librettos.

The beginning of opera almost coincides with the introduction of the modern calendar, Gregorian style, in all Roman Catholic countries. The non-Catholic parts of Germany followed suit in 1700, other countries even later. All dates are given here according to one and the same system, viz. the Gregorian style. In this respect a word must be said about England and Russia, disregarding some cases of minor importance.

In England the change of calendar took place in 1752. Wednesday, 2 September of that year was followed by Thursday, 14 September. So the dates given in this book of performances in England before September 1752 will be found to differ from those quoted, for instance, by Burney, by 11 days in the 18th century, by 10 days in the 17th. I should have liked to retain the familiar Burney dates, but in an international chronology they had to be sacrificed for the sake of conformity. Boyce's *The Chaplet* was first produced, according to the original play-bill, on Saturday, 2 December 1749, which was Saturday, 13 December in most of the rest of Europe. Obviously it could not be placed in front of Rameau's *Zoroastre* (see col. 211), which actually was performed eight days before and not three days after *The Chaplet*.

The same applies to Russia, where the Gregorian calendar was not introduced until 1917. All the dates of operatic performances in Russia are here given according to Western style, which is ahead of Russian style by 11 days in the 18th, 12 days in the 19th and 13 days in the 20th century. In some very few cases, where it could not be ascertained whether a date quoted from a review meant Russian or Western style, the figures are given in italics.

In each entry the date is followed by the name of the composer and the title
of the opera. Fuller details about the composers will be found in index II.
The name is printed within round brackets when the performance of the opera
took place after the composer's death; within square brackets when he was
the compiler or *arrangeur* rather than the real composer (see for instance
col. 159).

The titles of the operas are given in the form in which they first appeared
on the play-bills or in the librettos, even if this form is unfamiliar (see for
instance col. 448). It is also given in the original language, that is, the language
in which the opera was first performed. It was thought unnecessary to translate
Italian, French and German titles. To all other non-English titles a translation
has been added unless the title is a proper name. Russian titles appear in the
original characters, in an English transliteration, and in translation. In trans-
literating Russian names and titles the rules of the British Museum Catalogue
have been followed with some slight deviations.

Next comes the name oft he town in which the opera was first performed,
with the name of the theatre if the town was an important operatic centre (see
list of abbreviations, p. xv). Some towns had different names at different
periods, and sometimes both names had to be used. Obviously performances
in 18th century Russia cannot be stated to have taken place at Leningrad.

The notes appended to the heading begin in each case with the name of the
author or librettist, and the literary source, if any, from which the libretto was
derived. No effort has been spared to bring some light into this unexplored
province of literature, and the authorship of not a few librettos is established
here for the first time. Even more obscure is the bibliography of translations
and adaptations, and this is the first attempt to collect systematically the widely
scattered material. In general the results were rather surprising, although I
confined myself to what may be called independent translations, that is, such
as were used for performances in a foreign language or were issued as distinct
publications. Only in exceptional cases have I mentioned translations which
were printed opposite the original text (for use by the audience in the theatre)
when the opera was produced in the original language in a foreign country.

Concerning later revivals, the principles I followed were roughly these: the
older operas, of the 17th and the greater part of the 18th century, are recorded
as fully as possible. In the 19th century this proved to be tiresome and un-
instructive. The operas of Donizetti, Bellini and Verdi were performed in
hundreds of Italian towns every year throughout the century and there would
have been no point in enumerating all those productions. In some cases, such
as *Freischütz*, *Tristan*, *Otello* full records are given up to a certain date. Generally
only the first performances in other countries are indicated. By 'countries' I
mean cultural rather than political units; islands, for instance, are treated as
separate countries, and bi-cultural and bilingual towns like Nice, Trieste,

Strasbourg, Prague have received special attention. It goes without saying that the European boundaries referred to in remarks such as 'for the first time in Czechoslovakia' are those which were in force before the second world war.

Thus the notes, which range from a few lines to several pages, will be found to contain much information about the later history of a particular opera. It was manifestly impracticable to give the authority for every single date of the many thousands assembled here. Originally it was intended to add a complete bibliography of the books and other sources consulted. This plan had to be abandoned. Many of the more important sources, however, are quoted in the text.

There remains to me the pleasant duty of gratefully acknowledging the valuable help I received from many quarters. In the first place my thanks are due to Mr. Richard Capell who, in the *Daily Telegraph* of 15 October 1938, took the unusual course of reviewing the manuscript of the present book. I have to thank Mr. Otto Haas, London, for his constant advice and interest, and for putting at my disposal his rich stock of music and books on music. I am very much indebted to the authorities and the staff of the British Museum, especially to Mr. William C. Smith and to Mr. Cecil B. Oldman; to Mr. Rupert Erlebach, librarian of the Royal College of Music; to the librarians of the Bibliothèque de l'Arsenal and of the Bibliothèque Musicale de l'Opéra, Paris, of the Bibliothèque du Conservatoire, Brussels, and of the Gemeente Museum (Scheurleer collection), The Hague. For giving me access to books and other sources not elsewhere available I have to thank Mr. Paul Hirsch, Cambridge, and Mr. Michael D. Calvocoressi, London. I am very much obliged to Professor Otto Erich Deutsch, Cambridge, for letting me use his manuscript *Repertory of the Imperial Theatres of Vienna*, and for many valuable suggestions.

Furthermore, I wish to convey my thanks to many correspondents for information concerning operatic history in their respective countries. To the directors and librarians of the opera-houses at Antwerp (Koninklijke Vlaamsche Opera); Copenhagen; Geneva (M. Bretton); Kaunas; Ljubljana (Dir. Vilko Ukmar); Paris (Théâtre National de l'Opéra-Comique, M. L. Galliéni); Prague (Národni Divadlo); Riga (Dir. J. Poruks); Sofia (Dir. V. Vassileff); Stockholm; and Zagreb. To M. Ludvík Boháček, Prague; Dr. Peter Gradenwitz, Tel-Aviv; Mr. Herbert Graf, formerly of Berlin; Dr. Hemendra Nath Das Gupta, Girish Ghosh Lecturer, Calcutta University; Mr. Julius Mattfeld of the Library Division, Columbia Broadcasting System, New York; M. R. Aloys Mooser, editor of *Dissonances*, Geneva; Mme Jolantha von Pukánszky-Kádár, Budapest; and Mr. Wäinö Sola of the Suomalainen Oopera, Helsinki.

Finally, I want to express my gratitude to Professor Edward J. Dent, Cambridge, not only for honouring this book with his introduction, but also for his help in going through the proofs; to my publishers, Messrs. W. Heffer &

Sons, Ltd., Cambridge, for their enterprising spirit and splendid efficiency; last not least to my wife, Edith Loewenberg, for her never-failing help and encouragement throughout the many years it took to prepare the book.

ALFRED LOEWENBERG

London,
October 1942 (revised August 1954)

The late Alfred Loewenberg left an interleaved and heavily annotated copy of his *Annals*; this has served as the basis of the present revised edition. Some alterations and fairly numerous corrections have been made, and many new dates and other facts added from the author's notes. Further corrections from other sources have been accepted and incorporated, but essentially the *Annals* remain Loewenberg's work, presented here as far as possible in his own revision. No attempt has been made to carry the records beyond 1940.

Thanks are due to Mr. Theodore Besterman, whose initiative made possible the publication of the second edition, and to Mr. Frank Walker, who generously undertook the laborious task of revising and editing the manuscript of this edition.

CONTENTS

ABBREVIATIONS

Besides the names of the theatres (see list below) very few abbreviations have been used, and most of them need no explanation (names of the months, etc.).

A.M.Z.:	Allgemeine Musikalische Zeitung.	I.S.C.M.:	International Society for Contemporary Music.
Carn.:	Carnival season (usually beginning December 26 of the preceding year and lasting until February or March).	n.d.:	no date (undated publication).
		R.M.I.:	Rivista Musicale Italiana.
I.M.S.:	International Musical Society.	S.I.M.:	Société Internationale de Musique.

PRINCIPAL THEATRES

(T. and Th. are used for Theatre and its equivalents, Pal. for Palazzo. Where no theatre is mentioned, the principal theatre of the town is meant.)

Barcelona, L.	Liceo	Paris, B.P.	Bouffes-Parisiens.
Berlin, D.O.	Deutsches Opernhaus.	C.I.	Comédie-Italienne.
Fr.W.	Friedrich-Wilhelmstädtisches (Theater).	Ch.É.	(Théâtre des) Champs-Élysées.
		F.Dr.	Folies-Dramatiques.
Kgst.	Königsstädtisches (Theater).	F.P.	Fantaisies-Parisiennes.
Kurf.O.	Kurfürsten-Oper.	Fa.	Théâtre Favart.
O.	(Königliches) Opernhaus (later Staatsoper).	Fey.	Théâtre Feydeau.
		G.L.	Gaîté-Lyrique.
Sch.	Schauspielhaus.	O.	Opéra (Académie Royale de Musique, etc.).
Th.d.W.	Theater des Westens.		
Th.U.d.L.	Theater Unter den Linden.	O.C.	Opéra-Comique.
V.O.	Volks-Oper.	O.N.L.	Opéra National Lyrique.
Vict.Th.	Victoria-Theater.	Ren.	(Théâtre de la) Renaissance.
Bologna, T.C.	Teatro Comunale.	St.G.	(Théâtre de la Foire) Saint-Germain.
Brussels, F.P.	Fantaisies-Parisiennes.		
M.	(Théâtre de la) Monnaie.	St.L.	(Théâtre de la Foire) Saint-Laurent.
Florence, P.	(Teatro della)Pergola.		
T.C.	Teatro Comunale.	Th.deM.	Théâtre de Monsieur.
Genoa, C.F.	(Teatro) Carlo Felice.	Th.I.	Théâtre-Italien.
S.Ag.	Sant'Agostino.	Th.L.	Théâtre-Lyrique.
		Th.S.B.	Théâtre Sarah Bernhardt.
Lisbon, S.C.	San Carlos.	Tr.L.	Trianon-Lyrique.
London, C.G.	Covent Garden.	Prague, Cz.	Czech Theatre.
D.L.	Drury Lane.	G.	German Theatre.
Hm.	Haymarket.	Rome, Ap.	(Teatro) Apollo.
H.M.'s.	His (or Her) Majesty's.	Arg.	(Teatro) Argentina.
L.O.H.	London Opera House.	C.	(Teatro) Costanzi.
Ly.	Lyceum (English Opera House)	Capr.	(Teatro) Capranica.
O.C.	Opera Comique.	T.R.	Teatro Reale.
R.A.M.	Royal Academy of Music.	Tord.	(Teatro) Tordinona.
R.C.M.	Royal College of Music.	Turin, T.d.T.	Teatro di Torino.
R.E.O.	Royal English Opera (House).	T.R.	Teatro Regio.
S.'s Wells.	Sadler's Wells.	T.V.E.	Teatro Vittorio Emanuele.
St.J.'s	St. James's.	Venice, F.	(Teatro La) Fenice.
	(Where no theatre is mentioned, the King's Theatre, Haymarket, is meant.)	S.Ben.	San Benedetto.
		S.Cass.	San Cassiano.
Madrid, T.L.	Teatro Lirico.	S.G.Gr.	San Giovanni Grisostomo.
T.R.	Teatro Reale.	SS.G.e.P.	Santi Giovanni e Paolo.
Z.	(Teatro de la) Zarzuela.	S.Sal.	San Salvatore.
Milan, Can.	(Teatro della) Canobbiana.	S.Sam.	San Samuele.
Sc.	(Teatro alla) Scala.	Vienna, B.	Burgtheater.
T.d.V.	Teatro dal Verme.	Ca.	Carl-Theater.
T.L.	Teatro Lirico (Internazionale).	Jos.	(Theater in der) Josefstadt.
T.R.D.	Teatro Regio Ducal.	Kä.	Kärntnertor-Theater.
Naples, Fior.	(Teatro dei) Fiorentini.	Leop.	(Theater in der) Leopoldstadt.
S.B.	San Bartolomeo.	O.	Opernhaus (Hofoper, later Staatsoper).
S.C.	San Carlo.		
T.N.	Teatro Nuovo.	V.O.	Volks-Oper.
New York, M.	Metropolitan (Opera House).	W.	(Theater auf der) Wieden (later Theater an der Wien).

INTRODUCTION

The first attempt at a Dictionary of Operas was made by Leone Allacci, a learned Greek from the island of Chios, who became Librarian of the Vatican Library and published his *Drammaturgia*, a catalogue of all operas performed up to that date, in 1666. Since then a number of catalogues, dictionaries and histories of Opera have been published in various languages, but the present monumental work of Dr. Alfred Loewenberg is the first, as far as I know, to arrange the material year by year in chronological, rather than alphabetical, order. It starts with the first of all operas, *La Dafne*, composed by Jacopo Peri and produced at Florence in 1597, and ends with those produced in 1940. The compiler makes no pretence of naming every single opera that has ever been produced anywhere during these three and a half centuries; to do so would have doubled or trebled the size of his volume. How many operas have been put on the stage, especially during the 19th century, for one performance only, never to be repeated or remembered, it is impossible to compute. In the volume before us we shall find the names of many quite unfamiliar works, and some of those were failures from their birth. Yet even these deserved recording for some reason or other; and it may be said that every work named in these pages has been contributory, in however slight a way, to the general history of the musical drama.

For every opera named we are given the names of librettist and composer, as well as the name of the theatre and the town in which the first production took place; but besides these bare facts we are often supplied with a vast quantity of subsidiary information, especially as regards the source of the plot, subsequent revivals in other cities and translations into various languages. A reader who is already interested in operatic history and acquainted at least with the general outline of it will derive from browsing at random on these pages all sorts of new lights on the subject. The most obvious thing to be learned from this book is the course of the main stream of opera, beginning with what we might call "academic" opera in Florence, produced before a small audience of excessively cultivated people. And because the only people of that period who were in a position to become excessively cultivated were princes and cardinals and the courtiers attendant on them, opera struck root as an eminently aristocratic and courtly entertainment, becoming gradually more and more sumptuous and spectacular as the 17th century progressed. In spite of simultaneous currents in different directions, what we might call "dynastic" opera survived indeed right up to the end of the 18th century, even after the French Revolution had begun to change the face of all European society; the last representative of "dynastic" opera was Mozart's *La Clemenza di Tito* in 1791.

Commercial opera begins with the inauguration of the "Teatro Tron di San Cassiano" at Venice in 1637, the first opera open to the general public on payment having been Manelli's *Andromeda*, of which the music is lost. This date gives Dr. Loewenberg one of his characteristic opportunities and the reader one of the peculiarly fascinating delights of this book: the occasional summaries of unexpected information such as can only be tracked down with difficulty elsewhere. Here, under date 1637, we find a complete list of the numerous Venetian theatres, called by the names of their parishes, like the St. James's and St. Martin's in London of to-day, but known also by the names of the noble families which erected and supported them. Later on we find the same sort of excursus on the operas of Lully, with a list of the latest dates at which they remained in the Paris repertory, and yet further on there is an interesting synopsis of the recent Handel opera revival in Germany.

Dynastic opera was almost always in Italian, wherever it was performed, and for that reason it is Vienna which preserved dynastic opera the longest, Vienna being from a musical point of view much more an Italian city than a German one. In Vienna the spectacular Italian opera was deliberately maintained for the glorification of the reigning house, and no doubt it was Metastasio's choice of subjects such as *La Clemenza di Tito* which caused his librettos to be set to music over and over again for the entertainment of such courts as Stuttgart, Munich, Dresden and Berlin. Paris enjoyed its dynastic opera in French, and there is one solitary example of an English dynastic opera—*Albion and Albanius*, composed by a Frenchman. Dryden may have originally intended *King Arthur* to be something of the same sort, but as it eventually came to be, with the collaboration of Purcell, it was to the glorification of the country as a whole rather than of the monarch.

We can learn from these pages when opera first crossed the Alps, and when the idea first occurred of translating an opera into another language. The *Dafne* of Rinuccini was translated into German by Martin Opitz (a poet of considerable distinction) in 1627, but new music seems to have been composed for it by Schütz; that suggests that in those days the words of an opera were still considered more important than the music. Another early translation is that of Cambert's *Ariane*, made for the performance in London in 1674; but our author is careful to point out that the opera was sung in London in French, and that the translation was made merely for the convenience of readers. Lully's *Roland* was translated into Dutch, but not performed in that language. His *Armide* (1686) seems to have been the first opera ever performed in a second language; it was the first French opera performed in Italy (1690) and must have been sung in Italian, as it was given not only at Rome, but at Mantua and in other places as well, even as late as 1740. Lully's *Acis et Galatée* (his last opera, 1686) had the honour of being the first non-German opera performed at Hamburg (in French, 1689), and although no mention is made of any other opera by Lully having been given in Germany, it is an undoubted fact that Lully's music was immensely popular in that country in the form of instrumental suites.

Most of the German composers of this period set their operas to Italian words; it was only at Hamburg that opera in German had any great attraction, and that only for a short period. Thus the newly-built Italian opera-house at Hanover was inaugurated with Steffani's *Enrico Leone* (1689); later it was given in German at Hamburg, Brunswick, Augsburg and Stuttgart.

That same year 1689 brings us to *Dido and Aeneas* of Purcell, and it is interesting to see from this book how it remained almost unknown and un-performed (except in mutilated concert versions) until Stanford had it revived for the Purcell bi-centenary in 1895, after which it became a favourite opera for amateur and school performances in this country, and then, after 1924, was staged in New York, Münster, Stuttgart, Vienna, Paris, Basle, The Hague, Florence, and Budapest, the last performance being in Hungarian. *The Fairy Queen*, after the Cambridge revival of 1920, has been performed in German at Essen (1931) and in French at Brussels (1935).

It was not until 1701 that opera reached Berlin, which for centuries had remained far behind the other German courts in all cultural matters. This new undertaking was due to the instigation of Queen Sophia Charlotte, who herself played the harpsichord at the performance of Bononcini's *Polifemo* in 1702. Frederick the Great supported opera in Berlin at his own expense for many years, and insisted that the composers should all be German, but he was not so patriotic in the matter of language; it was taken for granted that the librettos could not be in anything but Italian.

The 18th century shows the complete domination of the lyric stage by opera in Italian, whether serious or comic, apart from Paris, and even in Paris the conservative French party had to admit defeat in the famous *Guerre des Bouffons*. In the following century Paris had its regular *Théâtre des Italiens*, which was much more expensive and consequently more fashionable than the native opera. The world triumph of Italian opera during the first half of the 18th century was due entirely to the attraction of the Italian voices, especially those of the *castrati*. This adoration of the artificial soprano singers is one of the most difficult things for the modern music-lover to understand, especially since the worship of Adelina Patti in the last quarter of the 19th century led every critic to think of florid singing as something essentially feminine, and indeed associated principally with females of light character such as *La Traviata*. The florid singing of the *castrati* was undoubtedly heroic in expression, and it was obviously associated closely in the minds of contemporary hearers with the florid style of trumpet-playing to which modern audiences are well accustomed in the oratorios of Handel and the concertos of J. S. Bach.

With the reign of Queen Anne begins the sad story of native English opera and the gradual domination of almost all English musical life by foreign musicians who were only too happy to quit the poverty and the servility of continental life for the streets of London, traditionally supposed to be paved with gold. Here, the economic basis of Italian opera was not the royal privy purse as in Berlin or Stuttgart, but the extravagance of a wealthy aristocracy, and for two hundred years the Italian opera continued to be the acknowledged rendezvous of exclusive society. But a new rival was undermining the dignity of the old-fashioned *opera seria*; both in Italy and in France a new type of comic opera had been developed which was eventually to dethrone the *castrati* and itself suffer a certain degradation into the opera *semi-seria* of the early romantic period. Napoleon put an end to the *castrati* by making the operation a criminal offence; but the public had already tired of them, and they survived in Italy only as church singers.

Dr. Loewenberg shows us very clearly how the comic types of opera spread rapidly over the whole continent. They fall into four main groups: (1) the early French *vaudevilles*, plays with songs set to popular airs, often intended as skits on the serious operas of the day; (2) the English ballad operas, which also had only a short vogue, but exercised a formative influence on the comic opera of Germany; (3) the Italian *opera buffa*, starting at Naples, imitated at Bologna and Venice and thence exported to the musical world in general; (4) the French *opéra-comique*, which could not come into being until after the *vaudeville* type had come to an end in 1762. The French *opéra-comique* always retained an essentially French character, although it had been initiated by Italian composers; it was much more of a play than an opera, and the music, despite the charm of such composers as Monsigny, Grétry and Dalayrac, was always rather a secondary consideration, whereas the Italian *opera buffa*, conventional and foolish to the last degree from the dramatic point of view, depended mainly on the attraction of the singing.

It can be understood at once that comic operas were easily translatable into other languages, whereas the old *opera seria* was hardly conceivable without the Italian language and the voices of the Italian *castrati*. We can see from Burney's *History of Music* how the Italian comic opera soon came to demand equal rights with the serious opera at the King's Theatre in the Haymarket, and the book before us shows how both French and Italian comic operas were translated not only into English and German, but into Danish, Swedish, Polish and other languages. The first opera that had what one might call a world-wide success was one which is now completely forgotten except by bibliographers, Orlandini's *Il Marito Giocatore e la Moglie Bacchettona*, originally an *intermezzo* between the acts of a serious opera, like the more famous *La Serva Padrona*. Orlandini's *intermezzo* came out at Venice in 1718, ten years before *The Beggar's Opera* and fifteen years before *La Serva Padrona*. Its cumbrous title was too much for foreign lips and ears, but under various other names it went to Munich, Breslau, Brussels, Paris, Trieste, Vienna, Lisbon and London, in which last city it was called *The Gamester*, but was sung in Italian—"the first intermezzo or comic interlude which was ever introduced between the acts of an Italian opera in England" (Burney); this was in 1737. It was given later at Prague, Hamburg, Dresden, Potsdam and Paris, always in Italian; in 1755 it reached Copenhagen, where it was sung first in Italian and then translated into Danish. St. Petersburg saw it in 1757, Edinburgh in 1763, and as late as 1777 it was performed in German at Berlin, where the music was attributed to one "Herr Bergulesi"! We may note that at this period it was the general practice in Germany to sing only the recitatives in German; the songs and duets, etc., were all sung in Italian, which must have saved the unhappy translators a great deal of labour.

With *The Beggar's Opera* begins the interesting history of English comic opera in the American colonies. Jamaica saw it in 1733 and New York in 1750. We need not pursue the subject here; early American opera has already been exhaustively treated by American musicologists.

The history of Pergolesi's famous little opera—the only one by which he is now remembered—is complicated and curious. It came out first at Naples in 1733, but did not make very rapid progress in Italy. Its first performance outside Italy was at Graz in 1739, in Italian, and in Italian it was further given at the usual operatic centres, Dresden, Hamburg, Prague, Paris (1746), Vienna, Potsdam, Leipzig, Copenhagen, London (1750, as *intermezzi* for Ciampi's *Adriano in Siria*), Barcelona, Dijon, Dublin, and various other places. The first translation of it was into French in 1754, when it had 150 performances in Paris, and was given in Germany, Sweden and America too; it was in fact the first opera sung in America in French (Baltimore, 1790). From 1758 onwards various English versions appeared. As regards German versions there is some obscurity, but Dr. Loewenberg is inclined to accept 1770 as the date of the first (Vienna). Dutch, Polish, Swedish and Russian translations were also made before the 18th century came to an end. During the first half of the 19th century the little opera seems to have dropped out of all repertories, but revivals began in 1862, first in French, later in Italian (Florence, 1870), in German after 1880 and finally in English, first at New York in 1918, then in London, at the Lyric Theatre, Hammersmith, in 1919. Recent years have seen many revivals in unfamiliar languages; it is interesting to note in Dr. Loewenberg's pages the operas which have had the largest number of performances in countries not usually associated much with opera. *La Serva Padrona* has been sung in Spanish, Hungarian, Portuguese, Croatian, Dutch and Hebrew. The next opera to enjoy these polyglot revivals in modern times was Gluck's *Orfeo*, which has even achieved a concert performance in Japanese.

Of greater historical importance are the innumerable translations of French comic opera into most of the northern languages at the moment when the works of Monsigny, Dalayrac and Grétry were the fashionable novelties. Dr.

Loewenberg does not record much in the way of English translations, because in those days the English procedure was to get a libretto written by some native dramatist and supply it with songs taken from any source that came handy. A few songs by French composers might chance to find a place along with Italian songs and possibly a few traditional folk-songs; the ballad operas had set the tradition, and it was not until well on into the 19th century that the English theatres began to regard an opera in English as an organic musical whole, the work of one composer, be he native or foreign.

The widespread popularity of the French comic operas did not long survive their own time, but Monsigny and his contemporaries were succeeded in turn by Boieldieu, Auber and Adolphe Adam, and the influence of their music has been profound and lasting, not only on the theatre, but on the concert-music of those countries which most historians regard as belonging to the German sphere. In Germany itself the old French repertory was still current, even in such pre-eminent theatres as those of Dresden and Munich, during the early years of the present century. Beethoven, playing in the orchestra of the theatre at Bonn, became acquainted with all this French music, and it left a permanent trace on his own inspiration. Weber, Schubert and even Wagner, were saturated with the French comic opera style, a style to which the only possible rival in those days was that of Paer and Rossini.

After 1800, operas come thick and fast in all countries, and our author's main difficulty must have been to decide what works deserved inclusion in this book. For many generations Paris was still to lead the way in opera, even for the Italians, for the political condition of Italy made it no very attractive territory for a young composer in pursuit of a career. Rossini's reputation was made mainly in Paris, London and Vienna, Bellini's in Paris and London, Donizetti's in Vienna and Paris. Vienna itself was quite unproductive; musically it was a poor imitation of Paris. True, Weber and Schubert were both writing operas, but as far as Vienna went, they were complete failures. German opera was in much the same condition as English opera is at this moment; its habitual repertory was entirely foreign, or else utterly trivial. An idealist like Weber might try to force *Don Giovanni* and *Fidelio* down the throats of his German audiences, but nobody wanted to listen to them, any more than English audiences want to hear the very distinguished works which some of our own composers have contributed to the stage.

During the first half of the century the political aspect of opera becomes singularly interesting, and this book brings together a number of cases, perhaps already well known in isolation, but hardly considered by historians as part of a connected whole. The previous century had already seen the most dangerous play of the age, *Le Mariage de Figaro*, slip through the censorship under the disguise of an Italian opera. Later generations began to realize that opera, when it became a democratic diversion, might be a danger to lawful authority.

Cimarosa, whose *Matrimonio Segreto* had won the honour of being "encored" in its entirety at the command of the Austrian Emperor in 1792, was imprisoned and condemned to death at Naples in 1799 for openly showing his enthusiasm for the French Republicans. Even *Fidelio* barely escaped the censorship at Vienna, and was saved only by a personal appeal to the Empress. A French full score of *Fidelio* exists, published in 1826, with the names of the singers who were to perform it. The performance never took place, according to Dr. Loewenberg; and the odd thing about the score is that the names of the characters are altered and the scene is transferred from Spain to Germany. What political mystery lay behind all this? Another French opera, *Les Visitandines*, by Devienne (1792), which made fun of nuns and friars, had a great vogue in Germany; in Hamburg and Berlin it could be performed without alteration, but in Vienna the translator had to turn the convent into a Protestant girls' school. Rossini's *Mosè in Egitto* (Naples, 1818) had to be given in London as *Pietro l'Eremita* at the King's Theatre, although it was accepted in the original form as an oratorio at Exeter Hall in 1878. Bellini's *Bianca e Fernando* (Naples, 1826) had to be called *Bianca e Gernando*, because Fernando was the name of the King of Naples! In 1828 we come to Auber's *La Muette de Portici* (called *Masaniello* in England), a performance of which in Brussels on 25 August 1830, started the revolution which led to the independence of Belgium. Rossini's *Guillaume Tell* (1829) had to appear in London as *Andreas Hofer*, or *The Tell of the Tyrol*. "On account of its political subject," says Dr. Loewenberg, "the opera had to be given in many countries in different disguises and with more or less essential alterations in the original libretto. . . . As late as in 1866 the censor at Palermo demanded changes in the text." At Milan, Tell became William Wallace; at Rome, "Rodolfo di Sterlinga"; at St. Petersburg and Moscow, Charles the Bold.

Donizetti's *Lucrezia Borgia* (Milan, 1833) was another opera which suffered curious changes, but these were probably due not to the censorship but to Victor Hugo's objections to his play being turned into an opera. He made similar difficulties over Verdi's use of *Le Roi s'amuse* (*Rigoletto*). *Rigoletto*, as is well known, had to have its characters changed before the Austrian censorship would pass it for Venice. Naples and Rome were always nervous of political trouble, and Madame Pasta, when she came to London with Bellini, told Lady Morgan that she had narrowly escaped being thrown into prison for pronouncing the word *libertà* on the stage. *Les Huguenots* (1836) was too much for Munich and Vienna; at Munich it was called *Die Anglikaner und Puritaner*, at Vienna, *Die Gibellinen in Pisa*. Florence preferred the "Anglican" version.

Paris on the whole took a liberal view of opera; but it may be remarked that three distinguished men of letters were arraigned before a tribunal for offences against public morals—Victor Hugo for *Marion de Lorme* in 1829 and *Le Roi s'amuse* in 1832, Alexandre Dumas *fils* for *La Dame aux Camélias* (1849), and Flaubert for *Madame Bovary* (1857), all within a period of thirty years.

Another subject which this book might provoke us to study in detail is the history of certain opera plots and the way in which the same story has been treated by a number of different composers. A typical example is that episode in Ariosto's *Orlando Furioso* which suggested the deception of Claudio in *Much Ado About Nothing*; Handel presented it in *Ariodante*, Méhul in *Ariodant*, J. S. Mayr in *Ginevra di Scozia*, besides settings by lesser composers. Even after Rossini's triumph, and during his own lifetime, other composers attempted (with no success) to re-set *Il Barbiere di Siviglia*. Dr. Loewenberg has shown extraordinary learning and research in discovering the literary origins of numerous operas.

The last few pages of the book bring us almost to the present day and may well make us wonder what is to be the prospect of opera in the future. The period 1920–33 was wonderfully productive of what one might call experimental operas, mainly in Germany and Italy. And there were successful operas too. Puccini's posthumous *Turandot* (Milan, 1926) is described by Dr. Loewenberg as "so far the last world success in the history of opera." In Germany, Richard Strauss continued his prosperous career, although probably Schreker, D'Albert and E. W. Korngold secured more performances for their various operas; we may doubt whether any of these, except perhaps D'Albert's unpleasant *Tiefland*, will ever be revived, even in their country of origin. Of the "experimental" type, Křenek's *Jonny spielt auf* made the most sensation; Alban Berg's *Wozzeck* very nearly became a world success, in spite of its indescribable horror. One of the best of all the modern German operas was *Die Bürgschaft*, by Kurt Weill. The most prolific composers of opera during that period were Malipiero and Stravinsky; Malipiero, too, enjoyed the honour of having one of his operas suppressed by the authorities in Rome because it made fun of prime ministers in a modern-dress fairy-tale. Milhaud and Honegger also contributed works of high artistic value. How many of these will return to the stage when the world is at peace? The trouble with most of these operas (and with many by other composers) is that they are not such as will form the basis of a standard repertory. Every opera-house requires indispensably a certain number of works which may be counted on to fill the theatre whenever they are performed; that is why *Cavalleria Rusticana*, *Bohème* and *Butterfly*, with some dozen older works, are to be seen all over the world. On the other hand, such an opera as Milhaud's magnificent *Christophe Colomb*, like *Les Troyens* of Berlioz or Busoni's *Doktor Faust*, can only be put on occasionally, with the probability of a considerable deficit, in a theatre generously State-supported, and running regularly as a huge and complete organization, about the functioning of which there can never be the slightest moment of anxiety. And the numerous smaller works, involving perhaps far less expense, but appealing only to an extremely cultivated public, can only be produced when the management is quite certain that there exists such a highly specialized public to patronize them.

Of our own operatic problem in England I will say nothing here, and I am not competent to speak of conditions in America. This book is printed in English, and we may indeed feel proud that an English firm has undertaken its publication in these difficult days; but it is a work of international importance and will eventually be indispensable to libraries, booksellers, operatic managers, musical critics and genuine lovers of opera in all countries.

EDWARD J. DENT

Cambridge,
    October 1942.

"There is some danger at the present time that we may be led to an under-estimation of the efforts of the Florentine Camerata. They sought Greek drama and found opera. And whether or not they consciously or unconsciously utilized the traditional or progressive elements of their time, no historical subtleties will ever succeed in proving that opera really existed before the Florentine Camerata stumbled on it. All the undercurrents of their time might have been converging towards opera, yet of themselves they would not have led to opera without the new and distinguishing element of dramatic musical speech."

(O. G. T. SONNECK, in *The Musical Antiquary*, Vol. III, p. 40.)

1597

J. PERI: *La Dafne*

Carnival. Florence, Pal. Corsi

Text by O. Rinuccini. Not divided into acts (consists of prologue and 6 scenes).

Libretto published in 1600; a new issue appeared in 1604.

Peri's music is lost. So is a contemporary setting by Caccini (which might have been used at a performance in August 1600). Of an earlier, seemingly incomplete setting by Jacopo Corsi, two fragments were discovered at the Brussels Conservatoire (MS.8750) by H. Panum in 1888 and first published in *Musikalisches Wochenblatt*, 19 July 1888.

When was *Dafne*, the first opera, first performed? Looking through books of reference and histories of music one will find the year 1594 indicated as often as the year 1597. The former date is founded on a rather ambiguous passage in the preface to Peri's *Euridice* score (1601); the latter date on a statement in Gagliano's *Dafne* score (1608).

The whole complicated matter has been made perfectly clear by O. G. T. Sonneck; see his essay "Dafne the first opera" in *Sammelbände der Internationalen Musikgesellschaft*, Vol. XV (1913–14), or the note on the *Dafne* libretto in the Library of Congress *Catalogue of Opera Librettos printed before 1800* (1914), pp.340-345. Sonneck's arguments in favour of Gagliano's statement that the first production was in the Carnival of 1597 seem to be quite convincing, and in the course of the past 25 years no new documents have been discovered which could upset his theory.

It is to be hoped, however, that at least the misleading date of 1594 will disappear from the books of reference altogether, because Peri's "fin l'anno 1594"—even if it really refers to a production and not merely to the date of commission or composition—means the beginning of our year 1595, as Sonneck pointed out.

There remains one question which Sonneck apparently did not consider. What did Gagliano mean when in 1608 writing down the words "il carnovale dell' anno 1597"? Carnival began at the end of December and lasted until February or the beginning of March. But in 16th century Florence the Julian Calendar was still in force by which the new year began on 1 March. Thus the greater part of Carnival was not in the beginning of the year, but at the end, and Gagliano's words could refer to the last months of the Julian year 1597, i.e. to January or February of our, the Gregorian, year 1598. In this case Peri's "per tre anni continui che nel carnovale si rappresentò" could mean performances of *Dafne* in the beginning of (Gregorian) 1598, 1599 and 1600. This assumption would carry us down to the year in which the libretto was printed and would be perfectly consistent with all other dates established by contemporary accounts.

Dafne was first produced, whenever it was, at Jacopo Corsi's house, in the presence of "Don Giovanni Medici e d'alcuni de' principali gentiluomini de la città". According to Rinuccini's account (in the preface to the *Euridice* libretto, 1600) it was given in an improved version ("miglior forma") again at Corsi's in the presence of the Grand Duchess and of the cardinals Dal Monte and Montalto (presumably before 18 January 1599) and repeated at the Palazzo Pitti 21 January 1599. Another performance at Corsi's took place in August 1600 (this time, perhaps, with Caccini's music), and a last revival at the Palazzo Pitti (probably with Peri's music) 26 October 1604, in honour of a visit of the Duke of Parma (libretto reprinted with new first sheet). These are the performances which are known to have taken place; but there may have been more of which we have no knowledge yet.

(For Gagliano's new setting of the libretto, see 1608; for a German version of the libretto, see 1627.)

1600

J. PERI: *L'Euridice*

6 October. Florence, Pal. Pitti

Text by O. Rinuccini. Not divided into acts (consists of prologue and 6 scenes).

The first opera the music of which is extant. Produced as part of the wedding festivities celebrated at Florence in honour of Henri IV, King of France, and Maria de' Medici.

Libretto published in 1600 (dedication to Maria de' Medici dated October 1600; in some copies 4 October 1600).

Score published in 1601 (dedication dated 6 February 1600 = 1601 n.s.) as *Le Musiche . . . Sopra l'Euridice*; from Peri's preface we learn that parts of the music as sung in October 1600 were by Caccini (who set the same libretto to music at the same time; for the production of his setting as a whole, see below, 1602).

Peri's music was again published at Venice in 1608; new editions 1863; *c.*1900 (in L. Torchi's *L'Arte musicale in Italia*, Vol. VI); 1919 (vocal score, edited by C. Perinello); and 1934 (facsimile of the first edition).

Peri's *Euridice* was revived at Bologna, Casa Marescotti, 27 April 1616.

The first modern revival was at a Milan concert, 13 May 1916, in a two-act version by G. Tebaldini. Other revivals took place at Naples, Politeama, 28 January 1920 (by the "Associazione Scarlatti"); Florence, Pal. Pitti 29 December 1923; Munich, University 23 January 1934 (German version by B. Beyerle).

G. CACCINI: *Il Rapimento di Cefalo*

9 October. Florence, Pal. Vecchio

Text by G. Chiabrera. Prologue, 5 acts, and licenza.

Libretto published in 1600 (reprinted in Vol. III of A. Solerti's *Gli Albori del Melodramma*, 1905).

Il Rapimento di Cefalo was, three days after *Euridice*, produced in the course of the wedding festivities for Henri IV and Maria de' Medici. We know from the younger Michelangelo's description that, besides Caccini, three other composers had a share in the score: Stefano Venturi del Nibbio, Luca Bati and Pietro Strozzi. They were not mentioned by Caccini when he published parts of his music, consisting of two choruses and three airs, in his *Le Nuove Musiche* in 1601 (facsimile edition by F. Mantica issued in 1930).

The first instance of a translation of an opera libretto occurs already at this early date: *Le Ravissement de Cefale*, a French version by N. Chrétien des Croix, was published at Rouen in 1608 and was dedicated by the translator to the newborn Dauphin, Jean-Baptiste-Gaston (later Duke of Orléans), "l'heureux fruit" of the marriage which had been celebrated by the production of the Italian original eight years before.

1602

G. CACCINI: *L'Euridice*

5 December. Florence, Pal. Pitti

Rinuccini's text, as composed by Peri in 1600.

Parts of Caccini's music had already been used at the performances of 1600, as we know from the preface in Peri's score. Caccini's score was published earlier (dedication dated 20 December 1600) than Peri's (dedication dated 6 February 1600–01). The production, however, of Caccini's setting as a whole did not take place before 5 December 1602, when his *Euridice* was performed in honour of the Cardinals Montalto and Dal Monte and the Marchese Peretti.

Caccini's score was published in 1600 (or rather, actually about January 1601) as *L'Euridice composta in Musica In stile rappresentativo*; it was reprinted at Venice in 1615; new editions 1863, 1880 and 1881 (in Vol. X of Eitner's *Publikationen der Gesellschaft für Musikforschung*).

No separate issue of the libretto was printed for *Euridice* in 1602. Nor was Caccini's setting ever revived.

1606

AGAZZARI: *Eumelio*

Carnival. Rome, Seminario Romano

Librettist unknown. *Dramma pastorale recitato . . . Con le Musiche dell' Armonico Intronato* (which was the composer's surname as a member of the "Accademia degli Intronati" of Siena). Prologue and 3 acts.

The score was published at Venice in 1606 (one single copy at the Biblioteca di S. Cecilia, Rome, extant). The preface informs us that the opera was written within a fortnight and performed by pupils of the Seminario Romano with great success. No libretto seems to have been printed.

The prologue published in *La Diana* (Siena) 1933.

1607

MONTEVERDI: *La Favola d'Orfeo*

Carnival. Mantua

Text by A. Striggio (*Rappresentata in Musica*). Prologue and 5 acts.

Libretto published in 1607. Score (*Favola in Musica*) published at Venice in 1609 (dedication dated 22 August) and in 1615. Of these two editions only eight copies are known to be extant (three of them being preserved in Italy, two in England, two in Germany, and one in Belgium). There are new editions by Eitner (1881), d'Indy (1904), Orefice (1909), Erdmann-Guckel (1913), Malipiero (1923 and 1930), Orff (1930), Benvenuti (1934), and Respighi (1935).

A facsimile of the 1609 score was edited by A. Sandberger in 1928.

The opera was dedicated to the Hereditary Prince of Mantua, Francesco Gonzaga. After the private production at the "Accademia degl' Invaghiti" (the exact date of which is unknown) *Orfeo* was repeated at the Court Theatre, Mantua on 24 February and 1 March 1607. At Cremona, Monteverdi's native town, *Orfeo* was given by the "Accademia degl' Animosi" on 10 August 1607 (parts only); stage productions probably took place at Turin in 1610 and about the same time at Florence and Milan (see Solerti, *Gli Albori del Melodramma*, Vol. 1, pp.70 and 139).

After an interval of nearly 300 years it was only in the 20th century that *Orfeo* was restored to living music. The following revivals are to be recorded:

PARIS, SCHOLA CANTORUM 25 February 1904 (in concert form, in French, translated and arranged by Vincent d'Indy; repeated there 2 March 1904, 27 January 1905, 26 February 1905).

MILAN, CONSERVATORIO 30 November 1909 (in concert form, under Giacomo Orefice; this version was repeated at Mantua, T. Sociale 5 April 1910 and the following days at Venice, Bologna, Florence, Turin and in other Italian towns; also at Monte Carlo 16 April 1910.

BRUSSELS 23 January 1910 (in concert form, under Sylvain Dupuis).

PARIS, TH. RÉJANE 2 May 1911 (this was the first modern stage performance, under the direction of Marcel Labey; repeated 11 April and 13 April 1913).

NEW YORK, M. 14 April 1912 (concert performance, Orefice's version); Chicago 4 January 1913.

BRESLAU 8 June 1913 (stage performance, German version by H. Erdmann-Guckel).

BUENOS AIRES 10 May 1920 (Orefice's version) and 23 July 1937 (Benvenuti's version).

LONDON 8 March 1924 (in concert form at the Institut Français, Cromwell Gardens, d'Indy's version, under Louis Bourgeois).

MANNHEIM 17 April 1925 (stage performance, new German version by C. Orff).

OXFORD 7 December 1925 (in English, translated by R. L. Stuart, orchestrated by J. A. Westrup and W. H. Harris).

CAIRO 1928 (in Italian).

COLOGNE Summer 1928 (d'Indy's version, translated into German by H. Jalowetz).

LENINGRAD Summer 1929 (Malipiero's version).

LONDON, SCALA 30 December 1929 (the Oxford 1925 version).

VIENNA 14 January 1931 (in concert form, Orff's version, translated by D. Günther).

LISBON Spring 1932 (d'Indy's version, in Portuguese, under I. Cruz).

MANTUA, LOGGIA DUCALE April 1933 (under A. Zanella).

PERUGIA 19 September 1934 (Oreficc's version).

ROME, T.R. 26 December 1934 (new version by G. Benvenuti, text adapted by A. Rossato).

MILAN, SC. 16 March 1935 (new version by O. Respighi, text adapted by C. Guastalla).

MODENA May 1935 (Respighi's version, text adapted by C. Guastalla).

ZURICH 10 February 1936 (concert performance, in Italian; music arranged by H. F. Redlich).

BUDAPEST April 1936 (in Hungarian; Respighi's version).

1608

GAGLIANO: *La Dafne*

January. Mantua, T. della Corte

Rinuccini's text (see 1597), slightly altered and enlarged. Gagliano's first opera.

The score was published in 1608 (dedication dated 20 October; reprinted in an abridged version by Eitner in Vol. x of the *Publikationen der Gesellschaft für Musikforschung*, 1881). The libretto does not seem to have been printed. The opera was performed twice in the course of the Carnival, and repeated at Florence, presumably in Carnival 1610.

A recent revival of Gagliano's opera took place at Moscow Spring of 1911 (rescored by one Professor von Glehn); see *Die Musik*, July 1911, p.55.

MONTEVERDI: *L'Arianna*

28 May. Mantua, T. della Corte

Text by O. Rinuccini (*Tragedia . . . Rappresentata in musica*). Not divided into acts (consists of prologue and 8 scenes).

Performed at the wedding of Francesco Gonzaga, Hereditary Prince of Mantua, with Margherita, Princess of Savoy.

The libretto was first published in 1608 and has been frequently reprinted since. Of the music, unfortunately only a fragment has been preserved, the celebrated *Lamento d'Arianna* (begins "Lasciatemi morire"), first published in the sixth book of Monteverdi's Madrigals, Venice, 1614.

The opera probably was repeated at Florence in Carnival 1614 and revived at Venice, Autumn 1639 (at the inauguration of the Teatro di San Moisè, the third Venetian opera-house).

Modern revivals of the one extant scene took place at Carlsruhe January 1926 and Paris, Petite Scène 31 May 1931.

Arianna is known to have been famous in Italy for many years. The tunes were sung and played everywhere. When revived at Venice in 1639, more than 30 years after its first appearance, the old opera had hardly to be altered at all (as a comparison of the librettos shows) and still proved much more successful than many of the "modern" works. The Lamento served as a model of its kind for centuries to come, ". . . quelques pages, les plus douloureuses et les plus vraies qu'il ait écrites, et que Gluck n'a pas surpassées . . ." (Romain Rolland).

1610

GIACOBBI: *Andromeda*

Carnival. Bologna, Salone del Podestà

Text by R. Campeggi (*Tragedia . . . Da recitarsi in Musica*). Prologue and 5 acts.

First opera produced at Bologna of which the composer is known. Libretto printed in 1610 (copies in the Liceo Musicale, Bologna, and in the British Museum). "Fatta recitare in Musica di stile rappresentativo nella Città di Bologna, per disporto delle sue bellissime Dame. Ne i giorni di Carnesciale, con apparato magnifico, l'Anno MDCX . . . Fece la Musica Girolamo Giacobbi Mastro di Capella di S. Petronio di Bologna."

The music is lost; one air, "Io ti sfido, o mostro infame," is known to have been famous all over Italy.

A work entitled *Andromeda*, which might have been Giacobbi's opera, was performed at Salzburg on 15 February 1618. This would be, if the identification is correct, the first known instance of an opera produced outside Italy.

1616

BELLI: *Il Pianto d'Orfeo*

Carnival. Florence, Pal. Gherardesca

Text by G. Chiabrera. Five intermezzi.

The text was published in 1615 in Chiabrera's *Favolette . . . da rappresentarsi cantando*, and, according to Allacci and other bibliographers, separately at Genoa in 1622 (no copy of the separate edition has been traced yet).

The music was published under the title of *Orfeo dolente* in 1616 (one single copy of this score has been preserved at Breslau). The title-page informs us that it was sung between the acts of a performance of Tasso's *Aminta*.

Tasso's *Aminta* was revived, with Belli's intermezzi, at Brussels on 3 March 1926 (French version by A. de Rudder, music arranged by A. Tirabassi); this version was also published at Brussels 1927.

For an analysis of the work see H. Riemann, *Handbuch der Musikgeschichte*, Vol. II, Pt. 2, p.288. The text was reprinted by A. Solerti in Vol. III of his *Gli Albori del Melodramma* (1905). See also Solerti's *Musica . . . alla Corte Medicea* (1905), pp.375–391, where the version of the text as contained in the score is reproduced.

A recent attempt of A. Tirabassi (*The Musical Quarterly*, January 1939) to claim for Belli's opera a priority over even Peri's and Caccini's works is based on arguments which are certainly not sufficient to upset the whole history of early Italian opera (see *ibid.*, July 1940).

BOSCHETTI: *Strali d'Amore*

14 February. Viterbo

Librettist unknown. No copy of the libretto traced yet. Five intermezzi.

Score published in 1618 (*Favola recitata in Musica Per Intermedij . . .*). Produced at Count Andrea Maidalchini's, Viterbo, between the acts

of a comedy. Dedication in the score dated 15 March 1618.

The first description of the work (which is on the Mars-Venus-Vulcan story) was given by A. W. Ambros in 1878 (*Geschichte der Musik*, Vol. IV, p.301). Only two copies of the score are known to be extant.

1619

LANDI: *La Morte d'Orfeo*

[*1 June*]. Rome

Text by the composer (and not, as often stated, by Alessandro Matthei to whom the work is dedicated). *Tragicomedia Pastorale*, 5 acts. Landi was the first composer who wrote his own libretto.

Score printed in 1619 (the only known copy of this edition is in the British Museum) and again in 1639. Parts of the music were reprinted by H. Goldschmidt in 1901.

Text reprinted by A. Solerti in Vol. III of his *Gli Albori del Melodramma*, 1905, from the score of 1619.

The opera is stated to have been produced before the Papal Court.

GAGLIANO: *Il Medoro*

25 September. Florence, Pal. Pitti

Text by A. Salvadori (*. . . rappresentato in musica*), founded on an episode in Ariosto's *Orlando furioso*. Three acts.

Libretto printed in 1619 and 1623 (only copies of this second edition seem to be extant). Music lost.

The opera was produced to celebrate the election of the Emperor Ferdinand II (Cosimo de' Medici's brother-in-law). An intended revival at Mantua in 1622 (often mentioned on the authority of E. Vogel's monograph, 1889) did not take place as we learn from the dedication in the 1623 libretto.

From a contemporary diary, Solerti revealèd the fact that Peri had a (presumably small) share in the music.

1620

VITALI: *L'Aretusa*

8 February. Rome, Pal. Corsini

Text by O. Corsini (*Favola in Musica*). Prologue and 3 acts.

Score published in 1620 (text reprinted by A. Solerti from the score).

The preface informs us that the opera was written and composed within 44 days; it also gives the cast; the name part was sung by the castrato Gregorio Lazerini.

1625

F. CACCINI: *La Liberazione di Ruggiero dall'Isola d'Alcina*

2 February. Florence, Villa Poggio Imperiale

Text by F. Saracinelli (*Balletto rappresentato in musica*), founded on an episode in Ariosto's *Orlando furioso*. Not divided into acts (consists of prologue and 3 scenes).

Performed at a visit of Wladislaw Sigismund, Prince of Poland, to the Grand Duchess of Tuscany. Both score and libretto were published in 1625.

The first extant example of an "opera ballo"; at the same time the first instance of an operatic work written by a woman composer (Francesca was the daughter of Giulio Caccini, see 1600 and 1602). Parts of the music were reprinted by H. Goldschmidt in 1901.

It has been stated that *La Liberazione di Ruggiero* was also produced in Poland at an early date. While there is no evidence that a production actually took place, it is true that there exists a printed Polish translation by S. S. Jagodyński, called *Wybawienie Ruggiera z Wyspy Alcyny*, published at Cracow in 1628. See K. Estreicher, *Bibliografia Polska*, Vol. XXVII (1929), p.124.

1626

D. MAZZOCCHI: *La Catena d'Adone*

Before *13 February*. Rome, Casa Evandro Conti

Text by O. Tronsarelli (*Favola boschereccia*), founded on an episode in G. B. Marini's poem *Adone*. Prologue and 5 acts.

Both score and libretto were published in 1626.

The opera was revived at Bologna, T. Malvezzi, in Autumn 1648 (with prologue and intermezzi by N. Zoppio Turchi). Parts of the music were reprinted by H. Goldschmidt in 1901.

The dedications in the libretto (which was printed only after the performance) are dated 30 March and 12 May 1626. The dedication in the score is dated 24 October 1626.

The first (or at least, an early) performance is referred to in a letter, dated 13 February 1626, which was discovered by A. Saviotti (see *Giornale Storico della Letteratura Italiana*, Vol. XLI, p.70). The writer, one Antonio Donato, gives this piece of early opera criticism: "Fu cosa meno che mediocre, ma onorata da Nepoti Pontefici e molti cardinali." Modern critics would not agree with him on the quality of the work which is one of the most important operas of that period.

The opera seems to have been repeated at Viterbo later in 1626 (libretto reprinted). There is also an edition of the libretto dated Venice 1627.

1627

SCHÜTZ: *Dafne*

23 April. Torgau

Text by M. Opitz (partly translated from Rinuccini's Italian libretto, see 1597). ". . . *Musicalisch in den Schawplatz zu bringen*. . . ." Prologue and 5 acts.

Written to celebrate the wedding of George, Landgrave of Hesse, with Sophia Eleonora, Princess of Saxony, and performed at Hartenfels Castle, Torgau, Saxony.

The libretto was printed in 1627. The music of this earliest German opera is lost. The date of the first (or at least, an early) performance is indicated in a contemporary account of the wedding festival. It has been suggested that the actual first performance took place on 31 March/10 April 1627, the night before the wedding, as in the prologue bride and bridegroom are apostrophized.

1628

GAGLIANO and J. PERI: *La Flora, o vero Il Natal de' Fiori*

11 October. Florence, Pal. Pitti

Text by A. Salvadori (*Favola . . . Rappresentata in musica recitativa*). Prologue and 5 acts.

Performed at the wedding of Odoardo Farnese, Duke of Parma, with Margherita of Tuscany.

Both score and libretto were published in 1628. Gagliano is the only composer mentioned on the title-page of the score, but a note in it informs us that "Le musiche furono tutte del Sig. Marco da Gagliano, eccetta la parte di Clori, la quale fu opera del Sig. Jacopo Peri. . . ."

Parts of the music were reprinted by H. Goldschmidt in 1901.

1629

CORNACCHIOLI: *Diana schernita*

Carnival. Rome

Text by G. F. Parisano (*Favola Boscareccia*). Five acts.

Score published in 1629. Libretto not traced yet. The work was performed at the private house of the German Baron Johann Rudolf von Hohenrechberg.

The only known work of Cornacchioli, who was a native of Ascoli. Dedication in the score dated 6 June 1629. At the end the remark: "Questa Fauola è tolta dalle Metamorfesi di Ouidio, & posta in questi versi dal Sig. Giac: Francesco Parisani d'Ascoli."

1632

LANDI: *Il S. Alessio*

23 February. Rome, Pal. Barberini

Text by G. Rospigliosi (the future Pope Clement IX). *Dramma Musicale*, prologue and 3 acts.

First opera produced at the theatre in the Palazzo Barberini. Repeated there February 1634 in honour of a visit of Alexander Charles, brother of King Wladislaw IV of Poland. Revived Bologna 1647 (probably Landi's work).

Score published in 1634 (the only opera score of that period which is not exceedingly rare).

For an account of *S. Alessio* see G. Pavan in *Musica d'oggi*, October 1921; also U. Rolandi in *La Rassegna Dorica*, 20 February 1932. Parts of the music were reprinted by H. Goldschmidt in 1901.

In most dictionaries 1634 is given as the year of the first production. The date of 23 February 1632, however, is established by the account of a French traveller, Jean-Jacques Bouchard, who witnessed the first performance. See Lucien Marcheix, *Un Parisien à Rome et à Naples en 1632, D'après un manuscrit inédit . . .* (at the Bibliothèque de l'École des Beaux-Arts, Paris), 1897, p.9–10.

1633

M. A. ROSSI: *Erminia sul Giordano*

January. Rome, Pal. Barberini

Text probably by G. Rospigliosi (who became Pope Clement IX in 1667), founded on an episode in Tasso's *Gerusalemme liberata. Dramma musicale*, prologue and 3 acts.

Score published in 1637. Libretto not printed. The opera seems to have been repeated several times during the following years. It was the composer's only work for the stage. Parts of the music were reprinted by H. Goldschmidt in 1901.

The year of the first performance is given as 1625 by Fétis, Clément, Riemann, and others (which is obviously a mistake); Schmidl's Dictionary has 1635, Rolland, Goldschmidt, and Prunières 1637. Again (as in the case of *La*

Catena d'Adone, see 1626) a contemporary letter, discovered by A. Saviotti at the Biblioteca Oliveriana, Pesaro (see *Giornale Storico della Letteratura Italiana*, Vol. XLI, p.70) gives to the earlier date of Carnival, 1633, a high degree of probability. The letter is dated 2 February 1633, and the writer, one Fabio Almerici, refers to the opera as *La Fuga d'Erminia*.

1637

MANELLI: *L'Andromeda*

February or *March*. Venice, S. Cass.

Text by B. Ferrari (. . . *rappresentata in musica*). Three acts.

Written for the inauguration of the T. Tron di San Cassiano which was the first public opera-house in any town.

The libretto was printed only about two months after the production, the approximate date of which we can guess from the date of the publisher's dedication (6 May 1637) and the remark "Andromeda che su le scene rinacque già son due mesi. . . ." The music is lost, like the rest of Manelli's operas. For a bibliography of his works see G. Radiciotti, *L'Arte musicale in Tivoli* (1921), p.49.

Venice remained for many years the only town with regular opera seasons every Carnival. It appears from the chronologies that in the course of the 17th century more than 350 operas were produced at the different Venetian theatres, a number which increased to more than 1,600 at the close of the 18th century (including revivals and operas previously given elsewhere). The following is a list of the principal Venetian opera-houses founded before 1800.

Name. First opera given there and subsequent data.

S. CASSIANO, 1637: *Andromeda*, by Manelli. Operas until about 1800.

SS. GIOVANNI E PAOLO, 1639: *Delia*, by Sacrati. Operas until 1748.

S. MOISÈ, 1640: *Arianna*, by Monteverdi. Operas until 1818.

NOVISSIMO, 1641: *La finta Pazza*, by Sacrati. Seven operas until 1647.

SS. APOSTOLI, 1649: *Orontea*, by Cesti. Five operas until 1687.

S. APOLLINARE, 1651: *Oristeo*, by Cavalli. Ten operas until 1660.

S. SALVATORE, 1661: *Pasife*, by Castrovillari. Became T. S. Luca 1799, T. Apollo 1833, T. Goldoni 1875.

S. ANGELO, 1677: *Elena*, by Freschi. Operas until about 1800.

S. GIOVANNI GRISOSTOMO, 1678: *Vespasiano*, by Pallavicino. Became T. Malibran 1835.

S. FANTINO, 1699: *Paolo Emilio*, by Pignatta. Operas until 1720.

S. SAMUELE, 1710: *L'Ingannator ingannato*, by Ruggeri. Existed until 1870.

S. BENEDETTO, 1755: *Zoe*, by Cocchi. Became T. Rossini 1868.

LA FENICE, 1792: *I Giuochi d'Agrigento*, by Paisiello. Still in existence under that name.

1638

MANELLI: *La Maga fulminata*

[*6 February*]. Venice, S. Cass.

Text by B. Ferrari. Three acts.

Also given at Bologna [20 April] 1641. Manelli's second opera, and the second opera which was produced at Venice. Music lost.

The Venice libretto is dedicated to Basil Feilding (2nd Earl of Denbigh) who from 1634–39 was British Ambasador Extraordinary to the Republic of Venice.

1639

VITTORI: *La Galatea*

Carnival. Rome, Pal. Barberini

Text by the composer (*dramma . . . posto in musica*). Prologue and 3 acts.

Score published Rome 1639, libretto Spoleto 1655. Vittori's only opera. Date of production unknown (the Carnival ended 8 March 1639). Parts of the music were reprinted by H. Goldschmidt in 1901.

A recent opinion on *La Galatea* may be quoted here: "*La Galatea* è uno dei migliori esemplari dell' opera romana del Seicento per magnificenza di scenario, per agilità dell' azione scenica, per opportuna collocazione di arie a solo e d'insieme, per impiego efficace di parti corali. L'ultimo atto è un vero capolavoro per nobiltà d'espressione e per grandiosità di disegno" (F. Vatielli in *R.M.I.*, Vol. XLIII, 1939).

SACRATI: *La Delia* o sia *La Sera Sposa del Sole*

Before *20 January*. Venice, SS.G. e P.
Text by G. Strozzi (*Poema dramatico*, first set to music by F. Manelli, Bologna 1630). Three acts.

Written for the opening of the second Venetian opera-house, the Teatro Grimani dei Santi Giovanni e Paolo. From a note in the libretto it appears that the production must have preceded the date of the dedication (20 January). For use at the actual performance, a scenario was printed in which, by the way, Manelli, and not Sacrati, was indicated as the composer. The libretto was reprinted in 1644 (which points to a possible revival in that year). The music is lost, like the rest of Sacrati's operas.

Also given at Milan 1647 by the Accademici Febiarmonici.

CAVALLI: *Le Nozze di Teti e di Peleo*

[*24 January*]. Venice, S. Cass.
Text by O. Persiani (*Opera scenica*). Prologue and 3 acts.

Cavalli's first opera. The first Venetian opera the music of which has been preserved (in the Contarini collection, Biblioteca di S. Marco, Venice; see note on Pallavicino, 1679).

B. FERRARI: *L'Armida*

February. Venice, SS.G. e P.
Text by the composer (after Tasso). Prologue and 3 acts.

The first opera of which Ferrari, composer, poet, operatic manager, and theorbo virtuoso, wrote the music as well as the words. The music is lost, like the rest of Ferrari's operas. Revived Piacenza 1650.

V. MAZZOCCHI and MARAZZOLI: *Chi soffre, speri*

27 February. Rome, Pal. Barberini
Text by G. Rospigliosi (the future Pope Clement IX). *Comedia musicale*, prologue and 3 acts.

The first comic opera. MS score extant (only one copy known, in the Biblioteca Vaticana, Rome). Libretto not printed (but preserved in MS). Only an *Argomento et allegoria* of the opera was published in 1639 (copy in the Library of Congress, Washington).

According to A. Salza (*R.M.I.*, Vol. XIV, p.477) *Chi soffre, speri* possibly is an enlarged version of an earlier opera called *Il Falcone*, and produced at the same theatre towards the end of 1637.

Mazarin and Milton were amongst the illustrious guests who witnessed the birth of comic opera. Milton alludes to the performance in a letter to Lucas Holstenius, dated Florence, 30 March 1639.

See further, U. Rolandi in *Nuova Antologia*, October 1927. Parts of the music were published by H. Goldschmidt in 1901.

MONTEVERDI: *L'Adone*

[*21 December*]. Venice, SS.G. e P.
Text by P. Vendramin (*Tragedia musicale*), founded on the poem by G. B. Marini. Prologue and 5 acts.

The first opera Monteverdi—then aged 72—wrote for a public theatre. Very successful, given during the whole Carnival of 1640 and repeated in the autumn of that year. The music is lost.

The music has been attributed to Monteverdi by all older and most modern historians, from Bonlini (1730) to Prunières (1926) and Malipiero (1929). Yet it should be mentioned that the opera is most definitely ascribed to Manelli by some authorities, notably by G. Radiciotti (in the bibliography of Manelli's works, contained in his *L'Arte musicale in Tivoli*, 1921) and by P. Camerini in *Piazzola* (1925), p.339.

As a matter of fact, Monteverdi's name is not mentioned in the original libretto which contains, on the other hand, a dedication by Manelli to Antonio Grimani (the proprietor of the theatre) and a letter by the librettist Vendramin to Manelli. The question would be of major importance if the music were extant.

1640

CAVALLI: *Gli Amori di Apollo e di Dafne*

Carnival. Venice, S. Cass.

Text by G. F. Busenello (*rappresentati in musica*). Prologue and 3 acts.

Cavalli's second opera. Revived Venice, SS. G. et P., Carnival 1647. Score preserved. The libretto was printed (reprinted?) in 1656.

B. FERRARI: *Il Pastor regio*

[23 January]. Venice, S. Moisè

Text by the composer (*dramma . . . rappresentato in musica*). Prologue and 3 acts.

Ferrari's second opera. Music lost. Also given at Bologna [18 May] 1641; Genoa (indicated by Allacci without date); Piacenza 15 April 1646; Milan 1646.

1641

CAVALLI: *La Didone*

Carnival. Venice, S. Cass.

Text by G. F. Busenello (*opera rappresentata in musica*). Prologue and 3 acts.

Text printed as late as 1656 (separately, and in Busenello's *Ore ociose*); in 1641 only an *Argomento e scenario* was published. One of Cavalli's more important works. Score preserved.

SACRATI: *La finta Pazza*

[14 January]. Venice, T. Novissimo

Text by G. Strozzi. Prologue and 3 acts.

No connection with *La finta Pazza Licori*, another libretto by Strozzi, set to music by Monteverdi in 1627. Sacrati's opera was written for the opening of the fourth Venetian opera-house ("Teatro Novissimo"); it was very successful there (performed 12 times in 17 days) and was perhaps revived at the same theatre in 1644 (as the libretto was reprinted in that year). It was also given at Piacenza 1644; Bologna 1647; Genoa 1647; Milan 1662.

La finta Pazza was also one of the first Italian operas ever performed in Paris (at the Salle du Petit Bourbon 14 December 1645). Strictly speaking, it was the second, having been preceded by an unknown Italian opera, performed at the Palais Royal in February or March of the same year 1645, as we know from a letter written by the singer Atto Melani (the brother of the composer Jacopo Melani) to his protector Prince Mattias de'Medici.

Ademollo who first published that letter (in his *I primi Fasti della Musica italiana a Parigi*, 1884) suggested that the unknown opera, mentioned by Melani, might have been *La finta Pazza*; consequently the date of 25 February 1645 for the Paris production of Sacrati's opera is given in many books of reference.

In 1913 H. Prunières published his *L'Opéra Italien en France avant Lulli* in which he demonstrated that it must have been a different work which was produced in Paris in Carnival 1645. But, on his part, Prunières conjectured that the unknown opera was *Nicandro e Fileno* (by Lorenzani, see 1681), the music of which, discovered by Prunières himself some years later, he attributed to Marazzoli. And, although Prunières corrected himself (*Revue Musicale*, August 1922), his conjecture left its traces in many books published not only between 1913 and 1922 but also later (as in E. J. Dent's *Foundations of English Opera*, 1928, p.45). We still do not know which Italian opera actually was performed in Paris in February 1645.

We may assume that, when H. Kretzschmar in *Jahrbuch der Musik-Bibliothek Peters*, 1903, p.82, expressly rectifies a "mistake" of Grimm's (which is no mistake but perfectly correct), he was a victim of the same confusion.

MONTEVERDI: *Il Ritorno d'Ulisse in Patria*

February. Venice, S. Cass.

Text by G. Badoaro. Prologue and 5 acts.

Of this opera only a scenario was printed in 1641; a MS of the libretto is in the Biblioteca di S. Marco, Venice, a MS of the score in the National-Bibliothek, Vienna. (The authenticity of the latter has been doubted by some authorities.) The score was published in 1923 (in *Denkmäler der Tonkunst in Österreich*, edited by R. Haas). From some differences between the Venice libretto and the Vienna score (which is in 3 acts) it would appear that the opera was altered for a Vienna production; but there is no evidence to show that a performance at Vienna actually took place.

The opera was revived in concert form at the Institut des Hautes Études, Brussels 9 January 1925 (fragments only; French version by C. van den Borren); on the stage: Paris, Petite Scène 16 May 1925 (French version by X. de Courville, reduced to 3 acts, music adapted and re-scored by Vincent d'Indy); and, once more, in concert form, by the Schola Cantorum Paris 25 February 1927. In London the work was broadcast 16 January 1928 (English version by D. M. Craig).

1642

LUIGI ROSSI: *Palazzo d'Atlante incantato*

22 February. Rome, Pal. Barberini

Text by G. Rospigliosi (the future Pope Clement IX). Three acts.

Apparently no libretto was printed. The above title is taken from a MS copy of the text (*Biblioteca Nazionale*, Florence). Different titles are to be found in MS copies of the score, viz. *Il Palagio d'Atlante: overo La Guerriera amante* (Bologna score) and *Il Palazzo incantato* (Rome score).

The opera seems to have been revived at Pesaro about 1670. Extracts from the music were published by H. Goldschmidt in 1901.

MONTEVERDI: *L'Incoronatione di Poppea*

Autumn. Venice, SS.G. e P.

Text by G. F. Busenello (*opera musicale*). Prologue and 3 acts.

Monteverdi's last opera. Revived at Venice, SS. G. e P. Carnival 1646; given at Naples 1651 (as *Il Nerone overo L'incoronatione di Poppea*), by the company of "I Febi Armonici" as one of the earliest operas there, if not the first.

Libretto printed in 1651 (at Naples) and 1656 (in Busenello's *Ore ociose*). For the Venice productions in 1642 and 1646 only scenarios were printed.

From the MS score at the Biblioteca di San Marco, Venice, the music was published by H. Goldschmidt in 1904 (in Vol. II of *Studien zur Geschichte der italienischen Oper im 17. Jahrhundert*). The Naples score has also been preserved. A facsimile edition of the Venice score was published in 1938 (edited by G. Benvenuti).

L'Incoronatione di Poppea is the first opera on a historical (instead of mythological, biblical, or poetical) subject. It has been revived frequently in recent times, first in concert form, by the Schola Cantorum, Paris 24 February 1905 (music arranged by V. d'Indy); at the Institut des Hautes Études, Brussels February 1922 (in Italian).

Stage productions took place at:

PARIS, TH. DES ARTS 5 February 1913 (in French).

NORTHAMPTON, MASS., SMITH COLLEGE 27 April 1926.

BUENOS AIRES 9 August 1927 (d'Indy's version) and 7 August 1938 (Benvenuti's version).

OXFORD, UNIVERSITY OPERA CLUB 6 December 1927 (in English, translated by R. L. Stuart).

NEW YORK, JUILLIARD SCHOOL OF MUSIC 23 February 1933 (in Italian).

FLORENCE, GIARDINO BOBOLI 3 June 1937 (music arranged by G. Benvenuti).

VIENNA, V.O. 25 September 1937 (in German, translated and orchestrated by E. Křenek).

PARIS, O.C. 23 December 1937 (in French, translated by C. van den Borren); this version had previously been heard at Brussels April 1923 (fragments only, in concert form, orchestrated by R. Moulaert).

1643

CAVALLI: *L'Egisto*

Autumn. Venice, S. Cass.

Text by G. Faustini (*Favola dramatica musicale*). Prologue and 3 acts.

Also given at Rome 1643 (at the French Ambassador's); Genoa 1645; Paris February 1040; Florence [27 May] 1646; Bologna, T. Formagliari 1647 (revived 1659); perhaps also Naples 1651 (unrecorded reprint of the libretto, published Venice and Naples 1651, in the British Museum). Libretto also reprinted Florence 1667; Modena 1667.

It has been stated by various authors that Cavalli wrote this opera for the Vienna court and that it was produced there in 1642. Apart from the fact that the autograph score of *L'Egisto* is in the Vienna National-Bibliothek, there is no evidence to show that the opera was produced there at all, let alone earlier than at Venice. Cavalli's 7th opera and the first he wrote for soloists only. He used the chorus again in his *Ercole amante*, 1662.

1644

STADEN: *Seelewig*

??. Nuremberg

Text by G. P. Harsdörffer. Prologue and 3 acts.

The full title reads: *Das Geistliche Waldgedicht, oder Freudenspiel, genant Seelewig, Gesangsweis auf Italienische Art gesetzet.* Published in Harsdörffer's *Frauenzimmer Gesprechspiele* (8 vols., 1641–1649), Vol. IV (1644), first the text, and on pp.489–622

the music, for voices and thorough bass. It was reprinted, in vocal score, by R. Eitner in 1881 (in Vol. XIII of *Monatshefte für Musik-Geschichte*).

In a note, Harsdörffer alludes to a performance (which presumably took place at some private house at Nuremberg). There are records of productions at Wolfenbüttel in 1654 and at Augsburg as late as 1698 (see *Die Musik*, III, p.345). Revivals took place at Cologne in 1912 (arranged by R. Schulz-Dornburg) and at Gera in 1924.

As the music of Schütz's *Daphne* (see 1627) is lost, *Seelewig* is regarded as the first extant example of German opera. The first German opera preserved in full score dates only from 1671 (*q.v.*).

1645

ROVETTA: *Ercole in Lidia*

Carnival. Venice, T. Novissimo

Text by M. Bisaccioni. Prologue and 3 acts.

The first and probably the only produced opera of Rovetta, who in 1643 had succeeded Monteverdi as maestro di cappella of S. Marco, Venice. (He himself was succeeded by Cavalli in 1668.) John Evelyn attended a performance of this opera (see his *Diary*, Bray's edition, I, p.204). Music lost.

COLONNA: *La Proserpina rapita*

5 January. Rome, Pal. Gallicano

Text by O. Castelli. Prologue and five acts.

A MS score of this opera was discovered in the Royal Music Library, British Museum, and identified by W. Barclay Squire (see his paper *An Opera under Innocent X*, in *Gedenkboek . . . Dr. D. F. Scheurleer*, 1925).

John Evelyn was present at a revival on 8 April 1645, and mentions the performance in his *Diary* (Bray's edition, I, p.177). Of the libretto no copy seems to have been traced yet.

"The whole work is not a masterpiece, but so few operas of the Roman School of the period have survived that its recovery is of considerable musical interest" (W. B. Squire).

1647

LUIGI ROSSI: *L'Orfeo*

2 March. Paris, Palais Royal

Text by F. Buti (*tragicomedia per musica*). Prologue and 3 acts.

The libretto was not printed; a manuscript of it is in the Biblioteca Barberini, Rome. Only an "abrégé," in French, was published in 1647. The score was discovered by Romain Rolland in the Biblioteca Chigi, Rome, in 1888, and parts of the music were printed in H. Goldschmidt's *Studien zur Geschichte der italienischen Oper im 17. Jahrhundert* (1901).

Not the first Italian opera produced at Paris, but the first which was commissioned and expressly written for the French capital. The dates of 26 February or 3 March (given in some books of reference) are to be rectified. See further, H. Prunières, *L'Opéra en France avant Lulli* (1913), pp.86–150.

1649

CAVALLI: *Giasone*

[*5 January*]. Venice, S. Cass.

Text by G. A. Cicognini (*dramma musicale*). Prologue and 3 acts.

Cavalli's most successful work; the libretto had to be reprinted at Venice three times in the course of two years, and there were further editions in 1654, 1664, and 1666. *Giasone* was subsequently given at Milan 1650; Florence 1650; Bologna December 1651; Naples 1653; Rome 1654; Piacenza 1655; Palermo 1655; Vicenza 1658; Ferrara 1659; Viterbo 1659; Genoa 1661; Ancona December 1664; Siena 1666 (altered); Brescia 1667.

There were revivals at Florence 1651, 1656, 1658, 1662 and 1680; Naples 1661, 1667 and 1672; Milan 1662; Venice, S. Cass. 23 February 1666; Rome, Tord. 24 January 1671 (as *Il novello Giasone*, with a new prologue and other additions by A. Stradella); and Bologna 1673. A last revival at Rome in 1676 according to Ademollo did not

take place owing to Pope Innocent XI's dislike of theatrical entertainments. The libretto, however, was printed beforehand (copies in the Conservatoire, Brussels, and in the British Museum). Sonneck, in his note on the Rome 1671 edition of *Giasone* (Washington Catalogue, p.557), misinterprets Wotquenne's remark (Brussels Catalogue, p.78); it was the 1676, not the 1671, revival which was prohibited (Innocent XI was not elected until 1676).

The music of *Giasone* has been preserved; parts of it were published by Eitner in Vol. XII of *Publikationen der Gesellschaft für Musikforschung* (1883).

CESTI: *Orontea*

[*20 January*]. Venice, SS. Apostoli

Text by G. A. Cicognini (*drama musicale*). Prologue and 3 acts.

Cesti's first opera. Written for the inauguration of the short-lived Teatro dei Santi Apostoli (which was the fifth Venetian opera-house). Very successful in Italy and one of the earliest Italian operas to be given in Germany. Revived at Venice, SS.G. e P. [10 January] 1666 and Carnival 1683. Outside Venice produced at Genoa 1660; Turin 1662; Milan 1662 and 1664; Ferrara 1663; Macerata [22 June] 1665; Bologna 1665 and 1669; Palermo 1667; Lucca Carnival 1668; Naples privately 1674 ("musica rinnovata" perhaps at the Princess of Avellino's, by the "Filomolpi"); Reggio 1674; Hanover February 1678 (probably first opera there, text revised); Wolfenbüttel August 1686.

There must have been other productions between 1649 and 1662, as in the Turin libretto is an allusion to the successful vogue of *Orontea* in all parts of Italy.

(For a French adaptation of the libretto, see 1688.)

LEARDINI: *La Psiche*

September. Mantua

Text by D. Gabrielli (*tragicomedia rappresentata in musica*). Prologue and 5 acts.

Written for the wedding of Charles II, Duke of Mantua, with Isabella Clara, Archduchess of Austria. Score preserved.

1650

DASSOUCY: *Andromède*

February. Paris, Petit Bourbon

Text by P. Corneille. Prologue and 5 acts.

This *Tragedie Representée avec les Machines* . . . may be and has been regarded as a forerunner of French opera. The music, it is true, plays but a subordinate part in the play; there are some airs and duets and several choruses. In a letter written in 1672, Dassoucy claims: "Il scait que c'est moi qui ay donné l'âme aux vers de l'Andromède de Mr. de Corneille." Only fragments of the music are extant. *Andromède* was revived at the Comédie-Française 19 July 1682, with new music by Charpentier. A Dutch translation by F. Ryk was published in 1699.

See J. Carlez, *Pierre et Thomas Corneille, Librettistes* (1881), pp.8–16; H. Prunières in his *L'Opéra italien en France avant Lulli* (1913) and in *Revue Musicale*, 1937–39 ("Les Aventures de M. Dassoucy"). Prunières mentions another early operatic attempt by the same composer, a pastoral play *Les Amours d'Apollon et de Daphné*, of which Dassoucy also wrote the words. The text was printed in 1650, but there is no record of a performance.

ZAMPONI: *Ulisse all'Isola di Circe*

24 February. Brussels

Text probably by A. Amalteo (who signed the dedicatory poem in the libretto). Prologue, 3 acts and licenza.

First opera ever produced at Brussels, celebrating the wedding of Philip IV, King of Spain, with the Archduchess Maria Anna of Austria. Repeated at Brussels 4 February 1655 in honour of a visit of Queen Christina of Sweden. Libretto printed in 1650 (copy at Dresden). Score preserved (at Vienna).

See R. Haas in *Zeitschrift für Musikwissenschaft*, Vol. III (1920–21), p.385, and Vol. V (1922–23), p.63; and H. Liebrecht in *Le Flambeau*, December 1921.

1651

CAVALLI: *L'Oristeo*

Carnival. Venice, S. Apollinare

Text by G. Faustini (*drama per musica*). Prologue and 3 acts.

Written for the inauguration of the short-lived Teatro Sant' Apollinare which was the sixth Venetian opera-house.

Revived Bologna [2 January] 1656 as *L'Oristeo travestito*, altered (*per così dire, mascherato*); according to Allacci with intermezzi by Niccolò Zoppio Turchi, but they do not appear in the Bologna libretto as described by Sonneck. Perhaps he was responsible for the numerous alterations.

CAVALLI: *Alessandro Vincitor di se Stesso*

[*20 January*]. Venice, SS.G. e P.

Text by F. Sbarra (*dramma musicale*). Prologue and 3 acts.

One of Cavalli's more successful works. Given at:

FLORENCE [15 January] 1653 (libretto British Museum; 15 January 1653 is the date of dedication; imprint 1654)

BOLOGNA 1655

MUNICH 28 February 1658 }
MILAN 1659 } (probably Cavalli's setting)
NAPLES [8 October] 1662 }

As hardly any of the above-mentioned librettos have the name of the composer, it should be mentioned that there exists a second setting by Cesti and Bigongiari (see Sonneck's Catalogue, p.56), produced at Lucca 3 February 1654. This Lucca edition is remarkable as a very early instance of a libretto with a printed cast. A new edition (*quarta impressione*), Rome 1664 (see Wotquenne's Catalogue p.11) was printed for reading purposes rather than for an actual revival, as it retains the Lucca cast; so was the Bologna edition of 1683, mentioned by Allaci.

1652

BERTALI: *Theti*

March. Mantua

Text by D. Gabrielli (*Favola dramatica*). Prologue and 5 acts.

Produced to celebrate the arrival of the Archduke Ferdinand Carl and his consort Anna de'Medici on their visit to Italy. Revived Vienna 13 July 1656.

One of the few operas of Bertali, the music of which is extant. Bertali had been appointed court conductor at Vienna in 1649 (succeeding Giovanni Valentini), and as opera performances began at Vienna about that year, he is the first holder of that important post with whom we have to deal. Felice Sances became his successor in 1669 (*q.v.*).

1653

BERTALI: *L'Inganno d'Amore*

[*20 February*]. Regensburg

Text by B. Ferrari. Prologue and 3 acts.

Besides the Italian libretto, a German argument *Innhalt und Verfassung der Comoedi Von Liebs Betrug* was published in 1653.

One of the earliest Italian operas performed in Germany. It was dedicated to the Emperor Ferdinand III and produced at the Imperial Diet. Music lost.

CAVALLI: *L'Orione*

[*15 June*]. Milan, T.R.D.

Text by F. Melosio. Prologue and 3 acts.

The first opera Cavalli was commissioned to write for a town other than Venice (to celebrate the election of Ferdinand IV as King of the Romans).

The opera does not seem to have been revived at Venice, although the text was reprinted there

(in 1683 according to Allacci; but also earlier, in 1673, as a copy in the British Museum proves). Libretto also published Genoa 1653.

MARAZZOLI and ABBATINI: *Dal Male il Bene*

About *July.* Rome, Pal. Barberini

Text by G. Rospigliosi (the future Pope Clement IX). *Dramma musicale.* Prologue and 3 acts. First and third act composed by Abbatini, second act by Marazzoli.

Libretto not printed. Music extant (partly published by H. Goldschmidt in 1901). Produced at the wedding of Maffeo Barberini, Prince of Palestrina, with Olimpia Giustiniani.

1654

CAVALLI: *Xerse*

[*12 January*]. Venice, SS.G. e P.

Text by N. Minato. Prologue and 3 acts.

One of Cavalli's most celebrated works. Given at Genoa 1656; Naples 1657; revived at Venice 1657 (with new prologue, intermezzi and other additions); Bologna 1657 (with alterations); Palermo 1658 (first opera ever produced there; with alterations and comic intermezzi); Verona 1665 and Milan 1665 (altered by C. Righenzi).

In Italian also given at Paris 22 November 1660 (at the Grande Galerie du Louvre, celebrating the wedding of Louis XIV and Maria Theresa of Austria; Lully provided the airs de ballet for this production).

CAVALLI: *Il Ciro*

[*30 January*]. Venice, SS.G. e P.

Text by G. C. Sorentino (according to the preface earlier given at Naples with music by some other, unknown, composer). Prologue and 3 acts.

According to the preface, Cavalli composed only those parts of the music made necessary by the textual alterations *per accomodarsi al costume* of Venice.

Also given at Genoa 1654; revived Venice, SS. G. e P. [4 February] 1665 (with additional music by A. Mattioli); Bologna Carnival 1666 (with intermezzi by G. P. Cremata) and 1671; Modena 1675; Perugia 1678; Pistoia 1697.

The prologue was published by E. Wellesz in 1913 (Vol. I of *Studien zur Musikwissenschaft*).

CAPROLI: *Le Nozze di Peléo e di Theti*

14 April. Paris, Petit Bourbon

Text by F. Buti. Prologue and 3 acts.

After Rossi's *Orfeo* (see 1647), this was the second Italian opera commissioned and written expressly for Paris. Libretto printed in 1654. Of the music only the airs de ballet are extant (whether they were composed by Caproli, or rather by some French composer, is an open question).

"L'Orfeo avait été un véritable opéra; les ballets qui s'y trouvaient n'avaient qu'un rôle en quelque sorte décoratif et étaient dansés par des professionels. Au contraire dans Le Nozze la fusion de l'opéra italien et du ballet de Cour français est aussi complète que possible. Le ballet, au lieu de se suffire à lui-même, tire sa raison d'être de la comédie et celle-ci fait participer le ballet à l'action dramatique" (Prunières).

Buti's text seems to be the earliest Italian libretto which was translated into English, as "*The Nuptials of Peleus and Thetis*. A new Italian Comedy, whence the preceding Mask was extracted; Made English by a nearer adherence to the Original, than to the French Translation," 1654. The translator was James Howell, Historiographer Royal to Charles II. (In the British Museum catalogued, with a question-mark, as a translation of D. Gabrielli's 5-act *Theti* text, see 1652.)

CIRILLO: *L'Orontea Regina di Egitto*

??. Naples

Cicognini's text (first composed by Cesti, see 1649). Three acts.

The first extant example of an opera by a Neapolitan composer, though possibly some of Cesti's music was retained. The libretto published in 1654 says the work was "arricchita di nuova musica da Francesco Cirillo". For an analysis of the score see N. d'Arienzo's *Dell' opera comica dalle origini a G. B. Pergolesi* (1887). It is not known whether the opera was produced at the Teatro S. Bartolomeo, at the Royal Palace, or elsewhere.

1655

CAVALLI: *L'Erismena*

January. Venice, Sant'Apollinare

Text by A. Aureli. Prologue and 3 acts.

Revised Venice, S. Salv. [13 February] 1670 (with alterations and without the prologue). Also given at Bologna, T. Formagliari 1661 and revived there 1668; Florence 1661; Milan [11 February] 1661; Genoa 1666; Lucca Carnival 1668; Forlì 1673 (with added intermezzi); and Brescia (undated libretto printed).

The scores of both the 1655 and the 1670 versions are extant.

LA GUERRE: *Le Triomphe de l'Amour sur des Bergers et Bergères*

22 January. Paris, Louvre

Text by C. de Beys. One act.

Libretto printed 1654 (copy Bibl. Mazarine, Paris) and again *c.*1661–62 (copy Bibl. Nat., Paris). Called in the second edition *Pastorale . . . mise en musique.*

Publicly rehearsed 15 December 1654, first performed at the Louvre 22 January 1655, probably in concert form.

Repeated, as indicated in the second edition, 26 March 1657 "Devant Leurs Majestez" with some alterations and, this time, probably with scenery.

In a dedicatory letter to Louis XIV (in his *Oeuvres en vers de divers Autheurs . . .*, *c.*1662) La Guerre says: "Il y a quelques années qu'ayant eu l'honneur de faire représenter devant Votre Majesté une Comédie française en Musique, intitulée Le Triomphe de l'Amour, Elle témoigna ne pas désagréer tout a fait la nouveauté de cette Pièce, dont j'avois inventé la manière et qui est en effet le premier ouvrage de cette sorte qui ait jamais paru en ce Royaume. . . ." Four years later, exactly the same claim was made by Perrin and Cambert (see 1659).

The discovery of this earliest example of French opera is due to H. Quittard (*La première comédie française en musique*, in *Bulletin Français de la S.I.M.*, April and May, 1908).

The music, like that of Cambert's *Pastorale* (see 1659) seems to be lost.

CESTI: *L'Argia*

4 November. Innsbruck

Text by A. Apolloni (*dramma musicale*). Prologue and 3 acts.

Produced at Innsbruck in the presence of Queen Christina of Sweden, in honour of her conversion to Catholicism. Also given at Rome 1657 and 1661 (libretto published; produced?); Naples 1667; Venice, S. Salv. [13 January] 1669 (altered and without the prologue); Milan [20 February] 1669; Siena 1670 (first opera there); Genoa and Reggio 1671; Udine 1673. For an account of the Innsbruck production see A. Sandberger in *Svensk Tidskrift för Musikforskning*, 1924.

1656

MARAZZOLI: *La Vita umana* ovvero *Il Trionfo della Pietà*

31 January. Rome, Pal. Barberini

Text probably by J. Rospigliosi. Prologue and 3 acts.

The libretto (published in 1656 as *Il Trionfo della Pietà*) has been attributed to Giulio Rospigliosi, the future Pope Clement IX. That it was written by his nephew Jacopo, appears from the *Historia . . . di Christina . . . di Svetia*, by Gualdo Priorato Conte Goleazzo, published at Rome in

the same year, 1656. Last opera produced at the the Barberini Theatre, in honour of Queen Christina of Sweden, to whom the score (*Dramma musicale*) is dedicated. It was printed in 1658, apart from Bontempi's *Paride* (see 1662), the last Italian opera of the 17th century which was published. It is only about 100 years later that we find printed scores of Italian operas again. (See the astonishingly small list compiled by O. G. T. Sonneck in his *Miscellaneous Studies in the History of Music*, 1921, pp.305-7.) While printed scores of Italian operas are an exception, they are the rule with French operas; nearly all of them were published, until 1775 almost exclusively by the firm of Ballard.

LOCKE and others: *The Siege of Rhodes*

September. London, Rutland House

Text by W. D'Avenant. ("Made a Representation by the Art of Prospective in Scenes, And the Story sung in Recitative Musick. At the back part of Rutland-House in the upper end of Aldersgate-Street.") Five entries.

Libretto printed in 1656 (dedication dated 17/27 August). From D'Avenant's preface we learn that "The Musick was compos'd and both the Vocal and Instrumental is exercis'd by the most transcendent of England in that Art, and perhaps not unequal to the best Masters abroad; but being Recitative, and therefore unpractis'd here; though of great reputation amongst other Nations, the very attempt of it is an obligation to our own."

At the end of the libretto, the composers are enumerated as follows:

The Composition of Vocal Musick was perform'd

	First Entry		Mr. Henry Lawes
	Second Entry		Capt. Henry Cook
The	Third Entry	by	Capt. Henry Cook
	Fourth Entry		Mr. Matthew Lock
	Fifth Entry		Mr. Henry Lawes

The Instrumental Musick was compos'd by Dr. Charles Coleman, and Mr. George Hudson.

The text was reprinted in 1659, and again in 1663 and 1670, followed by a second part, "as they were lately (probably 28 June/8 July 1661, first part, and 29 June/9 July, second part; cf. Pepys, 2 July 1661) represented at His Highness the Duke of York's Theatre in Lincolns-Inn Fields". In the 1663 edition no composers are mentioned.

The Siege of Rhodes is rightly to be claimed as the first English opera. It was regarded as such as early as 1695, in the preface to *The Fairy-Queen* (see 1695): "That Sir William Davenant's *Siege of Rhodes* was the first Opera we ever had in England, no Man can deny; and is indeed a perfect Opera. . . ."

The music of *The Siege of Rhodes* unfortunately seems to be lost.

MELANI: *Il Potestà di Colognole*

c.26 December. Florence, P.

Text by G. A. Moniglia (*Dramma Civile Rusticale*). Three acts.

Written for the inauguration of the "Teatro degli Immobili in Via della Pergola," Florence.

Original libretto in the Rolandi collection, Rome. The score in the Biblioteca Chigi, Rome (discovered by Rolland), has the title *La Tancia overo Il Podestà di Colognole*.

The text was reprinted in 1689 in Moniglia's *Poesie Dramatiche*. In the preface to this edition Moniglia states that the opera was repeated at Florence (Teatro de' SS. Accademici Infuocati) in honour of the Archduke Ferdinand Carl of Austria, and that it was performed also at Bologna, Pisa and in other towns of Tuscany.

The revival at Florence was in Autumn 1661 (dedication dated 6 October 1661), the production at Bologna in 1673 (according to Allacci). No Pisa nor any other edition recorded by Allacci.

Contains a parody of the incantation scene in Cavalli's *Giasone* (published in *Atti dell' Acc. del R. Ist. Musicale di Firenze*, XXXIII (1895), Suppl. no.3). See for an analysis of the opera, H. Goldschmidt's *Studien zur Geschichte der italienischen Oper im 17. Jahrhundert* (1901), where also parts of the music are reprinted.

1657

P. A. ZIANI: *Le Fortune di Rodope, e di Damira*

Carnival. Venice, S. Apollinare

Text by A. Aureli. Prologue and 3 acts.

Ziani's first extant opera and one of his best works. Also given at Bologna Carnival 1658 (revived 1670); Milan 1660; Leghorn [15 May] 1661; Turin 1662 (as one of the first operas ever given there); Ferrara 1662; Palermo 1669; Reggio 1674.

This was the only opera produced at Venice in 1657 and the last which was given at the T. S. Apollinare.

KERLL: *L'Oronte*

February. Munich

Text by G. G. Alcaini. Prologue and 3 acts.

Written for the inauguration of the first Munich opera-house. Music lost, like the rest of Kerll's Italian operas.

The building of the first Munich opera-house was pulled down in 1802. Later opera-houses were the Residenz-Theater (opened with Ferradini's *Catone in Utica*, see 1753) and the Hof- und Nationaltheater (opened 12 October 1818, burnt down 14 January 1823, re-opened 2 January 1825).

J. J. LOEWE?: *Amelinde*

20 April. Brunswick

Text by Anton Ulrich, Duke of Brunswick (*Singe-Spiel*). Prologue, 5 acts, and epilogue.

The full title reads: *Amelinde, Oder: Dy triumphirende Seele, Wy sy nach vielerley versuchenden Anfechtungen überwindet, und Göttlicher Gnade fähig wird*. Of this early German opera only the libretto is extant. The music probably was by Loewe.

1658

LUCCIO: *Il Medoro*

[11 January]. Venice, SS.G. e P.

Text by A. Aureli (founded on an episode in Ariosto's *Orlando furioso*). Prologue and 3 acts.

The last of Luccio's four operas and the only one which is extant (MS score at Venice; airs printed).

Kretzschmar calls attention to the overture and to the ghost-raising scene of this opera.

(The name of the composer appears in different publications as Luzzo, Lucio, or Luccio. The works listed by Eitner, VI, pp.237 and 258, belong to one and the same composer.)

CAVALLI: *L'Hipermestra*

18 June. Florence, P.

Text by G. A. Moniglia. Prologue and 3 acts.

Written to celebrate the birth of the Infante of Spain, son of King Philip IV. This was the third opera performed at the Teatro della Pergola.

In the preface to the libretto Cavalli is called "egli che viene oggi reputato il primo compositore d'Italia, particolarmente sopra lo stile drammatico". The libretto was reprinted at Bologna in the same year.

1659

CAMBERT: *Pastorale*

April. Issy

Text by P. Perrin. Five acts.

The full title reads: "Première Comedie Française en Musique, Representée en France. Pastorale. Mise en Musique par Monsieur Camber...." First produced privately at M. de la Haye's at Issy, near Paris (the house is now the Séminaire de Saint-Sulpice), and after eight or ten performances there also given at Vincennes before Louis XIV (still in April 1659), on Mazarin's suggestion.

Perrin gives a detailed account of the *Pastorale* and its production in a letter to the Archbishop of Turin, dated 30 April 1659, which he printed as a preface to a new edition of the libretto in his *Les Oeuvres de Poesie* (Paris 1661). The letter has been reprinted in Pougin's *Les vrais Créateurs de l'Opéra français* (1881). It is a very interesting document and of high importance for the early history of French opera.

The music of this, Cambert's first opera, is lost.

The text was first printed in 1659 (*permission d'imprimer* dated 16 March) and again in 1661 (see above).

The *Pastorale d'Issy*, as it is commonly called, was for a long time regarded as the first French opera until Henry Quittard pointed out the priority of La Guerre's *Le Triomphe de l'Amour* (see 1655).

MARIANI: *Amore vuol Gioventù*

??. Viterbo

Text by L. Cortesi (*Scherzo drammatico*). Three acts.

Also given at Bologna 1664. Of this early comic opera (three characters only) no libretto seems to be known. The score has been preserved in the Biblioteca di S. Marco, Venice.

J. J. LOEWE: *Orpheus aus Thracien*

30 August. Wolfenbüttel

Text by Anton Ulrich, Duke of Brunswick (*Tragisches Gedicht*). Prologue and 3 acts.

The music of this second opera of Loewe (cf. 1657) is also lost.

Only the libretto is extant, the full title of which reads: *Orpheus aus Thracien, Der Calliope und des Apollinis Sohn, wie er seine Eurydice nach ihrem Tode unter der Erden gesuchet, gefunden, und wieder verlohren, auch selbst elendiglich umbkommen.*

1660

P. A. ZIANI: *L'Antigona delusa da Alceste*

[*15 January*]. Venice, SS.G. e P.

Text by A. Aureli (*drama per musica*). Prologue and 3 acts.

One of the older Ziani's most successful operas. Given at Bologna 1661; Milan [15 April] 1662; Naples 1669; Venice, S. Salv. Carnival 1670 (revived); Hanover February 1679 (as *L'Alceste*, text revised by O. Mauro, with additional music by M. Trento) and June 1681 (with a new prologue by Valente, music by P. A. Fiocco).

HIDALGO: *Celos aun del Ayre matan*

5 December. Madrid, Buen Retiro

Text by P. Calderón de la Barca (*Festa . . . Cantada*). Three acts.

The libretto appears to have been first printed in 1662. The earliest Spanish opera (on the subject of Cephalus and Procris; the title means "Jealousy, even of air, is deadly") which has been partly preserved. The music of the first act ("Primera Jornada"), for voices and bass, was discovered by J. Subirá in the musical library at the Duke of Alba's palace (Biblioteca del Palacio de Liria), Madrid (see his *La Música en la Casa de Alba*, 1927, pp.57–82). Subirá edited a vocal score in 1933.

The date of production was established by E. Cotarelo y Mori (see *Boletín de la Academia Española*, December 1932, p.756). For an analysis of the work see O. Ursprung in *Festschrift Arnold Schering*, 1937.

1661

KERLL: *L'Erinto*

Carnival? Munich

Text by P. P. Bissari. Prologue and 3 acts.

Written to celebrate the birth of the Bavarian Princess Maria Anna Christina. Revived at Munich in August 1671 in honour of a visit of the Archbishop of Salzburg, Maximilian Gandolph. Music lost.

(As the Princess was born on 7 November 1660, the first production probably was in the following Carnival.)

CESTI: *La Dori* ovvero
La Schiava fedele

Carnival. Florence, T. dei Sorgenti

Text by A. Apolloni. Prologue and 3 acts.

One of the chief works and one of the most successful Italian operas of the 17th century. It was revived at Florence [24 or 25 October] at the same theatre in the same year and subsequently given at Venice, S. Salv. [1 January]

1663 (revived SS.G. e P. [16 January] 1667, with the sub-title *Lo Schiavo reggio*, and again in Carnival 1671); Ferrara 1663; Vienna 1664 (celebrating the peace with the Turks); Macerata 27 January 1665 (first opera there); Lucca Carnival 1665; Parma 1665; Bologna 1667 and Carnival 1672; Reggio 1668; Florence 1670; Rome, Tord. 31 December 1671 (with a new prologue and other additions by A. Stradella); Mantua 1672 (as *Il regio Schiavo*); Naples, Pal. Reale 6 November 1675 (revived S.B. 23 December 1688, with a prologue and other additions, partly by A. Scarlatti); Munich March 1680 (with a new prologue by G. A. Bernabei; text altered by V. Terzago).

Parts of the opera were published by Eitner in 1883 (Vol. XII of *Publikationen der Gesellschaft für Musikforschung*).

MELANI: *Ercole in Tebe*

8 July. Florence, P.

Text by G. A. Moniglia. Prologue and 5 acts.

Written for the wedding of Cosimo III de' Medici with the Princess Marguérite Louise d'Orléans.

A detailed description of this magnificent "Festa teatrale" (the production of which cost nearly 100,000 Tuscan pounds) is to be found in Ademollo's *I primi Fasti del Teatro di Via della Pergola in Firenze* (1884).

The libretto was later adapted "all' uso di Venetia" by A. Aureli and set to music by Boretti in 1670.

1662

CAVALLI: *Ercole amante*

7 February. Paris, Tuileries

Text by F. Buti. Prologue and 5 acts.

According to the libretto, originally written for the wedding of Louis XIV with Maria Theresa of Austria, which had taken place already on 9 July 1660. The belated production served for the inauguration of the "Théâtre des Machines" at the Tuileries palace. The only opera Cavalli wrote expressly for Paris. Lully provided the music for the accompanying ballets.

A French translation, probably by C. Lilij, was printed with the Italian libretto, Paris 1662, and also published separately at Antwerp in the same year (copies in the British Museum).

Not counting the Fontainebleau production of Lorenzani's *Nicandro e Fileno* in 1681, this was the last Italian opera performed in Paris for 67 years (Orlandini's *Il Marito Giocatore* in 1729 being the next), and the last Italian opera seria even for 149 years (up to the production of Paisiello's *Pirro* in 1811).

The first period of Italian opera at Paris, terminated by *Ercole amante*, can be summarized as follows:

(1) An unknown Italian opera   February 1645
(2) *La finta Pazza*, by Sacrati (see 1641)
                        14 December 1645
(3) *Egisto*, by Cavalli (see 1643)   February 1646
(4) *Orfeo*, by Rossi   2 March 1647
(5) *Le Nozze di Peleo*, by Caproli   14 April 1654
(6) *Xerse*, by Cavalli (see 1654) 22 November 1660
(7) *Ercole amante*, by Cavalli   7 February 1662

BONTEMPI: *Il Paride*

3 November. Dresden

Text by the composer (*opera musicale*). Five acts.

Written for the wedding of Erdmute Sophia, Princess of Saxony, with Christian Ernst, Margrave of Brandenburg-Bayreuth. Score printed in 1662.

First Italian opera produced at Dresden, on a provisional stage at the palace. Some years later, 27 January 1667, a regular opera-house was inaugurated with the same composer's *Il Teseo*. It was replaced by a new theatre in 1719 (see Lotti's *Giove in Argo*, 1717) and eventually by the Hoftheater, built by Semper (opened 12 April 1841; burnt down 21 September 1869; re-opened 2 February 1878).

1663

ROVETTINO: *Gl'Amori d'Apollo e di Leucotoe*

[*8 January*]. Venice, SS.G. e P.

Text by A. Aureli. Three acts.

Of the three operas of Rovettino (who in 1690 succeeded Legrenzi as maestro di cappella of S. Marco, Venice), the only one which is extant. It contains the earliest known example of an accompanied recitative (*recitativo stromentato*).

DRAGHI: *Achille in Sciro*

18 November. Vienna

Text by O. Ximenes. Prologue, 3 acts and licenza.

Draghi's first extant opera, out of a total of 172, most of them written for the Vienna court, between 1661–99.

1664

CAVALLI: *Scipione Africano*

[*9 February*]. Venice, SS.G. e P.

Text by N. Minato. Three acts.

Revived at the same theatre Carnival 1678 (with alterations by G. B. Viviani, text revised by T. Fattorini). Also given at Naples 6 November 1667; Florence 1669; Ferrara 1669; Bologna 1670; and Rome 8 January 1671 (with a prologue and intermezzi, *Lesbo e Ceffea*, by A. Stradella), at the inauguration of the Teatro "Tordinona" (= Torre di Nona), which was the first public opera-house at Rome. It was founded by Giacomo d'Alibert, pulled down in 1697, rebuilt in 1733 and, after a fire on 29 January 1787, again in 1795, then renamed "Teatro Apollo".

(See on the early history of the theatre, A. Cametti in *Nuova Antologia*, 1 February 1931.)

Scipione Africano also given at Perugia 1677 as *Il Trionfo della Continenza*; and Milan, T.R.D. [1 February] 1692.

1665

CAVALLI: *Mutio Scevola*

[*26 January*]. Venice, S. Salv.

Text by N. Minato. Prologue and 3 acts.

Also given at Bologna 1665 and 1667. Cavalli's thirty-ninth opera. Minato's libretto occurs again towards the end of the century, in anonymous settings at Milan, T.R.D. [20 January] 1690, Rome (1695), Naples (1698) and Turin (1700).

1666

SARTORIO: *Seleuco*

[*16 January*]. Venice, S. Salv.

Text by N. Minato. Three acts.

Revived at the same theatre [16 January] 1668; at Milan 1671. The first extant opera of Sartorio, who from 1666–75 was court conductor at Hanover.

CESTI: *Il Tito*

[*13 February*]. Venice, SS.G. e P.

Text by N. Beregani (*melodrama*). Three acts.

Revived Rome, Tord. [12 February] 1672 (with a prologue by A. Stradella); Lucca September 1676.

The libretto was dedicated to Maria Mancini, who mentions the opera in her memoirs: "J'y fus particulièrement favorisée par l'opéra de Tite qui me fut dédié, qui est assurément une des jolies pièces qu'on aie encore représenté au théâtre Grimani, où je voulus bien assister cinq fois de suite y prenant beaucoup de plaisir, et ayant même voulu cinq ans après qu'on la représentât de nouveau à Rome à la Tour di None."

1667

SARTORIO: *La Prosperità di Elio Seiano* and *La Caduta di Elio Seiano*

Carnival. Venice, S. Salv.

Text of both operas by N. Minato. Three acts each.

The first example of an operatic "cycle"; the two parts were performed in turns on successive nights later in the season, beginning probably on 3 February, when the dedication in the libretto of the second part was dated.

It should be noted that the dedication in the libretto of the first part is dated 15 January 1666, which is either a misprint or old style ("more Veneto"), as the libretto itself has the imprint 1667 and is listed as having been produced in Carnival 1667 by all chronologists of the Venetian stage.

The first part was revived at Pisa 1670; Rome, Tord. 24 January 1672 (with intermezzi and a prologue added), and probably also at Lucca 14 January 1675 and Bologna 1679.

CESTI: *Il Pomo d'Oro*

Carnival. Vienna

Text by F. Sbarra (*Festa teatrale*). Prologue and 5 acts.

Written to celebrate the wedding of the Emperor Leopold I with the Infanta Margherita of Spain. Revived at Vienna 12 July 1668 (for the Empress's birthday). Libretto printed in 1667 and 1668; in the latter year also a detailed argument, in German, was published; in 1672 there followed a German translation by J.G.Meyer. Of the music, only the prologue and the first, second and fourth acts are extant. They were published in Vols. III and IV of *Denkmäler der Tonkunst in Österreich* in 1896 and 1897 (edited by G. Adler).

The exact date of the first production cannot be established (see Adler's introduction); the wedding was on 12 December 1666, and the Carnival ended 2 February 1667.

It has been stated that *Il Pomo d'Oro* was revived at Madrid as late as 1703. But, according to Cotarelo y Mori, the play then produced was a mythological comedy of the same title and not Cesti's opera (which with its huge apparatus was not likely to be revived anywhere after the occasion for which it was written).

CESTI: *Le Disgrazie d'Amore*

Carnival. Vienna

Text by F. Sbarra (*dramma giocosomorale*). Prologue and 3 acts.

After *Il Pomo d'Oro* this was Cesti's second opera produced at Vienna in that Carnival. The prologue was composed by the Emperor Leopold I himself.

The libretto was reprinted at Rome later in the same year (dedication dated 14 December 1667), but (in spite of Ademollo's contrary statement) obviously rather for the book-shelf than for purposes of production. Score preserved.

1668

BORETTI: *Eliogabalo*

[*10 January*]. Venice, SS.G. e P.

Text by A. Aureli. Three acts.

Also given at Genoa 1670; Bologna, T. Formagliari 1671 (with intermezzi by G. L. Pocchettini); Rome, Tord. 4 January 1673 (one of the operas performed there in honour of Queen Christina of Sweden; with a prologue added for the occasion); Milan 1674.

1669

SANCES: *Apollo deluso*

9 June. Vienna

Text by A. Draghi (the composer, who also wrote librettos occasionally). Three acts and licenza.

Parts of the music were composed by the Emperor Leopold I (some airs published by G. Adler in *Musikalische Werke der Kaiser*, 1893). One of the few operas of Sances, who about the time of the production of *Apollo deluso* became court conductor at Vienna, succeeding Bertali (who had died I April 1669).

CAVALLI: *Il Coriolano*

??. Piacenza

Text by C. Ivanovich. Three acts.

Cavalli's forty-first and last opera. Music lost.

According to Allacci the opera was performed to celebrate the birth of Odoardo, son of the Duke Ranuccio II Farnese. The production is, however, not recorded in L. Balestrieri's *Feste e spettacoli alla corte dei Farnesi* (1909).

1670

MELANI: *Girello*

20 January. Florence, T. Cocomero

Text by F. Acciaiuoli (*Dramma Musicale Burlesco*). Prologue and 3 acts.

The story of this celebrated comic opera is rather complicated. The text was first published at Ronciglione (near Rome) in 1668 (a copy of this earliest edition is in the British Museum). The preface mentions a production at Rome "nello scorso Carnevale" (viz. at Palazzo Colonna in the beginning of February 1668) and in a notice to the reader, the anonymous author protests against the reproach of obscenity. The composer of that earliest production is unknown. Perhaps the music was written by Acciaiuoli himself, who was a poet and a musician as well as a producer and manager and inventor of theatrical machines. Next, there were productions at Macerata and Bologna in 1669, but it is only in 1670 that we know for certain that Melani's music was used as the Florence libretto mentions him ("Con la musica del Sig. Jacopo Melani, raro ingegno del nostro secolo"). Further productions, all of them anonymous, are recorded at Siena 1672; Naples, S.B. 1673; Milan, T.R.D. Carnival 1674; Ferrara [22 October] 1674; Modena 1675; Reggio 1676; Lucca September 1676 (not 1696); Venice, S. Moisè Carnival 1682; revived Bologna, T. Malvezzi Carnival 1696 and Florence, T. dei Sorgenti (?) 1697.

The music of *Girello* has been preserved in two anonymous scores at Naples and Modena respectively. But is it Melani's music? According to Ademollo the scores correspond to the original 1668 libretto rather than to those of the productions at Florence 1670, Naples 1673, and Modena 1675. For the Modena production Alessandro Stradella is known to have composed the prologue and it might have been used at Rome in 1668 already.

At Venice, 1682, the opera was sung by singers off-stage and performed by wax puppets. It has been stated that the music in 1682 was newly composed by one "Francesco Antonio Pistocchino," who has been identified with the well-known composer F. A. Pistocchi. But, as a matter of fact, the 1682 libretto is anonymous, as are all the others, and the music was attributed to Pistocchi only 50 years later by Bonlini. There is no sufficient evidence to show that Pistocchi ever composed *Il Girello*.

This was made clear by Ademollo as early as 1890 (see his paper "La Storia del Girello," in *Gazzetta Musicale di Milano*); but the music is still ascribed to Pistocchi in many books and catalogues, and his name is sometimes mentioned even in connection with earlier productions, such as 1672 (when Pistocchi was a boy of 13) and 1675.

DRAGHI: *Leonida in Tegea*

9 June. Vienna

Text by N. Minato. Three acts and licenza.

Written for the birthday of the Emperor Leopold I, who himself contributed two airs.

Revived Venice, S. Moisè [9 February] 1676 (with additional music by M. A. Ziani) and once more Vienna Carnival 1694.

SANCES: *Aristomene Messenio*

22 December. Vienna

Text by N. Minato. Three acts and licenza.

Written for the birthday of Queen Marianna of Spain. Sances's last opera.

1671

CAMBERT: *Pomone*

3 March. Paris, O.

Text by P. Perrin (*opera ou représentation en musique*); in later editions *pastorale*. Prologue and 5 acts.

With *Pomone* the Paris Opéra (then called "Académie Royale des Opera" and situated at the Salle du Jeu de Paume de la Bouteille, Rue des Fossez-de-Nesle, near Rue Guénégaud) was inaugurated. On 28 June 1669, Perrin had obtained the royal privilege of "faire chanter de pareilles Opera ou représentations en musique en vers françois, dans toute l'estendue de nostre royaume, pendant douze années". The date of the inauguration has been given as 18 or 19 March 1671, by elder historians. The date of 3 March has been fairly well established, from contemporary documents, by Nuitter and Thoinan (1886), and is generally accepted now.

Rehearsals or private performances of *Pomone* had taken place in June 1670 at the Sèvres palace of Marquis Alexandre de Rieux de Sourdéac who, besides Cambert and Perrin, must be mentioned as one of the first promoters of French opera and as its first producer.

The earliest literary allusion to *Pomone* occurs in 1677, in Saint-Evremond's comedy *Les Opera* (II, 4): "Pomone est le premier Opera françois qui ait paru sur le Théâtre. La Poésie en étoit fort méchante, la Musique belle." That scene in Saint-Evremond's comedy (which was never performed) contains similar comments on all the early French operas and is an important source of information (see Cambert's *Ariane*, 1674). The play was translated into German by J. C. Gottsched (as *Die Opern*, 1740) and in his version the remarks on French operas are turned into similar ones on the early German operas produced at Hamburg.

Altered by Grabu, *Pomone* was also performed at the Whitehall Theatre, London, in July 1674 (in French).

Of the music, only the prologue, the first act and a fragment of the second act have been preserved (in an unfinished printed edition; re-issued, in vocal score, by J. B. Weckerlin in 1881).

PERANDA and BONTEMPI: *Dafne*

3 September. Dresden

(German) text attributed to one of the composers, Bontempi, partly founded on M. Opitz's libretto of the same title (see 1627). Five acts.

The earliest German opera which is extant in fulls core (Dresden, Landesbibliothek). Original libretto apparently not printed, but preserved in MS.

The opera was revived at Dresden on 9 February 1672; 8 January 1673; 10 February 1678; and 23 February 1679.

For a full account see R. Engländer's paper in *Acta Musicologica*, vol. XIII (1941).

1672

PROVENZALE: *Il Schiavo di sua Moglie*

??. Naples?

Text by A. Perrucio e Fardella. Prologue and 3 acts.

The first of the two operas of Provenzale which are extant (see 1678). The MS score in the Biblioteca di Santa Cecilia, Rome, is dated 1671. But the libretto, hitherto unknown, was printed in 1672. See *Catalogo della Libreria Floncel*, Paris, 1774, no.2851. For an account of the opera see H. Goldschmidt in *Sammelbände of the I.M.S.*, Vol. VII (1905–06).

U. Prota–Giurleo (*Francesco Cirillo e l'introduzione del melodramma a Napoli*, Grumo Nevano, 1952, Appendix, p.31) gives Naples, S.B., as place of performance, and December 1671 (misprinted 1771] as the date. But these details are based only on assumptions.

PAGLIARDI: *Caligula delirante*

Carnival. Venice, SS.G. e P.

Text by D. Gisberti (originally called *La Pazzia*

in Trono, composed by Cavalli in 1660). Three acts.

Successful in Italy: given at Naples, Pal. Reale 29 January 1673 and subsequently at S.B.; Rome, Tord. 24 January 1674 (as *Il Caligola*, with alterations); Bologna, T. Formagliari 1674 (with intermezzi *Le Gare di Sdegno, d'Amore e di Gelosia*, text by F. M. Bordocchi, music by P. Franceschini); Milan T.R.D. [30 May] 1675 (libretto altered A. Lonati); Vicenza Carnival 1675 as *La Pazzia in Trono overo Caligula delirante*; Pesaro 1675. Revived Venice, SS.G. e P. Autumn 1680 (with additions); Rome, Capr. Carnival 1692; Lucca 5 February 1696.

According to Bonlini's and Groppo's catalogues it was the first opera produced at Venice in the Carnival of 1672. The dedication in the libretto, however, is dated 18 December 1672, which is either a misprint or would point to the Carnival of the following year.

CAMBERT: *Les Peines et les Plaisirs de l'Amour*

January or *February.* Paris, O.

Text by G. Gilbert. Prologue and 5 acts.

The full title reads: *Opéra, pastorale héroique des Peines et des Plaisirs de l'Amour, en vers lyriques . . . Representée en musique. . . .* Of the music only the prologue and the first act have been preserved (re-issued in vocal score by J. B. Weckerlin in 1881).

The last opera of Cambert produced in Paris before he went to London in September 1673.

The date of the first production has not been fixed yet. The original libretto gives only the year, 1672. The performance must have taken place before 1 April 1672, as on that date the "Théâtre du Jeu de Paume de la Bouteille" was closed by Royal decree. (This disposes of the date of 8 April 1672, given by Léris and many others.) According to Nuitter and Thoinan, the production was in February or in the beginning of March, according to Mélèse in January. The first act was revived privately at Malmaison 24 June 1928 (under F. Raugel).

SARTORIO: *L'Adelaide*

[*19 February*]. Venice, S. Salv.

Text by P. Dolfino. Three acts.

Sartorio's chief work, "von der wundervollen Ouverture ab eine Kabinettsleistung an Erfindung" (Kretzschmar). Revived at Brussels 27 August 1681 (in Italian).

LULLY: *Les Festes de l'Amour et de Bacchus*

15 November. Paris, O.

Text by P. Quinault (in collaboration with Molière and I. de Benserade). Prologue and 3 acts.

This pastorale was Lully's first opera, being more or less a pasticcio made up from music of his earlier ballets (such as *Le Bourgeois Gentilhomme*, *Georges Dandin*, and others).

The performance took place at the Salle du Jeu de Paume de Bel-Air, in Rue de Vaugirard, after Cambert's first theatre had been closed down earlier in the year and the opera privilege, after an inextricable chain of intrigues, had passed (March 1672) from Perrin and Cambert to Lully, to remain with him until his death.

The opera was also given at Amsterdam 5 July 1688 and revived in Paris 1689; 1696; August 1706; 1716; and 13 February 1738 (parts only). Revived in French at Düsseldorf 1710; Lille 1720.

Score published 1717. In the same year appeared a Dutch translation by D. Buijsero.

SARTORIO: *L'Orfeo*

[*14 December*]. Venice, S. Salv.

Text by A. Aureli. Prologue and 3 acts.

Also given at Naples, Pal. Reale Autumn 1682; Brunswick August 1690 (in Italian; a German translation by J. C. Lorber was printed for that occasion). Revived as *Orfeo o sia Amore spesso inganna* (with many alterations) at Bologna, T. Formagliari 23 January 1695; Turin [20 April] 1697; Genoa Carnival 1706.

A production at Vienna in 1672 (as *Orfeo ed Euridice*, earlier than at Venice?) is recorded by Köchel rather vaguely.

1673

LULLY: *Cadmus et Hermione*

27 April. Paris, O.

Text by P. Quinault. Prologue and 5 acts.

The first French tragédie-lyrique, performed at the Th. du Jeu de Paume de Bel-Air and transferred to the new home of the Opéra, at the Palais-Royal, in 1674. Louis XIV was present at the first night, and according to the *Gazette de France* the Royal party "sortit extraordinairement satisfaite de ce superbe spectacle". Revived at St. Germain en Laye 5 June 1678; Paris October 1679; 4 December 1690; 21 September 1703; 28 August 1711; and 22 August 1737. Given at Amsterdam 1687 (in French; a Dutch translation by T. Arendsz was published in that year); at Brussels November 1734 (in Flemish). The last Paris revival was followed by a parody, *Pierrot Cadmus*, by D. Carolet, produced O.C. 31 August 1737.

The score was printed in 1719.

See W. J. Lawrence, *The French Opera in London. A Riddle of 1686* in *The Times Literary Supplement*, 28 March 1936, on a possible production of *Cadmus et Hermione* in London, 11–21 February 1686, probably at Dorset Garden, in French. Lawrence's assumption is based on a letter by Peregrine Bertie to the Countess of Rutland, and on an allusion in the prologue of Jevon's *The Devil of a Wife* (first acted at Dorset Garden, 4–14 March 1686).

PAGLIARDI: *Lisimaco*

[*10 December*]. Venice, SS.G. e P.

Text by C. Ivanovich. Three acts.

Revived Turin, Carnival 1681; Florence, T. Cocomero Carnival 1689.

The librettist, a native of Dalmatia, was the first to write a book which deals with the history of opera at Venice, viz. *Minerva al Tavolino. Lettere diverse . . . con Memorie teatrali di Venezia*, 1681 (second edition 1688). It was followed by G. C. Bonlini's *Le Glorie della Poesia, e della Musica* only about 50 years later, in 1730.

1674

LULLY: *Alceste* ou *Le Triomphe d'Alcide*

19 January. Paris, O.

Text by P. Quinault. Prologue and 5 acts.

The first opera performed at the Palais Royal, the new home of the Académie Royale de Musique which Lully succeeded in securing for his enterprise after Molière's death in 1673.

Mme de Sévigné, who was present at the rehearsals, announces the opera in a letter, dated 8 January 1674: "On joue jeudi l'Opéra qui est un prodige de beauté: il y a des endroits de la musique qui ont mérités mes larmes. . . ." Louis XIV first heard *Alceste* at the Palais Royal on 14 April 1674; it was given at Versailles 4 July 1674; Fontainebleau August 1677; St. Germain 1678, and revived at Paris September 1682; 25 November 1706; 16 January 1716; 30 November 1728; 22 January 1739; and, without prologue, 15 November 1757.

Given at Lyons 1696 and 1699; Brussels 12 October 1705 (revived January 1725); Lille 1720.

Parodies: *Alceste*, by P. F. Dominique and J. A. Romagnesi, C.I. 21 December 1728 and revived there, with alterations, 9 February 1739; *La Noce interrompue*, by C. S. Favart, C.I. 26 January 1758.

Score first published in 1708.

DRAGHI: *La Lanterna di Diogene*

5 February. Vienna

Text by N. Minato. Three acts. One air was composed by the Emperor Leopold I.

The copy of the libretto at the Brussels Conservatoire contains a MS note (published by Wotquenne) from which we learn that *La Lanterna di Diogene* was a satirical opera "à clef," each of the 26 characters representing members of the European high society, from Leopold I, Louis XIV, Charles XI of Sweden down to various Dukes, Counts and Ambassadors. The twenty-seventh character of the opera *Tirreo Eunuco* was politely described by the unknown commentator as an "incerta persona."

CAMBERT?: *Ariane*, ou *Le Mariage de Bacchus*

9 April. London, D.L.

Text by P. Perrin. Prologue and 5 acts. Music lost.

Libretto extant, in a French and in an English edition, copies of both of which are in the British Museum. The title-page of the French libretto reads: "Ariane, ou Le Mariage de Bacchus Opera: Compose par le Sieur P.P. et mis en Musique par le Sieur Grabut, Maitre de la Musique du Roi. Represente par l'Academie Roiale de Musique, ou Theatre-Roial".

The title of the English edition reads, slightly divergently: "An Opera, or, a vocal representation; First compos'd by Monsieur P.P. Now put into Musick by Monsieur Grabut .. and acted by the Royall Academy of Musick at the Theatre-Royal in Covent-Garden".

We know that Perrin had written this libretto as early as 1659; he refers to it in the prefatory letter to the 1661 edition of his *Pastorale* (see 1659). We also know that Cambert had set the text to music and that his setting was rehearsed at the Hôtel de Nevers, Paris, in 1669, but that it was not printed or produced owing to the death of Mazarin.

In Saint-Evremond's comedy *Les Opera* (cf. note on *Pomone*, 1671) the following dialogue concerns *Ariane*:—

"Celui-ci est écrit à la main. Lisez, monsieur Guillaut."

"C'est l'Ariane de Cambert, qui n'a pas été représentée: mais on en vit les répétitions. La poësie fut pareille à celle de Pomone, pour être du même auteur, et la musique fut le chef-d'œuvre de Cambert. J'ose dire que les plaintes d'Ariane, et quelques autres endroits de la pièce ne cèdent presque en rien à ce que Baptiste [viz. Lully] a fait de plus beau".

Five years after the Paris rehearsals *Ariane* was produced in London, as the opening opera of the short-lived "Royall Academy of Musick," at the Theatral Royal, Bridges Street, Covent Garden (the second building of Drury Lane Theatre; the first building, opened in 1663, was destroyed by fire 15/25 January 1672). From the notice to the reader in the English edition of the text, it becomes absolutely clear that *Ariane* was sung in French, and that the English version was "a meer Translation, and nothing else" and that it was "thought absolutely necessary for the satisfaction of those, who being unacquainted with the French tongue, and who being Spectators, would find themselves necessitated to see the most pressing of their Senses go away from the Theatre ungratified, by their not understanding the Subject that brought them thither".

The exact date of the first production of *Ariane* in London has been established by A. Nicoll (see *The Times Literary Supplement*, 21 September 1922). *Ariane* seems to have been that mysterious and much discussed "Italian opera" which Evelyn mentions in his Diary, 5 January 1674. He probably attended a rehearsal of *Ariane* (see also W. J. Lawrence, *ib.*, 26 September 1929).

Cambert's and Grabu's activities in London have been dealt with in recent papers by A. Tessier and W. H. G. Flood (see *La Revue Musicale*, December 1927 and August 1928). The question of the composer of *Ariane* as produced in London, 1674, is still unsolved. It is hardly credible that Cambert should have chosen for the opening of the London Academy, founded by himself, another setting of *Ariane* than his own. On the other hand, there is the evidence of the title-pages, where Grabu is mentioned as the composer very definitely, and even more so in the English libretto which emphasizes the fact of a new setting.

The explanation that Grabu altered and adapted Cambert's original music, is not very satisfactory, but it is the only one which now can be offered. Possibly the lost music of *Ariane* may be discovered some day and give a clue as to the real composer.

1675

LEGRENZI: *Eteocle e Polinice*

January. Venice, S. Salv.
Text by T. Fattorini. Three acts.
Score extant. Also given at Naples 1680; Milan

1684; Modena, T. Fontanelli 4 November 1690.

Another opera by Legrenzi, called *La Divisione del Mondo*, and produced at the same theatre later in the same Carnival [4 February] 1675, is stated to have been one of his best works. A manuscript score of *La Divisione del Mondo* was sold in 1880, from the Gehring collection (no.1360).

LULLY: *Thésée*

12 January. Saint-Germain
Text by P. Quinault. Prologue and 5 acts.
Revived at Saint-Germain 16 February 1677 and January 1678.

First given at Paris April 1675, and revived there 29 October 1679; October 1688; November 1698; 17 November 1707; 5 December 1720; 29 November 1729; 10 December 1744; 3 December 1754 (without the prologue); 13 (not 8) December 1765; 1 February 1767; 23 March 1770; and 23 February 1779 (with some new accompaniments by J. Grenier and one air re-set by him).

Thus, *Thésée* remained in the repertory for well over 100 years, longer than any other of Lully's operas[1]. The score was first printed in 1688.

Also given at Brussels 18 May 1682 (revived with a new prologue by P. A. Fiocco 10 November 1697, and 1 January 1713); Wolfenbüttel 19 August 1687 (in French); Lyons 1692; Ghent June 1698; probably also at the Hague in 1701; Lille 1718.

The 1744 revival was followed by two parodies, *Arlequin Thésée* by A. J. de Valois d'Orville,

[1] *Thésée*		from 1675 to 1779	= 104 years
Amadis	„	1684 „ 1771	= 87 „
Alceste	„	1674 „ 1757	= 83 „
Armide	„	1686 „ 1764	= 78 „
Proserpine	„	1680 „ 1758	= 78 „
Acis	„	1686 „ 1762	= 76 „
Atys	„	1676 „ 1747	= 71 „
Roland	„	1685 „ 1755	= 70 „
Festes de l'Amour	„	1672 „ 1738	= 66 „
Persée	„	1682 „ 1746	= 64 „
Cadmus	„	1673 „ 1737	= 64 „
Phaeton	„	1683 „ 1742	= 59 „
Isis	„	1677 „ 1732	= 55 „
Bellérophon	„	1679 „ 1728	= 49 „
Psyché	„	1678 „ 1713	= 35 „

C.I. 30 January 1745, and *Thésée* by C. S. Favart, P. Laujon and Parvi, O.C. 17 February 1745.

Quinault's text was several times re-set in the 18th century; first by Mondonville (Fontaine-bleau 7 November 1765, Paris 13 January 1767); the failure of Mondonville's setting was imme-diately followed by a successful revival of Lully's original; secondly, by Gossec (Paris 1 March 1782). Both composers kept parts of Lully's music, including the famous air *Faites grâce à mon âge en faveur de ma gloire*. There is a third new setting by J. Grenier (text reduced by P. F. de Remuzat), probably produced at Marseilles in 1782 (libretto Bibl. Soleinne).

LOCKE: *Psyche*

9 March. London, Dorset Gardens

Text by T. Shadwell (founded on a French tragédie-ballet by Molière, Pierre Corneille and Quinault, produced at Paris in 1671). Prologue, 5 acts and epilogue.

The 1675 libretto is called "A Tragedy"; the music was published in the same year as "The English Opera; or the Vocal Musick in Psyche, with the Instrumental therein Intermix'd".

In the preface Shadwell states: "And by his excellent Composition, that long known able and approved Master of Musick, Mr. Lock, . . . has done me a great deal of right; though, I believe, the unskilful in Musick will not like the more solemn part of it . . ."; he also informs us that "All the Instrumental Musick (which is not mingled with the Vocal) was composed by that Great Master, Seignior Gio: Baptista Draghi. . . ."

Psyche was revived at Dorset Gardens in 1690 (libretto reprinted) and at D.L. 20 June 1704, as *Psyche or Love's Mistress*.

As to the date of the first production, there has always been much uncertainty since Downes in his *Roscius Anglicanus* (1708) stated that it was given in February 1673-74. The discovery of the now accepted date (which corresponds to the year in which text and music were printed) is due to A. Nicoll (see *The Times Literary Supplement*, 21 September 1922). The laconic statement in Evelyn's *Diary* under 5 January 1674: "I saw an

Italian opera in music, the first that had been in England of this kind," is now believed to refer to the French *Ariane*, not to the English *Psyche* (although why Evelyn calls it Italian remains a puzzle; the explanation that he meant to say "after the Italian manner" is not very satisfactory).

Psyche may be called the earliest surviving example of an English opera. For a discussion of it, see chapter VI of E. J. Dent's *Foundations of English Opera* (1928).

GIANNETTINI: *Medea in Atene*

[*14 December*]. Venice, S. Moisè

Text by A. Aureli. Prologue and 3 acts.

Giannettini's first and most successful opera. Revived at Venice, S. Angelo [30 December] 1677 (with additions); Milan 1681; Lucca 9 Jan-uary 1683; Parma 1688 (as *Teseo in Atene*, with additional music by B. Sabadini).

In Italian also Brussels 24 January 1682 (at the opening of the Opéra du Quai au Foin); Wolfen-büttel 1686; February 1688 and 1692.

In German (translated by C. H. Postel), Ham-burg Carnival 1695; Augsburg Summer 1697; Stuttgart 3 October 1700; and perhaps also Leip-zig October 1701 (a different translation).

C. PALLAVICINO: *Galieno*

[*23 December*]. Venice, SS.G. e P.

Text by M. Noris. Three acts.

Revived Naples, S.B. [17 February] 1685; Mi-lan T.R.D. [1 February] 1687.

1676

LULLY: *Atys*

10 January. Saint-Germain

Text by P. Quinault. Prologue and 5 acts.

First given at Paris April 1676; Fontainebleau August 1677; revived St. Germain 15 January 1678 and 7 January 1682; revived Paris Novem-ber 1689; August 1690; 31 December 1699; 29 November 1708; 28 November 1709; 23 Decem-ber 1725; 7 January 1738; and 7 November 1747 (not 1740 as Lajarte has it); there were further concert performances at Versailles June 1749 and June 1751, and (without prologue) Fontainebleau 17 November 1753.

In French also given at the Hague 1687; Marseilles February 1689; Lyons 7 August 1689 (revived December 1742); Brussels 19 November 1700; Lille 1720.

The popularity of *Atys* (which was called *L'Opéra du Roi* because of its being a favourite with Louis XIV) is also indicated by no less than seven parodies, viz. *Atys*, by P. F. Dominique, O.C. [3 February] 1710; *Arlequin Atys*, by C. F. B. de Pontau, C.I. 22 January 1726; *La Grand-Mère amoureuse*, by L. Fuzelier and d'Orneval, Foire St. G. 10 February 1726 (by marionettes); *Atys*, by A. Piron, O.C. 19 February 1726; *Atys travesti*, by D. Carolet, Th. des Marionettes, Foire St. G., March 1736; *Cybelle amoureuse*, by A. J. Sticotti, C.I. January 1738 (according to Léris); performance not recorded by Gueullette, Origny, or in the *Mercure de France;* libretto printed after 10 February 1738 without indication of performance; so it was probably replaced by *Atys*, by J. A. Romagnesi, C.I. 27 February 1738.

Score first published in 1689; 2nd edition 1720. It was in *Atys* that Lully introduced the doublebass into the opera orchestra (played by Teobaldo di Gatti, cf. 1701). A Dutch translation by G. T. Domis was published in 1723. (For Piccinni's setting of Quinault's libretto, see 1780.)

LEGRENZI: *Germanico sul Reno*

[*27 January*]. Venice, S. Salv.
Text by G. C. Corradi. Three acts.

Also given at Modena, T. Ducale 1677; Milan, T.R.D. 1677 and Bologna Summer 1680.

PASQUINI: *La Donna ancora è fedele*

19 April. Rome, Pal. Colonna
Text by D. F. Contini. Three acts.

Pasquini's first opera and one of the few extant ones. Also given at Macerata [17 February] 1680. Scarlatti set the same libretto in 1698. From the preface to the libretto it appears that the opera was written to celebrate the birthday of Prince Lorenzo Onofrio Colonna, the husband of Maria Mancini.

FRANCESCHINI: *L'Arsinoe*

[*26 December*]. Bologna, T. Formagliari.
Text by T. Stanzani. Three acts.

Franceschini's best opera. Also given at Venice, S. Angelo Autumn 1677; Pesaro 1678 and Carnival 1681; Innsbruck 12 January 1686.

For an English version of the text, see 1705.

1677

FRESCHI: *Helena rapita da Paride*

Carnival. Venice, S. Angelo
Text by A. Aureli. Prologue and 3 acts.

Freschi's first and most successful opera. Also given at Verona 1680 (as *L'Enone schernita*, without the prologue); Milan, T.R.D. 1681; Modena, T. Ducale 1681 (with prologue and intermezzi by Conte G. B. Rosselli); Hanover June 1681 (text revised by Valenti); Lucca Carnival 1683; Bassano 1684. Revived Venice, S. Moisè [18 January] 1687 (with alterations and additions by F. Navarra); Rovigo Carnival 1707 (still Freschi's setting?).

Helena was the first opera produced at Sant' Angelo the ninth Venetian opera-house. Kretzschmar quotes from it the *Lamento di Paride* as one of the latest and most beautiful imitations of Monteverdi's *Lamento d'Arianna* (see 1608).

LULLY: *Isis*

5 January. Saint-Germain
Text by P. Quinault. Prologue and 5 acts.

First given at Paris, April 1677; Marseille 9 March 1701; revived Paris 14 February 1704; 15 September 1717; and 14 December 1732.

At its first appearance *Isis* (which later was surnamed "l'opéra des musiciens") was rather a failure, due perhaps to the fact that in the quarrel scene between Juno and the nymph Io occurs what was supposed to be an allusion to Madame de Montespan, the King's mistress. Quinault, anyway, was for two years banished from court and wrote his next libretto for Lully only in 1680.

A parody, *La Vache Io*, by Charpentier, was produced at the Foire St. L. in 1718; another, by L. Fuzelier, *A Fourbe Fourbe et demi, ou le Trompeur trompé*, at the Th. des Marionettes, Foire St. G. 3 February 1733.

The score of *Isis* was first published in 1699; re-published 1719.

LEGRENZI: *Totila*

February. Venice, SS.G. e P.

Text by M. Noris. Three acts.

H. Kretzschmar (*Geschichte der Oper*, p.104) calls attention to the high musical value of this opera.

1678

STRADELLA: *La Forza dell'Amor paterno*

Carnival. Genoa, T. del Falcone

Librettist unknown. Three acts.

The first and only opera of Stradella which is known to have been produced during his lifetime (cf. 1686).

The remarkable history of this opera can be told in a number of quotations (translated for the sake of conformity):

1789: C. Burney, *History*, IV, p.105: "For being in possession of the drama he set for Genoa previous to his murder, which is entitled *La Forza dell' Amor paterno*, and dated Genoa MDCLXXVIII, it appears that the dedication of this opera to Signora Teresa Raggi Saoli, was written by Stradella himself".

1866: A. Catelani, *Delle Opere di A.S.*, p.38: "As for *la Forza dell' Amor paterno* I do not know what to say: Burney asserted that he had seen and possessed the libretto. Until now, he is the only fortunate one. For my part, I have renewed inquiries *ad infinitum*, over land and sea, as you might say: but I did not find the

libretto, not a trace in a thousand catalogues, not even a record of its having been produced".

1906: H. Hess, *Die Opern A.S.'s*: "Burney's indication seems to prove correct, after all. Although no actual trace of the work itself has been found yet, there are some corresponding records referring to a production. . . ."

1927: The MS score (partly in autograph) was discovered and identified by A. Gentili in the Mauro Foà collection, now in the National Library, Turin. See his report in *Accademie e Biblioteche d'Italia*, Vol. I (1927–28), pp.40–42 and in *Il Pianoforte*, Vol. VIII, no.5/6 (May–June 1927). "My satisfaction then, may be imagined in recognising in the Foà collection the whole of the opera and in being able to establish it as the original score from Stradella's own hand. My considered opinion is that this opera must be regarded not only as its author's masterpiece, but also as one of the most precious gems in the vast operatic output of the 17th century".

1932: A vocal score, edited (*trascritta e armonizzata*) by A. Gentili, was published by Ricordi.

There remains the question of the libretto, which seems to be unknown even to Gentili. Burney's statement was quite correct. His copy was in the British Museum in 1866 as well as in 1906, when Catelani and Hess were writing, and it is there to-day. This completes the story of Stradella's opera:

LA FORZA / DELL'AMOR / PATERNO. / DRAMMA PER MUSICA. / Da recitarsi nel Teatro del Falcone / L'ANNO M.DC. LXXVIII. / CONSACRATO / All'illustrissima Signora / TERESA RAGGI / SAOLI./ Genoa, Franchelli, n.d. Dedication signed by Alessandro Stradella.

The characters are Seleuco, Stratonica, Antioco, Lucinda, Arbante, Eurindo, Rubia. No cast.

C. PALLAVICINO: *Il Vespasiano*

Carnival. Venice, S.G.Gr.

Text by G. C. Corradi. Three acts.

Successful in Italy. Repeated at the same theatre, Carnival 1680 and also given at Genoa 1680 and/or

1682 (with additional music by C. F. Pollarolo); Ferrara 1682 (with additional music by G. F. Tosi); Modena Autumn 1685; Milan 1685; again at Ferrara 1687 (with alterations); Rome, Tord. 24 January 1693 (text altered by S. Stampiglia); Bologna 3 February 1695; Pesaro Autumn 1718 (this revival was arranged in honour of the Pretender James Francis Stuart, then residing at Pesaro).

Il Vespasiano was written for the inauguration of the Teatro Grimano di San Giovanni Grisostomo, which was the tenth opera-house at Venice. After 1747 it was devoted chiefly to the drama, but it became an opera-house again in the 19th century. Re-opened 25 December 1832; called Teatro Malibran since 8 April 1835; restored 26 July 1890 and again 17 December 1919 (re-opened with Verdi's *Otello*).

THEILE: *Der erschaffene, gefallene und aufgerichtete Mensch*

12 January. Hamburg

Text by C. Richter. Prologue and 5 acts.

Written for the inauguration of the first German opera-house, the Hamburg "Theater am Gänsemarkt." Revived at Frankfort in 1698, and seemingly at Viborg (Viipuri), Finland, as late as about 1768 (by a travelling German troupe under the management of C. G. Seuerling; communication from Mr. Wäinö Sola, Helsinki).

Libretto extant (as of all operas produced at Hamburg in the 17th and early 18th century). Music lost, as is the music of Theile's second and last opera, *Orontes*, produced at Hamburg later in the same year.

During the 72 years of its existence, more than 280 operas were produced at the Hamburg opera-house, German original operas, German versions of Italian and French operas, from 1703 onwards chiefly operas which contained German as well as Italian airs, and after September 1738 purely Italian operas (under Mingotti's management). The last production of the German company was a pasticcio, *Der Jahrmarkt von Saint-Germain*, 2

January 1738. The building was pulled down 7 January 1750, and the Italian troupe continued from 18 November 1751 at another building, the "Reithaus".

LULLY: *Psyché*

19 April. Paris, O.

Text by T. Corneille and B. de Fontenelle. Prologue and 5 acts.

Of all of Lully's operas *Psyché* was the least successful. It was revived at Paris only twice, 8 June 1703 and 22 June 1713.

It was also given at Wolfenbüttel, August 1686 (in French), and at Modena 1687 (in French, with Italian interpolations). Score published in 1720.

Parts of *Psyché* had a modern hearing at the Th. des Arts, Rouen, on 7 June 1911.

Lully had dealt with the same subject before; a tragédie-ballet of the same title by Molière, Pierre Corneille and Quinault, to which he had written the music, had been produced at the Tuileries on 17 January 1671. It was on that earlier non-operatic *Psyché* that Locke and Shadwell founded their English opera (see 1674).

PROVENZALE: *Difendere l'Offensore o vero La Stellidaura vendicante*

??. Naples. Pal. Reale

Text by A. Perruccio e Fardella. Three acts.

The second and last of Provenzale's two extant operas (cf. 1671). Revived at Naples in 1685.

No copy of the original edition of the libretto has been traced yet. According to Allacci (1755), there are editions of 1678, 1679, and 1685 (and a prose version, 1690), and the same dates are given in A. Mongitore's *Bibliotheca Sicula* (1707-14). F. Galiani (*Del Dialetto Napoletano . . .*, 1779) mentions a 1674 edition. According to B. Croce the production was at the Palazzo Regio; in G. Gimma's *Elogi Accademici*, 1703, a performance at the Palace of Prince Cursi Cicinelli is mentioned.

U. Prota-Giurleo (*Francesco Cirillo e l'introduzione del melodramma a Napoli*, Grumo Nevano, 1952, Appendix, p.31) gives the date and place of first performance as 2 September 1674, in Prince Cursi Cicinelli's villa at Mergellina.

The earliest known libretto is that of the revival of 1685, which contains the cast but does not mention the theatre (see Florimo, IV, p.576, and Croce, I Teatri di Napoli, 1891, p.191).

The score of La Stellidaura (like that of Il Schiavo di sua Moglie) has been preserved in the Biblioteca di Santa Cecilia, Rome. It was examined by Romain Rolland (see his Histoire de l'Opéra en Europe avant Lully et Scarlatti, 1895, pp.187–96) and by Hugo Goldschmidt (see Sammelbände of the I.M.S., Vol. VII, 1905–06). The two eminent historians contradict each other in a highly curious way. Rolland calls the score a manuscript without title, without list of characters, date, or author's name; nevertheless, he gives the date of 1670 (perhaps on the authority of a misprint in B. Croce's quotation from Mongitore!), while Goldschmidt claimed that 1678 was indicated in the score as the year of production.

It may be mentioned that in 1895 Rolland suggested the possibility that Francesco Provenzale, the founder of the Neapolitan School and important forerunner of Scarlatti, might be identical with one Francesco della Torre who, from 1678–85, was manager of the Teatro San Bartolomeo at Naples and might have been a composer himself as he signed, along with Perruccio, the dedication of an opera libretto, Chi tal nasce tal vive, overo L'Alessandro Bala (score preserved at Monte Cassino; produced Naples, 20 December 1678). The suggestion was founded on purely external evidence, not on reasons of style, etc. (as Goldschmidt maintains, who, by the way, also substituted the name of the hero, Alessandro Bala, for that of the supposed composer, Francesco della Torre!). Rolland's assumption has not been accepted by historians, it has even been rejected as a "fantastica ipotesi" by a recent writer on Provenzale (G. Pannain in R.M.I., 1925). Yet a copy of Chi tal nasce . . . at the Naples Conservatorio is, in the recently published catalogue, now actually attributed to Provenzale. Prota-Giurleo also accepts Chi tal nasce . . . as a work by Provenzale.

1679

M. A. ZIANI: *Alessandro Magno in Sidone*

Carnival. Venice, SS.G. e P.

Text by A. Aureli. Three acts.

Ziani's first opera. Also given at Vicenza 1681 and revived at Venice in Carnival 1683 (at the Teatro di Canal Regio as La Virtù sublimata dal Grande, ovvero Il Macedone continente).

PASQUINI: *Dov' è Amore è Pietà*

6 January. Rome, Capr.

Text: an abridged version of Moniglia's Hipermestra (see 1658). Three acts. Music lost.

In the libretto Pasquini is mentioned as "che trà i Compositori più eccellenti di Musica non è in Roma il secondo" and it is stated that he set the old text to music within a few days, "alla moderna usanza di bizzarre, e spiritose ariette".

The opera was written for the inauguration of the Teatro Capranica, the second public opera-house at Rome (cf. 1664). Operas were given there, with many interruptions, for 202 years, the last being Verdi's Ernani on 1 March 1881. Today, the T. Capranica is a cinema.

J. W. FRANCK: *Die drey Töchter Cecrops*

January. Ansbach

Text by M. A. von Königsmarck. Prologue and 5 acts.

Given at Hamburg in 1680 (in a reduced version, perhaps with some new music by Strungk, to whom the opera was attributed by J. Mattheson in Der Musikalische Patriot, 1728) and revived at Ansbach 14 April 1683. Franck's authorship has been definitely established by the discovery of the original libretto, which mentions his name.

One of the earliest German operas extant in full score. Discovered by A. Sandberger about 1910, it was published only in 1938 (as Vol. 38 of Denkmäler der Tonkunst in Bayern, edited by G. F.

Schmidt; see his account in *Archiv für Musikfor-schung*, Vol. IV).

LULLY: *Bellérophon*

31 January. Paris, O.

Text by T. Corneille (who alone is mentioned in all earlier editions of the text; he seems to have had two famous collaborators, Fontenelle and Boileau, who claimed their respective shares much later). Prologue and 5 acts.

Very successful, given for about nine months running; performed at St.-Germain 3 January 1680 and revived at Paris 10 December 1705; 11 January 1718; 6 April 1728; Versailles 15 February 1749 (in concert form); and (not recorded so far) once more Versailles 27 November 1773, reduced to 4 acts, music arranged by Berton and Granier, at the wedding of the Comte d'Artois, the future King Charles X.

Given at Lyons 20 June 1688; at Brussels 8 November 1696 (with a new prologue by P. A. Fiocco; revived 14 November 1708).

Parts of the music were revived at the Th. des Arts, Rouen, on 7 June 1911.

A parody *Arlequin Bellérophon*, by P. F. Dominique and J. A. Romagnesi, was produced at the C.I., Paris 7 May 1728.

In the last act Lully introduced a "prélude avec trompettes". *Bellérophon* was the first of Lully's operas the score of which was published (1679; 2nd edition 1714).

A. SCARLATTI: *Gli Equivoci nel Sembiante*

February. Rome, Capr.

Text by D. F. Contini. Three acts.

Scarlatti's first opera. Score preserved. Also given at Bologna 1679 (as *L'Errore innocente*); Monte Filottramo, near Macerata 1680; Naples, at Duke of Maddaloni's March 1680, and Pal. Reale 21 December 1681 (with a prologue added); Vienna Carnival 1681 (as *Amor non vuol Inganni*, with intermezzi by G. B. Pederzuoli, *Il Giudice di Villa*); Ravenna 1685.

See on the Vienna production of Scarlatti's opera, A. Lorenz in *Zeitschrift für Musikwissenschaft*, IX, p.86 (November 1926).

Of 115 operas written by Scarlatti between 1679 and 1721, about 80 are known by their titles and 35 have been preserved in full score.

C. PALLAVICINO: *Le Amazoni nell'Isole fortunate*

[*11 November*]. Piazzola (near Padua)

Text by F. M. Piccioli. Prologue and 3 acts.

This and Freschi's *Berenice* (see 1680) were two famous operas expressly written for the private theatre of the Venetian procurator Marco Contarini (1633–89). He plays an important part in the history of music as a collector of MS opera scores, chiefly by Venetian composers. His collection is now in the Biblioteca di S. Marco, Venice, where the 112 scores (*Codices Contariniani*) were identified and catalogued by Taddeo Wiel in 1888. An astonishing number of "lost" works came to light, amongst them no less than 28 scores by Cavalli.

1680

AGOSTINI: *Il Ratto delle Sabine*

Carnival. Venice, S.G.Gr.

Text by G. F. Bussani. Three acts.

Of Agostini's operas the only one which is extant. Revived Bologna Carnival 1689.

M. A. ZIANI: *Damira placata*

Carnival. Venice, S. Moisè

Text by F. Acciaiuoli (*Drama da rappresentarsi nel loco ov' era il Teatro Zane a S. Moisè. . . . Consacrato al genio de'curiosi*). Three acts.

The opera was produced on a provisional stage, by wooden puppets, "figure di legno al naturale di estraordinario artificioso lavoro", as Bonlini tells us. The singers sang behind the scenes. In a similar way, Acciaiuoli's *Ulisse in Feaccia* (music by A. del Gaudio) and his *Girello* (see 1670) were produced at the same place in

1681 and 1682, with wax puppets; and *Il Leandro* (text by Badovero, music by Pistocchi) had preceded them in 1679. Ziani's score is extant. (See on puppet operas, W. J. Lawrence, in *The Musical Quarterly*, Vol. x (1924), p.236.)

DRAGHI: *La Patienza di Socrate con due Moglie*

6 January. Prague

Text by N. Minato (*Scherzo dramatico per musica*). Three acts.

First opera ever produced at Prague. (See P. Nettl, *Beiträge zur böhmischen and mährischen Musikgeschichte*, 1927.) The ballet music was composed by J. H. Schmelzer. Score preserved.

LULLY: *Proserpine*

3 February. Saint-Germain

Text by P. Quinault. Prologue and 5 acts.

First given at Paris 15 November 1680 and revived there November 1681; Marly 1683; Paris 31 July 1699; 7 March 1715; 28 January 1727; 31 January 1741; and 14 November 1758 (without the prologue). Also given at Antwerp Autumn 1682 (first opera there); in French also, Wolfenbüttel 1685; Amsterdam 15 September 1688 and 1703.

The score was first published in 1680; 2nd edition 1714.

The last three revivals of *Proserpine* were followed by parodies, viz. *Les Noces de Proserpine*, by A. R. Le Sage and d'Orneval, O.C. 31 March 1727; *Farinette*, by C. S. Favart, O.C. 9 March 1741; and *Petrine*, altered from *Farinette* by J. M. Sedaine, C.I. 13 January 1759. (For Paisiello's new setting of Quinault's text see 1803.)

A. SCARLATTI: *L'Honestà negli Amori*

6 February. Rome, Pal. Bernini

Text by "Felice Parnasso" (pseudonym of G. F. Bernini?). Three acts.

The opera is dedicated to and was performed before Queen Christina of Sweden, then residing at Rome. Revived Siena 1690 (with additional music by G. Fabbrini).

J. W. FRANCK: *Aeneas*

??. Hamburg

Text probably by the composer. Prologue and 3 acts.

The full title reads: *Aeneas des Trojanischen Fürsten Ankunfft in Italien.* Airs from this opera were printed in 1680. After Theile and Strungk, Franck was the third composer working for the new German opera-house at Hamburg (*c.*15 operas, 1679–86).

STRUNGK: *Esther*

??. Hamburg

Text by J. M. Köler. Prologue and 5 acts.

The full title reads: *Die Liebreiche, durch Tugend und Schönheit Erhöhete Esther.* Thirty-six airs from this opera were printed in 1684. After Theile, Strungk was probably the second composer working for the new German opera-house at Hamburg (*c.*8 operas, 1678–93).

FRESCHI: *Berenice vendicativa*

[*8 November*]. Piazzola (near Padua)

Text by G. M. Rapparini. Three acts.

Produced at Contarini's private theatre (cf.1679) with a very splendid and prodigal display of stage effects (see Grove, III, p.694, 3rd edition, 1927). The production of *Berenice* has been frequently cited as an example of operatic baroque by writers on the history of opera since 1681, when its gorgeous scenery was first described by two eye-witnesses, C. Ivanovich (*Minerva al Tavolino*, Venice 1681, Vol. I, p.17) and J. Chassebras de Cramailles (*Histoire de mes Conquetes, Mercure Galant*, February 1681). See, for instance, A. Burgh, *Anecdotes of Music*, II, p.383 (1814); *Edinburgh Review*, May 1820; *Allgemeine Musikalische Zeitung*, 1821, etc.

Freschi's music is extant. That the opera with its choruses of many hundreds, with its elephants, and stables full of horses, was not given on other stages, seems only natural.

In this year, 1680, appeared the first Dutch opera, *De Triomferende Min. Vredespel. Gemengt met Zang-en Snaarenspel, Vliegwerken en Baletten*, text by D. Buijsero, music by Carolus Hacquart. The libretto, containing the airs, was printed (copies Hague, Coll. Scheurleer, and London, British Museum). The opera was written to celebrate the peace of Nymwegen (1679); but it was not produced until 240 years later (see 7 July 1920) on which occasion the text was reprinted.

1681

STEFFANI: *Marco Aurelio*

12 or 13 February. Munich

Text by V. Terzago (the brother of the composer). Three acts.

Steffani's first opera. Score preserved.

LORENZANI: *Nicandro e Fileno*

September. Fontainebleau

Text by F. Mancini-Mazarini, Duc de Nevers (Cardinal Mazarin's nephew). *Poemetto dramatico per Musica.* Three acts.

Lorenzani's first opera; apparently the only Italian opera produced in France between 1662 (see note on Cavalli's *Ercole amante*) and 1729. Anonymous undated libretto printed. Score recovered by H. Prunières (see *Revue Musicale*, August 1922).

"Le Roy a permis au duc de Nevers de faire un opera, et Lulli a fait tout son possible pour l'empescher, mais inutilement." (*Nouvelles Extraordinaires*, Leyden 25 September 1681.)

"Dans son ensemble, cette partition est d'une réelle importance pour l'histoire de l'opéra en France et représente un essai des plus intéressants pour opposer à la tragédie en musique de Lully un opéra italien adapté au goût des spectateurs français". (Prunières.)

FRESCHI: *Olimpia vendicata*

[*20 November*]. Venice, S. Angelo.
Text by A. Aureli. Three acts.

Also given at Pavia 1684 (with additional

music by M. Martinenghi), Naples December 1686; Parma 1687 (as *Olimpia placata*, with additional music by B. Sabadini); Bologna, T. Formagliari 1688 and T. della Sala 1694; Rome, Capr. 9 February 1692 (as *Amor vince lo Sdegno*, with a new third act by an unknown composer).

1682

DRAGHI: *La Chimera*

Carnival. Vienna

Text by N. Minato (*Drama fantastico musicale*). Three acts.

Revived at Vienna Carnival 1692. First performed in 1682 according to Allacci, Köchel, Weilen. A suspicion that the date of 1672 in Wotquenne's *Catalogue* (1901, p.41) was a misprint has been confirmed by the Brussels Conservatoire.

J. W. FRANCK: *Diocletianus*

6 March. Hamburg

Text by L. von Bostel. Prologue and 3 acts.

Perhaps also produced at Ansbach, though certainly not in 1679 (as H. Mersmann, *Beiträge zur Ansbacher Musikgeschichte*, 1916, p.17, claims), but only between 1682 and 1686 as an Ansbach "inventarium de Anno 1686" (quoted by Mersmann) states that *Diocletiano* was "in Partitura auss Hamburg gesandt".

One of Franck's most important works. Airs from it were printed in 1682.

LULLY: *Persée*

18 April. Paris, O.

Text by P. Quinault. Prologue and 5 acts.

Given at Versailles in July of the same year and revived at Paris 10 April 1687; 9 February 1703; 20 November 1710; 8 November 1722; 14 February 1737; 15 November 1746 and 1765 (with additions by B. de Bury and P. M. Berton).

Revived at Versailles 1 March 1747 (with a new prologue, text by C. A. Leclerq de La Bruère, music by B. de Bury) and 17 May 1770 (reduced to 3 acts, text altered by N. R. Joliveau, with additional music by B. de Bury, A. Dauvergne, F. Rebel and F. Francœur), to celebrate the wedding of the Dauphin Louis (XVI) with Marie Antoinette. Another 3-act version, by Marmontel, was composed by Philidor in 1780.

Given at Brussels as early as November 1682 (revived 6 November 1685 and 28 December 1706); Amsterdam 21 August 1688 (*airs à chanter* published); Lyons Winter 1696-7. The score was first printed in 1682; 2nd edition 1722.

Parodies: *Persée le Cadet*, anonymous (in monologues) Foire St. G. 4 February 1709; *Arlequin Persée* by L. Fuzelier, C.I. 18 December 1722; *Le Mariage en l'Air* by D. Carolet, O.C. 13 March 1737; *Polichinelle Persée* (by marionettes) Foire St. G. 1737.

Date of first performance April 18 (not 17) according to the *Mercure Galant*.

1683

LULLY: *Phaéton*

9 January. Versailles

Text by P. Quinault. Prologue and 5 acts.

First given at Paris 27 April 1683 and revived there November 1692; 12 January 1702; 5 January 1710; 11 November 1721; 21 December 1730; and 13 November 1742. At Versailles 6 May 1749 and 3 August 1750 (in concert form).

Also given at Avignon, July 1687 (first opera there); Lyons, 3 or 7 January 1688 (first opera there); Brussels 24 January 1696; Ghent 1708; Hague 15 December 1710; Lille 1718; Marseilles 17 May 1720 (in concert form).

Phaéton was one of Lully's most successful works; its popularity (it was surnamed "l'opéra du peuple") called forth the following parodies at the C.I.: *Arlequin Phaéton*, by J. Palaprat, 4 February 1692 (Dutch translation by Emanuel van der Hoeven published 1724); *Parodie de Phaéton*, by Macharti, 11 December 1721; *Arlequin Phaéton*, by P. F. Dominique and J. A. Romagnesi, 22 February 1731; *Arlequin Phaéton*, by F. Riccoboni, 21 January 1743. A fifth parody, by G. Bailly, was published in 1758.

The score was first published in 1683.

Louis XV was present at the 1721 revival (the first time that he visited the Opéra.)

Date of first production 9 January (not 6 January, as usually given) has been established by P. Mélèse from contemporary papers.

LEGRENZI: *Il Giustino*

January. Venice, S. Salv.

Text by N. Beregani. Three acts.

Legrenzi's last great success. Also given at Naples, Pal. Reale 6 November 1684 (with an added prologue); Genoa 1689; Milan [29 January] 1689 and 1691 (text altered); Brescia 1691; Bologna 1691 and [29 January] 1692; Lucca 29 December 1693; Rome, Tord. 8 January 1695 (text altered by S. Stampiglia); Verona 1696; Modena, T. Fontanelli 9 January 1697.

A. SCARLATTI: *Il Pompeo*

[25 January]. Rome, Pal. Colonna

Text by N. Minato (first set to music by Cavalli in 1666). Three acts.

One of Scarlatti's early serious operas.

Also given at Naples, Pal. Reale, [30 January] 1684; Ravenna [10 May] 1685; Leghorn 1688; Palermo 1690; Bologna 9 February 1692.

1684

LULLY: *Amadis*

18 January. Paris, O.

Text by P. Quinault. Prologue and 5 acts.

The opera was to be produced first at Versailles (Louis XIV himself had suggested the subject of the opera), but owing to the death of the Queen, *Amadis* was first publicly performed at Paris, and at Versailles only one year later, viz. 5 March 1685.

Revived in Paris 8 April 1687; 31 May 1701; 1 March 1707; 26 April 1718 (as *Amadis de Gaule*); 4 October 1731; 8 November 1740; 6 November 1759; and 26 November 1771 (additions by Laborde and Berton).

Also given at Amsterdam 1687; Brussels January 1695 (with prologue by P. A. Fiocco) and 4 October 1709.

The score was first published in 1684; 2nd edition 1721. A Dutch translation by T. Arendsz appeared in 1687.

A modern revival was at the Twentieth Century Theatre, London, on 14 June 1938 (by amateurs; English version by O. Daunt).

There were two early satires (rather than parodies) produced at the Th. I. in the same year, viz: a comedy by N. de Fatouville, *Arlequin Empereur dans la Lune*, 5 March 1684, and *Amadis Cuisinier*, May 1684. Later parodies include *La Naissance d'Amadis*, by F. Regnard, C.I. 10 February 1694; *Arlequin Amadis*, by P. F. Dominique and J. A. Romagnesi, C.I. 27 November 1731; *Polichinelle Amadis* (anonymous), Th. des Marionettes, Foire St. G., March 1732; *Amadis*, by J. A. Romagnesi and F. Riccoboni, music by Blaise, C.I. 19 December 1740; *Amadis*, by A. J. Labbet de Morambert, C.I. 31 December 1759; *Amadis*, by A. J. Sticotti, 1760, not performed.

J. C. Bach set the same text to music 95 years later (see 1779).

C. PALLAVICINO: *Massimo Puppieno*

[*28 December*]. Venice, SS.G. e P.

Text by A. Aureli. Three acts.

Very successful in Italy: repeated with additions Venice, same theatre, 1685; Milan 18 June 1685; Trent 1688; Verona 1689; Genoa 1690; Bologna 9 January 1692; Ferrara 1692; Fano 1694; Lucca 20 August 1695; Florence Carnival 1699; Rome Carnival 1718. Music lost.

c.1684?

BLOW: *Venus and Adonis*

??. London

Librettist unknown. Prologue and 3 acts. Date and place of first performance unknown.

From a MS. score in the British Museum (Add. MS.22100) we know that in this "Masque for the Entertainment of the King" (the only work Blow

wrote for the stage) the part of Venus was sung by Mary Davies, the actress who became the mistress of Charles II in 1667 (see Pepys's *Diary*, 14 January 1668), and the part of Cupid by Lady Mary Tudor, their daughter. As the title was bestowed on her in December 1680, and she became, by marriage, Lady Derwentwater in August 1687, the performance must have taken place between those two dates, as generally stated.

The margin, however, can be narrowed down, considering that Charles II died on 6 February 1685, and that his mistress and his natural child are not likely to have sung the masque under his successor. On the other hand, it seems preferable to suggest the latest possible year, as Lady Mary Tudor was born in 1763 and so, in 1684, was only a child of eleven, which is rather young even for the part of Cupid.

The libretto does not seem to have been printed. The score was published in 1902 by G. E. P. Arkwright, as no.xxv of his *Old English Edition*, and again in 1939, edited by A. Lewis.

Venus and Adonis was revived at Glastonbury 5 April 1920; London, Old Vic 1 June 1920 (by the Glastonbury company) and Scala Th. 13 July 1926; Liverpool 17 February 1928; Oxford 9 March 1937; London, R.C.M. 19 June 1938.

1685

LULLY: *Roland*

8 January. Versailles

Text by P. Quinault. Prologue and 5 acts.

First given at Paris 8 March 1685, and revived there 12 February 1705; 15 November 1709; 15 December 1716; 11 November 1727; 19 December 1743; and 11 November 1755 (additions by L. Aubert). Given at Lille 1720; Brussels 19 November 1721.

A Dutch version by T. Arendsz was published at Amsterdam in 1686. The metres of the translation prove that it was intended to go with Lully's music. But there is no record of a production.

Parodies: *Pierrot Furieux, ou Pierrot Roland*, by L. Fuzelier, O.C. 3 February 1717; *Arlequin Ro-*

land, by P. F. Dominique and J. A. Romagnesi, C.I. 31 December 1727; *Roland*, by C. F. Panard and A. J. Sticotti, C.I. 20 January 1744; *Bolan ou Le Médecin amoureux*, by J. Bailly, C.I. 27 December 1755. Léris mentions one more, *Polichinelle Gros-Jean*, performed at the Th. des Marionettes (1744).

The first production was on 8 January (not 18 as indicated in later editions of the libretto). Again, as in *Amadis*, Louis XIV had suggested the subject himself. The score was first printed in 1685.

Piccinni used the same libretto 93 years later (see 1778).

GAULTIER: *Le Triomphe de la Paix*

28 January. Marseilles

Text by the composer (according to A. Fabre, *Les Rues . . . de Marseille*, III, p.295). Prologue and 3 acts.

The text was printed in 1685, but no copy of it has been traced yet. The music is also lost.

This was the first opera ever produced at Marseilles. See on Gaultier (who was a pupil of Lully), L. de La Laurencie's paper in Vol. XIII (1911–12) of the *Sammelbände of the I.M.S.*

(The wrong date of 1682 for the opening of the Marseilles opera-house is due to Castil-Blaze or Fétis and still occurs in books of reference.)

C. PALLAVICINO: *Penelope la Casta*

[28 January]. Venice, S.G.Gr.

Text by M. Noris. Three acts..

Also given Milan 1696.

Bonlini (1730) says: "Questo Drama . . . è uno di quelli che ha più incontrato nel genio universale de'Spettatori", meaning Noris's libretto, which was reset by Perti (Rome 1696), Scarlatti (Naples 1696) and Chelleri (Venice 1716).

GRABU: *Albion and Albanius*

13 June. London, Dorset Gardens

Text by J. Dryden (*an opera*). Prologue, 3 acts and epilogue.

Libretto published in 1685, score in 1687. Besides *Ariane* (the authorship of which is doubtful, see 1674) Grabu's only opera, as far as we know. For a detailed account of the work, its musical importance and its political meaning, see E. J. Dent, *Foundations of English Opera* (1928), pp.160–70. In his most interesting preface, Dryden pays high tribute to his musical collaborator; his coining of the term "Songish Part" (as opposed to the recitative part of opera) is worth mentioning once more.

A. SCARLATTI: *Olimpia vendicata*

23 December. Naples, Pal. Reale

Text by A. Aureli (first composed by Freschi, see 1681). Three acts.

This opera contains a very early instance of accompanied recitative (quoted by E. J. Dent, *Scarlatti*, p.46).

The date of first performance has been very ingeniously detected and established by A. Lorenz (*Alessandro Scarlatti's Jugendoper*, Vol. I, 1927, pp.93–96).

STEFFANI: *Servio Tullio*

[30 December]. Munich

Text by V. Terzago (the brother of the composer). Prologue and 3 acts.

Written for the wedding of the Elector Max Emanuel with Maria Antonia, the daughter of the Emperor Leopold I.

For an analysis of *Servio Tullio*, see A. Neisser's monograph (1902).

1686

BERNABEI: *L'Ascanio*

January. Munich

Text by F. R. Sbarra. Three acts.

One of the 15 operas the younger Bernabei wrote for the Munich court, where he succeeded his father in 1688. Produced some days after *Servio Tullio* (see [30 December] 1685) as indicated in the preface.

J. W. FRANCK: *Cara Mustapha*

January. Hamburg

Text by L. von Bostel. Prologue and 3 acts.

The full title reads: *Der Glückliche Gross-Vezier Cara Mustapha Erster Theil, nebenst der grausamen Belagerung, und Bestürmung der Kayserlichen Residentz-Stadt Wien*; a sequel, called *Der Unglückliche Gross-Vezier Cara Mustapha* . . . followed a few nights later. Airs from the two operas were printed in 1686 (some of them reprinted by F. Zelle in 1889). The last traceable work Franck wrote for Hamburg before he came to London *c.*1690 (see W. B. Squire, in *The Musical Antiquary*, July 1912).

C. PALLAVICINO: *L'Amazone Corsara*

[*1 February*]. Venice, SS.G. e P.

Text by G. C. Corradi. Three acts.

Sub-title: *L'Alvilda, Regina de Goti.* Successful in Italy, revived at Venice Carnival 1688 and subsequently given at Bologna 17 January 1688; Naples, Pal. Reale 6 November 1689; Vicenza 1690; Turin, T.R. Carnival 1696; Verona 1697; Rovigo 1697.

LULLY: *Armide*

15 February. Paris, O.

Text by P. Quinault (after Tasso). Prologue and 5 acts.

This last of Lully's tragédies-lyriques was regarded to be his masterpiece by his contemporaries as well as by later generations. Score first published in 1686; then in 1710 and once more in 1718. In January 1687 there was a performance in honour of the ambassadors from Siam. Revived in Paris 27 November 1703; 26 December 1713; June 1714; 9 November 1724; 7 January 1746 (previously, 30 December 1745 at Versailles); 17 February 1747; 3 November 1761; and 4 December (not 3 October) 1764 (this latest revival preceded Gluck's new setting of the same libretto by less than 13 years). Outside Paris given at Avignon September 1687; Lyons 15 February 1689; 1698 and 29 April 1730; Brussels 20 Jan-

uary 1695 (with a new prologue by P. A. Fiocco); Hague 1701; Marseilles 10 March 1701.

Also performed at Rome in 1690, as the first French opera ever given in Italy. Italian translation (by S. Stampiglia?) published in that year. According to F. Torrefranca (*Festschrift für Johannes Wolf*, 1929) performed at some private palazzo rather than in public. According to Salvioli perhaps also given at Mantua in 1695. *Armide* must have been rather well-known in Italy, as the president De Brosses mentions in his letters a private performance at Cardinal Ottoboni's as late as about 1740.

A German translation by J. J. Eschenburg was published in 1766.

According to an old tradition *Armide* is also said to have been produced at Madrid in 1693, as the first opera at the Spanish court. The statement first occurs in Bonnet-Bourdelot's *Histoire de la Musique et de ses Effets* (1715), p.379, was repeated by Arteaga in *Le Rivoluzioni del Teatro Musicale Italiano* (1783), I, p.241, and by many other writers since. According to E. Cotarelo y Mori (*Origines . . . de la Opera en España*, 1917) neither *Armide* nor any other of Lully's operas was ever given in Spain.

Parodies on *Armide*, of the same title, were produced at the C.I., Paris 21 January 1725 (by J. Bailly, part of the music by J. J. Mouret) and 11 January 1762 (by P. Laujon). A third, anonymous one, was printed in 1747.

Armide was revived, in concert form, at Paris 24 November 1905 (by the Schola Cantorum); Florence 12 May 1911 (by the Associazione dei Musicologi; orchestration revised by C. Cordara); and, on the stage, at Monte Carlo 6 April 1918 and Geneva December 1939.

For Gluck's setting of Quinault's text, see 1777.

LULLY: *Acis et Galatée*

6 Septembre. Anet

Text by J. G. de Campistron (*pastorale héroïque*). Prologue and 3 acts.

Lully's last work. Score published in 1686. First produced at a fête galante given by the Duke of Vendôme to the Dauphin; given at Paris 11 days later (17 September 1686) and revived 5 June 1689; 10 June 1695 (according to the *Mercure Galant*, 20 June 1695 at Trianon "pour le Roi de Angleterre"); 13 June 1702; 5 October 1704; 18 August 1718; 13 September 1725; 19 August 1734 (with new *divertissement, Les Plaisirs champêtres*, by Rebel *père*); 18 August 1744; 23 January 1749 (at Versailles, with the prologue from *Phaëton*); 6 June 1752 (after 1 August 1752 on the same bill with Pergolesi's *La Serva Padrona*); and 7 September 1762 (without the prologue).

Also given at Hamburg December 1689 (in French; first opera there by a non-German composer and sung in a foreign language) and at Brussels 7 November 1695 (with a prologue by P. A. Fiocco).

In German (translator not mentioned), Hamburg 1695 and Stuttgart 1698.

A parody by C. S. Favart, called *Tircis et Doristée* was produced at the C.I. 4 September 1752 and at Laxenburg, near Vienna 10 May 1756 (Champée signed the Vienna score as copyist, not as composer, as claimed by Mantuani and Eitner).

Acis et Galatée was revived at Amsterdam 23 November 1933 (in French, under Pierre Monteux, by the Wagnervereeniging, on which occasion the libretto was reprinted, edited by H. Prunières). In London the opera was broadcast on 29 March 1937 (in French).

(STRADELLA): *Il Trespolo Tutore balordo*

[*October*]. Modena

Text by G. C. Villifranchi (altered from a prose comedy by G. B. Ricciardi). Three acts.

The libretto was first published at Bologna 1679, under the title *Amore è Veleno, e Medicina degl' Intelletti o vero Trespolo Tutore* (and again in 1682 and 1686 as *Il Tutore balordo*); from Villifranchi's dedication to Ricciardi, dated 11 June 1679, it appears that this edition was not printed for a special occasion, and his allusions to previous productions at Rome, Genoa and Naples—with or without music—are rather vague.

The 1686 production at the T. Fontanelli, Modena, is the earliest (and only one) to be connected with Stradella's score, which is extant.

(An anonymous libretto of the same title, preserved at Vienna, has probably nothing to do with Stradella's opera; see Weilen, no.945; according to him perhaps performed at Vienna 4 March 1737.)

GABRIELI: *Il Mauritio*

[*25 December*]. Venice, S. Salv.

Text by A. Morselli. Three acts.

The most successful of Gabrieli's 11 operas; also given at Milan 1687 and/or 1689; Bergamo [12 January] 1689; Modena, T. Fontanelli 30 October 1689; Padua May 1691; Vicenza 1691; Rome, Tord. February 1692 (with alterations by S. Stampiglia); Bologna 31 December 1696; Udine 1696.

1687

C. PALLAVICINO: *La Gierusalemme liberata*

[*3 January*]. Venice, SS.G. e P.

Text by G. C. Corradi (founded on Tasso's poem). Three acts.

Given some weeks later, 2 February 1687 at Dresden (German translation in libretto by C. Bernhardi). Revived at Hamburg Spring 1694 (in Italian) and releated there 1695 in German (as *Armida*, translated by G. Fiedler; this German version contains, for the first time at Hamburg, also one Italian air).

The score was published in 1916 as Vol. LV of *Denkmäler Deutscher Tonkunst*, edited by H. Abert.

STEFFANI: *Alarico il Baltha*

18 January. Munich

Text by L. Orlandi. Three acts.

Full title: *Alarico il Baltha, cioè l'Audace, Rè de Gothi*. Written for the birthday of the Bavarian Electress Maria Antonia.

The score was published in 1912 as Vol. XI of *Denkmäler der Tonkunst in Bayern*, edited by H. Riemann.

BIBER: *Chi la dura la vince*

[*30 June*]. Salzburg

Text by F. M. Raffaelini. Three acts.

Biber's only extant opera. See on this earliest *Arminius* opera C. Schneider in *Archiv für Musikwissenschaft*, Vol. VIII (1926), p.281. The date of the election of the Archbishop Johann Ernst von Thun (to whom the work is dedicated) gives a *terminus a quo* for the date of production.

COLASSE: *Achile et Polixène*

7 November. Paris, O.

Text by J. G. de Campistron. Prologue and 5 acts.

Overture and first act were Lully's last composition (d. 22 March 1687). Colasse finished the work of his master, thus setting up a tradition held by French opera composers throughout the centuries. Also given at Hamburg December 1692 (in French) and revived at Paris 11 October 1712.

The score was published in 1687.

A French opera *Andromaque*, produced at Amsterdam 20 July 1688, probably was Colasse's work (in which Andromache is one of the chief characters); there is no French 17th-century opera of that title.

1688

A. SCARLATTI: *La Rosmene* overo *L'Infedeltà fedele*

Carnival. Naples, Pal. Reale

Text by G. D. de Totis. Three acts.

According to A. Lorenz one of Scarlatti's best works. Also given at Florence 1689; Rome 1690; Ferrara 1694.

LORENZANI: *Orontée*

23 August. Chantilly.

Text by M. Leclerc (adapted from Cicognini's Italian libretto, see 1649). *Tragédie en Musique*, prologue and 5 acts.

Produced at a fête given by the Prince of Condé in honour of a visit of the Grand Dauphin.

Lorenzani's only French opera (cf. 1681). Libretto printed in 1688. Of the music only some airs de ballet are extant. An account of *Orontée* will be found in *Revue Musicale*, June 1928 (A. Tessier).

LÖHNER: *Theseus*

15 November. Nuremberg

Text by the composer (translated from an Italian libretto by Aureli, *Teseo tra le Rivali*, composed by Freschi in 1685). Three acts.

Forty-four airs from this opera were printed in 1688. See A. Sandberger in *Archiv für Musikwissenschaft*, Vol. I (October 1918).

1689

COLASSE: *Thétis et Pélée*

11 January. Paris, O.

Text by B. de Fontenelle. Prologue and 5 acts.

Colasse's chief work and one of the most successful French operas between Lully and Rameau.

Revived in Paris 1697, 27 April 1699; 16 April 1708 (with additions by A. Campra and B. Stuck); 13 May 1712; 4 November 1723; 19 January 1736; and 29 November 1750 (Fontenelle is said to have been present at this revival, nearly 62 years after the first production. He died, a centenarian, in 1757); Fontainebleau 14 November 1754 (without the prologue). Given at Brussels in 1709 (revived 12 May 1726); Lille [1720].

Parodies: *Arlequin Thétis*, by A. R. Lesage, O.C. 30 July 1713; *Thétis et Pélée*, by P. C. Roy, Sceaux August 1714; *Les Noces d'Arlequin et de Silvia, ou Thétis et Pélée déguisés*, by P. F. Dominique, C.I. 19 January 1724; *Les Amants inquiets*, by C. S. Favart, C.I. 9 March 1751 and Versailles 22 January 1755.

Score published in 1689, 1708 and 1716. Fontenelle's text was reset by Laborde (Fontainebleau 10 October 1765), who retained some parts of Colasse's original music.

STEFFANI: *Henrico Leone*

30 January. Hanover

Text by O. Mauro. Three acts.

Written for the inauguration of the Hanover Italian opera-house.

Steffani's most successful work. Given in a German translation by G. Fiedler at Hamburg 1696; Brunswick August 1697 (revived August 1699; 2 February 1716 [with Italian airs, some from Steffani's *Tassilone*, and additions by G. C. Schürmann]; August 1729); Augsburg 1698; Stuttgart 11 October 1701 (as *Mechthilde*).

Date of first performance indicated in a letter of the Italian composer Antonio Giannettini (see E. J. Luin, *Antonio Giannettini e la Musica a Modena*, 1931).

(C. PALLAVICINO): *L'Antiope*

14 February. Dresden

Text by S. B. Pallavicino (the son of the composer). Three acts.

Pallavicino's last work (d. 29 January 1688), completed by Strungk. (See F. Berend, *N. A. Strungk*, 1913, for an analysis of the opera and the share of the two composers.)

PURCELL: *Dido and Aeneas*

December? London

Text by N. Tate. Prologue and 3 acts.

The only known copy of the original (undated) libretto (in the R.C.M., London) has no proper title, it simply reads: *An Opera Perform'd at Mr. Josias Priest's Boarding School at Chelsey. By Young Gentlewomen. The Words made by Mr. Nat. [sic; should be Nah. = Nahum] Tate. The Musick composed by Mr. Henry Purcell.*

The date of the first performance of the most famous English opera is still uncertain. For a long time, in fact since Hawkins (1776) up to 1904, it was believed to have been written about 1677. Only W. B. Squire's and W. H. G. Flood's researches (see *Sammelbände of the I.M.S.*, Vol. v, 1903–04, and *Musical Times*, June and November, 1918) have fixed the date of "second half of 1689, probably Christmas" with a high degree of prob-

ability. Surely, a mis-dating by no less than 12 years of a work of such outstanding importance is a unique case in the history of opera.

The score was published for the first time in 1841, edited by G. A. Macfarren for the Musical Antiquarian Society. There are later editions by E. F. Rimbault 1872 (vocal score); W. H. Cummings 1889 (as Vol. III of the collected edition of Purcell's works); A. Bodanzky 1924; E. J. Dent 1925.

Some public performances, after Purcell's death, took place about February 1700, 9 February 1704 and 19 April 1704, when *The Loves of Dido and Aeneas* ("a Mask, in Four Musical Entertainments") was given as an interlude at the Lincoln's Inn Fields Theatre. Parts of the music were heard at concerts occasionally in the 18th century. But it was only after a lapse of more than 195 years that *Dido and Aeneas* reached the stage again. The following revivals are to be recorded:

LONDON, R.A.M. 10 July 1878 (in concert form, by the Gluck Society).

LONDON, ST. J.'S HALL 1 March 1888 (in concert form, by the Bach Choir; Cummings' version).

LONDON, LY. 20 November 1895 (on the stage, by the R.C.M., in celebration of the bicentenary of Purcell's death, additional accompaniments by C. Wood).

DUBLIN 14 December 1895 (in concert form, by the University Society).

LONDON, HAMPSTEAD CONSERVATOIRE 17 May 1900 (by the Purcell Operatic Society).

LONDON, CORONET TH. 25 March 1901 (by the Purcell Operatic Society).

LONDON, GUILDHALL SCHOOL 17 March 1910.

LONDON, HYDE PARK 3 July 1920 (by the League of Arts).

LONDON, SCALA TH. 31 December 1929.

LONDON, SADLER'S WELLS 6 November 1931.

LONDON, NEW TH. 1 July 1941.

GLASTONBURY August 1915.

CLIFTON 14 October 1924.

ALTON, HANTS. 10 February 1926.

BRISTOL 21 October 1926.

GLASGOW 13 April 1932 and 24 April 1940.

OXFORD 10 November 1937.

Revivals outside Great Britain:

NEW YORK, TOWN HALL 13 January 1924 (in concert form, Bodanzky's version); on the stage: Juilliard School of Music 18 February 1932 and 29 March 1939 (Dent's version).

HOMBURG (near FRANKFORT) 12 June 1924 (in concert form).

MÜNSTER 14 March 1926 (on the stage, Dent's version; German translation by A. Mayer).

PARIS, PETITE SCÈNE 21 March 1927 (in French, translation by P. Landormy).

VIENNA 27 March 1927 (at the Redoutensaal, in German; music arranged from Dent's version by H. Gál).

STUTTGART 15 July 1927 (in German, Dent's version).

BASLE 9 June 1931 (in German, Dent's version).

THE HAGUE November 1934 (Gál's version).

BUDAPEST 6 December 1938 (in Hungarian, translated by K. Nádasdy; music arranged by J. Ádám).

NANTES February 1939 (in concert form).

FLORENCE May 1940 (Dent's version, translated M. Labroca, orchestrated by V. Gui).

1690

A. SCARLATTI: *La Statira*

5 January. Rome, T. Tordinona

Text by P. Ottoboni (the nephew of Pope Alexander VIII). Three acts.

Score preserved. Written for the reopening of the Tordinona theatre (closed 1675–89).

STEFFANI: *La Superbia d'Alessandro*

??. Hanover

Text by O. Mauro. Prologue and 3 acts.

Repeated at Hanover in 1691 as *Il Zelo di Leonato*, without the prologue, and with alterations.

Successful in a German version by G. Fiedler, *Der hochmüthige Alexander*: Hamburg 1695; Brunswick August 1699; Stuttgart 18 September 1700.

KUSSER: *Julia*

August. Brunswick

Text by F. C. Bressand. "In einem Schauspiel singend vorgestellt". Three acts.

Kusser's first traceable opera. Music lost. Leibniz mentions the opera in a letter to the Landgrave of Hesse-Rheinfels, dated 14 September 1690.

KRIEGER: *Der grossmüthige Scipio*

2 November. Weissenfels

Text: a German version by an unknown translator of Minato's *Scipione Africano* (see 1664). Prologue and 3 acts.

Airs from this opera were printed in 1692.

Krieger was court conductor at Weissenfels from 1680–1725. Of the numerous operas written by his successor, J. A. Kobelius, nothing is left.

A. SCARLATTI: *Gli Equivoci in Amore* overo *La Rosaura*

December. Rome, French Embassy

Text by G. B. Lucini. Three acts.

Written for a double wedding of the Colonna, Ottoboni, and Barberini families. Repeated Rome 1692 by the Accademici Uniti; an intended production at Tord. 1691 did not take place.

Two acts of this opera were published by R. Eitner in 1885 (in Vol. XIV of the *Publikationen der Gesellschaft für Musikforschung*).

OTTOBONI?: *Il Colombo* overo *L'India scoperta*

28 December. Rome, T. Tordinona

Text by the composer. Three acts.

The earliest *Columbus* opera, written (and perhaps composed) by Cardinal Pietro Ottoboni, the nephew of Pope Alexander VIII. Music lost. See on this opera Ademollo and Wotquenne, who cite amusing criticisms from the *Mémoires* of Philippe Emmanuel de Coulanges (1820 edition, p.227) and a poem by the Duke of Nevers ending thus:

Le grand bruit de la peste, en tous lieux répandu,
A fait cesser cette musique;
Cet opéra sauvage est enfin défendu
Et nous ne verrons plus ce monstre dramatique.

1691

PURCELL: *King Arthur* or *The British Worthy*

May or *June*. London, Dorset Gardens

Text by J. Dryden (*A dramatick opera*). Prologue, 5 acts and epilogue.

Regarded by Dryden as a sequel to his *Albion and Albanius* (see 1685).

Only one air was printed in Purcell's lifetime, and extracts followed in the 18th and 19th centuries. The score was first published in 1843, edited by E. Taylor for the Musical Antiquarian Society. Further editions by G. E. P. Arkwright (1889), W. H. Cummings (1897), J. A. Fuller Maitland (1897), and D. Arundell (1928, as Vol. XXVI of the collected edition of Purcell's works).

King Arthur was very successful and frequently revived. Given at London, D.L. 13 March 1706; London, Goodman's Fields Th. 30 December 1735 (as *Merlin or The British Inchanter and King Arthur, the British Worthy;* this version is attributed to William Giffard, the manager of Goodman's Fields Theatre; see on this production Thomas Gray's letter to Walpole of 3 January 1736); York 24 January 1747; Dublin 17 March 1750 and 7 February 1763; London, D.L. 13 December 1720; 12 November 1772; 19 October 1781 (text altered by D. Garrick, additional music by Arne); 22 November 1784 (as *Arthur and Emmeline*, additions by Linley); Dublin 1789 (Arne's version, as *Arthur and Emmeline*); London, Royalty 5 April 1790; New York 24 April 1800 (with Purcell's music?); *Arthur and Emmeline* revived London, C.G. 2 November 1803 and 26 October 1819 (music arranged by Bishop), also Lyceum 2 July 1827 (music arranged by W. Hawes); D.L. 16 November 1842.

Modern revivals, mostly in concert form:

BIRMINGHAM 6 October 1897 (Fuller Maitland's version).

PARIS (privately) 9 May 1922 (French version by I. Delage-Prat).

FALMOUTH 3 December 1924 (on the stage).

CAMBRIDGE 14 February 1928 (on the stage).

NEW YORK, UNIVERSITY 24 April 1935 (in concert form).

LONDON, QUEEN'S HALL 11 December 1935 (in concert form).

STEFFANI: *Orlando generoso*

December. Hanover

Text by O. Mauro. Three acts.

In German (translated by G. Fiedler) Hamburg January 1696 and revived there in 1707; 29 January 1720, "erneuert, doch mit Beibehaltung der Fiedlerschen Übersetzung, wenigstens in Recitativ" (Mattheson); Brunswick August 1697 (in German) and February 1698 (in Italian).

Airs from this opera were printed in 1699 at Lübeck.

1692

PERTI: *Il Furio Camillo*

Carnival. Venice, S. Salv.

Text by M. Noris. Three acts.

The most successful of Perti's 24 operas. Also given at Bologna 17 January 1693; Milan, T.R.D. [25 January] 1693; Genoa 1693; Rome, Tord. February 1696 (text altered by S. Stampiglia); Mantua 1700.

The music seems to be lost.

STEFFANI: *Le Rivali concordi*

20 February. Hanover

Text by O. Mauro. Three acts.

In German (as *Die vereinigten Mit-Buhler oder Die siegende Atalanta*, translation by G. Fiedler)

Hamburg 1698 and probably Stuttgart 18 September 1699 (as *Le Rivali concordi oder die versöhnten Nebenbuhler*).

PURCELL: *The Fairy-Queen*

April. London, Dorset Gardens

Text: an anonymous adaptation, perhaps by E. Settle, of Shakespeare's *A Midsummer Night's Dream*. Prologue and 5 acts.

Only some songs were published in Purcell's lifetime. The original score was lost as early as in October 1700, when there appeared in the *London Gazette* the well-known advertisement offering 20 guineas reward for its recovery. Perhaps it was recovered through this advertisement, for advertisements in the Daily Courant show that one act was performed at D.L. 1 February 1703. The score was re-discovered more than 200 years later, by J. S. Shedlock, in the library of the R.A.M., London. Edited by Shedlock in 1903 and again in 1914, as Vol. XII of the collected edition of Purcell's works.

Revivals:

LONDON, ST. GEORGE'S HALL 15 June 1901 (in concert form, under Shedlock).

LONDON, MORLEY COLLEGE 10 June 1911 (in concert form, under G. Holst).

CAMBRIDGE 10 February 1920 (first production on the stage since 1692, under C. B. Rootham).

LONDON, RUDOLF STEINER HALL 23 June 1927.

CAMBRIDGE 10 February 1931.

ESSEN 27 June 1931 (open-air performance, in German, translation by E. Schulz-Dornburg).

BRUSSELS 28 June 1935 (in French, translated by J. Rousseau and J. Weterings).

A German arrangement by H. Stieber was published in 1936.

KUSSER: *Ariadne*

15 February. Brunswick

Text by F. C. Bressand. Five acts.

Revived at Brunswick 28 August 1692 and 1715. Airs from this opera were printed at Stuttgart in 1700 (as *Heliconische Musen-Lust*).

KUSSER: *Jason*

1 September. Brunswick

Text by F. C. Bressand. Five acts.

Also given at Hamburg 1695 and Stuttgart 1698 (as *Die unglückliche Liebe des tapfern Jasons*, reduced to 3 acts); 7 November 1700; and 1702. Revived at Brunswick August 1715 and August 1724 (as *Die an des Jasons Untreue sich rächende Medea*; 1715 reduced to 3 acts; 1724 additional music by Schürmann, 3 acts).

The music of *Jason* seems to be lost. An anonymous score in the Staatsbibliothek, Berlin, was for a long time thought to be Kusser's work, copied by Keiser. But it has been proved to be a different opera, *Jason oder die Eroberung des güldenen Fliesses*, Hamburg 25 November 1720, music chiefly by Schürmann. See G. F. Schmidt, *Frühdeutsche Oper* (1933–34), Vol. I, pp.44 and Vol. II, p.8; W. Schulze, *Quellen der Hamburger Oper* (1938), pp.41–44.

1693

STEFFANI: *La Libertà contenta*

3 February. Hanover

Text by O. Mauro. Three acts.

In German (as *Der in seiner Freyheit vergnügte Alcibiades*, translated by G. Fiedler) given at Hamburg 1697; Stuttgart 28 April 1699 (with a prologue, perhaps by Kusser, added) and 28 April 1701; Brunswick February 1700.

STRUNGK: *Alceste*

18 May. Leipzig

Text by P. Thiemich (founded on Aureli's *Antigona delusa da Alceste*, see 1660). Prologue and 3 acts.

Written for the inauguration of the Leipzig opera-house. Repeated at Naumburg and Weissenfels in the same year, 1693 (as *Hercules*). Music lost, as is the music of *Nero*, the second opera Strungk wrote for Leipzig in Autumn of the same year.

See on the early history of the first Leipzig opera-house F. Berend's dissertation on Strungk (1913) and G. F. Schmidt in the *Sandberger Fest-schrift* (1919). About 100 German operas were given there until 1720, most of them anonymous and all except one lost. Strungk, Boxberg, Telemann, Grünewald, Hofmann, Heinichen, J. G. Vogler are the few composers mentioned in the libretti.

BRONNER: *Echo und Narcissus*

??. Brunswick

Text by F. C. Bressand. Three acts.

Also given at Hamburg 1694. The first of Bronner's 7 operas, none of which is extant. See F. Chrysander in *Jahrbücher für Musikwissenschaft* (1863), pp.210–227.

ERLEBACH: *Die Plejades* oder *Das Siebengestirne*

??. Brunswick

Text by F. C. Bressand. Three acts.

Also given at Hamburg 1694 and revived at Brunswick February 1699. Erlebach's only opera. Music lost.

CONRADI: *Gensericus*

??. Hamburg

Text by C. H. Postel. Prologue and 3 acts.

Full title reads: *Der grosse König der Africa-nischen Wenden Gensericus, als Rom- und Kartha-gens Überwinder.*

Of Conradi's 8 operas the only one which is extant, at least in a revised version in which it was revived at Hamburg 20 June 1722 under the new title of *Sieg der Schönheit* (text altered by C.F. Weichmann, additional music by Telemann). In his *Der Musikalische Patriot* (1728) Mattheson states: "Dieser Sieg bestund in dem alten Gensericus ... mit einigen Neuerungen: von Telemannischer Composition. Hrn. Postels Poesie wurde verbessert durch Hn. Weichmann". See also Mattheson's review in his *Critica Musica*, Vol. I, Pt. 3 (July 1722) which is the first opera review in the first German musical periodical.

In Telemann's version the opera was also given at Brunswick February 1725; 18 August 1728 and February 1732; revived at Hamburg 18 November 1734.

Conradi was, after Theile, Strungk, Franck, and Förtsch, the fifth composer writing for the Hamburg German opera.

M. A. CHARPENTIER: *Médée*

4 December. Paris, O.

Text by T. Corneille. Prologue and 5 acts. Charpentier's only opera produced at the Académie.

Never revived in Paris, although considered by some critics to equal even Lully's operas. Also given at Lille 17 November 1700. The score was printed in 1694.

1694

POLLAROLO: *Ottone*

Carnival. Venice, S.G.Gr.

Text by G. Frigimelica Roberti. Five acts.

In Italian also given at Udine 1696; Brunswick August 1697; and, with alterations, Venice Carnival 1716.

KUSSER: *Erindo* oder *Die unsträfliche Liebe*

Carnival? Hamburg

Text by C. F. Bressand. Three acts.

Also given at Augsburg 1698 (as *Die unsträf-liche Liebe*). Forty-four airs from *Erindo* were printed in 1695 and reprinted in 1938 (edited by H. Osthoff).

(The first production was, according to W. Schulze, rather in the beginning of 1694 than in the Autumn of 1693 as has been assumed.)

Revived, in concert-form, Hamburg December 1939.

A. SCARLATTI: *Pirro, e Demetrio*

[28 January]. Naples, S.B.

Text by A. Morselli (first composed by Tosi in 1690). Three acts.

One of Scarlatti's most famous works. Repeated at Rome, Capr., in the same year, 1694 (not 1696); Siena, Acc. Rozzi 1695, with prologue and intermezzi by D. Franchini; Florence, Acc. dei Sorgenti 1696; Milan, T.R.D. Carnival 1695; perhaps also Mantua 1700; revived Florence Carnival 1711, as *La Forza della Fedeltà* and Fano [9 January] 1716, under the same title, with additional airs by other composers, arranged by A. Massarotti). At Naples, an intermezzo (characters: Amor and Ruffino, his secretary) was performed between Acts II and III.

Outside Italy given at Brunswick August 1696 (in Italian) and February 1700 (in German, translated by G. Fiedler). Perhaps also Leipzig October 1696.

London, Hm. 25 December 1708, as *Pyrrhus and Demetrius*, English version by O. MacSwiney, music arranged by N. F. Haym, with additions from Scarlatti's *Rosaura*, see 1690. Sung partly in English and partly in Italian (London début of the famous Italian singer Nicolo Grimaldi, called Nicolino). Very successful in London, given 61 times until 1717. Last revived 21 March 1716, wholly in Italian. Also given Dublin Spring 1711.

E. C. DE LAGUERRE: *Céphale et Procris*

15 *March*. Paris, O.

Text by J. F. Duché. Prologue and 5 acts.

Unsuccessful, but worth recording as the first work of a woman composer to be produced at the Paris Opéra. It was her only work for the stage. Score printed 1694. A Dutch translation of the text by G. T. Domis was published at Amsterdam in 1710.

KEISER: *Basilius*

Spring? Hamburg

Text by F. C. Bressand (founded on an Italian libretto by F. Parisetti). Three acts.

The full title reads: *Der königliche Schäfer, oder Basilius in Arcadien*.

One of Keiser's earliest operas. Music lost. It has been generally thought to be actually his first

opera, on the authority of Mattheson, who stated in his *Ehrenpforte* that *Basilius* had been heard at Brunswick or Wolfenbüttel before it was given at Hamburg. Chrysander (1863) hesitatingly accepted that statement, but according to G. F. Schmidt (*Neue Beiträge*, ... 1929) the opera made its appearance at Brunswick only about February 1696 (as *Basilius*). Mattheson probably confounded Keiser's opera with the Italian original (*Il Rè Pastore overo il Basilio in Arcadia*) which had indeed been produced at Brunswick in 1691 (with music by Alveri) and of which Bressand made a German translation (see F. Chrysander in *Jahrbücher für musikalische Wissenschaft*, 1863, pp.204–205).

Whether it was in fact Keiser's first opera will be difficult to decide, as the date of the first performance of *Basilius* at Hamburg is not known, and two other operas by him were produced at Brunswick in the same year, 1694, viz. *Procris und Cephalus* (date unknown) and *Die wiedergefundenen Verliebten* (sometimes also believed to be his first work for the stage) on 14 October.

1695

POLLAROLO: *Gl'Inganni felici*

25 *November*. Venice, S. Angelo

Text by A. Zeno. Three acts.

The first setting of Zeno's first libretto. Also given at Verona 1697; Naples, S.B. Autumn 1699; Brescia 1707; Vicenza 1709. Music lost. "L'Autore di questo dramma, ora celeberrimo per tanti altri, e per l'erudizione singolare di cui è fornito; fu certamente il primo a nobilitare il nostro Teatro" (Groppo).

MEDER: *Nero*

Before 28 *November*. Danzig

Text: the same German version, by an unknown translator, of an Italian libretto by G. C. Corradi, which Strungk had composed two years earlier (see 1693). Three acts.

The first German opera ever produced at

Danzig. Music lost. (An Italian opera, *Le Nozze d'Amore e di Psiche*, text by V. Puccitelli, music by M. Scacchi, had been given there as early as 15 February 1646.) The composer's attempt to introduce opera as a regular institution was suppressed by the municipal council. Meder's next opera had to be performed at Schottland, a small place outside Danzig territory (1698). (See J. Bolte in *Vierteljahrsschrift für Musikwissenschaft*, 1891).

STEFFANI: *I Trionfi del Fato* overo *Le Glorie d'Enea*

December. Hanover

Text by O. Mauro. Three acts.

According to Kretzschmar, Steffani's most important opera. Given at Hamburg 25 November 1699 (in German, as *Il Triumfo del Fato oder Das maechtige Geschick bei Lavinia und Dido*, translated by G. Fiedler). Revived Brunswick February 1716 (in Italian, as *Enea in Italia*).

1696

KEISER: *Circe* and *Penelope*

February. Brunswick

Text by C. F. Bressand. Two parts, in 3 acts each.

Full titles: *Circe oder Des Ulysses erster Theil* and *Penelope oder Des Ulysses zweiter Theil*.

Both parts were repeated at Brunswick February 1697 and also given at Hamburg in 1702, the second part under the title of *Penelope und Ulysses, ander Theil*. The first part also perhaps Leipzig October 1697 and January or October 1699. The second part was revived at Brunswick in August 1708 as *Ulysses Wiederkunfft*.

Keiser's *Ulysses*, written 26 years later for Copenhagen (see 1722), is a different work altogether.

M. A. (or G.) BONONCINI: *Il Trionfo di Camilla Regina de' Volsci*

26 December. Naples, S.B.

Text by S. Stampiglia. Three acts.

Bononcini's most successful opera; given at

Vienna 1697? (according to Allacci and Gerber); Rome, Capr. [8 January] 1698, as *La Rinovata Camilla Regina de Volsci*; Mantua 1698; Piacenza 1698; Venice, S. Salv. [4 October] 1698; Ferrara 1699 (and according to Burney 1707); Genoa Carnival 1700 (and 1703, and Autumn 1710?); Siena 1700; Turin, T.R. Carnival 1701; Leghorn 1701; Lucca February 1702; Milan 1702; Udine 1704 (as *La Fede in Cimento*); Rovigo October 1705 (as *La Fede in Cimento*) and 1706; London, D.L. 10 April 1706 (see below); Padua Carnival 1707 (as *La Fede in Cimento*); Bologna 1709 (as *Amore per Amore*) and 30 December 1718 (as *La Fede in Cimento*); Dublin March 1711; Udine 1715; Leghorn May 1715.

There has always been much uncertainty about this opera, beginning with the composer and the year and place of its first production. It is often attributed to the older Bononcini, Giovanni, e.g. in a MS score preserved at Münster (see E. J. Dent, *Scarlatti*, p.65); in the *Avvisi di Napoli*, reporting the performance of 1696: "posta egregiamente in musica dall'eccellente Sonator di Violone Sig. Giovanni Bononcini, Bolognese"; in two MSS. in the British Museum (Add. MSS. 14185 and 14186); also by the anonymous author of *A Critical Discours on Opera's and Musick in England* (1709), who says: "Compos'd by Gio. Buononcini, and prepared for the English Stage by Ni . . . o Ha . . . m". See also Burney, IV, p.210, note. Most of the earlier librettos do not mention the composer, but M. A. Bononcini's name is given in the Venice 1698 libretto; also in a MS score in Vienna.

As to the first production, there is no evidence for the often repeated statement that *Camilla* was first produced at Vienna in 1693 (even the 1697 production there is doubtful). The Naples libretto is the earliest known (copy in the Brussels Conservatoire). Neither Florimo nor Croce mentions the production at Naples; but apart from the fact that the libretto gives the full cast, there is further evidence for the production to be found in the preface to the libretto of Alessandro Scarlatti's *Emireno*, from which we also learn the approximate date, as it is stated there that *Camilla* was produced between an anonymous *Comodo An-*

tonino (text by F. M. Paglia; according to Croce 18 November 1696) and Scarlatti's *Emireno* (probably Carnival 1697).

In London, *Camilla* was produced at D.L. 10 April 1706 in an English version by O. MacSwiney[1], music adapted by N. F. Haym (but according to Sonneck not altered or enlarged, but practically intact). Very successful in London; first given wholly in English, but from 17 December 1707 half English and half Italian, when Valentini and "The Baroness" sang their parts in the latter language (Burney, IV, p.205). Revived in London (in English) at Lincoln's Inn Fields Th. 13 January 1717, 7 March 1719 and 30 November 1726. Also given at Dublin Spring 1711 (see above). There were no less than 113 performances between 1706 and 1728, which is by far the greatest number an Italian opera reached in London in the course of the whole 18th century; most of the performances, it is true, were wholly in English.

1697

PISTOCCHI: *Il Narciso*

March. Ansbach

Text by A. Zeno (*Pastorale per musica*). Five acts.

The first opera Pistocchi wrote for a German court (for the inauguration of the Italian operahouse at Ansbach) and the first setting of Zeno's libretto. The composer himself sang the name part. Revived Munich Carnival 1701. Music lost.

DESMARETS: *Vénus et Adonis*

17 March. Paris, O.

Text by J. B. Rousseau. Prologue and 5 acts.

Revived in Paris 17 August 1717; given at Lunéville 15 November 1707; Lille 1720; Ham-

---

[1] He signed the dedication in the printed libretto. From an agreement between Haym and Christopher Rich, dated 14 January 1705, and published by A. Nicoll, *A History of Early Eighteenth Century Drama* (1929), p.274, it appears that the English version originally had been prepared by an otherwise unknown Mr. Northman.

burg April 1725 (in French, with a "teutschem comiquen Vorspiel").

Score published in 1697.

KEISER: *Der geliebte Adonis*

Spring? Hamburg

Text by C. H. Postel. Three acts.

This is the earliest of Keiser's operas the score of which has been preserved. Parts of the opera were revived at Hamburg 14 January 1878 (at the bicentenary celebrations of the Hamburg opera, as *Klage um den toten Adonis*, music arranged by J. N. Fuchs).

DESTOUCHES: *Issé*

7 October. Fontainebleau

Text by A. Houdar de La Motte (*pastorale héroïque*). Prologue and 3 acts.

Destouches's most successful work. Repeated at Trianon 17 December and at the Paris Opéra 30 December 1697, and revived there 14 October 1708 (enlarged to 5 acts); 7 September 1719; 3 February 1721; 19 November 1733; 14 November 1741; Versailles 26 November 1749, without the prologue; Paris 23 December 1756; finally at Versailles 18 December 1773 (with alterations by Berton).

In French also Lyons 1709; Hague 27 December 1710; Brussels 22 December 1711.

In German (as *Isse oder Die vergnügende Liebe*) Wolfenbüttel 12 September or 4 October 1710 (music arranged [partly newly composed?] by Schürmann).

Revived in concert form by the Schola Cantorum, Paris 27 November 1908.

The first performance at Fontainebleau is recorded in the *Journal* of the Marquis de Dangeau: "On chanta un petit opéra dont un mousquetaire a fait la musique; le roi et les courtisans convinrent qu'elle est aussi bonne que celle de Lully et qu'elle n'est point volée".

The score was published in 1708 and 1724. Two parodies were produced at the C.I., Paris, viz. *Les Amours de Vincennes*, by P. F. Dominique, 12 October 1719; and *Les Oracles*, by J. A. Romagnesi, 21 December 1741.

CAMPRA: *L'Europe galante*

24 *October*. Paris, O.

Text by A. Houdar de La Motte. Prologue and 4 entrées.

L'Europe galante is the first outstanding example of "opéra-ballet", a French favourite form during the 18th century. Marmontel (*Eléments de Litté-rature*) defines it as "un spectacle composé d'actes détachés quant à l'action, mais réunis sous une idée collective". Each act or entrée may be called a little opera in itself where the action is reduced to a strict minimum, where the subject often becomes a mere pretext for the development of music, and above all, dance (P. M. Masson, *Rameau*, 1930, p.21).

In such "spectacle coupé" the single entrées are easily interchangeable; new ones could be substituted almost *ad libitum*. About the middle of the century the "idée collective" was often lost sight of, and the earlier "Festes de . . ." and "Amours de . . ." titles become, more honestly, "Fragments de . . ."

L'Europe galante consists of a prologue, *Les Forges de l'Amour*, and of four entrées, *La France*, *L'Espagne*, *L'Italie*, and *La Turquie*.

Revived in Paris 18 May 1706; 20 August 1715; February 1716 (with cantata *Œnone* added); 20 June 1724; 22 February 1725 (with another entrée *La Provençale*, in place of *L'Espagne*); 14 June 1736; 9 May 1747; 26 August 1755 (with additions by L. Aubert); 17 June 1766 (parts); and 16 February 1775 (the last entrée only).

Also given probably at the Hague in 1701; Ghent 1706 (with a prologue by P. A. Fiocco); Lille [1718]; Brussels 4 November 1726. Score published in 1724.

Given at Hamburg 21 February 1724 (in French, in an abridged version), as the first act of a 3-act pasticcio, called *Der Beschluss des Carnevals*. The second act was a French comedy (without music) and the third act was a German comic opera by Telemann, with the Italian title, *Il Capitano*. "Surely one of the oddest mixtures imaginable!" (Sonneck), even in the pasticcio-minded 18th century.

A. SCARLATTI: *La Caduta de' Decemviri*

November. Naples, S.B.

Text by S. Stampiglia. Three acts.

According to B. Croce, Scarlatti's best score written to Stampiglia's worst libretto. Also given at Palermo 1698 (with a prologue *L'Alcide*); and probably Leghorn 1699; Florence Carnival 1700; Genoa Autumn 1701; Siena Carnival 1704 (composer not mentioned in librettos of these performances).

DURÓN: *Veneno es de Amor la Embidia*

(Envy is the Poison of Love)

17 *November*. Madrid

Text by A. de Zamora. Three acts.

One of the very few surviving examples of early Spanish zarzuela. See for an analysis E. Cotarelo y Mori, in *Boletín de la Academia Española*, 1932, pp.767 *sqq*.

1698

KEISER: *Augustus*

9 *June*. Hamburg

Text by C. H. Postel. Three acts.

The lengthy title reads: *Der bey dem allgemeinen Welt-friede von dem grossen Augustus geschlossene Tempel des Janus*. The opera was written to celebrate the peace of Ryswick (1697) and the glory of the Emperor Leopold I in general. Although a *pièce d'occasion*, it was revived at Hamburg in 1712 and even as late as 10 October 1729 (with prologue by Telemann); also, in an adaptation, at Copenhagen 30 November 1722, as *Der von Othino, dem Urheber des Dänischen Reichs geschlossene Tempel des Janus* (not 10 October 1746, as E. H. Müller, *Angelo u. Pietro Mingotti*, 1917, p.XXII, supposes). Score preserved.

"Hr. Keiser machte die Music, Hr. Postel die Verse. Diese beiden Verfasser verstunden sich sehr wol, und brachten viel schönes zu Wege. Diese Opera bewiess es sonderlich" (Mattheson).

BOXBERG: *Sardanapalus*

??. Ansbach

Text by the composer. Prologue and 3 (?) acts.

Of Boxberg's operas (most of them written for Leipzig) the only one which is extant. The score was discovered by A. Sandberger (see H. Mersmann, *Beiträge zur Ansbacher Musikgeschichte*, 1916). An anonymous opera of the same title, produced at Leipzig in 1708, is (according to G. F. Schmidt) a different work.

KEISER: *Orpheus*

??. Brunswick

Text by F. C. Bressand. Five acts.

Consisting of two parts, called *Die sterbende Eurydice oder Orpheus erster Theil*, and *Die verwandelte Leyer des Orpheus*, respectively, under which titles it was given at Brunswick February 1699, and Hamburg 1702 (as two 3-act operas). Revived Brunswick February 1700 (as *Orpheus und Euridice*, 3 acts) and February 1770 (in the same form); Hamburg 1709 (in 5 acts, as *Die biss in und nach dem Todt unerhoerte Treue des Orpheus*) and 1726 (as *Die wunderbare Beständigkeit der Liebe oder Orpheus*); Brunswick August 1727 (in 3 acts, remodelled by Schürmann).

A. SCARLATTI: *Il Prigioniero fortunato*

14 December. Naples, S.B.

Text by F. M. Paglia. Three acts.

Also given at Mantua 1699; Florence Autumn 1699; Palermo 1702.

1699

POLLAROLO: *Faramondo*

Carnival. Venice, S.G.Gr.

Text by A. Zeno. Three acts.

Given at Pratolino later in the same year (with alterations); Bologna 24 June 1709 (as pasticcio). In German (translated by G. Fiedler) Brunswick August 1699 and February 1701 (no composer mentioned, but probably Pollarolo's opera).

Revived Brussels 4 November 1727 (in Italian).

DESTOUCHES: *Amadis de Grèce*

25 March. Paris, O.

Text by A. Houdar de La Motte. Prologue and 5 acts.

Revived in Paris 3 November 1711 (with alterations); 9 March 1724; 7 March 1745; and, in concert form, Versailles 30 April 1749 and 16 January 1751.

Given at Brussels 2 January 1711; Lille [1718]; Lyons in 1742.

Score published 1699.

A parody, *Amadis le Cadet*, by L. Fuzelier was produced at the C.I., Paris 24 March 1724.

1700

KEISER: *La Forza della Virtù* oder *Die Macht der Tugend*

Carnival. Hamburg

Text by C. F. Bressand (translated from an Italian libretto by D. David, first set to music by Pollarolo in 1693). Three acts.

Successful at Hamburg, given there nearly all the year through. Score preserved. Airs from the opera were printed in 1701.

A. SCARLATTI: *L'Eraclea*

Carnival? Naples, S.B.

Text by S. Stampiglia. Three acts.

Given at Parma in the same year (music by Scarlatti and Sabadini).

L'Eraclea contains the earliest known example of a vocal operatic septet (quoted in E. J. Dent's monograph, pp.56–58).

PISTOCCHI: *Le Risa di Democrito*

February. Vienna

Text by N. Minato (first set to music by Draghi in 1670). Three acts.

Also given at Bologna 16 January 1708 (revived in 1727), at Forlì 1710, and at the Stadttheater, Vienna, as late as in September 1737 (eleven years after Pistocchi's death) and once more in 1742.

DESTOUCHES: *Omphale*

10 November. Paris, O.

Text by A. Houdar de La Motte. Prologue and 5 acts.

One of Destouches's chief works. Given at Lyons in 1713; at Brussels 4 November 1715; revived at Paris 21 April 1721; 27 January 1733; 13 January 1735; and 14 January 1752 (at Marly 10 May 1751).

In German (translated and arranged by G. P. Telemann), Hamburg 24 April 1724.

Parodies: *Hercule filant*, by L. Fuzelier,. C.I. 15 May 1721; *Polichinelle Alcide ou Le Héros en Quenouille*, by D. Carolet, Th. des Marionettes, Foire St. G. 26 February 1733; *La Fileuse*, by J. J. Vadé, O.C. 8 March 1752; *Fanfale*, by C. S. Favart and P. A. L. de Marcouville, C.I. 8 March 1752. A fifth parody, by J. Bailly, was published in 1758, not performed.

After the last revival, the Baron F. M. de Grimm published (February 1752) his famous *Lettre sur Omphale* (against the French tragédie-lyrique in general), thus opening the notorious "Guerre des Bouffonnistes et Anti-Bouffonnistes" before the Italian buffo troupe had actually started their performances at the Paris Opéra (on 1 August 1752 with Pergolesi's *La Serva Padrona*).

The original libretto of *Omphale* gives 10 November 1701 (instead of 1700) as the date of the first performance, and this has been followed by all authorities and books of reference. P. Mélèse, however, in his recently published *Répertoire Analytique* (1934), enters the opera under 1700, on the authority of the *Journal du Marquis de Dangeau*, who records several rehearsals at Fontainebleau in October 1700, and also the general rehearsal there on 4 November 1700. There is no review of the opera in the *Mercure Galant*. Whether, after the rehearsal, the Paris production was postponed for more than a year, or the date of 1701 in the libretto is a misprint, it is difficult to decide.

CAMPRA: *Hésione*

21 December. Paris, O.

Text by A. Danchet. Prologue and 5 acts.

After two opéra-ballets in 1697 and 1699, this was Campra's first tragédie-lyrique.

Given at Brussels in 1710; Lille [1720]. Revived in Paris 19 July 1709 (with new airs); 13 September 1729; 1 March 1743; Versailles and Compiègne, May 1750; and Versailles 20 November 1752 (in concert form).

Score published 1700 and 1701.

A parody of the same title, by P. F. Dominique and J. A. Romagnesi, was produced at the C.I. 22 October 1729.

1701

POLLAROLO: *Le Pazzie degli Amanti*

February. Vienna

Text by F. Passarini. Three acts.

The only opera the Venetian composer wrote for Vienna. Revived Rovigo Autumn 1711; Venice Carnival 1719.

KEISER: *Stoertebecker und Joedge Michaels*

??. Hamburg

Text by Hotter. Three acts.

A second part followed later in the same year. In the preface to the libretto the unusual character of the subject is emphasized (Störtebecker was a 14th-century Hamburg pirate).

The music, apart from a single instrumental minuet, is lost.

ARIOSTI: *La Fede ne Tradimenti*

12 July. Berlin

Text by G. Gigli (first set to music by Fabbrini in 1689)[1]. Three acts.

One of the very few operas produced at Berlin before the reign of Frederick the Great. The performance took place at the Lietzenburg (now Charlottenburg) palace. Score preserved in the British Museum.

[1] As the result of a comparison, C. Sachs suggests that the text might have been written by Queen Sophia Charlotte, in French, and that it was translated into Italian by O. Mauro.

GATTI: *Scylla*

16 September. Paris, O.

Text by J. F. Duché. Prologue and 5 acts.

Given since 20 December 1701 in an altered version and with a new prologue.

The last and best opera of Gatti who, after Lully and Lorenzani, was the third Italian composer who contributed to the French operatic stage.

Score published.

Scylla was revived in Paris, 1 October 1720 and 11 September 1732. A parody by L. Fuzelier, *Le Cheveu*, was produced at the O.C. 25 September 1732.

ALDROVANDINI: *Mitridate in Sebastia*

December. Genoa, T. del Falcone

Text by G. Maggi. Three acts.

Also given at Turin, T.R. Carnival 1702; Florence Carnival 1704; and (with additional music by G. Vignola) Naples, S.B. December 1706.

1702

G. BONONCINI: *Polifemo*

Summer. Berlin

Text by A. Ariosti. One act (17 scenes).

The first opera produced at Berlin which is extant; the performance took place at the Lietzenburg Palace (now Charlottenburg, called after Queen Sophia Charlotte, who played the cembalo part at the production of Bononcini's opera).

Exact date of first performance unknown, but it appears from the Queen's letter to Steffani that it must have taken place after 25 July; see C. Sachs, *Musik und Oper am Kurbrandenburgischen Hof*, 1910 (where the libretto was printed for the first time).

In a new arrangement by G. Kaernbach, *Polifemo* was broadcast from Berlin on 6 August 1937; vocal score published 1938.

CAMPRA: *Tancrède*

7 November. Paris, O.

Text by A. Danchet (after Tasso). Prologue and 5 acts.

Campra's chief work. Given at Brussels in 1708. Revived in Paris 20 October 1707 (with alterations); 8 June 1717 (with added ballet *Les Fêtes Corinthiennes*, music by Campra); 3 (not 30) March 1729 (with new alterations); 23 October 1738; after Campra's death (1744); Versailles 10 December 1748 (without the prologue); Paris 22 February 1750 and 5 October 1764.

The part of the heroine Clorinde (sung by Mlle. Maupin) is written for contralto for the first time in French opera.

A parody by N. Barbier, *La Vengeance de Colombine ou Arlequin beau-frère du Grand Turc*, was produced at Lyons as early as 13 July 1703; two others *Pierrot Tancrède ou La Méprise de l'Amour* (by L. Fuzelier, C. F. Panard and C. F. B. de Pontau) and *Arlequin Tancrède* (by P. F. Dominique and J. A. Romagnesi) were produced at the O.C. and at the C.I., Paris, 10 and 19 March 1729, respectively.

1703

GASPARINI: *Il Più fedel frà i Vassalli*

[*3 February*]. Venice, S. Cass.

Text by F. Silvani. Three acts.

Gasparini's second and most successful opera. Given at Milan, T.R.D. Carnival 1703 (revived 26 December 1720); Bologna 31 May 1710 (pasticcio); London 23 December 1711 (as *Antioco*)[1]; Padua 1714; Udine 1715; Venice Carnival 1716 (revived at the T.S. Angelo, with alterations); Durlach 1716 (in Italian; probably Gasparini's setting).

BADIA: *La Psiche*

21 February. Vienna

Text by P. A. Bernardoni (*Poemetto drammatico*). One act.

[1] Gasparini actually wrote an opera *Antioco*, text by A. Zeno and P. Pariati, first produced at Venice in 1705. Comparison of the libretti shows that the work given in London was not that *Antioco*, but that it is identical with *Il più fedel frà i Vassalli*, the hero in question being an Egyptian prince, and not Antiochus I, King of Syria, as in the opera of 1705.

One of the 27 operas of Badia who, from 1696 to 1738, was court conductor at Vienna.

KEISER: *Die verdammte Staat-Sucht, oder Der verfuehrte Claudius*

Spring? Hamburg

Text by H. Hinsch. Three acts.

The first opera produced at Hamburg which contains besides 56 German airs, 11 in Italian, thus indicating the beginning of the decadence of style there.

Revived at Hamburg 1706; 21 November 1718 and 17 July 1726 as *Claudius, Roemischer Kayser* (with alterations).

FEDELI: *Almira*

??. Brunswick

Text by G. Pancieri (first composed by Boniventi in 1691). Three acts.

The composer spent the greater part of his life at various German courts (Dresden, Berlin, Cassel). Exact date of first production unknown. See on this opera G. F. Schmidt, *Die frühdeutsche Oper . . .* (1933), Vol. I, p.38.

1704

F. CONTI: *Alba Cornelia*

Carnival. Milan, T.R.D.

Text by S. Stampiglia. Three acts.

Revived Vienna February 1714 (with intermezzi *Milo e Lesbina*); Breslau 19 February 1726; Brussels Carnival 1728.

KEISER: *Nebucadnezar*

Carnival. Hamburg

Text by C. F. Hunold, called Menantes. Three acts.

The full title reads: *Der Gestuertzte und wieder Erhoehte Nebucadnezar, König zu Babylon unter dem grossen Propheten Daniel.*

Revived Hamburg 28 July 1728 (music revised by Telemann).

GASPARINI: *La Fede tradita e vendicata*

[5 January]. Venice, S. Cass.

Text by F. Silvani. Three acts.

One of Gasparini's most successful operas. Given at Florence Carnival 1705; Verona 1705; Lucca Carnival 1706; Leghorn 1707; Naples, S.B. December 1707 (text altered by C. de Petris, additional music by G. Vignola); Brescia 1709; Rome, Capr. Carnival 1712; Bologna 15 August 1712 (with additional music by Orlandini); London 9 March 1713 (as *Ernelinda*, pasticcio); Modena 26 December 1713; Venice, S. Moisè, Autumn 1715; Turin, T. Carignano, Carnival 1719; Brunswick February 1726 (as *Rodoaldo Re di Norvegia*); Prague 1727 (Gasparini mentioned for the last time).

By degrees, Gasparini's original music seems to have been displaced by additions from a rival setting by Orlandini which was first produced at Genoa, S. Agostino Autumn 1709 (copy of the libretto Bibl. Soleinne; in the Catalogue, no.4728, one Cesare Buonazzoli is mentioned as the author; he rather seems to have been the manager of the Genoa theatre who signed the dedication).

There are further anonymous productions of *La Fede tradita e vendicata* at Graz Autumn 1736, and Prague 1738. In the meantime, however, Silvani's text had been reset by Vivaldi (1726) and Bioni (1729).

DESMARETS and CAMPRA: *Iphigénie en Tauride*

6 May. Paris, O.

Text by J. F. Duché and A. Danchet. Prologue and 5 acts.

Revived in Paris 12 March 1711; 15 January 1719; 16 December 1734; in concert form, Versailles 13 July 1746 and Compiègne 6 June 1750; and once more Paris, O. 16 November 1762 (music revised by P. M. Berton).

Given at Lyons in 1712 and February 1714; Lille [1720]; Brussels 11 August 1726.

Score published without date; re-published 1721 and 1723.

This was the earliest opera on the subject. The first Italian *Ifigenia in Tauride*, by Domenico Scarlatti, was produced at Rome on 15 February 1713 (text by C. S. Capeci).

GRÜNEWALD: *Germanicus*

October. Leipzig

Librettist unknown. Three acts.

Given at Naumburg and Hamburg in 1706 (as *Die errettete Unschuld oder Germanicus, Römischer General*) and (according to Gottsched) revived at Leipzig in 1710 and 1720.

MATTHESON: *Cleopatra*

20 October. Hamburg

Text by F. C. Feustking. Three acts.

The full title reads: *Die betrogene Staats-Liebe, oder Die unglückselige Cleopatra, Königin von Egypten.* Score preserved.

In this opera Mattheson sang and conducted alternately! It was after a performance of *Cleopatra* on 5 December 1704, when Handel refused to give up his seat at the cembalo, that the well-known duel between the two composers took place.

1705

GASPARINI: *Ambleto*

Carnival. Venice, S. Cass.

Text by A. Zeno and P. Pariati. Three acts.

The first *Hamlet* opera. (Shakespeare is not mentioned amongst the sources in the libretto; see L. Collison-Morley in *The Athenæum* 31 December 1910.) Also given at Verona 1707; Naples, S.B. 1711; London 9 March 1712.

Domenico Scarlatti's opera on the same subject (sometimes stated to be the first) was produced at Rome in 1715 only (same text).

(Gasparini's setting was first given in Carnival 1705, according to the libretto; in Carnival 1706 or even 1707 according to other authorities.)

HANDEL: *Almira*

8 January. Hamburg

Text by F. C. Feustking (founded on an Italian librettob y G. Pancieri, set to music by Boniventi in 1691). Three acts.

The full title reads: *Der in Krohnen erlangte Glückswechsel, oder Almira, Koenigin von Castilien.*

Handel's first opera, containing 41 German and 15 Italian airs.

Revived Hamburg 7 February 1732 (with alterations; probably revised by Telemann).

Modern revivals, in a new version by J. N. Fuchs, were at Hamburg 14 January 1878 (bicentenary of the Hamburg Opera); Leipzig 25 June 1879; Hamburg 23 February 1885 (Handel bicentenary).

Keiser, being jealous of his young rival's success, set the same libretto in 1706 (text altered by B. Feind: *Der durchlauchige Secretarius, oder Almira, Koenigin in Castilien*; produced Autumn 1706; some airs printed). Handel wrote three more German operas for Hamburg (*Nero*, 1705, and *Florindo* and *Daphne*, 1708), which are lost.

CLAYTON?: *Arsinoe, Queen of Cyprus*

27 January. London, D.L.

Text: an English version, probably by P. A. Motteux,[1] of an Italian libretto by T. Stanzani (composed by Franceschini, see 1676). *An opera, after the Italian manner: All sung*. Three acts. (The words "All sung" were omitted on the title page of later editions of the libretto. The editors probably realized that the English public had soon got accustomed to recitative and needed no explanation any longer.)

Although it was, strictly speaking, an English opera, the history of Italian opera in England begins with *Arsinoe*, as there is a steady development, from the mere translation of an Italian libretto to the actual insertion of Italian airs in *Camilla* (see 1696; in London 1706), to *Almahide* (see 1710; with English intermezzi) and *L'Idaspe fedele* (1710, see *Gli Amanti generosi* 1705). Burney

[1] First attributed to him by Whincop in 1747.

gives a detailed account of those early years and in the light of modern research they have been dealt with by A. Nicoll (*Anglia*, Vol. XLVI) and others.

Whether Clayton composed the music of *Arsinoe* or merely utilized a collection of Italian airs, is still an unsolved problem. It should be noted, however, that in the preface to the libretto, which he signed himself, he does not claim to have composed the music.

The preface has been reprinted in Sonneck's *Catalogue*. Burney closes his most unfavourable account of *Arsinoe* with this passage: "It is scarce credible, that in the course of the first year this miserable performance which neither deserved the name of a drama by its poetry, nor an opera by its music, should sustain twenty-four representations, and the second year eleven". The anonymous author of *A Critical Discourse upon Opera's in England* ... (1709) is even more severe: "There is nothing in it but a few Sketches of antiquated Italian Airs, so mangled and sophisticated, that instead of *Arsinoe*, it ought to be called the Hospital of the old Decrepid Italian opera's".

GREBER: *The Loves of Ergasto*
20 April. London, Hm.

Text probably by A. Amalteo: *Gli Amori piacevoli d'Ergasto (favoletta per musica)* Vienna 1661. A *pastorale*, prologue and 3 acts.

Produced at the inauguration of the Queen's Theatre, Haymarket, the first opera to be given at the house which was to become the regular home of Italian opera in London for more than 150 years.

There has always been much uncertainty about this work, its title, the date of its first performance, and the language in which it was sung.

The title given here is that of the printed libretto and that under which it was advertised for a second (and apparently last) performance on 24 April (5 May) 1705. Cibber (writing 34 years later) called it "a translated opera, to Italian musick", and gives the title as *The Triumph of Love*; and later still there is a permanent confusion with two almost contemporary English operas

with similar titles, viz. *The Temple of Love*, text by Motteux, music by G. F. Saggione, produced at the same theatre, 7/18 March 1706; and *Love's Triumph*, text by Motteux (after Ottoboni), music by Cesarini, Giovanni del Violone and Gasparini, produced at the same theatre, 26 February (8 March) 1708. The date of the first production, at the opening night of the new theatre, is quite correctly given in Downes's *Roscius Anglicanus* (1708), and was then "corrected" by later writers.

As to the language, there seems to be no doubt that the opera was sung in Italian, thus antedating *Almahide* (which is generally believed to be the first example) by five years (see 1710). The cast of *The Loves of Ergasto* is unknown, apart from the "Italian boy" (Burney, IV, p.200); but Downes, the earliest critic, clearly says, ". . . . opened his theatre with a foreign opera, performed by a new set of singers arrived from Italy", and Congreve's epilogue "at the Opening . . . with an Italian Pastoral" (*Works*, 1710, Vol. III) stresses the fact that the fare offered on that occasion was something entirely new.

Moreover, there is the libretto of *The Loves of Ergasto*; for what other reason should it have been printed in English and Italian on alternate pages than to give the public the opportunity of following what they heard in a foreign language? The fact that the opera was so unsuccessful as to be given only twice, and that it was both preceded and followed, at Drury Lane and at the Haymarket, by eight other operas, all of which were sung in English (before *Almahide* cleared the way for the final victory of Italian opera), may have contributed to Burney's not mentioning its significance as the first Italian opera in London.

The historical importance of the work is even greater, as the score has been preserved (at the Vienna National-Bibliothek, under the Italian title of *Gli Amori d'Ergasto*). Eitner, followed by all books of reference, dates the score *c*.1701, whereas Weilen (Catalogue no.581) gives the date of *c*.1707–08, on the authority of an allusion in the prologue (not to be found in the London libretto) to the bride of the Emperor Charles VI, Elisabeth Christina of Brunswick-Wolfenbüttel, who was in Vienna from May 1707 to April 1708.

So it seems that Greber, who had come to London with the singer Francesca Margherita de l'Epine in 1692, and is not known to have left before 1705, wrote the opera for London, not for Vienna, where it was produced (or intended to be produced) only about two years later with a new prologue expressly written for that occasion. A comparison of the London libretto and the Vienna score might throw further light on the history of *The Loves of Ergasto*.

(For details on the London production, see W. J. Lawrence in *The Musical Quarterly*, Vol. VII (1921) and A. Nicoll in *Anglia*, Vol. XLVI (1922).

MANCINI: *Gli Amanti generosi*
??. Naples, S.B.

Text by G. P. Candi (first set to music by Vinacese, Venice 1703). Three acts.

Mancini's opera became better known as *L'Idaspe fedele*, under which title it was produced in London, Hm. 3 April 1710 (dedication dated 6 Marzo 1709–10, and signed by Cav. Nicolino Grimaldi, who sang the title part).

Very successful; performed 46 times until 1716 (revived 2 December 1711, with additional songs, and 18 May 1715). In this work English songs and singers have definitely disappeared, and the victory of purely Italian opera is complete.

"Nicolini's combat with a lion in the Haymarket" was the subject of Addison's famous satire in the thirteenth *Spectator* of 15–26 March 1711 (1710, old style). The essay was published nearly one year after the first performance of *Idaspe*, and not about the time of its production (a fact which has not always been realized by historians).

Burney gives 23 May as the date of the first London performance, which is obviously a misprint for 23 March (3 April, n.s.). In the British Museum copy of the 1712 edition of the libretto there is a hand-written note: "Produced ... more properly March 2ᵈ when it was rehearsed for Nicolini's benefit". This fact of a sort of public dress rehearsal is corroborated by the newspapers (cf. A. Nicoll in *Anglia*, Vol. XLVI, p.277).

There is a little-known reference to *Idaspe* in Z. C. von Uffenbach's *Merkwürdige Reisen* (1753), Vol. II, p.440.

A parody, *Harlequin-Hydaspes: or, The Greshamite*, a Mock-Opera in 3 acts, by Mrs. Aubert, was produced at the Lincoln's Inn Fields Th. 7 June 1719, three years after the run of the original was finished. As indicated in the libretto of *Harlequin-Hydaspes*, most of the songs were taken from *Idaspe*, but there were also songs from other London operas of those years, from *Almahide* (see 1710), *Pyrrhus* (see 1694), from Handel's *Rinaldo* (see 1711) and *Amadigi* (see 1715), and from an anonymous *Clearte* (1716).

KEISER: *Octavia*
5 August. Hamburg

Text by B. Feind. Three acts.

The full title reads: *Die roemische Unruhe, oder Die edelmuehtige Octavia*.

One of Keiser's better works, written in competition with Handel's second (lost) opera, *Die durch Blut und Mord erlangete Liebe, oder Nero* (text by F. C. Feustking; the same subject as in *Octavia*). The score was printed in 1902 as a supplement to the Handel *Gesamtausgabe* (edited by M. Seiffert).

LACOSTE: *Philomèle*
20 October. Paris, O.

Text by P. C. Roy. Prologue and 5 acts.

The most successful opera of Lacoste, who was a chorus singer, and later became conductor at the Opéra. Revived in Paris 8 October 1709; 27 April 1723; and 19 October 1734. Given at Lille [1720]; Brussels 10 January 1727; Lyons 26 April 1730 and 1742.

Score published 1705.

A parody of the same title, by A. Piron, was produced at the C.I., Paris 12 June 1723.

1706

F. CONTI: *Clotilda*
February. Vienna

Text by G. B. Neri (first composed by Ruggeri in 1696). Three acts.

In English, London, Hm. 13 March 1709 (adapted by J. J. Heidegger; a pasticcio, which also contained airs by Scarlatti and Bononcini, some of them sung in Italian) and again 27 May 1711.

MARAIS: *Alcione*

18 February. Paris O.

Text by A. Houdar de La Motte. Prologue and 5 acts.

Very successful in Paris; revived there 17 April 1719; 9 May 1730; 21 September 1741; 19 October 1756 (with many alterations and additions by L. Aubert); and 30 April 1771 ("partition complétement transformée", according to Lajarte; see his *Les Transformations d'un Opéra au dixhuitième siècle*, *Chronique Musicale*, 15 April 1874).

The opera was famous for its *tempeste symphonique*, one of the first essays in operatic realism. Score published 1706.

A parody by J. A. Romagnesi (*Alcionne*) was produced at the C.I. on 26 October 1741 (with music by Blaise).

KEISER: *Masagniello Furioso*, oder *Die Neapolitanische Fischer-Empoerung*

June. Hamburg

Text by B. Feind. Three acts.

Revived at Hamburg in 1714 and 18 June 1727 (new version; music revised by Telemann).

The first opera on this subject, 122 years before Auber's *Muette de Portici* (see 1828).

SCHÜRMANN: *Telemaque*

June or *July.* Naumburg

(German) text by J. C. Frauendorf (?). Four acts.

Revived in a much altered 3-act version, as *Telemachus und Calypso*, Brunswick August 1717; February 1720; and February (?) 1723; at Hamburg 26 November 1721.

M. A. ZIANI: *Meleagro*

16 August. Vienna

Text by P. A. Bernardoni. Three acts and licenza. Also given at Brescia 1710.

1707

STEFFANI: *Arminio*

Carnival. Düsseldorf

Librettist unknown. Five acts.

The first of the three operas Steffani wrote for Düsseldorf before finally sacrificing his musical career to his diplomatic activities.

A. SCARLATTI: *Il Mitridate Eupatore*

Carnival. Venice, S.G.Gr.

Text by G. Frigimelica Roberti. Five acts.

The first of Scarlatti's operas produced at Venice. Revived probably Reggio 1713; Milan, T.R.D. [15 January] 1717.

CLAYTON: *Rosamond*

15 March. London, D.L.

Text by J. Addison. Three acts.

Clayton's second and last experiment in English opera. Failure, performed three times only. (For Arne's setting of the same libretto see 1733.) Addison, in his satirical *Spectator* essays, is silent on this his own unfortunate contribution to the history of opera. The anonymous author of *A Critical Discourse upon Opera's in England* (London 1709) reviews *Rosamond* as follows: "In short, this Opera is no better than a confus'd Chaos of Musick, where there is ev'ry thing, and nothing, and for my part I think the only thing to be lik'd in it, is that it's short: and I believe, if a Reward was to be ordain'd for him that made the worst Musick in all the World, the Author of Rosamond wou'd have reason to say he had not lost his Labour, since he wou'd have an undoubted Title to the Gratification".

[PEPUSCH]: *Thomyris, Queen of Scythia*

12 April. London, D.L.

Text by P. A. Motteux. Three acts.

The music consisted of airs by A. Scarlatti, G. Bononcini (these two named in the printed score), Steffani, Gasparini, and Albinoni (these three mentioned by Hawkins). Pepusch adapted and arranged the music and wrote the recitatives. *Thomyris* is the first perfect example of a London pasticcio. It was sung partly in English and partly in Italian. Very successful, performed 42 times until 1728 (revived D.L. 28 November 1709; Lincoln's Inn Fields 20 May 1717 and 20 November 1728, in English).

There can be hardly a doubt as to Motteux's authorship as he is mentioned on the title-page of all editions of *Thomyris*. Yet the anonymous author of *A Critical Discourse upon Opera's in England* (London 1709) most decidedly attributes it, along with *Clotilda* (see 1706), to the "Swiss Count whose Earldom lies in the Land of the Moon", meaning not Motteux but obviously J. J. Heidegger. In a later paragraph the author calls *Thomyris* and *Clotilda* plainly "the Swiss Operas".

GRAUPNER: *Dido, Koenigin von Carthago*

Spring. Hamburg

Text by H. Hinsch. Three acts.

The first opera Graupner wrote for Hamburg. Score preserved. See on Graupner W. Nagel's study in *Sammelbände of the I.M.S.*, Vol. x (1908–09).

KEISER and GRAUPNER:
Der angenehme Betrug oder *Der Carneval von Venedig*

Summer. Hamburg

Text by Meister and M. Cuno. Three acts.

One of Keiser's most successful works, frequently revived until 1735. Some of the airs were sung in Italian.

The greater part of the music has been preserved and a selection was published in *Denkmäler Deutscher Tonkunst*, Vol. xxxviii (1912), edited by M. Schneider.

There was a modern revival at Hamburg in March 1931 (music arranged by F. Tutenberg).

1708
Prunella

23 February. London, D.L.

Text by R. Estcourt (*an interlude. . . . The sense and musick collected from the most famous masters*). Four acts.

Isolated example of English musical intermezzi and probably the first English operatic satire on Italian opera.

Prunella was performed (for the author's benefit) at a revival of George Villiers, Duke of Buckingham's comedy, *The Rehearsal* (originally produced in 1671), apparently between the acts. Some of the airs are indicated as to be sung to tunes from Clayton's *Arsinoe* (see 1705), Bononcini's *Camilla* (see 1696), and from *Thomyris* (see 1707).

"Some of the songs in the above-mentioned operas are parodied in it. It was a strange medley, and could not, we think, be very entertaining" (*Biographia Dramatica*).

" . . . some of the songs are sung by the characters in the Rehearsal—it was meant as a burlesque on the Italian Opera—it might amuse in representation, but it is dull in perusal . . ." (Genest).

LITERES: *Accis y Galatea*

19 December. Madrid, Buen Retiro

Text by J. de Cañizares. Two acts.

Early Spanish "zarzuela heroica", "casi uno ópera por el gran número de recitativos, arietas y cuatros que tiene" (Cotarelo y Mori). It was produced at the Buen Retiro Palace. Pedrell published one air from it in Vol. ii of his *Teatro lírico Español anterior al Siglo xix* (1897). An anonymous work of the same title, produced at Lisbon 22 October 1711 (in Spanish) may have been Literes's opera.

1709
M. A. ZIANI: *Chilonida*

21 April. Vienna

Text by N. Minato (first set to music by Draghi in 1677). Three acts and licenza.

Ziani's setting was written for the birthday of the Empress Amalia Wilhelmina. Repeated Vienna, Carnival 1710.

ASTORGA: *Dafni*

21 April. Genoa, S. Agostino

Text by E. Manfredi (first set to music by Aldrovandini in 1696), with alterations by F. M. Paglia (first set in this form by A. Scarlatti in 1700). *Drama Pastorale per Musica.* Three acts.

Only the first act is extant.

Also given at Barcelona June 1709; Parma Carnival 1715 (composer not mentioned; according to Volkmann rather Astorga's than Scarlatti's setting); Breslau September 1726.

For a detailed account of the history of *Dafni* see H. Volkmann's monograph on Astorga. Volkmann suggests Carlo de Petris as the author who adapted Manfredi's *Dafni* for Scarlatti and Astorga. Paglia however is mentioned in the original libretto which was unknown to Volkmann; see Giuseppe Dura, *Catalogo di Libri antichi e rari*, Naples 1861, no.11892.

KEISER: *Desiderius, Koenig der Longobarden*

26 July. Hamburg

Text by B. Feind. Five acts.

Written to celebrate the birthday of the Emperor Joseph I.

A. OREFICE: *Patrò Calienno de la Costa*

October. Naples, Fior.

Text by "Agasippo Mercotellis"[1]. Three acts.

Music lost. Libretto preserved. According to M. Scherillo this was the first Neapolitan comic opera (analysis of the libretto in his *L'Opera buffa*

[1] According to Scherillo an anagrammatic pseudonym of one (unknown) "Giasoppe Martoscelli"; according to B. Croce the libretto is founded upon an unpublished comedy, *La Perna*, by Nicolò Corvo. The work was referred to in the *Avvisi di Napoli*, 8 October 1709, as "una graziosa e piaciutissima Commedia in Musica, tutta in lingua napoletana".

Napoletana, 1916). A still earlier example is *La Cilla*, text by F. A. Tullio, music by M. A. Faggioli, produced 1706 and revived at the palace of Prince Chiusano, Naples 26 December 1707.

Patrò Calienno de la Costa incorporated also arias by an anonymous "azzellente Autore", possibly Alessandro Scarlatti.

A. OREFICE and MANCINI: *L'Engelberta* o sia *La Forza dell'Innocenza*

4 November. Naples, Pal. Reale

Text by A. Zeno and P. Pariati (first set to music by Fiorè and by Gasparini in 1708). Three acts.

The composers had an equal share; Orefice composed the first and part of the second act, Mancini the rest. Score preserved. Intermezzi, *Melissa schernita*, were performed between the acts and at the end of the opera.

HANDEL: *Agrippina*

26 December. Venice, S.G.Gr.

Text by V. Grimani. Three acts.

Probably Handel's only opera produced in Italy in the course of his three years' journey there, the performance of *Rodrigo* (Florence? 1708?) still being doubtful.[1] Successful at Venice, given there for 27 nights during the Carnival season. In Italian also given at Naples S.B. 15 February 1713 (with additional music by Mancini); Hamburg 3 November 1718 and 5 November 1722; Vienna 1719.

1710

G. BONONCINI?: *Almahide*

21 January. London, Hm.

Librettist unknown; the libretto is founded upon Dryden's *Almanzor and Almahide*, the second part of his *The Conquest of Granada by the Spaniards* (1672). Three acts.

[1] Cf. *Music and Letters*, Vol.xx, nos.1 and 4 (January and October 1939).

The historical importance of *Almahide* is emphasized by Burney as follows: "Neither the poet nor composer is mentioned in the book of the words or printed copy of the Musick, which seems all of one style, and that style more like Bononcini's than any other composer of the times. This was the first opera performed in England, *wholly in Italian* and by Italian singers; who were Nicolini, Valentini, Cassani, Margarita, and Isabella Girardeau. There were, indeed, intermezzi between the acts, in English, and sung by Dogget, Mrs. Lindsey and Mrs. Cross; but the opera was wholly Italian in poetry, Music and performance". (As to the question whether *Almahide* really was the first Italian opera in London, see note on Greber's *The Loves of Ergasto*, 1705.)

The score, published by Walsh in 1710 as *Songs in the new opera call'd Almahide*, states on the title-page: "The Songs done in Italian & English as they are Perform'd at ye Queens Theatre". There are 35 Italian airs, and the intermezzi as mentioned by Burney; 8 English songs, duets, etc., sung by Dogget, Mrs. Lindsey and Mrs. Cross in the characters of Floro, Blesa and Eliza. *Almahide* was given 24 times until 1712.

CAMPRA: *Les Festes Vénitiennes*

17 June. Paris, O.

Text by A. Danchet. Prologue and 3 entrées, called *La Feste des Barquerolles*, *Les Sérenades et les Joueurs* and *L'Amour saltimbanque*.

The following new entrées were added later: *La Feste marine*, 8 July 1710 (instead of *La Feste des Barquerolles*); *Le Bal*, 8 August 1710; *Les Devins de la Place Saint-Marc*, 5 September 1710; *L'Opéra*, 14 October 1710; *Le Triomphe de la Folie*, December 1710.

After 14 October 1710 (51st performance) given as *Le Carnaval de Venise*.

Given at Lyons in 1711. Revived in Paris in manifold variations of the single entrées, 11 October 1712; 10 July 1721; 14 June 1731; 19 July 1740; 16 June 1750; and 28 August 1759 (with additions by P. M. Berton). The 1740 revival was followed by a parody by C. S. Favart, called *Les Festes Villageoises*, and produced at the O.C.

30 August 1740; an earlier anonymous parody, *Les Fêtes Parisiennes*, had been given by a troupe of rope-dancers on 3 February 1711.

HEINICHEN: *Paris und Helena* oder *Der glückliche Liebeswechsel*

??. Naumburg

Text, an altered German version, by an unknown author (B. Feind?), of an Italian libretto, *La Forza dell' Amore*, first produced with music by Keiser at Hamburg in 1709. Three acts.

Score preserved.

1711

KEISER: *Croesus*

Carnival? Hamburg

Text by L. von Bostel (founded on an Italian libretto by Minato, 1678, and first set to music by Förtsch in 1684). Three acts.

The full title reads: *Der hochmuethige, gestuerzte und wieder erhabne Croesus*.

One of Keiser's best works. Revived in a new version, Hamburg 6 December 1730. Both versions extant. The opera was published in Vol. xxxix of *Denkmäler Deutscher Tonkunst*, 1912 (edited by M. Schneider).

A parody by J. P. Praetorius, called *Buchhöfer Der Stumme Prinz Atis*, was produced at Hamburg in 1726. According to the preface it was meant to be a parody after the French model, with music partly from the original.

The exact date of the first production of *Croesus* is unknown; as the MS score bears the date of 1710, the libretto the date of 1711, one might assume that it was performed early in 1711.

CHELLERI: *L'Innocenza giustificata*

Carnival? Milan, T.R.D.

Text by F. Silvani (first set to music by Vinacese in 1698). Three acts.

The only opera of Chelleri which is partly extant. In Italian (as *L'Innocenza difesa*) also given at Venice Carnival 1722; Cassel 1726; Brunswick 1731.

In German (as *Judith, Gemahlin Kayser Ludewigs des Frommen oder Die siegende Unschuld*, translated by J. G. Hamann), Hamburg 27 November 1732 (with recitatives and three new airs by Telemann and three airs from Handel's *Lotario*, see 1729; the airs were sung in Italian); given at Hamburg until 1737.

F. CONTI: *Il Trionfo dell'Amore e della Costanza*

21 January. Vienna

Text by F. Ballerini. Three acts.

In German (translated by J. J. Hoe), Hamburg January 1718 (music adapted by Keiser; some airs were sung in Italian); in German also Copenhagen 28 November 1722. In Italian, Breslau Winter 1725.

MATTHESON: *Henrico IV*

9 February. Hamburg

Text by J. J. Hoe. Five acts.

The full title reads: *Die geheimen Begebenheiten Henrico IV, Königs von Castilien und Leon, oder Die getheilte Liebe.*

Airs from this opera were printed in 1711.

HANDEL: *Rinaldo*

7 March. London, Hm.

Text by G. Rossi (from a sketch, after Tasso, by A. Hill, who then provided the printed English translation). Three acts.

The first opera Handel wrote for London. In the preface to the libretto Rossi calls the composer the "Orfeo del nostro secolo".

Rinaldo was more or less a pasticcio containing several airs from Handel's earlier operas. The famous *Lascia ch'io pianga* derives from this opera. Very successful in London; given 15 times during the first season, again 22 times until 1715, and revived, with alterations, 16 January 1717 and 17 April 1731.

Also given at:

DUBLIN April 1711 (by Nicolino's troupe as the first Italian opera in Ireland).

HAMBURG November 1715 (in German, translated by B. Feind); frequently revived until 1730.

NAPLES, PAL. REALE 1 October 1718 (in Italian, with additional music by L. Leo).

RUGGERI: *Elisa*

November. Venice, S. Angelo

Text by D. Lalli. Three acts.

After 74 years of operatic activity at Venice, this was the first comic opera ever produced there. Music lost.

For a discussion of the libretto, see M. Scherillo, *L'Opera buffa napoletana* (1916), p.490.

FASCH: *Lucius Verus*

27 November. Zeitz

Text, a German version, by an unknown author, of Zeno's *Lucio Vero* (first composed by Pollarolo in 1700). Three acts.

The most successful opera of Fasch, who is more important as a composer of instrumental music. Lost, like the rest of his operas.

Revived at Zeitz 27 November 1713 (as *Berenice*), and once more at Zerbst January 1739.

1712

CAMPRA: *Idoménée*

12 January. Paris, O.

Text by A. Danchet. Five acts.

Revived at Paris 5 April 1731. (Varesco's Italian *Idomeneo*, composed by Mozart in 1781, was derived from Danchet's libretto.)

Score published (n.d.).

GALLIARD: *Calypso and Telemachus*

25 May. London, Hm.

Text by J. Hughes. Three acts.

Revived Lincoln's Inn Fields Th. 10 March 1717.

This was, for many years, the last attempt at English grand opera. (For an account, see Burney, IV, p.232). Airs printed.

Hughes closes his preface (in which he calls his opera "an Essay for the Improvement of Theatrical Musick in the English Language, after the Model of the Italians") with the following tribute to Galliard: "I cannot conclude without acknowledging the Pleasure I have had, to find the Words of this Opera so naturally express'd in the Musick, that I believe the Gentleman who has compos'd it, has offer'd a much more prevailing Argument than any I cou'd urge, to shew that the English Language is capable of the most agreeable Graces of Harmony. I have mention'd this without his Leave, yet cou'd not refrain from doing him a Justice, which I perswade [sic] my self will be confirm'd by the Opinion of the most disinterested Judges."

"Dr. Arnold told me Mr Handell had so high an opinion of Calypso and Telemachus as to have declared he would sooner have composed it than any one of his own Operas. W.K. 1813" (handwritten note by William Kitchener in his copy of the *Songs*, sold in Julian Marshall's Sale, 29 July 1884 (sale catalogue no.442).

MARTINEZ DE LA ROCA:
Los Desagravios de Troya
(The Relief of Troy)
June or *July*. Zaragoza

Text by J. F. Escuder. Prologue and 3 acts.

The only Spanish opera of the 18th century (and even up to about 1840) which was printed in full score. See E. Cotarelo y Mori, *Historia de la Zarzuela* (1934), pp.78–80.

The opera was written in honour of the birth of a Spanish prince, and privately produced at the palace of Count de Montemar, field-marshal and governor of Zaragoza. The dedication in the score is dated 28 July 1712.

HANDEL: *Il Pastor fido*
3 December. London, Hm.

Text by G. Rossi (from Guarini's pastoral play, 1585). Three acts.

Revived in a new version, London, Hm. 29 May 1734 and C.G. 20 November 1734 (with a

new prologue in the "Temple of Erato, President of Musick").

DESTOUCHES: *Callirhoé*
27 December. Paris, O.

Text by P. C. Roy. Prologue and 5 acts.

One of the best of Destouches's later works. Given at Lyons 14 March 1715; Brussels 9 December 1721. Revived in Paris 3 January 1732, 22 October 1743, and 9 November 1773 (with alterations by Dauvergne) at the O. and once more as late as 2 March 1875 at the Th. Taitbout (re-scored by P. Lacome).

Score published 1712.

1713

FEO: *L'Amor tirannico* ossia *Zenobia*
18 January. Naples, S.B.

Text by D. Lalli (first set to music by Gasparini in 1710). Three acts.

Feo's first extant opera.

HANDEL: *Teseo*
21 January. London, Hm.

Text by N. F. Haym. Five acts.

Given 14 times during the season, but never revived.

HEINICHEN: *Calfurnia*
[*26 January*]. Venice, S. Angelo

Text by G. Braccioli. Three acts.

With and after Handel, Heinichen was one of the first German composers to write operas for Italian towns. A second work of his was produced at the same theatre in the same Carnival.

Calfurnia was also given at Hamburg February 1716 (in German, as *Die roemische Grossmuht oder Calfurnia*, translated by J. U. König; some of the airs were sung in Italian).

SALOMON: *Médée et Jason*
24 April. Paris, O.

Text by A. de La Roque (later attributed to S. J. de Pellegrin). Prologue and 5 acts.

The first and more successful of the two operas of Salomon, who was a gambist in the Paris Opéra orchestra. Revived in Paris 17 October 1713, with alterations; 29 April 1727; 22 November 1736; and 22 February 1749. Given at Brussels 14 September 1726.

Score published 1713.

A parody of the same title (by P. F. Dominique, F. Riccoboni, and J. A. Romagnesi) was produced at the C.I. 28 May 1727 and revived there 10 December 1736 (altered by D. Carolet).

1714

D. SCARLATTI: *Amor d'un Ombra e Gelosia d'un Aura*

20 January. Rome

Text by C. S. Capeci. Three acts.

The last of eight operas composed by Scarlatti for the private theatre of Queen Maria Casimira of Poland (who lived in Rome from March 1699 until June 1714). Also produced in London 10 June 1720 (as *Narciso*, text altered by P. A. Rolli) with additional numbers (two songs and two duets) by Thomas Roseingrave, who (according to Burney, IV, p.266) had brought over the score from Italy.

LEO: *Pisistrato*

13 May. Naples, S.B.

Text by D. Lalli (1711). Three acts.

Leo's first opera. Score preserved.

SCHWEITZELSPERGER: *Die romanische Lucretia*

??. Durlach

Librettist unknown. Prologue and 3 acts.

Probably repeated at Durlach in 1715 and 1716 and also given at Coburg 1718 and Nuremberg Spring 1719 (with alterations).

The only extant opera of Schweitzelsperger and of some 50 German operas (by Trost, Blinzig, Käfer, and others) produced at the court of Baden-Durlach between 1712-31.

See on Schweitzelsperger and his *Lucretia* score L. Schiedermair in *Sammelbände of the I.M.S.*, Vol. XIV (1912-13).

MOURET: *Les Festes de Thalie*

19 August. Paris, O.

Text by J. de Lafont. Prologue and 3 entrées.

In this successful opéra-ballet the comic element was first introduced into the sphere of French opera. Originally it consisted of three 1-act comic operas called *La Folie*, *La Femme*, and *La Veuve*, respectively. An epilogue, *La Critique des Festes de Thalie*, was added on 9 October 1714, the third act was replaced by *La Veuve coquette* on 12 March 1715, and a fourth entrée, *La Provençale*, was added on 17 September 1722 in place of *La Critique*. In various combinations revived at Paris 25 June 1722; 2 June 1735; 29 June 1745; and 24 September 1754. *La Femme* on 13 August 1765; *La Provençale* on 10 August 1745; 6 February 1755; 31 January 1758; 18 August 1769; and 16 February 1775; at Versailles 22 February 1764. The opera was given at Brussels as early as 2 October 1714 (revived 1 September 1740).

A parody on *Les Festes de Thalie*, by P. Laujon and Parvi, with music by Blaise, called *La Fille, la Femme, et la Veuve*, was produced at the C.I. on 21 August 1745 (after which parodies of grand operas were prohibited there for six years).

There were also two successful parodies of single acts, the music of both was written by Duni, viz. (1) *La Fille mal gardée ou Le Pédant amoureux* (parody of *La Provençale*, text by C. S. Favart, Madame Favart, and Lourdet de Santerre), produced at the C.I. 4 March 1758. In French also Amsterdam and Hague 1760; Brussels 7 January 1761; Vienna 4 February 1764; Frankfort 10 April 1764. Dutch versions by J. T. Neyts (Rotterdam 1764) and by J. F. Cammaert (Brussels 1767) printed. (2) *La Veuve indécise* (parody of *La Veuve coquette*, text by J. J. Vadé), produced at the O.C. 24 September 1759; Vienna 1761 (with new airs); Amsterdam 16 September 1761 (revised by L. Anseaume).

See on *Les Festes de Thalie* and its parodies, R. Viollier in *Revue de Musicologie*, Vol. XIX (May 1935).

F. CONTI: *I Satiri in Arcadia*

28 August. Vienna

Text by P. Pariati (*Favola pastorale*). Three acts.

In German (as *Cloris und Tirsis*, translated by Dr. Gazal), Hamburg 23 January 1719 (with Italian airs); Copenhagen 18 December 1721. An anonymous German opera, *Die Satyren in Arcadien* (perhaps a version of Conti's work), was produced at Leipzig in 1719.

PORPORA: *Arianna e Teseo*

1 October. Vienna

Text by P. Pariati. Three acts.

Revived Vienna Carnival 1717; Venice Autumn 1727; Florence 9 August 1729. No connection with *Ariadne in Naxus*, text by Rolli, produced London, Lincoln's Inn Fields Th. 9 January 1734.

MOURET: *Ragonde*

December. Sceaux

Text by P. Néricault Destouches.

The full title reads: *Le Mariage de Ragonde et de Colin ou La Veillée de Village.* The second successful opéra-ballet by Mouret, produced in 1714. It consisted of three intermèdes, called *La Veillée, Les Lutins,* and *La Noce et le Charivari,* and was privately produced at one of the "Grandes Nuits" at the palace of the Duchess of Maine at Sceaux.

First given at the Paris Opéra only four years after the composer's death as *Les Amours de Ragonde,* 31 January 1742 (then called *comédie en musique* and somewhat altered).

Revived Paris 12 February 1743; Versailles 24 March 1745 and 27 February 1748 (instead of Destouches, Nicolas de Malesieux[1] is mentioned as the author in the 1748 libretto); again Paris 11 February 1752; 5 February 1769; and 22 February 1773 (these latest two revivals not recorded by Lajarte).

Given at Lyons 1742; Brussels 10 March 1748; Bordeaux 1758.

[1] He had been one of the chief literary contributors to the theatrical performances at Sceaux—hence the mistake in the later libretto.

1715

A. SCARLATTI: *Il Tigrane* overo *L'egual Impegno d'Amore e di Fede*

16 February. Naples, S.B.

Text by D. Lalli (originally called *L'Amor di Figlio non conosciuto,* set to music by Albinoni, Venice 1715). Three acts.

Scarlatti's most famous opera; it is stated in the libretto that this was his 106th work for the stage. In *Tigrane,* horns were introduced into the opera orchestra for the first time.

Repeated at Innsbruck in the same year; at Leghorn Carnival 1716.

Date of first performance given in the Naples *Avvisi* of 19 February 1715 (Piovano).

KEISER: *Fredegunda*

March. Hamburg

Text by J. U. König (founded on an Italian libretto by F. Silvani, set to music by Gasparini in 1704). Five acts.

One of Keiser's most popular works; given at Hamburg until 1738.

An early description of *Fredegunda* is given in E. L. Gerber's *Historisch-Biographisches Lexicon der Tonkünstler* (1791).

HANDEL: *Amadigi di Gaula*

5 June. London, Hm.

Text probably by J. J. Heidegger (who signed the dedication; cf. Burney, IV, p.255). Three acts.

Given in London 19 times until 1717. Hamburg September 1717 and 6 February 1719 (in German, as *Oriana,* translated by J. Beccau, additional airs by Keiser; the airs were sung in Italian). There is a printed Dutch translation by K. Elzevier (n.d.). Revived Osnabrück 7 January 1929 (new German version by H. Dütschke).

ORLANDINI: *Amore e Maestà*

Summer. Florence, T. Cocomero

Text by A. Salvi. Three acts.

Given in an altered version by P. A. Rolli (as *Arsace*), with additional music by F. Amadei,

London, Hm. 12 February 1721; this version was translated into German by J. Mattheson (who also composed the German recitatives) and given at Hamburg on 18 May 1722 (frequently revived until 1736).

The original (presumably without Amadei's additions) was revived at Turin Carnival 1726 and Florence, P. Carnival 1732 (as *Arsace*).

Date and place of the first production are recorded by F. Piovano in *Sammelbände of the I.M.S.*, Vol. IX (1907–08), p.272. The original libretto is recorded by R. Uccelli, *Contributo alla bibliografia della Toscana*, 1922. See also Allacci, cols. 62 and 116, and Sonneck's *Catalogue*, p.157. That Orlandini did not compose his opera expressly for London becomes clear, moreover, from the remark in the London libretto: "This Opera was Originally set to Musick by Signor Orlandini, excepting those Songs mark'd with a Star, which are compos'd by Signor Philippo Amadei".

1716

BERTIN DE LA DOUÉ: *Ajax*

20 April. Paris, O.

Text by Mennesson. Prologue and 5 acts.

The most successful of Bertin de la Doué's five operas. Revived at Paris 16 June 1726 (début of the famous dancer, Marie-Anne Cupis, called Camargo); 2 August 1742; and 14 October 1770 (with additions by L. J. Francœur).

In French also given at Lille 1723; Brussels December 1723; Stockholm 9 April 1724; Lyons 1742.

Score published 1716.

A parody by L. Fuzelier, called *L'Amant brutal*, was produced at the O.C. on 3 July 1726.

POLLAROLO: *Ariodante*

Autumn. Venice, S.G.Gr.

Text by A. Salvi (originally called *Ginevra Principessa di Scozia* and set to music by Perti in 1708). Three acts.

Faustina Bordoni's first appearance was in this opera. Repeated Venice Autumn 1718 (text altered by G. Boldini); Treviso 1722.

VIVALDI: *Arsilda, Regina di Ponto*

Autumn. Venice, S. Angelo

Text by D. Lalli. Three acts.

One of Vivaldi's earliest operas. Up to 1927, of more than 40 operas, only two were known to be extant; *Arsilda* was one of them. But a good many more have been discovered since in the Mauro Foà Collection purchased by the Biblioteca Nazionale, Turin, in that year.

GERVAIS: *Hypermnestre*

3 November. Paris, O.

Text by J. de Lafont. Prologue and 5 acts.

It has been stated, without sufficient evidence though, that the Duke Philip of Orléans collaborated in this opera.

Revived at Paris April 1717 (fifth act remodelled by S. J. de Pellegrin); 1 June 1728; 18 August 1746; and 1 October 1765. Given at Lyons in 1742.

A parody by P. F. Dominique and J. A. Romagnesi, called *La bonne Femme*, was produced at the C.I. on 28 June 1728.

LOTTI: *Alessandro Severo*

26 December. Venice, S.G.Gr.

Text by A. Zeno (first setting of the libretto). Three acts.

The last opera Lotti wrote in Italy before he went to Dresden in 1717.

Revised Brussels 6 July 1729 (in Italian).

1717

KEISER: *Die grossmüthige Tomyris*

July. Hamburg.

Text by J. J. Hoe (founded on an Italian libretto by D. Lalli, *L'Amor di Figlio non conosciuto*, set to music by Albinoni in 1715). Three acts.

Brunswick August 1719; revived there in August 1720; February 1721; February 1724; and once more in August 1749 (with additional Italian airs by Hasse and others). Probably also given at Durlach 1721 and revived at Hamburg 5 May 1721 and 3 November 1723.

LOTTI: *Giove in Argo*

25 October. Dresden

Text by A. M. Lucchini. Three acts.

The first opera Lotti wrote for Dresden. Produced at the Redoutensaal ("Sala di Ridotto") as the new opera-house ("Regio Elettoral Teatro") was not ready yet. It was inaugurated on 3 September 1719 with the same opera.

Between the acts of *Giove in Argo* the intermezzi *Vespetta e Milo* (text by S. Stampiglia and F. Ballerini, music by A. Scarlatti and F. Conti) were produced, one of the first instances of that sort of performance in Germany.

(Date of first performance according to Fürstenau and Schatz; the dedication in the libretto is dated November 1717.)

CAMPRA: *Camille, Reine des Volsques*

9 November. Paris, O.

Text by A. Danchet. Prologue and 5 acts.

Revived at Paris, after an interval of 44 years, 22 September 1761 (without the prologue; music revised by P. M. Berton).

1718

ORLANDINI: *Antigona*

January. Venice, S. Cass.

Text by B. Pasqualigo. Five acts.

One of Orlandini's most successful serious operas. Revived at Venice, S. Angelo Carnival 1721 and S. Cass. 7 November 1724; Turin, T.R. Carnival 1727; and Bologna 14 June 1727 as *La Fedeltà coronata* (reduced to 3 acts).

In Italian, also given at Brunswick February and August 1724; Wolfenbüttel 17 April 1725; Brunswick again (with German recitatives and

choruses) August 1732; at Breslau 1 October 1728 (as *Antigone vendicata*).

SCHÜRMANN: *Heinrich der Vogler*

[*1 August*]. Brunswick

Text by J. U. König. (The title reads in full: *Heinrich der Vogler, Hertzog zu Braunschweig, nachmahls erwehlter Teutscher Kayser*.) Three acts.

Hamburg 6 November 1719 and revived 18 July 1735. Revived at Brunswick February 1721; August 1726 as *Henricus Auceps* (with some additional airs by Graun) and August 1730 (under the original title). Given by a German company at Stockholm 29 January 1734.

A second part, by the same authors, was produced at Brunswick [11 January] 1721.

PORPORA: *Temistocle*

1 October. Vienna

Zeno's text (first set to music by M. A. Ziani in 1701). Three acts.

Revived at Brussels 28 September 1729.

The opera by Porpora of this title performed in London 5 March 1743 was an entirely different work (libretto by Metastasio).

CALDARA: *Ifigenia in Aulide*

4 November. Vienna

Text by A. Zeno. Three acts.

One of the earliest operas Caldara wrote for Vienna. Revived there 22 November 1723.

(It has been stated that the opera was first produced at Vienna four years earlier, viz. 4 November 1714. According to Weilen's Catalogue, M. A. Ziani's *Andromeda* was given on that day.)

A. SCARLATTI: *Il Trionfo dell' Onore*

26 November. Naples, Fior.

Text by F. A. Tullio. Three acts.

The first extant example of a comic opera of the Neapolitan School. Two scenes from it were published by E. J. Dent in *Sammelbände of the I.M.S.*, Vol. XI (1909–10). The opera was revived at Loughton, Essex 23 July 1937 (in English, translated and produced by G. Dunn; open-air performance) and once more 20 July 1939; also revived at Siena 18 September 1940 (revised by V. Mortari).

ORLANDINI: *Il Marito Giogatore e la Moglie Bacchettona*

24 December. Venice, S. Angelo

Text by A. Salvi. Three parts.

These famous intermezzi were first performed between the acts of F. Chelleri's opera seria *Amalasunta*. Besides several revivals on Italian stages (Florence 1720; Rome, T. Alibert Carnival 1721; Ferrara Carnival 1722; Genoa Spring 1723 (as *Serpilla e Bacocco*); Lucca Carnival 1724 and Autumn 1740; Bologna 1725 (as *Il Giuocatore*) and Carnival 1748 (as *Bacocco o sia il Giuocatore*); Naples, S.B. 1 October 1725; Palermo 1726, etc., between the acts of various opere serie by other composers) they were also given at:

MUNICH 27 October 1722 (under the title of *Serpilla e Bacocco*, as intermezzi in Albinoni's *I veri Amici*).

BRESLAU November 1727 (in Bioni's *Attalo ed Arsinoe*).

BRUSSELS 4 November 1728 (in Orlandini's *Lucio Papirio Dittatore*).

PARIS, O. 7 June 1729 (as *Bajocco e Serpilla*).

TRIESTE August 1730 (as *Serpilla e Bacocco*).

MOSCOW 25 March 1731.

VIENNA 8 April 1733 (in Giacomelli's *La Caccia in Etolia*).

ST. PETERSBURG 1733 and 21 October 1757.

LISBON 1736 (in Schiassi's *Alessandro nell'Indie*).

LONDON 12 January 1737 (as *The Gamester*, sung in Italian; the first "intermezzo, or comic interlude, which was ever introduced between the acts of an Italian opera in England" [Burney, IV, p.400]. The opera was Hasse's *Siroe*).

HAMBURG 15 February 1741 and again 3 August 1744, 24 February 1746, 4 July 1753 and 1767.

PRAGUE 1744 (under the original title; no composer mentioned).

DRESDEN 29 August 1746.

AUGSBURG 1746.

POTSDAM Summer 1748 and again 16 October 1751.

PARIS, O. 22 August 1752 (as *Il Giocatore*, revived, after 23 years, by Bambini's buffo troupe, with additional music by Pergolesi, Buini and, probably, Auletta).

HANOVER 20 September 1753.

COPENHAGEN 5 February 1755, 19 December 1755, and 4 February 1757 (in Italian) and again 1758 (in Danish, with recitatives by J. C. Kleen).

MAYENCE 1758.

EDINBURGH 27 June 1763.

BERLIN 28 April 1777 (with German recitatives; the play-bill mentions as the composer "Herrn Bergulesi").

Following the productions at the Paris Opéra, two French parodies were performed at the C.I., viz.: (1) *Le Joueur*, 21 July 1729; text (a mixture of French and Italian) by P. F. Dominique and J. A. Romagnesi, music, it seems, partly from the original, partly composed by J. J. Mouret; also given at Fontainebleau 7 January 1730. (2) *Baiocco et Serpilla*, 6 March 1753; text (wholly in French now) partly rewritten by C. S. Favart, music by C. Sodi. This latter parody was (in French) also given at Stockholm 20 January 1757, Hague 1758, Amsterdam 1761, and Brussels 1766; revived Paris, Variétés-Amusantes, 16 July 1797. In Swedish (translated by C. Envallsson), Stockholm 21 April 1784 (given there until 1798) and Gothenburg 13 March 1795 (revived 10 December 1810). There was a recent revival of Sodi's setting at the Mercury Th., London, 25 July 1940 (as *The Gamester*, English version by G. Dunn), produced by the "Intimate Opera Company".

On the complicated history of this opera the following authorities should be consulted: A. Wotquenne, *Catalogue de la Bibliothèque du Conservatoire Royal de Bruxelles*, Vol. I, pp.458–60 (1898); L. de La Laurencie in *Revue Musicale* (*Bulletin Français de la S.I.M.*), 1912, no.6–8; G. Calmus in *Monthly Magazine of the I.M.S.*, 1912–13, p.114; O. G. T. Sonneck, *ibid.*, p.170; O. G. T. Sonneck in *The Musical Antiquary*, 1913, p.160;

O. G. T. Sonneck, *Catalogue . . . Washington*, pp.730-34 (1914).

No composer is mentioned in the original Venice libretto. Orlandini's name occurs for the first time in the London 1737 libretto. A MS score at Wolfenbüttel names Leonardo Vinci as the composer. Sonneck's verdict in 1913 was: ". . . therefore I do not think that we should longer hesitate, at least at present, to attribute *Il Giocatore* to Giuseppe Maria Orlandini"; but in 1914: ". . . consequently we must further assume that both Vinci and Orlandini composed the same text at a very early date, but we cannot as yet definitely attribute the earliest setting, that for Venice 1718-19, to either one or the other".

Since then, the score has been attributed again to Orlandini by G. Pavan (*R.M.I.*, 1922, p.433) and by H. Liebrecht (*Histoire du Théâtre Français à Bruxelles*, 1923, p.157), who mentions scores bearing Orlandini's name at Vienna and Rostock; to Vinci by G. F. Schmidt (*Zeitschrift für Musikwissenschaft*, VI, p.523).

The "méprises invraisemblables" (Wotquenne) which have been made in dealing with the history of *Il Giocatore* we need not enumerate again. They have not ceased since, either. J. G. Prod'homme, for instance, in his *L'Opéra* (1925), p.75, gives for the 1729 production at the Paris Opéra the names of the librettists of the 1729 parody "Romagnesi et Dominique," and the name of the composer of the 1752 parody "Sodi (ou Auletta?)".

As several of the above performances were anonymous, it must be mentioned that there are at least four later settings of the libretto, by G. Scarlatti, Florence Carnival 1747; Hasse, Frankfort 5 April 1755; Paisiello, Turin 1774 (according to Florimo); Schacht, Regensburg 1775 (libretto British Museum).

G. BONONCINI: *Griselda*

26 December. Milan, T.R.D.

Zeno's text (first composed by Pollarolo in 1701). Three acts.

London 5 March 1722 (text altered by P. A. Rolli) and revived there 2 June 1733. This opera

and the same composer's *Crispo* (see 1721) are the subject of discussion in Richard Steele's comedy, *The Conscious Lovers* (1723), II, 2. Rolli translated the comedy into Italian (1724) and does not fail to emphasize in a note his collaboration with Bononcini.

1719

A. SCARLATTI: *M. Attilio Regolo*

Carnival. Rome, Capr.

Text by M. Noris (first composed by **Pagliardi** in 1693). Three acts.

Revived Bologna October 1724.

F. CONTI: *Don Chisciotte in Sierra Morena*

11 February. Vienna

Text by A. Zeno and P. Pariati (*Tragicommedia per musica*), after Cervantes. Five acts.

(In later editions of the text the title was changed into *Don Chisciotte in Corte della Duchessa.*)

Also given at Brunswick February 1720 (in Italian).

In German (as *Don Quixotte in dem Mohrengebuerge*, translated by J. S. Müller) Brunswick, August 1721 (revived February 1733 [with some Italian airs] and February 1738) and Hamburg 5 October 1722 (with some airs sung in Italian; given there until 1737).

Revived Vienna 9 April 1826 (private performance at Hofrat von Kiesewetter's; see *A.M.Z.*, 1826, p.360, and Grove, III, p.21, 3rd edition, 1927).

SCHÜRMANN: *Die getreue Alceste*

February. Brunswick

Text by J. U. König (founded on Quinault's French libretto, see 1674). Three acts.

Hamburg 3 July 1719, as *Alceste* (given until 1723); Brunswick August 1721.

FUX: *Elisa*

25 August. Laxenburg, near Vienna

Text by P. Pariati (*Festa teatrale*). One act.

The only opera of Fux which was published in his lifetime. Written for the birthday of the Empress Elizabeth Christina.

Revived Vienna 31 August 1729; in this year the score was published at Amsterdam—probably the only printed full score of an Italian opera seria between 1662 (Bontempi's *Paride*) and 1756 (Sarti's *Ciro riconosciuto*).

Gerber says that the Emperor Charles VI conducted the 1729 revival at the cembalo.

LOTTI: *Teofane*

13 September. Dresden

Text by S. B. Pallavicino. Three acts.

Written for the wedding of Prince Frederick Augustus of Saxony and Maria Josepha, Archduchess of Austria.

Lotti's last opera. A German translation by C. F. Teucher was published in the same year.

TORRI: *La Merope*

12 October. Munich

Zeno's text (first composed by Gasparini in 1711). Three acts.

Torri's best and most successful opera. Repeated at Munich 9 June 1720 and 24 January 1723. Also given at Brussels December 1728 (in Italian).

The third act was printed in *Denkmäler der Tonkunst in Bayern*, Vol. XIX–XX (1920), edited by H. Junker.

CALDARA: *Lucio Papirio Dittatore*

4 November. Vienna

Text by A. Zeno (written for Caldara). Three acts.

In Italian also given at Brunswick 9 February 1721 and Brussels 4 December 1728.

1720

STUCK: *Polidore*

15 February. Paris, O.

Text by J. L. I. de La Serre (founded on a tragedy by S. J. de Pellegrin, 1706). Prologue and 5 acts.

The last opera of Stuck, who was one of the earliest violoncellists in the orchestra of the Paris Opéra. Revived there 21 April 1739.

Score published 1720.

PORTA: *Numitore*

13 April. London, Hm.

Text by P. A. Rolli. Three acts.

Handel's "Royal Academy of Music" was inaugurated with this opera. Porta's most successful work.

In Italian also given at Brunswick 1723 (as *Rhea Sylvia*); in German as *Die helden-muethige Schaefer Romulus und Remus*) Hamburg 2 November 1724 (with additional music by J. P. Kuntz; recitatives sung in German, airs partly in German, partly in Italian).

HANDEL: *Il Radamisto*

8 May. London, Hm.

Text by N. F. Haym. Three acts.

The first opera of Handel which was produced at the newly-founded "Royal Academy of Music." Repeated there, with alterations, 8 January 1721 and 6 December 1721, and once more in January or February 1728. This latter revival, mentioned by Burney, IV, p.259, but not recorded in F. Colman's *Opera Register* (see p.93), nor by Fassini and Nicoll, I was not able to verify from the newspapers as the parts in question are missing in the British Museum set.[1] That the revival actually took place is confirmed by the printed libretto, with full cast, a copy of which has been found in the National Library of Scotland, Edinburgh.

Given at Hamburg 28 January 1722 (in German, as *Zenobia, oder Das Muster rechtschaffener*

---

[1] January and February of the *Daily Courant*, the only paper in which the Italian operas were advertised then.

ehelichen Liebe, translated by J. Mattheson, who also composed the German recitatives; the airs were sung in Italian; revived 20 January 1736).

Revived in a new German version by J. Wenz: Göttingen 22 June 1927; and once more Düsseldorf 14 May 1937 (translated by H. Buths).

TORRI: *Lucio Vero*

12 October. Munich

Zeno's text (first composed by Pollarolo in 1700). Three acts.

Revived at Munich 3 January 1723.

G. BONONCINI: *Astarto*

30 November. London, Hm.

Text by P. A. Rolli (altered from an earlier libretto by Zeno and Pariati, first set to music by Albinoni in 1708). Three acts.

The first opera Handel's rival wrote in London. "V.E. è stata una delle principali Cause non solo di promovere nella Reale Accademia, quest' Opera; ma pur' anche il di lei rinomato Compositore, il quale l'à di nuove Bellezze accresciuta per mostrare tutta la dovuta attenzione a suoi Protettori" (from Rolli's dedication to Richard, Earl of Burlington; it appears from it that the latter had seen *Astarto* some years ago at the T. Capranica, Rome, which must have been Predieri's setting in 1714).

Bononcini's opera was also given at Hamburg 20 October 1721 (in Italian) and was revived in London, Lincoln's Inn Fields 9 March 1734.

1721

A. SCARLATTI: *La Griselda*

January. Rome, Capr.

Zeno's text (first set to music by Pollarolo in 1701). Three acts.

Scarlatti's 114th opera and the last which is extant.

ORLANDINI: *Nerone*

January. Venice, S.G.Gr.

Text by A. Piovene. Three acts.

In German (translated by J. Mattheson who also added six airs of his own), Hamburg 17 November 1723 and given there until 1738 (the airs were sung in Italian). In Italian also, Vienna 3 April 1731 (probably Orlandini's setting).

TELEMANN: *Der gedultige Socrates*

28 January. Hamburg

Text by J. U. König (founded on Minato's *La Patienza di Socrate con due Moglie*, see 1680). Three acts.

The first opera Telemann wrote for Hamburg.

Revived Crefeld 16 June 1934 (revised by J. Baum).

G. BONONCINI: *Crispo*

February. Rome, Capr.

Text by G. Lemer. Three acts.

Successful in London 31 January 1722 (text revised by P. A. Rolli); given for 21 nights. (Cf. note on *Griselda*, 1718.)

F. MATTEI (AMADEI?), G. BONONCINI and HANDEL: *Il Muzio Scevola*

26 April. London, Hm.

Text by P. A. Rolli. Three acts.

None of the composers is mentioned in the libretto. Burney (IV, p.258) and Hawkins (V, p.277) assumed that Ariosti[1] joined hands with Bononcini and Handel in this opera, but Chrysander proved that the third composer was one Filippo Mattei, called Pippo (who perhaps is identical to Filippo Amadei, Orlandini's collaborator in *Arsace*, see 1715).

[1] Ariosti's name as the composer of the first act still occurs in modern publications, e.g. in T. Vallese's *Paolo Rolli in Inghilterra*, 1938.

Mattei wrote the first act, Bononcini[1] the second act, Handel the third act.

In Italian also Hamburg 7 January 1723 (performed with a prologue in German).

The third act, i.e. Handel's share, was revived at Essen on 9 June 1928 (German version by R. Steglich).

HASSE: *Antioco*

11 August. Brunswick

Text by A. Zeno and P. Pariati (first set to music by Gasparini in 1705). Three acts.

Hasse's first opera. Only some airs are extant. The statements that Hasse's first opera was either called *Antigonus* (or *Antigono*) or that it was written to a German libretto have been refuted long ago. But since Burney (*Present State*, I, p.343) and Gerber, they obstinately recur even in modern books and papers. The Italian–German libretto of *Antioco*, which is extant, proves that the opera was composed to an Italian text and was sung either wholly in Italian (according to G. F. Schmidt) or else with Italian airs and German recitatives (according to R. Haas and H. J. Moser).

PORSILE: *Meride e Selinunte*

28 August. Laxenburg, near Vienna

Text by A. Zeno. Five acts.

The first greater work of Porsile, who was court conductor at Vienna from 1720–40. Intermezzi, *Rosina e Lesbo*, were produced with the opera.

HANDEL: *Il Floridante*

20 December. London, Hm.

Text by P. A. Rolli. Three acts.

Revived London 10 May 1727 and 14 March 1733. In German (as *Der thrazische Printz Flori-*

[1] See on *Muzio Scaevola* also W. H. Cummings in *The Musical Times*, 1911, p.18. It should be mentioned that Bononcini had composed a whole opera of his own on the same subject for Vienna in 1710 (produced there 10 July 1710; text by N. Minato); score preserved. One wonders if Bononcini used parts of his old music again and how far Rolli's libretto is indebted to Minato's earlier text.

dantes, translated by J. Beccau), Hamburg 28 April 1723 (the airs were sung in Italian).

1722

VINCI: *Li Zite 'n Galera*

Carnival. Naples, Fior.

Text by B. Saddumene. Three acts.

Vinci's first extant opera. Autograph score at Naples dated 20 November 1721. Not Saddumene's first original libretto as has been stated; preceded by *Don Ciccio*, also set by Vinci and produced at the same theatre in 1721. (Libretto in the British Museum; music apparently lost.)

KEISER: *Ulysses*

November. Copenhagen

(German) text by F. M. Lersner (founded on a French libretto by Guichard, composed by Rebel père in 1703). Three acts.

Score preserved. Written for the birthday of King Frederick IV of Denmark. The only opera Keiser wrote for Copenhagen, where, from Christmas 1721 to January 1723, a German operatic company acted at the court theatre.

(See T. Krogh in *Aarbog for Musik*, 1924, and in *Festschrift für Johannes Wolf*, 1929.)

1723

HANDEL: *Ottone, Re di Germania*

23 January. London, Hm.

Text by N. F. Haym (altered from Pallavicino's *Teofane*, see 1719). Three acts.

Successful in London; first produced for Francesca Cuzzoni's début; revived 16 February 1726; 22 April 1727; 24 November 1733; and 21 December 1734 (43 performances in all).

In Italian also, Brunswick August 1723 (with intermezzi *Barlafuso e Pipa*) and February 1725 (with additional airs by Lotti).

In German (translated by J. G. Glauche), Hamburg 15 May 1726 (music adapted by Telemann;

the airs were sung in Italian; given there until 1729).

There exists an edition of the libretto printed at Paris in 1724 (copy recently acquired by the Library of Congress) with French synopses. Probably there is a connection with an intended visit of the London opera company to Paris in the Summer of 1723 which however came to nothing. See *Le Mercure*, April 1723, p.770: "Quelques Acteurs Italiens de l'Opera de Londres doivent venir à Paris, & donner douze representations dans le cours du mois de Juillet prochain. . . ."

Revived (in a new German version by O. Hagen) at Göttingen 5 July 1921; Graz 19 December 1923; Berlin 6 September 1926, etc.

An English translation of Hagen's version by P. E. Pinkerton was published in 1928.

ARIOSTI: *Cajo Marzio Coriolano*
2 March. London, Hm.
Text by N. F. Haym. Three acts.

This was probably the first opera Ariosti wrote for London. *L'Odio e l'Amore* (1721), which Burney attributed to him was, according to Chrysander, by G. Bononcini. Revived in London 5 April 1732.

FEO: *Siface*
13 May. Naples, S.B.
Text by P. Metastasio (altered for Feo from an earlier libretto by D. David, *La Forza della Virtù*, set to music by Pollarolo in 1693). Three acts.

One of Feo's best works.

Date of first performance according to the MS score at the Conservatorio S. Pietro a Majella, Naples; corroborated by G. Pavan (*R.M.I.*, Vol. XXVIII, 1922, pp.427 and 432), who also reveals Metastasio's source which was unknown to Schatz and Sonneck (although Bonlini, p.199, gave a hint as early as 1730, and a copy of David's text actually is in the Schatz Collection; see Sonneck's *Catalogue*, pp.526 and 1005).

As Schatz rightly claimed, Feo was the first composer of *Siface* and not Porpora (see 1725); consequently, Metastasio's *Siface* text precedes that of *Didone abbandonata* (see 1724).

HANDEL: *Flavio, Re de' Longobardi*
25 May. London, Hm.
Text by N. F. Haym (partly founded on Corneille's *Cid* and altered from an earlier Italian libretto by S. Ghigi, set to music by Pollarolo in 1706). Three acts.
Revived in London 29 April 1732.

BLAMONT: *Les Festes grecques et romaines*
13 July. Paris, O.
Text by L. Fuzelier (*ballet héroïque*). Prologue and 3 acts, called *Les Jeux Olympiques*, *Les Bacchanales*, and *Les Saturnales*, respectively.

A fourth act, *La Fête de Diane*, was added on 9 February 1734 (but dropped in later revivals). Very successful in Paris.

Revivals at the Opéra were on 11 June 1733; 4 July 1741; 5 June 1753; 4 May 1762 (*Les Saturnales* only, with alterations); 28 August 1770 (with alterations by Dauvergne).

Given at Brussels in 1741. Fuzelier claims in the preface to a later edition to have introduced into French tragédie-lyrique for the first time "les événemens de l'histoire," following the Italian example of Scarlatti and Bononcini, and calls his work "un ballet d'une espece toute nouvelle".

Given at Moulins 1742 in concert form; prologue and *Les Bacchanales* revived Versailles 26 March 1748; *Les Saturnales* revived Versailles 13 February 1749; Prologue revived Fontainebleau 11 October 1764.

A parody, by Fuzelier himself, called *Les Saturnales*, three acts, was produced at the C.I. 2 September 1723; reduced to one act as *Les Débris des Saturnales*, 6 September 1723; another, *Les Festes des Environs de Paris*, by P. T. Gondot, 4 July 1753.

FUX: *Costanza e Fortezza*
28 August. Prague
Text by P. Pariati. Three acts.

Written to celebrate the coronation of the Emperor Charles VI as King of Bohemia and the birthday of the Empress Elizabeth Christina. Produced at the Hradzhin palace. Sometimes wrongly claimed to have been the first opera ever produced at Prague (but see 1680). The score was printed as Vol. VII of *Denkmäler der Tonkunst in Österreich* (1910), edited by E. Wellesz.

The opera was revived at:

NORTHAMPTON, MASS. 7 May 1938 (by Smith College students, under W. Josten, in an English version by G. P. Smith).

PRAGUE 1 July 1938 (by students of the Prague Conservatoire under O. Jeremiáš).

VINCI: *Silla Dittatore*

1 October. Naples, Pal. Reale

Text probably by Vincenzo Cassani (*Il Tiranno Eroe*, Venice 1710, originally set to music by Albinoni). Three acts.

Vinci's first extant opera seria. Written to celebrate the birthday of the Emperor Charles VI. Publicly performed at the Teatro S.B. 17 October 1723 (according to the *Mercure de France*).

TORRI: *Griselda*

12 October. Munich

Zeno's text (first set to music by Pollarolo in 1701). Three acts.

Name part created by Faustina Bordoni (the first part she sang in Germany).

Revived at Munich Carnival 1735. For a comparison of Scarlatti's and Torri's *Griselda* operas, see H. Junker in *Sandberger-Festschrift* (1919).

1724

SARRO: *Didone abbandonata*

5 February. Naples, S.B.

Text by P. Metastasio. Three acts.

The first setting of Metastasio's first *dramma per musica* (not counting some smaller works and his *Siface*, altered from an earlier libretto by D. David), which established his fame as the leading librettist of the 18th century (there are far more than a thousand settings of his librettos; no complete bibliography yet available). Sarro's opera was repeated at Turin, T.R. Carnival 1727

and Venice, Autumn 1730 (text altered by G. Boldini). (Date of first performance according to the *Mercure de France*. E. Gabrici, *Metastasio in Napoli* [1918], p.75, gives 8 February.)

HANDEL: *Giulio Cesare in Egitto*

2 March. London, Hm.

Text by N. F. Haym. Three acts.

Along with *Rodelinda* (see 1725) perhaps Handel's most successful opera.

Revived in London 28 January 1730 and 12 February 1732; and once more, with Rubinelli and Mara, 1 March 1787, according to Edgcumbe "a medley from his Italian works". The 1787 libretto says: "The music entirely by Handel, and selected from various operas set by that incomparble [*sic*] composer, under the direction of Dr. Arnold"; and "The original, however, offering a great number of incongruities, both in the language and the conduct, several material alterations have been thought absolutely necessary, to give the piece a dramatic consistency, and to suit it to the refinement of a modern audience".

Outside London given at Brunswick August 1725, 1727 and August 1733 (in Italian, as *Giulio Cesare e Cleopatra*); Hamburg 21 November 1725 (in German, translated by T. Lediard, with additions by J. G. Linike, who also composed the German recitatives; the airs were sung in Italian; given there until 1737); Vienna 1731 (in Italian; Haym's libretto reduced and altered).

There seems to exist an edition of the libretto printed at Paris in 1724, similar to that of Handel's *Ottone*. See *Catalogo della Libreria Floncel*, Paris 1774, nos.2717 and 7826.

Modern revivals (German version by O. Hagen): Göttingen 5 July 1922; Berlin, V.O. 4 June 1923; Copenhagen 5 March 1924 (by the Berlin company); Zurich 23 March 1924; Basle 3 September 1924; Vienna, Academy of Music, 29 May 1926 and O. 3 May 1928; and on many other German stages.

Also Northampton, Mass., Smith College 14 May 1927 (in English); London, Foundling Hospital 23 June 1927 (in English, in an abridged concert version) and Scala Th. 6 January 1930; New York, Juillard School 21 January 1931 (in English); Amsterdam 1 December 1933 (by the Dutch Opera Studio); Strasbourg January 1935 (in French, translated by L. Mancini); Pozńan 1936 (in Polish).

TELEMANN: *Der neu-modische Liebhaber Damon*

June. Hamburg

Text probably by the composer (*Ein scherzhaftes Singespiel*). Three acts.

Presumably first produced between 3 June and 3 July, as it is not recorded in Willers's repertory (see *Archiv für Musikwissenschaft*, Vol. VI), where the performances between those two dates are missing.

CALDARA: *Gianguir*

4 November. Vienna

Text by A. Zeno (written for Caldara). Five acts.

In German (translated by J. S. Müller) Hamburg 6 February 1728 (in a free adaptation as *Pharao und Joseph*; the airs were sung in Italian).

HANDEL: *Tamerlano*

11 November. London, Hm.

Text by A. Piovene (first set to music by Gasparini in 1710), adapted by N. F. Haym. Three acts.

Revived in London 24 November 1731.

In German (translated by J. P. Praetorius) Hamburg 27 September 1725 (music adapted by Telemann; the airs were sung in Italian); between the acts intermezzi were performed, probably Telemann's *Die ungleiche Heyrath*, see 1725.

Tamerlano was revived at Carlsruhe 7 September 1924 (new translation and arrangement by A. Rudolph and H. Roth) and Leipzig 7 June 1925.

1725

HANDEL: *Rodelinda*

24 February. London, Hm.

Text by A. Salvi (first set to music by Perti in 1710), altered by N. F. Haym. Three acts.

Revived London 15 May 1731.

In German (translated by C. G. Wendt) Hamburg 29 November 1734 (the airs were sung in Italian).

Modern revivals:

GÖTTINGEN	26 June 1920	(new German version by O. Hagen).
ZURICH	13 June 1923	
BERLIN, V.O.	29 January 1924	

NORTHAMPTON, MASS., SMITH COLLEGE 9 May 1931 (in English).

LONDON, OLD VIC 5 June 1939 (in English).

The so-called "Handel Renaissance" movement in Germany started with *Rodelinda*; the following is a short list of revivals (for details see the entries under each year):

Rodelinda	1725	GÖTTINGEN	1920
Ottone	1723	GÖTTINGEN	1921
Orlando	1733	HALLE	1922
Giulio Cesare	1724	GÖTTINGEN	1922
Serse	1738	GÖTTINGEN	1924
Tamerlano	1724	CARLSRUHE	1924
Admeto	1727	BRUNSWICK	1925
Siroe	1728	GERA	1925
Ariodante	1735	STUTTGART	1926
Ezio	1732	GÖTTINGEN	1926
Radamisto	1720	GÖTTINGEN	1927
Poro	1731	BRUNSWICK	1928
Muzio Scaevola	1721	ESSEN	1928
Alcina	1735	LEIPZIG	1928
Amadigi	1715	OSNABRÜCK	1929
Arminio	1737	LEIPZIG	1935
Partenope	1730	GÖTTINGEN	1935
Scipione	1726	GÖTTINGEN	1937
Tolomeo	1728	GÖTTINGEN	1938

TELEMANN: *Die ungleiche Heyrath oder Das herrsch-süchtige Camer Mädgen*

27 September. Hamburg

Text by J. P. Praetorius (founded on an Italian libretto by P. Pariati, *Pimpinone*, set to music by Albinoni in 1708). Three parts.

Early instance of German intermezzi after the Italian pattern, though there is some doubt whether Telemann did more than set the new

German recitatives and add some German arias to Albinoni's Italian arias. Sung in a mixture of German and Italian. First produced at Hamburg probably between the acts of Handel's *Tamerlano*. The MS score has the title *Pimpinone*.

Revived Erlangen 29 September 1925 and Bamberg February 1929 (revised by G. Becking).

Score printed in 1936 (*Reichsdenkmale*, Vol. VI, edited by T. W. Werner).

VINCI: *Astianatte*

2 December. Naples, S.B.

Text by A. Salvi (first set to music by M. A. Bononcini in 1701). Three acts.

The best of Vinci's serious operas. (Date of first performance indicated in the *Mercure de France*.)

PORPORA: *Siface*

26 December. Milan, T.R.D.

Metastasio's adaptation of David's text (stated by the author, many years later, to have been written expressly for Porpora; but see 1723). Three acts.

Also given at Venice, Carnival 1726 and, with alterations, as *Siface Re di Numidia* Rome, Capr. 7 February 1730.

In German (translated by J. P. Praetorius), Hamburg Winter 1727 (the airs sung in Italian).

1726

LEO: *Il Trionfo di Camilla Regina de' Volsci*

8 January. Rome, Capr.

Text by S. Stampiglia (first set to music by M. A. Bononcini, see 1696). Three acts.

One of Leo's most famous serious operas.

VINCI: *Siroe, Re di Persia*

January. Venice, S.G.Gr.

Text by P. Metastasio. Three acts.

The first setting of Metastasio's second original libretto. "Questo Drama, universalmente gradito ha reso immortale il Nome del suo celebre Autore" (Bonlini).

Revived at the same theatre, Carnival 1731 (text altered by G. Boldini, additional music by Galuppi and Pescetti); Prague 1734; Parma Carnival 1753; Milan, T.R.D. 1759.

SCHÜRMANN: *Ludovicus Pius* oder *Ludewig der Fromme*

February. Brunswick

(German) text by C. E. Simonetti. Three acts.

Repeated at Brunswick, August 1727 and February 1734. Also produced by a German company at Stockholm 19 November 1733.

(Schürmann used for his opera some pieces by Campra, Destouches and Graun.) The score was printed in 1890 (as Vol. XVII of Eitner's *Publikationen älterer Musikwerke*, edited by H. Sommer).

PORSILE: *Spartaco*

21 February. Vienna

Text by G. C. Pasquini (scenario by A. Zeno). Three acts.

Faustina Bordoni sang in this opera before she came to London in May 1726.

HANDEL: *Scipione*

23 March. London, Hm.

Text by P. A. Rolli (founded on Zeno's *Scipione nelle Spagne*, first set to music by Caldara in 1710). Three acts.

Rolli says in the libretto: "The first Hint of this Drama, and some Lines in it, are borrow'd; but what, otherwise, relates either to the Plot itself, or the Diction thro' the Whole, is entirely new".

Revived London 14 November 1730; Göttingen 1937 (translated by E. Dahnk-Baroffio).

HASSE: *Il Sesostrate*

13 May. Naples, S.B.

Text by A. Carasale. Three acts.

Hasse's first greater success (though limited to Naples).

Intermezzi, *Miride e Damari*, were sung between the acts.

According to the original libretto, first performed on Maria Theresa's birthday, 13 May (not 26 August, the date usually given).

HANDEL: *Alessandro*

16 May. London, Hm.

Text by P. A. Rolli. Three acts.

Faustina Bordoni's London début (in the part of Rossane).

In German (translated by C. G. Wendt), Hamburg 18 November 1726; Brunswick 17 August 1728 (airs and final chorus sung in Italian; cf. the account in J. F. A. von Uffenbach's *Tagebuch* (1728), edited by Max Arnim, 1928; given as *Der hochmüthige Alexander*, perhaps not Wendt's translation).

KEISER: *Der laecherliche Printz Jodelet*

??. Hamburg

Text by J. P. Praetorius (founded on P. Scarron's comedy, *Jodelet ou Le Maître Valet*, 1645, and on an older Hamburg libretto, set to music by Franck in 1680). Five acts.

One of Keiser's best comic operas. Exact date of first performance unknown. The opera appears in Willers's repertory list (see *Archiv für Musikwissenschaft*, Vol. VI, 1924) only on 25 February 1727 as "not acted", and then (revived) 26 January 1733. Probably also given at Vienna 21 September 1738. The opera was printed in 1892 in Eitner's *Publikationen älterer Musikwerke*, Vol. XVIII (edited by F. Zelle) and revived at Hamburg in 1930.

RISTORI: *Calandro*

2 September. Pillnitz, near Dresden

Text by S. B. Pallavicino. Three acts.

The first extant opera of Ristori, and one of the earliest Italian comic operas produced in Germany. Revived at Dresden Carnival 1728 (Frederick the Great, then Crown Prince, attended this revival); also produced at Moscow 11 December 1731 (in Italian).

REBEL and FRANCOEUR: *Pirame et Thisbé*

17 October. Paris O.

Text by J. L. I. de La Serre. Prologue and 5 acts.

The first of 10 operas by the two French composers, who were inspectors of the Paris Opéra from 1746–57, and directors from 1757–66; their names have become inseparable in the history of opera.

Pirame et Thisbé was revived at Marly 1 March 1734 and in Paris on 26 January 1740, 23 January 1759 (without prologue) and 5 February 1771. Given at Lyons in January 1741; Montpellier 1755; Amiens 1766 (in concert-form).

Score published 1726.

Each Paris production was followed by parodies, viz. *Pirame et Thisbé* (by J. A. Romagnesi, F. Riccoboni and P. F. Dominique), C.I. 13 November 1726; *Pirame et Thisbé* (by C. S. Favart), O.C. 3 March 1740; *Le Qui pro quo ou Polichinelle Pirame* (anonymous), by marionettes, Foire St. G., December 1740; *Pirame et Thisbé* (by F. Riccoboni, a revised version of the 1726 parody), C.I. 5 March 1759.

1727

GRAUN: *Sinilde*

3 February. Brunswick

Text by J. U. König (founded on an Italian libretto by F. Silvani, *Il miglior d'ogni Amore per il peggiore d'ogni Odio*, set to music by Gasparini in 1703). Three acts. Full title: *Die in ihrer Unschuld siegende Sinilde.*

Graun's first opera. Revived at Brunswick August 1729 and August 1736 (in both cases as *Sancio oder die in ihrer Unschuld siegende Sinilde*).

The same text was set to music by Telemann later in the same year.

CALDARA: *Don Chisciotte in Corte della Duchessa*

6 February. Vienna

Text by G. C. Pasquini (*Opera serioridicola*), after Cervantes. Five acts.

In German (adapted by G. C. Schürmann), Brunswick 9 February 1728 (revived 11 August 1738).

HANDEL: *Admeto, Re di Tessaglia*

11 February. London, Hm.

Text: an altered version (by Haym? or Rolli?), of an earlier Italian libretto by A. Aureli, *L'Antigona delusa da Alceste*, set to music by P. A. Ziani (see 1660). Three acts.

Very successful in London; it was given in 1727 for 19 nights running and revived 5 June 1728; 18 December 1731 (with alterations); and 12 March 1754 (latest revival of any Handel opera in his lifetime).

Also given at Brunswick, August 1729, February 1732 and August 1739 (with German recitatives, translated probably by G. C. Schürmann) and at Hamburg 23 January 1730 (in German, translated by C. G. Wendt, given there until 1736).

Revived Brunswick 14 October 1925 (arrangement and new German version by H. Dütschke; his translation had been printed as early as 1906).

G. BONONCINI: *Astianatte*

17 May. London, Hm.

Text by N. F. Haym (altered from an earlier libretto by A. Salvi, first set to music by Bononcini's brother, Marc'Antonio Bononcini in 1701). Three acts.

The last opera Bononcini wrote for London. The notorious battle on the stage between the two rival singers, Faustina Bordoni (Ermione) and Francesca Cuzzoni (Andromaca), took place during the last performance of *Astianatte* (last night of the season, 6/17 June).

MOURET: *Les Amours des Dieux*

14 September. Paris, O.

Text by L. Fuzelier (*ballet-héroïque*). Prologue and 4 entrées (called *Neptune et Amymone, Jupiter et Niobé, Apollon et Coronis,* and *Ariane et Bacchus*). Successful in Paris.

Revived 18 June 1737; 12 May 1746 [not 1747]; 16 August 1757 (with two additional airs by

Gossec, text by Marmontel, and without the second entrée); 18 August 1767 (the third entrée only). Given at Amiens 1735 (in concert form); Lyons 1739 (the second entrée only); Brussels 1741.

VINCI: *La Caduta dei Decemviri*

1 October. Naples, S.B.

Stampiglia's text (first set to music by Scarlatti, see 1697). Three acts.

One of Vinci's best works; written to celebrate the birthday of the Emperor Charles VI.

ARIOSTI: *Teuzzone*

1 November. London, Hm.

Text by A. Zeno (first set to music by Magni and Monari in 1706). Three acts.

Ariosti's last opera. Given for three nights only.

HANDEL: *Riccardo I, Re d'Inghilterra*

22 November. London, Hm.

Text (*quasi tutto*) by P. A. Rolli. Three acts.

In German (as *Der misslungene Braut-Wechsel oder Richardus I, Koenig von England,* translated by C. G. Wendt) Hamburg 3 February 1729 (with additional German airs by Telemann, while Handel's airs were sung in Italian); another German version by an unknown translator (*Richardus genannt das Löwen-Herz, König in Engelland*) was given (with Italian airs) at Brunswick in the same month, February 1729 (revived February 1734).

1728

BUINI: *Il Malmocor*

Carnival. Bologna, T. Marsigli Rossi

Text probably by the composer (*tragichissimo drama per musica*). Three acts.

The title is *Malmocor,* not *Malmosor* as quoted by most authorities. The dedication in the libretto is dated 12 December 1727.

At Bologna the opera was produced with intermezzi, *La Serva astuta,* between the acts. Revived Venice Spring 1731 as *Artanaganamenone.*

See on this opera G. Rossi, *Varietà Letterarie* (1912), pp.165–186.

On Buini see E. J. Dent's study in *Sammelbände of the I.M.S.*, Vol. XIII (1911–12). Dent says that "not a single note of his music appears to have survived anywhere". But at least one air, inserted into the Paris 1752 revival of Orlandini's *Giocatore* (see 1718), has been discovered since (see L. de La Laurencie in *Revue Musicale*, June 1912, p.26).

[PEPUSCH]: *The Beggar's Opera*

9 February. London, Lincoln's Inn Fields

Text by J. Gay. Three acts.

The music consists of 69 numbers adapted by Pepusch to popular airs; he also arranged and orchestrated the score and composed one of the songs and the overture (which is founded on the air *One evening, having lost my way* occurring in the third act).

Notes on the sources of the tunes, by W. H. G. Flood, will be found in the appendix to L. Melville's *Life and Letters of John Gay* (1921). It appears that of the 69 airs, 28 are Old English, 15 Old Irish, 5 Old Scottish, and 3 Old French songs. The rest of 18 songs can be attributed to individual composers, namely Purcell (3), Barret, Clarke, Handel, Carey (2 each), and Bononcini, Eccles, Geminiani (?), Wilford, Pepusch, Frescobaldi and Ramondon (1 each).

Given for 62 nights during the first season, which was the longest run of any play on the English stage before 1822. Very successful all over England and in all English-speaking countries. From a note in Pope's *The Dunciad* we learn that *The Beggar's Opera* was acted even at Minorca, then a British possession.

First given at Dublin, March 1728; Dover *c.* March 1728; Norwich April 1728; Bath May 1728; Newcastle *c.*May 1728 (by two rival companies); Canterbury and Bristol June 1728; Sandwich July 1728; Deal August 1728; Glasgow August 1728; Haddington 9 November 1728; Bury, Colchester and Ipswich November 1728; Edinburgh 1728; Drogheda June 1729; Richmond 25 June 1730. Given in Jamaica in 1733

(see W. R. Chetwood, *A General History of the Stage*, 1749, p.40); New York 3 December 1750; Annapolis, Md. 22 June 1752; Philadelphia 24 August 1759 and, according to W. E. Schultz (*Gay's Beggar's Opera*, 1923) before 1800 in America also produced at Boston, Providence, Newport, Baltimore, Richmond, Williamsburg, Norfolk and Charleston.

The Beggar's Opera Tragediz'd ("in Roman Shapes") Hm. 14 June 1734.

The London performances up to 1749 are recorded in A. Nicoll's *A History of Early 18th Century Drama*, p.331, and the London revivals up to 1876 in W. D. Adams's *A Dictionary of the Drama*, p.135.

Different versions were produced at:

DUBLIN 2 January 1765 (additional music by Giordani).

C.G. 17 October 1777 (altered by E. Thompson).

D.L. 8 November 1777 (new accompaniments by Linley).

C.G. 14 December 1813 (in an abridged 2-act version).

A version with additions by T. A. Arne was published (perhaps the C. G. version 1777).

Later revivals in London were at C.G. 9 December 1878 (Macheath: Sims Reeves); Avenue Th. 3 November 1886 (orchestrated by G. Fox); Lyric, H'smith 5 June 1920 (arranged and orchestrated by F. Austin). This production had a run of 1,463 nights (until 15 December 1923; the longest run an opera ever had) and was revived at the same theatre on 23 June 1925; 22 May 1926; 14 February 1928; 11 March 1929; 13 May 1930; and at the Criterion 6 March 1935. Again Brighton 16 January 1940; London, Hm. 5 March 1940 and New Th. 21 February 1941. A modern adaptation by W. Garstang, *The Students' Opera* was produced by the Leeds University Dramatic Society 18 December 1924 (adapted to Austin's version of the music).

American 19th and 20th century revivals were at New York 4 June 1849; 20 December 1854; 31 October 1860; 28 November 1870; Philadelphia 15 November 1854; New Haven, Yale University 3 May 1912. New York, Greenwich

Village Th. 29 December 1920 (the Hammersmith version); subsequently given at Montreal, Toronto, Ottawa, Indianopolis, and at Chicago 20 March 1921; Los Angeles 7 November 1921; S. Francisco 21 November 1921. Again revived New York, 48th Street Th. 28 March 1928.

First given in French (but by an English company) London, Little Hm. 10 May 1749 and 27 February 1750 (as *L'Opéra du Gueux*, translated by A. Hallam); another French version, by C. P. Patu, was published in 1756; a third version, published in 1767, is attributed in *Cat. Bibl. Soleinne* to Mme Thiroux d'Arconville. There is no record of a French production in Paris. *The Beggar's Opera* was first given there in English at the Th. Caumartin 22 December 1921 (the Hammersmith version).

A German adaptation by E. E. Buschmann, *Die Strassenräuber*, was published in 1770, and in a new version as *Die Schleichhändler* in 1775. It was written *Zum Behuf des Hamburgischen Theaters*, but it does not seem to have been acted.

In a modern German version by K. Heiffert *The Beggar's Opera* was first produced at Cologne University in 1930 and at Aachen 8 February 1931, etc. (For another German adaptation by B. Brecht, with new music by Weill, see 1928.)

Polly, the sequel to the *Beggar's Opera*, although written and ready to be performed in 1729, was not acted until 48 years later (see 1777). An imitation, *Macheath Turn'd Pirate or Polly in India*, was however acted at London, Hm. 10 June 1737.

HANDEL: *Siroe, Re di Persia*
28 February. London, Hm.

Metastasio's text (first set to music by Vinci, see 1726), altered by N. F. Haym. Three acts.

Also given at Brunswick August 1730 and 9 February 1735.

Revived Gera 25 December 1925 (in German, adapted by R. Meyer).

HANDEL: *Tolomeo, Re di Egitto*
11 May. London, Hm.

Text by N. F. Haym. Three acts.

Revived in London 30 May 1730 and 13 Jan-

uary 1733. Revived Göttingen 19 June 1938 (in German, translated by E. Dahnk-Baroffio).

TELEMANN: *Miriways*
26 May. Hamburg

Text by J. S. Müller. Three acts.

Repeated there in 1730 (*not* revived there 31 May 1745, as claimed by E. H. Müller, *Angelo u. Pietro Mingotti*, 1917, p.x, from a Hamburg playbill, without year).

1729

The Gentle Shepherd
9 February. Edinburgh, Taylor's Hall

Text by A. Ramsay (*A Scots pastoral comedy*). Five acts.

The music consists of 21 ballad airs.

First published in 1725 as a pastoral comedy (containing 4 songs only). Changed into a ballad opera in 1728 after *The Beggar's Opera* had been produced at Haddington. First performed in 1729 probably by pupils of the Haddington Grammar School, where it was repeated 7 September 1729. First given in London, D.L., 1 May 1730 as *Patie and Peggy, or The Fair Foundling*, reduced to one act (with prologue and epilogue) and adapted by T. Cibber. His preface is dated 20 April (1 May) 1730, and the newspapers show that the first production took place on that night (different dates are given by some authorities).

The first professional production of the original was at Edinburgh, Canongate Th. 29 April 1758. Frequently revived in Scotland both by amateurs and professionals. Dublin 1758.

Given in a new English adaptation by R. Tickell, with additional music by Linley, London, D.L. 29 October 1781.

There are other versions by C. Vanderstop (published 1777), W. Ward (1785), M. Turner (1790), A. Allan (1798), A. Maclaren (1811). The latest revival in London was at C.G. 27 June 1817 (revised by G. Bethune, with Linley's music and new additions by Bishop).

Given at Montego Bay, Jamaica 20 March 1784; New York 7 June 1786 (a libretto had bene published already in 1750), and Philadelphia 4 February 1791 (in Tickell's 1781 version); New York 5 June 1795 (orchestrated by B. Carr).

The Gentle Shepherd was revived at Glasgow 13 November 1876 (at the Gaiety Th.) and once more Glasgow 3 September 1923 and Edinburgh 10 September 1923 (adapted and arranged by W. Eaton, music selected and composed by W. Robins).

HASSE: *Tigrane*

4 November. Naples, S.B.

Text by F. Silvani (originally called *La Virtù trionfante dell' Amore e dell' Odio* and set to music by M. A. Ziani in 1691). Three acts.

Between the acts, Hasse's first intermezzi, *La Serva scaltra ovvero La Moglie a Forza*, were produced.

Revived at Naples, S.C. 4 November 1745 (with additional music by A. Palella).

Erroneously considered to be the first opera Hasse wrote in Italy, owing to a mistake by Florimo, who gave the date of production as 1723. The cast he gives, however, is identical with that in the libretto of 1729, while quite different singers were engaged at Naples in 1723.

TELEMANN: *Flavius Bertaridus Koenig der Longobarden*

23 November. Hamburg

Text by the composer and C. G. Wendt (translated from an Italian libretto by S. Ghigi, set to music by Pollarolo in 1706). Three acts.

Telemann's last extant opera.

HANDEL: *Lotario*

13 December. London, Hm.

Text altered from A. Salvi's *Adelaide* (first set to music by Orlandini earlier in the same year), not from M. Noris's *Berengario* as Burney says. Three acts.

Three airs from this opera were used at the Hamburg 1732 production of Chelleri's *Innocenza giustificata* (see 1711).

CAREY: *The Contrivances*

16 August. London, D.L.

Text by the composer. One act.

Given 14 years previously (20 August 1715) at the same theatre as *The Contrivances; or, More Ways than One*. Genest calls it "a very good ballad Farce" and it appears in G. Tufts's chronological list of ballad operas (in *The Musical Antiquary*, January 1913) under 1715. But the first edition of the play shows that there was practically no music in it then. The 13 songs, etc., were added only in 1729, viz. one year after, not fourteen years before *The Beggar's Opera*.

The Contrivances is no ballad opera, in the accepted sense of the word, either, as it is expressly stated in the title of the score (published by the author in 1729) that both words and music were by Carey. It is called "A comi-farcial Opera" in a Dublin 1731 edition and "Ballad Opera" in the 1743 edition of Carey's *Dramatick Works*. (Neither the 1715 nor the 1729 editions contain any description as to the genre of the piece.)

Given at Dublin 1731 and 26 February 1733; Philadelphia 20 April 1767 (libretto published already in 1762); New York 11 January 1768; Montego Bay, Jamaica 10 May 1777.

Frequently revived in London until 1750, and C.G. 25 March and D.L. 3 April 1761; C.G. 23 April 1773; C.G. 6 May 1785. The latest revival seems to have been at Bath on 16 June 1819.

1730

VINCI: *Artaserse*

4 February. Rome, T. delle Dame

Text by P. Metastasio. Three acts.

The first setting of this famous libretto. Vinci's last opera (he died 28 May 1730). Given at Naples later in the same year and revived there 20 January 1738 (libretto altered by L. S. Stampiglia, who added a prologue which was set to music by Leo) and 5 November 1743; Vienna 28 August 1730; Leghorn Carnival 1731; Ferrara Autumn 1731; Camerino Carnival 1733; London 16 January 1734 (as *Arbace*); Florence Carnival 1740;

Ferrara Carnival 1745 (music by Vinci and Hasse); Dresden 23 August 1746; Parma Carnival 1754.

HASSE: *Artaserse*

February. Venice, S.G.Gr.

Metastasio's text (see above). Three acts.

Hasse set the libretto at the same time as Vinci. His setting was produced at the T.S. Giovanni Grisostomo as the last opera of the Carnival season. The opera exists in several different versions (as Mennicke and Sonneck pointed out).

The following productions are to be recorded: Genoa Spring 1730 (probably Hasse's setting); Lucca Autumn 1730; London 10 February 1734 (music chiefly by Hasse and by R. Broschi); Graz Spring 1738 (German translation in the libretto by F. J. Pircker); Madrid 25 October 1738 (probably Hasse's setting); Modena Carnival 1739; Ljubljana Carnival 1740; Dresden 9 September 1740 (second version); Bologna 1745; Brunswick February 1751 (probably Hasse's setting); Lübeck 6 November 1752; London 29 January 1754 (revived with alterations); Naples, S.C. 20 January 1760 (third version) and Summer 1762; Warsaw 3 August 1760 (libretto Bodleian Library, Oxford); Ferrara 26 December 1764; Lodi 1765; London 20 February 1766 (for the third time there; third version).

For an analysis of the different versions see O.G.T. Sonneck in *Sammelbände of the I.M.S.*, Vol. XIV (1912–13).

HANDEL: *Partenope*

7 March. London, Hm.

Text by S. Stampiglia (first set to music by Manzo in 1699). Three acts.

Revived London, C.G. 9 February 1737. Also given at Brunswick February 1731 (in Italian; revived 12 September 1731; February 1732; 1 October 1732; 1 August 1733); Hamburg 28 October 1733 (in German, translated by C. G. Wendt; with recitatives by Keiser; the airs were sung in Italian; given there until 1736).

Revived Göttingen July 1935 (new German version by E. Dahnk-Baroffio).

1731

CALDARA and REUTTER: *La Pazienza di Socrate con due Moglie*

17 January. Vienna

Text by N. Minato (*Scherzo dramatico*, first set to music by Draghi, see 1680). Three acts.

Caldara wrote the beginning of the first and the third act, Reutter the rest of the opera.

HANDEL: *Poro, Re dell' Indie*

13 February. London, Hm.

Text: an altered version of Metastasio's *Alessandro nell' Indie* (first set to music by Vinci in 1729). Three acts.

Revived London, C.G. 19 December 1736. Also given at Hamburg 25 February 1732 (in German, translated by C. G. Wendt, as *Triumph der Grossmuth und Treue, oder Cleofida, Koenigin von Indien*; recitatives by Telemann; the airs were sung in Italian; given there until 1736); Brunswick August 1732 (in Italian, with a prologue, *Apollo festeggiante*).

Revived Brunswick 21 April 1928 (new German version by H. Dütschke) and, by the Brunswick company, also given at Copenhagen.

PORTA: *Farnace*

Spring. Bologna, T. Malvezzi

Text by A. M. Lucchini (first set to music by Vinci in 1724). Three acts.

Porta's setting was revived at Munich Carnival 1740 (where he had become court conductor in 1738).

The Devil to Pay; or The Wives Metamorphos'd

17 August. London, D.L.

Text by C. Coffey (in collaboration with J. Mottley, founded on a farce, *The Devil of a Wife, or A Comical Transformation*, 1686, attributed to T. Jevon, but perhaps written by T. Shadwell; see A. E. Richards in *Publications of the Modern*

Language Association of America, Vol. xxi, 1906, pp.808–830). Ballad opera, originally in 3 acts, reduced to one act by T. Cibber in 1732.[1] The music consists of 16 songs, of which one is marked as having been composed by Seedo.

Very successful on English stages. Given at Dublin 6 March 1732; Edinburgh 18 January 1734; Charleston, S.C. 16 March 1736; New York 8 January 1751; Annapolis, Md. 31 July 1752; Glasgow 1761; Philadelphia 19 December 1766; Kingston, Jamaica 30 October 1779; Cape Town 1802. Frequently revived; the latest revival in London was at C.G. 9 May 1828.

Given in German (translated by C. W. von Borcke) by Schönemann's troupe, probably with the English original music, at Berlin 24 January 1743; Hamburg 29 June 1747; Leipzig 26 January 1750. (Borcke was Prussian Ambassador to London and the first German translator of Shakespeare's *Julius Caesar*. Of his translation of *The Devil To Pay* only some fragments are extant.)

A French translation by C. P. Patu was published in 1756.

A sequel, called *The Merry Cobler*, also by Coffey, was produced at D.L., London 17 May 1735 (unsuccessful).

The Devil To Pay plays an important part in the history of comic opera. The German Singspiel movement originates from it and there were also successful French and Italian imitations. See the settings by Standfuss 1752 and 1759; Philidor 1756; Hiller 1766; Portugal 1797; Paer 1800; Solié 1809. The latest version probably was Balfe's *The Devil's In It*, see 1852.

HASSE: *Cleofide*

13 November. Dresden

Metastasio's text (*Alessandro nell'Indie*, see above), altered by M. A. Boccardi. Three acts.

Also given (mostly as *Alessandro nell' Indie*) at Milan Carnival 1732; Munich 1735; Venice Carnival 1736; revived Carnival 1738 and Carnival 1743; Graz Carnival 1738; Verona Carnival

[1] First produced in one act at Goodman's Fields Theatre, London 19 December 1731.

1740; Pressburg Summer 1741; Vienna, Kä. 8 December 1746; Lucca Autumn 1759; Berlin January 1777.

CALDARA: *Il Demetrio*

4 November. Vienna

Text by P. Metastasio (written for Caldara). Three acts.

In Italian also given at Brunswick February 1734 (as *Il Demetrio Re della Sina*); Bologna Carnival 1742 (Caldara's setting?).

1732

BROSCHI: *Merope*

Carnival. Turin, T.R.

Zeno's text (first set to music by Gasparini in 1712). Three acts.

The most successful opera of Broschi (the brother of the famous singer Farinelli).

Also given at Lucca Autumn 1733, etc.; London 19 January 1737; Jaromeriz, Moravia Autumn 1737.

HASSE: *Cajo Fabricio*

12 January. Rome, Capr.

Zeno's text (first set to music by Caldara in 1731). Three acts.

Given, with the usual alterations, at Naples, S.B. Winter 1733 (with intermezzi *La Contadina*); Dresden 8 July 1734; Jaromeriz, Moravia Autumn 1734 (as *Pirro*); Venice Carnival 1735; Salzburg 1737; Leghorn Carnival 1740; Lucca Carnival 1740; Bologna 1743 (probably Hasse's setting); Graz Carnival 1743 (probably Hasse's setting); Frankfort 7 April 1755; Berlin September 1766.

Hasse's setting, with recitatives by Handel, probably also London 15 December 1733.

HASSE: *Il Demetrio*

January. Venice, S.G.Gr.

The second setting of Metastasio's text (see 1731). Three acts.

Given in an altered version as *Cleonice*, Vienna February 1734 and Venice, S. Angelo Carnival 1740; as *Demetrio* repeated at Venice, S. Cass. Carnival 1737 and S.G.Gr. Carnival 1747.

Also given at Parma 1736; Madrid 16 February 1738 (at the inauguration of the first Italian opera-house in Spain, the Teatro de los Caños del Peral); Reggio Summer 1739; Dresden 8 February 1740 (altered); Lucca Carnival 1741; Hamburg 4 November 1744 (pasticcio, the greater part of the music by Scalabrini); Gorizia Carnival 1745; Ferrara Carnival 1746; Turin Carnival 1748; Frankfort 7 April 1755 (probably Hasse's setting).

There was a revival at Mantua as late as in Carnival 1770 (Mozart attended the performance of 10 January, on his first Italian journey).

HANDEL: *Ezio*

26 January. London, Hm.

Metastasio's text (first set to music by Auletta in 1728). Three acts.

The libretto mentions neither Handel nor Metastasio; it does mention Mr. Humphreys, who provided the printed translation. Unsuccessful (given for 5 nights only).

Revived (in a German version by F. Nothold) at Göttingen 30 June 1926; Münster 2 December 1926 (first festival of the German Handel Society); Berlin, D.O. 31 January 1928.

F. CONTI: *L'Issipile*

February. Vienna

Text by P. Metastasio (written for Conti). Three acts.

Conti's last opera. In Italian also given at Brunswick February 1733 and August 1736 (probably Conti's setting); Jaromeriz, Moravia 4 October 1733.

In German (translated by C. G. Wendt, as *Sieg der kindlichen Liebe oder Issipile*) Hamburg 20 February 1737 (airs sung in Italian).

HANDEL: *Sosarme Re di Media*

26 February. London, Hm.

Text: an altered version of *Alfonso Primo* by M. Noris (first set to music by Pollarolo in 1694). Three acts. Revived London 8 May 1734.

MONTÉCLAIR: *Jephté*

28 February. Paris, O.

Text by S. J. de Pellegrin (. . . *tirée de l'Ecriture Sainte*). Prologue and 5 acts.

Montéclair's chief work. The first opera on a biblical subject produced at the Paris Académie Royale de Musique; it was temporarily banned by the Archbishop of Paris. Successful and frequently revived until 1740 and again 3 March 1744 and 6 February 1761. Marseilles 1735; Versailles 9 September 1750 (in concert form).

Jephté contains, as a concession, the usual ballets, and a prologue with characters from Greek mythology. (See for details J. Carlez, *Un Opéra biblique au XVIIIᵉ Siècle*, 1879.) *Les Amusements à la Mode*, by F. Riccoboni and J. A. Romagnesi, C.I. 21 April 1732, includes a parody on *Jephthé*.

Date of first performance according to the printed score; the original libretto has 4 March. The *Mercure de France*, exceptionally, does not give the date.

HANDEL: *Acis and Galatea*

28 May. London, Little Hm.

Text by J. Gay (*An English Pastoral Opera*). Three acts.

Originally written as a masque, probably in 1719, and performed so, at Cannons, probably in 1721. Adapted for the stage, parts of it were given at Lincoln's Inn Fields Th. 6 April 1731. Produced in its entirety at the Little Hm. Th. on the above date (unauthorized) and a few weeks later (21 June 1732) by Handel himself at the Hm.

Given at Dublin 1735 (at Aungier Street Th.) and 31 January 1742 (in concert form, at Fishamble Street Th., conducted by the composer); Dublin again 17 December 1742. The original seems to have been given in Swedish at Stockholm as early as 19 January 1734, in concert form; at Stockholm also 10 May 1773 (in Swedish, translated by L. S. Lalin, with additions by H. F. Johnsen and others); a Swedish parody by C. I. Hallman, music by C. Stenborg, called *Casper och Dorothea*, was produced at Stockholm 31 August 1775 and Gothenburg 9 February 1776.

Frequently revived in London, viz. Little Hm. 2 April 1753 (in English, for Sra. Frasi's benefit); Ranelagh House 9 June 1757; Marylebone Gdns. 27 May 1773; Queen's, Tottenham Street 3 February 1831 (additional accompaniments by Cipriani Potter); D.L. 20 June 1838; D.L. 5 February 1842 (with a prologue by T. S. Cooke); Crystal Palace 21 October 1865 (in concert form); Princess's 2 August 1899; Great Queen Street Th. 10 March 1902 (produced by Gordon Craig, with Mozart's accompaniments[1]); Bishopsgate Inst. 2 December 1926 (in concert form).

Outside London revived at Durham 17 October 1792; New York 14 February 1839 (in concert form), and 21 November 1842 (on the stage); Edinburgh 1 May 1840; Dublin 6 June 1853; Carlsruhe 8 March 1888 (in German, translated and arranged by F. Mottl); Cologne 25 October 1898 (in a concert version by F. Chrysander); Munich May 1903 (by the *Orchesterverein*); Munich 7 June 1922 (stage production); Copenhagen 13 December 1935 (in Danish, translated by M. Dam); lately, Falmouth 23 June 1941.

A Spanish translation by R. Benedito was published in 1935.

PERGOLESI: *Lo Frate 'nnamorato*

23 September. Naples, Fior.

Text by G. A. Federico (*Commeddeja pe mmusica*), written in Neapolitan dialect. Three acts.

Repeated, with alterations, at the same theatre Carnival 1734 and revived T.N. Winter 1748.

PESCETTI: *Demetrio*

26 December. Florence, P.

Metastasio's text (first set to music by Caldara, see 1731). Three acts.

Revived London 23 February 1737 as the first and most successful of several operas Pescetti produced in London, where he was composer to the King's Th. from 1737 to 1740. Galuppi became his successor (see 1741).

---

[1] Originally written for private performances at Vienna in November and December 1788.

1733

d'ALMEIDA: *La Pazienza di Socrate*

Carnival. Lisbon

Minato's text (first set to music by Draghi, see 1680, and again by Caldara and Reutter, see 1731). Three acts.

The first (Italian) opera by a Portuguese composer which is partly extant (the third act only). Libretto printed. Produced at the Paço da Ribeira.

CALDARA: *Sancio Panza, Governatore dell' Isola Barattaria*

27 January. Vienna, B.

Text by G. C. Pasquini (*comedia per musica*), after Cervantes). Three acts.

(Thus the island of Barattaria occurs in the title of an opera 156 years before Sullivan's *Gondoliers*, see 1889.)

HANDEL: *Orlando*

7 February. London, Hm.

Text by G. Braccioli (first set to music by Ristori in 1713). Three acts.

Revived as *Orlandos Liebeswahn* (German version by H. J. Moser), Halle 28 May 1922 and Krefeld 1934.

T. A. ARNE: *Rosamond*

18 March. London, Lincoln's Inn Fields

Addison's text (first set to music by Clayton, see 1707). Three acts.

Arne's first opera. Of the music only six songs and one duet have been preserved. Successful on English stages.

Revived in London, D.L. 19 March 1740, 11 February 1745 and 22 April 1765; at C.G. 26 April 1754. Given at Dublin 18 May 1743 (reduced to 2 acts) and revived there 31 December 1755.

HASSE: *Siroe Rè di Persia*

2 May. Bologna, T. Malvezzi

Metastasio's text (first set to music by Vinci, see 1726). Three acts.

Given at Florence 1736; London 4 December 1736 (see Burney, IV, p.400); Padua June 1737; Madrid [24 March] 1739; Parma Carnival 1742; Rimini 1743; Naples, S.C. 5 November 1747; Lucca Autumn 1748. In a revised version: Warsaw Carnival 1763; Vienna 1763; Dresden 3 August 1763; Siena 1765.

PERGOLESI: *La Serva Padrona*

28 August. Naples, S.B.

Text by G. A. Federico. (The text has often wrongly been attributed to J. A. Nelli, whose 3-act comedy of the same title, published 1731, has nothing to do with the libretto.) Two parts. Intermezzi, first performed between the acts of Pergolesi's serious opera, *Il Prigionier superbo* (librettist unknown). The original text as contained in the libretto of *Il Prigionier superbo* has been reprinted by B. Croce in the second edition of his *I Teatri di Napoli*, 1916.

Pergolesi's most famous work. It soon (not so very soon though) became known in Italy (Rome, T. Valle February 1738; Parma 1738; San Giovanni in Persiceto, September 1739 and Bologna later in the same year; Lucca 1740; Venice 1740, 1741, 1742, 1745; Florence 1742; Padua Spring 1747; Reggio Carnival 1748, etc.) and made its way across the Alps, with travelling companies, within six years. In Italian given at:

GRAZ Easter 1739 (the German translation in the printed libretto by J. L. von Ghelen).

DRESDEN 8 February 1740 (as intermezzi in Hasse's *Demetrio*).

GORIZIA Carnival 1742.

HAMBURG 31 October 1743; revived 1744; 1745; 1746.

PRAGUE 1744.

PARIS, C.I. 4 October 1746 (with an overture by Paganelli).

VIENNA, KÄ. 15 October 1746 (as intermezzi in Wagenseil's *La Clemenza di Tito*).

AUGSBURG 1746.

POTSDAM 15 March 1748.

LEIPZIG 21 May 1748.

COPENHAGEN 1749, November 1752; 11 December 1754; 14 November 1755; 24 November 1756; 7 December 1757.

LONDON, HM. 7 April 1750 (as intermezzi in Ciampi's *Adriano in Siria*).

BARCELONA Summer 1750.

NUREMBERG 19 July 1751.

BERLIN 1752.

SCHWETZINGEN Summer 1752.

PARIS, O. 1 August 1752 (with an overture by Telemann, on the same bill with Lully's *Acis et Galatée*).

Lübeck 15 May 1753; Brunswick 30 April 1753; Frankfort 24 May 1753; Danzig July 1753; Hanover 3 September 1753; Liége Autumn 1754; Dijon 8 February 1756; Mayence 1758; Bamberg 1760; Edinburgh 21 June 1763; York October 1763; Dublin 28 April 1764; Maestricht 17 December 1764; Gotha 30 January 1767; Kremsmünster 1774; Riga 1777, etc.

First given at PARIS, in Italian, in 1746 and 1752, as indicated above. The 1752 production at the Opéra caused the famous *Querelle des Bouffons*, the struggle between the defenders of French tragédie-lyrique and the adherents of Italian opera buffa, fought out in some 60 pamphlets published between 1752 and 1754 (cf. note on *Omphale*, 1700). A complete list of those pamphlets (Grimm, Holbach, Rousseau, Diderot are amongst the authors) will be found in L. Reichenburg's *Contribution à l'histoire de la Querelle des Bouffons* (Philadelphia 1937).

A French prose translation of *La Serva Padrona* is printed opposite the Italian text in the Paris libretti of 1746 and 1752, entitled *La Soubrette Maîtresse*.

The first translation of *La Serva Padrona* intended for performance was the French version by P. Baurans ("que l'on m'a assuré être gouverneur des enfants de Mr. Delaporte, intendant de Grenoble", according to his contemporary, T. S. Gueullette), called *La Servante Maîtresse*, and first produced at Paris, C.I. 14 August 1754 (given there *c*.150 times within one year). Also given at Versailles 4 December 1754; Brussels 12 July 1755; Aachen 30 August 1757; Vienna and Hague

1758; Frankfort 19 April 1760; Amsterdam 1760; Dresden 1764; Smolna (Russia) *c.*November 1773; Berlin 22 April 1776; St. Petersburg 21 December 1776 (by amateurs; probably in French); Munich 17 March 1783; Gothenburg 22 April 1783; Stockholm May 1783; Cassel 14 April 1784; Baltimore 12 June 1790 (first opera in America that was sung in French); New York 9 December 1790; Cologne 1795/6; Charleston, S.C. 15 May 1797; Philadelphia 25 May 1798; Kingston, Jamaica 20 December 1800.

First given in LONDON, in Italian, in 1750, as indicated above. The performance was on 27 March (7 April, n.s.) and not on 27 April (o.s.) as some books of reference have it. In Italian, revived at the Hm. 24 March 1763 and 23 April 1776. First given in English at Marylebone Gardens, London 8 June 1758, as *The Servant Mistress*, adapted by S. Storace the Elder and J. Trusler. Transported to the Little Hm. 29 March 1759, advertised as "with addition of a new act and a new character as originally performed at Naples". Frequently revived during the following years. It was a special favourite with summer audiences at Marylebone Gardens; given there on 16 June 1770 with additional songs by S. Arnold, as counterpoise to a rival production at Ranelagh House, where a version by Dibdin was performed on 28 May 1770 (*The Maid the Mistress*, text by I. Bickerstaffe, music by Dibdin; transported to D.L. 12 April 1771 under the new title of *He wou'd if he cou'd; or, An old Fool worse than any*); revived Royalty Th. 28 January 1788.

An English version by D. E. Baker is printed in the libretto of the Italian production of *La Serva Padrona* at Edinburgh, 1763. The last English 18th-century adaptation, by J. O'Keeffe, was produced at C.G. 14 February 1783 (with Arnold's additions).

There is much uncertainty and confusion about the early German versions of *La Serva Padrona*. According to J. H. F. Müller (*Genaue Nachrichten,* ... 1772) there was given at Vienna, Kä. 6 January 1770, *La serva padrona, nachgeahmt von Kurz* (i.e. J. J. F. von Kurz, called Bernardon). The music of this version has been attributed to the composer I. Gspan[1]. But a Nuremberg playbill of 5 February 1778 (quoted by G. Dieke, *Kindertheater,* 1934) says: "La serva padrona, Die Dienerin eine Frau, übersetzt von Ignatius Gspan". Perhaps Kurz had Pergolesi's opera in his repertory, translated by himself and adapted to the German words by Gspan (who may have added some music of his own). But it is not quite clear whether Kurz's version originally had any music at all, or was "imitated as a comedy".

Next we find *Lachet wer lachen kann oder die Dienerin eine Frau,* translated by one Pauli, produced at Munich 26 February 1783 (recorded by P. Legband). As a matter of fact, Piccinni (who did not write an opera of such title) is mentioned as the composer; but that might easily be a slip, as often occurs in 18th-century bills. What was probably another German version of Pergolesi's opera was printed (and probably performed) at Schleswig in 1785 under the title *Wie sie pfeift, so muss er tanzen*; see *Bibliotheca Danica*, Vol. IV (1902), col.420, entered under the "author's" name of *Padiona, Serva* [*sic*]; the same misunderstanding occurs in the Index Vol. (1913), p.195. So far these German versions have not been mentioned in the Pergolesi bibliography. H. M. Schletterer stated (Waldersee's *Sammlung Musikalischer Vorträge,* 1880) that *La Serva Padrona* was first produced in German at Bremen in 1803. But the Bremen historian, J. H. Behncken, had recorded that performance as early as 1856, clearly stating that it was Paisiello's opera of the same title. Schletterer's blunder, unfortunately, has been taken over by every later writer on Pergolesi, down to the latest edition of Radiciotti's standard biography (1935). Undoubtedly a German version of *La Serva Padrona* was *Zofenherrschaft,* translated by C. A. Herklots, produced Berlin 19 March 1810 (with an overture by P. C. Guglielmi) and Darmstadt 19 September 1810 (as *Die gebietrische Magd*).

An anonymous Dutch version, *De Kamenier van Fortuin* (translated from the French) was published in 1772 and performed at Amsterdam

[1] He joined Bernardon's troupe as musical director 1 October 1770.

1773; another one, by B. Ruloffs, *Pandolfus en Zerbina of De Meid Meesteres*, in 1793.

An anonymous Polish version (translated from the French) was produced at Warsaw in 1780 (first recorded performance 11 March 1781). The Italian original was given there on 28 May 1781, Kurz's German version already in 1774.

A Swedish version, by C. Envallsson (also translated from the French), was produced at Stockholm 3 October 1781 and Gothenburg 5 August 1783.

According to N. Findeizen, Pergolesi's opera was produced in Russian at Moscow in 1789; according to O. Chayanova's monograph on the Moscow Maddoks Theatre this again was Paisiello's *Serva Padrona* (translated by Prince A. I. Golintsin). Pergolesi's opera, in Italian, had been given at Moscow on 26 June 1782.

La Serva Padrona is one of the oldest operas still in the reportery. After a short period of oblivion in the first half of the 19th century it has been frequently revived in many countries ever since:

BADEN BADEN 11 August 1862 (in French).

PARIS, O.C. 13 August 1862 (in French, music revised by F. A. Gevaert); revived there 22 February 1900; 13 October 1910; Tr. L. 20 November 1920; O.C. 2 April 1929; 23 December 1937.

BRUSSELS, M. 19 December 1862 (in French); revived Th. Molière 16 November 1905; M. 4 November 1921.

FLORENCE 20 June 1870 (in Italian); revived 24 March 1893 and 25 April 1911.

NAPLES 14 May 1871 (in Italian); by the Società Filarmonica.

LONDON, ROYALTY 7 March 1873 (in French); Lyric, H'smith 29 January 1919 (in English, translated by G. Crawford); Mercury 15 June 1939 (in English, translated by G. Dunn).

HAMBURG 25 April 1880 (in German, translated by H. M. Schletterer).

LEIPZIG 1 July 1880 (in German); revived 8 October 1893.

STOCKHOLM 13 September 1881 (in Swedish, translated by E. A. Wallmark, already published 1864); revived 14 October 1939.

WEIMAR 15 January 1888 (in German).

MILAN 27 November 1892 (in Italian).

CARLSRUHE 3 November 1893 (in German).

HANOVER 19 April 1894 (in German).

RIGA 1894 (in German).

STUTTGART 3 May 1898 (in German).

COPENHAGEN 1 September 1900 (in Danish, translated by J. Dam).

MUNICH 28 December 1901 (in German); revised by F. Wüllner.

VENICE April 1907 (in Italian); revised by E. Wolf-Ferrari.

VIENNA 29 May 1909 (in German); revised by R. Kleinmichel; revived 27 March 1927 and 14 May 1930.

LAUCHSTEDT 29 May 1910 (in German); revised by H. Abert.

JESI 2 October 1910 (in Italian), at the Pergolesi bicentenary festival.

RIO DE JANEIRO 5 August 1912 (in Italian).

BASLE 7 May 1914 (in German, Abert's version).

NEW YORK, LYCEUM 7 May 1917 (in English, translated by S. Rosenfeld); Juilliard School 18 February 1932 (in English); M. 23 February 1935 (in Italian); Little Th. 11 January 1938 (in English, translated by G. Dunn).

BARCELONA 8 November 1922 (in Spanish), by the Asociación de Música de Camera.

BUENOS AIRES 1924 (in Spanish).

BUDAPEST 26 May 1926 (in Hungarian, translated by V. Lányi).

FALMOUTH 13 December 1927 (in English, translated by M. and E. Radford).

BERLIN, D.O. 23 March 1929 (in German).

ZAGREB 15 December 1930 (in Croatian).

TURIN 20 November 1931 (in Italian); San Remo 5 March 1933, etc.

LENINGRAD Spring 1933 (in Russian, translated by M. A. Kuzmin).

MALTA 6 January 1934 (in Italian).

TEL AVIV 8 May 1934 (in Hebrew, translated by M. Freidmann).

LISBON Spring 1937 (in Portuguese, translated by M. Oliveira).

HAGUE Spring 1938 (in Dutch).

(For Paisiello's opera of the same title, see 1781)

RAMEAU: *Hippolyte et Aricie*

1 October. Paris, O.

Text by S. J. de Pellegrin. Prologue and 5 acts.

Rameau's first opera (an earlier *Samson*, text by Voltaire, was never performed; text published 1745).

Given at Lyons 1735 and again February 1743.

Revived at the Opéra 11 September 1742 (with alterations); 25 February 1757; 4 October 1758; and 24 March 1767 (with additions by P. M. Berton, Boyer and Gaviniès).

The first production and some of the revivals were followed by parodies, viz. *Le Badinage*, by L. de Boissy, C.Fr. 23 November 1733, and, at the C.I., *Hippolyte et Aricie*, by J. A. Romagnesi and F. Riccoboni, 30 November 1733, and *Hipolyte et Aricie*, by C. S. Favart and Parmentier, music by Blaise, 11 October 1742 (revived 16 March 1757).

Modern revivals: Geneva 28 March 1903 (under Jaques-Dalcroze); Paris, O. 13 May 1908 (music revised by V. d'Indy); Basle 20 May 1931 (in German, translated by L. Jansen).

1734

VIVALDI: *L'Olimpiade*

Carnival. Venice, S. Angelo

The second setting of Metastasio's text (first set to music by Caldara in 1733). Three acts.

One of the many operas of Vivaldi, the scores of which were recovered by A. Gentili in the Foà Collection, Turin, in 1927.

L'Olimpiade was, after 205 years, revived at the Vivaldi Festival, Siena 19 September 1939 (music arranged by V. Mortari).

ARAJA: *La Forza dell'Amore e dell'Odio*

Carnival. Milan, T.R.D.

Anonymous text by C. F. P. Three acts.

Given at St. Petersburg 9 February 1736 as the first Italian opera seria there (precisely 100 years before Glinka's *Life for the Czar*). Score preserved at Vienna; dated 1739.

It has been stated that Araja wrote this opera expressly for the Russian court theatre. But the fact that he brought it with him from Milan is proved by the 1734 libretto, which is extant (Paris, Bibliothèque de l'Opéra). The opera is mentioned in some books of reference under the title of *Abiazare* (which is the female chief character in *La Forza dell'Amore e dell'Odio*).

The Russian translation, by V. K. Tredyakovsky, as printed in the St. Petersburg libretto, is entitled *Sila Lyubi i Nenavisti*. The first opera Araja composed expressly for St. Petersburg was Metastasio's *Semiramide riconosciuta*, produced there (as *Il finto Nino overo Semiramide riconosciuta*) one year after *La Forza*, viz. 9 February 1737. J. von Stählin published German translations of both *La Forza* and *Semiramide* in 1736.

Araja was the first of the great number of famous Italian composers at the Russian court in the 18th century; his successors include Manfredini (1759–66); Galuppi (1765–68); Traetta (1768–76); Paisiello (1776–83); Sarti (1784–86 and again 1792–96); Cimarosa (1787–91); Martin y Soler (1788–94) and Cavos (1797–98, when Italian opera was prohibited by Paul I).

HANDEL: *Ariadne in Crete*

6 February. London, Hm.

Text attributed to F. Colman, but seems rather to be a thorough revision, or re-writing, by Colman or another, of Pariati's *Arianna e Teseo*. Three acts.

An *Arianna in Creta* given at Brunswick in August 1737 and February 1738 may have been Handel's opera.

On F. Colman, the father of George Colman the Elder, see the latter's biography by E. R. Page (1935), pp.1–8. To Francis Colman is attributed the handwritten *Opera Register* in the British Museum which closes after the entry of *Ariadne*, for which he is said to have written the text. As Colman died at Pisa, 20 April 1733, he did not live to see the production of the opera, nor can he have written the last section of the *Opera Register* (if he wrote it at all). The unknown author who wrote, or at least finished, the manuscript enters

Ariadne in Crete under a wrong date (confounding it with the rival opera at Lincoln's Inn Fields, Porpora's *Ariadne in Naxus*): *Janry pmo Ariadne in Crete a new Opera & very good & perform'd very often—Sigr Carestino sung surprisingly well: a new Eunuch—many times perform'd.*

The libretto of *Ariadne in Crete* is attributed to Francis Colman by all writers on Handel since Chrysander. The earliest authority for this attribution seems to be Richard Brinsley Peake (*Memoirs of the Colman Family*, 1841, Vol. I, p.14) and his evidence does not seem too convincing as he mixes up Handel's and Porpora's *Ariadne* operas. The characters in Handel's opera are exactly the same as in Pietro Pariati's libretto *Arianna e Teseo* (first Vienna 1714; later Florence 1729, where Colman may have got hold of the text and may have sent it to Handel). The texts of some of the arias are identical.

KEISER: *Circe*

1 March. Hamburg

Text by J. P. Praetorius (translation from a libretto written in Dutch and French by J. J. Mauricius, Dutch minister at Hamburg). Five acts.

Keiser's last opera; contains 21 German and 23 Italian airs, the latter partly by Vinci, Handel, and Hasse.

PERGOLESI: *La Contadina astuta*

25 October. Naples, S.B.

Text by T. Mariani. Two intermezzi, sung between the acts of Pergolesi's *Adriano in Siria* (Metastasio's text).

The serious opera was unsuccessful; but the intermezzi enjoyed a long vogue after the composer's death, under many different titles and with the usual alterations and additions, according to the requirements and abilities of the different buffo troupes. The following productions are to be recorded:

ROME 1737 (as *Livietta e Tracollo*) and [2 February] 1748 (as *La finta Polacca*).

MILAN, T.R.D. 1739 (as *Il Ladro finto Pazzo*).

VENICE, S.SAM. Spring, 1741 (as *Il finto Pazzo*, airs by other composers added, libretto altered by

Goldoni); S. Moisè, Autumn 1744 (as *Il Tracollo*); S. Moisè, Carnival 1746 (as *Livietta*).

BOLOGNA 1746 (as *Il Tracollo*).

DRESDEN 5 August 1747 (as *Il finto Pazzo*).

PRAGUE 1747/48 (as *Il finto Pazzo*).

MADRID January 1748 (as *La Contadina astuta*).

VIENNA 1748 (as *Il Tracollo*) and 6 January 1759 (as *Il finto Pazzo*).

LEIPZIG 15 May 1748 (as *Il finto Pazzo*).

POTSDAM 1748 (as *Il finto Pazzo*).

HAMBURG 29 January 1749 (as *Il finto Pazzo*).

BRUNSWICK 1749 (as *Il finto Pazzo*).

COPENHAGEN 1749 (as *Il Tracollo*) and 16 February 1757 (same title).

VENICE, S.CASS. Carnival 1750 (as *Il Ladro convertito per Amore*).

ST. PETERSBURG, PETERHOF 2 August 1750 (as *Tracollo*).

PARIS, O. 1 May 1753 (as *Tracollo, Medico ignorante*).

BARCELONA [27 January] 1754 (as *Tracollo*).

SCHWETZINGEN Summer 1754 (as *Tracollo*).

EDINBURGH 11 July 1763 (as *Tracollo*).

YORK October 1763 (as *The amorous Robber*, by Italian singers).

One wonders whether an English burletta, *La Strattagemma* [sic] or *The Stratagem*, produced in London, Marylebone Gardens 26 July 1759, was not a version of *La Contadina astuta*. Unfortunately, not more than the title and the attribution to Pergolesi appear from the advertisement, and no libretto seems to have been printed. Two years later, the same title recurs for a "tragicomic burletta," produced at the Little Haymarket Th. 23 June 1761; but this time, however, the music of *The Stratagem* is attributed to Hasse.

A French parody on Pergolesi's intermezzi (as produced at the Paris Opéra in 1753), *Tracollo Charlatan*, was given at the C.I., Paris, 17 November 1756 (text by J. Lacombe, music by Sodi).

La Contadina astuta was revived in the original Italian at Treviso 24 April 1917; Trieste 11 June 1925; Rome, T. Quirinetta 20 April 1927, etc. In an English version by M. and E. Radford at the Duke's Th., London 16 March 1933 (by the R.A.M.).

1735

PERGOLESI: *Olimpiade*

8 January. Rome, T. Tordinona

Metastasio's text (first set to music by Caldara in 1733). Three acts.

The best of Pergolesi's serious operas. Unsuccessful in Rome; also given at Venice November 1738; Munich 1738; Siena Summer 1741; London 1 May 1742 (as *Meraspe overo L'Olimpiade*), text altered by P. A. Rolli; more or less a pasticcio, no composer's name mentioned in the libretto.

"Our fifth Opera was the Olimpiade, in which they retain'd most of Pergolesi's Songs & yet 'tis gone already, as if it had been a poor thing of Galuppi's. Two nights did I enjoy it all alone, snugg in a Nook in the Gallery, but found no one in those regions had ever heard of Pergolesi, nay, I heard several affirm it was a Composition of Pescetti's: now there is a 6th sprung up by the name of Cefalo & Procri." (Thomas Gray's letter to John Chute, 24 May, 1742).

Olimpiade was revived at the T. della Fortuna, Fano, in March 1937 (under R. Falk).

(Date of first production, 8 [or 9] January, according to A. Cametti, not 31 January as usually given).

GIACOMELLI: *Cesare in Egitto*

January. Milan, T.R.D.

Text by G. F. Bussani (first set to music by Sartorio in 1677). Three acts.

Also given at Venice in Autumn of the same year, and Naples, S.B. May 1736.

The best of Giacomelli's *c.*13 operas produced between 1724 and 1739.

HANDEL: *Ariodante*

19 January. London, C.G.

Text by A. Salvi (originally called *Ginevra Principessa di Scozia* and first set to music by Perti in 1708), from Ariosto's *Orlando Furioso*. Three acts.

Revived Stuttgart 28 September 1926 (German version by A. Rudolph).

LEO: *Demofoonte*

20 January. Naples, S.B.

Metastasio's text (first set to music by Caldara in 1733). Three acts.

The most successful of Leo's serious operas. Revived Naples, S.C. 19 December 1741.

HANDEL: *Alcina*

27 April. London, C.G.

Text by A. Marchi (first set to music by Albinoni in 1725), from Ariosto's *Orlando Furioso*. Three acts.

Given in London 24 times until 1737. In Italian also Brunswick February 1738 (some airs sung in German) and August 1738 (wholly in Italian).

Revived Leipzig 14 June 1928 (German version by H. Roth).

Alcina was the first of Handel's operas published in the German Handel *Gesamtausgabe* (1869).

DUNI: *Nerone*

21 May. Rome, T. Tordinona

Text by F. Silvani, with alterations. Three acts.

Of the music only some airs are extant. Duni's first opera, chiefly remembered for the fact that the Romans preferred it very much to Pergolesi's *Olimpiade* (see above) and received it enthusiastically. Duni is reported to have told Pergolesi at the rehearsals of *Olimpiade*: "Vi sono troppe finezze al di sopra dell' intelligenza del volgo nella vostra opera. Queste bellezze passeranno incomprese, e voi non riescirete punto. La mia opera, ve lo confesso, non sarà paragonabile alla vostra; ma più semplice, sarà più felice".

RAMEAU: *Les Indes galantes*

23 August. Paris, O.

Text by L. Fuzelier (*ballet héroïque*). Prologue and 3 entrées, called *Le Turc généreux*, *Les Incas du Pérou*, and *Les Fleurs*, *Feste persane*. A fourth entrée, *Les Sauvages*, was added on 10 March 1736.

With modifications, *Les Indes galantes* was revived at Paris 10 March 1736; 28 May 1743; 8 June 1751; and 14 July 1761. *Les Incas du Pérou* at

Versailles 30 January 1765; Paris 5 December 1771. *Les Sauvages* at Versailles 16. February 1765; Choisy 10 October 1769; Paris 16 July 1773.

Les Fleurs had a modern revival at the O.C. 30 May 1925.

The second entrée was given at Parma on 18 December 1757 (in Italian, as *Gl'Incà del Perù*, translated by C. I. Frugoni).

Favart wrote a parody, *L'Ambigu de la Folie, ou Le Ballet des Dindons*, produced at the O.C. 31 August 1743; reduced to 3 entrées, this was revived at the C.I. 26 July 1751 and again 8 August 1761 under the title of *Les Indes dansantes*. A new parody on the fourth entrée (*Les Sauvages*) was added on 2 September 1751 (C.I.) under the title of *Les Amours champestres*; it was also given at Vienna in 1755 and, with new music by P. van Maldere, at Schönbrunn 5 October 1758. Its text was used for the modern Gluck pasticcio, *Die Maienkönigin*, music partly from Gluck's *L'Isle de Merlin* (see 1758).

Another parody, *Les Indes chantantes*, by J. A. Romagnesi and F. Riccoboni, with music by Mouret, was produced at the C.I. 17 September 1735 (revived there 12 August 1743). The same day a parody by D. Carolet was produced at the O.C.: *Les Amours des Indes*, consisting of *Le bon Turc* and *Le jaloux Poltron*; one week later, 24 September 1735, a parody on the third entrée followed: *Le Déguisement postiche*.

HASSE: *Tito Vespasiano* ovvero *La Clemenza di Tito*

24 September. Pesaro

Metastasio's text (partly founded on Corneille's *Cinna* and first set to music by Caldara in 1734). Three acts.

Hasse's setting was written for the inauguration of the Teatro Publico, Pesaro.

Also given at Dresden 17 January 1738 (revived 11 January 1740 and 26 July 1746); Naples, S.C., 4 November 1738 (with additional music by Antonio Palella); Madrid [14 May] 1739 (Spanish translation in libretto by P. F. Quazza); Moscow 9 June 1742; Berlin 11 January 1743 and 22 July 1744; Brunswick August 1743 (with recitatives

and two choruses in German, translated probably by Schürmann; repeated there February 1744); Hamburg, with a prologue by Paolo Scalabrini, 8 December 1745 (revived 14 October 1748); St. Petersburg 1 January 1747; Copenhagen 18 December 1748; Palermo Carnival 1764; Cremona Carnival 1770 (Mozart attended a performance on his first Italian journey).

At Moscow the opera was given at the coronation of the Empress Elizabeth, with a prologue, *La Russia afflitta e riconsolata*, text by J. von Stählin, music by D. dall' Oglio. See on this production J. von Stählin's *Beylagen zum neuveränderten Russland* (1770), which is the earliest account of the history of opera in Russia. A short paragraph on the Moscow production appeared in the July 1742 issue of the *Mercure de France*—quite a remarkable achievement of early journalism.

PREDIERI: *Il Sogno di Scipione*

1 October. Laxenburg, near Vienna

Text by P. Metastasio (*Azione teatrale, allusiva alle sfortunate campagne delle armi Austriache in Italia*). One act.

Revived Vienna 4 November 1739.

(Mozart set the same text in 1772.)

PERGOLESI: *Il Flaminio*

Autumn. Naples, T.N.

Text by G. A. Federico. Three acts.

Pergolesi's last work for the stage; as it does not appear from the title, it should be mentioned that it is a comic opera.

Successful at Naples, revived there Winter 1737, 1739 and Winter 1749. Also given at Siena Carnival 1742.

1736

CALDARA: *Achille in Sciro*

13 February. Vienna, B.

Text by P. Metastasio. Three acts.

Written to celebrate the wedding of Maria Theresa (then Archduchess) with Stephen Francis, Duke of Lorraine.

HANDEL: *Atalanta*

23 May. London, C.G.

Librettist unknown. Three acts.

"As it is Perform'd . . . on Occasion of an Illustrious Wedding", namely that of Frederick Prince of Wales, son of George II, to Princess Augusta of Saxe-Gotha. Ten performances.

RISTORI: *Le Fate*

10 August. Dresden

Text by S. B. Pallavicino. One act.[1]

Written to celebrate the return of the Elector Frederick Augustus II from Warsaw where he was crowned King of Poland. Ristori was commissioned to write the coronation opera because Hasse was on leave in Italy at that time.

1737

AULETTA: *Orazio*

Carnival. Naples, T.N.

Text by Antonio Palomba (his first libretto), partly in Neapolitan dialect. Three acts.

This work had a truly extraordinary career. Revived at Florence in 1740 and 1742 (without Auletta's name and with music by other composers); Venice, S. Moisè Autumn 1743 (with additions by Alessandro Maccari and others, but misattributed in the libretto to Latilla and Pergolesi); Genoa Carnival 1744; Graz Carnival 1745; Leipzig Spring 1745; Hamburg 17 June 1745 (at Graz, Leipzig and Hamburg misattributed to Latilla and Pergolesi); Milan 1746 (without composer's name); Bologna 25 August 1747 (under Auletta's name); Vienna 20 August 1748; Venice Spring 1748 (under Auletta's name); Reggio 1748 (under Auletta's name); London 10 December 1748 (under Auletta's name); Copenhagen 1749; Brussels 20 September 1749 (attributed on one page of the libretto to Auletta and on

---

[1] The libretto (Washington, Library of Congress) is in one act; the MS score (according to Ristori's biographer, K. R. Mengelberg) has three acts.

another to Galuppi); Parma 1749; Lucca 1752 (without composer's name); Leiden 1752; Paris, O. 19 September 1752 (in a much condensed version, as *Il Maestro di Musica*; the libretto does not name the composer, the *Mercure de France* says the airs are by different authors; the score was published in the following year under Pergolesi's name); Ravenna 1754; Trieste Carnival 1756 (attributed to "varii celebri Autori"); Munich 1758; Florence Carnival 1760 (reduced to intermezzo dimensions, as *La Scolara alla moda*, and attributed to "diversi celebri Autori").

A proportion of Auletta's music survived throughout, but after the opera had been in circulation a few years most of the airs were by other composers—it had become a *pasticcio*. This was probably what happened to most other such opere buffe.

The Paris version, which includes four numbers by Auletta, one by G. M. Capelli and others by unidentified composers, had a career of its own as *Il Maestro di Musica*, misattributed to Pergolesi.

Translated into French by P. Baurans, it was given as *Le Maître de Musique* at Paris, C.I. 31 May 1755 and, in a revised version, 7 March 1757; revived Versailles 14 March 1764 and Paris, C.I. April 1776.

In French also given at Brussels 1755; Hague 1758 and 1 February 1774.

After an interval of more than 150 years, *Il Maestro di Musica* was revived (in German, as *Der getreue Musikmeister*, translated and orchestrated by A. Schering) at Lauchstedt 6 July 1924; Prague May 1929; Frankfort 1 February 1930; Basle 17 April 1931; also Vienna 8 February 1938 (at the "Insel" Theatre; Schering's version, partly re-written by H. F. Koenigsgarten).

An Italian reconstruction by F. Caffarelli, (who edited a new vocal-score in 1935) at Rome, Palazzo Doria Pamfilj 27 April 1935, Jesi (Pergolesi's native town) 22 March 1936 (by the Amici della Musica da Camera); Buenos Aires August 1936.

Revived in English by Columbia University students, New York 17 April 1936.

HANDEL: *Arminio*

23 January. London,C.G.

Text by A. Salvi (first set to music by A. Scarlatti in 1703), with alterations. (Burney's statement as to the origin of the libretto is not correct.) Three acts.

Performed six times only.

Revived Leipzig 23 February 1935 (German version and arrangement by H. J. Moser and M. Seiffert).

HANDEL: *Giustino*

27 February. London, C.G.

Text: an altered version of N. Beregani's libretto, first set to music by Legrenzi (see 1683). Three acts. Performed nine times.

Given at Brunswick August 1741 (with Italian airs and German recitatives and choruses; translated by C. E. Simonetti and G. C. Schürmann; the latter also contributed some additional music).

LAMPE: *The Dragon of Wantley*

27 May. London, Hm.

Text by H. Carey (*A burlesque opera*). Three acts.

A satire on Italian opera seria, directed particularly against Handel's *Giustino* (see above); but the opera is said to have been a favourite with Handel all the same.

Concerning the date of first performance see *Notes and Queries*, Vol. 171 (1936), p.41, and Emmett L. Avery, *Fielding's Last Season with the Haymarket Theatre*, in *Modern Philology* (Chicago), Vol. 36, 1938/39.

Very successful in London; C.G. 6 November 1737 and given there 67 times during the first season and frequently revived. First given at Dublin 6 February 1738. The latest revival at C.G. was on 18 March 1782. Of the libretto no less than 14 editions were published within one year. In a dedicatory letter to Lampe (inserted in later editions) Carey says: "It is a Burlesque Opera: And Burlesque cannot be too low. Lowness (figuratively speaking) is the Sublimity of Burlesque: If so, this opera is, consequently, the tip-top Sublime of its Kind. Your Musick, on the

other hand, is as grand and as pompous as possible by which Means the Contrast is the stronger, and has succeeded accordingly". A sequel called *Margery, or A worse Plague than the Dragon*, by the same authors, was produced at C.G. on 20 December 1738 and at Dublin 5 February 1739. It was later altered and reprinted as *The Dragoness*, and was revived as *Lady Moore or The Dragoness* at C.G. 28 April 1755.

A parody by an unknown author, called *The Pigeon-Pye, or A King's Coronation: proper materials for forming an Oratorio, Opera or Play according to the Modern Taste, to be represented in opposition to the Dragon of Wantley*, was published in 1738.

HANDEL: *Berenice*

29 May. London, C.G.

Text by A. Salvi (first set to music by Perti in 1709). Three acts.

Unsuccessful, given for four nights only. Brunswick February 1743 (with Italian airs and German recitatives and opening chorus, music arranged by G. C. Schürmann).

LATILLA: *Gismondo*

Summer. Naples, Fior.

Text in Neapolitan dialect by G. A. Federico. Three acts.

Very successful in a Tuscan version as *La finta Cameriera*. Mostly under that title, given at Rome, Valle 1738, Florence 1738 (revived Spring 1742); Modena and Faenza 1741; Genova Spring 1742; Vicenza Carnival 1743; Venice, S. Angelo Spring 1743; Bologna Carnival 1743 (revived 1749); Vienna, Kä. 1744; Hamburg 20 August 1744 (in condensed form, as intermezzi, *La Giardiniera Contessa*, 2 parts) and 21 November 1745 (as *La finta Cameriera*); Graz Carnival 1745; Leipzig Spring 1745; Naples and Milan, T.R.D. 1745; Turin, T. Carignano Carnival 1747; Reggio and Mantua 1747; Parma and Munich 1749; London 1 February 1749 (as *Don Calascione*; Latilla not mentioned); Brussels August 1749 (by the same company and under the same title as in London); Copenhagen 1749 (revived 1 October 1755 as *La Giardiniera*, no composer mentioned;

and 12 November 1756); Barcelona 1750; Brunswick 2 August 1751; Paris, O. 30 November 1752; Leiden 1752; Pavia 1753; Trieste Autumn 1754; Dresden August 1762 and Gotha 2 November 1765 (as *La Giardiniera fatta Contessa per le Stravaganze di Don Calassione*).

RAMEAU: *Castor et Pollux*

24 October. Paris, O.

Text by P. J. J. Bernard. Prologue and 5 acts.

Rameau's chief work. Frequently revived at the Paris Opéra; given there 254 times until 1785. When, in 1791, Candeille set the same libretto again, he kept parts of the original music. Given also on many French provincial stages and (in French) at Parma 6 December 1758 (Italian translation in the libretto by J. A. Sanvitale) and Cassel 1776.

Parodies: *Castor et Pollux*, by J. A. Romagnesi and F. Riccoboni, C.I. 14 or 24 December 1737; *Les Jumeaux*, by J. N. Guerin de Frémicourt and others, C.I. 9 March 1754; *Castor et Pollux*, by P. T. Gondot, Brussels 14 January 1754 and as *Les Gémeaux*, Paris, C.I. 10 May 1777; *Le bon Frère*, by P. J. B. Nougaret, published 1779; *Christophe et Pierre-Luc*, by J. E. Despréaux, Trianon May 1780.

Castor et Pollux has been revived several times in the 20th century. First in concert form by the Schola Cantorum, Paris 29 January 1903. On the stage: Montpellier 23 January 1908; Paris, O. 21 March 1918 (recitatives and dances orchestrated by A. Bachelet) and 20 October 1930; Glasgow 27 April 1927 (by amateurs, for the first time in English, translated by G. F. MacCrone); Geneva 28 September 1930 (by the Paris Opéra company); Oxford 22 November 1934 (in English, translated by D. Arundell and T. W. J. Taylor); Florence 27 April 1935 (at the Maggio Musicale Fiorentino, by the Paris Opéra company); Buenos Aires 30 July 1936 (in French).

SARRO: *Achille in Sciro*

4 November. Naples, S.C.

Metastasio's text (first set to music by Caldara in 1736), adapted by L. S. Stampiglia. Three acts.

Written for the inauguration of the Teatro San Carlo, Naples. (The theatre was burnt down on 13 February 1816 and reopened on 12 January 1817.)

LEO: *L'Olimpiade*

19 December. Naples, S.C.

Metastasio's text (first set to music by Caldara in 1733), adapted by L. S. Stampiglio. Three acts.

Given at Lisbon later in the same month. Revived Naples 19 December 1743.

1738

GALUPPI: *Alessandro nell'Indie*

Carnival. Mantua

Metastasio's text (first set to music by Vinci in 1729). Three acts.

Galuppi's first greater success (in the list of his operas this is no.15). Given in many Italian towns (until 1762) and at Stuttgart 30 August 1752 and Munich 12 October 1755.

HANDEL: *Faramondo*

18 January. London, Hm.

Zeno's text (first set to music by Pollarolo in 1699), with alterations. Three acts.

Unsuccessful (8 nights only) and never revived.

LATILLA: *Madama Ciana*

February. Rome, T. Pallacorda

Text by G. Barlocci (according to Schatz originally called *Donna Marzia*). Three acts.

Given, under many different titles, and with alterations at Lisbon Carnival 1740; Venice, S. Cass. Autumn 1744 (with some new airs by Galuppi); Milan June 1745; Turin Carnival 1747 (as *L'Ambizione delusa*) and 1748 (as *Ciana*); Vienna 15 July 1748 (as *La Nobiltà immaginaria*); Leghorn Autumn 1748; Bologna January 1749; Ferrara Spring 1749, and Munich 13 July 1749 (as *Ciana*); London 24 January 1750; Paris, O. 23 September 1753 (as *Gli Artigiani arrichiti*, reduced to 2 acts).

HANDEL: *Serse*

26 April. London, Hm.

Text altered from an earlier libretto by N. Minato (first set to music by Cavalli, see 1654). Three acts.

Handel's only opera with a comic plot (if not a comic opera in the strict sense of the word). The famous *Largo* (*Ombra mai fu* . . .) occurs in *Serse*. Performed 5 times only. Revived at:

GÖTTINGEN 5 July 1924 (in German, translated by O. Hagen).

VIENNA, SCHÖNBRUNN 30 May 1925 (in German, translated by O. Hagen).

BUDAPEST 12 May 1928 (in Hungarian, translated by P. Ottlik).

NORTHAMPTON, MASS. 12 May 1928 (in English, translated by T. N. Wilder).

NEW YORK, JULLIARD SCHOOL 15 December 1932 (in English, translated by T. N. Wilder).

CHICAGO, UNIVERSITY 16 February 1935 (in English, translated by T. N. Wilder).

LOUGHTON, ESSEX 15 June 1935 (in English, translated by G. Dunn).

LONDON, DUKE'S 28 November 1935 (in English, translated by G. Dunn, by the R.A.M.).

CORSELLI: *Alessandro nell' Indie*

9 May. Madrid, Buen Retiro

Metastasio's text (first set to music by Vinci in 1729). Three acts.

Corselli's setting was written for the celebration of the wedding of Charles IV, King of Naples (later King of Spain) and Princess Maria Amalia of Saxony. Produced at the Palacio Real Buen Retiro (first Italian opera there).

1739

RINALDO DI CAPUA: *Vologeso, Re dei Parti*

Carnival. Rome, Arg.

Text: an altered version of Zeno's *Lucio Vero*. Three acts.

The earliest of Rinaldo di Capua's serious operas. Also given at Malta in 1740. Of the music only some airs have been preserved.

d'ALMEIDA: *La Spinalba* o vero *Il Vecchio matto*

Carnival. Lisbon

Librettist unknown (*Dramma comico*). Three acts.

The first (Italian) opera of a Portuguese composer which has been preserved as a whole (score at the Bibliotheca da Ajuda, Lisbon). The opera was produced at the Paço da Ribeira.

RAMEAU: *Les Fêtes d'Hébé* ou *Les Talents lyriques*

21 May. Paris, O.

Text by A. G. de Montdorge. Prologue and 3 entrées, called *La Poësie, La Musique,* and *La Danse* (or sometimes referred to, after their principal characters, as *Sapho, Tirtée,* and *Aeglé*).

Very successful opéra-ballet, revived in Paris 27 July 1747; 18 May 1756; 5 June 1764; 6 July 1770 (the third entrée only); 27 October 1772 and 3 November 1775 (the second entrée only). The third entrée also revived Fontainebleau 6 November 1753; Versailles 18 January 1764. The second entrée also revived Versailles 22 February 1764.

Also given at Lyons 1740; Brussels 1741.

Revived Brussels 21 March 1910 (the first entrée only); Monte Carlo 24 January 1914; Dijon 2 March 1939.

Favart wrote parodies on all three entrées; the first two, called *Les Amours de Gogo* and *Sansonnet et Tonton* were forbidden by the police; the third, *L'Amour impromptu*, was produced at the O.C. 10 July 1756. Other parodies include: *Les Talents comiques*, by C. F. Panard, O.C. 8 July 1739; *Les Talents comiques*, by A. J. de Valois d'Orville, O.C. 10 August 1747; and *Le Prix de l'Amour*, by J. L. Araignon, music by C. F. Clément, C.I. 27 September 1756.

LEO: *Amor vuol Sofferenza*

Autumn. Naples, T.N.

Text by G. A. Federico. Three acts.

The best of Leo's comic operas. Successful in Italy. Given at Florence 1742; Palermo Autumn 1746; Bologna 3 February 1748 (as *La finta Frascatana*); Padua 1748 and London 11 January 1749 (as *La finta Frascatana*).

Revived (as *La finta Frascatana*) Naples, T.N. Autumn 1744 (with additional music by M. Capranica) and once more Carnival 1750 (with additional music by Logroscino and G. Ferradini; libretto British Museum).

Known also as *Il Cioè*, "Cioè" being the constantly repeated favourite word of Fazio, a popular comic character (cf. Cocchi's *Li Matti per Amore*, 1754). See on this opera E. J. Dent's study in *Sammelbände of the I.M.S.*, Vol. VIII (1906–07).

The President De Brosses wrote in one of his famous letters from Italy (dated Naples, 14 November 1739) to M. de Neuilly: "Quelle invention! quelle harmonie! quelle excellente plaisanterie musicale! je porterai cet opéra en France. . . ."

RAMEAU: *Dardanus*

19 November. Paris, O.

Text by C. A. Leclerc de La Bruère. Prologue and 5 acts.

A parody by C. S. Favart, C. F. Panard, and Parmentier, called *Arlequin Dardanus* was produced at the C.I., Paris 14 January 1740. In the 18th century *Dardanus* was revived at the Opéra on 23 April 1744 (new version; two acts rewritten); 15 April 1760 (with new alterations); 20 April 1762; and 4 February 1768 (without prologue) (more than 100 times until 1770); at Fontainebleau 8 October 1763 and 9 November 1769.

Modern revivals: Paris 26 April 1907 (in concert form, by the Schola Cantorum); Dijon 1907; Algiers February 1934 (on the stage).

Sacchini used a reduced version of the same libretto for his opera of the same title (see 1784).

1740

BERNASCONI: *Temistocle*

Carnival. Salzburg

Metastasio's text (first set to music by Caldara in 1736). Three acts.

Bernasconi's setting was also given at Padua 6 June 1740 and Venice, S.G. Gr. Carnival 1744 and revived at Munich (where Bernasconi became Porta's successor as court conductor in 1755), February 1754.

JOMMELLI: *Ricimero, Rè dei Goti*

16 January. Rome, Arg.

Text: an altered version of A. Zeno's and P. Pariati's *Flavio Anicio Olibrio* (first performed with music by Gasparini in 1707). Three acts.

See on the *Ricimero* libretto M. Fehr's study in *Zeitschrift für Musikwissenschaft*, Vol. 1 (1918–19). Jommelli's first extant opera.

PÉREZ: *Siroe*

4 November. Naples, S.C.

Metastasio's text (first set to music by Vinci in 1726). Three acts.

Pérez's first extant opera seria. Revived at Lisbon Autumn 1752 and once more 1756.

1741

HANDEL: *Deidamia*

21 January. London, Lincoln's Inn Fields

Text by P. Rolli. Three acts.

Handel's last opera. Unsuccessful; given for three nights only and never revived.

La Chercheuse d'Esprit

20 February. Paris, O.C.

Text by C. S. Favart and A. R. de Voyer d'Argenson, Marquis de Paulmy (founded on Lafontaine's tale *Comment l'Esprit vient aux Filles*). One act.

Composer unknown. The score has been attributed to Duni (who came to Paris only in

1757). Very successful (ran for 200 nights), and frequently revived in Paris.

In French also given at Brussels 14 May 1743; Munich 1749; London, Little Hm. 28 November 1749 and 23 December 1786; Turin Spring 1753; Cassel 1781.

Anonymous German versions were published in 1749 and 1750; a Dutch translation by H. van Elvervelt was published at Amsterdam in 1758. Revived at Paris at the
VARIÉTÉS 15 February 1822 (text altered by T. M. Dumersan and W. Lafontaine).
VAUDEVILLE 13 March 1822 (in a rival version by N. Gersin and J. J. Gabriel, with some new airs by J. D. Doche). 2 June 1863 (text altered by C. Hérald, music arranged by J. F. Pillevesse).
OPÉRA COMIQUE 22 February 1900 (arranged and orchestrated by J. B. T. Weckerlin).

JOMMELLI: *Ezio*

29 April. Bologna, T. Malvezzi

Metastasio's text (first set to music by Auletta in 1728). Three acts.

Jommelli's first greater success. Given in different versions at Naples 4 November 1748; Vienna, Schönbrunn 4 October 1749; Stuttgart 11 February 1751 and 11 February 1758. Revived Bologna, T.C. 31 January 1768; Lisbon 6 June 1771 (according to the score at Naples) and/or 31 March 1772 (according to the libretto).

PÉREZ: *Demetrio*

13 June. Palermo

Metastasio's text (first set to music by Caldara in 1731). Three acts.

Revived Venice, S. Sam. Spring 1751. Very successful at Lisbon; first given there in 1753 and revived Carnival 1765 and Autumn 1768.

GRAUN: *Rodelinda, Regina de' Longobardi*

13 December. Berlin, Schloss

Text by G. G. Bottarelli (altered from an earlier libretto by A. Salvi, the same utilized by Haym for Handel's *Rodelinda*, see 1725). Three acts.

The first of 27 operas Graun wrote for the Prussian court from 1741–56. Revived Berlin, O. 24 July 1744 and 19 December 1777.

GALUPPI: *Penelope*

23 December. London, Hm.

Text by P. A. Rolli. Three acts.

The first of four operas Galuppi wrote for London, where he spent two seasons. Revived London 17 December 1754 (probably as pasticcio as the libretto does not mention Galuppi's name any more).

JOMMELLI: *Merope*

26 December. Venice, S.G. Gr.

Zeno's text (first set to music by Gasparini in 1711). Three acts.

Also given at Bologna December 1744; Vienna 13 July 1749; Barcelona 4 December 1751, Pesaro Carnival 1753; Stuttgart 11 February 1756.

GLUCK: *Artaserse*

26 December. Milan, T.R.D.

Metastasio's text (first set to music by Vinci, see 1730). Three acts.

Gluck's first opera. (Thus in the same year 1741 there was in January the first production of Handel's last, and in December the first production of Gluck's first opera.)

Of the music only small parts have been preserved.

1742

HASSE: *Lucio Papirio*

18 January. Dresden

Zeno's text (first set to music by Caldara, see 1719). Three acts.

Frederick the Great was present at the second night on 19 January. Also given at Brunswick August 1744 (with German recitatives, translated and probably composed by Schürmann); Naples, S.C., 4 November 1746; Berlin 24 January 1766 and January 1784.

GLUCK: *Demetrio*

2 May. Venice, S. Sam.

Metastasio's text (first set to music by Caldara, see 1731). Three acts.

Gluck's second opera. Only 6 airs are extant. (The opera is sometimes quoted as *Cleonice*.)

HASSE: *Didone abbandonata*

7 October Hubertusburg, near Dresden

Metastasio's text (first set to music by Sarro, see 1724). Three acts.

Naples, S.C. 20 January 1744; London 6 April 1748 (chiefly by Hasse); Berlin 29 December 1752 and December 1769; an intended further revival at Berlin in January 1780 was cancelled on account of the death of Princess Louisa Amalia.

GRAUN: *Cleopatra e Cesare*

7 December. Berlin, O.

Text by G. G. Bottarelli (founded on P. Corneille's *La Mort de Pompée*). Three acts.

Written for the inauguration of the Berlin opera-house (which was burnt down, after exactly 100 years of existence, 18 August 1842, and was rebuilt and reopened 7 December 1844, with Meyerbeer's *Ein Feldlager in Schlesien*).

GLUCK: *Demofoonte*

26 December. Milan, T.R.D.

Metastasio's text (first set to music by Caldara in 1733). Three acts.

Gluck's first greater success. Also given at Reggio May 1743 (with additional airs by F. Maggiore); Florence 1743; Bologna 26 December 1743; Vienna 6 October 1744 (Gluck's setting?); Ferrara Carnival 1745. Revived Milan 13 May 1747; Florence 1749. Airs preserved; overture and recitatives lost.

1743

TERRADELLAS: *Merope*

Carnival. Rome, T. delle Dame

Zeno's text (first set to music by Gasparini in 1711). Three acts.

Given at Florence, P. in the same Carnival and revived there 26 December 1749; also Leghorn Carnival 1744 and Ancona Carnival 1746.

JOMMELLI: *Demofoonte*

13 June. Padua.

Metastasio's text (first set to music by Caldara in 1733). Three acts.

One of Jommelli's most successful works; given at Parma Spring 1749; Milan T.R.D. January 1753; Lodi Carnival 1754; London 9 December 1755; Stuttgart 11 February 1764 (repeated at Ludwigsburg 11 February 1765 and 1769; last revived at Stuttgart 10 January 1778); Naples, S.C. 4 November 1770 (with alterations; Mozart was present at the first night); Lisbon 6 June 1775.

GLUCK: *Il Tigrane*

9 September. Crema

Text: Goldoni's version of F. Silvani's *La Virtù trionfante dell'Amore e dell'Odio* (1691), as first set by G. Arena in 1741. Three acts.

Only parts of the music are extant.

Discovery and reconstruction of this opera are due to F. Piovano; see his admirable paper "Un Opéra inconnu de Gluck" in *Sammelbände of the I.M.S.*, Vol. IX (1907–08). See on the origin of the libretto also G. Ortolani in the City of Venice edition of Goldoni's Works, Vol. XXXIII (1934), pp.311–314.

HASSE: *Antigono*

10 October. Hubertusburg, near Dresden

Text by P. Metastasio (written for Hasse). Three acts.

Given at the Dresden Court Theatre 20 January 1744 and at Hamburg 10 September 1744 (Hasse's setting, according to Mattheson; according to the libretto the greater part of the music was by Scalabrini); Naples, S.C. 19 December 1744 (music adapted by A. Palella); Brunswick 31 January 1746 (sung partly in German, translated by Schürmann?); Milan, T.R.D. Carnival 1747; Parma Carnival 1753 (as *Alessandro Re d'Epiro*).

GRAUN: *Artaserse*

2 December. Berlin, O.

Metastasio's text (first set to music by Vinci, see 1730). Three acts.

Also given at Brunswick, August 1745 (as *Artabanus*, with German recitatives, translated by Schürmann, and additional airs) and 23 August 1747; and Stuttgart 30 August 1750 (at the inauguration of the new opera-house there).

1744

TERRADELLAS: *Artaserse*

Carnival. Venice, S.G. Gr.

Metastasio' stext (first set to music by Vinci, see 1730). Three acts.

Terradellas's chief work, given on several Italian stages.

GLUCK: *La Sofonisba*

[*13 January*] Milan, T.R.D.

Silvani's text (first set to music by Caldara in 1708), with most of the airs taken from different librettos of Metastasio's. Three acts.

GLUCK: *Ipermestra*

21 November. Venice, S.G. Gr.

Text by P. Metastasio (written for Hasse earlier in the same year). Three acts.

The first of Gluck's operas of which all the airs and recitatives are extant in full score.[1] Also given at Prague Autumn 1750; Munich 1751 (according to Piovano probably Gluck's setting); St. Petersburg 3 March 1760 (according to some authors; according to R. A. Mooser *extrémement douteux*).

HASSE: *Semiramide riconosciuta*

26 December. Venice, S.G. Gr.

Metastasio's text (first set to music by Vinci in 1729). Three acts.

[1] British Museum, Add. MSS 16014.

Also given at S. Giovanni in Persiceto 1745; Graz Carnival 1746; Leipzig 6 May 1746; Prague Summer 1746 (revived 1760); Dresden 11 January 1747; London 18 May 1748; Brunswick August 1748 (recitatives and some airs in German, translated by Schürmann?); Warsaw 7 October 1760.

1745

REBEL and FRANCOEUR: *Zélindor Roi des Silphes*

17 March. Versailles

Text by F. A. P. de Moncrif. Prologue and 1 act.

First produced at the Paris Opéra 10 August 1745 and frequently revived there until 1752 and again 17 June 1766; Versailles 18 December 1752; Bellevue 4 March 1753; Fontainebleau 19 October 1769; Paris 11 May 1773.

Given in an Italian version by C. I. Frugoni at Parma Autumn 1757.

A parody, *Zéphire et Fleurette* (text by P. Laujon and C. F. Panard, revised by Favart), was produced at the C.I., Paris 23 March 1754.

RAMEAU: *Platée*

31 March. Versailles

Text by J. Autreau and A. J. de Valois d'Orville (*ballet-bouffon*). Prologue and 3 acts.

Given at the Paris Opéra only four years later, 4 February 1749 (text altered by Ballot de Sovot and revived there 9 February 1750 and 21 February 1754. Known also with the sub-title *Junon jalouse.* Modern revivals:

MUNICH, KAIM-SAAL, 26 January 1901 (by the Munich "Orchesterverein").

MONTE CARLO 5 April 1917 (in French).

COMO 29 January 1921 (by the "Amici della Musica", Italian version by A. Finzi and P. Clausetti).

MILAN, T. CARCANO 31 January 1921 (by the "Amici della Musica", Italian version by A. Finzi and P. Clausetti).

"Cet ouvrage de carnaval est très-curieux à étudier. C'était la première incursion de l'Ecole française dans le genre de musique bouffonne, où excellaient les vieux maîtres italiens" (Lajarte). The 1754 revival struck the final blow at the Italian artists who had been producing their inter-mezzi at the Paris Opéra for 18 months. They gave their last performance on 7 March 1754.

FIORILLO: *L'Olimpiade*

May. Venice, S. Sam.

Metastasio's text (first set to music by Caldara in 1733). Three acts.

Revived in August 1749 at Brunswick, where Fiorillo became court conductor in 1754 (as Schürmann's successor).

HASSE: *Arminio*

7 October. Dresden

Text by G. C. Pasquini. Three acts and licenza.

The second Dresden performance took place at the request of Frederick II, after the battle of Kesselsdorf, 19 December 1745. Revived at Dres-den 8 January 1753. Also given at Berlin 18 Jan-uary 1747 (revived 24 December 1773); Vienna 13 May 1747 (with ballet music by Holzbauer); Brunswick 22 August 1747 (with German reci-tatives, translated by Schürmann?); Warsaw 3 August 1761.

An earlier *Arminio* opera by Hasse, produced at Milan 28 August 1730, is a different work altogether (text by A. Salvi).

PÉREZ: *Alessandro nell' Indie*

26 December. Genoa, S. Agostino

Metastasio's text (first set to music by Vinci in 1729). Three acts.

Revived Naples, S.C. 4 November 1749. Given at Lisbon 31 March 1755 (at the inaugu-ration of the Royal Opera di Tejo) and revived there at the S. Carlos theatre as late as Carnival 1806. Also given at Cadiz [17 December] 1764.

1746

JOMMELLI: *Don Trastullo*

Carnival. Rome, T. della Pace

Librettist unknown. Two parts.

Successful intermezzi, given on many Italian stages (at Rome, Tord. 7 February 1756 as *La Cantata e Disfida di Don Trastullo*) and at Madrid, Buen Retiro 23 September 1757; Munich 1758 and Carnival 1763; Warsaw c.1766; London 9 April 1767 (for one night only; not recorded by Burney or by Nicoll).

GRAUN: *Demofoonte, Rè di Tracia*

17 January. Berlin, O.

Metastasio's text (first composed by Caldara in 1733). Three acts.

Revived Berlin Carnival 1774 (with altera-tions). Three airs in this opera were composed by King Frederick II.

GLUCK: *La Caduta de' Giganti*

18 January. London, Hm.

Text by F. Vanneschi. Two parts.

The first of the two operas Gluck wrote for London. It was when hearing *La Caduta de' Gi-ganti* that Handel is said to have made the well-known remark "He knaws no more of contra-punto as mein cook, Waltz".

Six airs from the opera were published by Walsh.

JOMMELLI: *Cajo Mario*

6 February. Rome, Arg.

Text by G. Roccaforte. Three acts.

Successful in Italy; Florence, P. Autumn 1747; Bologna Carnival 1751 and Carnival 1758; Mo-dena December 1751; Leghorn Carnival 1754; Verona Carnival 1762; Cesena Carnival 1770.

Revived Prague 1772 as *Il Cajo Mario Console e Patricio.*

GLUCK: *Artamene*

15 March. London, Hm.

Text by B. Vitturi (first set to music by Albinoni in 1740), altered by F. Vanneschi. Three acts.

Like *La Caduta de' Giganti* (see above), *Artamene* was more or less a pasticcio from earlier operas, chiefly from *Tigrane*, *Sofonisbe*, and *Ipermestra* (1743 and 1744). See on Gluck's two London operas W. B. Squire in *The Musical Quarterly*, Vol. 1 (1915).

Six airs from *Artamene* were published by Walsh.

LECLAIR: *Scylla et Glaucus*

4 October. Paris, O.

Text by d'Albaret. Prologue and 5 acts.

The only opera of the famous violinist. Unsuccessful. Extracts were revived in concert form at Lyons (Leclair's native town) on 21 March 1909.

SCHÜRER: *La Galatea*

8 November. Dresden

Text by P. Metastasio (written in 1722, first composer unknown). Two acts.

Repeated at Pillnitz 28 June 1747 (at the Bavarian-Saxon double wedding; see note on Gluck's *Le Nozze d'Ercole e d'Ebe*, 1747).

1747

LOGROSCINO: *Il Governatore*

Carnival. Naples, T.N.

Text by D. Canicà. Three acts.

The best-known of Logroscino's comic operas. The score was discovered by E. J. Dent at Münster about 1904. The finale of the first act was published by H. Kretzschmar (*Jahrbuch der Musikbibliothek Peters*, 1908, reprinted in Kretzschmar's *Gesammelte Aufsätze*, Vol. II, appendix).

JOMMELLI: *La Didone abbandonata*

28 January. Rome, Arg.

Metastasio's text (first set to music by Sarro in 1724). Three acts.

One of Jommelli's most important works. Vienna 8 December 1749; Stuttgart April 1751 and revived there in a new version 11 February

1763 and again 10 January 1777 and 25 September 1782. An analysis of the opera is given in W. Heinse's novel, *Hildegard von Hohenthal* (1795-96).

SCHÜRER: *Doris*

13 February. Dresden

Librettist unknown. *Ein musikalisches Schaeferspiel*. Two acts.

An isolated instance of a German pastoral opera in the very period when Italian opera was the fashion all over Germany, several years before the introduction of German Singspiel.

TERRADELLAS: *Bellerofonte*

4 April. London, Hm.

Text by F. Vanneschi. Three acts.

" ... crescendo is used in this opera, seemingly for the first time; and new effects are frequently produced by pianos and fortes" (Burney, IV, p.456).

COCCHI: *La Maestra*

Spring. Naples, T.N.

Text by A. Palomba. Three acts.

Cocchi's most successful comic opera. Given at Bologna Septembre 1747; Turin 1748; Modena 1748; Venice, S. Moisè Autumn 1748 as *La Scuola moderna, o sia La Maestra di buon Gusto*; text altered by C. Goldoni, probably with new music by Ciampi, who is mentioned in a 1749 Verona libretto (*La Maestra di Scuola*). Cocchi's setting was revived at Naples, Fior. Carnival 1751 (with additional music by Latilla and Cordella); Venice Carnival 1754; Sinigaglia July 1754; Bologna 8 January 1757; Milan, T.R.D. Autumn 1757; Rome, Capr. Carnival 1760.

Outside Italy given at London 11 March 1749; Potsdam Summer 1749 (anonymous); Paris, O. 25 January 1753 (as *La Scaltra Governatrice*); Barcelona [13 August] 1753 (anonymous); Brussels Winter 1753; Trieste Carnival 1755; Prague 1756; Dresden 4 August 1756; St. Petersburg 5 November 1759 (anonymous); Nuremberg 8 January 1763; Berlin 23 December 1763 (as *La Maestra di Scuola*).

GLUCK: *Le Nozze d'Ercole e d'Ebe*

29 June. Pillnitz, near Dresden

Librettist unknown (the text was first set to music by Porpora, Venice 18 February 1744). Two acts.

The production of this serenata was part of the wedding festivities in honour of the double marriage of Max Joseph, Elector of Bavaria, with Maria Anna, Princess of Saxony, and of Frederick Christian, Prince of Saxony, with Maria Antonia Walpurgis, Princess of Bavaria (the composer, see 1754 and 1760). Hasse, Scalabrini, and Schürer contributed the rest of the wedding operas. The score was published in 1914 (Vol. xiv of *Denkmäler der Tonkunst in Bayern*, edited by H. Abert).

PORPORA: *Filandro*

18 July. Dresden

Text by V. Cassani (*dramma comico-pastorale*), originally called *L'Incostanza schernita* and first set to music by Albinoni in 1727. Three acts.

The first opera produced at Dresden under Hasse's direction which was not composed by Hasse (but by his former teacher and now rival, Porpora). There were a sinking and a rising star in the cast too: Faustina Hasse as "Orsinda" and Porpora's pupil, Regina Mingotti, as "Corina".

BOISMORTIER: *Daphnis et Chloé*

28 September. Paris, O.

Text by P. Laujon (*pastorale*). Prologue and 3 acts.

The last and best of Boismortier's three operas. Revived Paris, O. 4 May 1752. A parody by P. T. Gondot, *Les Bergers de Qualité*, was produced at the C.I. 5 June 1752.

HASSE: *Leucippo*

7 October. Hubertusburg, near Dresden

Text by G. C. Pasquini (*favola pastorale*). Three acts.

Also given at Brunswick 1747 (revived February 1765); Salzthal 28 August 1748 (as *Dafne e Leucippo*); Vienna 28 August 1748; Venice May 1749; Dresden 7 January 1751 (revived 1761); Prague Spring 1752; Frankfort 19 September 1754; Mannheim 1757; Pressburg 1759; Berlin 7 January 1765.

GALUPPI: *L'Olimpiade*

26 December. Milan, T.R.D.

Metastasio's text (first set to music by Caldara in 1733). Three acts.

The most successful of Galuppi's serious operas. Given at Mannheim 17 January 1749 (revived 19 November 1756); Naples, S.C. 18 December 1749 (revived with alterations 30 May 1750); Prague Spring 1750; London 10 February 1756 (text altered by F. Vanneschi, additional airs by F. Giardini); Cadiz [24 December] 1762; Siena 24 July 1763.

1748

LOGROSCINO: *Giunio Bruto*

January. Rome, Arg.

Librettist unknown (of this title only a 17th century text is recorded by Allacci). Three acts.

No copy of the libretto is known. Date and place of first (?) performance are given in the MS score at Münster. *Il Governatore* (see 1747), *Giunio Bruto* and *Olimpiade* (Rome, 1753; recently discovered in a private collection at Cambridge) are the only extant operas of Logroscino, out of a total of more than 25 which are known by title.

HASSE: *Demofoonte*

9 February. Dresden

Metastasio's text (first set to music by Caldara in 1733). Three acts.

One of Hasse's greatest successes. Venice Carnival 1749; Mannheim January 1750; Naples S.C. January 1750; Vicenza Carnival 1754. With alterations: Naples 4 November 1758; Warsaw 7 October 1759; Malta Autumn 1765.

GLUCK: *Semiramide riconosciuta*

14 May. Vienna, B.

Metastasio's text (first set to music by Vinci in 1729). Three acts.

Gluck wrote this opera to celebrate the birthday of the Empress Maria Theresa. Revived Hamburg 19 October 1936 (translated by H. Swedlund, with additional music from Gluck's *Poro*, 1744).

GRAUN: *Ifigenia in Aulide*

13 December. Berlin, O.

Text by L. de Villati (probably written in collaboration with Frederick II, founded on Racine's tragedy). Three acts.

Successful in Berlin where it was last revived in January 1768. Also performed at Brunswick August 1749 (recitatives and some airs in German, translated by Schürmann?).

An earlier, German, opera by Graun on the same subject (text by G. C. Schürmann) had been produced at Brunswick 16 August 1728 (revived 5 February 1731 and 16 August 1734) and Hamburg 3 December 1731.

CIAMPI: *Bertoldo, Bertoldino e Cacasenno*

27 December. Venice, S. Moisè

Text by C. Goldoni (founded on Italian 16th century legends). Three acts.

Frequently given with slightly different titles, as *Bertoldo*, *Bertoldo in Corte*, *Bertoldo alla Corte*; in London as *Bertoldo, Bertoldino e Cacasenno alla Corte del Re Alboino* (1754) and as *Bertoldo* (1762). The complicated history of this famous comic opera has been fully investigated by O. G. T. Sonneck (*Sammelbände of the I.M.S.*, Vol. XII, 1910–11). More recent contributions to its problems are to be found in the City of Venice edition of Goldoni's Works (Vol. XXVII, pp.291–297) and in A. Iacuzzi's *European Vogue of Favart* (1932).

The following productions are to be recorded: Verona Carnival 1750; Padua 11 June 1750; Milan, T.R.D. Spring 1750; Brunswick *c.*1750; Bologna Summer 1751; Strasbourg 1751; Paris, O. 9 November 1753; Potsdam 30 March 1754; Amsterdam 1754; London, C.G. 9 December 1754 (revived 11 January 1762); Ferrara and Pesaro Carnival 1755; Genoa Summer 1755; Piacenza Spring 1758; Trieste Carnival 1760; Prague 1760; St. Petersburg 4 May 1761. Revived as a pasticcio, Treviso Autumn 1791.

When, in 1753, Ciampi's opera was produced in Paris by Bambini's buffo troupe and proved a great success, the minor Paris theatres, after their custom, soon followed suit with French parodies. One of them, Favart's *Le Caprice amoureux*, is recorded here as an independent work (see 1755) because it was in Favart's rather than in Goldoni's version that the opera was imitated during the second half of the century.

The other parody was called *Bertholde à la Ville* and produced at the O.C. Paris 9 March 1754, Brussels 28 June 1755 and Hague 1760. Its author was L. Anseaume (perhaps in collaboration with G. C. de Lattaignant, or with J. J. Vadé and Farin de Hautemer), and A. N. La Salle d'Offemont arranged the music from the Italian original and from French popular airs. There is also a Dutch version of *Bertholde à la Ville* by J. T. Neyts (n.d.).

1749

JOMMELLI: *Artaserse*

4 February. Rome, Arg.

Metastasio's text (first set to music by Vinci, see 1730). Three acts.

Also given at Mannheim Carnival 1751 and Stuttgart 30 August 1756 (in Italian).

GLUCK: *La Contesa dei Numi*

9 April. Copenhagen

Text by P. Metastasio (written in 1729 to celebrate the birth of the Dauphin, son of Louis XV, and produced at Cardinal Polignac's, Rome 26 November 1729 with music by Vinci); the Danish translation in the libretto by T. Clitau. One act.

Gluck chose the same text when the birth of the Danish Prince Christian, later King Christian VII, was to be celebrated. Parts of the opera were revived at Copenhagen, in concert form, 1 April 1871 and February 1902.

JOMMELLI: *Demetrio*

Spring. Parma

Metastasio's text (first set to music by Caldara, see 1731). Three acts.

Also given at Madrid, Buen Retiro 23 September 1751; Mannheim 4 November 1753; Pressburg 1760.

GALUPPI: *L'Arcadia in Brenta*

14 May. Venice, S. Angelo

Text by C. Goldoni (the first comic libretto he wrote for Galuppi. An earlier setting by Ciampi, produced at Piacenza 1746 or at Bassano Autumn 1747 is very doubtful. No libretto earlier than 1749 has come to light yet). Three acts.

Galuppi's first great success as a composer of comic operas. Given on Italian stages until 1769; Rome Carnival 1759, reduced to 2 acts; Como 1765, as *La nuova Arcadia*.

In Italian also Barcelona 1751; Leyden 1752; London, C.G. 18 November 1754; Hamburg 2 April 1755; Dresden 23 May 1755; Cologne 21 February 1757; St. Petersburg 9 February 1759; Pressburg Spring 1759; Munich 1760. Last revived Bonn Carnival 1771.

An undated Italian-French libretto is mentioned in *Cat. Bibl. Soleinne* (no.4744).

CIAMPI: *Il Negligente*

Autumn. Venice, S. Moisè

Text by C. Goldoni. Three acts.

Successful in Italy; given at Lodi Carnival 1752 as *Il Trascurato*; at Florence Autumn 1752 as *Lo Spensierato*. In Italian also given at London as early as 1 December 1749; Frankfort 5 October 1754 (German translation in libretto by M. Soralli); Trieste Autumn 1756; Oporto 15 May 1762 (first Italian opera there, produced at the Theatro do Corpo da Guarda; Portuguese libretto *O Descuidado* printed; music attributed to Pergolesi by T. Braga and by Vasconcellos).

RAMEAU: *Zoroastre*

5 December. Paris, O.

Text by L. de Cahusac. Prologue and 5 acts.

Revived at the O. on 20. January 1756 (new version, 3 acts partly re-written) and (with alterations by Berton) 26 January 1770. Given at Dresden 7 February 1752 in an Italian version by

G. Casanova (the famous adventurer) and in an almost completely new setting by J. A. Adam.[1] A parody by T. G. Taconet, called *Nostradamus*, was produced at the O.C. in 1756. The original was once more revived, in concert form, by the Schola Cantorum, Paris 26 November 1903.

BOYCE: *The Chaplet*

13 December. London, D.L.

Text by M. Mendez (*A musical entertainment*). Two acts.

Successful on English stages. Frequently revived in London in the 18th century; given at D.L. 129 times until 1773. Also given at Dublin 1757; Philadelphia 4 June 1767; New York 14 March 1768. As early as 1818 *The Quarterly Musical Magazine and Review* wrote: "Dr. William Boyce wrote a musical entertainment called the Chaplet which now lies amongst the things forgotten; it is in one act. The dialogue is carried on in recitative, and there are airs, duets, and one chorus. Some of them are, we believe, transferred to the Burletta of Midas, *Push about the brisk bowl* is one of these. There is nothing in the whole thing to save it from oblivion". Still, *The Chaplet* was revived again on 24 March 1936 by the Arts Theatre Club, London.

GALUPPI: *Il Conte Caramella*

18 December. Verona

Text by C. Goldoni (partly founded on Addison's comedy, *The Drummer or The Haunted House*, 1716). Three acts.

Given on many Italian stages and at Barcelona [18 June] 1754; Prague 1755; Dresden 18 July 1755; Trieste Carnival 1756; Moscow 27 June 1759; St. Petersburg 21 September 1759; Nuremberg 7 February 1763 and 5 November 1763 (as *Lo Spettro con Tamburo*); Grafeneck, near Stuttgart 4 November 1765 (as *Il Tamburo notturno*; Potsdam 23 September 1766.

(Date and place of first performance according to Schatz, Piovano, and all other authorities. The

[1] For an account of the Dresden production see the *Mercure de France*, May 1752.

earliest libretto known, however, is that for the production at Venice, S. Sam. 13 November 1751.)

In this year, 1749, there was published an important German opera libretto, *Thusnelde, ein Singspiel in 4 Aufzügen, mit einem Vorbericht von der Möglichkeit und Beschaffenheit guter Singspiele*, by Johann Adolf Scheibe. His text was never set to music; but it may be regarded as the literary starting point of the 18th century German national opera movement, and as the prototype of works like Schweitzer's *Alceste* (see 1773) and Holzbauer's *Günther von Schwarzburg* (see 1777).

1750

GLUCK: *Ezio*

Carnival. Prague

Metastasio's text (first set to music by Auletta in 1728). Three acts.

Also given at Leipzig 1751 and revived at Vienna December 1763.

German translation by J. A. von Ghelen published Vienna 1765.

HASSE: *Attilio Regolo*

12 January. Dresden

Text by P. Metastasio (written in 1740 at Vienna but not performed there because of the death of the Emperor Charles VI). Three acts.

Hasse's opera (which was the first setting of the libretto) was revived at Berlin December 1775.

GALUPPI: *Il Mondo della Luna*

29 January. Venice, S. Moisè

Text by C. Goldoni (the first setting of this famous libretto which was later composed by Piccinni, Haydn, Paisiello and many others). Three acts.

Successful in Italy. In Italian also given at Barcelona Spring 1751; Brussels Winter 1753; Brunswick January 1753 (revived February 1760); Dresden 7 October 1754; Hamburg 23

January 1755; Prague 1755; Moscow Summer 1758; London 22 November 1760; Breslau 1796.

In German produced at Oels (undated libretto printed).

GALUPPI: *Il Mondo alla Roversa* o sia *Le Donne che comandano*

14 November. Venice, S. Cass.

Text by C. Goldoni (*Dramma bernesco*). Three acts.

In Italian also given at Trieste 1752; Barcelona 1752; Brussels December 1753; Prague 1754; Leipzig 5 May 1754; Dresden 25 June 1754 (revived 1768); Hamburg 22 November 1754; Laibach 1757 (as *L'Impero delle Donne*); Munich 1758; Moscow 1759.

The only opera of Galuppi which was published in his lifetime (vocal score, Leipzig, Breitkopf, 1758). For a recent account of the work see G. G. Bernardi in *Musica d'Oggi*, June 1934.

1751

TERRADELLAS: *Sesostri Re d'Egitto*

Carnival. Rome, T. delle Dame

Text by A. Zeno and P. Pariati (first set to music by Gasparini in 1709). Three acts.

Terradellas's last opera. The story that Jommelli was so jealous of the success of *Sesostri* as to poison his rival Terradellas (who died 20 May, 1751) first occurs in *A.M.Z.*, 1800, no.24, and was taken over by very many books and magazines. It seems that Friedrich Rochlitz, editor of the Leipzig periodical, simply invented it as no trace of the legend is to be found in 18th century sources.

HASSE: *Il Ciro riconosciuto*

20 January. Dresden

Metastasio's text (first set to music by Caldara in 1736). Three acts.

Also given at Prague in the same Carnival; Stuttgart 11 February 1752; Warsaw Carnival 1762. This was the last opera in which Faustina Hasse appeared in public.

JOMMELLI: L'Ifigenia

9 February. Rome, Arg.

Text by M. Verazi. Three acts.

Also given at Mannheim 4 November 1751; Naples 18 December 1753; Barcelona Spring 1755; Prague 1762; Cassel August 1766.

This is the *Ifigenia in Aulide* subject; an *Ifigenia in Tauride* by Jommelli (Naples 20 January 1771 and Lisbon Carnival 1776) is also extant.

ABOS: Tito Manlio

30 May. Naples, S.C.

Probably G. Roccaforte's text (first set to music by Manna in 1742). Three acts.

Of Abos's serious operas the only one which is extant. Also given at Modena 26 December 1753; London 10 April 1756; Florence, P. 26 December 1759.

In a contemporary letter quoted by B. Croce the libretto is called "un ben raccolto mazzetto di scelti fiori del Salvi"; Salvi, however, is not known to have written a "Tito Manlio" text. In the British Museum Catalogue the London libretto is attributed to Matteo Noris; but his *Tito Manlio* (first set to music by Pollarolo in 1696) is strikingly different from that used by Abos.

TRAETTA: Il Farnace

4 November. Naples, S.C.

Text: an altered version of Zeno's *Mitridate* (first set to music by Caldara in 1728). Three acts.

Traetta's first opera.

BERTONI: Le Pescatrici

26 December. Venice, S. Sam.

Text by C. Goldoni. Three acts.

Bertoni's most successful comic opera. Given on many Italian stages and in Italian also at Brussels *c.*December 1753; Dresden 5 September 1754; Prague 1757; Bonn May 1758; London 28 April 1761; Barcelona [28 May] 1761 (revived 1769); Logroño, Spain 1764; Brunswick August 1766 (as *Le tre Pescatrici*).

In Spanish (translated by R. de la Cruz) Madrid 26 October 1765.

1752

HAYDN: Der neue krumme Teufel[1]

Spring. Vienna, Kä.

Text by J. J. F. von Kurz (founded on Lesage's *Le Diable boiteux*). Two acts.

Haydn's first opera. The music unfortunately seems to be lost, astonishingly, as the work was rather successful; there must have been many copies and one or the other might emerge some day.

Revived at the same theatre 24 November 1770 as *Asmodeus der krumme Teufel*; at the Leop. Th. 4 November 1782 (as *Der krumme Teufel*) and once more at the suburban Fasan Theatre 28 September 1783. Also given at Pressburg 29 October 1764; Nuremberg 12 August 1766; Frankfort 1767; Prague 17 November 1771; Berlin 15 February 1774 (as *Der hinkende Teufel*); Warsaw 1774; Donaueschingen 1778-9; Dresden June 1782; Munich 7 January 1783, and on many minor stages until the end of the century. The opera is last mentioned in the *Gothaer Taschenbuch für die Schaubühne*, 1798, p.271.

A comedy founded on Lesage's novel had been produced at Vienna on 16 July 1738. See on the first period of Viennese German Singspiel, V. Helfert in *Zeitschrift für Musikwissenschaft*, Vol. V (1922-23) and R. Haas in *Studien zur Musikwissenschaft*, Vol. XII (1925).

BONNO: L'Eroe Cinese

13 May. Vienna, Schönbrunn

Text by P. Metastasio. Three acts.

Written for Bonno and first produced by *giovani distinte dame e cavalieri*. Also given at Barcelona 23 September 1755 and Parma 1 May 1764. On Bonno, who in 1774 became Gassmann's

---

[1] Title from the earliest extant libretto (undated; copy Stadtbibliothek, Vienna); according to R. Haas (*Studien zur Musikwissenschaft*, Vol. XII [1925], p.55) this edition belongs probably to a revival in 1758, and the original title possibly was *Der krumme Teufel*. An Italian intermezzo *Il Vecchio ingannato* is contained in the second act of *Der neue krumme Teufel*; at Pressburg 1764 the intermezzo was called *Le Avventure di Lesbina*.

successor as court conductor at Vienna, see E. Wellesz's study in *Sammelbände of the I.M.S.*, Vol. XI (1909–10).

STANDFUSS: *Der Teufel ist los, oder Die verwandelten Weiber*

6 October. Leipzig

Text by C. F. Weisse (founded on C. Coffey's *The Devil to Pay*, see 1731). Two acts.

Within a few months Haydn's Viennese operetta was followed by the first North German Singspiel—surely more than a mere coincidence. Standfuss's music has been preserved only in Hiller's revised version of the opera (see 1766). His setting was also heard at Hamburg and Königsberg 1756; Frankfort 26 September 1757 (revived 20 November 1770); Berlin 31 January 1761; Nuremberg Winter 1764-5; and revived at Lübeck 27 September 1776. He also composed the music for a sequel *Der lustige Schuster* (see 1759).

J. J. ROUSSEAU: *Le Devin du Village*

18 October. Fontainebleau

Text by the composer (*intermède*). One act.

First produced at Fontainebleau with a pasticcio overture and recitatives by Jélyotte and Francoeur. Produced at the Opéra, Paris 1 March 1753 with Rousseau's original recitatives and with a newly composed overture. Given there more than 400 times until 1829 (20 April 1779 in an altered version, with 6 new airs).

Some days after the production at the Paris Opéra, on 4 March 1753 given at the palace of Bellevue, at the private theatre of Mme de Pompadour who played the part of Colin.

Revived in Paris at the Comédie-Française 29 May 1838; Th. du Vaudeville 30 August 1864 (partly re-orchestrated by J. Cadaux); Galerie Vivienne 24 December 1896; O.C. 27 June 1912 (previously at Ermenonville 23 June 1912; music revised by J. Tiersot); Petite Scène 5 May 1923.

Outside Paris given (in French) at Brussels 1753; Lyons 1754; The Hague 28 March 1754; Stockholm 9 February 1758; Frankfort November-

ber 1759; Vienna Autumn 1760; Turin Spring 1761; Liége 10 January 1771; Warsaw May 1778; Hamburg 28 June 1782 (on the same bill with *Les Amours de Bastien et Bastienne*, see below); Gothenburg 2 May 1783; Stockholm June 1783; Amsterdam 1787; New York 21 October 1790; Cologne 1795-6; St. Petersburg 1797; Berne 10 June 1809; Cassel Spring 1811; Quebec 26 May 1846 (by the Société des Amateurs Canadiens); Algiers September 1901 (by the Petit Athénée).

A Dutch version by J. F. Cammaert was published at Brussels in 1758 (reprinted 1762). Produced in Dutch at The Hague in 1769 (if not earlier). Revived Amsterdam December 1932 (by the Dutch Chamber Opera).

An English version, by Charles Burney, *The Cunning-Man (a musical entertainment, imitated and adapted to the original music)* was produced in London, D. L. 21 November 1766 and Dublin 1767.

Apart from Burney's adaptation, there was an anonymous English version, *The Village Conjurer*, published in 1767 (in Vol. II of Rousseau's *Miscellaneous Works*).

A German version by C. Dielitz was published in 1820. Produced in German only much later: Vienna 5 March 1909 (by amateurs); Leipzig 21 March 1911 (Dielitz's translation revised by P. Prina, music arranged by R. Gound); Zurich 29 June 1912.

The great success of *Le Devin du Village* soon called forth a parody. It was written by C. S. Favart (in collaboration with his wife and Harny de Guerville and called *Les Amours de Bastien et Bastienne*). Produced at the C.I., Paris 4 August 1753 (50th performance as early as 19 December 1753). In French also, Fontainebleau 3 November 1753; Brussels November 1753; Laxenburg (near Vienna) 16 June 1755; Vienna 5 July 1755; Frankfort 27 March 1764; Hamburg 28 June 1782; Gothenburg 4 May 1783; Sielce (Poland) 7 September 1788; Lazienk (near Warsaw) Summer 1791 (music arranged by Gaetano). Revived Paris, Petite Scène 5 May 1923 (along with *Le Devin du Village*).

Les Amours de Bastien et Bastienne was first given in German at Berlin, Donner'sches Haus 29 May

1763 (see M. Dubinski in *Die Musik*, August 1912, p.142). Another German version, by F. W. Weiskern, was first produced at Vienna, Kä. 5 May 1764 (according to J. H. F. Müller, *Genaue Nachrichten . . .*, 1772; later authorities give 5 April 1764) and subsequently at Brünn 1770; Prague 11 February 1772; Berlin 22 October 1773, etc. Revived Vienna, Jos. 29 May 1779 and Leop. 29 October 1781; Munich 29 January 1784 (as *Bastien und Bastienne, oder In der Liebe muss gezankt sein*).

For Mozart's new setting of Weiskern's adaptation, see 1768.

Abert (I, 141, note) quotes a 1764 edition of Weiskern's version. In the British Museum there is a copy of a 1774 edition with additions by J. H. F. Müller (cf. *Music and Letters*, October 1942).

Another parody on *Le Devin du Village* was J. J. Vadé's *La nouvelle Bastienne*, produced at the O.C., Paris 17 September 1754; it was much less successful than Favart's work.

GLUCK: *La Clemenza di Tito*

4 November. Naples, S.C.

Metastasio's text (first set to music by Caldara in 1734). Three acts.

Gluck introduced the air *Se mai senti spirarti* from this opera afterwards into *Iphigénie en Tauride* (see 1779) where it became *Oh malheureuse Iphigénie*.

G. SCARLATTI: *I portentosi Effetti della Madre Natura*

11 November. Venice, S. Sam.

Text by C. Goldoni. Three acts.

Outside Italy given at:

TRIESTE 1754 (in Italian).

MUNICH 1758 (in Italian).

HAGUE I March 1760 (in Italian; production recorded by D. F. Scheuerleer and J. Fransen; an Italian-French libretto of 1754, translated by one Dampenet, is mentioned in *Cat. Bibl. Soleinne* VI, 406).

NUREMBERG 4 January 1763 (in Italian).

BERLIN 19 December 1763 (in Italian).

FRANKFORT 3 October 1764 (in German, as *Die wunderbare Wirkung der Natur*).

BRUNSWICK February 1765 (in Italian).

MADRID 12 June 1766 (in Spanish, translated by R. de a Cruz, additional music by P. Esteve).

BLAVET: *Le Jaloux corrigé*

18 November. Berny

Text by C. Collé. One act.

First performed at the Comte de Clermont's palace. Paris, O. 1 March 1753 (on the same bill with Rousseau's *Le Devin du Village*, see above). In French also Mannheim 1754. The score consists chiefly of airs from the Italian intermezzi then being performed in Paris (*La Serva Padrona, Il Giocatore* and *Il Maestro di Musica*). Blavet composed the recitatives and the vaudeville finale. See on this early French comic opera L. de La Laurencie in *L'Année Musicale*, 1912.

GALUPPI: *La Calamita de Cuori*

26 December. Venice, S. Sam.

Text by C. Goldoni. Three acts.

Given at Rome, Capr. February 1757 in a reduced 2-act version (*ridotta a farsetta*) and at Bologna January 1759 in a still shorter one-act version (*ridotta ad intermezzo* as *Gli quattro Amanti in un Amante solo*). Revived Reggio 30 April 1768 and Modena May 1768 (as *La Straniera riconosciuta*).

Outside Italy given at Prague 1754; Leipzig 15 May 1754; Dresden 18 July 1754; Hamburg 13 November 1754; Moscow 9 February 1759 (in Italian; Russian translation by E. Bulatnitsky published in same year); London 3 February 1763 (with an overture by J. C. Bach); Bonn 16 December 1764; Lisbon and Warsaw 1766; Aranjuez Spring 1769.

1753

JOMMELLI: *Attilio Regolo*

8 January. Rome, T. delle Dame

Metastasio's text (first set to music by Hasse, see 1750). Three acts.

Also given in London 23 April (not 11 May) 1754 (first Jommelli opera in London) and revived 15 May 1762; revived Naples, S.C. 23 March 1761.

MONDONVILLE: *Titon et l'Aurore*

9 January. Paris, O.

Text by Abbé de La Marre, retouched by C. A. F. de Voisenon; the prologue by A. Houdar de La Motte (*pastorale-héroïque*). Prologue and 3 acts.

Revived in Paris 22 February (not January) 1763 and 12 January 1768; Fontainebleau 18 October 1764; Marseilles 1777.

In French also Brussels October 1754; Gothenburg 24 January 1763; Cassel 1767.

In Italian (translated by C. I. Frugoni) Parma Autumn 1758.

Parodies: (1) *Totinet*, by L. Poinsinet and M. Portelance, O.C. 23 February 1753. (2) *Raton et Rosette ou La Vengeance inutile*, text by C. S. Favart, music partly from Mondonville's opera, partly by Sodi, C.I. 28 March 1753. In French also Fontainebleau 27 October 1753; Vienna 14 September 1755; Ulriksdal (Sweden) 1 September 1756; Hague 1760. Revived Paris, C.I. 20 June 1773. There is also a Dutch translation by J. T. Neyts (n.d.). In Swedish (translated by C. Envallsson), Stockholm 2 April 1799. (3) *Le Rien*, by J. J. Vadé, O.C. 10 April 1753. (4) *Titonet*, by J. Bailly, published 1758, not performed.

HASSE: *Solimano*

5 February. Dresden

Text by G. A. Migliavacca. Three acts.

One of Hasse's most famous works, produced with the utmost splendour (see *Curiosa Saxonica*, 1753, p.66). A revival at Pesaro 1772 is doubtful.

GRAUN: *Silla*

27 March. Berlin, O.

Text by King Frederick II of Prussia (written in French, founded on Duché's *Scylla*, see 1701), translated into Italian by G. P. Tagliazucchi. A German translation by F. W. Eichholz was published at Halberstadt in 1753. Three acts.

Revived Berlin January 1783.

An English translation by S. Derrick (*Sylla*) was published in London 1753. (It does not seem to have been intended for a production in London. None of Graun's operas was ever produced in England.)

RINALDO DI CAPUA: *La Zingara*

19 June. Paris, O.

Librettist unknown. Two acts.

Rinaldo di Capua's most famous work and the only one which has been preserved as a whole. It is unlikely that the 1753 Paris performance of this popular intermezzo was the first production; but it is the earliest of which we know. According to Ortolani the work probably dates from 1739.

In Italian also given at Pesaro Carnival 1755; Mayence 1758; York October 1763 (?*The Fortune Teller*, by Italian singers; see S. Rosenfeld, *Strolling Players in the Provinces*, 1939, p.160).

It was, however, in its French version that *La Zingara* made headway; this was called *La Bohémienne* (adapted by C. S. Favart, additions from Pergolesi and others) and produced at Paris, C.I. 28 July 1755.[1] In French also Brussels and Liège 1756; Hague 1758; Vienna 1758 (as *L'Egyptienne*); Nuremberg 2 February 1763; Frankfort 5 April 1764; Dresden 1 May 1764; Stockholm October 1768; Warsaw September 1778; Gothenburg 27 April 1783.

In Swedish (translation by C. H. Flintberg), Stockholm 28 September 1780; Gothenburg 12 September 1783.

In Russian perhaps Moscow 25 June 1788 (no composer mentioned).

There are two Dutch versions of the libretto, by J. T. Neyts and by J. Nomsz (n.d.).

Two English pieces, the one by an unknown author, with music by Barthélemon (*La Zingara, or The Gipsey*, London, Marylebone Gardens 25 [not 21] August 1773), the other by C. Dibdin,

[1] There was an unsuccessful rival version by Moustou, also called *La Bohémienne*, produced at the O.C. Paris 14 July 1755 (music arranged by C. F. Clément).

with music by Arnold (*The Gipsy*, London Hm. 3 August 1778), have, according to Iacuzzi, nothing in common with Favart's version.

La Zingara was revived, with a new German libretto, music arranged by R. von Mojsisovicz, at the Conservatoire, Graz 27 May 1927 and at Fürth 12 November 1927 (as *Die chinesischen Mädchen*).

For details on the music of *La Zingara* and *La Bohémienne* see P. Spitta in *Vierteljahrsschrift für Musikwissenschaft*, Vol. III (1887) and Sonneck's *Catalogue*, pp.1168, 1169.

SELLITTI: *Il Cinese rimpatriato*

19 June. Paris, O.

Librettist unknown. One act.

Produced on the same bill with *La Zingara*, with an overture by Jommelli (which, according to La Laurencie, did its best to sound Chinese).

There are two different French adaptations: *Le Chinois poli en France*, by L. Anseaume, produced at Paris, O.C. 20 July 1754; Brussels 23 August 1755; Vienna, Laxenburg 2 June 1756; and *Les Chinois*, by C. S. Favart and J. A. Naigeon, additional music from Pergolesi and Cocchi, Paris C.I. 18 March 1756 (revived 28 February 1760); Brussels 17 July 1756; Hague 1759; Amsterdam 1760. Dutch version by J. T. Neyts printed (n.d.).

DAUVERGNE: *Les Troqueurs*

30 July. Paris, O.C.

Text by J. J. Vadé (after Lafontaine). One act. Called by the *Mercure de France* "premier Intermède que nous ayons eu en France dans le goût purement Italien".

In French also given at Brussels November 1753; Stockholm 1754; Hague and Vienna 1758; Frankfort 20 May 1760; Nuremberg 15 January 1763; St. Petersburg 1 May 1765; Dresden 1765. A parody by Farin de Hautemer, *Le Troc*, was published in 1756.

There is a printed Dutch version by J. T. Neyts (n.d.).

Revivals: Paris, Th. du Rire 25 March 1899; Brussels, Th. Molière 14 December 1905; Paris, Petite Scène 30 January 1925.

FERRANDINI: *Catone in Utica*

12 October. Munich

Metastasio's text (first set to music by Vinci in 1727). Three acts.

Written for the inauguration of the new Munich opera-house "Teatro Nuovo presso la Residenza", afterwards known as the "Residenz-Theater").

DAUVERGNE: *La Coquette trompée*

13 November. Fontainebleau

Text by C. S. Favart (*comédie en musique*). One act.

Revived Paris, O. 8 August 1758 (as the third act of a 4-act opéra-ballet, called *Les Festes d'Euterpe*).

AGNESI: *Ciro in Armenia*

26 December. Milan, T.R.D.

Text probably by the composer. Three acts.

The most important work of Maria Teresa d'Agnesi-Pinottini, one of the earliest Italian women composers of operas.

1754

MARIA ANTONIA WALPURGIS: *Il Trionfo della Fedeltà*

Summer. Dresden

Text by the composer (with alterations by Metastasio). Three acts.

The first opera of the Saxon Princess; Hasse composed parts of the music. Revived Munich 6 February 1761; Bonn 1769; Padua 14 June 1772.

The score was published in 1756. A German translation of the libretto (by J.C. Gottsched?) appeared in F. W. Marpurg's *Historisch-Kritische Beyträge*, Vol. III, pt.4 (1757); other German versions appeared at Leipzig 1754 (*Der Triumph der Treue*) and Dresden 1767 (*Der Sieg der Treue*). The opera is not identical, as has been assumed, with a pasticcio of the same title, produced at Charlottenburg August 1753.

A French translation, by De Marolle, was published in 1765.

GLUCK: *Le Cinesi*

24 September. Schlosshof, near Vienna

Text by P. Metastasio (*trattenimento drammatico*, originally set to music by Caldara—not by Reutter —in 1735 and in a revised form by Conforto in 1751).[1] One act.

Produced at the Prince of Saxe-Hildburghausen's Palace of Schlosshof (between Vienna and Pressburg) and repeated at the Burgtheater, Vienna, on 17 April 1755. Also given in Italian at St. Petersburg 18 or 19 February 1761.

GALUPPI: *Il Filosofo di Campagna*

26 October. Venice, S. Sam.

Text by C. Goldoni. Three acts.

Galuppi's most famous work and the most popular Italian comic opera between Pergolesi's *La Serva Padrona* (1733) and Piccinni's *La buona Figliuola* (1760). The Venice 1754 production is the first of which a libretto is extant. An earlier performance at Milan in the summer of 1750 is recorded by Paglicci-Brozzi (*Il Regio Ducal Teatro di Milano nel Secolo XVIII*, p.120) and has been accepted by Schatz and Sonneck; but the first known Milan libretto dates from 1755. Another production which may have been Galuppi's opera is mentioned in the unpublished diary of D. M. Galeati (Bibl. Com., Bologna) under the date of 19 August 1754: ". . . nel Teatro Formagliari si

---

[1] The editor of the standard edition of Metastasio's *Opere* (Paris, Herissant, 1780–82) is responsible for two wrong statements concerning *Le Cinesi*, namely that the little work had been first set by Reutter, and that the author altered it for Gluck. As a matter of fact, Caldara was the first composer, and the revised version (with four, instead of three, characters) was made for Niccolò Conforto, whose setting, as *La Festa Cinese*, was heard at Aranjuez 30 May 1751, three years before Gluck.

recitava . . . poi si recitò . . . il Filosofo in Villa". But no Bologna 1754 libretto is extant either.

Very successful all over Italy; given in a reduced two-act version as *La Serva astuta* at Rome Carnival 1757 and Venice 18 November 1761; given at Bassano Carnival 1763 as *La Campagna*.

Outside Italy given at Frankfort 21 April 1755 (and 1 April 1764 as intermezzo); Dresden 13 June 1755; Prague 1755; Mannheim 1756 (revived Schwetzingen March 1771); Munich 1758; Barcelona 1758; St. Petersburg 16 September 1758; Pressburg 1759; Brussels June 1759 (as *Il Tutore burlato*).

London 6 January 1761 (revived 21 April 1768, "but not heard with the same pleasure", according to Burney, and again 16 January 1770 and 8 February 1772).

Dublin Carnival 1762 (presumably as *Il Tutore burlato*; this production is always quoted as *The Guardian trick'd* for the simple reason that the British Museum copy of the libretto lacks the first, Italian, title-page).

Vienna 1763 and 1768; Bonn 3 January 1764; Zaragoza 1764; Carlsbad Summer 1765; Berlin 18 July 1765; Warsaw 1766; Stralsund January 1769; Salamanca *c.* 1769; Hermannstadt 1770 (as *La Serva astuta*; Galuppi's opera?); Moscow 1774; Reval and Riga 1777; Stockholm 9 November 1780 (as *Il Filosofo ignorante di Campagna*).

In Spanish (translated by R. de la Cruz) Madrid 26 January 1766 and Barcelona [20 June] 1769.

A German adaptation (*Der Philosoph auf dem Lande*, nachgeahmt von Kurz) was given at Vienna, Kä., on 12 May 1770 (according to J. H. F. Müller, *Genaue Nachrichten . . .*, 1772).

An English adaptation *The Wedding Ring*, text and music by Charles Dibdin, was produced at D.L., London, on 1 February 1773.

Il Filosofo di Campagna was revived at the Liceo Benedetto Marcello, Venice 28 February 1907 (at Goldoni's bicentenary festival, under the direction of Wolf-Ferrari); at Treviso 20 April 1927 (in the reduced *Serva astuta* version, music arranged by G. G. Bernardi); and at Casa Rezzonico, Venice 26 July 1938 (music arranged by V. Mortari).

MONDONVILLE: *Daphnis et Alcimadure*

29 October. Fontainebleau

Text by the composer (*pastouralo Toulouzeno*, in Languedoc dialect). Prologue in French, *Les Jeux floraux*, text by C. A. F. de Voisenon. Prologue and 3 acts.

Given at the Paris Opéra on 29 December 1754 and revived there in French on 10 June 1768 and 17 March 1773. The French version, according to Grimm (1768), is also by the composer. Given at Montpellier (in the patois of that town) on 25 August 1758 (in concert form); Versailles 12 and/or 19 December 1764.

Parodies: *Jerosme et Fanchonette ou La Pastorale de la Grenouillère*, by J. J. Vadé, O.C. 18 February 1755; *Les Amours de Mathurine*, by J. Lacombe, C.I. 10 June 1756; *L'heureuse Feinte* (anonymous), published 1756.

COCCHI: *Li Matti per Amore*

Autumn. Venice, S. Sam.

Text: an altered version of G. A. Federico's *Amor vuol Sofferenza* (see 1739). Three acts.

Given at Vicenza Spring 1755; at Modena, T. Rangoni Summer 1755 as *Il Signor Cioè*. In Italian also Munich 1761; Nuremberg 19 January 1763; Berlin Carnival 1764, etc.

(The libretto has often been attributed to Goldoni who, perhaps, altered the original text for Venice.)

1755

V. PALLAVICINO and FISCHIETTI: *Lo Speziale*

Carnival. Venice, S. Sam.

Text by C. Goldoni. Three acts.

Pallavicino composed the first act, Fischietti the rest of the opera.

Given at Rome Carnival 1757 in a reduced *farsetta* version; revived at Mantua 21 January 1764 with sub-title *La finta Ammalata*; at Treviso Spring 1770 as *Il Bottanico Novellista*.

Outside Italy given at Dresden July 1755; Prague 1756; St. Petersburg Carnival 1758; Munich 1759; Copenhagen Autumn 1759 (Danish translation in the libretto by R. Soelberg); Trieste 1760; Cadiz 1762; Sevilla 1764; London 6 May 1769.

(For Haydn's setting of the same libretto see 1768; for a German version see 1771.)

GRAUN: *Montezuma*

6 January. Berlin, O.

(Original French) text by King Frederick II, Italian version by G. P. Tagliazucchi. Three acts.

Repeated Berlin Carnival 1771. Revived Saarbrücken 13 October 1936 (German version by F. Neumeyer.)

The score was published as Vol. xv of *Denkmäler deutscher Tonkunst* in 1904 (edited by A. Mayer-Reinach.)

HASSE: *Ezio*

20 January. Dresden

Metastasio's text (first set to music by Auletta in 1728). Three acts.

Also given in London 12 April 1755. (Hasse is mentioned as the composer in the libretto; according to Burney the music was by Pérez.)

(An earlier setting by Hasse of the same libretto, produced Naples 1730, is lost.)

SMITH: *The Fairies*

3 February. London, D.L.

Text by the composer (from *A Midsummer Night's Dream*). Prologue and 3 acts.

(The text has often been attributed to Garrick, who repudiated the authorship in a letter to James Murphy French, December 1756.) Also given at New York 29 May 1786 and Philadelphia 29 June 1787. According to Pohl, this was the first attempt to introduce recitative into English opera.

"Garrick has produced a detestable English opera, which is crowded by all true lovers of their country. To mark the opposition to Italian opera, it is sung by some cast singers, two Italians, a French girl, and the chapel boys; and to regale with sense, it is Shakspeare's *Midsummer Night's Dream*, which is forty times more non-sensical than the worst translation of any Italian opera-books". (Horace Walpole, letter to Richard Bentley, 23 February 1755.)

JOMMELLI: *Pelope*

11 February. Stuttgart

Text by M. Verazi. Three acts.

The first of Jommelli's Stuttgart operas which is extant. Revived Lisbon Carnival 1768.

[DUNI]: *Le Caprice amoureux* ou *Ninette à la Cour*

12 February. Paris, C.I.

Text by C. S. Favart (a French version or "parody" of Goldoni's *Bertoldo, Bertoldino e Cacasenno,* see 1749). Originally in 3 acts; reduced to 2 acts 8 March 1756 (date according to the *Mercure de France*).

From O. G. T. Sonneck's study in *Sammelbände of the I.M.S.,* Vol. XII (1910–11) it appears that Duni was not the composer of this opera which really was a pasticcio from Ciampi, Latilla, Cocchi, Sellitti, Jommelli, Vinci, etc. Duni certainly arranged the score for Favart. He is, however, called the composer in most books of reference, and he was regarded as such as early as 1776 (on the title-page of the Copenhagen libretto of the same opera).

Duni's autograph score, preserved at Vienna, bears the title *Le Retour au Village.*

In French also given at Brussels 30 January 1756; Liége and Hague 1759; Vienna 1760; Amsterdam 1761; Frankfort 24 May 1762; Pressburg 11 July 1764; Dresden 2 December 1765; St. Petersburg 26 December 1765; Copenhagen 24 October 1767; Smolna 23 January 1776; Warsaw August 1778.

In Danish, Copenhagen 12 March 1776 (as pasticcio; translated by N. K. Bredal).

In Swedish, Stockholm 29 October 1793 and Lund 16 September 1795 (as pasticcio; translated by J. M. Lannerstjerna).

A Dutch translation by J. F. Cammaert was published in 1757 (reprinted 1762); performed in Dutch Amsterdam 1773.

A German translation by C. L. R[euling] was published at Prague in 1769; performed in German Mayence *c.*1765; Pressburg 1778; Agram 29 August 1784; Budapest 26 July 1796.

English adaptations were *The Capricious Lovers* (text by R. Lloyd, music by G. Rush), London, D.L. 28 November 1764; and *Phillis at Court* (an alteration of the same text, music by T. Giordani), Dublin 25 February 1767 (see W. J. Lawrence in *The Musical Quarterly,* Vol. VIII, p.397).

(For an Italian version of the libretto see 1765; for Weisse's German version of the libretto, see 1767.)

A new version of the original libretto by Creuzé de Lesser (new music by Berton) was produced at the O.C., Paris 21 December 1811; another version, by F. V. A. d'Artois de Bournonville and E. T. M. Ourry at the Vaudeville 28 October 1822; another one, by J. H. Dupin and T. M. F. Sauvage, at the Th. Porte St. Martin on 26 November 1822 (music arranged by A. Piccinni); and a fourth version, by N. Brazier, P. F. A. Carmouche and Joslin, at the Variétés 19 December 1822.

ARAJA: *Cephal i Prokris*

Цефалъ и Прокрисъ

10 March. St. Petersburg

Text by A. P. Sumarokov. Three acts.

Excerpts from this very early Russian opera (the MS score of which has been preserved) were published by V. Morkov in 1862.

A French translation by De Henninger was printed in 1755.

UTTINI: *Il Re Pastore*

24 July. Stockholm

Metastasio's text (first composed by Bonno in 1751). Three acts.

Produced at the palace of Drottningholm. The best of Uttini's Italian operas and the only one of which the score was printed. See on his activity in Sweden E. Sundström in *Svensk Tidskrift för Musikforskning*, Vol. XIII (1931).

JOMMELLI: *Enea nel Lazio*

30 August. Stuttgart

Text by M. Verazi. Three acts.

Revived Ludwigsburg 6 January 1766; Lisbon Carnival 1767.

GALUPPI: *Le Nozze*

14 September. Bologna, T. Formagliari

Text by C. Goldoni. Three acts.

Successful in Italy: Milan, T.R.D. Autumn 1756; Venice Carnival 1757, etc. Given at Perugia Carnival 1759 and on many other stages as *Le Nozze di Dorina*.

Outside Italy given at Mannheim 1757; Prague 1760; Barcelona [23 August] 1760; London 1 February 1762; Bonn 13 May 1764; Vienna 1764; Lisbon 1766; Dresden 1766; Warsaw 1766.

(The first production at Bologna was at the T. Formagliari, not at the T. Marsigli Rossi, according to a note in D. M. Galeati's unpublished diary, 13 September 1755, and according to the original libretto.) This Goldoni text became famous again when Sarti set it 27 years later under the new title of *Fra due litiganti il terzo gode* (see 1782).

GLUCK: *L'Innocenza giustificata*

8 December. Vienna, B.

Text by Count G. Durazzo (airs by Metastasio). One act (2 parts).

Repeated in August 1756 and revived Summer 1768 in a revised version as *La Vestale*. See on this opera A. Einstein's paper in *The Monthly Musical Record*, September 1936. ("Orfeo stands in much the same relation to L'Innocenza giustificata as Lohengrin does to Rienzi".) The score was published in 1937 (Vol. LXXXII of *Denkmäler der Tonkunst in Österreich*, edited by A. Einstein). According to L. T. Belgrano an opera called *L'Innocenza giustificata* was also given at Genoa,

T. Falcone Spring 1760. It may have been Gluck's as no other opera of that title is known.

SCOLARI: *La Cascina*

27 December. Venice, S. Sam.

Text by C. Goldoni. Three acts.

Scolari's most popular comic opera. Given at Bassano Carnival 1763, as *La Campagna*; in Italy until 1772.

In Italian also produced at Dresden 30 June 1756; Trieste Carnival 1757; St. Petersburg Autumn 1758; Barcelona [7 April] 1761 (with some airs by Brusa); Dublin 19 December 1761; Nuremberg 15 November 1762; London 8 January 1763 (as pasticcio, text arranged by G. G. Bottarelli); Berlin December 1763; Pressburg 26 December 1764; Warsaw 1765; Lisbon Carnival 1766; Gotha 18 September 1767 (German translation in the libretto by A. S. Perrin); Vienna 1768 (as pasticcio).

1756

CAFARO: *La Disfatta di Dario*

20 January. Naples, S.C.

Text by N. G. Morbilli, Duke of Sant'Angelo. Three acts.

Cafaro's first opera and the first setting of this favourite libretto.

Revived Florence, P. Autumn 1757, etc.

FISCHIETTI: *La Ritornata di Londra*

7 February. Venice, S. Sam.

Text by C. Goldoni. Three acts.

Successful in Italy; given at Parma Autumn 1757, as *La Virtuosa ritornata da Londra*; at Genoa [22 December] 1758 and Modena 12 January 1760 as *Il Ritorno di Londra*. Outside Italy given at Dresden 22 July 1756; Prague Carnival 1757; St. Petersburg 25 February 1758; Lübeck 24 July 1758; Hague 1759; Barcelona [6 May] 1761; Munich 1761; Copenhagen Carnival 1762; Nuremberg 8 November 1762; Berlin October 1764; Córdoba 1769; Potsdam 26 July 1776.

GLUCK: *Antigono*

9 February. Rome, Arg.

Metastasio's text (first set to music by Hasse, see 1743). Three acts.

Gluck used in this opera parts from his earlier works.

HASSE: *Olimpiade*

16 February. Dresden

Metastasio's text (first set to music by Caldara in 1733). Three acts.

Revived Warsaw Carnival 1761; Turin 26 December 1764.

GRAUN: *Merope*

27 March. Berlin, O.

(Original French) text by King Frederick II (after Voltaire), Italian version by G. P. Tagliazucchi. Three acts.

Graun's last opera. It was also the last opera produced at Berlin before the Seven Years' War, and the first which was given there after the war (revived 19 March 1764 and once more Carnival 1773).

[PHILIDOR]: *Le Diable à quatre* ou *La double Métamorphose*

19 August. Paris, O.C.

Text by J. M. Sedaine (from Coffey's *The Devil to Pay*, see 1731), adapted by Baurans. Three acts.

Philidor arranged (and not composed) the music, which consists of popular airs.

In French also given at Laxenburg (near Vienna) 28 May 1759 (with additional airs by Gluck); Liége 8 December 1759; Hague and Amsterdam 1760; Brussels 16 January 1762; Dresden 1765; Copenhagen 1768. Revived Versailles 29 February 1764; Paris, C.I. 14 February 1790.

In German (adapted by F. W. Weiskern), Vienna, Kä. 29 April 1767.

In Swedish (translated by C. Envallsson), Stockholm 3 June 1787 (pasticcio).

A Polish version by J. Baudouin, with new music by Gaetano, was produced at Warsaw 18 November 1787.

CONFORTO: *Nitteti*

23 September. Madrid, Buen Retiro

Text by P. Metastasio. Three acts.

The first setting of this famous libretto which was Metastasio's last great success, and written expressly for Madrid, where his friend, the singer Farinelli was then manager of the court theatres. Conforto's setting was produced at the Buen Retiro palace, for the celebration of the birthday of King Ferdinand VI.

The remark in the Herissant edition of Metastasio's *Opere* ". . . scritto dall' autore in Vienna, per la Real corte cattolica; ed ivi . . . rappresentato la prima volta . . ." is somewhat misleading. A. Della Corte in his *I primi musicisti di Metastasio* (appendix to his biography of Paisiello, 1922) makes no efforts to settle that point.

GLUCK: *Il Re Pastore*

8 December. Vienna, B.

Metastasio's text (first set to music by Bonno in 1751). Three acts.

Gluck's setting was written for the birthday of the Emperor Francis I.

BRUSA: *Le Statue*

27 December. Venice, S. Sam.

Text by G. B. Brusa (the son of the composer). Three acts.

Repeated Rome, T. Valle Carnival 1758; Trieste Carnival 1758; Turin, T. Carignano Autumn 1763. In Italian also Nuremberg 26 January 1763 and probably Potsdam 29 July 1768.

The score of this *dramma giocoso per musica* by the rather unknown Venetian composer was discovered by A. Della Corte and is analysed in his *L'Opera comica italiana nell' '700*, Vol. I, pp.126-135.

1757

PÉREZ: *Solimano*

Carnival. Lisbon, Th. de Salvaterra

Librettist unknown. Three acts.

Pérez's most important opera (cf. H. Kretzschmar, *Geschichte der Oper*, pp.188-189). Revived Lisbon 31 March 1768; Palermo 1779.

HAMAL: *Voëgge di Chôfontaine*
(The Trip to Chaudfontaine)

23 January. Liége

Text by S. J. de Harlez, P. G. de Vivario, P. R. de Cartier, and J. J. Fabry. *Opera burless' es treuz act.*

Comic opera written in the Liége dialect; one of a series of four Walloon operas (the others were *Li Ligeoi ègagy*, *Li Fiesse di Houte-si-Plou*, and *Les Ypoconte*).

First produced in concert form at the Hôtel-de-Ville, the first act 23 January, the second act 16 February, the third act 25 February 1757. The whole 19 September 1767, at the inauguration of the Liége Theatre, and again 15 June 1776. Music preserved. Vocal score published 1858 (edited by L. Terry).

The first act was revived at Liége on 13 April 1867; the whole opera, in a French version by H. de Fleurigny, Brussels Th. Molière 10 March 1890 and Paris, Nouveautés 2 June 1890.

(See on this opera C. Bellaigue's study in *Revue des Deux Mondes*, 15 September 1921.)

DUNI: *Le Peintre amoureux de son Modèle*

26 July. Paris, O.C.

Text by L. Anseaume. Two acts.

Successful on French stages.

Outside Paris given at The Hague and Liége 1759; Turin Spring 1761; Brussels 27 September 1761; Stockholm 8 November 1764; Warsaw 8 May 1765; Copenhagen 1767; Cassel 26 January 1784.

In German (translated by J. H. Faber), Frankfort 1773.

In Russian (translated by V. G. Voroblevsky), Moscow 18 February 1779.

In Swedish (translated by C. Envallsson), Stockholm 31 August 1782.

A "Parade et parodie" on Duni's opera, called *Gilles, Garçon Peintre, z'Amoureux-t-et-Rival*, text by A. A. H. Poinsinet, music by J. B. de La Borde, was produced at the O.C., Paris 2 March 1758; and at Copenhagen 1772 (in French).

TRAETTA: *La Didone abbandonata*

Autumn. Venice, S. Moisè

Metastasio's text (first set to music by Sarro, see 1724). Three acts.

Successful in Italy (Milan, T.R.D. January 1763; Naples, S.C. January 1764, with prologue by Majo; Parma 1764, etc.).

G. SCARLATTI: *L'Isola disabitata*

20 November. Venice, S. Sam.

Text by C. Goldoni. Three acts.

The most successful opera of the younger Scarlatti.

Given at Genoa T. Falcone, [14 August] 1760 as *La Chinese smarrita*. In Italian also given at Vienna 1757 (revived 12 May 1763, reduced to 1 act, and 9 December 1773); Trieste Carnival 1759; Barcelona 4 November 1761; Klagenfurt 1765; Prague Summer 1767; Dresden 10 November 1767.

FISCHIETTI: *Il Mercato di Malmantile*

26 December. Venice, S. Sam.

Text by C. Goldoni. Three acts.

It seems that the music originally was to be written by G. Scarlatti as his name occurs in the original libretto overpasted with a slip bearing Fischietti's name. Very successful in Italy and abroad; given at Barcelona [8 April] 1760; Cadiz Spring 1762; Valenzia Autumn 1768.

London 10 November 1761 and, with new songs (by Galuppi?), 14 April 1762; revived 28 January 1769.

Dublin Carnival 1762; Nuremberg 3 November 1762; Lisbon Carnival 1763; Vienna 15 May 1763 (according to Zinzendorf's diary); Frankfort 7 April 1764; Warsaw 1765; Dresden 6 February 1766 (revised by the composer); Hanover 26 February 1770; Bonn 1772, etc.

In Spanish, Madrid Carnival 1764 (as *La Feria de Valdemoro*, translation by J. Clavijo y Fajardo).

1758

MAJO: *Ricimero, Rè dei Goti*

Carnival. Parma

Librettist unknown. Three acts.

Majo's first opera. Successful in Italy; Rome Carnival 1759; Naples 1760, etc.

HOLZBAUER: *Nitteti*

Carnival. Turin, T.R.

Metastasio's text (first set to music by Conforto, see 1756). Three acts.

In Italian also, Mannheim 4 November 1758. One of the few Italian operas of Holzbauer which are extant.

DAUVERGNE: *Enée et Lavinie*

14 February. Paris, O.

Text adapted by Paradis de Moncrif from an old libretto by B. de Fontenelle (first set to music by Colasse in 1690). Five acts.

The most successful of Dauvergne's serious operas; revived in Paris 6 December 1768 (rectify Lajarte who says that it was never revived).

An anonymous parody *L'Embarras du Choix* was produced at the O.C. on 13 March 1758.

In French opera one of the earliest examples of re-setting an old libretto, a practice so common in Italy; see *Mercure de France*, December 1765.

GLUCK: *L'Isle de Merlin* ou *Le Monde renversé*

3 October. Vienna, Schönbrunn

Text by L. Anseaume (altered from a vaudeville by A. R. Lesage and d'Orneval, originally produced at the Théâtre de la Foire St. Laurent, Paris, in 1718 under the title *Le Monde renversé*, and with Anseaume's alterations in 1753). One act.

Large parts of the music of *L'Isle de Merlin* were used for *Die Maienkönigin*, a modern Gluck pasticcio, text by M. Kalbeck (founded on *Les Amours champêtres*, see 1735, note on Rameau's *Les Indes galantes*), music arranged by J. N. Fuchs.

First performed at Vienna 13 May 1888, and subsequently given at Stuttgart 12 January 1899; Weimar 13 December 1899, etc.; Dresden 31 October 1902; Berlin 26 April 1912; Graz 8 October 1914.

In German also, Prague 7 January 1900; Riga 23 January 1904; Zurich February 1909; Philadelphia 1 December 1927.

Translations from Kalbeck's version produced at:

STOCKHOLM 16 March 1896 (in Swedish).

BUDAPEST 19 March 1913 (in Hungarian, translated by D. Kosztolányi).

KAUNAS 23 September 1922 (in Lithuanian).

COPENHAGEN 17 April 1933 (in Danish, translated by H. H. Seedorff Pedersen).

TRAETTA: *L'Olimpiade*

Autumn. Verona

Metastasio's text (first set to music by Caldara in 1733). Three acts.

Revived Florence 15 October 1767; St. Petersburg 2 May 1769.

FISCHIETTI: *Il Signor Dottore*

Autumn. Venice, S. Moisè

Text by C. Goldoni. Three acts.

Successful in Italy; last revived Pavia 1787.

In Italian, also given at Trieste 26 December 1759; Brunswick 1760 and February 1766; Munich 1760; Barcelona [6 September] 1761; Prague 1762; Lisbon Carnival 1763 (as *Il Dottore*); Cadiz [23 January] 1764; Vienna, Laxenburg 6 June 1764; Warsaw 1766; London 12 March 1767 (revived 1 May 1770); Dresden Winter 1768 (revised by the composer); Bonn 1772.

TRAETTA: *Buovo d'Antona*

27 December. Venice, S. Moisè

Text by C. Goldoni (founded on the Anglo-Norman 13th century romance of *Bevis of Hampton*). Three acts.

Traetta's first extant comic opera.

In Italian also given at Turin, T. Carignano 1759; Bologna [11 October] 1759; Barcelona [22

May] 1760; Sevilla 1764 (first Italian opera there); Verona Spring 1765; Palma, Mallorca [26 May] 1767; Dresden 1772.

In the Zatta edition of Goldoni's plays it is stated (Vol. XLI, 1794) that *Buovo d'Antona* was first produced at Florence in 1750 (without mentioning a composer). Consequently, the date of 1750 (sometimes misprinted as 1756) for the production of Traetta's opera has been taken over by Florimo, Wotquenne, Dent and many others. But as long as a (possibly misprinted) date, given so many years after the vogue of the opera was over, remains the only evidence for a production in 1750, it seems to be safer to adopt the date of the earliest extant libretto (which mentions Traetta as the composer). The year 1758 is also given in a biographical note on Traetta in Forkel's *Musikalischer Almanach*, 1783, p.109. See also G. Ortolani in *Opere complete di Carlo Goldoni*, Vol. XXXI, p.552; "... si tratta, come spesso, d'un errore evidente ..."; and "Troppe volte le affermazioni dell' edizione Zatta risultano fantastiche".

SCALABRINI:
Den Belønnede Kiaerlighed eller De Troe Elskende
(Love rewarded or The faithful Lovers)

29 December. Copenhagen

Text by J. Windtmølle (translation from an anonymous Italian libretto *L'Amor premiato o Gli Amanti fedeli*). Three acts.

Scalabrini's first Danish opera (*Comisk Syngespil*) and one of the earliest operas produced at the Danish National Theatre. Music lost.

1759

GASSMANN: *Gli Uccellatori*

Carnival. Venice, S. Moisè

Text by C. Goldoni. Three acts.

Gassmann's first great success; given on many other Italian stages.

In Italian, also Trieste Carnival 1760; Barcelona [6 August] 1760; Madrid 10 December

1764; Prague Spring 1765 (with additional music by G. Rust); Carlsbad Summer 1765; Dresden 29 October 1765; Warsaw Autumn 1765; Palma, Mallorca [6 August] 1767; Vienna Autumn 1768; London 18 December 1770.

In Spanish (translated by R. de la Cruz), Madrid 20 January 1764.

STANDFUSS: *Der lustige Schuster*

18 January. Lübeck

Text by C. F. Weisse (founded on C. Coffey's *The Merry Cobbler*, 1735). Three acts.

The second part of *Der Teufel ist los* by the same authors (see 1752). Also given at Frankfort 1762; Dresden 9 February 1765; and, in a revised version by Hiller (cf. note on his *Die verwandelten Weiber*, 1766), Leipzig Summer 1766; Hamburg 22 August 1769; Weimar 5 May 1771; Berlin 20 July 1771; Budapest 1774; Altdorf 1777; Salzburg 5 November 1780. On minor German stages revived even in the 19th century (Hanover 1809; Görlitz 1820; Münster 31 August 1873!). Given in Swedish (translator not mentioned) at Gothenburg 1 April 1783.

An anonymous opera which, judging from the title, might have been a Russian version of *Der lustige Schuster* was produced at Moscow 12 January 1789.

MONSIGNY: *Les Aveux indiscrets*

7 February. Paris, O.C.

Text by La Ribadière (after Lafontaine). One act.

In French, also given at Brussels May 1759, Frankfort 1760 and Copenhagen 1769. In German Frankfort *c.*1775. In Russian, Moscow 1787 (translated by V. A. Levshin).

A parody of the same title, by Toussaint Gaspard Taconet, was produced at Versailles 19 February 1759 and Paris, Th. Nicolet 1764.

LARUETTE: *Cendrillon*

21 February. Paris, O.C.

Text by L. Anseaume. One act.

The first of the many operas dealing with the *Cinderella* subject (see Isouard, 1810; Steibelt,

1810; Rossini, 1817; Rozkošny, 1885; Massenet, 1899; Wolf-Ferrari, 1900). Date of first performance according to the *Mercure de France*; the printed libretto has 20 February. Also given at Brussels 1766 or earlier.

PHILIDOR: *Blaise le Savetier*

9 March. Paris, O.C.

Text by J. M. Sedaine (after Lafontaine). One act.

Philidor's first opera. Very successful in Paris. In French also given at Brussels January 1760; Hague 1760; Amsterdam 26 May 1762; Turin Spring 1765; Hanover 17 July 1769; Cassel 21 July 1784.

In German (translated by J. H. Faber), Frankfort 1772; revived Munich 19 May 1785. In Swedish (adapted by C. Envallsson), Stockholm 21 April 1797. Dutch version by J. T. Neyts published (n.d.). A German adaptation *Der Dorfbalbier* by C. F. Weisse, music by Hiller, was produced at Leipzig in 1771. An English version *The Landlord outwitted or The Cobler's Wife*, S.'s Wells 23 June 1783 and 10 May 1784; and as *Who pays the Rent, or The Landlord outwitted*, 8 May 1797. An English adaptation *The Cobler; or A Wife of Ten Thousand*, text and music by C. Dibdin, was produced in London, D.L. 9 December 1774.

TRAETTA: *Ippolito ed Aricia*

9 May. Parma

Te: . by C. I. Frugoni (an Italian version of Pellegrin's French libretto, set by Rameau, see 1733). Five acts.

Traetta made use of some of Rameau's original music (see M. Cooper, *Gluck*, 1935, p.26). Revived Parma Spring 1765.

(Date of first performance indicated in the *Mercure de France*.)

GLUCK: *Cythère assiégée*

Summer. Schwetzingen

Text by C. S. Favart (from Longus's *Daphnis et Chloë*). One act.

Originally the text had been written by Favart and C. B. Fagan as *Le Pouvoir de l'Amour, ou Le Siège de Cythère* in 1743. In 1748 it was altered by Favart alone and performed as *La Cythère assiégée* at Brussels 7 July 1748; Paris, O.C. 12 August 1754; and Vienna 1757. The composers of those earlier versions are not known. Gluck's setting was first produced at Schwetzingen, near Mannheim (exact date unknown) and, according to A. Einstein, at Vienna in the same year, 1759, perhaps even earlier than at Schwetzingen. Zinzendorf in his diary mentions a performance at Vienna on 17 February 1762. Also given at Lyons 17 March 1762 (in concert form). Remodelled as a 3-act opéra-ballet: Paris, O. 1 (not 11) August 1775 (with additional music by Berton, text by Moline). In German (translated by K. L. Gieseke), Vienna, W. 19 January 1796 (with additional music by F. A. Hoffmeister).

Revived Magdeburg 24 January 1929 (new German version by L. K. Mayer).

LARUETTE: *L'Yvrogne corrigé*

24 July. Paris, O.C.

Text by L. Anseaume and Lourdet de Santerre (founded on a fable by Lafontaine). Two acts.

Gluck composed the same text some months later (see 1760). Date of first performance according to the *Mercure de France*. The printed libretto has 23 July 1759. Revived Hague 1760.

GLUCK: *L'Arbre enchanté* ou *Le Tuteur dupé*

3 October. Vienna, Schönbrunn

Text by L. H. Dancourt (altered from an earlier French vaudeville by J. J. Vadé, called *Le Poirier*, itself based on Lafontaine's tale *La Gageure des trois Commères*, produced at Paris, O.C. 7 August 1752). One act.

In French, also Hague 31 January 1771. Remodelled by Gluck (text altered by Moline), Versailles 27 February 1775 (given there in honour of a visit of Marie Antoinette's brother, the Archduke Maximilian); also performed at Rożana (Poland), at Prince Sapieha's, 12 September 1784.

In Danish (translated by A. G. Thoroup), Copenhagen 21 September 1792.

In Russian, Moscow 30 June 1793.

In German (translated by K. L. Gieseke), Vienna, W. 31 May 1794.

Revived Paris, F.P. 27 April 1867 (text altered by C. Nuitter) and subsequently at:

PRAGUE 1868 (in German) according to Wotquenne.

BRUSSELS, TH. MOLIÈRE 18 January 1906 (in French).

FRANKFORT 1921 (in German).

WIESBADEN January 1926 (in German; music arranged by A. Rother).

BERLIN 3 July 1936 (in German; at the Hochschule für Musik).

AMSTERDAM January 1937 (by the Dutch Chamber Opera).

Vocal score edited by Max Arend, with German version by Käthe Arend-Andrasch, published 1914.

1760

PICCINNI: *La buona Figliuola*

6 February. Rome, T. delle Dame

Text by C. Goldoni (founded on Samuel Richardson's *Pamela or Virtue Rewarded,* 1740). Three acts.

Goldoni had treated the subject as a comedy in 1750 and re-wrote it as an opera libretto in 1756 when it was first set by Duni (Parma 26 December 1756 and, in French, Paris, C.I. 8 June 1761). There is also a setting by Perillo, given at Venice ten days after the Rome production of Piccinni's opera.

Piccinni's 18th opera and his greatest success; given all over Italy; at Rome, Capr. February 1762, as *La buona Figliuola Zitella,* reduced to a "farsetta"; at Reggio May 1763, Modena, T. di Corte 18 June 1763, and Florence Autumn 1763 as *La Baronessa riconosciuta;* at Naples, T.N. Summer 1778 with many alterations.

Outside Italy:

BARCELONA [19 March] 1761 (in Italian); subsequently given at Sevilla 1764; S. Ildefonso

Summer 1767 (with three additional airs by Marescalchi); Valencia [4 January] 1769; Aranjuez Summer 1769. In Spanish (translated by A. Bazo), Madrid 1765, with additional music by P. Esteve; Barcelona 1770; Valladolid 1772.

NUREMBERG 7 June 1762 (in Italian; according to an advertisement, quoted by F. E. Hysel), apparently for the first time in Germany.

BONN 23 March 1764 (in Italian, revived 13 May 1772).

VIENNA 19 May 1764 (in Italian, at the Palace of Laxenburg; at the Burgtheater, Summer 1768 and 9 April 1777); in French, Kä. 22 January 1776; in German, Kä. 5 December 1784.

WARSAW 1765 (in Italian) and 22 January 1783 (in Polish, translated by W. Boguslawski); in Polish also, Wilna 4 April 1799.

DRESDEN 16 November 1765 (in Italian; given there until 1781).

INNSBRUCK 1765.

LONDON, HM. 25 November 1766 (according to advertisement; Burney gives 9 December 1766), in Italian; revived there almost every season until 1785, and again, 28 May 1789; 5 May 1796; and 21 June 1810, for Catalani's benefit, "from the original score, with no alteration whatever".

LONDON, C.G. 3 December 1766 (in English, as *The Accomplish'd Maid,* translated by E. Toms, who calls his version the "first attempt of bringing an entire musical composition on the English stage"; another translation, by T. Holcroft, *The Maid of the Vale,* was given at Dublin in 1775, with new music by Michael Arne; the Covent Garden libretto was reprinted at Philadelphia in 1777, apparently the first opera of Italian origin published in America; but there is no record of an American production.

BERLIN December 1768 (in Italian) and 8 September 1777 (in German, translated by J. J. Eschenburg; this version was given on every German stage: Berlin 8 September 1777 at Döbbelin's Th. and 10 March 1787 at the National Th.; St. Petersburg 15 January 1778; Hamburg 14 January 1779; Vienna 5 December 1784; Riga Autumn 1785, etc.).

COPENHAGEN Autumn 1769 and 2 January 1777 (in Italian, Danish translation in the libretto by F. A. Friis) and 1772 (in French).

MANNHEIM 4 November 1769 (in Italian) and 2 May 1782 (in German).

PARIS, C.I. 17 June 1771 (in French, translated by J. F. Cailhava d'Estandoux, music arranged by D. Baccelli; revived there 29 January 1777 under Piccinni's supervision; this version was also given at Brussels 1771; Maestricht and Copenhagen 1772; Vienna 22 January 1776; Liége 19 June 1779; Cassel 16 July 1784). In Italian: Paris, O. 7 December 1778 and Th. de M. 3 February 1790.

CEUTA (MOROCCO) 6 July 1773 (in Italian; see R. Twiss, *Travels Through Portugal and Spain*, 1775, p.274).

BASTIA (CORSICA) Carnival 1775 (in Italian).

ESZTERHÁZA Autumn 1776 (in Italian).

DUBLIN 17 May 1777 (in Italian; Michael Kelly's début; see his *Reminiscences*, Vol. I, p.17).

RIGA 1777 (in Italian).

ST. PETERSBURG 31 May 1779 (in Italian).

KREMSMÜNSTER 1781 (in Italian).

STOCKHOLM 28 March 1781 (in Italian) and 10 September 1788 (in Swedish, translated by C. Envallsson).

KOUSKOVO 13 June or 13 July 1782 (in Russian? Russian version by I. A. Dmitrevsky, published in that year).

An undated Dutch adaptation by J. T. Neyts was published about 1770.

P. L. Ginguené, Piccinni's first biographer (1800) reports, with some reserve, a production of *La buona Figliuola*, by Italian Jesuits, at the Chinese Court, Peking, before 1778!

La buona Figliuola was revived, under the title of *La Cecchina* and with alterations, at Bari (the composer's native town) 7 February 1928 (celebrating the bicentenary of Piccinni's birth, under the direction of La Rotella).

MARIA ANTONIA WALPURGIS: *Talestri, Regina delle Amazoni*

6 February. Nymphenburg, near Munich

Text by the composer. Three acts and licenza.

The second and last opera of the Saxon Princess. Revived Dresden 24 August 1763 and 3 December 1767 (début of G. E. Mara). Score published 1765.

A French translation, by De Marolle, was published in 1765.

A German adaptation as a tragedy without music was published at Zwickau in 1766.

TRAETTA: *I Tintaridi*

April. Parma

Text by C. I. Frugoni (an Italian version of Bernard's *Castor et Pollux*, see 1737). Five acts.

In Italian also given at Vienna 1760; revived Florence 3 January 1768.

(*Tintaridi* is the correct form of the title, not *Tantaridi* or *Tantiridi* (Goldschmidt), nor *Tindaridi* (Riemann), nor *Tindari* (Schmidl).

GLUCK: *L'Yvrogne corrigé*

April. Vienna, B.

Text by L. Anseaume (first set to music by Laruette, see 1759). Two acts.

In German, Vienna, B. December 1781 (as *Der letzte Rausch*, by a company of children; anonymous translation published Mannheim 1780); Gotha 14 May 1784 (as *Die Trunkenbolde in der Hölle*).

Revived Paris, Petite Scène 7 June 1922 (in French); Nantes 13 March 1928; by the Petite Scène also produced at Barcelona Spring 1928; Amsterdam November 1928; Brussels 26 November 1928; Swinemünde Summer 1928 (new German version by W. M. Treichlinger); London, Birkbeck College 12 March 1931 (in English, translated by G. Dunn). Kiel 7 May 1936 (new German version by B. Engelke).

DURÁN: *Antigono*

10 July. Barcelona

Metastasio's text (first set to music by Hasse, see 1743). Three acts.

Durán's setting seems to be the first opera by a Catalan composer expressly written for the Barcelona stage.

PHILIDOR: *Le Soldat Magicien*

14 August. Paris, O.C.

Text by L. Anseaume (founded on a story by A. Le Métel d'Ouville). One act.

In French also given at Amsterdam 11 April 1761; Brussels 13 May 1761; Hague 29 December 1761; Bonn March 1764; Copenhagen 1767; Hanover 17 July 1769.

In Dutch, Amsterdam 1768 (translations by J. T. Neyts and J. F. Cammaert printed).

In German (translated by J. J. Eschenburg): Brunswick and Hamburg 1770 (by Ackermann's company); Hanover 12 May 1773; Cologne 14 July 1780; Berlin 25 April 1785, etc.

Another German version, by 'F. W. M.', published at Mannheim in 1771, was probably used by Marchand's company at Frankfort. Sonneck attributes this translation to F. L. W. Meyer, but this can hardly be correct, as Meyer was born in 1758.

In Danish (translated by L. Knudsen), Copenhagen 29 April 1783.

In Polish (translated by L. Pierozyński), Warsaw 11 March 1787 (some new music by Gaetano) and Wilna 9 April 1799.

Revived Paris, Tr. L. 17 January 1920.

HASSE: *Alcide al Bivio*

8 October. Vienna

Text by P. Metastasio. One act.

Written for the wedding of the Archduke Joseph and the Princess Isabella of Bourbon and performed at the Redoutensaal of the Hofburg (together with *Tetide*, a serenata by Gluck which is not extant).

In Italian also given at Copenhagen 2 February 1774 (Danish translation in the libretto by F. A. Friis); Leipzig 23 December 1777 (under J. A. Hiller) and Vienna 11 March 1781 (in concert form).

Vocal score published 1763.

Revived for the centenary of Hasse's death at Dresden 29 December 1883 (in German, as *Die Wahl des Herkules*, translated by K. F. Niese) on the same bill with one of Hasse's intermezzi,

Rimario e Grilantea, the actual first production of which is not dateable.

GAVINIÈS: *Le Prétendu*

6 November. Paris, C.I.

Text by F. Riccoboni. Three acts.

The only opera by the famous French violinist.

In French also given at Frankfort 28 February 1761; Vienna 15 January 1763; Brussels 1767.

LAMPUGNANI: *Amor Contadino*

12 November. Venice, S. Angelo

Text by C. Goldoni. Three acts.

Lampugnani's last traceable opera. Given on some Italian stages and (in Italian) also at Munich 1761; Prague Summer 1763; Copenhagen Autumn 1763 (Danish translation in the libretto by R. Soelberg); Lisbon Carnival 1764.

GALUPPI: *L'Amante di tutte*

15 November. Venice, S. Moisè

Text by A. Galuppi (the son of the composer). Three acts.

Very successful in Italy (Bologna, Verona, Turin 1762, Milan, Parma 1763, Florence 1764, etc.; given at Rome, Tord. 7 January 1762 as *Il Matrimonio in Villa ossia L'Amante di tutte*) and abroad: Barcelona [4 May] 1762; Prague 1763; Copenhagen Autumn 1763 (as *La Moglie bizarra*, Danish translation in the libretto by R. Soelberg); Gorizia Carnival 1764; Dresden 1 May 1766 (revived 30 September 1775); Ljubljana [22 November] 1766; Cadiz 20 January 1767; Vienna 1767 (as *Il Vecchio geloso*); San Ildefonso (Spain) Summer 1768; Valencia Autumn 1768; Rostock November 1768; Stralsund January 1769; Mannheim Carnival 1770; Lübeck 17 August 1773 (as *Il Vecchio geloso*); Warsaw 17 January 1776; Stockholm 7 February 1781; Lisbon as late as Autumn 1807.

In German, Leipzig 27 June 1769 (see C. H. Schmid, *Schreiben über die Leipziger Bühne*, 1770).

In Polish, Warsaw 6 April 1783 (translator unknown).

(Date of first performance from Gradenigo's unpublished *Notatorj*.)

T. A. ARNE: *Thomas and Sally, or The Sailor's Return*

28 November. London, C.G.

Text by I. Bickerstaffe. Two acts.

Successful on English stages: given at Dublin 27 April 1761 (not December 1759); York Spring 1764; Newcastle Summer 1764; Edinburgh 19 January 1765; Philadelphia 14 November 1766; New York 21 December 1767; Kingston, Jamaica 2 October 1779.

In *Thomas and Sally*, clarinets were introduced into the English opera orchestra for the first time.

Frequently revived in London; recent revivals were Lyric Th., Hammersmith, 10 April 1926; Arts Theatre Club 24 March 1936; Cambridge 27 July 1937; New York, Little Th. 4 January 1938 and London, Mercury Th. 15 June 1939 (by the "Intimate Opera Company"); London, New Th. 1 July 1941.

DUNI: *L'Isle des Foux*

29 December. Paris, C.I.

Text by L. Anseaume and P. A. Lefèvre de Marcouville (founded on Goldoni's *Arcifanfano, Rè dei Matti*). Two acts.

In French, also given at Vienna 4 July 1761; Brussels 14 February 1762; Copenhagen 1770; Moscow on or before 24 September 1775 (on which day Bourrée de Corberon attended a performance); Liége 3 February 1784.

1761

PICCINNI: *Le Vicende della Sorte*

3 January. Rome, Valle

Text by G. Petrosellini (founded on Goldoni's *I portentosi Effetti della Madre Natura*, see 1752). Three acts.

Very successful in Italy and abroad: Lisbon 6 June 1766; Dresden 2 December 1766; Brunswick 1768 (in 2 acts); London 6 November 1770 (pasticcio; Giordani, Sacchini, Barthélemon are named as composers in the printed score).

Revived Bologna Palazzo Felicini 21 August 1769 (as *Le Vicende del Caso*); Rome Capr. 8 January 1774.

In German (translated by J. C. Bock), Leipzig 30 June 1780; another German title or version was *Das Spiel des Zufalls*, produced at Munich 1 May 1785 (Piccinni mentioned as composer). Another German translation, by J. A. von Ghelen, was published at Vienna in 1761.

TRAETTA: *Armida*

3 January. Vienna, B.

Text by Count G. Durazzo (founded on Quinault's *Armide*, see 1686), versification by G. Migliavacca. One act.

One of Traetta's most important works. Given also at Naples, S.C. Spring 1763; revived Venice, S. Salv. 27 May 1767 (this latter production, according to Salvioli and Haas, with a new text by F. Sarego, a statement which is not borne out by the entries of both the 1761 and 1767 librettos in the Library of Congress *Catalogue*).

GALUPPI: *Li Tre Amanti ridicoli*

18 January. Venice, S. Moisè

Text by A. Galuppi (the son of the composer). Three acts.

Successful in Italy; also given in Italian at Trieste 1762; Prague Autumn 1763; Brunswick February 1765; Vienna and Münster 1765; Dresden 27 November 1766; London 5 November 1768 (with some new music by F. Alessandri; text altered by G. G. Bottarelli); Copenhagen Autumn 1771; Bonn 1774.

(Date of first performance according to Gradenigo's unpublished *Notatorj*.)

MONSIGNY: *Le Cadi dupé*

4 February. Paris, O.C.

Text by P. R. Lemonnier (set by Gluck later in the same year). One act.

Monsigny's setting was also given at Amsterdam 12 December 1761; Dresden 1765 (revived

29 September 1767); Brussels 1766; Copenhagen January 1767; Hanover 31 July 1769; Liége 1 December 1770; Turin Spring 1774; Cassel 21 November 1783; Moscow 29 January 1785.

In Swedish (translated by C. Envallsson and C. Stenborg), Stockholm 19 April 1781; Gothenburg 30 September 1783.

In Russian, Moscow 25 May 1794.

A Dutch version by J. T. Neyts was published c.1762; a German version by J. H. Faber in 1772; a Danish version by L. Knudsen in 1785.

JOMMELLI: *L'Olimpiade*

11 February. Stuttgart

Metastasio's text (first set to music by Caldara in 1733). Prologue and 3 acts.

Revived Lisbon 31 March 1774. The only opera of Jommelli of which the score was printed (in 1783): cf. Rudolf Krauss, *Die Buch- und Notendruckerei der Hohen Karlsschule*, in *Württembergische Vierteljahrshefte*, Vol. xx (1911).

PHILIDOR: *Le Jardinier et son Seigneur*

18 February. Paris, O.C.

Text by J. M. Sedaine (after a fable by Lafontaine). One act.

In French also, Brussels 1767, Copenhagen 1772 and Cassel 15 September 1784.

The existence of a new genre of dramatic music, namely French opéra-comique, different from the older type *en vaudevilles* and developing alongside of grand opéra, had now become a fact well recognized in the public mind, as we may conclude from the remark in the *Mercure de France* (March 1761), *à propos* the production of *Le Jardinier et son Seigneur* . . . "La Musique qui est devenue la partie intéressante d'un Opéra-comique. . . ."

PICCINNI: *La buona Figliuola maritata*

10 June. Bologna, T. Formagliari

Text by C. Goldoni. Three acts.

A sequel to *La buona Figliuola* (see 1760), but not nearly as successful. Given at Reggio 1762 and Modena, T. di Corte, 12 July 1763 as *La*

Baronessa maritata; at Florence Spring 1765 as *La buona Moglie*; at Naples, T.N. Summer 1765 as *La Cecchina maritata* (text revised by P. Mililotti). In Italian, also given at Barcelona [25 September] 1763; Brunswick 1763; Vienna 1764; Warsaw 1765; Dresden 5 December 1765; London 31 January 1767 (cf. Burney, IV, p.492; revived 2 May 1771); Valencia Carnival 1769; Madrid 1769; Paris, O. 15 April 1779.

Yet another sequel, *La buona Figliuola supposta Vedova* (text by A. Bianchi, music by Latilla), was produced at Venice, S. Cass. Carnival 1766.

PHILIDOR: *Le Maréchal ferrant*

22 August. Paris, O.C.

Text by A. F. Quétant (and, according to Des Boulmiers, Servières and Anseaume). One act.

One of Philidor's most popular works; given at Fontainebleau 3 November 1762 and all over France. In French, also given at Amsterdam 1762; Vienna 26 June 1763; Frankfort 25 March 1764 and probably earlier; St. Petersburg 7 October 1764 (first French opera in Russia); Turin Spring 1765; Dresden 1765; Geneva 1766; Copenhagen February 1767; Brussels 1767; Aachen 23 July 1768; Ghent 19 March 1769; Hamburg 10 February 1769; Liége 30 October 1770; Warsaw 1 February 1778; Munich 7 April 1783; Cassel 2 October 1784; Cologne 1796-7; Kingston, Jamaica 15 February 1802.

In German (translated by J. André), Frankfort Autumn 1771; Munich 12 April 1776; Vienna Spring 1776; Pressburg 1 March 1779, etc. In a new German version by H. A. O. Reichard, Gotha 7 October 1776; Bonn 21 March 1779; Hamburg 1779; Carlsruhe 1781; Hanover 28 June 1787; Cologne 11 June 1880; Pyrmont 7 July 1781; Riga 16 November 1785; Bremen 19 December 1785; Berlin 3 September 1787, etc. In German also Amsterdam 2 June 1796.

In Danish (translated by J. H. Wessel), Copenhagen 15 December 1778.

In Russian, Moscow 1780.

In Swedish (translated by C. Envallsson, music adapted by C. Stenborg), Stockholm 11 July 1781 and, with alterations, 23 September 1786.

In Polish (translated by J. Baudouin), Warsaw 15 December 1781.

In English, Boston 25 March 1793.

A Spanish version (*El Borrado burlado*, text and music by Conde de Peñaflorida) was produced at Vergara 11 September 1764.

Dutch translations by J. N. Neyts and by J. Menkema were published in 1769 and 1784 respectively.

There was a contemporary parody on *Le Maréchal ferrant*, called *Le Forgeron*, by G. Delautel, part of the music by the author, produced at the Th. Nicolet, Paris, in April 1762.

Philidor's opera was revived in Paris, Tr. L. 20 November 1920.

MONSIGNY: *On ne s'avise jamais de tout*

14 September. Paris, O.C.

Text by J. M. Sedaine (after Lafontaine's tale of the same title). One act.

Performed at Fontainebleau 2 December 1761.

In French also given at Brussels 25 February 1762; Hague 12 May 1762; Vienna 17 August 1762; Amsterdam 1762; St. Petersburg 9 December 1764; Geneva 1766; Dresden 18 July 1766; Turin Spring 1774.

In German (translated by J. H. Faber), Frankfort 1772; Augsburg 31 August 1779; Warsaw 11 October 1782.

In Swedish (translated by C. Envallsson), Stockholm 28 May 1790.

A Dutch version by J. F. Cammaert was published in 1763.

Revived Brussels, Th. Molière 15 February 1906; Paris, "Th. de Monsieur" (Th. des Mathurins), December 1910; Paris, Petite Scène 26 February 1928. In German, as *Das Lebenselixier*, new German text by L. Metzl, music arranged by H. Gál, Baden (near Vienna), June 1936.

Vocal score (edited by C. Lecocq) re-issued in 1910.

[AUDINOT]: *Le Tonnelier*

28 September. Paris, O.C.

Text by the composer (after Lafontaine). One act.

Audinot was rather the compiler than the composer of the first version; see the account in Charles Maurice's *Histoire anecdotique du Théâtre et de la Littérature*, I, p.373; according to a note by Weckerlin in the Paris Conservatoire copy of the score, J. C. Trial, Philidor, Gossec, Audinot and Schobert all contributed to *Le Tonnelier*.

This comic opera only became a great success four years later, in a new version (text revised by F. A. Quétant, music re-arranged by Gossec). First produced Paris, C.I. 16 March 1765; in French also, Geneva 1766; Copenhagen March 1767; Brussels 20 April 1767; Lübeck 17 May 1769; Vienna 15 January 1776; Warsaw 12 February 1778; St. Petersburg 2 January 1779; London 6 June 1783 (privately, 40 Great Marlborough St., in concert form); Gothenburg 26 April 1784; Moscow 25 November 1784; New York 7 October 1790 (first opera which was sung in French there); Aachen 17 August 1794; Hamburg 29 December 1794; Cologne 1795-6.

In German, Hamburg Summer 1771; (translated by C. F. Schwan); Weimar 3 August 1772; Gotha 12 July 1774; Leipzig 30 September 1774; Hague 1774; Altenburg 19 August 1775, etc.; (translated by J. H. Faber), Frankfort 1775; Dresden 9 November 1775; Vienna, Fasan Th. 12 May 1776 and B. 29 June 1780; Troppau 1781; Berlin 2 November 1781; Riga 13 December 1782; Cassel 1783; Stockholm June 1783; Amsterdam c.1793.

In Polish (translated by J. Baudouin), Warsaw 7 September 1779; Cracow 24 June 1790.

In Danish (translated by H. Gram), Copenhagen 27 October 1780; revived 7 March 1858.

In Swedish (translated by C. Envallsson), Stockholm 17 January 1781.

In Russian (translated by F. V. Gensh), Moscow 17 August 1783; (perhaps earlier at Kouskovo 1780; a Russian translation by V. G. Voroblevsky was published, n.d.).

There are four different Dutch translations, by

J. F. Cammaert (1768); J. T. Neyts (n.d.); A. Soulage (1786); and B. Ruloffs (1792). Burney attended a Flemish production at Brussels in July 1772. In Flemish also Oudenarde 1796-7.

An English adaptation, *The Cooper*, text and music by T. A. Arne, was produced in London, Hm. 10 June 1772; also Boston 3 April 1793.

Gossec's version was frequently revived in France; at Lyons as late as 23 February 1927 (re-scored by M. Reuchsel).

GLUCK: *Le Cadi dupé*

December. Vienna, B.

Text by P. R. Lemonnier (set by Monsigny about the same time, see above). One act.

Exact date of first performance unknown; from a letter written by Count Durazzo to Favart we know that it must have been before 12 December. In Zinzendorf's diary a performance on 13 December is recorded.

In German (translated by J. André) Berlin 1 December 1783; Hamburg, December 1783.

After an interval of nearly a century, Gluck's opera was revived in a new arrangement by J. N. Fuchs, at Hamburg 14 January 1878 (text revised by W. Hock) and Vienna 9 March 1881 (text revised by F. Krastel); subsequently given on many other German stages, viz. Mannheim 19 April 1882; Cassel 6 May 1882; Berlin 31 May 1882; Munich 6 October 1882; Graz 25 April 1883; in German, also Prague 3 April 1887; Rotterdam 1887; Manchester 22 April 1893 (by amateurs); Strasbourg 15 February 1900; again revived, Lauchstedt 29 May 1909; Vienna (Schönbrunn) 14 May 1930.

In Hungarian (translated by E. Abrányi), Budapest 4 October 1881.

In the original French, Paris, Petite Scène 14 March 1926; Nantes 13 March 1928.

In Dutch, Amsterdam, July 1930 (at the Conservatoire).

In English, Rochester, N.Y., Eastman School of Music 16 May 1932.

In Hebrew (translated by Z. Israel), Jerusalem 1935.

1762

J. C. BACH: *Alessandro nell'Indie*

20 January. Naples, S.C.

Metastasio's text (first set to music by Vinci in 1729). Three acts.

The last opera Bach wrote for the Italian stage before he settled in London in Autumn 1762.

Midas

22 January. Dublin

Text by K. O'Hara (*An English burletta*). Three acts.

The music of this famous parody on Italian opera seria consists of popular tunes, selected by the author, but "in its frequent resort to concerted music bridged the gap between ballad opera and comic opera" (W. J. Lawrence).

According to O'Keeffe (*Recollections* 1826 I, p.53), William Brownlow "a musical amateur and fine player on the harpsichord helped settling the music for Midas". It was written on the instance of Lord Mornington, father of the Duke of Wellington, and first produced at Crow Street Th., Dublin, as a counter-attraction to Scolari's *La Cascina* (see 1755), produced at the rival theatre in Smock Alley on 19 December 1761 (cf. R. Hitchcock, *An historical View of the Irish Stage*, Vol. II, 1794, p.93). First given in London, C.G. 22 February 1764 (reduced to 2 acts 5 February 1766; reduced to one-act interlude, Richmond 8 September 1766) and frequently revived since, viz. D.L. 25 October 1802; C.G. 17 September 1812; Ly. 4 August 1817; Surrey Th. 16 July 1851; Brighton 30 July 1859; and as late as 4 June 1923 at Trinity College Hall, Cambridge.

Given at Philadelphia on 24 November 1769 (revived 1 May 1840); New York 3 May 1773 (frequently revived); Montego Bay, Jamaica 12 April 1777; Boston 25 April 1794.

Given by an English company also at St. Petersburg 11 January 1772 (according to Findeizen it was Grétry's *Le Jugement de Midas*, which, considering the rest of the repertory of that troupe, seems very unlikely).

T. A. ARNE: *Artaxerxes*

2 February. London, C.G.

Text: an English translation, by the composer, of Metastasio's *Artaserse* (1729). Three acts.

Arne's most famous opera, very successful on English stages. Last revived at C.G. 30 September 1814 (with additional music by Bishop) and 16 October 1839. First given at Dublin 18 February 1765; Edinburgh 1769 (with the addition of three favourite Scots airs, text by Robert Ferguson; revived 1 July 1830); New York 31 January 1828 (re-orchestrated by C. E. Horn).

GALUPPI: *Il Marchese Villano*

2 February. Venice, S. Moisè

Text by P. Chiari. Three acts.

In Italy given under several different titles, viz. *Il Marchese Giorgino* (Turin, T. Carignano Autumn 1763); *Il Marchese Tulipano* (Sinigaglia 9 February 1764 and Milan, T.R.D. Autumn 1764); *La Lavandara* (Autumn 1770); *La Lavandara astuta* (Mantua Autumn 1771).

Outside Italy given at Prague 1766; Dresden 22 July 1766; Warsaw 1766; Vienna, Schönbrunn 12 September 1767 (celebrating the engagement of Ferdinand IV of Naples to Maria Josepha of Austria; German translation by J. A. von Ghelen published) and Kä. 29 May 1776 (Italian-German libretto published; additions by other composers); Ludwigsburg Spring 1770; Corfu Autumn 1771 (as *Il Matrimonio per Inganno*); Potsdam 9 July 1773; Graz Carnival 1778.

In German (as *Der Landjunker und sein Sohn*, translated by J. H. Burmann), Frankfort 18 September 1784. Another German adaptation, possibly, was *Kaspar der bäuerische Landedelmann*, Vienna, Leop. 13 January 1782 (no composer mentioned, but the original title was *Il Marchese Villano*).

BLAISE: *Annette et Lubin*

15 February. Paris, C.I.

Text by M. J. B. Favart, her husband C. S. Favart, and J. B. Lourdet de Santerre (founded on one of Marmontel's *Contes Moraux*). One act.

This little work had previously been performed in January 1762 at the wedding of one M. de Mailly. Blaise partly compiled and partly composed the music. Very successful in France; first performed at Fontainebleau 27 October 1762. Revived in Paris as late as October 1910 at the Th. des Mathurins and 1 February 1930 at the Th. de l'Avenue. Vocal score reprinted in 1910 (edited by R. Montford).

In French, also performed at Amsterdam and The Hague 1762; Frankfort 23 March 1764; St. Petersburg 14 January 1765; Dresden 5 February 1765; Turin Spring 1765; Geneva, Copenhagen and Brussels 1766; Rheinsberg 27 August 1766; Hamburg 2 December 1766; Vienna 1768; Regensburg c.1773 (with additional music by J. Touchemoulin); Warsaw 25 July 1778; Gothenburg 6 May 1784; Moscow 9 December 1784; Charleston, S.C. 16 July 1794.

In Dutch (translated by P. F. Lynslager), Amsterdam 1779; another translation, by J. T. Neyts, already published Rotterdam 1764 and Amsterdam 1768.

In Swedish (translated by N. Öhrwall), Gothenburg 7 May 1782 and Stockholm 2 May 1786.

In Polish (translator unknown), Warsaw 20 October 1787.

In some other countries the original music was replaced:

> *Lucas und Hannchen*, text by J. J. Eschenburg, music by J. F. G. Beckmann: Brunswick 1768; Cologne Spring 1772; Hanover 28 April 1777.
>
> *Nanetta e Lubino*, text by C. F. Badini, music by G. Pugnani, London 8 April 1769; Warsaw 19 February 1781; and (according to Regli and others); Turin, T. Carignano 1784 (but this production seems doubtful).
>
> *Annette and Lubin*, text and music by C. Dibdin: London, C.G. 2 October 1778.

The libretto of Hiller's *Die Liebe auf dem Lande* (see 1768) is partly founded on *Annette et Lubin*.

Marmontel himself turned his story into an opera which was performed, with music by J. B. de Laborde, at Maréchal de Richelieu's private theatre on 30 March 1762 and at Brussels 18 October 1767 (as *La nouvelle Annette et Lubin*); also at Cassel 26 November 1783. More than a quarter of a century after its first production *Annette et Lubin* was still popular enough to inspire two sequels: (1) *La Vieillesse d'Annette et Lubin* (text by L. A. Bertin d'Antilly, music by P. D. A. Chapelle), Paris, C.I. 1 August 1789 and Brussels 18 January 1796. (2) *La Vengeance du Bailli* (text by C. S. Favart and his son C. N. J. Favart, music by L. E. Jadin), Paris, Th. de M. 30 April 1791.

About the same time, J. P. E. Martini (to whom Font incorrectly attributes the 1762 music) set the original libretto again; his opera was produced at Fontainebleau 6 February 1789; publicly at the O.C., Paris 18 April 1800 and at the French theatre, St. Petersburg 29 June 1800.

Annette et Lubin was the first new work produced at the Comédie-Italienne, Paris, after its amalgamation with the Opéra-Comique (which hitherto had been performing at the fairs of St. Laurent and St. Germain). The new company started on 3 February 1762, with a double-bill consisting of Monsigny's *On ne s'avise jamais de tout* and Philidor's *Blaise le Savetier* at the old home of the Comédie-Italienne at the Hôtel de Bourgogne. They moved to the Salle Favart (Hotel Choiseul, Place des Italiens) in 1783.

HASSE: *Il Trionfo di Clelia*

27 April. Vienna, B.

Text by P. Metastasio (written for Hasse). Three acts.

Written and produced to celebrate the confinement of the Archduchess Isabella of Bourbon.

Also given at Warsaw 3 August 1762 and Naples, S.C. January 1763.

PHILIDOR: *Sancho Pança dans son Isle*

8 July. Paris, C.I.

Text by A. A. H. Poinsinet (after Cervantes). One act.

Performed at Fontainebleau 27 October 1762. In French also: Copenhagen and Brussels 1767; Lübeck 11 December 1769; Liége 13 November 1770; Cassel 28 January 1784; Cologne 1796-7.

In German (translated by J. J. Eschenburg), Brunswick 19 December 1769; Hamburg Autumn 1770; Hanover 10 May 1773; Berlin 2 July 1773; Mannheim 1 August 1779, etc. Another German translation by F. W. Eichholz was published at Halberstadt in 1776.

In Russian (translated by V. A. Levshin), Moscow 3 October 1785.

The opera was revived by the Petite Scène, Paris 7 June 1922; and at Madrid Summer 1929 (in Spanish).

GLUCK: *Orfeo, ed Euridice*

5 October. Vienna, B.

Text by R. de' Calzabigi (*Azione teatrale per Musica*). Three acts.

Notwithstanding *Alceste* (see 1767) and the two *Iphigénie* settings (see 1774 and 1779) *Orfeo* remains the composer's *meilleur titre de gloire* as his first reform opera. Calzabigi claimed his share in the famous letter to the *Mercure de France* (published 21 August 1784): "J'espère que vous conviendrez, Monsieur, d'après cet exposé, que si M. Gluck a été le créateur de la Musique dramatique, il ne l'a pas créée de rien. Je lui ai fourni la matière ou le chaos si vous voulez; l'honneur de cette création nous est donc commun".

First produced Vienna, Burgtheater 5 October 1762; following performances were 10 and 21 October, 11 November, 12 December; 13 February 1763, 24 July; then (after a single performance, in French, at the Kä. 30 June 1781) revived, B. 31 December 1781, again in Italian. After that the opera was not given again at Vienna until 1862 (see below).

After Vienna, *Orfeo* is stated to have been produced at Frankfort in April 1764 at the coronation of the Archduke Joseph as King of the Romans. This production, however, seems somewhat doubtful. See for details (also of all further performances), *The Musical Quarterly*, July 1940.

18th century productions:

PARMA 24 August 1769 as the last act of a mixed spectacle called *Le Feste d'Apollo*, produced for the celebration of the wedding of Ferdinando, Prince of Parma, to Princess Maria Amalia, daughter of the Empress Maria Theresa.

LONDON 7 April 1770 (in Italian), text altered by G. G. Bottarelli, additional music by J. C. Bach and P. Guglielmi; repeated 30 April 1771; then 9 March 1773 in its original form, 25 May 1773 once more in the Bach-Guglielmi version. Twelve years later, 12 May 1785, revived for the singer Tenducci, this time with additional music by J. C. Bach, Handel and Anfossi, text altered by A. Andrei. First produced in English C.G. 28 February 1792 (with additions by Handel, J. C. Bach, Sacchini, Weichsel and Reeve!).

BRESLAU, ZWINGER 29 August 1770 (in concert form; German version by J. J. Eschenburg).

BOLOGNA, T.C. May 1771 and Casino Nobile 16 February 1788 (in Italian).

FLORENCE, T. COCOMERO 13 September 1771 and T. Porta Rossa 7 March 1773 (in concert form).

MUNICH 5 February 1773 (in Italian, with additional music by J. C. Bach and G. Guadagni).

STOCKHOLM 25 November 1773 (in Swedish, translated by G. Rothman, music arranged by F. Uttini); revived 11 May 1786 (new Swedish translation, from the French version, by A. F. Ristell).

NAPLES, PAL. REALE 25 January 1774 (in its original form) and S.C. 4 November 1774 (with J. C. Bach's additions).

PARIS, O. 2 August 1774 (in French, translated by P. L. Moline, with alterations); given there 297 times until 28 July 1848. A parody, by P. L. Moline and L. F. A. Dorvigny, called *Roger-Bontems et Javotte*, was produced at the C.I., Paris, 13 May 1775; another *Le petit Orphée* by J. Rouhier-Deschamps, music by P. D. Deshayes, at Le Havre 18 March 1785 and Paris, Variétés 13 June 1793 (not 1792, as indicated in the libretto).

HAMBURG Winter 1775-6, in concert form.

BRUSSELS 19 August 1776 (in French; last revived there 15 February 1938).

ESZTERHÁZA 1776 (in Italian).

WARSAW 25 November 1776 and 25 November 1789 (in Italian).

HAGUE 1779 (in French).

COPENHAGEN 24 April 1779 (in concert form, probably in French).

BRÜNN 12 December 1779 (first stage-performance in German; translator not mentioned; see *Litteratur-und Theater-Zeitung* 1780, p.96).

BARCELONA 1780 (Italian libretto printed; production not otherwise recorded).

ST. PETERSBURG 1782 (Italian libretto printed; production not otherwise recorded).

MAYENCE 4 November 1782 (in German, by J. Böhm's company and possibly in his translation).

FRANKFORT January 1783 (in German, by J. Böhm's company and possibly in his translation; subsequently also produced at Aachen, and Düsseldorf).

LILLE 2 March 1783 (in French).

HANOVER *c.* May 1783 (in Italian).

DUBLIN 3 January 1784 (at the Smock Alley Th., for the first time in English, translated by F. Gentleman, music adapted by F. Tenducci); a burletta by R. Houlton, music by T. Giordani, was produced at the Capel Street Th., Dublin 14 June 1784.

PADUA 1784 (in Italian).

SALZBURG 5 April 1786 (in Italian; concert performance).

CASSEL 22 August 1787 (in German, by J. Böhm's company).

AVIGNON 1790 (in French).

CHARLESTON, S.C. 24 June 1794 (in French, announced as "by Paisielo"; Gluck's opera? See O. G. T. Sonneck, *Early Opera in America*, p.206).

SIENA Summer 1795 (in Italian, concert performance at the Accademia dei Ravvivati).

MADRID 1 January 1799 (in Italian).

19th and 20th century productions:

LISBON Spring 1801 (in Italian, text altered by G. Caravita; additional music by M. A. Portugal; revived there not before 31 January 1893).

CLAUSENBURG before 1804 (in Hungarian, translated by J. Kónyi; according to Z. Ferenczi. Kónyi's translation had been published as early as 1774; see *Bibliographia Hungariae* II, p.941).

BRUNSWICK 1806 (in French).

BERLIN 20 April 1808 (in German, translated by J. D. Sander from the French version; revived 25 October 1818, 13 November 1841, etc.) and 3 April 1821 (in Italian).

BRESCIA 12 September 1808 (in concert form, by the Società Filamonica).

MILAN 24 May 1813 (in concert form at the Conservatorio; repeated there 1862 and 25 April 1879).

DRESDEN 19 April 1838 (apart from a concert performance at Breslau in 1831, this was the first German production after Berlin). Most German stages produced *Orfeo* only after 1850; Weimar 16 February 1854 with a prelude and finale by Liszt; Mannheim 16 December 1860; Munich 11 July 1861.

PARIS, TH. L. 19 November 1859 (in French, music revised by Berlioz); the next revivals at Paris were at the Gaîté 9 May 1889 (in Italian) and O.C. 5 May 1896 (in French).

LONDON, C.G. 27 June 1860 (Berlioz's version); 6 November 1890 (original version); Ly. 10 December 1892 (in English, by the R.C.M.); C.G. 17 May 1898 (for the first time in French); 22 June 1905; Savoy 12 April 1910 (in English); C.G. 1 July 1920 and 20 June 1937.

DUBLIN 21 September 1860 (in Italian).

MANCHESTER 12 December 1861 (in concert form, English version by H. F. Chorley).

VIENNA 15 November 1862 (for the first time there since 1781, in concert form; further concert performances 8 April 1870 and 6 April 1873); revived on the stage as late as 2 February 1882 (in German).

NEW YORK 25 May 1863 (at the Winter Garden, in English, translated by F. M. Raymond); Academy of Music 8 January 1886 (in English); M. 30 December 1891, 11 December 1895, 23 December 1909, 22 May 1936, 29 November 1939 (in Italian); revived in English Provincetown Playhouse 29 April 1926; May-

fair Th. 21 February 1927; Juillard School 1935.

BADEN-BADEN 17 August 1863 (in French).

PRAGUE 17 December 1864 (for the first time in Czech, translated by J. J. Kolár and J. Kopp); revived there 6 November 1884 (new Czech version by V. J. Novotný); revived at Brünn 30 June 1883 (in German).

ST. PETERSBURG 2 June 1867 (in Italian, privately, at court, under Rubinstein) and 27 April 1868 (in Russian).

RIGA 30 December 1869 (in German).

WEIMAR 6 March 1870 (first performance of the Berlioz version in Germany).

CAMBRIDGE 22 May 1876 (in English, Chorley's translation, in concert form by St. John's College Musical Society).

GRAZ 26 March 1877 (in German).

ROTTERDAM January 1880 (in German).

BUDAPEST 8 March 1883 (in Hungarian, translated by E. Abrányi) and 30 January 1904 (translated by S. Várady).

BOSTON 11 April 1885 (in German).

ROME, COST. 26 October 1888 (first stage performance in Italy in the 19th century); subsequently Florence, P. 16 February 1889; Venice, F. 17 March 1889; Milan, T. Manzoni 10 April 1889; Turin, T. Vittorio Emanuele May 1889; Naples 24 June 1889; Trieste 5 December 1889; Genoa 13 April 1890, etc.

BARCELONA, T.L. September 1889 (in Italian); Catalan version by J. Pena published 1910.

TRIESTE 1889 (in German).

CAMBRIDGE 13 May 1890 (in English; Chorley's version revised).

BASLE 5 March 1894 (in German; possibly for the first time in Switzerland).

COPENHAGEN 30 September 1896 (in Danish, translated by J. Lehmann).

BUENOS AIRES 5 January 1899 (in Italian); revived 3 June 1924.

AMSTERDAM October 1902 (in Dutch).

ANTWERP 15 March 1904 (in French) and 4 November 1911 (in Flemish).

MARSEILLES 29 March 1904 (in French).

OSLO (CHRISTIANIA) 8 October 1907 (in Norwegian).

HELSINKI 21 April 1914 (in Finnish).

LAUCHSTEDT 19 June 1914 (revival of the 1762 version, new German translation by H. Abert).

FALMOUTH 28 November 1923 (new English version by M. and E. Radford).

SOFIA 30 September 1927 (in Bulgarian, translated by V. Bobchevsky).

LONDON, OLD VIC 29 November 1933 (new English version by E. J. Dent).

TOKYO 3 February 1935 (in concert form, in a Japanese translation by Ono).

RIO DE JANEIRO August 1935 (in Italian).

CAIRO 1937 (in German).

JERUSALEM 7 February 1939 (concert performance, in Italian).

Open-air productions took place at the Amphithéâtre, Orange, 11 July 1903; at the Théâtre du Jorat, Mézières (Switzerland) 1 July 1911 (music arranged by G. Doret and C. Saint-Saëns); at the Arènes, Béziers, 30 June 1928; and at the Park de Procé, Nantes, 28 June 1930.

TRAETTA: *Sofonisba*

4 November. Mannheim

Text by M. Verazi (according to M. Fehr only a new version of A. Zeno's *Scipione nelle Spagne*, first produced with music by Caldara at Barcelona in 1710). Three acts.

Although one of Traetta's best works it does not seem to have been given on any other stage. The opera was published in *Denkmäler der Tonkunst in Bayern* (edited by H. Goldschmidt) in 1914.

MONSIGNY: *Le Roi et le Fermier*

22 November. Paris, C.I.

Text by J. M. Sedaine. Three acts.

Successful in Paris (last revived O.C. 23 October 1806), first given at Versailles 15 February 1763.

In French also given at Vienna Autumn 1763; Warsaw Carnival 1766; Geneva 1766; Dresden 16 July 1766; Brussels 1767; Ghent 12 March 1769; Lübeck 27 November 1769; Liége 22 November 1770; St. Petersburg 3 February 1776; Cassel 1782.

In German (translation by C. G. Pfeffel published Frankfort 1766), performed Cologne Spring 1772; (with new dialogue by J. H. Faber published Frankfort 1773), performed Frankfort 13 September 1774 or earlier; Munich 19 April 1781; Carlsruhe 1781.

In Danish (translated by C. D. Biehl), Copenhagen 25 November 1777.

In Swedish (translated by C. Envallsson), Stockholm 24 January 1784.

A Dutch version, by J. F. Cammaert, was published at Brussels in 1764; another, by J. T. Neyts, about the same time (n.d.).

PICCINNI: *Il Cavaliere per Amore*

Winter. Naples, T.N.

Text by G. Petrosellini. Two acts.

In Italian also, Lisbon Carnival 1764; Vienna Carnival 1766; Dresden 22 February 1766; Bialystok (Poland) Spring 1766 (at the private theatre of the Hetman Branicki). Revived Munich Summer 1772; Warsaw 19 April 1775; Moscow 27 September 1782.

Given in an enlarged 3-act version, *Il Fumo villano* (text altered by A. Palomba, with additional music by B. Ottani), at Venice Autumn 1766 and Copenhagen Autumn 1769 (Danish translation in the libretto by F. A. Friis).

T. A. ARNE: *Love in a Village*

8 December. London, C.G.

Text by I. Bickerstaffe. Three acts.

Music partly composed, partly selected. Overture by C. F. Abel. Besides Arne, 15 other composers had their share in the score; but out of 43 numbers 19 are Arne's, 6 of them expressly composed for *Love in a Village*, which, therefore, has been called the first English comic opera, after the preceding period of 35 years of, more or less pure, ballad opera. (See M. Silburn, in *The Musical Times*, July 1920).

First given at Dublin 8 July 1763; York Spring 1764; Newcastle Summer 1764; Edinburgh 1765; Philadelphia before 22 January 1767; New York 11 January 1768; Kingston, Jamaica 9 October 1779; Calcutta 24 February 1791.

Frequently revived in London; the latest productions were at the Princess's Th. 4 March 1844 and 16 November 1848; Surrey 17 September 1853; Guildhall School of Music 10 May 1923 and Everyman 21 December 1923 (music arranged by J. Herbage); Leeds 27 March 1926; Lyric, Hammersmith 19 April 1928 (music arranged by A. Reynolds).

DUNI: *Le Milicien*

29 December. Versailles

Text by L. Anseaume. One act.

First given at the C.I., Paris 1 January 1763 and in French also, Brussels 1767; Hamburg 10 February 1769; Vienna 15 January 1776; Warsaw 30 July 1777; Liége 30 January 1779. Revived Paris, Th. de la Cité, 28 October 1795; Hamburg 1795; Antwerp 27 August 1807.

In German (translated by J. H. Faber), Frankfort 1772; Munich 6 January 1783; Carlsruhe 6 December 1786.

In Swedish (translated by C. Envallsson), Stockholm 23 November 1782.

In Polish, Warsaw 2 January 1783; Cracow 29 April 1790; Wilna 26 February 1799.

There are three printed Dutch versions, by J. T. Neyts (n.d.), J. F. Cammaert (1770), and P. F. Lynslager (1779 and 1782).

1763

RUTINI: *I Matrimoni in Maschera*

Carnival. Cremona, T.N.

Text, according to Piovano, perhaps by F. Casori. Three acts.

Sonneck (*Catalogue*, p.739) gives "Venice, Autumn 1765" as place and date of first performance. But there are earlier productions on record:
CREMONA as above.
BOLOGNA, T. FORMAGLIARI 30 July 1763 (as *Il Matrimonio in Maschera*).
FLORENCE, T. VIA S. MARIA Autumn 1763 (as *Gli Sposi in Maschera*).
FERRARA Carnival 1764 (as *Li Matrimonj in Maschera*; libretto British Museum).

NOVARA Carnival 1764 (as *Li Matrimoni in Maschera*).
TRIESTE Spring 1764 (as *Il Matrimonio in Maschera*).
ROVIGO Autumn 1764 (as *Il Tutore burlato*, additional music by Scolari).
MODENA, T. RANGONI January 1765 (as *Gli Sposi in Maschera*).

Rutini's name only occurs in the libretti for the performances at Novara, Trieste and Modena. There is a libretto at Münster of a work, *Amore in Maschera o sia il Tutore burlato*, performed still earlier, at Rome, T. Valle, Carnival 1762, which is obviously related, at any rate in subject, with Rutini's opera. But this was a set of "intermezzi in musica", not a three act opera. The early history of *I Matrimoni in Maschera* remains somewhat dubious.

Given then at Venice, S. Cass., Autumn 1765 (the first performance which is recorded by Sonneck) and other Italian stages; at Pistoia with yet another title, *Li Sposi per Inganno* (pasticcio).

Outside Italy: Dresden 6 January 1767; Aranjuez Spring 1767; Prague Summer 1767; Copenhagen Autumn 1768 (as *Il Tutore burlato*; Danish translation in the libretto by F. A. Friis); Munich Summer 1772; Valencia [25 August] 1774 (pasticcio). *Die Verheyratung in der Maske*, one act, Brunswick 26 January 1779, performed by children, was probably a reduced version of Rutini's opera.

The most successful of Rutini's comic operas. Score preserved. See for an analysis, A. Della Corte, *L'Opera comica Italiana* (1923), Vol. I, p.254.

d'AVOSSA: *La Pupilla*

Carnival. Naples, Fior.

Text by A. Palomba. Three acts.

Avossa's only extant opera. Given at Venice, S. Moisè Autumn 1765 as *Il Ciarlone;* Turin, T. Carignano 1766 and 1774 as *La Pupilla scaltra*. In Italian also Barcelona 1765, Lisbon 1766 and Prague 1768 (as *Il Ciarlone*); Stralsund January 1769; Copenhagen Autumn 1769 (as *La Pupilla ed il Ciarlone;* Danish translation in the libretto by F. A. Friis); Vienna 1770 (as *Il Ciarlone*); Munich Carnival 1775.

VENTO: *L'Egiziana*
Carnival. Venice, S. Moisè

Librettist unknown. Three acts.

Vento's only extant opera. Given at Milan, T. R.D., in Autumn of the same year, and (with additional music by Gassmann) at Vienna Summer 1769 and Florence Spring 1771 (as *La Zingara*).

VAN MALDERE: *La Bagarre*
10 February. Paris, C.I.

Text by J. F. Guichard and A. A. H. Poinsinet. One act.

The only opera of the Belgian composer that was produced in Paris; given at Brussels later in the same year.

PICCINNI: *Le Contadine bizarre*
February. Rome, Capr.

Text by G. Petrosellini. Three acts.

Successful in Italy; given at Verona Autumn 1764 as *La Schiocchezza in Amore*; Rome, Capr. 5 February 1765 as *Le Contadine astute*; Bologna September 1765 as *La Contadina bizarra*; Sinigaglia July 1769 as *Le Villanelle astute*. Last revived in Italy, Bergamo 26 December 1776 (as *Le Villane astute*).

In Italian also, Trieste Carnival 1764; Klagenfurt 1765; Lisbon Autumn 1765; Dresden 28 October 1766; Vienna Carnival 1767; Prague Summer 1767; Breslau 7 September 1768; Berlin December 1768; London 7 November 1769; Bastia (Corsica) 1774 (as *Le Villanelle astute*).

In Spanish (translated by R. de la Cruz), Madrid [20 August] 1773.

(Date of first production according to G. Pavan; Venice Autumn 1763 is usually given.)

J. C. BACH: *Orione* o sia *Diana vendicata*
19 February. London, Hm.

Text by G. G. Bottarelli. Three acts.

Bach's first London opera. Very successful,

given there for three months' run and revived 24 May 1777.

PHILIDOR: *Le Bûcheron* ou *Les trois Souhaits*
28 February. Paris, C.I.

Text by J. F. Guichard and N. Castet (founded on a tale by Perrault). One act. Given at Versailles 15 March 1763, etc. Outside France:
VIENNA 1765 and 1768 (in French).
DRESDEN 1765 and 2 April 1766 (in French).
GENEVA AND BRUSSELS 1766 (in French).
COPENHAGEN 1767 (in French) and 3 December 1782 (in Danish, translated by L. Knudsen).
GHENT 14 March 1769.
HAMBURG Autumn 1770 (in German, translated by J. H. Faber).
FRANKFORT 1773 (in German, translated by J. H. Faber).
BERLIN 20 February 1774 (in German, translated by J. A. C. Koch).
WARSAW August 1778 (in French) and 1780 (in Polish, translated by L. Pierozyński).
LIÉGE 8 June 1779 (in French).
MUNICH 7 August 1781 (in German).
CASSEL 8 December 1783 (in French).
MOSCOW 15 or 22 July 1787 (in Russian).

There are two printed Dutch translations by J. F. Cammaert (1770) and by J. T. Neyts (n.d.). An Italian version by G. Brunati was published in 1805. For a German version of the libretto see 1778.

The opera was revived at Brussels, Th. Molière, 8 March 1906.

SACCHINI: *Alessandro nell' Indie*
Spring. Venice, S. Salv.

Metastasio's text (first set to music by Vinci in 1729). Three acts.

Successful in Italy. Turin Carnival 1766; Naples, S.C., 2 June 1768, etc.

GLUCK: *Il Trionfo di Clelia*
14 May. Bologna, T.C.

Metastasio's text (first set to music by Hasse, see 1762). Three acts.

Gluck's setting was written for the inauguration of the new Teatro Comunale, Bologna; it does not appear to have been produced on any other stage.

SACCHINI: *L'Olimpiade*

June. Padua

Metastasio's text (first set to music by Caldara in 1733). Three acts.

Given on Italian stages until about 1790. In Italian also, Salzburg 1 May 1768. In French (translated by N. E. Framery), Paris, C.I. 2 October 1777 (originally intended for production at the Opéra, but withdrawn after some rehearsals; revived C.I. 15 January 1778 and 24 April 1780); Fontainebleau 24 October 1777; Ghent 21 December 1778; Liége 21 December 1779.

In German, Bonn 16 March 1783; Frankfort 6 May 1783; Mannheim 28 November 1784; Carlsruhe 14 February 1785; Mayence 21 December 1785 (one of the very few Italian serious operas of that time which were translated into German); also given at Winterthur November 1793 (in concert form).

DUNI: *Les deux Chasseurs et la Laitière*

21 July. Paris, C.I.

Text by L. Anseaume (after two fables by Lafontaine). One act.

Very popular in France and abroad. In French also Brussels 1763 and 1766; Vienna, Laxenburg 8 May 1764; Amsterdam 1764; St. Petersburg 12 November 1764; Stockholm 7 January 1765; Warsaw 8 May 1765; Dresden 1765; Turin Spring 1765; Hamburg 4 December 1766; Copenhagen 30 December 1766; Lübeck 17 May 1769; Liége 6 November 1770; Moscow 24 November 1775 (according to the diary of Bourrée de Corberon); Smolna February 1776; Stockholm June 1783; Cassel 16 January 1784; New York 9 November 1790 (Sonneck) or 10 November 1790 (Odell); London 20 Janua · 1792 (at the Th. of Varieties, Savile Row); Charleston, S.C. 8 February 1794; Cologne 1795-6; Philadelphia 17 December 1796.

In German (first translated by C. F. Schwan), Mannheim 1771; Weimar 15 November 1771; Cologne Spring 1772; Berlin 5 August 1772; Hanover 23 June 1773; Hamburg 1773; Gotha 20 September 1774; Leipzig 8 October 1774; Altenburg 26 August 1775; Frankfort 18 September 1776 if not earlier; Regensburg 15 May 1778; Bonn 28 February 1779; Munich 6 August 1779; Augsburg 13 August 1779; Vienna, Jos. 23 August 1779 (revived Leop. 20 December 1803); Carlsruhe 1881; Bremen 15 October 1883. In German also, Hague 1774; Warsaw 6 May 1781; Riga 29 October 1782; Pressburg 1789.

In Russian (translated by Z. Krizhanovsky), St. Petersburg 1779.

In Swedish (translated by C. Stenborg), Stockholm 15 November 1780; Gothenburg 16 November 1781.

In Polish (translated by J. Baudouin), Warsaw 19 July 1781; Cracow 5 November 1789.

In Danish (translated by L. Knudsen), Copenhagen 6 November 1781.

There are printed Dutch versions by J. F. Cammaert, 1764, J. T. Neyts, 1768 and 1770, and P. F. Lynslager, 1778, 1783 and 1794. Given in Dutch at The Hague as late as 1820.

A translation into Provençal dialect, called *La Laytayro dé Naubernad*, was published at Toulouse in 1783.

Frequently revived in Paris: O.C. 3 August 1865 (text revised by J. Adenis); Galerie Vivienne 15 October 1896; and Petite Scène 25 April 1920.

(Date of first production according to the libretto; according to Bachaumont's *Mémoires secrets*, it was 23 July; according to the *Mercure de France* it was 25 July 1763.)

TRAETTA: *Ifigenia in Tauride*

4 October. Vienna, Schönbrunn

Text by M. Coltellini. Three acts.

In Italian also, Florence 1 February 1767 (under Gluck's direction); Milan, T.R.D. 26 December 1767; St. Petersburg April 1768; Copenhagen 25 October 1774 (probably Traetta's opera); Mantua 1777; Naples, S.C. January 1778. Revived Florence, P. 21 March 1782 (as a cantata, two parts); Vienna, B. 22 December 1784 (in concert form); Eszterháza 1786 (with one additional air by Haydn). Burney (IV, p.505) mentions a private performance in London, at Mrs. Blaire's "lately" (i.e. before 1789). Performed as an oratorio, *S. Ifigenia in Etiopia*, Florence 19 March 1773.

Earlier performances of Traetta's opera in 1758 and 1759 are recorded in Sonnleithner's *Collectaneen*. But the 1763 libretto (no earlier edition is known) reads: "Sebbene il presente dramma sia stato composto espressamente dall'autore per questa occasione". See on this question (which is of some bearing because of the possible priority to Gluck's *Orfeo*) Goldschmidt's introduction to Traetta's works in *Denkmäler Deutscher Tonkunst*, p.14; also R. Haas, *Gluck und Durazzo*, p.70 and A. Einstein, *Gluck*, p.46.

BORONI: *L'Amore in Musica*

15 October. Venice, S. Moisè

Text perhaps by C. Goldoni (see on his possible authorship G. Ortolani in *Opere complete di Carlo Goldoni*, Vol. XXXII, p.143). Three acts.

Outside Italy given at Vienna 1764; Dresden 12 September 1765; Prague, Carlsbad, Warsaw 1765; Lisbon 1766; Ludwigsburg 22 August 1770; Brunswick 1777.

1764

PICCINNI: *Gli Stravaganti*

1 January. Rome, Valle

Librettist unknown. Two acts.

Successful in Italy; given at Parma in the same Carnival as *La Schiava riconosciuta*, which is the better-known title of this opera. In Italian also given at:

LISBON 6 June 1765.

DRESDEN 15 October 1765 (as *La Schiava*; revived 12 October 1776 and 12 April 1780).

LONDON 21 October 1766 (as *Gli Stravaganti osia I Matrimoni alla Moda*, pasticcio, arranged by G. G. Bottarelli, "in which there were several

airs by Piccinni" [Burney]; and in its original form, as *La Schiava* 7 November 1767; revived 22 February 1770; 12 March 1772; 1 April 1777; and 24 February 1784).

Vienna, B. before 19 February 1768; Brunswick 1768; Copenhagen Autumn 1768 (Danish translation in the libretto by F. A. Friis; revived 6 March 1776); Valencia Autumn 1768; Barcelona [22 April] 1769; Dresden 1770; Mannheim 19 November 1771; Warsaw 16 October 1775; Regensburg Carnival 1777; Aachen 28 August 1781; Danzig August 1782; Cracow 1 January 1788.

In German (as *Die Sclavin und der grossmüthige Seefahrer*, translated by J. J. Eschenburg). Mannheim January 1773; Leipzig 13 August 1777; Munich November 1777; Cologne Summer 1779; Vienna, Jos. 28 June 1779 (B. 7 August 1781, translated by G. Stephanie); Salzburg 22 October 1780; Warsaw 21 April 1781; Bonn 1 December 1782; Bremen 22 December 1783; Riga 7 June 1785; Carlsruhe 2 November 1785; Berlin 20 November 1786; Prague 1787; Agram 15 October 1789; Amsterdam Winter 1791.

An anonymous French 1-act version, *L'Esclave ou Le Marin généreux*, was probably first performed at Zweibrücken 1773 (where the libretto—copy Bibl. Soleinne—was printed in that year); in French also, Hague 1782; St. Petersburg 1800.

In Swedish (translated from the French by C. Manderström), Stockholm (31 May 1779 according to the libretto; produced only) 31 July 1783.

PHILIDOR: *Le Sorcier*

2 January. Paris, C.I.

Text by A. A. H. Poinsinet. Two acts.

Philidor introduced one air from Gluck's *Orfeo* ("Chiamo il mio ben così") into his *Sorcier* ("Nous étions dans cet âge"); see on this plagiarism the introduction to the Pelletan edition of Gluck's *Orfeo* (1898). First given at Versailles 21 March 1764; in French also, at Amsterdam 1764; Vienna 1765; Turin Spring 1765; Copenhagen and Brussels 1767; Hamburg 6 February 1769; Hanover 31 July 1769; Liége 24 November 1770; Hague 24 January 1774; Smolna 16 February

1775; Berlin 24 January 1777; Warsaw July 1778; St. Petersburg 1798.

In German (translated by J. H. Faber); Hamburg 1771; Frankfort 1772; Hague 1774; Dresden January 1777; Munich 4 May 1779, etc. Another German version, by C. F. Henisch, was published at Prague in 1772.

There are Dutch translations by J. T. Neyts (n.d.) and by J. F. Cammaert (1769). Revived Paris, F.P. 9 February 1867 (text revised by J. Adenis, music revised by Poise; reduced to 1 act).

GLUCK: *La Rencontre imprévue*

7 January. Vienna, B.

Text by L. H. Dancourt (from an earlier French vaudeville by Lesage and d'Orneval, 1726). Three acts.

The last and best of Gluck's French comic operas.

In French also, Bordeaux 1766 (as *Ali et Rézia*); Brussels 19 May 1766; Amsterdam, Hague and Mannheim 1768; Copenhagen 1772; Liége 23 December 1776; Cassel 1780; Lille 17 November 1783; Marseilles 1784; Paris, C.I. 1 May 1790 (music arranged by J. P. Solié).

In German (translated by J. H. Faber, as *Die unvermuthete Zusammenkunft oder Die Pilgrimme von Mecca*), Frankfort 16 April 1771; Vienna, Kä. Spring 1776 (revived B. 26 July 1780, Leop. 10 November 1789 and Kä. 28 June 1807); Munich 9 March 1779; Augsburg 16 July 1779; Ulm 6 December 1781; Hamburg 1781; Carlsruhe 1781; Nuremberg Autumn 1782; Bonn 16 September 1783; Berlin 27 October 1783 (first Gluck opera there); Mayence 1784; Riga 5 August 1785; Schwedt 23 December 1785; Pressburg 14 July 1786; Pyrmont and Cologne 1786; Hanover 11 May 1789; Brunswick 22 August 1789; Brünn 31 January 1792; Graz 14 December 1793; Berne Spring 1804, etc.

In Danish (translated by P. T. Vandall), Copenhagen 26 November 1776.

In Swedish (translated by C. Envallsson), Stockholm 20 June 1786.

There is also a printed Dutch version by J. T. Neyts (n.d.)

Revivals. In French: Paris, O.C. 20 December 1906 (as *Les Pèlerins de la Mecque*); Paris, Tr.L. 6 November 1923.

In German: (text revised by C. Hagemann) WIESBADEN October 1922.

BASLE 26 September 1924.

BERLIN, O. 18 February 1928.

VIENNA June 1931.

STETTIN 16 February 1932 (new German version by C. Rittberg).

In English (translated by G. Dunn), Loughton, Essex 21 July 1939.

The score was first published in 1931, edited by M. Arend.

RUSH: *The Royal Shepherd*

24 February. London, D.L.

Text by R. Rolt (an English version of Metastasio's *Il Re Pastore*). Three acts.

Given in an altered version by F. Tenducci at Dublin July 1765 and Edinburgh 30 January 1769; and (as *Amintas*) London, C.G. 15 December 1769 (with additional music by Guglielmi, Arnold, and Th. C. Carter).

MONSIGNY: *Rose et Colas*

8 March. Paris, C.I.

Text by J. M. Sedaine (founded on Lafontaine's tale *Le Van*). One act.

One of Monsigny's most popular works, Fontainebleau 13 October 1764, etc. Very successful in Paris; given at the C.I. until 21 February 1794; revived at the Th. de l'Egalité 3 November 1794; O.C. 12 May 1862 (revised by Gevaert) and at the Tr.L. 12 January 1918; revived at the Conservatoire, Amsterdam June 1929. Outside France given at:

WARSAW 27 August 1765 (in French) and 7 September 1781 (in German).

GENEVA AND BRUSSELS 1766 (in French).

COPENHAGEN March 1767 (in French) and 28 October 1777 (in Danish, translated by N. K. Bredal).

LIÉGE 27 October 1770 (in French).

HAMBURG 9 November 1770 (in German, translated by J. H. Faber); Mannheim 1771; Frankfort 3 April 1771, etc.

AMSTERDAM 4 February 1774 (in French) and [6 May] 1783 (in Dutch, translated by P. F. Lynslager); an earlier version, by J. T. Neyts, had been published in 1769; Hague Spring 1774 (in German).

VIENNA 8 January 1776 (in French) and 9 May 1778 (in German).

MOSCOW 29 August 1784 (in Russian, translated by M. V. Sushkova) and 4 January 1785 (in French); revived 6 June 1809.

BERLIN 17 October 1786 (in German).

STOCKHOLM 21 July 1790 (in Swedish, translated by C. Stenborg; revived there as late as 15 October 1927).

An English version, text and music by C. Dibdin, was produced at C.G. London on 18 September 1778.

FISCHIETTI: *Vologeso, Re de' Parti*

4 October. Prague

Text by A. Zeno (a later version of his *Lucio Vero*, 1700). Three acts.

The composer was then musical director of Bustelli's troupe. In 1765 he became Hasse's successor at Dresden.

BATTISHILL and M. ARNE: *Almena*

2 November. London, D.L.

Text by R. Rolt. Three acts.

Another English serious opera by Rolt, produced at D.L. in 1764 (see above, *The Royal Shepherd*). Also given at Dublin *c.* 1765; with alterations, D.L. 7 February 1766.

MAJO: *Ifigenia in Tauride*

4 November. Mannheim

Text by M. Verazi. Three acts.

SACCHINI: *Lucio Vero*

4 November. Naples, S.C.

Zeno's text (first set to music by Pollarolo in 1700). Three acts.

Revived at Naples 13 August 1785. Also given in London 20 November 1773 (Sacchini is mentioned by Burney and most other authorities; the libretto says "Music by several eminent composers").

KOHOUT: *Le Serrurier*

20 December. Paris, C.I.

Text by A. F. Quétant. One act.

In French also, Brussels 1767; Copenhagen 1769; Vienna 24 January 1776. In Swedish (translated by C. Envallsson), Stockholm 3 October 1797. In German (translated by J. H. Faber), Frankfort Autumn 1771. Dutch translation by J. T. Neyts published (n.d.).

An early instance of a French comic opera written by a Czech composer. The score was printed in 1765. *Le Serrurier* was revived at the Prague Conservatoire on 24 June 1929 (see J. Branberger in *Der Auftakt*, February 1929).

1765

SACCHINI: *La Contadina in Corte*

Carnival. Rome, Valle

Librettist unknown to Schatz-Sonneck. P. Gradenigo (in his unpublished *Notatorj*, Venice, Museo Correr) attributes a libretto of the same title, but in 3, instead of 2 acts, set by Rust and performed at Venice in 1763 and at Lisbon in 1765, to Gasparo Gozzi.[1]

One of the various versions of the *Bertoldo* story (see 1749); given at Rovigo Carnival 1779 as *La Contadina ingentilita*.

[1] A comparison of the two libretti (see A. Iacuzzi, *The European Vogue of Favart*, pp.259–266) shows that the text as composed by Sacchini was reduced and considerably altered. But Sacchini returned to the original 3-act version in 1771 when the opera was given at Ludwigsburg and about the same time in London. Matters are even more complicated than Iacuzzi states. He does not discuss the two extant London libretti, the second of which (1782) seems to represent a third version (two acts, but six instead of four characters). Both the Ludwigsburg 1771 and the London 1782 libretto affirm that the music was "entirely new"; but we may take such statements *cum grano salis*.

In Italian also: Prague Carnival 1767 (according to Teuber), 1777 (according to Haas and Kamper); Vienna 1767 (revived 19 April 1782); Dresden 17 January 1767; Pressburg 1768; Ljubljana Carnival 1769; Hanover 6 February 1770; Bamberg 18 June 1770; Copenhagen Carnival 1771 (Danish translation in libretto by R. Soelberg); London 14 March 1771 (revived 14 December 1779 and 2 March 1782); Ludwigsburg Spring 1771; Madrid 1771 (as *La Sandrina*); Bonn March 1772; Munich April 1772; Schwetzingen July 1772; Graz 1776; Trieste 5 April 1779; Warsaw 22 January 1781; Brunswick *c.* Carnival 1783; St. Petersburg 1784 (?); Gothenburg 30 April 1793; Stockholm 12 November 1793; Christiania 2 May 1794.

A German translation, *Das Bauermädchen am Hofe*, Munich 1777, preserved at Regensburg, is, according to S. Färber, signed "L. J. F.", perhaps a misprint for "C. J. F.", (the Munich translator, C. J. Förg).

In Polish (translated by W. Boguslawski), Warsaw 19 October 1783.

PICCINNI: *Il Barone di Torreforte*
10 January. Rome, Capr.

Librettist unknown. Two acts.

In Italian also: Dresden 12 June 1766 (revived 23 January 1781); Würzburg [22 September] 1769; Hanover 22 March 1770; Bonn 1772; Palermo Autumn 1775; London 22 February 1781.

In Spanish (translated by R. de la Cruz), Madrid 4 February 1768 and Barcelona 1774.

In German, Hanover 22 March 1770.

The same text was set by Joseph Michl and produced at Munich 23 March 1772 (in Italian) and in a German translation by C. J. Förg at Munich 1777 and Mannheim 24 June 1779.

GLUCK: *Il Telemaco o sia L'Isola di Circe*
30 January. Vienna, B.

Text by M. Coltellini (altered from an earlier Italian libretto by C. S. Capeci which was first composed by A. Scarlatti in 1718). Two acts.

It has often been stated that *Telemaco* was first produced at Rome in 1750, in an original 3-act version. The evidence for and against this legendary original *Telemaco* has been summed up by M. Cooper and A. Einstein in their recent books on Gluck. It should be pointed out that as early as 1890 A. Ademollo wrote in the *Gazzetta Musicale di Milano* (p.398): "Di tale rappresentazione non si trova nè il libretto, nè alcun documento. Di più, nel 1750, Anno Santo, i teatri di Roma restarono tutti chiusi, come sempre negli Anni Santi."

The score of the 1765 *Telemaco* has been preserved.

ARNOLD: *The Maid of the Mill*
31 January. London, C.G.

Text by I. Bickerstaffe (founded on Richardson's *Pamela*). Three acts.

Successful ballad opera which had a run of 29 nights in its first season. The printed score mentions—besides Arnold who arranged the music —no less than 18 composers from whose works the music was compiled. The overture was written by T. A. Erskine, Earl of Kelly.

Revived London, C.G. 20 October 1797 in a reduced 2-act version and 18 October 1814 with some new music by Bishop and others.

Given at Dublin, Crow Street Th. 25 March 1765 (as pasticcio) and Smock Alley Th. the next night (with new music by Giordani). R. Hitchcock (*Irish Stage*, 1794) gives a slightly different account as to the dates: "Both managers thought it an object worth their utmost attention. The words of the opera were published and equally free for both. But the music was in manuscript and the sole property of the Covent-garden manager. From him Mr. Barry purchased it and consequently imagined he had in this instance securely triumphed over his antagonist. In this dilemma Mr. Mossop found an unexpected resource, in the great abilities of Signior Giordani. It is a fact well established, that though the parts were writing out in Dublin for Mr. Barry, yet did Signior Giordani sit down and new compose the entire opera of the *Maid of the Mill* in full score, with all the accompaniments, in less than a fortnight; and it was written out, studied, the scenes painted, and the opera brought out, two nights before they were able to accomplish it at Crowstreet".

The Maid of the Mill was also given at New York 4 May 1769; Philadelphia 5 January 1770, etc.; Brighton 31 July 1770 (first opera there); Kingston, Jamaica 13 November 1779. Also produced by a travelling English troupe at St. Petersburg 16 May 1772.

A parody, *The Man of the Mill*, by "Seignior Squallini", was published in 1765.

BATES: *Pharnaces*

15 February. London, D.L.
Text by T. Hull (founded on an Italian libretto by A. M. Lucchini). Three acts.

One of the few attempts to follow up the great success of Arne's *Artaxerxes* (see 1762). Bates's only grand opera.

PHILIDOR: *Tom Jones*

27 February. Paris, C.I.
Text by A. A. H. Poinsinet and B. Davesne (founded on Fielding's novel). Three acts.

Regarded by some authors as Philidor's *chef-d'œuvre*. First given at Versailles 20 March 1765 and repeated at the C.I. 30 January 1766 with some alterations. Subsequently given at Geneva 1766; Brussels 26 July 1766; Dresden 3 December 1766; Amsterdam 1767; Vienna 1768; Copenhagen 1769; Lübeck 4 December 1769; Florence, T. Via S. Maria September 1776 (libretto Washington; one of a series of French opéra-comiques produced at Florence under the direction of Rutini; see Floquet's letter to Grétry, dated 13 September 1776, in *Mercure de France*, November 1776); Turin Spring 1778; Cassel 23 January 1784; St. Petersburg 20 July 1800. Revived at Paris, Fa. 15 February 1795.

In German, Frankfort 16 September 1769 (translated by F. J. Sebastiani; one of the earliest German translations of French *opéra-comique*; later versions were by J. H. Faber (published Mannheim 1772; Frankfort 1773) and by F. W. Gotter (Mayence 1776; Hamburg 26 April 1779; Munich 6 July 1779, etc.); in German, also Hague 1774; Riga 24 March 1784.

In Russian (translated by Princess Volkonsky and V. A. Levshin), Moscow before 1786 (at Prince Volkonsky's private theatre).

In Swedish (translated by C. Envallsson), Stockholm 3 November 1790.

There are printed Dutch versions by J. T. Neyts, n.d.; by J. N. Esgers, Hague 1779; and by C. Lorié, Amsterdam 1785.

Tom Jones was revived by amateurs ("Société du 18e Siècle") at the Salle Villiers, Paris in June 1914.

An English opera, text by J. Reed, music composed and compiled by Arnold (London, C.G. 14 January 1769) is an independent work, using Poinsinet's text only to a very small degree and not a single number of Philidor's music.

SACCHINI: *Il finto Pazzo per Amore*

Spring. Rome, Valle
Text by T. Mariani (first composed by Sellitti, Naples 1735). Two acts.

Given at Pavia Spring 1775 as *Il Soldato per Forza impazzito per Amore*. Last revived Varese Autumn 1797.

In Italian also, Dresden 1769; Pressburg 1770; Prague 12 September 1781.

In German (translated by G. Stephanie), Vienna, B. 6 April 1779 (revived Leop. 10 May 1787); Hamburg 1780; Riga 26 June 1784.

Given at Warsaw 10 January 1775 (in Italian); 25 September 1779 (in Polish, translated by W. Boguslawski); 31 May 1781 (in German).

BLAISE: *Isabelle et Gertrude* ou *Les Sylphes supposés*

14 August. Paris, C.I.
Text by C. S. Favart (founded on Voltaire's *Gertrude ou L'Éducation d'une Fille*). One act.

The authors introduced three airs by Gluck into their "mince partition" (as Clément-Larousse call it).

In French also given at Brussels 1 May 1766; Dresden 1766; Copenhagen 1767; Mannheim 1767; Lübeck 11 December 1769; Cassel 1780 and 26 April 1784.

Last revived in Paris by the Petite Scène May 1914 and 25 April 1920.

The same libretto was set by young Grétry in 1766; it was his first French opera, produced at Geneva in December 1766.

DUNI: *La Fée Urgèle*, ou *Ce qui plaît aux Dames*

26 October. Fontainebleau

Text by C. S. Favart (after a tale by Voltaire which, itself, is founded on Chaucer's *The Wife of Bath's Tale*). Four acts.

Given at Paris, C.I. 4 December 1765 and last revived there at the Gymnase 6 January 1821 (reduced to one act and with new choruses by L. Aimon).

In French also Geneva 1766; Brussels 12 December 1766; Amsterdam and Hague 1767; Copenhagen 1770; Vienna, Kä. November 1780; Moscow 13 November 1874 (revived 22 December 1810); Cologne 1796-7. Revived at Antwerp 10 March 1824.

In German (translated by J. H. Faber), Mannheim 1772; Frankfort Spring 1772.

In Danish (translated by J. H. Wessel), Copenhagen 30 January 1782.

In Polish (translated by J. Baudouin), Warsaw 5 April 1783.

An English adaptation of the libretto is D. Garrick's *A Christmas Tale*, produced London, D.L. 27 October 1773 (with new music by Dibdin); Dublin 7 March 1777.

P. GUGLIELMI: *Il Ratto della Sposa*

Autumn. Venice, S. Moisè

Text by G. Martinelli. Three acts.

Guglielmi's 18th opera and his first great success. Given at Padua Carnival 1775 as *Il Vecchio deluso*; at Siena 11 February 1778 as *La Sposa rapita*.

In Italian also given at Dresden 22 May 1766; Trieste [10 September] 1766; Barcelona [2 June]

1767; Lisbon 6 June 1767; London 26 March 1768; Breslau 6 September 1768; Berlin December 1768; Valencia Autumn 1769; Ludwigsburg Summer 1770; Copenhagen Autumn 1770 (Danish translation in the libretto by R. Soelberg); Bonn 1772; Gorizia Carnival 1776; Vienna 9 June 1777 (as *Il Vecchio deluso*; probably Guglielmi's opera).

1766

SACCHINI: *L'Isola d'Amore*

Carnival. Rome, Valle

Librettist unknown. Two acts.

The most successful of Sacchini's comic operas, particularly in the French and German versions.

In Italian also given at Dresden 9 February 1768; Oggerstein near Mannheim 1769, and Schwetzingen June 1772; Vienna Summer 1769 (additional music by Gassmann); Mannheim January 1772 and 1775; Munich Carnival 1773; Lisbon 20 April 1774; Regensburg 1775; London 12 March 1776; Eszterháza Summer 1776; as *La Colonia*, re-translated from the French version by G. A. Riva, Colorno, near Parma 9 October 1775.

In Spanish (translated by R. de la Cruz), Madrid 12 September 1774; Barcelona 1777.

In French (as *La Colonie*, translated by N. E. Framery), Paris, C.I. 16 August 1775 (revived Th. de l'Egalité 23 September 1794); Fontainebleau 4 November 1775; Brussels 10 January 1776; Vienna c. January 1776; Cassel 2 July 1777; Warsaw June 1778; Smolna 25 June 1778; Parma, Conte de Flavigny's April 1784; Cologne 1796-7; Moscow 1 May 1809.

In Danish (translated from the French version by N. K. Bredal), Copenhagen 15 April 1777.

In German (translated from the French version by J. André), Mannheim 21 February 1779; Berlin 2 May 1779 (revived 13 April 1790); Breslau 2 December 1779; Hamburg 8 February 1780; Frankfort 11 April 1780; Vienna, B. 7 May 1780; Augsburg 19 May 1780; Cologne 5 July 1780; Munich 18 August 1780; Bonn 6 October

1780; Cassel 7 September 1781; Riga 29 October 1783; Carlsruhe 29 October 1784; Schwedt 7 October 1785; Solothurn 12 July 1789; Pressburg November 1793.

In Polish (translator unknown), Warsaw 1780.

In Dutch (translated from the French version, translator unknown), Amsterdam 1782.

In Swedish (translated from the French version by C. Envallsson), Stockholm 7 May 1783; Gothenburg 16 April 1784; Malmö 23 September 1804.

In Russian (translated from the French version by V. G. Voroblevsky), Moscow 16 November 1780 (revived 25 September 1794) and St. Petersburg 23 November 1790.

PICCINNI: *La Pescatrice* ovvero *L'Erede riconosciuta*

9 January. Rome, Capr.

Librettist unknown (the text has nothing to do with Goldoni's *Pescatrici*). Two acts.

Given at Venice Autumn 1771 in an enlarged 3-act version with additional music by S. Perillo; at Turin, T. Carignano 1781 and Genoa 1782 as *La Pescatrice innocente*.

In Italian also, Vienna 23 January 1769; Dresden 31 January 1773; Munich April 1773; Warsaw 16 January 1775; Regensburg Carnival 1777, etc.

In German (translated by C. J. Förg) Munich 1771-2 and 11 September 1777; Salzburg 1778; Nuremberg 7 July 1779 (by Schikaneder's company); Regensburg 27 December 1779; Augsburg 13 April 1780; Gotha 24 April 1784; Carlsruhe 6 December 1784; Pforzheim 6 June 1787, etc. In German, also Warsaw 23 June 1781; Pressburg 1788; Riga 1790. (C. A. Vulpius had another German translation, called *Der Liebestrank*, ready by 1787; but it does not seem to have been acted.)

JOMMELLI: *Il Vologeso*

11 February. Ludwigsburg

Text: a later version of Zeno's *Lucio Vero* (1700), first set to music by Rinaldo di Capua in 1739. Three acts.

Lisbon Carnival 1769.

A scene from this opera was sung at a London concert as late as 5 May 1823; parts of the opera were revived at the inauguration of the new Stuttgart Hoftheater even on 14 September 1912. (See for a description of the opera, W. Heinse's novel *Hildegard von Hohenthal*, 1795-96.)

PAISIELLO: *Le finte Contesse*

February. Rome, Valle

Text by P. Chiari (originally called *Il Marchese Villano* and first set to music by Galuppi, see 1762), reduced to 1 act.

Given at Milan July 1770 as *La Lavandara astuta* (pasticcio, additions by Piccinni); also Pisa Carnival 1786. Revived in an enlarged 2-act version St. Petersburg 1777 (at Oranienbaum Palace) and 1 November 1779 (at Kamenoy Ostrov) as *Il Matrimonio inaspettato*.

Under this title as well as under two others, viz. *Il Marchese Tulipano* (Florence) and *La Contadina di Spirito* (Vienna) the opera was then given all over Europe; yet another sub-title *La Contessa di Sarzana* was used at Trieste. Given at: Naples, Palace of Portici June 1781; Florence, P. Spring 1783; Vienna 6 April 1785; London 24 January 1786 (with additional music by Cherubini; a pasticcio *Il Marchese Villano*, with music by Piccinni and Paisiello had been given there already 26 March 1778); Hamburg 1 May 1787; Versailles 17 July 1787; Rome, Capr. 7 January 1788; Eszterháza 1788; Madrid 25 August 1788; Trieste January 1789; Warsaw 6 January 1790; Lisbon 1790; Barcelona 9 December 1791; Prague 1792; Paris, Th. I. 13 December 1801.

There were almost as many German alternative titles. Given at:

PRESSBURG 18 November 1785 (as *Das listige Bauernmädchen*, translated by J. Chudy).

PYRMONT 1 August 1786 (as *Ritter Tulipan auf Rosenstock, Nelkenhain und Hollerblüth, oder Das listige Bauernmädchen*).

NUREMBERG 1787 (as *Das witzige Landmädchen oder Der geadelte Landmann*).

COLOGNE 1787-8; Hanover 18 April 1792 and Bremen 22 October 1792 (as *Das listige Bauernmädchen oder Die unvermutete Heirat*).

VIENNA, TH.A.D. LANDSTRASSE Spring 1790.

MUNICH 20 December 1793 (as *Das listige Bauern-mädchen oder das Tulipanengeschlecht*).

The opera was frequently revived in German in the beginning of the 19th century (Poznán 1 February 1805; Würzburg 13 February 1809; Hanover 1 May 1809; Darmstadt 13 August 1809, Berlin 19 December 1811, Hamburg 28 February 1813; Bremen 13 May 1814; Mayence 17 May 1815; Graz 15 November 1827) and was given at Stuttgart as late as 1843.

In French (translated by C. J. A. Gourbillon), Paris, Th. de M. 28 January 1789 (revived Th. Porte Saint-Martin 9 September 1802); Lille 15 November 1789; Ghent 1792; Liége 1 August 1795; Brussels 2 January 1796; Kingston, Jamaica 20 December 1800; Antwerp 15 January 1805 (revived 10 July 1812); Moscow 28 August 1809; Lyons October 1816; Le Havre 18 February 1817.

In Swedish (translated by C. Envallsson), Stockholm 13 November 1794.

In Russian (translated by V. A. Levshin), St. Petersburg 26 April 1795 (revived April 1811); Moscow 22 June 1798 (revived 4 May 1806 and 5 May 1820).

In Polish (translated by L. Osiński), Warsaw 1804.

In Dutch (translated by C. van der Vijver), Amsterdam [21 October] 1807.

MONSIGNY: *Aline, Reine de Golconde*

15 April. Paris, O.

Text by J. M. Sedaine (founded on a story by S. J. de Boufflers). Three acts.

Revived in Paris 4 October 1768; 26 May 1772; 4 July 1779; and 16 July 1782. In French also Brussels 4 July 1774; Liége 18 January 1783.

A German translation by F. L. W. Meyer was published at Berlin 1782.

An Italian version by A. Andrei, music by Rauzzini, was produced in London 18 March 1784.

In Russian, Moscow 21 December 1786 and 1793.

A parody by P. T. Gondot, called *Nanine, Sœur de Lait de la Reine de Golconde* was published in 1768.

The story became a favourite subject with opera composers: see Uttini 1776; Schulz 1787; Berton 1803; Donizetti 1828.

BARTHÉLEMON: *Pelopida*

24 May. London, Hm.

Very probably G. Roccaforte's text (first set to music by G. Scarlatti in 1763). Three acts.

The first opera of Barthélemon who, since 1764, had been leader of the orchestra at the King's Theatre. Extracts from the opera were performed at a Dublin concert 10 October 1771.

J. A. HILLER: *Die verwandelten Weiber, oder Der Teufel ist los*

28 May. Leipzig

Text by C. F. Weisse. (For his first, 2-act version, of the libretto, set by Standfuss, see 1752; this new 3-act version was influenced by Sedaine's French libretto of 1756, *q.v.*).

Very successful all over Germany: Hamburg 21 July 1766, etc., Berlin 13 July 1771. In German also, St. Petersburg 11 February 1779; Graz 10 February 1793; Temesvar 28 February 1802; Vienna, Leop. 19 December 1809. Parts of the opera were given at Hamburg as late as 19 February 1855.

(For a sequel *Der lustige Schuster oder Der zweite Teil vom Teufel ist los*, see 1759; this was also revised and partly re-composed by Hiller, but it can hardly be called a new opera and is treated here as a new version of Standfuss's original setting. Hiller's new version was also given at Leipzig in 1766; exact date unknown, probably a few weeks after *Die verwandelten Weiber*.)

GOSSEC: *Les Pêcheurs*

7 June. Paris, C.I.

Text by A. N. de La Salle d'Offémont. One act.

One of Gossec's best works. In French also given at Brussels 10 September 1767; Smolna

8 March 1777; Cassel 20 February 1784; Cologne 1796-7. Last revived Antwerp 11 March 1805 and Brussels 31 July 1815.

In Swedish (translated by C. Envallsson), Stockholm 6 September 1789; Gothenburg 28 October 1790; Malmö 12 July 1808.

In Dutch (translated by B. Ruloffs), Amsterdam [6 May] 1793; Oudenarde 1796-7.

DUNI: *La Clochette*

24 July. Paris, C.I.

Text by L. Anseaume (founded on a tale by Lafontaine). One act.

In French also Amsterdam 1766; Brussels 18 January 1767; Copenhagen 1767; Vienna 1768; Warsaw 10 February 1778; Liége 10 June 1780; Munich 21 March 1783; Gothenburg 25 April 1783; Stockholm June 1783; Cassel 30 October 1784; Hamburg 1795; Cologne 1795-6.

In Swedish (translated by D. G. Björn), Gothenburg 16 December 1783 and Stockholm 18 February 1786.

In Russian, Kouskovo 1780 and Moscow 19 September 1792.

A Dutch version by J. T. Neyts was published in 1768; another by J. G. Doornik in 1783.

Vocal score reprinted in 1910, edited by C. Lecocq. Revived Paris, Variétés amusantes, 29 August 1794 and "Th. de Monsieur" (Th. des Mathurins) 22 December 1910.

TRAETTA: *Le Serve Rivali*

Autumn. Venice, S. Moisè

Text by P. Chiari. Three acts.

Very successful in Italy: Florence, T. Cocomero Spring 1767; repeated Venice, S. Moisè Autumn 1767; Bologna November 1767; Novara Carnival 1769; Milan, T.R.D. Summer 1769, etc.

In Italian also, Vienna 1767; Lisbon and Brunswick 1768; Dresden 11 October 1768; London 3 June 1769 (revived 19 December 1780); Bonn 1773; Warsaw 4 February 1775.

In German as *Die Nebenbuhlerinnen*, Cologne 27 September 1785; Cassel 5 January 1787; Pyrmont 7 August 1787.

JOMMELLI: *Il Matrimonio per Concorso*

4 November. Ludwigsburg

Text by G. Martinelli. Three acts.

In Italian also, Milan, T.R.D. Autumn 1768; Lisbon 6 June 1770. At Stuttgart still given during the 'eighties.

HILLER: *Lisuart und Dariolette* oder *Die Frage und die Antwort*

25 November. Leipzig

Text by D. Schiebeler (partly founded on Favart's *La Fée Urgèle*, see 1765).

On the origin of the libretto see G. Schmidtmann's dissertation on Schiebeler, 1909). Originally in 2 acts; given also at Vienna 6 January 1767. An enlarged 3-act version was produced at Leipzig 7 January 1767; Salzthal 1 August 1769; Hamburg 1769; Berlin 26 July 1771, etc.

1767

P. GUGLIELMI: *La Sposa fedele*

Carnival. Venice, S. Moisè

Text by P. Chiari. Three acts.

The most successful of Guglielmi's earlier operas. Given at Florence, Carnival 1774 as *La Rosinella o La Sposa fedele* and Spring 1779 as *La Sposa costante*; at Genoa, S.Ag. Summer 1776 as *La Fedeltà in Amore*.

Outside Italy, in Italian, given at Dresden 1768; Copenhagen Autumn 1768 (Danish translation in the libretto by F. A. Friis); Vienna 1769 (revived 19 April 1777); London 31 March 1770 (as *La Costanza di Rosinella*; repeated 31 October 1775 under its original title, as a pasticcio); Munich Summer 1772; Cadiz 1772; Lisbon Autumn 1773; Warsaw 4 January 1775; Prague 1775; Madrid Summer 1776; Graz, Carnival 1778; Eszterháza 3 May 1778, etc.

Successful also in a German translation by J. J. Eschenburg, as *Robert und Kalliste, oder Der Triumph der Treue*: Berlin 8 April 1775; Dresden 25 February 1776; Vienna 20 June 1776; Hamburg 25 September 1776; Hanover 10 January 1777; Frankfort 14 June 1777; St. Petersburg 29 January 1778; Strasbourg 28 February 1779; Augsburg 11 June 1779; Bonn 9 December 1781; Warsaw 22 June 1782; Riga 29 November 1782; Prague Easter 1783; Munich 1 July 1783; Laibach 31 May 1784; Cologne Autumn 1784; Carlsruhe 21 February 1785; Bremen 18 October 1785; Cassel 28 April 1787; Pyrmont 26 June 1787; Pressburg 1788; Graz 14 March 1789; Wolfenbüttel 25 August 1789; Budapest 27 December 1789; Amsterdam 1792, etc. Given on German stages until about 1800.

HAYDN: *La Cantarina*
Carnival. Eszterháza

Librettist unknown (the text is different from Goldoni's intermezzo of the same title, set to music by Galuppi in 1756). Two acts.

Revived Bielefeld 21 March 1939 (in German, as *Die kleine Sängerin*, translated and arranged by M. See).

M. ARNE: *Cymon*
2 January. London, D.L.

Text by D. Garrick (*A dramatic romance*, founded on Dryden's poem *Cymon and Iphigenia*). Prologue, 5 acts, and epilogue.

Arne's most successful work; Dublin 4 March 1771 (accompaniments by W. Clagget); Philadelphia 3 March 1773; New York 3 May 1773; Edinburgh 1783, etc. Frequently revived in London; the latest revivals were at:

C.G. 20 November 1815 (reduced to 3 acts, with additions by Bishop, also airs by Stevenson, Braham and Paer).

C.G. 14 December 1815 (reduced to 2 acts); and 21 October 1817; 11 October 1820 and 7 April 1827).

.Y. 1 April 1850 (reduced to 1 act, adapted by J. R. Planché as *Cymon and Iphigenia*).

MYSLIVECZEK: *Il Bellerofonte*
20 January. Naples, S.C.

Text by G. Bonechi (according to B. Croce, who quotes a letter by Bonechi, saying that his work

had previously been successfully produced in Russia, viz., with music by Araja in 1750). Three acts.

The first success of the Czech composer; given at Siena [6 May] 1767 and later in the same year also produced at Prague. (The opera was not written for Parma as stated by Eitner and many other authorities.)

J. A. HILLER: *Lottchen am Hofe*
24 April. Leipzig

Text by C. F. Weisse (after Goldoni and Favart, see 1749 and 1755). Three acts.

Successful on German stages; Berlin 1 July 1769, etc.; in German also, Prague 1 April 1771; St. Petersburg 1778; Riga 1778 (as *Lotte und Gürgel*); Salzburg 18 February 1781. Given in Germany until the end of the 18th century. Revived Darmstadt 31 March 1936 (new version by F. Herburger and A. Anzengruber).

Given at Vienna, Kä. 10 June 1769 "umgeändert als Lustspiel von Heufeld". A new setting of Favart's text (see 1755) by H. M. Berton (first produced Paris 21 December 1811) was given with parts of Hiller's music when performed (in a German version by G. F. Treitschke) at Vienna, W. 19 October 1815.

GASSMANN: *L'Amore Artigiano*
26 April. Vienna, B.

Text by C. Goldoni (first set to music by Latilla in 1760). Three acts.

Gassmann's setting was very successful all over Europe. Given at:

BOLOGNA [10 April] 1768 and on many other Italian stages: Burney attended a performance at Milan 17 July 1770; revived Milan, Sc. 1 May 1782.

VALENCIA Autumn 1769 (in Italian).

DRESDEN 2 January 1770 (in Italian).

COPENHAGEN Autumn 1770 (in Italian; Danish translation in the libretto by R. Soelberg) and 4 January 1781 (in Danish, translated by L. Knudsen).

SCHWETZINGEN May 1772 (in Italian).

PRAGUE 1774 (in Italian) and Summer 1783 (in German).

MUNICH Carnival 1775.

WARSAW 22 January 1775 (in Italian) and 22 April 1787 (in Polish, translated by W. Boguslawski).

GRAZ Spring 1778 (in Italian) and 18 December 1792 (in German).

LONDON 3 March 1778 (in Italian; not 3 August 1775).

VIENNA, B. 29 September 1779 (for the first time in German, translator not mentioned); revived Leop. 30 April 1790 (translated by J. A. von Ghelen); and in yet another version by K. F. Lippert, Kä. 29 December 1801 (as pasticcio).

NICE Carnival 1781 (in Italian).

BONN 15 October 1781; Frankfort 13 April 1782; Hamburg 28 August 1782, etc. (in German).

DUBLIN 1782 (in Italian).

BERLIN 16 June 1783 (in German).

RIGA 18 December 1783 (in German).

ST. PETERSBURG 1785 (in Italian).

PRESSBURG 1788 (in German; revived 16 December 1797).

BUDAPEST 1788 (in German).

PAISIELLO: *L'Idolo Cinese*

Spring. Naples, T.N.

Text by G. B. Lorenzi. Three acts.

Successful at Naples; given 6 April 1768 at the court theatre of Caserta as the first comic opera there. In Italian also, Paris, O. 10 June 1779 (with additional music by Piccinni and others); St. Petersburg 30 August 1779 (at Tsarskoye Selo; French and Russian translations by A. G. Volkov and Levachoi published on that occasion). Revived Naples Fondo 1783.

MOZART: *Apollo et Hyacinthus* seu *Hyacinthi Metamorphosis*

13 May. Salzburg

(Latin) text by R. Widl. Called a *Lateinische Komödie*. Strictly speaking, not an opera, but musical intermezzi (9 numbers) in Widl's Latin tragedy, *Clementia Croesi*. Such Latin plays were performed at Salzburg University at the end of each term. (Even this was not the first stage-work of the eleven-year-old boy; *Die Schuldigkeit des ersten Gebotes*, the first act of which was set by Mozart, had been given at Salzburg University on 12 March 1767.)

Apollo et Hyacinthus was revived at

ROSTOCK 29 April 1922 (in German, translated by H. C. Schott and G. Scholz, music arranged by P. G. Scholz and J. Turnau).

MUNICH April 1932 (in German, translated by E. Mann, music arranged by K. Schleifer).

SALZBURG August 1935 (new version by R. Tenschert, arranged for puppets); this version was also given at Linz 16 April 1937.

GOSSEC: *Toinon et Toinette*

20 June. Paris, C.I.

Text by J. A. J. Des Boulmiers. Two acts.

In French also, Amsterdam and Hague 1768; Liége 2 February 1771; Copenhagen 1771; Brussels 27 May 1776; Cassel 14 January 1784.

In German (translated by J. H. Faber), Frankfort 1774; Cologne 22 June 1775; (translated by G. Stephanie), Vienna, Kä. 1 June 1776 and B. 9 February 1779, etc.

In Dutch (translated by P. J. Uylenbroek), Amsterdam November 1783; an earlier Dutch version, by J. T. Neyts, had been published at Alkmaer in 1768, and a third anonymous one in the same year. Burney attended a performance in Flemish at Brussels in July 1772 (music arranged by Vitzthumb).

In Danish (translated by A. G. Thoroup), Copenhagen 25 November 1785.

In Swedish (adapted and translated by C. Envallsson), Stockholm 11 September 1804 (pasticcio); also Malmö 22 April 1807 and Lund 22 July 1807.

NAUMANN: *L'Achille in Sciro*

5 September. Palermo

Metastasio's text (first set to music by Caldara, see 1736). Three acts.

Naumann's first preserved opera.

HASSE: *Partenope*

9 Septembre. Vienna, B.

Text by P. Metastasio. Two acts.

Written to celebrate the betrothal of King Ferdinand IV of Naples to the Archduchess Maria Josepha (d. 15 October 1767). Also given at Naples, S.C. 20 September 1767 and Berlin 18 July 1775.

(According to the diary of Khevenhüller[1] *Partenope* had been produced two years earlier at Innsbruck, 6 August 1765, at the wedding of the Archduke Leopold; but it was *Romolo ed Ersilia*, by the same authors, which was performed on that occasion.)

PHILIDOR: *Ernelinde Princesse de Norvège*

24 November. Paris, O.

Text by A. A. H. Poinsinet (founded on an Italian libretto by M. Noris, *Ricimero, Rè de Vandali*, 1684). Three acts.

Philidor's chief work in the province of grand opera. Given at Paris 24 January 1769 as *Sandomir, Prince de Dannemarck* and revived (with the original title) Versailles 11 December 1773 and Paris, O. 8 July 1777 (enlarged to 5 acts, text revised by J. M. Sedaine).

Given at Brussels 4 October 1772 (first version) and 4 November 1774 (second version).

A parody by J. E. Despréaux, called *Berlingue*, was produced at Choisy 13 September 1777 and another, called *Sans-Dormir*, at the C.I., Paris 12 October 1777.

Vocal score reprinted in 1883 (edited by César Franck).

GLUCK: *Alceste*

26 December. Vienna, B.

Text by R. de' Calzabigi (*Tragedia per musica*). Three acts.

[1] *Aus der Zeit Maria Theresias. Tagebuch des Fürsten Johann Josef Khevenhüller-Metsch.* Vol. VI (1764–67), 1917, pp.120 and 263. The anticipation of the 1767 title in a diary entry of 1765 remains a curious fact which can be explained only by assuming that the title of the opera was supplied from memory at a later date.

After *Orfeo* (see 1762) Gluck's second "reform opera"; the preface to the score (published Vienna 1769) is one of the most remarkable documents for the theory of opera. The date of 16 December (instead of 26) 1767 for the first performance at Vienna, still frequently occurring, is wrong, and owes its existence to an old misprint; see C. F. Pohl, *Haydn*, Vol. II (1882), p.119.

Alceste was revived at Vienna, in Italian, on 21 September 1770; again Schönbrunn 25 November 1781 and Vienna, B. 3 December 1781; also Vienna, Prince Auerperg's February 1786. Outside Vienna given at Paris, O. 23 April 1776 (in French, translated by F. L. G. Lebland du Roullet; with some adjustments in the last act by Gossec); given there more or less regularly until 1826; revived 21 October 1861 (revised by Berlioz) and 12 October 1866 (313 performances in all). Then revived at the O.C. 28 May 1904 and again at the O. 8 February 1926 and 23 November 1936. A parody by P. A. A. de Piis, P. Y. Barré, J. B. D. Desprès and L. P. P. Resnier, called *La Bonne Femme ou Le Phénix*, was produced at the C.I. on 7 July 1776. Another, *Céleste*, by Bardon, was published in 1784.

In French also given at Cassel 6 April 1778 (first performance in Germany); Brunswick 1801.

In Italy, Padua 1777; Bologna, T.C. 9 May 1778 and Casino Nobile February 1788; Naples, Fondo Autumn 1785; Florence, P. 26 December 1786. (Calzabigi's text was also used by Guglielmi, whose setting was produced at Milan 26 December 1768, exactly one year after Gluck's.)

In Italian also given at Copenhagen 1 February 1775 (Danish translation in the libretto by R. Soelberg); Lille 12 April 1783; Hanover c.November 1783; London 30 April 1795 (for Brigitta Banti's benefit; a selection had been given previously at a "fête" at the King's Th. 10 April 1780, with Antonia Bernasconi for whom Gluck originally had written the part of Alceste); Berlin 4 March 1796 and 15 January 1804; St. Petersburg 1798; Moscow Carnival 1803; Trieste 1804.

In Swedish (translated by C. J. Hertzenhjelm and J. H. Kellgren, music arranged by L. S. Lalin), Stockholm 26 February 1781.

In German, Frankfort 31 July 1784 (translated by J. Böhm); Cologne Autumn 1784 (Böhm's translation); Cassel 23 March 1787; Mayence 9 April 1791 (translated by H. G. Schmieder); Berlin 15 October 1817 (translated by C. A. Herklots); Budapest 1 November 1817; Munich 8 July 1840; Dresden 17 February 1846; Prague 17 November 1846; Leipzig 18 June 1853; Carlsruhe 28 June 1855; Rotterdam April 1864.

In Russian, Kouskovo, Count Cheremetyev's, after 1785.

Some of the more recent revivals of *Alceste* were at:

VIENNA 4 October 1885 and 6 March 1916 (in German).

BOLOGNA, T.C. 7 October 1888 (in Italian, re-translated from Herklots's German version by A. Zanardini).

BARCELONA, T.L. September 1889 (in Italian, re-translated from Herklots's German version by A. Zanardini).

COPENHAGEN 15 November 1898 (in concert form).

PRAGUE 6 February 1901 (in German).

PARIS, O.C. 28 May 1904 (in French).

LONDON, H.M'S 2 December 1904 (by the R.C.M., in English, translated by C. Aveling).

BRUSSELS 14 December 1904 (in French; for the first time there).

STUTTGART 18 November 1923 (new German version by H. Abert).

PARIS, O. 8 February 1926 and 23 November 1936 (in French).

ZURICH 10 March 1926 (in German).

TURIN, T. DI TORINO 12 May 1926 (in Italian).

OXFORD 6 December 1926 (in English).

BUENOS AIRES 21 June 1934 (in French).

FLORENCE, BOBOLI GDNS. 1 June 1935 (in Italian).

ROME, T.R. 16 January 1937 (in Italian).

LONDON, C.G. 6 May 1937 (in French).

BASLE 1 June 1939 (in German).

The first American opera libretto was printed in 1767, *The Disappointment, or, The Force of Cre-* *dulity, a new American Comic Opera of two acts. By Andrew Barton*. It was announced for production at Philadelphia 20 April 1767, but withdrawn as it contained "personal reflections". Reprinted (in 3 acts) 1796. The music consists of popular airs. See O. G. T. Sonneck, in *Sammelbände of the I.M.S.*, Vol. VI (1904–5).

1768

GASSMANN: *La Notte critica*

5 January. Vienna, B.

Text by C. Goldoni (first set to music by Boroni, 1766, and Piccinni, 1767). Three acts.

In German (translated by J. J. Eschenburg) Vienna, B. 10 January 1783.

DUNI: *Les Moissonneurs*

27 January. Paris, C.I.

Text by C. S. Favart. Three acts.

In French also, Amsterdam 1768; Liége 8 December 1768; Copenhagen 12 June 1769; Erlangen 1769.

In German (translated by J. H. Faber) Frankfort 1772; another German version, by G. K. Pfeffel was given at Rostock 5 June 1776 (modified by P. F. Ilgener; see Sonneck's *Catalogue*, p.974 and A. Iacuzzi, *The European Vogue of Favart*, p.184).

An anonymous English translation *The Reapers, or The Englishman out of Paris*, was published in 1770; see also Shield's *Rosina*, 1782.

A Spanish version by R. de la Cruz was set by Esteve (*La Espigadera*, Madrid 20 July 1778).

An anonymous Dutch translation was published in 1785.

JOMMELLI: *Fetonte*

11 February. Ludwigsburg

Text by M. Verazi. Three acts.

Lisbon 6 June 1769. Given at Stuttgart until 1773. An earlier *Fetonte* opera by Jommelli (performed Stuttgart 11 February 1753; different libretto) is not extant.

The score was published in the *Denkmäler Deutscher Tonkunst* series in 1907 (edited by H. Abert).

DIBDIN: *Lionel and Clarissa*

25 February. London, C.G.

Text by I. Bickerstaffe. Three acts.

Given in a new version as *Lionel and Clarissa, or A School for Fathers*, London, D.L. 8 February 1770; Dublin 2 April 1770 (first version already 1769); Philadelphia 14 December 1772; Kingston, Jamaica 14 April 1781; Edinburgh 23 February 1786 (if not earlier); New York 21 February 1794 (first recorded performance; probably given there already c.1773); Boston 14 November 1796.

The greater part of the music was composed by Dibdin; as to the additions by other composers, see Sonneck's *Catalogue*, p.687.

Frequently revived on English stages; in London as late as 22 May 1924 at Birkbeck Institute and 28 October 1925 at the Lyric, Hammersmith (music arranged by A. Reynolds; ran for 171 nights).

TRAETTA: *L'Isola disabitata*

[*26 April*]. Bologna, T.C.

Metastasio's text (first set to music by Bonno in 1752). Two acts.

Of the music only one air is extant. Given also at St. Petersburg Carnival 1769; Copenhagen 8 January 1773 (Danish translation in the libretto by F. A. Friis); Warsaw 1 June 1781 (composer not mentioned; rather Traetta's than G. Scarlatti's setting); Prague Autumn 1783.

GALUPPI: *Ifigenia in Tauride*

2 May. St. Petersburg

Text by M. Coltellini (first set to music by Traetta, see 1763). Three acts.

The only opera Galuppi wrote for Russia where he was court conductor, 1766–68. Score preserved.

J. A. HILLER: *Die Liebe auf dem Lande*

18 May. Leipzig

Text by C. F. Weisse (founded on Favart's *Annette et Lubin*, see 1762, and Anseaume's *La Clochette*, see 1766). Three acts.

Hamburg 1769; Berlin 13 August 1771 and all over Germany; in German also, St. Petersburg 5 November 1778; Vienna 7 June 1779; Riga 30 April 1784.

For a Danish version, see 1810.

RODRIGUEZ DE HITA: *Briseida*

11 July. Madrid, T. del Principe

Text by R. de la Cruz (*zarzuela heróica*). Two acts.

Parts of the music were revived in concert form at the Ateneo, Madrid in 1896 (under F. Pedrell).

GRÉTRY: *Le Huron*

20 August. Paris, C.I.

Text by J. F. Marmontel (founded on Voltaire's *L'Ingénu*). Two acts.

Grétry's first success; given in Paris until 1807; the 100th performance there was on 17 March 1776.

In French also, Amsterdam 1768; Liége 26 January 1769; Copenhagen 1769; Cassel 19 November 1783; Parma Carnival 1787.

In German (translated by C. L. Reuling) Vienna 1770; Prague 1770; Frankfort 1772–73; Mayence 1776; revived Vienna, Kä. April 1776 and Leop. 25 October 1783; Bonn 1783.

In Danish (translated by C. H. Pram), Copenhagen 6 January 1780.

A Dutch version by J. T. Neyts was published in 1769.

MOZART: *Bastien und Bastienne*

September? Vienna

Text: F. W. Weiskern's German version of Favart's parody on Rousseau's *Le Devin du Village* (see 1752). One act.

The performance took place at the garden theatre of Anton Mesmer, the once famous hypnotist, probably in September 1768. It was the only production of this little Singspiel until 122 years later. The *Bastien und Bastienne* produced at Vienna suburban theatres 3 August 1775 and 29 May 1779 is attributed to Mozart in E. K. Blümml's and G. Gugitz's *Alt-Wiener Thespiskarren* (p.481). But there is no evidence that this was not rather the Weiskern version of Favart's parody, which seems to be much more likely (see 1752).

Bastien und Bastienne was revived by the *Gesellschaft der Opernfreunde* at the Architektenhaus, Berlin on 2 October 1890. One year later, with a new text by M. Kalbeck, it was produced at Vienna, O. 25 December 1891 and subsequently at Brünn 14 April 1892, Graz 28 November 1892, Hamburg 29 November 1892, Berlin 5 December 1892, Basle 19 December 1892 and in most German theatres. Another new version, by R. Simons, was given at Vienna, V.O. 31 October 1905.

Translated from Kalbeck's version also given at:

BUDAPEST 20 November 1892 (in Hungarian, translated by A. Radó).

STOCKHOLM 28 September 1893 (in Swedish, translated by E. Grandinson).

LONDON, DALY's 26 December 1894 (in English, translated by C. Bache) and C.G. 2 May 1907 (in German); broadcast 17 March 1933 (English version by E. Blom).

PARIS, O.C. 9 June 1900 (in French, translated by H. Gauthier-Villars and G. Hartmann); revived at the Théâtre Club Arlequin 9 January 1932.

BRUSSELS 29 December 1900 (in French).

ANTWERP 2 February 1901 (in Flemish).

PRAGUE 1905 (in Czech, translated by V. J. Novotný).

ZAGREB 1 June 1911 (in Croatian; by amateurs).

MANCHESTER 21 October 1912 (in English, translated by S. Langford).

VENICE, LICEO 1914 (in Italian, translated by C. Rossi).

MADRID Spring 1915 (in Spanish, translated by A. Gil y Gordaliza, with recitatives by Manuel M. Faixá).

NEW YORK 26 October 1916 (in English, translated by A. Mattulath) and 5 February 1939 (translated by H. Hagen).

TRIESTE, CONSERVATORIO 14 June 1923 (in Italian).

ROME, T. DI MARCELLO 21 January 1927 (in Italian).

NANTES 13 March 1928 (in French).

BARCELONA April 1928 (in French).

SALZBURG 6 August 1928 (in Russian, by the Leningrad Conservatoire).

GENEVA March 1933 (in French).

HAGUE April 1938 (by the Dutch Chamber Opera).

JERUSALEM 1 March 1939 (in Hebrew, translated by E. Troche).

RODRIGUEZ DE HITA: *Las Segadoras* (The Reapers)

3 October. Madrid, T. del Principe

Text by R. de la Cruz (*zarzuela burlesca*). Two acts.

Successful at Madrid. Also given at Barcelona 1773. Music preserved.

HAYDN: *Lo Speziale*

Autumn. Eszterháza

Text by C. Goldoni (first set to music by V. Pallavicini and Fischietti, see 1755). Three acts.

Repeated Vienna 22 March 1770 (privately at Freiherr von Sumerau's).

Revived (in a German version by R. Hirschfeld), Dresden 22 June 1895; Vienna, Ca. 3 November 1895; Hamburg 5 November 1895; Basle 19 March 1897, etc. Again Vienna, O. 10 February 1899 and 29 May 1909 (reduced to one act, scoring revised); Amsterdam 24 January 1911.

In 1932 (being the year of the 200th anniversary of Haydn's birth) the opera was seen again on many German stages (Vienna 9 April 1932, etc.). Since 1925 produced in many countries by the Vienna Sängerknaben. Translated from Hirschfeld's version, *Lo Speziale* was given in London, King's Th., Hammersmith 3 September 1925 (English version by A. Skalski and K. Lark); at the Neighborhood Playhouse, New York 16 March 1926 (English version by A. Macdonald, music arranged by H. Barlow); at Budapest 24 April 1932 (Hungarian version by E. Unger).

DIBDIN: *The Padlock*

3 October. London, D.L.

Text by I. Bickerstaffe (founded on Cervantes's story *El Celoso extremeño*). Two acts.

Very successful on English stages. Given at New York as early as 29 May 1769; Philadelphia 8 November 1769, etc. Dublin 26 February 1770; Edinburgh *c.* January 1775; Montego Bay, Jamaica 19 March 1777; Calcutta 1789; Cape Town 27 May 1815; Bombay November 1820. Also given by a touring English company at St. Petersburg 21 November or 17 December 1771. During the 19th century revived on many European and American stages by the touring Negro actor Ira Aldridge (in the part of Mungo, which was, in 1768, created by Dibdin himself).

Given at Vienna, Ca. 19 February 1853 (in English) and 18 April 1857 (in German, as *Das Vorhängeschloss*, translated by C. Juin). Anonymous French version published 1822.

DUNI: *Les Sabots*

26 October. Paris, C.I.

Text by J. M. Sedaine and J. Cazotte. One act.

In French also, Copenhagen 1769; Liége 17 December 1776. In Swedish Gothenburg 21 November 1786. There are two printed Dutch versions by J. T. Neyts (n.d.) and by J. C. Honig (1812). The opera was revived at the O.C., Paris on 6 July 1866.

HASSE: *Piramo e Tisbe*

November. Vienna, B.

Text by M. Coltellini (*Intermezzo tragico*). Two acts.

The last intermezzo of Hasse and one of the few extant ones. Repeated Laxenburg Palace September 1770 and also given at Potsdam March 1771; Dresden 1775; Copenhagen 1778. Revived Cologne Autumn 1939 (in German).

ESTEVE: *Los Jardineros de Aranjuez*

25 December. Madrid, T. de la Cruz

Text by the composer (*opera comico-buffo-dramatica*). Two acts.

Early extant example of Spanish comic opera.

1769

SACCHINI: *Il Cidde*

Carnival. Rome, Arg.

Text by G. Pizzi. Three acts.

In Italian also, London 19 January 1773 (libretto altered by G. G. Bottarelli); Lisbon Autumn 1773.

Revived in a French version as *Chimène ou Le Cid* (translated by N. F. Guillard) Fontainebleau 18 November 1783 and Paris, O. 9 February 1784; also Brussels 3 May 1801. Given at Paris 50 times until 1790; revived Paris, O. 5 April 1808.

The statement, given by some authors, that this opera was first produced as *Chimena* at Rome in 1762 or 1764, lacks verification.

GRÉTRY: *Lucile*

5 January. Paris, C.I.

Text by J. F. Marmontel (from his tale *L'École des Pères*). One act.

Given at Fontainebleau 18 October 1769; in Paris until 1793 (100th performance 8 July 1773).

In French also, Copenhagen, Amsterdam and Hague 1769; Liége 25 November 1770; Laxenburg, near Vienna 23 September 1772; Turin Spring 1774; Florence September 1776; Warsaw July 1778; Cassel 17 December 1783.

In German (translated by J. H. Faber), Frankfort 1772; Cologne Spring 1772; Hague 1774; Vienna, Kä. May 1776 and B. 29 June 1778; Gotha 6 November 1778; Munich November 1778; Augsburg 1 July 1779; Carlsruhe 1781; Bonn 5 June 1782, etc.

In Swedish (translated by A. M. Malmstedt), Stockholm 19 June 1776 (music adapted by L. S. Lalin); revived Malmö 28 October 1804.

In Danish (translated by N. K. Bredal), Copenhagen 4 September 1778 (at Fredensborg palace) and 27 October 1778 (at the Royal Theatre).

In Dutch, Amsterdam Winter 1783 (see *De Tooneelspel-Beschouwer*, 1783); there are printed versions by J. T. Neyts (n.d.) and by P. J. Uylenbrock (1781).

In Polish (translated by F. Zablocki), Warsaw 19 February 1788.

Lucile contains the famous quartet, "Où peut-on être mieux qu'au sein de sa famille". The opera was revived at Liége as late as 17 April 1920.

MONSIGNY: *Le Déserteur*

6 March. Paris, C.I.

Text by J. M. Sedaine. Three acts.

Monsigny's most famous work. Given in Paris until the end of the 19th century; revived at St. Cloud 28 October 1843 and at the O.C. 30 October 1843 (re-scored by Adam); F.P. 8 October 1867; O.C. 23 June 1893 and 26 October 1911. Outside Paris given at:

AMSTERDAM 1769 (in French); 11 May 1772 (in Dutch, translated by J. T. Neyts) and 1776 (in German); another Dutch version, by B. Ruloffs, was published in 1782 and 1784.

HAMBURG and BRUNSWICK 1770 (in German, translated by J. J. Eschenburg); Frankfort 8 April 1771, etc. There are at least two more German versions, by C. F. Schwan (published Mannheim 1770; used at Altenburg 13 September 1775) and by M. von Brahm (published Vienna 1770; used for a performance, apparently without music, at Vienna, Kä. 19 November 1770).

COPENHAGEN 1770 (in French) and 28 November 1775 (in Danish, translated by N. K. Bredal).

LIÉGE 4 December 1770 (in French).

BERLIN 12 May 1772 (in German; given there until 1822).

DRESDEN 1772 (in French, as *Alexis ou le Déserteur*) and October 1775 (in German).

LONDON, D.L. 2 November 1773 (in English, adapted by C. Dibdin, who also added some music of his own and two numbers by Philidor); Dublin 10 February 1774.

HAGUE 8 February 1774 (in French) and later in the same year in German.

VIENNA, SCHÖNBRUNN 22 October 1775 (in French) and Kä., April 1776 and B. 28 November 1779 (in German; last revived there 24 November 1813, in a new version by W. Ehlers).

TURIN Spring 1776 (in French).

STOCKHOLM 15 May 1777 (in Swedish, as *Alexis*, translated by C. Stenborg); also in Swedish at

Malmö 19 August 1804; Lund 7 Septembre 1808.

WARSAW 1778 (in French) and 17 January 1788 (in Polish, translated by L. Pierozyński).

CASSEL 1779 (in French).

KOUSKOVO 18 February 1781 (in Russian, translated by V. G. Voroblevsky; a later translation, by V. Levshin, was published in 1793).

RIGA 14 January 1783 (in German).

ST. PETERSBURG 23 January 1785 (in French); and 20 October 1789 (in Russian, Voroblevsky's translation).

MOSCOW 22 February 1785 (in French) and 1799 (in Russian); revived 22 February 1807 and 22 January 1819.

NEW YORK 8 June 1787 and Philadelphia 11 July 1787 (in English, the London version).

PRESSBURG 1788 and Budapest 25 September 1789 (in German).

BOSTON 24 April 1793 and Philadelphia 14 May 1798 (in French).

CARVALHO: *L'Amore industrioso*

31 March. Lisbon, Th. d'Ajuda

Text by G. Casori (first set to music by Rutini in 1765). Three acts.

Carvalho's first (Italian) opera; successful at Lisbon, where it was first produced on the birthday of Queen Marianna Vittoria. Score preserved.

MOZART: *La finta Semplice*

1 May. Salzburg

Text by M. Coltellini (founded on an earlier libretto of the same title by Goldoni, which was first set by Perillo in 1764). Three acts.

The opera had been written for Vienna in 1768, but the production there was frustrated; see Abert-Jahn, I, p.128, and Leopold Mozart's formal complaint to the Emperor, in chapter I of H. G. Farmer's and H. Smith's *New Mozartiana* (Glasgow 1935). More than 150 years after its first production at the Archbishop's palace, Salzburg, *La finta Semplice* was revived in a German version by A. Rudolph (as *Die verstellte Einfalt*) at Carlsruhe 2 October 1921; also given at the

Akademie-Th., Vienna 10 February 1925; Breslau December 1927; Prague December 1928.

In Danish (as *Rosinas Skaelmsstykker*, translated from Rudolph's version by G. Hetsch), Copenhagen 21 April 1923.

DIBDIN: *The Ephesian Matron*

12 May. London, Ranelagh House

Text by I. Bickerstaffe (*A comic serenata, after the manner of the Italian*). One act.

First produced at Ranelagh House at a "Jubilee Ridotto or Bal Paré" (the date is given here for the first time). Repeated Little Hm. 31 August 1769; D.L. 8 May 1771; Dublin December 1778.

Revived London, Court Th. 3 May 1926; Duke's 16 March 1933 (by the R.A.M.); Art Theatre Club 24 March 1936; R.C.M. 19 June 1938; Fortune 23 April 1940. Revived in a German version by G. R. Kruse at the Lessing Museum, Berlin on 25 February 1932.

MEYER VON SCHAUENSEE: *Hans Hüttenstock*

??. Lucerne

Text by the composer. Two acts. Performed at the annual meeting of the "Helvetische Konkordiagesellschaft", probably at the Engelberg convent, Lucerne. First extant example of a comic opera written by a Swiss composer.

RODRIGUEZ DE HITA: *Las Labradoras de Murcia*

16 Septembre. Madrid, T. del Principe

Text by R. de la Cruz (*zarzuela burlesca*). Two acts.

Revived in concert form Madrid 28 May 1896 (revised by F. Pedrell).

GRÉTRY: *Le Tableau parlant*

20 September. Paris, C.I.

Text by L. Anseaume (*comédie-parade*). One act.

Very successful on French stages. First given at Fontainebleau 7 November 1770 and frequently revived in Paris: at the O.C. until 1865; Th. L.

1 June 1854; O. Nat. Lyrique 23 October 1876; Galerie Vivienne 4 April 1895; "Th. de Monsieur" (Th. des Mathurins) October 1910; Bordeaux 6 April 1880; Brussels 25 March 1909.

In French also given at Brussels 1769; Copenhagen 1770; Liége 17 November 1770; Vienna, Laxenburg 10 September 1772; Turin Spring 1774; Harlem 27 June 1774; Moscow 3 November 1775 (revived 29 April 1809); Warsaw August 1778; Munich 14 March 1783; Geneva 17 January 1784; Cassel 8 May 1784; Charleston, S.C. 17 June 1794; Philadelphia 17 December 1796; Madrid July 1859; Baden-Baden 14 August 1861.

In German (translated by F. W. M.), Mannheim 1771; (translated by H. A. O. Reichard), Cologne 20 April 1722; Berlin 31 May 1774; Gotha 13 January 1775 (music adapted and two additional airs by A. Schweitzer); Vienna, Kä. May 1776; Munich 1776; Hamburg 15 December 1780; Riga 21 February 1783; Pressburg 7 November 1785, etc.

In Spanish (translated by R. de la Cruz), Madrid July 1777 and, in a new version, 3 July 1781.

In Danish (translated by J. H. Wessel), Copenhagen 30 November 1779.

In Russian (translated by A. Y. Khilkov), Moscow 15 June 1780.

In Polish (translated by J. Baudouin), Warsaw 1782.

In Swedish, Stockholm 10 April 1782 (translated by C. Envallsson) and 15 January 1799 (translated by C. G. af Leopold); Malmö 6 May 1807.

In Dutch (translated by B. Ruloffs), Amsterdam October 1783. Another Dutch translation by J. T. Neyts published (n.d.).

1770

SCHWEITZER: *Elysium*

18 January. Hanover

Text by J. G. Jacobi (*Ein Vorspiel mit Arien*). One act.

Written as a *pièce d'occasion* for celebrating Queen Charlotte's birthday, but later on given on other stages as well; Hamburg 19 July 1770; Dessau 24 September 1774 (first opera there); Berlin 17 August 1775; Lucerne 1776, etc.

In German also, St. Petersburg 1776; Riga 10 August 1784. Last revived Magdeburg 17 March 1797; Königsberg April 1806.

An anonymous French translation was published at Paris in 1771.

J. A. HILLER: *Die Jagd*

29 January. Weimar

Text by C. F. Weisse (founded on C. Collé's *La Partie de Chasse de Henri IV* which, itself, is based upon Sedaine's *Le Roi et le Fermier*, see 1762, and, further back, upon R. Dodsley's *The King and the Miller of Mansfield*, 1736). Three acts.

Hiller's most popular work; given at St. Pölten 1 January 1771, Hamburg 14 February 1771, Berlin 18 June 1771, and all over Germany.

In German also, Pressburg December 1775; Vienna, Kä. June 1776; St. Petersburg 25 April 1779; Warsaw 9 December 1781; Riga 1 November 1782; Lucerne 1787; Amsterdam c.1793.

J. F. Reichardt, in his *Über die Deutsche Komische Oper* ... (1774) gives a detailed description of *Die Jagd*.

Frequently revived during the 19th and even in the 20th century, viz.:

LEIPZIG 11 March 1805, 28 January 1826 (for Weisse's centenary), 18 November 1857, and 28 January 1891.

OSNABRÜCK 20 November 1830 (revised by Lortzing).

DRESDEN 27 February 1837 (given there until 1866).

KÖNIGSBERG 25 November 1855.

BERLIN, FR. W. 14 September 1857 and 11 October 1890 (revised by E. Pohl, re-scored by G. Lehnhardt).

HAMBURG 16 May 1858 and 15 January 1878.

BREMEN February 1905 (Lortzing's version).

LEIPZIG September 1912.

DRESDEN October 1915 (revised by V. Eckert).

GRÉTRY: *Silvain*

19 February. Paris, C.I.

Text by J. F. Marmontel (founded on Gessner's *Erast*). One act.

Given in Paris until 1827. In French also, Amsterdam and Hague 1770; Liége 12 January 1771; Bonn 1771; Copenhagen 1771; Harlem 3 July 1774; Smolna 24 April 1781; Cassel 21 January 1784; Lazienk Summer 1791; Brussels 30 December 1794; Cologne 1795–96; Hamburg 1797 or earlier; St. Petersburg 4 February 1800.

In German, Frankfort 1772 (translated by J. H. Faber); Hanover 7 May 1773 (as *Walder*); Berlin 26 May 1773 (as *Erast und Lucinde*, translated by J. J. Eschenburg); Hamburg 21 July 1773; Vienna, Kä. May 1776 and, in a new translation, B. 18 November 1778; St. Petersburg 1 March 1778 (Eschenburg's version); Munich October 1778.

In Danish (translated by N. K. Bredal), Copenhagen 15 February 1775.

In Dutch, Amsterdam September 1783; there are printed Dutch versions by H. Asschenbergh, 1777; by J. T. Neyts (n.d.); by J. A. Backer, 1785; and by P. J. Kasteleyn, 1786.

In Russian (translated by V. Levshin), Moscow, Prince Volkonsky's 9 March 1788.

In Swedish (translated by A. M. Malmstedt), Stockholm 27 July 1791.

(For a German opera on the same subject, see Benda's *Walder*, 1776.)

COIGNET and J. J. ROUSSEAU: *Pygmalion*

May. Lyons

Text by J. J. Rousseau (*Scène lyrique*). One act.

The earliest account of this first "melodrame" or "monodrame" is contained in Coignet's letter to the *Mercure de France*, January 1771 (in answer to a report that the whole of *Pygmalion* was composed as well as written by Rousseau):

"... mais ce n'est point un opéra: il l'a intitulé, Scène Lyrique. Les paroles ne se chantent point, & la Musique ne sert qu'à remplir les intervalles des repos nécessaires à la déclamation. ... Je dois cependant à l'exacte vérité d'annoncer, que dans les vingt-six ritournelles qui composent la Musique de ce drame, il y en a deux que M. Rousseau a faites lui-même. Je n'aurois pas besoin de les indiquer à quiconque verra ou entendra cet ouvrage; mais comme tout le monde ne sera pas à portée d'en juger, par la difficulté de représenter ce spectacle, je déclare que l'Andante de l'ouverture, & que le premier morceau de l'interlocution qui caractérise le travail de Pygmalion, appartiennent à M. Rousseau. . . ."

After private performances at Lyons, Hôtel de Ville, and Paris (at Madame de Brionne's), *Pygmalion* was publicly produced at the Comédie-Française, Paris, on 30 October 1775; given there once 11 September 1780, with new music by Baudron (in place of Coignet's share).

Revived at the Variétés amusantes 2 April 1793; Th. de l'Egalité 11 October 1794; Th. de la Cité 26 September 1805.

Parody by Guillemain Arlequin, *Marchand de Poupées ou le Pygmalion moderne*, Variétés amusantes 24 May 1779.

In French also given at: Brussels 1772; Venice, S.Sam. Carnival 1774; Hague 29 January 1774; Milan, T.R.D. 1775; Palermo 1776; Brescia 1776; Warsaw April 1777; St. Petersburg 13 July 1777 (privately); Cassel and Dresden 1779; Naples 1781; Hamburg June 1782; Gothenburg 29 April 1783; Madrid January 1788; New York 9 (Sonneck) or 10 (Odell) November 1790 (perhaps in English) and 3 March 1796 (in French); Vienna 4 January 1791; Charleston, S.C. 8 February 1794; Copenhagen 1805; Berlin 16 August 1808 and 13 April 1832.

In Polish, Warsaw 23 November 1777 (translated by T. K. Wegierski); there is another printed Polish version by J. Baudouin (n.d.).

In German (translated by O. H. von Gemmingen), Mannheim 29 March 1778; German versions of Rousseau's text were set by Aspelmayr, Schweitzer, Benda, etc. (see 1779).

For Italian versions, see Cimadoro's setting, 1790.

Spanish versions by P. Suárez y Pánez, and by J. D. Rojo, both published 1788; by F. Duran, published (3rd edition) 1816.

Anonymous English version published 1779. In the preface there is an allusion to performances (in French) at Lord "Villers" (Villiers's?) private theatre at Boulney (?), with Le Texier as Pygmalion, and Miss Hodges (to whom the translation is dedicated) as Galatea. There is another English version, by William Mason, written in 1775 but not published until 1811 (in Vol. II of his *Works*).

Russian version by V. I. Maikov published 1779.

Dutch versions published 1788 (anonymous), 1790 (by J. van Walré) and 1796 (by J. van Balen).

Danish version by N. T. Bruun published 1814.

E. Istel's theory (see Beihefte of the *I.M.S.*, Vol. I, 1901) that there exists a second version of *Pygmalion* wholly composed by Rousseau, has not been generally accepted. There was a scenic revival of the Berlin score (according to Istel, Rousseau's setting), at Munich on 4 May 1904 (with an older German translation by G. von Leon, originally published 1788). The Coignet-Rousseau version was last revived at the Comédie-Française, Paris 29 June 1912 (music revised by L. Léon and O. Letorey).

JOMMELLI: *Armida abbandonata*

30 May. Naples, S.C.

Text by F. S. de' Rogati (after Tasso). Three acts.

One of Jommelli's best works. Lisbon 31 March 1773; Florence, P. 1775; revived Naples 13 August 1780 (last Jommelli production in Italy). Mozart attended one of the 1770 performances at Naples.

GASSMANN: *La Contessina*

3 September. Neustadt, Moravia

Text (founded on an earlier libretto of the same title by Goldoni), generally attributed to M. Coltellini (who is, for instance, mentioned as the author in the Milan and London librettos); but according to Lazzeri (*La Vita . . . di Calzabigi*, 1907, p.215) and G. Ortolani (in the City of Venice edition of the works of Goldoni, Vol. XXVII, 1929, p.159) it was written by R. de' Calzabigi (MS of the libretto preserved; see also H. Michel in *Gluck-Jahrbuch*, IV, 1918, p.113). Three acts.

First performed at Neustadt (Uničov), Moravia, at a meeting of the German Emperor, Joseph II and King Frederick II of Prussia. Subsequently performed (in Italian) at Vienna 1770; Dresden 2 January 1772 (with additional music by Schuster); Florence, T. Cocomero Spring 1772; Turin, T. Carignano Autumn 1772 and Lisbon Carnival 1774 as *Il Superbo deluso*; London 11 January 1774; Milan, T.R.D. Autumn 1774; Modena, T. di Corte, November 1774; Trieste Carnival 1775; Copenhagen 26 March 1778; Bologna Summer 1778 (pasticcio, additions from Astaritta and Cimarosa); Parma Carnival 1779 (pasticcio); Rimini Carnival 1780 (same pasticcio as at Bologna).

Successful also in different German versions; as *Das gräfliche Fräulein* (translated by L. Schmidt) Prague Summer 1783; Nuremberg 25 August 1784; Cologne 14 November 1786. As *Die junge Gräfin* (translated by J. A. Hiller), Riga 14 September 1784. As *Die Gräfin oder Der übel-angebrachte Stolz*, Vienna, Leop. 30 May 1786; revived there 28 March 1797 and 16 January 1803 as *Johann in sechs Gestalten*.

The score was printed in *Denkmäler der Tonkunst in Österreich* (1919), in J. A. Hiller's translation, edited by R. Haas.

The opera was revived at Klagenfurt 18 March 1924 and Mannheim 20 September 1924 (revised by L. K. Mayer).

E. W. WOLF: *Das Rosenfest*

4 September. Weimar

Text by G. E. Heermann (founded on a French libretto by Favart, produced with music by Blaise, Duni, and Philidor at Fontainebleau 25 October 1769 and at the C.I., Paris 14 December 1769). Three acts.

Wolf's most successful Singspiel. Leipzig 21 September 1770; Berlin 2 July 1771; Hanover 12 July 1773; Hamburg 1773, etc. In German also, St. Petersburg 1 February 1778.

313

PACHECO: *En Casa de Nadie no se meta Nadie o El buen Marido*

28 September. Madrid, T. del Principe

Text by R. de la Cruz. Two acts.

Early *zarzuela jocosa*. Score preserved.

(The proverbial title freely translated means *Mind your own Business; or, The good Husband.*) Pacheco's only work for the stage. See J. Subirá, *La Musica en la Casa de Alba* (1927), p.335.

GRÉTRY: *Les deux Avares*

27 October. Fontainebleau

Text by C. G. Fenouillot de Falbaire. Two acts.

After two private performances publicly produced at the C.I., Paris on 6 December of the same year, and, with alterations, 6 June 1773.

In French also, Brussels 1771; Copenhagen 1772; Leghorn 8 June 1773; Hague 20 February 1774; Liége 19 November 1775; Vienna 10 January 1776; Florence September 1776; Stuttgart 14 December 1776; Warsaw 1776; Geneva 7 February 1784; Cassel 20 February 1784, etc. St. Petersburg 18 November 1800.

In German (translated by J. H. Faber), Frankfort 1771 (libretto printed in that year; performance not recorded); Vienna, Kä. May 1776 and B. 12 May 1779 (revived Vienna, W. January 1805, translated by J. von Seyfried, with additional music by A. J. Fischer); Munich 30 June 1776; Gotha 11 September 1776; Dresden May 1777; Pressburg August 1777; Hamburg 26 February 1778; Augsburg 9 July 1779; Cologne 22 June 1780; Bonn 3 December 1780; Riga 20 December 1782; Carlsruhe 22 April 1785; Berlin 11 December 1787 (revived 2 August 1858); Budapest 8 January 1812.

In Danish (translated by N. K. Bredal), Copenhagen 29 October 1774.

In Swedish (translated by C. Manderström), Stockholm 15 May 1778; Gothenburg 12 March 1782 (with additional music by B. Schindler).

In Polish (translated by J. Baudouin), Warsaw 25 September 1781.

314

In Russian (translated by V. G. Voroblevsky), Kouskovo *c.*1780; (translated by F. V. Gensh), Moscow 5 March 1783; (translated by Z. Krizhanovsky) St. Petersburg 17 July 1789.

In Dutch, Amsterdam 9 May 1772. There are three printed Dutch translations, by J. T. Neyts (n.d.), J. F. Cammaert (1772) and B. Ruloffs (1787).

An English adaptation by K. O'Hara (*The Two Misers*), music by Dibdin, was produced in London, C.G. 21 January 1775; (also Dublin 1781 with the sub-title *The Mufti's Ghost*); Baltimore 14 March 1783; New York 17 July 1786; and Philadelphia 9 April 1791. There are also German and Italian adaptations. When, 90 years later, Agnelli, a pupil of Donizetti, set the original text again, he kept parts of Grétry's music (Marseilles 22 March 1860; Brussels 26 April 1867). Grétry's opera was revived at:

PARIS, O.C. 23 June 1893 (in French).

CARLSRUHE 2 October 1894 (in German).

MOSCOW 1909 (in Russian).

CASSEL 1926 (in German).

GENEVA March 1932 (in French, by students).

VERSAILLES 12 May 1939 (in French; by pupils of the Paris Conservatoire at the Th. Montansier).

GLUCK: *Paride e Elena*

3 November. Vienna, B.

Text by R. de' Calzabigi (the third and last libretto he wrote for Gluck; but see note on Salieri's *Les Danaides*, 1784). Five acts.

Unsuccessful; outside Vienna only given at Naples [17 December] 1777. Khevenhüller wrote in his diary " . . . welche aber wegen ihres ungleichen und in etwas wunderlichen Gusto nicht besondere Approbation gefunden hat".

Revived Prague 9 February 1901 and Hamburg 11 March 1905 (in German; revised by J. Stransky, in a reduced 2-act version). Again Tübingen 22 June 1937 (in concert form) and Weimar 30 November 1937 (on the stage).

(Date of first performance 3 November, not 30 November as sometimes stated.)

GRÉTRY: *L'Amitié à l'Épreuve*

13 November. Fontainebleau

Text by C. S. Favart and C. H. F. de Voisenon (founded on a tale by Marmontel). Two acts.

Paris, C.I. 24 January 1771. Reduced to one act: Versailles 29 December 1775 and Paris, C.I. 1 January 1776. Enlarged again (3 acts); Fontainebleau 24 October 1786 and Paris, C.I. 30 October 1786 (as *Les vrais Amis ou L'Amitié à l'Épreuve*). In French also, Brussels 1771; Copenhagen 1772; Berlin 1773; Hague 29 January 1774; Liége 6 January 1776; Cassel 3 April 1784.

In German (translated by J. H. Faber), Frankfort 29 April 1772; (translated by H. A. O. Reichard), Gotha 22 November 1775; Munich 1775; Amsterdam 1776; Dresden 1777; Mannheim 19 May 1778; Regensburg 21 January 1780; Berlin 12 February 1780; Vienna, B. 22 January 1781 (translated by G. Stefanie?); Bonn 2 April 1782; Münster 22 July 1782; Hamburg 30 December 1782.

In Danish (translated by N. K. Bredal), Copenhagen 25 October 1775.

In Russian (translated by V. G. Voroblevsky), Kouskovo 10 July 1779.

A Dutch version by J. T. Neyts was published about 1772; another Dutch version, by B. Ruloffs, was published in 1782.

An anonymous English adaptation called *The Peruvian* with new music by J. Hook was produced at C. G., London 18 March 1786.

The opera was revived at Erfurt May 1938 (in German, adapted by B. Laass).

MOZART: *Mitridate, Re di Ponto*

26 December. Milan, T.R.D.

Text by V. A. Cigna-Santi (founded on G. Parini's Italian translation of Racine's tragedy, and first set to music by Q. Gasparini in 1767). Three acts.

The first opera Mozart wrote for the Italian stage. Successful; ran for 20 nights, but never revived.

1771

GAZZANIGA: *La Locanda*

Carnival. Venice, S. Moisè

Text by G. Bertati. Three acts.

One of Gazzaniga's most popular works; given all over Italy and, in Italian, also at Lisbon 1772; Dresden 1772; Vienna 22 September 1772; Munich Carnival 1773; Trieste Carnival 1773; Ljubljana Carnival 1773; Cadiz July 1773; Bastia, Corsica 1775; Copenhagen 20 December 1775 (Danish translation in the libretto by R. Soelberg); Klagenfurt Spring 1778; Graz Summer 1778; Eszterháza 22 November 1778; St. Petersburg 6 January 1779.

Also given as *Il Matrimonio per Inganno* at Pavia June 1773; Warsaw 1774; Eszterháza c. 1775; as *Il Re dei Mamalucchi* at Prague 1775; Varese Autumn 1778; as *Il Mamalucco* at Pesaro Carnival 1776.

PICCINNI: *Le finte Gemelle*

2 January. Rome, Valle

Text by G. Petrosellini. Two acts.

In Italy also given as *Le due finte Gemelle* and as *Le Germane in Equivoco* (Sinigaglia Summer 1774); last revived Pesaro Carnival 1800. In Italian also given at Vienna 20 April 1772 (with additions); Mannheim 7 November 1772; Dresden 2 January 1773; Munich Carnival 1773; Lisbon Summer 1773 (in an enlarged 3-act version); Paris, O. 11 June 1778 (opening night of the second Italian buffo company in Paris, led by Piccinni; performed there on the same bill with Mozart's ballet, *Les petits Riens*, which was recovered by V. Wilder in 1872); Warsaw Spring 1784.

MYSLIVECZEK: *Motezuma*

January. Florence, P.

Text by V. A. Cigna-Santi (first composed by Majo in 1765). Three acts.

This opera by the Czech composer was revived at the State Conservatory, Prague in Summer 1931.

MARTINI: *L'Amoureux de quinze Ans* ou *La double Fête*

18 April. Paris, C.I.

Text by P. Laujon. Three acts.

Martini's first successful opera. Originally written for Chantilly, to celebrate the wedding of the Duc de Bourbon, but not performed there. Given Fontainebleau 12 October 1771; revived Paris, Fa. 29 October 1794; in the French provinces until 1812.

In French also given at Brussels 2 September 1774; Haarlem 7 July 1774; Cassel 1780 and 25 August 1784; Smolna 1783.

In German, Vienna, B. 29 December 1778 (translated by G. Stephanie, according to contemporary accounts; by L. A. Hoffmann, according to Goedeke); Mayence 3 February 1790 (translated by C. A. Vulpius). There is a printed Dutch translation by J. T. Neyts (n.d.).

J. A. HILLER: *Der Aerndtekranz*

Spring. Leipzig

Text by C. F. Weisse. Three acts.

Successful in Germany: Berlin 17 February 1772; Königsberg 1773; Hanover 17 June 1773; Hamburg 4 August 1773; Dresden 8 January 1776; Vienna, Kä. Spring 1776, etc. In German also, Amsterdam 1776; Riga 8 December 1784; Lucerne 1787. Last given at Berlin 4 October 1794; Breslau 2 July 1802; Leipzig 18 March 1805.

The exact date of the first performance is unknown, but it must have been between 3 April (when Koch's company came from Weimar) and 29 May (when they went to Berlin).

A song from this Singspiel is the theme of Max Reger's *Hiller-Variationen*, op. 100.

SALIERI: *Armida*

2 June. Vienna, B.

Text by M. Coltellini (after Tasso); first set by G. Scarlatti, 1766. Three acts.

Also given at:

COPENHAGEN 20 November 1773 (in Italian; Danish translation in the libretto by F. A. Friis) and 30 January 1781 (in Danish, translated by A. G. Thoroup).

ST. PETERSBURG 1774 (in Italian); Russian translation by I. A. Dmitrevsky and French translation by Deville published on that occasion.

HAMBURG Winter 1775–76 (in concert form).

MAYENCE 1783–84 (in German, translated by C. F. Cramer).

BRUNSWICK 1785 (in Italian).

BERLIN 16 April 1787 (in concert form, in German, translated by C. F. Cramer).

WINTERTHUR 1 December 1790 (in concert form; frequently revived there until 1808).

DANZIG May 1798 and 5 March 1800 (in concert form).

ROELLIG: *Clarisse* oder *Das unbekannte Dienstmädgen*

8 October. Hamburg

Text by J. C. Bock (founded on Marmontel's dramatization of his story, *La Bergère des Alpes*). Three acts.

Successful in North Germany; Lübeck 9 December 1772; Hanover 30 April 1773, etc.

HASSE: *Ruggiero* o vero *L'eroica Gratitudine*

16 October. Milan, T.R.D.

Text by P. Metastasio. Three acts and licenza.

Hasse's last opera. Also given at Naples, S.C. 20 January 1772.

MOZART: *Ascanio in Alba*

17 October. Milan, T.R.D.

Text by G. Parini (*Festa teatrale*). Two acts.

These two works, the last opera of the 72-years-old Hasse and the youthful serenata of the 15-years-old Mozart, were written for the wedding of the Archduke Ferdinand and the Princess Maria Ricciarda Beatrice of Modena. These two days in October 1771 may be said to separate two epochs of opera. The often quoted two sayings, referring to this event, may be once more repeated here; Hasse's (apocryphal) words, "Questo ragazzo ci farà dimenticar tutti", and Leopold Mozart's letter to his wife (19 October 1771), "Mir ist leid, die Serenata des Wolfgang hat die opera von Hasse so niedergeschlagen, dass ich es nicht beschreiben kann".

GRÉTRY: *L'Ami de la Maison*

26 October. Fontainebleau

Text by J. F. Marmontel. Three acts.

Publicly performed Paris, C.I. 14 May 1772 (not 2 December 1771, as indicated in one issue of the libretto; nor 14 March 1772) and given there until 1829.

Outside Paris given at:

BRUSSELS 1772 (in French).

FRANKFORT 1772 (in German, translated by J. H. Faber).

COPENHAGEN 1773 (in French) and 23 October 1776 (in Danish, translated by N. K. Bredal).

VIENNA, KÄ. May 1776 and B. 26 May 1778 (in German).

TURIN Spring 1776 (in French).

WARSAW 1776 (in French) and 18 August 1781 (in German).

LIÉGE 7 January 1777 (in French).

GOTHA 8 August 1777 (in German, new translation by H. A. O. Reichard).

MUNICH November 1778 (in German).

CASSEL 1780 and 7 June 1784 (in French).

BERLIN 16 October 1780 (in German).

RIGA 3 June 1783 (in German).

GENEVA 4 May 1785 (in French).

Russian translation by V. G. Voroblevsky published Moscow 1779.

GRÉTRY: *Zémire et Azor*

9 November. Fontainebleau

Text by J. F. Marmontel (founded on P. C. Nivelle de La Chaussée's comedy *Amour par Amour*, 1742). *Comédie Ballet.* Four acts.

Subsequently performed in public, Paris, C.I. 16 December 1771. One of Grétry's most successful works; given in Paris until 1836 and revived at the O.C., 29 June 1846 (re-orchestrated by Adam) and 15 September 1862.

Zémire et Azor soon became an international success. Given at:

BRUSSELS 1772 (in French).

FRANKFORT 23 May 1772 (in German, translated by J. H. Faber).

MANNHEIM Summer 1772 (in German) and January 1776 (in Italian, translated by M. Verazi).

COPENHAGEN 1772 (in French) and 7 January 1777 (in Danish, translated by N. K. Bredal).

HAGUE 1774 (in German).

LIÉGE 20 November 1774 (in French).

HANOVER 1774 (in French).

BRUNSWICK 1774 (in French).

HAMBURG December 1774 (in French) and 27 August 1777 (in German).

MOSCOW 16 June 1775 (in Russian, translated by M. V. Sushkova).

VIENNA, SCHÖNBRUNN 10 October 1775 (in French) and Kä. May 1776 and B. 13 October 1779 (in German); revived Leop. 21 January 1790; W. 8 January 1818 (music arranged by Seyfried).

GOTHA 29 January 1776 (in German, translated by H. A. O. Reichard); another German version, by Moritz August von Thümmel, was published in 1776 (composed by Neefe, performed Leipzig 5 March 1776); another anonymous one (possibly by Bock) at Münster 1777; still another in a vocal score, translated and edited by Hiller 1783.

TURIN Spring 1776; Florence September 1776; Parma, at Comte de Flavigny's Carnival 1782 (in French).

WARSAW October 1776 (in French); 13 October 1781 (in German); and 9 May 1782 (in Polish, translated by Kuszewski).

AMSTERDAM 1776 (in German); January 1784 (in Dutch, translated by P. Pijpers); there are earlier printed Dutch versions by J. T. Neyts (n.d.) and B. H. v. A. (Brussels 1772).

LONDON, D.L. 5 December 1776 (in English, adapted by G. Collier, music arranged by Linley); Hm. 23 February 1779 (in Italian, Verazi's translation); revived 8 March 1781 (Verazi's translation altered by C. F. Badini)

and 23 July 1796 (new translation by L. da Ponte). Collier and Linley's version revived C. G. 1812, with additions by Bishop, Welsh and Cooke.

ST. PETERSBURG 27 June 1777 (in French); 10 August 1777 (in Italian, at Oranienbaum palace); 19 January 1778 (in German); and 8 October 1784 (in Russian).

DROTTNINGHOLM 22 July 1778 and Stockholm 12 October 1778 (in Swedish, translated by A. M. Malmstedt, music adapted by D. L. Wasenholtz and P. Frigelius).

CASSEL 1778 and 15 December 1783 (in French).

BERLIN 16 October 1778 (in German); also Munich c. December 1778; Augsburg 10 August 1779; Cologne 1781; Hanover 15 January 1781, etc.

PRESSBURG 7 February 1780 (in German).

PRAGUE 1781 (in German).

GRAZ Carnival 1782 (in Italian).

RIGA 14 October 1782 (in German).

GENEVA 7 January 1784 (in French).

BUDAPEST 1787 (in German).

NEW YORK 1 June 1787 (in English, Linley's adaptation).

PHILADELPHIA 28 July 1787 (in English, Linley's adaptation).

MADRID 26 January 1791 (in Italian).

HAVANA 17 December 1791 (in French?)

CHARLESTON, S.C. 6 August 1794 and Philadelphia 1 June 1798 (in French).

BOSTON 31 March 1797 (in English; not Linley's adaptation).

LISBON Spring 1797 (in Italian).

DUBLIN 1801 (Linley's version).

Zémire et Azor was revived at Brussels 12 May 1909, and Liége 19 May 1930. In English, London, Arts Theatre Club 12 May 1935 and Fortune Th. 23 April 1940 (by amateurs, music arranged by Leighton Lucas).

For German operas on the same subject, see 1776 (Baumgarten) and 1819 (Spohr). A German sequel *Der Ring der Liebe oder Zemirens und Azorens Ehestand*, with music by Umlauff, was produced at Vienna 3 December 1786.

NEEFE: *Die Apotheke*

13 December. Berlin

Text by J. J. Engel (founded on Goldoni's *Lo Speziale*, see 1755, and originally written for Hiller). Two acts.

The first new Singspiel to be produced at Koch's "Theater in der Behrenstrasse", Berlin. Rostock 13 November 1772; Bonn 10 April 1782; Bremen 20 November 1782; Carlsruhe 17 November 1784, etc. In German also, St. Petersburg 26 February 1778.

DELLER: *Il Maestro di Capella*

31 December. Vienna, B.

Text by A. Palomba (originally called *Orazio* and first set to music by Auletta in 1737; see col. 187). Three acts.

Deller's best-known work; of the music only parts are extant.

Der Kapellmeister oder der verwirrte Opern-Verwalter von Neapel, Cologne Spring 1772, was probably a German version of this; also as *Der verwirrte Operndirektor*, Hague 1774.

1772

GAZZANIGA: *L'Isola di Alcina*

Carnival. Venice, S. Moisè

Text by G. Bertati (after Ariosto). Three acts.

One of Gazzaniga's greatest successes; given in many Italian towns and at Lisbon Autumn 1772; Dresden 20 March 1773; Schwetzingen May 1773; Vienna 4 April 1774; Bastia, Corsica Autumn 1774; Prague 1775; London 28 March 1776 and 17 April 1777; Copenhagen 6 March 1777 (Danish translation in the libretto by R. Soelberg); Dublin 12 April 1777; Graz Autumn 1778; Eszterháza 1779 (with one additional air by Haydn).

Given at Warsaw 10 June 1775 (in Italian) and 8 March 1790 (in Polish, translated by L. Pierozyński).

SACCHINI: *Armida*

Carnival. Milan, T.R.D.

Text by G. de Gamerra (after Tasso). Three acts.

In Italian also given at Florence, T. in Via S. Maria Autumn 1772; in London 22 April 1780 (as *Rinaldo*) and revived there 17 February 1791 at the opening of the new Pantheon Opera House in Oxford Street (text altered by G. Tonioli, music arranged by Mazzinghi); Lisbon 1798.

In French (as *Renaud*, adapted by J. J. Leboeuf, who used for his French text Pellegrin's libretto *Renaud*, set by Desmarets in 1722; music arranged by Framery), Paris, O. 28 February 1783 (given there 156 times until 1800 and revived 16 March 1815); Liége 24 January 1784; Copenhagen 1786 (in concert form).

(Leboeuf's version was re-translated into Italian by G. Cinque for the Russian composer P. Skokov, whose setting was produced at Naples, S.C. 4 November 1788.)

ZANETTI: *Le Lavarandine*

Carnival. Rome, Capr.

Text by F. Mari. Two acts.

The most popular opera of this otherwise unimportant composer and the only one which is still extant.

In Italian also, Lisbon 1773 and Dresden December 1774.

Successful in a German version by J. C. Bock: Hamburg 17 May 1779; Leipzig 6 October 1779; Frankfort 25 April 1781; Vienna, B. 11 July 1781; Pyrmont 15 July 1781; Bonn 4 November 1781; Riga 18 July 1783; Carlsruhe 29 October 1785; Berlin 11 December 1786; Prague 1790, etc.

SALIERI: *La Fiera di Venezia*

29 January. Vienna, B.

Text by G. G. Boccherini. Three acts.

In Italian also given at Mannheim 22 November 1772; Bonn 1774; Warsaw 25 February 1775; Dresden 4 November 1775; Turin, T. Carignano Autumn 1776; Copenhagen 10 April 1777 (Danish translation in the libretto by R. Soelberg);

Graz Summer 1778; Florence, P. Spring 1779; Milan 21 August 1779 (at the inauguration of the new T. della Canobbiana); Kremsmünster 1780; Munich Carnival 1786.

In German (translated by H. C. Pleissner), Hamburg 16 July 1781; Frankfort 14 April 1784; Bremen 13 December 1784; Schwedt 30 May 1786; Cassel 2 March 1787; Hanover 1 February 1790; Breslau 19 March 1790; Budapest 6 August 1790; Vienna, Leop. 13 July 1791; Berlin 25 February 1799, etc. Another German version, by J. N. Rothmann, was published c.1780 (n.d.).

In Russian, St. Petersburg 25 May 1791; Moscow 26 November 1795 (revived 6 May 1807 and 4 June 1821).

SARTI: *Deucalion og Pyrrha*
19 March. Copenhagen

Text by C. A. Thielo, airs by N. K. Bredal (based on a French comedy by G. F. Poullain de Saint-Foix). One act.

The most successful of Sarti's Danish operas; given at Copenhagen 20 times until 1785 and in a Swedish version by W. von Rosenheim at Stockholm 21 October 1790. The music does not seem to have been preserved.

MOZART: *Il Sogno di Scipione*
1 May. Salzburg

Metastasio's text (first set to music by Predieri, see 1735). One act.

Mozart's setting of this *Serenata drammatica* was written to celebrate the installation of the new Archbishop of Salzburg, Hieronymus von Colloredo. (Date of first performance according to A. Kutscher; E. Anderson gives 29 April.)

E. W. WOLF: *Die Dorfdeputierten*
15 June. Berlin

Text by G. E. Heermann (founded on Goldoni's comedy, *Il Feudatario*). Three acts.

Successful in Germany; Vienna, Kä. June 1776; in German also, St. Petersburg 5 February 1778. A Hungarian translation by Szerelemhegyi was published before 1796.

SCHWEITZER: *Die Dorfgala*
30 June. Weimar

Text by F. W. Gotter. Two acts.

Also in 2 acts: Hamburg 21 January 1779.

Enlarged to 3 acts: Gotha 9 December 1774; Leipzig 5 May 1775; Altenburg 1 September 1775; Dresden February 1776; Berlin 25 March 1784; Schwedt 29 August 1785.

Reduced to 1 act: Frankfort 6 September 1777; Mayence 1778; Mannheim 26 December 1779; Bonn 26 May 1780; Cologne 29 June 1780; Pyrmont 1 August 1781; Cassel 10 September 1781; Berlin 16 July 1802.

In German also, St. Petersburg 27 August 1778.

GALVÁN: *Las Foncarraleras*
(The Maids of Fuencarral)
25 September. Madrid, T. del Principe

Text by R. de la Cruz. Two acts.

One of the few extant examples of Spanish 18th-century zarzuela.

DÉZÈDE: *Julie*
28 September. Paris, C.I.

Text by J. M. Boutet de Monvel. Three acts.

Dézède's first opera. In French also, Brussels 1773; Haarlem 28 June 1774; Vienna 1775; Moscow August 1775; Liége 16 January 1776; Cassel 30 June 1784.

In German (first translated by J. H. Faber; there is another German version by G. F. W. Grossmann), Frankfort 18 April 1776; Amsterdam 1776 (there is also a printed Dutch version by J. T. Neyts, n.d.); Munich 29 January 1779; Bonn 21 February 1779; Vienna, B. 23 August 1779; Frankfort 4 April 1780; Hamburg January 1782; Bremen 6 October 1783; Cologne Spring 1787; Brunswick 29 June 1789; Hanover 19 April 1790.

In Danish (translated by J. H. Wessel), Copenhagen 7 November 1783.

In Swedish (translated by C. Manderström), Stockholm 25 March 1786; Gothenburg 3 November 1796.

(Date of first performance according to *Mercure de France*; the libretto gives 22 September 1772.)

MOZART: *Lucio Silla*

26 December. Milan, T.R.D.

Text by G. de Gamerra, with alterations by Metastasio. Three acts.

The last opera Mozart wrote in Italy.

Revived Prague 14 December 1929 (German version by A. Rudolph).

1773

ANFOSSI: *L'Incognita perseguitata*

9 January. Rome, T. delle Dame

Text by G. Petrosellini (first set to music by Piccinni in 1764). Three acts.

Although Piccinni's setting was fairly successful (outside Italy also given at Lisbon 31 March 1766 and Dresden 3 December 1768) the glory of *L'Incognita perseguitata* remains with Anfossi's music; this opera was his first great success; given at Milan Summer 1773 and all over Italy; at Bologna Autumn 1773 and Carnival 1786 and Naples, T.N. Autumn 1778, as *Giannetta*; at Forlì 1779 as *La Giannetta perseguitata*. Also given at:

VIENNA 31 August 1773 (as *Metilda ritrovata*).

MANNHEIM 21 November 1773.

DRESDEN 4 January 1774 (as *La Giannetta perseguitata*).

MUNICH Carnival 1774.

TRIESTE Carnival 1775.

WARSAW 23 March 1775 (as *La Metilde ritrovata*).

COPENHAGEN 1 November 1775 (as *La Giannetta*; Danish translation in the libretto by R. Soelberg).

ESZTERHÁZA 1779 (as *Metilde ritrovata*).

ST. PETERSBURG 10 July 1779 (as *La Giannetta*).

BARCELONA 30 May 1786.

In French (translated by P. L. Moline, music adapted by J. N. A. Le Froid de Méreaux), Fontainebleau 25 October 1776 (or, according to a later edition of the libretto, 12 November 1776; an intended production at the C.I., Paris, did not

take place); a French version by C. Compan was produced at Versailles on 8 June 1781; another French adaptation, by B. F. de Rozoy (music arranged by J. B. Rochefort) was given at Paris, O. 21 September 1781 and at Cassel 19 July 1784. In French also Aachen 17 August 1794.

In German (translated by G. Stephanie), Vienna, B. 21 August 1780 (revived 8 April 1795); and probably Schwedt 21 April 1786. A German translation by Stierle is mentioned in the *Gothaer Theater-Kalendar*, 1783, p.210 (probably for Augsburg 15 May 1780, *Die verfolgte Unbekannte*).

In Spanish (translated by Fermin del Rey), Madrid 10 September 1787.

UTTINI: *Thetis och Pelée*

18 January. Stockholm

Text by J. Wellander (founded on a play by King Gustaf III). Five acts.

The first Swedish grand opera. Given 30 October 1775 in a reduced 3-act version; revived 13 February 1791. One act was revived on 18 January 1923 at the 150th anniversary festival of the Stockholm opera-house.

A parody by C. I. Hallman, with music by C. Stenborg, called *Petis och Thelée*, was produced at Stockholm 27 September 1779 and Gothenburg 15 November 1779.

ANDRÉ: *Der Töpfer*

22 January. Hanau, near Frankfort

Text by the composer. One act.

André's first opera.

Frankfort 29 October 1773 (revived in 2 acts 7 November 1780); Weimar 20 January 1774; Gotha 29 July 1774; Leipzig 14 October 1774; Berlin 14 February 1775, etc.; Dessau 4 December 1776; Hamburg 1778; Salzburg 8 January 1781; Munich 9 January 1781; Regensburg 1781; Dresden July 1782; Bremen 30 October 1783.

Goethe was so much impressed by the little work that he wrote his first Singspiel, *Erwin and Elmire*, for André (1775).

GRÉTRY: *Le Magnifique*

4 March. Paris, C.I.

Text by J. M. Sedaine (founded on a tale by La-fontaine). Three acts.

In French also, Versailles 26 March 1773 (the libretto says 19 March); Hague 27 January 1774; Vienna 1775; Liége 20 January 1776; Turin Spring 1776; Cassel 24 November 1783; Parma, at Comte de Flavigny's Carnival 1788; Brussels 8 March 1792; Gachina 31 October 1799; Moscow 31 December 1810.

In German (translated by J. H. Faber), Frankfort 27 April 1775; Vienna, B. 11 May 1776; Munich October 1778; Augsburg 29 March 1780; Carlsruhe 1781; Cologne December 1784.

A Dutch version, by J. T. Neyts, was published about 1775; another, by H. Asschenbergh in 1786.

SCHWEITZER: *Alceste*

28 May. Weimar

Text by C. M. Wieland. Five acts.

Intended by the authors as the first step towards a German national opera.[1] The vocal score was printed in 1774 and 1786, the full score in 1779. First performed by Seyler's troupe at Weimar and subsequently given at: Frankfort Spring 1774; Gotha 16 August 1774; Schwetzingen 13 August 1775; Altenburg 15 September 1775; Mannheim November 1775; Lucerne 1775; Königsberg 1776 (in concert form); Dresden 1776; Danzig 4 November 1777 (in concert form); Breslau 14 January 1779; Munich 1779; Berlin 31 May 1780; Hamburg 23 April 1781; Leipzig 8 August 1781; Magdeburg January 1782 (in concert form); Fürth 12 October 1782; Nuremberg 30 October 1782; Neustrelitz 28 April 1783; Passau 1 November 1783; Bozen 19 March 1784; Vienna, Neustift 1784; Mayence 18 November 1785; Cassel 1785 if not earlier; Prague 1792. Italian translation by G. U. Pagani Cesa published 1830.

[1] "... das erste Stück unserer Bühne in Metastasios Geschmack". (C. H. Schmid, *Chronologie des deutschen Theaters*, 1775.)

A parody, *Euridice*, by F. H. von Einsiedel, with music by Seckendorf, was performed at Weimar 3 September 1779.

The opera was revived at Weimar on 9 June 1933.

SALIERI: *La Locandiera*

8 June. Vienna, B.

Text by D. Poggi (founded on Goldoni's comedy). Three acts.

In Italian also, Warsaw 12 January 1775; Florence 27 July 1775; Dresden 1776; Copenhagen 30 October 1777; Paris, Th. Feydeau 29 February 1792 (as *La Locandiera scaltra*, with additions by Cherubini).

In German (translated by L. Zehnmark), Vienna 12 November 1782; Pressburg 2 September 1785.

DÉZÈDE: *L'Erreur d'un Moment,* ou *La Suite de Julie*

14 June. Paris, C.I.

Text by J. M. Boutet de Monvel (as the title says, a sequel to *Julie*, by the same authors, see 1772). One act.

In French also Vienna 1775; Moscow 17 December 1775; Liége 19 January 1777 and Cassel 17 December 1783.

A German translation by J. M. Kellner, *Julie oder der kurze Irrthum*, was published at Wetzlar in 1777; performed Cologne 1779 (also with title *Das zerstörte Versprechen*).

In Russian (translated by A. Y. Khilkov), Moscow 1782.

In Swedish (translated by C. Manderström), Stockholm 4 November 1787; Gothenburg 13 March 1789.

Dutch version by J. T. Neyts printed (n.d.).

In 1805 the same libretto was set by the then 23-years-old Auber (his first work for the stage; produced by amateurs).

NAUMANN: *Armida*

June. Padua

Text by G. Bertati (after Tasso). Three acts.

Naumann's first greater success; in Italian also given at Prague 1776 and Vienna 15 October 1777.

In German (translated by J. C. Bock), Leipzig 6 July 1780; Dresden Winter 1780; Berlin 27 December 1782; Schwedt 2 December 1785; Breslau 24 January 1786.

HAYDN: *L'Infedeltà delusa*

26 July. Eszterháza

Librettist unknown (*Burletta per musica*). Two acts.

Revived Vienna 14 May 1930 (as *Liebe macht erfinderisch*, German version by H. Goja, music revised by G. Kassowitz).

GRÉTRY: *La Rosière de Salency*

23 October. Fontainebleau

Text by A. F. J. Masson de Pézay (*opéra lyri-comique*). Four acts.

Paris, C.I. 28 February 1774 and, in a reduced 3-act version (now called *pastorale*) 18 June 1774.

The date of the first, Fontainebleau, produc-tion, not hitherto recorded, is given in the original libretto (copy Paris, Bibliothèque Nationale).

In French also, Brussels 20 May 1774; Smolna 30 July 1775; Turin Spring 1776; Cassel 1777; Parma, at Comte de Flavigny's Carnival 1790; St. Petersburg 1798.

In German (translated by J. H. Faber), Frank-fort 1775; Augsburg 20 August 1779; Vienna 9 September 1779; Pressburg 3 April 1780; Co-logne 7 August 1780; Munich 11 September 1780; Bonn 18 October 1780; Pyrmont 17 July 1781; Regensburg 1781; Warsaw 15 September 1782; Bremen 15 October 1784; Hanover 22 January 1794.

In Italian (as *La Festa della Rosa*, translated by M. Verazi), Schwetzingen July 1776.

In Danish (translated by C. D. Biehl), Copen-hagen 4 September 1779, at Fredensborg Palace and 17 September 1779 at the Royal Theatre.

In Swedish (translated by C. J. Lindegren), Stockholm 31 January 1798.

Given as a pantomime at Charleston, S.C. on 1 July 1795.

There are printed Dutch versions by J. T. Neyts (n.d.), by B. D. A[sten] (1775), and by H. Ogelwight (1792).

Revived Moscow 14 May 1810 (in French).

MONSIGNY: *La belle Arsène*

6 November. Fontainebleau

Text by C. S. Favart (*comédie-féerie*; his last lib-retto), founded on Voltaire's poem *La Bégueule*. Three acts.

Given at Paris, C.I. 14 August 1775 in an enlarged 4-act version. Last revived Paris, O.C. 1 October 1794 and 21 September 1808.

In French also, Liége 18 February 1776; Brus-sels 19 February 1776, etc. Cassel 24 May 1777; Turin Spring 1778; Smolna 15 December 1782; Parma Carnival 1789; Cologne 1795–96; Mos-cow 15 May 1809; Berne 6 July 1809; Stock-holm June 1813.

In Danish (translated by T. C. Walter), Copen-hagen 30 January 1777 and (in a new translation by A. G. Thoroup) 4 September 1781 (at Fre-densborg Palace) and 10 December 1781 (at the Royal Theatre).

In German (translated by J. H. Faber), Düssel-dorf 27 November 1778; Mannheim 20 March 1779; Frankfort 15 April 1779; Cologne Sum-mer 1779; Berlin 25 August 1779 (translated by J. André); Bonn 9 March 1780; Munich 4 July 1780; Hamburg 27 October 1780; Hanover 8 January 1781; Warsaw 25 November 1781; Riga 30 September 1782 (first opera given at the new Vietinghoff theatre); Neustrelitz 5 May 1783; Bremen 1 December 1783; Schwedt 16 August 1785; Rostock 20 June 1786; Vienna, Kä. 4 Au-gust 1786; Cassel 24 January 1787; Pyrmont 22 July 1787; Dresden 29 May 1788.

In Swedish (translated by A. M. Malmstedt), Drottningholm 22 July 1779 and Stockholm 13 January 1780.

In Russian, St. Petersburg 1785 (revived 22 June 1815); Moscow January 1802 (revived 26 May 1806).

In Dutch (translated by B. Ruloffs), Amster-dam [10 October] 1788; there was another Dutch version, by J. T. Neyts, published (n.d.).

In Polish (translated by F. Zablocki), Warsaw 17 October 1788.

In Italian (translated by L. da Ponte), London 12 December 1795 (music arranged by Mazzinghi).

The vocal score of *La belle Arsène* was reprinted in 1909.

A parody, *La Lingère*, by Mague de Saint-Aubin, was produced at La Rochelle December 1777; Paris, Th. des Petits Comédiens du Bois de Boulogne July 1781; Saint-Cloud 21 October 1781.

HOLLY: *Der Kaufmann von Smyrna*

13 November. Berlin

Text by C. F. Schwan (founded on a comedy by Chamfort and first set to music by Vogler in 1771). One act.

The most successful of Holly's operas; given at Vienna, Kä. June 1776 as *Wohltaten gewinnen die Herzen* and B. 13 February 1781 as *Der Sklavenhändler von Smyrna*.

The same libretto was set by Stegmann and first performed in the same year, 1773, at Königsberg (exact date unknown) and elsewhere in Germany; also given at Copenhagen 2 January 1776 (in Danish, translated by P. T. Vandall; given there until 1817); in German, St. Petersburg 20 February 1778 and Riga 25 February 1785; Hamburg, as late as 24 July 1793 and 13 May 1808.

GOSSEC: *Sabinus*

4 December. Versailles

Text by M. P. G. de Chabanon (founded on his tragedy *Eponine*, 1762). Five acts.

Gossec's first *tragédie-lyrique* (unsuccessful). Paris, O. 22 February 1774.

GRÉTRY: *Céphale, et Procris*, ou *L'Amour conjugal*

30 December. Versailles

Text by J. F. Marmontel. Three acts.

Paris, O. 2 May 1775 and (with alterations) 23 May 1777.

In French also, Cassel 1783 (and again 26 April 1802; Germain translation by J. D. von Apell published on that occasion).

Revived Brussels 30 April 1930 (and again 8 September 1930 at the eighth I.S.C.M. festival).

1774

ANFOSSI: *La finta Giardiniera*

Carnival. Rome, T. delle Dame

Text by R. de' Calzabigi (the same libretto Mozart set to music in 1775; for a comparison of Anfossi's and Mozart's settings, see E. J. Dent, *Mozart's Operas*, p.45). Three acts.

In Italian also given at Würzburg [26 August] 1774; Dresden 7 February 1775; London 7 March 1775 (as *La Marchesa Giardiniera*, with additions by T. Giordani); Vienna 13 June 1775; Warsaw 17 December 1775; Paris, O. 12 November 1778; Eszterháza Autumn 1780; Lisbon Carnival 1786.

In German (as *Die edle Gärtnerin*) Frankfort 12 September 1782.

In French (translated by Balle), Paris, Th. de M. 5 February 1789.

In Polish (translated by W. Boguslawski), Warsaw 14 February 1790.

PICCINNI: *Alessandro nell'Indie*

12 January. Naples, S.C.

Metastasio's text (first set to music by Vinci in 1729). Three acts.

The best of Piccinni's Italian serious operas; revived at Naples, Fondo 12 January 1792 after the composer's return from Paris. (An earlier setting by Piccinni of the same libretto had been performed at Rome, Arg. 21 January 1758. Both scores extant.)

T. C. WALTER: *Den Prøvede Troskab* (Faithfulness Proved)

31 January. Copenhagen

Text by C. D. Biehl. Three acts.

Not the first Danish opera, but the first written by a Danish composer; given three times only.

PAISIELLO: *Il Duello*

Spring. Naples, T.N.

Text by G. B. Lorenzi. One act.

In Italian also given at Vienna 15 July 1775; Tsarskoye Selo 1782.

In French (as *Le Duel comique*, adapted and enlarged to 2 acts by P. L. Moline, additional music by J. N. A. Le Froid de Méreaux), Paris, C.I. 16 September 1776 and Fontainebleau 10 October 1777.

In German (translated by C. G. Neefe): Vienna, Kä. 17 April 1786; Mannheim 3 August 1786; Carlsruhe 6 January 1790; Budapest 18 July 1790.

In Polish, Wilna 16 May 1799.

Revived Taranto 26 November 1916 (music revised by C. De Nardis).

GLUCK: *Iphigénie en Aulide*

19 April. Paris, O.

Text by F. L. G. Lebland du Roullet (founded on Racine's tragedy). Three acts.

The first work Gluck wrote for the Paris Opéra. "Jamais le Public n'a montré tant d'empressement et d'enthousiasme que pour cet opéra qui doit faire époque dans la musique Françoise" (*Mercure de France*). Its success was interrupted after the 5th performance through the death of Louis xv. Resumed 10 January 1775 and given there 428 times until 1824; revived at the O.C. 18 December 1907.

A parody by J. E. Despréaux called *Momie* was given at Choisy in August 1778.

In French also, Lille 7 July 1782; Cassel 1782; Hamburg 1795; Ghent 1799; St. Petersburg 1801; Brunswick 1806.

In Swedish (translated by C. Manderström, music adapted by D. L. Wasenholtz and L. S. Lalin), Stockholm 29 December 1778 (with a prologue by Uttini, text by J. H. Kellgren).

In Dutch (translated by P. Pijpers), Amsterdam 1801.

In German (translated by J. D. Sander), Magdeburg 1790; Schwerin 3 January 1806; Munich 1807 (revived 29 January 1816, partly re-orchestrated by Winter); Vienna 14 December 1808;

Berlin 25 December 1809; Cassel 3 June 1819; Stuttgart 23 December 1820.

In 1846 Richard Wagner revised the opera by improving the translation, changing the orchestration and composing some new recitatives for the third act (into which he even introduced a new character, Artemis). This version was first produced at Dresden 24 February 1847 and given on many German stages (including Vienna 12 October 1867 and Berlin 11 June 1914). Also Strasbourg 11 March 1900. Revived Zurich 17 October 1936.

In Italian (translated by G. Schmidt), Naples, S.C. 15 August 1812.

In Danish (translated by A. Hertz; Wagner's version), Copenhagen 27 April 1861 and Christiania 20 October 1875.

In Czech (translated by J. Böhm) Prague 9 April 1872 (revived 29 May 1921). Given at Brussels for the first time as late as 26 April 1910 (in French) and even later in England and America: Oxford 20 November 1933 (in English, translated by J. Troutbeck); Philadelphia 22 February 1935 (in French); Glasgow 14 April 1937 (in English, by the Scottish National Academy of Music).

In Croatian, Zagreb 6 July 1933.

In Hungarian, Budapest October 1937.

ANFOSSI: *Il Geloso in Cimento*

25 May. Vienna, B.

Text by G. Bertati. Three acts.

Given also as *La Vedova galante* (Graz Winter 1779), *La Vedova scaltra* (Castelnuovo 1785) and as *La Vedova bizarra* (Naples, Fior. 1788). Reduced to 2 acts, Venice, S. Moisè Autumn 1784.

In Italian also, Venice, S. Sam. November 1774; Turin and Rome 1775, etc. Trieste May 1775; Dresden November 1775; Copenhagen 31 January 1776 (Danish translation in the libretto by R. Soelberg); Warsaw July 1776; Prague 1776; London 4 February 1777; Dublin 1778; Eszterháza 10 September 1778; Paris, O. 18 January 1779 (with additions by Giardini); St. Petersburg 13 April 1779; Brunswick 1781; Barcelona 12 June 1783; Cracow 2 May 1790.

In German (as *Die Eifersucht auf der Probe*, translated by J. J. Eschenburg), Hamburg 12 January 1781; Berlin 3 March 1781 (revived 29 August 1806); Vienna, Kä. 27 September 1783 and Leop. 22 March 1787; Bonn 6 July 1783; Riga 13 January 1784; Cologne Autumn 1784; Schwedt 22 November 1785; St. Petersburg 1785; Linz 18 April 1786; Cassel 12 March 1787; Hanover 7 June 1787; Prague 1787; Rostock 23 June 1788; Dresden July 1788; Munich May 1789; Pyrmont 10 July 1790; Amsterdam 1792; another German version, by L. Zehnmark, was used at Pressburg 12 June 1786 and Budapest 7 July 1790.

In Polish (translated by L. Pierozyński) Warsaw 15 July 1787.

JOMMELLI: *Il Trionfo di Clelia*

6 June. Lisbon, Th. d'Ajuda

Metastasio's text (first set to music by Hasse, see 1762). Three acts.

Jommelli's last opera (he died on 25 August 1774), written for the birthday of King Joseph 1 of Portugal.

DIBDIN: *The Waterman;* or, *The First of August*

8 August. London, Hm.

Ballad opera, text and music (partly composed and partly compiled) by Dibdin. Two acts.

Very successful on English stages; frequently revived in London during the 19th century, and as late as 23 May 1911 at C.G. for Santley's benefit and farewell performance. Given at Dublin 31 December 1776; Edinburgh 11 January 1777; Spanish Town, Jamaica February 1789; Philadelphia 8 April 1791; New York 22 May 1793 (last revived 1 July 1872). A new edition of the vocal score by S. N. Sedgwick and E. M. Lee was published in 1928.

(Date of first performance checked from the newspapers. It is differently given in some books of reference.)

PAISIELLO: *Il Credulo deluso*

September. Naples, T.N.

Text: an altered version of Goldoni's *Il Mondo della Luna* (see 1750). Three acts.

The month of the first production is recorded in the Venetian *Giornale Enciclopedico*, February 1775 (apropos of the Venice production of another opera on the same subject by Astaritta):

"Si rappresenta attualmente questo Dramma anche a Napoli, colà pure accomodato all' uso odierno Napolitano, che forse è più stravagante del Lombardo; e tanto ne piacque la Musica del S. Maestro Paisiello, che dal mese di Settembre dell' anno prossimo scorso sino ad ora se n'è continuata la rappresentazione".

Given in a reduced 2-act version, text altered by M. Coltellini, at St. Petersburg 5 October 1783 (as *Il Mondo della Luna*); Naples, Fondo 10 October 1784; Vienna 20 October 1786.

In French (translated by M. J. Mattieu de Lépidor, as *Orgon dans la Lune ou le Crédule trompé*), Versailles before 11 June 1777; Hague 21 January 1780 and Paris, Th. d. M. 27 April 1789.

Revived Parma 26 June 1813; and lately, celebrating the Paisiello bicentenary, Naples May 1940 (the revival, at least, was announced).

J. C. BACH: *Lucio Silla*

4 November. Mannheim

Text by G. de Gamerra (first set to music by Mozart, see 1772), with alterations by M. Verazi. Three acts.

C. S. Terry, on the authority of F. Walter, assumes the date of performance to have been 20 November 1776. The original Italian libretto is undated, but the German translation bears the date of 1774 and leaves no doubt that the opera was first produced at Mannheim in celebration of the name-day of the Elector, 4 November, of that year.

Revived Kiel 22 March 1929 (in German, translated and arranged by F. Tutenberg).

MARTINI: *Henri IV*

14 November. Paris, C.I.

Text by F. B. de Rozoy. Three acts.

First given at Versailles 16 December 1774; in French also, Vienna 1775; Brussels 20 September 1775, etc.; in French also, St. Petersburg 9 December 1784.

A German version was published at Frankfort *c.*1776, an anonymous Dutch version in 1778.

Revived, Paris, C.I. 21 November 1789; Antwerp 7 August 1806; and, with alterations, as *Henri IV, ou La Bataille d'Ivry*, Paris, O.C. 23 April 1814, "pour l'heureux retour des Fils de Henri IV au Trône de France" as indicated in the libretto.

Revived in Russian (translated by A. P. Veshnyakov), St. Petersburg 4 December 1820.

An anonymous Dutch translation was published in 1778. A Swedish version by J. S. Ahlgren, with new music by G. H. Küster, was given at Stockholm 19 December 1870.

PAISIELLO: *La Frascatana*

November. Venice, S. Sam.

Text by F. Livigni. Three acts.

Very successful in Italy and all over Europe. Naples, T.N. Winter 1774 (revived there with additional music by Paisiello, November 1786); Milan, T.R.D. Autumn 1775 and Sc. Autumn 1780, etc. In Italian also produced at:

VIENNA 29 April 1775.

TRIESTE May 1775.

PRAGUE 1776.

DRESDEN 1776.

COPENHAGEN 31 October 1776.

LONDON 5 November 1776.

DUBLIN Spring 1777.

ESZTERHÁZA 31 May 1778.

GRAZ Summer 1778.

PARIS, O. 10 September 1778.

ST. PETERSBURG 4 November 1778.

CASSEL 1779.

BARCELONA 26 March 1780.

WARSAW 27 January 1781.

BRUNSWICK 1782

GHENT June 1783.

MADRID 24 November 1787.

CRACOW 12 March 1789

LISBON 1793.

Revived in London 5 April 1781; 15 May 1788; 5 June 1794; 9 January 1808; revived in Paris 15 October 1806.

A pasticcio from *La Frascatana* and *Le due Contesse* (see 1776), called *Il finto Spettro* (text by M. Verazi) was produced at Mannheim 26 November 1776; it was the last opera which was sung in Italian there.

In German (translated by J. F. Schmidt), Augsburg 30 July 1779; Pressburg 8 February 1780; Frankfort 1 June 1781; Berlin 19 November 1781; Graz and Laibach 1782; Riga 9 May 1783; Vienna, Neustift 3 August 1783 and Kä. 9 September 1783; Prague 1787; Budapest 29 September 1787; Amsterdam 21 June 1796. Another German version, by M***, called *Der Vormund oder Das Mädchen von Frascati*, was given at Mannheim 14 January 1783. Translated also from the French version (see below), as *Die Infantin von Zamora*: Weimar October 1785; Graz 1 January 1794 (earlier given there in 1782, see above, in a translation by A. L.).

In French (as *L'Infante de Zamora*, adapted by N. E. Framery) first at Strasbourg Autumn 1780 (see letter in *Litteratur- und Theaterzeitung*, 16 December 1780); subsequently produced at Versailles 1781 and all over France; Lille 26 May 1782; Ghent July 1782; Liége 7 December 1782; Cassel 28 November 1783; eventually Paris, Th. de M. 22 June 1789; revived Antwerp 23 January 1806.

In Russian (translated by V. A. Levshin), St. Petersburg 1780.

In Danish (translated by L. Knudsen), Copenhagen 2 April 1782.

In Polish (translated by W. Boguslawski), Warsaw 13 July 1782; Cracow 13 February 1790.

A Dutch translation (from the French version) by B. Zurmühlen was published 1784.

In Swedish (translated from the French version by J. D. Valerius), Stockholm 10 October 1799.

La Frascatana was revived by the Società Filarmonica, Turin 19 June 1937 (under G. Gedda).

1775

PAISIELLO: *La Discordia fortunata*

Carnival. Venice, S. Sam.

Text by "Abate F. B. A. F.". Three acts.

Given at Dresden 20 November 1776 and Prague Autumn 1784 as *L'Avaro deluso*; at Rome, Tord. January 1780 in a reduced 2-act version; at Pesaro Carnival 1780 as *Il Quadro parlante*. In Italian also, Vienna 6 July 1785.

In German (translated by C. A. Vulpius), Weimar 26 April 1786; (translated by J. L. Schmidt), Aachen 26 March 1787; (translated by P. Trautmann), Prague 1787. Hanover 17 April 1787; Budapest 1788 (Vulpius's translation); Hamburg 28 August 1789, etc.

MOZART: *La finta Giardiniera*

13 January. Munich

Calzabigi's text (first set to music by Anfossi, see 1774), with alterations by M. Coltellini. Three acts.

After the very successful Munich production the opera was translated into German by the actor Stierle for the touring troupe of the manager Johann Böhm. The first traceable performance of this German version took place at Augsburg on 1 May 1780 (as *Die verstellte Gärtnerin*); also given in the same year at Nuremberg. But it is likely to have been given earlier in 1780, or even late in 1779, at Salzburg where Böhm's troupe had a season before they went to Augsburg and where Mozart also spent those months. Next we find the opera performed at Frankfort on 2 April 1782 (as *Sandrina oder Die verstellte Gräfin*). This was the first performance of any Mozart opera in Central or Northern Germany; another translation (by H. G. Schmieder?) *Das verstellte Gärtnermädchen* was given at Mayence in August 1789 (play-bill of the second performance, 22 August 1789, preserved).

After Mozart's death *La finta Giardiniera* was given, in the original Italian, once more at Prague on 10 March 1796; and, in German again, as *Die schöne Gärtnerin* at Oels (Silesia) 25 February 1797 (see *Schlesische Provinzialblätter*, February 1797, p.199); then it disappeared from the stage for 95 years.

It was revived, in a new translation by M. Kalbeck, on the same bill with *Bastien und Bastienne* at:

Vienna, O. 25 December 1891 (music revised by J. N. Fuchs); subsequently at Bremen 30 September 1892; Leipzig 28 November 1892; Basle 1 March 1893; Berlin 2 December 1893; Graz 11 December 1896, etc.

20th Century Revivals

In German:

MAYENCE 21 October 1915 (revised by R. and L. Berger).

DARMSTADT 25 November 1915 (revised by O. Bie; one act).

BERLIN 17 February 1916 (O. Bie's version).

CARLSRUHE 27 January 1918 (revised by A. Rudolph).

MUNICH 14 January 1935 (revised by S. Anheisser).

BASLE 14 March 1935 (the Mayence 1915 version).

In Hungarian (as *Mirandolina*, adapted to a new libretto by S. Hevesi, founded on Goldoni's comedy), Budapest 27 November 1924.

In English (translated by H. Dowd), New York, Mayfair Th. 18 January 1927; London, Scala 7 January 1930 (with recitatives by L. Heward).

In the original Italian (music revised by V. Garulli), Trieste July 1928; Milan, T.d.V. 6 November 1928.

G. BENDA: *Ariadne auf Naxos*

27 January. Gotha

Text by J. C. Brandes (founded on a cantata by H. W. von Gerstenberg and originally written for Schweitzer, who did not finish his composition). *Ein Duodrama mit Musick*. One act.

The first and most successful German "melo-drama" (a spoken play with orchestral accompaniment throughout). Published 1778 (vocal score) and 1781 (full score). New edition of the vocal score published 1920 (edited by A. Einstein).

In German also produced at Leipzig 24 April 1775; Altenburg 11 September 1775; Berlin 23 August 1776; Hamburg 6 September 1776; Hanover 27 December 1776, etc.; Vienna, Jos. 11 July 1779 and B. 4 January 1780; St. Petersburg 2 September 1779; Salzburg 29 September 1780; Warsaw 19 May 1781; Riga 16 October 1782; Pressburg 24 January 1798.

Benda's *Ariadne* was one of the very few German musical dramas before Mozart to be translated into other languages. Produced at:

BERLIN 10 February 1777 (in French, translated by Prince Frederick Augustus of Brunswick-Oels).

WARSAW 8 March 1778 (in French, "traduit de l'Allemand par un Prince du Sang d'une des plus illustres maisons du Nord", probably the same translation as used at Berlin).

COPENHAGEN 29 May 1778 (in Danish, translated by B. G. Sporon).

PARIS, C.I. 20 July 1781 (in French, translated by J. B. Dubois de Jancigny[1]).

NAPLES, FIOR. 16 December 1783 (in Italian, translated by H . . . ; see Cramer's *Magazin der Musik*, 1784, pp.64–70).

GORIZIA 1786 (in Italian, translated by A. de' Giorgi-Bertóla).

STOCKHOLM 22 December 1786 (in Swedish, translated by J. P. Stolpe); revived Gothenburg 9 October 1806; Malmö 21 July 1807; Lund 24 July 1807.

BUDAPEST 18 May 1802 (in Hungarian).

PRAGUE 22 December 1875 (in Czech); revived Brno 1935.

Frequently revived on German stages: Munich 18 December 1832 (music revised by H. L. von

---

[1] He wrote the introductory essay in the French libretto; the anonymous translation is attributed both to him and to Cuinet Dorbeil; see Catalogue of the Bibliothèque Nationale, Paris, Vol. 18, p.968, and Vol. 34, p.609.

Spengel); Berlin 13 June 1833; Königsberg 25 November 1855; Breslau 17 January 1898; Weimar 16 June 1916; Lauchstedt 6 July 1924; Regensburg 23 February 1925; Aussig 1931.

The German melodrama movement initiated by Benda in 1775, soon found adherents, such as Neefe, Reichardt, Vogler, Winter, Danzi, Cannabich, Zumsteeg and interest even on the part of Mozart, who admired *Ariadne* (see his letter to Leopold Mozart, dated Mannheim, 12 November 1778). The whole movement, however, lasted only for about twenty years. See for details E. Istel, *Die Entstehung des deutschen Melodramas* (1906).

GRÉTRY: *La fausse Magie*

1 February. Paris, C.I.

Text by J. F. Marmontel. Two acts.

Given at the C.I., with alterations, 18 March 1776; in Paris until 1828 and revived at the O.C. 16 July 1863 (re-orchestrated by E. Prévost).

In French also produced at Hague 1775; Liége 23 December 1775; Brussels 10 May 1776; Stuttgart 13 June 1776; Cassel 1777; Turin Spring 1778; Geneva 4 October 1784; Charleston, S.C. 3 June 1795; Hamburg 1795; Cologne 1796–97; Gachina (Russia) 4 September 1798; Hanover 27 July 1805; Moscow 20 April 1809; Vienna 27 June 1809.

In Danish (translated by N. K. Bredal), Copenhagen 30 January 1778.

In German (as *Die abgeredete Zauberey*, translated by G. Stephanie), Vienna, B. 27 October 1778; (as *Das Blendwerk*, translated by F. L. W. Meyer), Mannheim 25 February 1779; (as *Der Zauberspiegel*, translated by J. André and C. F. von Bonin), Berlin 18 January 1781. Yet another German version, by J. N. Rothmann was published in 1781.

In German also, Warsaw 1 June 1782; Riga 30 June 1783.

In Dutch, Amsterdam 1785; in Flemish already, Mecheln 1783.

In Swedish (translated by C. Envallsson), Stockholm 16 July 1792.

G. BENDA: *Der Dorfjahrmarkt*

10 February. Gotha

Text by F. W. Gotter. One act.

The vocal score was published in 1776 as *Der Dorfjahrmarkt*, the libretto in 1778 as *Der Jahrmarkt*. Full score first published in 1930, in *Denkmäler Deutscher Tonkunst*, edited by T. W. Werner. This very popular Singspiel originally had one act. Divided into two acts and with some additional music by J. A. Hiller it was given at Leipzig 25 April 1775; Dresden 26 October 1775; Hanover 8 May 1776; Hamburg 4 July 1776; Berlin 18 June 1778; Vienna, B. 15 April 1779; Mannheim 13 February 1780; Riga 23 October 1782, etc.

In Danish (translated by S. Sønnichsen and N. H. Weinwich), Copenhagen 21 November 1788.

Revived Würzburg 5 December 1915 (revised by L. Landshoff); Hanover May 1931 (according to the *D.D.T.* edition).

RAUZZINI: *Piramo e Tisbe*

16 March. London, Hm.

Text by M. Coltellini. Two parts.

The first and best opera Rauzzini wrote for London (revived there 29 March 1781).

In Italian also, Vienna 31 December 1776; Brunswick Spring 1782; Prague Summer 1783; Warsaw Spring 1784.

In German (translated by L. Zehnmark), Vienna, B. 7 December 1794.

(Date of first performance checked from newspapers; different dates are given by Nicoll and Terry.)

MOZART: *Il Re Pastore*

23 April. Salzburg

Metastasio's text (first set to music by Bonno in 1751). Two acts.

Mozart's setting was produced in honour of a visit of the Archduke Maximilian, son of Maria Theresa, to Salzburg.

Revived Salzburg 27 January 1906 and Munich March 1906 (in Italian, celebrating Mozart's 150th birthday); Dessau 9 May 1933 (in a German translation by S. Anheisser).

G. BENDA: *Medea*

1 May. Leipzig

Text by F. W. Gotter. *Ein mit Musik vermischtes Drama.* One act.

Benda's second melodrama, hardly less successful than *Ariadne* some months earlier. Vocal score published 1778 and 1785.

Subsequently produced at Gotha 6 June 1775; Altenburg 6 September 1775; Dresden 6 November 1775; Hamburg 10 December 1776; Berlin 26 March 1777; Frankfort 31 May 1777; Vienna, B. 5 December 1778, etc.; Graz 7 July 1818.

In German also, St. Petersburg 8 February 1781; Warsaw 16 April 1781; Flensburg 1781; Riga 12 March 1783; Berne March 1811; Moscow 24 February 1821; Strasbourg 15 June 1825.

In French, Warsaw 4 March 1785.

In Danish (translated by F. Schwartz), Copenhagen 17 October 1788 (published already 1782).

In Hungarian (translated by M. Ernyi), Budapest 19 May 1802.

In Russian, Moscow 1802.

In Polish (translated by F. Zablocki), Warsaw 1806.

A Czech version by K. H. Tham was published in 1787; produced in Czech (not in Tham's translation), Prague 22 December 1875.

An Italian version, with new music by G. Poffa, was given at Trieste 21 November 1783; in Italian also Forlì Spring 1784; Gorizia Summer 1786; Milan 1792.

A French version by J. J. G. Berthevin, with new music by J. S. Démar, was published (and performed?) at Orléans in 1798 (*Bibl. Soleinne*, no.3005); two earlier French translations, by De Rosières, Vienna 1778, and by A. Berquin, Paris 1781, were published.

An anonymous Swedish version appeared 1784 in *Afton-Bladed* (Stockholm).

Frequently revived in Germany: Munich 12 February 1885 (revised by J. R. Schachner); Gotha 21 March 1888 and 22 February 1896; Regensburg 23 February 1925; Berlin 25 March 1934. Revived in Czech, Brno 1935.

HAYDN: *L'Incontro improviso*

29 August. Eszterháza

Text: an Italian version, by K. Friberth, of Dancourt's *Rencontre imprévue* (set by Gluck, see 1764). Three acts.

Produced in honour of a visit of the Archduke Ferdinand, son of Maria Theresa, to Eszterháza.

Revived Lauchstedt Summer 1936 (in German, as *Unverhofftes Begegnen*, translated by H. Schultz).

PAISIELLO: *Socrate immaginario*

October. Naples, T.N.

Text by G. B. Lorenzi, on a plan by F. Galiani. Originally in two acts.

After a command performance at court, 23 October 1775 the opera was banned by King Ferdinand I (being "ritrovato indiscreto") and allowed to be acted again only in March 1780 (now in 3 acts). Subsequently given at Florence, P. Spring 1780, etc.; Dresden 1781; Milan, Sc. Autumn 1783; Malta Carnival 1784; Lisbon Carnival 1788; and revived at Naples (with some alterations) in 1796, 1801, and 1814; at Milan in 1801 and 1814.

A modern revival took place at the T. degli Independenti, Rome 20 February 1926 (as a spoken comedy, without the greater part of Paisiello's music). A new edition of the vocal score (edited by G. Barini) was published in 1931. Revived again Naples, Politeama 6 or 10 October 1936.

One of Paisiello's best works. ". . . il capolavoro poetico dell' opera buffa, come il Matrimonio segreto n'è il capolavoro musicale. Queste due produzioni mostrano quanto l'ingegno napoletano possa nel genere comico" (Scherillo).

M. Kelly was present at the "first representation" (meaning that of the 1780 revival as he arrived at Naples only 30 May 1779. See his *Reminiscences*, I, p.49; the famous Casacciello then sang the name-part, which in 1775 had been created by Gennaro Lucio).

ANFOSSI: *L'Avaro*

Autumn. Venice, S. Moisè

Text by G. Bertati. Three acts.

Milan 3 August 1776; Bologna and Turin 1776; Florence Carnival 1777; Parma Carnival 1777; Alessandria April 1777; revived Venice, S. Moisè Carnival 1778; Vicenza and Cremona Carnival 1778, etc. Given at Florence Spring 1777, as *La Fedeltà nelle Angustie*.

In Italian also, Vienna 1776; Trieste 26 December 1776; Copenhagen 31 January 1777 (Danish translation in the libretto by R. Soelberg); Graz Carnival 1779; Warsaw Autumn 1779; Dresden 1780; Brunswick 1782 and Hanover 1783 (as *Il Sordo e l'Avaro*); Frankfort February 1783 (as *I due Avari*); London 14 June 1783; Lille 4 March 1788; Madrid 1791. Revived Milan, Sc. March 1791; Trieste Carnival 1805.

In French (as *Le Tuteur avare*, translated by J. L. Gabiot de Salins, additional music by Cambini), Paris, Th. Beaujolais 1 March 1788; Versailles 15 August 1788; Liége 16 December 1789.

In German (as *Der Geizige oder Die Liebe ist sinnreich*), Hanover 14 June 1790; Pyrmont 28 June 1790.

In Spanish (translated by L. F. Comella), Madrid 9 December 1796.

LINLEY: *The Duenna;* or, *The Double Elopement*

21 November. London, C.G.

Text by R. B. Sheridan. Three acts.

Music partly composed, partly compiled by Thomas Linley, father and son.

One of the most successful English comic operas of the 18th century: "63 nights was the career of the Beggar's Opera; but the Duenna was acted no less than 75 times during the first season, the only intermissions being a few weeks at Christmas, and the Fridays on every week; the latter on account of Leoni, who, being a Jew, could not act on those nights" (G. Hogarth, II, p.350).

Given at York 9 April 1776; Birmingham 12 August 1776; Dublin, Th. R., Crow St. 31 January 1777 (in a pirated version as *The Governess*) and New Th., Fishamble St. 21 February 1777 (in the original form); Kingston, Jamaica, 27 November 1779; New York 10 July 1786; Philadelphia 3 July 1787; Baltimore 5 September 1787; Charleston, S.C. 13 March 1795 (orchestrated by T. Bradford); etc. A parody by I. Pottinger was published 1776.

An Italian version of the libretto, *La Governante*, by C. F. Badini, was composed by Bertoni and produced in London, Hm. 15 May 1779; according to the libretto some of the original songs were retained.

A French translation (without the lyrics), by A. H. Lapierre de Châteauneuf, *La Duègne et le Juif Portugais*, was published in 1827.

The Duenna was given at Calcutta 1915 in Bengali, at Bombay 1925 in Marathi.

Frequently revived on English stages; Norwich 1922; Birmingham May 1923 (arranged by C. F. Smyly) and 26 December 1924; arranged by A. Reynolds: London, Lyric Th. (Hammersmith) 23 October 1924 and again 22 April 1931 (ran for 141 nights).

1776

PAISIELLO: *Le due Contesse*

2 January. Rome, Valle

Text by G. Petrosellini. Two parts.

Successful in Italy. Milan, Sc. Spring 1782, etc.

In Italian also produced at Vienna 17 November 1776; Dresden and Graz 1777; London 4 November 1777; St. Petersburg 1778; Paris, O. 9 July 1778; Warsaw 1779; Prague 1783; Barcelona 24 July 1783; Madrid 25 July 1788.

In German (translated by C. J. Förg), Munich 18 May 1779; Frankfort 15 May 1782; Cologne Autumn 1784; Hamburg 1785; Mannheim 29 September 1785; Carlsruhe 20 October 1785; Budapest 2 February 1787, etc.

In French (adapted by N. E. Framery), Versailles and Strasbourg before 5 July 1781 (according to Framery's letter to Paisiello as quoted by Schizzi); Amsterdam 15 November 1785 (libretto British Museum); Liége 9 February 1787.

In Russian, St. Petersburg 1782.
In Polish, Wilna 17 February 1810.

ANFOSSI: *La vera Costanza*

2 January. Rome, T. delle Dame

Text by F. Puttini. Three acts.

Repeated at Rome in the same year at T. Pallacorda; Bologna Autumn 1776; Turin 1776; Florence Carnival 1777; Milan Autumn 1777, etc.

Given at Venice 20 November 1776 as *La Pescatrice fedele*; at Florence, T. Cocomero Spring 1777 and Milan Autumn 1777 as *Il Principe di Lago Nero*.

In Italian also, Vienna 12 January 1777; Trieste 25 January 1777; Dresden February 1777; London 20 January 1778; Copenhagen 31 January 1778 (Danish translation in the libretto by R. Soelberg); St. Petersburg 25 November 1778; Brunswick February 1783; Prague 1785.

UTTINI: *Aline Drotning uti Golconda*

11 January. Stockholm

Text: a Swedish translation, by C. B. Zibet, of Sedaine's French libretto (see 1766). Three acts.

Uttini's last opera. Revived at Stockholm 30 November 1778 and 14 May 1781.

FRIDZERI: *Les Souliers mors-dorés ou La Cordonnière Allemande*

11 January. Paris, C.I.

Text by A. de Ferrières. Two acts.

The most popular of Fridzeri's comic operas.

In French also, Brussels 4 September 1776; Cassel 9 January 1784; Baltimore 30 March 1796; Philadelphia 24 December 1796. Revived Nantes 14 August 1806.

In Polish (translated by A. Michniewski), Warsaw July 1776; Cracow 17 December 1789.

In Russian, Moscow 22 January 1779.

In Dutch (translated by P. F. Lijnslager), Amsterdam 1779.

In German (translated by J. André), Munich 13 April 1779; Bonn 9 February 1783; for a German opera on the same subject, see 1779.

In Swedish (translated by C. Envallsson), Stockholm 8 February 1785 (as pasticcio).

A Danish adaptation, *Silkeskoene*, by T. Thaarup, music by Schall, was produced at Copenhagen on 28 March 1794.

J. SCHUSTER: *La Didone abbandonata*

[*12 January*]. Naples, S.C.

Metastasio's text (first set to music by Sarro, see 1724). Three acts.

The best of Schuster's Italian serious operas.

Revived in 1779 at Venice and Naples (see M. Kelly's *Reminiscences*, I, p.72).

As to the date of the first performance, no season is indicated by Florimo, Croce, or by Engländer in his study on Schuster. The score at the Naples Conservatorio has the handwritten note "li 12 del 1776."

BERTONI: *Orfeo, ed Euridice*

January. Venice, S. Ben.

Calzabigi's text (first set to music by Gluck, see 1762). One act.

First produced on the same bill with another 1-act opera by Bertoni, *Aristo e Temira*; repeated Padua 2 May 1776 in concert form; Venice, S. Ben. 3 June 1776 and revived Venice, F. 13 May 1795.

In Italian also, London 31 May 1780 (for one night only, "in the manner of an oratorio"); Cassel 1781; Hanover 1783; Berlin 31 January 1788 (enlarged to 3 acts; additional music by Reichardt; Gluck's *Orfeo* was not given at Berlin before 1808); Eszterháza 1788.

Bertoni's setting (considered now as a rather clumsy imitation of Gluck) was published in full score in 1776. The interesting preface has been reprinted several times (e.g. in the Pelletan edition of Gluck's *Orfeo*, 1898).

G. BENDA: *Walder*

23 February. Gotha

Text by F. W. Gotter (from Marmontel's *Silvain*, see 1770; *Ein ländliches Schauspiel mit Gesang*). One act.

Dresden July 1776; Frankfort 29 May 1777; Hamburg 19 December 1777; Berlin 4 March 1780, etc.

In German also, Pressburg August 1792.

BAUMGARTEN: *Zemire und Azor*

18 May. Breslau

Text: a German version, by K. E. Schubert and the composer, of Marmontel's French libretto (see 1771). *Romantisch-komische Oper*. Four acts.

Given by the Breslau company also at Vienna, Kä. June 1776; Mayence 1776.

GRÉTRY: *Les Mariages Samnites*

12 June. Paris, C.I.

Text by B. F. de Rozoy (founded on a tale by Marmontel). Three acts.

A new version of the first opera Grétry had written for Paris (1768, performed privately at the Prince de Conti's).

Revived with alterations (the dialogue in verse instead of prose), Paris, C.I. 22 May 1782. In French also, Brussels 4 November 1776; Cassel 19 June 1779; Geneva 6 March 1784.

In German (translated by J. André and F. L. W. Meyer), Frankfort 1776 or 1777; Schwedt 1780; Mannheim 17 February 1782; Berlin 1 June 1782; Münster 27 July 1782; Bonn 10 November 1782; Vienna, W. March 1806 (re-orchestrated by Seyfried).

In Danish (translated by A. G. Thoroup), Copenhagen 30 January 1784.

In Russian, Kouskovo 11 July 1787.

The march from this opera is the theme of Mozart's piano variations K. 352 (1781).

A parody *Céphalide, ou Les autres Mariages samnites*, text by Prince Charles Joseph de Ligne, music by Vitzthumb and Cifolelli, was given at Brussels on 30 January 1777.

G. BENDA: *Romeo und Julie*

25 September. Gotha

Text by F. W. Gotter (after Shakespeare). Three acts.

This was the first *Romeo and Juliet* opera of a long series to follow[1] and the only German one. Very successful on German stages: Dresden February 1777; Frankfort 3 June 1777; Hamburg 10 May 1778; Berlin 8 February 1779; Regensburg February 1779 (orchestrated by T. von Schacht); Mannheim 11 March 1779; Stuttgart 1780; Breslau 1 December 1780; Bonn 8 May 1782; Prague Summer 1783; Vienna, Kä. 27 August 1783; Bremen 13 October 1783; Riga 20 July 1784; Munich 12 November 1784; Cassel 28 February 1787; Pyrmont 3 July 1787; Hanover 23 November 1787; Cologne 1787–88; Dresden 26 June 1788; Celle 18 September 1789; Bremen 11 December 1793; Graz 26 September 1794.

In German also, Pressburg 1787; Temesvar 8 December 1801; St. Petersburg 1810, and according to R. Schlösser, at Amsterdam, Solothurn, and Odense.

The opera was revived at the State Conservatoire, Prague in Summer 1931.

DIBDIN: *The Seraglio*

14 November. London, C.G.

Text by the composer. Two acts.

Successful in London; also given at Philadelphia 19 May 1794 and New York 21 September 1797. Some airs were contributed by S. Arnold and by J. A. Fisher.

SARTI: *Le Gelosie villane*

November. Venice, S. Sam.

Text by T. Grandi (founded on Goldoni's comedy, *Il Feudatario*). Three acts.

Sarti's first great success as a composer of comic opera. Given at Pistoia 3 January 1779 and on other Italian stages as *Il Feudatario*. Milan, Sc. Spring 1779 (first comic opera there). Revived Venice, S. Angelo 23 August 1798 as *Il Feudatario* and Turin, Carignano 1799 as *Il Feudatario burlato*.

[1] See Steibelt 1793; Zingarelli 1796; Vaccai 1825; Bellini 1830; Marchetti 1865; Gounod 1867; d'Ivry 1878; Barkworth 1916; Zandonai 1922.

In Italian also given at Vienna 8 October 1777 (revived 21 April 1793, perhaps with Mozart's final chorus K. 615, composed in 1791).

Dresden 14 January 1778; Eszterháza 1779; Trieste 5 October 1779; St. Petersburg 6 October 1779 (revived 1 December 1798); Graz Winter 1780; Brunswick *c.* Summer 1782; Frankfort February 1783; Potsdam 29 March 1783 and Berlin 18 January 1784; Barcelona 26 January 1784 (revived 16 July 1807); London 15 April 1784 (revived 1 February 1794 as *I Contadini bizzarri*; 8 June 1797; and 10 January 1801); Warsaw 24 February 1785; Versailles September 1787 and Paris, Th. d. M. 14 April 1790 (revived 14 March 1805); Madrid 19 January 1788; Lisbon Summer 1793; Lugano 1807.

In German (translated by H. C. Pleissner), Bonn 13 July 1783; Frankfort 8 August 1783; Linz 5 August 1786; Budapest 23 April 1790; Berlin 5 October 1791, etc.

In Polish (translated by L. Pierozyński), Warsaw 27 May 1786 (revived 1810) and Wilna 14 February 1799.

BORTNYANSKY: *Creonte*

26 November. Venice, S. Ben.

Librettist unknown. Two acts.

One of the earliest examples of an opera written for the Italian stage by a Russian composer (the only forerunner, it seems, being *Demofoonte*, performed at Leghorn Carnival 1773, composed by M. S. Berezovsky).

1777

HOLZBAUER: *Günther von Schwarzburg*

5 January. Mannheim

Text by A. Klein. Three acts.

Holzbauer's only German opera. Modestly called "Singspiel", but it was a new attempt to create a German grand national opera (with recitatives).

Given at Mannheim until 1785; also Mayence 1778; Münster 17 August 1782; Frankfort 14

September 1782; Bonn 17 November 1782; Brünn 11 January 1783; Breslau 1783; Cologne Autumn 1784; Cassel August 1785; Pressburg 1788; Hanover 4 June 1789 (celebrating the birthday of King George III); Budapest 3 September 1792.

The score was printed in 1776 and reprinted in 1902 (Vol. VIII–IX of *Denkmäler Deutscher Tonkunst*, edited by H. Kretzschmar). It was the first German opera ever published in full score.

ANFOSSI: *Il Curioso indiscreto*

February. Rome, T. delle Dame

Librettist unknown. Three acts.

In Italian also given at Dresden 4 April 1778; Paris, O. 13 August 1778; Barcelona 26 April 1780; Trieste 3 October 1780; Prague Spring 1782; Vienna 30 June 1783; London 18 December 1784; Madrid 1 October 1791; Warsaw 30 October 1792 (as *Il Curioso burlato*).

In French (translated by P. U. Dubuisson), Paris, Th. Montansier 23 September 1790.

For the Vienna performance of Anfossi's opera, Mozart wrote the two soprano airs *Vorrei spiegarvi, oh dio* (K. 418) and *No, no che non sei capace* (K. 419).

DÉZÈDE: *Les trois Fermiers*

24 May. Paris, C.I.

Text by J. M. Boutet de Monvel. Two acts.

In French also given at Cassel 1778; Liége 24 June 1779; Vienna 1780; Smolna November 1780; Stockholm 28 May 1783; St. Petersburg 13 September 1798.

In German (translated by W. G. Becker and C. G. Neefe): Frankfort 21 April 1779; Mannheim 2 May 1779; Berlin 24 April 1780; Bonn 21 May 1780; Cologne 6 June 1780; Hamburg 25 September 1780; Munich 28 November 1780; Münster 18 July 1782; Riga 13 February 1783; Bremen 9 December 1784; Schwedt 30 December 1784; Vienna, Kä. 28 October 1785; Mainz 26 November 1785, etc.; revived Berlin 10 March 1809.

In Danish (translated by J. H. Wessel), Copenhagen 4 September 1780 at Fredensborg Palace and 30 October 1780 at the Royal Theatre.

In Swedish (translated by C. Envallsson), Stockholm 2 January 1794; Gothenburg 24 May 1796; another version, by C. J. Lindegren, was produced at Stockholm 10 February 1797 (with additional music by Dupuy).

Dutch translation by H. J. Roullaud published 1787.

SCHMITTBAUER: *Lindor und Ismene*

4 June. Lüneburg

Text by J. von Soden. One act.

Libretto first published in 1771; a second edition, with alterations and under the title *Ein Grab in Arkadien!* followed in 1779, a third edition, called *Arkadien*, 1788, in Vol. I of Soden's collected plays. (All three editions in the Library of Congress, Washington; see Sonneck's *Catalogue*, pp.686–87.) The MS score of the opera has been preserved (at Darmstadt); for a detailed account of it see L. Schiedermair, in *Sammelbände of the I.M.S.*, Vol. XIV (1913), pp.542–50.

Place and date of first performance according to G. Fischer, *Musik in Hannover* (1903), p.39. Produced by J. F. Stöffler's company under the direction of Franz Anton von Weber, the father of Carl Maria von Weber. An earlier production at Hanover in 1771 (by Seyler's troupe?), as maintained by Schatz, I could not verify. Fischer's date is supported by the facts that Schmittbauer is not mentioned as the composer of *Lindor und Ismene* in the Gotha *Theaterkalender* before 1777, and that the Darmstadt score has the date of 1778.

Soden's remark in the 1779 preface "auf der hannöverischen Bühne" might be regarded as fitting for Lüneburg as well; for Lüneburg belonged to (the electorate of) Hanover. In the 1788 edition this prefatory note was extended to "auf der hannöverischen Bühne und anderen . . ." which would cover productions at Cologne 6 July 1779; Rostock 17 May 1780; Nuremberg 7 November 1782; Bozen 15 March 1784; Carlsruhe 25 April 1785. An opera *Lindor und Ismene* was also performed by a German troupe at St. Petersburg on 15 November 1778 (see Findeizen, II, p.115, who mentions as the composer Schweitzer with a question-mark). It was, however, probably not Schmittbauer's opera, but a setting of the same text by Nikolaus Mühle which was produced there (see *Gothaer Theaterkalender*, 1780, p.258) as well as at Danzig 21 September 1781 (see L. Gomperz, *Kritische Bemerkungen über das Theater*, p.105).

(PEPUSCH and) ARNOLD: *Polly*

19 June. London, Little Hm.

Text by J. Gay (*An Opera, being the second part of the Beggar's Opera*). Three acts.

The preface to the libretto is dated 15 March 1729; text and songs were published in that year, but the opera was not allowed to be acted until 48 years later (with alterations in the original text by G. Colman the Elder and 6 new airs by Arnold).

Revived:

LONDON, LITTLE HM. 11 June 1782.

LONDON, D.L. 16 June 1813 (for this unsuccessful revival M. Kelly wrote some new airs).

LONDON, KINGSWAY 30 December 1922 (text rewritten by C. Bax, music arranged by F. Austin. This revival had a run of 324 nights).

LONDON, CHELSEA PALACE 31 March 1923 (text adapted by W. E. B. Henderson and R. B. Salisbury, lyrics by N. Slee, music arranged by H. Bath).

Also revived New York, Cherry Lane Playhouse 10 October 1925.

STENBORG: *Konung Gustaf Adolphs Jagt*

25 June. Stockholm

Text by A. F. Ristell (founded on C. Collé's comedy *La Partie de Chasse de Henri IV*). Three acts.

The earliest attempt at Swedish historical opera (*comedie . . . blandad med sang*). First given at Gothenburg 6 December 1779.

HAYDN: *Il Mondo della Luna*

3 August. Eszterháza

Goldoni's text (first set to music by Galuppi, see 1750). Three acts.

Revived Schwerin 20 March 1932 (in German, translated by W. M. Treichlinger, music arranged by M. Lothar); this version was also given at Berlin, Hochschule für Musik 1 July 1932; Basle 6 January 1933.

RIGHINI: *Il Convitato di Pietra* o sia *Il Dissoluto*

21 August. Vienna, Kä.

Librettist unknown to Sonneck; the text is (on what authority?) attributed to A. de' Filistri da Caramondani in C. Schmidl's *Dizionario*; both the Vienna and Prague libretti are anonymous. Three acts.

One of the earliest Italian *Don Giovanni* operas, ten years before Mozart. Also produced at Prague 1777; Eszterháza Summer 1781 (probably Righini's opera); Brunswick 1782; Hanover 1783 or 1784.

Further *Don Giovanni* operas of this period are:

Il Convitato di Pietra, anonymous text (2 acts), music by G. Callegari; Venice, S. Cass. Carnival 1777.

Il Convitato di Pietra, text by G. B. Lorenzi (1 act), music by Tritto; Naples, Fior. Carnival 1783.

Albertini's opera, see 1783; Gazzaniga's and Mozart's operas, see 1787.

Il nuovo Convitato di Pietra, text by G. M. Foppa (2 acts), music by F. Gardi; Venice, S. Sam. 5 February 1787; also Bologna 1791; Milan, Teatro privato de' due Muri Summer 1791 (performed by amateurs); Corfu Carnival 1795; Milan, Can. Summer 1796.

Il Convitato di Pietra, Lorenzi's text, music by V. Fabrizi; Fano 1788; Leghorn 1789; Barcelona 8 July 1790; Bologna Carnival 1791; Lucca Autumn 1792; Lisbon 1796; Madrid 12 November 1796, etc.

Additional pasticci with similar titles were produced at Rome, Valle Autumn 1789; Venice,

S. Cass. Carnival 1792 (1 act; text different from all others); Bastia, Corsica Spring 1797.

SARTI: *Medonte, Rè di Epiro*

8 September. Florence, P.

Text by G. de Gamerra. Three acts.

Apart from *Giulio Sabino* (see 1781) Sarti's most important serious opera. Given all over Italy (until the end of the century) and (in Italian) also at London 14 November 1782 (revived 8 December 1798); Trieste 26 March 1786 (revived 12 November 1796); Madrid 27 January 1787; Vienna 9 February 1794.

GLUCK: *Armide*

23 September. Paris, O.

Quinault's text (first set to music by Lully, see 1686). Five acts.

At the Paris Opéra given until 1837 and revived there 12 April 1905 (392 performances up to 1913). Given at Versailles 14 June 1784.

Parodies: *L'Opéra de Province*, by P. A. A. de Piis, P. Y. Barré, J. P. D. Desprès and L. P. P. Resnier, Paris, C.I. 17 December 1777 (revived 18 October 1780); *Madame Terrible*, by P. L. Moline, Meaux 6 September 1778. Early productions after Paris:

COPENHAGEN 1 May 1779 (in concert form; parts only).

HANOVER 18 January 1782 (in Italian).

CASSEL 4 April 1783 (in French).

STOCKHOLM 24 January 1787 (in Swedish, translated by A. F. Ristell, with a prologue by G. J. Vogler, text by C. G. af Leopold, and with ballet music by J. M. Kraus).

BERLIN 20 May 1805 (in German, translated by J. von Voss; given there until 1889).

VIENNA, W. 9 January 1808 and Kä. 3 April 1808 (in German).

BRUSSELS 23 December 1823 (in French); revived 7 November 1905.

Some revivals:

DRESDEN 5 March 1843 (Wagner conducting).

CARLSRUHE May 1853 (in German, recitatives by Jos. Strauss, translation revised by E. Devrient).

PRAGUE 11 April 1866 (in Czech, translated by J. Böhm) and 9 March 1898 (in German).

BASLE 3 December 1880 (for the first time in Switzerland?).

NAPLES, S.C. 11 March 1890 (for the first time in Italy, translated by A. Zanardini).

WIESBADEN 15 May 1902 (in German, revised by G. von Hülsen and J. Schlar).

BÉZIERS 28 August 1904 (open-air performance).

LYONS 12 November 1904 (in French).

LONDON, C.G. 6 July 1906 (in French; for the first time in England, apart from a concert selection given at a Norwich Festival on 18 September 1860); revived C.G. 1 May 1928 (in German).

NEW YORK 14 November 1910 (in French).

MILAN, SC. 17 December 1911 (new Italian translation by A. Lega).

FALMOUTH 24 November 1936 (for first time in English, translated by M. and E. Radford); also Glasgow 14 April 1939.

FLORENCE May 1941 (in German).

MONSIGNY: *Félix, ou L'Enfant trouvé*

10 November. Fontainebleau

Text by J. M. Sedaine. Three acts.

Monsigny's last opera; like Rossini, Monsigny lived on for more than 39 years without writing another work for the stage.

Paris, C.I. 24 November 1777; given at the O.C. until 1825. Revived at the Opéra Populaire 22 December 1847 (re-scored by Adam).

In French also, Liége 12 November 1782; Cassel 16 June 1784; Amsterdam and Hague 1784; Cologne 1796–97; Berne 1 January 1807; Moscow 4 June 1810.

In German (translated by J. André), Mannheim 6 April 1783; Berlin 5 January 1784 (revived 2 November 1801, with additions by B. A. Weber); Vienna, Kä. 16 October 1785; Riga 14 May 1790.

There are printed Dutch versions, anonymous 1784, and by P. Pijpers, 1790. A Danish version by R. Frankenau was published in 1808.

1778

G. BENDA: *Der Holzhauer* oder *Die drei Wünsche*

2 January. Gotha

Text: a German version, by F. W. Gotter, of Guichard's and Castet's *Le Bûcheron* (see 1763). One act.

In German also, Hamburg 4 May 1778, etc.; Bonn 13 December 1780; Berlin 20 April 1781; Munich September 1782; Riga 8 July 1785.

An opera of this title was given at Moscow on 15 July 1787 (in Russian); as no composer is mentioned, it may have been Philidor's original.

BERTONI: *Quinto Fabio*

January. Milan, T. Interinale

Text: an altered version of Zeno's *Lucio Papirio Dittatore*, 1719. Three acts.

Given on many Italian stages; Padua 12 June 1778; Venice, S. Ben. 25 November 1784; Rome, Arg. 7 January 1786, etc.; also London 22 January 1780 and 7 March 1782; Trieste 22 February 1785.

NAUMANN: *Amphion*

26 January. Stockholm

Text by G. G. Adlerbeth (from a French libretto by A. L. Thomas). Prologue and 1 act.

Naumann's first Swedish opera; a German vocal score in 3 acts was published in 1784; in German (translated by J. L. Neumann), produced at Schwedt 22 August 1785. A number of private and concert performances in Germany between 1785 and 1798 are recorded in Engländer's biography of Naumann; the opera was last given in concert form at Leipzig 12 March 1812.

Parts of the music of *Amphion* were used in the English pantomime, *The Picture of Paris* (text by R. Merry and C. Bonnor), produced London, C.G. 20 December 1790 (the rest of the score by W. Shield).

PICCINNI: *Roland*

27 January. Paris, O.

Quinault's text (first set to music by Lully, see 1685), altered and reduced to three acts by J. F. Marmontel.

Piccinni's first French opera; in Paris given until 1793.

In French also, Copenhagen 1 May 1779 (in concert form, parts only); Cassel 1781 and 1 June 1784; Lille 5 September 1781; Liége 4 June 1782.

In Swedish (translated by A. F. Ristell, music adapted by L. S. Lalin), Stockholm 22 July 1781 at Drottningholm Palace and 10 December 1781 publicly.

A German translation, by J. D. von Apell, was published at Göttingen in 1802.

Parodies: *La Rage d'Amour*, by L. F. A. Dorvigny, Paris, C.I. 19 March 1778; *Romans*, by J. E. Despréaux, Marly 30 May 1778; *Donnerpamp* (Swedish), by C. I. Hallman, music by C. Stenborg and J. D. Zander, Stockholm 26 January 1783 and Gothenburg 17 December 1784.

J. E. HARTMANN: *Balders Død*

7 February. Copenhagen

Text by J. Evald (*Heroisk Syngespil*). Three acts. Given at Copenhagen until 1832.

German versions by F. Münter and by C. H. Reichel, published 1780 and 1782 respectively. Produced in German, Regensburg 27 July 1788 (by Schikaneder's troupe, in the open air!). English version by G. Borrow published 1889. There occur in *Balders Død*, a hundred years before Wagner, ensembles of the Valkyries.

UMLAUFF: *Die Bergknappen*

17 February. Vienna, B.

Text by P. Weidmann. One act.

Opening opera of the newly-founded German *Nationalsingspiel* at the Burgtheater. There had been a private performance for the Emperor Joseph II on 16 January. Also given at Hamburg 1780; Regensburg 1781; Mannheim 4 July 1784; Riga Autumn 1785; Prague 1791.

An anonymous Polish translation was published at Warsaw in 1779.

The score of *Die Bergknappen* was published in 1911 (in the *D.T.Ö.* series, edited by R. Haas). For a contemporary account of the first season of the Nationalsingspiel, see J. H. F. Müller, *Abschied von der . . . Schaubühne* (1802), p.253.

J. SCHUSTER: *Der Alchymist*
March. Dresden

Text by A. G. Meissner (also set by André, Berlin 11 April 1778 and revived there 5 November 1787). One act.

Schuster's most successful work: Hamburg 27 January 1779; Mannheim 23 March 1779; Vienna, Jos. 20 April 1779 (André or Schuster?) and Kä. 17 April 1786 (Schuster); Riga 19 November 1782, etc.

Revived at Dresden 14 October 1796; 16 March 1798; and May 1933 (revised by R. Engländer).

J. C. BACH: *La Clemenza di Scipione*
4 April. London, Hm.

Librettist unknown. Three acts.

According to the review in the *Public Advertiser*, "The Poetry is said to be the Production of a Foreign Minister residing at our Court; a Person of Taste and Learning who softens the Cares of Negociation, by sacrificing in secret to the Muses".

Bach's last Italian opera. Revived London 28 March 1805 (Elizabeth Billington's benefit).

(First production 1778, not 1775, as wrongly stated by Pohl, Schwarz, and others.)

TRAETTA: *Il Cavaliere errante*
Spring. Venice, S. Moisè

Text by G. Bertati (*Dramma eroicomico*). Two acts.

Traetta's last preserved opera. Successful in Italy: Florence, P. 20 April 1778; Parma 26 December 1779; Turin, T. Carignano 1785 (as *Stordilano, Principe di Granata*); Padua, 22 July 1786, etc.

In Italian also, Vienna 1779; Paris, O. 5 August 1779; Dresden 1780; Eszterháza Summer 1782 (as *Il Cavaliere errante nell' Isola incantata*). According to A. Schatz (*Vierteljahrsschrift für Musik-*

wissenschaft, v, p.251) revived at Dresden as late as 16 May 1804 (in German, as *Amanda, die mächtige Fee, oder: Zauberey über Zauberey*).

SACCHINI: *L'Amore Soldato*
5 May. London, Hm.

Text by A. Andrei (altered from an earlier libretto by N. Tassi, originally called *L'Amor tra l'Armi* and first set by G. M. Rutini in 1768). Three acts.

In Italian also, Paris, O. 8 July 1779; Eszterháza 1779; Florence May 1781.

GAZZANIGA: *La Vendemmia*
15 May. Florence, P.

Text by G. Bertati (partly founded on an earlier libretto of the same title by Goldoni). Two acts.

Originally given earlier in the same year, January 1778, as an intermezzo, *Il Marchese di Verde Antico*, at the T. Capr., Rome, with music by Gazzaniga and Piticchio.

One of Gazzaniga's most successful works; in Italy given until 1804.

In Italian also, Trieste 26 December 1778; Eszterháza Spring 1780; Prague 1780; Brunswick 1782; Dresden 1783; Warsaw 7 September 1785; London 9 May 1789[1]; Paris, Th. Feydeau 1 June 1791 (with additional music by Cherubini and Mengozzi); Madrid 1792; Barcelona 13 September 1792; Lisbon 24 June 1794. Revived Milan, Sc. 4 November 1796 and Autumn 1804.

In German, Cassel 23 October 1790; Hanover 4 February 1791 and perhaps Prague 1791 (anonymous opera, *Die Weinlese* performed in that year).

GRÉTRY: *Le Jugement de Midas*
27 June. Paris, C.I.

Text by T. d'Hèle. Three acts.

In French also, Liége 28 May 1779; Hague 1779; Cassel 1779; Vienna 1780; Parma, at Comte

---

[1] At the London production of *La Vendemmia*, the duet (Count-Susanna) *Crudel perchè finora* from Mozart's *Le Nozze di Figaro* was sung by Benucci and Anna Storace; probably the first piece of any Mozart opera which was heard on the London stage.

de Flavigny's Carnival 1784; Hamburg 1795; New Orleans 11 June 1808.

In German (translated by C. G. Neefe), Bonn 21 February 1781; Riga 19 May 1783; (translated by C. F. von Bonin and J. André), Berlin 9 July 1781. There are two more German versions, by J. N. Rothmann (published 1781) and by B. C. d'Arien.

The opera was revived at Paris, Petite Scène 18 May 1924; Amsterdam Conservatoire January 1938.

KAMIEŃSKI: *Nedza Uszcześliwiona*
(Misery Made Happy)

11 July. Warsaw

Text by W. Boguslawski (from a "cantata" by F. Bohomolec). Two acts.

The first Polish opera. Music (consisting of 11 airs and 2 duets) extant. Date (differently given in most books) according to L. Bernacki.

ASPELMAYR: *Die Kinder der Natur*

15 July. Vienna, B.

Text (according to Goedeke, v, p.323) by L. A. Hoffmann (founded on C. C. de Marivaux's comedy, *La Dispute,* 1747). Two acts.

Aspelmayr was the second German composer represented in the repertory of the Vienna *Nationalsingspiel* (after Umlauff, see above).

SALIERI: *Europa riconosciuta*

3 August. Milan, Sc.

Text by M. Verazi. Two acts.

Written for the inauguration of the new "Teatro alla Scala" (its predecessor, the Teatro Regio-Ducal, inaugurated 26 December 1717 with Gasparini's *Costantino,* having burnt down on 25 February 1776). Gluck had been invited to write the opening opera, but had refused.

MYSLIVECZEK: *Olimpiade*

4 November. Naples, S.C.

Metastasio's text (first set to music by Caldara in 1733). Three acts.

Regarded as the chief work of the Czech com-

poser. This was the first opera Michael Kelly heard at Naples; see his *Reminiscences,* I, p.44, where he spells the name of the "German" composer "Metzlevisic".

SARTI: *I Contrattempi*

November. Venice, S. Sam.

Text by N. Porta. Three acts.

Successful in Italy; Florence Spring 1781; Monza Autumn 1781; Turin, T. Carignano Autumn 1781; given at Novara Carnival 1782, Padua Autumn 1786 and Vicenza 26 December 1786 as *Gli Equivoci svelati.*

In Italian, also, Dresden 10 January 1782; Vienna 26 April 1784.

In German, Pressburg 1788; Budapest 9 June 1789.

GRÉTRY: *Les fausses Apparences* ou
L'Amant jaloux

20 November. Versailles

Text by T. d'Hèle, versification by F. Levasseur. Three acts.

Paris, C.I. 23 December 1778.

In French also, Hague 1779; Liége 27 November 1779; Vienna Summer 1780; Cassel 1780; Parma Carnival 1781; Smolna 5 July 1781; Brussels 18 May 1795; Hamburg 1795; St. Petersburg 28 September 1795.

In German: Vienna B. 12 October 1780 (translated by G. Stephanie); Berlin 17 December 1781 (translated by J. André and C. F. von Bonin); Bonn 10 February 1782; Münster 10 August 1782; Mannheim 8 September 1782 (translated by F. W. Gotter, music adapted by C. G. Neefe); Hamburg 6 February 1783 (translated by B. C. d'Arien); Carlsruhe 28 December 1785.

In Polish (translated by L. Pierozyński), Warsaw 7 Septembre 1787.

In Danish (translated by J. H. Wessel), Copenhagen 23 November 1787.

In Swedish (translated by C. Envallsson), Stockholm 26 March 1790.

Dutch version by A. K. published 1797.

Grétry's opera was revived at Paris, O.C. 18 September 1850; and, lately, at Liége 16 May 1930 and at the Conservatoire, Geneva 16 April 1931.

BORTNYANSKY: *Quinto Fabio*

26 December. Modena, T. di Corte

Text: the same version of Zeno's *Lucio Papirio*, which Bertoni had set to music earlier in 1778 (see above). Three acts.

Bortnyansky's second and last Italian opera. He afterwards wrote two French *opéras-comiques* (librettos by De La Fermière) for the Russian court, viz. *Le Faucon* (Gachina 22 October 1786) and *Le Fils rival ou La moderne Stratonice* (Pavlovsk 22 October 1787), the scores of which are extant.

SALIERI: *La Scola de'Gelosi*

27 December. Venice, S. Moisè

Text by C. Mazzolà. Two acts.

Successful in Italy; Bologna November 1779 and Autumn 1780 (as *L'Amore in contrasto*); Florence April 1780 and January 1787; Turin, T. Carignano Autumn 1780; Macerata Carnival 1781; Modena, T. di Corte 13 June 1781; Venice, S. Sam. Carnival 1783, etc.; given at Naples, T.N. Carnival 1785 in a new version (text altered by G. Bonito, additional music by F. Cipolla). Revived Milan, Sc. 15 November 1798.

In Italian also, given at: Trieste 26 December 1779; Eszterháza Summer 1780 (with one additional air by Haydn); Warsaw 20 January 1781; Dresden 17 February 1781; Brunswick *c.*Summer 1782; Frankfort February 1783; Vienna 22 April 1783; Prague 1783; London 11 March 1786; Cracow 16 April 1789; Madrid 1 March 1791; Paris 20 May 1791; Lisbon Spring 1795.

In Polish (translated by W. Boguslawski), Warsaw 28 January 1783; Cracow 27 June 1790; Wilna 2 December 1798.

In German (translated by L. Zehnmark), Riga 19 September 1783; Vienna, Neustift Th. 4 December 1783 and Kä. 19 November 1784; Budapest Summer 1784 (first opera ever given there); Hamburg 23 November 1785 (translated by C. F.

Bretzner) and 9 January 1787 (in a new translation as *Das Narrenhaus*); Schleswig 1786; Pressburg January 1787; Berlin 13 February 1787, etc.

In Russian, St. Petersburg 26 June 1789; Moscow 5 September 1797 (revived 2 February 1809).

In Spanish (translated by L. F. Comella), Madrid 12 November 1797.

CIMAROSA: *L'Italiana in Londra*

28 December. Rome, Valle

Text (according to *Gazzetta Toscana*, 1 January 1780) by G. Petrosellini. Two acts.

Cimarosa's twelfth opera and his first great success. Turin, T. Carignano Autumn 1779; Florence Carnival 1780; Novara Carnival 1780; Parma Summer 1780; Milan, Sc. 10 July 1780 and all over Italy.

In Italian also produced at: Pillnitz 20 September 1780 and Dresden 4 October 1780; Gorizia 1781; Graz Carnival 1781; Prague 1781; Warsaw 14 May 1781 and Cracow 7 February 1788; Trieste 27 September 1781; Ghent September 1782; Lugano 28 September 1782 (first opera ever given there, announced as by Paisiello); Aachen 7 November 1782; Barcelona 8 May 1783; Madrid 19 January 1785; Lisbon Carnival 1788; Cadiz 1792; Vienna 5 May 1783; Versailles July 1787; Paris, Th. de M. 9 September 1790 (with additions by Cherubini and Mingozzi; revived 17 October 1801). London 15 January 1788 (as *La Locandiera*, the scene changed from London to Amsterdam); St. Petersburg 1797.

In German (translated by C. F. Pleissner): Bonn 25 May 1783; Frankfort 13 September 1783; Nuremberg 31 August 1784; Salzburg 19 September 1784; Riga 18 May 1785 (as *Nantchen oder Das deutsche Mädchen in London*); etc. New German version by J. C. Bock: Pressburg 21 August 1786; Weimar 7 October 1786; Cologne 5 November 1786; Hanover 7 May 1787; Hamburg 3 July 1789, etc. Never given at Berlin.

In Polish (translated by W. Boguslawski), Warsaw 16 January 1783; Wilna 3 January 1799.

In Danish (translated by L. Knudsen), Copenhagen 14 October 1786.

In French (as *Livia, ou L'Italienne à Londres*, adapted by Pigeon de Saint-Paterne), Paris, Th. Montansier 13 April 1790; (translated by Neuville), Amsterdam December 1792.

In Swedish (translated by C. Envallsson), Stockholm 13 November 1795.

In Russian, St. Petersburg 4 June 1810.

The opera was revived at Geneva (seventh Festival of the I.S.C.M.) 8 April 1929 (reduced 1-act version by A. Lualdi).

1779

Melnik, Koldun, Obmanshchik i Svat
Мельник, Колдун, Обманщик и Сват

31 January. Moscow

Text by A. O. Ablesimov. Three acts.

(The title means *Miller, Wizard, Deceiver, and Marriage-Broker.*)

Frequently misattributed to Fomin. Ablesimov indicated in the libretto various popular melodies to be used in the work and these were harmonised for the performance at Moscow by an otherwise unknown violinist named Sokolovsky. Additions were made from time to time and it is possible that Fomin was responsible for the overture and a few new numbers added at St. Petersburg.

First given at St. Petersburg 14 February 1781. Very popular comic opera, frequently revived in Russia during the 19th century. Vocal score reprinted in 1894 (misattributed to Fomin).

Revived in Paris, Petite Scène 14 June 1929 (in French, translated by O. Choumansky, G. Alphaud, and X. de Courville, music revised by Cherepnin).

PAISIELLO: *Gli Astrologi immaginari*

14 February. St. Petersburg

Text by G. Bertati (founded on Marmontel's tale *Le Connoisseur*), originally in 3 acts and called *I Visionari* (first composed by Astaritta, Venice Autumn 1772; Dresden 3 September 1774; Lisbon Carnival 1775). Two acts.

Very successful all over Europe. Sometimes given under the original title, or as *I Filosofi im-*

maginari. Not to be confounded with *Il Socrate immaginario* (see 1775) which is a different work. Apart from *Il Barbiere di Siviglia* (see 1782), the most important opera Paisiello wrote for the Russian Court.

(The date of the first performance is given by the Empress Catherine II in a letter dated 5/16 February 1779. Schatz-Sonneck and other sources give 18 February 1779.)

In Italian also produced at Warsaw 30 April 1781; Moscow 25 April 1782; Venice, S. Sam. Autumn 1782; Ghent May 1783; Vienna 8 October 1783; Naples, Fior. 1784; Eszterháza 1784; Salzburg 1785; Barcelona 16 June 1785; Paris, Th. de M. 24 March 1789; Lisbon 1790; Dresden December 1793; Trieste Spring 1796; Milan, Sc. 5 November 1798.

In German (translated by G. Stephanie), Vienna, B. 22 May 1781; Frankfort 30 October 1781; Hamburg 29 January 1782; Berlin 27 March 1783; Munich 29 July 1783; Salzburg Autumn 1783; Trieste July 1784 (first opera ever sung in German there); Cologne Autumn 1784; Carlsruhe 5 October 1784; Riga 10 November 1784; Budapest 13 May 1786; Hanover 27 April 1787; Pforzheim 1 June 1787; Prague 1787; Pyrmont 8 July 1790; Cassel 13 November 1790; Pressburg 8 September 1792; Bremen 28 October 1792; Osnabrück 4 March 1793; Warsaw 17 September 1793; Cracow September 1796 (as *Der verjüngte Greis*, according to *Journal des Luxus und der Moden*); Agram 22 January 1799; Berne Spring 1804.

In Danish (translated by L. Knudsen), Copenhagen 21 December 1784.

In French (translated by P. U. Dubuisson), Paris, Th. Beaujolais 15 January 1789.

In Polish (translated by W. Boguslawski), Warsaw 18 April 1790.

In Hungarian (translated by A. Szerelemhegyi), Budapest 27 September 1793; Clausenburg 14 September 1806.

In Russian, Moscow 26 February 1794; St. Petersburg 19 September 1796.

The latest recorded productions were at Vienna 6 April 1802; Berlin 12 December 1806; Milan

Spring 1807; Parma Summer 1807; Padua Autumn 1808; Venice 11 June 1809; Stuttgart 21 June 1809; Moscow 18 September 1819 (in German); Lucerne 1819 (in German, by students).

SEYDELMANN: *Arsene*

3 March. Dresden

Text by A. G. Meissner (translated from Favart's French libretto, see 1773). Four acts.

The best work of the Saxon composer. Date of first performance according to Schatz; R. Cahn-Speyer gives Leipzig 15 April 1779 and Dresden 26 November 1781. Also given at Cologne 1785–86.

HAYDN: *La vera Costanza*

Spring. Eszterháza

Puttini's text (first set to music by Anfossi, see 1776), with alterations by P. Travaglia. Three acts.

Haydn's setting was originally written for the Vienna Hoftheater, but it was never produced there. It became fairly popular in a German version by F. X. Girzik: *Der flatterhafte Liebhaber oder Der Sieg der Beständigkeit*, given at Pressburg 30 January 1786; Budapest 7 July 1789; Vienna, Th. a.d.Landstrasse 13 April 1790; Brünn 14 January 1792.

In a French version by P. U. Dubuisson, as *Laurette*, given at Paris, Th.d.M. 21 January 1791. Probably translated from this French version it was then performed as *Laurette* at Cologne in July 1796 (in German).

According to O. Chayanova (see also *Der Freimüthige*, I, p.199) an opera of this title (which may have been Haydn's) was performed in Russian at Moscow in 1802.

GLUCK: *Iphigénie en Tauride*

18 May. Paris, O.

Text by N. F. Guillard. Four acts.

Very successful in France; given at the Opéra 408 times until 1829; revived Th.L. 26 November 1868; Ren. 7 December 1899; O.C. 18 June 1900; 20 April 1914; and 18 April 1931.

Parodies: (1) *Les Rêveries renouvelées des Grecs*, by C. S. Favart and J. N. Guerin de Frémicourt, music by F. J. Prot, Paris, C.I. 26 June 1779; also Cassel 1782; Toulouse 1784; Liége 7 January 1789; Brussels 22 August 1798; Stockholm 25 February 1800 (in Swedish, translated by C. Envallsson); Moscow 24 October 1807 (in French). Revived Ghent 19 February 1822; Paris, Variétés 6 December 1822. (Favart used for *Les Rêveries* an earlier piece of his, written in collaboration with C. H. F. de Voisenon, called *La petite Iphigénie* and produced in Paris, C.I. 21 July 1757 as a parody of C. Guymond de Latouche's tragedy *Iphigénie en Tauride*); (2) *Les bons Amis ou Il était Temps*, by L. F. A. Dorvigny, Variétés-Amusantes 2 July 1779 (no music); (3) *Iphise aux Boulevards* (anonymous), Th. des Elèves August 1779.

Early productions of Gluck's opera were at:

VIENNA, B. 23 October 1781 (in German, translated by J. von Alxinger) and 14 December 1783 (in Italian, translated by L. da Ponte); also at Prince Auersperg's, February 1786.

LILLE 3 March 1782.

STOCKHOLM 5 May 1783 (in Swedish, translated by A. F. Ristell).

RHEINSBERG 9 May 1783 (in French).

CASSEL 26 March 1784 (in French).

COPENHAGEN 6 February 1785 (concert performance, in French).

BERLIN 21 February 1788 (in concert form, in French) and 24 February 1795 (on the stage, new German version by J. D. Sander).

MAYENCE 24 May 1790 (in German).

FRANKFORT 27 July 1790 (in German).

MANNHEIM 18 January 1791 (in German).

HAMBURG 22 December 1793 (the first act only, in concert form); on the stage, complete, 21 June 1811.

HANOVER 7 February 1794 (in German).

BREMEN 18 December 1794 (in German).

LONDON 7 April 1796 (in Italian, Da Ponte's version).

WEIMAR 27 December 1800 (in German, translated by C. A. Vulpius).

BRUNSWICK 1802 (in French).

STUTTGART 1 October 1805 (in German).

MUNICH 21 October 1808 (in German).

BRESLAU 22 March 1810 (in German).

DANZIG 31 March 1811 (in German).

BUDAPEST 15 September 1814 (in German).

AMSTERDAM 1821 (in German).

Later productions:

LONDON, PRINCE's 9 July 1840 (in German) and H.M's 8 May 1866 (in Italian, translated by S. de Castrone, Marchese della Rajata; in English much later, see below).

PRAGUE 10 February 1843 (in German) and 6 June 1890 (in Czech, translated by V. J. Novotný).

COPENHAGEN 20 October 1847 (in Danish, translated by A. Hertz).

MANCHESTER 11 January 1860 (at a Hallé concert, for the first time in English, translated by H. F. Chorley).

BASLE 15 March 1877 (in German, for the first time in Switzerland?).

BRUSSELS 25 February 1883 (in concert form).

BARCELONA 15 April 1900 (in Italian).

ORANGE 12 August 1900 (open air performance at the Roman Theatre).

ALGIERS March 1901 (in French).

HAGUE January 1902 (in French).

LONDON, H.M's 18 February 1910 (in English, by R.C.M.).

NEW YORK, M. 25 November 1916 (in German; for the first time in America).

VICENZA 28 August 1922 (at the T. Olimpico, for the first time in Italy).

BASLE 5 September 1929 (in a German version, by G. Bundi).

FALMOUTH 16 February 1933 (in English, translated by M. and E. Radford).

LONDON, CENTURY TH. 3 February 1934 (same version).

CHRISTIANSUND c.December 1934 (in Norwegian).

MILAN, SC. 11 March 1937 (in Italian).

BUENOS AIRES 24 September 1937 (in German).

UMLAUFF: *Die puecefarbnen Schuhe* oder *Die schöne Schusterinn*

22 June. Vienna, B.

Text: a German version, by G. Stephanie, of Ferrières's French libretto (see 1776). Two acts.

Successful in Germany: Hamburg 16 December 1779, etc.; also Salzburg 24 September 1780; Warsaw 18 September 1781; Dresden 5 December 1781; Riga 19 August 1783; Vienna, Leop. 9 June 1783; Breslau 22 April 1785; Berlin 4 June 1785 (German version by J. André); Schwedt 6 February 1786; Carlsruhe 14 March 1786; Prague 5 September 1790; Budapest 11 September 1791.

Revived Vienna, Kä. 31 January 1785 and W. 27 April 1795; Berlin 26 July 1825.

CIMAROSA: *L'Infedeltà fedele*

20 July. Naples, Fondo

Text by G. B. Lorenzi. Three acts.

Written for the inauguration of the new "Real Teatro del Fondo di Separazione", Naples. According to the preface, Lorenzi tried to create a new genre half-way between opera seria and opera buffa.

Outside Italy only given at Dresden 5 October 1782.

DA SILVA: *La Galatea*

21 August. Lisbon, Th. di Queluz

Text by P. Metastasio (written in 1722; first composer unknown). Two acts.

Da Silva's setting was written for the celebration of the birthday of "Don Giuseppe, Principe del Brazile" (son of Maria I, Queen of Portugal). The score of this early opera by a Portuguese composer is extant.

G. BENDA: *Pygmalion*

20 September. Gotha

Text: a German version, by an unknown translator (Gotter?), of Rousseau's *scène lyrique* (see 1770). One act.

The vocal score of Benda's setting was published in 1780.

Also produced at Bonn 24 February 1780; Mannheim 28 January 1783; Weimar 29 January 1791; Pressburg March 1794 (Benda's?); Berlin 25 November 1797; Leipzig 2 June 1799; Breslau 2 July 1799; Vienna, Kä. 12 June 1801, etc. Given at Berlin until 1835.

In Russian, Moscow 24 February 1794.
In French, Poznán 17 February 1806.
Revived in Czech, Brno 1935.

Previously to Benda, two other German composers had tried their hands at a new setting of Rousseau's *Pygmalion*. First Aspelmayr, whose version in a German translation by J. G. von Laudes was performed at Vienna 19 February 1772 (and perhaps even earlier with the original French text); probably at Prague 1 October 1772; and, according to G. Becker, also on some Italian stages. Secondly Schweitzer, whose setting (translator probably J. F. Schmidt) was first performed at Weimar 13 May 1772 and subsequently at Leipzig 3 November 1774 and Gotha 15 November 1774. The music of both Aspelmayr's and Schweitzer's versions seems to be lost.

GLUCK: *Echo et Narcisse*

24 September. Paris, O.

Text by L. T. de Tschudy. Three acts.

Gluck's last opera. Unsuccessful; after a few performances in 1779 and 1780, revived in Paris only on 25 March 1806 in a reduced 2-act version by A. L. Beaunier, music arranged by H. M. Berton (10 performances until 1814). Given at Lille 17 March 1782.

Revived in the 20th century by the Elizabeth Duncan School at Darmstadt 11 October 1913 (revised by E. Duncan and M. Merz); and subsequently on some other German stages and at Zurich 27 October 1913 (German version by T. Rehbaum).

Revived in French privately, at Malmaison 4 July 1926 (under F. Raugel).

KOSPOTH: *Adrast und Isidore,* oder *Die Serenate*

16 October. Berlin

Text by C. F. Bretzner (founded on Molière's *Le Silicien*). Two acts.

Given in Berlin until 1802; Schwedt 7 January 1785; Breslau 23 July 1790. Bretzner's text was also composed by F. Preu (Dresden 22 February 1779; Hamburg 23 August 1779; Budapest 6 No-

vember 1786) and by F. A. von Mitscha (Vienna, B. 26 April 1781).

P. GUGLIELMI: *La Villanella ingentilita*

8 November. Naples, Fior.

Text by S. Zini. Three acts.

After 12 years (see *La Sposa fedele*, 1767) in the course of which Guglielmi wrote no less than 25 unsuccessful works, this was the first opera of a more fortunate period lasting until 1790.

Given at Florence, P. Spring 1782 as *I due Fratelli sciocchi;* new 2-act version Milan, Sc. 9 August 1783 (*I Fratelli Pappamosca*); revived Naples Autumn 1784; Rome, T. Pallacorda Carnival 1790 (as *La Villanella incivilita*).

Outside Italy: Lisbon Carnival 1786; Marseilles Autumn 1789. Probably identical with an opera *La Villanella fortunata*, which was produced by a travelling company at Breslau 6 January 1792; Lübeck 8 July 1792; Gothenburg 23 April 1793; Stockholm 1 October 1793; and Christiania 20 May 1794.

GRÉTRY: *Les Événements imprévus*

11 November. Versailles

Text by T. d'Hèle. Three acts.

Paris, C.I. 13 November 1779 and, with alterations, 12 October 1780.

In French also, Cassel 1781; Liége 31 December 1781; Amsterdam 12 April 1791.

In German (as *Die unvermutheten Zufaelle,* translated by G. Stephanie), Vienna, B. 1 September 1781; Frankfort 2 January 1783; (as *Unverhofft kommt oft,* translated by J. André), Berlin 17 April 1782; Hamburg 6 December 1782; Mannheim 29 June 1783; Bonn 23 July 1783, etc.

In Danish (translated by L. Knudsen), Copenhagen 2 January 1784.

In Swedish (translated by C. Stenborg), Stockholm 27 October 1800.

An English adaptation by G. Colman, additional music by M. Kelly and W. Hawes, *Gay Deceivers; or More Laugh than Love*, was given in London, Little Hm. 22 August 1804 (revived 10

May 1828) and in New York on 5 November 1819. An English translation of the original, *Unforeseen Events*, was published in T. Holcroft's *Theatrical Recorder*, II (1806).

HAYDN: *L' Isola disabitata*

6 December. Eszterháza

Metastasio's text (first set to music by Bonno in 1754). Two parts.

In Italian also, Vienna 19 March 1785 (in concert form); Berlin 1786.

In German, perhaps Pressburg 24 April 1780 (Haydn's setting? The anonymous performance is recorded in A. Heppner's book on the Pressburg stage; considering the place and the year it seems not unlikely that it was Haydn's opera. A German translation of Metastasio's text, by A. G. Meissner, had been published in 1778 and might have been used).

Revived Vienna 29 May 1909 (in German, reduced to one act, scoring revised); Washington, Library of Congress 9 March 1936 (in Italian); Florence, P. 21 May 1938 (in Italian). Vocal score published 1938.

J. C. BACH: *Amadis de Gaule*

14 December. Paris, O.

Quinault's text (first set to music by Lully, see 1684), reduced to three acts by A. M. D. de Vismes.

Bach's last (unsuccessful) opera, the only one he wrote for Paris. "Les Gluckistes ont trouvés qu'il n'avait ni l'originalité de Gluck, ni ses sublimes élans; les Piccinistes, que son chant n'avait ni le charme, ni la variété de la mélodie de Piccini" (Grimm, *Corresp. litt.* x, p.236).

MYSLIVECZEK: *Armida*

26 December. Milan, S.C.

Text: an Italian version, by G. A. Migliavacca, of Quinault's *Armide* (first set to music by Lully, see 1686). Three acts.

Mysliveczek's last opera.

GRÉTRY: *Aucassin et Nicolette*, OU *Les Moeurs du bon vieux Temps*

30 December. Versailles

Text by J. M. Sedaine (founded on the French 13th century story). Four acts.

Paris, C.I. 3 January 1780 and repeated there 7 January 1782 in a reduced 3-act version with some new music.

In French also, Liége 25 February 1783; Cassel 27 August 1784; Geneva 22 June 1785; Cologne 1796–97; Berne 3 October 1801.

In German (translated by J. André), Hamburg 17 September 1787; Berlin 3 August 1791. There was another German translation by C. G. Neefe, 1785.

1780

CARUSO: *L'Albergatrice vivace*

Carnival. Venice, S. Sam.

Librettist unknown. Two acts.

The most successful of Caruso's more than 50 operas. Given on many Italian stages (Milan, Sc. 25 July 1781, etc.) and at Warsaw 24 January 1781; Dresden 1782; London 16 December 1783 (with additions by other composers); Hanover 1783 or 1784; Potsdam 20 September 1785.

SALIERI: *La Dama Pastorella*

January. Rome, Valle

Text by G. Petrosellini. Two acts.

This opera became more popular 10 years later when Da Ponte revised the libretto for Vienna. Produced there under the new title *La Cifra* 11 December 1789.

In Italian also given at Dresden 1790; Milan, Sc. 16 October 1790; Barcelona 30 May 1791; Warsaw 2 March 1793; Lisbon Spring 1796; London 10 March 1798.

In German (as *Der Aufschluss* or as *Die Entzifferung*, translated by H. G. Schmieder), Hanover 5 June 1792; Mannheim 24 June 1793 (translated by H. Beck); Hamburg 7 October 1793; Vienna 19 December 1805; Frankfort 1

June 1807; (as *Das Kästchen mit der Chiffer*, translated by C. A. Vulpius), Berlin 25 February 1793; (as *Das entdeckte Geheimnis*, translated by K. L. Gieseke), Vienna, W. 8 April 1795.

In Spanish (translated by L. F. Comella), Madrid 8 July 1799.

SCHWEITZER: *Rosamund*

20 January. Mannheim

Text by C. M. Wieland. Three acts.

Schweitzer's last work. The opera was ready to be performed on 11 January 1778 when the sudden death of the Bavarian Elector, Maximilian Joseph, on 30 December 1777, and the departure of his successor, Carl Theodor, to Munich frustrated the production. Two years later the interest in the new development of German national opera raised by *Alceste* and *Günther von Schwarzburg* had somewhat diminished; *Rosamund* was given at Mannheim four times only and did not reach any other stage.

J. E. HARTMANN: *Fiskerne*

31 January. Copenhagen

Text by J. Evald. Three acts.

Very successful at Copenhagen; given there until 1814 and revived 31 January 1880 (in concert form, by the Cäciliaföreningen).

In this opera occurs the Danish National Anthem *Kong Christian*.

There are printed German versions of the libretto by C. F. Cramer (1780) and C. F. Sander (1786); Swedish translation by G. E. Lundgren published 1875.

PICCINNI: *Atys*

22 February. Paris, O.

Quinault's text (first set to music by Lully, see 1676), altered and reduced to 3 acts by J. F. Marmontel.

Given in Paris 64 times until 1792.

In French also, Copenhagen 1795 (parts, in concert form); St. Petersburg 1798.

In Swedish (translated by A. F. Ristell), Stockholm 1 November 1784 (music adapted by L. S. Lalin).

PAISIELLO: *La finta Amante*

4 June. Mogilev

Librettist unknown. Two acts.

The opera was written for a meeting of Catherine II and Joseph II which took place at Mogilev, on the Dnieper, White Russia, on 4 June. The opera was probably produced on that night.

In Italian also given at: Moscow 24 May 1782; Vienna, Laxenburg Palace 20 June 1784 and B. 7 July 1784; Cracow 3 April 1788; Naples, Fior. August 1788 and S.C. 13 August 1788 (revived Fondo Autumn 1825); Palermo 1793; St. Petersburg 19 September 1799; Paris 19 May 1804.

In Russian (translated by Z. Krizhanovsky), St. Petersburg 1784; Moscow 15 April 1787.

In German (translated by J. André) perhaps Carlsruhe 22 March 1786 (see L. Schiedermair, *Die Oper an den Badischen Höfen*, p.533); Mannheim 8 April 1788; Baden 1789; Frankfort 14 September 1793.

GRÉTRY: *Andromaque*

6 June. Paris, O.

Text by L. G. Pitra (founded on Racine's tragedy). Three acts.

Grétry's first *tragédie-lyrique* (unsuccessful). According to Grimm, a parody on *Andromaque*, by J. B. Henri Gourgault Dugazon, was performed at Mlle Guimard's private theatre in August 1780.

In Swedish (translated by A. F. Ristell, J. H. Kellgren, and A. N. Edelcrantz), Drottningholm Palace 22 July 1785 and Stockholm 3 November 1785.

BEECKE: *Claudine von Villa Bella*

13 June. Vienna, B.

The first of the numerous settings of Goethe's *Schauspiel mit Gesang* (1776). Three acts.

Frankfort 3 February 1784; Bonn 10 February 1784, etc.

CIMAROSA: *Il Falegname*

Summer. Naples, Fior.

Text by G. Palomba. Three acts.

Milan, Sc. 11 August 1781; Florence Carnival

1782; Mantua Spring 1782; Bologna October 1782; Venice, S. Moisè Autumn 1784; Turin, T. Carignano Autumn 1785, etc. (Given at Treviso, Zara, and Udine, Summer 1789 as *L'Artista*; in Italy until 1803, mostly in a reduced 2-act version).

In Italian also: Prague 1782; Graz Carnival 1783; Vienna 25 July 1783 (revived with alterations 15 July 1789); Brunswick 1784; Dresden 1787; Charlottenburg July 1789; Warsaw 31 December 1792; Madrid 12 November 1793.

NEEFE: *Adelheit von Veltheim*
23 September. Frankfort

Text by G. F. W. Grossmann. Four acts.

The most successful work of Neefe who was Beethoven's first teacher at Bonn. Given at Bonn 11 October 1780; Pyrmont 19 July 1781; Cassel 20 August 1781; Vienna, B. 31 August 1781 (by a company of children); Berlin 2 July 1782; Münster 8 July 1782; Bremen 17 December 1783; Breslau 2 December 1784, etc. (in Germany given until about 1800).

In German also, Trieste 17 June 1787 (with music?); Schleswig 1789.

One of the earliest German operas on a Turkish subject and in that respect the immediate forerunner of Mozart's *Entführung* (see 1782).

KOSPOTH: *Der Irrwisch* oder *Endlich fand er sie*
2 October. Berlin

Text by C. F. Bretzner. Three acts.

One of the favourite German Singspiel librettos of that time; there are settings by Holly, Preu, Mühle, Dieter, all *c*.1780; see also Umlauff's setting, 1782.

Kospoth's opera was given in Berlin until 1796. In German also, Bremen 26 August 1784; Riga Autumn 1785; Schwedt 30 September 1785; Hanover 27 December 1787.

HAYDN: *La Fedeltà premiata*
15 October. Eszterháza

Text: an altered version of G. B. Lorenzi's *L'Infedeltà fedele* (see 1779). Three acts.

Written for the inauguration of the new theatre at Eszterháza. In German (as *Die belohnte Treue*; translator unknown), Vienna 18 December 1784; Pressburg 3 June 1785; Budapest 5 June 1789; Graz 11 October 1792.

ANFOSSI: *I Viaggiatori felici*
October. Venice, S. Sam.

Text by F. Livigni. Two acts.

One of Anfossi's most successful comic operas.

Given on many Italian stages: Florence, P. 17 April 1781; Turin, T. Carignano Autumn 1781; Bologna Autumn 1781; Milan, Sc. Carnival 1784 and Autumn 1787, etc. In Italian also at Trieste 23 May 1781; Prague December 1781; Dresden 21 November 1781; London 11 December 1781 (revived 28 May 1785 and 1 March 1803); Brunswick 1782; Hanover 1782; Vienna 29 December 1783; Corfu Autumn 1784; Madrid 1787; Paris, Th. de M. 30 June 1790 (three additional airs by Cherubini); Warsaw 18 September 1790; Lisbon Spring 1794.

In German (translated by F. X. Girzik), Pressburg 27 May 1785 and Budapest 16 October 1789; (translated by K. L. Giescke), Graz 1788; (translated by C. F. D. Schubart), Stuttgart 1 September 1789.

FLOQUET: *Le Seigneur bienfaisant*
14 December. Paris, O.

Text by M. A. J. Rochon de Chabannes. Three acts, called *Le Pressoir ou Les Fêtes de l'Automne*; *L'Incendie*; and *Le Bal*; a prologue or first act *Le Retour du Seigneur dans ses Terres* was added for a revival on 23 December 1782. Given at Bordeaux 1794 as *Le Général bienfaisant*.

Floquet's most successful work and of some historical interest as an attempt to introduce a bourgeois subject into the heroic repertory of the Paris Opéra.

JACKSON: *The Lord of the Manor*
27 December. London, D.L.

Text by J. Burgoyne (founded on Marmontel's *Silvain*, see 1770). Three acts.

Successful on English stages. First given at Dublin 23 March 1781; Edinburgh 24 July 1781. Libretto also published Philadelphia 1790 and 1791.

Given in New York 2 February 1818 and 27 December 1826; revived in London, C.G. 24 October 1812 (with additional music by J. C. Doyle, Bishop, Welsh, Reeve and Davy); D.L. 20 December 1820; Ly. 12 November 1834; and Strand 21 November 1853.

(Burgoyne's preface contains interesting ideas on the development and possibilities of English opera.)

1781

CIMAROSA: *Il Pittor Parigino*

4 January. Rome, Valle

Text by G. Petrosellini. Two acts.

Originally in two acts; a later, 3-act version, *Il Barone burlato* was first given at Naples Winter 1784 (text altered by G. Bonito, additional music by F. Cipolla.

Very successful in Italy; Bologna Autumn 1781; Parma Carnival 1782; Turin Spring 1782; Milan, Sc. 10 August 1782; Venice, S. Sam. Autumn 1783, etc. In Italy until 1808.

In Italian also given at Prague and Dresden 1782; Leipzig Summer 1782; Barcelona 20 April 1783; London 25 January 1785 (text altered by A. Andrei); Vienna 18 May 1785 (revived 24 May 1792, "die Musik verbessert und vermehrt", probably the 1784 version); Warsaw 25 November 1785; Corfu Carnival 1787; Eszterháza 1789; Antwerp 30 August 1804; Paris 1 August 1805.

In German (as *Der Maler von Paris*, translated by F. X. Girzik), Pressburg 28 July 1786; Hanover 4 July 1788; Budapest 8 August 1792; (as *Der Onkel aus Amsterdam*, translated by G. C. Claudius), Oels 13 May 1797.

SARTI: *Giulio Sabino*

January. Venice, S. Ben.

Text by P. Giovannini. Three acts.

The most successful of Sarti's serious operas. Florence, P. Autumn 1781; Pisa Spring 1782; Imola Summer 1782; Bologna September 1782;

Forlì Spring 1783; Modena 1 January 1784; Reggio 1784; Perugia Carnival 1784; Naples, S.C. 13 August 1786, etc.

In Italian also given at: Esterháza, Brunswick and Barcelona in 1783; Hanover January 1784; Warsaw 15 March 1785; Vienna, Kä. 4 August 1785 (revived 14 September 1805 with additional music by Weigl, Salieri and Gyrowetz); Trieste 1 March 1788; London 5 April 1788; Madrid 16 December 1797; Lisbon 13 May 1798; Berlin 3 January 1803 (as *Epponina*, with additions by Gürrlich).

In German (translated by J. N. Schueller), Pressburg 2 January 1786 and Budapest 26 November 1792; another German translation, by N. A. Heiden, was published at Nuremberg in 1781 (performed?).

The opera contains a famous funeral march which has been compared to the one in Beethoven's *Eroica*.

KAMIEŃSKI: *Zośka czyli Wiejskie Zaloty* (Sophia, or Country Courtship)

21 January. Warsaw

Text by S. Szymański. One act.

Popular Polish ballad-opera, Kamieński's most successful work; given 76 times until 1859 (but not "consecutively". Riemann's *Musiklexikon* and many other books of reference repeat a slip in L. von Trocki's pamphlet, *Die Entwicklung der Oper in Polen*, 1867, p.24; see *ibid.*, p.11). Text printed 1784. Music extant.

The year of the first performance was 1779 according to Dmuszewski-Karasowski; 1780 according to A. Zalewski's *Kronika* (1807). 21 January 1781 is the date of the first recorded performance (advertisement). Given at Cracow on 17 October 1790.

PICCINNI: *Iphigénie en Tauride*

23 January. Paris, O.

Text by A. Du Congé Dubreuil. Four acts.

The opera seems to have been commissioned by the management of the Opéra at the same time as Gluck's *Iphigénie en Tauride* (see 1779), taking advantage of the struggle between Gluckistes and Piccinnistes. According to Lajarte, "le pauvre Piccinni a été encore une fois dupe des intrigues et du mauvais vouloir de l'administration". Still, his opera was performed more than 30 times (revived 17 June 1785 and 6 November 1790).

In French also given at Copenhagen 25 February 1787 (in concert form); in concert form also St. Petersburg 29 December 1791. Parts of it were revived at Paris, O. on 26 March 1916.

CHAMPEIN: *La Mélomanie*

23 January. Paris, C.I.

Text by Grenier and Duveyrier. One act.

Champein's best work, given at the O.C. until 1829.

In French also, Liége 27 November 1783; Hague 27 March 1784; Rouen 29 March 1784; Cassel 25 September 1784; Marseilles 31 October 1787 (at the inauguration of the Grand-Théâtre); Aachen 10 August 1794; Hamburg 1795; Charleston, S.C. 16 June 1795; St. Petersburg 31 August 1795; Baltimore 14 March 1796; Philadelphia 30 December 1796; Cologne 1796–97; Moscow 8 February 1809; Berne 23 April 1810.

In German (translated by H. G. Schmieder), Frankfort 5 August 1785; (translated by C. G. Neefe), Hanover 7 September 1790; Hamburg 1799; (translated by C. A. Herklots), Berlin 1 June 1813.

In Dutch, Amsterdam 1786 (revived Hague 1814); in Flemish, Oudenarde 1795.

In Danish (translated by A. G. Thoroup), Copenhagen 15 February 1791.

In Swedish (translated by C. Envallsson), Stockholm 15 December 1796.

A Russian version of the libretto by A. V. Khrapovitsky was set by Martin y Soler: produced St. Petersburg 18 January 1790.

MOZART: *Idomeneo*

29 January. Munich

Text by G. B. Varesco (founded on Danchet's French libretto, see 1712). Three acts.

In Mozart's lifetime, the opera was, after Munich, only given once more; (private) performance at Prince Auersperg's, Vienna, in March 1786. The duet K.489 and the rondo K.490 were added for that occasion. A private performance, in Italian, presumably in concert form, took place at Budapest in 1803; see *Bibliographia Hungariae*, Vol. II, p.201.

Next, *Idomeneo* was produced in German on a few stages in the beginning of the 19th century: Cassel 1 January 1802 (translated by J. D. von Apell); Nuremberg 1803; Hamburg 31 March 1804 (in concert form); Vienna 13 May 1806 (translated by G. F. Treitschke); Berlin 3 August 1806; Frankfort 4 November 1807; Stuttgart 14 November 1810; Leipzig 1811 (in concert form); Bucharest 1818; Königsberg 12 December 1821; Riga 1825 (in concert form).

On many important stages the opera was produced about the middle of the 19th century: Weimar 16 February 1840; Munich 12 January 1845 (translated by L. Lenz; announced as first performance at Munich!); new German translation by K. F. Niese: Dresden 15 January 1854; Berlin 15 October 1855; Mannheim 27 January 1861; Leipzig 3 February 1869; Darmstadt 22 October 1871; Cassel 28 November 1877.

New arrangement by J. N. Fuchs: Vienna 25 October 1879; Hamburg 17 January 1880; Rotterdam 4 December 1880; Prague 17 October 1887.

The opera was revived in a new arrangement by E. Lewicki at Carlsruhe 4 April 1917 and Dresden 4 March 1925.

Many revivals took place in 1931, celebrating the 150th anniversary of the first performance. It was given in new arrangements by A. Rother at Dessau 19 February 1931; by Richard Strauss and L. Wallerstein at Vienna 16 April 1931; Zurich Spring 1932; Berlin 11 November 1932, etc.; by W. Meckbach, Brunswick 31 May 1931; and by E. Wolf-Ferrari and E. L. Stahl at Munich 15 June 1931.

The Italian original was revived at the Mozart Festival, Basle 13 May 1931.

Idomeneo was very seldom given outside the German speaking countries. Parts of the music were used in a French pasticcio, *Louis XII ou La Route de Reims* by J. F. S. Maizony de Lauréal and J. H. Vernoy de Saint-Georges, music from *Idomeneo, Tito*, etc., arranged by P. Crémont and A. Vergne, produced at Paris, Odéon 7 June 1825 (*A l'occasion du Sacre de Sa Majesté Charles X*) and in an English pasticcio *The Casket* by M. R. Lacy, produced in London, D.L. 10 March 1829.

In Paris, parts of *Idomeneo* were heard at the Conservatoire in February 1846; the whole opera at a Schola Cantorum concert 27 November 1902 and, recently, in Italian, Conservatoire 21 February 1931 and Th. des Champs-Elysées 28 October 1933 (by the Société des Études Mozartiennes).

The third act was staged at the Th. des Arts, 12 December 1912 (in French, translated by L. Laloy).

Recent productions:

PRAGUE 5 December 1931 (in Czech, translated by J. Fiala).

BRUSSELS 25 January 1932 (the Strauss-Wallerstein version in French, translated by P. Spaak).

GLASGOW 12 March 1934 (in English, translated by M. and E. Radford).

LONDON, TWENTIETH CENTURY TH. 12 March 1938 (in English, M. and E. Radford's version).

CAMBRIDGE 2 May 1939 (in English, M. and E. Radford's version).

The opera does not seem to have been produced in America so far. Nor was it ever given in Italy, although P. Lichtenthal made an arrangement for Italian stages as early as 1843 (see *A.M. Z.*, Vol. XLV, p.809).

NAUMANN: *Elisa*

21 April. Dresden

Text by C. Mazzolà. Two acts.

In Italian also given at Prague 1788; at Dresden until 1790.

In Danish (translated by L. Knudsen), Copenhagen 30 January 1795.

SALIERI: *Der Rauchfangkehrer*

30 April. Vienna, B.

Text by L. von Auenbrugger. (Sub-title: *Die unentbehrlichen Verräther ihrer Herrschaften aus Eigennutz.*) Three acts.

Salieri's contribution to the "National-Singspiel"; the first of his two German operas. Also given at Frankfort 14 November 1782; Berlin 12 August 1783 (adapted); Prague Summer 1783; Salzburg Autumn 1783; Mannheim 10 April 1785; Riga October 1785; Carlsruhe 2 May 1786; Hanover 29 May 1787; Budapest 14 July 1787; Pressburg 1788; Munich September 1788, etc.

Revived Vienna, Leop. 9 October 1786 (with original title) and Th.a.d. Landstrasse, 10 May 1790, as *Die listigen Kaminfeger oder Die bestraften Spröden.*

ANDRÉ: *Belmont und Constanze* oder *Die Entführung aus dem Serail*

25 May. Berlin

Text by C. F. Bretzner (according to W. Preibisch founded on G. Martinelli's Italian libretto, *La Schiava liberata*, performed with music by Jommelli at Ludwigsburg 18 December 1768, with music by Schuster at Dresden 2 October 1777; according to E. J. Dent founded on the English pasticcio, *The Captive*, text by I. Bickerstaffe, performed London, Hm. 21 June 1769). Three acts.

Bretzner's text was written for André. When Stephanie and Mozart used his libretto in 1782, Bretzner published his notorious protest in the *Berliner Litteratur und Theater-Zeitung* ("Ein gewisser Mensch namens Mozart . . .").

André's setting was also given at Munich 16 November 1781; Leipzig 1781; Hamburg 13 June 1782; Carlsruhe 16 October 1784; Schwedt 14 January 1785.

ZINGARELLI: *Montezuma*

13 August. Naples, S.C.

Text by V. A. Cigna-Santi (first composed by Majo in 1765). Three acts.

Zingarelli's first opera. There is no record of a later production at Vienna (as claimed by all writers on Zingarelli) when the opera "was highly praised by Haydn"; but there possibly was one at Eszterháza in 1786.

PAISIELLO: *La Serva Padrona*

10 September. St. Petersburg

G. A. Federico's text (first set to music by Pergolesi, see 1733). Two parts.

Paisiello's setting was written in order to celebrate the name-day of the Grand Duke Alexander of Russia, and produced at the Ermitage.

"Per non avere qui nè poeta nè libri sono stato costretto di mettere in musica la Serva padrona fatta tanti anni fa del fu Pergolesi, come lei sa; e andò in scena il dì trenta dello scorso con un successo mirabile, per il quale S.M.I. l'Imperatrice ha fatto un presente alli due attori: cioè alla donna che ha fatto la parte di Serpina eccellentemente le ha donato un fiore da testa di brillanti, all'uomo che ha fatto la parte di Uberto (che con difficoltà si può far meglio) gli ha donato un anello di brillanti, e a me una scatola con un contorno di brillanti" (letter by Paisiello to F. Galiani, published by S. Panareo in 1910).

In Italian also given at Moscow 26 June 1782; Warsaw 9 January 1785[1]; Vienna 26 March 1786 (privately, at Prince Auersperg's) and Kä. 18 June 1794; Madrid 25 September 1786; Bologna Autumn 1786; Lille 6 November 1786; Cracow 9 November 1788; Paris, Th. de M. 12 March 1789 (revived Th. I. 21 November 1801); Lisbon 1790; Prague 1791 (according to O. Kamper by "Passetto"); Trieste 6 August 1793; London 29 May 1794; Schwerin 1794; Breslau 7 November 1799; Lyons 18 July 1805.

In French St. Petersburg 7 November 1782.

In Russian (translated by Prince A. I. Golintsin), St. Petersburg 31 July 1789; Moscow 1789 (revived 12 September 1817).

[1] An earlier performance on 28 May 1781, as recorded by L. Bernacki, *Teatr, Dramat i Muzyka za Stanislawa Augusta*, Vol. II, p.300, must have been Pergolesi's opera.

In Polish (translated by W. Boguslawski), Warsaw 30 October 1791.

Said to have been sung in Czech, by Italian singers, at Prague 1795.

In German, Bremen December 1803 (as *Das Dienstmädchen als Gebieterin*; see note on the German productions of Pergolesi's *Serva Padrona*, 1733).

Revivals: Milan 27 October 1826; London, H.M.'s 21 June 1858 (in concert form) and 5 July 1858 (on the stage); New York 13 November 1858; Philadelphia 29 January 1859; Dublin 10 March 1860; Paris 25 December 1868; Padua, T. Concordi Spring 1871; Naples 26 May 1878 (by the Società Filarmonica); and lately, Rome, T. Eleonora Duse 10 June 1927 and Cairo 1936.

ALESSANDRI: *Il Vecchio geloso*

Autumn. Milan, Sc.

Text (according to U. Rolandi) by G. Bertati (partly founded on Molière's *L'École des Maris*). Two acts.

The most successful of Alessandri's comic operas; given at Padua 1782 and Leghorn 1784 as *Il Marito geloso*.

In Italian also, Trieste Carnival 1783; Fiume 1783; Vienna 7 May 1784; Prague 1784.

In German (translated by F. X. Girzik), Pressburg 26 July 1785; Linz 5 June 1786; Budapest 19 July 1789; Brünn 12 July 1792.

CIMAROSA: *Giannina e Bernadone*

November. Venice, S. Sam.

Text by F. Livigni. Two acts.

Very successful in Italy and abroad; Varese Autumn 1782; Leghorn Carnival 1783; Novara Spring 1783; Turin Autumn 1783; Bologna Spring 1784; Siena Summer 1784; Palermo 1784; Parma Carnival 1785; Naples, T.N. Spring 1785, etc.; given at Venice, S. Angelo Carnival 1786; reduced to an intermezzo as *Il Villano geloso*. First given at Milan, Sc. 24 June 1790.

In Italian also produced at Prague Autumn 1783; Trieste January 1784; Vienna 24 September 1784; Dresden 4 January 1785; Warsaw 6

January 1785; Barcelona 25 August 1786; Drott-
ningholm 1786 and Stockholm 20 February 1787;
Malta Carnival 1787; London 9 January 1787;
Versailles Summer 1787; Madrid 18 October
1788; Marseilles 1790; Lisbon Spring 1791; St.
Petersburg 1794; Paris, Th.I. 18 July 1801; Corfu
Autumn 1824.

In Polish (translated by L. Pierozyński),
Warsaw 10 January 1787; Wilna 21 February
1799.

In Swedish (translated by C. Stenborg and C.
Envallsson), Stockholm 15 December 1796.

A German translation, *Hanchen und Bernardon*,
was published at Salzburg in 1788.

Frequently revived in Italy: Florence, T. degli
Arrischiati 18 May 1870; Naples January 1882,
by the Società Filarmonica dei Nobili; 23 September 1882 at the T. Fior. and 14 December
1895 at the T. Mercadante; Rome May 1905
(privately at Villa Torlonia); and lately, Turin,
T.R. 2 March 1932.

ARNOLD: *The Banditi;* or
Love's Labyrinth

28 November. London, C.G.

Text by J. O'Keeffe. Two acts.

Given at the same theatre one year later, 2 November 1782, in an enlarged 3-act version as *The
Castle of Andalusia*, which is the better known
title of this successful comic opera (music, as
usual, partly compiled, partly composed). Also
given at Dublin 11 January 1782 (with additional
songs by F. Tenducci); Edinburgh 12 July 1783;
New York 21 April 1788; Philadelphia 5 November 1788, etc. Revived London, C.G. 15 May
1807 (in 2 acts, as *Which is the Master?*); Hm. 26
July and C.G. 1 November 1817 (reduced to 2
acts by J. Winston, additional music by Bishop);
again C.G. 20 June 1826.

CIMAROSA: *Il Convito*

27 December. Venice, S. Sam.

Text by F. Livigni. Two acts.

Revived Milan, Sc. 4 November 1796. In
Italy given until after 1800.

In Italian also, Trieste Carnival 1783; Dresden
1783; Warsaw 27 January 1785; Marseilles Autumn 1790; Lisbon Autumn 1796; Paris, Th.I.
3 June 1803.

In German (as *Der Schmaus*, translated by J. H.
Burmann), Frankfort 2 October 1784; Mayence
14 December 1785; Mannheim 27 April 1786;
Carlsruhe 28 October 1786; Salzburg 1787 (as
Das Gastmahl); Hanover 13 November 1789;
Berne Spring 1804.

(In London the opera was performed with new
music by Bertoni, text altered by A. Andrei, on
2 November 1782.)

1782

GRÉTRY: *La double Epreuve* ou
Colinette à la Cour

1 January. Paris, O.

Text by J. B. Lourdet de Santerre (*comédie-
lyrique*). Three acts.

A new successful version of Favart's *Ninette à
la Cour* (see 1755). Revived Paris 2 August 1791;
24 January 1810; 115 performances until 1816.

In French also, Ghent 29 March 1783; Cassel
22 December 1783; Liége 14 February 1784;
Geneva April 1785; last revived Paris, O. 24
January 1810.

In German (as *Die doppelte Erkenntlichkeit*,
translated by F. X. Huber, additional music by
Süssmayr), Vienna 28 February 1796.

UMLAUFF: *Das Irrlicht* oder
Endlich fand er sie

17 January. Vienna, B.

Bretzner's text (first published 1779 and already
set by Kospoth, see 1780, and by at least three
other composers, with alterations). Three acts.

Umlauff's setting was also given at Mannheim
5 February 1786; Riga 25 May 1786; Hamburg
Autumn 1787; etc., and revived at Vienna, W.
2 April 1796; Poznán 31 October 1803.

WINTER: *Helena und Paris*

5 *February*. Munich

Text by C. J. Förg. Three acts.

Winter's first greater success: given at Vienna 20 November 1784; Carlsruhe 9 May 1785; Mannheim 5 December 1786; Pressburg 1788; Budapest 2 October 1789; Frankfort 30 June 1792; Berlin 6 February 1797, etc. In Italian, Florence, P. Carnival 1784. In the preface to the libretto Winter pays tribute to Holzbauer as one of the first German composers to have achieved glory "in dem erhabnen Fache von Theatermusik".

CIMAROSA: *La Ballerina amante*

Summer. Naples, Fior.

Text (according to the MS score at Naples) by C. A. Casini. Two acts.

Milan, Sc. August 1783, etc. Given at Rovigo Autumn 1789 as *L'Amante ridicolo*; in Italy until about 1804.

In Italian also, Malta Carnival 1784; Trieste 26 December 1784; Prague Spring 1785; Barcelona 14 October 1785; Dresden and Eszterháza 1786; Madrid 24 October 1787; Lisbon 30 June 1793 (inauguration of the Real Theatro de San Carlos); St. Petersburg 23 January 1796.

MOZART: *Die Entführung aus dem Serail*

16 *July*. Vienna, B.

Bretzner's text (first set to music by André, see 1781), altered by G. Stephanie. Three acts.

Mozart's first German opera on a larger scale and his first great success. There were 34 performances at Vienna until 4 February 1788 when the "National-Singspiel" at the Burgtheater came to an end.

The first productions in German outside Vienna were at:

PRAGUE Autumn 1782.

WARSAW 8 May 1783.

BONN 22 June 1783.

FRANKFORT 2 August 1783.

LEIPZIG 25 September 1783.

MANNHEIM 18 April 1784.

CARLSRUHE 16 October 1784.

COLOGNE 24 October 1784.

SALZBURG 17 November 1784.

DRESDEN 12 January 1785.

RIGA 1 March 1785.

MUNICH 1 April 1785.

WEIMAR 4 April 1785.

AACHEN 24 April 1785.

CASSEL 26 May 1785.

PRESSBURG 13 June 1785.

AUGSBURG 19 August 1785.

NUREMBERG 25 August 1785.

MAYENCE 3 December 1785.

ROSTOCK 5 July 1786.

ALTONA 17 July 1786.

HANOVER 12 April 1787.

HAMBURG 18 June 1787.

BRESLAU 24 August 1787.

CARLSRUHE 17 September 1787.

COBLENZ 23 November 1787.

GRAZ 15 June 1788.

BERLIN 16 October 1788.

LÜBECK 7 January 1789; Bamberg 14 April 1789 (in concert form).

AMSTERDAM January 1791 (privately, according to H. C. Rogge, already 1789).

BUDAPEST 19 June 1791; Hermannstadt and Temesvar 1792, etc.

STUTTGART 19 September 1795 (Stuttgart was the last of the greater German stages, where the *Entführung* was given because Dieter's setting of the same text, see 1784, barred its way).

BERNE 1803; Basle 13 January 1809; Winterthur 21 August 1826.

Translated into other languages the *Entführung* was given at:

WARSAW 25 November 1783 (in Polish, translator unknown; in German earlier, see above).

AMSTERDAM 1797 (in Dutch, translated by G. Brender à Brandis; in German earlier, see above).

PARIS 26 September 1798 (at the Lycée des Arts, French version by P. L. Moline); Th. de la Cité 16 November 1801 (in German, first opera ever sung there in that language; see note on *Das Sonnenfest der Braminen*, 1790); Th. L. 11 May 1859 (in French, translated by Prosper-Pascal); O. 4 December 1903 (the Brussels 1902 version, see below, recitatives by P. Vidal).

MOSCOW 8 February 1810 (in Russian, translated by S. Kuvichinsky) and St. Petersburg 30 December 1816 (translated by A. I. Sheller); Moscow 29 June 1820 (in German); revived Leningrad 28 March 1925.

COPENHAGEN 1 April 1813 and Christiania 1832 (in Danish, translated by N. T. Bruun).

STOCKHOLM 21 September 1814 (in Swedish, translated by M. Altén).

LONDON, C.G. 24 November 1827 (in English, as *The Seraglio*, translated by W. Dimond, with additional airs by C. Kramer); D.L. 23 June 1841 (in German); H.M.'s 30 June 1866 (in Italian, translator not mentioned; with recitatives by Arditi); C.G. 9 June 1881 (in Italian, with recitatives by Benedict); H.M.'s 20 June 1910 (in English, translated by J. Troutbeck and P. Greenbank).

GHENT 14 June 1829 (in German) and 27 January 1860 (in French); Brussels August 1829 (in German) and 15 February 1902 (in French, translated by M. Kufferath and L. Solvay).

PRAGUE 8 November 1829 (in Czech, translated by J. Jungmann; in German much earlier, see above).

NEW YORK 16 February 1860 (by the Brooklyn Operatic Circle, in Italian according to J. Mattfeld who gives the title as *Belmonte and Constanze;* Odell gives the title as *Il Seraglio* and does not mention the language. But since no Italian version of *Die Entführung* had been staged yet anywhere at that date and the conductor was Carl Anschütz and the singers American or German, and as other productions of the "Operatic Circle" included *Der Freischütz* and *Fidelio*, both in German, it seems much more likely that *Die Entführung*, too, was sung in German). Subsequently given at the German Opera House, New York 10 October 1862; Philadelphia 4 March 1863; in English: New York, Hotel Astor 8 January 1910;

Rochester, N.Y. 1 November 1926; New York, Guild Th. 4 April 1927.

BUDAPEST 21 March 1882 (in Hungarian, translator not mentioned; in German much earlier, see above); revived 15 March 1913 (new Hungarian version by S. Hevesi).

ALEXANDRIA 6 February 1889 (in Greek, according to reports in contemporary journals).

DUBLIN 11 July 1921 (in English; for the first time in Ireland).

ZAGREB 2 March 1922 (in Croatian).

RIGA 18 March 1924 (in Lettish; in German much earlier, see above).

HELSINKI 5 February 1926 (in Finnish).

BUCHAREST December 1927 (in Rumanian).

BARCELONA 3 January 1928 (in German; for the first time in Spain).

SOFIA 14 March 1928 (in Bulgarian).

LJUBLJANA 20 November 1929 (in Slovenian, translated by F. Bučar).

TEL-AVIV 2 May 1935 (in Hebrew, translated by Z. Israel).

FLORENCE, P. 18 May 1935 (in German; for the first time in Italy).

BUENOS AIRES 23 August 1938 (in German).

HAYDN: *Orlando Paladino*

August. Eszterháza

Text by N. Porta after Ariosto (an altered version of a libretto by C. F. Badini, called *Le Pazzie d'Orlando* and performed with music by Guglielmi in London 23 February 1871. Porta altered the text for Prague, where Guglielmi's opera was produced as *Orlando Paladino* in 1775). Three acts.

The most successful of Haydn's operas. Full list of performances: In the original Italian Dresden 28 November 1792. In German (as *Roland der Pfalzgraf*, translated by F. X. Girzik): Pressburg 22 May 1786; Prague 1791; Brünn 26 October 1791; Vienna, W. 9 January 1792; Budapest 21 May 1792; Mannheim 5 August 1792; Donaueschingen 13 January 1793; Frankfort 22 September 1793; Cologne 18 November 1793; Graz 26 November 1793; Nuremberg 14 January 1796 (as *Der wütende Roland*); Berlin 18

April 1798; Hanover 28 June 1798; Bremen 4 October 1798; Oels 29 October 1799; Leipzig January 1800; Munich 5 December 1800; Augsburg 1802; Ballenstedt 3 October 1802; Königsberg 2 December 1803; Hamburg 22 March 1805; Breslau 20 December 1805 (new translation by J. G. Rhode); St. Petersburg *c.* December 1813 (in German). Revived Leipzig 31 March 1932 (as *Ritter Roland*, revised by E. Latzko).

ANDRÉ: *Der Liebhaber als Automat* oder *Die redende Maschine*

11 September. Berlin

Text by the composer (founded on a French libretto by Cuinet Dorbeil, set to music by Rigel in 1781). One act.

André's most successful Singspiel. Given in Berlin until 1796; also on many other German stages and Riga 1790; Prague 1791; Amsterdam 1792; Vienna, W. 19 April 1793.

SARTI: *Fra due Litiganti il terzo gode*

14 September. Milan, Sc.

Text: an altered version of C. Goldoni's *Le Nozze* (first set to music by Galuppi, see 1755). Three acts.

Sarti's setting became very popular and will always be remembered because of Mozart's quoting it in the last act of *Don Giovanni*.

Given at Venice, S. Moisè Autumn 1782 as *I Pretendenti delusi;* Naples, T. Fondo 10 December 1784 as *Le Nozze di Dorina;* Padua Carnival 1792 as *I due Litiganti;* Naples 1798 as *Dorina contrastata* (pasticcio). In Italian also produced at Vienna 28 May 1783 (German translation in the libretto by Schönborn); Leipzig 10 June 1783; Prague 1783; Trieste 27 December 1783; London 6 January 1784 (as *I Rivali delusi*) and 26 February 1793 (as *Le Nozze di Dorina*, with additional airs by Martin and Storace); Dresden 1784; Barcelona 9 December 1784; Warsaw 2 January 1785; Stuttgart 1785; Graz Winter 1785; Fiume Carnival 1786 (as *Fra tre Litiganti alcun non gode*); Regensburg 1786; Lille 8 November 1786; Berlin Autumn 1787; Madrid 5 June 1789; Paris, Th.d.M. 14 September 1789 (with additions by

Zingarelli, G. G. Ferrari and Viotti); (revived 6 January 1791 at the inauguration of the Th. Feydeau; Th.I. 13 April 1802 and 2 August 1809 as *Le Nozze di Dorina ossia I tre Pretendenti*); Lisbon Autumn 1793.

In German (as *Wenn sich zwey streiten, freut sich der dritte,* translated by L. Zehnmark) Vienna, Fasan Th. 10 May 1784 and Kä. 27 November 1784 and Leop. 17 January 1789; Cologne 2 January 1785 and 8 October 1786; Pressburg 4 July 1785; Mayence 12 November 1785; Munich 4 August 1786; Schwedt 3 November 1786; Strasbourg 14 July 1787; Salzburg 1787; Budapest 9 August 1787; Warsaw 23 October 1793; (as *Wer's Glück hat führt die Braut heim oder Im Trüben ist gut fischen,* translated by J. André; see *Ephemeriden . . .,* 1785, p.199) Hamburg 10 February 1785; Frankfort 12 May 1785; Mannheim 29 December 1785; Carlsruhe 14 October 1786; Vienna, Kä. 14 September 1787; Hanover 14 January 1788; Berlin 14 July 1788; Dresden July 1788; Riga 1790; Pyrmont 2 July 1790; Cassel 25 August 1790; Amsterdam 1791; Innsbruck 1793; Bremen 1803–04; Berne Spring 1804. Another German version by P. Trautmann was used at Prague 1787.

Revived Hamburg 3 April 1811 (with new dialogue by J. F. Schink; see K. L. Costenoble, *Tagebücher,* Vol. II, p.104; the undated libretto in the Library of Congress, Schatz no. 9459, probably belongs to this revival and not to the 1785 production); Berlin 5 March 1812.

In Polish (translated by L. Pierozyński) Warsaw 1789.

In French as *Hélène et Francisque,* translated by P. U. Dubuisson, Paris, Th. Montansier 20 April 1790 and Th. National 25 September 1793.

In Danish (translated by L. Knudsen) Copenhagen 7 April 1795.

EDELMANN: *Ariane dans l' Isle de Naxos*

24 September. Paris, O.

Text by P. L. Moline. One act.

The best work of the Alsatian composer, who was guillotined in 1794. Given at the Paris O.

until 1825. In French also, New York 21 March 1791 (see Sonneck, *Early Opera in America*, p.201); St. Petersburg 1793; Brussels 13 May 1796 (as *Ariane abandonnée*).

In Russian, Moscow 25 February 1799.

In German, St. Petersburg 1810.

PAISIELLO: *Il Barbiere di Siviglia* ovvero *La Precauzione inutile*

26 September. St. Petersburg

Text by G. Petrosellini (founded on Beaumarchais's comedy, 1775). Four acts.

Written 33 years before Rossini's opera of the same title, Paisiello's *Barbiere* was, in its time, not less successful and popular than its follower, and recent revivals show that the older setting has not been completely obliterated even now.

The exact date of the first performance at the Ermitage, not yet to be found in any book of reference, has been communicated by Paisiello himself in an (undated) letter, written probably in the beginning of 1783 to F. Galiani, his former collaborator in *Il Socrate immaginario* (see S. Panareo, *Paisiello in Russia*, 1910, p.37). See for further details *Music and Letters*, Vol. xx, No.2 April 1939).

In Italian also produced at Vienna 13 August 1783; Caserta 22 November 1783 (at the royal palace); Trieste 26 December 1785; Milan, Sc. Autumn 1786; Venice, S. Sam. 28 January 1787; Naples, Fior. 1787 (reduced to 3 acts and with additions by Paisiello); etc. Given at Venice, S. Moisè 5 January 1800 in a reduced 1-act version.

Prague Carnival 1784; Warsaw 2 October 1785; Barcelona 3 August 1786; London 11 June 1789 (revived 26 January 1793; 5 June 1798; 9 June 1807); Paris, Th. de M. 22 July 1789; Lisbon Summer 1791 and 21 June 1799; Madrid 16 January 1796; Mexico 4 December 1806 (first Italian opera ever given there).

In French (translated by N. E. Framery, with dialogue from Beaumarchais), Versailles 14 September 1784; Lille 26 June 1785; Cassel 29 August 1785; Liége 31 January 1786; (in a new French version by P. L. Moline) Paris, O.C. 16

March 1793; Brussels 8 November 1793; St. Petersburg 1797; New Orleans 12 July 1810.

In German (translated by J. N. Schueller), Pressburg 14 October 1785; (translated by G. F. W. Grossmann) Mannheim 20 November 1785, etc.; Berlin 30 August 1788 (given there until 1826); Vienna, W. 2 August 1796.

In Spanish, Madrid 3 December 1787 (revived 12 August 1800).

In Russian (translated by M. V. Popov), St. Petersburg 27 August 1790; Moscow 29 August 1797.

Anonymous Dutch translation published 1792.

In Swedish (translated by J. D. Valerius), Stockholm 8 June 1797.

In Polish, Wilna 12 November 1805.

Productions (in English) at Philadelphia, Charleston, S.C., and Baltimore in 1794 as claimed by H. E. Krehbiel, H. C. Lahee, and many other writers are very doubtful.

Revivals: Paris, F.P. 15 May 1868 and O.C. 27 June 1889 (in French, new translation by V. Wilder, re-orchestrated by T. C. Constantin). Turin, T. Balbo September 1875; Venice, T. Malibran January 1876 and 13 May 1903; Genoa, Politeama September 1878; Naples 23 June 1879, etc. Berlin, Kroll's 19 April 1913 (in German, revised by R. Falk). Antwerp December 1913 (in Flemish). Monte Carlo 31 March 1918 (in Italian); Milan, Scala 27 April 1939 (in Italian).

NAUMANN: *Cora och Alonzo*

30 September. Stockholm

Text by G. G. Adlerbeth (founded on Marmontel's novel, *Les Incas*). Three acts.

The opera had been finished in 1779 and in 1780 a German vocal score was published (translated by J. L. Neumann). Previously to the Stockholm production a concert performance had taken place at the Hôtel de Pologne, Dresden 15 March 1780. At Stockholm the opera was given at the inauguration of the new operahouse; it was frequently revived there until 1832, and once more, 30 September 1882, at the 100th anniversary of the inauguration.

Successful also on German stages: Schwedt 25 September 1786; Berlin 25 April 1787 (in concert form); Hanover 4 June 1788; Pressburg 1788, etc. To the list of German productions as given by Engländer in his monograph on Naumann may be added performances at Winterthur 18 November 1789 (in concert form) and Aachen 31 July 1791.

In Danish (translated by T. Thaarup), Copenhagen 30 January 1788; previously given there in concert form 1784.

CARVALHO: *Penelope nella Partenza da Sparta*

17 December. Lisbon, Real Camara

(Italian) text by G. Martinelli. One act and licenza.

Performed on the birthday of Queen Maria I. One of the best works of the Portuguese composer.

SHIELD: *Rosina*

31 December. London, C.G.

Text by F. Brooke (founded on Favart's *Les Moissonneurs*, see 1768). Two acts.

Popular ballad opera; Dublin 18 March 1783; Edinburgh 24 January 1784; Belfast 1784; Montego Bay, Jamaica 23 April 1785; New York 19 April 1786; Philadelphia 19 January 1787, etc. Revived in London until 1831, and as late as 12 January 1923 by the Mayfair Dramatic Club at the Guildhall School of Music.

1783

BERNARDINI: *Il Conte di Bell'Umore*

Carnival. Rome, Pallacorda

Text by the composer. Two acts.

Bernardini's most successful comic opera. Given all over Italy; at Varese Autumn 1792 as *Il Conte brillante*, with additional music by Carlo Uboldi; in Italian also given at Leipzig Summer 1783; Barcelona 4 September 1783; Prague Autumn 1783; Lisbon Carnival 1785 and Spring 1791; Graz Spring 1785; Trieste Summer 1791; Madrid 6 May 1795.

CIMAROSA: *Chi dell'altrui si veste, presto si spoglia*

Carnival. Naples, Fior.

Text by G. Palomba. Three acts.

Successful in Italy; Milan, Sc. Autumn 1784, etc.

In Italian also produced at Eszterháza 1786; Madrid 25 December 1787; Dresden 1789; Barcelona 9 December 1789; London 7 January 1790 (as *Ninetta*, with additional music by F. Giardini); Lisbon 1792; St. Petersburg 30 May 1798; Gachina 11 September 1798; Cagliari, Sardinia Carnival 1804.

Revived at Rome, T. Valle Summer 1813 (reduced to 2 acts); Naples, T.N. April 1825 (as *Nina e Martuffo*, reduced to one act).

CIMAROSA: *I due Baroni di Rocca Azzurra*

February. Rome, Valle

Text by G. Palomba. Two acts.

Successful in Italy; Milan, Sc. Spring 1786, etc. Revived Modena 11 May 1802 as *La Sposa in Contrasto*.

In Italian also given at Eszterháza 1787; Barcelona 27 June 1789; St. Petersburg c.1789 (?); Vienna 6 September 1789; Dresden 1790; Lisbon Carnival 1791; Warsaw 1 September 1792; Corfu, Autumn 1793; Paris 14 July 1802 (with additions by Fioravanti); London 1 January 1803.

For the Vienna production Mozart wrote the aria K.578 (*Alma grande e nobil Core*).

ALBERTINI: *Don Juan, albo Ukarany Libertyn*

23 February. Warsaw

Text by W. Boguslawski (translated from an Italian libretto)[1]. Three acts.

Polish *Don Giovanni* opera, four years before Mozart; successful in Poland, given at Warsaw

---

[1] Perhaps the anonymous text *Il Convitato di Pietra*, composed by Righini (see 1777), it being the only three-act version on record. I was unable to see a copy of Boguslawski's libretto.

until about 1812. Libretto published 1783; parts of the music are preserved.

In Italian, perhaps Florence, P. 9 April 1792 (see note on Mozart's *Don Giovanni*, col.454).

DÉZÈDE: *Blaise et Babet* ou *La Suite des trois Fermiers*

4 *April*. Versailles

Text by J. M. Boutet de Monvel (a sequel to his *Les trois Fermiers*, see 1777). Two acts.

Paris, C.I. 30 June 1783; given at the O.C. until 1827.

In French also, Stockholm 1784; Cassel 23 October 1784; Liége 23 November 1784; St. Petersburg, Ermitage 22 January 1792; Charleston, S.C. 23 July 1794; Brussels 9 March 1795; Hamburg 5 June 1795; Cologne 1795–96; Baltimore March 1796; Philadelphia 7 January 1797; Port Louis, Mauritius 19 July 1797 (first opera ever given there); Hanover 28 December 1803.

In German (as *Blaise und Babet*), Carlsruhe 14 April 1787; (as *Töffel und Dortchen*, translated by H. von Mayer), Mannheim 10 August 1788; Hamburg 13 October 1788, etc.; Amsterdam 1790; Berlin 9 September 1797. Last revived Hamburg 16 January 1814.

In Dutch (translated by H. J. Roullaud), Amsterdam 1788 (revived Hague 1808).

In Danish (translated by J. H. Wessel), Copenhagen 18 May 1790.

In Swedish (translated by C. J. Lindegren), Stockholm 29 November 1797.

In Russian, Moscow 1804.

Italian translation by G. Piazza published 1801.

SHIELD: *The Shamrock;* or, *The Anniversary of St. Patrick*

7 *April*. London, C.G.

Text by J. O'Keeffe. *A pastoral Romance*. Two acts.

Revived at the same theatre some months later (4 November 1783) in an altered version as *The poor Soldier*, which proved a great success. Very popular on English stages. Dublin 16 January 1784 and, in a revised version, 1785. Montego

Bay, Jamaica 9 April 1785; New York 2 December 1785 (18 times within six months); Philadelphia 22 January 1787; Calcutta 1 May 1789.

In English also, Hamburg 9 March 1795 (where a short-lived English theatre, under the management of one Williamson from Edinburgh, existed in that year). Revived in London, C.G. 20 September 1809 and D.L. 19 February 1816. A sequel to *The poor Soldier* by the same authors (*Patrick in Prussia; or, Love in a Camp*) was produced in London, C.G. 17 February 1786 (revived D.L. 15 February 1814); both Edinburgh and New York 9 April 1787; Philadelphia 5 July 1787, etc.

The music consists of Irish airs, selected by O'Keeffe; overture, accompaniments and additional airs by Shield. The original version does not seem to have been preserved (although, according to the play-bill, at least the words of the songs were printed).

The music of *The poor Soldier* was published probably in 1783 (1782 according to the British Museum Catalogue, which seems unlikely).

Date of first performance of *The Shamrock*, 7 April 1783 (not May 7 as stated by W. J. Lawrence in *The Musical Antiquary*, Vol. IV, p.185).

SCHUBAUR: *Die Dorfdeputierten*

8 *May*. Munich

G. E. Heermann's text (first set to music by E. W. Wolf, see 1772). Three acts.

The only Singspiel of Schubaur the score of which is still extant. Very successful on German stages; given until 1815; Mannheim 19 November 1783, etc.; Salzburg 17 April 1785; Riga 23 August 1785; Budapest 26 March 1787; Pressburg 1788; Amsterdam 1791; Berlin 23 September 1796; Basle 3 March 1809.

P. GUGLIELMI: *La Quakera spiritosa*

Summer. Naples, Fior.

Text by G. Palomba. Three acts.

Reduced to 2 acts: Milan, Sc. August 1785.

In Italian also produced at Dresden 1785; Eszterháza 1787; Vienna 13 August 1790 (text revised by L. da Ponte).

In German (translated by F. X. Girzik), Pressburg 1788.

PICCINNI: *Didon*

16 October. Fontainebleau

Text by J. F. Marmontel. Three acts.

The most successful of Piccinni's French operas; publicly performed at Paris, O. 1 December 1783 (given there until 1836; the 250th performance was on 8 February 1826); Lille 27 June 1790.

In French also, Copenhagen 20 April 1794 (in concert form); Rheinsberg 1 October 1795; Hamburg 1796; Liége 20 February 1802; St. Petersburg 1804; Stockholm 2 April 1805; Antwerp 19 January 1819.

In German (translated by H. G. Schmieder), Mayence 12 February 1792 and Frankfort 15 April 1792; (translated by C. A. Herklots), Berlin 18 March 1799; Breslau 15 August 1800; revived Berlin 6 November 1807 (with ballet music by B. A. Weber); Darmstadt 26 December 1825.

At Solothurn 1794 adapted to a German libretto *Das siegende Christentum.*

MARTINI: *Le Droit du Seigneur*

17 October. Fontainebleau

Text by F. G. Desfontaines and Laval. Three acts.

Paris, C.I. 29 December 1783. In French also, Amsterdam 1784; Cassel 9 March 1785; Liége 21 February 1786; Hamburg 1795-96.

In German (translation by B. C. d'Arien), Cassel 25 August 1787; Hamburg 13 March 1789; Berlin 16 October 1790, etc.

In Swedish (translated by J. D. Valerius), Stockholm 6 June 1799.

A Danish version by A. G. Thoroup was published in 1790.

GRÉTRY: *La Caravane du Caire*

30 October. Fontainebleau

Text by E. Morel de Chédeville (the King, Louis XVI, is said to have had a share in the libretto). Three acts.

Paris, O. 15 January 1784 (given there for more than 500 nights, until 1829).

A parody *Le Marchand d'Esclaves*, by J. B. Radet, P. Y. Barré and J. R. Lecouppey de la Rozière, was produced at the C.I. 27 January 1784; another, *Les Reconnaissances ou La Foire de Beaucaire*, at the Variétés Amusantes 2 August 1784.

In French also, Geneva 22 June 1785; Charleston, S.C. 3 August 1795; Hamburg 1796; Cologne 1796-97; Liége 15 December 1796; Brunswick 1803; Hanover 14 August 1803; St. Petersburg November 1804; Berne 12 February 1806.

In Italian (translated by G. Carpani), Monza Autumn 1795 (with additional music by W. Pichl); Lisbon 14 May 1807 (with one air by A. J. do Rego).

In Swedish (translated by J. M. Lannerstjerna), Stockholm 1 November 1796 (with a prologue by L. Piccinni).

In German (translated by F. X. Huber), Vienna, W. 4 October 1804; Brünn 16 March 1812.

In Russian (translated by I. F. Timkovsky), Moscow 28 November 1816; St. Petersburg 17 November 1817.

A Dutch version by P. Pijpers was published in 1788.

CHERUBINI: *Lo Sposo di tre, Marito di Nessuna*

Autumn. Venice, S. Sam.

Text by F. Livigni. Two acts.

Cherubini's first comic opera. Apparently not given on any other stages then, but revived 143 years later at Dresden 27 November 1926 (as *Don Pistacchio, der dreifach Verlobte*, German version by H. Tessmer and A. Reucker).

BIANCHI: *La Villanella rapita*

Autumn. Venice, San Moisé

Text by G. Bertati (founded on Favart's *Le Caprice amoureux*, see 1755). Two acts.

Bianchi's most popular work; Milan, Sc., September 1785, etc.

In Italian also given at Trieste January 1785; Dresden 1785; Prague Autumn 1785 (as *La Sposa rapita*); Vienna 25 November 1785; Eszterháza 1786; Barcelona 27 April 1787; Madrid 29 April 1788; Paris, Th. de M. 15 June 1789 (pasticcio; revived 18 February 1802); London 27 February 1790; St. Petersburg 1795; Lisbon Spring 1796.

In French (translated by P. U. Dubuisson), Paris, Th. Français Comique et Lyrique Summer 1790.

In Swedish (translated by G. G. Adlerbeth), Stockholm 24 July 1802 (pasticcio).

In Russian (translated by A. I. Sheller), St. Petersburg 16 December 1816.

In German, Budapest 1 February 1792.

In Vienna, Bianchi's opera was performed with two inserted pieces by Mozart, a quartet and a trio (K. 479, 480). Mozart's additions were also used in Paris, London, Madrid and St. Petersburg, and, probably, elsewhere as well.

PICCINNI: *Le faux Lord*

6 December. Paris, C.I.

Text by G. M. Piccinni, the son of the composer. Two acts.

Piccinni's last greater success.

In French also given at Cassel 17 January 1785; Amsterdam 1785; Liége 31 October 1796.

In Danish (translated by C. D. Biehl), Copenhagen 4 October 1785.

In German (translated by J. André), Hamburg August 1787; Mannheim 24 February 1788.

In Russian, St. Petersburg 28 July 1790.

In Swedish (translated by J. D. Valerius), Stockholm 16 November 1798.

CARUSO: *Gli Amanti alla Prova*

26 December. Venice, S. Moisé

Text by G. Bertati. Two acts.

One of the best-known of Caruso's numerous operas and one of the few extant ones.

Successful in Italy. Given at Ancona Carnival 1786, as *I tre Amanti in Prova;* Naples, T. Fondo Autumn 1787 as *Gli Amanti dispettosi;* revived Milan, Sc. 5 March 1796. In Italian also, Barcelona 9 December 1786; Madrid 8 April 1798.

1784

P. GUGLIELMI: *Le Vicende d'Amore*

Carnival. Rome, Valle

Librettist unknown. Two acts.

In Italian also, Vienna 16 June 1784; Prague Autumn 1784; Dresden 1785; Lübeck July 1787; Brunswick Carnival 1791.

In German (as *Der verliebte Zwist*, translated by G. F. W. Grossmann), Cassel 2 April 1791; Hanover 4 May 1791.

ZANDER: *Niugg spar och Fan tar,* eller *Åldrarnes Dårskaper*

17 February. Stockholm

Text by C. Envallsson (partly founded on Plautus's *Mostellaria*). Two acts.

The proverbial title means *The Niggard Saves, the Devil Takes, or The Follies of Old Age.*

Zander's best comic opera, given at Stockholm 40 times until 1819 (revived 14 September 1819). Given at Gothenburg 21 February 1792; at Malmö 6 December 1805.

HAYDN: *Armida*

26 February. Eszterháza

Text by J. Durandi (first set to music by Anfossi in 1770), after Tasso. Three acts.

Durandi's authorship has been doubted by some authorities; but see G. de Gregory, *Vita di Jacopo Durandi* (1817), p.24: "... per il nuovo dramma del carnovale del 1770, aderì egli replicate instanze, e compose l'Armida, dramma con musica del maestro Anfossi, stampato in Torino nell 1770 e quindi ristampato nell 1805, epoca in cui fu di nuovo rappresentato, ed a consolazione del nostro poeta venne dall' armonioso Hayden messo per la seconda volta in musica, e dal pubblico Torinese applaudito".

Haydn's last performed opera; on his *L'Anima del Filosofo,* libretto by C. F. Badini, written for London in 1791, but not performed, see H. Botstiber, pp.340–45; autograph score Berlin; a selection was published in 1805 (vocal score) and 1807 (full score) as *Orfeo ed Euridice*, and given in concert form at Leipzig 29 September 1807 (parts) and Königsberg 29 October 1808.

Armida was given in German (translated by F. X. Girzik), Pressburg 3 November 1786 (according to A. Heppner) or 16 October 1785 (according to Pohl and Wendschuh); Budapest 8 April 1791; Vienna, W. 25 March 1797 (in concert form). Revived at Turin 26 December 1804 (in Italian, in 2 acts).

GRÉTRY: *Théodore et Paulin*

5 March. Versailles

Text by P. J. B. Choudard Desforges. Three acts.

Better known by its later title, *L'Épreuve villageoise;* given at Paris, C.I. 18 March 1784 as *Théodore et Paulin* and, reduced to two acts, 24 June 1784 as *L'Épreuve villageoise;* in Paris until 1831 and frequently revived afterwards, viz. O.C. 25 May 1853 (re-orchestrated by Auber); 3 September 1866; 24 May 1888; Th.L. 11 September 1863; Galerie Vivienne 15 April 1896; Tr. L. 12 January 1918.

In French also given at Liége 14 December 1784; Cassel 27 May 1785; Brussels 6 August 1794; Cologne 1795–96; Gachina 20 September 1798; Moscow 6 May 1809; Berne 5 July 1809; New York 14 September 1827; Baden-Baden 17 July 1863.

In German, Hanover 8 September 1790; revived Graz 29 March 1895 (new German version by F. von Hausegger, music arranged by S. von Hausegger); another German version by Schletterer was published 1897.

Dutch translation by P. F. Lynslager published Amsterdam 1788.

(For a sequel, see 1787.)

SHIELD: *Robin Hood;* or, *Sherwood Forest*

17 April. London, C.G.

Text by L. MacNally. Three acts.

Successful on English stages: Dublin 30 December 1784; Charleston, S.C. 16 February 1793; Philadelphia 10 March 1794; New York 30 April

1794; Baltimore 6 November 1794 (with additional music by A. Reinagle); revived D. L. 13 March 1813 (with additional music by J. Addison).

According to W. T. Parke (*Musical Memoirs*) the overture was written by C. F. Baumgarten.

SALIERI: *Les Danaïdes*

26 April. Paris, O.

Text by F. L. G. Lebland du Roullet and L. T. de Tschudy (founded on and partly translated from an Italian libretto by Calzabigi, called *Ipermestra*, written for Gluck in 1778 and published in 1784). Five acts.

The opera was announced and produced as a common work by Gluck and Salieri and it was only after the twelfth performance that Gluck made a public statement to the effect that *Les Danaïdes* was entirely his pupil Salieri's work.

Successful in Paris; given at the O. 127 times until 7 January 1828, since 22 October 1817 in a 4-act version (text altered by A. F. Desaugiers; additional music by Spontini).

A parody by M. J. Gentil de Chavagnac and M. A. M. Desaugiers, called *Les petites Danaïdes, ou 99 Victimes*, was produced at Paris, Th. Porte St. Martin 14 December 1819 and (in French) London, Hm. 18 July 1831.

Salieri's opera was also given in German (translated by J. W. T. Franz), Mannheim 30 October 1796, and in Danish (translated by N. T. Bruun), Copenhagen 1805 (in concert form).

Calzabigi protested against the breach of his author's rights in a famous letter to the *Mercure de France* (21 August 1784). For details, see J. G. Prod'homme in *The Musical Quarterly*, Vol. III (1917), p.263. The correspondence in the *Mercure de France* is reprinted in G. Lazzeri's book on Calzabigi (1907).

CIMAROSA: *L'Olimpiade*

10 July. Vicenza

Metastasio's text (first set to music by Caldara in 1733). Three acts.

Written for the inauguration of the Teatro Eretenio, Vicenza.

Milan, Sc. 7 September 1788, etc. (in Italy given until 1807).

In Italian also produced at Trieste 24 April 1786; London 8 May 1788; Corfu Carnival 1791; Lisbon Summer 1798.

PAISIELLO: *Il Re Teodoro in Venezia*

23 August. Vienna, B.

Text by G. B. Casti (*Dramma eroicomico*). Two acts.

One of Paisiello's best and most successful works and a favourite opera for the next 30 years; it deals with the story of Baron Theodore de Neuhoff, who was King of Corsica in 1736, and died in London 1756.

In Italian also produced at Prague Autumn 1784; Warsaw 16 January 1785; Florence, P. Carnival 1785; Naples Fior. 1785; Stuttgart and Brunswick 1785; Milan, Sc. September 1786; Berlin 1787 (libretto printed; performed?); London 8 (not 18) December 1787; Paris, Th. de M. 21 February 1789 (revived 4 April 1804); Madrid 10 December 1789; Dresden May 1791 (as *Gli Avventurieri*, music partly adapted to a new libretto by C. Mazzolà); in the original version revived Dresden 1812; Barcelona 25 August 1792. Last revived, Bologna Spring 1825.

In German (translated by J. Böhm), Vienna, Kä. 4 February 1785; revived W. 18 March 1796 (in a new version by E. Schikaneder) and 3 September 1813 (in a new version by J. von Seyfried); Pressburg 16 May 1785 (at the inauguration of Count Erdödy's opera-house; German version by F. Teyber); Budapest 21 December 1787. On most German stages Böhm's version was used: Schwetzingen 21 July 1785 and Mannheim 24 July 1785; Cologne Autumn 1785; Mayence 10 December 1785; Berlin 7 August 1786 (revived 6 November 1799 and Kgst. 11 October 1824), etc. In a new German version by B. C. d'Arien: Munich March 1788 and Hamburg 14 April 1788; translated by C. A. Vulpius, Weimar 30 January 1794. Another German translation by P. W. G. Hansleutner was published Stuttgart 1786.

In German also given at Zurich 29 July 1788 (in concert form; first opera ever heard there).

In French (in 3 acts, translated by P. U. Dubuisson), Brussels 1786; Fontainebleau 28 October 1786; Versailles 18 November 1786; Lille 13 June 1790; Paris, Th. Montansier 28 October 1790 and Odéon 24 August 1797; Ghent 1791; Hamburg December 1803; Antwerp 9 February 1815. Another French version (in 2 acts), by P. L. Moline, recitatives by L. C. A. Chardiny, was used at Paris, O. 11 September 1787.

In Danish (translated by A. G. Thoroup), Copenhagen 23 October 1795.

In Polish (translated by W. Boguslawski), Lvóv 1798 and Warsaw 1799.

DIETER: *Belmont und Constanze,* oder *Die Entführung aus dem Serail*

27 August. Stuttgart

A new setting of Bretzner's text (see 1781 and 1782), two years after Mozart. Three acts.

Dieter's composition was very successful at Stuttgart (where Mozart's opera was not given before 1795).

HOLLAND: *Agatka, czyli Przyjazd Pana*

(Agatha, or The Lord's Arrival)

17 September. Nieświez (Poland)

Text by Prince M. Radziwill. *Operetka.* Three acts.

First produced at the Prince's private theatre at a visit of King Stanislaw Poniatowski; publicly performed Warsaw 30 October 1785; Lvóv June 1796. One of the first extant examples of Polish opera.

Given at Warsaw until the end of the 18th century, since 1799 in a reduced 2-act version.

SACCHINI: *Dardanus*

18 September. Versailles

La Bruère's text (first set to music by Rameau, see 1739), altered and reduced by N. F. Guillard. Four acts.

Sacchini's first original French opera. Paris, O. 30 November 1784; reduced to 3 acts: Fontaine-bleau 20 October 1785 and Paris, O. 13 January 1786 (given there until 1808).

CIMAROSA: *I due supposti Conti* ossia *Lo Sposo senza Moglie*

10 October. Milan, Sc.

Text by A. Anelli. Two acts.

Florence, P. Carnival 1785; Parma Summer 1785; Venice, S. Sam. Autumn 1785; Padua 7 October 1785; Bologna Carnival 1786; Turin and Verona 1786, etc.

Given at Rome, Valle Spring 1786, with the sub-title *Lo Sposo ridicolo*.

In Italian also produced at Trieste Carnival 1786; Barcelona 30 May 1787; Dresden 1787; Vienna 12 May 1789; Madrid 10 August 1789; Marseilles 1790; Lisbon 1791; Cadiz 1792; St. Petersburg 20 April 1798.

Revived Milan (at the inauguration of the T. Lentasio) 17 January 1805 as *Lo Sposo senza Moglie*.

GRÉTRY: *Richard Cœur-de-Lion*

21 October. Paris, C.I.

Text by J. M. Sedaine. Three acts.

Grétry's most famous opera; enlarged to 4 acts, Paris, C.I. 21 December 1785, but a few days later again altered and reduced to 3 acts; given on French stages throughout the whole 19th century and still revived now and then.

Re-scored by Adam: Paris, O.C. 27 September 1841; Th.L. 23 May 1856; O.C. 18 October 1873. Some of the latest revivals were at Paris, O.C. 13 October 1910; Tr.L. 2 February 1918; Liége 16 August 1908 and 16 May 1930; Brussels 28 October 1933.

In French also, Ghent 29 October 1786; Liége 5 January 1787, etc.; St. Petersburg 2 July 1795; Warsaw 22 March 1819; London, St.J's. 26 February 1849; Baden-Baden 18 July 1864.

In English (rival versions), London, C.G. 16 October 1786 (translated by L. MacNally, music adapted by Shield) and D.L. 24 October 1786 (translated by J. Burgoyne, music adapted by Linley); the latter version was also given at Dublin 1786; Edinburgh 7 April 1792; Boston 23 January 1797 (partly re-scored by Trille Labarre); Philadelphia 23 March 1798; New York 21 May 1800 (partly re-scored by V. Pelissier; revived 13 April 1836).

In Italian (translated probably by G. Carpani, according to De Tipaldo, *Biografie*), Monza Autumn 1787; Lisbon Carnival 1792.

In German (first translated by J. André): Hamburg 30 July 1787 (and "nach der Londoner Ver-änderung", translation altered by F. L. Schröder, 6 December 1790); Vienna Kä. 7 January 1788 (frequently revived; W. 1802 (additions by A. Fischer) and 28 November 1810 (re-orchestrated by I. von Seyfried); Berlin 9 February 1790 (revived 3 March 1806 with additions by B. A. Weber and J. Weigl); Poznán 22 September 1805; Prague 1807; Budapest 11 February 1811. The latest revivals on German stages were at Mannheim 1849 (orchestrated by L. Hetsch); Breslau 25 January 1858; Königsberg 18 October 1861; Leipzig 12 December 1862; Munich 25 August 1866; Carlsruhe 2 December 1888 and 19 November 1898.

In Danish (translated by L. Knudsen), Copenhagen 31 January 1791.

In Dutch (translated by B. Ruloffs), Amsterdam [24 February] 1791.

In Swedish (translated by C. Envallson), Stockholm 21 December 1791 and (translated by C. J. Lindegren) 30 January 1797; Malmö 11 May 1807; Lund 21 August 1807; Gothenburg 19 November 1807. Revived Stockholm 25 November 1857 (new Swedish version by C. W. A. Strandberg; re-scored by J. Foroni).

In Polish (translated by J. Baudouin), Warsaw 14 April 1809.

In Spanish, Madrid 3 May 1812.

In Russian (translated by V. A. Levshin), St. Petersburg 9 November 1815; Moscow 30 October 1817.

1785

DÉZÈDE: *Alexis et Justine*

14 January. Versailles

Text by J. M. Boutet de Monvel. Two acts.
Paris, C.I. 17 January 1785.

In French also Liége 15 November 1785; Charleston, S.C. 10 July 1795; Cologne 1795–96; St. Petersburg 6 July 1798.

In German (translated by C. G. Neefe), Mannheim 7 October 1787; Carlsruhe 14 February 1789; Berlin 31 March 1789; Munich August 1795, etc.

Anonymous Dutch version published 1796.

GRÉTRY: *Panurge dans l'Isle des Lanternes*

25 January. Paris, O.

Text by E. Morel de Chédeville and the Comte de Provence (Louis XVIII), after Rabelais (but, according to Quérard, more or less copied from a MS by the late F. Parfaict, the historian of the Paris theatres). Three acts.

"Une nouvelle tentative pour étendre les limites du genre comique sur le Théâtre d'Opéra" (*Mercure de France*).

In Paris given 248 times until 1824; in French also, Lyons 12 September 1787; Hague 1789; Brussels 21 January 1793; Hamburg December 1796; Gachina November 1799; St. Petersburg 17 February 1800; Cassel Spring 1813.

In Swedish (translated by J. D. Valerius), Stockholm 16 December 1799.

Dutch translation by C. Loots published 1804.

WINTER: *Der Bettelstudent* oder *Das Donnerwetter*

2 February. Munich

Text by P. Weidmann (originally published as a comedy in 1776 and first produced at Vienna, B. 6 October 1776), founded on Cervantes's story *La Cueva de Salamanca.* Two acts.

Winter's music was added for the Munich production.

Very popular on German stages: Vienna, Leop. 19 July 1785, etc. In German also, Warsaw 29 September 1793; Budapest 13 May 1801; Berlin 23 June 1802.

In Czech, Prague 17 April 1785 (translated by V. Tham; if not merely performed as a comedy, it would have been the first "opera" ever sung in that language); revived 16 September 1791.

In Swedish (translated by H. A. Kullberg), Stockholm 13 December 1833 and (in a new version by E. W. Djurström), 31 March 1855 (music arranged by A. Säfström).

Given in Germany until the middle of the 19th century, but from about 1800 with many additions by other composers (W. Müller, etc); as a *Quodlibet* (arranged by L. Schneider; published 1838; 2nd edition Berlin 1851) given at Weimar as late as 30 November 1882.

As *Der reisende Student* also given at the German theatre, New York 25 October 1842 and Hoboken 15 June 1853, the former being probably, the latter definitely, Schneider's version.

CHERUBINI: *La finta Principessa*

2 April. London, Hm.

Text by F. Livigni (first set to music by Alessandri in 1782). Two acts.

The first of two operas Cherubini wrote for London where he held the post of composer at the King's Theatre for two seasons before he went to Paris.

LIMA: *Le Nozze d'Ercole, e d'Ebe*

13 April. Lisbon

(Italian) text by an unknown author. Two acts.

Performed at the double wedding of two Spanish and two Portuguese princes and princesses at the palace of the Spanish Ambassador to Lisbon, Fernando Nuñez.

STORACE: *Gli Sposi malcontenti*

1 June. Vienna, B.

Text by G. Brunati. Two acts.
Storace's first opera.

In Italian also, Prague 1786; Leipzig Summer 1786; Dresden 1789.

In German (translated by J. W. Cowmeadow), Hanover 11 May 1792; Berlin 12 December 1793; Breslau 4 June 1795.

In French (translated by P. U. Dubuisson), Paris 12 April 1790 (at the opening of the Théâtre de la Demoiselle Montansier); repeated 29 August 1793 at the Th. National.

P. GUGLIELMI: *La Virtuosa in Mergellina*

Summer. Naples, T.N.

Text by S. Zini. Two acts.

Successful in Italy: given at Cremona Carnival 1791 as *Chi la dura la vince ossia La finta Cantatrice;* at Venice Autumn 1791 as *La Virtuosa bizzara.*

In Italian also, Malta Carnival 1787; Lisbon Carnival 1790 and 17 December 1793; Warsaw 9 April 1792; Barcelona 22 June 1792; Madrid 21 January 1797; London 7 April 1807.

SCHENK: *Die Weinlese*

12 October. Vienna, Leop.

Text: an altered version, by W. C. D. Meyer, of Weisse's *Aerndtekranz* (see 1771). Three acts.

Schenk's first opera and one of the first successes at Marinelli's new "Theater in der Leopoldstadt", Vienna (opened in 1781). Given there until 1803; given also at Vienna, W. *c.* 9 July 1791 (as *Der Erntekranz oder das Schnitterfest*).

SALIERI: *La Grotta di Trofonio*

12 October. Vienna, B.

Text by G. B. Casti. Two acts.

In Italian also given at Dresden 1786; Trieste 14 January 1787; Paris, Th. de M. 15 March 1790 (with 2 airs by Cherubini); Parma Carnival 1791; Lisbon 1795; Gorizia Carnival 1795; Barcelona 1796; Stuttgart 23 October 1809.

Even more successful on German stages where it was produced in several different translations: PRESSBURG 17 April 1786 and Budapest 16 July 1789 (translated by F. X. Girzik).

FRANKFORT 25 October 1786; Mannheim 19 November 1786 and Cassel 5 February 1787 (translated by C. G. Neefe).

PRAGUE 1787 (translated by P. Trautmann).

HAMBURG 5 December 1787; Vienna 3 September 1789; Munich October 1789; Berlin 19 March 1794; Riga 3 October 1794, etc.

In Danish (translated by C. D. Biehl), Copenhagen 8 January 1789.

An English adaptation by P. Hoare, *The Cave of Trophonius*, music arranged by Storace, was given in London, D.L. 3 May 1791 (see M. Kelly's *Reminiscences*, II, p.3).

SARTI: *I finti Eredi*

30 October. St. Petersburg

Text by G. Bertati (originally called *Il Villano geloso* and first set, in 3 acts, by Galuppi in 1769). Two acts.

The first opera Sarti wrote in Russia.

Also given at Prague 1786; Vienna 1 August 1786; Dresden 1787; Turin 1791; Milan, Sc. 26 February 1792; Padua October 1793; Madrid 9 June 1794; Lisbon 11 September 1794; Trieste 26 December 1795; Florence Autumn 1796; Palermo September 1797; Venice September 1799, etc. Revived Barcelona 12 October 1803.

FABRIZI: *Li due Castellani Burlati*

Autumn. Bologna, T. Marsigli-Rossi

Text by F. Livigni (first set to music by Valentini earlier in the same year). Two acts.

The first and one of the best of Fabrizi's comic operas and about the only one of which the score has survived. Given on many Italian stages (at Parma Carnival 1786 as a pasticcio from Valentini's and Fabrizi's settings) and at Barcelona 27 June 1786; Dresden 1788; Madrid 30 April 1789; London 2 February 1790; Lisbon Summer 1797 (reduced to 1 act).

GAZZANIGA: *La Moglie capricciosa*

Autumn. Venice, S. Moisè

Text by F. Livigni. Two acts.

Successful in Italy; given there until after 1800.

In Italian also, Dresden 18 March 1786; Trieste 26 December 1787; Madrid 21 January 1790; Lisbon Summer 1791; Vienna 26 April 1792; Warsaw 5 March 1793.

In German: Bautzen 27 October 1796 (probably earlier elsewhere).

PICCINNI: *Pénélope*

2 November. Fontainebleau

Text by J. F. Marmontel. Three acts.

The last of Piccinni's French serious operas which was produced. Paris, O. 9 December 1785 and with alterations 16 October 1787.

Unsuccessful (14 performances), but still of enough interest to call forth three parodies, viz. *Constance* by J. B. Radet, P. Y. Barré and J. R. Lecouppey de la Rozière, C.I. 6 January 1786; *Syncopé, Reine de Mic-Mac*, by J. E. Despréaux, Versailles 31 January 1786; and *Jean de Retour*, by P. G. Parisau, Variétés Amusantes 9 February 1786.

P. GUGLIELMI: *Enea e Lavinia*

4 November. Naples, S.C.

Text by V. de Stefani. Three acts.

One of the most important of Guglielmi's serious operas; repeated at Naples 13 August 1788 and also given at Milan, Sc. 28 July 1789, Venice, Genoa, etc.; Madrid 25 August 1790.

DALAYRAC: *La Dot*

8 November. Fontainebleau

Text by F. G. Desfontaines, a revised version of his earlier libretto *Le Billet de Mariage*. Three acts.

One of Dalayrac's first greater successes. Paris C.I. 21 November 1785 (given at the O.C. until 1828); in French also, Liége 15 November 1786; Brussels 2 November 1795; St. Petersburg 7 August 1795; Hamburg 13 September 1797 or earlier; Gachina 5 October 1798.

In Italian (translated by G. Carpani), Monza Autumn 1789 (additional music by W. Pichl).

1786

MARTIN Y SOLER: *Il Burbero di buon Cuore*

4 January. Vienna, B.

Text by L. da Ponte (founded on Goldoni's comedy, *Le Bourru bienfaisant*). Two acts.

Martin y Soler's first greater success: Venice Autumn 1798; Rome, Valle Spring 1790; Bologna, T. Zagnoni May 1790, etc.

In Italian also: Prague 1786; Dresden 3 October 1789; Trieste 26 December 1789; Paris, Th. Feydeau 22 February 1791; Madrid 30 May 1792; London 17 May 1794 (with additional music by Haydn, Trento and G. G. Ferrari); Barcelona 14 October 1794; St. Petersburg 30 May 1796.

Revived Vienna 9 November 1789 (with two additional airs by Mozart, K.582, 583, written for Louise Villeneuve).

SACCHINI: *Oedipe à Colone*

4 January. Versailles

Text by N. F. Guillard. Three acts.

Sacchini's chief work; first produced at the Paris O. 1 February 1787 (after Sacchini's death) and frequently revived there until 1844 (583 performances).

In French also, Liége 2 March 1796; Hamburg 20 April 1796 (revived 1799 and 1811); Cologne 1796–97; Copenhagen 1798 (in concert form); St. Petersburg 6 May 1799; Antwerp 14 February 1805.

In German (translated by C. A. Herklots), Hanover 21 May 1790; Berlin 16 October 1797; Munich 15 July 1800; Vienna 3 August 1802, etc. Last given in Germany: Weimar 17 February 1820 and Cassel 1 May 1826.

In Swedish (translated by C. G. Nordforss), Stockholm 1 November 1800 (given there until 1836).

In Italian (translated by G. Schmidt?), Naples, S.C. 14 May 1808.

In Russian (translated by R. M. Zotov), St. Petersburg 13 September 1816.

Dutch translations by P. J. Uylenbroek and by J. Kinker were published in 1795 (reprinted 1799) and 1807 respectively.

The opera was revived in concert form at Frankfort in April 1862 and at the Conservatoire, Brussels 7 December 1881; on the stage, Antwerp Autumn 1909 (in Flemish); Paris, O. 27. February 1916 (parts only).

TARCHI: *Ariarate*

January. Milan, Sc.

Text by F. Moretti. Three acts.

The most successful of Tarchi's numerous Italian operas (see 1800 for the best work of his French period). Given at Bologna May 1786; Trieste 9 April 1787; Palermo 2 June 1787; Naples, S.C. 4 November 1787, etc. In Italian also, Warsaw 11 January 1787.

NAUMANN: *Gustaf Wasa*

19 January. Stockholm

Text by J. H. Kellgren (scenario by King Gustaf III). Three acts.

Given at Stockholm 134 times until 1823 and frequently revived during the 19th century (since 12 April 1859 partly re-orchestrated by I. Lachner); parts of it even were revived as late as 18 January 1923.

(A Danish translation of the libretto, by F. H. Guldberg, was published in 1796; a Dutch version by J. Meerman in 1806.) The scenario by Gustaf III was published first in French (translated by J. B. Dechaux), Stockholm 1804; in German (translated by C. F. Rühs), Berlin 1805; in the original Swedish, Stockholm 1806.

A parody by E. Schröderheim, *Gustava Göck*, was performed at Court 1787, published 1850.

NAUMANN: *Orpheus og Euridice*

31 January. Copenhagen

Text by C. D. Biehl (partly founded on Calzabigi's libretto). Three acts.

The first grand opera in the Danish language; given at Copenhagen until 1791. German vocal score (translated by C. F. Cramer) published

1787. Given in concert form at Winterthur 30 November 1791 (in German, orchestrated by T. Müller); Stettin Winter 1798–99.

A Danish parody by P. L. Heiberg, *Michel og Malene*, adapted to Naumann's music, was published in 1789.

MOZART: *Der Schauspieldirektor*

7 February. Vienna, Schönbrunn

Text by G. Stephanie. *Komödie mit Musik.* One act. The music consists of an overture, two airs, a trio and the finale.

Written for a garden-party given by the Emperor Joseph II at Schönbrunn and performed together with Salieri's divertimento teatrale, *Prima la Musica e poi le Parole* (text by G. B. Casti). A correspondent to the Berlin periodical, *Ephemeriden der Literatur und des Theaters* (1786, p.189), mentions in his report of the Schönbrunn production the name of every singer as well as Stephanie's—but not Mozart's.

Publicly performed Vienna, Kä. 18 (not 11) February 1786 and W. 5 August 1797; also at Salzburg 1797–98 and Graz 4 April 1799. According to the preface to a later edition of Stephanie's *Singspiele*, it was also performed at Hamburg (before 1792; see Sonneck's *Catalogue*, pp.969–70; but this production is not recorded by Schütze, Meyer or by any other writer on the Hamburg stage). In a new arrangement by M. Stegmayer (*Quodlibet für den Carneval*) revived Vienna, W. 20 February 1814 (with additional music by Dittersdorf and others); also performed at Strasbourg 17 September 1814; Agram 24 May 1827.

After a long period of oblivion, the libretto was revised by L. Schneider, who replaced Stephanie's original imaginary characters by Mozart himself, Schikaneder (the "Schauspieldirektor"), Mozart's sister-in-law, Aloysia Lange, etc. This version was first produced at Berlin 25 April 1845 and Vienna, Leop. 2 December 1845 (as *Mozart und Schikaneder*) and has been generally accepted since; given at Riga 17 November 1845; Prague 7 August 1846; Basle 18 January 1858; Vienna, Kä. 28 August 1858. Another version, by R. Genée, called *Der Kapellmeister*, was produced at Kroll's, Berlin 22 May 1896. The original version was revived at Vienna, V.O. 17 February 1916.

Translated into other languages, mostly from L. Schneider's version, *Der Schauspieldirektor* was performed at:

PARIS, B.P. 20 May 1856 (as *L'Imprésario*, translated by L. Battu and Lud. Halévy) and Tr.L. 2 February 1918 (as *Le Directeur de Théâtre*, new translation by P. Bérel); the 1856 version was, by the B.P. company, also produced in London (see below) and at Berlin, Kroll's 26 June 1858.

STOCKHOLM 27 January 1857 (in Swedish, translated by J. C. Stjernström).

LONDON, ST. JAMES's 30 May 1857 (in French, by the Bouffes-Parisiens); Crystal Palace 11 August 1860 (in concert form, in Italian); Crystal Palace 14 September 1877 (as *The Manager*, translated by W. Grist); Crystal Palace 18 October 1892 and Olympic 25 October 1892 (in Italian, as *L'Impresario*, with recitatives by A. Mascheroni); H.M.'s 23 July 1910 (in English).

NEW YORK 9 November 1870 (in German) and 26 October 1916 (in English, as *The Impresario*, translated by H. E. Krehbiel).

PRAGUE 12 March 1875 (in Czech; revived 11 April 1916 and 9 January 1937).

COPENHAGEN 1 September 1877 (in Danish, translated by H. P. Holst).

AMSTERDAM July 1930 (in Dutch, at the Conservatoire).

Lately revived in English, S. Francisco March 1933 (translated by S. Neustadt); and Cambridge 27 July 1937 and London, Sadler's Wells 23 March 1938 (translated by E. Blom); his version had previously been broadcast from London on 17 March 1933.

On Vulpius's *Die theatralischen Abenteuer* (made up from the *Schauspieldirektor* and from Cimarosa's *L'Impresario in Angustie*), see col.433.

PAISIELLO: *Le Gare generose*

Spring. Naples, Fior

Text by G. Palomba. Two acts.

The exact date of the first performance is un-known. According to the libretto it was given "per prim' opera in quest' anno", and this was in Spring according to G. Pavan. Very successful in Italy and abroad; on many stages given as *Gli Schiavi per Amore*. Milan, Sc. 13 August 1791, etc.

In Italian also, Vienna 1 September 1786; Prague January 1787; London 24 April 1787 (Anna Storace's London début; revived 27 May 1790 and 14 March 1797); Versailles August 1787; Madrid 5 July 1789 and Barcelona 4 November 1790; Moscow 1790 or 1791; Lisbon Carnival 1792; Warsaw 7 July 1792; Dresden 3 October 1793; St. Petersburg 6 October 1798.

In German (as *Der Wettstreit der Grossmuth*, translated by F. X. Girzik), Pressburg 1787; Bozen February 1789; Budapest 27 May 1789; Vienna, Th. a.d. Landstrasse 22 May 1790; and (in another translation by H. G. Schmieder, *Die beyden Flüchtlinge*), Mayence 1789 (according to Schatz-Sonneck); Mayence 12 January 1791 (according to the repertory as given in *Journal des Luxus und der Moden*); Hamburg 30 June 1791; Hanover 16 November 1791, etc.

In French (as *Le bon Maître ou Les Esclaves par Amour*, translated by C. J. A. Gourbillon and P. G. Parisau), Paris, Th. de M. 20 March 1790. Another French version (*Le Maître généreux*, translated by P. U. Dubuisson) was produced at Paris, Th. Montansier 28 May 1790 and Th. Nat. 20 August 1793; Amsterdam December 1792; Hamburg 1796; Antwerp 14 January 1804.

PASHKEEVICH?: *Fevey*
Февей

30 April. St. Petersburg

Text by the Empress Catharine II (from a Russian story, *O Karevice Feveya*). Four acts.

First produced at the Ermitage; publicly performed St. Petersburg 8 December 1790.

The vocal score was printed in 1789 under Pashkeevich's name. Later authorities (Longinov, in *Molva*, 1857, p.43) attribute the music to an otherwise completely unknown composer, Brisk (not Briks, as Riemann has it), under whose name the music was reprinted in 1895.

MOZART: *Le Nozze di Figaro*

1 May. Vienna, B.

Text by L. da Ponte (founded on Beaumarchais's comedy, *La folle Journée, ou Le Mariage de Figaro,* 1785). Four acts.

When first produced in Vienna, the opera was not a very great success; there were nine performances in 1786, none in 1787 and 1788. Revived only 29 August 1789, with two new airs for Adrianna Ferrarese (Susanna), *Al desio di chi t'adora* and *Un moto di gioia mi sento.* For an account of the first production, see Michael Kelly's *Reminiscences,* Vol. I, pp.258–262.

Early productions in Italian were at:

PRAGUE December 1786.

MONZA Autumn 1787 (see below).

FLORENCE Spring 1788 (see below).

POTSDAM Autumn 1790.

LEIPZIG 26 May 1793.

First performed in German at:

PRAGUE, ROSENTHAL TH. June 1787 (according to an advertisement quoted by Teuber, II, p.244; translated possibly by V. Maschek).

DONAUESCHINGEN 23 September 1787 (at the Prince of Fürstenberg's private theatre; according to the play-bill, translated by Secretair Held and Kammersänger Walter).

LEIPZIG 3 August 1788.

GRAZ 9 August 1788.

FRANKFORT 11 October 1788 (translated by C. A. Vulpius).

HANOVER 18 May 1789 (translated by A. F. von Knigge: "Der Dialog ist von meiner Tochter [Philippine Eregine von Knigge]. Sie hat dabei das französische Stück genützt und manche launichte Stelle, die im Italienischen weggelassen war, wieder hereingebracht. Der Text der Arien ist von mir . . ." (Knigge's *Dramaturgische Blätter,* 23 May 1789).

BRUNSWICK 11 August 1789.

CELLE 14 September 1789.

BONN AND COLOGNE 1789 (Vulpius's translation).

STUTTGART 23 July 1790 (Vulpius's translation).

BERLIN 14 September 1790 (500th performance 24 September 1908).

MANNHEIM 24 October 1790.

HAMBURG 4 April 1791 (Knigge's translation).

AACHEN 15 May 1792.

VIENNA, W. 28 December 1792 (translated by K. L. Gieseke).

WEIMAR 24 October 1793.

MUNICH January 1794.

BRESLAU 31 October 1794.

DRESDEN 30 April 1795.

VIENNA, KÄ. 10 July 1798 (Knigge's translation).

On another early German translation (Passau 1789) see A. E. Cherbuliez, in *Bericht über die musikwissenschaftliche Tagung . . . in Salzburg,* 1931, p.150 ff.

In Italy the opera was first performed at Monza Autumn 1787 and Florence, P. Spring 1788. See on these rather odd productions (at Monza the 3rd and 4th act was re-written by Angelo Tarchi!) A. Einstein, in *The Monthly Musical Record,* July 1935. They passed nearly unnoticed; G. Piccini, in his *Il Teatro della Pergola* (1912) does not even mention the Florence performance, while U. Morini (*La R. Accademia degli Immobili ed il suo Teatro La Pergola,* 1926) attributes the opera to Paisiello. *Figaro* was then given at Turin, T. Carignano Autumn 1811, as *Il Matrimonio di Figaro;* at Naples, Fondo March 1814; Milan, Sc. 27 March 1815; Florence, T. degl' Intrepidi Spring 1818 and P. Autumn 1821; Leghorn Carnival 1823; Milan, Canobbiana 8 October 1825; Turin, T. Carignano Autumn 1826, etc.

At the Fiorentini Theatre, Naples, an altered version of Da Ponte's libretto was produced in 1792, called *La Serva onorata* (music by Piccinni); the text was also used by Paer for his *Il nuovo Figaro* (Parma January 1794).

France and Belgium:

PARIS, O. 20 March 1793 (in French, translated by F. Notaris; spoken dialogue, from Beaumarchais, instead of recitative; five performances only).

PARIS, TH.I. 23 December 1807 (in Italian).

NÎMES 31 December 1818 (French version by F. H. J. Castil-Blaze).

NANTES 17 January 1822 (French version by F. H. J. Castil-Blaze).

BRUSSELS 11 April 1822 (French version by F. H. J. Castil-Blaze).

GHENT 29 November 1822 (French version by F. H. J. Castil-Blaze).

LILLE 20 January 1823 (French version by F. H. J. Castil-Blaze).

ANTWERP 26 February 1826 (French version by F. H. J. Castil-Blaze).

PARIS, ODÉON 28 June 1826 (French version by F. H. J. Castil-Blaze).

PARIS, TH.L. 8 May 1858 (translated by J. Barbier and M. Carré).

ANTWERP 4 December 1900 (in Flemish).

MONTE CARLO 23 February 1911 (new French version by P. Ferrier).

PARIS, O.C. 5 March 1919 (Ferrier's version).

PARIS, O.C. 1 July 1939 (new French version by A. Boschot).

To the different Paris productions may be added the pasticcio, *Figaro ou Le Jour des Noces*, text by F. V. A. and L. C. A. d'Artois de Bournonville, music arranged by Blangini (from Mozart's *Figaro* and Rossini's *Barbiere*), given at the Th. des Nouveautés 16 August 1827. The English equivalent was *The Two Figaros*, by J. R. Planché (founded on a French comedy by H. A. Richaud Martelly): London, Olympic 30 November 1836 and New York 16 November 1837, music, as in the French pasticcio, from Mozart's and Rossini's operas.

Other Countries:

AMSTERDAM 8 July 1794 (in German); 12 May 1809 (in Italian); 6 February 1817 (in French); 1825 (in Dutch).

MADRID 20 May 1802 (in Spanish, translated by V. R. de Arellano).

BUDAPEST 20 March 1812 (in German) and 11 September 1858 (in Hungarian, translated by M. F. = Miklós Feleki?).

LONDON, HM. 18 June 1812 (in Italian); C.G. 6 March 1819 (in English, adapted by T. Holcroft, music arranged by Bishop); D.L. 12 May 1841 (in German); C.G. 15 March 1842 (new English version by J. R. Planché; with spoken dialogue).

COPENHAGEN 9 January 1821 (in Danish, translated by N. T. Bruun); 14 June 1825 (in German); 25 May 1842 (in Italian); 7 January 1844 (new Danish version by N. C. L. Abrahams).

STOCKHOLM 23 January 1821 (in Swedish, translated by B. H. Crusell; Crusell's translation only published 1851; new Swedish translation by S. C. Bring published 1911).

DUBLIN 27 January 1821 (in English) and 6 March 1838 (in Italian).

NEW YORK 10 May 1824 (in English, Bishop's version); 24 October 1831 (in French); 23 November 1858 (in Italian); 18 December 1862 (in German).

EDINBURGH 4 December 1832 (in Italian).

ST. PETERSBURG December 1836 (in German); Carnival 1851 (in Italian); and 8 October 1901 (in Russian, translated by M. I. Chaikovsky); revived Leningrad 19 May 1936.

CHRISTIANIA 1838 (in Danish).

HELSINKI 30 October 1840 (in German) and 20 September 1922 (in Finnish, translated by T. Muroma).

BUCHAREST 1843 (in German) and October 1937 (in Rumanian); revived 6 November 1938 in German, by the Frankfort Opera Company.

ZAGREB July 1844 (in German) and 26 October 1917 (in Croatian, translated by A. Kassowitz-Cvijić); revived in German 19 May 1938, by the Frankfort Opera Company.

RIO DE JANEIRO 1848 (in Italian).

PRAGUE 14 November 1852 (for the first time there in Czech, translated by E. Ujky).

SYDNEY 19 August 1862 (in English).

WARSAW 31 December 1885 (in Polish).

SOFIA 23 September 1911 (in Bulgarian, translated by A. Naidenov) and 8 May 1938 (in German by the Frankfort Opera Company).

BARCELONA 2 February 1916 (in Italian) and 16 January 1923 (in German); Catalan translation by J. Pena published 1927.

LONDON, OLD VIC 15 January 1920 (new English version by E. J. Dent).

LJUBLJANA 28 November 1926 (in Slovenian, translated by I. Šorli).

BUENOS AIRES 29 June 1928 (in German).

BELGRADE 15 May 1938 (in German).
ATHENS 6 December 1938 (in German).

DALAYRAC: *Nina*, ou *La Folle par Amour*

15 May. Paris, C.I.

Text by B. J. Marsollier (founded on a story in F. T. M. de Baculard d'Arnaud's *Délassements de l'Homme sensible*). One act.

Very successful in France; last revived Paris, O.C. 5 January 1852.

A parody, *Nani ou La Folle de Village*, by P. J. C. Lecocq Darcourt was published in 1787 and produced at Valenciennes 3 September 1788.

In French also, Liége 24 November 1786, etc.; Aachen 21 July 1794; Charleston, S.C. 23 July 1794; Cologne 1796–97; St. Petersburg 5 November 1798; Moscow 10 October 1808.

In German (translated by B. C. d'Arien), Hamburg 31 January 1787 and Munich October 1787; (translated by H. G. Schmieder), Mannheim 17 June 1787; Munich October 1787; (translated by J. André), Berlin 3 May 1788 and Potsdam 22 September 1788 (first opera sung in German there); Vienna, Leop. 11 June 1790 and W. 29 July 1806; Budapest 30 January 1796; Rotterdam Spring 1797; Berne Spring 1804.

In English (translated by J. Wolcot, music adapted by W. T. Parke, additions by Shield; see Parke's *Musical Memoirs*, I, p.95), London, C.G. 24 April 1787. There are three more English versions, viz. *Nina; or The Love distracted Maid* (anonymous) and *Nina; or The Madness of Love* (by G. M. Berkeley), both published 1787. The third, by W. Dunlap, was used at a revival in New York 4 February 1805.

In Italian (translated by G. Carpani), Monza Autumn 1788 and Milan, Canobiana March 1789; but soon replaced in Italy by Paisiello's setting (see 1789).

In Russian, Kouskovo 28 November 1790.

In Swedish (translated by C. Stenborg), Stockholm 8 December 1792; Malmö 17 April 1807; Lund 15 August 1808.

Dutch translation published 1789; performed in Flemish Oudenarde 1795.

P. GUGLIELMI: *L'Inganno amoroso*

12 June. Naples, T.N.

Text by G. Palomba. Two acts.

Successful in Italy; given at Rome, T. Valle Carnival 1787 in a reduced version as *Gli Equivoci nati da Somiglianza;* Venice, S. Moisè Autumn 1788 as *Le Nozze disturbate;* Monza Autumn 1788 and Bologna Carnival 1791, as *Le due Gemelle;* Parma Carnival 1792 as *L'Equivoco amoroso;* Savona 1793 as *Li due Equivoci per Somiglianza;* Padua Carnival 1794 as *Le due finte Gemelle.* Given in Italy until 1809; in Italian also, Vienna 9 April 1787; Barcelona 30 May 1789 (revived 25 August 1803); Paris, Th. de M. 29 May 1790 (additions by Paisiello); Marseilles March 1791; Trieste 26 December 1791; Madrid 4 April 1793; Lisbon Spring 1796; St. Petersburg 29 August 1798.

A German version by J. B. Krebs, *Die Zwillingsbrüder*, was produced at Stuttgart c.1810.

DITTERSDORF: *Doctor und Apotheker*

11 July. Vienna, Kä.

Text by G. Stephanie (said to be founded on a French play, *L'Apothicaire de Murcia,*which bibliographically seems to be untraceable). Two acts.

Dittersdorf's most successful opera. Frequently revived on German stages up to the present time.

Given at Pressburg 15 September 1786; Cassel 13 April 1787; Hamburg 7 May 1787; Berlin 25 June 1787 (113 times until 1853, revived 31 December 1890, 1 November 1899 and 26 April 1912).

In German also, Budapest 26 November 1787; Schleswig 1788; Prague 1790; Riga 1790; Agram 1790 (or earlier; see *Journal des Luxus und der Moden*, 1790, p.513); Amsterdam 1792; Warsaw 10 August 1793; Poznán 29 October 1803; Berne Spring 1804.

In English (adapted by J. Cobb, additional music by S. Storace), London, D.L. 25 October 1788 (running for 36 nights); also given at Dublin 22 July 1789; Boston 1795; Charleston, S.C. 26 April 1796 (music arranged by B. Bergman); Philadelphia 20 May 1796; New York 3 March 1798.

In Danish (translated by L. Knudsen), Copenhagen 17 November 1789.

In Russian (translated by F. Rozanov), Moscow 1788.

In French (translated by Beaunoir), Brussels 2 May 1794 (music adapted by C. F. H. Duquesnoy); Hamburg 1796.

In Swedish (adapted by C. Envallsson), Stockholm 6 June 1795 (at an earlier production 28 October 1791 new music by J. D. Zander had been used); revived Gothenburg 29 April 1828 and Stockholm 1 February 1858 (new Swedish translation by F. T. Hedberg).

In Dutch (translated by I. J. A. Gogel), Amsterdam 1796; revived Hague 1809.

In Hungarian (translated by J. Kiss), Debreczen 27 July 1799.

Revived in German, Munich 22 May 1823 (with additional numbers by Poissl); Basle 4 January 1852 (first time in Switzerland?); New York 30 June 1875. Some of the latest revivals in Germany were at Halle 1 January 1918; Munich December 1924; Coblenz March 1938 (revised by H. Burkard).

J. C. VOGEL: *La Toison d'Or*
5 September. Paris, O.

Text by P. Desriaux. Three acts.

Vogel's first opera. The score is dedicated to Gluck, who praised the opera highly shortly before his death. Revived with alterations as *Médée à Colchos*, Paris, O. 17 June 1788 (nine days before the composer's death at the age of 32).

Date of first performance according to the *Mercure de France*, to the *Mémoirs sécrets* and to the printed score. The libretto has August 29 1786 and a second libretto published under the title *Médée à Colchos ou la Toison d'Or* was issued with the date of 27 September 1786.

CIMAROSA: *Le Trame deluse*
September. Naples, T.N.

Text by G. M. Diodati. Two acts.

Successful in Italy; Milan, Sc. 19 August 1787 (revived 2 November 1818); given at Bologna Autumn 1799, as *Li Raggiri scoperti;* last revived Rome, Arg. 30 April 1822.

In Italian also given at Vienna 7 May 1787; Madrid 5 July 1788; Dresden 3 January 1789; Barcelona 14 October 1789; Corfu Carnival 1790; Lisbon 13 May 1790 (revived Spring 1797); Marseilles Autumn 1790; London 14 February 1792; Warsaw 6 June 1792; Paris, Th. Feydeau 16 June 1792.

In German, Pressburg 1788 and Budapest 28 July 1789 (as *Die betrogenen Betrüger*); Weimar 24 October 1794; Oels 16 January 1796; Vienna, W. 18 June 1796 (as *Die vereitelten Ränke*, translated probably by C. A. Vulpius); Hanover 4 February 1802; Bremen 1802–03; Berlin 11 January 1808.

In Spanish, Madrid 23 October 1802 (as *Las Tramas burladas*).

Date of first performance according to a note in the autograph score at Naples.

SCHUBAUR: *Die treuen Köhler*
29 September. Munich

Text by G. E. Heermann (first set to music by E. W. Wolf in 1773). Two acts.

Schubaur's last opera. Stuttgart 16 October 1788, etc. Revived Vienna, W. 26 April 1797. Vocal score printed. (The libretto is founded upon a historical event, the kidnapping of two Saxon princes in 1455; see P. A. Merbach in *Neues Archiv für Sächsische Geschichte und Altertumskunde*, 1929.)

DITTERSDORF: *Betrug durch Aberglauben*
3 October. Vienna, Kä.

Text by F. Eberl. Two acts.

Successful on German stages: Pressburg and Cologne 1787; Frankfort 23 September 1787; Hamburg 7 July 1788; Hanover 22 October 1788; Mannheim 16 November 1788; Berlin 17 January 1789; Carlsruhe 19 January 1789; Stuttgart 1 May 1789; Budapest 12 June 1789; Munich September 1789; Prague 1790, etc. Revived Vienna 4 September 1796; Stuttgart 30 October 1808.

In Danish (translated by A. G. Thoroup), Copenhagen 15 March 1796.

First performed 3 October, not 30 October as Riedinger has it.

CIMAROSA: *L' Impresario in Angustie*

October. Naples, T.N.

Text by G. M. Diodati. One act.

In its original form this farce was given on the same bill with the two-act opera *Il Credulo* by the same authors (see the original libretto in Sonneck's *Catalogue*, p.332).

The difficulties in dating the first performance have been pointed out by Sonneck. According to Diodati's statement in the preface to the *Impresario* libretto, it was produced "appresso all altra mia *Le Trame deluse*", which would mean about October.

Given at Milan, Sc. 3 October 1789 and all over Italy (until about 1825); in Italian also, Trieste 6 December 1788; Paris, Th. de M. 6 May 1789 (enlarged to 2 acts, additions by Guglielmi and Giordani); Barcelona 13 July 1789; Eszterháza 1790; Lisbon Carnival 1792; Warsaw 29 September 1792; Vienna 24 October 1793; Ljubljana Spring 1794; Dresden Spring 1794; St. Petersburg 1794 or 20 February 1795. Revived Paris, Th. I. 12 March 1802.

In French (as *Le Directeur dans l'Embarras*, translated by P. U. Dubuisson), Paris, Th. Beaujolais 23 December 1789; Ghent 1791; Hamburg c. January 1795; Rotterdam 25 April 1796; Berne 26 February 1806; Moscow 19 April 1809; Antwerp 6 January 1821. Another French version, *La Comédie à la Campagne*, translated by F. A. Duvert, music adapted by P. C. Crémont, was produced at the Odéon, Paris, 16 August 1825.

In German (as *Der Direkteur in der Klemme*, translated by Pilger), Aachen 8 May 1791 and Cologne 25 September 1791. Another version, by no less a translator than Goethe (who had been present at a performance of the Italian original at Rome on 31 July 1787), was produced at Weimar 24 October 1791 (as *Die theatralischen Abenteuer;* see M. Morris in *Goethe-Jahrbuch*, Vol.

XXVI, 1905). Some years later, a 2-act version, adapted by C. A. Vulpius to music from Cimarosa's opera and Mozart's *Schauspieldirektor* (both of them originally produced in the same year and treating very similar subjects), was given at Weimar (14 October 1797) and subsequently on many other German stages; in German also, Laibach 15 January 1811 and St. Petersburg 1813. Revived Hamburg 24 June 1814, Berlin 18 July 1817 and (Kgst.) 10 August 1824. A new German translation by E. Latzko was published 1932.

In Danish (translated by F. G. Sporon), Copenhagen 15 December 1795.

In Swedish (translated from the French version by C. G. Nordforss), Stockholm 28 April 1799.

In Polish (translated by W. Boguslawski), Lvóv 1796 and Warsaw 1799.

In Dutch (translated from the French version by W. van Ollefen), Amsterdam 1800.

In Russian (translator not mentioned), Moscow 25 October 1820.

In the original Italian, Cimarosa's opera was revived at Turin, T.R. 28 February 1933, and Milan, Sc. 9 March 1938 (music revised by A. Toni).

DALAYRAC: *Azémia, ou Le nouveau Robinson*

17 October. Fontainebleau

Text by A. E. X. de Lachabeaussière (*opéra-comique ou roman lyri-comique*). Three acts.

Publicly performed Paris, C.I. 3 May 1787 (with the new sub-title *Les Sauvages*, and with a new third act); given until 1828.

In French also, Liége 3 October 1789; Brussels 17 June 1795; Cologne 1796–97; Hamburg and Gachina 1797; Moscow 5 February 1810; New York 20 September 1827.

In German (translated by H. G. Schmieder), Mayence 26 May 1789; Hamburg 21 September 1789; Berlin 7 June 1790; Munich 8 April 1791; Cologne 20 November 1791; Graz 18 April 1793 (translated by J. Perinet); Vienna, Leop. 7

July 1795 and Kä. 22 July 1805; Budapest 6 June 1797; Berne Spring 1804; St. Petersburg 1808; Basle 16 January 1809.

Dutch translation by E. G. Beaumont published Rotterdam 1790; another by H. Ogelwight published Amsterdam 1791.

In Swedish (translated by W. von Rosenheim), Stockholm 6 June 1793 and (in another version by C. Envallsson) 13 June 1793 (at two different theatres); Gothenburg 25 February 1796; Malmö 27 April 1807; Lund 10 August 1807.

In Russian (translated by V. A. Levshin), Kouskovo c.1794 and Moscow 1803.

In Danish (translated by N. T. Bruun), Copenhagen 29 October 1810.

In Dutch, Amsterdam 1817.

LEMOYNE: *Phèdre*

26 October. Fontainebleau

Text by F. B. Hoffman. Three acts.

Lemoyne's chief work. Publicly performed Paris, O. 21 November 1786 (given there 36 times until 1792 and revived 5 December 1795 and 2 November 1813).

In Russian (translated by P. N. Semenov), St. Petersburg 30 December 1818 (additional music by Steibelt).

GRÉTRY: *Les Méprises par Ressemblance*

7 November. Fontainebleau

Text by J. Patrat. Three acts.

Paris, C.I. 16 November 1786. In French also, Amsterdam 9 April 1791; Brussels 8 December 1799 (as *Les deux Grenadiers*). Revived Paris, O.C. 24 September 1817 and 29 July 1858; in Swedish, Stockholm 7 March 1877 (as *De bägge Grenadiererna*, orchestration revised by J. Dente).

Patrat later had the music suppressed and his text produced as a comedy, under the title of *Les deux Grenadiers ou Les Quiproquos;* in this form performed, Th. de la Cité 7 October 1793. Dutch translation of this version published 1805.

GRÉTRY: *Le Comte d'Albert*

13 November. Fontainebleau

Text by J. M. Sedaine (founded on a fable by Lafontaine). Two acts; produced on the same bill with a third act called *Suite du Comte d'Albert.* Revived as *Albert et Antoine ou Le Service récompensé*, Fa. 7 December 1794.

Paris, C.I. 8 February 1787. In French also, Liége 21 November 1787; Amsterdam 1788; Cologne 1796–97; St. Petersburg 27 April 1800; Hanover 11 June 1805; Moscow 29 April 1809; Antwerp 17 September 1812.

In German (translated by H. G. Schmieder), Mayence 20 June 1789; Berlin 2 January 1799.

In Swedish (translated by C. J. Lindegren), Stockholm 16 May 1799.

In Russian (translated by A. P. Veshnyakov), St. Petersburg 23 December 1822.

An English adaptation by P. Hoare, with some new music by M. Kelly, called *A Friend in Need is a Friend indeed*, was produced in London, D.L. 9 February 1797.

MARTIN Y SOLER: *Una Cosa rara o sia Bellezza ed Onestà*

17 November. Vienna, B.

Text by L. da Ponte (founded on a story *La Luna della Sierra*, by Luis Velez de Guevara). Two acts.

Martin y Soler's most popular work and one of the great operatic successes of that period. Frequently revived until about 1825. In Italian also given at:

DRESDEN 1787.

PRAGUE Autumn 1787.

MILAN, S.C. 13 October 1787.

VENICE 26 December 1787.

TRIESTE January 1788.

ROME, VALLE 12 April 1788.

DRESDEN 12 April 1788.

LJUBLJANA 1788.

ST. PETERSBURG Autumn 1788.

LONDON 10 January 1789.

MADRID 23 September 1789.

WARSAW 3 January 1790.

BARCELONA 2 September 1790.

PARIS, TH. FEYDEAU 2 November 1791.

LISBON 25 April 1794

CAGLIARI, SARDINIA Autumn 1805.

Revived in London 13 June 1805 and 16 May 1816; revived Paris 29 August 1812.

In German (as *Cosa rara, der seltne Fall, oder Schönheit und Tugend*, translated by F. Eberl), Vienna, Leop. 26 June 1787; (as *Eine seltne Verschwisterung: Tugend und Schönheit beysammen*, translated by F. X. Girzik) Pressburg 1787 and Budapest February 1788; (as *Lilla, oder Schönheit und Tugend*, translated by J. André) Cologne Spring 1787, Hamburg 9 January 1788, Mannheim 8 June 1788, Munich July 1788, Schleswig 1788, Berlin 3 August 1788, Carlsruhe 16 September 1788; (as *Lilla, oder die seltene Treue*) Prague 4 September 1789, Leipzig 24 September 1789.

In German also, Amsterdam 19 May 1792; Temesvar 7 March 1802; Berne Spring 1804; Poznán 3 October 1805.

A German sequel, *Der Fall ist noch weit seltener! oder: Die geplagten Ehemänner* (text by E. Schikaneder, music by B. Schack), was given at Vienna, W. 10 May 1790; Prague 1792; Hamburg 1 October 1792; Budapest 11 September 1793.

In Russian (translated by I. A. Dmitrevsky), St. Petersburg 12 June 1789 (revived 26 June 1803); Moscow 30 April 1795 (revived 27 April 1806; 26 December 1816; 29 August 1823).

In Danish (translated by L. Knudsen), Copenhagen 15 November 1791.

In Polish (translated by W. Boguslawski), Warsaw 1794; Wilna 13 February 1810.

In French (as *Les Accordées de Village*, translated by J. Patrat), Paris, Th. Montansier 3 November 1797, Th. de la Cité 14 December 1797; Ghent 1800.

For an English adaptation, see Storace's *Siege of Belgrade*, 1791.

Una Cosa rara was revived at Halle December 1921 (in German, André's version revised by L. Sachse); Barcelona 21 April 1936 (in Italian, at the fourteenth Festival of the I.S.C.M.).

ANFOSSI: *Le Gelosie fortunate*

Autumn. Venice, S. Sam.

Text by F. Livigni. Two acts.

Milan, Sc. 10 February 1788, etc.

In Italian also given at Barcelona 23 July 1787 (revived 12 May 1791); Vienna 2 June 1788 and with alterations 13 June 1789; Eszterháza 1789; Madrid 22 October 1791; Trieste Summer 1794; Bastia, Corsica Spring 1797.

Performed at Vienna with one inserted air by Mozart (*Un bacio di mano*, K.541). Performed at San Francesco d'Albaro, near Genoa Autumn 1790 with additions by Paisiello.

FOMIN: *Novogorodskoy Bogatir Boyeslavich*

Новогородской Богатырь Боеславичь

(Boyeslavich the Hero of Novgorod)

8 December. St. Petersburg

Text by the Empress Catharine II. Five acts.

First produced at the Ermitage; publicly performed Moscow 16 February 1795.

STORACE: *Gli Equivoci*

27 December. Vienna, B.

Text by L. da Ponte (founded on Shakespeare's *Comedy of Errors*. *Dramma buffo . . . ad imitazione della comedia inglese di Shakespeare, che ha per titolo: Les meprises*). Two acts.

Given at Leipzig Summer 1793 as *Li quattro Gemelli;* in Italian also, Prague 1793; Dresden 18 November 1797. In German, Pressburg 1788.

Later on Storace introduced parts of the music into his English operas *No Song, no Supper* (1790) and *The Pirates* (1792). See on *Gli Equivoci*, one of the earliest Shakespearean operas, H. Boas in *Sammelbände* of the *I.M.S.*, Vol. xv (1913–14), p.330, and A. Einstein in *The Monthly Musical Record*, March–April, 1936.

1787

CHAMPEIN: *Les Dettes*

11 January. Paris, C.I.

Text by N. J. Forgeot. Two acts.

Given in Paris until 1826.

In French also, Liége 20 January 1788; Charleston, S.C. 21 July 1795; Hamburg 1795; Cologne 1795–96; Hanover 20 January 1804; Moscow 28 July 1810.

In Dutch (translated by H. Ogelwight), Amsterdam July 1791.

(Date of first performance according to *Mercure de France;* the libretto gives 8 January 1787.)

PAISIELLO: *Pirro*

12 January. Naples, S.C.

Text by G. de Gamerra. Three acts.

Successful in Italy (last revived Naples, S.C. 25 December 1811; Parma 5 December 1812). Given at Rome, Ap. Summer 1798 in a reduced 2-act version.

In Italian also given at Trieste 24 April 1789; Warsaw 16 January 1790; Leipzig Summer 1793; Madrid 14 October 1793; Prague 1794; London 13 June 1809 (in preparation already in 1791, semi-public dress rehearsals 23 February, 10 and 22 March; not produced then as the licence was refused by the Lord Chamberlain); Paris 19 January 1811 (first Italian opera seria there for 125 years, since Cavalli's *Ercole amante* in 1662!).

(According to Paisiello himself, *Pirro* was the first serious opera which contains finales.)

VOGLER: *Castore e Polluce*

12 January. Munich

Text: a reduced 3-act version of C. I. Frugoni's *I Tintaridi* (see 1760).

Successful at Munich. Revived (in Italian) Prague 1798 and 1801; Vienna 22 December 1803 (in concert form); Munich 14 January 1806 (with alterations, at the wedding of Eugène Beauharnais with Princess Augusta of Bavaria).

The chorus of the furies from *Castore e Polluce* was introduced into a *Don Giovanni* performance

at Munich as late as 1824 (*A.M.Z.*, 1824, p.585; see also C. M. von Weber's letter of 22 March 1811).

Date of first production according to Schatz, Rudhart, Zenger.

DITTERSDORF: *Democrito corretto*

24 January. Vienna, B.

Text (according to G. Gugitz) by G. Brunati (founded on J. F. Regnard's comedy *Démocrite*, 1700). Two acts.

The Italian production was a failure, but the opera became fairly popular on the German stage. The earliest German version (1788) was called *Silene* (by Dittersdorf himself? see A. E. Brachvogel, *Geschichte der Königlichen Theater zu Berlin*, Vol. II, 1878, p.134); produced perhaps at Pressburg 1788 as *Der gebesserte Democrit*.

In a German version by H. G. Schmieder the opera was then given at

MAYENCE 1790 (as *Democrit*).

MANNHEIM 26 May 1791 as *Der eingebildete Democrit*.

AACHEN 5 June 1791 and Cologne 3 October 1791 as *Democrit am Hofe*.

FRANKFORT 10 July 1791 as *Democrit*.

HAMBURG 27 July 1791 as *Democrit der Zweyte* (translation altered by F. L. Schröder; in 3 acts).

MUNICH 13 June 1794 as *Der neue Democrit*.

(Date of first performance according to Pohl and others: Riedinger has 1 January; Schatz-Sonneck 27 January, perhaps following Krebs's "Wednesday, 27 January"; yet 27 January was a Saturday.)

BULANT: *Zbitenshchik*
Збитеньщикъ
(The Seller of Mead)

28 January. Moscow

Text by Y. B. Knyazhnin. Three acts.

Very popular Russian comic opera. First given at St. Petersburg 22 May 1789, and frequently revived on Russian stages until after 1850. The text (first printed in 1789) is an imitation of the *Barber of Seville*, which, in Paisiello's setting, had been very successful in Russia (see 1782). A MS score of the opera was shown at the International Theatre Exhibition, Vienna, 1892.

Dates of the first performances according to N. Findeizen's "Очерки по истории музыки в России . . ." (1929), Vol. II, p.107. Different dates, probably misprinted, are given in the same author's article on early Russian opera in *The Musical Quarterly*, 1933.

SCHALL: *Claudine af Villa Bella*

29 January. Copenhagen

Text, a Danish version, by N. H. Weinwich, of Goethe's *Singspiel* (see 1780). Three acts.

The first of Schall's seven Danish operas.

GAZZANIGA: *Don Giovanni Tenorio o sia Il Convitato di Pietra*

5 February. Venice, S. Moisè

Text by G. Bertati. One act.

Forming the second act of *Il Capriccio drammatico* (music perhaps by Valentini, who is mentioned in a later libretto, Forlì, 1789). Wiel and Schatz have made it clear that *Il Capriccio drammatico* is only a slightly altered version of Bertati's *La Novità* (Venice, S. Moisè Autumn 1775), which then served as introductory act to *L'Italiano a Parigi* (music of both by Alessandri).

Very successful in Italy; Bologna Spring 1788; Milan, Sc. 3 October 1789; Turin and Forlì 1789, etc. (given at Milan, T. Lentasio, as late as 11 April 1821). In Italian also Paris 10 October 1791 (Cherubini, then conductor at the Th. Feydeau, introduced some pieces from Mozart's *Don Giovanni* into Gazzaniga's work and one quartet of his own); Lisbon Carnival 1792; London 1 March 1794 (see below); [Madrid 12 November 1796, Gazzaniga's according to Carmena y Millan; in reality Fabrizi's opera, according to the libretto].

The opera is of special interest as the immediate forerunner of Mozart's *Don Giovanni;* particularly so since Chrysander first drew attention to the fact that Da Ponte, Mozart's librettist, obviously knew Bertati's text, and not only knew but used

it. When in 1794 poet to the King's Theatre, Da Ponte concocted a new one-act version from Bertati's and from his own libretto; this "tragicomic opera," *Il Don Giovanni*, was produced in London on 1 March 1794 with parts of Gazzaniga's music and additional airs by Sarti, Federici and Guglielmi. Mozart's opera came to London no less than 23 years later. It is, however, likely that at least Mozart's "Catalogue Song" was heard in London in 1794 as the text is literally to be found in the libretto. (See Chrysander's study in *Vierteljahrsschrift für Musikwissenschaft*, Vol. IV [1887], which deals thoroughly with the whole Gazzaniga-Mozart question.)

DITTERSDORF: *Die Liebe im Narrenhause*

12 April. Vienna, Kä.

Text by G. Stephanie. Two acts.

Successful on German stages; given at Pressburg 1787; Cologne 1787–88; Hamburg 8 December 1788 (as *Orpheus der Zweyte*, text altered by F. L. Schröder, music adapted by J. F. Hönicke); Hanover 2 November 1789; Stuttgart 5 April 1790; Munich November 1790; Berlin 16 May 1791, etc. In German also, Budapest 4 June 1790; Amsterdam 1792; Warsaw 28 September 1793. Revived Stuttgart 26 November 1808; Würzburg 27 October 1813.

CIMAROSA: *Il Fanatico burlato*

Spring. Naples, Fondo

Text by S. Zini. Two acts.

(The title in a MS score at the Florence Conservatorio is *La Burla felice overo Il Fanatico burlato*.) According to the libretto given "per prim' opera di quest' anno", which was in Spring according to Cambiasi. Successful in Italy; Milan, Sc. 30 March 1788, etc. Revived Naples, T.N. Carnival 1808; Florence, P. October 1809.

Outside Italy given at Vienna 10 August 1788; Barcelona 27 April 1789; Paris, Th. de M. 28 November 1789; Corfu Autumn 1790; Lisbon 1794.

In German as *Der adelsüchtige Bürger*, Mann-heim 13 October 1791.

ÅHLSTRÖM: *Frigga*

31 May. Stockholm

Text by C. G. af Leopold (founded on a comedy by King Gustaf III of Sweden). One act.

Revived Stockholm 18 April 1803 (in an en-larged 2-act version). See T. Norlind's study in *Svensk Tidskrift för Musikforskning*, Vol. VIII (1926).

SALIERI: *Tarare*

8 June. Paris, O.

Text by P. A. Caron de Beaumarchais. Prologue and 5 acts.

Salieri's chief work. Given in Paris 131 times until 1826; revived 3 August 1790 with some additions; 16 July 1799; and 3 February 1819 in a reduced 3-act version arranged by A. F. De-saugiers).

In French also, Liége 24 January 1789; St. Petersburg 1789 (revived 1 July 1803); Copen-hagen 1799 (the prologue only, in concert form); Hanover 23 March 1804; Hague 1805; Bruns-wick 1806; the second version Brussels 24 Feb-ruary 1821.

A parody by F. L. de Bonnefoy de Bonyon, called *Lanlaire ou Le Chaos*, was produced at the C.I., Paris 27 July 1787; another, *Bagare*, by Magne de Saint-Aubin, was given in another theatre four days later, and a third, *Errata*, by F. L. B***, was published in the same year.

Even more successful than the French original was an Italian adaptation by Da Ponte (original-ly in 5 acts) *Axur, Re d'Ormus;* first performed Vienna, B. 8 January 1788, celebrating the wed-ding of the Archduke (later Emperor) Francis II; this version was also given at: Prague and Leipzig 1788; Dresden 21 November 1789 (reduced to 2 acts); Warsaw 2 January 1790; Lisbon 17 De-cember 1790 and Spring 1799; Milan, Sc. 16 May 1792 and Summer 1797; Barcelona 1800; Paris, Th.I. 6 March 1813; Rio de Janeiro 17 Decem-ber 1814.

Into German the opera was first translated by F. X. Girzik (Pressburg 1788 and Budapest 3 November 1789) and by W. Müller (published Carlsruhe 1788; not intended for the stage).

On most stages a 4-act version by H. G. Schmieder was used: Frankfort 14 August 1790; Hanover and Potsdam 23 September 1791 and Berlin 24 October 1791; Cassel 3 September 1791; Stuttgart 8 October 1791; Hamburg 28 December 1791; Amsterdam 28 May 1794; Vienna 8 December 1797, etc.

Given at Brünn in 1810 in a new translation called *Atar*. Frequently revived in Germany; some of the latest productions were at Prague 20 January 1815 and 1827 (re-scored by Trieben-see); Weimar 26 December 1835; Munich 14 January 1842; Frankfort 1844; Leipzig 24 March 1846; Altona 1851; Stuttgart as late as 27 Sep-tember 1863 (re-scored by P. von Lindpaintner and K. Eckert, new translation by F. J. Schütky).

In Polish (translated by W. Boguslawski), Warsaw 24 September 1793; Poznán 13 July 1801; Wilna 8 September 1801.

Anonymous Dutch translation published 1793.

In Russian, Moscow 21 November 1817.

An English translation by C. James was pub-lished as early as 1787; but the opera was only produced at the Ly., London 15 (not 14) August 1825 ("compiled from the German, French, and Italian scores and arranged to the English words by Mr. Hawes"; English version by S. J. Arnold.).

SCHULZ: *Aline, Reine de Golconde*

Summer. Rheinsberg

Sedaine's text (first set to music by Monsigny, see 1766). Three acts.

Performed at the private French opera-house of Prince Heinrich of Prussia where Schulz was conductor. The exact date of the production is unknown; the performance is alluded to in the preface of the vocal score, published in 1790. The opera was very popular afterwards in a Danish adaptation by T. Thaarup (*Aline Dronning i Gol-conda*); first performed at Copenhagen 30 Jan-uary 1789 and given there until 1818.

BERTON: *Les Promesses de Mariage*

4 July. Paris, C.I.

Text by P. J. B. Choudard Desforges (a sequel to his *Théodore et Paulin*, composed by Grétry, see 1784). Two acts.

The first of the younger Berton's numerous operas.

DALAYRAC: *Renaud d'Ast*

19 July. Paris, C.I.

Text by J. B. Radet and P. Y. Barré (founded on Lafontaine's tale, *L'Oraison de Saint-Julien*). Two acts.

In Paris, given until 1828; in French also, Liége 15 November 1789; St. Petersburg 22 July 1795; Cologne 1796–97; Hanover 24 January 1804; Moscow 19 December 1807; Stockholm April 1813.

In German:

HANOVER 16 June 1788 (as *Reinald*, translated by H. G. Schmieder).

MAYENCE November 1788 (as *Reinald*, translated by H. G. Schmieder).

HAMBURG 12 January 1790 (as *Reinald*, translated by H. G. Schmieder).

AMSTERDAM 1790 (as *Reinald*, translated by H. G. Schmieder).

BERLIN 27 July 1791 (as *Reinald*, translated by H. G. Schmieder).

VIENNA, W. 27 August 1791 (as *Georg von Asten*, translated by K. L. Gieseke).

MUNICH 3 November 1799 (as *Georg von Asten*, translated by K. L. Gieseke).

VIENNA, LEOP. 3 October 1799 (as *Der Liebhaber in der Klemme*, translated by J. Perinet) and 1 December 1801 (translated by Sedtler).

In Italian (translated by G. Carpini), Monza Autumn 1789.

In Danish (translated by O. C. Olufsen and F. Schwartz), Copenhagen 16 April 1793.

In Swedish (translated by C. Envallsson), Stockholm 6 June 1796.

In Russian, Moscow 26 December 1799.

In Flemish, Oudenarde 1799.

A Dutch translation by J. van Walré was published in 1803.

HÄFFNER: *Electra*

22 July. Stockholm

Text by A. F. Ristell (from a French libretto by Guillard, set to music by Lemoyne in 1782). Three acts.

The first and most important of Häffner's three Swedish operas; first performed at the Palace of Drottningholm; given at the Royal Theatre, Stockholm 10 December 1787.

ARNOLD: *Inkle and Yarico*

4 August. London, Little Hm.

Text by G. Colman, the younger. Three acts.

One of Arnold's most popular works. Dublin 5 December 1787; Kingston, Jamaica 2 August 1788; New York 6 July 1789; Philadelphia 17 May 1790; Calcutta 10 February 1791; Boston 1794.

Frequently revived on English stages; at New York as late as 22 April 1844. (Date of first performance verified from the play-bill; the libretto has 11 August).

PHILIDOR: *La belle Esclave* ou *Valcour et Zéila*

18 September. Paris, Th. Beaujolais

Text by A. J. Dumaniant. One act.

One of Philidor's last works; also given at Marseilles 1 March 1788; Liége 19 September 1789, etc.

MARTIN Y SOLER: *L'Arbore di Diana*

1 October. Vienna, B.

Text by L. da Ponte. Two acts.

Written to celebrate the wedding of the Archduchess Maria Theresa with Prince Anton of Saxony. Nearly as successful as *Una Cosa rara* by the same authors (see 1786).

In Italian also given at Prague 16 January 1788; Leipzig 25 May 1788; Milan, Sc. 1 October 1788; Trieste 26 December 1788; Passau 31 January 1789; Madrid 4 November 1789; Warsaw 25 February 1790; Barcelona 25 August 1791; Rotterdam 1795; London 18 April 1797.

In German (translated by F. Eberl), Vienna, Leop. 17 July 1788 and Kä. 29 August 1802; (translated by F. X. Girzik), Pressburg 1788; Budapest 26 August 1789; (translated by B. C. d'Arien), Hamburg 10 November 1788; (translated by C. G. Neefe), Bonn 3 January 1789.

Berlin 24 February 1789; Prague 26 April 1791 (revived 25 June 1808); Amsterdam 1792; Weimar 10 October 1793 (translated by C. A. Vulpius); Schleswig 1799; Temesvar 3 December 1801; Basle 23 January 1809. Revived Stuttgart 2 January 1819 (new German version by F. K. Hiemer).

In French (translated by P. U. Dubuisson), Paris, Th. Montansier 6 May 1790; Ghent 1799.

In Russian (translated by I. A. Dmitrevsky), St. Petersburg 15 September 1789; Moscow 1792; revived Moscow 1 December 1808 and St. Petersburg 13 October 1818.

In Polish (translated by J. N. Kaminski), Lvóv 1798; Wilna 30 December 1798; Warsaw 31 August 1799.

Anonymous Dutch translation published (n.d.).

PAISIELLO: *La Modista Raggiratrice*

Autumn. Naples, Fior.

Text by G. B. Lorenzi (founded on an older libretto by G. A. Federico, *Filippo*, 1735, and first set to music by Tritto in 1784). Three acts.

Very successful in Italy; Milan, Sc. 7 June 1790, etc.; given at Rome, T. Valle June 1788 as *La Scuffiara amante o sia Il Maestro di Scuola Napoletano;* at Pavia Carnival 1789 and Lodi Summer 1789 as *La Cuffiara astuta ossia L'onesta Raggiratrice;* at Gorizia Carnival 1790 as *La Modista ossia La Scuffiaja*, with some alterations; at Naples 1792 and Milan, Sc. 26 May 1808 as *La Scuffiara* (with new additions); at Florence, P. Spring 1800 as *La Scuffia Raggiratrice*.

Outside Italy: Vienna 23 April 1788; Warsaw 25 September 1789 (by amateurs); Madrid 26 July 1791; Lisbon Carnival 1792; Leipzig Summer 1793; London 16 April 1796 (revived 16 February 1819; Paisiello's setting according to the libretto, not Tritto's, as Nicoll has it); Paris, Th. I. 11 July 1802.

Revived Naples, T.N. Autumn 1843 and again Fior. 15 April 1883 ("riveduta, corretta e rinnovata, nè si sa da chi", as a reviewer wrote); Rome 1 January 1892.

MOZART: *Il Dissoluto punito o sia Il D. Giovanni*

29 October. Prague

Text by L. da Ponte (*Dramma giocoso*), partly founded on Bertati's *Don Giovanni o sia Il Convitato di Pietra* (see above). Two acts.

Given at Prague 532 times within 100 years (during the same period given at Berlin 491 times, at Vienna 472 times); given at Prague for the first time in German 8 November 1807 (but according to O. Teuber already in 1791 at the "Vaterländische Bühne im Hiberner Kloster"); given at Prague for the first time in Czech 9 April 1825 (see the preface to J. N. Stěpánek's translation) and revived in a new Czech version by V. J. Novotný 27 September 1884; 100th Czech performance 12 June 1894.

After Prague, first produced at Vienna, B. 7 May 1788 (in Italian, with three additional numbers: the airs, *Mi tradì* and *Dalla sua pace* and the duet, *Per queste tue manine*); given at Vienna for the first time in German: W. 5 November 1792 (translated by C. H. Spiess); Kä. 11 December 1798 (translated by K. F. Lippert).

In Italian also performed at Leipzig 15 June 1788 (by the Prague company; called on the play-bill, *Ein grosses Singspiel*).

Productions in German up to 1802

[The following list is, with additions and corrections, founded on the studies by C. Engel (*Die Don Juan-Sage auf der Bühne*, 1887), R. von Freisauff (*Mozart's Don Juan*, 1887), A. Schatz (review of Freisauff's book in *Vierteljahrsschrift für Musikwissenschaft*, 1888) and P. A. Merbach (in *Die Scene*, Vol. VII, parts 7–9, 1917); for details on the earliest German productions see also the various papers by O. Bacher.]

MAYENCE 13 March 1789, and FRANKFORT 3 May 1789 (translated by H. G. Schmieder); these dates have been established by O. Bacher; the wrong date of 23 May 1789 for the first German performance of *Don Giovanni* (Sonneck, Abert, etc.) should be rectified.

MANNHEIM 27 September 1789 (translated by C. G. Neefe).

BONN 13 October 1789 (translated by C. G. Neefe).

HAMBURG 27 October 1789 (translated by F. L. Schröder).

GRAZ 30 November 1789 (this performance is doubtful; announced, but not reviewed. First recorded performance at Graz 28 May 1795).

BRÜNN December 1789.

AUGSBURG 1790.

SOEST 26 June 1790.

SCHWERIN 5 July 1790.

BERLIN 20 December 1790 (Schröder's translation; 500th performance 25 November 1887); in Italian: Kgst. 24 April 1843.

HANOVER 4 March 1791.

CASSEL 16 April 1791 (given there in French in April 1811).

PRAGUE 1791 (at the "Vaterländische Bühne im Hiberner Kloster", according to O. Teuber).

PYRMONT 8 July 1791.

MUNICH 7 August 1791.

COLOGNE 7 October 1791.

BRESLAU 20 January 1792 (Schmieder's translation).

WEIMAR 30 January 1792 (in Italian: 4 September 1813).

GLOGAU 26 July 1792.

BREMEN 24 October 1792.

VIENNA, W. 5 November 1792 (translated by C. H. Spiess).

BRUNSWICK 10 March 1793.

MÜNSTER March 1793.

PASSAU May 1793 (but see A. E. Cherbuliez, in *Bericht über die musikwissensehaftliche Tagung . . . in Salzburg*, 1931, p.150 ff. where a Passau 1789 score is mentioned).

DÜSSELDORF, AACHEN, KÖNIGSBERG 1793.

LÜBECK 17 October 1793.

OELS 11 January 1794.

AMSTERDAM 9 June 1794 (according to Rogge and Scheurleer; Schatz has 8 March 1794, Merbach 11 November 1794).

GOTHA AND OEDENBURG 1794.

RUDOLSTADT 10 September 1794.

DANZIG 11 September 1794.

ERFURT 22 September 1794.

SCHLESWIG 1 December 1794.

KIEL 12 January 1795.

MAGDEBURG January 1795.

STETTIN 30 January 1795.

NUREMBERG 20 April 1795.

ERLANGEN May 1795.

FRANKFORT (ODER) 1795.

LAUCHSTEDT 3 August 1795.

DRESDEN 16 September 1795 (new German version by C. A. Zschiedrisch; in Italian: 28 May 1814).

LEIPZIG 3 January 1796 (in Italian earlier, see above).

STUTTGART 28 March 1796.

POTSDAM 1796.

FREIBURG 1796.

SALZBURG 18 January 1797.

DESSAU 27 January 1797.

BAUTZEN 6 April 1797.

GÖRLITZ 1797.

REVAL 1797 (in Estonian much later, see below).

ST. PETERSBURG 1797 (according to *Theaterjournal* 1797, I, p.196).

BUDAPEST 28 December 1797 (according to *Allgemeine Deutsche Theaterzeitung*, Pressburg; according to J. Kádár only 1801. But according to *Gothaer Theaterkalender* 1790, p.131, in preparation there already in 1790, translated probably by F. X. Girzik).

KARLSBAD 23 June 1798.

NACHOD 1 July 1798.

LINZ 2 November 1798.

VIENNA, KÄ. 11 December 1798 (translated by K. F. Lippert).

PRESSBURG 26 December 1798.

SAGAN 1 January 1799.

ALTENBURG 2 May 1799.

NAUMBURG 23 June 1799.

AURICH AND MINDEN 1799.

RIGA 1799 (in Lettish much later, see below).

BALLENSTEDT January 1799.

GREIFSWALD 13 February 1800.

INNSBRUCK 22 April 1800.

ALTONA 29 November 1800.

COBURG 18 March 1801.

ELBING 9 June 1802.

In 1801 F. Rochlitz's translation (founded on Neefe and Schröder) was published which served as a standard version for *c.* 50 years; more recent German versions are by G. H. F. T. Sever (1854); W. Viol (1858); L. Bischoff (1860); A. von Wolzogen (1860 and 1869); C. H. Bitter (1866); B. Gugler (1869); T. Epstein (1870); F. Grandaur (1871); K. F. Niese (1872); M. Kalbeck (1886); H. Levi (1896); E. Heinemann (1904); K. Scheidemantel (1913); A. Bodanzky (1914), etc.

"Don Giovanni" in other countries
Poland

WARSAW 14 October 1789 (in Italian) and 1817 (in Polish, translated by K. Brodziński).

POZNÁN 24 October 1803 (in German).

LEMBERG 27 February 1879 (in Polish; but certainly given earlier there in German).

Russia

ST. PETERSBURG 1797 (in German, see above; no performance earlier than 1800 is recorded by Findeizen. In *Journal des Luxus und der Moden* and in Iffland's *Almanach fürs Theater* a performance in Spring 1809 is mentioned. The earliest extant play-bill dates from 14 May 1828).

ST. PETERSBURG 3 May 1828 (in Russian, translated by R. M. Zotov; date according to Stasov and Cheshikhin; Freisauff and Schatz give 2 September 1828).

MOSCOW 7 June 1825 (in Italian).

ST. PETERSBURG Carnival 1831 (in Italian).

KIEV 1876 (in Russian, translated by A. Grigoryev).

Holland

AMSTERDAM 9 June 1794 (in German, see above; copy of the libretto Coll. Portheim, Vienna).

AMSTERDAM 18 October 1803 (in French; the Kalkbrenner version, see below, under Paris).

AMSTERDAM 26 March 1804 (in Dutch, translated by H. Ogelwight).

AMSTERDAM 31 January 1809 (in Italian; the French translation in the libretto [copy Coll. Hirsch, British Museum] by F. C. Müller).

HAGUE 11 May 1804 (in Dutch) and 7 December 1815 (in French); the Castil-Blaze version 1835; 20 May 1829 (in German).

ROTTERDAM 27 May 1810 (in German); 11 February 1836 (in French); 23 March 1843 (in Italian).

See on the productions of *Don Giovanni* in Holland, H. C. Rogge in *Tijdschrift der Vereeniging voor Noord-Nederlands Musiekgeschiedenis*, Vol.II (1887), p.237.

A new Dutch translation by C. van der Linden was published in 1903.

Hungary

BUDAPEST 28 December 1797 (? in German, see above).

KRONSTADT 8 October 1826 (in Hungarian, translated by E. Pály; his version published Kassán 1829).

CLAUSENBURG 14 December 1826 (in Hungarian, translated by E. Pály.

BUDAPEST 24 November 1827 (in Hungarian, translated by E. Pály.

BUDAPEST 29 May 1839 (new Hungarian version by J. Szerdahelyi; since 1917 a modern translation by Z. Harsányi has been used).

France

PARIS, O. 17 September 1805 (30. Fructidor An XIII, in French, adapted by J. Thuring and D. Baillot, music arranged by C. Kalkbrenner; this mutilated version was given 28 times until 27 January 1807. The Empress Josephine was present at the first night; Napoléon heard the opera about the same time at Ludwigsburg on 4 October 1805).

PARIS, TH. I. 2 September 1811 (in Italian; under Spontini's direction).

PARIS, ODÉON 24 December 1827 (in French, as *Le Festin de Pierre*, adapted by F. H. J. Castil-Blaze, with dialogue from Molière's play; 4 acts).

PARIS, TH. I. 26 May 1831 (in German, by a company from Aachen).

PARIS, O. 10 March 1834 (in French; new 5-act version by H. Blaze de Bury and E. Deschamps. Revived 21 March 1841, 2 April 1866, etc.; 100th performance 4 November 1872. Since 1866 given with a ballet, music from Mozart, arranged by Auber).

PARIS, TH. L. 8 May 1866 (new translation by H. Trianon, music adapted by J. F. E. Gautier).

PARIS, O.C. 17 November 1896 (new translation by L.V. Durdilly).

PARIS, O.C. 9 December 1912 (new translation by P. Ferrier).

PARIS, CH.E. 28 May 1924 (in German, by the Vienna O. company).

PARIS, O. 14 March 1934 (new translation by A. Boschot).

LILLE 10 October 1805 (in French; the Kalkbrenner version).

NANTES 14 November 1814 (in French).

LYONS 10 December 1822 (in French; first production of the Paris 1827 version) and 9 October 1841 (in German).

ROUEN 4 June 1841 (in German); 24 January 1866 (in Italian); and 19 January 1898 (in French).

MARSEILLES 15 September 1842 (in German) and 16 May 1867 (in French).

BORDEAUX 26 April 1869 (in French).

MONTE CARLO 14 February 1907 (in Italian).

Belgium

GHENT 5 October 1806 (in French; the Kalkbrenner version).

BRUSSELS 1 April 1807 (in French; the Kalkbrenner version).

ANTWERP 3 December 1807 (in French; the Kalkbrenner version).

LIÉGE 23 May 1839 (in German).

BRUSSELS 9 August 1844 (in German).

BRUSSELS 20 March 1861 (in Italian).

BRUSSELS 17 May 1867 (in French, the Paris 1834 version).

ANTWERP 1 October 1898 (in Flemish, translated by E. Keurvels).

Denmark, Sweden, Norway

COPENHAGEN 5 May 1807 (in Danish, translated by L. Kruse).

COPENHAGEN 23 February 1845 (new Danish version by N. C. L. Abrahams).

COPENHAGEN 1 June 1858 (in German).

STOCKHOLM 6 December 1813 (in Swedish, translated by C. G. Nordforss).

STOCKHOLM 27 January 1856 (new Swedish version byW. Bauck); another Swedish version by S. C. Bring published 1911.

CHRISTIANIA 6 January 1836 (in Norwegian; revived 7 May 1902 at the Nationalteatret).

Italy

According to Freisauff, Schatz, Abert, and others, Mozart's opera was produced at Florence, P. as early as 9 April 1792. According to U. Morini the opera produced then was Albertini's *Don Giovanni* (see 1783), while G. Pavan does not mention any performance at all. No libretto seems to be extant. But there is a strong argument against so early a *Don Giovanni* production in Italy in Franz Niemtschek's biography of Mozart (1798), p.68: "In Florenz habe man den 1ten Akt des Don Juan nach neun misslungenen Proben, für unausführbar erklärt!! Diese Nachrichten hörte der Verfasser aus dem Munde eines Teutschen berühmten Opernkomponisten d. Hrn. W**, der sich in Italien lange aufhielt, und den Zustand der Musik daselbst genau kennt, weil er für einige grosse Bühnen Opern schrieb". (The opera composer alluded to probably is Peter von Winter.)

Apart from the doubtful Florence production the first performances of *Don Giovanni* in Italy were at:

BERGAMO Carnival 1811.

ROME, VALLE 11 June 1811.

NAPLES, FONDO 14 October 1812 and Autumn 1816; S. C. 6 July 1834.

MILAN, SC. 17 October 1814; T. Rè. 1 January 1820.

TURIN, T. D'ANGENNES Autumn 1815; T. Carignano Autumn 1828; T. R. Carnival 1859.

FLORENCE, T. DE' RISOLUTI Summer 1817; P. April 1818.

BOLOGNA, T. BADINI December 1817.

PARMA, T. DUCALE 26 December 1821.

GENOA, T. DEL FALCONE May 1824; C. F. Spring 1867.

BOLZANO (BOZEN) 19 April 1827 (in German).

VENICE, S. BEN. 8 April 1833.

MALTA September 1833.

TRIESTE 26 December 1842, etc.

CAGLIARI, SARDINIA 13 January 1883.

Switzerland
(productions in German):

BERNE 15 April 1812.

ST. GALLEN 1812.

ZURICH 1822 (in concert form).

WINTERTHUR 28 November 1827 (in concert form).

BASLE 4 February 1835.

GENEVA 1856; in French 7 April 1874.

On 8 November 1850 Richard Wagner conducted a *Don Giovanni* performance at Zurich "mit neuer Bearbeitung des Dialogs und mit Recitativs" by himself.

Great Britain, Ireland, etc.

London.—On amateur performances of *Don Giovanni* and other Mozart operas in London between 1806 and 1811 see the anonymous articles, *Autobiography of an Amateur Singer* in *The Harmonicon*, 1831, pp.106 and 135; see also 1830, p.113, note. Cf. F. O. Souper in *The Monthly Musical Record*, January 1935.

On the professional stage:

LONDON, HM. 12 April 1817 (not 20 May 1817; in Italian; given 23 times during the first season).

LONDON, C.G. 30 May 1817 (in English, as *The Libertine*, translated by I. Pocock, music adapted by Bishop).

LONDON, ADELPHI 5 July 1830 (in English, adapted by W. Hawes).

LONDON, HM. 11 July 1832 (in German).

LONDON, D.L. 5 February 1833 (in English, translated by S. Beazley).

LONDON, PRINCESS'S 1 October 1849 (in English; author of this new version not mentioned; probably J.W. Mould, who edited the work as Vol.VI of his *The Standard Lyric Drama* in 1850).

LONDON, OLD VIC. 24 November 1921 (translated by E. J. Dent).

The 300th performance at C.G. was on 15 July 1914.

DUBLIN 7 January 1828 (in Italian).

EDINBURGH 21 July 1830 (in English, translated and adapted by T. H. Reynoldson).

EDINBURGH 27 November 1832 (in Italian).

CALCUTTA 4 February 1833 (in English, scenes only; see Hemendranath Das Gupta, *The Indian Stage* (1935), pp.264–65).

MELBOURNE 1861 (in English).

SYDNEY September 1862 (in English).

CAIRO 1870 (in Italian).

U.S.A.:

NEW YORK, PARK TH. 23 May 1826 (in Italian).

PHILADELPHIA 25 December 1827 (in Italian).

PHILADELPHIA 6 November 1837 (in English, advertised as "First time in America, in a faithful translation").

SAN FRANCISCO 1855 (in Italian).

NEW YORK, STADT TH. 2 April 1856 (in German).

NEW YORK, CHATHAM TH. 29 May 1862 (in English, Bishop's version).

CHICAGO 1859 (in Italian).

Latin America, Spain, and Portugal
(all productions in Italian):

BUENOS AIRES 8 February 1827 (Spanish translation in the printed libretto by J. M. S.).

MADRID, T. DE LA CRUZ 15 December 1834 (revived T. R. 20 April 1864).

LISBON 6 January 1839 (revived 1 December 1868).

BARCELONA 18 December 1849 (Catalan translation by J. Pena published 1931).

MEXICO 23 June 1852 (revived 1 November 1895).

LIMA, PERU Carnival 1854 (see M. Hauser, *Reisebriefe*, p.93).

SANTIAGO, CHILE 1870 (see R. Briseño, *Estadística Bibliográfica de la Literatura Chilena*, Vol.II, p.97).

RIO DE JANEIRO Summer 1880.

Other Countries

REVAL (TALLINN) 1797 (in German) and 1929 (in Estonian, translated by G. Tuksam).

RIGA 1799 (in German) and 12 February 1921 (in Lettish, translated by L. Laicens).

LAIBACH (LJUBLJANA) 15 November 1815 (in German, C. H. Spiess's translation) and 24 January 1925 (in Slovenian).

AGRAM (ZAGREB) 1830 (in German) and 19 January 1875 (in Croatian, translated by E. J. Tomić); 1 June 1920 (new translation by M. Nehajev).

HELSINKI 6 November 1840 (in German) and 27 March 1878 (in Finnish, translated by A. Törneroos).

SOFIA 7 April 1930 (in Bulgarian, translated by B. Danovsky).

KAUNAS 5 December 1933 (in Lithuanian, translated by S. Santvaras).

BUCHAREST c. January 1834 (in German) and Spring 1936 (in Rumanian).

1788

REICHARDT *Andromeda*

2 *January*. Berlin, O.

Text by A. de' Filistri da Caramondani. One act. Reichardt's first Italian opera.

CHERUBINI: *Ifigenia in Aulide*

February. Turin, T.R.

Text by F. Moretti (firs set to music by Zingarelli in 1787). Three acts.

The last opera Cherubini wrote in Italy; given in the same year 1788 at Parma, Milan and Florence; in Italian also, London 24 January 1789.

TRITTO: *Le Avventure amorose*

Spring. Rome, Valle

Text by "Timido P.A." Two acts.

The most successful of Tritto's numerous operas. Given at Genoa Spring 1789 as *Le Avventure galanti;* at Bologna 14 January 1792 as *Le Vicende amorose;* at Turin 1792, Padua 13 June 1792 and Trieste 13 August 1793 as *I Raggiri d'Amore;* outside Italy: Paris 26 January 1789 (opening of the Th. de Monsieur, later Feydeau); Barcelona 4

July 1791 and Madrid 4 November 1791 (as *Le Avventure galanti*); Dresden 6 November 1793 (as *I Disprezzatori delle Donne*); Lisbon Carnival 1797 (as *Le Vicende amorose*).

Date of first performance and original title according to Formenti's *Indice dei Spettacoli*, 1788–89, quoted in C. L. Curiel's *Il Teatro S. Pietro di Trieste* (1937). Schatz-Sonneck give *Le Vicende amorose* as the original title and April 1787, as the date of the first performance.

DANZI: *Die Mitternachtsstunde*

April. Munich

Text by M. G. Lambrecht (founded on Dumaniant's comedy, *La Guerre ouverte*). Three acts.

The most successful of Danzi's numerous operas and the only one which was published.

Revived Munich February 1798; Frankfort 12 February 1799; Hamburg c. February 1799; Berlin 1 October 1799; Mannheim 29 June 1800; Nuremberg 1801; in German also Budapest 10 August 1803; St. Petersburg 1808; last given Munich 29 June 1815.

P. GUGLIELMI: *La Pastorella nobile*

19 April. Naples, T.N.

Text by S. Zini. Two acts.

One of Guglielmi's most successful works. Given at Milan, Sc. September 1789 and all over Italy; the latest revival was at Venice, S. Ben. 28 June 1809.

In Italian also produced at Barcelona 25 August 1789 and Madrid 18 June 1791; Paris, Th. de M. 12 December 1789 (additions by Martin y Soler and Cherubini; revived 4 April 1807 as *L'Erede di Belprato;* given until 1822); Nice Carnival 1790; Vienna 24 May 1790 (additions by Weigl); Corfu Autumn 1790; Dresden 12 February 1791; Lisbon 13 May 1791; London, Pantheon 17 December 1791 (revived Hm. 10 February 1801); Prague 1792; Palma, Mallorca Autumn 1793; St. Petersburg 1797.

In German (as *Die Schöne auf dem Lande*, translated by H. G. Schmieder), Frankfort 25 October

1791; Cologne 27 October 1793; (as *Die adeliche Schäferin*, translated by K. L. Gieseke), Brünn 14 November 1791; Breslau 1 June 1792, Graz 30 October 1792, etc.; (as *Der Lohn weiblicher Sittsamkeit*, translated by G. F. W. Grossmann), Hanover 10 February 1795 and (as *Das adlige Landmädchen*), 15 April 1796; and (in yet another German version by K. F. Lippert) Vienna 17 May 1798.

(SACCHINI): *Arvire et Evelina*

29 April. Paris, O.

Text by N. F. Guillard (founded on W. Mason's *Caractacus*, produced London, C.G. 6 December 1776, with incidental music by Arne). Three acts.

Sacchini's last opera, performed two years after his death, completed by J. B. Rey. Successful in Paris; given at the O. 87 times until 1811 and revived there 13 September 1820 (reduced to 2 acts by N. S. G. Saulnier, music adapted by Berton).

In Italian (as *Evelina*, translated by L. da Ponte), London 10 January 1797.

In Danish (translation by R. Frankenau), Copenhagen 30 January 1799; the first act had been previously heard there in concert form in 1791 (in French).

DALAYRAC: *Sargines, ou L'Elève de l'Amour*

14 May. Paris, C.I.

Text by J. M. Boutet de Monvel (founded on a story in F. T. M. Baculard d'Arnaud's *Epreuves du Sentiment*). Four acts.

In French also, Cassel 26 August 1790; Liége February 1793; Brussels 16 July 1794; St. Petersburg 1804; Trier 13 December 1804; Berne 12 July 1809; Moscow 26 November 1810.

In German (translated by H. G. Schmieder), Frankfort 5 September 1790; Mannheim 10 April 1791, etc. At Hamburg March 1800 as *Otto von Waldburg*.

In Swedish (translated by C. Envallsson), Stockholm 29 April 1795.

PAISIELLO: *L'Amor contrastato*

Summer. Naples, Fior

Text by G. Palomba. Two acts.

Better known by its later titles, *La Molinara*, or *La Molinarella*. Given at Venice Carnival 1789 in an enlarged 3-act version; Milan, Sc. March 1791, etc.

In Italian also produced at Madrid 16 May 1789 (revived 20 June 1792 and 23 May 1809); Barcelona 30 May 1790; Paris, Th. de M. 31 October 1789 (with nine additional numbers by Cherubini; revived Th. I. 2 September 1801 and 1 July 1809); Eszterháza Summer 1790; Dresden 1790; Vienna 13 November 1790 (frequently revived until 1833); Trieste 28 December 1790; London, Pantheon 21 May 1791 (revived Hm. 6 December 1794, 22 March 1803, 8 March 1817); Prague 1791; Warsaw 28 April 1792; Innsbruck 16 July 1792; Lisbon Autumn 1793; St. Petersburg 1795 and 9 December 1798 (revived 1831); Amsterdam 1806.

In German (as *Die Launen der Liebe*), Brünn 30 November 1791; very popular in a German version by C. F. Bretzner (as *Die schöne Müllerin*), Frankfort 26 December 1792; Hanover 8 April 1793; Hamburg 26 April 1793; Berlin 16 October 1793, etc.; in German also, Rotterdam Spring 1796; Berne Spring 1804; Amsterdam 1805; St. Petersburg 1809; Copenhagen 10 June 1825; Budapest 4 July 1825. Last revived Dresden 7 December 1861; Berlin, Fr.W. 27 April 1862.

German vocal score published 1890.

In Russian (translated by N. S. Krasnopolsky), St. Petersburg 8 June 1812; (translated by A. F. Merzlyakov), Moscow 7 November 1816.

Beethoven used two arias from this opera for variations: *Quant' è più bello* and the better known *Nel cor più non mi sento* (*Mich fliehen alle Freuden*), both 1796.

SALIERI: *Il Talismano*

10 September. Vienna, B.

Text by L. da Ponte. Three acts.

Altered from an earlier libretto by Goldoni, which had been written for the inauguration of the new Teatro della Canobbiana, Milan; produced with music by Salieri (first act) and Rust (second and third acts) in September 1779 as the first new opera there; also given at the Scala in July 1785 and on some other Italian stages. For Vienna, Da Ponte modernized the libretto, and Salieri wrote entirely new music. This second setting apparently was never heard in Italy, but was the more successful in Central Europe.

In Italian also given at Prague 1788; Dresden and Brunswick 1789; Warsaw 12 January 1790.

In a German version by F. Eberl: Vienna, Leop. 30 April 1789; Budapest 5 July 1789; Warsaw 8 December 1793.

In a German version by H. G. Schmieder: Mayence 20 February 1790; Carlsruhe 22 November 1790; Munich 14 June 1793; Hamburg 1794; Berne Spring 1804.

In a German version by A. F. von Knigge: Hanover 4 June 1790; Berlin 20 May 1796; Breslau 4 January 1799; Schleswig 1805.

CHERUBINI: *Démophoon*

5 December. Paris, O.

Text by J. F. Marmontel (based on Metastasio's *Demofoonte*). Three acts.

Cherubini's first French opera; given for eight nights only. Never revived anywhere, apart from a concert at Coblenz 29 November 1926, when extracts from the opera were performed.

P. RITTER: *Der Eremit auf Formentara*

14 December. Mannheim

Text by A. von Kotzebue. Two acts.

Ritter's most successful opera. Given on many German stages and, in German, also at Brünn 12 October 1791; Budapest 9 December 1791; Schleswig 1792. Revived Agram 20 March 1804 (Ritter's setting?); Hanover 4 May 1804.

Dutch translation by V... published Rotterdam 1791.

1789

DALAYRAC: *Les deux petits Savoyards*

14 January. Paris, C.I.

Text by B. J. Marsollier. One act.

One of Dalayrac's greatest successes. Given in Paris until 1836 and revived at St. Cloud 22 July 1847 (by pupils of the Paris Conservatoire).

In French also given at Liége 17 September 1789; Geneva 17 December 1789; Aachen 24 August 1794; St. Petersburg 4 February 1795; Hamburg 4 March 1795; Cologne 1796–97; Philadelphia 16 January 1797; Moscow 5 February 1810; London, St. J.'s 19 April 1844.

Even more popular in Germany (first translation by H. G. Schmieder), Mayence 12 May 1790; Mannheim 25 July 1790; Hanover 7 September 1790; Hamburg 7 October 1791; Berlin 9 November 1791; Brünn 21 June 1792; Breslau 14 September 1792; Bremen 31 October 1792; Vienna, Leop. 13 December 1792 (translated by J. Perinet) and W. the very next night, 14 December 1792, in Schmieder's translation; (revised by A. J. Fischer, Kä. 14 August 1804); Graz 11 July 1793; Budapest 30 March 1794; Poznán 23 November 1803; Berne Spring 1804; Prague 26 June 1814; Moscow 20 November 1819.

Given in Germany throughout the 19th century; last revived Carlsruhe 2 October 1894 and 16 May 1902.

In Dutch (translated by H. Asschenbergh and H. G. Roullard), Amsterdam 1790; revived Hague 1822; in Flemish, Oudenarde Winter 1797–8.

In Italian (translated by G. Carpani), Monza Autumn 1791; S. Pier d'Arena (near Genoa) Autumn 1793; Lisbon 11 January 1796. Another Italian version, by G. Brunati, was published in 1798.

In Danish (translated by A. G. Thoroup), Copenhagen 18 September 1792.

In Swedish (translated by C. Envallsson), Stockholm 6 June 1794; Malmö 13 May 1807; Lund 24 August 1807.

In Russian, Moscow 1801.

In Polish (translated by K. Hebdowski), Warsaw 1809.

In English (translated by M. Lonsdale), London, S's Wells 29 June 1789 and 8 July 1795. An English adaptation by F. Reynolds, *The Duke of Savoy; or, Wife and Mistress*, additional music by Bishop, was given in London, C.G. 29 September 1817; the original, in English, London, Queen's 13 February 1835; in French, St. J.'s 19 April 1844.

GIORDANI: *La Disfatta di Dario*

7 February. Milan, Sc.

Text: an altered version of Morbilli's libretto (first set to music by Cafaro, see 1756). Three acts.

The most successful opera of Giordani and one of the very few that have been preserved. Revived Lisbon 17 December 1806.

MARTIN Y SOLER: *Gore Bogatir Kosometovich*

Горе Богатыр Косометович

(Mock-Hero Kosometovitch)

9 February. St. Petersburg

Text by the Empress Catharine II. Five acts.

First performed at the Ermitage; publicly, St Petersburg 28 April 1789.

See on the political background of this satirical opera (directed against Gustavus III of Sweden), A. Brückner in *Baltische Monatsschrift*, Vol.XVI (1867), p.307; and R. A. Mooser in *R.M.I.*, Vol. XL (1936).

J. SCHUSTER: *Rübenzahl o sia Il vero Amore*

14 February. Dresden

Text by C. Mazzolà. Two acts.

The first opera on this favourite German subject, composed by a German composer to Italian words. Given at Prague 1789 as *Il Trionfo dell' Amore sulla Magia* and at Warsaw 10 February 1790 as *Il Degorgone ossia Il Trionfo dell' Amore sulla Magia*.

In German (translated by J. Perinet), Vienna, Leop. 13 October 1794; Bautzen 21 February 1799; Görlitz 1800; Agram 6 November 1804.

GRÉTRY: *Raoul Barbe Bleue*

2 March. Paris, C.I.

Text by J. M. Sedaine. Three acts.

This *Comédie en prose, mêlée d'ariettes* seems to be the first of the very many *Blue-Beard* operas, a favourite theme from the 18th century up to Dukas (1907), Bartók (1918), and Reznicek (1920).

In French also, Brussels and Amsterdam 1791; Hamburg 24 January 1797; St. Petersburg 22 October 1798; Moscow 24 October 1808.

In German (as *Der Blaubart*, translator not mentioned), Oels 5 January 1799; (translated by H. G. Schmieder); Altona 9 September 1800; Berlin 23 March 1801 (revived 22 March 1844 and 27 July 1865); Vienna, W. 14 August 1804 (Schmieder's translation revised by J. Sonnleithner; music revised by A. J. Fischer; revived Kä. 12 April 1821 and 2 October 1833); Prague 19 June 1814 (revived 10 May 1840); Helsinki 6 December 1833; Bucharest 1834; Basle 1 December 1841. Last revived Carlsruhe 10 April 1890 (revised by F. Mottl).

In Polish (translated by J. Baudouin), Warsaw 2 February 1805.

Dutch translation by N. G. Brinkman published 1807.

In Russian (translated by A. V. Luknitsky), St. Petersburg 13 February 1815; Moscow 2 January 1817.

In Hungarian (translated by F. S. Deáky), Clausenburg 23 February 1822.

In Czech (translated by S. K. Machaček), Prague 18 December 1831.

KUNZEN: *Holger Danske*

31 March. Copenhagen

Text by J. E. Baggesen (founded on Wieland's *Oberon*). Three acts.

Regarded as the outstanding Danish national opera of the 18th century, but given 6 times only.

A parody by Heiberg, *Holger Tydske*, was published in 1789.

Revived in concert-form by the Cäciliaföreningen, Copenhagen 19 February 1912.

A German translation by C. F. Cramer was published in 1789.

CORDEIRO DA SILVA: *Bauce e Palemone*

25 April. Lisbon, Th. d'Ajuda

(Italian) text by G. Martinelli. One act.

The best work of the Portuguese composer.

CHAMPEIN: *Le nouveau Don-Quichotte*

25 May. Paris, Th. de M.

Text by Boissel (from Cervantes). Two acts.

Along with *La Mélomanie* (see 1781), Champein's most successful work; produced under the pseudonym of Zaccharelli.

In French also, Brussels 29 June 1792 (revived 13 January 1816 as *Manquinados*); Hamburg 3 August 1803; St. Petersburg January 1806; Moscow 6 May 1809.

In Swedish (translated by J. D. Valerius), Stockholm 16 November 1804.

In Russian (translated by A. V. Luknitsky), St. Petersburg 2 December 1811.

LEMOYNE: *Les Prétendus*

2 June. Paris, O.

Text by M. A. J. Rochon de Chabannes (*comédie-lyrique*). One act.

In Paris given 294 times until 1827, and revived at St. Cloud 22 July 1847 (by pupils of the Paris Conservatoire).

In French also, Amsterdam 13 April 1791; Brussels 29 August 1791; Hamburg 1798–99; St. Petersburg 29 July 1799; Berne 13 September 1802; Hanover 7 January 1804; Moscow 4 February 1809.

In German (as *Drei Freier auf einmal*, translated by H. G. Schmieder), Frankfort 25 September 1791; Mannheim 14 March 1793, etc.; Berlin 29 October 1804.

In Danish (translated by R. Frankenau), Copenhagen 4 November 1803.

In Swedish (translated by C. G. Nordforss), Stockholm 26 April 1810.

PAISIELLO: *Nina* o sia *La Pazza per Amore*

25 June. Caserta, Royal Palace

Text by G. Carpani (translated from Marsollier's French libretto, see 1786), with spoken dialogue, and with additions by G. B. Lorenzi. One act.

First produced at Caserta in honour of a visit of Queen Maria Carolina of Sicily.

Publicly produced at Naples, Fior. 1790 (enlarged to 2 acts and with new additions by Lorenzi and Paisiello) and all over Italy. Given with recitatives first at Parma Carnival 1793 and Naples, Fior. 1795; given on Italian stages until about 1845. In Italian also:

BARCELONA 4 November 1789.

VIENNA 13 April 1790 (with additional music by Weigl, text revised by L. da Ponte; frequently revived until 24 April 1830).

PARIS, TH. FEYDEAU 4 September 1791 (with recitatives and one air by Cherubini; revived Th.I. 30 August 1802 and 10 February 1824).

DRESDEN 7 January 1792.

WARSAW 12 May 1792.

TRIESTE [4 September] 1792.

LISBON Spring 1794.

PRAGUE 1794 (said to have been sung there in Czech, by Italian singers, in 1796).

ST. PETERSBURG 1794 or 1795.

LONDON 27 April 1797 (revived 26 May 1825 for Pasta's benefit).

AMSTERDAM Carnival 1808.

In German, Mannheim 29 October 1793; Munich December 1796.

In Spanish (translated by L. F. Comella), Madrid 9 December 1795 (probably with Paisiello's music).

In Russian, St. Petersburg 29 August 1796 and Moscow 12 September 1797.

In Polish (translated by W. Pekalski), Warsaw 1809.

Revived Turin, T. Carignano 9 May 1910, (by the Associazione dei Musicologi Italiani); Naples, T. Sannazaro 28 May 1921; Milan, T. Manzoni 31 March 1940 (text revised by R. Simoni, music arranged by C. Gatti).

DITTERSDORF: *Hironimus Knicker*

7 July. Vienna, Leop.

The text, by different authors attributed to Eberl, Schikaneder, Vulpius, or Stephanie, seems to have been written by the composer himself. Two acts.

From a passage in Dittersdorf's autobiography may be concluded that he originally composed this opera as well as *Das rothe Kaeppchen* (see 1790) and others for the private theatre of the Prince-Bishop of Breslau, Count Schaffgottsch, at Johannisberg in Silesia, where it was perhaps performed in or about 1787; perhaps also at Brünn December 1788.

No libretto earlier than 1792 seems to be known; Sonneck (p. 593) claims the Hamburg 1792 libretto to be approximately the original one; but Schütze's remark in his *Hamburgische Theatergeschichte* (1794, p.94): ". . . eine alte, von einem allzeitfertigen Skribenten neubearbeitete Oper . . .", seems to indicate that, although with new modifications, Vulpius's Weimar version (1791) was used at Hamburg as well.

Apart from *Doctor und Apotheker*, Dittersdorf's most popular opera; given on every German stage between 1790 and 1810 and frequently revived afterwards.

A miser being the chief character, the title had to be changed sometimes: out of consideration for the Archbishop Hieronymus Colloredo (Mozart's Archbishop!) it became at Salzburg *Chrisostomus Knicker;* and was, according to the *Journal des Luxus und der Moden*, later on (November 1792) given there as *Hokus Pokus oder Die Lebensessenz* (text and music altered by A. F. von Hofmann), which is peculiar because Dittersdorf actually wrote an opera of the title *Hokus Pokus* in 1791. At Brunswick, in 1811, *Hieronymus Knicker* became *Lucius Knicker* for Jerome Bonaparte's sake.

The earliest performances were at Breslau 26

February 1790; Stuttgart 29 April 1791; Cologne 18 September 1791; Brünn 13 October 1791; Weimar 24 November 1791 (text altered by C. A. Vulpius); Berlin 15 July 1792 (revived Kgst. 3 November 1824); Hamburg 19 November 1792; Hanover 6 February 1793; Munich 12 April 1793, etc.

In German also given at Budapest 19 October 1790; Amsterdam 1792; Warsaw 21 June 1796; Temesvar 28 January 1802; Berne July 1804; Poznán 16 February 1805; Moscow 12 February 1820; Helsinki 23 August 1832.

Some of the latest performances were at Berlin, Fr. W. 29 June 1851; Leipzig 3 April 1852; Basle 18 January 1858; Dresden 16 July 1863.

Dutch translation by H. Molkenboer published 1796.

REICHARDT: *Claudine von Villa Bella*

29 July. Berlin

Goethe's text (first set to music by Beecke, see 1780). Three acts.

First performed at the Schlosstheater, Charlottenburg; publicly Berlin, O. 3 August 1789. Revived Königsberg May 1932 (remodelled by J. Müller-Blattau).

(J. C. VOGEL): *Démophon*

22 September. Paris, O.

Text by P. Desriaux (founded on Metastasio's *Demofoonte;* another French adaptation had been set by Cherubini 10 months earlier, see 1788). Three acts.

Vogel's second and last opera, produced 15 months after his death.

In French also, Copenhagen 1792 (the first act only, in concert form); Brunswick 1805.

In German (translated by I. F. Castelli), Vienna W. 11 May 1808 (additions by J. von Seyfried).

KRAUS: *Soliman den II., eller De tre Sultaninnorna*

22 September. Stockholm

Text by J. G. Oxenstjerna (translated from a French libretto by C. S. Favart, 1761). Three acts.

The most successful opera of Kraus, who, in 1788, had succeeded Uttini as court conductor at Stockholm. Given there 31 times until 1817; Gothenburg 20 May 1808; Lund 22 July 1808.

REICHARDT: *Brenno*

16 October. Berlin, O.

Text by A. de' Filistri da Caramondani. Three acts.

The best of Reichardt's Italian operas. Full score published 1789.

Revived, in an abridged concert version, Berlin 24 January 1798 (in German; first time that music to German words was sung at the Berlin O.) and Danzig 21 April 1800. Revived in Italian Berlin 11 January 1802. The overture was a favourite in Berlin concerts for many years; played as late as as 16 January 1847.

PANECK: *Die christliche Judenbraut*

18 October. Budapest

Text by F. X. Girzik. Two acts.

Very successful on German stages; Prague Summer 1790; Vienna, Th.a.d. Landstrasse 11 October 1790 (and W. 27 December 1796); Breslau 25 November 1791; Brünn 9 September 1792; Weimar 1 November 1792; Lübeck 23 January 1793; Graz 27 April 1793; Salzburg 1793; Munich 28 January 1794; Oels 29 August 1795 (music arranged by Dittersdorf); Nuremberg *c.*1795; Cologne 1795–96; Hanover 30 June 1796; Bremen *c.*November 1796; Carlsruhe 9 February 1798; Temesvar 13 December 1801. Given at Königsberg as late as 1816.

A sequel *Der Durchmarsch oder Der Alte muss bezahlen* was produced at Vienna, Leop. 30 November 1808 (text by J. Perinet, music by V. Tuczek). The vocal score of *Die christliche Judenbraut* was printed. In a list of current music, otherwise not critical, published in the *Gothaer Theater-Kalender*, 1799, T. F. K. Arnold calls it "ein in jeder Rücksicht erbärmliches Produkt, welches ich blos deshalb angeführt habe weil es noch in allen Orten ausgepocht und ausgepfiffen wurde, da es hingegen in der Leopoldstadt und auf dem Kärnthner Thortheater zu Wien nicht genug

aufgeführt werden kann" (the two stages, by the way, on which the *Judenbraut* was *not* given!).

Date of first performance according to J. Ká-dár. An earlier production at Pressburg in 1788 (Schatz) seems doubtful.

DALAYRAC: *Raoul, Sire de Créqui*

31 October. Paris, C.I.

Text by J. M. Boutet de Monvel. Three acts.

Revived Paris, Fa. 9 November 1794 as *Bathilde et Éloi.*

In French also, Brussels 4 February 1791; Aachen 24 August 1794; Cologne 1796–97; St. Petersburg 1800; Hanover 1803; Moscow 30 August 1810; New Orleans 1810.

In German (translated by H. G. Schmieder), Mayence 17 December 1791 (music adapted by Stegmann); Riga 12 February 1793; (translated by J. Perinet), Vienna, Leop. 10 September 1793; (translated by C. A. Herklots), Munich October 1794; Hamburg 1794; Berlin 13 March 1795; Schleswig 1795; Hanover 8 June 1795; Oels 29 October 1795; Bremen 6 November 1795; Breslau 13 July 1797.

Revived Berlin 19 November 1804; Vienna, Kä. 22 May 1805 (with additional music by B. A. Weber); Würzburg 18 June 1809.

In Swedish (adapted by O. Kexél), Stockholm 28 January 1793.

In Italian (translated by G. Carpani), Monza Autumn 1791; Lisbon 17 December 1795.

In Russian (translated by S. N. Glinka), Moscow 1804.

In Polish (translated by W. Pekalski), Warsaw 1810.

A Dutch translation by B. A. Fallee was published in 1807; another by Kup (n.d.).

The opera was revived, for a single night, at the O.C., Paris 5 July 1889.

P. GUGLIELMI: *La bella Pescatrice*

Autumn. Naples, T.N.

Text by S. Zini. Two acts.

First performed at Naples, T.N., "per second opera di quest' anno"; according to Piovano

(*R.M.I.*, Vol. XVII, p. 825) this was only in Autumn.

Given at Rome Carnival 1790 as *La Villanella incivilita;* Milan, Sc. 11 August 1790, etc. In Italy until 1807; in Italian also, Madrid 3 July 1790 and Barcelona 3 August 1790; Paris, Th. de M. 23 December 1790 (additions by Mengozzi); Lisbon Carnival 1791 (revived 19 January 1798); London, Pantheon 24 March 1791 (revived Hm. 7 April 1801); Vienna 26 April 1791 (revived 15 July 1798); Dresden 5 November 1791 (revived 1811); Linz 1792.

In German (translated by F. H. von Einsiedel), Weimar 5 January 1792.

In Russian, St. Petersburg 26 May 1792.

CIMAROSA: *La Vergine del Sole*

6 November. St. Petersburg

Text by F. Moretti (first composed by Sarti, as *Idalide*, in 1783). Three acts.

One of the two operas Cimarosa wrote expressly for the Russian court.

In Italian also given at Bologna 7 February 1790, etc., sometimes as *Idalide;* Warsaw 3 July 1790; Madrid 4 November 1790; Lisbon 25 July 1802. Revived St. Petersburg 1804; Rome, Valle May 1810.

WRANITZKY: *Oberon, König der Elfen*

7 November. Vienna, W.

Text by K. L. Gieseke (founded on Wieland's poem and a libretto, *Hüon und Amande*, by F. S. Seyler, 1789). *Romantisch komische Oper*, 3 acts.

Very successful all over Germany until 1826 when it was replaced in the repertory by Weber's opera; occasionally revived even after 1826.

Exact date of first production has been established by O. E. Deutsch. All later dates, as 6 May 1790 (K. Glossy), 23 May 1791 (Goedeke) are to be rectified. The statement that the opera was expressly written for the coronation of Leopold II and *first* produced at Frankfort was taken over from Jahn by nearly every author (including Schatz-Sonneck).

After Vienna produced at Frankfort 15 October 1790, " mit einigen neu hineingemachten Gesängen von Schmieder, in Musik gesetzt von Stegmann und Walter" (*Journal des Luxus und der Moden,* December 1790); Mannheim 20 November 1790; Budapest 25 November 1790; Hanover 10 February 1791; Hamburg 17 October 1791; Prague 1791; Berlin 15 February 1792, etc. Given at Weimar 28 May 1796 in an altered version by C. A. Vulpius.

In German also, Warsaw 31 October 1793; Amsterdam 8 June 1796; Pressburg 2 December 1797; Temesvar 5 November 1801; Berne 1803; Poznán 2 December 1804.

In Dutch, Amsterdam *c.*1797; Dutch translation published 1796, 1797 and 1802.

In Russian (translated by Yankovich), St. Petersburg 9 May 1798; Moscow 1802.

In Polish (translated by B. Kudlicz), Warsaw 1810.

Revived Berlin, Kgst. 14 June 1826 (obviously taking advantage of the London success of Weber's opera before it could be produced in Germany); revived Hamburg as late as 25 March 1847 (with Weber's overture played before Wranitzky's opera).

(On the origin of the libretto, see G. Bobrik, *Wielands . . . Oberon auf der deutschen Singspielbühne,* 1909; and R. Fellinger in *Die Musik,* September 1934.)

PAISIELLO: *I Zingari in Fiera*

21 November. Naples, Fondo

Text by G. Palomba. Two acts.

Very successful in Italy; Milan, Sc. 18 September 1790 (revived 3 January 1804), etc.; in Italian also produced at Madrid 19 October 1790; Barcelona 9 December 1790; Lisbon 1791; Vienna 18 September 1791; Charlottenburg 8 October 1791; Dresden 1792; Warsaw 22 December 1792; London 14 May 1793 (revived 4 January 1800 and 27 Mai 1803); Pavlovsk 1796; St. Petersburg 4 September 1800; Paris, Th. I. 3 May 1802; Cagliari, Sardinia Carnival 1808.

In German, Mannheim 4 August 1791 (as *Die Zigeunerin oder Der gefoppte Astrolog*); Weimar

24 November 1792 (as *Die Zigeunerin*, translated by F. H. von Einsiedel).

In Russian, Moscow Spring 1804.

The opera was revived at Naples, Fior. 1 July 1883.

STORACE: *The Haunted Tower*

24 November. London, D.L.

Text by J. Cobb. Three acts.

Storace's first English opera (the music "selected, adapted and composed").

Very successful in London, given 50 times during the first season. Dublin 14 January 1793; Edinburgh 9 February 1793; Charleston, S.C. 24 April 1793; Philadelphia 2 December 1794; New York 9 January 1795 (with additional music by V. Pelissier); Spanish Town, Jamaica 6 February 1816. Revived London, D.L. 24 February 1816; C.G. 3 February 1832; and once more as late as 26 May 1922 at the Guildhall School of Music (by the Mayfair Dramatic Club).

LEMOYNE: *Nephté*

15 December. Paris, O.

Text by F. B. Hoffman (founded on T. Corneille's tragedy, *Camma*). Three acts.

It was in *Nephté* that, for the first time at the Paris Opéra, a composer was called before the curtain. Given in Paris 40 times until 1791. Revived Brussels 12 November 1804.

ANFOSSI: *Zenobia di Palmira*

26 December. Venice, S. Ben.

Text by G. Sertor. Two acts.

The most successful of Anfossi's serious operas and one of his last works.

In Italian also produced at Madrid 9 December 1790; Warsaw 17 January 1791; Leipzig Summer 1792; London 20 December 1794; Gachina 26 October 1797 (Anfossi's or Paisiello's setting?); Trieste November 1797; Moscow Carnival 1803; Barcelona 22 December 1806 (Anfossi's or Paisiello's setting?).

1790

GRÉTRY: *Pierre le Grand*

13 January. Paris, C.I.

Text by J. N. Bouilly. Four acts.

In French also given at Rotterdam 3 February 1792; Brussels 8 August 1792; Hanover 14 April 1805; Berne 5 February 1806. Revived Paris, O.C. 31 January 1801 and 7 May 1814.

In German (translated by C. A. Herklots), Berlin 16 October 1794; Hamburg Spring 1795.

In Dutch (translated by B. Ruloffs), Amsterdam 1799 (revived 1811).

CIMADORO: *Pimmaglione*

26 January. Venice, S. Sam.

Text: an Italian version, by A. S. Sografi, of Rousseau's *Pygmalion* (see 1770). One act.

According to Dassori, first performed Venice 1788; the earliest known libretto, however, mentions Venice, T. San Samuele, 26 January 1790, as place and date of the production. Not recorded by Wiel. Sonneck gives the date but not the theatre.

Successful in Italy: Padua March 1790 (in concert form by the Accademia dei Signori Scolari; libretto British Museum; revived Padua at the Sala Verde 29 April 1791 and at the T. Obizzi January 1811); Trieste 20 May 1790; Parma 23 November 1793 (translated by G. Perini); Florence and Ferrara 1794; Milan, Sc. 20 November 1795; Naples 1795; Lucca 21 January 1796; Ancona 1796; Rome, T. Apollo Carnival 1797 and Valle Autumn 1808; Turin Carnival 1801; Verona 13 May 1809, etc. One of the latest revivals in Italy was at Rome, Arg. 30 November 1822.

Outside Italy given at Vienna, B. 15 July 1791 (revived Kä. 6 July 1804, in Italian, and Leop. 21 September 1814, in German); Brünn 2 February 1792; Paris 4 May 1792 (revived 28 April 1814); Regensburg March 1793; Passau June 1793; Barcelona 5 June 1794; Madrid 12 November 1796; London 8 June 1797; Frankfort Spring 1800 (music by Cimadoro and Paer); Lisbon

Summer 1801; Dresden 24 February 1802 (as intermezzo in the pasticcio *Il Giorno natalizio*, music by J. Schuster and others; see *Journal des Luxus und der Moden*, 1802, p.280).

Pimmaglione was later on frequently revived by the singer Marianna Sessi in various towns, as Amsterdam 1816; Brussels 29 June 1816; Berlin 6 July 1817; Hanover 26 September 1817; Hamburg 3 January 1818; Stockholm 30 May 1818; St. Petersburg 5 August 1818; Moscow 24 April 1819; Dresden 6 November 1820; Leipzig 25 November 1820; Munich February 1821; Wilna 29 May 1821; Prague Spring 1822; Strasbourg 12 November 1823, etc.; sung by her at Hamburg as late as 22 January 1836.

Besides Sografi's, there were several other Italian versions of Rousseau's *Pygmalion*, viz. by F. S. de' Rogati (published Naples 1773); by S. Zannowich, published Paris 1773; by G. Perini (published Milan 1777; produced with Cimadoro's music, Parma 1793, see above;) by G. Tamagni (produced Fermo Carnival 1780; music by?); by A. Pepoli (produced at his private theatre, Padua 12 July 1793; music by Pepoli himself); by C. Conci (produced Pavia Summer 1799, with music by T. Gilardoni). Sografi's version was also set by B. Asioli (first produced Turin 1789, probably at the private theatre of Marchese Gherardini; music printed; revived at Paris as late as 2 April 1829). Finally, there were settings by F. Sirotti (produced Milan, Sc. Carnival 1793) and by F. Gnecco (Genoa Spring 1794). See also Cherubini's *Pimmalione*, 1809.

MOZART: *Così fan tutte* o sia *La Scuola degli Amanti*

26 January. Vienna, B.

Text by L. da Ponte (the third and last libretto he wrote for Mozart). Two acts.

In Italian also produced at Prague 1791 (exact date unknown; in any case before Mozart's death, on 5th December of that year, as the libretto says: ". . . Mozzart, maestro di Capella in actual servizio di S. Maestà Cesarea"); Leipzig Summer 1791; Dresden 5 October 1791.

German adaptations:

No other opera, perhaps, has been subjected to so many different versions and attempts to "improve" the libretto. The first German performance was at Frankfort 1 May 1791 (as *Liebe und Versuchung*, translated by H. G. Schmieder and C. D. Stegmann). Given at Amsterdam 1791, in German, as *So machen's die Mädchen*. Also given at Mayence 11 June 1791 and Brünn 24 April 1792. Next came Berlin 3 August 1792 (as *Eine macht's wie die Andere oder Die Schule der Liebhaber;* translator unknown); Hanover 10 October 1792 (as *So machen's die Mädchen alle*, 4 acts; so also at Cologne, Aachen and Düsseldorf 1793); Passau 3 January 1793 (as *So macht's jede*); Mannheim 12 May 1793 (as *Die Wette*); Augsburg 10 January 1794 (same title as at Berlin); Vienna, W. 14 August 1794 (as *Die Schule der Liebe oder So machen sie's alle*, translated by K. L. Gieseke).

The first German translation, which was more generally accepted, was C. F. Bretzner's version, *Weibertreue, oder Die Mädchen sind von Flandern* (in 2 acts); first performed at Leipzig 1794; Breslau 16 January 1795; Bautzen 3 September 1795; Hanover 23 September 1795; Bremen 16 October 1795; Hamburg 3 February 1796; Graz 18 August 1796, etc. A second version by Bretzner, in 4 acts, called *Die Wette oder Mädchenlist und Liebe*, was given at Stuttgart 16 May 1796 and Hamburg 6 July 1796. Two more 18th-century versions were *Die Wette oder Weibertreue keine Treue*, Munich May 1795, and *So sind sie alle, alle* (translated by C. A. Vulpius), Weimar 10 January 1797. Bretzner's 2-act version was given at Vienna, Leop. 1 July 1802 as *Die zwei Tanten aus Mailand, oder Die Verkleidungen*.

Of the numerous 19th and 20th century versions, the following may be mentioned:

VIENNA, B. 19 September 1804 as *Mädchentreue* (translated by G. F. Treitschke).

BERLIN 9 September 1805 as *Mädchentreue* (translated by G. F. Treitschke).

PRAGUE 1808 as *Mädchentreue* (translated by G. F. Treitschke).

BRESLAU 10 April 1806 as *Mädchenrache* (translated by J. G. Rhode; see *Der Freimüthige*, IV, p.312).

VIENNA, W. 20 January 1814 as *Die Zauberprobe* (a revised version of G. F. Treitschke's translation).

PRAGUE 7 March 1815 as *Die Zauberprobe* (a revised version of G. F. Treitschke's translation).

STUTTGART 7 January 1817 as *Mädchen sind Mädchen* (translated by J. B. Krebs).

BERLIN, O. 25 March 1820 and Munich 1824 as *Die verfängliche Wette* (translated by C. A. Herklots).

BERLIN, KGST. 29 December 1825 as *So machen es alle* (translated by K. von Holtei).

VIENNA, KÄ. 31 October 1840 as *So machen es alle* (translated by K. von Holtei).

WEIMAR 13 November 1830 as *Der Weiberkenner oder Wer hat die Wette gewonnen?*

MAYENCE 11 October 1838 as *Die Guerillas* (translated by J. D. Anton).

BERLIN 15 December 1846 as *So machen es alle* (a revised version of Herklots's translation by L. Schneider).

VIENNA 19 February 1863 as *Weibertreue.*

DRESDEN 19 September 1856 (translated by K. F. Niese; at Dresden for the first time in German).

CARLSRUHE 9 September 1860 as *So machen's alle* (translated by E. Devrient, recitatives arranged by W. Kalliwoda).

Mention may also be made of a pasticcio *Winzer und Sänger*, text by J. P. Lyser (published in *Mozart-Album*, 1856), music chiefly from *Così fan tutte* (3 numbers from *Idomeneo*), produced at the Tivoli, Hamburg 2 June 1856. F. Hirth does not mention the performance in his monograph on Lyser (p.521).

An attempt to drop Da Ponte's original text altogether and to adapt the music to a new libretto, founded on a comedy by Calderón, was made by the singer K. Scheidemantel: Dresden 6 June 1909 (as *Die Dame Kobold*).

Outside the German speaking countries, *Così fan tutte* was given in the original Italian at:

TRIESTE June 1797 (as *La Scuola degli Amanti*).

BARCELONA 4 November 1798 (at Madrid as late as 22 May 1878).

VARESE Autumn 1805.

MILAN, SC. 19 September 1807 and Spring 1814 (both as *La Scuola degli Amanti*).

NAPLES, FONDO Carnival 1815 (revived 1870).

TURIN, CARIGN. Autumn 1814 (as *La Scuola degli Amanti*); 23 September 1816, etc. Revived Turin, T. Gerbino Summer 1872.

Given at Venice, T. Fenice 14 September 1934 in German (by the Vienna O. company).

COPENHAGEN 19 October 1798 (as *Veddemaalet eller Elskernes Skole*, translated by A. G. Thoroup).

COPENHAGEN 19 December 1826 (as *Flugten fra Klostret*, adapted to a new libretto by A. G. Oehlenschläger).

COPENHAGEN 12 April 1887 (as *Det gør de alle*, translated by E. Bøgh).

PARIS, TH. I. 28 January 1809 (in Italian; date according to the libretto; Castil-Blaze, Pougin, Prod'homme give 1 February or 11 February respectively; Napoléon had the opera privately performed at Compiègne on 1 September 1811).

PARIS, O. 5 January 1813 (in French, adapted to a new libretto *Le Laboureur Chinois*, by E. Morel de Chédeville, J. M. Deschamps, and J. B. D. Desprès; 1-act pasticcio, music from *Così fan tutte*, and from other works by Mozart, Haydn and Mayr, arranged by Berton).

PARIS, TH. L. 31 March 1863 (in French, as *Peines d'Amour perdues;* this time the *Così fan tutte* music was adapted to a new text by J. Barbier and M. Carré, founded on Shakespeare's *Love's Labour's Lost*).

PARIS, O.C. 20 April 1920 (for the first time translated from the original by L. V. Durdilly and J. Chantavoine).

(See, for details on the Paris productions, J. G. Prod'homme in *Le Ménestrel*, 19 June 1925.)

LONDON, HM. 9 May 1811 (in Italian).

LONDON, LY. 29 July 1828 (in English, as *Tit for Tat; or The Tables Turned*, translated by S. J. Arnold?; music arranged by W. Hawes).

LONDON, PRINCE'S 30 January 1841 (in English, as *The Retaliation;* by amateurs).

LONDON, LY. 14 April 1841 (in English, as *The Retaliation;* by amateurs).

LONDON, ST. GEORGE'S HALL 16 January 1873 (in Italian).

LONDON, SAVOY (R.C.M.) 16 July 1890 (in English, translated by M. E. Browne).

LONDON, KINGSWAY TH. 23 March 1927 (in English, translated by M. E. Browne).

BRISTOL 18 October 1926 (Browne's version revised by E. J. Dent).

The 1828 version was also given at Dublin 13 April 1831.

ST. PETERSBURG 1813 (in German) and Carnival 1831 (in Italian).

STOCKHOLM 14 May 1830 (in Swedish, translated by N. E. W. af Wetterstedt from Bretzner's German version; revived there only 15 February 1940).

PRAGUE 30 October 1831 (for the first time in Czech, translated by S. K. Machaček).

BRUSSELS 29 January 1875 (in Italian) and 8 February 1923 (in French, translated by P. Spaak).

BASLE 31 January 1883 (in German, L. Schneider's version; for the first time in Switzerland?; Zurich only 24 February 1899).

NEW YORK, M. 24 March 1922 (in Italian; apparently for the first time in America) and Juilliard School of Music 28 February 1940 (in Italian).

RIGA 21 November 1925 (in Lettish).

LJUBLJANA 25 December 1926 (in Slovenian).

LEMBERG 1927 (for the first time in Polish; at the Conservatoire).

BUDAPEST 9 January 1930 (in Hungarian, translated by V. Lányi; previously produced there at the Conservatoire in 1927).

BRATISLAVA 1933 (in Slovakian).

BUENOS AIRES 17 July 1934 (in Italian).

ANTWERP 22 January 1938 (in Flemish).

STORACE: *No Song, no Supper*
16 April. London, D.L.

Text by P. Hoare. Two acts.

The music "chiefly composed" by Storace, who took a trio and a sextet from his *Equivoci* (see 1786) and some pieces from Grétry and other composers. Very successful on English stages; Dublin 15 March 1791; Philadelphia 30 November 1792 (given there until 1851); New York

15 February 1793 (given there until 1847); in English also, Hamburg 20 February 1795 (see note on *The Shamrock,* 1783); Cape Town 9 October 1815.

Revived in London, Ly. 19 October 1809 and D.L. 14 June 1817; revived at Manchester as late as 11 July 1870.

ZINGARELLI: *Antigone*
30 April. Paris, O.

Text by J. F. Marmontel. Three acts.

Zingarelli's only French opera. Unsuccessful (only given twice). In Italian, Leghorn Carnival 1791.

R. KREUTZER: *Jeanne d'Arc à Orléans*
10 May. Paris, C.I.

Text by P. J. B. Choudard Desforges and Cousin. Three acts.

This seems to be the first opera on this favourite subject (see Balfe 1837; Hoven 1840; Verdi 1845; Mermet 1876; Chaikovsky 1881). Kreutzer's first opera. Revived Antwerp 15 February 1822.

DITTERSDORF: *Das rothe Kaeppchen*
26 May. Breslau

Text by the composer, founded on Livigni's *Giannina e Bernadone,* see 1781 (and not by C. A. Vulpius, as Riedinger has it, nor by K. L. Giesecke to whom it has also been attributed). Three acts.

(According to Riedinger first produced at Vienna, Leop. 1788, and perhaps even earlier at Johannisberg. As far as the Leopoldstadt theatre is concerned Hadamowsky's Catalogue shows that the opera was not given there at all; as to Johannisberg, see note on *Hironymus Knicker,* 1789).

Given at Weimar 7 June 1791 (text revised and reduced to 2 acts by C. A. Vulpius); Prague 1791; Cologne 9 October 1791; Berlin 20 December 1791; Vienna, W. 23 February 1792; Hanover 11 April 1792; Munich 4 May 1792; Bremen 19 October 1792; Hamburg 1792; Nuremberg 1793; Rostock 16 June 1794; Dessau 31 July 1794; Salzburg Spring 1795; Graz 29 June 1797; Carlsruhe 15 December 1797, etc.; in German also, Amsterdam 1792; Budapest 6 August 1800; Paris 21 November 1801; Poznán 9 September 1805; St. Petersburg 1809; Solothurn 20 January 1811.

In Danish (translated by L. Knudsen), Copenhagen 19 May 1794.

In Dutch (translated by C. Loots), Amsterdam 1796; revived 1817.

Frequently revived in Germany throughout the 19th century; some of the latest revivals were at Riga October 1857; Berlin 23 April 1861; Stuttgart 6 March 1868; Munich 17 November 1868; Dessau 13 January 1899.

Beethoven published variations on a theme from this opera (*Es war einmal ein alter Mann*) in 1794.

DALAYRAC: *La Soirée orageuse*

29 May. Paris, C.I.

Text by J. B. Radet. One act.

In French also given at Amsterdam 16 April 1791; Brussels 8 June 1791; Hamburg 1795; Cologne 21 September 1797; Gachina (near St. Petersburg) 3 October 1798. Revived Paris, O.C. 5 July 1889.

In Swedish (translated by C. Envallsson), Stockholm 7 October 1793.

In German (as *Die stürmische Nacht*), Vienna, Leop. 14 August 1795; St. Petersburg 1809; Moscow 25 November 1820.

Dutch translation published 1799; performed in Flemish already at Oudenarde 26 September 1796 and Courtrai 16 December 1796.

P. GUGLIELMI: *La Serva innamorata*

Summer. Naples, Fior.

Text by G. Palomba. Two acts.

Successful in Italy (last revived Venice Summer 1817).

In Italian also, Vienna 15 February 1791 (as *La Giardiniera innamorata*); Barcelona 4 November 1792; Lisbon Summer 1794; Trieste 26 December 1794; Madrid 12 April 1795; Paris, Th. I. 28 December 1804; Amsterdam 1808.

BERTON: *Les Rigueurs du Cloître*

28 August. Paris, C.I.

Text by J. Fiévée. Two acts.

Brussels 1 March 1793, etc. Berton's first more important work; of historical interest as the earliest instance of those "rescue operas" which ruled the repertory of Central Europe from the time of the French Revolution until about 1820, Beethoven's *Fidelio* and Cherubini's *Les deux Journées* being the climax of that movement.

MÉHUL: *Euphrosine ou Le Tyran corrigé*

4 September. Paris, C.I.

Text by F. B. Hoffman. Five acts.

Reduced to 4 acts on 11 September 1790; since 22 August 1795 given in the final, 3-act version. Méhul's first performed opera. Given in Paris until 1829 and revived 26 February 1900 at the Th. L. de la Renaissance as *Euphrosine et Coradin* (text revised by P. Ferrier).

In French also, Brussels 10 October 1792; St. Petersburg 1798; Hanover 2 August 1803; Moscow 17 October 1808; Berne 27 May 1809.

In German, Frankfort 29 April 1792; (translation by K. L. Gieseke) Vienna, W. 19 September 1795; Hamburg Spring 1797; Mayence 1797; Munich December 1798; Schleswig 1802; Budapest 16 September 1811; St. Petersburg 1815; revived Berlin 9 December 1825 (new German version by May). Another German translation, by G. E. Lüderwald, was published at Riga (n. d.).

In Dutch (translation by P. G. Witsen Geysbeek), Amsterdam [1 November] 1798.

In Russian (translated by A. I. Sheller), St. Petersburg 11 October 1815; Moscow 24 April 1816.

W. MÜLLER: *Das Sonnenfest der Braminen*

9 September. Vienna. Leop.

Text by K. F. Hensler (*heroisch-komisches Original-Singspiel*). Two acts.

The first great success of Müller who, since 1786, had been conductor at the Th. in der Leopoldstadt.

Subsequently given at Prague 1792; Graz 1 January 1793; Hamburg 3 July 1793 (with additional music by C. D. Stegmann); Brünn 1794; Nuremberg 1794; Weimar 31 January 1795 (text altered by C. A. Vulpius); Berlin 16 October 1795; Breslau 4 December 1795; Bremen December 1796; Hanover 27 February 1797; Carlsruhe 27 January 1798; Oels 12 May 1798; Aachen 8 September 1799; Cologne, Düsseldorf and Crefeld 1799; Munich October 1800; Temesvar 27 December 1801; Berne 1803; Poznán 27 October 1805.

In German also produced at the Th. de la Cité, Paris 3 December 1801. This was the last production of the short-lived first German opera-season in Paris, under the management of one Haselmeyer. The season was in Autumn 1801 (not 1802 as stated by Castil-Blaze; see *A.M.Z.*, 10 February 1802). The productions were: 16 November 1801, *Die Entführung aus dem Serail;* 21 November, *Das rote Käppchen;* 25 November, *Das Neusonntagskind;* 29 November, *Der Spiegel von Arkadien;* 30 November, *Der Tyroler Wastel;* and 3 December, *Das Sonnenfest der Braminen.* The theatre had been named "Théâtre Mozart" for the occasion.

In Dutch (translated by S. Bos), Amsterdam 1798.

In Polish (translated by W. Boguslawski), Warsaw 23 November 1800.

SCHULZ: *Høst-Gildet*

(The Harvest Home)

16 September. Copenhagen

Text by T. Thaarup. One act.

Given at Copenhagen until 1835 (since 21 January 1791 in a new version). A German translation by F. H. W. Froelich was published in 1795.

PASHKEEVICH, SARTI, and CANNOBIO: *Nachalnoye Upravlenie Olega*

Начальное Управленіе Олега

(The early Reign of Oleg)

26 October. St. Petersburg

Text by the Empress Catharine II. Five acts.

First produced at the Ermitage; publicly performed 2 November 1790.

First Russian opera published in full score (1791). The opera was written "in imitation of Shakespeare, not observing the traditional rules of the stage".

Interesting notes by Sarti on his *Oleg* music are reprinted in G. Pasolini Zanelli's biography of the composer (1883); for an account of this opera see also Count Valentin Eszterházy's letters (edited by Ernest Daudet, 1907), p.326 and 333.

A German translation, by Ch. F. Völkner, was published in 1792.

BEFFROY DE REIGNY: *Nicodème dans la Lune* ou *La Révolution pacifique*

7 November. Paris

Text by the composer (*Folie en prose mêlée d'ariettes et de vaudevilles*). Three acts.

This satirical play (hardly to be called an opera) had a run of 363 nights at the small "Théâtre Français comique et lyrique" (Boulevard St. Martin; existing only from 26 June 1790 to 25 January 1794) and was revived at the Théâtre de la Cité on 31 December 1796 for another 200 nights. (For a sequel see 1791.)

An imitation by Deduit, *Nicodème dans le Soleil,* was performed at the Théâtre de M. Yon, Boulevard du Temple, 11 June 1791; another by Maillet, *Le Retour de Nicodème de la Lune* at the Délassements Comiques at about the same time.

BIANCHI: *La Vendetta di Nino*

12 November. Naples, S.C.

Text by F. Moretti (founded on M. Cesarotti's Italian version of Voltaire's *Semiramis*). Two acts.

Outside Italy given at

MADRID 9 December 1793 (in Italian) and 4 November 1800 (in Spanish, translated by V. R. de Arellano, music adapted by M. Ronzi).

LONDON 26 April 1794 (as *La Semiramide*, text altered by L. da Ponte; Brigitta Banti's London début; revived 8 February 1800).

PARIS, TH.I. 19 August 1811 (as *Semiramide*); revived 2 October 1815.

1791

STORACE: *The Siege of Belgrade*

1 January. London, D.L.

Text by J. Cobb. Three acts.

Storace partly composed the music, partly compiled it form Martin's opera *Una Cosa rara* (see 1786) and other works. Kelly, II, I : "There was a good deal of beautiful original music in it, by Storace, who, with his great taste and knowledge of effect, had also selected some from Martini"; Parke: "The first stage musical performance of moment to be given at our national theatres"; and "This opera presented a marked instance of the rapid transition which the English opera had made from the simplicity of the ballad farce to the captivating splendours of the Italian drama. The music, which was excellent throughout, procured the author for his copyright one thousand pounds".

Letter in *Journal des Luxus und der Moden*, 15 January 1791: "Ich war gestern nicht wenig verwundert, als ich in der hier sehr beliebten Operette: The Siege of Belgrade fast alle Arien der Cosa rara fand. Ein gewisser Signore Storace versteht die Kunst aus vielen Italiänischen Opern eine Original-Englische zusammenzustoppeln. Sänger und Sängerinnen sind gut und schmelzen die rauhen Töne ihrer Sprache so ziemlich in die Accente der Liebe".

Very successful in London, given there for 50 nights during the first season; given at Dublin 27 January 1792; New York 30 December 1796; Philadelphia 1801; Edinburgh 15 December 1810; the last revivals took place when Braham first

appeared on the American stage (Philadelphia 10 December 1840; New York 21 December 1840).

R. KREUTZER: *Paul et Virginie*

15 January. Paris, C.I.

Text by E. G. F. de Favières (founded on Saint-Pierre's story, first published in 1787). Three acts.

Revived Paris, O. 12 June 1806 (changed into an opéra-ballet); revived at the O.C. 14 August 1846.

In French also, Rotterdam 22 November 1791; Liége 19 December 1791; Brussels 31 January 1792; Amsterdam 1792; Aachen 3 August 1794; Cologne 1795-96; Hamburg 23 October 1795; St. Petersburg 18 June 1800; Hanover 24 December 1803; Berne 8 July 1809; Moscow 15 January 1810.

In German (translated by H. G. Schmieder), Amsterdam 1793; Berlin 21 January 1794, etc.; (translated by I. F. Castelli, as *Die Familie auf Isle-de-France*) Vienna, W. 1805; St. Petersburg 1818.

In Swedish (translated by D. G. Björn), Stockholm 15 May 1794.

Dutch translation by P. G. Witsen Geysbeek published 1797.

In Danish (translated by N. T. Bruun), Copenhagen 19 May 1815.

In Russian (translated by P. N. Kobyakov), St. Petersburg 6 November 1809 and Moscow 28 May 1812.

The opera was given as a pantomime at Boston 10 May 1797.

F. L. BENDA: *Louise*

16 January. Königsberg

Text by E. F. Jester. Three acts.

The most successful opera of Georg Benda's son.

In German also, Riga 10 June 1794; Hamburg 1794; revived at Königsberg as late as 1820.

MARTIN Y SOLER and PASHKEEVICH: *Fedul s Detmi*
Федул с Дѣтьми
(Fedul and his Children)
27 *January*. St. Petersburg

Text by the Empress Catharine II. One act.

First performed at the Ermitage; publicly, St. Petersburg 2 March 1791; Moscow 7 January 1796 (revived 1 January 1807, 13 November 1821 and once more as late as 6 December 1896). Vocal score published in 1895. Of the music, six numbers were written by Martin and five by Pashkeevich.

BORGHI: *La Morte di Semiramide*
9 *February*. Milan, Sc.

Text by A. S. Sografi. Three acts.

Borghi's best opera. Bologna October 1791, etc.

In Italian also, Trieste 4 October 1795; Vienna 14 May 1797; Lisbon Spring 1799.

MÉHUL: *Cora*
15 *February*. Paris, O.

Text by Valadier (founded on Marmontel's novel, *Les Incas*). Four acts.

Unsuccessful; given for five nights only.

DITTERSDORF: *Der Gutsherr* oder *Hannchen und Gürge*
2 *March*. Vienna, W.

Text by J. F. Jünger. Two acts.

Very successful on German stages; sometimes called *Der Schiffspatron;* Frankfort 6 June 1792; Munich 6 July 1792; Breslau 30 November 1792; Bremen 3 December 1792; Hanover 23 January 1793; Graz 19 March 1793; Cologne 15 December 1793; Aachen and Düsseldorf 1793; Hamburg 28 April 1794; Carlsruhe 6 January 1798, etc.

In German also, Warsaw and Lemberg 1793; Budapest 17 July 1796; Temesvar 18 February 1802; Poznán 3 November 1803.

The last revivals seem to have been at Darmstadt 30 March 1807 and Vienna, Leop. 7 May 1816.

DALAYRAC: *Camille* ou *Le Souterrain*
19 *March*. Paris, C.I.

Text by B. J. Marsollier (founded on Mme de Genlis's *Adèle et Théodore*). Three acts.

Successful in France. Last revived Paris, O.C. 3 August 1841.

In French also, Brussels 25 April 1792; St. Petersburg May 1792 (previously given by amateurs at Aleksandrovsk; see *Souvenirs of Mme Vigée-Lebrun*, English edition, 1879, Vol. II, p.20); Cologne 1796–97; Moscow 31 October 1808; Berne 5 June 1809; New York 8 September 1827.

In Dutch (translated by A. C. Brinkman), Amsterdam 1796; in Flemish, Oudenarde 1 October 1798.

In Swedish (translated by C. Envallsson), Stockholm 29 May 1797 and (in another version by C. J. Lindegren) 6 May 1800.

In Italian (translated by G. Carpani), Monza Autumn 1794; Lisbon 29 November 1799.

In Danish (translated by N. T. Bruun), Copenhagen 28 March 1805.

In Russian (translated by D. I. Vyelyashev-Volyntsov), Moscow 30 January 1812; St. Petersburg 13 December 1813.

An English adaptation by P. Hoare, *The Captive of Spilburg*, with new music by Kelly and Dussek, was produced in London, D.L. 14 November 1798 and New York 25 March 1801.

NAUMANN: *La Dama Soldato*
30 *March*. Dresden

Text by C. Mazzolà. Two acts.

The most successful of Naumann's comic operas.

In Italian also Prague 1792.

In German (translation by C. A. Vulpius published Leipzig 1793 as *Was thut die Liebe nicht*), Vienna, Leop. 14 August 1794 (as *Der weibliche Soldat*); Schwerin 1795; Mannheim 16 August 1795; Königsberg 31 January 1796; Oels 30 July 1796; Dresden 17 September 1802; Leipzig 1803; Hamburg 14 September 1804; Amsterdam 28 October 1807; Berlin 26 May 1812. Last revived Weimar 2 February 1831.

A one act version by Schmieder was announced in the *Journal für Theater und andere schöne Künste*, 1797, p.114.

GRÉTRY: *Guillaume Tell*

9 April. Paris, C.I.

Text by J.M. Sedaine. Three acts.

Important revolution opera.

In French also Ghent 1794; New Orleans *c.* 1817. Revived Paris, O.C. 24 May 1828 (text revised by J. P. Pellissier, music re-scored by Berton); Marseilles 16 October 1828; Le Havre 6 December 1828, etc., but this new run of Grétry's work was cut short by Rossini's *Tell* (1829). Grétry's opera was produced once more by a French company in New York 12 August 1831.

CANDEILLE: *Castor et Pollux*

14 June. Paris, O.

P.J.J. Bernard's text (first set to music by Rameau, see 1737). Five acts.

Candeille re-scored and retained some pieces of Rameau's original music. Successful in Paris; Louis XVI and Marie Antoinette attended a performance on 20 September 1791 (the last time they went to the Académie Royale de Musique). Revived in Paris 18 October 1796 and 28 December 1814.

PAISIELLO: *La Locanda*

16 June. London, Pantheon

Text: a reduced version of G. Bertati's *La Locanda* (first set to music by Gazzaniga, see 1771) by G. Tonioli. Two acts.

First given in Italy at Naples, Fior. January 1792 (as *Il Fanatico in Berlina*, with an additional third act, text by G. B. Lorenzi); Genoa, S.Ag. 28 May 1792 (not 1791); given at Palermo Summer 1792 as *Le Avventure della Locanda;* Milan, Sc. 14 August 1792; Turin, T. Carignano Autumn 1792, etc.

In Italian also Barcelona 24 April 1792; Vienna 10 July 1792; Trieste 26 December 1792; Leipzig

Summer 1793; Lisbon Spring 1795 (as *Lo Strambo in Berlina*); Bastia, Corsica Spring 1797; Oporto 1799; Amsterdam 1808; Paris 22 July 1814. Revived in London, Hm. 28 February 1792 and 22 May 1802.

In German (as *Die Abenteuer im Gasthof oder Die lächerlichen Reisenden*, translated by K. L. Gieseke), Vienna, W. 9 April 1796; Graz 30 April 1798; Temesvar 25 February 1802.

In Polish, Wilna February 1811.

NASOLINI: *La Morte di Cleopatra*

22 June. Vicenza

Text by A. S. Sografi. Two acts.

Very successful in Italy, where it was given until 1817.

In Italian also Trieste 24 April 1792; Berlin March 1797 (at Countess Lichtenau's private theatre); Madrid 6 October 1798; Lisbon Summer 1800; London 4 March 1806; Oporto 8 November 1807; Paris 1 December 1813 (Napoléon attended the first night).

CHERUBINI: *Lodoïska*

18 July. Paris, Th. Feydeau

Text by C. F. Fillette Loraux. Three acts.

One of Cherubini's chief works. Rather more appreciated in Germany than in France.

In German (translated by C. A. Herklots), Berlin 13 May 1797; Schleswig 1799; Dessau Spring 1800; Hamburg *c.* September 1800; Vienna, W. 23 March 1802 (Kä. 24 January 1814; Jos. 10 December 1828); Budapest 1803; Munich 1813; Hermannstadt and Lemberg 1814; Riga Autumn 1842. Last revived Leipzig 21 November 1854.

In Italian, Dresden May 1802.

In Polish (translated by W. Boguslawski), Warsaw and Wilna 1804; Poznán June 1805.

In Danish (translated by N. T. Bruun), Copenhagen 31 October 1815.

In English, New York 4 December 1826 (music arranged by R. Honey).

R. KREUTZER: *Lodoïska*

1 August. Paris, C.I.

Text by J. E. B. Dejaure. Three acts.

As it was often the case in these years, the two rival houses of opéra-comique produced operas on the same subject. In France, Kreutzer's setting was the more popular one.

In French also given at Amsterdam February 1793; Brussels 19 June 1793; Cologne 1796–97; Hamburg 1797; Brunswick 24 June 1809; Hanover 15 March 1804; St. Petersburg 1804; Berne 24 June 1809; Moscow 5 November 1810.

In Italian (translated by G. Carpani), Monza Autumn 1793; Lisbon 17 December 1796 (music arranged by Leal Moreira).

In Swedish (translated by J. P. Stolpe), Stockholm 2 November 1795 (with an epilogue by Lindegren, music by Haeffner).

In Russian (translated by V. A. Levshin), St. Petersburg 22 June 1814 and Moscow 24 October 1816.

In Dutch (translated by B. Ruloffs), Amsterdam 1796.

In London, *Lodoïska* was performed as a pasticcio, music selected from Cherubini, Kreutzer and Andreozzi, arranged by Storace and adapted to an English libretto by J. P. Kemble (D. L. 9 June 1794 and New York 13 June 1808). (Kelly, Vol. II, p.66: "I was in Paris at the first representations of *Lodoiska* at both theatres; but, partiality apart the Drury Lane piece surpassed them both"). Also C.G. 15 October 1816; Dublin 1816.

MOZART: *La Clemenza di Tito*

6 September. Prague

Metastasio's text (first set to music by Caldara in 1734), reduced and altered by C. Mazzolà. Two acts.

Written and performed within 18 days to celebrate the coronation of the Emperor Leopold II as King of Bohemia. After the special occasion for which it was composed the opera became known to a greater public only some years after Mozart's death. First given at Vienna, Kä. 29 December 1794 and B. 31 March 1795 (also W.

8 September 1798 and 25 March 1799) and at Hamburg 7 February 1796 and Berlin 28 February 1796 (in concert form, for the benefit of the composer's widow).

In German (translated mostly by F. Rochlitz):

DRESDEN 26 May 1796.

CASSEL March 1797.

BUDAPEST 11 June 1798.

ALTONA 1798.

BRÜNN 4 October 1798.

BAUTZEN 3 December 1798.

BRESLAU 19 March 1799.

GRAZ 18 July 1799.

FRANKFORT 22 August 1799 (translated perhaps by J. J. Ihlee).

WEIMAR 21 December 1799 (translated by C. A. Vulpius).

LEIPZIG, January 1801.

MUNICH 10 February 1801.

DESSAU 10 August 1801.

BERLIN 16 October 1801.

BREMEN December 1801.

HANOVER 24 February 1802.

MANNHEIM 8 August 1802 (additions from Cimarosa, Weigl, Winter).

STUTTGART 7 November 1803.

POZNÁN 20 March 1806.

SALZBURG 1 May 1807.

KÖNIGSBERG 29 April 1808.

PRAGUE 1808.

COLOGNE September 1808.

HAMBURG 30 September 1808.

BASLE 18 January 1809.

PRESSBURG 20 November 1809, etc.

In a German version by J. von Seyfried produced at Vienna, W. 22 September 1801; Kä. 12 April 1804 (in Italian, with some additional music by Weigl) and 2 January 1811 (in German).

Given at Munich in Italian 21 July 1805 (with additional airs by Winter, Cannabich, Weigl and Mayr) and in German 14 February 1824 as *König Garibald* (the libretto gives the date as 16 February), adapted to a new libretto by C. M. Heigel, additional music by J. H. Stuntz (celebrating the 25th jubilee of King Max Joseph of Bavaria).

Revived at Prague 17 December 1848 (celebrating the Emperor Francis Joseph's accession to the throne).

Frequently revived in Germany, particularly in Mozart jubilee years such as 1856 and 1906. The most recent revivals were at Leipzig December 1916 and Mannheim November 1919 (new German version by A. Rudolph).

Outside Austria and Germany *La Clemenza di Tito* was produced in London, Hm. 27 March 1806 (in Italian, for Elizabeth Billington's benefit, text altered by S. Buonaiuti); first Mozart opera in London; revived 3 March 1812; 2 March 1816; 1 May 1821. Given in German at the Prince's Th. 16 July 1840.

LISBON Autumn 1806 (in Italian).

AMSTERDAM 1809 (in Italian); 20 December 1823 (in German) and 1840 (in Dutch).

NAPLES, S.C. 13 May 1809 (in Italian).

PARIS, TH.I. 20 May 1816 (in Italian).

MILAN, T. RÈ 26 December 1816 (in Italian).

MILAN, SC. 26 December 1818 (in Italian).

ST. PETERSBURG 24 April 1817 (in Russian, translated by A. I. Sheller) and 20 August 1818 (in Italian).

MOSCOW 23 July 1818 (in Russian).

COPENHAGEN 29 January 1823 (in Danish, translated by N. T. Bruun); revived 8 September 1860.

STOCKHOLM 23 June 1823 (in Swedish, translated by A. Lindeberg).

PRAGUE 19 November 1891 (for the first time there in Czech, translated by V. J. Novotný).

FALMOUTH 12 November 1930 (for the first time in English, translated by M. and E. Radford).

LONDON, WEST CENTRAL HALL 28 February 1931 (in English, translated by M. and E. Radford).

A Serbian translation by J. Grčić was published in 1891 (for a concert performance at Novi Sad?).

Apparently not yet produced in America.

I. WALTER: *Der Spiegelritter*

11 September. Frankfort

Text by A. von Kotzebue. Three acts.

Popular in Germany; given at Hanover 21 February 1793; Mannheim 10 March 1793; Bre-

men 10 October 1793; Hamburg 26 October 1795; Berlin 26 January 1796; Oels 10 December 1796, etc.

A Dutch translation by A. Fokke Simonsz appeared in 1807.

MOZART: *Die Zauberflöte*

30 September. Vienna, W.

Text by E. Schikaneder. Two acts.

The actor and writer Karl Ludwig Gieseke (real name, Johann Georg Metzler) who played in the first performance the small part of the first slave (d. 1833 as professor of mineralogy in Dublin), seems to have had a rather important share in the libretto (cf. F. Grandaur in *Neue Zeitschrift für Musik*, 1891; E. von Komorzynski in *Alt-Wiener Kalender für das Jahr 1922* and E. J. Dent's *Mozart's Opera The Magic Flute; its History and Interpretation*, 1911).

Die Zauberflöte was a great success right from the beginning. Schikaneder announced the 83rd night on 23 November 1792 as the 100th performance, the 135th night on 22 October 1795 as the 200th performance. On 1 January 1798 he announced the 300th performance. Altogether, the opera was given at the Theater auf der Wieden 223 times until 6 May 1801. (See on Goethe's project of a sequel to *Die Zauberflöte*, the pamphlet by Victor Jung, 1900. For an actual sequel, Winter's *Das Labyrint*, see 1798.)

A belated continuation, *Sarastro* by K. E. Goepfart, text by G. Stommel, was given in concert form at Hengelo (Holland) on 9 December 1891.

After Vienna, *Die Zauberflöte* was first produced at Prague 25 October 1792; given there in Italian (translated by G. de Gamerra, as *Il Flauto magico*, with recitatives by J. B. Kucharž) Carnival 1794; in Czech perhaps in the same year; translation by "R. B. A." (A. Nejedly, A. J. Puchmajer, and Š. Hněwkowský) published 1794 and re-issued 1931. Given at Prague in a Czech version by J. K. Chmelenský 11 January 1829; in a new version by J. Böhm 5 December 1874.

Productions in German:

ZITTAU 1792 (in concert form).

AUGSBURG 21 January 1793.

LEIPZIG 25 January 1793.

PASSAU 31 January 1793.

BUDAPEST 3 March 1793 (in German).

GRAZ 29 May 1793.

BRÜNN June 1793.

GODESBERG, NEAR BONN June 1793.

MAGDEBURG 1793 (fragments only) and 18 March 1799 (complete).

MUNICH 11 July 1793.

WARSAW 27 July 1793 (in German).

DRESDEN 7 August 1793 (in German) and 2 April 1794 (in Italian).

FRANKFORT 16 August 1793.

LINZ 25 August 1793.

HAMBURG 15 November 1793 (200th performance 29 November 1836).

WEIMAR 16 January 1794 (in 3 acts, libretto revised by C. A. Vulpius).

KÖNIGSBERG January 1794.

MANNHEIM 29 March 1794 (Vulpius's version).

BRUNSWICK 17 April 1794 (in German) and 6 August 1804 (in French, translated by A. Bursay).

FREIBURG 24 April 1794.

STETTIN 24 April 1794.

HANOVER 25 April 1794.

OLOMOUC 3 May 1794.

BERLIN 12 May 1794 (500th performance 3 September 1905); in Italian, Kgst. 24 February 1849.

AMSTERDAM 31 May 1794 (in German).

NUREMBERG 14 May 1794.

ELBING June 1794.

MAYENCE 1794.

COLOGNE 1794 and 29 April 1796.

ALTONA 1794 and 28 August 1798.

LAUCHSTEDT 3 July 1794.

AACHEN 10 July 1794.

DESSAU 11 August 1794.

RUDOLSTADT 26 August 1794.

BAUTZEN 26 August 1794.

HALBERSTADT 29 August 1794 (by amateurs).

ERFURT 27 September 1794.

BREMEN 3 October 1794.

DANZIG 19 October 1794.

DÜSSELDORF 4 November 1794.

LÜBECK 17 November 1794.

SCHLESWIG 29 December 1794.

KIEL 14 January 1795.

BRESLAU 25 February 1795.

ROSTOCK 19 May 1795.

STRALSUND 22 June 1795.

OELS 1 August 1795.

GREIFSWALD 20 October 1795.

OEDENBURG 12 December 1795.

STUTTGART 18 December 1795.

TEMESVAR 1796 (in German).

CASSEL 5 December 1796.

BERNE 12 December 1796.

NEUSTRELITZ 2 January 1797.

PRESSBURG 26 February 1797.

OSNABRÜCK 13 March 1797.

BALLENSTEDT 22 December 1797.

LEMBERG 1797 (in German).

REVAL 1797 (in German).

ST. PETERSBURG 1797 (in German).

KREFELD Spring 1798.

HERMANNSTADT 29 June 1798.

CRACOW 1799, etc.

First given at the Vienna Hoftheater 24 February 1801 (400th performance there 18 November 1893); at Vienna Leop. first 2 November 1810.

In other languages, *Die Zauberflöte* was given in Italian and in Czech at Prague and Dresden, see above; at:

AMSTERDAM 3 April 1799 (in Dutch, translated by J. C. Meyer); in German earlier, see above; in French 18 October 1803; in Italian 30 December 1809.

MOSCOW 1801 (in Russian, at Maddoks's Th. according to Chayanova; see also A. von Kotzebue's journal, *Der Freimüthige*, I, p.199). Earlier dates as given by Findeizen (Moscow 1794?) and by Stasov (St. Petersburg 1799) lack verification. (Anonymous Russian translation published St. Petersburg 1799.) Given at St. Petersburg 1797 in German (see above; production recorded in *Theaterjournal*, I, p.196) and 5 June 1818 (in Russian, translated by A. I. Sheller).

PARIS, O. 20 August 1801 (in French, as *Les Mystères d'Isis*, text by E. Morel de Chédeville; "Le Citoyen Lachnith a composé le récitatif, et formé la partition" (he used parts from Mozart's *La Clemenza di Tito*, *Le Nozze di Figaro*, and *Don Giovanni*). This mutilated version had its 100th performance on 23 October 1818 and was given 134 times until 2 May 1827. Also given at Nantes 2 March 1815. See the analysis in G. Servières's *Episodes d'Histoire Musicale*, 1914.

PARIS, TH. I. 21 May 1829 (in German, by a company from Aachen).

PARIS, TH. L. 23 February 1865 (in French, translated by C. Nuitter and A. Beaumont).

PARIS, O.C. 3 April 1878 (in French, translated by C. Nuitter and A. Beaumont).

PARIS, O.C. 31 May 1909 (new translation by A. Bisson and P. Ferrier).

PARIS, O. 22 December 1922 (new translation by J. G. Prod'homme and J. Kienlin, first given Brussels 1912, see below).

WARSAW 29 January 1802 and Poznán July 1805 (in Polish, translated by W. Boguslawski); in German earlier at Warsaw, Lemberg, Cracow, see above; revived Lemberg 21 June 1923 (new Polish version by A. Kiczman).

LONDON, HM. 6 June 1811 (in Italian, translated by G. de Gamerra).

NORWICH 1 June 1829 (in English, adapted by C. H. Mueller).

LONDON, C.G. 27 May 1833 (in German; a selection already King's Th. 18 June 1829).

LONDON, D.L. 10 March 1838 (in English, adapted by J. R. Planché).

DUBLIN 29 September 1868 (in Italian).

CAMBRIDGE 1 December 1911 (new English version by E. J. Dent).

STOCKHOLM 30 May 1812 (in Swedish, translated by H. A. Kullberg).

COPENHAGEN 23 March 1816 (in Danish, translated by N. T. Bruun, the second act only; both acts 30 January 1826 in Danish, 20 May 1826 in German; concert performances of the first act already 24 February 1798 and 14 May 1801.

MILAN, SC. 15 April 1816 (in Italian; revived there as late as 12 May 1923).

BUCHAREST 1818 (in German).

BRUSSELS August 1829 (in German, by the Aachen company coming from Paris).

BRUSSELS 10 February 1880 (in French, the Paris 1865 version).

BRUSSELS 20 December 1912 (new French version by J. G. Prod'homme and J. Kienlin).

NEW YORK 17 April 1833 (in English, adapted by C. E. Horn); 23 January 1855 (in German); 21 November 1859 (in Italian).

H. C. Lahee (*Annals of Music in America*) records a performance of *Die Zauberflöte* at Philadelphia as early as 7 March 1832. This statement, given without reference, has been taken over by many writers including J. G. Prod'homme, and A. Einstein (in the third edition of Köchel's *Verzeichnis*). No such performance can be substantiated from the books dealing with the history of the Philadelphia stage, not even from the daily account book of the Philadelphia theatre as edited by R. D. James in 1932.

HELSINKI 15 April 1841 (in German) and 12 January 1877 (in Finnish, translated by A. Törneroos).

CLAUSENBURG 3 December 1843 (in Hungarian, translated by E. Pály; parts only); the whole opera, Budapest 17 February 1877, translated by G. Böhm). An earlier Hungarian version by S. László had been published in 1804. Since 1913, a modern translation by Z. Harsányi has been used.

ANTWERP 14 March 1896 (in Flemish).

ZAGREB 18 February 1899 (in Croatian, translated by A. Harambašić).

MONTE CARLO 26 March 1921 (in Italian).

BUENOS AIRES 16 May 1923 (in Italian).

RIGA 28 November 1923 (in Lettish).

BARCELONA 15 January 1925 (in German); Catalan translation by J. Pena published on that occasion.

LJUBLJANA 22 December 1927 (in Slovenian).

SOFIA 1 May 1931 (in Bulgarian, translated by B. Danovsky).

A performance in Egypt, at the Pyramids, took place in April 1912 (produced by K. Guttenberger-Peler).

BEFFROY DE REIGNY:
Les deux Nicodèmes ou Les Français dans la Planète de Jupiter

21 November. Paris, Th. Feydeau

Text by the composer. Two acts.

A sequel to his *Nicodème* (see 1790); after a few nights banned by the police for political reasons. Other sequels were *Le vrai Nicodème* (1791); *Les trois Nicodèmes* (1791); *Nicodème aux Enfers* (1792). For details see C. Westercamp's monograph on Beffroy de Reigny (1930).

DALAYRAC: *Philippe et Georgette*

28 December. Paris, C.I.

Text by J. M. Boutet de Monvel. One act.

Given in Paris until 1827.

In French also, Ghent 1794; Brussels 8 June 1795; Cologne 1796–97; St. Petersburg 30 April 1800; Hanover 31 December 1803; Moscow 1 October 1808; Vienna 30 July 1809.

In Dutch (translated by A. C. Brinkman), Amsterdam 1796.

In German (translated by C. A. Herklots), Hamburg 2 October 1798; revived Berlin 14 February 1805 (new German version by A. W. Schlegel, who is mentioned as the translator in *A.M.Z.*; with additions by B. A. Weber).

In Danish (translated by E. de Falsen), Copenhagen 9 April 1799.

In Swedish (translated by J. D. Valerius), Stockholm 28 January 1800.

1792

CIMAROSA: *Il Matrimonio segreto*

7 February. Vienna, B.

Text by G. Bertati (founded on *The Clandestine Marriage*, by G. Colman and D. Garrick, 1766). Two acts.

Cimarosa's most successful work. Apart from Mozart, the only Italian opera buffa between Pergolesi and Rossini which is still in the repertory in Italy as well as in other countries. The first opera Cimarosa wrote for Vienna after his return from Russia. It is said to have been repeated the same night on the Emperor Leopold II's special request.

Given at Vienna 133 times until 1884. In Italian also Prague 1792; Leipzig 20 June 1792; Dresden 3 October 1792; Monza December 1792 (for the first time in Italy); Milan, Sc. 17 February 1793 and all over Italy; given at Palermo 1793 and Siena Carnival 1795 as *Lo Sposalizio segreto;* given at Turin Autumn 1803 as *Il Matrimonio notturno.* Barcelona 22 May 1793; Madrid 21 September 1793 (revived 1 May 1878); Lisbon Summer 1794 (revived 17 November 1868). London 11 January 1794 (revived 21 April 1798, 25 January 1803, 10 May 1814, 30 May 1818, 16 July 1829; H.M.'s 14 July 1842 and 14 June 1849; C.G. 21 June 1849; H.M.'s 23 June 1860, Ly. 14 February 1871, etc.). Trieste 15 March 1794; Ljubljana Summer 1794; St. Petersburg 1794 or 20 February 1795 (revived Carnival 1850); Charlottenburg 2 October 1796. Paris, Th.I. 10 May 1801 (given there 332 times until 1872). Amsterdam 1806 and Carnival 1808. Mexico December 1831; New York 4 January 1834; Philadelphia 17 April 1834; Berlin, Kgst. 26 June 1841; Bucharest 1847; Calcutta 1870 (libretto British Museum); Malta 1872.

In German: Berlin 5 November 1792 (translated by F. L.W. Meyer); Mannheim 18 August 1793 (translated by H. Beck); Hanover 28 May 1794; Passau 1794; Oels 21 May 1796; Weimar 3 December 1796 (translated by C. A. Vulpius); Cologne 1796–97; Budapest 30 August 1797; Munich 30 March 1798 (translated by K. L. Gieseke); Breslau 16 October 1798; Rostock 7 May 1801; Bremen 1803–04; Hamburg 28 December 1804; Vienna 10 June 1806 (for the first time there in German); Laibach 15 January 1811; Graz 26 March 1825 (translated by J. C. Grünbaum); Dresden 10 June 1849 (first time there in German); Stuttgart May 1850; Vienna 15 October 1850; Munich 6 April 1851, etc. (new German translation by A. Lewald, recitatives by Lindpaintner). **Another German translation, by C. Lebrün, was published 1838.**

In French (translated by P. L. Moline), Ghent 1793; Brussels 4 June 1798; Antwerp 27 December 1804; (translated by F. H. J. Castil-Blaze) Nîmes 1817; Strasbourg 6 October 1824; Hague October 1838; (translated by Moras and F. Santallier) Le Havre February 1862.

In Spanish (translated by L. F. Comella), Madrid 7 September 1795.

In Danish (translated by F. G. Sporon), Copenhagen 26 September 1797; revived 30 May 1854 (new translation by T. Overskou).

In Swedish (translated by C. Envallsson), Stockholm 11 February 1800; revived 1 December 1851 (new translation by C. W. A. Strandberg).

In Polish (translated by J. Adamczewski), Warsaw 27 December 1805; revived 21 November 1840 (new translation by K. K. Kurpiński).

In Dutch (translated from the French version by B. A. Fallee), Amsterdam 1808.

In Russian, St. Petersburg 24 May 1822.

In English (translated by H. F. Chorley), London, C.G. 1 November 1842 and Dublin 6 May 1843; (translated by W. Grist) London, Crystal Palace 13 December 1877.

In Czech (translated by B. Peška), Prague 17 December 1872.

Some revivals after 1880:

VIENNA 15 March 1884 (revised by J. N. Fuchs).

LONDON, SHAFTESBURY 12 November 1891 (in Italian), and St. George's Hall, 25 November 1896 (in English).

ST. PETERSBURG 29 September 1895 (in Russian, translated by N. Yurin).

HAMBURG 11 May 1909 (new German version by T. Rehbaum, music revised by W. Kleefeld).

BUENOS AIRES 12 August 1911 (in Italian).

PRAGUE 22 April 1914 (in Czech).

MONTE CARLO 16 March 1916 (in Italian).

BARCELONA 9 November 1916 (in Italian).

PARIS, TR.L. 12 March 1921 and O.C. 10 October 1931 (new French version by D. Muller).

BIRMINGHAM 20 June 1921 (new English version by R. Gatty).

LONDON, COURT TH. 26 June 1928 (English version by R. Gatty).

BASLE 22 March 1927 (new German version by L. Jansen)

BERLIN 6 October 1928 (in German, Jansen's version).

WASHINGTON 23 April 1933 (at the Juilliard School of Music; in English, Gatty's version, recitatives by A. Stœssel).

BUCHAREST in or before 1934–35 (in Rumanian).

NEW YORK, M. January 1937 (Gatty's version).

SCHALL: *Kinafarerne*
(Travellers to China)

2 March. Copenhagen

Text by P. A. Heiberg. Two acts.

Successful at Copenhagen; given there until 1830.

GAVEAUX: *L'Amour filial*

7 March. Paris, Th. Feydeau

Text by C. A. Demoustier. One act.

Gaveaux's first opera, originally called *Les deux Suisses*, sub-title *La Jambe de Bois*. Successful in Paris.

In French also, Brussels 29 June 1795; Rotterdam July 1795; Cologne 1795–96; Wilna 18 June 1802; Hanover 26 April 1804; Berne 3 June 1809; Moscow 7 August 1809. Revived Liége 20 February 1814 (as *Les deux Suisses*).

In German (translated by C. A. Herklots), Berlin 16 October 1796; Hamburg 1796, etc.

In Danish (translated by R. Frankenau), Copenhagen 31 October 1797.

In Spanish, Madrid 25 December 1802 (probably Gaveaux's opera).

In Swedish, Stockholm 24 June 1807 (advertised as by Dalayrac).

In Polish (translated by Sekolowski), Warsaw 1808.

In Flemish, Oudenarde 1795.

There are printed Dutch versions by G. Brender à Brandis and by J. C. van Son, both 1799. Revived in Dutch at The Hague as late as 1832.

MÉHUL: *Stratonice*

3 May. Paris, C.I.

Text by F. B. Hoffman (*comédie-héroïque*). One act.

Revived at the O. 20 March 1821 (recitatives by Méhul's nephew, Louis Joseph Daussoigne). Given in Paris until 1827.

In French also, Lyons 1792; Brussels 15 August 1796 (the second version 16 August 1825); Cologne 1796–97; St. Petersburg 1798; Berne 19 July 1810; Moscow 22 December 1810.

In German (translated by C. A. Herklots), Berlin 23 August 1815.

In Russian (translated by F. F. Kokoshkin), St. Petersburg 1 May 1820.

A parody by J. B. D. Desprès and J. A. P. de Ségur, called *Nice*, was produced at the Th. du Vaudeville, Paris 6 June 1792.

PAISIELLO: *I Giuochi d'Agrigento*

16 May. Venice, F.

Text by A. Pepoli. Three acts.

Written for the opening of the new "Teatro la Fenice." Also given at London 5 February 1793 and Lisbon 4 November 1799. Revived Venice, F. 7 February 1801.

DEVIENNE: *Les Visitandines*

7 July. Paris, Th. Feydeau

Text by L. B. Picard. Three (produced in two) acts.

One of the most successful French operas of the revolution period.

Frequently revived in Paris, viz.:

O.C. 2 March 1825 (as *Le Pensionnat de jeunes Demoiselles*, text altered by J. B. C. Vial).

ODÉON 30 June 1825 (as *Les Français au Sérail*, text altered by H. Albertin).

TH. L. 11 February 1852; Folies Bergère 2 March 1872; Galerie Vivienne 11 November 1895; O.C. 15 May 1900; Th. L. 17 January 1920.

Outside France produced at:

GHENT 1793 (revived 1879).

BRUSSELS 23 August 1794; revived 27 September 1818 (as *Belfort et Euphémie*) and 25 April 1852.

COLOGNE 1796–97; Hamburg 1797; Brunswick 1801.

BERNE 24 June 1809.

ANTWERP 1 February 1827 (as *Le Pensionnat de jeunes Demoiselles*).

ST. PETERSBURG Spring 1805 (as *Belfort et Euphémie ou La Pension de Nevers*).

DUBLIN 1824 (as *Le Pensionnat de Nevers;* French-English libretto Allen A. Brown Collection, Boston).

In German (as *Die Heimsucherinnen*), Schleswig 10 March 1794 (translator unknown; libretto printed; see *Bibliotheca Danica*, Vol. IV, p.406); as *Liebe wagt alles* (translated by H. G. Schmieder), Hamburg 4 May 1798; (as *Die Herrnhutherinnen*), Vienna 26 November 1804; (as *Die Liebe im Kloster*, translated by C. A. Herklots), Berlin 3 October 1808.

In Swedish (translated by D. G. Björn), Stockholm 22 February 1794; Malmö 13 April 1807; Lund 3 August 1807.

In Dutch (translated by H. Ogelwight), Amsterdam 1796 (revived there 1799 and Hague 1814).

In Danish (translated by E. de Falsen), Copenhagen 5 May 1797 (given there until 1854).

In Spanish (as *La Quinta de Escorondón*), Madrid 24 June 1803.

An anonymous parody, *Les Putins cloîtrées*, was published 1793 and 1796.

STEGMANN: *Heinrich der Löwe*

15 July. Frankfort

Text by H. G. Schmieder (*Ein allegorisches Singspiel*). Two acts.

Written for the coronation of the Emperor Francis II. Also given at Vienna, W. 23 August 1792; Hamburg 2 February and 2 March 1794 (in concert form).

Revived Königsberg 1802 and November 1823 (with new dialogue by Struve).

ZINGARELLI: *Il Mercato di Monfregoso*

22 September. Milan, Sc.

Text: an altered and reduced version of Goldoni's *Il Mercato di Malmantile* (see 1757). Two acts.

Zingarelli's best comic opera; last revived in Italy: Milan, Sc. September 1801; Naples, Fondo 9 October 1803.

In Italian also given at Prague 1793; Vienna 13 June 1793; Leipzig Summer 1793; Barcelona 14 May 1794; Lisbon Summer 1795; Madrid Spring 1796.

In German (as *Der Jahrmarkt von Woltershausen*, translated by J. F. Schlotterbeck), Stuttgart Summer 1804.

NASOLINI: *Eugenia*

13 October. Venice, S. Ben.

Text by G. M. Foppa (from Beaumarchais's drama). Three acts.

Outside Italy given at Dresden Carnival 1794; Lisbon Autumn 1794; Barcelona 12 November 1794; Madrid 9 December 1795.

PAER: *Il Tempo fa Giustizia a tutti*

Autumn. Parma

Text by A. Brambilla. Two acts.

The first of Paer's operas which had a greater success.

Given at Piacenza Spring 1793, Padua 26 December 1793 and Genoa, T. Falcone Carnival 1797 as *Le Astuzie amorose* and all over North Italy. Also Corfu Carnival 1795.

Revived (as *La Locanda dei Vagabondi*) Modena, T. Rangoni 20 July 1804; Barcelona 20 November 1806; Bologna 26 December 1809; Dresden 1813; and once more Florence, T. degli Arrischiati 30 April 1872.

PAISIELLO: *L'Elfrida*

4 November. Naples, S.C.

Text by R. de' Calzabigi. Two acts.

Given in a new version, with a happy instead

of a tragic end, at Bologna Carnival 1796 and (as *(Adelvolto)* Verona Carnival 1797.

In Italian also given at Madrid 25 August 1794; Trieste October 1797; Corfu Carnival 1798; London 19 May 1798 (last revised 6 February 1813); Lisbon 17 December 1804.

In German (translated by J. O. H. Schaum), Berlin 16 October 1802.

STORACE: *The Pirates*

21 November. London, Little Hm.

Text by J. Cobb. Three acts.

Again, as in his *No Song, no Supper* (see 1790), Storace used parts of his *Equivoci* music, but also introduced a quintet from Guglielmi's *La bella Pescatrice* (according to Kelly) and airs by Anfossi and Bianchi (according to Parke); the additions are not indicated in the printed score.

Revived with additional music by Braham, Cooke, Mercadante and Balducci, orchestration revised by Cooke, London, D.L. 29 November 1827 as *Isidore de Merida; or, The Devil's Creek;* this version was also given in New York on 9 June 1828 (music arranged by C. E. Horn).

(Date of first performance verified from the newspapers; Genest has 11 November, Kelly 20 November.)

1793

DALAYRAC: *Ambroise* ou *Voilà ma Journée*

12 January. Paris, C.I.

Text by J. M. Boutet de Monvel. One act.

Successful in Paris; given at the O.C. until 1827.

In French also, St. Petersburg 26 October 1793; Brussels 15 February 1796 (revived 7 December 1840); Hanover 16 August 1803; Moscow 15 October 1808; Berne 17 July 1809; Vienna 26 August 1826.

In German, Vienna, W. 6 March 1812.

In Russian (translated by P. N. Kobyakov),

St. Petersburg 19 December 1809 and Moscow 10 November 1814.

In Swedish (translated by C. G. Nordforss), Stockholm 11 December 1812; Gothenburg 14 June 1816.

In Dutch (translated by C. Vreedenberg), Amsterdam 1816.

LESUEUR: *La Caverne*

16 *February*. Paris, Th. Feydeau

Text by P. Dercy (founded on an episode in Lesage's *Gil Blas*). Three acts.

One of the earliest examples of "bandit" opera, a species characteristic of that period. According to H. Kretzschmar, *La Caverne* is ". . . vielleicht dasjenige Kunstwerk, das uns den tiefsten Blick auf Geist und Herz der Schreckenszeit gestattet. Es gibt keine zweite Oper mit solch dumpfängstlicher Stimmung, solcher fieberhaften Erregung und solcher wilden Energie".

In French also, Liége 2 September 1795; Brussels 18 December 1795; Rotterdam 9 November 1796; Cologne 1796–97; Brunswick Spring 1804; St. Petersburg May 1805; Moscow 28 October 1809; Cassel May 1812.

Dutch translation by P.G. van Witsen Geysbeek published 1799.

In German, Vienna, W. 14 June 1803 (as *Die Höhle bey Cosiro*, translated by J. von Seyfried) and Kä. 24 June 1803 (as *Die Räuberhöhle*, translated by K. F. Lippert); Berlin 29 June 1807; Stuttgart 1817 (as *Alfonso und Seraphine*); Prague Summer 1819. Another translation by H. G. Schmieder, *Die Räuberhöhle*, published Hamburg 1804.

In Russian (translated by N. V. Vsevolozhsky), St. Petersburg 10 August 1818; Moscow 6 May 1819 (with additional music by Maurer).

SCHULZ: *Indtoget* (Entry)

26 *February*. Copenhagen

Text by P. A. Heiberg. Two acts.

Given at Copenhagen 49 times until 1827.

MÉHUL: *Le jeune Sage et le vieux Fou*

28 *March*. Paris, O.C.[1]

Text by F. B. Hoffman. One act.

In French also, Liége 30 September 1795; Cologne 1796–97; Brussels 1 March 1799, etc.

In Swedish (translated by C. G. Nordforss), Stockholm 9 October 1805.

In Russian, St. Petersburg January 1812.

Revived at the Arts Theatre Club, London 8 May 1929 (as *There's no Fool like a young Fool*, English version by H. Graham).

PORTUGAL: *La Confusione nata dalla Somiglianza* ossiano *I due Gobbi*

Spring. Rome, Pallacorda

Text by C. Mazzini (founded on a comedy by L. Del Buono). Two acts.

The first great success of Portugal, the only Portuguese composer whose (Italian) operas were given all over Europe. Milan, Sc. 14 February 1796, etc.

In Italian also, Dresden 4 December 1793; Trieste 14 January 1794 (revived Spring 1815); Barcelona 16 June 1794; Vienna 28 June 1794; Prague 1794; Corfu 26 December 1794; London 15 March 1796; St. Petersburg 1798; Cagliari, Sardinia Autumn 1802; Amsterdam 1806.

In German (translated by C. A. Herklots), Berlin 3 August 1795; Hamburg 6 May 1796, etc. Another German version (by K. L. Gieseke) was used at Budapest 25 March 1801 and Graz 24 January 1803. Given on German stages until 1819: Herklots's translation, Hanover 25 July 1819; Gieseke's translation, Nuremberg 29 November 1819.

The opera does not seem to have been given at Lisbon, the composer's native town.

[1] On 11 February 1793 the Paris "Comédie-Italienne" takes the new name of Théâtre de l'Opéra-Comique National" under which it becomes now generally known. Between 1783 and 1801 it was also often called "Salle Favart" or "Théâtre de la Rue Favart" as different from the rival house in Rue Feydeau (late "Théâtre de Monsieur"). In 1801 the two companies were amalgamated.

KUNZEN: *Die Weinlese*

3 May. Frankfort

Text by J. J. Ihlee. Three acts.

The most successful work of the German-Danish composer.

In German also given at Prague 1794; Hamburg 28 August 1795; Breslau 11 November 1796; Hanover 31 July 1797; Bremen September 1797; Oels 2 December 1797; St. Petersburg 1803; Berne April 1804; Berlin 16 November 1807, etc. Revived (in a reduced 2-act version) Berlin, Kgst. 28 June 1825; Leipzig 2 August 1826.

In Danish (as *Vinhøsten eller Hvem fører Bruden hjem*, translated by R. Frankenau), Copenhagen 22 December 1796 (given there until 1832).

CIMAROSA: *I Traci amanti*

19 June. Naples, T.N.

Text by G. Palomba. Two acts.

Successful in Italy; given at Padua 6 October 1795 as *Il Padre alla Moda;* another alternative title was, according to Cambiasi, *Lo Sbarco di Mustanzir*). In Italy given until 1818. Outside Italy: Madrid 15 July 1794; Lisbon Carnival 1796 (as *Gli Turchi amanti*); London 16 February 1796; Dresden 1796; Vienna 30 April 1800; Paris 31 November 1809 (according to the libretto; Castil-Blaze gives 22 November 1809).

(Date of first performance according to the autograph score at Naples).

STEIBELT: *Roméo et Juliette*

10 September. Paris, Th. Feydeau

Text by J. A. P. de Ségur. Three acts.

Steibelt's most successful work (particularly popular in Russia, where Steibelt succeeded Boieldieu as conductor of the French opera company in 1811). Last revived in Paris, O.C. 19 January 1822.

In French also, Liége 29 November 1796; Cologne 1796–97; Brussels 17 March 1799 (revived 14 March 1815); St. Petersburg 1809; Moscow 28 May 1810; New Orleans 6 August 1810.

In Danish (translated by N. T. Bruun), Copenhagen 18 April 1806 (previously given there in French, 1798, in concert form).

In Russian (translated by A. G. Volkov), Moscow 2 January 1809; St. Petersburg 19 September 1817.

In Swedish (translated by C. G. Nordforss), Stockholm 30 January 1815.

In German, St. Petersburg 16 February 1818.

(This opera was the first in which a Chinese gong was used in the orchestra.)

ARNOLD: *The Children in the Wood*

1 October. London, Little Hm.

Text by T. Morton. Two acts.

Successful on English stages and Dublin 10 February 1794; Philadelphia 24 November 1794 (given there until 1833; additional music by B. Carr; New York 26 December 1794 (with additional music by B. Carr), etc.

W. MÜLLER: *Das Neusonntagskind*

10 October. Vienna, Leop.

Text by C. Perinet (founded on P. Hafner's comedy *Der Furchtsame*, 1774). Two acts.

Very successful all over Austria and Germany: Graz 20 February 1794; Pressburg 3 April 1794; Budapest 21 April 1794; Salzburg Autumn 1794, etc.; also Nuremberg 1794 and Mayence 1795 (as *Der Geisterseher*); adapted for the North German stage by E. Grossmann, Hamburg 3 February 1795; Hanover 3 July 1795; Bremen 20 October 1795; Weimar 29 March 1796 (text altered by C. A. Vulpius); Berlin 6 May 1796; Mannheim 26 February 1797; Oels 18 March 1797; Breslau August 1797; Carlsruhe 16 March 1798; Aachen 9 May 1798; Munich 14 January 1800, etc.

The last (154th) Vienna performance was on 26 July 1829; given at Weimar as late as 11 March 1846; Würzburg 20 February 1849; Berlin, Fr.W. 24 May 1852; Breslau 29 April 1862.

In German also, Rotterdam Spring 1796; Temesvar 22 November 1801; Paris, Th. de la Cité 25 November 1801; Berne Spring 1804; Poznán

16 September 1805 (as *Der Geisterseher*); St. Petersburg 1808; Moscow 9 September 1820.

In Dutch (translated by G. C. de Greuve), Amsterdam 1799; (translated by G. Vreedenberg) Amsterdam 1813 and Hague 1829.

In Polish (translated by W. Boguslawski), Warsaw 1802.

WINTER: *I Fratelli Rivali*

November. Venice, S. Ben.

Text by M. Butturini. Two acts.

In Italian also given at Prague 25 October 1794; Dresden October 1795 (revived September 1816); Vienna 16 November 1795; Madrid 30 May 1797; London 18 February 1800.

In German (translated by M. Stegmayer), Frankfort 1798; Mannheim 15 September 1799; (translated by F. X. Girzik) Budapest 11 May 1800, etc. Revived Munich 16 July 1819; Stuttgart 1820.

BOIELDIEU: *La Fille coupable*

2 November. Rouen

Text by J. F. A. Boieldieu, the father of the composer. Two acts.

Boieldieu's first opera. Score preserved.

SCHULZ: *Peters Bryllup*
(Peter's Wedding)

12 December. Copenhagen

Text by T. Thaarup. Two acts.

Given at Copenhagen until 1835.

1794

PORTUGAL: *Lo Spazzacamino Principe*

4 January. Venice, S. Moisè

Text by G. M. Foppa (founded on a French comedy by Maurin de Pompigny, 1785). One act.

One of Portugal's most successful works. Given at Lisbon later in the same year (1794) in Portuguese (as *O Basculho da Chaminé*) and 27 May 1799 in Italian.

In Italian also given at Dresden Spring 1794; Vienna 5 September 1795; Barcelona 6 May 1796; Bastia, Corsica Spring 1797; St. Petersburg 22 November 1797; Ljubljana Spring 1799; London 17 June 1800. Last revived Milan 14 March 1819.

In Russian (translated by I. A. Dmitrevsky), Moscow 26 November 1798 (revived 3 November 1808).

In German (as *Schornsteinfeger Peter*, in a 2-act version by C. A. Zschiedrisch), Dresden 22 May 1799; Hamburg 9 May 1800, etc.; Warsaw 1810.

WEIGL: *La Principessa d'Amalfi*

10 January. Vienna, B.

Text by G. Bertati. Two acts.

Weigl's first greater success. Haydn wrote to the young composer on 11 January: ". . . da molto tempo non ò ascoltato musica con più attenzione che la sua *Principessa di Amalfi* di ieri: chiara di pensiero, alta, piena di sentimento; in poche parole, un capolavoro".

In Italian also given at Prague 1794; Leipzig 15 June 1794; Dresden 13 December 1794; Charlottenburg 19 June 1796; Milan, Sc. April 1803; Paris 14 November 1805; Venice, F. Autumn 1807, etc.

In German (translated by F. X. Girzik), Budapest 28 April 1795; (translated by C. A. Vulpius) Weimar 6 January 1798; revived Graz 2 March 1807.

PORTUGAL: *Demofoonte*

8 February. Milan, Sc.

Metastasio's text (first set to music by Caldara in 1733). Three acts.

In a reduced 2-act version given at Lisbon 15 August 1808 (revived 25 April 1819) and Rio de Janeiro 17 December 1811 (as one of the first operas ever produced there).

STEFANI: *Cud, czyli Krakowiaki i*
Gorale

1 March. Warsaw

Text by W. Boguslawski. Two acts.

(The title means: *The Miracle; or, The Craco-vians and the Mountain-Folk.*)

For a contemporary account see J. G. Seume's *Einige Nachrichten über die Vorfälle in Polen im Jahr 1794,* 1796, pp.15–17.

Very successful in Poland; given at Warsaw 144 times until 1859. Lemberg 1796; Poznán 7 July 1801; Cracow 22 September 1809. A sequel, *Zabobon (Superstition),* mostly called *Nowe Kra-kowiacy* (3 acts, text by J. N. Kaminski, music by Kurpiński) was first produced at Warsaw in 1816; also Lemberg 22 November 1816 (in Polish) and 11 March 1829 (in German, translated by F. Pohlenburg); Wilna 25 September 1827, etc. This sequel was, since 1826, often performed on the same bill with the original. Revived at Warsaw as late as 8 March 1913 (second part) and 24 July 1929 (first part).

Also produced (in Polish) at the Exhibition Th., Vienna 11 September 1892.

HEWITT: *Tammanny; or, The*
Indian Chief

3 March. New York, John Street Th.

Text by A. J. Hatton. Three acts.

One of the earliest American operas. Given at New York 13 March 1795 in a reduced 2-act version as *America rediscovered.* Also Philadelphia 18 October 1794; Boston 4 January 1796. Music lost. Of the text, the lyrics only are extant.

W. MÜLLER: *Die Schwestern*
von Prag

11 March. Vienna, Leop.

Text by C. Perinet (founded on P. Hafner's comedy *Die reisenden Comödianten,* 1774). Two acts.

Even more popular than his *Neusonntagskind* (see 1793), given on every German stage; Nurem-berg 1794–96; Salzburg Spring 1795; Cologne,

Aachen, Düsseldorf and Crefeld 1797; Hamburg Carnival 1799–1800; Oels 6 July 1799; Berlin 24 March 1800, etc.

In German also Budapest 9 October 1794; Pressburg 15 January 1795; Schleswig 1798; Te-mesvar 29 November 1801; Agram 2 May 1802; Poznán 12 August 1804; St. Petersburg 1808; Prague Carnival 1809; Moscow 3 February 1821; Gothenburg 26 December 1827; Helsinki 28 March 1838; New York 30 November 1859.

In Hungarian (translated by P. J. Kotsi), Clau-senburg 16 February 1803; Budapest 17 February 1808.

In Polish (translated by J. Drozdowski), Warsaw 1803; Wilna 1808

In Russian (translated by A. I. Sheller), St. Pe-tersburg 10 October 1814; Moscow 11 December 1817.

In Dutch, Hague 1830.

Some of the latest revivals were at Hamburg 12 April 1849; Berlin 16 March 1852; Vienna 8 January 1859; Munich 31 December 1863; Kö-nigsberg 26 January 1870.

A *Nachgestaltung* by C. Czarniawski was pub-lished in 1935 (produced Baden, near Vienna June 1935).

Beethoven used the air *Ich bin der Schneider Ka-kadu* from this opera for his Variations, op.121a (1824).

GAVEAUX: *La Famille indigente*

24 March. Paris, Th. Feydeau

Text by B. A. Planterre (*Fait historique, mêlé de Chant,* founded on an idyl by S. Gessner). One act.

In French also, Brussels 8 February 1796; Rot-terdam 2 September 1796; Cologne 1796–97, etc.

In Danish (translated by N. T. Bruun), Co-penhagen 17 September 1802.

ZINGARELLI: *Gerusalemme distrutta*

Lent. Florence, P.

Text by A. S. Sografi. Two acts.

Revived Florence, T. de' Infocuati 27 Novem-ber 1803 as *La Distruzione di Gerusalemme.* Revived in 1807 for a private performance at Casa Lante, Rome, and revived Rome, T. Valle 14 March 1810; Naples, T. Fondo 1811; Milan, Sc. 22 February 1812, etc.

In Italian also at Paris 4 May 1811 and Vienna, W. 22 May 1817.

In German (translated by F. K. Hiemer), Stuttgart 6 November 1814; Darmstadt November 1815.

ISOUARD: *L'Avviso ai Maritati*

Spring. Florence, P.

Text by F. Gonella. Three acts.

The first opera of the Maltese composer. Successful in Italy; given also at Lisbon 1794; Dresden Carnival 1795; Madrid 2 August 1795.

CIMAROSA: *Le Astuzie femminili*

16 August. Naples, Fondo

Text by G. Palomba (for unknown reasons Riemann, Clément-Larousse, Nicoll and others name Metastasio (!) as the author of the libretto). Two acts.

Successful in Italy; first given at Milan, Sc. 12 March 1803.

Outside Italy given at Barcelona 12 September 1795; Lisbon 2 December 1797; Paris 21 October 1802; London 21 February 1804.

In German (translated by C. A. Herklots), Berlin 9 September 1799.

Revived Naples, T. Filarmonico 10 February 1871 (text revised by E. Golisciani, recitatives by C. Rossi) and London, C.G. 15 July 1871; Bologna, T. Brunetti Summer 1871; Florence, T. Arrischiati Autumn 1871; Paris 5 February 1874; Rome, Capr. November 1878; Florence, T. Niccolini 14 January 1893.

Again revived (orchestrated by O. Respighi; produced by Diaghilev, as an opera-ballet, choreography by Massine) Paris, O. 27 May 1920; London, C.G. 22 June 1920; Naples 30 May 1921; Monte Carlo 24 December 1923; Florence, P. 20 May 1939.

(Date of first performance according to the autograph score at Naples.)

ANDREOZZI: *La Principessa Filosofa ossia Il Contravveleno*

6 October. Venice, S. Ben.

Text by A. S. Sografi (*Commedia ridotta ad uso melodrammatico*). Two acts.

The most popular of Andreozzi's numerous operas (a list of which will be found in *R.M.I.*, Vol. XVI, p.263).

Outside Italy given at Madrid 5 October 1797; Lisbon Summer 1800; London 5 May 1801 (text altered by S. Buonaiuti).

SÜSSMAYR: *Der Spiegel von Arkadien*

14 November. Vienna, W.

Text by E. Schikaneder. Two acts.

The most successful work of Mozart's pupil and one of the best achievements of the German "Zauber-Oper". In Vienna given 113 times until 1804; last revived there 26 August 1826.

In German also given at Pressburg 12 September 1795; Frankfort 20 September 1795; Passau 1796; Hamburg Summer 1796; Berlin 3 August 1796; Munich March 1797; Hanover 2 June 1797; Bremen October 1797; Salzburg, Cologne, Düsseldorf and Crefeld 1797; Aachen May 1798, etc. Also Lemberg 1797; Schleswig and Budapest 1800; Paris, Th. de la Cité 29 November 1801; Temesvar 14 January 1802; Berne 1803; Warsaw 3 November 1804; Poznán 18 November 1804; St. Petersburg 1804; given at Weimar 2 February 1796 as *Die neuen Arkadier* (text altered by C. A. Vulpius).

In Italian (!), Prague 7 September 1795 (in German there 9 March 1809).

In Russian, St. Petersburg 5 May 1814; Moscow 7 May 1818.

There are also printed French (by F. G. Haussner, 1801) and Polish (by W. Kratzer, n.d.) versions.

CHERUBINI: *Elisa* ou *Le Voyage au Mont-Bernard*

13 December. Paris, Th. Feydeau

Text by J. A. de Révéroni Saint-Cyr. Two acts.

Like *Lodoïska* (see 1791), more successful in Germany than in France.

In German (translated by C. A. Herklots), Berlin 10 October 1799; Vienna, W. 18 December 1802; Budapest 16 September 1805, etc.

In Spanish, Madrid 10 February 1803.

In Russian, Moscow 1803; St. Petersburg 10 October 1814.

Revived in an abridged German version (by E. Pasqué and F. Langer) as a prologue to *Les deux Journées* (see 1800), Mannheim 25 March 1903.

LEAL MOREIRA: *A Vingança da Cigana* (The Gipsy's Vengeance)

December. Lisbon, S.C.

Text by "Lereno Secinuntino, Arcade Romano" (pseudonym of the Brazilian poet Domingos Caldas Barbosa). One act.

This *drama jocoserio* was the first opera which was sung in Portuguese at the new Theatro San Carlos, Lisbon (opened 30 June 1793). Score preserved.

STORACE: *The Cherokee*

20 December. London, D.L.

Text by J. Cobb. Three acts.

Given at Boston 24 June 1799. Revived London, D.L. 30 April 1802 as *Algonah*, with additional music by M. Kelly (see his *Reminiscences*, Vol. II, p.79, where he erroneously gives 20 November as the date of the first performance; and Vol. II, p.188, where he simply says "The drama by Cobb, the music by myself", without even mentioning the fact that *Algonah* was only a new version of his friend Storace's *The Cherokee*.

The opera was lately revived at Leeds 27 October 1926 (score arranged by A. Tyrer).

CIMAROSA: *Penelope*

26 December. Naples, Fondo

Text by G. M. Diodati. Two acts.

Successful in Italy; also given at Lisbon 30 September 1804; Paris 8 May 1815 (according to the libretto; Castil-Blaze gives 31 December 1815);

London 11 January 1817 (Giuditta Pasta's London début); St. Petersburg 21 November 1818.

1795

MARTIN Y SOLER: *La Scola de Maritati*

27 January. London, Hm.

Text by L. da Ponte. Two acts.

Date of the first performance verified from the newspapers; Sonneck gives 17 May 1794 (the date of the London production of *Il Burbero di buon Cuore*). According to most authorities since Fétis, this opera had been originally produced at St. Petersburg about 1788 under the title of *Gli Sposi in Contrasto*. In fact, there is no record of its ever having been given in Russia (see also R. A. Mooser in *R.M.I.*, Vol. XL, 1936, p.441), and no reason to doubt Da Ponte's statement that he wrote the libretto in and for London within three weeks.

Subsequently given, under the original title or as *La Capricciosa corretta*, at Venice, S. Moisè 5 October 1795; Crema 26 December 1795; Genoa and Bologna Spring 1796; Florence, P. 7 May 1796 (revived Spring 1811); Milan, Sc. 7 June 1796; Turin and Udine 1796; Palermo 1797; Padua Autumn 1797; Naples, T. Fondo 1798; Ancona 1798; Rome February 1800; Brescia Summer 1806, etc.

In Italian also:

DRESDEN 1796 (as *La Capricciosa corretta*).

VIENNA 11 October 1796 (as *Gli Sposi in Contrasto*).

MADRID 16 April 1797 (as *La Capricciosa corretta*).

LISBON Summer 1797 (as *La Capricciosa corretta*).

PRAGUE 20 January 1802 (as *La Capricciosa corretta*).

PARIS 2 June 1806 (as *La Moglie corretta*); revived 25 March 1815.

AMSTERDAM 1807 (as *La Moglie corretta*).

Revived in London 26 January 1798 and 14 July 1801.

In German (first?), Bautzen 28 January 1798; Weimar 25 May 1799 (translation revised by C. A. Vulpius; as *Die Eigensinnige*); revived Frankfort 1824.

DALAYRAC: *Adèle et Dorsan*

27 April. Paris, O.C.

Text by B. J. Marsollier. Three acts.

In French also, Liége 8 November 1798; Brussels 25 October 1799; St. Petersburg 1800, Berne 8 May 1802. Reduced to 2 acts Paris, Fey. 8 October 1801.

WEDEL: *Serenaden* eller *De sorte Naeser*

(The Serenade or The black Noses)

15 May. Copenhagen

Text by C. H. Pram. Three acts.

The most successful of Wedel's three "Syngestykke"; given at Copenhagen until 1804.

MARTIN Y SOLER: *L'Isola del Piacere*

26 May. London, Hm.

Text by L. da Ponte. Two acts.

Unsuccessful in London, given three times only. On the second night (28 May) an intermezzo, *Le Nozze de Contadini Spagnoli*, was introduced. Revived in London 11 June 1801.

In Italian also given at Venice, S. Moisè 23 January 1797 (as *L'Isola piacevole*); Florence, T. in Via Santa Maria and Udine Summer 1797, etc.; Madrid 25 July 1799 (in Italian) and 3 October 1801 (in Spanish, translated by L. F. Comella); Lisbon 26 January 1801 (in Italian).

In German:

VIENNA, W. 26 April 1800 (as *Die Insel der Liebe*, translated by M. Stegmayer; additions by I. von Seyfried; also Leop. 21 October 1809).

BUDAPEST *c.*1800 (as *Die Insel der Liebe*, translated by M. Stegmayer).

AACHEN 9 August 1802 (as *Die Insel der Liebe*).

MANNHEIM 12 December 1802 (as *Die Entdeckungsfahrer*, translated by S. G. = Stefan Grua?).

LEIPZIG 24 October 1804 (as *Das Liebesfest in Katalonien*, Stegmayer's translation).

HAMBURG 16 September 1805 (as *Das Fest der Liebe oder Die beiden Eifersüchtigen*).

In Hungarian (as *Szerelem Szigete*, translated by A. Láng), Neumarkt (Maros-Vásárhely) 10 August 1806 and Clausenburg 21 September 1806.

HOFFMEISTER: *Der Königssohn aus Ithaka*

27 June. Vienna, W.

Text by E. Schikaneder. Two acts.

The most successful of Hoffmeister's operas.

Given at Prague 5 April 1796 (revived 1824); Hamburg 26 January 1797 (very much altered); Weimar 11 February 1797 (as *Telemach, Prinz von Ithaka*, text revised by C. A. Vulpius); in German also, Budapest *c.*1800; Temesvar 16 December 1801.

In Polish (translated by W. Boguslawski), Warsaw 17 March 1803.

SALIERI: *Palmira, Regina di Persia*

14 October. Vienna, Kä.

Text by G. de Gamerra (from an intended French opera *La Princesse de Babylone*, by Martin after Voltaire, 1788). Two acts.

In Italian, Prague 1796; St. Petersburg 12 September 1796; Dresden 18 March 1797; Rome, T. Pallacorda Spring 1805.

In German (translated by J. J. Ihlee), Frankfort 7 April 1797; (translated by J. F. Schlotterbeck), Stuttgart 27 June 1797 (celebrating the arrival of the English Princess Charlotte Augusta Matilda, daughter of George III and married to King Frederick II of Württemberg); (translated by C. A. Herklots), Berlin 10 January 1798 (revived 15 October 1826); Budapest 20 August 1798; (translated by C. A. Vulpius), Weimar 2 March 1799; Altona 5 October 1799; Schleswig 1800; Hamburg 13 November 1801; (Ihlee's translation) Vienna, W. 24 February 1803 (revived 18 April 1815).

In Polish (translated by W. Boguslawski), Warsaw 1804; Wilna 1809.

Parts of the opera were revived in concert form at Leipzig on 1 March 1838.

S. PALMA: *La Pietra simpatica*

Autumn. Naples, Fior.

Text by G. B. Lorenzi (founded on Marmontel's tale, *Le Connoisseur*). Two acts.

The most successful of Palma's comic operas; "una poesia ed una musica geniale e dotta" (Napoli-Signorelli). Milan, Sc. 26 August 1797, etc. Given at Parma Autumn 1811, with additions by G. Alinovi.

In Italian also given at Vienna 6 May 1796; Barcelona 26 April 1798; Trieste 26 December 1798; Paris 30 June 1801 (with additions by M. Trento).

BRUNI: *Toberne* ou *Le Pêcheur suédois*

3 December. Paris, Th. Feydeau

Text by C. Patrat. Two acts.

In French also given at Brussels 29 June 1796; Hague September 1796; Cologne 1796–97; Berne 26 September 1801; Moscow 6 June 1809.

In German (translated by C. A. Herklots), Berlin 22 March 1797; Vienna, W. 14 March 1801; Hermannstadt 30 August 1804.

Dutch translation by H. Ogelwight published 1798.

In Swedish (translated by C. G. Nordforss), Stockholm 11 January 1798 at the Arsenal Th. and 9 November 1798 at the Royal Th. Given at Stockholm (where the opera was of special local appeal) until 1837. Also Malmö 27 June 1808.

In Russian (translated by P. N. Arapov), St. Petersburg 29 July 1822; Moscow 15 January 1823.

PAER: *L'Intrigo amoroso*

December. Venice, S. Moisè

Text by G. Bertati. Two acts.

In Italy also given as *Il Male vien dal Buco* (Ferrara 1797; Venice, S. Angelo 26 June 1797); *Saed ossia Il Serraglio* (Turin 1798); and *Gl'Intrighi del Serraglio ossia Il Male vien dal Bene* (Bologna 17 September 1797; Milan, Sc. 14 August 1800).

In Italian also Vienna 26 April 1798; Lisbon Summer 1798; Dresden 17 April 1799; Barcelona 13 June 1799; Prague 28 April 1802.

(It appears from the *Giornale dei Teatri di Venezia* that the opera was first produced about the middle of December, before the beginning of the Carnival stagione on 26 December, the date usually given.)

CIMAROSA: *I Nemici generosi*

26 December. Rome, Valle

Text (according to the Catalogue of the Cimarosa Exhibition, Vienna 1901) by F. Petrosellini. Originally in 2 acts.

Reduced to 1 act (as *Il Duello per Complimento*, Venice, S. Moisè 24 September 1797).

In Italian also, Vienna 2 July 1796 (revived 1 October 1804); Dresden 18 January 1797; Barcelona 9 December 1797; Corfu Carnival 1798; St. Petersburg 1798; Paris 9 August 1801 (revived 31 March 1808 and 17 February 1818); Cagliari, Sardinia Autumn 1805.

1796

GAVEAUX: *Le petit Matelot* ou *Le Mariage impromptu*

7 January. Paris, Th. Feydeau

Text by C. A. G. Pigault-Lebrun. One act.

Gaveaux's most popular work, a special favourite in Germany.

In French also, Brussels 28 August 1796; Hamburg 4 September 1797; St. Petersburg 5 December 1798; Berne December 1800; Hanover 18 September 1803. Given by French amateurs at Cape Town 11 October 1808.

In German (translated by C. A. Herklots), Berlin 20 May 1797; Oels 3 March 1798; Breslau 23 April 1798; Bremen Autumn 1798; Hamburg 1798; Krefeld 20 May 1799; Graz 1800; Munich March 1800; Vienna, W. 1801 and Kä. 29 June 1805; Berne 1803; Poznán 25 September 1805; Prague Summer 1810; given at Hamburg as late as in 1866.

In Swedish (translated by C. G. Nordforss), Stockholm 28 October 1799; Malmö 7 September 1806.

In Danish (translated by R. Frankenau), Copenhagen 10 November 1800 (given until 1832).

In Russian (translated by I. I. Valberkh), Moscow 1801; St. Petersburg Autumn 1808; revived Moscow 23 May 1809 in French, 6 March 1810 in Russian, and 25 September 1819 in German.

In Spanish (translated by V. R. de Arellano), Madrid 24 February 1802 and Mexico 1825.

In Dutch (translated by C. Vreedenberg), Amsterdam and Hague 1828.

Italian translation by G. Ricchi published 1805.

NASOLINI: *Merope*

21 January. Venice, S. Ben.

Text by M. Butturini. Three acts.

In Italian also, Trieste October 1799 (libretto altered by G. Artusi; revived there Spring 1808); London 28 March 1802 (as *Merope e Polifonte*, with Elizabeth Billington and Brigitta Banti; very successful; see Kelly's *Reminiscences*, II, p.186); Paris 21 December 1811 (Napoléon attended a command performance at his private Théâtre des Tuileries 1 December 1811); Munich 1 September 1812 (additional music by Poissl and Mayr; libretto reduced to 2 acts and adapted by J. Schlett).

Produced in a German version by F. K. Hiemer at Stuttgart 29 September 1813 and Frankfort June 1818 (with Nasolini's and Poissl's music).

MAYR: *Lodoiska*

26 January. Venice, F.

Text by F. Gonella. Three acts.

Successful in Italy; given at Milan, Sc. 26 December 1799 in a reduced 2-act version.

In Italy until 1819. In Italian also, Vienna 31 May 1798 (additional music by Weigl); Lisbon 4 November 1798; Dresden May 1802; Paris, Th. des Tuileries 16 April 1811.

ZINGARELLI: *Giulietta e Romeo*

30 January. Milan, Sc.

Text by G. M. Foppa (after Shakespeare). Three acts.

Zingarelli's most important work which kept the stage until *c.*1825–30, when Vaccai's and Bellini's operas on the same subject appeared. Given

at Leghorn 1807 with the sub-title *Le Tombe di Verona.*

In Italian also given at:

VIENNA 7 April 1797; (28 April 1804 with additions by Weigl; last revived there in 1830).

LISBON 1798.

TRIESTE November 1800.

PARIS, TH.I. 16 December 1812 (but previously at Napoléon's private Théâtre des Tuileries 9 March 1809).

BERLIN 30 July 1817.

MOSCOW 8 May 1819.

MUNICH August 1819 (with many additions by Winter).

LONDON 21 June 1824.

NEW YORK 26 July 1826.

BUENOS AIRES 3 August 1826.

In German, Bozen 1798; Berlin 7 August 1812 (translated by C. A. Herklots); Hamburg 28 March 1817; Munich 22 August 1819, etc.

In Polish, Wilna 22 April 1810.

STEGMANN: *Der Triumph der Liebe*

4 April. Hamburg

Text by E. F. Jester. Four acts.

(Sub-title in the printed vocal score *Das kühne Abentheuer.*)

The most successful of Stegmann's operas.

Revived Hamburg 24 November 1806 (as *Die Roseninsel*, libretto revised by K. L. Costenoble). Last given at Königsberg February 1821.

CARR: *The Archers*, or *Mountaineers of Switzerland*

18 April. New York, John Street, Th.

Text by W. Dunlap (dealing with the *William Tell* story; founded on an anonymous libretto, *Helvetic Liberty, or, The Lass of the Lakes*, published London 1792 and reprinted Philadelphia 1794). Three acts.

Given three times in New York and, in 1797, twice at Boston.

The first American opera of which parts of the music (three pieces) are extant.

SOLIÉ: *Le Secret*

20 April. Paris, O.C.

Text by F. B. Hoffman. One act.

Solié's most successful work.

In French also Brussels 10 October 1796, etc.; Cologne 1796–97; Hamburg 1797; Hanover 1803; Berne 19 February 1806; New Orleans 4 September 1808; Vienna 6 August 1809; Moscow 30 June 1810.

In German, Hamburg December 1799; Schleswig 1800; Bremen Autumn 1800; Hanover 17 April 1801; (translated by C. A. Herklots), Berlin 23 September 1803; (translated by C.A. Vulpius), Weimar 15 July 1805; (translated by M. Stegmayer), Budapest 1 January 1807; Munich 1807; Vienna, W. August 1808 (revived 8 October 1839); in German also Poznán 19 July 1804; Moscow 5 August 1819; Amsterdam 27 September 1824. Given on German stages until about 1860.

In Flemish, Oudenarde Winter 1797–98.

In Russian (translated by S. N. Glinka), Moscow 1799; St. Petersburg 23 October 1809.

In Dutch (translated by P. G. van Witsen Geysbeek), Amsterdam 1801; Hague 1809.

In Spanish, Madrid 3 December 1801; Mexico 1824.

In Swedish (translated by J. D. Valerius), Stockholm 19 June 1800; Gothenburg 31 March 1803; Malmö 15 August 1804; Lund 3 July 1807.

In Danish (translated by A. G. Thoroup), Copenhagen 13 December 1803.

In Polish (translated by J. Drozdowski), Warsaw 1806.

Italian translation by A. Piazza published 1797.

HAIBEL: *Der Tiroler Wastel*

14 May. Vienna, W.

Text by E. Schikaneder. Three acts.

The only extant Singspiel of Mozart's future brother-in-law.

Very successful on German stages: Graz 20 February 1797; Prague June 1797; Budapest 1798; Agram November or December 1799; Dresden 31 July 1801; Laibach 1806; Hamburg 23 Octo-

ber 1810 (as *Die Tiroler in Wien*); Berlin, Kgst. 16 February 1825.

In German also, Paris, Th. de la Cité 30 November 1801; Poznán 25 July 1804; St. Petersburg 1808; Berne 13 May 1811. Given at Vienna (100th performance 25 May 1798) until 1837, at Weimar until 1841, at Lübeck until 1842; revived Basle 17 February 1850.

A sequel *Österreichs treue Brüder oder die Scharfschützen in Tyrol* by the same authors, was produced at Vienna, W. 25 October 1796, and Pressburg 26 March 1797.

WINTER: *Das unterbrochene Opferfest*

14 June. Vienna, Kä.

Text by F. X. Huber. Two acts.

Winter's most famous work and about the most successful German opera between *Zauberflöte* (1791) and *Freischütz* (1821).

Given at Berlin 1 March 1797; Munich 19 August 1797; Hamburg 1 September 1797 (as *Myrrha und Elvira*, text altered by C. A. Vulpius), etc.

In German also Budapest 11 December 1797; Brünn 21 December 1797; Pressburg 1 December 1798; Temesvar 19 November 1801; Poznán 2 September 1805; Prague 1807; St. Petersburg 1808; Berne 11 March 1812; Amsterdam 29 November 1823; London, Hm. 28 May 1834.

In Italian, Dresden 25 April 1798; Florence, T. dei Risoluti Summer 1818.

In Polish (translated by W. Boguslawski), Warsaw 5 November 1802; Poznán July 1805.

In Swedish (translated by C. G. Nordforss), Stockholm 16 November 1812.

In Russian (translated by Aleksandrov), Moscow 10 February 1817; at St. Petersburg two days later in a different version by A. I. Sheller.

In Danish (translated by N. T. Bruun), Copenhagen 29 January 1818.

In French, Antwerp 31 March 1818; Paris, Odéon 21 October 1824 (translated by J. H. de Saur and L. de Saint-Géniès, music arranged by P. Crémont and Vogt); there are earlier printed

French versions by J. D. von Apell (Cassel 1802) and by A. van Hoogstraaten (Amsterdam 1805).

In English (translated by H. Napier), London, Ly. 7 August 1826 (music arranged by W. Hawes).

Given on German stages until the end of the 19th century; last revived Leipzig 25 August 1917.

DALAYRAC: *Marianne*

7 July. Paris, O.C.

Text by B. J. Marsollier. One act.

Successful in Paris; given at the O.C. until 1825. In French also, Brussels 26 October 1796; Berne January 1801, etc.

In Danish (translated by K. L. Rahbek), Copenhagen 13 September 1798.

In German (translated by C. A. Herklots), Berlin 28 November 1803.

Italian version by D. Bresciani published 1797; Dutch version by P. J. Uylenbroek published 1800.

PORTUGAL: *La Donna di Genio volubile*

5 October. Venice, S. Moisè

Text by G. Bertati (founded on a comedy by Goldoni). Two acts.

Given at the same theatre 4 November 1796 with a new second act, and at the T.S.Sam. 16 November 1800 reduced to one act. Bologna 1797; Modena, T. Rangoni 28 December 1797; Rome, Ap. Spring 1798; Milan, Sc. June 1799, etc. In Italy until 1815; in Italian also, Trieste Summer 1797; Corfu Carnival 1798; Dresden 8 December 1798; Lisbon 23 January 1799; Vienna 21 October 1799; Barcelona 18 November 1799; Dubrovnik (Ragusa) 1803; Paris, Th.I. 19 January 1804 (revived 2 October 1813 and 26 August 1819); Oporto 19 November 1805; Amsterdam Carnival 1806.

In Spanish (translation probably by L. F. Comella), Madrid 9 December 1801.

SCHENK: *Der Dorfbarbier*

30 October. Vienna, B.

Text by J. and P. Weidmann (originally produced as a comedy at the same theatre 18 June 1785). One act.

Schenk's most popular work, given on every German stage. Berlin 13 March 1798; Hamburg 4 January 1799 (in 2 acts); Breslau 19 September 1799; Oels 29 March 1800; Hanover 30 June 1800; etc.

In German also Agram 23 September 1802; Poznán 10 November 1803; Schleswig 1804; Eisenstadt 1805; St. Petersburg 1808; Budapest 7 January 1812; Prague 22 September 1816; Moscow 2 October 1819; Amsterdam 20 April 1825; Gothenburg 23 April 1827; New York 15 December 1847.

In Hungarian (translated by P. J. Kotsi), Budapest 4 July 1808; Clausenburg 26 July 1812. In Polish (translated by M. Wagrowski), Warsaw 1810. In Czech (translated by V. Filípek), Prague 29 February 1859.

Some of the latest revivals: Frankfort 25 December 1889; Vienna 23 February 1890; Breslau 17 January 1898; Prague 11 February 1898; Berlin, D.O. 23 March 1929. In Swedish, Stockholm 27 October 1893. Score published in the *D.T.Ö.* series in 1927 (edited by R. Haas).

A sequel, *Adam in der Klemme*, music by Diabelli, was produced at Vienna, Kä. 25 April 1809.

KUNZEN: *Hemmeligheden* (Secrecies)

22 November. Copenhagen

Text by A. G. Thoroup (from a French libretto by Quétant, *Les Femmes et le Secret*, set to music by Vachon in 1767). One act.

The most successful of Kunzen's Danish works; given at Copenhagen 49 times until 1851. (According to T. Krogh, given in Germany as *Können sie schweigen;* I was not able to find a record of a performance.)

GRESNICK: *Les faux Mendians*

23 November. Paris, Th. Louvois

Text by J. A. Lebrun-Tossa. One act.

This opera of the Belgian composer was first given at Liége 16 January 1800 and revived there at the eighth festival of the I.S.C.M. on 3 September 1930.

(Clément-Larousse give 23 November 1797, as the date of the first performance. According to the printed score and the libretto it was in *Frimaire, An V*, viz. November 1796.)

PELISSIER: *Edwin and Angelina,* or: *The Banditti*

19 December. New York, John Street Th.

Text by E. H. Smith (founded on O. Goldsmith's ballad, 1764). Three acts.

This second American opera of the year 1796 was given only once. Two songs are preserved. Libretto printed.

CIMAROSA: *Gli Orazi ed i Curiazi*

26 December. Venice, F.

Text by A. S. Sografi. Three acts.

The most successful of Cimarosa's serious operas. Milan, Sc. 26 December 1797, etc. Last revived in Italy at Florence, P. October 1841.

In Italian also produced at Vienna 30 June 1797 (last revived W. 16 March 1822); Lisbon 17 December 1798; Prague 1799; Trieste 1 October 1800; Paris 3 March 1804 (the first act only); 18 January 1810 (private performance for Napoléon); 16 June 1813 (publicly; revived 14 August 1823); St. Petersburg Carnival 1805; London 2 May 1805 (frequently revived until 11 March 1841); Dresden May 1805; Munich 13 July 1806 (with additions by Danzi), etc.; Barcelona 4 November 1807.

In Polish (translated by L. Osiński), Warsaw 1812.

In Russian (translated by A. I. Sheller), St. Petersburg 11 March 1815.

In Spanish (translated by D. Solis), Madrid 10 June 1816.

VAL. FIORAVANTI: *Il Furbo contro al Furbo*

29 December. Venice, S. Sam.

Text probably by the composer. Two acts.

Fioravanti's first greater success. Given at Parma Carnival 1798 as *L'Arte contro l'Arte*; at Trieste Autumn 1802, as *Chi la fa, chi la disfa e chi l'imbroglia*; at Modena, T. Rangoni 26 December 1804, as *Il Ciabattino incivilito*. Milan, Sc. March 1798, etc.

In Italian also, given at Trieste March 1797; Vienna 10 June 1797 (as *Il Ciabattino ringentilito*); Corfu Autumn 1797; Barcelona 13 May 1799; Lisbon Autumn 1800; Dubrovnik (Ragusa) 1804; London 1 March 1808 (revived 19 January 1813).

1797

GRÉTRY: *Lisbeth*

10 January. Paris, O.C.

Text by E. G. F. de Favières (founded on a story by Florian). Three acts.

In French also given at Ghent 1799; Liége 25 October 1799; Brussels 23 January 1800; Berne 28 February 1801, etc. On French stages until about 1813.

In Swedish (translated by J. W. Spetz), Stockholm 6 September 1803.

Italian translation by G. Savorgnan published 1797.

See on this opera (in which Favières introduced the Swiss poet and painter Salomon Gessner) E. Closson in *Revue Musicale*, Vol. v, no.6 (April 1924).

GRÉTRY: *Anacréon chez Polycrate*

17 January. Paris, O.

Text by J. H. Guy. Three acts.

Given in Paris until 1825; 100th performance 9 December 1814. In French also, Brussels 10 March 1803; Brunswick Summer 1804.

In Swedish (translated by J. D. Valerius), Stockholm 18 January 1803.

In German (translated by C. A. Herklots), Berlin 3 August 1809.

A Dutch version by C. A. van Raij was published in 1812.

The opera was revived at Tournai as late as 16 December 1900.

BRUNI: *Le Major Palmer*

26 January. Paris, Th. Feydeau

Text by C. A. G. Pigault-Lebrun. Three acts.

In French also, Brussels 10 November 1797; Moscow 12 January 1811.

In German (translated by C. A. Herklots), Berlin 16 October 1798; Dessau Spring 1800 (with an additional quartet by B. A. Weber); Vienna, W. September 1805; Budapest 15 September 1806.

In Swedish (translated by J. D. Valerius), Stockholm 19 September 1800.

In Spanish (translated by F. Enciso Castrillón) Madrid 28 January 1804.

In Polish, Wilna 16 November 1810.

BOIELDIEU: *La Famille Suisse*

11 February. Paris, Th. Feydeau

Text by C. Godard d'Aucour de Saint-Just. One act.

The first of Boieldieu's operas which was produced in Paris; also given at Brussels 22 November 1797.

PAER: *Il Principe di Taranto*

11 February. Parma

Text: an altered version of F. Livigni's *La finta Principessa* (see 1785). Two acts.

Milan, Sc. September 1797, etc. Revived Naples, T.N. Spring 1807 as *La Contadina fortunata*; Modena, T. in Via Emilia 24 September 1809; Vigevano Autumn 1810; Parma Carnival 1812.

In Italian also given at Madrid 13 July 1797; Dresden 24 March 1798 (revived 16 June 1821); Vienna 6 November 1798; Prague 22 December 1799; Paris 14 May 1803; London 23 December 1806 (revived 16 January 1810).

CHERUBINI: *Médée*

13 March. Paris, Th. Feydeau

Text by F. B. Hoffman. Three acts.

Not very successful in Paris and never revived there. Two parodies were produced there the same month, *La Sorcière*, by C. A. Sewrin, at the Th. de la Cité 27 March 1797, and *Bébée et Jargon*, by P. Villiers and P. A. Capelle, at the Th. Montansier the very next night. Revived in French, Brussels 31 March 1814.

In German (translated by C. A. Herklots), Berlin 17 February 1800; (translated by G. F. Treitschke) Vienna 6 November 1802; Budapest 23 December 1803; Brünn 24 November 1817.

In Danish (translated by T. Overskou), Copenhagen 14 February 1826.

Given in London, H.M.'s for the first time as late as 6 June 1865 (in Italian, translated by S. de Castrone della Rajata, recitatives by Arditi); an earlier production was prevented by Cherubini himself, as appears from the following passage: "Outre cela le caractère de la musique est trop sévère pour le goût des Anglais. . . . Si Mr. Watten s'obstinait à vouloir le donner . . . je serais obligé de faire mettre un article dans les papiers publiques pour prévenir tout le monde que cet opéra aurait été représenté contre mon gré" (unpublished letter by Cherubini of 25 April 1815).

Frequently revived on German stages; Prague 7 February 1840; Frankfort 1 March 1855 (with recitatives by F. Lachner); Rotterdam 1866; Munich 12 April 1872; Berlin 30 October 1872; Vienna 26 November 1880; Hamburg 20 October 1896; and lately Erfurt 14 March 1925 (revised by H. Schüler and H. Strobel).

Given for the first time in Italy at Milan, Sc. 30 December 1909 (new Italian version by C. Zangarini, with Lachner's recitatives).

KUNZEN: *Dragedukken*
(The good Fairy)

14 March. Copenhagen

Text by E. de Falsen. Four acts.

Given at Copenhagen until 1821. Also Christiania 11 April 1804; revived Copenhagen 15 June 1832 (the second act only); Bergen 6 October 1852.

BERTON: *Ponce de Léon*

15 March. Paris, O.C.

Text by the composer (*Opéra-bouffon*). Three acts.

In French also, Ghent 1798; Brussels 2 September 1801; St. Petersburg 1804.

In Danish (translated by L. Kruse), Copenhagen 24 May 1803.

MÉHUL: *Le jeune Henri*

1 May. Paris, O.C.

Text by J. N. Bouilly (originally called *La Jeunesse de Henri IV*, and written for Grétry). Two acts.

The opera itself was unsuccessful; but it was famous for its *ouverture de chasse*, which had to be played three times at the first night, and was a concert favourite throughout the 19th century.

DALAYRAC: *La Maison isolée* ou *Le Vieillard des Vosges*

11 May. Paris, O.C.

Text by B. J. Marsollier. Two acts.

Successful in Paris; revived Odéon 20 August 1827; F.Dr. 6 May 1832 as *Les Voleurs des Vosges*, reduced to one act.

In French also, Ghent 1798; Hanover 1 August 1803; Moscow 15 October 1810.

In Swedish (translated by C. G. Nordforss), Stockholm 6 May 1802; Gothenburg 12 July 1805; Malmö 1 July 1808; revived at Stockholm as late as 4 February 1860.

In Dutch (translated by B. C. van Goeris), Amsterdam 1802 (revived 1819).

In Russian, St. Petersburg 5 August 1819; Moscow 22 December 1819.

In German (translated by L. Angely), Weimar 17 February 1823; Berlin, Kgst. 25 October 1824.

PARADIS: *Rinaldo und Alcina*

Summer. Prague

Text by L. von Baczko (published in 1794), after Ariosto. Three acts.

On Maria Theresia von Paradis, the blind pianist and composer, see F. Niecks in *The Monthly*

Musical Record, January 1913. Her opera does not seem to have been successful; a rather rude letter in the *Journal des Luxus und der Moden* (1797, p.566) reads: "Von dem sonderbaren Opernwerk nach welchem Sie fragen, und welches diesen Sommer bei uns gesehen und gehört worden ist, darf ich Ihnen nur sagen, dass der Verfasser der Oper und der Komponist, beide blind sind. . . . Zum Unglück für die Oper, war das Publikum nicht auch blind".

SOR: *Telemaco nella Isola di Calipso*

25 August. Barcelona, T. Principal

Text: a reduced version of an older libretto by C. S. Capeci (first set to music by A. Scarlatti in 1718), according to Schilling the one used by Cipolla in 1785 (see Sonneck's *Catalogue*, p.1056). Two parts.

The only opera of the famous Spanish guitarist who, later on, wrote a few ballets for the Paris Opéra and spent some years in London. The music of *Telemaco* does not seem to have been preserved.

WEIGL: *L'Amor marinaro*

15 October. Vienna, B.

Text by G. de Gamerra. Three acts.

In Italian also, Dresden 18 July 1798; Ljubljana Spring 1799; Bologna Autumn 1805; Florence, P. 1 December 1810; Milan, T. Carcano Spring 1811; Parma 26 December 1813; Modena Carnival 1814; Naples, Fondo 1819.

In German (as *Der Korsar oder Die Liebe unter den Seeleuten*), Mannheim 11 May 1800; Berlin 10 November 1800 (revived Kgst. 30 November 1827); Budapest 13 October 1800; Prague 16 October 1814; Vienna, Kä. 28 July 1821 (revived Jos. 4 June 1833). A translation by Bürde called *Der Korsar aus Liebe* was used at Breslau 17 April 1801 and Hanover 26 September 1805.

In English (as *The Pirate of Genoa*, translator unknown), London, Ly. 5 September 1828.

In Polish, Wilna 18 May 1818.

Beethoven used the air *Pria ch'io l'impegno* for the variations of his clarinet trio, op.11 (1798).

PORTUGAL: *Le Donne cambiate*

22 October. Venice, S. Moisè

Text by G. M. Foppa (one of the latest versions of the *Devil to pay* story, see 1731). Two acts.

Successful in Italy, where it was sometimes produced as *Il Ciabattino*, *Il Diavolo a quattro*, or *Il Calzolaio*. Milan, Sc. March 1801, etc. At Ancona 1802 as *L'allegro Ciabattino* (probably Portugal's opera).

In Italian also, given at Dresden 2 October 1799 (with a new finale by Gestewitz); Trieste 26 December 1799; Lisbon Spring 1804; Paris 27 March 1806; London, Pantheon 27 February 1812.

In Portuguese (as *O Sapateiro*), Lisbon 1802 and revived 25 June 1814 (as *O Mestre Biajo Sapateiro*).

In Polish (translated by L. Osiński), Warsaw 1810.

MEDERITSCH and WINTER: *Babylons Pyramiden*

25 October. Vienna, W.

Text by E. Schikaneder. Two acts.

First act composed by Mederitsch, second act by Winter. One of the better works of the *Zauberflöte* school. Also given at Budapest 2 May 1804; Prague 23 June 1815.

There occurs in the second act a "Todverkündigung" which according to Bücken is well worth comparing to that in *Die Walküre*.

I. WALTER: *Doktor Faust*

28 December. Bremen

Text by H. G. Schmieder (*Eine Original-Oper*), based on the original version of Goethe's tragedy. Four acts.

Hanover 11 June 1798, etc. On this earliest *Faust* opera, see P. Spitta's study in his *Zur Musik* (1892).

Revived Regensburg 1819 (with new libretto by C. A. Mämminger).

1798

DALAYRAC: *Gulnare* ou *L'Esclave persane*

9 January. Paris, O.C.

Text by B. J. Marsollier. One act.

In French also, Ghent 1798; Brussels 16 January 1799; Hanover 24 August 1803; Moscow 7 October 1809; Berne 26 February 1819; revived at the Odéon, Paris 18 May 1828.

In German (translated by H. G. Schmieder), Berlin 12 August 1801.

In Swedish (translated by J. D. Valerius), Stockholm 19 October 1801.

In Spanish, Madrid 23 February 1802.

In Russian (translated by D. N. Barkov), St. Petersburg 25 November 1818.

In Polish (translated by L. A. Dmuszewski), Warsaw 3 December 1820.

Dutch translation by M. G. Engelman published 1807.

A German version of the libretto, by F. K. Lippert, was composed by Süssmayr (produced Vienna 5 July 1800).

KAUER: *Das Donauweibchen*

11 January. Vienna, Leop.

Text by K. F. Hensler (*Ein romantisches komisches Volksmärchen mit Gesang nach einer Sage der Vorzeit*). Three acts.

Kauer's most popular work. A second part (by the same authors) was given at the same theatre on 13 February 1798, a third part, *Die Nymphe der Donau* (text by T. Berling, music by Bierey) at Altona 25 July 1801; Vienna, Leop. 4 February 1803; Hamburg 15 March 1803; a fourth part, *Hulda, die Nixenkönigin, oder das Fest der Treue* (music by C. F. Ebers), at Poznán 22 July 1804. There was also an interlude *Das Nixenreich oder Drei Tage in den Fluten* (text by H. G. Schmieder, music by Friedrich Adam Hiller, the son of the Singspiel composer), produced Schleswig and Bremen 1802; Altona 14 April 1803; Vienna 10 August 1805. And, finally, there was a "Seitenstück" by Hensler and Kauer, called *Das Wald-*

weibchen, produced Vienna, Leop. 1 April 1800 and Hamburg 3 February 1804.

At the Leopoldstadt theatre the first part was given until 1839, the second part until 1821. On suburban stages of Vienna we find the first part as late as in 1875. At Berlin the first three parts were produced on 13 April 1801, 3 February 1802 and 25 April 1805 respectively. During the first half of the 19th century the *Donauweibchen* was frequently revived in Germany (the first two parts at Hamburg on 1 February and 8 March 1849).

Adapted to local use we find versions like *Die Saalnixe*, etc. (see, for instance, *Journal für Literatur, Kunst, Luxus und Mode*, 1823, p.639).

Outside Austria and Germany, *Das Donauweibchen* was given at:

AMSTERDAM 18 October 1801 (in German) and Autumn 1805 (in Dutch, translated by A. Fokke Simonsz).

TEMESVAR 26 November 1801 (in German).

BERNE 1803 (in German).

BUDAPEST 1804 (in German).

HAGUE 19 December 1809 (in Dutch).

LEMBERG 21 March 1814 (in Polish, as *Syrena z Dniestru*, translated by D. Jakubowicz and J. N. Kamiński, with additional music by K. Lipiński, the famous violinist; this was an adaptation of the second part; the first part followed on 30 May 1814).

GOTHENBURG 22 April 1827 and STOCKHOLM 24 February 1844 (in Swedish, translated by E. W. Djurström).

COPENHAGEN 27 July 1827 (in German).

HELSINKI 20 June 1830 (in German).

NEW YORK 17 December 1859 and 30 January 1867 (in German).

RIGA 12 February 1870 (in German).

Particularly successful in a Russian version by N. S. Krasnopolsky (parts 1, 2, 3) and Shakhovsky (part 4)—Krasnopolsky's text being adapted from Hensler, while Shakhovsky's is entirely new—as *Lesta, Dnyeprovskaya Rusalka* (*Lesta, the Dnyepr Nymph*), with additional music by Cavos and Davydov:

First part (music by Kauer and Davydov), St. Petersburg 7 November 1803; Moscow 1804.

Second part (music by Kauer, Davydov and Cavos), St. Petersburg 17 May 1804; Moscow 1805.

Third part (music by Davydov alone), St. Petersburg 6 November 1805; Moscow 1 November 1807.

A fourth part, with music by Cavos, was given at St. Petersburg on 12 January 1807 and at Moscow on 23 May 1824; this fourth part was revived at St. Petersburg in 1852–54.

PAER: *La Virtù al Cimento*

January. Parma

Text by A. Anelli (founded on Boccaccio's story; originally called *Griselda*, and first set to music by Piccinni, Venice, S. Sam. 8 October 1793; rectify Engländer in *Neues Archiv für Sächsische Geschichte und Altertumskunde*, 1929, p.219). Two acts.

One of Paer's best and most successful works: Milan, Sc. 24 May 1799, etc.; in Italy given until 1832, mostly as *Griselda*.

In Italian also Vienna 29 November 1799; Dresden September 1800; Barcelona 4 November 1801; Paris 18 June 1803; Oporto 13 May 1806; Lugano 4 October 1806 (inauguration of the first theatre there); Amsterdam 1807; Lisbon 29 May 1808; London 13 January 1816.

In German (translated by Bürde), Breslau 19 March 1802; (translated by J. J. Ihlee), Frankfort 23 August 1802; Hamburg 23 March 1804; Hanover 3 January 1816; (translated by M. G. Lambrecht) Munich 21 October 1804. In German also, St. Petersburg Spring 1814.

In Polish (translated by J. F. Królikowski), Wilna 15 October 1809 and Warsaw 1818.

In Swedish (translated by C. G. Nordforss), Stockholm 28 February 1810.

In Russian (translated by P. A. Katyenin), St. Petersburg 3 November 1817.

In Spanish, Madrid 4 October 1817.

In French, Antwerp 20 November 1817.

PORTUGAL: *Fernando nel Messico*

16 January. Venice, S. Ben.

Text by F. Tarducci. Three acts.

Written for Elizabeth Billington.

In Italian also, Trieste 2 October 1799 (libretto altered by G. Artusi); London 31 March 1803; Lisbon Summer 1805 (altered and reduced to two acts).

DALAYRAC: *Alexis ou L'Erreur d'un bon Père*

24 January. Paris, Th. Feydeau

Text by B. J. Marsollier. One act.

In French also Brussels 17 July 1798; Aachen 17 August 1800; Vienna 6 September 1809; Berne 17 February 1819.

In German (translated by C. A. Herklots), Berlin 27 December 1802; (translated by J. von Seyfried), Vienna, W. September 1805; Budapest 6 June 1806; Prague Summer 1807.

In Danish (translated by N. T. Bruun), Copenhagen 30 September 1803.

An Italian translation by G. Ricchi was published in 1804; a Dutch translation by J. M. Naret Koning in 1830.

Revived Buenos Aires 19 September 1831 (in French).

DELLA MARIA: *Le Prisonnier ou La Ressemblance*

29 January. Paris, O.C.

Text by A. Duval (founded on Kotzebue's comedy *Der Gefangene*). One act.

Della Maria's most popular work. Given in Paris until 1839.

In French also, Brussels 25 June 1798 (revived 15 December 1822); Amsterdam 1798; Rotterdam 24 April 1799; Hanover 22 December 1803; Moscow 6 October 1808; Vienna 20 June 1809.

In Dutch (translated by P. J. Uylenbroek), Amsterdam 1798 (revived 1816).

In German, Mannheim 9 June 1799; Frankfort 23 January 1800 (translated by J. J. Ihlee; given

there until 1846); Oels 15 February 1800 (translated by A. von Kotzebue); Berlin 15 August 1800 (translated by C. A. Herklots); Vienna, W. 13 May 1801 (translated by K. Vio; revived 2 October 1815), etc. Poznán 30 July 1804 (Kotzebue's translation); Moscow 8 January 1820.

In Swedish (translated by C. Envallsson), Stockholm 25 April 1799; Lund 22 September 1808.

In English, London, Hm. 17 July 1799 (in two acts, as *The Castle of Sorrento*, adapted by G. Colman and H. Heartwell, music arranged and enlarged by Attwood; a one-act translation by Heartwell had been published earlier in the same year, but was not acted, being "too simple for an English stage").

In Danish (translated by J. Baggesen), Copenhagen 30 January 1801.

In Russian (translated by D. N. Barkov), Moscow 1802 (revived 1 December 1819); St. Petersburg 12 May 1814.

In Hungarian (translated by F. S. Deáky), Clausenburg 23 December 1822.

Italian translation by T. de Lellis published 1804.

There are two more German versions, by Ch. M. Franke, Leipzig 1800, and by J. D. von Apell, Cassel 1801.

KUNZEN: *Erik Ejegod*

30 January. Copenhagen

Text by J. Baggesen (originally written for J. A. P. Schulz). Three acts.

Given at Copenhagen until 1827.

GAVEAUX: *Léonore ou L'Amour conjugal*

19 February. Paris, Th. Feydeau

Text by J. N. Bouilly (*Fait historique*). Two acts.

Brussels 29 June 1799. The first setting of the *Fidelio* story; for Paer's and Beethoven's operas see 1804 and 1805; for an account of Gaveaux's opera see G. Servières's *Episodes d'Histoire Musicale* (1914).

WEIGL: *Das Dorf im Gebuerge*

17 April. Vienna, B.

Text by A. von Kotzebue. Two acts.

Oels 11 January 1800; Hamburg 14 August 1811; Berlin 20 May 1814; Hanover 21 May 1815, etc.; in German also, Budapest 1825; last revived Königsberg 28 January 1833; Basle 9 December 1842.

In Polish (translated by K. Brodziński), Warsaw 1818.

Anonymous Dutch version published 1807.

BOIELDIEU: *Zoraïme et Zulnar*

10 May. Paris, O.C.

Text by C. Godard d'Aucour de Saint-Just. Three acts.

Boieldieu first greater success. In French also given at Brussels 28 November 1799; Brunswick 1803; Cassel 1811. Revived, with some alterations, Paris 25 June 1824.

In Spanish, Barcelona 18 September 1802.

In Russian (translated by P. N. Kobyakov), St. Petersburg 30 December 1813; Moscow 19 February 1818.

In Danish (translated by N. T. Bruun), Copenhagen 29 January 1821.

WINTER: *Das Labirint* oder *Der Kampf mit den Elementen*

12 June. Vienna, W.

Text by E. Schikaneder. Two acts.

A sequel to his *Zauberflöte* libretto, but not very successful. Outside Vienna produced only on few German stages: Berlin 18 July 1803; Frankfurt 30 March 1806; Nuremberg 16 October 1807; Königsberg 1821; Clausenburg 23 December 1822 (parts only); Budapest 24 November 1828.

Revived at Kiel 23 October 1930 as *Papagenos Hochzeit* (arranged by G. Hartmann).

REICHARDT: *Die Geisterinsel*

6 July. Berlin, O.

Text by F. W. Gotter and F. H. von Einsiedel (founded on Shakespeare's *Tempest*). Three acts.

The libretto was originally intended for Mozart, then offered to Dittersdorf; eventually first set by Friedrich Fleischmann, whose opera was first produced at Weimar 19 May 1798 (see W. Deetjen in *Shakespeare Jahrbuch*, vol.64, 1923).

Reichardt's opera also given at Leipzig 14 January 1800; Dessau 7 March 1800, etc.

Revived Berlin 3 August 1825.

DELLA MARIA: *L'Opéra-Comique*

9 July. Paris, O.C.

Text by J. A. P. de Ségur and E. Mercier-Dupaty. One act.

After *Le Prisonnier*, the composer's second great success of that year; in Paris given until 1839; in French also Brussels 17 November 1798 (revived 24 December 1840); Hanover 21 November 1803; Moscow 27 October 1808; Vienna 9 July 1809.

In Spanish (translated by V. R. de Arellano), Madrid 19 May 1801.

In German (translated by F. K. Hiemer), Stuttgart 13 July 1801; Mannheim 19 March 1802; (translated by H. G. Schmieder), Budapest 1 January 1802; (translated by G. F. Treitschke), Breslau 24 February 1802; Berlin 15 October 1803; Vienna 28 January 1804, etc.

In Danish (translated by A. G. Thoroup), Copenhagen 6 May 1802; Christiania 12 February 1806; revived Copenhagen 3 March 1849 (new translation by N. V. Dorph).

In Swedish (translated by C. G. Nordforss), Stockholm 22 July 1803; Lund 20 August 1807; Malmö 19 January 1810.

In Polish (translated by J. Adamczewski), Warsaw 1806.

In Russian, St. Petersburg 4 June 1822.

Dutch translation by J. de Quack published 1802.

CHERUBINI: *L'Hôtellerie portugaise*

25 July. Paris, Th. Feydeau

Text by E. Aignan. One act.

In German (translated by G. F. Treitschke), Vienna 22 September 1803; Leipzig December

1803; Berlin 16 April 1804, etc. Revived Carlsruhe 3 November 1893 (revised by F. Mottl); Magdeburg July 1917 (re-modelled by B. Engelke).

DALAYRAC: *Léon* ou *Le Château de Montenero*

15 October. Paris, O.C.

Text by F. B. Hoffman. Three acts.

In French also, given at Brussels 24 March 1800; Brunswick c.1802; Stockholm 14 July 1803; Hanover 26 April 1804; Moscow 28 September 1808; Berne 1 June 1809.

In German (translated by J. J. Ihlee), Frankfort 1801; Berlin 17 September 1802 (with additions by B. A. Weber); Aachen 1802; Breslau 12 August 1803; Munich 1803; Vienna, W. December 1804; Budapest 2 December 1805; Prague Summer 1807; Hamburg 7 December 1812.

In Swedish (translated by J. D. Valerius), Stockholm 16 December 1805.

In Polish (translated by K. Hebdowski), Warsaw 1809.

In Russian (translated by D. I. Vyelyashev-Volyntsov), Moscow 27 February 1812; St. Petersburg Spring 1812.

In Spanish, Madrid 25 July 1812.

In Danish (translated by N. T. Bruun), Copenhagen 28 May 1813 (given until 1852).

MAYR: *Che Originali*

18 October. Venice, S. Ben.

Text by G. Rossi. One act.

This *farsa* was the first great success of the German-Italian composer; frequently produced as *Il Fanatico per la Musica, Il Pazzo per la Musica, La Musicomania, Il Trionfo della Musica;* Milan, Sc. 7 March 1801, etc.

In Italy until about 1830; outside Italy, in Italian, given at:

BARCELONA 3 June 1802.

VIENNA 9 May 1803.

DRESDEN November 1803 (as *La Musicomania*).

PARIS, TH.I. 7 October 1805 (revived 9 December 1815).

AMSTERDAM November 1805 (music arranged and enlarged by Pucitta).

LONDON 19 June 1806 (pasticcio; frequently revived until 28 February 1824).

ANTWERP 29 June 1818.

BERLIN 7 June 1822; Hamburg 6 July 1822, etc.

LISBON 27 April 1822.

EDINBURGH 3 January 1828.

NEW YORK 20 April 1829 (pasticcio; revived 3 November 1847!).

PHILADELPHIA 5 May 1829 (first Italian opera there).

DUBLIN Autumn 1829.

ST. PETERSBURG 1830.

In Spanish, Madrid 20 June 1806; Buenos Aires 1813.

ZUMSTEEG: *Die Geisterinsel*

7 November. Stuttgart

Text by F. W. Gotter and F. H. von Einsiedel (the third setting of their Shakespearean libretto in this year). Three acts.

Zumsteeg's most important work. Schleswig 1800; Hamburg 18 November 1803; Breslau 9 April 1805; Leipzig 1806; Würzburg 29 June 1808; Königsberg 1809; Mannheim 28 January 1817. Revived at Stuttgart 10 June 1814 and once more as late as 26 September 1889.

(For a detailed analysis of this *Tempest* opera see T. F. K. Arnold's *Gallerie der berühmtesten Tonkünstler* . . . part 1, pp.44–96.)

DELLA MARIA: *L'Oncle Valet*

9 December. Paris, O.C.

Text by A. Duval. One act.

In French also given at Brussels 9 June 1799, etc.

In Swedish (translated by J. D. Valerius), Stockholm 10 August 1802.

In German (translated by G. F. Treitschke), Vienna, Kä. 2 November 1803 and W. the very next night; (translated by C. A. Herklots), Berlin 2 January 1806; Hamburg 12 January 1806, etc. Revived Berlin 21 August 1817 (new translation by May).

PORTUGAL: *Non irritare le Donne ovvero Il chiamantesi Filosofo*

27 December. Venice, S. Moisè

Text by G. M. Foppa. One act.

In Italian also, Paris 1 May 1801 (at the opening of the new Théâtre-Italien, under Dlle Montansier's management).

Revived Trieste Carnival 1807 (as *Il Filosofo*, enlarged to two acts, additional music by N. Giuliani); Venice, S. Ben. 9 March 1822.

Date of first performance according to Carvalhaes and all other authorities; 1798 libretto printed. But according to the *Gazzetta dei Teatri di Venezia* (contained in the *Teatro Moderno Applaudito*), at the T. S. Moisè the operas *Furberia e Puntiglio* (by Bernardini) and *Fedeltà ed Amore alla Prova* (by Gazzaniga) were given that night. Portugal's opera only occurs at the T. S. Benedetto 16 October 1799.

DEVIENNE: *Les Comédiens ambulans*

28 December. Paris, Th. Feydeau

Text by L. B. Picard. Two acts.

In French also, Ghent 1799; Brussels 19 April 1800, etc.

In German (translated by G. F. Treitschke), Vienna 23 January 1805; Würzburg 29 February 1808, etc.

In Danish (translated by N. T. Bruun), Copenhagen 19 May 1810.

1799

SALIERI: *Falstaff osia Le tre Burle*

3 January. Vienna, Kä.

Text by C. P. Defranceschi (from Shakespeare). Two acts.

In Italian also, Dresden 26 October 1799.

In German (translated by C. A. Herklots), Berlin 16 December 1799.

(Beethoven used the air *La stessa, la stessissima* from this opera for piano variations in 1799.)

VAL. FIORAVANTI: *Le Cantatrici villane*

January. Naples, Fior.

Text by G. Palomba. Two acts.

Fioravanti's greatest success and one of the most popular Italian comic operas of that period.

Given in a reduced 1-act version (text adapted by G. M. Foppa) as *Le Virtuose ridicole* at Venice, S. Moisè 28 December 1801. First given at Milan, Sc. 19 April 1802.

In Italian also:

BARCELONA 9 August 1802.

LISBON 12 October 1803, Oporto 19 November 1805.

DRESDEN 1804.

VIENNA 1 September 1804 (frequently revived until 23 May 1840).

AMSTERDAM Carnival 1806 (in German 5 January 1825).

PARIS, TH.I. 30 January 1806 (frequently revived until 1842).

ST. PETERSBURG 1829, Odessa Summer 1839.

LONDON 27 May 1842.

BERLIN, KGST. 16 May 1844.

Very successful also on German stages (as *Die Sängerinnen auf dem Lande*, translated by J. C. Grünbaum): Frankfurt 4 May 1806; Hamburg 2 January 1810; Berlin 19 December 1810; Berne 3 February 1812; Munich 1812; St. Petersburg 1813; Prague 30 January 1814; Vienna, Leop. 10 September 1814, etc.

In Russian (translated by G. Vyen), St. Petersburg May 1804; Moscow 2 September 1808.

In Spanish, Madrid 15 July 1809.

In Polish (translated by J. F. Królikowski), Wilna 1807 and Warsaw 1818.

Copenhagen 5 June 1827 (in German) and 1 September 1828 (in Danish, translated by J. L. Heiberg).

Last revived in Italy at Florence, T. Niccolini 4 September 1870.

Some of the more recent revivals in German were at Basle 21 January 1842; Coburg 1 June 1852; Dresden 9 March 1861 and 2 September 1877; Königsberg 13 November 1873; Hamburg 8 March 1880.

Berlin, Fr. W. 11 October 1890 (revised by E. Pohl, re-orchestrated by G. Lehnhardt); Gladbach April 1930 and Erfurt 3 September 1931 (new German version by A. Haelssig).

The date of the first performance is wrongly given as 1803 by many authorities. The original libretto reads "per quart'opera del corrente anno 1798"; Fioravanti states in his autobiographical sketch (Turin, Biblioteca Civica; first publication in *Il Tiberino*, 23 March 1840), that it was given "nel Carnevale 1798—entrando il '99".

DALAYRAC: *Adolphe et Clara* ou *Les deux Prisonniers*

10 February. Paris, O.C.

Text by B. J. Marsollier. One act.

Very successful in Paris; last revived at the O.C. 3 May 1849; at the Galerie Vivienne 11 November 1895.

In French also, Brussels 4 August 1799 (revived 11 January 1852); Berne 3 October 1801; Hanover 22 June 1803; Königsberg 1805; Moscow 28 September 1808; Vienna 18 June 1809; Stockholm 24 October 1812; Berlin, Kgst. 4 June 1825; Mexico 1826; New York 23 August 1827; Buenos Aires 26 November 1827.

In German (translated by C. A. Herklots), Schleswig 1800; Berlin 9 March 1801; Munich 1801; Vienna, W. 1801 and Kä. 4 June 1810; Breslau 23 November 1801; (translated by F. K. Hiemer), Stuttgart 20 March 1801; Hamburg 23 October 1801; Berne 1804; Poznán 27 January 1805; Vienna 4 June 1810; Prague 6 February 1814. Another German translation by W. Lohmann published 1808. Revived Berlin, Fr. W. 22 July 1852 (translated by L. Schneider).

In Spanish (translated by E. Tapia), Madrid 29 January 1801.

In Swedish (translated by C. G. Nordforss), Stockholm 3 March 1801; Malmö 6 March 1807; Lund 14 August 1807.

In Danish (translated by J. Baggesen), Copenhagen 17 December 1801.

In Dutch (translated by H. H. Klijn), Amsterdam 1802; revived Amsterdam 1826; Hague 1829.

In Russian, Moscow 30 September 1811.

Italian translation by G. Ricchi published 1804.

Given in London 26 October 1805 by a German troupe at the Sanssouci Theatre; an English two-act version by J. Kenney, music by M. P. King (*Matrimony*) was produced in London, D.L. 20 November 1804; New York 17 May 1805; Dublin 26 January 1806.

PAER: *Camilla* ossia *Il Sotterraneo*

23 February. Vienna, Kä.

Text by G. Carpani (translated from Marsollier's French libretto, see 1791). Three acts.

In Italian also given at Prague 1799; Dresden 1800; Parma Carnival 1802; Paris 15 September 1804; Bologna 1805; Milan, Sc. 27 October 1807; Amsterdam 1808; Madrid 17 November 1809 (as *Il Sotterraneo*); Naples, T. Fondo Summer 1810; London 12 May 1812 (revived 3 April 1819).

In German (translated by J. J. Ihlee), Frankfort 4 July 1799; Budapest c.1800; Breslau 12 March 1800 (translated by Bürde); Berlin 11 February 1801; Schleswig and Munich 1801; Aachen 1802; Weimar 23 January 1802 (translated by C. A. Vulpius); Hamburg 18 December 1803; Bremen 1803–04; Hanover 26 August 1807; Vienna, W. 5 June 1808; Berne 7 February 1812; Prague 17 August 1814. Revived in German, Carlsruhe May 1846.

In Polish (translated by W. Boguslawski), Warsaw 1810.

In Russian (translated by R. M. Zotov), St. Petersburg 27 December 1824.

In Italy popular during the first half of the 19th century; last revived at the T. Niccolini, Florence 24 October 1870.

BERTON: *Montano et Stéphanie*

15 April. Paris, O.C.

Text by J. E. B. Dejaure (founded on an episode in Aristo's *Orlando furioso*). Three acts.

The libretto had first been offered to Grétry; see on the origin and production of the work the chapter "Berton" in Adolphe Adam's *Derniers Souvenirs d'un Musicien* (1859).

After a few performances prohibited by the police; given with a new third act (text by G. M. Legouvé) 4 May 1800 (at the O.C. until 1827); in French also Ghent 1799; Brussels 8 July 1800; Berne 29 January 1806; Hamburg 24 February 1809.

In German (as *Rosamunde*, translated by J. von Seyfried), Vienna, W. 2 May 1810; revived in German, Weimar 16 February 1845.

In Danish (translated by N. T. Bruun), Copenhagen 24 May 1821.

In Russian, St. Petersburg 29 January 1836.

Italian translation by G. Ferretti published 1806.

MAYR: *Adelaide di Guesclino*

1 May. Venice, F.

Text by G. Rossi (founded on Voltaire's tragedy). Two acts.

In Italian also, Prague 1802; Vienna 24 March 1802 (with additional music by A. Cartellieri); Dresden 1807; Amsterdam January 1817.

In German, Frankfort Spring 1804; Hamburg 1 December 1815; Würzburg 7 May 1819.

MÉHUL: *Adrien*

4 June. Paris, O.

Text by F. B. Hoffman (founded on Metastasio's *Adriano in Siria*). Three acts.

The opera was to be given in March, 1792 as *Adrien, Empereur de Rome* (libretto printed), but the production was not allowed then. Méhul took the overture from an earlier opera *Horatius Coclès*.

Given in Paris until 1803; outside France, only Rheinsberg 23 May 1801 (in French).

A parody *Rien ou Peu de chose*, by Lapierre de Châteauneuf, was performed in Paris, Gaîté 1 July 1799.

SPONTINI: *La finta Filosofa*

Summer. Naples, T.N.

Text by D. Piccinni (a new version of *L'Eroismo ridicolo*, by the same authors. Produced at the same theatre in Carnival, 1798). Three acts.

The earliest opera of Spontini which became known outside Italy: Paris 10 February 1804; Dresden 1805.

SÜSSMAYR: *Soliman der Zweite* oder *Die drei Sultanninen*

1 October. Vienna, Kä.

Text by F. X. Huber (based on a French libretto by Favart, 1761). Two acts.

Popular on German stages; Berlin 15 April 1800; Breslau 31 October 1800; Budapest, *c.* 1800; Hamburg 1 September 1801; Temesvar 17 December 1801; Schleswig 1802; Prague 1810; Berne 2 March 1812; Hanover 26 March 1817, etc. Revived Vienna, Leop. 5 November 1813. Given on German stages until about 1828.

Beethoven published variations on a theme from this opera (*Tändeln und Scherzen*) in 1799.

MÉHUL: *Ariodant*

11 October. Paris, O.C.

Text by F. B. Hoffman (the same subject as in Berton's *Montano et Stéphanie*, see above). Three acts.

According to Bücken this opera is an important landmark in the development of Leitmotiv technique.

In French also, Liége 9 January 1802; Brussels 27 January 1803.

In Russian (translated by D. I. Vyelyashev-Volyntsov), Moscow 1803.

In German (translated by J. von Seyfried), Vienna, W. 16 February 1804 (with additions by I. von Seyfried); Berlin 1 June 1816.

In Swedish (translated by C. G. Nordforss), Stockholm 18 January 1808.

W. MÜLLER: *Die Teufelsmühle am Wienerberg*

12 November. Vienna, Leop.

Text by K. F. Hensler (*Ein österreichisches Volksmärchen mit Gesang nach einer Sage der Vorzeit*). Four acts.

One of the most popular of Müller's works, given all over Central Europe.

In German, Agram 7 June 1802; Berne 1803; Poznán 9 August 1804 (as *Die Schwarzthaler Mühle am Wienerberge*); Mannheim 6 January 1805; Altona 29 June 1806; Bremen 1807-08 (as *Die Teufelsmühle am Blocksberge*); Brünn 1808; Berlin 18 December 1824; Helsinki 15 December 1837; New York June 1858 and 12 February 1873.

In Russian (translated by Sokolsky), Moscow 14 November 1816.

In Czech (translated by J. N. Stěpánek), Prague 14 February 1830 (revived 25 February 1844).

A sequel *Otto von Löwenstein*, produced at Vienna, Leop. 24 June 1815, was given for ten nights only. The first part was revived at the Kaiserjubiläums-Stadttheater, Vienna, on 20 November 1899 (celebrating the 100th anniversary of the first performance).

(KRAUS): *Aeneas i Carthago*

18 November. Stockholm

Text by J. H. Kellgren. Prologue and 5 acts.

Kraus's most important work, performed 7 years after his death (although finished already in 1872).

In French, St. Petersburg c.1806 (concert performance under Neukomm).

A parody by J. D. Valerius, *Skön Kirstin och Matts Hane*, was produced at Stockholm on 29 April 1802.

BERTON: *Le Délire* ou *Les Suites d'une Erreur*

7 December. Paris, O.C.

Text by J. A. de Révéroni Saint-Cyr. One act.

In French also, Brussels 24 April 1801; Moscow 8 October 1808; Vienna 14 September 1826; revived Paris, O.C. 26 May 1843.

Given at Madrid in two different Spanish versions, 9 December 1801 (translated by D. Solis) and 29 April 1806 (translated by F. Enciso Castrillón); in Spanish also, Buenos Aires 1828.

In Russian (translated by P. N. Semenov), St. Petersburg 25 May 1812; Moscow 23 September 1816.

In German, Vienna 4 February 1831.

1800

CHERUBINI: *Les deux Journées*

16 January. Paris, Th. Feydeau

Text by J. N. Bouilly (*comédie lyrique*). Three acts.

Cherubini's most important work; even more successful in Germany than in France. Given at the O.C., Paris until 1830 and revived 7 April 1842.

In French also, Brussels 10 December 1800; Brunswick 1801; Hague 29 August 1801; Berne 5 October 1801; Hanover 9 August 1803; St. Petersburg 1804; Moscow 12 October 1808; New Orleans 12 March 1811; New York 23 July 1827.

In German (as *Der Wasserträger*, translated by H. G. Schmieder), Frankfort 5 July 1801; Berlin 15 March 1802, etc. Given at Vienna, W. 13 August 1802 (as *Graf Armand*) and Kä. the very next night (as *Die Tage der Gefahr*, translated by G. F. Treitschke). In German also Berne 1803; Budapest 20 April 1804; Agram 18 August 1804; Prague 17 October 1813; Amsterdam 5 November 1823; Bucharest 21 December 1830; Helsinki 9 April 1834; Reval 1896. (For a German sequel see 1806.)

In English (as *The Escapes; or The Water Carrier*, translated by T. Holcroft, music arranged by Attwood), London, C.G. 14 October 1801; revived C.G. 6 November 1824; Princess's 27 October 1875; and by the R.C.M., Savoy 24 June 1886 and H.M.'s 21 November 1911. In English also, Boston 20 January 1872; New York 10 February 1872, etc. (translated by A. Baildon).

In Danish (translated by N. T. Bruun), Copenhagen 14 April 1803.

In Swedish (translated by E. U. Nordforss), Stockholm 2 December 1803.

In Polish (translated by W. Boguslawski), Warsaw, May 1804; Wilna 1806.

In Russian (translated by V. A. Levshin), Moscow 1804; St. Petersburg 19 February 1813.

In Czech (translated by S. K. Machaček), Prague 25 April 1824.

In Hungarian (translated by F. S. Deáky), Clausenburg 24 April 1827.

In Italian (translated by G. Zaffira), London, D.L. 20 June 1872 (with recitatives by Costa).

An anonymous Dutch translation was published at Amsterdam in 1801, an Italian translation by P. Andolfati in 1804.

The chief work of Cherubini (who was himself an Italian) does not seem to have been produced in Italy at all.

Still revived in Germany now and then; in a new version by E. Pasqué, music arranged by F. Langer, it was produced at Mannheim 25 March 1903 (with a prologue made up from Cherubini's *Elisa*, see 1794); a new German version by E. Bloch was published in 1932. Revived at Prague 18 November 1932 (in Czech, Machaček's translation revised by F. V. Autrata); revived at Leningrad Spring 1933 (in Russian).

WINTER: *Marie von Montalban*

28 January. Munich

Text by K. Reger (founded on J. N. Komareck's tragedy of the same title, 1792, which was a sequel to K. M. Plümicke's *Lanassa*, the German version of A. M. Lemierre's *La Veuve de Malabar*). Four acts.

One of Winter's most important operas; the finale of the last act is said to have influenced Beethoven's *Fidelio*.

In German also, Berlin 29 December 1800; Vienna 26 July 1803; Prague January 1809, etc. The latest revivals were at Frankfort 17 July 1815; Dresden 22 February 1821; Hanover 1 December 1822.

In Polish (translated by W. Boguslawski), Warsaw 1805.

FOMIN: *Amerikantsi*
Американцы

19 February. St. Petersburg

Text by A. I. Klushin. Two acts.

The vocal score of this Russian comic opera was published in 1893.

B. A. WEBER: *Mudarra*

10 March. Berlin, O.

Text by C. A. Herklots. Four acts.

The most important work of the Berlin conductor; unsuccessful. Also Breslau 28 July 1800.

LEBRUN: *Marcelin*

22 March. Paris, Th. Feydeau

Text by F. Bernard-Valville. One act.

In French also, Liége 5 July 1801, etc.

In Spanish (as *El Marcelino*), Madrid 25 August 1801.

In German (as *Pachter Robert*, translated by J. von Seyfried), Vienna, W. 19 October 1803; Leipzig Spring 1805; Berlin 15 October 1805; Budapest 6 June 1806; Munich 1808; St. Petersburg 1808; Prague Spring 1821; Vienna, Kä. 20 September 1822, etc. Given on German stages until 1831.

In Swedish (translated by C. G. Nordforss), Stockholm 20 June 1804.

REICHARDT: *Lieb' und Treue*

31 March. Berlin, O.

Text by the composer (who used for his Lieder poems by Goethe, Herder, Salis, and folk songs). One act.

The first "Liederspiel" (a sort of German equivalent to the French "vaudeville"). See *A. M.Z.*, 22 July 1801, where Reichardt explains the meaning of the new form invented by him; see also *Journal des Luxus und der Moden*, 1800, p.481. The Liederspiel was given in Berlin until 1816.

Also Breslau 5 September 1800; Königsberg 1800; Bremen 1804–05; Schaffhausen 22 August 1809; Hamburg 26 June 1811, etc.

TARCHI: *D'Auberge en Auberge*
ou *Les Préventions*

26 April. Paris, O.C.

Text by E. Mercier-Dupaty. Three acts.

The most successful of Tarchi's six French comic operas.

In French also, Brussels 9 April 1802; Brunswick 1803.

In German (as *Die zwey Posten*, translated by G. F. Treitschke), Vienna 18 January 1804; Munich 19 August 1808, etc.

In Danish (translated by N. T. Bruun), Copenhagen 9 January 1806.

An English translation by J. Wild (*From Inn to Inn*) was published in 1805; it does not seem to have been acted.

A Dutch translation by A. Fokke Simonsz was published in the same year.

The subject became a favourite with Italian librettists and composers: *Di Locanda in Locanda e sempre in Sala*, text by L. Buonavoglia, music by Mayr (Venice 5 June 1805); *Amor tutto vince*, see 1805; *Di Posta in Posta*, text by L. Romanelli, music by V. Lavigna (Milan 2 July 1808).

KUNZEN: *Min Bedstemoder*

15 May. Copenhagen

Text by E. de Falsen (after Prince Hoare's *My Grand-Mother*). Two acts.

Given at Copenhagen until 1834.

SALIERI: *Cesare in Farmacusa*

2 June. Vienna, Kä.

Text by C. P. Defranceschi. Two acts.

In Italian also, Prague Carnival 1801 and Dresden February 1802.

In German, translated by J. J. Ihlee, Frankfort 1801; translated by G. F. Treitschke: Prague 15 January 1802; Hamburg 12 August 1803; Budapest 26 October 1803; Berlin 16 October 1804; Vienna, W. November 1808.

BOIELDIEU: *Béniowski ou Les Exilés du Kamchattka*

8 June. Paris, O.C.

Text by A. Duval (founded on a play by A. von Kotzebue). Three acts.

Given at the O.C. until 1828; since 20 July 1824 in a new version.

In French also, Liége 13 March 1802; Brunswick March 1803; Brussels 11 December 1803.

In German (translated by G. F. Treitschke), Vienna 20 June 1804.

In Polish (translated by B. Kudlicz), Warsaw 1813.

Parodies: *Je ne sais qui ou Les Exaltés de Charentin*, by P. Y. Barré, J. E. Despréaux, M. Dieulafoy and A. de Chazet, Th. du Vaudeville 16 June 1800; *Betowski ou L'Isle des Cygnes*, by F. P. A. Léger, P. A. Villiers, and R. C. G. de Pixérécourt, Th. des Troubadours 7 July 1800.

MAYR: *Il Carretto del Venditore d'Aceto*

28 June. Venice, S. Angelo

Text by G. M. Foppa (founded on a play by Mercier). One act.

In Italian also given at Dresden November 1802; Vienna 17 September 1803; Barcelona 22 December 1803; Amsterdam 1808; London, Pantheon 27 February 1812; Lisbon 22 July 1814; Madrid 30 July 1821.

In Portuguese, Lisbon 17 August 1810.

In German (translated by I. K. Kollmann), Vienna, Leop. 25 June 1816; Graz 8 February 1828; Würzburg 19 October 1829.

BOIELDIEU: *Le Calife de Bagdad*

16 September. Paris, O.C.

Text by C. Godard d'Aucour de Saint-Just. One act.

One of the most successful works of Boieldieu's pre-Russian period. Given at the O.C. until 1836 and revived there 27 April 1851 and 18 December 1875; revived at the Fantaisies-Parisiennes 16 March 1867.

In French also, Ghent 1800; Brussels 6 March 1801; Hague 7 November 1801; Hanover 30 August 1803; Brunswick 1803; St. Petersburg 1804 and Moscow 10 October 1808; Berne 15 June 1809; Vienna 2 July 1809; Stockholm April 1813; New York 27 August 1827.

In Spanish (translated by E. Tapia), Madrid 4 July 1801.

In German (translated by J. A. Bergk and F. Laun), Hamburg 14 May 1802; (translated by

C. A. Herklots) Berlin 18 March 1803; Vienna, W. July 1804; Budapest 1 January 1810; Prague 7 August 1814, etc. Revived Frankfort 14 September 1876 and 20 April 1878; Breslau February 1890; Königsberg 11 March 1939 (new German version by F. Schröder).

In Danish (translated by T. Thaarup), Copenhagen 30 January 1804.

In Russian (translated by E. Lifanov), St. Petersburg January 1806; Moscow 12 May 1811.

In Polish (translated by L. A. Dmuszewski), Warsaw 1807.

In Swedish (translated by C. G. Nordforss), Stockholm 23 May 1808.

In English (adapted by T. J. Dibdin), London, Hm. 11 May 1809; New York 14 October 1829.

An anonymous Dutch translation was published in 1802; an Italian translation by A. Zanchi in 1804.

REICHARDT: *Tamerlan*
16 October. Berlin, O.

Text by J. O. H. Schaum (translated from a French libretto by E. Morel de Chédeville). Four acts.

The opera had been written for Paris in 1786; but it was not performed there, the composer suddenly being forced to return to Berlin after the death of Frederick the Great. See Reichardt's pamphlet, *An das musikalische Publikum seine französischen Opern Tamerlan und Panthée betreffend* (1787). The original libretto was eventually set to music by Winter, see 1802.

SALIERI: *Angiolina ossia Il Matrimonio per Susurro*
22 October. Vienna, Kä.

Text by C. P. Defranceschi (founded on Ben Jonson's *Epicoene*). Two acts.

In Italian also given at London 29 December 1801 (as *Angelina*, text altered by L. da Ponte); Prague 10 February 1802; Dresden March 1803; Bologna May 1807; Paris 5 April 1809; Florence, T. Cocomero Autumn 1807 and T. dei Risoluti, Summer 1815.

In German, Breslau 28 May 1802; Berlin 16 October 1803.

In Polish (translated by W. Merlini), Wilna 16 May 1811; Cracow December 1821.

DALAYRAC: *Maison à vendre*
23 October. Paris, O.C.

Text by A. Duval. One act.

Of Dalayrac's numerous comic operas, this was probably the most successful one; frequently revived at different Paris theatres during the 19th century; and lately O.C. 26 October 1911; Tr. L. 19 January 1924; O.C. 5 April 1932. Revived at The Hague as late as April 1940.

In French also, Brussels 24 March 1801; Brunswick 1806; Moscow 20 October 1808; Berne 17 June 1809; Vienna 24 August 1809; Stockholm June 1813; New York 13 July 1827; Calcutta 28 September 1836.

In Spanish (translated by F. Enciso Castrillón), Madrid 9 July 1801; Buenos Aires July 1821 (Bosch) and/or 21 September 1826 (Kelly).

In German (translated by F. K. Hiemer), Stuttgart 5 March 1802; Mannheim 31 October 1802, etc.; Schleswig 1806; Hanover 25 May 1807.

In English (adapted and enlarged to 2 acts by J. Cobb, with some new music by M. Kelly), London, D.L. 17 November 1802 and New York 25 May 1803.

In Danish (translated by R. Frankenau), Copenhagen 30 November 1802.

In Swedish (translated by C. G. Nordforss), Stockholm 11 July 1808; Gothenburg 10 December 1813; revived Stockholm 14 September 1860 (new Swedish version by F. Arlberg).

In Dutch (translated by C. A. van Ray), Amsterdam 1809.

In Russian (translated by Adamovich), Moscow 15 January 1824.

An Italian translation by G. Piazza was published at Venice in 1804.

C. M. VON WEBER: *Das Waldmädchen*
24 November. Freiberg (Saxony)

Text by C. von Steinsberg. Two acts.

Weber's first performed opera. Given also at

Chemnitz 5 December 1800 (as *Das stumme Waldmädchen*) and Vienna, Leop. 4 December 1804 (as *Das Mädchen im Spessarter Walde*); it should be mentioned that the latter has been attributed to Wenzel Müller, in W. Krone's book on that composer (1906) as well as in F. Hadamowsky's *Das Theater in der Wiener Leopold-stadt* (1934). The opera was probably given either under the name or with additional music by Müller, who then was conductor at the Leopold-stadt Theatre (and was, some years later, to be succeeded by Weber at Prague).

See on this opera Weber's *Autobiographische Skizze* (1818): "Ich schrieb die vom Ritter von Steinsberg gedichtete Oper: das Waldmädchen, welche in November 1800 auch da gegeben wurde und sich dann später weiter verbreitete als mir lieb sein konnte (in Wien 14 mal gegeben, in Prag ins Böhmische übersetzt und in Peters-burg mit Beifall gesehen)". As to the perform-ances at Prague and St. Petersburg, mentioned by Weber, no trace of them could be discovered; nor could they be verified by Weber's son as early as in 1864.

Of the music, two fragments only have been preserved. For the new version, *Silvana*, see 1810.

PAER: *Poche, ma buone*, ossia *Le Donne cambiate*

18 December. Vienna, Kä.

Text by G. M. Foppa (first set to music by Portu-gal, see 1797). Two acts.

The alternative title in a MS score at the Florence Conservatorio is *La Moglie ravveduta*.

In Italian also, Prague 25 January 1802; Dres-den 30 April 1817.

Very successful in a German version by M. Stegmayer (as *Der lustige Schuster*, or *Die Weiber-kur*): Frankfort 13 March 1802; Bremen 1804–05; Leipzig 13 December 1805; Berlin 25 May 1807; Basle 9 March 1809; Vienna, W. 27 April 1809 (additions by I. von Seyfried and J. G. Lickl); Prague August 1810; St. Petersburg 1810; Berne 12 February 1812; Hanover 26 January 1825; Amsterdam 7 March 1825.

In Czech (translated by J. N. Stěpánek), Prague 21 January 1844.

Frequently revived in Germany during the first half of the century; the latest revival was at Kroll's, Berlin 15 August 1858.

It was probably also a German version of Paer's opera that was given at the German Stadt-Theater, New York, on 31 December 1859.

A vocal score, edited by R. Kleinmichel, was published as late as 1890.

1801

(CIMAROSA): *Artemisia*

17 January. Venice, F.

Text by "Jamejo Cratisto" (pseud.) *Dramma tra-gico per musica.* From *Giornale dei Teatri di Venezia* (contained in *Il Teatro Moderno Applaudito*) it appears that the author was Count Giovanni Battista Colloredo.

Cimarosa's last opera (performed a few days after his death); only two of the three acts were finished.

Given also at Rome Carnival 1806; Lisbon Summer 1806; Florence Autumn 1806 and Sum-mer 1813; Parma Carnival 1807; Dresden and Naples 1807.

Cimarosa had written an opera on the same subject some years earlier: *L'Artemisia, Regina di Caria*, produced Naples, S.C. June 1797. This was a setting of a different libretto, by M. Mar-chesini.

BERTON: *Le grand Deuil*

21 January. Paris, O.C.

Text by J. B. Vial and C. G. Etienne. One act.

Outside Paris given at:

BRUSSELS 16 December 1801 (in French).

VIENNA, W. 3 February 1804 (in German).

BRUNSWICK SUMMER 1804 (in French).

COPENHAGEN 1 October 1804 (in Danish, trans-lated by L. Kruse).

BERLIN 20 January 1806 (in German).

MOSCOW 14 January 1808 (in Russian).

ST. PETERSBURG 1810 (in German).

HAMBURG 14 January 1812 (in German).
WARSAW 1813 (in Polish, translated by B. Kudlicz).
KÖNIGSBERG 1820 (in German).

NICCOLINI: *I Baccanali di Roma*

21 January. Milan, Sc.
Text by L. Romanelli. Two acts.

Niccolini's most important opera; first great success of Angelica Catalani.

Outside Italy, given at Lisbon 24 June 1804 and St. Petersburg 4 August 1804.

HÄFFNER: *Renaud*

29 January. Stockholm
Text by N. B. Sparrschöld (translated from J. J. Leboeuf's French version of Gamerra's *Armida*, see 1772). Three acts.

The last opera of the Swedish composer.

MÉHUL: *L'Irato ou L'Emporté*

18 February. Paris, O.C.
Text by B. J. Marsollier (*comédie-parade*). One act.

Very successful in Paris; given at the O.C. until 1833 and revived there 28 May 1852; Th. L. 16 November 1868; Galerie Vivienne 15 October 1896, and again O.C. 20 December 1899 and 17 October 1917.

In French also, Liége 9 August 1801; Brussels 6 July 1802 (revived 13 February 1902); Hanover 29 August 1803; Brunswick 1803; Moscow 20 October 1808; revived Lyons June 1931.

In German (as *Der Tollkopf*, translated probably by H. G. Schmieder), Altona 7 August 1802; Hamburg 10 August 1802; Berlin 22 June 1804, etc.; St. Petersburg 1810; (as *Die Temperamente*, translated by J. von Seyfried), Vienna, W. 9 July 1803; revived Weimar 26 September 1832 (as *Der zänkische Onkel*, translated by C. Götze).

In Spanish, Madrid 21 July 1803.

In Polish (translated by Matuszewski), Warsaw 1805.

In Swedish (translated by C. G. Nordforss), Stockholm 25 August 1808.

In Dutch (translated by V. Vreedenberg), Amsterdam 1809.

The score is dedicated to "Général Bonaparte, Premier Consul de la République Française".

HIMMEL: *Frohsinn und Schwärmerei*

9 March. Berlin, O.
Text by C. A. Herklots. One act.

Popular "Liederspiel" (see Reichardt, 1800), given on many German stages. Hamburg 15 April 1806, etc.

ORLANDI: *Il Podestà di Chioggia*

12 March. Milan, Sc.
Text by A. Anelli. Two acts.

Successful in Italy; given at Venice, S. Luca 22 August 1801 as *Il Deputato di Rocca;* at Milan, T. Lentasio, March 1807 as *Il Podestà di Foggia.*

In Italian also, Lisbon Spring 1804; Vienna 23 October 1805; Paris 3 December 1806.

REICHARDT: *Jery und Bätely*

30 March. Berlin, O.
Goethe's text (first produced with music by C. S. von Seckendorff at Weimar 12 July 1780; first published 1790). One act.

Given in Berlin until 1825; produced by Goethe himself at Weimar 9 June 1804; Hamburg 16 September 1811; Breslau 9 January 1816.

Revived Hamburg 1881; Weimar 16 June 1916.

R. KREUTZER: *Astianax*

12 April. Paris, O.
Text by J. E. B. Dejaure. Three acts.
Given in Paris until 1816.

MAYR: *Ginevra di Scozia*

21 April. Trieste
Text by G. Rossi (after Ariosto). Two acts.

Written for the inauguration of the Teatro Nuovo, Trieste.

Milan, Sc. 26 December 1802, etc.; in Italy given until 1831.

In Italian also Vienna 27 October 1801 (with some additional music by Weigl); Berlin February 1804; Munich 13 July 1805 (revived Autumn 1818); Weimar 11 November 1811; Corfu Carnival 1828.

In German, Frankfort 26 December 1802 (as *Ariodante*); Lübeck 21 July 1806; Budapest 12 October 1807.

In Polish (translated by W. Boguslawski), Warsaw 1809; Wilna 22 March 1810.

EBERL: *Die Königin der schwarzen Inseln*

23 May. Vienna, Kä.

Text by J. Schwaldopler (after Wieland). Two acts.

The only surviving opera of the famous Viennese pianist; overture printed.

PAER: *Achille*

6 June. Vienna, Kä.

Text by G. de Gamerra. Two acts.

In Italian also Prague 1803; Dresden 7 April 1804; Paris, Th. des Tuileries 31 January 1808 (first act) and 19 March 1808 (second act); Mannheim 24 May 1812; Forlì Spring 1816; Milan, Sc. 26 December 1816.

In German, Frankfort 11 April 1802 (revived 6 April 1823 and 4 January 1835); Stuttgart December 1805; Berlin 15 October 1810; St. Petersburg 1810; Budapest 12 August 1812; Hanover 24 April 1815; Copenhagen 4 March 1820; Prague 1825; Riga 1825.

In Polish (translated by J. Adamczewski), Warsaw 3 December 1808 (with additional music by J. Elsner).

TEYBER: *Alexander*

13 June. Vienna, W.

Text by E. Schikaneder (*Grosse heroische Oper*). Two acts.

Written for the inauguration of the "K.K. priv. Theater an der Wien" which succeeded

Schikaneder's old "Freyhaus" theatre "auf der Wieden".

Produced with a prologue by Schikaneder, *Thespis Traum*.

FARINELLI: *Teresa e Claudio*

9 September. Venice, S. Luca

Text by G. M. Foppa (founded on a comedy by Greppi). Two acts.

One of the best and most successful operas of Farinelli.

Outside Italy given at Vienna 23 September 1802 (as *L'Amore irritato della Difficoltà*, with additional music by Weigl); Barcelona 4 November 1803; Lisbon Winter 1804; Amsterdam 1808; London 13 April 1809; Munich Summer 1817.

DALAYRAC: *Léhéman ou La Tour de Newstadt*

12 December. Paris, O.C.

Text by B. J. Marsollier. Three acts.

In French also, Brussels 14 June 1802 (revived 17 January 1819); Brunswick 1803.

More successful in Germany where it was one of the favourite "rescue operas" of that period (first translated by G. L. P. Sievers).

Given at Vienna, W. May 1803 (revived 6 July 1824); Berlin 7 June 1803; Munich 1803 (as *Macdonald*, translated by C. M. Heigel; revived 25 July 1811 and 2 November 1819); Budapest 29 August 1803 (revived 30 July 1827); Schleswig 1804; St. Petersburg 27 September 1810; Hamburg 27 May 1812; last revived Weimar 4 September 1830.

In Swedish (translated by C. G. Nordforss), Stockholm 13 May 1805.

In Polish (translated by J. Baudouin), Warsaw 1807.

In Russian (translated by R. M. Zotov), St. Petersburg 3 February 1823; Moscow 7 December 1824.

A Dutch translation by C. A. van Raij was published in 1813, a Danish translation by N. T. Bruun in 1814.

TRENTO: *Quanti Casi in un Giorno!*

December. Venice, S. Ben.

Text by G. Artusi. One act.

Trento's most successful work; given at Leghorn Carnival 1803 as *Gli Assassini.*

Outside Italy given at Lisbon 1803; Barcelona 4 June 1805 (as *Roberto Capo d'Assassini*); Amsterdam Carnival 1806; London 3 February 1807 (as *Roberto l'Assassino*); Dresden 1808; Paris 29 August 1808 (as *La Foresta di Nicobar*); revived Munich January 1819; Cremona Carnival 1823.

1802

MAYR: *I Misteri Eleusini*

16 January. Milan, Sc.

Text by G. Bernardoni. Two acts.

Given at Venice Spring 1804 as *Polibete.*

Revived at Milan, Sc. 28 February 1807, with additions; Naples, S.C. 22 November 1809.

In Italian also, Lisbon 7 November 1807; Paris 15 January 1814 (the first act at Napoléon's private "Théâtre des Tuileries" 6 January 1814); Madrid 19 November 1821 (as *Antinoo in Eleusi*).

DALAYRAC: *L'Antichambre* ou *Les Valets entre eux*

26 February. Paris, O.C.

Text by E. Mercier-Dupaty. One act.

Given there in 1802 only once; far more successful in a new version as *Picaros et Diégo* 3 May 1803 which held the boards until 1837.

In French also, Brussels 25 November 1803; St. Petersburg 1804; Moscow 7 October 1809.

In German (as *Die Glücksritter*, translated by C. A. Herklots), Berlin 26 September 1804.

In Spanish (translated by F. Enciso Castrillón), Madrid 1 January 1807.

In Swedish (translated by J. E. Brooman), Stockholm 18 October 1813.

SCHALL: *Domherren i Milano,* eller *De uventede Gaester*

16 March. Copenhagen

Text by N. T. Bruun (after a French play by A. Duval, *Le Souper imprévu, ou Le Chanoine de Milan*). Two acts.

The most successful of Schall's operas, given at Copenhagen until 1833.

MÉHUL: *Une Folie*

5 April. Paris, O.C.

Text by J. N. Bouilly. Two acts.

The most successful of Méhul's comic operas.

In French also Brussels 6 September 1802; Ghent 16 July 1803; Hanover 4 August 1803; Brunswick 1803; Berne 5 March 1806; New Orleans 30 January 1808; Moscow 12 June 1809; Vienna 22 June 1809; Florence April 1839 (by amateurs, at Prince Poniatowsky's).

In German (five different versions):

BERLIN 28 March 1803 (as *Je toller, je besser*, translated by C. A. Herklots).

HAMBURG 4 May 1804 (as *Je toller, je besser*, translated by C. A. Herklots).

WEIMAR 2 June 1804 (as *Je toller, je besser*, translated by C. A. Herklots).

VIENNA, W. 24 May 1803 (as *Die beiden Füchse*, translated by J. von Seyfried).

BERNE SUMMER 1804 (as *Die beiden Füchse*, translated by J. von Seyfried).

POZNÁN 17 August 1804 (as *Die beiden Füchse*, translated by J. von Seyfried).

MUNICH 17 July 1807 (as *Die beiden Füchse*, translated by J. von Seyfried).

PRAGUE 1807 (as *Die beiden Füchse*, translated by J. von Seyfried).

LUCERNE 1810 (as *Die beiden Füchse*, translated by J. von Seyfried).

MOSCOW 30 September 1820 (as *Die beiden Füchse*, translated by J. von Seyfried).

MANNHEIM 3 July 1803 (as *Vetter Jacob*, translated by F. K. Hiemer).

FRANKFORT 29 January 1804 (as *List und Liebe*, translated by J. J. Ihlee).

STUTTGART 8 April 1804 (as *List und Liebe*, translated by J. J. Ihlee).

SCHLESWIG 1804 (as *Wagen gewinnt*, translated by G. F. Treitschke).

VIENNA, KÄ. 22 June 1809 (as *Wagen gewinnt*, translated by G. F. Treitschke).

In Spanish (translated by M. Bellosartes), Madrid 1 January 1803.

In Swedish (translated by C. G. Nordforss), Stockholm 1 February 1804; Lund 29 July 1808; Malmö 2 December 1810.

In Hungarian, Clausenburg 14 February 1806.

In Russian (translated by V. A. Levshin), Moscow 17 July 1807; St. Petersburg Summer 1810.

In Polish (translated by W. Pekalski), Warsaw 1808; Wilno 18 January 1811.

Never given at Copenhagen (see Dupuy, 1806).

A Dutch translation of the libretto (by C. Vreedenberg) was published in 1803.

An English version by G. Colman, *Love Laughs at Locksmiths,* was given in London, Little Hm. 25 July 1803 (new music by M. Kelly; see his *Reminiscences,* Vol. II, p.197: "The original music was very good but not calculated for an English audience; I therefore recomposed the whole music"). Kelly's version was also given in Dublin February 1804; New York 23 May 1804 (revived 28 September 1849) and on many other American stages as well as at Cape Town in 1838.

Another English translation, probably by J. Wild, was published in 1804.

Méhul's original was revived at the O.C. on 20 November 1843, at the Gaîté on 6 December 1874; at Buenos Aires by a French company in 1852; in German, Frankfort 13 March 1840 and January 1864; Berlin, Kroll's 5 August 1851; Dresden 25 June 1854; Königsberg 23 May 1874; Prague November 1934.

CATEL: *Sémiramis*

4 May. Paris, O.

Text by P. Desriaux (based on Voltaire's tragedy). Three acts.

Catel's first opera. Given in Paris until 1810.

In German (translated by I. F. Castelli), Vienna, W. 23 October 1806; Budapest 18 April 1808; Prague Autumn 1810; Berlin 27 October 1824.

The overture of this opera was a concert favourite until *c.*1850.

BERTON: *Le Concert interrompu*

31 May. Paris, O.C.

Text by B. J. Marsollier and E. G. F. de Favières. One act.

In French also Ghent 1802; Brussels 9 November 1803; Hamburg July 1805, etc.

In Spanish, Madrid 9 December 1804.

In German, Berlin 26 January 1807.

In Danish (translated by N. T. Bruun), Copenhagen 11 December 1807.

In Swedish (translated by C. G. Nordforss), Stockholm 3 February 1813.

In Polish (translated by W. Boguslawski), Warsaw 1816.

MÉHUL: *Le Trésor supposé* ou *Le Danger d'écouter aux Portes*

29 July. Paris, O.C.

Text by F. B. Hoffman. One act.

In Paris last revived on 16 July 1824.

In French also, Ghent 1802; Brussels 1 January 1803; Hanover 12 March 1804; Brunswick Spring 1804; Berne 28 June 1809; Vienna 2 November 1809; Stockholm April 1813; Calcutta 12 October 1836.

In German (translated by J. von Seyfried), Vienna, W. 10 August 1803; (translated by D. Jäger), Berlin 7 October 1803; Munich 1807; (translated by G. L. P. Sievers), Hamburg 30 December 1807.

In German also, Prague Summer 1807; St. Petersburg 1809; Moscow 25 December 1819. Last revived Munich 22 June 1852; Dresden 19 January 1857.

In Danish (translated by N. T. Bruun), Copenhagen 17 May 1804; revived Bergen 7 October 1855.

In Swedish (translated by C. G. Nordforss), Stockholm 22 February 1805; Gothenburg 8 July 1805.

In Spanish (translated by F. Enciso Castrillón), Madrid 12 May 1805.

In Russian (translated by A. V. Luknitsky), St. Petersburg 17 February 1807; Moscow 26 February 1807.

In Hungarian (translated by J. Horváth), Clausenburg 30 March 1807.

In Polish (translated by B. Kudlicz), Warsaw 1812.

An Italian translation by P. Grappelli was published in 1805; another by G. M. Foppa (from Seyfried's German version) in 1808.

A Dutch translation by J. de Quack and B. A. Fallee was published in 1813.

WINTER: *Tamerlan*

14 September. Paris, O.

Text by E. Morel de Chédeville (based on Voltaire's *Orphelin de la Chine;* originally written for Reichardt in 1786; see 16 October 1800). Four acts.

Winter's only French opera. Revived in Paris 1 February 1815.

In German (translated by J. von Sonnleithner), Vienna 9 April 1805 (in concert form) and W. 19 June 1812 (with additions by I. von Seyfried); Budapest 18 October 1814; Würzburg 19 October 1814.

VAL. FIORAVANTI: *La Capricciosa pentita*

2 October. Milan, Sc.

Text by L. Romanelli. Two acts.

Very successful in Italy; given at Turin, T. Carignano Autumn 1806 as *La Sposa corretta;* at Venice Autumn 1810 as *Capriccio e Pentimento;* revived Venice 25 December 1832.

Outside Italy: Vienna 26 June 1805; Paris 5 September 1805 (revived 21 October 1817 as *La Sposa stravagante*); Amsterdam 1807; London 6 January 1809 (under the original title) and revived 7 February 1815 (as *L'Orgoglio avvilito*, rather

confusingly as Fioravanti actually wrote an opera of that title, produced at Milan in January 1803. A comparison of the libretti shows that the London *Orgoglio* has nothing to do with the Milan *Orgoglio*, and is identical with *La Capricciosa pentita*); Lugano 1810; Munich 11 October 1816.

TRITTO: *Gli Americani*

4 November. Naples, S.C.

Text by G. Rossi. Two acts.

One of Tritto's best works. Lisbon 4 November 1803. New version (*Gonzalvo*), Naples 13 August 1805; revived Padua June 1819.

MÉHUL: *Joanna*

23 November. Paris, O.C.

Text by B. J. Marsollier. Two acts.

In German, Vienna, W. 14 December 1803 (very successful there); Budapest 1 January 1805; Würzburg 6 August 1809.

PAER: *I Fuorusciti di Firenze*

27 November. Dresden

Text by A. Anelli. Two acts.

The first opera Paer wrote for Dresden; one of his most successful works.

In Italian also, Prague December 1802; Vienna 31 July 1804; Parma Carnival 1805; Naples 13 October 1810; Milan, Sc. 8 February 1814; Paris 20 March 1819; Barcelona 5 July 1819.

In German (translated by C. W. Franke), Breslau 2 October 1804; Leipzig 19 October 1804; Hamburg 3 February 1807; Weimar 19 December 1807; Prague 1808; Berlin 17 June 1813; Munich 1814, etc.

In Danish (translated by A. G. Oehlenschläger), Copenhagen 30 October 1823.

In English (as *The Freebooters*, translated by H. Napier, music arranged by W. Hawes), London, Ly. 20 August 1827; New York 24 December 1827; Edinburgh 8 March 1830.

Date of first performance according to *Journal des Luxus und der Moden*, 1803, p.40. In most books of reference the Vienna 1804 production is wrongly stated to have been the original one.

ISOUARD: *Michel-Ange*

11 December. Paris, O.C.

Text by E. J. B. Delrieu. One act.

Isouard's first greater success; in Paris given until 1829.

In French also, Ghent 1802; Brussels 28 March 1803; Hamburg Summer 1803; Brunswick Spring 1804; Hanover 3 July 1805.

In Dutch (translated by C. Vreedenberg), Amsterdam 1803.

In German (translated by C. A. Herklots), Munich 1803; Vienna, Leop. 1 June 1804; Berlin 21 January 1805, etc.; revived Mannheim 28 June 1835.

In Spanish, Madrid 13 June 1804.

In Polish (translated by L. A. Dmuszewski), Warsaw 1812.

In Danish (translated by N. T. Bruun), Copenhagen 1 January 1820.

1803

BOIELDIEU: *Ma Tante Aurore ou Le Roman impromptu*

13 January. Paris, O.C.

Text by C. de Longchamps (on the title-page of the libretto: ". . . sifflé en trois actes le 23 nivôse, applaudi en deux le 25 du même mois . . ."). Given at the O.C. until 1836; revived Th. L. 18 October 1851; Galerie Vivienne 5 April 1894; Tr. L. 15 January 1921.

In French also Ghent 1803; Brunswick and Hamburg 1803; Brussels 18 March 1803; Hanover 10 March 1804; St. Petersburg 1804; Stockholm 1805; Berne 19 February 1806; Moscow 24 October 1808; Vienna 13 August 1809; New Orleans 1810; New York 18 July 1827.

In German (translated by M. G. Lambrecht), Vienna, W. 11 April 1804; (translated by C. A. Herklots); Altona 6 July 1806; Berlin 23 March 1807.

In Spanish (translated by F. Enciso Castrillón), Madrid 21 December 1803.

In Danish (translated by T. Thaarup), Copenhagen 19 March 1812.

In Swedish (translated by C. G. Nordforss), Stockholm 29 April 1813.

In Russian, Moscow 31 January 1822.

Parodies: *La Nièce de ma Tante Aurore ou La Manie des Romans*, by J. A. Jaquelin, Th. des Jeunes Artistes 8 March 1803; *La Famille de ma Tante Aurore ou La Matinée romanesque*, by P. Thénard, Brest 29 December 1803.

RIGHINI: *Gerusalemme liberata ossia Armida al Campo de Franchi. La Selva incantata*

17 January. Berlin, O.

Text by A. de' Filistri da Caramondani (after Tasso).

Righini's most important work (consisting of two 2-act operas).

One of the last Italian works produced at the Berlin O. Revived Berlin 15 October 1811 (in German, translated by C. A. Herklots) and 17 December 1815 (in Italian).

In Swedish (translated by C. G. Nordforss), Stockholm 26 January 1831; an earlier Swedish version had already been published at Gothenburg in 1819 (for a concert performance?).

LAVIGNA: *La Muta per Amore ossia Il Medico per Forza*

24 January. Milan, Sc.

Text by G. M. Foppa. One act.

The first and most successful opera of Lavigna, who was maestro al cembalo at the Scala, and later became the teacher of Verdi.

MÉHUL: *Héléna*

1 March. Paris, O.C.

Text by J. N. Bouilly and J. A. de Révéroni Saint-Cyr. Three acts.

In French also, Brunswick Spring 1804; Brussels 19 August 1804; Moscow 16 October 1809.

In German (translated by G. F. Treitschke), Vienna 22 August 1803; Berlin 14 November 1803; Schleswig 1804; Budapest 16 December 1807; Munich 1810; Prague 4 January 1815 (one additional air by Weber); revived Dresden 22 April 1817 (additions by Paer and Nasolini); Vienna, Jos. 1 September 1827.

In Danish (translated by N. T. Bruun), Copenhagen 20 November 1806.

In Polish (translated by J. Adamczewski), Warsaw 1807.

In Russian, Moscow 4 March 1812.

Italian translation by F. G. Galli published 1805.

(The overture to this opera anticipates the famous trumpet-call in *Fidelio*.)

C. M. VON WEBER: *Peter Schmoll und seine Nachbarn*

March? Augsburg

Text by J. Türk (founded on a novel by C. G. Kramer). Two acts.

Weber's second opera, written at Salzburg in 1801–02; exact date of production unknown; failure. Libretto lost; score preserved and printed in 1926; the opera was revived at Lübeck December 1927 (new dialogue by K. Eggert).

PAISIELLO: *Proserpine*

29 March. Paris, O.

Quinault's text (first set to music by Lully, see 1680), reduced to 3 acts and altered by N. F. Guillard.

The only French opera of Paisiello, then "Premier Maître de Chapelle et Compositeur au Service de S.M. le Roi de Naples; actuellement employé pour composer et diriger la Musique particulière du Premier Consul".

Unsuccessful (14 performances) and never revived.

ISOUARD: *Les Confidences*

31 March. Paris, O.C.

Text by A. G. Jars (not by F. B. Hoffman as some books of reference have it). Two acts.

In French also, Brussels 2 October 1803; Hamburg 1804; Berne 5 March 1806.

In German, Vienna 23 July 1804 (as *Die Verwechslungen*, translated by M. G. Lambrecht); Berlin 24 September 1805 (as *Die vertrauten Nebenbuhler*, translated by C. A. Herklots).

In Spanish (translated by F. Enciso Castrillón), Madrid 16 January 1805.

In Danish (translated by N. T. Bruun), Copenhagen 14 May 1805.

In Polish (translated by K. Brodziński), Warsaw 1816.

PAER: *Sargino ossia L'Allievo dell' Amore*

26 May. Dresden

Text by G. M. Foppa (founded on Monvel's French libretto, see 1788). Two acts.

One of Paer's most successful works.

In Italian also, Prague 15 September 1804; Vienna 25 February 1807; Amsterdam 1809; Milan, Sc. 5 March 1814; Naples, T. Fondo 1815; Trieste 8 April 1828.

In German (translated by C. M. Heigel), Munich 13 July 1804; (translated by J. J. Ihlee), Hanover 2 September 1804; Frankfort 9 September 1804; Vienna, W. 4 February 1806; Berlin 3 February 1808; Prague 1808; Hamburg 13 October 1809, etc. Also Amsterdam 20 November 1824; Budapest 26 January 1829; Antwerp 5 August 1831; Bucharest 19 January 1834; last given Lemberg 5 June 1838; Cassel 24 October 1839; Riga 1843.

In Swedish (translated by C. G. Nordforss), Stockholm 19 May 1806.

In Polish (translated by W. Boguslawski), Warsaw 1811.

In Russian, St. Petersburg 29 December 1815.

In Danish (translated by N. T. Bruun), Copenhagen 31 January 1820.

(Date of first performance according to *A.M. Z.*, v, p.622. Engländer in *Neues Archiv für Sächsische Geschichte und Altertumskunde*, 1929, gives June 6th on p.209, June 26th on p.220.)

WINTER: *La Grotta di Calipso*

31 May. London, Hm.

Text by L. da Ponte. Two acts.

The first opera Winter wrote for London; very successful there (with Elizabeth Billington).

In German, Munich 17 April 1807.

CANNABICH: *Palmer und Amalia*

August. Munich

Text: a German version, by an unknown translator, of Pigault-Lebrun's French libretto (see 1797). Three acts.

Unsuccessful: ". . . da man ohnehin in diesem Werke die Quintessenz Mozartischer und Cherubinischer Melodien zur Genüge antrifft. Für das seltene Vergnügen aber, ohngefähr ein Dutzend Opern mit einem Male zu hören, wird hiermit dem Verfasser des Werkes gebührender Dank abgestattet" (*A.M.Z.*, 1803, no.49).

PAVESI: *Un Avvertimento ai Gelosi*

27 August. Venice, S. Ben.

Text by G. M. Foppa. One act.

The first of Pavesi's numerous operas.

Successful in Italy; given at Naples, T. N. Spring 1805 as *La Scuola de' Gelosi;* Milan, Sc. 6 November 1813.

In Italian also Barcelona 2 August 1804; Amsterdam 1808; Paris 27 May 1809; Cagliari, Sardinia Carnival 1811; Munich 31 August 1816; Lisbon 1819; Madrid 29 October 1821.

BERTON: *Aline, Reine de Golconde*

2 September. Paris, O.C.

Text by J. B. C. Vial and E. G. F. de Favières (a new version of Sedaine's libretto, see 1766). Three acts.

Berton's most successful work. Given at the O.C. until 1830 and revived at the Opéra National (Boulevard du Temple) 16 November 1847 (re-scored by Adam).

In French also, Brussels 4 January 1804; Brunswick 1804; Hanover 3 June 1806; Berne 12 June 1809; Stockholm 2 April 1811 (privately); New Orleans Spring 1825; and probably New York 29 August 1827.

In German (translated by C. A. Herklots), Berlin 3 March 1804; (translated by G. F. Treitschke), Vienna 6 March 1804; Frankfort 7 April 1805; Munich 1807; Hamburg 11 September 1807, etc. Bamberg 26 October 1808 (E. T. A. Hoffmann's début as conductor); Budapest 14 April 1813; Prague 19 April 1814; Helsinki 26 February 1838. Last revived in German: Königsberg 25 December 1851.

In Spanish, Madrid 4 November 1804.

In Polish (translated by K. Hebdowski), Warsaw 1808; Cracow 14 September 1809.

In Swedish (translated by C. G. Nordforss), Stockholm 18 April 1811.

In Russian (translated by D. I. Vyelyashev-Volyntsov), St. Petersburg 15 May 1815; Moscow 5 October 1815.

In Hungarian (translated by J. Kiss), Clausenburg 29 January 1836.

Never given at Copenhagen as J. A. P. Schulz's opera on the same subject (see 1787) was very successful there.

The libretto was again used by Boieldieu, whose setting was produced at the French Opera, St. Petersburg 17 March 1804.

FEDERICI: *Zaira*

3 September. Milan, T. Carcano

Text by M. Bocciardini. Two acts.

There is much that is dubious in the history of this opera. Written for the inauguration of the new Teatro Carcano, Milan, as generally stated. But from a remark in Sorge's *Teatri di Palermo* it would appear that the opera originally was performed at the T. di Santa Cecilia, Palermo, in 1799; and Florimo records an opera by Federici under the title of *Il Trionfo della Religione* as having been produced at Naples, T. N. in 1802, which has the same characters as *Zaira*. The original Milan bill of 1803 attributes the opera not to Vincenzo Federici, as generally stated, but to the much less well-known Francesco Federici of Genoa.

Outside Italy (in Italian) given at Vienna 25 July 1805; Dresden 20 May 1807; Lisbon 22 June 1808; Madrid 22 January 1809; London 26 December 1810; Paris 20 June 1817.

In Polish, Warsaw 1810.

CHERUBINI: *Anacréon* ou *L'Amour fugitif*

4 October. Paris, O.

Text by R. Mendouze. Two acts.

Unsuccessful: outside Paris only given at the Redoutensaal, Vienna, on 14 April 1805 (in concert form; German version by M. Stegmayer).

This opéra-ballet contains a famous overture and the beautiful air *Jeunes filles aux regards doux.*

ISOUARD: *Le Médecin Turc*

19 November. Paris, O.C.

Text by P. Villiers and A. Gouffé. One act.

Given at the O.C. until 1827; in French also, Brussels 21 February 1804; Brunswick 11 June 1804; Moscow 16 May 1807; Berne 15 July 1809.

In German, Vienna, Kä. May 1804; Frankfort September 1805, etc.

In Spanish (translated by F. Enciso Castrillón), Madrid 14 October 1804.

In Russian (translated by A. V. Luknitsky), St. Petersburg 19 November 1810.

In Polish (translated by L. A. Dmuszewski), Warsaw 1816.

MAYR: *Alonso e Cora*

26 December. Milan, Sc.

Text by G. Bernardoni. Two acts.

In Italian also, Vienna 1 June 1804; in German, Frankfort April 1805.

Revived in a new version by F. Berio di Salsa, as *Cora*, Naples S.C. March 1815, and in German, Vienna 3 October 1822 (with additional music by Weigl).

FARINELLI: *I Riti d'Efeso*

26 December. Venice, F.

Text by G. Rossi. Two acts.

Given in Italy until 1822. In Italian also, Vienna 19 December 1804 (with 2 airs by Weigl); Lisbon 13 May 1806; London 7 March 1815.

1804

DALAYRAC: *La jeune Prude,* ou *Les Femmes entre elles*

14 January. Paris, O.C.

Text by E. Mercier-Dupaty. One act.

Given in Paris until 1827; in French also Brussels 25 September 1804; Berne 23 June 1809; Moscow 24 February 1810.

In German (as *Die Spröde auf der Probe*), Vienna 29 December 1804.

In Russian, Moscow 1805.

In Polish (translated by W. Pekalski), Warsaw 30 December 1821.

A Dutch version by M. G. Engelman was published in 1810.

DALAYRAC: *Une Heure de Mariage*

20 March. Paris, O.C.

Text by C. G. Etienne. One act.

Last revived in Paris, O.C. 17 December 1849 and Tr. L. 15 January 1921.

In French also, Brussels 1 August 1804; Brunswick Summer 1804; St. Petersburg March 1805; Hamburg 8 August 1805; Moscow 1 October 1808; Berne 31 May 1809; Stockholm April 1813; New York August 1830.

In German, Berlin 14 February 1805, etc.

In Spanish, Madrid 21 February 1805.

In Danish (translated by N. T. Bruun), Copenhagen 23 December 1806.

In Swedish (translated by C. G. Nordforss), Stockholm 25 February 1809.

In Polish (translated by W. Boguslawski), Warsaw 1813.

A Dutch version by C. van der Vijver was published in 1807.

WINTER: *Il Trionfo dell' Amor fraterno*

22 March. London, Hm.

Text by L. da Ponte. Three acts.

In German, Munich 13 January 1805; Vienna December 1806 (in concert form).

In French, Paris, O. 19 August 1806 (as *Castor et Pollux*, music adapted to a libretto by E. Morel de Chédeville which was founded on the older text by P. J. J. Bernard, see 1737).

The statement in Gugitz's Da Ponte bibliography that the libretto was not printed, is not correct.

PUCITTA: *La Burla fortunata* ossia *I due Prigionieri*

9 April. Venice, S. Moisè

Text by G. D. Camagna (founded on Marsollier's *Adolphe et Clara*, see 1799). One act.

In Italian also, Zara 1805; Amsterdam 1806; Paris 10 June 1811 (as *Adolfo e Chiara*); London 26 May 1814; Munich 26 July 1816; Vienna 16 March 1817; Barcelona 8 January 1821. Revived Milan, T. Carcano July 1833.

In Spanish (as *El Matrimonio reunido*, translated by F. Enciso Castrillón), Madrid 2 January 1818; Mexico 1826.

GENERALLI: *Pamela nubile*

12 April. Venice, S. Ben.

Text by G. Rossi. One act.

Generali's first great success.

Outside Italy: Vienna 29 July 1805 (as *La Virtù premiata per Amore*); Barcelona 16 January 1806 (revived 22 December 1817); Amsterdam Carnival 1806; Dresden 1810; Paris 8 December 1810; Munich 4 October 1816; Lisbon Winter 1819. Revived Milan, Sc. 18 October 1823.

WINTER: *Il Ratto di Proserpina*

3 May. London, Hm.

Text by L. da Ponte. Two acts.

Written for E. Billington and J. Grassini (see Kelly's *Reminiscences*, II, p.216). Winter used parts of the music from his *Opferfest*, 1796.

Revived London 20 July 1815; Paris 7 December 1816.

In German (translated by J. Schlett), Munich 15 January 1808.

HIMMEL: *Fanchon, das Leiermädchen*

15 May. Berlin, O.

Text by A. von Kotzebue (founded on a French vaudeville by J. M. Pain and J. N. Bouilly). Three acts.

Very popular in Germany; in Berlin given until 1853. Breslau 9 November 1804; Poznán 18 February 1805; Hamburg 19 July 1805; Hanover 9 September 1805; Munich 1805; Königsberg 1805; Prague May 1807; Vienna, W. 13 July 1808 (revived Kä. 18 June 1817; 3 December 1834; and Leop. 3 November 1846); in German also St. Petersburg 12 February 1806; Viipuri (Finland) 20 October 1825. Last revived Königsberg 3 November 1855 and 9 December 1909.

In Dutch (translated by A. Fokke Simonsz), Amsterdam 1806.

In Danish (translated by N. T. Bruun), Copenhagen 29 October 1814.

In Polish (translated by W. Boguslawski), Warsaw 1820.

In Swedish (translated by J. E. Remmer), Stockholm 28 October 1822; Gothenburg 27 April 1827.

VOGLER: *Samori*

17 May. Vienna, W.

Text by F. X. Huber. Three acts.

Important work of the famous theoretician, but unsuccessful.

Darmstadt 30 June 1811; Breslau 11 March 1818.

Most Viennese authors (M. Voll, T. von Frimmel, K. Glossy) give May 7 as the date of the first performance and so does Thayer. May 17 is given by the reviewers in the *Allgemeine Musikalische Zeitung* and other journals.

C. F. Becker, one of the first compilers of a kind of reference-book for musical dates (1849) has 18 May, and he usually is just one or two days wrong.

GAVEAUX: *Un Quart-d'Heure de Silence*

9 June. Paris, O.C.

Text by Guillet. One act.

In French also, Brussels 3 January 1805, etc.

In Spanish (translated by F. Enciso Castrillón), Madrid 30 May 1806.

In Russian (translated by S. N. Glinka), Moscow 31 December 1807; St. Petersburg 13 December 1824.

In Polish (translated by K. Brodziński), Warsaw 1817.

For a German version of the text, see 1805.

A Swedish version by C. G. Nordforss, with new music by J. B. Struwe, was given at Stockholm 21 March 1810.

GAVEAUX: *Le Bouffe et le Tailleur*

21 June. Paris, Th. Montansier

Text by P. Villiers and A. Gouffé. One act.

Given at the O.C. until 1836; revived 10 December 1895 at the Galerie Vivienne and 17 March 1899 at the Th. L. de la Renaissance.

In French also, Brussels 7 January 1805 (frequently revived in Belgium until about 1890); Stockholm June 1813; Berne 6 March 1819; Berlin, Kgst. 25 May 1825; Vienna 9 August 1826; New York 20 August 1827; London, St. J.'s 22 January 1849.

In Russian (translated by P. A. Vyazemsky), St. Petersburg 24 September 1813. Given at Moscow on 22 October 1808 in French, 10 May 1816 in Russian, and 22 January 1820 in German.

In Swedish, Stockholm 24 November 1813.

In Polish (translated by A. Zolkowski), Warsaw 1816.

A Dutch version by J. de Quack and B. A. Fallee was published in 1812.

For a German opera on the same subject, see 1814.

MAYR: *Elisa*

5 July. Venice, S. Ben.

Text by G. Rossi (founded on Saint-Cyr's French libretto, see 1794). Two acts.

In Italian also, Barcelona 25 August 1807; Amsterdam 1808; Dresden 1810; Munich Summer 1816; London 25 May 1820 (privately performed at the Dutch Ambassador's as *Il Monte di San Bernardo*, in concert form); Madrid 11 January 1823.

In Polish (translated by A. Rutkowski), Warsaw 1810 (with additional music by J. Elsner).

LESUEUR: *Ossian* ou *Les Bardes*

10 July. Paris, O.

Text by P. Dercy and J. M. Deschamps. Five acts.

The first new opera at the Académie Impériale de Musique; given there until 1817. Napoléon, to whom the score is dedicated, attended the second performance on 13 July; it was the first opera he heard as Emperor; he had suggested the subject himself (the German writer J. G. Sulzer, in his *Theorie der schönen Künste*, 1771–74, was the first to recommend Ossian as a subject suitable for operatic treatment).

Parts of Lesueur's work were revived at the Paris Opéra on 25 May 1916.

There were at least three parodies of *Ossian* produced at the minor Paris theatres in 1804: *Bombarde, ou Les Marchands de Chansons*, by Alexis Daudet, J. Servières and F. P. A. Léger, Th. Molière, 19 July 1804; *Ossian Cadet, ou Les Guimbardes* by E. Mercier-Dupaty, A. de Chazet, and C. F. Moreau, Vaudeville Th. 30 July 1804; *Oh! que c'est sciant, ou Oxessian*, by F. Cornu and M. A. M. Desaugiers, Th. Montansier 3 September 1804.

PORTUGAL: *L'Oro non compra Amore*

Autumn. Lisbon, S.C.

Text by G. Caravita (founded on Bertati's *Villanella rapita*, see 1783). Two acts.

In Italian also, Milan, Sc. 5 November 1808, etc. Rio de Janeiro 17 December 1811 (revived 22 August 1817); Paris 23 December 1815; Munich 14 November 1817; last revived at Lisbon 31 January 1825.

In Spanish, Madrid 18 June 1819.

PAER: *Leonora* ossia *L'Amore coniugale*

3 October. Dresden

Text probably by the Dresden singer, G. Cinti (Italian version of Bouilly's French libretto, see 1798). Two acts.

On the debated question whether Beethoven knew Paer's opera before writing *Fidelio*, see T. Frimmel, *Beethoven-Handbuch*, II, pp.3–6.

In Italian also given at Prague 1805; Vienna March 1806 (privately at Prince Lobkowitz's; see *Journal des Luxus und der Moden*, 1806, p.287 and p.440); Fontainebleau 8 November 1809; Florence, P. Spring 1812; Naples, T. Fondo Summer 1816.

In German (translated by F. Rochlitz, as *Leonore oder Spaniens Gefängnisse bei Sevilla*); Vienna 8 February 1809; Stuttgart 19 November 1809; Frankfort 4 June 1810; Berlin 11 July 1810; Munich 1813, etc. Revived Dresden 14 March 1821 (seven years after the final version of *Fidelio*).

GNECCO: *Filandro e Carolina*

October. Rome, Valle

Text by the composer. One act.

Successful in Italy. Given with alterations, Genoa February 1810 (as *Clementina e Roberto*), and revived there Spring 1825.

In Italian also, Fiume Autumn 1805 (enlarged to 2 acts); Dresden 1806 (as *Filandro e Alfonsina*); Barcelona 6 September 1806; Lisbon Spring 1807; Madrid 26 August 1808; Nice Carnival 1811; Trieste Spring 1811; Paris 11 October 1817.

SPONTINI: *Milton*

27 November. Paris, O.C.

Text by V. J. Etienne de Jouy and M. Dieulafoy (*fait historique*). One act.

In French also, Brussels 1 April 1805; Hague 1805.

In German (translated by G. F. Treitschke), Vienna 24 September 1805; Berlin 24 March 1806, etc. Revived Aachen 20 November 1829; Weimar 13 October 1834; Vienna 17 February 1839.

In Spanish (translated by F. Enciso Castrillón), Madrid 4 November 1805.

The printed score contains an Italian translation by G. L. Balochi.

1805

B. A. WEBER: *Die Wette*

21 January. Berlin, O.

Text, a German version of Guillet's French libretto *Un Quart-d'Heure de Silence* (see 1804). One act.

Given at Hamburg 17 June 1808 as *Nur ein Viertelstündchen geschwiegen;* Munich 1812; in German also, Prague 8 April 1815.

WINTER: *Zaira*

29 January. London, Hm.

Librettist unknown. (Perhaps the text was written by Filippo Pananti, who at that time was "poeta in titolo, un piccolo Metastasio" at the King's theatre; see his letter of 7 February 1806, published in *Giornale Storico della Letteratura Italiana*, 1892. *Zaira* might have been his work, as the librettos of all other operas produced in London between 1805–07 are accounted for. But according to Lipowsky the text was by Da Ponte, founded on Voltaire's tragedy.) Two acts.

The most important of Winter's London operas (overture taken from *Maria von Montalban*, 1800). Revived there 17 February 1816.

In German, Munich 27 May 1816; Berlin 19 October 1816.

Zaira was also to be performed in Paris on 5 March 1812, but withdrawn.

WEIGL: *Die Uniform*

15 February. Vienna, Kä.

Text by G. F. Treitschke (translated from an Italian libretto by G. Carpani). Two acts.

Stated to have been previously produced at Schönbrunn, in Italian, the Empress Maria Theresa singing the part of "Pauline". It was not possible to establish the date of that performance. The autograph score at Vienna, however, is dated

1800. The opera was for some years very successful in Germany; Frankfort 16 September 1805; Berlin 9 December 1805; Hamburg 19 August 1806; Hanover 1810, etc. In German also, Budapest 14 March 1808; Prague 1808.

In the original Italian, Dresden January 1806 (revised by Paer); Milan 2 April 1809 (revived Spring 1821); Turin, T. Carignano November 1810.

In Russian (translated by R. M. Zotov), St. Petersburg 18 April 1817.

ISOUARD: *L'Intrigue aux Fenêtres*
26 February. Paris, O.C.

Text by J. N. Bouilly and E. Mercier-Dupaty. One act.

Given at the O.C. until 1827; Brussels 24 June 1805.

In German (translated by G. F. Treitschke), Frankfort 16 September 1805; Vienna 17 January 1806; (translated by Haug) Stuttgart May 1806; (translated by K. Reinhard) Munich 1806; (Treitschke's translation again) Berlin 16 April 1807 (with additions by F. L. Seidel and B. A. Weber), etc. Last revived Hamburg 7 September 1832.

In Spanish (translated by F. Enciso Castrillón). Madrid 14 October 1805.

In Russian (translated by A. V. Luknitsky), St. Petersburg 7 June 1807.

In Polish (translated by L. Osiński), Warsaw 1807.

In Swedish (translated by C. G. Nordforss), Stockholm 23 November 1807.

In Danish (translated by N. T. Bruun), Copenhagen 1 October 1813.

Dutch translation by C. A. van Raij published 1812.

SPONTINI: *Julie ou Le Pot de Fleurs*
12 March. Paris, O.C.

Text by A. G. Jars. One act.

In French also, Brussels 15 August 1805.

In German (translated by G. F. Treitschke), Vienna 24 September 1806; Berlin 5 December 1808, etc. Revived Magdeburg 26 June 1825.

HOFFMAN: *Die lustigen Musikanten*
6 April. Warsaw

Text by C. Brentano. Two acts.

Given at Warsaw (which then was part of Prussia, and where E. T. A. Hoffmann worked as an assistant judge) by a German company (see *Zeitung für die elegante Welt*, 1805, p.406). Score preserved at Paris Conservatoire. The opera was revived at Hamburg 7 March 1924.

P. C. GUGLIELMI: *La Scelta dello Sposo*
24 April. Venice, S. Moisè

Text by L. Buonavoglia. One act.

Given at Rome, Ap. 28 December 1805 in an enlarged 2-act version (as *La Vedova contrastata*, text altered by F. Tarducci). Milan, Sc. 6 December 1807, etc. Revived Palermo 1821 as *I Concorrenti alle Nozze;* Venice Carnival 1836 as *I tre Pretendenti delusi.*

Outside Italy, produced at Lisbon Spring 1806 (as *La Contessina contrastata*); Barcelona 22 August 1806 (revived 5 October 1820); Amsterdam 1808; Dresden 13 September 1808; Paris 21 April 1810 (as *La Vedova capricciosa*); Vienna 24 September 1812 (under the original title) and 29 March 1817 (as *La Vedova contrastata*); Munich July 1816; Hermannstadt and Kronstadt Summer 1821; Odessa October 1821; Stuttgart Autumn 1826.

In German (translated by C. W. Haeser), Prague 1808.

In Spanish (translated by F. Enciso Castrillón), Madrid 18 August 1817.

According to Piovano, produced in London 1829, a statement which I was unable to verify.

ISOUARD: *Le Déjeuner de Garçons*
24 April. Paris, O.C.

Text by A. F. Creuzé de Lesser. One act.

In French also, Brussels 19 November 1806.

In Danish (translated by N. T. Bruun), Copenhagen 6 November 1809.

In German (translated by C. A. Herklots), Berlin 25 June 1813.

In Russian (translated by I. I. Valberkh), St.

Petersburg 21 November 1814 and Moscow 14 December 1815.

GARCIA: *El Poeta Calculista*

28 April. Madrid

Text by the composer; monodrama (*Tonadilla*) which the famous singer wrote for himself. One act.

Produced at the Teatro de los Caños del Peral. In Spanish also, Paris 15 March 1809.

(See J. Tiersot in *The Musical Quarterly*, Vol. XIII, 1927.)

BOIELDIEU: *La jeune Femme Colère*

30 April. St. Petersburg

Text by Claparède (a singer of the French opera company at St. Petersburg), founded on a comedy by Etienne. One act.

The first successful work of Boieldieu's Russian period. First produced at the Ermitage; publicly 6 May 1805.

In French also, Brussels 22 December 1805; Moscow 27 October 1808; Berne 29 May 1809; Rouen 3 January 1811; Paris, O.C. 12 October 1812 (given there until 1840); Stockholm May 1813.

In German (translated by J. Sonnleithner), Vienna 8 March 1809; Berlin, Kgst. 11 August 1828, etc.

In Swedish (translated by C. G. Nordforss), Stockholm 21 March 1808 (music arranged by J. B. Struwe); Malmö 7 February 1810.

In Russian (translated by R. M. Zotov), St. Petersburg 1 November 1821.

In Danish (translated by I. Nielsen), Copenhagen as late as 17 September 1863.

PAER: *Sofonisba*

19 May. Bologna, T. del Corso

Text by D. Rossetti (altered and reduced from an earlier libretto by G. F. Zanetti, set to music by Jommelli in 1746). Two acts.

Written for the inauguration of the Teatro del Corso. In Italy given until 1820.

In Italian also, Dresden 15 March 1806; Vienna

25 May 1806 (in concert form); Amsterdam 14 June 1815 (parts only).

In German, Frankfort 15 March 1808; Munich 8 February 1814; Pressburg January 1816 (as *Massinissa*, translation G. Reinbeck); Hamburg 20 December 1816; Budapest 21 September 1818 (Reinbeck's translation).

WEIGL: *Vestas Feuer*

10 August. Vienna, W.

Text by E. Schikaneder (his last libretto). Two acts.

Also given at Frankfort Spring 1807; Budapest 10 July 1809; Würzburg 15 September 1809, etc.

This rather unimportant opera (see the review in *A.M.Z.*, Vol. VII, p.767, and the description in E. Komorzynski's *Schikaneder*) is of some interest because Schikaneder originally wrote the libretto for Beethoven. A fragment of his setting (81 pages; MS. in the library of the Gesellschaft der Musikfreunde, Vienna) was identified by R. Biberhofer in 1930. Both Beethoven's fragment and Weigl's autograph score were on view at the Vienna Haydn Exhibition, 1932. When Schikaneder became aware that Beethoven was not interested in the plan any longer, he gave the text to Weigl, who was less fastidious about the quality of librettos.

GNECCO: *La Prova d'una Opera seria*

16 August. Milan, Sc.

Text by the composer. Two acts.

According to G. Pavan, an enlarged version of a one-act farsa, called *La prima Prova dell' Opera Gli Orazi ed i Curiazi*, text by G. Artusi, and first produced at Venice, S. G. Gr. 8 July 1803. One of the most successful Italian comic operas of that time. Given at Naples, T.N. 1807 as *L'Apertura del Nuovo Teatro* (reduced to one act). In Italy until about 1850.

In Italian also, Barcelona 29 May 1806; Lisbon Summer 1806; Paris 4 September 1806 (revived 27 November 1810 and 28 October 1831); Brussels 4 April 1810; Dresden 1815; Munich 22 July 1818; London 23 June 1831 (frequently revived there until 18 June 1860); Berlin, Kgst. 14 August 1841; Dublin 2 September 1841; Copenhagen Carnival 1843; Oran, Algeria Spring 1843; Klagenfurt Autumn 1845; St. Petersburg 1846; Stockholm 1849 (Swedish translation in libretto by N. E. W. af Wetterstedt).

In German, Breslau 1832; Vienna 12 October 1839.

DALAYRAC: *Gulistan* ou *Le Hulla de Samarcande*

30 September. Paris, O.C.

Text by C. G. Etienne and A. E. X. Poisson de Lachabeaussière. Three acts.

The most important of Dalayrac's later works. At the O.C. given until 1829 and revived 10 August 1844 (re-scored by Adam). Revived at Beauvais February 1930.

In French also, Brussels 11 April 1806; Berne 5 July 1809; Moscow 8 February 1812; New York 1 August 1827 (according to J. Mattfeld; Odell does not record the performance).

In German, Vienna 2 August 1806 (with additional music by I. von Seyfried); Frankfort 31 August 1806; Prague Summer 1807; Budapest 8 June 1807; Munich 1808; Berlin, Kgst. 20 March 1830.

In Spanish, Madrid 23 October 1810.

In Polish (translated by L. A. Dmuszewski), Warsaw 1812; Wilna 2 October 1827.

P. C. GUGLIELMI: *Amor tutto vince*

Autumn. Naples, Fior.

Text by G. Palomba (founded on Dupaty's *D'Auberge en Auberge*, see 1800). Two acts.

Very successful in Italy; given at Florence Spring 1807 as *Di una Locanda all' altra*; Pavia Carnival 1814 as *Il Papirio*; other alternative titles were *Don Papirio* and *La Donna di più Caratteri*.

In Italian also produced at Munich 29 June 1817; Berne 12 July 1820.

Revived (in 3 acts) Florence, T. degli Arrischiati 30 March 1872 and Rome, T. Rossini 12 January 1875.

BEETHOVEN: *Fidelio* oder *Die eheliche Liebe*

20 November. Vienna, W.

Text: a German version, by J. Sonnleithner, of Bouilly's French libretto, *Lénore ou L'Amour conjugal* (see 1798; see also Paer's *Leonora*, 1804). Originally in three acts. In 1806 the opera was altered and reduced to two acts by S. von Breuning. In 1814 it was given its final form by G. F. Treitschke (2 acts).

There were not more than three performances in 1805. In its second version, *Fidelio* was produced at the same theatre 29 March 1806; this time, there were only two performances. The final version was given at the Kä. on 23 May 1814 (c.550 times to date).

As to the four overtures of the opera: the socalled *Leonore* no.2 was played at the first production in 1805; the *Leonore* no.3 in 1806; the *Fidelio* overture (in E major) in 1814 (for the first time 26 May; on 23 May the *Prometheus* or the *Ruinen von Athen* overture had been substituted). The *Leonore* no.1 overture was written for a performance at Prague in May 1807; which did not take place.

First produced at Prague, under Weber's direction 27 November 1814 (according to Weber's stage-diary; Thayer gives the date of 21 November; Teuber 26 November); Leipzig 15 February 1815 and Dresden 12 April 1815 (in the 1805 version); Berlin 11 October 1815 (685 performances until 1937); Graz 5 February 1816; Carlsruhe 10 March 1816; Budapest 6 May 1816; Hamburg 22 May 1816; Cassel 3 June 1816; Breslau 12 July 1816; Weimar 4 September 1816; Brünn 24 February 1817; Stuttgart 20 July 1817; Danzig 13 September 1818; Elbing 6 May 1819; Königsberg December 1819; Munich 1 July 1821, etc.; most German stages produced the opera in the 'thirties.

In German also produced at Riga 22 June 1818; St. Petersburg Spring 1819; Amsterdam 13 November 1824; Paris, Th. I. 30 May 1829; Strasbourg 6 May 1832; London, Hm. 18 May 1832; Zurich January 1834 (in concert form); Basle 27 February 1837; Liége 28 May 1838; Mitau (Latvia) 24 June 1839 (under Richard Wagner); Helsinki 22 June 1841; Moscow Autumn 1842; Marseilles July 1844; Brussels 5 August 1844; New York 29 May 1856; Boston 1 April 1857; Stockholm 31 May 1863; Barcelona 11 January 1921.

The 1805 version, reconstructed by E. Prieger (published 1905) was revived at Breslau 1 March 1886 (in concert form); Berlin 20 November 1905 (on the stage, under Richard Strauss). At Trier (Trèves) on 8 October 1912, *Fidelio* was produced with German recitatives by J. Doebber.

PARIS, TH. I. 30 May 1829 (in German); Conservatoire 22 June 1845 (in concert form); Th. I. 31 January 1852 (in Italian, the London version); Th. L. 5 May 1860 (in French, translated by J. Barbier and M. Carré); O.C. 30 December 1898 (in French, the Brussels 1889 version). The first French adaptation is the one contained in the full score published by Jacques Hippolyte Aristide Farrenc and intended for a production at the Odéon, Paris, probably in 1826, which did not take place. The names of the translators, etc. are not known. "Paroles de MM. N . . . and . . ., Arrangées pour la Scène Française par MM. J. T. et A. F." The last initials probably are those of the publisher, Aristide Farrenc. (Cf. the *Introduction*, p. xxiii.)

COPENHAGEN 17 September 1829 (in Danish, translated by C. N. Rosenkilde).

STOCKHOLM 14 April 1832 (in Swedish, translated by B. H. Crusell).

LONDON, HM. 18 May 1832 (in German); C.G. 12 June 1835 (in English, translated by W. McGregor Logan); H.M.'s 20 May 1851 (in Italian, translated by S. M. Maggioni, recitatives by Balfe); C.G. 27 May 1851 (in Italian, under Costa); D.L. 20 April 1852 (in English, translated by J. W. Mould); Ly. 2 November 1876 (in English, translated by T. Oliphant). Revived Sadler's Wells 3 November 1937 (new English version by E. J. Dent).

NEW YORK 9 September 1839 (in English); 29 December 1856 (in German); 10 March 1882 (in Italian).

PHILADELPHIA 21 October 1839 (in English).

BUDAPEST 28 December 1839 (in Hungarian, translated by K. Lengey); in German earlier, see above.

HELSINKI 22 June 1841 (in German) and 13 October 1876 (in Finnish).

MOSCOW Autumn 1842 (in German) and 14 April 1880 at the Imperial College of Music (in Russian, translated by O. A. Lepko).

MARSEILLES July 1844 (in German) and 13 January 1854 (in French).

BRUSSELS 5 August 1844 (in German); 1 December 1847 (for the first time in French, translated by F. H. J. Castil-Blaze); 11 March 1889 (new French version by G. Antheunis, recitatives by Gevaert).

DUBLIN 14 September 1854 (in Italian).

ST. PETERSBURG Carnival 1863 (in Italian) and 9 October 1905 (in Russian); in German much earlier, see above.

PRAGUE 21 January 1870 (in Czech, translated by M.B.); in German much earlier, see above; in a new Czech version by V. J. Novotný, 2 December 1887.

CHRISTIANIA Spring 1876 (in Norwegian).

EDINBURGH 25 November 1876 (in Italian).

NEW ORLEANS 11 December 1877 (in Italian).

ROME, AP. 4 February 1886 (for the first time in Italy and for four nights only); revived Turin 10 February 1927; Milan, Sc. 7 April 1927, etc.

MEXICO 12 April 1891 (in English!).

MADRID November 1893 (in Italian, for the first time in Spain); Barcelona 11 January 1921 (in German).

ANTWERP 23 March 1895 (in Flemish).

ZAGREB 15 March 1898 (in Croatian, translated by A. Harambašić).

MONTE CARLO 5 April 1898 (in French).

GENEVA 17 March 1899 (in French).

WARSAW 1919 (in Polish).

RIGA 12 May 1925 (in Lettish, translated by E. Virza); in German much earlier, see above.

LJUBLJANA 10 May 1927 (in Slovenian, translated by F. Bučar).

BUENOS AIRES 17 June 1927 (in Italian).

BUCHAREST October 1931 (in Rumanian).

TUCZEK: *Lanassa*

13 December. Budapest

Text by the composer (founded on K. M. Plü-micke's German version of Lemierre's tragedy, *La Veuve de Malabar*). Three acts.

Tuczek's most successful German opera. Revived Budapest 15 February 1813.

Also given at Vienna, Leop. 4 July 1810; Würzburg 27 March 1815.

1806

CORRI: *The Travellers; or, Music's Fascination*

22 January. London, D.L.

Text by A. Cherry (*An operatic drama*). Five acts.

Corri's most successful work; libretto reprinted 8 times in 1806.

Philadelphia 26 December 1808 (American adaptation by J. N. Barker).

Revived London, D.L. 13 May 1823 and 25 April 1836.

"An opera on a novel plan . . . the music of which professed to describe the styles of the four quarters of the world" (Parke, II, p.5).

MÉHUL: *Les deux Aveugles de Tolède*

28 January. Paris, O.C.

Text by B. J. Marsollier. One act.

In French also, Brussels 1 December 1806; Stockholm May 1813.

In German, Vienna 31 October 1806; Weimar 23 September 1809; Munich 1810; Berlin 10 November 1812. Last revived, Frankfort 10 November 1850.

In Russian (translated by A. V. Luknitsky), Moscow 26 November 1807; St. Petersburg 24 January 1808.

In Spanish, Madrid 24 November 1810.

In Swedish (translated by J. H. Callou de Villeneuve), Stockholm 28 October 1833.

BIEREY: *Rosette, das Schweizer Hirtenmädchen*

3 February. Leipzig

Text by C. F. Bretzner. Two acts.

Bierey's most successful work: Hamburg 4 July 1806 (as *Drei Freier um eine Braut*); Hanover 5 June 1809; Berlin 22 July 1812; Budapest 4 May 1818, etc. Last revived Weimar 6 December 1828.

GAVEAUX: *M. des Chalumeaux* ou *La Soirée de Carnaval*

17 February. Paris, O.C.

Text by A. F. Creuzé de Lesser. Three acts.

In French also, Brussels 29 May 1806; Berne 31 May 1809; Moscow 14 May 1810.

In Swedish, Stockholm 27 June 1808; Gothenburg 19 May 1815.

In Dutch, Amsterdam 1808.

In German, Berlin 23 December 1814.

Revived Paris, O.C. 26 January 1843; Galerie Vivienne 26 February 1897.

CHERUBINI: *Faniska*

25 February. Vienna, Kä.

Text by J. Sonnleithner. Three acts.

Cherubini's only German Singspiel. The libretto appears to have originally been written in Italian, by an unknown author, based upon R. C. G. de Pixérécourt's French melodrama *Les Mines de Pologne* (1803).

Cherubini (who knew no German) seems to have composed the music to the Italian words (which are to be found in the published score) and Sonnleithner's German adaptation was written afterwards.

Faniska was, in German, also given at Breslau 16 July 1806; Hamburg 14 October 1806; Munich October 1806; Berlin 2 February 1807; Budapest 23 February 1807; Prague 3 May 1807 (at the inauguration of the first regular German opera-house there); Amsterdam 1809; St. Petersburg 1815.

Last revived in Germany: Frankfort 8 September 1860.

In Russian (translated by A. I. Sheller), St. Petersburg 7 December 1815; Moscow 4 June 1817.

In Dutch, Amsterdam 1834 or earlier.

The work was never produced either in France or in Italy.

HIMMEL: *Die Sylphen*
14 April. Berlin, O.

Text by L. Robert (the brother of Rahel Varnhagen), based on Gozzi's comedy *La Donna Serpente;* the same comedy on which the text of Wagner's *Die Feen* (see 1888) is founded; see also Casella's opera (1932). Three acts.

Himmel's opera was revived in concert form at Frankfort 25 April 1863 (by the "Operngesangverein").

BLANGINI: *Nephtali* ou *Les Ammonites*
15 April. Paris, O.

Text by E. Aignan. Three acts.

Blangini's best work. Brussels 15 December 1808.

In German (translated by J. von Seyfried, with additional music by J. von Seyfried), Vienna, W. 17 December 1812 and Kä. 16 May 1816.

MÉHUL: *Uthal*
17 May. Paris, O.C.

Text by J. M. B. Bins de Saint-Victor (*imité d'Ossian*). One act.

One of Méhul's most important works. In order to create a gloomy and mysterious effect, Méhul wrote his score without violins.

In French also given at Brussels 17 March 1807.

A parody by J. M. Pain and P. A. Vieillard, called *Brutal, ou Il vaut mieux tard que jamais* was produced at the Th. du Vaudeville, Paris 31 May 1806.

The opera was particularly successful in Germany: Stuttgart 30 November 1806 (translated by F. K. Hiemer); Berlin 3 October 1808 (translated by C. A. Herklots); Vienna 15 January 1810; Prague 19 October 1813, etc.

Revived Munich 30 May 1875 and (new translation by O. Devrient), Carlsruhe 18 October 1891; Munich 31 October 1894; Elberfeld 8 April 1900; Dessau 15 April 1904 and 10 April 1906.

In Danish (translated by C. Borgaard), Copenhagen 7 July 1846.

DUPUY: *Ungdom og Galskab* eller *List over List*
(Youth and Folly, or Trick upon Trick)
19 May. Copenhagen

Text by N. T. Bruun (translation from Bouilly's *Une Folie*, see 1802). Two acts.

The most successful Danish opera of that period; given at Copenhagen 170 times until 1880 and revived 26 December 1910. The 200th performance was on 5 March 1911.

In Swedish (translated by C. G. Nordforss), Stockholm 31 October 1814.

In German (as *List und Liebe*, translated by G. Hartmann), Kiel 23 October 1930.

CLASING: *Mischelli und sein Sohn*
30 May. Hamburg

Text by A. Kirchner (a singer at the Hamburg opera). Three acts.

A German sequel to Cherubini's *Deux Journées*. Also given at Hanover 9 November 1806.

DALAYRAC: *Deux Mots* ou *Une Nuit dans la Forêt*
9 June. Paris, O.C.

Text by B. J. Marsollier. One act.

Dalayrac's last great success; given at Paris, O.C. until 1828 and revived there on 30 August 1862.

In French also, Brussels 7 December 1806; Moscow 10 December 1810.

In German (translated by C. A. Herklots), Berlin 16 April 1807; Prague Summer 1807; Vienna, W. 9 July 1807 (revived 12 May 1823); Munich 1807; St. Petersburg 18 August 1811; Hamburg 30 October 1811; Budapest 6 August 1815; Basle 16 October 1835. Revived in German: Prague February 1861; Königsberg 26 December 1873.

In Polish (translated by W. Pekalski), Warsaw 1808.

In Russian (translated by I. I. Valberkh), St. Petersburg 4 December 1809; Moscow 23 February 1812.

In Czech (translated by J. N. Štěpánek), Prague 1815.

In Swedish (translated by C. G. Nordforss), Stockholm 14 March 1816.

In Danish (translated by N. T. Bruun), Copenhagen 19 December 1818.

In Hungarian (translated by F. S. Deáky), Clausenburg 8 March 1823; Budapest 18 January 1828.

In English, Philadelphia 18 May 1839 (as *Two Words, or A Night on the Forest;* probably Dalayrac's opera).

A Dutch version by G. A. Engelman and C. van der Vijver was published in 1806.

An Italian translation by G. Bonfio was published in 1807.

MÉHUL: *Gabrielle d'Estrées* ou *Les Amours d'Henri IV*

25 June. Paris, O.C.

Text by C. Godard d'Aucour de Saint-Just. Three acts.

In French also, Brussels 26 December 1806; Moscow 16 January 1812.

In German (translated by G. F. Treitschke), Vienna, W. 15 June 1807 (additions by I. von Seyfried); revived Frankfort 1 January 1822.

In Polish (translated by W. Pekalski), Warsaw 1809.

BERTON: *Les Maris Garçons*

15 July. Paris, O.C.

Text by C. Gaugiran-Nanteuil. One act.

Given in Paris until 1828; in French also, Brussels 3 October 1806; Berne 1807; Moscow 15 October 1808.

In Polish, Warsaw 1909.

In Swedish (translated by C. G. Nordforss), Stockholm 7 September 1812.

In Russian (translated by D. N. Barkov), St. Petersburg 1 May 1820.

In Danish (translated by T. Overskou), Copenhagen 31 May 1825.

GYROWETZ: *Agnes Sorel*

4 December. Vienna, Kä.

Text by J. Sonnleithner. Three acts.

Gyrowetz's first great success: Hamburg 14 August 1807; Prague 6 February 1808; Berlin 15 October 1809 (revived Kgst. 1 March 1834); Munich 1811, etc.

In German also, Budapest 29 April 1812; St. Petersburg January 1814; Strasbourg 26 September 1818; Berne 12 February 1823; Bucharest 26 January 1834.

In Polish (translated by J. Pawlowski), Warsaw 1816.

In Danish (translated by N. T. Bruun), Copenhagen 16 May 1817.

In Hungarian (translated by F. S. Deáky), Clausenburg 27 April 1820; Budapest 23 January 1828.

Agnes Sorel was given as festival opera for the Vienna Congress on 4 March 1815, at a theatre specially erected in the Augarten (Gyrowetz conducting).

DALAYRAC: *Koulouf,* ou *Les Chinois*

18 December. Paris, O.C.

Text by R. C. G. de Pixérécourt. Three acts.

In French also, Brussels 9 February 1808.

In German (translated by G. F. Treitschke), Vienna 20 August 1808.

In Swedish (translated by C. G. Nordforss), Stockholm 13 November 1809.

In Polish (translated by L. A. Dmuszewski), Warsaw 1813.

A Danish version by N. T. Bruun was published in 1820.

MAYR: *Adelasia e Aleramo*

26 December. Milan, Sc.

Text by L. Romanelli. Two acts.

In Italy given until 1820.

In Italian also, Vienna 23 June 1807; Trieste Spring 1808; Munich 9 June 1808; London 10 January 1815.

In German (translated by C. A. Herklots), Budapest 24 October 1808; Berlin 3 August 1811.

(The largo of the introduction to this opera is taken from the *Don Giovanni* overture.)

BOIELDIEU: *Télémaque*

28 December. St. Petersburg

Text by P. Dercy (first set to music as *Télémaque dans l'Isle de Calypso* by Lesueur in 1796). Three acts.

First performed at the Ermitage; three days later publicly.

Translated into Russian by A. I. Sheller, it was given at St. Petersburg on 11 September 1815.

In German (translated by F. K. Hiemer), Stuttgart 23 October 1814.

In Polish, Warsaw 24 August 1828.

Never given in Paris; Boieldieu introduced parts of the music into his *Jean de Paris* (see 1812).

1807

P. C. GUGLIELMI: *Guerra aperta ossia Astuzia contro Astuzia*

January. Rome, Valle

Text by B. Mezzanotte (from a French comedy by A. J. Dumaniant). Two acts.

Given in Italy until 1830.

In Italian also, London 12 November 1809 (as *La Scomessa*, text altered by S. Buonaiuti); Dresden 13 January 1810; Malta 1812; Vienna 22 March 1817; Corfu Autumn 1825.

NICCOLINI: *Traiano in Dacia*

3 February. Rome, Arg.

Text by M. A. Prunetti. Two acts.

Very successful in Italy.

In Italian also, Vienna 26 May 1810 (43 performances); Munich Spring 1818.

In German (translated by F. K. Hiemer), Stuttgart 18 May 1812; Darmstadt 26 December 1812; Budapest 23 September 1813; Lemberg 13 April 1825.

MÉHUL: *Joseph*

17 February. Paris, O.C.

Text by A. Duval (*drame mêlé de chants*). Three acts.

Méhul's chief work.

In French also, Brussels 6 January 1808; Hamburg 29 March 1809; Berne 9 June 1809; Amsterdam 1830, etc.

In German:

MUNICH 6 January 1809 (translated by M. G. Lambrecht).

VIENNA, W. 5 December 1809 (Kä. 14 June 1815).

BUDAPEST 6 August 1810 (translated by F. J. Hassaureck).

BERLIN 22 November 1811 (translated by C. A. Herklots).

BERNE 24 February 1812.

PRAGUE 26 September 1813.

ST. PETERSBURG 1815 and Moscow 5 August 1820.

DRESDEN 30 January 1817 (Weber's début as conductor there; with a finale by F. Fränzl).

AMSTERDAM 4 September 1824 (Dutch translation by M. G. Engelman published in 1808 already).

HELSINKI 19 November 1830.

BUCHAREST *c.*January 1834.

WINTERTHUR November 1840 (in concert form).

LONDON, D.L. 7 April 1841 (in concert form).

In Russian (translated by Brant), Moscow 20 January 1812; St. Petersburg 24 September 1813.

In Polish (translated by W. Boguslawski), Warsaw 1812.

In Danish (translated by N. T. Bruun), Copenhagen 10 October 1816; Christiania Autumn 1829.

In Hungarian (translated by A. Láng), Clausenburg 23 December 1822; Budapest 7 November 1827.

In Italian (translated by F. S. Kandler), Milan 30 March 1823 (privately performed as an oratorio at Marchese Castelbarco's).

In Czech (translated by J. K. Chmelenský), Prague 17 November 1824; Brno 6 January 1839.

In English (translated by J. Webb), Birmingham 4 October 1826 (concert performance).

In Flemish, Ghent 6 December 1841. (Flemish translation by J. Dubuisson published 1874). Revivals:

Paris: at the O.C. the opera was revived on 11 September 1851, 18 August 1866, 5 June 1882 and 24 November 1910; Th.L. 21 January 1862; O. 26 May 1899 (recitatives by Bourgault-Ducoudray).

Windsor Castle 1 January 1856 (concert performance; English version by W. Bartholomew, recitatives by W. G. Cusins).

Stockholm 15 October 1856 (in Swedish, translated by C. G. Nordforss and C. F. A. Holmström; production planned and libretto printed in 1817 already).

New York May 1857 (in German).

Orange 21 August 1869 (in French; open air performance).

Prague 1 February 1892 (in Czech, new translation by V. J. Novotný).

In Croatian (translated by A. Harambašić), Zagreb 8 April 1899.

In German, Vienna 17 August 1908 (recitatives by F. von Weingartner); Dessau 21 February 1909; Berlin 27 March 1909, etc. (recitatives by M. Zenger); Tsingtao May 1909; Basle 21 April 1912.

In Italian, Milan, Sc. 23 February 1899 (first and only stage production in Italy; new translation by A. Galli).

In Spanish, Barcelona, Novedades September 1900 (for the first time in Spain).

Dublin, Antient Concert Rooms, 29 April 1908 (concert performance in English, translated by G. Emerson Scott).

London, C.G. 3 February 1914 (in German; first and only stage production in England).

In Estonian, Tallinn 1919.

A Serbian translation by J. Grčić was published in 1889.

GYROWETZ: *Ida, die Büssende*

26 February. Vienna, W.

Text by F. I. von Holbein. Four acts.

Hamburg 19 January 1808; Berlin 2 March 1808, etc.

In German also, Budapest 28 November 1808; Prague 12 September 1819.

In Polish (translated by B. Kudlicz), Warsaw 1811 (with additional music by J. Elsner).

ISOUARD: *Les Rendez-vous bourgeois*

9 May. Paris, O.C.

Text by F. B. Hoffman. One act.

Very successful in Paris; last revived at the O.C. on 26 February 1895, 18 November 1915 and 14 October 1933.

In French also, Brussels 9 August 1807; Berne 19 June 1809; Brunswick 1810; Moscow 1 December 1810; Vienna 18 August 1826; New York 25 July 1827; Berlin 7 June 1828; London, St. J.'s 20 June 1836; Turin April 1858; Barcelona 20 November 1869.

In German (as *Alle fürchten sich*, translated by I. F. Castelli), Vienna, W. 30 March 1808; (as *Das Krähwinkler Rendez-vous*, translated by H. G. Schmieder) St. Petersburg 1810; (as *Die Hasen in der Hasenheide*, translated by L. Angely) Berlin, Kgst. 5 March 1827 (this version was popular for many years; revived Vienna, Ca. 21 April 1861); (as *Das Landhaus am Walde oder Einer fürchtet sich vor dem Anderen*, translated by H. Zunz) Stuttgart c.February 1828; (as *Das Stelldichein*, translated by K. Blum) Berlin, O. 31 October 1839 (revived 17 March 1889).

In Russian (translated by Y. I. Lizogub), St. Petersburg 4 June 1810; Moscow 15 December 1817.

In Swedish (translated by C. G. Nordforss), Stockholm 7 February 1814.

In Dutch (translated by M. G. Engelman), Amsterdam 1818 and Hague 1820.

In Polish (translated by L. Matuszyński), Warsaw 27 June 1821 (revived c.1860, with additional music by Moniuszko).

WEIGL: *Kaiser Hadrian*

21 May. Vienna, Kä.

Text by J. C. Mayer. Three acts.

Frankfort 15 April 1808; Stuttgart 11 December 1808; Munich 29 January 1809; Hamburg 13 July 1810, etc.

In German also, Budapest 21 August 1809.

GYROWETZ: *Die Junggesellen-Wirtschaft*

18 June. Vienna, Kä.

Text by G. F. Treitschke. One act.

Leipzig 1808; Stuttgart 8 May 1809, etc. In German also, Budapest 18 November 1811. Still popular in Germany during the 1820's.

In French (as *Le Ménage de Garçon*), Liége 26 November 1821.

CAVOS: *Ilya Bogatir*

Илья-Богатырь

(Ilya the Hero)

22 September. St. Petersburg

Text by I. A. Kruilov. Four acts.

One of the better works of the Russian composer. Revived Moscow 7 August 1823.

VAL. FIORAVANTI: *I Virtuosi ambulanti*

26 September. Paris, Th.I.

Text by G. L. Balochi (translated from Picard's *Les Comédiens ambulans*, see 1798). Two acts.

This was the first important Italian opera written expressly for the Paris Théâtre-Italien (then called Théâtre de l'Impératrice). One of Fioravanti's most successful works.

In the original Italian, also given at London 31 May 1808 (as *La Virtuosa in Puntiglio*); Naples, Fior. Spring 1816; Dresden 15 April 1820; Florence November 1821 (as *I Soggetti di Teatro*).

In German (translated by C. A. Herklots), Frankfort 16 February 1808; Berlin 30 August 1808; Hamburg 13 October 1812, etc.; Leipzig 11 February 1814 (by Sekonda's troupe; E. T. A.

Hoffmann conducting); Munich 1820; Vienna, W. 31 January 1822; Budapest 1823; Prague 28 October 1837. Last revived Berlin, Fr.W. 26 February 1852.

In Russian, St. Petersburg 6 May 1816.

In Polish (translated by J. Kruszyński), Warsaw 1817.

WEIGL: *Adrian von Ostade*

3 October. Vienna, Kä.

Text by G. F. Treitschke. One act.

Very successful on German stages: Stuttgart 26 December 1808; Hamburg 1 June 1810; Berlin 7 October 1812; Budapest 28 June 1813; Prague 4 June 1814, etc.; Basle 17 February 1843; last revived Hamburg 16 January 1878.

In Russian (translated by A. I. Sheller), St. Petersburg 30 October 1820.

RÖSLER: *Elisene, Prinzessin von Bulgarien*

18 October. Prague

Text by I. F. Castelli (founded on L. C. Caigniez's melodrama, *La Forêt d'Hermanstadt*, 1805). Three acts.

First original opera produced at the new German opera-house, Prague (see 1806). Vienna, Leop. 10 March 1809; Munich 16 April 1809, etc. Revived Prague 20 April 1815 (in German) and 28 September 1827 (in Czech, translated by S. K. Machaček).

(See on this opera J. F. Reichardt's *Vertraute Briefe*, no.41, 15 April 1809.)

PERSUIS and LESUEUR: *Le Triomphe de Trajan*

23 October. Paris, O.

Text by J. A. Esménard. Three acts.

Written and produced in order to celebrate Napoléon's return from Prussia. Given in Paris 119 times until 1827 (100th performance 9 October 1814).

BIEREY: *Wladimir, Fürst von Novgorod*

25 November. Vienna, W.

Text by M. Stegmayer. Three acts.

Hamburg 7 November 1808; Breslau 8 November 1808; Prague January 1809; Budapest 28 May 1810, etc. Revived Vienna 31 August 1824.

In Czech (translated by S. K. Machaček), Prague 26 October 1828.

SPONTINI: *La Vestale*

16 December. Paris, O.

Text by V. J. Etienne de Jouy. Three acts.

Spontini's chief work. The text had originally been written for Boieldieu and was subsequently refused by Méhul. Given at the Paris Opéra 213 times until 1857; 100th performance 7 June 1816, 200th performance 4 January 1830, last revival 17 March 1854; given there once more 24 January 1909, in Italian, by the company of the Scala, Milan (see below).

A parody, called *La Marchande des Modes*, was produced at the Th. du Vaudeville, Paris 13 January 1808; in French also at Rudolstadt 1811.

In French also given at Antwerp 6 September 1809; Brussels 15 March 1810; St. Petersburg 7 November 1812; Philadelphia 30 October 1828 (by a French troupe from New Orleans).

In German (translated by J. von Seyfried), Vienna 12 November 1810; (translated by C. A. Herklots), Berlin 18 January 1811 (100th performance 6 October 1839); Stuttgart 4 August 1811; Munich 14 January 1812; Hamburg 29 March 1815.

In German also, Brünn 19 August 1811; Prague October 1811; Budapest 26 June 1812; St. Petersburg January 1814; Amsterdam 1829; London, C.G. 9 June 1842.

In Italian (translated by N. Perotti), Dresden 1810; (translated by G. Schmidt), Naples, S.C. 8 September 1811 (revived 8 September 1813 and Spring 1818), etc.; Milan 26 December 1824; London, Hm. 2 December 1826; St. Petersburg 1829.

In Russian (translated by A. G. Volkov), St. Petersburg 18 April 1814; Moscow 9 October 1823.

In Spanish, Madrid 10 July 1817.

In Polish (translated by L. A. Dmuszewski), Warsaw 21 February 1821.

In Swedish (translated by A. Lindeberg), Stockholm 3 January 1823 (with a prologue by Berwald).

In Hungarian, Budapest 21 April 1840.

In Danish (translated by N. T. Bruun), Copenhagen 18 September 1844.

In Flemish (translated by E. Hiel), Antwerp 16 December 1909.

Some of the latest revivals: in Italian, Milan 16 December 1908 and Paris 24 January 1909; Buenos Aires 21 May 1910; Barcelona 30 November 1910 (Catalan version by J. Pena published on that occasion); New York, M. 13 November 1925 (first time there); Florence 4 May 1933. In French, Brussels 18 December 1924 and 27 November 1936. In German (new translation by H. Schaeffer), Düsseldorf March 1937.

An open-air performance took place at the Arènes, Béziers, on 26 August 1906 (in French).

1808

SUTOR: *Apollo's Wettgesang*

27 March. Stuttgart

Text by F. K. Hiemer (founded on d'Hèle's French libretto, *Le Jugement de Midas*, see 1778). Three acts.

Sutor's best work, successful in Germany: Hamburg 25 July 1811; Hanover 8 June 1817; Munich 14 July 1818; Dresden 11 September 1820, etc. In German also, Budapest 18 September 1826.

WEIGL: *Il Rivale di se stesso*

18 April. Milan, Sc.

Text by L. Romanelli (from a German play by F. J. W. Ziegler, 1790). Two acts.

In Italian also, Parma 17 February 1810; Paris 20 September 1810; Dresden 1812; Vienna 29 October 1812; Lisbon Spring 1820. Revived at Milan, Sc. 18 April 1818.

BOIELDIEU: *Les Voitures versées*

26 April. St. Petersburg

Text by E. Mercier-Dupaty (originally given in Paris, as a vaudeville, in 1806). Two acts.

The most successful work of Boieldieu's Russian period.

In French also produced Moscow 29 October 1808 and, with some alterations, Paris, O.C. 29 April 1820 and Brussels 3 August 1820.

Given in Paris until 1836 and revived at the O.C. 7 May 1852; 27 April 1868; and once more 5 April 1932.

In Russian (translated by R. M. Zotov), St. Petersburg 21 September 1818 and Moscow 6 February 1823.

In German (translated by G. Döring), Frankfort Autumn 1821; (translated by J. Kupelwieser), Prague Autumn 1821; Riga 1825; Vienna 6 September 1826; Budapest 26 May 1827; Berlin, Kgst. 18 October 1827.

In Danish (translated by T. Overskou), Copenhagen 12 March 1829.

Revivals: Munich 5 May 1902 (by the Orchesterverein); Berlin 5 November 1913 (as *Der Satansweg*, new translation by G. Droescher); Breslau 25 December 1913 and Graz March 1918 (as *Das Loch in der Landstrasse*, another new translation by E. Freund); Paris, O.C. 5 April 1932 (in French).

R. KREUTZER: *Aristippe*

24 May. Paris, O.

Text by P. F. Giraud and M. T. Leclercq (*comédie-lyrique*). Two acts.

Successful in Paris; at the Opéra given until 1830; 100th performance 5 June 1822; Brussels 7 January 1818.

ISOUARD: *Un Jour à Paris* ou *La Leçon singulière*

24 May. Paris, O.C.

Text by C. G. Etienne. Three acts.

Given in Paris until 1826; Brussels 23 November 1808; in French also Hamburg 14 December 1809; Cassel Spring 1811; Rudolstadt 1811.

In German (translated by C. A. Herklots), Berlin 20 March 1809; Vienna, W. 26 November 1811 (additions by I. von Seyfried); Riga 1822; Graz 23 February 1827.

ORLANDI: *La Dama Soldato*

20 September. Milan, Sc.

Text by C. Mazzolà (first set to music by Naumann, see 1791). Two acts.

In Italy given until 1837.

In Italian also, London 13 May 1813; Lugano 1815; Munich September 1816; Barcelona 3 June 1817; Vienna, W. 24 March 1818.

In German (as *Die weibliche Schildwache*, translated by J. B. Krebs), Stuttgart January 1824; Würzburg 18 January 1827.

WEIGL: *Das Waisenhaus*

4 October. Vienna, Kä.

Text by G. F. Treitschke (but see below). Two acts.

One of Weigl's most popular works.

In German also given at Budapest 12 March 1809; Frankfort 26 March 1809; Hamburg 22 June 1809; Munich 28 July 1809; Berlin 24 November 1809; Amsterdam 1810 and 1811; Prague 1816; Dresden 4 June 1817, etc.

In Czech (translated by S. K. Macháček), Prague 12 March 1826.

There seems to be something dubious about Treitschke's authorship. An opera on the same subject (text by F. Moll) had been composed by the Strasbourg conductor, Stanislaus Spindler, in 1807 (produced Strasbourg 1 December 1807 and Carlsruhe 10 October 1808, in German, and revived Strasbourg 23 February 1825, in French). See *Journal des Luxus und der Moden*, 1808, p.801; see also *A.M.Z.*, 1819, p.699, and Spohr's *Selbstbiographie* (1860), Vol. I, p.243. A. Schmidt (*Denksteine*, 1848, p.186) establishes Treitschke's priority by the simple means of post-dating the production of Spindler's opera by 10 years!

GENERALI: *Le Lagrime di una Vedova*

26 December. Venice, S. Moisè

Text by G. M. Foppa. One act.

Successful in Italy; first given at the Scala, Milan 21 April 1817; in Italian also, Barcelona 25 January 1816; Munich 26 August 1816; Paris 20 April 1819; Lisbon 4 September 1820; Hermannstadt and Kronstadt Summer 1821; Vienna 6 September 1824.

In German (as *Witwentrauer*, translated by J. C. Grünbaum), Vienna 12 February 1824 (revived 7 August 1840).

NICCOLINI: *Coriolano*

26 December. Milan, Sc.

Text by L. Romanelli. Two acts.

In Italian also given at Vienna 10 September 1810 and Lisbon 15 June 1818.

1809

BISHOP: *The Circassian Bride*

23 February. London, D.L.

Text by C. Ward. Three acts.

Produced the night before the fire of Drury Lane; the score was burnt but Bishop re-wrote the opera from memory and published it.

WEIGL: *Die Schweizerfamilie*

14 March. Vienna, Kä.

Text by I. F. Castelli. Three acts.

Weigl's most famous work; given on every German stage during the 19th century and popular in many other countries as well.

After Vienna first produced at Prague Autumn 1809; Budapest 30 January 1810; in Germany first Dessau January 1810; Munich 28 January 1810; Hamburg 16 February 1810; Berlin 21 November 1810, etc.

In German also given at St. Petersburg August 1811; Berne 19 February 1812; Amsterdam 30 June 1824; Copenhagen 13 January 1827; Brussels 5 August 1829; Paris, Th.I. 3 June 1830; Helsinki 12 October 1830; Lucerne 26 August 1831 (see Mendelssohn's letter to E. Devrient); Zurich 3 April 1832 (in concert form); London, Hm. 25 July 1832; Bucharest Autumn 1833; Philadelphia 5 May 1840; New York 17 December 1845 (revived 6 February 1874).

In Italian (translated by A. Wagner), Dresden Autumn 1811; Milan 2 November 1816 (in 2 acts).

In French (translated by C. A. Sewrin and Alissan de Chazet), privately produced at Saint-Cloud 27 October 1812 (as *La Vallée Suisse;* it was the favourite opera of the Empress Marie-Louise); publicly Liége 27 February 1813 and Paris, Odéon 6 February 1827 (as *Emmeline ou La Famille Suisse,* music arranged by P. Crémont).

In Danish (translated by H. H. Schønberg), Copenhagen 23 September 1814.

In Polish (translated by W. Boguslawski), Warsaw 1815; Wilna 22 November 1825.

In Russian (translated by N. I. Grech), St. Petersburg 22 December 1814; Moscow 17 April 1817.

In Swedish (translated by M. Altén), Stockholm 27 October 1815.

In Hungarian (translated by I. Déry), Clausenburg 9 March 1822; Budapest 17 September 1827.

In Czech (translated by S. K. Machaček), Prague 28 December 1823 (apart from isolated attempts in the 18th century, first opera ever sung in that language).

In London, an operatic drama *Lilla* (text by J. R. Planché) was produced at C.G. 21 October 1825 which contained parts of the *Schweizerfamilie* music; the whole opera was given (in English, as *The Swiss Family; or, Home, Sweet Home*) at the Surrey Th. 27 June 1828 (by a "Juvenile Opera Company") and at the Hm. 25 July 1832 (by a German company).

The latest revivals of the opera seem to have taken place at Königsberg on 9 February 1902 (reduced to one act, revised by G. Hartmann and P. Frommer) and Munich 13 October 1918.

LESUEUR: *La Mort d'Adam et son Apothéose*

21 March. Paris, O.

Text by H. F. Guillard (based on Klopstock's drama). Three acts.

Lesueur's last performed opera; unsuccessful (16 performances).

WEYSE: *Sovedrikken* (The Sleeping-Draught)

21 April. Copenhagen

Text by A. G. Oehlenschläger (founded on a German libretto by C. F. Bretzner). Two acts.

Very successful at Copenhagen; given 100 times until 30 May 1874, since 6 October 1821 in an enlarged 4-act version, and revived 12 September 1914.

EULE: *Der Unsichtbare*

7 July. Hamburg

Text by K. L. Costenoble. One act.

Successful in Germany: Breslau 9 January 1810; Stuttgart 26 January 1810, etc; Berlin 25 April 1822; Dresden 15 July 1823; Prague 11 January 1828; Basle 29 November 1837; the latest revivals were at Leipzig 17 January 1846; Berlin, Fr.W. 6 February 1853; Dresden 11 July 1863; Darmstadt 5 February 1869.

WINTER: *Colmal*

15 September. Munich

Text by M. von Collin (after Ossian). Three acts.
One of Winter's best works, but unsuccessful.
Libretto published in Collin's *Dramatische Dichtungen*, Vol. II (1813), as *Calthon und Colmal*.

PAER: *Agnese di Fitz-Henry*

October. Ponte d'Altaro (near Parma)

Text by L. Buonavoglia (founded on Amelia Opie's tale *The Father and Daughter*, 1801). Two acts.

First produced at Villa Scotti, Ponte d'Altaro, near Parma; publicly Parma, T.S. Caterina Spring 1811, by amateurs; Naples, Fior. 1812 and

1814 (with spoken dialogue, text revised by L. Giannetti); Rome, Valle Spring 1813; Trieste Spring 1813; Milan, Sc. 2 July 1814 and all over Italy where it was given until about 1850, simply as *Agnese*. For an early appreciation see C. Gervasoni, *Nuova Teoria di Musica* (1812), p.212.

In Italian also given at: Dresden 1812; Weimar 30 January 1813; Munich 18 August 1816; Barcelona 14 October 1816; London 15 May 1817 (revived 27 June 1820 and 28 July 1832); Paris 24 July 1819; Odessa September 1821 and about the same time at Moscow; Lisbon 17 December 1823; Vienna 17 February 1825; Santiago, Chile 1830; Liverpool 1831, as *Il Padre e la Figlia;* Dublin 17 December 1831; Mexico January 1832; Edinburgh 24 December 1832; Cagliari, Sardinia September 1835; Ajaccio, Corsica Carnival 1840.

In German (translated by C. A. Herklots), Berlin 27 January 1815; Vienna, W. April 1820; Budapest 7 August 1820; Amsterdam 1 December 1823.

In Russian (translated by I. N. Svichinsky), St. Petersburg 11 February 1822; Moscow 18 July 1823.

In Danish (translated by N. T. Bruun), Copenhagen 1 September 1823.

In Polish (as *Aniela*), Warsaw 24 July 1830.

SPONTINI: *Fernand Cortez* ou *La Conquête du Mexique*

28 November. Paris, O.

Text by J. A. Esménard and V. J. Etienne de Jouy (founded on A. Piron's tragedy). Three acts.

Given at the Paris O. *c.*250 times until 1840, since 28 May 1817 in a revised version. The 100th performance was on 12 February 1823. A parody called *Relâche pour la Répétition générale de Fernand Cortez, ou Le grand Opéra en Province*, by C. F. Moreau, M. N. Balisson de Rougemont, and P. A. Vieillard, was produced at the Th. du Vaudeville, Paris 21 December 1809.

Outside Paris given at:

DRESDEN March 1812 (in Italian, translated by N. Perotti).

VIENNA 26 May 1812 (in German, translated by I. F. Castelli); second version 3 October 1818.

PRAGUE 9 September 1813 (in German; Weber's début as conductor there).

BERLIN 15 October 1814 (in German, translated by J. O. H. Schaum); second version 20 April 1818 (new translation by May); given there 161 times until 1894.

BUDAPEST 4 January 1815 (in German).

ST. PETERSBURG 21 January 1820 (in Russian, translated by D. N. Barkov) and November 1838 (in German).

NAPLES, S.C. 4 February 1820 (in Italian, translated by G. Schmidt; Rossini conducting).

BRUSSELS 27 August 1822 (in French).

RIGA 1824 (in German).

STOCKHOLM 13 June 1826 (in Swedish, translated by P. A. Granberg).

COPENHAGEN 19 January 1827 (in Danish, translated by N. T. Bruun).

WARSAW 6 December 1845 (in Polish, translated by J. Jasiński).

AMSTERDAM March 1846 (in German).

Never performed in London where an opera on the same subject by Bishop (text by J. R. Planché, produced C.G. 5 November 1823), although unsuccessful barred the way to the original.

Revivals:

ROME 4 May 1877 (by the Società Musicale Romana; new Italian version by A. Zanardini).

NEW YORK, M. 16 January 1888 (in German, for the first time in America).

LEIPZIG 10 May 1888 (in German).

PRAGUE 29 November 1900 (in German).

MILAN, SC. 26 December 1916 (in Italian).

SOLIÉ: *Le Diable à quatre* ou *La Femme acariâtre*

30 November. Paris, O.C.

Text by A. F. Creuzé de Lesser (a new version of Sedaine's libretto, see 1756). Three acts.

Successful in Paris; last revived at the O.C. in 1835 and at the Th.L. 15 October 1853 (re-scored by Adam).

In French also, Berne 4 July 1810; Brussels 13 April 1814; New York 17 August 1827.

In Swedish (translated by G. F. Åbergsson), Stockholm 11 December 1811.

In Russian (translated by F. F. Kokoshkin), St. Petersburg 22 November 1813; Moscow 29 December 1814.

In Dutch (translated by M. G. Engelman), Amsterdam 1820.

CHERUBINI: *Pimmalione*

30 November. Paris, Th. des Tuileries

Text by S. Vestris (partly founded on Sografi's Italian version of Rousseau's *Pygmalion*, see 1770 and 1790). One act.

Cherubini wrote this little Italian opera for Napoléon's private theatre, wehre it was performed twice in 1809 and once more in 1812.

1810

MORLACCHI: *Le Danaide*

11 February. Rome, Arg.

Text by S. Scatizzi (altered from Metastasio's *Ipermestra*). Two acts.

Morlacchi's first success. Dresden February 1812 (revived December 1814 and December 1818). New version, Perugia 1816; Milan 2 March 1819.

ISOUARD: *Cendrillon*

22 February. Paris, O.C.

Text by C. G. Etienne. Three acts.

Very successful in Paris and abroad. Given at:

BRUNSWICK 1810 (in French).

BRUSSELS 13 June 1810 (in French).

EISENSTADT, HUNGARY 9 September 1810 (in German, translated by H. Schmidt).

FRANKFORT 1 January 1811 (in German, translated by H. Schmidt).

STOCKHOLM 23 February 1811 (in Swedish, translated by C. G. Nordforss).

VIENNA, W. 2 April 1811 (in German).

MOSCOW 27 May 1811 (in French).

BERLIN 14 June 1811 (in German, translated by C. A. Herklots); Munich 1811; Hamburg 26 February 1812, etc. At Königsberg 1812 German translation by F. E. Jester as *Prinzessin Aschenbrödel*.

WARSAW 1811 (in Polish, translated by W. Pekalski).

BUDAPEST 13 February 1812 (in German).

BERNE 4 April 1812 (in German).

AMSTERDAM 1812 (in Dutch, translated by C. A. van Raij; an earlier translation by H. van Overvest Kup had been published at Rotterdam in 1810).

BRÜNN 21 September 1812 (in German).

COPENHAGEN 20 October 1812 (in Danish, translated by N. T. Bruun).

PRAGUE I January 1814 (in German) and 17. October 1830 (in Czech, translated by J. N. Stěpánek).

LEMBERG 1814 (in German).

MADRID 9 January 1815 (in Spanish).

AGRAM 16 September 1826 (in German).

NEW YORK 13 July 1827 (in French).

CLAUSENBURG 26 July 1834 (in Hungarian, translated by F. S. Deáky).

HELSINKI 22 January 1841 (in German).

Last revived in German: Königsberg 11 December 1872; Mannheim 14 January 1883. In French: Paris, O.C. 23 January 1877; Galerie Vivienne 17 February 1896.

Steibelt set the same libretto later in the same year (see below). In most countries Isouard's opera was, after 1820, displaced by Rossini's even more successful *Cenerentola* (see 1817).

BISHOP: *The Maniac; or, The Swiss Banditti*

13 March. London, Ly.

Text by S. J. Arnold. Three acts.

Bishop's first success as an opera composer; 26 performances.

R. KREUTZER: *Abel*

23 March. Paris, O.

Text by F. B. Hoffman. Three acts.

Revived (in a reduced 2-act version as *La Mort d'Abel*), Paris, O. 17 March 1823.

(The opera had been previously performed before the Empress at Malmaison on 26 March 1807.)

KUNZEN: *Kaerlighed paa Landet*

23 March. Copenhagen

Text by N. T. Bruun (translated from Weisse's *Die Liebe auf dem Lande*, see 1768). Three acts.

Successful at Copenhagen; given there 18 times until 1818.

J. N. HUMMEL: *Mathilde von Guise*

26 March. Vienna, Kä.

Text: a German version, by an unknown translator, of a French libretto by Mercier-Dupaty, set by Solié in 1808. Three acts.

The most successful opera of the famous pianist. Vocal score printed.

Revived, in a new version, Weimar 17 February 1821; Prague Spring 1822; Riga 1825 (in concert form); Berlin 3 August 1833.

PUCITTA: *La Vestale*

3 May. London, Hm.

Text: an Italian version of Etienne de Jouy's French libretto (see 1807). Two acts.

The best of the numerous operas Pucitta wrote for London and for Angelica Catalani. Vocal score printed. Also given at Lisbon Carnival 1816; Milan, T. Rè July 1816, etc. Buenos Aires 23 July 1828.

CATEL: *Les Bayadères*

8 August. Paris, O.

Text by V. J. Etienne de Jouy. Three acts.

Catel's chief work. Given at the Paris Opéra 140 times until 1828 (100th performance 13 November 1818); Brussels 25 January 1820.

In German (translated by I. F. Castelli), Vienna 14 October 1813; (translated by C. A. Herklots), Berlin 11 March 1814; Munich 31 January 1817.

In Russian (translated by A. I. Sheller), St. Petersburg 30 October 1820.

A parody by J. T. Merle, E. T. M. Ourry, and A. de Chazet, called *Les Baladin*, was produced at the Variétés, Paris, on 5 September 1810; another, by M. Dieulafoy and N. Gersin, called *La Manufacture d'Indiennes, ou Le Trionfe du Schall et les Queues du Chat*, was produced at the Th. du Vaudeville on 8 September 1810.

KIENLEN: *Claudine von Villa Bella*

9 September. Munich

Goethe's text (first set to music by Beecke, see 1780). Three acts.

The most successful of Kienlen's works; given also at Stuttgart 10 March 1811 and Berlin 30 April 1818. The music seems to be lost.

See E. Holzer's study in *Die Musik*, VIII (1909), p.145. Date of first performance, unknown to Holzer, Zenger, etc., according to *Journal des Luxus und der Moden*, 1810, p.630.

GENERALI: *Adelina*

16 September. Venice, S. Moisè

Text by G. Rossi (*melodramma sentimentale*). One act.

The most successful of Generali's comic operas.

Given in Italy until 1837; in a reduced version as *Luisina*, Sinigaglia July 1811; Venice, S. Moisè Autumn 1811; Crema May 1814, and Urbino Carnival 1815. First given at the Scala, Milan 10 November 1816.

In Italian also given at:

PARIS 20 June 1812.

MUNICH 1 June 1815.

VIENNA 26 November 1816.

BERNE 20 July 1820.

ODESSA October 1821.

BARCELONA 25 February 1824.

LONDON 19 March 1825.

LISBON 1826.

ST. PETERSBURG Autumn 1829.

MEXICO 1834.

In German (translated by F. K. Hiemer), Stuttgart 23 March 1818, etc.; Amsterdam 1820.

C. M. VON WEBER: *Silvana*

16 September. Frankfort

Text by F. K. Hiemer (a new version of Steinsberg's *Das Waldmädchen*, see 1800). Three acts.

Weber's first greater success: Berlin 10 July 1812; Prague 2 February 1817; Graz 5 January 1818; Budapest 1820; Riga 1823; Lemberg 1850.

Revived Dresden 29 July 1855; Berlin, Kroll's 1 December 1858; Hamburg 5 January 1885 (text re-written by E. Pasqué, prologue, 4 acts, and epilogue); music arranged by F. Langer; this version was given at Berlin, Kroll's 17 July 1889 and on many other German stages; also Basle 29 January 1886; Rotterdam 1890; Riga 1891.

Silvana was the first of Weber's operas which was translated into other languages:

LONDON, SURREY 2 September 1828 (in English, translated by C. A. Somerset).

PRAGUE 18 November 1832 (in Czech, translated by J. N. Stěpánek).

PARIS, ATHÉNÉE 3 April 1872 (in French, translated by V. Wilder and E. Mestépès).

HAGUE January 1873 (in French, translated by V. Wilder and E. Mestépès).

ANTWERP 17 February 1880 (in French) and 2 October 1897 (in Flemish).

PAVESI: *Ser Marcantonio*

26 September. Milan, Sc.

Text by A. Anelli. Two acts.

Very successful in Italy until about 1840, when Donizetti's *Don Pasquale* (see 1843) displaced it. Given at Parma 15 November 1811 as *Bettina e Marcantonio*.

In Italian also, Paris 10 July 1813 (the first act already 15 July 1811 at Napoléon's private theatre); Barcelona 14 October 1815; Munich 20 September 1816; Dresden 20 October 1817; Vienna, W. 5 February 1818; Odessa October 1821; Corfu Autumn 1831.

In Spanish, Madrid 13 May 1817.

In German, Vienna, W. August 1821; Stuttgart Autumn 1828 (translated by J. B. Krebs); Cassel 16 September 1829, etc.; revived Vienna, Kä. 15 November 1842.

FRÄNZL: *Carlo Fioras*
oder *Der Stumme in der Sierra Morena*

16 October. Munich

Text by W. Vogel. Three acts.

Successful in Germany: Berlin 12 February 1813, etc.

In German also, Prague 19 December 1813; Hanover 1 October 1815; St. Petersburg December 1817.

Revived (under the title of *Carlos Romaldi* and arranged as a melodrama with choruses, additional music by Lannoy), Vienna, W. 22 August 1822; again Berlin, Kgst. 12 January 1827 and Vienna, Jos. 8 August 1827.

In Russian (translated by I. N. Svichinsky), St. Petersburg 10 February 1820 and Moscow 5 September 1821.

STEIBELT: *Cendrillon*

26 October. St. Petersburg

Text by C. G. Etienne (set to music by Isouard earlier in the same year, see above). Three acts.

Successful in Russia; originally produced at St. Petersburg by the French troupe and subsequently also in German 8 February 1811 (translated by H. G. Schmieder) and Russian 12 May 1814 (translated by A. V. Luknitsky).

In Russian also, Moscow 23 February 1816.

ROSSINI: *La Cambiale di Matrimonio*

3 November. Venice, S. Moisè

Text by G. Rossi (*farsa*, founded on a comedy by C. Federici). One act.

Rossini's first performed opera.

Outside Italy, given at Barcelona 26 April 1816; Trieste 1822 (enlarged to two acts); Vienna 2 October 1834 (in German, as *Der Bräutigam aus Canada*, translated by J. C. Grünbaum) and 3 May 1837 (in Italian).

After an interval of many years, the opera was revived at Venice 10 April 1910; and again Turin 5 May 1927; Bologna 11 January 1934; Genoa February 1934; Pesaro 29 February 1936.

In Italian also, Vienna, Stadttheater 22 Sep-

tember 1937 and New York, 44th St. Theatre 8 November 1937.

The duet, *Dunque io son*, from this *farsa* was afterwards introduced into *Il Barbiere di Siviglia*.

BLANGINI: *Le Sacrifice d'Abraham*

14 November. Cassel

Text by Colonel Saint-Marcel.[1] Three acts.

In 1809 Blangini had been appointed court composer to Napoléon's brother Jerome, King of Westphalia, whose birthday was celebrated by the production of this opera (originally written for Paris).

1811

BOIELDIEU: *Rien de trop* ou
Les deux Paravents

6 January. St. Petersburg

Text by J. M. Pain (originally performed in Paris 1808 as a vaudeville). One act.

Paris, O.C. 19 April 1811; Brussels 11 August 1811; in French also Cassel Spring 1812; Stockholm May 1813.

In German, Vienna 8 April 1812.

In Polish (translated by W. Boguslawski), Warsaw 1819.

MORLACCHI: *Raoul di Crequi*

April. Dresden

Text by L. Romanelli (an Italian version of Monvel's French libretto, see 1789; first set to music by Mayr in 1809). Two acts.

The first opera Morlacchi wrote for Dresden and one of his best works. "Questo musicale dramma viene riputato il suo capo d'opera, essendo una musica di un genere affatto nuovo: tutto il dramma è in un sol pezzo di musica senza recitative al cembalo, senza ritornelli, e senza soliloquj, con otto spezie di coristi e con balli intrecciati ai cori ed ai finali . . ." (Gervasoni).

[1] According to *A.M.Z.* Probably A. H. P. Tardieu de Saint-Marcel, "ancien garde du corps du comte d'Artois" (Quérard) who collaborated with Blangini on another occasion.

C. M. VON WEBER: *Abu Hassan*

4 June. Munich

Text by F. K. Hiemer. One act.

Stuttgart 10 July 1811; Vienna, W. 28 May 1813 (O. only 17 November 1872); Berlin 28 July 1813; Prague Summer 1819, etc.; slightly altered Dresden 10 March 1823; Riga 1824, etc.

In German also, New York 8 September 1877; Rotterdam 1882.

In Danish (translated by T. Overskou), Copenhagen 11 March 1824.

In English (translated by W. Dimond, music adapted by T. S. Cooke), London, D.L. 4 April 1825; this version was also given at New York 5 November 1827; Philadelphia 21 November 1827 and Dublin 10 April 1828.

In French (translated by C. Nuitter and A. Beaumont), Paris, Th.L. 11 May 1859.

In Italian (translated by S. de Castrone, Marchese della Rajata), London, D.L. 12 May 1870 (recitatives by Arditi).

In Swedish (translated by A. Lindgren), Stockholm 1880 (revived 17 April 1901).

In Hungarian (translated by E. Abrányi), Budapest February 1882.

In Flemish, Antwerp 26 November 1898.

Still given on German stages; last revived at Berlin 18 December 1936.

Outside Germany some of the latest revivals were at Basle 21 October 1924; New York 23 March 1934 and Biltmore Th. 9 June 1936 (new English version by A. Houghton); Cambridge 22 February 1938 (new English version by W. Dean); Amsterdam October 1934 (by the Dutch Chamber Opera); Johannesburg March 1942.

MOSCA: *I Pretendenti delusi*

7 September. Milan, Sc.

Text by L. Prividali. Two acts.

Successful in Italy.

In Italian also given at Barcelona 22 June 1816; Munich 19 February 1818; Dresden 19 May 1821; London 9 April 1822; Vienna 21 March 1825.

In Spanish, Madrid 18 August 1818.

Mosca claimed to have used in this opera orchestra crescendo for the first time, earlier than Rossini, to whom the innovation afterwards was attributed.

ISOUARD: *Le Billet de Loterie*

14 September. Paris, O.C.

Text by A. F. Creuzé de Lesser and J. F. Roger. One act.

In Paris given until 1833. In French also, Liége 21 December 1811; Brussels 23 January 1812; Cassel 25 April 1812; New Orleans 1816, etc.

In German (translated by I. F. Castelli), Vienna 5 February 1812; Prague 21 November 1813; Weimar 21 December 1814; Berlin 19 March 1817 (translated by C. A. Herklots; given until 1850), Munich 1822, etc. In German also, Agram 13 December 1838 (translated by G. Freund).

Revived Lemberg 11 March 1859 (in Polish); Amsterdam, Conservatoire June 1929 (in Dutch).

GYROWETZ: *Der Augenarzt*

1 October. Vienna, Kä.

Text by J. E. Veith (founded on a French libretto by A. Croizette and A. F. Chateauvieux, *Les Aveugles de Franconville* set by Lebrun and performed Paris 28 April 1802); according to F. I. von Holbein (preface in his *Theater*, Vol. II, 1812) plagiarized from his own *Die beiden Blinden*, published 1812. Two acts.

One of Gyrowetz's most successful works; given in Vienna 93 times (until 1817). Budapest 13 January 1812; Würzburg 3 April 1812; Pressburg 5 May 1812; Munich 28 July 1812; Berlin 14 August 1815 and all over Germany.

A French adaptation by A. Chalas and E. de Montglave, *La jeune Aveugle*, was given at the Odéon, Paris 2 March 1826.

A Czech version by J. K. Chmelenský was published (not produced) at Prague in 1833.

ISOUARD: *Le Magicien sans Magie*

4 November. Paris, O.C.

Text by A. F. Creuzé de Lesser and J. F. Roger. Two acts.

In French also, Brussels 27 February 1812; Cassel Summer 1812.

In German Vienna, W. 22 April 1812.

In Dutch (translated by B. A. Fallee and C. A. van Raij), Amsterdam 1813.

In Polish (translated by W. Boguslawski), Warsaw 1819.

In Russian (translated by D. N. Barkov), St. Petersburg 24 July 1820; Moscow 8 February 1822.

An English version of the text, by W. H. Hamilton, was set by Blewitt and given at Dublin 1 March 1815.

ZINGARELLI: *Berenice, Regina d'Armenia*

12 November. Rome, Valle

Text by J. Ferretti (founded on Zeno's *Lucio Vero*). Two acts.

Zingarelli's last opera. The often repeated statement that it had a run of more than 100 performances is, according to Cametti, much exaggerated. Copy of the libretto (unknown to Cametti), recorded in *Cat. Bibl. Soleinne.*

SPOHR: *Der Zweikampf mit der Geliebten*

15 November. Hamburg

Text by J. F. Schink. Three acts.

Spohr's first performed opera; on his earlier *Alruna*, see *Journal des Luxus und der Moden*, 1809, p.317; and E. Schmitz in *Journal of the I.M.S.*, Vol. XIII (1911–12).

Revived Cassel 7 February 1840. French vocal score (translated by H. Brovellio) published (*c.*1825).

Spohr afterwards introduced one air from this opera into his *Faust* (see 1816).

TOMAŠEK: *Seraphine*

15 December. Prague

Text by J. Dambeck. Three acts.

The only opera by the Bohemian composer to be produced. Neither the libretto seems to have been printed, nor the music to have been preserved.

ROMBERG: *Die Ruinen von Paluzzi*

27 December. Hamburg

Text by J. F. Schink. Three acts.

The best opera of the famous violinist. Vocal score printed.

1812

ROSSINI: *L'Inganno felice*

8 January. Venice, S. Moisè

Text by G. M. Foppa. One act.

Rossini's first great success.

Outside Italy (in Italian), also given at Barcelona 14 December 1815; Munich 25 June 1816; Vienna 26 November 1816 (first Rossini opera in Vienna; revived 4 May 1836); Lisbon 1817; Dresden 3 January 1818; London 1 July 1819 (revived 5 July 1827); Paris 13 May 1819; Berne 17 July 1820; Rio de Janeiro 1 December 1824; Buenos Aires 8 June 1826; Santiago June 1830 (first opera in Chile); St. Petersburg 1830; Vera Cruz August 1831; New York 11 May 1833; Prague Spring 1833; Berlin, Kgst. 26 October 1850.

In German (as *Der glückliche Betrug*) Weimar 1818; (as *Die Getäuschten*, translated by F. K. Hiemer), Frankfort November 1818; Stuttgart 14 May 1819; Berlin 27 September 1820; (as *Glückliche Täuschung*, translated by J. C. Grünbaum), Vienna 30 October 1823; Budapest 9 January 1826; Agram 1833.

In Spanish, Madrid 20 January 1820.

In Polish (translated by K. Brodziński), Warsaw February 1820.

In Danish (translated by N. T. Bruun), Copenhagen 5 March 1826.

In Hungarian, Clausenburg 28 May 1834 and Budapest 12 September 1835.

Revived by the Società Filarmonica, Naples 29 January 1872.

A French vocal score (*Le Traître démasqué*, translated by L. Danglas) was published at Brussels (n.d.).

WEYSE: *Faruk*

30 January. Copenhagen

Text by A. G. Oehlenschläger. Three acts.

Given at Copenhagen until 1834.

ISOUARD: *Lully et Quinault* ou
Le Déjeuner impossible

27 February. Paris, O.C.

Text by P. C. Gaugiran-Nanteuil. One act.

Given at Paris until 1833; in French also, Brussels 31 May 1812; Cassel Summer 1812; New Orleans before 1825; Vienna 18 July 1826; New York 1 September 1827.

In German (translated by J. von Seyfried), Vienna, W. 23 September 1813.

In Polish (translated by B. Kudlicz), Warsaw 1814.

In Danish (translated by N. T. Bruun), Copenhagen 5 September 1820.

(A Swedish 2-act version of the text by L. E. Granberg was composed by Berens and produced at Stockholm 15 November 1859.)

ROSSINI: *Ciro in Babilonia* o sia
La Caduta di Baldassarre

14 March. Ferrara

Text by F. Aventi. Two acts.

Given in Italy until 1827.

In Italian also, Munich 27 October 1816; Vienna, W. 18 June 1817; Weimar 20 March 1819; Dresden 2 October 1822; London, D.L. 30 January 1823 (in concert form).

BOIELDIEU: *Jean de Paris*

4 April. Paris, O.C.

Text by C. Godard d'Aucour de Saint-Just. Two acts.

One of Boieldieu's most famous works; the well-known cavatine *Ah! quel plaisir d'être en voyage* was taken from his *Télémaque* (see 1806).

Given at the O.C. until 1862 and revived at the Galerie Vivienne, 13 December 1893.

A parody by A. L. D. Martainville and T. M. Dumersan, called *Jean de Passy*, was produced at the Variétés 2 May 1812.

In French also given at Antwerp 30 July 1812; Brussels 21 December 1812, etc.; Berne 23 January 1819; New Orleans 1819; New York 6 August 1827; Amsterdam 1834; Rio de Janeiro Autumn 1846.

In German: Vienna, Kä. 28 August 1812 (translated by I. F. Castelli); Vienna, W. 29 August 1812 (translated by J. von Seyfried); Monrepos 28 September 1812 and Frankfort 11 November 1812 (translated by F. K. Hiemer); Berlin 25 March 1813 (translated by C. A. Herklots); Hamburg 21 January 1813; Munich 29 January 1813; Brünn 15 March 1813; Budapest 1813; St. Petersburg January 1814; Prague 8 January 1814; Berne 11 March 1823; Helsinki 25 May 1830; Bucharest 7 November 1830; Amsterdam October 1836. The latest revival in Germany was at Greifswald 30 January 1931.

In English, London, C.G. 12 November 1814 (translated by I. Pocock, music arranged by Bishop who added several numbers of his own); this version was also given in New York 25 November 1816 (before the French original was given there on 6 August 1827). In English also, St. Louis 3 October 1837; Melbourne 1862. Revived London, Olympic 31 July 1869 (music arranged by W. F. Taylor).

In Polish (translated by S. Regulski), Warsaw 1813.

In Danish (translated by N. T. Bruun), Copenhagen 1 February 1815.

In Spanish, Madrid 11 May 1816.

In Italian, Naples, Fondo Spring 1816.

In Russian (translated by Prince P. N. Shalikov), Moscow 9 January 1818; St. Petersburg 10 November 1819.

In Swedish (translated by J. D. Valerius), Stockholm 21 May 1819.

In Hungarian (translated by E. Pály), Clausenburg 1 November 1825; Budapest 3 November 1827.

In Czech (translated by J. N. Stěpánek), Prague 7 January 1827.

Dutch translation by J. C. Honig published Amsterdam 1813.

GYROWETZ: *Federica ed Adolfo*

6 April. Vienna, Kä.

Text by G. Rossi. Two acts.

Gyrowetz's first performed Italian opera; (an earlier *Semiramide*, written for London in 1791, had been destroyed in the fire of the "Pantheon" on 14 January 1792). Unsuccessful.

In Polish (translated by K. Tymowski), Warsaw 1816.

ROSSINI: *La Scala di Seta*

9 May. Venice, S. Moisè

Text by G. Rossi (founded on a French libretto by Planard, *L'Échelle de Soie*, set to music by Gaveaux in 1808). One act.

This farsa was outside Italy only given at Barcelona 4 August 1823 and at Lisbon 24 January 1825. Overture still popular.

CATEL: *Les Aubergistes de Qualité*

17 June. Paris, O.C.

Text by V. J. Etienne de Jouy. Three acts.

Given in Paris until 1825; Brussels 13 July 1813.

In German (translated by J. von Seyfried), Vienna, W. 5 February 1813; (translated by F. K. Hiemer), Stuttgart 27 June 1813; Prague 19 September 1813; Agram 15 May 1815; Dresden 25 September 1817, etc. Revived Vienna 21 December 1831.

In English (as *The Innkeepers* adapted, by C. Cummins), Leeds September 1829.

PERSUIS: *Jérusalem délivrée*

15 September. Paris, O.

Text by L. P. Baour Lormian (after Tasso). Five acts.

Persuis's most important work.

A parody by C. F. Moreau, E. T. M. Ourry, and E. G. M. Théaulon de Lambert, called *Jérusalem déshabillée* was produced at the Vaudeville, Paris, on 3 October 1812.

In German (translated by J. von Seyfried), Vienna, W. 11 February 1815; Carlsruhe August 1820.

A Dutch translation by A. Loosjes was published at Haarlem in 1813.

ROSSINI: *La Pietra del Paragone*

26 September. Milan, Sc.

Text by L. Romanelli. Two acts.

Outside Italy (in Italian), also given at Munich July 1817; Oporto February 1821; Paris 5 April 1821; Lisbon 30 May 1821; Barcelona 9 June 1821; Cagliari, Sardinia Carnival 1836; Mexico 1836.

In German (as *Weiberproben*, translated by J. von Seyfried), Vienna, W. 30 April 1821; Graz 25 February 1822; (as *Der Probierstein*), Berlin, Kgst. 5 October 1827.

A pasticcio *Un curioso Accidente*, arranged by A. Berrettoni and consisting chiefly of pieces from *La Pietra del Paragone*, was given at the Th.I., Paris 26 November 1859. The original was last revived at Warsaw 9 March 1866 (in Italian), and Florence, T. Pagliano 1 September 1868.

ROSSINI: *L'Occasione fa il Ladro*

24 November. Venice, S. Moisè

Text by L. Prividali. One act.

Barcelona 18 July 1822; Lisbon 6 February 1826; St. Petersburg 1830; Lugano October 1833.

In German, Vienna 27 August 1834.

Revived Pesaro 10 July 1892 (at the Liceo Rossini); Turin April 1913 (by the "Circolo degli Artisti"); Trieste June 1924 (at the T. Filodrammatico); London, Little Th. 14 January 1929 (in English, by marionettes).

WEIGL: *Der Bergsturz*

19 December. Vienna, Kä.

Text by J. A. F. Reil (founded on an actual event, a landslip near Goldau in September 1806). Three acts.

Weimar 18 November 1815; Darmstadt 15 September 1816; Leipzig 15 July 1818, etc.

MEYERBEER: *Jephta's Gelübde*

23 December. Munich

Text by A. Schreiber. Three acts.

Meyerbeer's first opera; given only twice.

1813

MEYERBEER: *Wirth und Gast,* oder *Aus Scherz Ernst*

6 January. Stuttgart

Text by J. G. Wohlbrück. Two acts.

Re-modelled Vienna 20 October 1814 (as *Die beiden Kalifen*); given also at Prague 22 October 1815; and Dresden 22 February 1820 (as *Alimelek*).

ROSSINI: *Il Signor Bruschino* ossia *Il Figlio per Azzardo*

End of January. Venice, S. Moisè

Text by G. M. Foppa (founded on a French comedy by Alissan de Chazet and E. T. M. Ourry). One act.

This little work was unsuccessful and soon forgotten when *Tancredi* and *L'Italiana in Algeri* came out in the same year. It was, however, frequently revived later on:

MILAN, CANOBBIANA 2 June 1844 (in Italian).

PARIS, B.P. 28 December 1857 (as *Bruschino*, French version by P. A. A. Pittaud de Forges and J. Offenbach).

MADRID, Z. 1 June 1858 (in Spanish, translated by L. de Olona and M. Pina).

BERLIN, KROLL'S 13 June 1858 (in French, by the Bouffes-Parisiens).

BRUSSELS 9 October 1859 (in French, by the Bouffes-Parisiens).

BERLIN, FR.W. 24 August 1862 (in German, translated by J. C. Grünbaum).

BOLOGNA, T. CONTAVALLI 19 May 1901 (in Italian).

MILAN, T. D. V. 5 June 1917 (in Italian).

WIESBADEN 16 February 1932 (new German version by L. Landshoff and K. Wolfskehl).

NEW YORK, M. 6 December 1932 (in Italian).

FLORENCE 6 May 1937, etc.

ROSSINI: *Tancredi*

6 February. Venice, F.

Text by G. Rossi (*melodramma eroico*, founded on Tasso's *Gerusalemme liberata* and Voltaire's tragedy *Tancredi*). Two acts.

Rossini's first world success; given on every Italian and on most foreign stages; in London until 1858, in Berlin until 1859, in Paris until 1862. The latest revival probably was at Dresden 27 October 1871 (in German). *Tancredi* was also the first of Rossini's operas which was translated into other languages. The first performances were at:

MUNICH August 1816 (in Italian) and 1821 (in German).

VIENNA 17 December 1816 (in Italian) and 12 March 1818 (in German).

DARMSTADT 26 December 1816 (for the first time in German, translated by F. K. Hiemer).

STUTTGART 20 February 1817 (translated by F. K. Hiemer).

PRAGUE April 1817 (in German, translated by J. C. Grünbaum) and 12 May 1825 (in Czech, translated by J. Doucha).

BARCELONA 5 May 1817 (in Italian).

ST. PETERSBURG Autumn 1817 (in German); Spring 1829 (in Italian); and December 1839 (in Russian).

MAYENCE 21 September 1817 (in German, Grünbaum's version, at the inauguration of the new "Grossherzoglich-Hessische Nationalbühne").

BERLIN, O. 5 January 1818 (in German, translated by C. A. Herklots) and O. 12 February 1821 and Kgst. 21 July 1841 (in Italian).

BUDAPEST 26 January 1818 (in German) and 30 October 1827 (in Hungarian).

WARSAW 1818 (in Polish, translated by K. Brodziński); Wilna 17 August 1827.

AMSTERDAM December 1818 (in German) and 1835 (in French).

LONDON 4 May 1820 (in Italian) and Princess's 17 April 1843 (in English; translator not mentioned).

COPENHAGEN 30 October 1820 (in Danish, translated by N. T. Bruun) and November 1844 (in Italian).

PARIS, TH.I. 23 April 1822 (in Italian) and Odéon 7 September 1827 (in French, translated by E. d'Anglemont and J. P. F. Lesguillon, music arranged by J. F. A. Lemière de Corvey).

LISBON 18 September 1822 (in Italian).

MOSCOW 26 November 1825 (in Italian).

MEXICO 29 December 1825 (in Spanish) and 4 August 1832 (in Italian).

NEW YORK 31 December 1825 (in Italian).

CORFU Carnival 1826.

RIO DE JANEIRO 22 January 1826 (in Italian).

STRASBOURG February 1826 (for the first time in French, translated by Dussert; see *A.M.Z.*, 1826, p.687).

AGRAM 6 May 1827 (in German).

CLAUSENBURG 19 May 1827 (for the first time in Hungarian, translated by E. Pály).

BUENOS AIRES 31 May 1828 (in Italian).

BOSTON 2 September 1829 (in Italian; first Italian opera there).

STOCKHOLM 18 September 1829 (in Swedish, translated by J. L. Åbergsson; the first act already 25 October 1817, in concert form).

SANTIAGO, CHILE 1830 (in Italian).

LIMA 1831 (in Italian).

PHILADELPHIA 15 September 1831 (in Italian).

BUCHAREST 29 December 1833 (in German).

HELSINKI 28 February 1834 (in German).

BRUSSELS 24 March 1834 (in French, the Paris version).

DUBLIN 27 September 1834 (in Italian).

BASLE 15 October 1834 (in German).

MAYR: *La Rosa rossa e la Rosa bianca*

21 February. Genoa, S. Agostino

Text by F. Romani (founded on a French libretto by R. C. G. de Pixérécourt, set to music by Gaveaux in 1809). Two acts.

Milan, T. Carc. July 1815, etc.; given at Naples, S.C. Spring 1819 and Venice Autumn 1819 as *Il Trionfo dell'Amicizia*. Outside Italy: Munich May 1817; Lisbon 13 February 1822; Paris 6 May 1823; Madrid 1 January 1824; London 16 February 1828.

La Rosa rossa e la Rosa bianca was the first text written by Felice Romani, who has been called the best Italian librettist between Metastasio and Boito. He wrote about 90 librettos, of which the musical settings amount to over 200. Incidentally,

the most famous French librettist of the 19th century, A. E. Scribe, wrote his first opera text in the same year, 1813 (see note on Auber's *Leicester*, 1823).

ISOUARD: *Le Prince de Catane*

4 March. Paris, O.C.

Text by R. R. L. Castel. Three acts.

In French also, Brussels 7 July 1814, etc.

In German (translated by J. von Seyfried), Vienna, W. 10 December 1813 (additions by I. von Seyfried); Prague 12 June 1814; Budapest 19 June 1815. Revived Graz 4 November 1826.

In Spanish, Madrid 2 August 1817.

In Russian (translated by A. I. Sheller), St. Petersburg 2 October 1817.

PLANTADE: *Le Mari de Circonstances*

18 March. Paris, O.C.

Text by F. A. E. de Planard. One act.

In Paris given until 1831; Brussels 13 October 1813 (revived 31 October 1836).

CHERUBINI: *Les Abencérages* ou *L'Étendard de Grenade*

6 April. Paris, O.

Text by V. J. Etienne de Jouy (founded on Florian's novel, *Gonzalve de Cordove*). Three acts.

There were not more than 20 performances. Napoléon attended the first night.)

In German (translated by C. A. Herklots), Berlin 11 March 1828 (music revised by Spontini).

ROSSINI: *L'Italiana in Algeri*

22 May. Venice, S. Ben.

Text by A. Anelli (originally written for L. Mosca and performed at the Scala, Milan 16 August 1808). Two acts.

After *Tancredi* Rossini's second great success in this year. Given at Rome as *Il Naufragio felice* (1815), and as *Il Pampaluco* (13 January 1816).

Outside Italy:

BARCELONA 29 August 1815 (in Italian).

MUNICH 18 June 1816 (in Italian; first Rossini opera in Germany).

MADRID 29 September 1816 (in Spanish).

PARIS 1 February 1817 (in Italian; first Rossini opera in Paris).

VIENNA, KÄ. 15 February 1817 (in Italian) and W. January 1821 (in German).

LISBON 22 June 1818 (in Italian).

STUTTGART 6 September 1818 (for the first time in German, translated by J. C. Grünbaum); Cassel 23 November 1818; Hanover 27 December 1818, etc.

BUCHAREST 8 September 1818 (in German).

LONDON, HM. 26 January 1819 (in Italian) and Princess's 30 December 1844 (in English).

GRAZ 6 February 1819 (in German).

AMSTERDAM Summer 1819 (in German).

WARSAW 1819 and 8 December 1826 (in two different Polish versions by K. Brodziński and by W. Boguslawski respectively).

BUDAPEST 11 October 1819 (in German) and 8 January 1828 (in Hungarian).

BERNE 14 July 1820 (in Italian).

HERMANNSTADT AND KRONSTADT May 1821 (in Italian).

PRAGUE Carnival 1823 (in German).

MEXICO 1824 (in Spanish) and November 1831 (in Italian).

BERLIN, KGST. 3 August 1825 (in German) and 22 November 1841 (in Italian).

BUENOS AIRES 9 July 1826 (in Italian).

CLAUSENBURG 11 February 1827 (for the first time in Hungarian).

AGRAM 1827 (in German).

ST. PETERSBURG 29 June 1829 (in Italian) and Spring 1837 (in German).

SANTIAGO, CHILE 1830 (in Italian).

RIO DE JANEIRO 9 October 1830 (in Italian).

LIÉGE 4 April 1831 (in French, translated by F. H. J. Castil-Blaze); a new French translation by the composer C. Lecocq was published in 1893.

NEW YORK 5 November 1832 (in Italian).

PHILADELPHIA 4 February 1833 (in Italian).

MARSEILLES 11 March 1833 (in French).

BRUSSELS 6 October 1835 (in French).

HAVANA February 1836 (in Italian).

DUBLIN 24 March 1838 (in Italian).

CONSTANTINOPLE Carnival 1839 (in Italian).

ORAN, ALGERIA Autumn 1842 (in Italian).

COPENHAGEN Carnival 1843 (in Italian).

Given on Italian stages until about 1900 and again since 1925.

Revived New York 5 December 1919 (in Italian); Turin 26 November 1925 (under V. Gui, at the inauguration of the Teatro di Torino, late T. Scribe); Paris, Ch.É. 21 May 1929 (in Italian).

FREIBURG 29 April 1931 (new German version by H. Röhr).

PRAGUE 31 December 1933 (for the first time in Czech).

LONDON, C.G. 16 May 1935 (in Italian).

BUENOS AIRES 1 July 1938 (in Italian).

BASLE 11 November 1938 (in German).

MÉHUL: *Le Prince Troubadour* ou *Le Grand Trompeur de Dames*

24 May. Paris, O.C.

Text by A. Duval. One act.

In French also, Brussels 9 January 1814; Liége 24 December 1814, etc.

In Russian (translated by A. I. Sheller), St. Petersburg 30 December 1816.

In German, Frankfort November 1814; Vienna 24 September 1819.

BOIELDIEU: *Le nouveau Seigneur de Village*

29 June. Paris, O.C.

Text by A. F. Creuzé de Lesser and E. G. F. de Favières. One act.

Popular in France; given at the O.C. until 1898 and revived on 12 December 1934.

In French also, Brussels 13 October 1813; Berne 20 January 1819; Vienna 22 July 1826; Berlin 22 May 1828; Rio de Janeiro Autumn 1846; London, St. J.'s 22 January 1849; Soerabaya 2 December 1867.

In German (translated by I. F. Castelli), Vienna 24 May 1814; Frankfort November 1814; Berlin 24 May 1815; Prague 3 August 1815; St. Petersburg 1815; Budapest 1815; Bucharest 20

November 1830, etc. Revived Munich 28 September 1853; Dresden September 1862.

In Polish (translated by L. A. Dmuszewski), Warsaw 1815.

In Swedish (translated by J. C. Puke), Stockholm 20 January 1818; revived 13 December 1861 (new translation by F. A. Dahlgren).

In Danish (translated by N. T. Bruun), Copenhagen 6 February 1819.

In Dutch (translated by M. G. Engelman), Amsterdam 1819; Hague 1831; Ostende 19 July 1840. Revived Amsterdam January 1935 (by the Dutch Chamber Opera).

In Russian (translated by A. I. Pisarev), Moscow 22 January 1824; (translated by R. M. Zotov) St. Petersburg 10 May 1825.

In English (as *My Lord is not my Lord*, adapted by G. Dance), London, D.L. 29 January 1840; New York 10 December 1849.

GYROWETZ: *Robert* oder *Die Prüfung*

15 July. Vienna, Kä.

Text by F. X. Huber. Two acts.

"... diese Oper hat Beethoven jedesmahl als sie gegeben wurde, besucht, und äusserte dem G. durch einen Händedruck, dass diese Oper vor allen andern ihm am besten gefiele". This passage occurs in the manuscript of Gyrowetz's autobiography, but was omitted in the printed edition (1848).

GARCIA: *Il Califfo di Bagdad*

30 September. Naples, Fondo

Text by A. L. Tottola (founded on the French libretto by Saint-Just, see 1800). Two acts.

The most successful opera of the famous singer. Given also in Paris 22 March 1817 and Mexico Carnival 1825.

MAYR: *Medea in Corinto*

28 November. Naples, S.C.

Text by F. Romani. Two acts.

Outside Italy given at Dresden 3 January 1821; Paris 14 January 1823; London 1 June 1826 (revived H.M.'s as late as 12 March 1850).

ROSSINI: *Aureliano in Palmira*

26 December. Milan, Sc.

Text by F. Romani. Two acts.

Given in Italy until 1831; at Vicenza Summer 1817 and Venice Autumn 1820 as *Zenobia*. Outside Italy, Barcelona 12 August 1822; Lisbon 10 October 1824; Corfu Autumn 1825; London 22 June 1826 (not 16 May 1826 as stated in the libretto); Buenos Aires 6 November 1829.

In German, Graz 22 March 1827.

Rossini introduced parts of the music into his *Barbiere di Siviglia* (see 1816).

1814

ISOUARD: *Joconde* ou *Les Coureurs d'Aventures*

28 February. Paris, O.C.

Text by C. G. Etienne. Three acts.

Given in Paris until the end of the century and revived at the Tr.L. 10 January 1918; revived at Beauvais 5 March 1931.

In French also, Liége 13 December 1814; Brussels 9 January 1815 (revived 21 April 1884); Berne 10 February 1819; Dublin 1824 (libretto Allen A. Brown Collection, Boston); New York 27 July 1827; Baden-Baden 1 August 1864.

In German (translated by J. von Seyfried), Vienna, Augarten Th. 12 March 1815 and Kä. 1 April 1815; Budapest 25 September 1815; Prague 2 January 1816; Munich 5 January 1816; Berlin 26 April 1816 (translated here by J. O. H. Schaum), etc. Revived Vienna 19 November 1855, etc.; Munich 2 December 1870 (as *Minnefahrten*, new German version by F. Grandaur).

In Polish (translated by W. Pekalski), Warsaw 1815.

In Russian (translated by P. A. Korsakov), St. Petersburg 7 February 1815; Moscow 22 December 1817.

In Spanish, Madrid 15 July 1816.

In Danish (translated by N. T. Bruun), Copenhagen 14 October 1817.

In Swedish (translated by C. G. Nordforss), Stockholm 14 January 1820; revived 7 April 1858 (new translation by H. O. Wieselgren).

In Norwegian, Christiania Autumn 1873.

In English (translated by C. Santley), London, Ly. 25 October 1876.

KLEINHEINZ: *Harald*

22 March. Budapest

(German) text by M. Stegmayer. Three acts.

Vienna, W. 24 August 1815 (as *Harald, der Kronenräuber*).

On Kleinheinz, see A. Sandberger's study in his *Ausgewählte Aufsätze zur Musikgeschichte*, Vol. II, p.226 (1924).

KUHLAU: *Røverborgen*
(The Brigands' Castle)

26 May. Copenhagen

Text by A. G. Oehlenschläger. Three acts.

Kuhlau's most successful opera (his famous *Elverhøj* not being an opera, but a play with incidental music); given at Copenhagen until 1880.

In German (translated by Oehlenschläger himself), Hamburg 22 March 1816; Cassel 28 July 1819 (as *Die Burg Rocheloup*); Leipzig 4 September 1822; Riga 1822; Breslau 26 February 1823.

POISSL: *Athalia*

3 June. Munich

Text by J. G. Wohlbrück (founded on Racine's tragedy). Three acts.

Stuttgart 21 May 1815; Frankfort 17 September 1815; Prague 21 May 1816; Berlin 25 February 1817, etc. Revived Munich 5 December 1828.

GUHR: *Die Vestalin*

3 June. Cassel

Text: J. von Seyfried's German version of Etienne de Jouy's French libretto (see 1807). Three acts.

Guhr's only opera; given at Cassel until 1821.

ROSSINI: *Il Turco in Italia*

14 August. Milan, Sc.

Text by F. Romani. Two acts.

Given at Vicenza 1816 as *Il Tutore deluso*, at Rome Autumn 1819 as *La Capricciosa corretta;* last revived in Italy, Florence, T. Niccolini 16 March 1882.

Outside Italy:

DRESDEN 30 November 1816 (in Italian).

MADRID 14 October 1818 (in Spanish).

STUTTGART 23 April 1819 (in German, translated by F. K. Hiemer).

VIENNA, W. March 1820 (in German, translated by J. von Seyfried) and Kä. 1 March 1825 (in Italian).

PARIS 23 May 1820 (in Italian).

BARCELONA 9 June 1820 (in Italian).

LISBON 10 July 1820 (in Italian).

LONDON, HM. 19 May 1821 (in Italian) and D.L. 1 May 1827 (in English, as *The Turkish Lovers*, adapted by M. R. Lacy).

MOSCOW 24 November 1821 (in Italian).

PRAGUE 3 January 1823 (in German).

ST. PETERSBURG 12 June 1823 (in Russian, translated by A. I. Sheller) and Spring 1829 (in Italian).

WARSAW 17 March 1824 (in Polish, translated by L. Osiński).

STOCKHOLM 21 April 1824 (in Swedish, translated by J. E. Remmer).

BASTIA, CORSICA Carnival 1825 (in Italian).

BERLIN, KGST. 1 March 1826 (in German, translated by K. von Holtei) and 18 September 1841 (in Italian).

NEW YORK 14 March 1826 (in Italian; revived 18 December 1840).

EDINBURGH 19 December 1827 (in Italian).

DUBLIN 7 October 1834 (in Italian).

BUCHAREST Carnival 1847 (in Italian).

ISOUARD: *Jeannot et Colin*

17 October. Paris, O.C.

Text by C. G. Etienne. Three acts.

Revived Paris, O.C. 17 June 1850 and 12 October 1857.

In French also, Brussels 7 December 1815; New York 10 August 1827.

In German (translated by I. F. Castelli), Vienna 9 November 1815; Brünn 13 August 1817; Breslau 1817; Berlin 3 August 1821.

In Polish (translated by W. Boguslawski), Warsaw 1817.

In Danish (translated by N. T. Bruun), Copenhagen 6 October 1818.

DRIEBERG: *Der Sänger und der Schneider*

23 November. Berlin, O.

Text: a German version (by the composer?) of Villiers's and Gouffé's French libretto (see 1804). One act.

Drieberg's most successful work; given on German stages until after 1850. Berne 19 February 1823; Vienna, W. 20 July 1824; Gothenburg 6 December 1832 (in German); Basle 23 November 1836; Agram 13 July 1839.

KURPINSKI: *Jadwiga, Królowa Polska*

(Jadviga, Queen of Poland)

23 December. Warsaw

Text by J. U. Niemcewicz. Three acts.

Successful on Polish stages. Wilna 1 November 1816, etc. Revived at Warsaw as late as October 1907.

1815

CATRUFO: *Félicie* ou *La jeune Fille romanesque*

28 February. Paris, O.C.

Text by E. Mercier-Dupaty. Three acts.

The most successful work of Catrufo, who began as a composer of Italian operas at Malta and ended as a singing teacher in London.

Given in Paris until 1825; in French also, Berne 24 February 1819.

In Polish (translated by Lipinski), Warsaw 1816.

In Russian (translated by N. V. Vsevolozhsky), St. Petersburg 15 December 1817.

For a Swedish version of the libretto, see 1821.

K. KREUTZER: *Die Alpenhütte*

1 March. Stuttgart

Text by A. von Kotzebue. One act.

The most popular of Kreutzer's early works. Given also at Würzburg 27 April 1815; Frankfort 11 May 1815; Donaueschingen 4 November 1819; Munich 25 August 1820; Vienna, Kä. 27 July 1822, etc. Revived Freiburg 23 November 1930.

POISSL: *Der Wettkampf zu Olympia* oder *Die Freunde*

21 April. Munich

Text by the composer (after Metastasio's *Olimpiade*). Three acts.

Stuttgart 3 November 1815; Darmstadt 14 July 1816; Dresden 16 March 1820, etc.

COCCIA: *Clotilda*

8 June. Venice, S. Ben

Text by G. Rossi (founded on a French melodrama by L. C. Caigniez). Two acts.

Coccia's most successful work; in Italy until about 1860. Given at Turin Spring 1822 as *La Foresta d'Hermannstadt*.

In Italian also, Lisbon 1818; Barcelona 19 August 1819; Munich 15 November 1819; Oporto 1820; Paris 20 May 1821; Dresden 5 January 1822; Palma, Mallorca Spring 1826; Mexico 1832; Odessa Summer 1839.

ROSSINI: *Elisabetta Regina d'Inghilterra*

4 October. Naples, S.C.

Text by G. Schmidt. Two acts.

Given at Venice December 1831 as *I Paggi de Leicester*.

Outside Italy, given at Barcelona 27 August 1817; Dresden 24 January 1818; London 30 April 1818; Munich 22 May 1818; Lisbon 11 December

1820; Paris 10 March 1822; Vienna, Kä. 30 May 1822; Odessa 1830; Mexico 1834.

In German, Vienna, W. 3 September 1818; Brünn 19 October 1818; Frankfort January 1819; Budapest 1 March 1819; Amsterdam Summer 1819; Graz 29 November 1819; Berlin 4 June 1824. Last recorded production, Würzburg 18 March 1841.

In Russian (translated by A. I. Sheller), St. Petersburg 27 April 1820.

Overture and finale of this opera were taken from *Aureliano in Palmira* (1813).

CAVOS: *Ivan Susanin*
Ивань Сусанинь
31 October. St. Petersburg

Text by Prince A. A. Shakhovskoy. Two acts.

Moscow 14 January 1822. Revived at St. Petersburg in 1852.

Cavos's best work; regarded for 20 years as a model of Russian national opera. When it was replaced in 1836 by Glinka's *Life for the Czar* (dealing with the same subject) Cavos said (according to Y. K. Arnold): "Les vieux doivent toujours céder la place aux plus jeunes. E poi—la sua musica è effettivamente migliore della mia, e tanto più che dimostra un carattere veramente nazionale".

BOCHSA: *La Lettre de Change*
11 December. Paris, O.C.

Text by F. A. E. de Planard. One act.

Bochsa's most successful work. Given in Paris until 1837.

In French also, Brussels 21 November 1816 (revived 25 February 1848); Berne 18 January 1819; Vienna 29 July 1826; New York 20 July 1827. Revived as late as 1867–68 at Ghent.

In German, Vienna 19 April 1819.

In English, London, Ly. 29 June 1820 and Dublin 6 February 1821 (as *The Promissory Note*, translated by S. Beazley?).

In Russian, St. Petersburg 30 September 1824.

ROSSINI: *Torvaldo e Dorliska*
26 December. Rome, Valle

Text by C. Sterbini. Two acts.

Given in Italy until 1840. Outside Italy: Barcelona 10 May 1818; Munich February 1820; Lisbon 7 August 1820; Paris 21 November 1820; Moscow 19 November 1825; St. Petersburg Spring 1829; Mexico 12 September 1831; Malta 1837; Ajaccio, Corsica December 1840; Oran, Algeria Autumn 1842.

In German (translated by F. von Biedenfeld), Vienna, W. 20 August 1821; Budapest 3 December 1821; Graz 4 December 1822; Prague 18 February 1823; Frankfort August 1824; Berlin, Kgst. 17 January 1829.

In Spanish, Madrid 23 June 1824.

1816

GENERALI: *I Baccanti di Roma*
14 January. Venice, F.

Text by G. Rossi. Two acts.

Milan, Sc. 29 January 1825, etc. Mostly given as *I Baccanali di Roma*.

In Italian also, Trieste Spring 1816; Lisbon September 1823; Corfu Carnival 1827; Prague 12 July 1827; Barcelona 10 November 1827; Havana Carnival 1840.

Performed as an oratorio, *Ozia*, Florence 14 February 1836.

In German, Munich 23 March 1817; Darmstadt 25 August 1818; Vienna, W. 12 June 1820; Budapest 20 January 1823.

WEYSE: *Ludlams Hule*
(The Cave of Adullam)
30 January. Copenhagen

Text by A. G. Oehlenschläger. Four acts.

Given at Copenhagen until 1861. An anonymous German translation was published in 1816.

ROSSINI: *Almaviva o sia L'Inutile Precauzione*

20 February. Rome, Arg.

Text by C. Sterbini (founded on Beaumarchais's *Le Barbier de Séville*). Two acts.

The title, *Il Barbiere di Siviglia*, was first used at the T. Contavalli, Bologna 10 August 1816. First produced at Rome 20 February 1816 (not 26 December 1816 as stated by Stendhal, nor 5 February 1816 as most books of reference have it). See for further details, *Music and Letters*, Vol. xx, no.2 (April 1939).

Outside Italy, given at:

LONDON, HM. 10 March 1818 (not 27 January 1818, in Italian) and C.G. 13 October 1818 (in English, translated by J. Fawcett and D. Terry, music arranged by Bishop).

BARCELONA 16 July 1818 (in Italian).

MUNICH 1 January 1819 (in Italian).

LISBON Carnival 1819 (in Italian).

NEW YORK 3 May 1819 (in English; most probably the C.G. version); 29 November 1825 (in Italian, at the opening of Garcia's first American season; first Italian opera ever given in New York); 19 October 1831 (in French); and 4 December 1863 (in German).

GRAZ 27 May 1819 (for the first time in German, translated by I. C. Kollmann).

VIENNA, W. 28 September 1819 (in German); Kä. 16 December 1820 (in German) and 14 April 1823 (in Italian).

PARIS, TH. I. 26 October 1819 (in Italian; this date is unanimously given by all authorities while the printed libretto has the date of 23 September 1819); in Castil-Blaze's French version (see below, under Lyons) produced at the Odéon 6 May 1824; T.L. 28 September 1851; Athénée 3 November 1871; O.C. 8 November 1884.

PRAGUE 29 September 1820 (in German); 2 February 1825 (in Czech, translated by S. K. Macháček); and 5 July 1843 (in Italian).

BRUNSWICK 3 October 1820 (for the first time in Northern Germany).

BRÜNN 18 December 1820 (in German).

KRONSTADT AND HERMANNSTADT May 1821 (in Italian).

MADRID 25 August 1821 (in Italian) and 1 October 1824 (in Spanish).

ODESSA 31 August 1821 (in Italian).

LYONS 19 September 1821 (for the first time in French, translated by F. H. J. Castil-Blaze; "d'après Beaumarchais et le drame italien, paroles ajustées sur la musique de Rossini").

BRUSSELS 3 October 1821 (in French).

MARSEILLES 18 December 1821 (in French).

DUBLIN 7 January 1822 (in English) and 14 October 1829 (in Italian).

PHILADELPHIA 1 March 1822; Baltimore 20 May 1822, etc. (in English).

BERLIN, O. 18 June 1822 (in German; given there more than 500 times until 1937) and Kgst. 8 May 1841 (in Italian).

ROTTERDAM 1822 (in French).

STRASBOURG 1822 (in French).

COPENHAGEN 14 September 1822 (in Danish, translated by T. Thaarup) and 10 May 1825 (in German); given in a new Danish version by N. C. L. Abrahams 4 March 1846.

ST. PETERSBURG 9 December 1822 (in Russian, translated by R. M. Zotov); 1823 (in German); 29 January 1829 (in Italian); revived Leningrad 6 March 1918.

RIGA 1823 (in German) and 11 February 1922 (in Lettish, translated by P. Licit).

AMSTERDAM October 1823 (in German); Spring 1825 (in Dutch); 1834 (in French).

EDINBURGH 21 June 1824 (in English) and 13 December 1827 (in Italian).

PRESSBURG 14 April 1825 (in German).

BUENOS AIRES 3 October 1825 (in Italian; first Italian opera ever given there).

STOCKHOLM 25 October 1825 (in Swedish, translated by B. H. Crusell) and 1848 (in Italian).

WARSAW 29 October 1825 (in Polish, translated by W. Boguslawski) and Summer 1843 (in Italian); Wilna 6 November 1827 (in Polish).

MEXICO 23 February 1826 (in Spanish) and 29 June 1827 (in Italian).

CLAUSENBURG 3 February 1827 (in Hungarian, translated by J. Szerdahelyi).

BUDAPEST 27 October 1827 (in Hungarian; earlier given there in German); October 1847 (in Italian).

HAVANA 1828 (in Italian).

SANTIAGO, CHILE Summer 1830 (in Italian).

BERNE 27 July 1830 (in Italian); Geneva 16 November 1831 (in French); Lugano 1832 (in Italian); Basle 28 November 1834 (in German).

CAGLIARI, SARDINIA Carnival 1831 (in Italian).

CORFU Autumn 1833 (in Italian).

BASTIA, CORSICA Autumn 1833 (in Italian).

BUCHAREST 20 February 1834 (in German); Autumn 1843 (in Italian); October 1922 (in Rumanian).

ATHENS August 1837 (in Italian; first Italian opera there).

HELSINKI Summer 1839 (in German) and 29 September 1874 (in Finnish, translated by A. Törneroos).

ALGIERS Carnival 1840 (in Italian).

CONSTANTINOPLE December 1841 (in Italian).

GUAYAQUIL, ECUADOR Spring 1843 (in Italian).

MALTA 1843 (in Italian).

GHENT 19 May 1844 (in Flemish).

TRINIDAD Autumn 1844 (in Italian).

BAHIA, BRAZIL June 1845 (in Italian).

RIO DE JANEIRO Autumn 1846 (in French) and about the same time in Italian.

SMYRNA Autumn 1847 (in Italian).

CHRISTIANIA (OSLO) August 1849 (in Italian) and 3 May 1913 (in Norwegian).

MELBOURNE 1856 (in English, translated by J. W. Mould).

BOGOTÁ, COLUMBIA 18 July 1858 (in Spanish).

PORT LOUIS, MAURITIUS 1 October 1860 (in French).

BATAVIA 11 September 1863 (in French).

QUEBEC 10 June 1864 (in Italian); see F. E. O. Monck, *My Canadian Leaves*, p.31.

CAIRO December 1869 (in Italian).

ZAGREB 2 December 1874 (in Croatian, translated by A. M. Bišćan).

CAPE TOWN 1875 (in Italian).

TIFLIS 1876 (in Italian).

KIEV 1876 (in Russian, translated by P. I. Kalashnikov).

LJUBLJANA 1905 (in Slovenian).

SHANGHAI 1918 (in Russian).

BELGRADE 1920 (in Serbian).

SOFIA 29 December 1922 (in Bulgarian).

TALLINN 1923 (in Estonian).

KAUNAS 12 April 1924 (in Lithuanian).

JERUSALEM 23 February 1927 (in Hebrew, translated by M. Freidmann).

RABAT, MOROCCO May 1935 (in French).

BOIELDIEU: *La Fête du Village voisin*

5 March. Paris, O.C.

Text by C. A. B. Sewrin. Three acts.

Very successful in Paris; last revived at the F.P. 11 November 1868; at the O.C. 15 January 1877; at the Galerie Vivienne 16 December 1895.

In French also, Ghent 31 July 1816; Brussels 27 December 1816 (revived 6 January 1883); Berne 6 March 1819; New York 16 July 1827; Florence April 1839 (by amateurs at Prince Poniatowsky's).

In German, Vienna 5 May 1817 (translated by I. F. Castelli); Berlin 28 October 1817 (translated by May); Budapest 10 May 1819.

In Russian (translated by D. N. Barkov), St. Petersburg 2 March 1818.

In Danish (translated by N. T. Bruun), Copenhagen 7 September 1821.

ISOUARD: *Les deux Maris*

18 March. Paris, O.C.

Text by C. G. Etienne. One act.

In French also, Ghent 9 June 1816, etc.

In German (translated by I. F. Castelli), Berlin 8 January 1819; Vienna 30 July 1819.

SCHALL: *De tre Galninger* eller *Kunster og Munterhed*

19 March. Copenhagen

Text by N. T. Bruun (founded on a French play by J. H. F. La Martelière, *Les trois Espiègles, ou Les Arts de la Folie*). Two acts.

Schall's last opera.

LEBRUN: *Le Rossignol*

23 April. Paris, O.

Text by C. G. Etienne. One act.

Very successful on French stages; given in Paris until 1852 (100th performance 30 June 1820); Brussels 15 November 1816 (revived 20 December 1845); given at Ghent until 1872.

In French also, New York 26 August 1833; London, D.L. 18 July 1846.

In English, London, Princess's Th. 24 April 1848 (music adapted by Loder).

This opera was famous for its flute solos ("Le Rossignol") played by the virtuoso, Jean Louis Tulou. It was during a performance of *Le Rossignol* (13 February 1820) that the Duke of Berry was assassinated at the Opéra.

CARAFA: *Gabriella di Vergy*

3 July. Naples, Fondo

Text by A. L. Tottola. Two acts.

The best of Carafa's Italian operas.

Outside Italy, given at Vienna 1 April 1824 and Barcelona 7 September 1829.

HOFFMANN: *Undine*

3 August. Berlin, Sch.

Text by F. de La Motte Fouqué (founded on his own tale of the same title). Three acts.

The chief musical work of the German novelist and composer; given in Berlin 14 times until 27 July 1817 when the destruction of the theatre by fire interrupted the course of performances. Apart from a production at Prague in Spring 1821, which was a complete failure, Hoffmann's opera was not revived until a hundred years later, at Aachen 30 June 1922 (libretto revised by H. von Wolzogen); Bamberg 24 January 1926; and again Leipzig 14 October 1933. The vocal score was first published in 1908. (edited by H. Pfitzner).

See on *Undine*, C. M. von Weber's article in *A.M.Z.*, March 19, 1817.

(For a new setting of Fouqué's libretto, see 1837; for Lortzing's opera on the same subject, see 1846.)

SPOHR: *Faust*

1 September. Prague

Text by J. K. Bernard. Two acts.

Apart from *Jessonda*, Spohr's chief work. It had been written for the Theater an der Wien, Vienna (where Spohr was conductor from 1813–16) but was not given there before 1818 (only the overture was played at a Vienna concert on 11 December 1814).

After Prague (where Weber conducted the first performance), *Faust* was given at Frankfort 15 March 1818; Vienna, W. 7 July 1818 (Kä. 7 August 1827); Budapest 19 November 1821; Königsberg 1825; Munich 1826; Berlin 14 November 1829.

In German also, Paris, Th.I. 20 April 1830; Amsterdam 1834; St. Petersburg December 1839; London, Prince's Th. 21 May 1840.

In Czech (translated by S. K. Machaček), Prague 2 February 1833.

In French (translated by Clérisseau and D. E. de Groot), Marseilles 10 March 1837.

In Italian (translated by S. M. Maggioni), London, C.G. 15 July 1852; this new version, for which the composer had added recitatives, was then produced in German at Munich 12 June 1853; Cassel 8 April 1854; Carlsruhe 1 March 1860; Dresden 5 October 1860.

English vocal score (translated by J. W. Mould) published 1852.

The opera was revived at Brunswick 10 April 1931 (revised by W. Kleefeld).

MÉHUL: *La Journée aux Aventures*

16 November. Paris, O.C.

Text by P. A. Capelle and L. Mézières-Miot. Three acts.

In Paris given until 1826; in French also, Liége 22 March 1817; Antwerp 23 March 1817; Brussels 27 November 1817; Berne 15 March 1819, etc.

In German (translated by T. Hell), Breslau September 1817; Vienna 11 April 1818; Hamburg 26 July 1826; Berlin 9 December 1839.

In Russian, St. Petersburg 31 May 1819; Moscow 3 February 1820.

In Danish (translated by C. J. Boye), Copenhagen 7 September 1824.

ROSSINI: *Otello* ossia *Il Moro di Venezia*

4 December. Naples, Fondo

Text by Marchese F. Berio di Salsa (after Shakespeare). Three acts.

Very successful in and outside Italy. First produced at:

MUNICH 13 September 1818 (in Italian) and 1821 (in German).

VIENNA, W. 19 January 1819 (in German, translated by F. von Biedenfeld); Kä. 29 April 1819 (in German, translated by J. C. Grünbaum) and 13 March 1823 (in Italian).

PRAGUE 25 April 1819 (in German) and 30 November 1825 (in Czech, translated by S. K. Machaček).

GRAZ 3 November 1819 (in German).

BUDAPEST 1819 (in German) and 19 November 1827 (in Hungarian).

LISBON 1820 (in Italian).

LEIPZIG 21 March 1820 (in German, Grünbaum's translation).

FRANKFORT 9 April 1820 (in German, Grünbaum's translation).

BERLIN, O. 16 January 1821 (in German) and Kgst. 15 October 1841 (in Italian).

BARCELONA 10 May 1821 (in Italian).

PARIS, TH. I. 5 June 1821 (in Italian); for productions in French, see below.

LONDON, HM. 16 May 1822 (in Italian) and Princess's 21 March 1844 (in English, translated by G. Soane).

RIGA 1823 (in German).

AMSTERDAM 1 November 1823 (in German); 1835 (in French); Autumn 1844 (in Italian).

LYONS 1 December 1823 (in French, translated by F. H. J. Castil-Blaze).

BRUSSELS 23 March 1824 (in French, translated by F. H. J. Castil-Blaze).

PARIS, ODÉON 25 July 1825 (in French, translated by F. H. J. Castil-Blaze).

NEW YORK 7 February 1826 (in Italian).

MEXICO 22 January 1827 (in Spanish).

BUENOS AIRES 22 August 1827 (in Italian).

WARSAW 14 June 1828 (in Polish, translated by D. Minasowicz) and Summer 1843 (in Italian).

ST. PETERSBURG February 1829 (in Italian), 1835 (in German) and 26 October 1860 (in Russian).

EDINBURGH 11 December 1832 (in Italian).

BUCHAREST 28 February 1834 (in German).

DUBLIN 23 September 1834 (in Italian).

BASLE 12 October 1835 (in German).

BRUSSELS 6 March 1839 (new French version by J. Lecomte and C. Bosselet).

AJACCIO, CORSICA Carnival 1840 (in Italian).

COPENHAGEN Summer 1841 (in German) and November 1841 (in Italian).

HELSINKI 17 October 1841 (in German).

TRINIDAD Autumn 1844 (in Italian).

PARIS, O. 2 September 1844 (in a third French version by A. Royer and G. Vaëz).

BRUSSELS 23 December 1846 (French version by A. Royer and G. Vaëz).

NEW ORLEANS February 1848

RIO DE JANEIRO 6 August 1855 (in Italian).

GOTHENBURG 28 April 1862 (in German).

VALPARAISO 1868 (in Italian).

The last revivals (in Italian) seem to have been at Cairo 2 November 1876; Madrid 26 February 1878; Vienna 29 April 1878; Berlin, Kroll's 26 October 1878; Rome, C. 19 December 1880.

Seven years later (1887) Verdi's *Otello* came out and Rossini's opera fell into oblivion altogether, apart from two German revivals of the older opera at Prague 3 June 1889 and Berlin, Kroll's 26 August 1889.

1817

P. C. GUGLIELMI: *Paolo e Virginia*

2 January. Naples, Fior.

Text by G. M. Diodati (founded on Saint-Pierre's story). Three acts.

The last and most successful of the 42 operas of the younger Guglielmi.

Last revived in Italy: Milan 3 January 1830 and Naples March 1832.

Outside Italy given at Dresden 29 April 1818 (libretto revised by Celani); Munich 26 April 1820; Odessa October 1821; Barcelona 18 June 1823.

ROSSINI: *La Cenerentola* ossia *La Bontà in Trionfo*

25 January. Rome, Valle

Text by J. Ferretti (founded on Etienne's French libretto, see 1810). Two acts.

Very successful all over Italy; also given at:

BARCELONA 15 April 1818 (in Italian).

MUNICH 30 August 1818 (in Italian).

LONDON, HM. 8 January 1820 (in Italian) and C.G. 13 April 1830 (in English, as *Cinderella; or The Fairy Queen and the Glass Slipper*, adapted by M. R. Lacy; this version also Edinburgh 7 February 1831; Dublin 1831, etc.); another, anonymous, adaptation was given at D.L. 9 January 1837.

VIENNA, W. 29 August 1820 (in German, translated by F. von Biedenfeld); Kä. 30 March 1822 (in German; Rossini conducting) and 17 May 1823 (in Italian).

BUDAPEST 30 October 1820 (in German).

LISBON 27 April 1821 (in Italian).

HERMANNSTADT AND KRONSTADT Summer 1821 (in Italian).

PARIS 8 June 1822 (in Italian).

AMSTERDAM 5 February 1824 (in German, translated by J. H. Dessaur).

CORFU Autumn 1824 (in Italian).

BERLIN, KGST. 20 October 1825 (in German, translated by K. von Holtei) and 29 December 1841 (in Italian).

MOSCOW 5 November 1825 (in Italian).

BUENOS AIRES 4 May 1826 (in Italian).

NEW YORK 27 June 1826 (in Italian) and 24 January 1831 (in English, the London C.G. version).

MEXICO August 1828 (in Italian).

ST. PETERSBURG February 1829 (in Italian) and 1831 (in Russian).

RIO DE JANEIRO 9 July 1829 (in Italian).

WARSAW 29 August 1829 (in Polish).

SANTIAGO, CHILE Summer 1830 (in Italian).

LIVERPOOL 1831 (in Italian).

BUCHAREST *c.* January 1834 (in German).

CALCUTTA November 1834 (in Italian).

MALTA 1835 (in Italian).

MENTONE Spring 1835 (in Italian, first opera there).

AJACCIO, CORSICA Autumn 1835 (in Italian, at the inauguration of the theatre there).

DUBLIN 3 January 1837 (in Italian).

ALGIERS Carnival 1839 (in Italian).

BRUSSELS May 1841 (in Italian) and 30 January 1869 (in French, translated by L. E. Crevel de Charlemagne).

CEPHALONIA 6 November 1841 (in Italian).

CONSTANTINOPLE Carnival 1843 (in Italian).

SYDNEY 12 February 1844 (in English, translated by R. Thompson; first opera ever produced in Australia).

COPENHAGEN Carnival 1846 (in Italian).

ATHENS Autumn 1852.

PRAGUE 4 February 1870 (in Czech, translated by J. V. Štulc).

A Greek translation by F. Crispi was published at Patras in 1879.

Revivals:

LONDON, SHAFTESBURY TH. 20 October 1891 (in Italian).

LIVERPOOL 11 May 1891 (in English, Lacy's version revised by T. Robertson).

LONDON, GRAND (ISLINGTON) 3 October 1892 (in English, Lacy's version revised by T. Robertson).

In Spanish (translated by Guillermo Perrín y Vico and Miguel de Palacios Brugeras, music adapted by Gerónimo Giménez) Madrid 23 February 1916.

In Italian: Pesaro 29 February 1920; Rome 9 March 1920; Paris, Ch. É. 30 May 1929; Florence 23 May 1933; London, C.G. 12 June 1934; Milan, Sc. 27 January 1937; Buenos Aires June 1939.

In German (as *Angelina*, new German translation by H. Röhr), Hamburg 16 May 1929; Zurich Autumn 1929; Vienna 25 June 1930; Prague September 1930; Berlin 26 April 1931.

In Czech, Prague 27 February 1932.

In Slovenian, Ljubljana 12 October 1935.

HÉROLD: *Les Rosières*

27 January. Paris, O.C.

Text by E. G. M. Théaulon de Lambert. Three acts.

The best of Hérold's early operas. Given at the O.C. until 1826; revived Th. L. 5 June 1860 and F.P. 23 October 1866.

In French also, Antwerp 30 June 1817; Brussels 17 July 1817, etc.

In German (translated by A. von Kotzebue), Frankfort Summer 1818, etc.

In Danish (translated by N. T. Bruun), Copenhagen 10 September 1819.

In Russian (translated by A. I. Sheller), St. Petersburg 22 June 1820.

WINTER: *Maometto II*

28 January. Milan, Sc.

Text by F. Romani. Two acts.

In Italian also, Naples, S.C. Summer 1818; Dresden 10 October 1818; in German (translated by K. Reger), Munich 28 March 1819; Darmstadt 11 March 1821. Revived Milan, Sc. 24 January 1826.

KUHLAU: *Trylleharpen*
(The Magic Harp)

30 January. Copenhagen

Text by J. I. Baggesen. Two acts. Failure.

CATEL: *Wallace,* ou *Le Ménestrel écossais*

24 March. Paris, O.C.

Text by J. V. Fontanes de Saint-Marcellin. Three acts.

Catel's chief work and his last success.

Antwerp 7 April 1818; Brussels 13 April 1818, etc. Revived Paris O.C. 4 December 1844 (libretto revised by J. H. Vernoy de Saint-Georges, music arranged by Boulanger).

In Russian (translated by D. N. Barkov), St. Petersburg 24 January 1821.

ROSSINI: *La Gazza Ladra*

31 May. Milan, Sc.

Text by G. Gherardini (founded on the French melodrama *La Pie voleuse,* by J. M. T. Baudouin d'Aubigny and L. C. Caigniez). Two acts.

Outside Italy produced at:

MUNICH November 1817 (in Italian) and 1826 (in German).

GRAZ 6 January 1819 (in German).

VIENNA, W. 3 May 1819 and Kä. 5 July 1820 (in German, translated by J. von Seyfried; in Italian 21 June 1822).

BUDAPEST 22 November 1819 (in German) and 18 December 1827 (in Hungarian).

BARCELONA 2 December 1819 (in Italian).

BRÜNN 24 March 1820 (in German).

LISBON 21 August 1820 (in Italian).

HANOVER 29 October 1820 (in German).

AMSTERDAM 1820 (in German).

ST. PETERSBURG 7 February 1821 (in Russian, translated by I. N. Svichinsky) and February 1829 (in Italian).

LONDON, HM. 10 March 1821 (in Italian); C.G. 4 February 1830 (in English, translated by E. Fitzball, as *Ninetta; or, The Maid of Palaiseau,* music adapted by Bishop); revived with alterations D.L. 13 October 1838, as *The Maid of Palaiseau.*

MADRID 30 May 1821 (in Italian) and 20 January 1825 (in Spanish).

PARIS, TH. I. 18 September 1821 (in Italian) and Odéon 2 August 1824 (in French).

BERLIN 11 April 1822 (in concert form) and 31 December 1824 (on the stage, in German); Kgst. 13 December 1846 (in Italian).

DUBLIN 6 July 1822 (in an English adaptation, *Annette,* music arranged by C. E. Horn) and Autumn 1829 (in Italian).

LILLE 15 October 1822 (in French, translated by F. H. J. Castil-Blaze).

BRUSSELS 27 November 1822 (in French, translated by F. H. J. Castil-Blaze).

CLAUSENBURG 23 December 1822 (in Hungarian, translated by E. Pály).

COPENHAGEN 19 February 1824 (in Danish, translated by N. T. Bruun).

WARSAW 22 February 1825 (in Polish, translated by L. Osiński, with new recitatives by Kurpiński).

RIGA 1825 (in German).

MEXICO 13 September 1825 (in Spanish) and 1833 (in Italian).

PHILADELPHIA October 1827 (in French).

EDINBURGH 10 January 1828 (in Italian).

BUENOS AIRES 29 November 1828 (in Italian).

RIO DE JANEIRO 30 June 1830 (in Italian).

SANTIAGO, CHILE 1830 (in Italian).

NEW YORK 28 August 1830 (in French); 18 November 1833 (in Italian); and 14 January 1839 (in English).

AGRAM 1831 (in German).

LIMA, PERU 3 November 1831 (in Italian).

BASLE 28 January 1835 (in German); Lugano 1836 (in Italian).

MALTA Autumn 1839 (in Italian).

STOCKHOLM 14 June 1843 (in Swedish, translated by N. E. W. af Wetterstedt).

CONSTANTINOPLE Summer 1845 (in Italian).

Given in Italy until 1858. Revived Paris, Th. L. 23 April 1852 (in French); London, C.G. 26 May 1860 and 5 July 1883 (in Italian); New York 6 February 1872 (in English) and 9 November 1883 (in Italian). St. Petersburg 2 January 1873 (in Italian); and lately, Breslau 24 November 1937 (new German version by A. Treumann-Mette).

POISSL: *Nittetis*

29 June. Darmstadt

Text by the composer (after Metastasio). Three acts.

Also given at Munich 2 January 1818; Berlin 1 December 1819, etc.

MEYERBEER: *Romilda e Costanza*

19 July. Padua

Text by G. Rossi. Two acts.

Meyerbeer's first Italian opera. Venice 8 October 1817, etc. In Italian also, Munich 8 November 1822.

In Danish (translated by C. J. Boye and K. L. Rahbek), Copenhagen 29 January 1822.

(The date of 19 July 1818 for the first production at Padua, given by Fétis, Clément-Larousse, Riemann, etc., is not correct; see *A. M. Z.*, Vol. XIX, p.612; G. R. Kruse in *Zeitschrift für Musikwissenschaft*, Vol. I, p.404, while rectifying the year, gives the wrong month instead.)

HÉROLD: *La Clochette* ou *Le Diable Page*

18 October. Paris, O.C.

Text by E. G. M. Théaulon de Lambert. Three acts.

Given in Paris until 1827. In French also, Ghent 9 September 1818; Brussels 27 July 1819, etc.; New York 28 October 1831.

In Polish (translated by L. A. Dmuszewski), Warsaw June 1818; Lemberg 7 January 1822.

In German (translated by G. F. Treitschke), Leipzig 19 December 1820; Vienna 20 June 1821 (with two inserted songs by Schubert); Prague Autumn 1821; Riga 1823; Berlin 27 May 1825; Budapest 1826, etc.; in Germany given until 1846 (Weimar).

In Russian (translated by Ksilandr), St. Petersburg 20 October 1819; Moscow 22 February 1821.

An anonymous Italian translation, *Il Campanello ovvero Il Diavolo Paggio*, was published at Milan as late as 1877.

ROSSINI: *Armida*

11 November. Naples, S.C.

Text by G. Schmidt (after Tasso). Three acts.

Rather unsuccessful in Italy (last revived Milan, Sc. 5 November 1836) and never performed in London, Paris, or New York; in the original Italian, outside Italy only given at Buenos Aires 5 February 1828.

Fairly popular in a German version by J. von Seyfried, Vienna, W. 11 December 1821; Budapest 11 March 1822; Prague 29 June 1823; Graz 18 February 1826; Hamburg 28 December 1827; Berlin, Kgst. 15 November 1832; Bucharest 17 August 1834.

In Hungarian, Budapest Spring 1838.

PACINI: *Adelaide e Comingio*

30 December. Milan, T. Rè

Text by G. Rossi (founded on a comedy by G. A. Gualzetti). Two acts.

Pacini's 15th opera and his first greater success. Given at Rome, Ap. 13 April 1819 as *Isabella e Florange;* at Naples Summer 1819 as *Adelaide maritata e Comingio Pittore.*

In Italian also, Barcelona 25 September 1822 (as *Comingio Pittore*); Madrid 18 May 1823; Oporto 1825; Berne November 1830; Mexico 1835.

In German, Munich 12 October 1820.

1818

ROSSINI: *Mosè in Egitto*

5 March. Naples, S.C.

Text by A. L. Tottola (*azione tragico-sacra*). Three acts.

The famous preghiera, *Dal tuo stellato soglio,* was added at a revival at the same theatre 7 March 1819. Given in an enlarged French act version by G. L. Balochi and V. J. Etienne de Jouy, as *Moïse et Pharaon, ou Le Passage de la Mer Rouge,* at the Paris Opéra on 26 March 1827. From about 1830 the opera was performed on Italian stages sometimes in the first, sometimes in the second version (*Mosè Nuovo*).

Given at:

BUDAPEST 18 December 1820 (for the first time in German, as *Elzia und Osiride,* translated by A. Fesztetics).

VIENNA, W. 28 March 1821 (in German, translated by J. von Seyfried) and Kä. 6 October 1824 (in Italian).

FRANKFORT Spring 1822 (in German).

LONDON, HM. 23 April 1822 (in Italian, as *Pietro l'Eremita*).

PARIS, TH. I. 20 October 1822 (in Italian).

LISBON 26 February 1823 (in Italian).

PRAGUE 12 April 1823 (in German).

DRESDEN 22 October 1823 (in Italian).

BARCELONA 23 June 1825 (in Italian).

PARIS, O. 26 March 1827 (in French, see above; given there 187 times until 1865; 100th performance 6 August 1838).

PERUGIA 4 February 1829 (first stage production of the second version in Italy; given earlier in concert form Rome 1827. Given at Parma 20 May 1829 as *Mosè e Faraone*).

ST. PETERSBURG Spring 1829 (as *Pietro l'Eremita,* first version) and 31 December 1853 (as *Zora,* second version).

HAMBURG 24 March 1831 (first production of the second version in German).

ZURICH 19 April 1831 (in concert form).

VIENNA I June 1831 (in German) and 4 April 1836 (in Italian).

LONDON, C.G. 22 February 1833 (this was an English version by M. R. Lacy, patched up from Rossini's opera and Handel's oratorio *Israel in Egypt,* called *The Israelites in Egypt; or The Passage of the Red Sea;* it was also given in New York on 31 October 1842, Philadelphia 16 December 1842, etc.).

AGRAM 1833 (in German).

MEXICO 4 June 1833 (in Italian).

HAVANA 1834 (in Italian).

NEW YORK 2 March 1835 (first version) and 7 May 1860 (second version, both in Italian); 31 October 1842 (in English, see above).

CAGLIARI, SARDINIA 30 August 1835 (in Italian).

BERLIN, KGST. 15 October 1835 (in German) and 18 April 1842 (in Italian).

BASLE 22 April 1836 (in German).

ALGIERS Carnival 1840 (in Italian).

LIÉGE 18 May 1842 (in German).

COPENHAGEN 20 September 1843 (in Danish, translated by N. C. L. Abrahams).

CONSTANTINOPLE Spring 1844 (in Italian).

MALTA 1849–50 (in Italian).

LONDON, C.G. 20 April 1850 (as *Zora;* the second version).

BRUSSELS 23 September 1850 (in Italian).

RIO DE JANEIRO 1858 (in Portuguese, translated by L. V. de Simoni).

WARSAW 1866 (in Italian).

TIFLIS Spring 1868 (in Italian).

BUENOS AIRES 26 October 1870 (in Italian).

SYDNEY September 1873 (in Italian).

KIEV 1877 (in Russian, translated by P. I. Kalashnikov).

Revived in German: Prague 14 January 1894; in Italian: Venice 26 December 1893; Milan, Sc. 12 September 1918; Florence 24 April 1935; Monte Carlo March 1937; Milan, Sc. 12 April 1937.

Mosè was frequently performed as an oratorio, in concert form; by the Società Filarmonica, Rome December 1827 (the Paris version, before it was first staged at Perugia); New York 22 December 1832 (at the Masonic Hall; also before the first stage-production); in London, Exeter Hall 24 May 1878 (by the Sacred Harmonic Society under Costa, English version by A. Matthison); at Bradford 30 November 1883 and Manchester 6 December 1883 (under Hallé).

An open-air performance, in French, took place at the Roman Theatre, Orange on 12 August 1888.

ELSNER: *Krøl Lokietek czyli Wiśliczanki*
(King Wladislaw, or The Vistula Maids)
3 April. Warsaw

Text by L. A. Dmuszewski. Two acts.

One of the better works of Elsner, who was the teacher of Chopin.

Lemberg 23 May 1819; Wilna 25 September 1821, etc.

WEIGL: *Nachtigall und Rabe*
20 April. Vienna, Kä.

Text by G. F. Treitschke (founded on Etienne's French libretto *Le Rossignol*, see 1816). One act.

Successful on German stages: Frankfort Summer 1818; Leipzig 31 August 1818; Budapest 4 January 1819; Prague Summer 1819; Berlin 12 September 1819; Munich 1820.

In German also, probably St. Petersburg 1839.

In English, London, Surrey 8 May 1828 (as *Die Nachtigall und der Rabe; or Damon and Phyllis*).

Revived Vienna, 7 August 1836; Munich 1 December 1866; and lately Hanover Summer 1937 (at Herrenhausen Park).

MORLACCHI: *Gianni di Parigi*
30 May. Milan, Sc.

Text by F. Romani (founded on Saint-Just's French libretto, see 1812). Two acts.

In Italian also given at Dresden 17 April 1819; Naples, S.C. Spring 1820; Barcelona 5 October 1825; Rome, T. Valle 10 May 1826 (reduced to 1 act).

Revived Genoa Autumn 1836.

In German (as *Die Prinzessin von Navarra*), Vienna, W. 25 October 1820.

MOSEL: *Cyrus und Astyages*
13 June. Vienna, Kä.

Text by M. von Collin (founded on Metastasio's *Ciro riconosciuto*). Three acts.

Probably the last German opera which was founded upon a libretto by Metastasio; Poissl's (see 1814, 1815, 1817) and Mosel's musical dramas were the last stragglers in the train of Schweitzer's *Alceste* (see 1773), before German opera took a new turn after Weber's *Freischütz* (see 1821).

BOIELDIEU: *Le petit Chaperon rouge*
30 June. Paris, O.C.

Text by E. G. M. Théaulon de Lambert. Three acts.

Last revived at the O.C. on 2 August 1860.

In French also, Antwerp 8 December 1818; Brussels 27 January 1819; Amsterdam March 1819, etc.; New Orleans January 1821; New York 31 August 1827; Philadelphia October 1827; Calcutta 19 August 1836.

In English (as *Rose d'Amour, or, Little Red Riding Hat*), London, C.G. 3 December 1818; another adaptation, by T. H. Reynoldson, was given at the Grecian Th. on 27 April 1844.

In German (translated by T. Hell), Breslau 24 March 1819; (translated by G. F. Treitschke), Vienna 27 March 1819; Budapest 5 July 1819; (translated by F. S. Krickeberg), Berlin 7 July 1819; Brünn 15 November 1819; Munich 1819; Prague Spring 1821; Riga 1822. Last revived,

Gotha 29 July 1893; Vienna 19 November 1895; Frankfort 27 November 1900.

In Russian (translated by R. M. Zotov), St. Petersburg 28 August 1819; Moscow 21 December 1820.

In Danish (translated by N. T. Bruun), Copenhagen 29 October 1819.

In Polish (translated by J. F. Królikowski), Warsaw 1820.

In Swedish (translated by C. G. Nordforss), Stockholm 22 February 1830.

In Flemish, Ghent 11 May 1845.

In Czech (translated by P.S.), Prague 12 March 1854.

An Italian version by C. Bassi was announced for performance at Milan in 1845 (libretto printed); not produced.

GYROWETZ: *Il finto Stanislao*

5 August. Milan, Sc.

Text by F. Romani. Two acts.

(Verdi used the same libretto 22 years later.) The only opera the Viennese composer wrote for Italy.

PACINI: *Il Barone di Dolsheim*

23 September. Milan, Sc.

Text by F. Romani (founded on a novel by Pigault-Lebrun). Two acts.

In Italy given until 1840, sometimes as *Federico II Re di Prussia* or as *Il Barone di Felcheim*.

In Italian also, Munich 15 October 1819 (as *La Colpa emendata dal Valore*); Barcelona 7 September 1820; London 22 January 1822; Madrid 17 August 1822; Lisbon 20 August 1824; Bastia, Corsica Autumn 1833; probably also Mexico (undated libretto printed).

In German, Vienna, W. 6 December 1821.

In Spanish, Madrid 22 July 1824.

BATTON: *La Fenêtre secrète* ou *Une Soirée à Madrid*

17 November. Paris, O.C.

Text by J. Desessarts d'Ambreville. Three acts.

Batton's first and best work. In French also, Brussels 7 June 1819.

In Danish (translated by N. T. Bruun), Copenhagen 10 August 1819.

ROSSINI: *Ricciardo e Zoraide*

3 December. Naples, S.C.

Text by Marchese F. Berio di Salsa (founded on the poem *Ricciardetto*, by N. Forteguerri). Two acts.

In Italian also given at Lisbon 13 July 1821; Vienna 8 July 1822 (reduced to 1 act); Madrid 19 November 1822; Dresden 12 April 1823; London 5 June 1823; Paris 25 May 1824; Malta 1825; Mexico 7 July 1833. Revived Milan, Sc. 13 October 1846.

In German (translated by J. C. Grünbaum), Vienna 3 October 1819; Stuttgart 1820; Budapest 1820; Munich 19 August 1821; Graz 6 November 1823, etc.

1819

F. BASILJ: *Gl' Illinesi*

26 January. Milan, Sc.

Text by F. Romani. Two acts.

The best of Basilj's comic operas.

Given at Rome 29 January 1820 as *Isaura e Ricciardo*. Romani is mentioned as the author in the original libretto; see the bibliographies by L. Lianovosani (1878), no.22, and by G. Bustico (*R.M.I.*, 1917), no.26. But according to A. Cametti (*La Musica Teatrale a Roma Cento Anni fa*, 1931) the text was written by C. Sterbini.

HÉROLD: *Les Troqueurs*

18 February. Paris, O.C.

Text by F. V. A. and L. C. A. d'Artois de Bournonville (founded on Vadé's libretto, see 1753). One act.

Given in Paris until 1825; Brussels 12 September 1819.

In Polish (translated by L. A. Dmuszewski), Warsaw 15 December 1820.

In German (translated by I. F. Castelli), Vienna 1 May 1820; Berlin, Kgst. 2 July 1825; in a new translation by C. A. L. von Lichtenstein: Berlin, O. 1 March 1831.

Revived Hanover 19 January 1852 (German version by E. Pasqué, *Der Weibertausch*); Berlin, Fr. W. 6 November 1880.

SPOHR: *Zemire und Azor*

4 April. Frankfort

Text by J. J. Ihlee (based on Marmontel's libretto, see 1771). Three acts.

Next to *Faust* and *Jessonda* Spohr's most successful work.

In German also, Amsterdam *c.* January 1820; Munich 1821; Vienna 20 December 1821, etc.

In French (adapted by H. Brovellio), Lille 18 April 1826.

In Swedish (translated by B. H. Crusell), Stockholm 1 December 1828.

In English, London, C.G. 5 April 1831 (as *Azor and Zemira; or The Magic Rose*, translated by W. Ball, music adapted by G. Smart); also Dublin 1831.

Revived (in concert form), Cassel 24 February 1862 and Berlin 17 November 1885.

ROSSINI: *Eduardo e Cristina*

24 April. Venice, S. Ben.

Text by G. Schmidt (originally set to music by Pavesi as *Odoardo e Cristina* and produced at Naples, S.C. 1 December 1810); altered for Rossini by A. L. Tottola and G. Bevilacqua-Aldovrandini. Two acts.

A great part of the music is taken from earlier unsuccessful works: 9 numbers come from *Adelaide di Borgogna* (Rome, Arg. 27 December 1817), 7 from *Ermione* (Naples, S.C. 27 March 1819), and 3 from *Ricciardo e Zoraida* (see 1818).

Outside Italy given at Munich 26 January 1821; Ljubljana May 1821; Lisbon 13 December 1822; Vienna 4 May 1824; Barcelona 10 November 1824; Corfu Autumn 1824; Santiago, Chile 1830; St. Petersburg 1831; New York 25 November 1834.

In German (translated by J. von Seyfried), Budapest 25 October 1820; Vienna, W. 16 October 1821; Bucharest November 1830; Graz 21 September 1833.

KURPINSKI: *Zamek na Czorsztynie czyli Bojomir i Wanda*
(The Castle of Czorsztyn, or Bogumir and Vanda)

11 May. Warsaw

Text by J. K. Krasiński. Two acts.

One of the best works of the Polish composer. Lemberg 8 November 1819; Cracow 24 August 1820, etc.

CARNICER: *Adele di Lusignano*

15 May. Barcelona, T. Principal

Text by F. Romani (first set to music by Carafa in 1817). Two acts.

Carnicer's first (Italian) opera.

MEYERBEER: *Emma di Resburgo*

26 June. Venice, S. Ben.

Text by G. Rossi. Two acts.

Successful in Italy.

In Italian also given Dresden 29 January 1820; Barcelona 31 January 1829.

In German (translated by May), Berlin 11 February 1820; Vienna, W. February 1820; Budapest 20 February 1821; Brünn 19 March 1921, etc.

In Polish (translated by K. Godebski), Warsaw 6 April 1821.

ROSSINI: *La Donna del Lago*

24 September. Naples, S.C.

Text by A. L. Tottola (founded on Scott's *The Lady of the Lake*). Two acts.

Very successful in Italy and abroad; given in London until 1851; in Paris until 1854; at Trieste as late as in Autumn 1860.

The first performances were at:
DRESDEN 29 September 1821 (in Italian).
MUNICH 8 December 1821 (in Italian).

LISBON 22 January 1822 (in Italian).

VIENNA 11 February 1822 (in German, as *Das Fräulein vom See*) and 25 July 1823 (in Italian).

MALTA 1822 (in Italian).

BUDAPEST 2 January 1822 (in German).

LONDON, HM. 18 February 1823 (in Italian) and D.L. 4 January 1827 and C.G. 31 January 1843 (in different anonymous English versions, that at C.G. by M. Lemon, the music adapted by Tully).

BARCELONA 17 May 1823 (in Italian).

ST. PETERSBURG 1824 (in German) and 22 April 1830 (in Italian).

PARIS, TH. I. 7 September 1824 (in Italian) and Odéon 31 October 1825 (in French, translated by J. B. Viollet d'Épagny and A. Rousseau, music arranged by Lemière de Corvey).

GRAZ 13 September 1824 (in German).

AMSTERDAM 15 December 1824 (in German) and before 1834 in Dutch.

BRÜNN 12 March 1827 (in German).

LIÈGE 16 April 1827 (in French).

COPENHAGEN 29 January 1828 (in Danish, translated by J. L. Heiberg).

NEW YORK 25 August 1829 (in French) and 16 December 1833 (in Italian).

STOCKHOLM 5 October 1831 (in Swedish, translated by J. L. Åbergsson).

BERLIN 15 October 1831 (in German).

BRUSSELS 5 March 1832 (in French).

MEXICO 10 December 1833 (in Italian).

PHILADELPHIA 21 April 1834 (in Italian).

DUBLIN 24 January 1837 (in Italian).

HAVANA Carnival 1840 (in Italian).

AJACCIO, CORSICA Autumn 1840 (in Italian).

RIO DE JANEIRO 1843 (in Italian).

VALPARAISO 1844 (in Italian).

STUNZ: *La Rappressaglia*

2 October. Milan, Sc.

Text by F. Romani (originally called *Il Contraccambio*, first set to music by Cordella and produced at Rome in Carnival of that year). Two acts.

The first and most successful opera of the Bavarian composer.

In Italian also, Barcelona 23 August 1821; Munich 13 June 1823.

In German (as *Das Schloss Lowinsky*, translated by J. von Seyfried), Vienna, W. 18 March 1824; Stuttgart 19 May 1824; Budapest 12 July 1824; Berlin, Kgst. 3 August 1827 (as *König Stanislaus oder Widervergeltung*).

SPONTINI: *Olimpie*

22 December. Paris, O.

Text by M. Dieulafoy and C. Brifaut (from Voltaire's tragedy). Three acts.

Unsuccessful in Paris (given 11 times only); revived after revision 28 February 1826.

In German (translated by E. T. A. Hoffmann), Berlin 14 May 1821 (as the first of his operas Spontini himself conducted there as Prussian Generalmusikdirektor); given in Berlin until 1870. In German also Dresden 12 November 1825 (with additions by Weber); Darmstadt 26 December 1858.

Revived (first and only time in Italy), Rome 12 December 1885 (in concert form by the Società Musicale Romana).

ROSSINI: *Bianca e Falliero* ossia *Il Consiglio dei Tre*

26 December. Milan, Sc.

Text by F. Romani (from A. Manzoni's tragedy, *Il Conte di Carmagnola*). Two acts.

Given at Lucca Summer 1829 with the subtitle *Il Foscarini*.

Outside Italy, Lisbon 3 July 1824; Vienna 19 February 1825; Barcelona 13 January 1830. Last revived Cagliari, Sardinia Autumn 1846.

1820

AUBER: *La Bergère Châtelaine*

27 January. Paris, O.C.

Text by F. A. E. de Planard. Three acts.

Auber's first greater success; given in Paris 55 times until 1828; Brussels 9 October 1820.

In German (translated by F. L. Rhode), Frankfort 6 May 1821.

In Russian, St. Petersburg 10 June 1824.

PIXIS: *Almazinde* oder *Die Höhle Sesam*

11 April. Vienna, W.

Text by H. Schmidt (first set to music by Bierey in 1814). Three acts.

The first opera of the famous pianist; given also at Prague May 1820.

WEIGL: *Baals Sturz*

13 April. Vienna, Kä.

Text by G. E. von Hofmann. Three acts.

Given at Stuttgart August 1821 as *Daniel in der Löwengrube*, the original title which the Vienna censor had objected to (see K. Glossy in *Jahrbuch der Grillparzer-Gesellschaft*, Vol.25 (1915), pp.244 f., 317 f. In German also, Budapest November 1821.

"Es ist dies nicht nur die gelungenste Arbeit dieses Komponisten, sondern eines der herrlichsten Produkte unseres Zeitalters" (*A.M.Z.*, 17 May 1820).

F. E. FESCA: *Cantemire*

27 April. Carlsruhe

Text by A. von Dusch. Two acts.

Fairly successful in Germany; Weber was the first to draw attention to Fesca as a gifted composer; see his article in *A.M.Z.*, 19 August 1818.

SCHUBERT: *Die Zwillingsbrüder*

14 June. Vienna, Kä.

Text by G. E. von Hofmann (*Posse mit Gesang*). One act.

Schubert's first performed work for the stage (the dates of 14 January 1820 and 11 June 1820, as given in some books of reference are not correct).

Revived Vienna 25 January 1882 (revised by J. N. Fuchs; again 22 November 1928); Strasbourg 4 February 1897; Lauchstedt 26 June 1938 (by the Leipzig University Collegium Musicum).

Of Schubert's numerous operas, *Die Zwillingsbrüder* and *Die Zauberharfe* (see next entry) are the only two which were produced in his lifetime; several more were given after his death; see 1854 (*Alfonso und Estrella*); 1861 (*Die Verschworenen*); 1896 (*Der vierjährige Posten*); 1897 (*Fierrabras*); 1918 (*Fernando*); and 1928 (*Die Freunde von Salamanca*).

SCHUBERT: *Die Zauberharfe*

19 August. Vienna, W.

Text by G. E. von Hofmann (*Zauberspiel mit Musik*). Three acts.

The music consisted of two overtures, five melodramatic pieces, and six choruses. Schubert introduced one overture from the unsuccessful work later on into *Rosamunde, Fürstin von Cypern*, a 4-act play by H. von Chézy (who wrote the *Euryanthe* libretto for Weber in 1823); *Rosamunde* was produced at Vienna, W. 20 December 1823 with incidental music by Schubert (the famous ballets and entr'actes). The *Zauberharfe* music was revived with A. Wilbrandt's play, *Das Märchen vom Untersberg*, Vienna 31 May 1884 (adapted by J. N. Fuchs), with Shakespeare's *Twelfth Night*, Hamburg 1885 (adapted by H. Kruse), and with F. Raimund's play, *Die gefesselte Phantasie*, Carlsruhe 13 March 1898 (adapted by F. Mottl), also at Berlin, Sch. 7 October 1921 and Vienna, B. 12 September 1936.

PACINI: *La Schiava in Bagdad* ossia *Il Papucciajo*

28 October. Turin, T. Carignano

Text by V. Pezzi (who is mentioned in later editions of the libretto) and not by F. Romani, to whom it is generally attributed. Romani's *Il Califfo e la Schiava* (first set by Basilj, Milan, Sc. 21 August 1819) is a different text. Two acts.

Pacini's opera was given outside Italy at Madrid 27 August 1825 (in Spanish) and (in Italian): Barcelona 16 December 1822; London 30 December 1826; St. Petersburg Spring 1830; revived Cagliari, Sardinia November 1839.

MEYERBEER: *Margherita d'Anjou*

14 November. Milan, Sc.

Text by F. Romani (founded on a French melodrama by R. C. G. de Pixérécourt). Two acts.

In Italian also, Munich February 1822; Dresden 20 March 1824; Barcelona 10 May 1825; London 12 January 1828; Madrid 14 March 1836; Lisbon 22 October 1837.

In French (in 3 acts, translated by T. Sauvage, music arranged by P. Crémont), Paris, Odéon 11 March 1826; Brussels 21 December 1826; Amsterdam Spring 1835; Hague 25 January 1839.

In German, Graz 26 March 1831; Berlin, Kgst. 22 November 1831; Prague December 1831; Budapest February 1832; Laibach 24 January 1833, etc.

ROSSINI: *Maometto II*

3 December. Naples, S.C.

Text by C. della Valle, Duke of Ventignano. Two acts.

This first version was also produced at Vienna 22 January 1823 (in German, translated by J. C. Grünbaum) and Lisbon 26 October 1826 (in Italian).

In 1826, Rossini adapted the *Maometto* music to a new French libretto by L. A. Soumet and G. L. Balochi (in 3 acts), called *Le Siège de Corinthe*, and added some new numbers. It was in this French version that the opera became a great success. First produced at:

PARIS, O. 9 October 1826 (given there until 1844; 100th performance 4 February 1839).

FRANKFORT 16 July 1827 (in German, translated by J. Kupelwieser).

BARCELONA 24 July 1827 (in Italian, as *L'Assedio di Corinto*, translated by C. Bassi).

BRUSSELS 21 August 1827 (in French).

BUDAPEST 3 December 1827 (in German).

PARMA 26 January 1828 (first production of the second version in Italy; previously the work had been heard at a concert of the Accademia Filarmonica, Rome 27 December 1827. Given at Venice, S. Ben. Spring 1828 as *L'Assedio di Granata;* at Genoa Spring 1828 in a different

Italian version by G. B. Scotti); Naples, S.C. 4 October 1828.

GRAZ 2 July 1828 (in German).

DRESDEN 3 January 1829 (in Italian).

PARIS, TH. I. 4 February 1829 (in Italian).

BRÜNN 31 December 1829 (in German).

BERLIN 25 January 1830 (in German).

ST. PETERSBURG 14 February 1830 (in Russian); December 1835 (in German); and Carnival 1855 (in Italian).

PRAGUE March 1831 (in German) and 3 December 1843 (in Czech, translated by E. Ujky).

VIENNA 4 July 1831 (in German).

MEXICO 1832 (in Italian).

CORFU Autumn 1833 (in Italian).

LONDON, HM. 5 June 1834 (in Italian) and D.L. 8 November 1836 (in English, translated by J. R. Planché, music arranged by T. S. Cooke).

NEW YORK 6 February 1835 (in Italian).

OPORTO 1837 (in Italian).

ALGIERS 1840 (in Italian).

BASLE 14 January 1842 (in German).

CONSTANTINOPLE 1844 (in Italian).

COPENHAGEN 28 October 1845 (in Danish, translated by T. Overskou).

Given in Italy until 1867. Last revived in Germany: Cologne 6 March 1880.

PACINI: *La Gioventù di Enrico V*

26 December. Rome, Valle

Text by J. Ferretti (partly founded on Shakespeare's *Henry IV*). Two acts.

The libretto is attributed to Ferretti by A. Cametti (who seems to be the most reliable authority), to G. Tarducci by Chiappari and Salvioli. Most books of reference wrongly attribute it to F. Romani (who wrote a libretto of the same title 14 years later for Mercadante).

Given at Milan, T. Rè 1 July 1823 (as *La bella Tavernaia ossia Le Avventure d'una Notte*); last revived Cagliari, Sardinia Carnival 1848.

In Italian also, Munich January 1822; Lisbon 22 August 1823; Madrid 24 February 1824; Zara, Carnival 1826; Bastia, Corsica Autumn 1833.

In Danish (translated by T. Overskou), Copenhagen 28 October 1831.

1821

GRAZIOLI: *La Festa della Riconoscenza o sia Il Pellegrino bianco*

25 January. Rome, Ap.

Text by J. Ferretti. Two acts.

The best of Grazioli's numerous operas; in Italian also given at Malta 1822; Trieste 1823; Lisbon 17 October 1823. Revived Naples, T. Rossini 1870.

In German (translated by L. Ritter von Rittersberg), Prague 24 September 1825.

ROSSINI: *Matilde di Shabran o sia Bellezza e Cuor di Ferro*

24 February. Rome, Ap.

Text by J. Ferretti (an Italian version of Hoffman's *Euphrosine*, see 1790). Two acts.

Paganini conducted the first performance. Successful in Italy; sometimes given as *Corradino*, or as *Bellezza e Cuor di Ferro*.

In Italian also given at Malta Carnival 1822; Vienna 7 May 1822 (revived 14 May 1856); London, Hm. 3 July 1823 (revived C.G. 18 April 1854); Bastia, Corsica Autumn 1825; Lisbon December 1825; Dresden 14 January 1826; Barcelona 28 April 1827; Madrid 7 November 1827; St. Petersburg February 1829; Rio de Janeiro 10 February 1829; Paris 15 October 1829; Odessa 1830; Corfu Autumn 1833; New York 10 February 1834; Philadelphia 28 April 1834; Cagliari, Sardinia 7 November 1835; Mexico 1837; Cephalonia Carnival 1841; Bona, Algeria Carnival 1844; Geneva May 1845; Brussels 21 September 1850. Last revived Florence 7 November 1892.

In German, Budapest 1823; Berlin 17 June 1827; Hamburg 22 June 1827; Prague 1827; Graz 6 September 1828; Bucharest 1834, etc. Revived Cologne 12 March 1852.

In Spanish, Madrid 7 January 1826.

C. M. VON WEBER: *Preciosa*

14 March. Berlin, O.

Text by P. A. Wolff. *Romantisches Schauspiel mit Musik* (founded on Cervantes's story *La Gitanella*). Four acts.

One of the border cases between Singspiel with spoken dialogue, and play with inserted musical numbers. Included here as surviving only by means of Weber's music.

Stated to have been first set by Goethe's friend, Carl Eberwein, but apparently not produced with his music. Further settings were by J. P. C. Schulz (Leipzig May 1812; Dresden 3 November 1812) and by I. von Seyfried (Vienna, W. 19 October 1812). Weber's music consists of ten numbers (choruses, ballets, melodramas, etc).

Successful in Germany; given at Berlin 115 times until 1890; frequently revived up to the present.

Outside Germany:

PRAGUE December 1821 (in German) and 20 November 1831 (in Czech, translated by J. K. Tyl).

COPENHAGEN 29 October 1822 (in Danish, translated by C. J. Boye).

RIGA 1823 (in German) and 1886 (in Lettish).

VIENNA, W. 5 July 1823 and B. 22 June 1825 (in German); Graz 6 January 1825.

BUDAPEST 1824 (in German) and 4 December 1827 (in Hungarian).

WINTERTHUR 1 October 1824 (in German); Berne 8 December 1826 (with puppets).

STOCKHOLM 20 October 1824 (in Swedish, translated by P. A. Granberg).

LONDON, C.G. 28 April 1825 (in English, translated probably by G. Soane or W. Ball, music arranged by W. Hawes) and St. J.'s 8 July 1853 (in German); revived D.L. 4 July 1881 (in German).

ST. PETERSBURG 3 October 1825 (in Russian, translated by A. Ivanov).

PARIS, ODÉON 17 November 1825 (in French, translated by T. Sauvage, music arranged by P. Crémont; one night only!); Th.I. 12 May 1842 (in German); Th.L. 16 April 1858 (new French version by C. Nuitter and A. Beaumont, with some numbers from Weber's *Silvana*).

AGRAM 15 May 1826 (in German).

CLAUSENBURG 30 January 1827 (in Hungarian, translated by F. Komlóssy).

WARSAW 17 March 1827 and Lemberg 21 December 1827 (in Polish, translated by J. D. Minasowicz).

GOTHENBURG 1 June 1827 (in German).

HAGUE 8 July 1834 (in Dutch, translated by F. J. Kerkhoven, the translation already published Amsterdam 1830).

NEW YORK, FRANKLIN TH. 9 March 1840 (in German; by amateurs).

CINCINNATI 13 October 1846 (in German).

BUCHAREST 1853 (in Rumanian, translated by Ed. Wachmann).

BERGEN, NORWAY 18 January 1857 (in Danish).

HELSINKI 12 May 1870 (in Finnish, translated by P. Cajander).

LJUBLJANA 1881 (in Slovenian, translated by J. Cimperman).

DORPAT (TARTU) 24 April 1883 (in Estonian).

ANTWERP October 1890 (in Flemish).

English version by L. C. Elson published Boston 1870; English vocal score (translated by J. Troutbeck) published London 1879. Revived in English, London, Twentieth Century Th. 1 June 1940.

PAER: *Le Maître de Chapelle* ou *Le Souper imprévu*

29 March. Paris, O.C.

Text by S. Gay (founded on A. Duval's comedy *Le Souper imprévu ou Le Chanoine de Milan*, 1796). One act.

This little opéra-comique, although it came rather late to most countries, proved to be a much more lasting success than Paer's ambitious Italian serious operas, so much admired in their time; given at the O.C. until 1914 and again 13 January 1933 and frequently revived at other Paris theatres, viz. Th.L. 28 September 1851; F.P. 18 November 1866; Nouveautés 1 April 1871; Tr.L. 27 January 1915 and 13 November 1931.

Outside Paris (in French), also given at Ghent 11 November 1821; Breslau April 1825; Berlin, Kgst. 1 June 1825; Vienna 20 September 1826; London, C.G. 13 June 1845, St. J.'s 15 January 1849, and O.C. 4 May 1872; Rio de Janeiro 1846; Buenos Aires 1852; New York 25 June 1852 (parts, in concert form, at the "Chinese Museum" already 1 August 1849); Turin April 1858; Madrid, Z. July 1859; Barcelona 30 June 1866; Lisbon 19 May 1878. Revived at The Hague as late as April 1940.

In German (as *Wie gerufen*), Dresden 2 June 1824 (in 2 acts).

Revived (new German version by H. Brennert and W. Kleefeld), Magdeburg 22 October 1903; Halle 30 April 1922, and again 8 June 1930.

In Italian (translated by A. Zanardini, recitatives by P. Floridia), Milan, T.L. 11 November 1895, etc.; Malta 1899; London, Prince of Wales's 16 February 1897; 22 May 1905 (at the inauguration of the Waldorf Theatre); and 20 May 1915 (by the Florence Ettlinger Opera School); Buenos Aires 21 December 1905; New York 9 December 1909.

In Spanish, Barcelona March 1924; Buenos Aires 1924.

In Danish (translation by P. Biørn), Copenhagen 1934.

AIBLINGER: *Rodrigo und Zimene*

1 May. Munich

Text by J. Sendtner (based on Corneille's *Cid*). Two acts.

The only (unsuccessful) German opera of the Munich conductor.

WEBER: *Der Freischütz*

18 June. Berlin, Sch.

Text by F. Kind (founded on a tale in J. A. Apel and F. Laun's *Gespensterbuch*, 1811). Three acts.

No other German opera had ever been so successful and conquered so many and even the smallest stages in so short a time. The 500th performance at Berlin was on 18 December 1884, the 800th on 11 February 1929; given there 852 times up to 1937.

The first productions in Germany, in 1821 and 1822, were at:

LEIPZIG 23 December 1821.

CARLSRUHE 26 December 1821.

BRUNSWICK 17 January 1822.

DRESDEN 26 January 1822.

HAMBURG 5 February 1822.

KÖNIGSBERG 25 February 1822.

CASSEL 1 March 1822.

HANOVER 12 March 1822.

FRANKFORT 31 March 1822.

DANZIG 31 March 1822.

STUTTGART 12 April 1822.

MUNICH 15 April 1822.

LÜBECK 29 April 1822.

WEIMAR 4 May 1822.

MANNHEIM 5 May 1822.

ELBING 25 June 1822.

DARMSTADT 4 August 1822.

NEUSTRELITZ 12 August 1822.

WÜRZBURG 21 August 1822.

NUREMBERG 26 August 1822.

AUGSBURG 30 August 1822.

BREMEN 26 September 1822.

COLOGNE 3 November 1822.

DÜSSELDORF 14 November 1822.

MAYENCE 16 November 1822, etc.

Productions in German, outside Germany, were at:

VIENNA 3 November 1821.

PRAGUE 29 December 1821.

BRÜNN 29 March 1822.

BUDAPEST 13 May 1822.

GRAZ 24 June 1822.

STRASBOURG Autumn 1822.

AMSTERDAM Autumn 1822.

RIGA 7 October 1822.

BERNE 14 March 1823.

ZURICH November 1823.

ST. PETERSBURG 19 January 1824.

WINTERTHUR 1 November 1824.

PARIS 12 May 1829.

VIIPURI 15 June 1829.

BRUSSELS 24 July 1829.

LONDON 9 May 1832.

BUDAPEST 19 September 1833.

BUCHAREST December 1833 or January 1834.

PHILADELPHIA 23 March 1840.

NEW YORK 22 January 1842.

AGRAM July 1844.

ODESSA 1845.

SAN FRANCISCO Summer 1854.

STOCKHOLM 21 June 1863.

An anonymous German parody, called *Samiel oder Die Wunderpille* was published in 1824 and (translated into Danish by P. D. Faber) at Aarhus in 1825; produced in a Swedish version by C. A. F. Berggren, Stockholm 1 August 1830. (See for other parodies, imitations, sequels, etc., P.A. Merbach in *Zeitschrift für Musikwissenschaft*, Vol. II, p.642.)

Translated into other languages, the opera was produced at:

COPENHAGEN 26 April 1822 (in Danish, translated by A. G. Oehlenschläger); Christiania 1836.

STOCKHOLM 23 April 1823 (in Swedish, translated by A. Lindeberg).

PRAGUE 6 May 1824 (in Czech, translated by J. N. Stěpánek); revived 24 February 1874 (new Czech version by J. Böhm).

ST. PETERSBURG 24 May 1824 and Moscow 18 July 1825 (in Russian, translated by R. M. Zotov); in Italian, St. Petersburg Carnival 1855.

LONDON 22 July 1824 (in English; see below).

PARIS 7 December 1824 (in French; see below).

CLAUSENBURG 19 March 1825 and Budapest 21 December 1827 (in Hungarian, translated by E. Pály).

WARSAW 4 July 1826; Wilna 5 September 1827; Lemberg 16 November 1827 (in Polish, translated by W. Boguslawski); revived Lemberg 17 September 1872 (new Polish version by A. Urbański).

AMSTERDAM 1827 (in Dutch).

FLORENCE 3 February 1843 (in Italian, translated by F. Guidi, recitatives by C. Romani).

RIO DE JANEIRO 1848 (in French) and 28 November 1865 (in Italian).

BARCELONA 4 August 1849 and Madrid 21 February 1874 (in Italian).

BERLIN, KGST. 5 December 1849 (in Italian, translated by J. A. Rossi; with Berlioz's recitatives).

VALPARAISO May 1854 (in Italian, with Berlioz's recitatives).

MILAN, T. CARCANO 24 June 1856 (in Italian, with Berlioz's recitatives).

BUENOS AIRES 14 September 1864 (in Italian, with Berlioz's recitatives).

MILAN, SC. 19 March 1872 (new Italian version by A. Boito, recitatives by F. Faccio); Rome, Ap. 26 November 1873; Venice, F. 19 March 1875; Turin 17 November 1877; Naples, T. Bellini 3 April 1880.

HELSINKI 30 December 1873 (in Finnish, translated by A. Törneroos; the second act only; the whole opera not before 1924.

ZAGREB 24 April 1875 (in Croatian, translated by P. Brani).

CAIRO February 1877 (in Italian).

MEXICO 1 April 1891 (in English!) and 29 September 1894 (in Italian).

RIGA 1893 (in Lettish); revived 8 October 1930 (new translation by E. Melngailis).

LJUBLJANA 28 December 1893 (in Slovenian, translated by A. Funtek).

ANTWERP 3 October 1893 (in Flemish).

LISBON 1894 (in Italian).

TALLINN 1919 (in Estonian).

BELGRADE 7 April 1924 (in Serbian; concert performance; Serbian translation by J. Grčić, B. Brančić, and M. Dimović published already 1900).

SOFIA 19 May 1930 (in Bulgarian, translated by H. Levensson).

The first London performance of Weber's opera took place at the English Opera House (Lyceum), on Thursday, 22 July (not 23), 1824 as *Der Freischütz; or, The seventh Bullet* (translation by W. McGregor Logan[1]), music adapted by W. Hawes. Several other adaptations followed in the

course of the next months, viz. a melodrame by J. H. Amherst (Royal Amphitheatre 30 August 1824) and three more operatic versions:

SURREY TH. 6 September 1824 (*Der Freischütz; or The Demon of the Wolf's Glen, and the seven charmed Bullets*, adapted by E. Fitzball).

C.G. 14 October 1824 (*Der Freischütz; or, The black Huntsman of Bohemia*, adapted by J. R. Planché and B. Livius).

D.L. 10 (not 11) November 1824 (*Der Freischütz*, adapted by G. Soane, additional music by Bishop).

A travesty, *Der Freischütz*, by Septimus Globus, Esq., was published in 1824; the half-title reads: "*Der Freischütz*, a new muse-sick-all and see-nick performance from the new German uproar. By the celebrated Funnybear". It seems to be identical with a parody produced at Edinburgh 26 May 1825 (as *Der Fryshot, or Number Seven*) as the words "muse-sick-all" and "see-nick" also occur on the Edinburgh play-bill.

The German original (apart from a selection sung at C.G. 3 June 1829) was first produced in London, Hm. 9 May 1832 by a German company under the direction of the French composer Chélard.[1] In Italian, as *Il franco Arciere*, the opera was heard at C.G. 16 March 1850 (with recitatives by Costa).

Given at:

EDINBURGH 29 December 1824 (in English; the Lyceum version).

DUBLIN 17 February 1825 (in English) and 4 October 1865 (in Italian).

CAPE TOWN 1831 (in English).

SYDNEY 25 August 1845 (in English).

NEW YORK 2 March 1825 (in English; sub-title, *The Wild Huntsman of Bohemia*, probably the

---

[1] Logan is mentioned as the translator in the vocal score published by the Royal Harmonic Institution in 1824. Considering the close connection of William Hawes with both the Lyceum and the Royal Harmonic Institution (see *Dict. Nat. Biog.*) there is every reason for assuming Logan's authorship. A. Nicoll (*A History of Early Nineteenth Century Drama*, Vol. II, p. 357) attributes the first English version of *Der Freischütz* to John Oxenford who, in 1824, was only a boy of twelve. Forty-two years later, Weber's opera was revived at Astley's (2 April 1866), and a comparison of the libretto ("rewritten by John Oxenford", *Lacy's Acting Edition*, Vol. LXIX) with the 1824 score shows not a small degree of indebtedness to Logan's version.

[1] It is generally stated that *Der Freischütz* was the first opera in London to have been sung in German. Strictly speaking, the statement is not quite correct. Dalayrac's *Adolphe et Clara* (see 1799), had been produced in German, by a company of children as early as 26 October 1805 at the Sanssouci Th. See on that early German season in London the magazine *London und Paris*, Vol. XVI (1805), pp.3–12, and XVII (1806), pp.93–108; and *Journal des Luxus und der Moden*, 1806, p.588.

C.G. version)[1]; 13 August 1827 (in French, Castil-Blaze's version, see below); 8 November 1827 (in English, the D. L. version); 29 January 1834 (the Lyceum version); 22 January 1842 (in German, by amateurs) and 8 December 1845 (by professionals); 21 October 1850 (in Italian).

PHILADELPHIA 18 March 1825 (not December 1824 as stated by W. B. Wood, *Recollections*, 1855, p.306) (in English, C.G. version, with additional music by H. W. Darley); 3 October 1827 (in French); and 23 March 1840 (in German).

BALTIMORE Spring 1825 (in English).

BOSTON 19 February 1828 (in English).

ST. LOUIS 10 August 1837 (in English).

HALIFAX, N.S. 9 January 1906 (in English).

PARIS, ODÉON 7 December 1824 (as *Robin des Bois ou Les trois Balles*, adapted by T. Sauvage and F. H. J. Castil-Blaze; this version was very successful; given in Paris more than 100 times and subsequently at Brussels 9 March 1825; Bordeaux 30 June 1825; Marseilles 20 July 1825; Rouen 19 August 1825; Nantes 29 September 1825; Lyons 17 October 1825; Lille 27 October 1825, etc.).

PARIS, TH. I. 12 May 1829 (in German).

PARIS, O.C. 15 January 1835 (the 1824 version).

PARIS, O. 7 June 1841 (new French version by E. Pacini and H. Berlioz, recitatives by Berlioz; last revived there 3 July 1876 and 27 October 1905 and given 231 times up to 1906).

PARIS, TH. L. 24 January 1855 (once more the 1824 version).

PARIS, TH. L. 19 December 1866 (new translation by H. Trianon and G. F. É. Gautier).

[1] There exists an adaptation of *Der Freischütz* by Washington Irving, written 1823–24 and published (as *The Wild Hunstman*) for the first time by the Boston Bibliophile Society in 1924. Irving's version was written on a Central European journey he undertook in the company of Barham Livius. The traces of their common work are easily to be detected in the printed edition of Livius's own version (produced at C.G., see above). In the preface Livius expresses his thanks to J. R. Planché "for whatever of poetic merit this opera may possess" and "to another friend, whose name, were he permitted, it would be his pride and his pleasure to declare, for various valuable hints and emendation".

PARIS, CHÂTEAU D'EAU 1 July 1891 (new translation by L. V. Durdilly).

PARIS, CH. E. 2 April 1913 (new translation by G. Servières).

PARIS, O. 29 October 1926 (new translation by A. Coeuroy).

(For details on the various Paris productions, see J. G. Prod'homme in *Le Ménestrel* October 1926.)

BRUSSELS 9 March 1825 (in French, Castil-Blaze's version).

BRUSSELS 24 July 1829 (in German).

BRUSSELS 20 April 1863 (in French, Berlioz's version).

LIÉGE 14 January 1867 (new French version by A. van Hasselt and J. B. Ronge).

AUBER: *Emma* ou *La Promesse imprudente*

7 July. Paris, O.C.

Text by F. A. E. de Planard. Three acts.

Given at the O.C. until 1836 and revived there 24 April 1846.

In French also, Liége 7 January 1822; Antwerp 3 March 1822; Brussels 23 July 1822, etc.

In German (translated by F. Ellmenreich), Berlin, Kgst. 3 August 1828 (reduced to one act); (translated by K. J. Braun von Braunthal), Vienna 20 October 1835.

MERCADANTE: *Elisa e Claudio* ossia *L'Amore protetto dall' Amicizia*

30 October. Milan, Sc.

Text by L. Romanelli (founded on F. Casari's play, *Rosella*). Two acts.

Mercadante's first great success; given all over Italy and at:

LONDON, HM. 12 April 1823 (in Italian) and Ly. 5 September 1835 (in English, as *No Plot without Danger*).

BARCELONA 16 April 1823 (in Italian).

PARIS, TH. I. 22 November 1823 (in Italian).

VIENNA, KÄ. 10 July 1824 (in Italian) and Jos. 24 July 1833 (in German).

LISBON 22 September 1824 (in Italian).

DRESDEN 5 February 1825 (in Italian).

BUDAPEST 28 February 1825 (in German) and 7 November 1835 (in Hungarian).

GRAZ 4 July 1827 (in German, translated by J. C. Grünbaum).

BERLIN, KGST. 18 October 1828 (in German, translated by J. C. Grünbaum).

ST. PETERSBURG Spring 1829 (in Italian) and 1831 (in Russian).

SANTIAGO, CHILE 1830 (in Italian).

CAGLIARI, SARDINIA Carnival 1831 (in Italian).

BUENOS AIRES 5 July 1831 (in Italian).

CORFU 1832 (in Italian).

MEXICO 1832 (in Italian).

NEW YORK 18 October 1832 (in Italian).

CLAUSENBURG January 1833 (in Hungarian, translated by J. Szerdahelyi).

PHILADELPHIA 23 January 1833 (in Italian).

AJACCIO, CORSICA Autumn 1835 (in Italian).

PRAGUE 10 October 1837 (in German).

DUBLIN 31 March 1838 (in Italian).

CEPHALONIA [15 December] 1838 (in Italian).

ALGIERS Carnival 1839 (in Italian).

CONSTANTINOPLE Summer 1842 (in Italian).

Last revived in Italy: Naples 13 May 1874 (by the Società Filarmonica).

DUPUY: *Felicie* eller *Den Romaneska Flickan*

19 December. Stockholm

Text by L. Hjortsberg (translated from Mercier-Dupaty's French libretto, see 1815). Three acts.

Dupuy's second and last opera.

In Danish (translated by C. N. Rosenkilde), Copenhagen 22 May 1823.

See on Dupuy, P. Long des Clavières, in *Schweizerisches Jahrbuch für Musikwissenschaft*, Vol. IV, 1929 (where the date of the Copenhagen production is wrongly given as 1803).

1822

DONIZETTI: *Zoraida di Granata*

28 January. Rome, Arg.

Text by B. Merelli. Two acts.

Donizetti's first greater success.

Revived, with alterations, at the same theatre 6 January 1824 (text revised by J. Ferretti); Lisbon Winter 1825.

MORLACCHI: *Tebaldo e Isolina*

4 February. Venice, F.

Text by G. Rossi. Two acts.

Morlacchi's most successful work; given at Naples Summer 1824 as *Rambaldo ed Isolina*.

In Italian also given at Barcelona 28 September 1824; Lisbon 6 October 1824; Dresden 5 March 1825; London 25 February 1826; Paris 31 July 1827; St. Petersburg Spring 1829; Mexico 27 October 1831; Havana 1834; Cagliari, Sardinia October 1835.

In German (translated by T. Hell), Leipzig 13 November 1826; Graz 19 July 1827; Prague 19 March 1829; Budapest 31 January 1835. (The German vocal score was arranged by Marschner.)

In Russian, St. Petersburg January 1841.

(ISOUARD): *Aladin* ou *La Lampe merveilleuse*

6 February. Paris, O.

Text by C. G. Etienne. Three acts.

Given at the O. 147 times until 1830; 100th performance 11 February 1825. In French also given at The Hague in 1834. This was Isouard's (d.1818) last work; it had been completed by A. M. Benincori, who did not live to see the production either (d. 30 December 1821).

ROSSINI: *Zelmira*

16 February. Naples, S.C.

Text by A. L. Tottola (founded on a French tragedy by P. L. Buirette de Belloy, 1762). Two acts.

The first of his operas Rossini himself conducted in Vienna and London.

In Italian also given at Vienna 13 April 1822; Lisbon 13 May 1823; London 24 January 1824; Barcelona 6 May 1824; Moscow 12 November 1825; Paris 14 March 1826; Berlin, Kgst. 3 February 1834; Mexico 1836.

In German, Munich 12 November 1822; Brünn November 1822; Lemberg 22 February 1823; Budapest 1823; Prague 25 April 1824; Graz 3 January 1825; Amsterdam 1825, etc.

SPONTINI: *Nurmahal*
oder *Das Rosenfest von Caschmir*

27 May. Berlin, O.

Text by C. A. Herklots (founded on Spicker's German translation of Moore's *Lalla Rookh*). Two parts.

Spontini's first German opera.

Revived Darmstadt 12 January 1834 and 6 May 1840; Berlin 23 October 1861.

(The bacchanale originally had been written for the 1817 revival of Salieri's *Danaides* [see 1784] at Paris.)

CARNICER: *Il Dissoluto punito*
o sia *Don Giovanni Tenorio*

20 June. Barcelona, T. Principal

Adapted from Da Ponte. Two acts.

The first *Don Juan* opera written by a Spanish composer, but to Italian words (cf. R. Mitjana, *Discantes y Contrapuntos*, 1905, pp.74–75).

ALYABYEV: *Lunnaya Noch,*
ili *Domovye*
Лунная Ночь или Домовые
(The Moon Night; or, The House Spirits)

1 July. St. Petersburg

Text by P. A. Mukhanov and P. N. Arapov. Two acts.

Moscow 3 July 1823. The most successful opera of the Russian composer, who is best-known by his songs, especially *The Nightingale*, which sometimes was used as "air de bravour" in the singing lesson of Rossini's *Barbiere di Siviglia*.

CARAFA: *Le Solitaire*

17 August. Paris, O.C.

Text by F. A. E. de Planard (founded on d'Arlincourt's novel). Three acts.

Carafa's most successful opera.

Given at the O.C. until 1833 and revived at the Th.L. 14 December 1855.

In French also, Brussels 9 January 1823; St. Petersburg 1824, etc.; New York 26 October 1827.

In German (translated by I. F. Castelli), Frankfort September 1823; Vienna 21 November 1826; Prague 28 November 1826; Budapest 9 February 1828; Berlin, Kgst. 30 August 1828, etc.

In Russian (translated by A. P. Veshnyakov), St. Petersburg 8 December 1823; Moscow 20 December 1824.

(MÉHUL): *Valentine de Milan*

28 November. Paris, O.C.

Text by J. N. Bouilly. Three acts.

Méhul's last work, completed by his nephew Daussoigne and posthumously performed. Unsuccessful in Paris. In French also, Brussels 15 April 1823.

In German (translated by G. Döring), Frankfort November 1823.

In Russian (translated by A. P. Veshnyakov), St. Petersburg 13 December 1824.

In Danish (translated by T. Overskou), Copenhagen 29 January 1829.

BISHOP: *Maid Marian;* or,
The Huntress of Arlingford

3 December. London, C.G.

Text by J. R. Planché (founded on T. L. Peacock's novel). *A Legendary Opera.* Three acts.

One of Bishop's best works (27 performances in London).

Also given at New York 9 January 1824 (as *Maid Marian; or, The Merry Days of Robin Hood*).

K. KREUTZER: *Libussa*

4 December. Vienna, Kä.

Text by J. K. Bernard. Three acts.

Kreutzer's first great success; subsequently produced at Budapest 3 March 1823; Brünn 29 March 1823; Prague 21 May 1823; Leipzig 29 August 1823; Frankfort 31 August 1823; Berlin 1 December 1823 (with additional music by K.

Blum); Munich 1824; Amsterdam 9 June 1824, etc.

In Danish (translated by C. N. Rosenkilde), Copenhagen 29 January 1824.

REICHA: *Sapho*

16 December. Paris, O.

Text by A. J. S. Empis and H. Cournol. Three acts.

The last opera of the famous pianist; unsuccessful, given for 12 nights only.

RUZSICSKA: *Béla Futása*
(Bela's Flight)

26 December. Clausenburg

Text by P. Csery (based on a play by A. von Kotzebue). Two acts.

Budapest 13 November 1827. This seems to be the earliest extant example of Hungarian opera; it was popular until about 20 years later, when Erkel's national operas were produced.

Revived Budapest 17 January 1836 and (according to Wurzbach) 24 February 1862.

(26 December is the earliest recorded performance; the opera seems to date from the preceding season.)

1823

AUBER: *Leicester* ou *Le Château de Kenilworth*

25 January. Paris, O.C.

Text by A. E. Scribe and A. H. J. Mélesville (founded on Scott's novel). Three acts.

In French also, Brussels 11 August 1823.

In German (translated by I. F. Castelli), Pressburg 25 October 1826; Vienna 30 October 1826; Graz 18 October 1827; Hamburg 18 February 1830; Berlin 15 May 1830, etc.

In Russian (translated by R. M. Zotov), St. Petersburg 14 October 1824 (with additional music by Cavos).

ROSSINI: *Semiramide*

3 February. Venice, F.

Text by G. Rossi (founded on Voltaire's tragedy). Two acts.

The last opera Rossini wrote in Italy. Very successful all over Europe.

In Italian also given at:

VIENNA, KÄ. 4 September 1823.
MUNICH March 1824.
LONDON, HM. 15 July 1824.
PARIS, TH. I. 8 December 1825.
LISBON Carnival 1826.
DRESDEN 4 January 1826.
OPORTO 27 January 1826.
BARCELONA 20 April 1826.
ODESSA 1826.
MALTA 1827.
ST. PETERSBURG February 1829.
MEXICO 20 February 1832.
BERLIN, KGST. 23 September 1833.
DUBLIN 9 October 1834.
HAVANA January 1835.
NEW ORLEANS 1 May 1837.
ALGIERS August 1837.
CORFU Carnival 1839.
BRUSSELS 5 May 1841.
VALPARAISO 1844.
COPENHAGEN Carnival 1845.
NEW YORK 3 January 1845 (parts already 29 April 1835).
AMSTERDAM October 1845.
CONSTANTINOPLE 2 November 1845.
RIO DE JANEIRO 1852.
BUENOS AIRES 13 June 1860.
CAIRO March 1870.

In German, Budapest 6 March 1826; Graz 27 August 1829; Hamburg 18 February 1830; Berlin 15 May 1830; Brünn 7 November 1831; Prague 12 April 1832; Vienna, Jos. 20 December 1832; Bucharest 11 November 1834; St. Petersburg 1837.

In Russian (translated by A. I. Sheller), St. Petersburg January 1836.

In English (translated by T. H. Reynoldson), London, C.G. 1 October 1842; Sydney and Melbourne 1866; New York 2 October 1884.

In French (translated by N. Lafont), Lyons 15 December 1844; (translated by F. J. Méry, recitatives adapted by Carafa), Marseilles 1 April 1854; Paris, O. 9 July 1860. Another French version by L. Montdutaigny was published in 1847.

In Czech, Prague 25 June 1864.

An anonymous Dutch translation was published at Amsterdam in 1827.

Last given in Paris 5 March 1874; Vienna 13 March 1877; Berlin (at the "Skating Rink") 6 June 1882; London, C.G. 23 June 1885 (with Adelina Patti); New York 25 January 1895. Revived at Lisbon 3 February 1904.

Revived at Rostock 18 March 1932 (new German translation by H. Bodenstedt, music revised by A. Secker and O. Petersen); at Florence 28 April 1940 (opening of the sixth Maggio Musicale Fiorentino).

BISHOP: *Clari; or, The Maid of Milan*

8 May. London, C.G.

Text by J. H. Payne (founded on Marmontel's tale, *Laurette*). Three acts.

New York 12 November 1823, etc. Given on minor London stages until 1854.

Revived at Seattle University in November 1928.

Bishop's most famous work, containing the song *Home, Sweet Home*. A sequel, called *Home Sweet Home or The Rantz des Vaches* (libretto by C. A. Somerset) was produced at C.G. 19 March 1829 and New York 25 May 1829. "An examination of the score of this work makes it apparent, that *Clari* having outlived its popularity, a fresh medium for the exploitation of Bishop's immortal balled was demanded . . ." (F. Corder, in *The Musical Quarterly*, Vol. IV, 1918). See on the vogue of *Clari* also, Willis T. Hanson's *The Early Life of John Howard Payne* (Boston 1913).

HÉROLD: *Le Muletier*

12 May. Paris, O.C.

Text by P. de Kock (after Boccaccio). One act.

Brussels 25 September 1823; revived Paris,

O.C. 29 August 1848 and 7 May 1858; F.P. 26 March 1868.

BERTON: *Virginie*

11 June. Paris, O.

Text by A. F. Desaugiers. Three acts.

The most successful of Berton's grand operas (given 32 times until 1827).

SPOHR: *Jessonda*

28 July. Cassel

Text by E. H. Gehe (founded on Lemierre's tragedy, *La Veuve de Malabar*). Three acts.

Spohr's chief work; given in Germany throughout the 19th century, and revived even in the 20th (Berlin, Morwitz-Oper 25 July 1907; Hanover 22 October 1909, etc.). First produced at Berlin 14 February 1825 (100th performance 1 May 1885).

In German also, Amsterdam 1829; Budapest 29 October 1832; Prague 18 March 1834; Vienna, Jos. 29 July 1836 and Kä. 22 October 1836; London, Prince's 18 June 1840; Lemberg 18 September 1841; Paris, Th. I. 28 April 1842; Basle 17 January 1845; Philadelphia 15 February 1864; Ghent 7 January 1881.

In Swedish (translated by A. Lindeberg), Stockholm 26 January 1826.

In Czech (translated by J. N. Stěpánek), Prague 1 March 1840.

In Italian (translated by S. M. Maggioni), London, C.G. 6 August 1853.

French (translated by H. Brovellio) and English (translated by W. Bartholomew) vocal scores published.

Never given in New York or in Italy.

CARAFA: *Le Valet de Chambre*

16 September. Paris, O.C.

Text by A. E. Scribe and A. H. J. Mélesville. One act.

Liége 21 November 1825; Brussels 26 September 1826 (revived 5 November 1841); revived Paris, O.C. 2 July 1858.

In German, Vienna 14 December 1830 and 19 October 1840.

AUBER: *La Neige* ou *Le Nouvel Eginard*

8 October. Paris, O.C.

Text by A. E. Scribe and G. Delavigne (originally written for Boieldieu). Four acts.

Given at the O.C. 176 times until 1841.

In French also, Brussels 5 February 1824; New York 30 July 1827.

In German (translated by I. F. Castelli), Vienna 19 March 1824; Prague 26 June 1824; Budapest 5 July 1824; Munich 30 July 1824; (translated by F. Ellmenreich) Frankfort September 1824; (translated by C. A. Herklots) Berlin 3 August 1824.

In German also, Riga 1825; Bucharest 1835; Basle 8 November 1837; Helsinki 15 December 1840. Revived Berlin, Kroll's 23 October 1858.

In English (as *The Frozen Lake*), London, C.G. 26 November 1824; previously Ly. 3 September 1824, adapted by J. R. Planché, music arranged by G. W. Reeve.

In Swedish (translated by N. E. W. af Wetterstedt), Stockholm 21 January 1825.

In Danish (translated by A. G. Oehlenschläger), Copenhagen 14 September 1825.

In Russian, St. Petersburg 11 January 1827.

In Czech (translated by J. K. Chmelenský), Prague 18 November 1827.

In Hungarian (translated by E. Pály), Clausenburg 20 August 1830.

Leicester (see above) and *La Neige* were the first results of the prolific partnership between Auber and A. E. Scribe which lasted until the latter's death in 1861. Of some 120 librettos written by Scribe, alone or in collaboration with others, and produced in Paris between 1813 and 1870, no less than 37 were set by Auber (who, on the other hand, set to music only 9 more librettos which were not by Scribe).

C. M. VON WEBER: *Euryanthe*

25 October. Vienna, Kä.

Text by H. von Chézy. Three acts.

Weber's only grand opera (without spoken dialogue). Subsequently given at Frankfort 8 March 1824; Prague 11 March 1824; Carlsruhe 21 March 1824; Dresden 31 March 1824; Munich 21 December 1825; Berlin 23 December 1825; Graz 1 February 1827, etc. and all over Germany.

In German also, produced at Budapest 30 December 1826; Paris, Th.I. 14 June 1831; London, C.G. 29 June 1833 (revived Prince's 3 June 1840 and D.L. 13 June 1882); Zurich November 1837; St. Petersburg Winter 1840; Riga October 1842; New York, M. 23 December 1887.

In French (translated by F. H. J. Castil-Blaze), Paris, O. 6 April 1831 (given 4 times only). Parts of the *Euryanthe* music had already been used in Castil-Blaze's pasticcio, *La Forêt de Sénart ou La Partie de Chasse*, produced at the Odéon, Paris 14 January 1826 and at Brussels 20 October 1826. *Euryanthe* was revived at the Th.L. 1 September 1857 (new French translation by A. de Leuven and J. H. Vernoy de Saint-Georges); again 17 March 1895 (at the Concerts d'Harcourt; the second act only; new French version by C. Grandmougin and E. d'Harcourt); the whole opera, in concert form, by the Schola Cantorum 31 January 1908.

In Swedish (translated by P. Westerstrand), Stockholm 3 December 1838.

In Russian, St. Petersburg April 1885.

In Flemish, Antwerp 6 October 1894.

In English (translated by W. Thornthwaite), London, Daly's 30 October 1900 (by the R.C.M.).

In Italian (translated by G. Macchi), Milan, Sc. 2 April 1902.

Frequently revived in Germany and Austria. The *Euryanthe* music was adapted to a new libretto by H. J. Moser (*Die sieben Raben*) at Berlin 5 March 1915.

Revived Basle 21 March 1924 in a version by R. Lauckner and D. F. Tovey.

[HAYDN]: *Die Ochsenmenuette*

13 December. Vienna, W.

Text by G. E. von Hofmann (dealing with an incident in Haydn's life). One act.

The music, compiled from Haydn's works, was arranged by I. von Seyfried, in Germany one of the earliest examples of that sort of pasticcio. Very successful on German stages, Berlin, Kgst. 4 August 1824[1] and O. 4 August 1848; Hamburg 11 May 1825; Hanover 26 May 1825; Prague 1831, etc. Revived Vienna, Kä. 12 September 1829 (in two acts); Leop. 22 September 1846; and W. 31 October 1857. In German also, New York 7 December 1858.

In Swedish (translated by C. G. Nordforss), Stockholm 26 April 1826.

Vocal score re-issued in 1927 (edited by G. Droescher).

Hofmann's libretto was founded upon a French comédie-anecdote mêlée de vaudevilles, by J. J. Gabriel and A. J. M. Wafflard (*Haydn ou Le Menuet du Bœuf*), produced at the Th. du Vaudeville, Paris 12 November 1812, in which there were five numbers by Haydn. There exists, however, a forerunner dating from a time when Haydn was still alive, *Le Menuet du Bœuf ou Une Leçon de Haydn*, by J. B. Constantin, printed (and produced?) at Verdun in 1805 (*Bibl. Soleinne*, no. 3053); here apparently the whole music was taken from Haydn's works.

B. KLEIN: *Dido*

15 October. Berlin, O.

Text by L. Rellstab. Three acts.

The only performed opera of the Berlin conductor; it had been previously given in concert form at Hofrat Parthey's on 9 April 1821; and was revived, also in concert form, at Berlin on 10 February 1855.

1824

VACCAI: *Pietro il Grande* ossia *Un Geloso alla Tortura*

17 January. Parma

Text by B. Merelli. Two acts.

Vaccai's first greater success.

In Italian also, given at Lisbon 25 August 1824;

[1] At the opening of the second Berlin opera-house, the Königstädtisches Theater (existed until 30 June 1851).

Dresden 6 January 1827; Barcelona 21 September 1828.

DONIZETTI: *L'Ajo nell' Imbarazzo*

4 February. Rome, Valle

Text by J. Ferretti (founded on a comedy by G. Giraud, first set to music by Pilotti in 1811). Two acts.

Successful in Italy.

In Italian also given at Vienna 2 April 1827 (first Donizetti opera there); Dresden 9 April 1828 (as *Il Governo alla Casa*); Barcelona 3 June 1828; Rio de Janeiro 14 July 1829; Lisbon 4 December 1837; Nice Carnival 1840; Berlin, Kgst. 26 July 1841; Corfu Autumn 1842; Copenhagen Spring 1844; Constantinople Spring 1844; London, H.M.'s 28 July 1846 (as *Don Gregorio*).

Last given in Italy, Milan 4 April 1866; Venice 12 February 1879.

MEYERBEER: *Il Crociato in Egitto*

7 March. Venice, F.

Text by G. Rossi. Two acts.

The last and most successful of Meyerbeer's Italian operas; Florence, P. 7 May 1824, etc. Given at Naples, S.C. 30 September 1826 as *Il Cavaliere d'Orville in Egitto*, at Rome Autumn 1836 as *Armando d'Orville*.

In Italian also London 30 June 1825; Munich July 1825; Paris 25 September 1825; Barcelona 22 December 1825; Dresden 14 November 1826; Oporto Spring 1827; Lisbon 25 April 1828; Havana 1828; Mexico 1837; Corfu Autumn 1838; Constantinople Carnival 1839.

In German (translated by J. Kupelwieser), Pressburg 7 October 1826; Munich 14 November 1826; Graz 1 September 1827; Budapest 8 March 1828; Prague 20 March 1828; Vienna 24 May 1829; Berlin, Kgst. 15 October 1832; Hamburg 15 April 1832 (with new dialogue by F. L. Schmidt); Bucharest 1835.

In Russian, St. Petersburg Spring 1841.

Revived Milan, Sc. 5 March 1859; Paris, Th.I. 27 March 1860; in German, Königsberg 14 April 1847 (translated by F. Ellmenreich); Graz December 1860.

AUBER: *Le Concert à la Cour* ou *La Débutante*

3 June. Paris, O.C.

Text by A. E. Scribe and A. H. J. Mélesville. One act.

Last revived at the O.C. 17 October 1851 (given there 246 times altogether).

In French also, Brussels 31 October 1824; Berlin 31 October 1835; Rio de Janeiro 1846; London, St. J.'s 26 February 1849.

In German (translated by C. A. Herklots), Berlin 11 October 1825; (translated by F. Ellmenreich) Budapest 31 March 1826; Prague 17 June 1826; Graz 31 July 1826; Munich 1826; Vienna, Jos. 10 January 1827 (with additional music by Riotte) and Kä. 9 March 1827; St. Petersburg 28 December 1836; last revived Frankfort 25 November 1857; Breslau 29 April 1862.

In Swedish (translated by P. U. Huldberg), Stockholm 7 February 1834.

In Danish (translated by T. Overskou), Copenhagen 28 October 1839.

In Hungarian (translated by E. Abrányi), Budapest as late as 3 March 1888.

PEELLAERT: *Agnes Sorel*

30 August. Brussels, M.

Text by J. N. Bouilly and E. Mercier-Dupaty (originally performed as a vaudeville in 1806). Three acts.

The opera had "six représentations, chiffre extraordinaire, à ce moment, pour une pièce bruxelloise" (Isnardon).

Also given at Ghent 19 January 1825, etc.

VACCAI: *La Pastorella Feudataria*

18 September. Turin, T. Carignano

Text by B. Merelli (founded on Planard's *Bergère Châteleine*, see 1820). Two acts.

In Italian also given at Dresden 20 April 1826; Lisbon 1826; Barcelona 20 December 1826; Paris, Th.I. 21 April 1827.

WÜRFEL: *Rübezahl*

7 October. Prague

Text by W. Marsano. Three acts.

Popular on German stages; Vienna, W. 10 March 1825; Leipzig 21 March 1825, etc.; Budapest 30 May 1829.

In Czech (translated by J. K. Chmelenský), Prague 30 January 1831.

KUHLAU: *Lulu*

29 October. Copenhagen

Text by C. F. Güntelberg (founded on a tale in C. M. Wieland's *Dschinnistan*). Three acts.

Danish romantic opera, given at Copenhagen until 1838.

A Swedish translation by P. U. Huldberg was published in 1835.

AUBER: *Léocadie*

4 November. Paris, O.C.

Text by A. E. Scribe and A. H. J. Mélesville (founded on Cervantes's story *La Fuerça de la Sangre*). Three acts.

Given in Paris 120 times until 1831; in French also, Ghent 9 March 1825; Brussels 23 March 1825, etc.

In English, London, D.L. 17 December 1825 (music arranged by B. Livius).

In German (translated by K. A. Ritter), Munich 12 July 1825; (in another version by F. Ellmenreich, as *Anatolie*), Vienna 20 October 1827; Prague 1827; Graz 30 November 1831, etc.

MIRECKI: *Evandro in Pergamo*

26 December. Genoa, S. Agostino.

Text by A. Peracchi (originally called *Argene e Dalmiro* and composed by Stuntz, Turin 26 December 1820). Two acts.

Probably the first opera written by a Polish composer for Italy; ran for 26 nights.

1825

LINDPAINTNER: *Der Bergkönig*

30 January. Stuttgart

Text by C. Hanisch. Three acts.

The same subject was treated by Spohr 2 months later.

In German also, Budapest 31 October 1825.

MARSCHNER: *Der Holzdieb*

22 February. Dresden

Text by F. Kind. One act.

The little work was not very successful at its first appearance; but it was frequently revived, viz.: Leipzig 13 January 1850 (at the Conservatoire); Berlin, Kroll's 21 April 1853 (as *Geborgt*); Barmen 8 May 1856 (by amateurs); Hamburg 18 January 1878; Hanover 9 May 1879; Königsberg 8 April 1902; Strasbourg January 1909; and, lately Amsterdam February 1935 (by the Dutch Chamber Opera); Berlin, D.O. 8 October 1937 (revised by H. Burkard and O. Rombach).

SPOHR: *Der Berggeist*

24 March. Cassel

Text by G. Döring. Three acts.

Written for the celebration of the wedding of Prince Bernhard Erich of Saxe-Meiningen and Princess Maria of Hesse-Cassel.

Also given at Leipzig 16 November 1825, etc.; Prague 24 June 1837.

AUBER: *Le Maçon*

3 May. Paris, O.C.

Text by A. E. Scribe and G. Delavigne. Three acts.

One of Auber's greatest successes; given at the O.C. 525 times until 1896. Given on German stages even until about 1930. Outside Paris produced at:

BRUSSELS 15 September 1825 (in French).

BERLIN 19 March 1826 (in German, translated by C. A. L. von Lichtenstein); another translation, by K. A. Ritter, was used at Würzburg 19 March 1828, etc.

BUDAPEST 15 June 1826 (in German) and 1 April 1846 (in Hungarian).

VIENNA 2 August 1826 (in German, translated by J. G. Seidl).

PRAGUE Autumn 1826 (in German) and 10 March 1850 (in Czech, translated by J. Pražský).

NEW YORK 1 August 1827 (in French) and 8 January 1857 (in German).

COPENHAGEN 1 September 1827 (in Danish, translated by T. Overskou).

LEMBERG 26 June 1828 (in Polish, translated by F. K. Blotnicki).

WARSAW 8 November 1828 (in Polish, translated by F. K. Blotnicki).

STOCKHOLM 3 April 1834 (in Swedish, translated by C. M. Craelius) and 22 June 1861 (in a new Swedish version by F. A. Dahlgren).

CLAUSENBURG 2 November 1834 (in Hungarian, translated by J. Szerdahelyi; translation published already Kassán 1830).

BASLE 13 March 1835 (in German).

BUCHAREST 1835 (in German).

ST. PETERSBURG January 1836 (in German).

RIGA 1837 (in German).

HELSINKI 28 June 1839 (in German).

RIO DE JANEIRO 1846 (in French).

LONDON, ST. J.'s 13 March 1850 (in French).

SPONTINI: *Alcidor*

23 May. Berlin, O.

(Original French) text by E. G. M. Théaulon de Lambert, German version by C. A. Herklots. Three parts.

Written for the celebration of the wedding of Prince Frederick of Holland and Princess Luise of Prussia.

Given in Berlin until 1836, but nowhere else.

ROSSINI: *Il Viaggio a Reims* ossia *L'Albergo del Giglio d'Oro*

19 June. Paris, Th. I.

Text by G. L. Balochi. Two acts.

The first work Rossini wrote for Paris (for the coronation of King Charles x). Complete failure, 3 nights only. Rossini used the greater part of the music for his *Comte d'Ory* (see 1828); after that, another resurrection, in Italian, took place at the Th. I. 26 October 1848 as *Andremo a Parigi ossia L'Albergo di Plombières* (without most of the *Comte d'Ory* additions).

Revived at Vienna 26 April 1854 (as *Il Viaggio a Vienna ossia L'Albergo di . . . ai Bagni di . . ., Melodrama d'Occasione, con Quadro allusivo*).

CORDELLA: *Gli Avventurieri*

6 September. Milan, Can.

Text by F. Romani. Two acts.

Successful in Italy; revived at the Scala, Milan 28 April 1840.

Also given at Lisbon 6 February 1826; Trieste Carnival 1827; Barcelona 19 September 1827.

DAVIES: *The Forest Rose;* or, *American Farmers*

7 October. New York, Chatham Th.

Text by S. Woodworth. Two acts.

Successful American pastoral opera, introducing the Yankee character of *Brother Jonathan* (*Jonathan Ploughboy*).

Revived New York 8 March 1849 and 16 May 1855.

LISZT: *Don Sanche* ou *Le Château d'Amour*

17 October. Paris, O.

Text by E. G. M. Théaulon de Lambert and De Rancé (founded on a story by Florian). *Opéra féerie.* One act.

The only opera of the (then 12 years old) composer; given 4 times only. Rodolphe Kreutzer is said to have helped with the orchestration. The score was for many years thought to be lost, but recovered in 1903; see J. Chantavoine in *Die Musik*, May 1904 (where the overture was printed for the first time).

VACCAI: *Giulietta e Romeo*

31 October. Milan, Can.

Text by F. Romani (after Shakespeare). Two acts.

Vaccai's greatest and last success; he wrote 9 more operas, all of which were failures.

In Italian also given at Barcelona 26 May 1827; Paris 11 September 1827; Lisbon Autumn 1828; London 10 April 1832; Mexico July 1841.

In German (translated by I. C. Kollmann), Graz 12 October 1833; Budapest 31 July 1845. After 1832, the last scene of this opera was frequently (in Italy nearly always) introduced into Bellini's *Capuleti e Montecchi* (see 1830); in this form parts of Vaccai's setting were revived at Hamburg as late as 8 September 1897.

PACINI: *L'ultimo Giorno di Pompei*

19 November. Naples, S.C.

Text by A. L. Tottola (not founded on the novel by E. Bulwer Lytton which was not published until 1834). Two acts.

Very successful in Italy; in Italian also given at Vienna 17 July 1827; Lisbon Autumn 1828; Madrid 7 September 1830; Paris 2 October 1830; London 17 March 1831; Mexico 31 July 1838.

In German (translated by G. Ott), Stuttgart Summer 1829; Vienna 18 August 1832 (at the Th. in der Josephstadt which was then re-opened as an opera-house under J. A. Stöger's management); Prague December 1834; Budapest 1 August 1835.

BOIELDIEU: *La Dame blanche*

10 December. Paris, O.C.

Text by A. E. Scribe (founded on Scott's *Guy Mannering* and *The Monastery*). Three acts.

Boieldieu's chief work, and one of the greatest successes of French opéra-comique. The 1,000th performance at the O.C. was on 16 December 1862, the 1,675th on 12 March 1914; last revived there 7 January 1926; revived at Brussels 20 October 1936.

Parodies: *Les Dames à la Mode* (on Boieldieu's opera and Rossini's *Donna del Lago*) by N. Gersin, N. Brazier, J. J. Gabriel, and A. Vulpian, Th. du Vaudeville 5 January 1826; *La Dame jaune*, at the same theatre, 9 March 1826; *La Dame noire ou Le Tambour et la Grisette*, by C. Honoré, Bordeaux February 1827.

La Dame blanche was first produced at Rouen, the composer's native town, on 25 February 1826 and subsequently given all over France.

Outside France, the first performances were at:

LIÉGE 13 March 1826 (in French).

BRUSSELS 6 April 1826 (in French).

VIENNA 6 July 1826 (in German, translated by I. F. Castelli); Graz 19 January 1827.

BERLIN, O. 1 August 1826 (in German, translated by C. A. L. von Lichtenstein) and Kgst. 2 November 1826 (translated by L. Angely); there were other German versions by F. Ellmenreich, J. B. Rousseau, and K. A. Ritter published about the same time. The latest German version, by G. Brecher, published 1931.

PRESSBURG 16 September 1826 and Budapest 23 October 1826 (in German).

LONDON, D.L. 9 October 1826 (in English, as *The White Lady*, translated by S. Beazley, music arranged by T. S. Cooke); C.G. 2 January 1827 (as *The White Maid*, translated by J. H. Payne); Hm. 9 June 1834 (in German); and St. J.'s 31 January 1849 (in French). Revived by the Carl Rosa Company between 1873–83 in a new English version by A. Matthison.

COPENHAGEN 30 October 1826 (in Danish, translated by T. Overskou).

NAPLES, FONDO Carnival 1827 (in Italian).

PRAGUE 9 January 1827 (in German) and 17 April 1853 (in Czech, translated by E. Ujky).

STOCKHOLM 31 January 1827 (in Swedish, translated by B. H. Crusell and N. E. W. af Wetterstedt) and 14 May 1863 (in German).

TRIESTE 7 July 1827 (in German).

WARSAW 23 August 1827 (in Polish, translated by W. Boguslawski).

NEW YORK 24 August 1827 (in French); 23 April 1828 and 21 May 1832 (in English, the D.L. and C.G. versions respectively); 15 January 1864 (in German).

AGRAM (ZAGREB) 2 January 1828 (in German) and 7 January 1900 (in Croatian, translated by V. Badalić).

MOSCOW 1828 (in Russian).

AMSTERDAM 1828 (in Dutch); 1834 (in French); October 1836 (in German).

CLAUSENBURG 15 August 1830 (in Hungarian, translated by E. Pály).

BUCHAREST January 1834 (in German) and 1 October 1840 (in French).

HELSINKI 14 April 1834 (in German).

BASLE 24 October 1834 (in German).

ST. PETERSBURG 1835 (in German) and 19 February 1864 (in Italian, translated by M. M. Marcello, recitatives by E. Bauer).

CHRISTIANIA 1835 (in Danish).

BATAVIA 10 October 1836 (in French; first opera ever given there); Soerabaya 29 October 1866.

RIGA 1837 (in German).

RIO DE JANEIRO 1846 (in French).

BUENOS AIRES 14 March 1852 (in French).

BADEN-BADEN 15 July 1864 (in French).

BARCELONA 23 June 1866 (in French).

LISBON 11 May 1878 (in French).

MEXICO 22 March 1879 (in French).

SARAJEVO 1882 (in German).

1826

MAURER: *Der neue Paris*

27 January. Hanover

Librettist unknown. One act.

In German also, Riga 18 October 1826.

In English (as *Not for me; or, The new Apple of Discord*, translated by H. Napier, music arranged by W. Hawes), London, Ly. 23 August 1828.

Produced in Russian (translated by N. I. Khmelnitsky), Moscow 3 July 1829 (as a vaudeville, with some new music by Verstovsky, probably partly in the original setting, as Maurer frequently collaborated with Verstovsky).

ŠKROUP: *Dráteník*
(The Tinker)

2 February. Prague

Text by J. K. Chmelenský. Two acts.

First opera ever written to Czech words.

Given at Brünn 21 November 1840; revived at Prague 28 January 1865; 10 July 1895; 20 February 1926; and 28 May 1938.

Škroup was the composer of the Czech national hymn *Kde domov můj?* (*Where is my Home?*) which first appeared in his incidental music to *Fidlovačka*, a farce by J. K. Tyl (performed 21 December 1834); the song was afterwards introduced into the finale of *Dráteník*.

MERCADANTE: *Caritea, Regina di Spagna*

21 February. Venice, F.

Text by P. Pola. Two acts.

Outside Italy: Barcelona 12 July 1828; London 26 July 1830; St. Petersburg 1831; Lisbon Summer 1834; Havana June 1836; Palma, Mallorca Carnival 1840; Mexico 6 September 1842. Mostly given as *Donna Caritea*.

In German, Graz September 1831; Brünn December 1833.

PEELLAERT: *Teniers ou La Noce flamande*

9 March. Brussels, M.

Text by J. N. Bouilly and J. M. Pain. One act.

Successful in Belgium; Ghent 17 April 1828; last revived at Brussels 2 December 1845.

FÉTIS: *La Vieille*

14 March. Paris, O.C.

Text by A. E. Scribe and G. Delavigne. One act.

The most successful opera of the famous writer on music; given at the O.C. until 1840 and revived there 11 October 1851.

In French also, Ghent 6 September 1826; Brussels 11 September 1826 (revived 20 December 1860); New York 20 July 1827; Calcutta 20 November 1838; Rio de Janeiro 1846.

In German (as *Die liebenswürdige Alte*, translated by L. Angely), Berlin, Kgst. 1 June 1827.

In English (as *Love in Wrinkles; or, The Russian Stratagem*, adapted by M. R. Lacy), London, D.L. 4 December 1828; (as *My old Woman*, adapted by G. Macfarren, music arranged by J. Blewitt) Surrey 14 January 1829.

WEBER: *Oberon; or, The Elf King's Oath*

12 April. London, C.G.

Text by J. R. Planché (founded on W. Sotheby's translation of C. M. Wieland's *Oberon*). Three acts.

Given in London 31 times during the first season and frequently revived afterwards; given at D.L. 19 April 1841 in German; at H.M.'s 3 July 1860 in Italian, translated by S.M. Maggioni, with recitatives by Benedict and additional music from other works of Weber.

Produced at Dublin 1 February 1827 (in English) and 8 October 1863 (in Italian); Edinburgh 26 August 1827 (in English); New York 9 October 1828 (in English); Philadelphia 9 March 1870 (in Italian); Melbourne and Sydney 1865 (in English).

Outside the English-speaking countries, given at:

LEIPZIG 23 December 1826 (in German, translated by T. Hell).

VIENNA, JOS. 20 March 1827 (text arranged by K. Meisl, music re-scored by Gläser); Kä. 4 February 1829 (in the original form).

BERLIN, O. 2 July 1828 (previously given there privately, at the publisher Schlesinger's in December 1826; see H. Dorn, *Aus meinem Leben*, Vol. II, p.101).

PRAGUE 4 October 1828 (in German) and 6 September 1889 (in Czech, translated by V. J. Novotný).

BUDAPEST 18 May 1829 (in German) and 29 January 1914 (in Hungarian, translated by S. Hevesi).

AMSTERDAM 1829 (in Dutch, translated by J. F. Majofski).

PARIS, TH.I. 25 May 1830 (in German); Th.L. 27 February 1857 (in French, translated by C. Nuitter, A. Beaumont and P. de Chazot); Ren. 10 April 1899 (new translation by L. V. Durdilly and M. Carré fils).

COPENHAGEN 31 January 1831 (in Danish, translated by A. G. Oehlenschläger); revived 18 December 1886 (new Danish version by S. Bauditz and P. Krohn).

RIGA 27 April 1832 (in German).

GRAZ 22 February 1834 (in German).

BASLE 15 April 1836 (in German).

LIÉGE 18 May 1838 (in German).

TOULOUSE May 1846 (in French, as *Huon de Bordeaux*, translated by F. H. J. Castil-Blaze; an earlier French version, by J. Ramoux, was written for Liége and published in 1832. According to *Annuaire Dramatique Belge*, 1842, p.151, produced at Marseilles in 1833, a statement I could not verify).

BRUSSELS July 1846 (in German); 16 November 1863 (in French, the Paris 1857 version); 23 November 1911 (new French version by M. Kufferath and H. Cain, with Wüllner's recitatives).

LEMBERG 1850 (in German).

STOCKHOLM 21 May 1858 (in Swedish, translated by C. W. A. Strandberg).

GHENT 20 February 1862 (in French).

ST. PETERSBURG 1863 (in Italian; the London 1860 version).

ROTTERDAM 28 January 1865 (in German).

ANTWERP 27 February 1872 (in French) and 17 January 1914 (in Flemish).

ROME 26 June 1882 (for the first time in Italy, in concert form, by the Società Musicale Romana).

AGRAM (Zagreb) 15 October 1901 (in Croatian, translated by A. Schneider).

MILAN, SC. 18 February 1913 (first stage production in Italy; new Italian version by A. Lega).

BUENOS AIRES 5 July 1913 (in Italian).

SOFIA 28 September 1936 (in Bulgarian).

Of the numerous revivals and arrangements in Germany, the following should be mentioned:

VIENNA 25 February 1881 (new German version by F. Grandaur, recitatives by F. Wüllner).

WIESBADEN 16 May 1900 (arranged by G. von Hülsen, J. Schlar and J. Lauff).

COLOGNE 10 April 1913 (new German version by G. Brecher, music revised by G. Mahler).

BASLE 15 November 1930 (new version by Weingartner).

Revived at the Metropolitan, New York 28 December 1918 (in English, music arranged by A. Bodanzky). Revived in Italian (with spoken dialogue), Rome, T.R. 12 December 1938; Milan, Sc. 26 March 1940.

BISHOP: *Aladdin*

29 April. London, D.L.

Text by G. Soane (*A fairy opera*). Three acts.

Bishop's only opera without spoken dialogue. Commissioned by Elliston, then manager of D.L., as a counter-attraction to *Oberon*, which was so successful at the rival house; but *Aladdin* was a complete failure and had to be withdrawn after a few nights.

Outside London, only given at Philadelphia 12 November 1830.

WOLFRAM: *Maja und Alpino* oder *Die bezauberte Rose*

24 May. Prague

Text by E. H. Gehe (founded on E. K. F. Schulze's poem *Die bezauberte Rose*, 1818). Three acts.

The most successful of Wolfram's operas. Dresden 7 September 1826; Berlin 13 December 1827, etc.

BELLINI: *Bianca e Gernando*

30 May. Naples, S.C.

Text by D. Gilardoni. Two acts.

Bellini's first publicly performed opera. The original title, *Bianca e Fernando*, had to be changed because Fernando had been the name of the late King of Naples.

Repeated Genoa 7 April 1828 (at the inauguration of the Teatro Carlo Felice; text revised by F. Romani); Rome 31 July 1837.

Outside Italy, only Barcelona 19 May 1830.

HÉROLD: *Marie*

12 August. Paris, O.C.

Text by F. A. E. de Planard. Three acts.

Very successful in Paris; last revived at the Th.L. 14 September 1855; O.C. 10 July 1865; Galerie Vivienne 6 December 1894.

Outside Paris given at:

VIENNA 18 December 1826 (in German, translated by I. F. Castelli).

BRUSSELS 18 January 1827 (in French).

BUDAPEST 15 March 1827 (in German).

HAMBURG 26 September 1827 (in German).

BERLIN, KGST. 7 November 1827 (in German).

NEW YORK 18 August 1829 (in French).

CLAUSENBURG 7 September 1830 (in Hungarian, translated by P. Szilágyi).

COPENHAGEN 25 September 1830 (in Danish, translated by T. Overskou).

STOCKHOLM 17 December 1832 (in Swedish, translated by J. E. Remmer).

PRAGUE 3 April 1840 (in German).

LONDON, PRINCESS'S 18 January 1849 (in English, as *Marie, the Foundling of the Lake*, music arranged by Loder).

BUCHAREST 1835 (in German).

[ROSSINI]: *Ivanhoé*

15 September. Paris, Odéon

Text by E. Deschamps and G. G. de Wailly (founded on Scott's novel). Three acts.

One of the numerous Rossini pasticcios; music from *Semiramide*, *Mosè*, *Tancredi* and *Gazza Ladra*, adapted to the new libretto by A. Pacini.

In French also, Ghent 10 January 1827; Lille 20 February 1827, etc.

In English (as *The Maid of Judah; or, The Knight Templars*, translated by M. R. Lacy), London, C.G. 7 March 1829; Dublin 30 June 1830; New York 27 February 1832; Philadelphia 6 March 1834.

In German, Coburg 1833.

Much confusion in books of reference has been caused by the fact that the famous composer Giovanni Pacini (1796–1867) also wrote an (Italian) *Ivanhoe* opera, performed Venice 19 March 1832 and (in German, translated by G. Ott) Vienna 14 February 1837. Apart from the subject, it has nothing to do with our (French) Rossini pasticcio, arranged by the less famous composer Antonio Pacini (1778–1866), father of Emiliano Pacini (1811–98), the librettist who translated *Freischütz*, *Trovatore*, etc., for the Paris Opéra.

C. CONTI: *Olimpia*

29 October. Naples, S.C.

Text by A. L. Tottola. Two acts.

Conti's best work; revived at Naples, S.C. on 9 October 1829.

AUBER: *Fiorella*

28 November. Paris, O.C.

Text by A. E. Scribe. Three acts.

Revived at the O.C. 9 June 1848 (118 performances). In French also, Ghent 14 March 1827; Brussels 5 April 1827; New York 22 August 1829.

In German (translated by I. F. Castelli), Berlin, Kgst. 14 March 1828; Pressburg 26 March 1828; Graz 26 April 1828; Budapest 25 September 1828; Prague 5 January 1829; Vienna, W. 19 February 1829 (as *Das Pilgerhaus*) and Kä. 5 March 1831 (as *Fiorella*). Another German translation by F. Ellmenreich was published c.1830.

In Danish (translated by T. Overskou), Copenhagen 13 February 1838.

1827

DONIZETTI: *Olivo e Pasquale*

7 January. Rome, Valle

Text by J. Ferretti (founded on a comedy by A. S. Sografi). Two acts.

Given in Italy until about 1870.

In Italian also produced at London 31 March 1832; Barcelona 6 February 1833; Bastia, Corsica Autumn 1833; Lisbon 20 January 1836; Nice Autumn 1839; Berlin, Kgst. 8 January 1845; Vienna 17 June 1847.

In German (translated by G. Ott), Graz 10 April 1830; Vienna, Jos. 5 October 1836.

PACINI: *Gli Arabi nelle Gallie* ossia *Il Trionfo della Fede*

8 March. Milan, Sc.

Text by L. Romanelli (founded on d'Arlincourt's novel *Le Renégat*). Two acts.

One of Pacini's most successful works.

In Italian also produced at Vienna 22 May 1827; Madrid 30 April 1829; Dresden 12 December 1829; London 12 May 1832; New York 20 January 1834; Philadelphia 23 April 1834; Lisbon Summer 1834; Clausenburg 9 January 1836 (parts only); Havana 29 January 1838; Odessa Autumn 1939; Nice Carnival 1842; Mexico 12 June 1842.

Revived (with seven additional numbers): Paris, Th.I. 30 January 1855 (as *L'Ultimo dei Clodovei ossia Gli Arabi nelle Gallie*).

MENDELSSOHN: *Die Hochzeit des Gamacho*

29 April. Berlin, Sch.

Text by C. A. L. von Lichtenstein (founded on an episode from Cervantes's *Don Quixote*). Two acts.

Mendelssohn's first performed opera; given only once. (On earlier attempts see G. Schünemann in *Zeitschrift für Musikwissenschaft*, Vol. v, p.506.)

Revived (in concert form): Frankfort 30 December 1860; Chicago 1 May 1875; Boston 19 March 1885 (English version by A. L. Blandy); Berlin 9 February 1886.

Lichtenstein is mentioned as the author (*zur beibehaltenen Musik ... umgearbeitet*) in the original libretto. Goedeke (III, p.1104), attributes the text to Friedrich Voigts; Devrient (*Erinnerungen*) to "Klingemann". Probably he did not mean Karl Klingemann, Mendelssohn's friend and collaborator in *Die Heimkehr aus der Fremde* (see 1851), but the elder August Klingemann whose *Don Quixote und Sancho Panza oder: Die Hochzeit des Gamacho* (music from different operas) had been produced at Berlin on 30 May 1811 (overture by Seidel). Lichtenstein perhaps based his version on Klingemann's *Dramatisches Spiel mit Gesang*, which had been published in 1815.

DONIZETTI: *Gli Esiliati in Siberia ossia Otto Mesi in due Ore*

13 May. Naples, T.N.

Text by D. Gilardoni (from a melodrama by R. C. G. de Pixérécourt which itself was founded upon the novel by S. Cottin, 1806). Three acts.

In Italian also given at Lisbon 4 March 1839 and Barcelona 15 October 1840.

In German (as *Die Macht der kindlichen Liebe*, translated by G. Ott), Graz 12 February 1829; Berlin, Kgst. 3 May 1832; Vienna 3 August 1832.

Revived (after Donizetti's death), Paris, Th.L. 31 December 1853 (in French, as *Elisabeth ou La Fille du Proscrit*, translated by A. de Leuven and L. L. Brunswick, music adapted by U. Fontana); this version, re-translated into Italian, was given at Milan, S. Radegonda 24 July 1854.

WEYSE: *Et Eventyr i Rosenborg Have* (An Adventure in Rosenborg Gardens)

26 May. Copenhagen

Text by J. L. Heiberg. One act.

Very successful in Denmark; frequently revived at Copenhagen; the 165th performance was on 27 February 1917!

CHÉLARD: *Macbeth*

29 June. Paris, O.

Text by C. J. Rouget de Lisle. Three acts.

The opera was a failure in Paris (5 nights only), but became successful in Germany (translated by C. M. Heigel); Munich 25 August 1828, etc.

In German also, London, Hm. 4 July 1832 (under Chélard); Budapest 21 October 1837. Revived Weimar 13 January 1861 (in an enlarged 5-act version).

DONIZETTI: *Il Borgomastro di Saardam*

19 August. Naples, Fondo

Text by D. Gilardoni (founded on a French play by A. H. J. Mélesville, J. T. Merle, and E. C. de Boirie, 1818). Two acts.

Successful in Italy. In Italian also, Barcelona 16 December 1829.

In German, Vienna, Jos. 16 September 1836; Berlin, Kgst. 3 August 1837.

In Hungarian (translated by K. Lengey) Budapest 1839.

(For a German opera on the same subject, see Lortzing's *Czaar und Zimmermann*, 1837).

SPOHR: *Pietro von Abano*

13 October. Cassel

Text by K. Pfeiffer (founded on a story by L. Tieck), originally written for Curschmann (see 1828). Two acts.

Revived Munich 13 April 1890.

BELLINI: *Il Pirata*

27 October. Milan, Sc.

Text by F. Romani. Two acts.

Bellini's first international success; still occasionally given in Italy; one of the latest revivals was at Rome on 1 January 1935.

In Italian also:

VIENNA 25 February 1828.

DRESDEN 31 October 1829.

LONDON 17 April 1830.

MADRID 9 May 1830.

PARIS 1 February 1832.

NEW YORK 5 December 1832.

LISBON 7 May 1834.

HAVANA 1834.

MEXICO 16 January 1835.

ALGIERS Spring 1839.

MALTA 1840.

BERLIN, KGST. 28 January 1843.

ST. PETERSBURG Spring 1843.

VALPARAISO 1845.

BUENOS AIRES 1 January 1850.

In German (translated by G. Ott): Graz 20 January 1830; Budapest 23 August 1830; Munich 31 October 1830; Prague Summer 1831; Berlin, Kgst. 31 August 1831; Amsterdam 1833 (here translated by F. Ellmenreich); Agram 1834; St. Petersburg 11 November 1836; Vienna 20 February 1840, etc.

In French (translated by E. Duprez, music adapted by P. Crémont): Lyons 24 February 1835; Toulouse 24 November 1835 (music arranged by J. Cadaux); Liége 8 February 1836; Amsterdam Spring 1836; Brussels 10 August 1838.

ONSLOW: *Le Colporteur* ou *L'Enfant du Bûcheron*

22 November. Paris, O.C.

Text by F. A. E. de Planard. Three acts.

The most successful of Onslow's three operas.

In French also given at Ghent 13 February 1828 (until 1863!); Liége 25 February 1828; Brussels 30 October 1828 (revived 17 May 1839), etc.

In German (as *Der Spion oder Alexis der Findling im Walde*, translated by J. Kupelwieser), Graz 9 August 1828; Budapest 9 March 1829; Prague May 1829, etc.; (as *Der Hausirer*, translated by C. A. L. von Lichtenstein), Berlin 19 August 1828.

In Danish (translated by J. L. Heiberg), Copenhagen 28 October 1828.

In English (as *The Emissary; or, The Revolt of Moscow*, adapted by B. Livius), London, D.L. 13 May 1831.

CARAFA: *Masaniello*, ou *Le Pêcheur napolitain*

27 December. Paris, O.C.

Text by C. Moreau and A. M. Lafortelle (the same subject as in Auber's *La Muette de Portici*, produced at the Opéra two months later).

Given at the O.C. 136 times and revived at the Th. Château d'Eau 10 August 1882. In French also, Ghent 19 March 1828; Amsterdam 1834, etc.

1828

DONIZETTI: *L'Esule di Roma* ossia *Il Proscritto*

2 January. Naples, S.C.

Text by D. Gilardoni. Two acts.

Given at Venice Spring 1831 as *Settimio ossia L'Esule di Roma*.

In Italian also, London 4 February 1832; Madrid 21 May 1832; Corfu Autumn 1832; Cagliari, Sardinia Autumn 1833; Ragusa Carnival 1838; Lisbon 13 June 1839; Nice Carnival 1840; Malta Summer 1841.

In German (translated by G. Ott), Graz 1 August 1832; Vienna, Jos. 26 September 1832; Prague March 1837.

MAURER: *Aloise*

16 January. Hanover

Text by F. I. von Holbein (founded on a novel by E. Wodomerius). Two acts.

The most successful opera of the well-known violinist.

In German also, Riga 22 July 1828; Hamburg 30 August 1828; Vienna 9 July 1829; Dresden 14 December 1834, etc. Revived Cassel 25 February 1869.

In Danish (translated by J. L. Heiberg), Copenhagen 29 January 1830.

AUBER: *La Muette de Portici*

29 February. Paris, O.

Text by A. E. Scribe and G. Delavigne. Five acts.

Auber's most famous work, and one of the greatest successes at the Paris Opéra; the 100th performance there was as early as 23 April 1840, the 500th 14 June 1880. Very successful in other countries as well, especially in Germany (at least five contemporary versions). It is well known that a performance (not the first performance though as sometimes stated) at Brussels 25 August 1830, gave the signal to the outbreak of the Belgian revolution, which led to the independence of the country.

Outside France produced at:

RUDOLSTADT 16 October 1828 (for the first time in German, translated by C. A. L. von Lichtenstein).

ANTWERP 27 November 1828 and Brussels 12 February 1829 (in French).

BUDAPEST 4 December 1828 (in German) and 14 August 1841 (in Hungarian, translated by P. Szilágyi; the translation already published Kassán 1833).

BERLIN 12 January 1829 (in German, Lichtenstein's translation); last revived there 24 April 1930.

HAMBURG 24 March 1829 (in German, translated by A. Lewald); there are other German versions by K. A. Ritter (Mannheim 14 June 1829) and by T. von Haupt (Dessau 21 April 1830).

VIENNA, JOS. 9 April 1829 (as *Die Stumme, oder Untreue und edle Rache*, translated by A. Prix); Kä. 12 February 1830 (Ritter's translation).

LONDON, D.L. 4 May 1829 (as *Masaniello; or, The Dumb Girl of Portici*, translated by J. Kenney, music adapted by T. S. Cooke and B. Livius); D.L. 24 March 1841 (in German); C.G. 23 June 1845 (in French) and 15 March 1849 (in Italian, translated by S. M. Maggioni).

PRAGUE 30 July 1829 (in German) and 8 January 1837 (in Czech, translated by J. K. Chmelenský). New Czech version by Mužík published 1891.

EDINBURGH 30 July 1829 and Dublin 2 December 1829 (in English).

AMSTERDAM 1829 (in Dutch, translated by C. Vreedenberg); 1834 (in French) and 1837 (in German).

COPENHAGEN 22 May 1830 (in Danish, translated by J. L. Heiberg).

WARSAW 15 January 1831 (in Polish, translated by J. D. Minasowicz).

AGRAM (ZAGREB) Summer 1831 (in German) and 27 February 1877 (in Croatian, translated by J. E. Tomić).

NEW YORK 15 August 1831 (in French); 28 November 1831 (in English); November 1854 (in German); and 18 June 1855 (in Italian).

TRIESTE Carnival 1832 (for the first time in Italian, translated by C. Bassi, additional music by Colla and Donizetti; subsequently given at Venice, S. Ben. 21 November 1834; Rome 30 May 1835; Naples 6 July 1836 (as *Manfredi Primo, Rè di Napoli*); Florence 8 September 1836; Milan 26 December 1838, etc.; given at Rome Spring 1847 as *Il Pescatore di Brindisi*; the first French opera which made a real success in Italy).

BUCHAREST 30 December 1833 (in German); Jassy February 1842 (in German).

ST. PETERSBURG 25 January 1834 (in German), 1847 (in Italian) and 8 December 1857 (in Russian); Moscow Carnival 1845 (in Italian) and 1858 (in Russian).

BASLE 8 December 1834 (in German).

MADRID 19 November 1835; Barcelona 17 March 1841 (in Italian).

STOCKHOLM 19 March 1836 (in Swedish, translated by B. H. Crusell).

BATAVIA Autumn 1836 and Soerabaya 26 October 1865 (in French).

ST. LOUIS 3 August 1837 (in English).

LISBON 4 April 1838 (in Italian).

HELSINKI 14 May 1841 (in German).

CAGLIARI, SARDINIA Carnival 1843 (in Italian).

CHRISTIANIA 28 April 1844 (in Norwegian).

SYDNEY 10 November 1845 (in English).

RIO DE JANEIRO 1846 (in French) and May 1891 (in Italian).

MONTEVIDEO October 1853 (in French).

BUENOS AIRES 23 March 1854 (in French) and 19 February 1874 (in Italian).

MEXICO August 1854 (in Italian).

SANTIAGO, CHILE 1858 (in French).

MALTA 1865 (in Italian).

CONSTANTINOPLE December 1869 (in Italian).

CAIRO 1870 (in Italian).

LJUBLJANA 1904 (in Slovenian; earlier given there in German).

MARSCHNER: *Der Vampyr*

29 March. Leipzig

Text by W. A. Wohlbrück. Two acts.

The first of Marschner's more important operas.

In German also, Budapest 29 December 1828; Prague 1829; Amsterdam 1834; Basle 4 February 1839; Riga 1839–40; Graz 27 January 1849.

Given at the Vienna O. as late as 15 October 1884; at Berlin, Kroll's as late as 8 July 1885 (O. 27 September 1890); and at Stuttgart (where Lindpaintner's opera of the same title, see below, was very successful) as late as 8 February 1891. Revived (in a new version by H. Pfitzner), Stuttgart 28 May 1924; Berlin 2 April 1927; Basle 7 April 1927, etc.

In English (translated by J. R. Planché, music arranged by W. Hawes), London, Ly. 25 August 1829.

In Russian, St. Petersburg 4 November 1833.

In French (translated by J. Ramoux and A. Aulagnier), Liége 27 January 1845.

Anonymous Dutch translation published Amsterdam 1835.

For the librettist's sources see Lindpainter, *Der Vampyr*, col.715.

DONIZETTI: *La Regina di Golconda*

12 May. Genoa, C.F.

Text by F. Romani (a new version of the 18th century subject, see 1766). Two acts.

First new opera at the Carlo Felice Theatre (opened 7 April 1828).

Outside Italy, given at Madrid 3 January 1842; Lisbon 12 June 1842; Cagliari, Sardinia Autumn 1842; Vienna 12 May 1843; Nice Autumn 1844; Barcelona 13 October 1849; St. Petersburg 18 January 1851. Revived Rome 3 December 1890.

VERSTOVSKY: *Pan Tvardovsky*

Панъ Твардовскій

5 June. Moscow

Text by K. S. Aksakov. Three acts.

St. Petersburg 9 February 1829 (revived 1852), etc. One of the more important works of the pre-Glinka period of Russian opera.

MORLACCHI: *Colombo*

21 June. Genoa, C.F.

Text by F. Romani. Two acts.

Second new opera at the Carlo Felice Theatre.

In Italian also, Dresden 2 May 1829; Leipzig 25 May 1830; revived Genoa Spring 1839; Sevilla June 1839.

MERCADANTE: *Gabriella di Vergy*

8 August. Lisbon, S.C.

Text by A. Profumo (partly taken from Tottola's libretto of the same title, see 1816). Two acts.

Given in a new version (text altered by E. Bidera) at Genoa Spring 1832; Milan 27 March 1837; Naples, S.C. Winter 1839, etc.

In Italian also, Barcelona 25 April 1837; Odessa Summer 1839; Trieste 5 October 1839; Cagliari,

Sardinia Autumn 1840; Dresden 11 February 1842; Malta 1852.

In German, Prague 15 December 1841.

ROSSINI: *Le Comte Ory*

20 August. Paris, O.

Text by A. E. Scribe and C. G. Delestre-Poirson. Two acts.

The first of Rossini's two French operas; it comprises the greater part of the music of *Il Viaggio a Reims* (see 1825) and 12 additional numbers.

Very successful in Paris; given at the Opéra 434 times until 18 January 1884 (last revived there 25 October 1880).

In French also, Liége 27 February 1829; Antwerp 17 March 1829; Brussels 24 August 1829; New York 22 August 1831; London, St. J.'s 20 June 1849; Baden-Baden 27 July 1863.

In Italian (translator not mentioned), London, Hm. 28 February 1829; Venice, S. Ben. 2 July 1829; Milan 10 May 1830; Barcelona 1 July 1830; Rome 11 October 1830 (revived 9 October 1890); Mexico 1833; Odessa 1839; St. Petersburg Carnival 1849; Malta 1870; Lisbon 20 March 1879.

In German (translated by F. von Biedenfeld), Berlin, Kgst. 11 February 1829; Graz 30 March 1829; Budapest 8 August 1829; Prague 24 October 1829; Vienna 3 November 1829; Bucharest 1834, etc. There were other German translations by T. von Haupt, and by K. A. Ritter published about the same time.

In Polish (translated by J. Slowaczyński), Warsaw 27 March 1830.

In Russian (translated by G. A. Elkan), St. Petersburg Winter 1838.

Revived Paris, Petite Scène 5 June 1926 (in French); Turin, T.R. March 1930 (in Italian).

LINDPAINTNER: *Der Vampyr*

21 September. Stuttgart

Text by C. M. Heigel. Three acts.

Munich 19 October 1828; Vienna 1 September 1829; Brünn 12 March 1832, etc. Given at Linz 20 April 1840 as *Isolde, Gräfin von Port d'Amour.* Last revived Stuttgart 21 December 1856.

The librettos of both Marschner's and Lindpaintner's operas are founded on J. W. Polidori's tale *The Vampyre* (first published in 1819 and then considered to be the work of Byron), by way of a French melodrame by C. Nodier, P. F. A. Carmouche, and A. de Jouffroy (Paris 1820), translated into German by L. Ritter in 1822.

RIES: *Die Räuberbraut*

15 October. Frankfort

Text G. Döring. Three acts.

Ries's most successful work. Leipzig 4 August 1829; Berlin 8 February 1831, etc.

In German also, Paris, Th.I. 22 June 1830; Amsterdam 1838.

In English (rival versions), London, Ly. 15 July 1829 (translated by E. Fitzball, music arranged by W. Hawes) and C.G. 22 October 1829 (translated by I. Pocock).

In French (translated by J. Ramoux), Liége 11 December 1839.

According to the Vienna *Allgemeine Theaterzeitung* (1829, p.470), Döring seems to have altered an earlier libretto, which was partly already composed by Ries. This accounts for the fact that, besides Döring, two other authors are mentioned as the librettist, viz., C. W. Haeser (Riemann) and J. J. Reiff (Goedeke, III).

CURSCHMANN: *Abdul und Erinieh* oder *Die Toten*

29 October. Cassel

Text by S. tor Hardt. One act.

The only opera of Curschmann who was a pupil of Spohr. Vocal score published 1836.

ŠKROUP: *Oldřich a Božena*

14 December. Prague

Text by J. K. Chmelenský. Three acts.

Early Czech historical opera. Škroup's second attempt (see 1826).

In German (translated by F. V. Ernst), Prague 12 February 1833; Coburg October 1835.

Revived Prague 7 November 1847 (in Czech).

1829

AUBER: *La Fiancée*

10 January. Paris, O.C.

Text by A. E. Scribe. Three acts.

Last revived at the O.C., Paris 10 February 1858 (273 performances altogether); outside Paris produced at:

BRUSSELS 8 April 1829 (in French).

BERLIN, KGST. 26 July 1829 (in German, translated by L. Angely) and O. 3 August 1829 (translated by C. A. L. von Lichtenstein); other German versions by T. von Haupt and by F. Ellmenreich were published about the same time. Given on German stages until 1861.

NEW YORK 21 August 1829 (in French) and 30 March 1832 (in English).

GRAZ 7 September 1829 (in German).

LONDON, D.L. 4 February 1830 (in English, as *The National Guard; or Bride and no Bride*, translated by J. R. Planché. This version was also given at Edinburgh 22 December 1830; New York 30 March 1832; and Philadelphia 13 May 1850).

PRAGUE September 1830 (in German).

BUDAPEST 17 January 1831 (in German).

VIENNA 21 April 1831 (in German, translated by K. A. Ritter).

COPENHAGEN 22 April 1831, Christiania 1834 (in Danish, translated by J. L. Heiberg).

ST. PETERSBURG 25 June 1832 (in Russian, translated by R. M. Zotov) and February 1834 (in German).

WARSAW 28 June 1832 (in Polish, translated by J. L. Piotrowski).

AMSTERDAM 1834 (in French).

TURIN, T. CARIGNANO Autumn 1835 (in Italian).

BASLE 13 November 1835 (in German).

BUCHAREST 1835 (in German).

SANTIAGO, CHILE 1851 (in French).

Given at Stockholm 30 May 1835 as a comedy (without music; Swedish version by O. U. Torsslow).

BELLINI: *La Straniera*

14 February. Milan, Sc.

Text by F. Romani (founded on d'Arlincourt's novel *L'Etrangère*, 1825). Two acts.

Very successful in Italy and abroad. In Italian also produced at:

DRESDEN 8 November 1830.

MADRID 3 December 1830.

LONDON 23 June 1832.

PARIS 4 November 1832.

CORFU Autumn 1833.

NEW YORK 10 November 1834.

VIENNA 20 May 1835.

LISBON 25 June 1835.

MEXICO 1837.

OPORTO 1837.

ALGIERS Carnival 1838.

CONSTANTINOPLE Carnival 1839.

ODESSA Spring 1839.

MALTA Carnival 1841.

PALMA, MALLORCA Carnival 1841.

BERLIN, KGST. 23 May 1842.

SANTIAGO, CHILE 1846.

RIO DE JANEIRO 2 December 1846.

WARSAW June 1855.

BUENOS AIRES 9 April 1864.

BUCHAREST 1876.

In German (translated by G. Ott): Graz 19 February 1831; Vienna 24 November 1831; Prague 26 January 1832; Berlin, Kgst. 3 February 1832; Budapest 30 July 1832; Amsterdam 1834; Bucharest 1834; Agram May 1835; Basle 10 February 1840. Given on German stages until 1884.

In Danish (translated by J. L. Heiberg), Copenhagen 4 December 1834.

In Hungarian (translated by J. Szerdahelyi), Budapest 1837.

In Swedish (translated by N. E. W. af Wetterstedt), Stockholm 23 January 1841.

Still given in Italy; one of the latest revivals was at the Scala, Milan 22 April 1935.

BOIELDIEU: *Les deux Nuits*

20 May. Paris, O.C.

Text by A. E. Scribe and J. N. Bouilly. Three acts.

Boieldieu's last opera.

In French also, Liége 1 February 1830; Antwerp 20 May 1831; Brussels 15 December 1831.

In English, London, C.G. 17 November 1829 (as *The Night before the Wedding*, translated by E. Fitzball, music adapted and enlarged by Bishop; see Fitzball's *Memoirs*, Vol. I, pp.183–192; this version was also given at Sydney on 4 May 1874).

In German (translated by I. F. Castelli), Budapest 21 December 1829; Hamburg 23 April 1830; Berlin, Kgst. 14 September 1830; Brünn 3 November 1830; Prague 15 March 1832; Vienna 17 May 1834.

In Danish (translated by J. L. Heiberg), Copenhagen 21 September 1832.

In Russian (translated by D. T. Lensky), St. Petersburg 1834.

SPONTINI: *Agnes von Hohenstaufen*

12 June. Berlin, O.

Text by E. Raupach. Three acts.

Spontini's last opera. The first act had already been given on 28 May 1827.

Revived Berlin 6 December 1837 (considerably altered).

ROSSINI: *Guillaume Tell*

3 August. Paris, O.

Text by V. J. Etienne de Jouy and H. L. F. Bis (founded on Schiller's drama). Four acts.

Rossini's last opera and (apart from his *Barbiere*) his greatest success. After *Guillaume Tell*, he voluntarily concluded his unprecedentedly successful career and spent the last 39 years of his life without writing another opera.

The 100th performance at the Paris O. was on 17 September 1834, the 500th on 10 February 1868; given there 868 times until 1912 and revived once more 23 April 1932. The original 4-act version was reduced to 3 acts on 1 June 1831. First given in Italian at the Th.I. 26 December 1836.

On account of its political subject, the opera had to be given in many countries in different disguises and with more or less essential alterations in the original libretto; see below, under London, Berlin, Milan, Rome, St. Petersburg, Warsaw, the various alternative titles. As late as in 1866 the censor at Palermo demanded changes in the text. At Riga the opera had to be given as *Karl der Kühne* right up to the end of the 19th century.

Outside Paris, the opera was first produced at:

BRUSSELS 18 March 1830 (in French).

FRANKFORT 24 March 1830 (in German, translated by T. von Haupt, music arranged by K. W. F. Guhr).

BUDAPEST 27 March 1830 and 3 April 1830 (in German; divided into 2 parts of 2 acts each); 9 May 1856 (in Hungarian, translated by L. Nádaskay).

LONDON, D.L. 1 May 1830 (as *Hofer; or The Tell of the Tyrol*, adapted by J. R. Planché, music arranged by Bishop); D.L. 3 December 1838 (new English version by A. Bunn; music again arranged by Bishop); H.M.'s 11 July 1839 (in Italian); C.G. 6 June 1845 (in French); the latest revival in London was at the London Opera House, Kingsway, 15 November 1911 (in French).

GRAZ 12 May 1830 (in German).

VIENNA 24 June 1830 and 22 July 1830 (in German, as at Budapest); very mutilated; with all the original music only 26 June 1848; in Italian 9 April 1853.

BERLIN, O. 18 October 1830 (as *Andreas Hofer*, translated from Planché's English version by C. A. L. von Lichtenstein); Kgst. 7 June 1838 (reduced to three acts, as in Paris); O. 6 October 1842 (for the first time in the original form; Haupt's translation).

BRÜNN 24 November 1830 (in German).

PRAGUE 30 December 1830 (in German) and 14 December 1866 (in Czech, translated by J. Böhm).

DRESDEN 28 January 1831 (acts 1–2, in Italian) and 29 January 1831 (acts 3–4, in Italian).

LUCCA 17 September 1831 (in Italian, translated by C. Bassi); Florence 27 October 1831; Naples, S.C. Spring 1833 as *Il Governatore Gessler e Guglielmo Tell*; etc. Given at Milan, Sc. 26

December 1836 as *Guglielmo Vallace;* at Rome 30 May 1840 as *Rodolfo di Sterlinga.*

NEW YORK 19 September 1831 (in English); 16 June 1845 (in French); 9 April 1855 (in Italian); and 18 April 1866 (in German).

AGRAM (ZAGREB) 1834 (in German) and 12 May 1887 (in Croatian, translated by J. E. Tomić).

ZURICH 1833 (in German).

AMSTERDAM 1834 (in German) and 1835 (in French).

MADRID 19 November 1834 (in Italian).

MEXICO 16 September 1836 (in Italian).

ST. PETERSBURG 11 November 1836 (in Russian, as *Karl Smily [Charles the Bold],* adapted by R. M. Zotov); June 1838 (in German); Carnival 1847 (in Italian, as *Carlo il Temerario*); Moscow Autumn 1842 (in German).

LISBON 25 November 1836 (in Italian).

COPENHAGEN Summer 1841 (in German, by a company from Neustrelitz) and 4 September 1842 (in Danish, translated by T. Overskou); Christiania (Oslo) 1851 (in Danish).

NEW ORLEANS 13 December 1842 (in French).

BUENOS AIRES 30 August 1854 (in French) and 19 November 1870 (in Italian).

WARSAW June 1855 (in Italian, as *Carlo il Temerario*).

STOCKHOLM 4 June 1856 (in Swedish, translated by C. W. A. Strandberg).

HELSINKI 22 July 1857 (in German).

HAVANA 1858 (in Italian).

SOERABAYA 16 November 1866 (in French).

MALTA 1870 (in Italian).

SYDNEY Autumn 1870 (in English).

RIO DE JANEIRO 20 June 1871 (in Italian).

BUCHAREST January 1876 (in French).

DUBLIN 4 April 1877 (in Italian).

LEMBERG 21 May 1878 (in Polish).

LJUBLJANA 1902 (in Slovenian).

An open-air production at the Arènes, Ermont (near Enghien) took place on 1 June 1902.

Some of the latest revivals outside France were at New York, M. 21 March 1931; Leningrad 1932 (in Russian); Berlin, O. 3 March 1934 (new German version by J. Kapp); Florence 9 May 1939 (at the fifth Maggio Musicale Fiorentino).

PIXIS: *Bibiana oder Die Kapelle im Walde*

8 October. Aachen

Text by L. Lax (founded on a novel by H. Cuno). Three acts.

In German also given at Paris, Th.I. 1 May 1830 and Prague 12 June 1830.

HALÉVY: *La Dilettante d'Avignon*

7 November. Paris, O.C.

Text by F. B. Hoffman and Léon Halévy (the brother of the composer). One act.

Halévy's first success; given at the O.C. 119 times until 1836.

In French also, Liége 16 December 1830; Brussels 28 August 1837.

MARSCHNER: *Der Templer und die Jüdin*

22 December. Leipzig

Text by W. A. Wohlbrück (founded on Scott's *Ivanhoe*). Three acts.

Berlin 3 August 1831, etc. In German also given at:

BUDAPEST 7 May 1832.

AMSTERDAM 1838.

PRAGUE 4 October 1839.

RIGA 1839–40.

ST. PETERSBURG 1840.

LONDON, PRINCE'S 17 June 1840.

GRAZ 7 March 1846.

BASLE 11 December 1846.

VIENNA 10 January 1849.

GOTHENBURG 27 January 1865.

NEW YORK 29 January 1872.

In Danish (translated by T. Overskou), Copenhagen 21 April 1834.

In Hungarian (translated by A. Radó), Budapest 8 March 1890.

Revived (in a new version by H. Pfitzner), Strasbourg 20 April 1912; Cologne 25 September 1913, etc.

CHÉLARD: *La Table et le Logement*

24 December. Paris, O.C.

Text by J. J. Gabriel and T. M. Dumersan. One act.

In German (as *Der Student*), Munich 19 February 1832.

In English (as *The Students of Jena; or, The Family Concert*, translated by J. R. Planché), London, D.L. 4 June 1833 (with Maria Malibran).

1830

AUBER: *Fra Diavolo ou L'Hôtellerie de Terracine*

28 January. Paris, O.C.

Text by A. E. Scribe. Three acts.

Two years after his most important grand opéra, *La Muette de Portici*, now Auber's most successful comic opera was produced; given at the O.C. 909 times until 1911.

Outside France:

BRUSSELS 15 July 1830 (in French).

BERLIN, KGST. 16 July 1830 (in German, translated by K. A. Ritter) and O. 3 August 1830 (translated by K. Blum); Kgst. 18 October 1848 (in Italian, recitatives by C. E. di Barbieri); Vict. Th. 24 May 1862 (in French).

GRAZ 9 August 1830 (in German).

HAMBURG 11 September 1830 (in German).

VIENNA 18 September 1830 (in German).

BUDAPEST 23 October 1830 (in German) and 29 September 1835 (in Hungarian).

ST. PETERSBURG 26 January 1831 (in Russian, translated by A. Rotchev and R. M. Zotov); February 1834 (in German); Carnival 1858 (in Italian). Revived Leningrad 25 September 1920.

LONDON, D.L. 1 February 1831 (as *The Devil's Brother*, music arranged by A. Lee); C.G. 3 November 1831 (translated by M. R. Lacy); St. J.'s 20 April 1849 (in French); Ly. 4 July 1857 (in Italian, translated by S. M. Maggioni, with recitatives and some new numbers).

BRÜNN 13 March 1831 (in German).

COPENHAGEN 19 May 1831 (in Danish, translated by T. Overskou); Christiania 1833.

AGRAM (ZAGREB) 1831 (in German) and 15 October 1887 (in Croatian, translated by A. M. Bišćan).

PRAGUE 4 August 1831 (in German) and 3 September 1843 (in Czech, translated by J. J. Kolár). Revived in new Czech translation 24 May 1910.

WARSAW 13 August 1831 (in Polish, translated by K. Forster).

NEW YORK 17 October 1831 (in French); 20 June 1833 (in English); 16 November 1858 (in German); 21 December 1864 (in Italian).

PHILADELPHIA 19 April 1833 (in English, translated by J. T. Reynoldson).

STOCKHOLM 17 May 1833 (in Swedish, translated by B. H. Crusell) and 10 June 1863 (in German).

CLAUSENBURG June 1833 (in Hungarian, translated by J. Szerdahelyi).

ZURICH 1833 (in German); Basle 8 October 1834, etc.

BUCHAREST 2 January 1834 (in German).

CALCUTTA 31 October 1836 (in French).

HELSINKI 19 November 1840 (in German) and 29 May 1874 (in Finnish, translated by A. Törneroos).

SYDNEY 14 August 1845 (in English).

BUENOS AIRES Spring 1852 (in French) and 30 June 1887 (in Italian).

BARCELONA 11 November 1853 (in Italian).

DUBLIN 6 August 1857 (in Italian).

OPORTO 30 August 1861 (in Portuguese).

MALTA 1866 (in Italian).

FLORENCE 5 January 1867 (in Italian).

CAIRO 1870 (in Italian).

TORONTO June 1874 (in English).

LISBON 17 March 1875 (in Italian) and 7 May 1878 (in French).

NAPLES, T. SANNAZARO 1 April 1875 (in Italian).

MEXICO 11 May 1879 (in French) and 23 February 1895 (in Spanish).

REVAL 26 October 1882 (in German).

RIO DE JANEIRO May 1891 (in Italian).

LJUBLJANA 1899 (in Slovenian).

MADRID 28 May 1919 (in Spanish, as *Zerlina*).

SOFIA 2 April 1924 (in Bulgarian; translation published already Varna 1905).

RIGA 8 November 1924 (in Lettish; earlier given there in German).

KAUNAS 23 September 1931 (in Lithuanian).

Still given in France, Germany, and other countries; revived in Italy, Turin 26 January 1929, etc.; in London, R.C.M. 20 November 1934 and Sadler's Wells 20 February 1935 (new English version by E. J. Dent).

BELLINI: *I Capuleti e i Montecchi*

11 March. Venice, F.

Text by F. Romani (founded on Shakespeare's *Romeo and Juliet;* first set to music by Vaccai, see 1825; Romani made some alterations for Bellini's new setting). Four parts.

Bellini introduced into this opera parts of his unsuccessful *Zaira*, written for the inauguration of the Teatro Regio, Parma (16 May 1829). Beginning with a performance at Bologna on 27 October 1832, *I Capuleti* was nearly always given with the last act substituted from Vaccai's *Giulietta e Romeo* (see 1825); the original form was restored as late as in December 1895, at Naples.

In Italian also produced at:

DRESDEN 1 October 1831.

MADRID 18 June 1832.

PARIS, TH.I. 10 January 1833.

LONDON 20 July 1833.

BERLIN, KGST. 5 June 1834.

CORFU 15 January 1835.

ODESSA Carnival 1835.

LISBON 9 February 1835.

HAVANA 12 January 1836.

MEXICO 1836.

DUBLIN 28 January 1837.

VIENNA 18 June 1839.

ATHENS Carnival 1841.

CEPHALONIA Carnival 1841.

COPENHAGEN 24 January 1841.

CONSTANTINOPLE Autumn 1841.

ST. PETERSBURG 1843.

BUCHAREST Autumn 1843.

RIO DE JANEIRO 1844.

VALPARAISO 1844.

TRINIDAD Autumn 1844.

BOSTON May 1847.

PHILADELPHIA 6 August 1847.

NEW YORK 28 January 1848.

BUENOS AIRES 23 October 1852.

In German (translated by J. C. Grünbaum), Berlin, Kgst. 18 June 1832; (tanslated by G. Ott) Graz 13 July 1832; Vienna, Jos. 23 November 1832 and Kä. 1 December 1832.

In German also, Brünn 10 April 1833; Prague 8 June 1833; Budapest 8 June 1833; Bucharest 18 March 1834; Amsterdam 1836; St. Petersburg 1836; Basle 20 April 1836; Riga 1837; Liége 22 May 1839; Helsinki 17 June 1839; Agram Autumn 1841; Gothenburg 26 January 1862.

(It may be mentioned that there are in the British Museum copies of two German versions, the one translated by J. C. Grünbaum [Berlin, n.d.], the other translation by F. Ellmenreich [Breslau, n.d.], which are practically identical.

In Hungarian (translated by J. Szerdahelyi), Clausenburg 29 May 1836 and Budapest 18 February 1839.

In Russian, St. Petersburg 1 March 1837.

In Czech (translated by V. A. Swoboda), Prague 13 May 1838.

In Danish (translated by N. C. L. Abrahams), Copenhagen 25 January 1845.

In French (translated by G. Oppelt), Ghent 9 November 1845; Antwerp 5 January 1851; (translated by C. Nuitter), Paris, O. 7 September 1859.

In Polish (translated by J. B. Wagner), Warsaw 10 April 1847.

Still given in Italy; one of the latest revivals was at Turin on 26 December 1934.

WOLFRAM: *Der Bergmönch*

14 March. Dresden

Text by K. B. von Miltitz. Three acts.

Successful on German stages: Prague 3 October 1831; Berlin 3 August 1832, etc.

SPOHR: *Der Alchymist*

28 July. Cassel

Text by "Fr. Georg Schmidt" (pseud. for K. Pfeiffer), based on a story by Washington Irving. Three acts.

In German also, Prague 23 November 1838.

In English (translated by T. H. Bayly, the songs by E. Fitzball; music arranged and enlarged by Bishop), London, D.L. 20 March 1832.

Spohr's opera was revived at Essen on 28 May 1925.

AUBER: *Le Dieu et la Bayadère* ou *La Courtisane amoureuse*

13 October. Paris, O.

Text by A. E. Scribe. Opéra-ballet. Two acts.

Given in Paris 146 times until 1866; 100th performance 4 June 1838, last revival 22 January 1866.

In French also, Brussels 7 February 1833, etc.

In German (translated by C. A. L. von Lichtenstein), Berlin 8 April 1831; Vienna 3 February 1832; Graz 4 February 1837; Prague 1848; Riga 1851. The latest revival seems to have been at Hamburg 19 March 1881.

In English (as *The Maid of Cashmere*, translated by E. Fitzball, music arranged by Bishop), London, D.L. 16 March 1833; (translated by J. H. Horncastle) Grecian Th. 1 March 1844; Bishop's version was also given at New York 3 October 1836 and on many other English and American stages.

In Danish (translated by T. Overskou), Copenhagen 28 May 1833.

In Russian, St. Petersburg 24 November 1835.

In Dutch, Amsterdam Spring 1836 (translation published 1835).

In Swedish (translated by E. A. Wallmark), Stockholm 14 March 1863.

DONIZETTI: *Anna Bolena*

26 December. Milan, T. Carcano

Text by F. Romani. Two acts.

It was with this his thirtieth opera that Donizetti entered the first rank of Italian composers, rivalling Rossini and Bellini.

Outside Italy, given at:

LONDON, HM. 8 July 1831 (in Italian; last revived D.L. 1 August 1871), and Princess's 12 January 1847 (in English, translated by C. Jefferys).

PARIS, TH.I. 1 September 1831 (in Italian; first Donizetti opera in Paris).

GRAZ 27 April 1832.

MADRID 21 August 1832 (in Italian).

VIENNA, JOS. 31 January 1833 (in German, translated by J. Kupelwieser).

BRÜNN 24 February 1833; Prague April 1834 (in German).

VIENNA, KÄ. 26 February 1833 (in German, translated by K. J. Braun von Braunthal) and 4 April 1835 (in Italian).

BUDAPEST 29 August 1833 (in German) and 1840 (in Hungarian, translated by R. Schodel-Klein).

BERLIN, KGST. 26 August 1833 (in German) and 1 July 1841 (in Italian).

MALTA 15 September 1833 (in Italian).

LISBON 23 February 1834 (in Italian).

DRESDEN 5 March 1834 (in Italian).

HAVANA 1834 (in Italian).

LE HAVRE 25 November 1835 (apparently for the first time in French, translated by F. H. J. Castil-Blaze); Lyons February 1839; Lille 24 February 1839, etc.

MEXICO February 1836 (in Italian).

ODESSA 1836 (in Italian).

ZANTE 1837 (in Italian).

ANTWERP 7 March 1838 (in French).

BRUSSELS 29 March 1838 (in French).

ST. PETERSBURG Spring 1838 (in German) and Carnival 1845 (in Italian).

NEW ORLEANS November 1839 (in French).

DUBLIN 11 September 1840 (in Italian); revived 13 September 1871.

GENEVA Autumn 1840 (in French).

NEW YORK 2 August 1843 (in French), 6 May 1844 (in English) and 7 January 1850 (in Italian).

PHILADELPHIA 7 October 1843 (in French), 11 April 1844 (in English, translated by J. R. Fry) and 3 December 1847 (in Italian).

ATHENS Autumn 1843 (in Italian).

STOCKHOLM 17 June 1844 (in Swedish, translated by N. E. W. af Wetterstedt).

HAGUE 1844 (in French).

CONSTANTINOPLE Carnival 1844 (in Italian).

SMYRNA Spring 1844 (in Italian).

COPENHAGEN Spring 1844 (in Italian).

RIO DE JANEIRO 1844 (in Italian).

WARSAW October 1844 (in Italian).

SANTIAGO, CHILE 1847 (in Italian).

LUGANO 1849 (in Italian).

BUENOS AIRES 17 December 1854 (in Italian).

The latest revivals in Italy were at Milan 20 January 1877; Brescia August 1879; and Leghorn 11 August 1881.

1831

CARNICER: *Colombo*

12 January. Madrid, T. del Principe

Romani's text (first set to music by Morlacchi, see 1828). Two acts.

First *Columbus* opera written by a Spanish composer.

BELLINI: *La Sonnambula*

6 March. Milan, T. Carcano

Text by F. Romani. Two acts.

Very successful all over the world, and still given in Italy.

The first performances were at:

LONDON, HM. 28 July 1831 (in Italian) and D.L. 1 May 1833 (in English, translated by S. Beazley, music adapted by Bishop; Maria Malibran's début on the English stage); 100th performance at C.G. 3 June 1889; given there until 1911.

PARIS, TH.I. 28 October 1831 (in Italian) and Th.L. 14 June 1867 (in French).

BUDAPEST 5 December 1832 (in German) and 19 June 1841 (in Hungarian, translated by F. S. Deáky).

MADRID 21 July 1834 (in Italian).

DRESDEN 27 September 1834 (in Italian).

VIENNA, JOS. 12 November 1834 (in German, translated by G. Ott) and Kä. 15 May 1835 (in Italian).

CORFU 9 December 1834 (in Italian).

PRESSBURG 20 December 1834 (in German).

PRAGUE May 1835 (in German) and 7 April 1865 (in Czech, translated by B. Peška).

NEW YORK 13 November 1835 (in English), 13 May 1844 (in Italian) and 4 January 1871 (in German).

BOSTON 28 December 1835; Philadelphia 11 February 1836; St. Louis 19 June 1838 (in English).

HAVANA January 1836 (in Italian).

MEXICO 1 February 1836 (in Italian).

BERLIN, O. 25 May 1836 (in German, translated by F. Ellmenreich) and Kgst. 7 March 1842 (in Italian).

DUBLIN 17 January 1837 (in Italian).

BASLE 10 March 1837 (in German; revived 12 March 1902).

ST. PETERSBURG 29 May 1837 (in Russian) and Spring 1843 (in Italian); revived 10 October 1897 (in Russian).

LISBON 6 October 1837 (in Italian).

ANTWERP 10 January 1839 (in French, translated by E. Monnier.

BORDEAUX March 1839 (in French, translated by E. Monnier.

BRUSSELS 26 June 1839 (in French, translated by E. Monnier; last revived 8 May 1933).

HELSINKI 7 July 1839 (in German), 1876 (in Swedish) and 8 February 1878 (in Finnish, translated by A. Törneroos).

ODESSA 19 September 1839 (in Italian).

AMSTERDAM 1839 (in German) and Carnival 1845 (in Italian).

PALMA, MALLORCA Carnival 1840 (in Italian).

NEW ORLEANS 14 January 1840 (in French).

ATHENS Spring 1840 (in Italian).

WARSAW 2 June 1840 (in Polish, translated by K. K. Kurpiński).

AJACCIO, CORSICA Carnival 1841 (in Italian).

CONSTANTINOPLE November 1841 (in Italian).

COPENHAGEN 4 November 1842 (in Italian) and 2 November 1864 (in Danish, translated by A. M. Rosenkilde).

STOCKHOLM 9 January 1843 (in Swedish, translated by N. E. W. af Wetterstedt).

MALTA Carnival 1844 (in Italian).

VALPARAISO 1844 (in Italian).

AGRAM (ZAGREB) July 1844 (in German) and 30 October 1877 (in Croatian, translated by J. E. Tomić).

BUCHAREST 17 February 1845 (in Italian).

SYDNEY 9 December 1845 (in English).

RIO DE JANEIRO 14 September 1846 (in Italian).

EDINBURGH 9 March 1847 (in English).

CHRISTIANIA 23 January 1848 (in Danish).

BUENOS AIRES 27 January 1850 (in Italian); last revived 26 July 1934.

CHICAGO 29 July 1850 (in Italian; first opera there).

SAN FRANCISCO 12 February 1851 (in Italian; first opera there).

MARSEILLES 25 May 1852 (in French).

MONTEVIDEO 1852 (in Italian).

TUNIS March 1935 (in Italian).

BERTIN: *Fausto*

8 March. Paris, Th.I.

Text by the composer (based on Goethe's tragedy). Four acts.

The first Italian *Faust* opera and probably the only one ever written by a woman composer; it was unsuccessful, but is reported to have been not unworthy of its great subject.

REISSIGER: *Die Felsenmühle zu Estalières*

10 April. Dresden

Text by K. B. von Miltitz. Two acts.

The best opera of Reissiger, who was Marschner's successor at Dresden; popular overture.

Successful on German stages: Berlin 3 August 1834; Prague 20 March 1840.

In Danish (translated by T. Overskou), Copenhagen 14 March 1833.

In Hungarian, Clausenburg 21 June 1834; Budapest 14 July 1835.

In Russian, Moscow 1835.

RAIMONDI: *Il Ventaglio*

19 April. Naples, Fondo

Text by D. Gilardoni (founded on Goldoni's comedy of the same title). Two acts.

Successful in Italy, especially at Naples where it was last revived on 11 June 1898.

Outside Italy given at Malta Spring 1840; Corfu Carnival 1844; and Athens Carnival 1856.

A sequel *Palmetella maritata* (text by A. Passaro) was given at Naples in 1837; unsuccessful, like most sequels.

HÉROLD: *Zampa* ou *La Fiancée de Marbre*

3 May. Paris, O.C.

Text by A. H. J. Mélesville. Three acts.

Very successful in Paris; the 300th performance at the O.C. was on 12 November 1863; given there 694 times until 1913.

The first performances outside France were at:

MAYENCE 17 November 1831 (in German, translated by F. Ellmenreich).

HAMBURG 25 November 1831 (in German, translated by F. Ellmenreich).

GRAZ November 1831 (in German, translated by J. Kupelwieser).

ANTWERP 8 December 1831, Brussels 10 April 1832, etc. (in French).

COPENHAGEN 20 January 1832; Christiania 31 May 1841 (in Danish, translated by T. Overskou).

BERLIN, O. 31 January 1832 (in German, translated by K. Blum) and Kgst. 23 April 1849 (in Italian).

BUDAPEST 10 March 1832 (in German) and 3 November 1836 (in Hungarian).

BRÜNN 9 April 1832 (in German, translated by J. von Seyfried).

VIENNA 3 May 1832 (in German, translated by J. von Seyfried).

PRAGUE 28 September 1832 (in German) and 14 February 1841 (in Czech, translated by J. N. Štěpánek; the first act only; the whole opera 15 October 1843).

LONDON, HM. 19 April 1833 (in German, with a new finale of the third act by J. N. Hummel); Olympic 10 June 1833 (in English, as *The Bridal Promise*, adapted by J. Oxenford); D.L. 21 March 1836 (in English, as *The Corsair*, adapted

by W. Ball); St.J.'s 16 January 1850 (in French);
C.G. 5 August 1858 (in Italian).

AGRAM (ZAGREB) 1833 (in German).

NEW YORK 12 August 1833 (in French); 29 March
1841 (in English, translated by W. H. Latham);
21 May 1862 (in German); and 17 December
1866 (in Italian).

NAPLES, FONDO 28 December 1833; Turin Autumn
1834; Florence January 1835; Milan 2 September 1835, etc. (in Italian, translated by G.
Schmidt); revived in a new translation by A.
Zanardini, with recitatives by A. Mariani,
Genoa Spring 1861; with recitatives by F.
Faccio, Milan, Sc. 19 January 1889.

MOSCOW Winter 1833 (in Russian, translated by
D. T. Lensky).

ST. PETERSBURG 3 June 1834 (in Russian); 1835
(in German); and 29 November 1876 (in
Italian).

WARSAW 9 March 1834 (in Polish, translated by
J. Jasiński).

CLAUSENBURG 21 June 1834 (in Hungarian, translated by J. Szerdahelyi).

AMSTERDAM 1834 (in French) and October 1836
(in German).

BUCHAREST 1834 (in German).

BASLE 18 February 1835 (in German).

STOCKHOLM 19 February 1838 (in Swedish, translated by P. Westerstrand) and 16 June 1863 (in
German).

LISBON 31 July 1839 (in Italian).

BARCELONA 8 October 1839 (in Italian).

HELSINKI 9 October 1840 (in German).

CHRISTIANIA 31 May 1841 (in Danish); Norwegian translation by A. M. Rosenkilde published
1848.

RIO DE JANEIRO Autumn 1846 (in French).

BUENOS AIRES 4 July 1854 (in French).

MADRID, Z. 1 September 1859 (in Spanish, translated by M. Pastorfido and N. Serra) and 31
December 1862 (in Italian).

Still occasionally revived in France and Germany; revived in English, Birmingham 20 September 1922.

AUBER: *Le Philtre*

20 June. Paris, O.

Text by A. E. Scribe. Two acts.

Given at the Paris Opéra 243 times until 1862;
100th performance 3 November 1837.

In French also, Brussels 5 January 1832 (given
until 1878); New York 9 August 1833; Amsterdam 1834; London, D.L. 10 August 1846.

In German (translated by C. A. L. von Lichtenstein), Berlin 15 October 1831; Vienna 3 April
1832; Brünn 15 October 1832; Graz 4 January
1834; St. Petersburg 1836 (pasticcio from Auber's opera and Donizetti's *Elisir d'Amore*, arranged by G. F. Keller).

In English, London, Olympic 27 October
1831 (as *The Love Spell, or The Flirts of the Village*,
music adapted by C. E. Horn); D.L. 3 November 1831 (as *The Love Charm, or The Village Coquette*, translated by J. R. Planché, music arranged by Bishop).

In Danish (translated by T. Overskou), Copenhagen 22 May 1832.

In Italian, Milan, T.L. 5 April 1900 (!); given
so late in Italy because Donizetti's *Elisir d'Amore*,
produced in 1832, barred the way to Auber's
opera on the same subject.

RIES: *The Sorceress*

4 August. London, Adelphi

Text by E. Fitzball (founded on C. F. van der
Velde's story *Arwed Gyllenstjerna*, 1822, translated into English 1827). Two acts.

After the great success his *Räuberbraut* (see
1828) had had in London, Ries had been asked
to write an opera for the English stage; it was a
complete failure.

"This opera was too heavy, and too Germanic,
and required, above all things, melody, without
which, no opera can ever succeed, whatever
merit else it may possess" (Fitzball's *Memoirs*,
Vol. I, p.213).

There is a German translation by J. B. Rousseau, *Liska, oder Die Hexe von Gyllensteen*; but the
opera was never given in Germany.

SCHNYDER VON WARTENSEE:
Fortunat

2 October. Frankfort

Text by G. Döring. Three acts.

The only opera of the German-Swiss composer which was performed and of which the vocal score was printed.

L. RICCI: *Chiara di Rosembergh*

11 October. Milan, Sc.

Text by G. Rossi (founded on Mad. de Genlis's novel *Le Siège de La Rochelle*). Two acts.

Very successful in Italy, where it was given until after 1880; one of the latest revivals was at Venice on 25 December 1878.

In Italian also:

BARCELONA 23 October 1832.

MADRID 3 December 1832

PARIS, TH. I. 6 November 1833.

LISBON 24 January 1834.

DUBROVNIK (Ragusa) 1834.

CORFU Autumn 1834.

HAVANA March 1836.

VIENNA 28 May 1836.

LONDON, LY. 24 January 1837.

MEXICO 1837.

ATHENS February 1840.

SMYRNA Summer 1840.

ALEXANDRIA Carnival 1842.

CONSTANTINOPLE Autumn 1843.

BERLIN, KGST. 15 October 1843.

NEW YORK 18 November 1844.

VALPARAISO 1845.

STOCKHOLM 1849.

WARSAW 1851.

BUENOS AIRES 23 December 1853.

In German (translated by G. Ott), Vienna 22 July 1834; Budapest 8 July 1843.

In Spanish (translated by A. Rodríguez), Madrid, Z. 10 June 1863.

AUBER AND OTHERS:
La Marquise de Brinvilliers

31 October. Paris, O.C.

Text by A. E. Scribe and F. H. J. Castil-Blaze. Three acts.

Also given at Brussels 2 August 1832. This opera is recorded here as an example of collective work, not unusual in France in those years; the nine joint composers, all of them more or less renowned, were: Auber, Batton, Berton, Blangini, Boieldieu, Carafa, Cherubini, Hérold, and Paer. The lion's share of the success went to Auber (who had contributed only one duet).

MEYERBEER: *Robert-le-Diable*

21 November. Paris, O.

Text by A. E. Scribe and G. Delavigne. Five acts.

Meyerbeer's first French opera; one of the greatest operatic successes of all times. The 100th performance at the Paris Opéra was already on 20 April 1834; the 500th on 1 March 1867; the 600th on 26 January 1877; altogether, the opera was given there 758 times until 9 August 1893 and revived at the Gaîté-Lyrique 17 November 1911.

Given in London in two different English versions on two consecutive days: at D.L. as *The Daemon; or, The Mystic Branch* 20 February 1832 (music adapted by Bishop), at C.G. as *The Fiend-Father; or, Robert of Normandy* 21 February 1832 (adapted by M. R. Lacy[1]); but even earlier an English parody (*romantic and magical burletta*) on the opera had been produced at the Adelphi Th. on 23 January of that year: *Robert le Diable, the Devil's Son*, by E. Fitzball and J. B. Buckstone. The French original was given at Hm. 11 June 1832, a German version at D.L. 18 June 1841, an Italian version by S. M. Maggioni at H.M.'s 4 May 1847.

Revived in English, Liverpool 8 February 1888. Last revived at C.G. 25 October 1890 (in Italian; 100th performance there). After Paris and London produced at:

[1] "I attended one such mongrel representation, and found in that piece of patchwork, *The Demon*, Meyerbeer's best intentions utterly destroyed; fine scenery and ignorant listeners could alone save this performance from complete failure. Drury Lane, in rivalry with Covent Garden, wanted to produce another version, and having better singers partially succeeded; still there was no Meyerbeer in it". (Moscheles, *Diary*.)

LIÉGE 26 March 1832; Antwerp 13 January 1833; Brussels 10 October 1833, etc. (in French).

BERLIN, O. 20 June 1832 (in German, translated by T. Hell); Kgst. 23 February 1848 (in Italian).

STRASBOURG 1 August 1832 (in another German version by E. Kneiff).

DUBLIN 26 November 1832 (in English) and 25 September 1869 (in Italian).

VIENNA, JOS. 22 June 1833 and Kä. 31 August 1833 (in German); revised V.O. 5 November 1921.

COPENHAGEN 28 October 1833 (in Danish, translated by T. Overskou).

NEW YORK 7 April 1834 (in English); 17 December 1841 (in Italian); 2 July 1845 (in French); and 16 September 1856 (in German).

BUDAPEST 14 April 1834 (in German) and 26 March 1836 (in Hungarian, translated by J. Szerdahelyi).

BRÜNN 23 August 1834 (in German).

ST. PETERSBURG 26 December 1834 (in Russian, translated by R. M. Zotov); November 1837 (in German); and Spring 1848 (in Italian).

THE HAGUE 1834 (in French).

AMSTERDAM 1834 (in French).

PRAGUE 24 July 1835 (in German) and 26 November 1864 (in Czech, translated by B. Peška).

BUCHAREST 1835 (in German) and 15 January 1853 (in Italian).

BASLE 14 March 1836 (in German; the Strasbourg version).

CALCUTTA 4 November 1836 (in French) and 1869 (in Italian).

LAIBACH November 1836 (in German).

WARSAW 16 December 1837 (in Polish, translated by L. A. Dmuszewski and J. Jasiński).

LISBON 2 September 1838 (in Italian, translated by C. Bassi) and 14 January 1882 (in Portuguese).

STOCKHOLM 10 May 1839 (in Swedish, translated by B. H. Crusell).

NEW ORLEANS November 1840 (in French).

FLORENCE, P. 26 November 1840 (in Italian, translated by F. Casuccini); given at Naples, S.C. 29 July 1856 as *Roberto di Piccardia*. Previously

the music had been used at the Canobbiana, Milan 24 March 1835, with a farce called *Baboon, Nano selvaggio*, "sacrilegamente accompagnata" (Cambiasi).

BARCELONA 6 September 1845 (in Italian).

ODESSA 12 December 1846 (in Italian).

VALPARAISO January 1847 (in Italian).

RIO DE JANEIRO January 1850 (in Italian).

HELSINKI 25 June 1850 (in German) and 4 May 1877 (in Finnish, translated by A. Törneroos).

BATAVIA Autumn 1850 and Soerabaya 23 November 1866 (in French).

CONSTANTINOPLE 27 October 1850 (in Italian).

ZAGREB (Agram) Spring 1852 (in Italian) and 29 April 1876 (in Croatian, translated by I. Trnski).

MALTA 1852 (in Italian).

MEXICO 1 October 1852 (in Italian).

CORFU February 1854 (in Italian).

BUENOS AIRES 9 July 1854 (in French) and 3 March 1869 (in Italian).

MELBOURNE 1866 (in English).

As a curiosity, it may be mentioned that the *Revue et Gazette Musicale*, 5 September 1841, records a production of *Robert le Diable* at Port Louis, Mauritius, and another on 29 September 1860. Yet, according to Seymour Hitié's *Théâtre à Maurice* (1917) Meyerbeer's opera was first given there on 28 February 1873.

BELLINI: *Norma*

26 December. Milan, Sc.

Text by F. Romani (founded on L. A. Soumet's tragedy of the same title). Two acts.

After *La Sonnambula* Bellini's second great success in that year and perhaps the most famous of all his operas. Given at Rome 18 January 1834 as *La Foresta d'Irminsul*.

Outside Italy given at:

VIENNA 11 May 1833 (in German, translated by J. von Seyfried) and 29 April 1835 (in Italian).

LONDON, HM. 20 June 1833 (in Italian); D.L. 24 June 1837 (in English, translated by J. R. Planché); C.G. 10 June 1842 (in German).

MADRID 16 January 1834 (in Italian) and Spring 1846 (in Spanish); Barcelona 4 June 1835 (in Italian).

BERLIN, KGST. 26 March 1834 and O. 12 January 1838 (in German); Kgst. 10 July 1841 (in Italian).

CORFU Autumn 1834 (in Italian).

BRÜNN 24 October 1834 (in German).

BUDAPEST 3 November 1834 (in German); 28 October 1837 (in Hungarian); and October 1847 (in Italian).

PRAGUE 20 February 1835 (in German) and 7 April 1839 (in Czech, translated by V. A. Swoboda).

LISBON Summer 1835 (in Italian).

ST. PETERSBURG November 1835 (in German); 15 October 1837 (in Russian); and 1844 (in Italian).

AGRAM (Zagreb) November 1835 (in German); Spring 1852 (in Italian); and 2 December 1876 (in Croatian, translated by D. Demeter).

PARIS, TH.I. 8 December 1835 (in Italian) and Th. L. 14 June 1864 (in French).

MEXICO 12 February 1836 (in Italian).

LEMBERG 5 April 1836 (in Italian).

CLAUSENBURG 23 May 1836 (in Hungarian, translated by J. Szerdahelyi).

HAVANA 12 August 1836 (in Italian).

BASLE 6 March 1837 (in German).

WILNA and MITAU Summer 1837 (in German).

LYONS 14 November 1837 (in Italian) and 18 December 1841 (in French, translated by E. Monnier).

RIGA 23 December 1837 (in German).

ALGIERS Carnival 1838 (in Italian).

LIÉGE 10 May 1838 (in German).

ODESSA Spring 1839 (in Italian).

AMSTERDAM May 1839 (in German); anonymous Dutch translation published Utrecht, n.d.

HELSINKI 9 June 1839 (in German) and 16 December 1874 (in Finnish, translated by A. Törneroos).

HAGUE October 1839 (in French, translated by E. Monnier) and September 1840 (in Italian).

PALMA, MALLORCA Carnival 1840 (in Italian).

COPENHAGEN 20 March 1840 (in Danish, translated by A. G. Oehlenschläger).

BRUSSELS April 1840 (in Italian) and 18 March 1842 (in French).

MOSCOW April 1840 (in Italian).

ATHENS Spring 1840 (in Italian).

MALTA Spring 1840 (in Italian).

PHILADELPHIA 11 January 1841 (in English, translated by J. R. Fry; the same night at two different theatres!) and 13 November 1843 (in Italian).

NANCY January 1841 (in French, translated by N. Lafont).

NEW YORK 25 February 1841 (in English) and 20 September 1843 (in Italian).

STOCKHOLM 19 May 1841 (in Swedish, translated by N. E. W. af Wetterstedt).

DUBLIN 31 August 1841 (in Italian).

CONSTANTINOPLE 18 November 1841 (in Italian; first Italian opera there).

JASSY 31 January 1842 (in German).

SMYRNA Summer 1842 (in Italian).

NEW ORLEANS 31 December 1842 (in Italian).

BUCHAREST 1842 (in German) and 15 September 1843 (in Italian, the first opera sung in Italian there). A Rumanian version by G. Asachi had been published at Jassy in 1838; first opera libretto ever printed in Rumanian.

WARSAW Summer 1843 (in Italian) and 8 May 1845 (in Polish, translated by J. Jasiński).

GUAJAQUIL, PERU Spring 1843 (in Italian).

GIBRALTAR Summer 1843 (in Italian).

RIO DE JANEIRO 17 January 1844 (in Italian) and 12 August 1858 (in Portuguese).

SANTIAGO, CHILE 1845 (in Italian).

BUENOS AIRES 26 June 1849 (in Italian).

NIZHNY NOVGOROD 8 May 1850 (in Russian).

SAN FRANCISCO February 1851 (in Italian).

SYDNEY 16 February 1852 (in English).

CARACAS, VENEZUELA November 1854 (in Italian).

SOERABAYA 2 November 1866 (in French).

CAIRO 1870 (in Italian).

ORANGE 23 August 1874 (in French; open-air performance at the Roman Theatre).

CAPE TOWN 1875 (in Italian).

CHRISTIANIA 1875 (in Norwegian).

LJUBLJANA 1896 (in Slovenian).

SOFIA 1901 (in Bulgarian? translated by S. Christov published 1901).

Still given in Italy and in other countries; some of the more recent revivals outside Italy were at:
VIENNA 22 September 1927 (in German).
NEW YORK, M. 16 November 1927 (in Italian).
LONDON, C.G. 28 May 1929 (in Italian).
TRIPOLIS November 1934 (in Italian).
BUCHAREST February 1935 (in Rumanian).
PRAGUE 20 February 1935 (in Czech).
PARIS, O. 11 June 1935 (in Italian).
BERLIN, D.O. March 1936 (new German version by W. Oehlmann).

1832

DONIZETTI: *Fausta*

12 January. Naples, S.C.
Text by D. Gilardoni (libretto completed by the composer). Two acts.

In Italian also given at Madrid 23 January 1833; Lisbon 1834; Havana 19 December 1837; Vienna 25 April 1841; London 29 May 1841; Valparaiso 1845.

Last revived: Milan 26 December 1859.
In German, Berlin, Kgst. 26 February 1835.

TAUBERT: *Die Kirmes*

23 January. Berlin, O.
Text by E. Devrient. One act.

Taubert's first and most successful opera. Revived Carlsruhe 11 November 1855; Berlin 21 February 1889.

MERCADANTE: *I Normanni a Parigi*

7 February. Turin, T.R.
Text by F. Romani. Three acts.
Successful in Italy. Also given at:
BARCELONA 1 August 1833 (in Italian).
VIENNA, JOS. 9 April 1834 (in German, translated by G. Ott).
BERLIN, KGST. 16 June 1835 (in German, translated by G. Ott).
LISBON 19 August 1836 (in Italian).
MEXICO 1837 (in Italian).

PALMA, MALLORCA Carnival 1840 (in Italian).
VIENNA, KÄ. 26 June 1844 (in Italian).

L. RICCI: *Il nuovo Figaro*

15 February. Parma
Text by J. Ferretti. Two acts.
Given in Italy until 1863.

In Italian also, Corfu Autumn 1833; Barcelona 18 December 1833; Madrid 3 April 1834; Lisbon 9 June 1834; Havana Spring 1836; London, Ly. 12 December 1837; Vienna 19 May 1838; Malta October 1838.

In German (translated by J. C. Grünbaum), Berlin, Kgst. 9 December 1834.

In Polish (translated by J. Checiński), Warsaw 23 March 1850.

In Spanish (translated by A. Rodríguez), Madrid, Z. 20 September 1862.

MARSCHNER: *Des Falkners Braut*

10 March. Leipzig
Text by W. A. Wohlbrück (founded on a story by K. Spindler). Three acts.

In German also Berlin 10 April 1838, etc. In English (as *Rob of the Fen*, translated by M. Lemon, music adapted by F. Romer), London, Ly. 7 July 1838.

(Marschner dedicated the opera to King William IV.)

BERGGREEN: *Billedet og Busten* (Portrait and Bust)

9 April. Copenhagen
Text by A. G. Oehlenschläger. Three acts.
Berggreen's only (unsuccessful) opera.

BREDAL: *Bruden fra Lammermoor*

5 May. Copenhagen
Text by H. C. Andersen (founded on Scott's *Bride of Lammermoor*). Four acts.

This Danish *romantisk Syngestykke* preceded Donizetti's *Lucia di Lammermoor* by three years.

DONIZETTI: *L'Elisir d'Amore*

12 May. Milan, Can.

Text by F. Romani (founded on Scribe's *Le Philtre*, see 1831). Two acts.

One of Donizetti's greatest successes; still given in Italy and sometimes revived in other countries. Given at the Teatro Rossini, Turin Autumn 1859 "tradot e ridot an dialet piemonteis da Anaclet Como d'Alba".

The first performances were at:

BARCELONA 5 May 1833 (in Italian).

MADRID 8 August 1833 (in Italian) and Z. 13 May 1863 (in Spanish, translated by C. Frontaura and M. Pastorfido).

CAGLIARI, SARDINIA Autumn 1833 (in Italian).

LISBON 6 January 1834 (in Italian).

LUGANO 1834 (in Italian).

BERLIN, KGST. 26 June 1834 (in German, translated by J. C. Grünbaum) and 22 May 1841 (in Italian); O. 3 August 1837 (in German).

VIENNA 9 April 1835 (in Italian) and 2 December 1837 (in German).

MEXICO 1836 (in Italian).

PRAGUE 22 October 1836 (in German) and 27 January 1840 (in Czech, translated by J. N. Stěpánek).

LONDON, LY. 10 December 1836 (in Italian) and Surrey Th. 29 May 1839 and D.L. 24 June 1839 (in English, translated by T. H. Reynoldson); revived 9 March 1934 at Birkbeck College.

DUBLIN 27 February 1838 (in Italian).

LEMBERG 10 March 1838 (in German).

MALTA 1838 (in Italian).

NEW YORK 18 June 1838 (in English) and 22 May 1844 (in Italian).

BUDAPEST July 1838 (in German).

PARIS, TH.I. 17 January 1839 (in Italian).

WARSAW 26 January 1839 (in Polish, translated by L. Osiński) and October 1844 (in Italian).

CORFU Spring 1839 and Carnival 1843 (in Italian).

ALGIERS Carnival 1840 (in Italian).

PRESSBURG Spring 1840 (in Italian).

CLAUSENBURG 7 May 1840 (in Hungarian, translated by F. S. Deáky).

BRUSSELS May 1840 (in Italian) and 15 March 1933 (for the first time in French, translated by P. Spaak).

ODESSA Summer 1840 (in Italian).

HAVANA November 1840 (in Italian).

BASLE 9 December 1840 (in German).

STOCKHOLM 10 December 1840 (in Swedish, translated by N. E. W. af Wetterstedt) and 1848 (in Italian).

AJACCIO, CORSICA Carnival 1841 (in Italian).

ST. PETERSBURG June 1841 (in Russian); 1842 (in German); and Autumn 1844 (in Italian); revived in Russian, Leningrad Spring 1934.

AGRAM (ZAGREB) Autumn 1841 (in German and in Italian) and 19 February 1887 (in Croatian, translated by J. E. Tomić).

ALEXANDRIA 9 October 1841 (in Italian; first opera there).

COPENHAGEN November 1841 (in Italian) and 16 June 1856 (in Danish, translated by T. Overskou).

SMYRNA Carnival 1843 (in Italian).

CONSTANTINOPLE Carnival 1844 (in Italian).

RIO DE JANEIRO 1844 (in Italian).

LA PAZ, BOLIVIA 1846 (in Italian).

BUENOS AIRES 1 January 1849 (in Italian).

HELSINKI 21 June 1849 (in German) and 12 December 1923 (in Finnish).

CHRISTIANIA August 1849 (in Italian).

JASSY 1851 (in Rumanian? libretto published in that year).

SAN FRANCISCO 1855 (in Italian).

MELBOURNE 1856 (in English).

SÃO LUIZ, BRAZIL 1856 (in Portuguese; libretto British Museum).

VALPARAISO 1864 (in Italian).

CAIRO December 1869 (in Italian).

BOSTON Spring 1887 (new English version by O. Weil).

SOFIA 28 December 1934 (in Bulgarian).

LJUBLJANA 14 October 1938 (in Slovenian, translated by R. Petelinova).

GENOVÉS: *El Rapto*

(The Robbery)

16 June. Madrid, T. de la Cruz

Text by M. J. de Larra. Two acts.

The only opera Genovés wrote to Spanish words. Score preserved; libretto lost.

RASTRELLI: *Salvator Rosa* oder *Zwey Nächte in Rom*

22 July. Dresden

Text by J. P. T. Lyser (founded on E. T. A. Hoffmann's *Signor Formica*). Two acts.

After the liquidation of Italian opera at Dresden this was the first new German opera there. Also given at Berlin, Kgst. 3 August 1833.

AUBER: *Le Serment* ou *Les faux Monnayeurs*

1 October. Paris, O.

Text by A. E. Scribe and E. J. E. Mazères. Three acts.

Given at the Paris O. until 1849; 100th performance 30 March 1849.

In French also, Liége 9 March 1833; Brussels 19 August 1834; Amsterdam Spring 1836.

In English (as *The Coiners; or, The Soldier's Oath*, adapted by M. R. Lacy), London, C.G. 23 March 1833.

In German (translated by "Dr. Petit"; pseud.?), Hamburg 5 November 1833; Graz 10 April 1834; Vienna, Jos. 29 July 1834 (with additional music by K. Kreutzer) and Kä. 29 October 1834; Budapest 29 November 1834; Berlin, Kgst. 28 March 1835; Prague May 1835; Bucharest 1835; last revived Coblenz 3 December 1899.

In Hungarian (translated by I. Balogh), Clausenburg 2 December 1834.

In Russian, St. Petersburg Spring 1840.

In Italian, Florence, P. Carnival 1852 (according to U. Morini).

In Czech (translated by K. S.), Prague 31 January 1866.

J. P. E. HARTMANN: *Ravnen* eller *Broderprøven*

(The Raven, or The Brother Test)

29 October. Copenhagen

Text by H. C. Andersen (founded on C. Gozzi's comedy, *Il Corvo*, 1761). Three acts.

Revived Copenhagen 23 April 1865 (in an enlarged 4-act version).

WOLFRAM: *Das Schloss Candra*

1 December. Dresden

Text by E. H. Gehe (*Heroische Oper*). Three acts.

Berlin 19 April 1833, Brünn October 1836, etc.

HÉROLD: *Le Pré aux Clercs*

15 December. Paris, O.C.

Text by F. A. E. de Planard. Three acts.

In France regarded as Hérold's best work and still given there.

One of the greatest successes at the O.C.: the 1,000th performance was on 10 October 1871, the 1,200th 10 September 1878, the 1,400th 17 April 1886; given there 1,589 times until 1898 and revived at the Tr. L. 25 February 1916 and 21 January 1925; at the O.C. 15 December 1932.

Outside France:

LIÉGE 8 April 1833.

BRUSSELS 15 April 1833, etc. (in French).

LONDON, ADELPHI 9 September 1833 (as *The Court Masque; or, Richmond in the Olden Time*, adapted by J. R. Planché, music arranged by W. Hawes).

LONDON, C.G. 1 April 1834 (as *The Challenge*, adapted by H. M. Milner, music arranged by T. S. Cooke).

LONDON, ST. J.'s 2 May 1849 (in French).

LONDON, C.G. 26 June 1880 (in Italian).

BERLIN 26 September 1833 (in German, translated by C. A. L. von Lichtenstein).

VIENNA, JOS. 17 October 1833 (in German, translated by J. Kupelwieser).

VIENNA, KÄ. 6 March 1834 (in German, translated by J. von Seyfried).

BUDAPEST 12 June 1834 (in German, translated by J. von Seyfried).

COPENHAGEN 28 October 1834 (in Danish, translated by T. Overskou).

BRÜNN 26 November 1834 (in German).

AMSTERDAM 1834 (in French).

ST. PETERSBURG January 1835 (in Russian, translated by Gorskoy).

PRAGUE February 1835 (in German) and 14 November 1873 (in Czech, translated by E. Züngel).

TURIN, T. D'ANGENNES May 1835 (in Italian, as *Il Duello ossia Il Prato degli Scrivani*).

BUCHAREST 1835 (in German).

STOCKHOLM 31 October 1836 (in Swedish, translated by G. G. Ingelman).

NEW YORK 3 July 1843 (in French).

RIO DE JANEIRO 25 September 1846 (in French).

BUENOS AIRES Spring 1852 (in French).

MADRID, Z. 1 September 1861 (in Spanish, translated by N. de la Escosura).

BADEN-BADEN 20 July 1863 (in French).

BARCELONA 20 November 1869 (in French).

NAPLES, T. FILARMONICO 15 June 1872 and T. Bellini 28 February 1880 (in Italian, translated by T. Cottrau).

LISBON 23 April 1878 (in French).

MEXICO 27 January 1881 (in French).

An English version by T. T. Barker, *The Field of Honor*, was published at Boston in 1880.

GLÄSER: *Des Adlers Horst*

29 December. Berlin, Kgst.

Text by K. von Holtei (founded on a story by Johanna Schopenhauer, the mother of the philosopher; the text originally was written for Meyerbeer). Three acts.

Gläser's most successful opera, given on every German stage.

Vienna 14 June 1833; Prague 7 December 1833; Basle 14 December 1835.

In German also, Amsterdam 1834; St. Petersburg 16 November 1836; Budapest 16 January 1837.

In Danish (translated by C. N. Rosenkilde), Copenhagen 29 May 1835.

In Swedish (translated by U. E. Mannerhjerta), Stockholm 20 February 1837.

In English (as *The Eagle's Haunt*) London, St. J.'s 5 May 1837.

First given at the Berlin O. 20 February 1855; the latest revivals were at Hamburg 19 March 1881; Mannheim 31 May 1882; Bremen 18 April 1883.

1833

DONIZETTI: *Il Furioso nell' Isola di San Domingo*

2 January. Rome, Valle

Text by J. Ferretti (founded on an episode in Cervantes's *Don Quixote*). Two acts.

Given all over Italy and, in Italian, also at:

BARCELONA 3 May 1834.

MALTA 1834.

CORFU Autumn 1834.

VIENNA 22 April 1835.

LISBON 1835.

MEXICO Spring 1836.

HAVANA 1836.

LONDON, LY. 17 December 1836.

NICE Spring 1837.

ODESSA Summer 1839.

BRUSSELS May 1840.

LUGANO 1840.

CONSTANTINOPLE Spring 1842.

ORAN, ALGERIA Autumn 1842.

ALEXANDRIA 1843.

RIO DE JANEIRO 1844.

BUCHAREST 1844.

BUENOS AIRES 2 December 1848.

PARIS, TH.I. 2 February 1862.

In German, Vienna 29 January 1835; Budapest 18 January 1836; Graz 18 March 1836; Berlin, Kgst. 1 March 1838.

In Russian, St. Petersburg February 1839.

In French (translated by G. Oppelt), Brussels 14 March 1844.

Last revived by the Società Filarmonica Drammatica, Trieste 8 December 1889.

COCCIA: *Caterina di Guise*

14 February. Milan, Sc.

Text by F. Romani. Two acts.

Coccia's best work.

In Italian also, Madrid 3 May 1835; Lisbon 7 March 1837; Vienna 15 April 1837; Odessa September 1839.

In German, Budapest 5 December 1835; Vienna, Jos. 14 April 1836.

K. KREUTZER: *Melusina*

27 February. Berlin, Kgst.

Text by F. Grillparzer (originally written for Beethoven). Three acts.

Brünn 9 August 1833; Vienna, Jos. 9 April 1835, etc.

AUBER: *Gustave III* ou *Le Bal Masqué*

27 February. Paris, O.

Text by A. E. Scribe. Five acts.

Given at the Paris Opéra 169 times until 1859; 100th performance 4 January 1837.

In French also, Brussels and Liége 19 February 1835; Hague and Amsterdam 1835, etc.

In English (translated by J. R. Planché, music arranged by T. S. Cooke), London, C.G. 13 November 1833; New York 21 July 1834; Edinburgh 7 February 1835; Sydney 23 October 1845.

In German (translated by C. A. L. von Lichtenstein), Frankfort 21 August 1834; Hamburg 29 October 1834, etc.; (translated by J. von Seyfried and G. E. von Hofmann) Vienna 26 September 1835; Graz 5 December 1835; Budapest 20 February 1836; Brünn 14 March 1836; Prague 5 April 1836, etc.; given at Weimar 16 February 1836 in a German version by M. J. Seidel, with a new finale by J. N. Hummel; Berlin, Kgst. 23 February 1837; Basle 26 February 1838; Agram July 1844; Helsinki 17 August 1856; Gothenburg 12 January 1865 (apart from this German production the opera was on account of its subject never produced in Sweden). Last revived in Germany, Hanover 5 October 1890.

In Hungarian (translated by J. Szerdahelyi), Budapest February 1839; Clausenburg 31 January 1845.

In Italian (translated by S. M. Maggioni?), London, H.M.'s 29 March 1851.

In Russian (as *Gonzago*), St. Petersburg 14 February 1860.

In Czech (translated by E. Züngel), Prague 26 January 1869.

For Verdi's opera on the same subject, see 1859.

BELLINI: *Beatrice di Tenda*

16 March. Venice, F.

Text by F. Romani. Two acts.

Very successful in Italy. Given at Trieste Autumn 1837, as *Il Castello d'Ursino.*

In Italian also:

LONDON 22 March 1836.
LISBON 8 May 1837.
VIENNA 15 June 1837.
MADRID and BARCELONA 12 December 1837.
MALTA Carnival 1840.
ATHENS Summer 1840.
ZANTE 30 December 1840.
PARIS, TH.I. 8 February 1841.
MEXICO September 1841.
HAVANA Autumn 1841.
BERLIN, KGST. 29 January 1842.
NEW ORLEANS 21 March 1842.
COPENHAGEN December 1842.
AGRAM March 1843.
LUGANO October 1843.
BONA, ALGERIA Carnival 1844.
NEW YORK 18 March 1844.
ST. PETERSBURG 29 November 1845.
STOCKHOLM Summer 1848.
BUENOS AIRES 8 April 1849.
BRUSSELS 9 October 1851.
BUCHAREST 1858.
CORFU 1862.

In German (as *Das Castell von Ursino*, translated by G. Ott), Vienna, Jos. 15 March 1836; Graz 1 June 1836; Prague 19 August 1836; Berlin, Kgst. 29 December 1836; Budapest 28 April 1838; on German stages until about 1855.

In Hungarian (translated by I. Jakab), Clausenburg 9 April 1840.

Frequently revived in Italy until *c.*1900 and once more at Catania (Bellini's native town), 1 January 1935.

DONIZETTI: *Parisina*

17 March. Florence, P.

Text by F. Romani (founded on Byron's poem). Three acts.

In Italian also, given at:

MADRID 27 August 1834.
LISBON 13 July 1836.
HAVANA [17 November] 1836.
PARIS 24 February 1838.
LONDON 1 June 1838.
DRESDEN 27 July 1839.
PALMA, MALLORCA 9 October 1839.
VIENNA 25 April 1840.
ODESSA Summer 1841.
BERLIN, KGST. 5 November 1841.
LIMA, PERU Spring 1843
MEXICO 1843.
SMYRNA Spring 1844.
VALPARAISO 1844.
BUDAPEST 25 January 1847.
MALTA 1848.
RIO DE JANEIRO June 1849.
NEW YORK 22 October 1850.
BUENOS AIRES 18 November 1852.

Last revived Naples, T. Bellini August 1895 and August 1896.

In German, Bucharest 1835; Graz 6 November 1841.

(HÉROLD): *Ludovic*

16 May. Paris, O.C.

Text by J. H. Vernoy de Saint-Georges. Two acts.

Hérold's last opera, completed by Halévy. Brussels 20 December 1833, etc.

In German (translated by J. Cornet), Leipzig November 1833; (translated by F. Genée), Berlin, Kgst. 12 December 1833; Vienna, Jos. 13 September 1834 (with additional music by K. Kreutzer); Prague 10 March 1838, etc.

In Danish (translated by T. Overskou), Copenhagen 24 May 1834; Christiania 1835.

In Russian, St. Petersburg February 1835.

MARSCHNER: *Hans Heiling*

24 May. Berlin, O.

Text by E. Devrient. Prologue and 3 acts.

Marschner's most important opera and one of the chief works of German pre-Wagnerian romanticism. Prague 30 December 1840; Graz 7 September 1844; Vienna 24 January 1846; Basle 6 January 1862.

In German also, Amsterdam *c.* March 1836; Budapest November 1856; Ghent 3 December 1880.

In Danish (translated by C. F. Güntelberg), Copenhagen 13 May 1836.

In Swedish (translated by C. W. A. Strandberg), Stockholm 11 October 1865.

In Czech (translated by A. E. Mužík), Prague 28 April 1889.

In Russian, Moscow 11 May 1901.

In Croatian (translated by V. Badalić), Zagreb 2 February 1902.

CARAFA: *La Prison d'Édimbourg*

20 July. Paris, O.C.

Text by A. E. Scribe and F. A. E. de Planard (founded on Scott's *Heart of Midlothian*). Three acts.

In French also, Amsterdam 1834; Liége 7 January 1835; Antwerp 21 April 1835, etc.

In German (translated by J. Kupelwieser), Vienna, Jos. 3 February 1835; (translated by J. D. Anton) Frankfort 26 April 1835; Basle 8 January 1836.

In Russian (translated by R. N. Zotov), St. Petersburg 25 December 1836.

In English (as *The Heart of Midlothian*), London, Princess's 18 April 1849 (with additional music by E. J. Loder).

For an Italian version of the libretto, see 1838.

CHERUBINI: *Ali Baba* ou
Les Quarante Voleurs

22 July. Paris, O.

Text by A. E. Scribe and A. H. J. Mélesville. Prologue and 4 acts.

Cherubini's last finished opera, partly utilizing the music of an earlier opera *Koukourgi*, written in 1793 for the Th. Feydeau but not performed. Given in Paris not more than 11 times.

In German (translated by J. C. Grünbaum), Dresden 22 November 1834; Berlin 27 February 1835, etc.

DONIZETTI: *Torquato Tasso*

9 September. Rome, Valle

Text by J. Ferretti. Three acts.

Successful in Italy; given at Naples, Fondo 4 April 1835 as *Sordello il Trovatore*. In Italy until 1881.

In Italian also produced at:

BARCELONA 21 February 1835.
LISBON 4 January 1837.
DUBLIN 19 April 1838.
ALGIERS February 1839.
VIENNA 3 April 1839.
ODESSA Spring 1839.
MARSEILLES June 1839.
LONDON 3 March 1840.
PALMA, MALLORCA Carnival 1841.
SANTIAGO, CUBA 1841.
BERLIN, KGST. 4 September 1841.
AGRAM Autumn 1841.
SMYRNA 1842.
LUGANO 1842.
RIO DE JANEIRO 1843.
COPENHAGEN Spring 1847.
BRUSSELS 3 February 1852.
MONTEVIDEO 1855.
BUENOS AIRES 3 November 1857.

In German, Vienna, Kä. 10 January 1837 (and three days later at the Jos.); Graz 31 March 1837.

LOBE: *Die Fürstin von Grenada*
oder *Der Zauberblick*

28 September. Weimar

Text by the composer and K. Sondershausen. Five acts.

The most successful of Lobe's five operas, all of them written for Weimar between 1821 and 1844. Leipzig 20 August 1834, etc.

KREBS: *Agnes Bernauer*

8 October. Hamburg

Text by A. Lewald. Four acts.

Krebs's most successful opera. Revived in a new version (as *Agnes der Engel von Augsburg*, with recitatives instead of dialogue), Dresden 17 January 1858 and again 25 October 1863.

See on the origin of this opera, Lewald's account in his *Europa*, 1836, Vol. IV, p.139.

DONIZETTI: *Lucrezia Borgia*

26 December. Milan, Sc.

Text by F. Romani (after Victor Hugo). Prologue and 2 acts.

On many Italian stages this opera had to be given in various disguises and under several titles: Florence 12 November 1838 as *Eustorgia da Romano*; Trieste Autumn 1838 as *Alfonso Duca di Ferrara*; Ferrara 14 April 1841 as *Giovanna I di Napoli*; Rome 26 December 1841 as *Elisa da Fosco*. In Paris, on the other hand, Victor Hugo (from whose drama Romani had taken plot and title) objected to the opera being performed in its original version and eventually succeeded; the libretto was changed and the title became *La Rinnegata*. (This version was also given in Italy, first at Turin in Carnival 1847.) Once more the story was changed when the music was adapted to a French libretto by E. Monnier (*Nizza de Grenade*), Versailles 1842. In other countries *Lucrezia Borgia* was given in its original form.

VIENNA 9 May 1839 (in Italian) and 24 November 1843 (in German, translated by J. Franke).
LONDON, H.M.'s 6 June 1839 (in Italian) and Princess's 30 December 1843 (in English, translated

by J. M. Weston). Last revived at C.G. 14 May 1888.

LUGANO 1839 (in Italian).

MADRID 4 July 1839 (in Italian). A Spanish parody by A. Azcona, called *La Venganza de Alifonso*, was given at Madrid on 24 December 1846.

BUDAPEST 31 August 1839 (in Hungarian, translated by I. Jakab) and 28 February 1840 (in German).

BERLIN, KGST. 14 December 1839 (in German, translated by W. H. Claepius) and 1 May 1841 (in Italian); O. 27 March 1840 (in German).

GRAZ 25 January 1840 (in German).

PRESSBURG Spring 1840 (in Italian).

LISBON 29 June 1840 (in Italian).

PARIS, TH.I. 27 October 1840 (since 14 January 1845 as *La Rinnegata*, see above).

HAVANA 1840 (in Italian).

CEPHALONIA Carnival 1841 (in Italian).

LYONS 5 May 1841 (in Italian) and 6 March 1843 (in French, as *Nizza de Grenade*; as *Lucrèce Borgia* only 10 January 1862).

MEXICO September 1841 (in Italian).

ODESSA November 1841 (in Italian).

COPENHAGEN November 1841 (in Italian) and 15 April 1859 (in Danish, translated by F. C. Hillerup).

ST. PETERSBURG January 1842 (in German); Autumn 1844 (in Italian); and 1855 (in Russian).

BRUSSELS 1 February 1842 (in French, as *Lucrèce Borgia*).

JASSY February 1842 (in German).

PRAGUE 16 March 1842 (in German) and 26 May 1861 (in Czech; revived 26 January 1884).

VERSAILLES 31 March 1842 (in French, as *Nizza de Grenade*, adapted by E. Monnier).

AMSTERDAM 1842 (in Italian).

ZAGREB March 1843 (in Italian) and 10 October 1874 (in Croatian).

WARSAW Summer 1843 (in Italian) and 13 April 1846 (in Polish, translated by L. Sygietyński).

ZURICH September 1843 (in German).

CORFU Autumn 1843 (in Italian).

ATHENS October 1843 (in Italian).

NEW ORLEANS 1843 (in Italian).

PALMA, MALLORCA Spring 1844 (in Italian).

ALGIERS Summer 1844 (in Italian).

NEW YORK 25 November 1844 (in Italian); 18 March 1856 (in German); and 13 October 1871 (in English).

MALTA Autumn 1844 (in Italian).

BUCHAREST 1845 (in Italian).

CONSTANTINOPLE Carnival 1845 (in Italian).

AMSTERDAM Autumn 1845 (in Italian) and March 1846 (in German).

SANTIAGO, CHILE 1847 (in Italian).

SMYRNA Autumn 1847 (in Italian).

STOCKHOLM July 1848 (in Italian) and 16 March 1853 (in Swedish, translated by A. Lindeberg).

BUENOS AIRES 5 April 1849 (in Italian).

HELSINKI 15 June 1849 (in German) and 26 February 1875 (in Finnish, translated by A. Törneroos).

CHRISTIANIA August 1849 (in Italian).

DUBLIN 17 September 1852 (in Italian).

SYDNEY 1855 (in English).

BOGOTÁ 29 July 1858 (in Spanish).

TIFLIS Autumn 1861 (in Italian).

CAPE TOWN 1875 (in Italian).

A Bulgarian translation by V. Shak was published at Sofia in 1891 (first opera libretto printed in that language).

Still given in Italy; one of the latest revivals was at Florence on 24 April 1933 (at the first Maggio Musicale Fiorentino).

1834

K. KREUTZER: *Das Nachtlager von Granada*

13 January. Vienna, Jos.

Text by K. J. Braun von Braunthal (founded on a play by F. Kind). Two acts.

Kreutzer's most popular work, very successful on German stages and still sometimes revived. An open-air performance took place at Zoppot in August 1909.

After Vienna, it was first given at Dresden 5 April 1834; Graz 2 May 1834; Budapest 13 October 1834; Prague 22 November 1834; Lemberg 17 October 1835; Linz 1835; Berlin, Kgst. 15

October 1836 (O. 4 August 1843); Vienna, Kä. 9 March 1837; Strasbourg September 1838; Basle 18 October 1839.

In German also, London, Prince's 13 May 1840; Riga 1840; Helsinki 31 January 1841; St. Petersburg 1841; Bordeaux 18 June 1841; Lyons 27 September 1841; Paris, Th.I. 3 May 1842; Liége 22 May 1842; Agram March 1844; Brussels 26 July 1844; Amsterdam 2 November 1848; Hoboken November 1853 (in concert form); New York 15 December 1862; Philadelphia 17 January 1863; Stockholm 28 May 1863.

In Czech (translated by J. N. Stěpánek), Prague 10 February 1839; revived 18 August 1889 (new Czech version by V. J. Novotný).

In Swedish (translated by F. Arlberg), Stockholm 29 February 1860.

In English, Boston March 1869.

In Croatian (translated by A. Šenoa), Zagreb 21 October 1876.

In Hungarian (translated by H. Bodorfi), Budapest 22 November 1888.

In Slovenian (translated by J. Cimperman), Ljubljana 1893.

In Flemish, Ghent March 1901.

In Lettish, Riga 1902.

MARLIANI: *Il Bravo*

1 February. Paris, Th.I.

Text by A. Berrettoni (founded on a novel by J. F. Cooper). Three acts.

In Italian also, Naples, S.C. 27 February 1836; Rome Spring 1842, etc.

In English (as *The Red Mask; or, The Council of Three*, adapted by J. R. Planché), London, D.L. 15 November 1834 (music arranged by T. S. Cooke; A. Nicoll, probably misinterpreting a passage in Planché's *Autobiography*, attributes the music to the singer John Templeton)[1].

In German (translated by J. D. Anton), Vienna, Jos. 12 May 1835; Prague December 1835, etc.

---

[1] *A History of Early Nineteenth Century Drama*, Vol. II, p.370. See J. R. Planché, *Recollections and Reflections*, pp.150 and 152.

C. LOEWE: *Die drei Wünsche*

18 February. Berlin, Sch.

Text by E. Raupach. Three acts.

The only performed Singspiel of the famous ballad composer, given three times at Berlin and twice at Weimar (first 2 February 1835).

L. RICCI: *Un' Avventura di Scaramuccia*

8 March. Milan, Sc.

Text by F. Romani. Two acts.

Very successful in Italy. Also given at:

VIENNA 10 June 1835 (in Italian).

LONDON, LY. 29 December 1836 (in Italian) and 23 August 1839 (in English, translated by E. Fitzball).

CAGLIARI, SARDINIA Carnival 1837 (in Italian).

MADRID 18 February 1837 (in Italian).

LISBON 11 February 1838 (in Italian).

DUBLIN 20 March 1838 (in Italian).

ZANTE Carnival 1840 (in Italian).

ODESSA Summer 1840 (in Italian).

MEXICO 5 February 1842 (in Italian).

VERSAILLES 24 June 1842 (in French, translated by P. A. A. Pittaud de Forges, music arranged by Flotow).

BADEN (near VIENNA) 3 August 1843 (in German).

MARSEILLES 23 May 1845 (in Italian).

GENEVA Autumn 1845 (in Italian).

CONSTANTINOPLE Carnival 1846 (in Italian).

PARIS, TH.I. 26 February 1846 (in Italian).

WARSAW 22 December 1846 (in Polish, translated by J. Jasiński).

BRUSSELS 10 July 1851 (in French).

BUENOS AIRES 20 August 1851 (in Italian).

VAN BREE: *Saffo*

22 March. Amsterdam

Text by J. van Lennep. Five acts.

Successful Dutch opera, given for 17 nights running. A. Dupont (*Répertoire Dramatique Belge*, Vol. I, p.197) wrongly calls this a French opera in 3 acts, performed at Antwerp, and says that the libretto was not printed; a copy is in the British Museum.

AUBER: *Lestocq* ou *L'Intrigue et l'Amour*

24 May. Paris, O.C.

Text by A. E. Scribe. Four acts.

Given at the O.C. until 1840; in French also, Brussels 28 October 1834; Amsterdam 1836.

In German (translated by C. A. L. von Lichtenstein), Berlin, Kgst. 15 January 1835; Magdeburg 3 February 1836 (conducted by Richard Wagner); Vienna, Jos. 12 November 1836 (as *Liebe und Intrigue*); Vienna, Kä. 13 March 1837 (as *Der treue Arzt*); Budapest 20 February 1837, etc. Revived Leipzig 8 August 1858; Brunswick 25 April 1860.

In English, London, C.G. 21 February 1835 (as *Lestocq; or, The Fête of the Hermitage*, translated by G. Macfarren, music arranged by T. S. Cooke).

In Danish (translated by C. N. Rosenkilde), Copenhagen 5 April 1836.

L. RICCI: *Gli Esposti* ossia *Eran due or sono tre*

3 June. Turin, T. d'Angennes

Text by J. Ferretti (founded on the comedy *Meneghin Pescena* by G. Fiorio). Two acts.

Very successful in Italy.

In Italian also given at Barcelona 18 August 1835; Cagliari, Sardinia Carnival 1836; Madrid 26 August 1836; Algiers January 1839; Agram 1841; Bastia, Corsica 1843; Locarno June 1846; Lisbon 20 November 1848; Valparaiso June 1852. Revived Florence 9 July 1870; Padua February 1880; Malta 1887.

In Portuguese (translated by L. V. de Simoni), Rio de Janeiro 20 April 1858.

In Spanish (translated by C. Frontaura), Madrid April 1867.

LODER: *Nourjahad*

21 July. London, Ly.

Text by S. J. Arnold, originally set to music by Kelly and performed at D.L. 25 November 1813 as *Illusion, or The Trances of Nourjahad*. The libretto has been wrongly attributed to Byron (*cf.* Ayrton's *Musical Library*). Three acts.

This was the first new opera at the "English Opera House" (under which name the Lyceum was re-opened on July 14 of that year).

PAER: *Un Caprice de Femme*

23 July. Paris, O.C.

Text by J. P. F. Lesguillon. One act.

Paer's last completed opera (performed 13 years after the preceding one).

Also given in Danish (translated by C. Hvid), Copenhagen 4 September 1838.

LAURO ROSSI: *La Casa disabitata*

16 August. Milan, Sc.

Text by J. Ferretti (founded on a comedy by G. Giraud). Two acts.

Rossi's first and greatest success. Given in a new version as *I falsi Monetari* (sometimes with the alternative title, *Don Eutichio e Sinforosa*), Turin, T. Sutera 26 December 1843; Milan, T. Rè 8 April 1844; Cagliari, Sardinia Autumn 1844, etc. Last revived in Italy: Milan, T. Carcano 26 December 1883 and Siena 22 March 1886.

Outside Italy: Madrid, Z. 20 July 1835 (in Italian) and 24 December 1859 (in Spanish, translated by M. Pastorfido); Mexico 1837 (in Spanish) and 1858 (in Italian); in Italian also, Nice Autumn 1844; Corfu Carnival 1845; Geneva 1 December 1845; Copenhagen Spring 1849; Lisbon 18 January 1852; Agram Autumn 1852.

BARNETT: *The Mountain Sylph*

25 August. London, Ly.

Text by T. J. Thackeray. Two acts.

Barnett's most important work; it has been called the first English opera since Arne's *Artaxerxes* in 1762, and there is some truth in that statement in as far as opera means only opera without spoken dialogue. *The Mountain Sylph* opens the long series of more or less successful English romantic operas, by Loder and Thomson (who also begin in 1834), Balfe (1835), Hullah

(1836), Rooke and Costa (1837), Benedict (1838), Hatton (1844), Wallace, Macfarren and Forbes (1845), Lavenu (1846), etc. Given on many English stages: Dublin May 1835; New York 15 September 1835 (music arranged by W. Penson); Philadelphia 28 January 1836; Edinburgh 21 January 1837; Sydney 12 May 1846, etc.

Frequently revived; by the Guildhall School of Music, London, as late as 5 July 1906.

JENSEN: *Robinson*

1 September. Copenhagen.

Text by G. Siesby. Three acts.

The only (unsuccessful) opera of Jensen, who was a pupil of Kuhlau.

ADAM: *Le Chalet*

25 September. Paris, O.C.

Text by A. E. Scribe and A. H. J. Mélesville. One act.

Adam's 10th French opera and his first great success. In Paris even more popular than his *Postillon de Longjumeau* (see 1836). The 1,000th performance at the O.C. was on 5 February 1873; the 1,400th on 8 July 1899. Still occasionally revived on French stages.

Outside France, given at:

BRUSSELS 19 December 1834 (in French).

ST. PETERSBURG 1835 (in Russian).

COPENHAGEN 14 September 1836 (in Danish, translated by C. Borgaard).

NEW YORK 22 September 1836 (in a mutilated English version, as *The Swiss Cottage*) and 7 July 1843 (in French); 29 October 1855 (new English version by E. Seguin).

STOCKHOLM 28 April 1837 (in Swedish, translated by B. H. Crusell).

NEW ORLEANS 22 November 1840 (in French).

LONDON, C.G. 6 June 1845 (in French); revived H.M.'s 26 December 1877 (in English, translator not mentioned) and C.G. 8 July 1899 (in French).

RIO DE JANEIRO Autumn 1846 (in French).

FRANKFORT 8 December 1846 (in German, translated by E. Hartenfels).

BUENOS AIRES 11 March 1852 (in French).

BERLIN, FR.W. 23 July 1853 (in German) and Vict. Th. 4 June 1862 (in French).

TURIN April 1858 (in French).

VIENNA 28 August 1858 (in German, translated by H. Proch).

MADRID, Z. July 1859 and Barcelona 14 July 1866 (in French).

OPORTO 6 July 1861 (in Portuguese) and Lisbon 29 May 1878 (in French).

SOERABAYA 15 February 1867 (in French).

PRAGUE 25 January 1871 (in Czech, translated by E. Züngel).

ORANGE 24 August 1874 (in French; open-air production at the Roman Theatre).

HELSINKI 31 March 1889 (in Finnish, translated by A. Törneroos).

For Donizetti's opera on the same subject see 1836. An anonymous Italian translation of the libretto was published in 1876. The opera was revived at Stuttgart September 1909 (in German); at Toulon December 1930 (in French).

J. THOMSON: *Hermann;* or, *The Broken Spear*

27 October. London, Cy.

Librettist unknown. "This young musician was elected professor of music in the University of Edinburgh on the foundation of that chair in 1838. His untimely death, which took place soon afterwards, deprived the world of a great and rising genius" (G. Hogarth).

DONIZETTI: *Gemma di Vergy*

26 December. Milan, Sc.

Text by E. Bidera (founded on A. Dumas's play *Charles VII chez ses Grands Vassaux*, 1831). Two acts.

In its time one of the most popular of Donizetti's operas, especially so in Italy; but it was a great success in other countries as well:

MADRID 4 August 1836.

LISBON 27 April 1838.

VIENNA 28 May 1838.

MALTA 1838.

MARSEILLES May 1839.
CORFU October 1839.
ALGIERS 3 December 1839.
PALMA, MALLORCA Spring 1840.
BRUSSELS 24 April 1840.
HAGUE September 1840.
NICE Autumn 1840.
HAVANA December 1840.
CEPHALONIA Carnival 1841.
ZANTE 26 January 1841.
LUGANO March 1841.
BERLIN, KGST. 6 May 1841.
ODESSA Summer 1841.
AGRAM Autumn 1841.
COPENHAGEN November 1841.
ATHENS 24 November 1841.
CONSTANTINOPLE January 1842.
LONDON 12 March 1842.
MEXICO 1 July 1842.
NEW YORK 2 October 1843.
TRINIDAD Autumn 1844.
PARIS 6 December 1845.
ST. PETERSBURG 1847.
BUENOS AIRES 21 April 1850.

In Hungarian (translated by I. Jakab), Budapest 1839 and Clausenburg 6 December 1842.

In German, Graz 17 June 1840; Budapest 12 June 1843.

In French, Lyons April 1860.

Last revived in Italian: Malta 5 December 1883; Mantua January 1888; Empoli 1 January 1901.

L. RICCI: *Chi dura vince*

27 December. Rome, Valle

Text by J. Ferretti. Two acts.

Outside Italy, given at:
CORFU Autumn 1840.
AGRAM Autumn 1841.
CAGLIARI, SARDINIA Autumn 1842.
ATHENS February 1843.
ORAN, ALGERIA Spring 1843.
COPENHAGEN Carnival 1844.
NICE January 1845.
VIENNA 6 May 1845.
BARCELONA 26 August 1845.

LISBON 21 January 1846.
LOCARNO June 1846.
MALTA 1849.
BUENOS AIRES 27 April 1854.

Last revived Milan 26 December 1878.

In French (as *La Petite Comtesse*, translated by G. Escudier, music arranged by the composer's brother, F. Ricci), Paris, Th. Taitbout 21 February 1876.

1835

BELLINI: *I Puritani di Scozia*

25 January. Paris, Th.I.

Text by C. Pepoli (founded on a play by F. Ancelot and X. B. Saintine, *Têtes Rondes et Cavaliers*, 1833). Three parts.

Bellini's last opera; he died on 24 September 1835, two days before the production of his rival's *Lucia di Lammermoor*.

Outside Paris, given at:
LONDON, HM. 21 May 1835 (in Italian) and Princess's 16 March 1843 (in English, translated by G. A. A'Beckett).

MILAN, SC. 26 December 1835; PALERMO 26 December 1835, etc. (Rome 6 February 1836 as *Elvira Walton*; Palermo Autumn 1840 as *Elvira ed Arturo*).

BERLIN, O. 10 February 1836 (in German, translated by C. A. L. von Lichtenstein) and Kgst. 2 June 1841 (in Italian).

VIENNA, KÄ. 16 May 1836 (in Italian) and Jos. 6 February 1837 (in German).

MADRID 26 September 1836 (in Italian).

BRÜNN 28 October 1836; Prague 18 March 1837 (in German).

BUDAPEST 10 December 1836 (in German).

DUBLIN 4 February 1837 (in Italian).

LISBON 17 April 1837 (in Italian).

COPENHAGEN 23 November 1838 (in Danish, translated by C. F. Güntelberg) and 21 November 1845 (in Italian).

LAIBACH December 1838 (in German).

BASLE 27 February 1839 (in German).

THE HAGUE 20 April 1839 (in French, translated by E. Monnier).

ALGIERS November 1839 (in Italian).

ST. PETERSBURG January 1840 (in Russian) and Spring 1843 (in Italian).

BRUSSELS 19 February 1840 (in French).

LILLE 3 May 1840 (in French).

MUNICH 12 November 1840 (in German, new translation by F. Ellmenreich).

HAVANA Carnival 1841 (in Italian).

ALEXANDRIA Carnival 1842 (in Italian).

MEXICO Carnival 1843 (in Italian).

PHILADELPHIA 22 November 1843 (in Italian).

NEW YORK 3 February 1844 (in Italian).

PALMA, MALLORCA September 1844 (in Italian).

MALTA 1845 (in Italian).

RIO DE JANEIRO 1845 (in Italian).

CONSTANTINOPLE December 1846 (in Italian).

BUENOS AIRES 25 July 1850 (in Italian).

STOCKHOLM 7 April 1851 (in Swedish, translated by A. F. Lindblad).

AGRAM January 1852 (in Italian).

WARSAW 1852 (in Polish, translated by J. Checiński).

AMSTERDAM 1853 (in Dutch).

SYDNEY Summer 1863 (in English).

HELSINKI 12 January 1898 (in Italian).

Still given in Italy; some of the latest revivals were at the Metropolitan, New York 18 February 1917; Florence 25 May 1933 (at the first Maggio Musicale Fiorentino); Barcelona December 1934; Catania 25 January 1935.

PERSIANI: *Inez de Castro*

28 January. Naples, S.C.

Text by S. Cammarano. Three acts.

Persiani's most successful opera, written for Maria Malibran. Given all over Italy and in Italian also, at Madrid 3 May 1837; Lisbon 10 December 1838; Paris 24 December 1839; London 30 May 1840.

COPPOLA: *La Pazza per Amore*

14 February. Rome, Valle

Text by J. Ferretti (founded on G. B. Lorenzi's Italian version of Marsollier's *Nina*, see 1786 and 1789). Two acts.

Coppola's most successful work. Given in Italy until 1872. In Italian also given at:

MEXICO Spring 1836.

VIENNA 9 April 1836.

LISBON 11 May 1836.

BARCELONA 31 May 1836.

LONDON, LY. 7 January 1837.

HAVANA 1837.

DUBLIN 17 March 1838.

ODESSA Spring 1840.

ATHENS Summer 1840.

LUGANO 1841.

COPENHAGEN November 1841.

BERLIN, KGST. 5 October 1842.

NEW YORK 5 February 1847.

PARIS, TH.I. 6 May 1854.

BUENOS AIRES 30 July 1855.

In French (as *Eva*, adapted by A. de Leuven and L. L. Brunswick, additional music by N. Girard); Paris, O.C. 9 December 1839.

In Portuguese, Rio de Janeiro 21 June 1858.

HALÉVY: *La Juive*

23 February. Paris, O.

Text by A. E. Scribe. Five acts.

Halévy's most famous work; given at the Paris Opéra 550 times until 1893; 100th performance 3 June 1840; 500th 26 May 1886. Revived Gaîté-Lyrique 21 November 1903; O. 3 April 1933. Last revived at Brussels 31 January 1938.

Outside France, given at:

BRUSSELS 23 December 1835, etc.

LEIPZIG 29 December 1835 (in German, translated by C. A. L. von Lichtenstein).

VIENNA 3 March 1836 (in German, translated by J. von Seyfried and G. E. von Hofmann).

BUDAPEST 25 July 1836 (in German) and 6 August 1842 (in Hungarian, translated by I. Jakab).

BERLIN, KGST. 28 November 1836 and O. 12 February 1847 (in German); last revived 29 November 1917.

BRÜNN 6 March 1837 (in German).

ST. PETERSBURG 23 October 1837 (in German); 14 December 1860 (in Russian, translated by N. I. Kulikov); 2 March 1872 (in Italian).

COPENHAGEN 25 May 1838 (in Danish, translated by T. Overskou).

RIGA 1838 (in German) and 15 February 1927 (in Lettish).

PRAGUE 25 July 1838 (in German) and 6 January 1854 (in Czech, translated by A. Č.).

NEW ORLEANS 13 February 1844 (in French).

HELSINKI 26 March 1844 (in German) and 14 December 1877 (in Finnish, translated by A. Törneroos).

NEW YORK 16 July 1845 (in French); 30 April 1860 (in Italian); 23 September 1864 (in German); 20 May 1921 (in Yiddish); 16 June 1922 (in Russian).

BASLE 29 October 1845 (in German).

LONDON, D.L. 29 July 1846 (in French); C.G. 25 July 1850 (for the first time in Italian, translated by P. Giannone); and Surrey 21 June 1854 (in English, translated by H. Drayton). As a drama, adapted from Scribe's libretto by J. R. Planché, *La Juive* had been given at D.L., London, as early as 16 November 1835 (incidental music by T. S. Cooke). This version was also given at New York 11 March 1836 (music arranged by W. Penson); Edinburgh 1 June 1836, etc.

MONTEVIDEO 3 October 1853 (in French).

BUENOS AIRES 17 April 1854 (in French) and Summer 1874 (in Italian).

WARSAW 8 February 1857 (in Polish, translated by J. Checiński) and Spring 1871 (in Italian).

GENOA 6 March 1858 (in Italian, translated by M. M. Marcello).

BARCELONA 1 March 1859 (in Italian, translated by M. M. Marcello).

GOTHENBURG 3 November 1864 (in German).

STOCKHOLM 6 June 1866 (in Swedish, translated by A. Lindeberg).

SOERABAYA 11 January 1867 (in French).

CONSTANTINOPLE 30 September 1869 (in Italian).

LISBON 29 October 1869 (in Italian).

CAIRO 1870 (in Italian).

SYDNEY Summer 1874 (in Italian).

MALTA 1877 (in Italian).

MEXICO 31 March 1883 (in French).

ZAGREB 5 May 1888 (in Croatian, translated by I. Orešković).

LIVERPOOL 27 October 1888 (new English version by W. Grist).

LJUBLJANA 1901 (in Slovenian).

OSLO 1921 (in Norwegian).

BELGRADE 1922 (in Serbian).

JERUSALEM 17 June 1924 (in Hebrew, translated by M. Freidmann); an earlier Hebrew version, by S. Mavrik, had been published at Wilna in 1886; another, by J. J. Lerner, at Warsaw in 1889.

KAUNAS 6 March 1927 (in Lithuanian).

SOFIA 23 December 1927 (in Bulgarian).

TALLINN 1931 (in Estonian).

BUCHAREST 1935 (in Rumanian).

DONIZETTI: *Marino Faliero*

12 March. Paris, Th.I.

Text by E. Bidera (founded on Byron's drama). Three acts.

In Italian also produced at:

LONDON 14 May 1835.

FLORENCE, T. ALFIERI April 1836.

MILAN 19 August 1837.

HAVANA November 1837.

MALTA 1838.

LISBON 15 October 1838.

VIENNA, KÄ. 20 April 1839.

BARCELONA 8 August 1839.

ZANTE Autumn 1839.

ODESSA Summer 1840.

CORFU 11 November 1840.

MEXICO 4 August 1841.

COPENHAGEN Carnival 1843.

LIMA, PERU Spring 1843.

BERLIN, KGST. 27 May 1843.

NEW YORK 15 December 1843.

CONSTANTINOPLE Carnival 1844.

ALGIERS Summer 1844.

VALPARAISO 1845.

BUCHAREST Autumn 1845.

LA PAZ, BOLIVIA 1847.

BRUSSELS 21 January 1851.

ATHENS Autumn 1853.

BUENOS AIRES 27 October 1853.

In German (as *Antonio Grimaldi*, translated by G. Ott), Pressburg 18 February 1838; Vienna, Jos.

21 April 1838; Lemberg June 1838; Graz 19 December 1838; (translated by W. H. Claepius) Berlin, Kgst. 15 October 1839; Prague 12 January 1840.

In Hungarian (translated by I. Jakab), Budapest April 1840.

In French (translated by L. Danglas), Ghent 12 March 1852; Marseilles 14 March 1857.

The latest revivals in Italy were at Verona 26 December 1887; Leghorn 6 May 1888; Florence 23 November 1892.

AUBER: *Le Cheval de Bronze*

23 March. Paris, O.C.

Text by A. E. Scribe (*opéra-féerique*). Three acts.

Given at the O.C. 106 times and revived at the Opéra (in a new version as opéra-ballet) on 21 September 1857.

In French also, Liége 28 December 1835; Hague 1835; Antwerp 7 December 1836; Brussels 7 March 1837; Amsterdam 1837, etc.; Rio de Janeiro Autumn 1846.

In English (translated by E. Fitzball, music arranged[1] by Rodwell), London, C.G. 14 December 1835; another translation, by A. Bunn, was given at D.L. on 5 January 1836 (with the original music); revived at the Alhambra, London 4 July 1881 as a *Grand Musical Spectacle* (new libretto by G. H. H. Paul); New York 23 October 1837 (in English) and 9 May 1842 (in French); Sydney 3 March 1850 (in English).

In German (translated by C. A. L. von Lichtenstein), Berlin 15 July 1835; Vienna 5 January 1836; Graz 28 June 1836, etc. Revived Munich 30 December 1869 and (revised by E. Humperdinck) Carlsruhe 10 November 1889; Berlin 5 May 1900; Prague 5 September 1900.

In Danish (translated by C. F. Güntelberg), Copenhagen 29 January 1836.

In Russian, St. Petersburg 29 January 1837; revived St. Petersburg 11 April 1878 and Moscow 28 January 1900 (new Russian version by G. A. Lishin).

---

[1] "Instead of being Auber's last opera, it was (at least a great part of it) Rodwell's last opera". (Bunn.)

In Polish (translated by J. Jasiński), Warsaw 12 August 1839.

In Italian, Milan, S. Radegonda 13 May 1875.

HÜTTENBRENNER: *Leonore*

22 April. Graz

Text by G. von Leitner (founded on G. A. Bürger's ballad). Two acts.

The most important opera of Schubert's friend Hüttenbrenner, who is now chiefly remembered as the egoistic keeper of the *Unfinished Symphony*.

Leonore was revived at Graz on 16 June 1837 (in a new 3-act version, text altered by I. C. Kollmann).

(First production 22 April, not 10 June as sometimes stated.)

LINDBLAD: *Frondörerna*
(The Frondists)

11 May. Stockholm

Text by N. J. Cervin-Stéenhoff (founded on a French play by A. H. J. Mélesville). *Historisk Komedi med Sång.* Three acts.

Revived Stockholm 1 December 1860 (with some new music) and again 19 September 1898.

See F. H. Törnblom in *Svensk Tidskrift för Musikforskning*, Vol. XVI (1935).

TRUHN: *Trilby*

22 May. Berlin, O.

Text by "L. W. Both" = L. Schneider (founded on a vaudeville by Scribe and Carmouche, 1823; the subject is that of Nodier's story). One act.

The same libretto was used by G. A. Schmitt, whose setting was produced at Frankfort 21 December 1845.

GOMIS: *Le Portefaix*

16 June. Paris, O.C.

Text by A. E. Scribe. Three acts.

The most successful opera of the Spanish composer (who after 1823 lived as a refugee in Paris and London).

In French also, Antwerp 21 December 1835.

In German (translated by J. Cornet, as *Gasparo, der Lastträger von Granada*), Brunswick January 1836; Berlin, Kgst. 16 March 1836; Hamburg 4 July 1836; Budapest 10 November 1836, etc.

In Danish (translated by C. F. Güntelberg), Copenhagen 8 March 1837.

CHÉLARD: *Die Hermannsschlacht*

12 September. Munich

Text by K. Weichselbaumer. Five acts.

Chélard's most important work; fairly successful in Germany.

DONIZETTI: *Lucia di Lammermoor*

26 September. Naples, S.C.

Text by S. Cammarano (founded on Scott's novel). Three acts.

The most famous of Donizetti's serious operas. Still given in Italy and other countries.

First performed at:

VIENNA 13 April 1837 (in Italian) and 28 January 1843 (in German).

MADRID 2 August 1837 (in Italian) and 13 February 1847 (in Spanish, music adapted to a new libretto by A. Azcona, called *El Sacristán de San Lorenzo*).

PARIS, TH.I. 12 December 1837 (in Italian); Ren. 6 August 1839 and O. 20 February 1846 (in French, translated by A. Royer and G. Vaëz).

LISBON 26 January 1838 (in Italian); a Portuguese parody by F. Palha, *O Andador das Almas*, was produced at Lisbon in 1850.

LONDON, H.M.'s 5 April 1838 (in Italian); Princess's 19 January 1843 (in English); D.L. 16 July 1845 (in French); 200th performance at C.G. on 4 June 1902.

MALTA 1838 (in Italian).

BADEN (near VIENNA) 25 August 1838 (in German, translated by G. Ott); Graz 12 September 1838.

BERLIN, KGST. 15 October 1838 (in German) and 15 May 1841 (in Italian); O. 16 June 1852 (in German).

PRAGUE 27 October 1838 (in German, translated by V. A. Swoboda) and 14 February 1864 (in Czech).

LEMBERG 29 December 1838 (in German).

LAIBACH (LJUBLJANA) February 1839 (in German) and 1907 (in Slovenian).

ALGIERS Spring 1839 (in Italian).

CORFU Spring 1839 (in Italian).

ODESSA Summer 1839 (in Italian).

BRUSSELS 5 September 1839 (in French).

ZANTE Autumn 1839 (in Italian).

AMSTERDAM December 1839 (in French) and Autumn 1844 (in Italian).

BUDAPEST 13 January 1840 (in German) and 4 August 1846 (in Hungarian, translated by B. Egressy).

ATHENS 23 January 1840 (in Italian, at the opening of the T. Sansoni).

PRESSBURG Spring 1840 (in Italian).

STOCKHOLM 26 May 1840 (in Swedish, translated from the French version by L. A. Weser) and 3 July 1848 (in Italian).

GENEVA Autumn 1840 (in French).

HAVANA 27 October 1840 (in Italian).

ST. PETERSBURG December 1840 (in Russian); 1842 (in German); and Spring 1843 (in Italian).

AJACCIO, CORSICA Carnival 1841 (in Italian).

LIMA, PERU 1841 (in Italian).

MEXICO 12 July 1841 (in Italian).

COPENHAGEN November 1841 (in Italian) and 8 December 1857 (in Danish, translated by T. Overskou).

NEW ORLEANS 28 December 1841 (in French).

ALEXANDRIA Carnival 1842 (in Italian).

BATAVIA 1 October 1842 (in French).

ZURICH May 1843 (in German).

NEW YORK 15 September 1843 (in Italian) and 17 November 1845 (in English, translated by G. Bowes and M. R. Lacy).

SANTIAGO, CHILE 1844 (in Italian).

PALMA, MALLORCA July 1844 (in Italian).

WARSAW October 1844 (in Italian) and 17 June 1845 (in Polish, translated by L. Sygietyński).

TRINIDAD 21 October 1844 (in Italian; first opera there).

BUCHAREST Autumn 1845 (in Italian) and 1903 (in Rumanian).

CONSTANTINOPLE November 1845 (in Italian).

DUBLIN 31 August 1846 (in Italian).

RIO DE JANEIRO 28 December 1846 (in Italian).

BUENOS AIRES 27 October 1848 (in Italian) and Spring 1852 (in French).

CHRISTIANIA August 1849 (in Italian).

HELSINKI 20 June 1850 (in German) and 21 November 1873 (in Finnish, translated by A. Törneroos).

TIFLIS Autumn 1853 (in Italian).

BOGOTÁ July 1858 (in Italian).

SOERABAYA 20 February 1865 (in French).

MELBOURNE 1865 (in English).

CAIRO Carnival 1870 (in Italian).

KIEV 1875 (in Russian, translated by A. Grigoryev).

ZAGREB 16 February 1878 (in Croatian, translated by J. E. Tomić).

CAPE TOWN 1895 (in Italian).

Some of the latest revivals were at:

VIENNA 19 January 1929 (in Italian).

SOFIA 29 April 1929 (in Bulgarian; translation published already at Shumen 1905).

ATHENS Summer 1933 (in Greek).

PRAGUE December 1934 (in German).

PARIS, O. 15 May 1935 (in Italian).

CARLSRUHE 2 July 1937 (new German version by H. Wolfram).

ROME 1 August 1937 (open-air performance at the Baths of Caracalla).

VERSTOVSKY: *Askoldova Mogila*
Аскольдова Могила
(The Tomb of Askold)

28 September. Moscow

Text by M. N. Zagoskin. Four acts.

Verstovsky's most successful work (the immediate forerunner of Glinka's *A Life for the Czar*). St. Petersburg 8 September 1841 (reached its 100th performance there in 1850, earlier than *A Life for the Czar*). Given on Russian stages throughout the 19th century; last revived at Moscow in 1897.

Produced also by a Russian company in New York 15 December 1869 (first Russian opera in America; English translation by O. Agrenev published on that occasion).

PRÉVOST: *Cosimo*

13 October. Paris, O.C.

Text by A. Villain de Saint-Hilaire and P. Duport. Two acts.

The most successful of Prévost's operas.

In French also, Brussels 1 January 1838; New York 22 July 1843.

In English, London, St. J.'s 7 May 1838.

Swedish version by L. A. Weser published 1837.

BALFE: *The Siege of Rochelle*

29 October. London, D.L.

Text by E. Fitzball (founded on Mme de Genlis's novel). Two acts.

Balfe's first English opera (on the production, see Fitzball's *Memoirs*, Vol. II, pp.17–27). Given in London for more than three months; last revived Princess's 8 October 1875. Dublin 4 May 1836; New York 9 April 1838; Sydney 3 August 1848. Revived Birmingham January 1892 and 3 February 1893.

In German (translated by A. J. Becher), Vienna, W. 24 October 1846.

RUOLZ: *Lara*

22 November. Naples, S.C.

Text by E. Bidera (after Byron). Three acts.

This opera was enthusiastically praised by Alexandre Dumas in the *Gazette Musicale*.

HALÉVY: *L'Éclair*

16 December. Paris, O.C.

Text by J. H. Vernoy de Saint-Georges and F. A. E. de Planard. Three acts.

Halévy's most successful comic opera, produced in the same year as *La Juive*. Given at the O.C. more than 300 times until 1879 and revived there 5 June 1899; still popular in France.

In French also, Antwerp 19 April 1836; Brussels 5 October 1836, etc; New Orleans 16 February 1837; Amsterdam 1837; Florence April 1839 (by amateurs, at Prince Poniatowsky's); New York 23 June 1843.

In German (translated by F. Genée), Berlin 3 August 1836; (translated by K. Holland), St. Petersburg 28 December 1836; (translated by F. Ellmenreich), Munich 24 November 1837; (translated by J. von Ribics), Prague 3 October 1840; Vienna, Jos. 23 November 1848 and Kä. 30 August 1849.

In Polish (translated by J. Jasiński), Warsaw 24 September 1836.

In Czech (translated by J. Svátek), Prague 9 August 1863.

In Russian, Moscow 6 February 1867.

In Italian, Naples 6 January 1884.

In Danish (translated by C. F. Güntelberg and E. Christiansen), Copenhagen 26 March 1886.

Revived (in F. Ellmenreich's translation), Hanover 22 October 1880 and on many other German stages; also at Rotterdam 1883; Strasbourg 30 March 1900, etc.; in a new German version by W. Kleefeld, as *Der Schicksalstag*, Halle 12 March 1922; Berlin, D.O. 21 February 1927.

COPPOLA: *Gli Illinesi*

26 December. Turin, T.R.

Text by F. Romani (first set to music by Basilj, see 1819, and *rafforzato e migliorato in gran parte* for Coppola). Two acts.

One of Coppola's better works; outside Italy given at Lisbon 16 September 1839.

1836

AUBER: *Actéon*

23 January. Paris, O.C.

Text by A. E. Scribe. One act.

Last revived at the O.C. on 30 June 1852.

In French also, Philadelphia 16 October 1843; Brussels 16 January 1846; London, St. J.'s 12 March 1849.

In German (translated by M. G. Friedrich), Vienna 3 July 1839.

(The title has merely symbolical meaning; the action is in 18th-century Sicily).

MARSCHNER: *Das Schloss am Ätna*

29 January. Leipzig

Text by A. Klingemann (originally called *Adelgunde*). Three acts.

Fairly successful in Germany; last revived Breslau 25 February 1848.

In Danish (translated by A. G. Oehlenschläger), Copenhagen 2 May 1837.

DONIZETTI: *Belisario*

4 February. Venice, F.

Text by S. Cammarano. Three acts.

Like most of Donizetti's operas of the thirties, successful all over the world.

In Italian produced at:

VIENNA 17 June 1836.
MADRID 22 November 1836.
LONDON 1 April 1837.
LJUBLJANA 1837.
LISBON 7 July 1837.
MALTA Carnival 1838.
ALGIERS 16 October 1838.
ODESSA Spring 1839.
ZANTE Spring 1839.
HAVANA February 1840.
ATHENS Spring 1840.
PRESSBURG Spring 1840.
LYONS 7 July 1840.
GHENT 27 June 1841.
MEXICO September 1841.
CONSTANTINOPLE Spring 1842.
ALEXANDRIA September 1842.
BERLIN, KGST. 12 November 1842.
RIO DE JANEIRO 1843.
PHILADELPHIA 29 July 1843.
BUCHAREST Autumn 1843.
PARIS, TH.I. 24 October 1843.
ST. PETERSBURG Carnival 1844.
NEW YORK 14 February 1844.
VALPARAISO 1844.
TRINIDAD Autumn 1844.
AMSTERDAM Autumn 1844.
COPENHAGEN Carnival 1845.
DUBLIN 3 September 1846.
BUENOS AIRES 26 July 1851.

MONTEVIDEO 1852.

The latest revivals in Italy were at Venice 3 November 1889; Pisa 8 August 1891; Leghorn 8 November 1891.

In German (translated by V. A. Swoboda), Prague 15 February 1838; Graz 31 August 1838; (translated by J. Hähnel) Berlin, Kgst. 28 April 1838 (and O. 28 December 1841); Lemberg September 1838; Budapest 3 November 1838; Vienna, Jos. 7 September 1839 and Kä. 12 November 1839; Zurich September 1840; Jassy 9 February 1842; Agram March 1844; Helsinki 5 July 1849; Gothenburg 1865; Reval 19 April 1883.

The latest revivals were at Vienna 11 February 1888; Frankfort 24 March 1888; Basle 20 October 1889; Coblenz 7 November 1899.

In Russian, St. Petersburg December 1839.

In Hungarian (translated by F. Gyergyai), Budapest 19 May 1841; Clausenburg 6 May 1842.

In French (translated by H. Lucas), Brussels 13 January 1843; Lille 23 April 1848.

In Czech (translated by J. N. Štĕpánek), Prague 1843.

In Polish (translated by J. Jasiński), Warsaw 27 June 1850.

MEYERBEER: *Les Huguenots*
29 February. Paris, O.

Text by A. E. Scribe (and E. Deschamps). Five acts.

Meyerbeer's most successful work. Given at the Paris O. 1,080 times until 1914 and revived there 13 January 1930 and 23 March 1936. 100th performance 22 July 1839; 500th 4 April 1872; 1,000th 16 May 1906. In Catholic countries plot and title had often to be changed (see below, under Munich, Vienna, Florence, Rome). It may be noted that in London as well as in New York, *Les Huguenots* was given in French, German, and Italian earlier than in English.

First produced at:

COLOGNE 21 March 1837 (in German, as *Margaretha von Navarra*); Leipzig 10 April 1837, etc. (in German, as *Die Hugenotten*, translated by I. F. Castelli).

HAGUE 11 November 1837 (in French).

BRUSSELS 15 November 1837 (in French; last revived 1 October 1934).

MUNICH 22 May 1838 (as *Die Anglicaner und Puritaner*, Castelli's version altered by C. Birch-Pfeiffer); under the original title 19 November 1848.

BASLE 18 January 1839 (in German); Geneva February 1839 (in French).

BUDAPEST 6 March 1839 (in German, translated by G. Ott) and 6 November 1852 (in Hungarian, translated by L. Nádaskay).

NEW ORLEANS 29 April 1839 (in French).

VIENNA, JOS. 6 July 1839 (as *Die Gibellinen in Pisa*, translated by G. Ott); Brünn 14 December 1839 (the same version).

VIENNA, KÄ. 19 December 1839 (as *Die Welfen und die Gibellinen*; the opera was given in Austria in its original form only after the 1848 revolution: Prague 6 May 1848; Vienna 17 July 1848, etc); in Italian, Vienna 18 March 1876.

LEMBERG 10 March 1840 and Cracow 2 December 1854 (in German).

PRAGUE 30 May 1840 (in German) and 13 January 1850 (in Czech, translated by B. Peška).

FLORENCE, P. 26 December 1841 (as *Gli Anglicani*, translated by F. Guidi); there are other Italian versions by C. Bassi, S. M. Maggioni, P. Perego, M. M. Marcello. Given at Rome 19 November 1864 (as *Renato di Croenwald*).

STOCKHOLM 10 May 1842 (in Swedish, translated by P. Westerstrand).

BERLIN 20 May 1842 (in German); revived in a new version by J. Kapp 1932.

LONDON, C.G. 20 June 1842 (in German); C.G. 30 June 1845 (in French); C.G. 20 July 1848 (in Italian); and Surrey 16 August 1849 (in English, translated by H. Russell). 200th performance at C.G. 20 July 1891; last revived there 30 May 1927 (in Italian).

ODESSA Autumn 1843 (in German).

NEW YORK 11 August 1845 (in French); 24 June 1850 (in Italian); 23 April 1866 (in German); 6 December 1869 (in English).

COPENHAGEN 28 February 1844 (in Danish, translated by T. Overskou).

HAVANA 1849 (in Italian).

ST. PETERSBURG Carnival 1850 (in Italian, as *I Guelfi e i Ghibellini*) and 2 February 1862 (in Russian, translated by P. I. Kalashnikov); given there in German, in concert form, March 1840 already; revived Moscow May 1934 (new Russian version by V. Yepanechnikov).

HELSINKI 11 June 1850 (in German) and 8 December 1876 (in Finnish, translated by A. Törneroos).

RIGA 1850 (in German as *Raoul und Valentine*) and 19 December 1923 (in Lettish).

BATAVIA 24 May 1851 and Soerabaya 28 December 1866 (in French).

LISBON 31 May 1854 (in Italian).

BARCELONA 17 January 1856 (in Italian).

DUBLIN 1 October 1857 (in Italian).

MADRID 9 February 1858 (in Italian).

WARSAW 11 July 1858 (in Polish, translated by J. B. Wagner).

ALGIERS November 1858 (in French).

SYDNEY 10 August 1863 (in English).

MEXICO November 1865 (in Italian).

CONSTANTINOPLE November 1866 (in Italian).

MALTA 1869 (in Italian).

BUENOS AIRES 18 June 1870 (in Italian).

CAIRO 1870 (in Italian).

RIO DE JANEIRO 14 September 1870 (in Italian).

CHRISTIANIA February 1876 (in Norwegian).

BUCHAREST March 1876 (in French).

ZAGREB 4 May 1878 (in Croatian, translated by H. Badalić).

LJUBLJANA 1904 (in Slovenian).

SOFIA 23 January 1922 (in Bulgarian).

TALLINN 1924 (in Estonian, translated by H. Laur).

JERUSALEM 12 December 1926 (in Hebrew, translated by A. Aschmann).

KAUNAS 22 January 1932 (in Lithuanian).

MERCADANTE: *I Briganti*

22 March. Paris, Th.I.

Text by J. Crescini (founded on Schiller's *Die Räuber*). Three acts.

In Italian also given at London 2 July 1836;

Venice, S. Ben. 30 September 1837; Milan 6 November 1837; Cagliari, Sardinia Autumn 1837; Lisbon 16 September 1838; Naples, S.C. Winter 1839; Madrid 12 December 1839; Malta Carnival 1840 (revived 1886); Corfu February 1844.

A French translation by L. Danglas was published in 1854.

R. WAGNER: *Das Liebesverbot* oder *Die Novize von Palermo*

29 March. Magdeburg

Text by the composer (founded on Shakespeare's *Measure for Measure*). Two acts.

Wagner's first performed opera, given for one night only; the second performance was announced but did not take place because "Bedlam broke loose behind the scenes" (E. Newman). (See Wagner's report in Vol. 1 of his *Gesammelte Schriften*).

The opera was first published in 1922 (vocal score) and 1923 (full score).

Revived Munich 24 March 1923; Berlin 20 January 1933 and on some other German stages.

BALFE: *The Maid of Artois*

27 May. London, D.L.

Text by A. Bunn. Three acts.

Written for Maria Malibran. Dublin 24 October 1840; New York 5 November 1847; Philadelphia 29 December 1847, etc.

Revived London, D.L. 8 October 1846 (with Ann Bishop).

DONIZETTI: *Il Campanello di Notte*

1 June. Naples, T.N.

Text by the composer (founded on a French vaudeville, *La Sonnette de Nuit*, by L. L. Brunswick, M. B. Troin, and V. Lhérie, 1835). One act.

Written within one week in order to save an impresario from bankruptcy. Successful in Italy; given sometimes as *Il Campanello dello Speziale* (Venice, S. Ben. 3 September 1853); in Italian also, London, Ly. 30 November 1837 and St. J.'s

14 November 1857; Dublin 3 March 1838; Barcelona 11 May 1855; Brussels 11 April 1862; St. Petersburg January 1864; Madrid 13 November 1869.

In Spanish, Madrid 24 December 1842; revived Circo 3 November 1862 (new Spanish version by M. Pastorfido).

In French (as *La Sonnette*, translated by J. Ruelle), Paris 2 December 1865 (at the opening of the Fantaisies-Parisiennes).

Revived New York, Lyceum 7 May 1917 (in English, translated by S. Rosenfeld); Breslau 12 October 1923 (in German, translated by W. Kleefeld); Budapest 26 May 1926 (in Hungarian, translated by V. Lányi).

COPPOLA: *Enrichetta Baienfeld*
ossia *La Festa della Rosa*

29 June. Vienna, Kä.

Text by J. Ferretti. Two acts.

In Italian also, produced at Milan 6 September 1836 and in some other Italian towns.

MONPOU: *Le Luthier de Vienne*

30 June. Paris, O.C.

Text by J. H. Vernoy de Saint-Georges and A. de Leuven. One act.

One of Monpou's better works. Liége 7 November 1836; Brussels 8 February 1838; Hague September 1838.

In Danish (translated by T. Overskou), Copenhagen 12 September 1839.

DONIZETTI: *Betly* ossia
La Capanna Svizzera

24 August. Naples, T.N.

Text by the composer (founded on Scribe's *Chalet*, see 1834). One act.

Given on an enlarged 2-act version at Palermo Autumn 1836.

In Italian also, Lisbon November 1837; London, Ly. 9 January 1838; Dublin 3 March 1838; Odessa Carnival 1841; Havana April 1842; Madrid 15 September 1842; Lugano 14 October 1846;

Philadelphia 25 October 1861; New York 28 October 1861; Buenos Aires 13 April 1895.

In English, London, Ly. 9 March 1841 (revived Gaiety 25 September 1870).

In Polish (translated by L. Matuszyński), Warsaw 15 August 1845; Lemberg 28 January 1859.

In French (translated by H. Lucas), Paris, O. 27 December 1853 (music arranged by Adam, the composer of *Le Chalet*, the French original of Donizetti's text).

Revived Naples, T.N. 13 October 1877; and once more Lugano May 1933.

ADAM: *Le Postillon de Longjumeau*
13 October. Paris, O.C.

Text by A. de Leuven and L. L. Brunswick. Three acts.

Outside France regarded as Adam's most popular work, while in Paris *Le Chalet* was more successful. The 500th night at the O.C. was on 24 October 1873; a centenary performance at Longjumeau took place on 17 May 1936.

Outside France, given at:

ANTWERP 22 February 1837; Brussels 22 May 1837, etc. (in French).

LONDON, ST. J.'s 13 March 1837 (in English, as *Postilion!*, translated by G. A. A'Beckett, music arranged by G. F. Stansbury); Grecian Th. 28 August 1843 (in English); D.L. 9 July 1845 (in French). Revived Empire 21 August 1886 (as *A Maiden Wife*); Edinburgh 10 December 1892; Dublin August 1893.

PRAGUE 11 May 1837 (in German, translated by V. A. Swoboda) and 27 June 1866 (in Czech, translated by B. Peška).

BERLIN 3 June 1837 (in German, translated by M. G. Friedrich).

BUDAPEST 30 September 1837 (in German) and 29 November 1904 (in Hungarian, translated by S. Várady).

LEMBERG 10 October 1837 (in German).

VIENNA 14 October 1837 (in German).

COPENHAGEN 28 October 1837 (in Danish, translated by Th. Overskou).

AMSTERDAM 1837 (in French) and February 1846 (in German).

ST. PETERSBURG January 1838 (in German).

WARSAW 5 May 1838 (in Polish, translated by J. Jasiński).

BASLE 16 November 1838 (in German, translated by F. Ellmenreich).

HELSINKI 17 July 1839 (in German) and 23 September 1930 (in Finnish).

STOCKHOLM 11 February 1839 (in Swedish, translated by L. A. Weser).

NEW YORK 30 March 1840 (in English); 16 June 1843 (in French); and 9 December 1870 (in German).

CHRISTIANIA 31 October 1841 (in Danish).

NEW ORLEANS 11 March 1845 (in English).

RIO DE JANEIRO Autumn 1846 (in French).

BADEN-BADEN 15 August 1862 (in French).

MILAN, S. RADEGONDA 17 March 1875 (for the first time in Italian; an Italian version of the libretto by C. Bassi had been set by Coppola in 1838).

SARAJEVO 1882 (in German).

ZAGREB 17 September 1899 (in Croatian, translated by M. Pogačić).

LJUBLJANA 1919 (in Slovenian).

BENEDICT: *Un Anno e un Giorno*

19 October. Naples, Fondo

Text by Marchese D. Andreotti. One act.

The last opera Benedict wrote in Italy before he settled in London.

In Italian also, London, Ly. 31 January 1837 (text altered by S. M. Maggioni).

Revived London, Ly. 9 March 1871.

BERTIN: *La Esméralda*

14 November. Paris, O.

Text by V. Hugo (from his novel, *Notre-Dame de Paris*, 1831). Four acts.

The first of a score of Esmeralda operas (see Mazzucato 1838; Dargomyshsky 1847; Battista 1851; Fry 1864; Campana 1869; A. G. Thomas 1883; F. Schmidt 1914).

Although this was, so to speak, the authorized operatic version of the famous novel, and although Louise Bertin as the daughter of the proprietor of

Le Journal des Débats enjoyed the highest protection from all quarters, her opera was a failure. Parts of it were revived at Paris, in concert form, on 6 July 1865. The vocal score was arranged by Liszt.

The statement in Riemann's *Musiklexikon* and elsewhere that the opera was also produced at Munich in a German version by Charlotte Birch-Pfeiffer is not correct. The German authoress had made a play out of Hugo's novel in 1830 already. Meyerbeer tried to secure a German production of Bertin's opera in 1838 (see his letter to Wilhelm Speyer of 6 July 1838, printed in Edward Speyer's biography of his father, 1925, p.201), but did not succeed.

HULLAH: *The Village Coquettes*

6 December. London, St. J.'s.

Text by Charles Dickens (the only opera libretto he ever wrote; see *The Musical World*, 16 February 1861, where a record of this little work will be found). Two acts.

The Village Coquettes was performed in Danish (as *Landligt Koketteri*, translator not mentioned) at Copenhagen 5 September 1862, apparently without music.

Revived London, King's Hall 19 June 1924 (by the Trinity College of Music, revised and with additional music by F. Bridge).

Vocal score re-issued in 1935.

GLINKA: *Zhizn za Tsarya*
Жизнь за Царя
(A Life for the Czar)

9 December. St. Petersburg

Text by Baron G. F. Rozen. Four acts and epilogue.

The first of Glinka's two operas. After the more or less successful attempts of the 18th and early 19th centuries Glinka's work opens the history of Russian opera proper.

A Life for the Czar was extremely popular all over Russia right up to the revolution of 1917 (and there have been attempts to adapt the music to new librettos since).

Every new season at St. Petersburg and Moscow was opened with a performance of it. First given at Moscow on 19 September 1842. The 100th performance at St. Petersburg was in 1851, the 300th on 1 May 1868, the 400th on 22 January 1874, the 500th on 27 November 1879, the 660th on 9 December 1896. Given at Kazan 7 September 1874, at the opening of the first opera-house there.

It took rather a long time before Glinka's opera was heard outside Russia and it has never become popular anywhere else; still, there are quite a number of productions to be recorded:

PRAGUE 29 August 1866 (in Czech; revived 1 June 1900).

REVAL (TALLINN) 15 March 1873 (in German).

MILAN, T. d. v. 20 May 1874 (in Italian, translated by Mad. Santagano Gorchakov).

RIGA 1878 (in German) and 1886 (in Lettish, first opera sung in that language).

HANOVER 12 December 1878 (in German, translated by R. Pohl).

TIFLIS 9 December 1880 (in Russian).

NICE 8 March 1881 (in Italian, at the private theatre of Baron Derwies) and 30 January 1890 (in French, translated by J. Ruelle and M. Delines).

LONDON, C.G. 12 July 1887 (in Italian).

BERLIN, VICT. TH. 6 May 1888 and Kroll's 20 May 1908 (in Russian).

COPENHAGEN June 1888 (in Russian).

MANCHESTER 9 July 1888 (in Russian, by the same touring company as in Berlin and Copenhagen; subsequently given in some other English towns).

HELSINKI 13 December 1888 (in Russian).

COBURG 22 October 1889 (in German).

PARIS, NOUVEAU TH. 19 October 1896 (in French; one air from the opera had been heard at a Berlioz concert in Paris as early as 16 March 1845).

POSEN (POZNAŃ) 25 December 1899 (in German, new translation by H. Schmidt).

HAMBURG 17 February 1900 (in German, Schmidt's translation).

MONTE CARLO 29 February 1916 (in Russian).

NEW YORK 4 February 1936 (parts only; in concert form, by the Schola Cantorum).

STUTTGART May 1937 (in German).

BERLIN, O. February 1940 (in German).

AUBER: *L'Ambassadrice*

21 December. Paris, O.C.

Text by A. E. Scribe. Three acts.

Given at the O.C. 417 times until 1873 and revived at the Galerie Vivienne, Paris, on 19 November 1897.

In French also, Brussels 27 July 1837; New Orleans 8 January 1841; Rio de Janeiro Autumn 1846.

In Danish (translated by T. Overskou), Copenhagen 1 September 1837.

In German (translated by C. A. L. von Lichtenstein), Berlin 15 October 1837; Graz 6 September 1838; Prague 20 April 1839; Vienna, Jos. 23 July 1839 and Kä. 24 January 1840, etc.; Zurich 1852. Another German translation by F. Ellmenreich was also used at some theatres.

London, St. J.'s 5 March 1838 (in English, translated by G. A. A'Beckett); Princess's 2 December 1847 (translated by ?); St. J.'s 27 January 1849 (in French).

New York 26 May 1843 (in French) and 27 January 1851 (in English, translated by G. Loder).

In Swedish (translated by U. E. Mannerhjerta), Stockholm 18 March 1846.

Madrid, Z. 14 September 1858 (in Spanish, translated by A. M. Segovia) and July 1859 (in French).

Revived Berlin, D.O. 24 October 1930 (as *Vertauschte Rollen*, new German version by A. Guttmann and M. Barthel).

The heroine of the opera, the prima donna Henriette, was supposed to be a portrait of Henriette Sontag.

1837

COSTA: *Malek Adel*

14 January. Paris, Th.I.

Text by C. Pepoli (founded on S. Cottin's novel, *Mathilde*, 1805). Three acts.

Costa used parts of the music of his earlier opera, *Malvina*, produced Naples, S.C. 7 February 1829. *Malek Adel* was also given in London on 18 May 1837.

LORTZING: *Die beiden Schützen*

20 February. Leipzig

Text by the composer (founded on Patrat's *Méprises par Ressemblance*, see 1786). Three acts.

Lortzing's first greater success: Prague 9 October 1838; Berlin 16 August 1839; Vienna, Jos. 6 September 1843 (O. only 15 October 1889); Basle 9 November 1845.

In German also Helsinki 13 July 1849; New York 13 December 1859.

Frequently revived in Germany; lately Magdeburg 17 April 1935 (as *Der vertauschte Sohn*, revised by A. Treumann-Mette).

In Czech (translated by E. Züngel), Prague 1883.

In English (as *The Random Shot*), London, St. George's Hall 31 March 1898 (by the London Academy of Music).

In Flemish, Antwerp October 1910.

French vocal score (*Les Méprises*, translated by L. Danglas) published Brussels 1865.

BARNETT: *Fair Rosamond*

28 February. London, D.L.

Text by C. Z. Barnett and F. S. Shannon. Four acts.

Barnett's second opera, less successful than his *Mountain Sylph* (see 1834).

MERCADANTE: *Il Giuramento*

10 March. Milan, Sc.

Text by G. Rossi (founded on Victor Hugo's *Angelo*). Three acts.

Mercadante's chief work; very successful in Italy; given at Rome, Valle [4 September] 1839 as *Amore e Dovere*; revived Florence 16 March 1883; Bassano 18 January 1884; at Altamura (Mercadante's native town) 17 August 1911.

In Italian also:

VIENNA 3 April 1838.

BARCELONA 7 November 1839.
LONDON 27 June 1840.
LISBON November 1840.
CAGLIARI, SARDINIA Carnival 1841.
GHENT 30 June 1841.
MALTA 1841.
CORFU Autumn 1841.
BRUSSELS May 1842.
MEXICO 1842.
HAVANA 1842.
AGRAM March 1843.
COPENHAGEN November 1843.
NICE Autumn 1844.
SANTIAGO, CHILE 1847.
NEW YORK 14 February 1848.
ST. PETERSBURG Spring 1848.
BUENOS AIRES 29 October 1851.
PARIS 22 November 1858.

In German (translated by G. Ott), Graz and Brünn Summer 1839; (translated by J. C. Grünbaum), Berlin 3 August 1839; Vienna 5 March 1842; Prague 24 March 1843 (as *Bianca und Elaisa*); Budapest 5 October 1844; Riga 2 February 1856.

In Hungarian (translated by I. Jakab), Budapest December 1838; Clausenburg 5 April 1846.

In Polish (translated by J. Jasiński), Warsaw 31 July 1845.

In French (as *Henriette d'Entragues, ou Un Pacte sous Philippe III*, translated by G. Oppelt), Brussels 9 February 1847.

In Swedish (translated by A. F. Lindblad), Stockholm 19 January 1852.

GIRSCHNER: *Undine*

20 April. Danzig

La Motte Fouqué's text (first set to music by Hoffmann, see 1816), revised by the author. Three acts.

Previously heard in concert form with piano accompaniment at Berlin 19 May 1830. Fouqué preferred Girschner's setting because of its greater "Gemütlichkeit". There was a heated dispute about this opera between the composer and F. H. Truhn; see *A.M.Z.*, 1837.

A. THOMAS: *La double Échelle*

23 August. Paris, O.C.

Text by F. A. E. de Planard. One act.

Thomas's first opera; given at the O.C. 187 times until 1845.

In French also, Antwerp 15 November 1837; New Orleans January 1841; Brussels 15 December 1842; London, St. J.'s 2 March 1849.

In German (translated by K. Blum), Berlin 15 October 1838; Vienna 31 October 1838, etc.

In English (as *The Matrimonial Ladder*, translated by G. Macfarren), London, Ly. 25 March 1841.

DONIZETTI: *Roberto d'Evereux,*
Conte d'Essex

2 October. Naples, S.C.

Text by S. Cammarano (founded on F. Ancelot's tragedy, *Elisabeth d'Angleterre*). Three acts.

Very successful in Italy; last revived Pavia Carnival 1882.

In Italian also, given at:

LISBON 13 July 1838.
BARCELONA 29 November 1838.
PARIS 27 December 1838.
HAVANA 1839.
BRUSSELS May 1840.
CORFU Autumn 1840.
MALTA Carnival 1841.
ODESSA Spring 1841.
BERLIN, KGST. 12 June 1841.
LONDON 24 June 1841.
LUGANO Autumn 1841.
COPENHAGEN November 1841.
MEXICO 1842.
ATHENS December 1842.
SMYRNA November 1843.
VIENNA 22 June 1844.
ST. PETERSBURG Carnival 1845.
CONSTANTINOPLE Summer 1845.
BASTIA, CORSICA Autumn 1847.
NEW YORK 15 January 1849.
AGRAM Carnival 1852.
BUENOS AIRES 26 May 1854.

In German (translated by G. Ott), Pressburg 17 November 1840.

In French (translated by E. Monnier), Hague 1840; Rouen 15 February 1841; Brussels 31 August 1842.

In Hungarian (translated by I. Jakab), Budapest 22 March 1841.

In Russian, St. Petersburg Spring 1843.

ROOKE: *Amilie;* or, *The Love Test*

2 December. London, C.G.

Text by J. T. Haines. Three acts.

Rooke's first opera (written as early as 1818; cf. note on Hatton's *Pasqual Bruno*, 1844). Successful on English stages: New York 15 October 1838; Dublin 10 November 1838; Philadelphia 19 November 1838.

Revived Melbourne 1862 and Sydney Summer 1863.

AUBER: *Le Domino noir*

2 December. Paris, O.C.

Text by A. E. Scribe. Three acts.

One of Auber's most successful comic operas; the 700th night at the O.C. was on 18 February 1866, the 1,000th on 3 April 1882. Still given on French stages as well as in other countries; last revived in Paris 10 June 1935 at the Th. Porte St. Martin.

Outside France:

LONDON, C.G. 16 February 1838 (in English, translated by J. Kenney and J. M. Morton); abridged versions had been given: Olympic 18 January 1838 (adapted by C. J. Mathews, music arranged by W. Penson); Adelphi 22 January 1838; and St. J.'s 29 January 1838. Other English versions: Little Hm. 10 June 1846 (by B. N. Webster); C.G. 20 February 1861 (new adaptation by H. F. Chorley); the French original: D.L. 10 August 1846 (by the Brussels company) and St. J.'s 15 January 1849 (opening of the first regular French opera season in London). Revived in English by the Guildhall School of Music 23 March 1904.

ANTWERP 4 April 1838 (revived 21 March 1931); Brussels 18 April 1838, etc. (in French).

BERLIN 16 June 1838 (in German, translated by C. A. L. von Lichtenstein).

AMSTERDAM 1838 (in French).

ST. PETERSBURG 1 January 1839 (in Russian).

COPENHAGEN 29 January 1839 (in Danish, translated by T. Overskou).

PRAGUE 19 February 1839 (in German) and 12 November 1869 (in Czech, translated by B. Peška); revived 14 February 1891 (new Czech version by Mužík).

CHRISTIANIA 29 May 1839 (in Danish); revived 9 September 1901 (in Norwegian).

NEW ORLEANS November 1839 (in French).

MADRID 22 February 1840 (in Italian) and December 1858 (in Spanish, translated by A. Arnao).

HELSINKI 6 January 1841 (in German) and 1 November 1876 (in Finnish, translated by A. Törneroos).

LISBON 8 December 1841 (in Portuguese) and 16 April 1878 (in French).

BUDAPEST 2 April 1842 (in Hungarian, translated by D. Lengyel).

NEW YORK 7 June 1843 (in French) and 18 July 1848 (in English).

STOCKHOLM 7 November 1845 (in Swedish, translated by N. E. W. af Wetterstedt; revived 6 November 1930).

VIENNA, W. 1 July 1846 and Kä. 28 July 1849 (in German); Graz 28 May 1850.

RIO DE JANEIRO Autumn 1846 (in French).

BASLE 12 March 1852 (in German).

BUENOS AIRES Spring 1852 (in French).

TURIN April 1858 (in French).

BADEN-BADEN 18 August 1862.

BARCELONA 7 July 1868 (in French).

WARSAW 1868 (in Polish, translated by L. Matuszyński).

ZAGREB 3 March 1874 (in Croatian, translated by J. E. Tomić).

BUCHAREST March 1876 (in French).

MALTA 1878 (in Italian, translated by A. Zanardini).

ROME 11 June 1891 (in Italian; apart from the French production at Turin, for the first time in Italy. For an Italian version of the libretto see Lauro Rossi's Il Domino nero, 1849).

LORTZING: *Czaar und Zimmermann, oder Die zwei Peter*

22 December. Leipzig

Text by the composer (founded on a French play by A. H. J. Mélesville, J. T. Merle and E. C. de Boirie, 1818). Three acts.

Lortzing's chief work; very successful in Germany, where it still holds the boards. Given at:

BERLIN 4 January 1839, etc.

COPENHAGEN Summer 1841 (in German, by the Neustrelitz company) and 18 September 1846 (in Danish, translated by A. Vibe).

PRAGUE 5 November 1841 (in German) and 6 Decembet 1846 (in Czech, translated by J. Pečírca).

BASLE 9 March 1842 (in German).

VIENNA, JOS. 4 August 1842 and Kä. 22 October 1842 (in German).

CHRISTIANIA 1842 (in Norwegian).

LIÉGE 20 October 1842 (in German).

STOCKHOLM 6 November 1843 (in Swedish, translated by J. M. Rosén) and 22 May 1863 (in German).

ZAGREB March 1844 (in German) and 20 February 1898 (in Croatian, translated by J. E. Tomić).

AMSTERDAM April 1845 (in German) and 24 November 1886 (in Dutch, translated by A. de Winter).

RIGA December 1845 (in German, as *Flandrische Abenteuer*, Maximilian I being substituted for Peter the Great).

STRASBOURG 1846 (in German) and 19 April 1860 (for the first time in French, translated by L. Danglas, as *Pierre le Grand à Saardam*).

BUDAPEST 15 January 1848 (in Hungarian).

HELSINKI 17 June 1849 (in German) and 23 September 1877 (in Finnish, translated by U. von Schrowe).

MILWAUKEE 8 April 1852 (in German).

NEW YORK 13 January 1857 (in German) and 8 February 1882 (in English).

BRUSSELS 9 October 1864 (in German) and 13 May 1867 (in French).

LONDON, GAIETY 15 April 1871 (in English, as *Peter the Shipwright*, translated by J. M. Maddox); revived Ly. 25 March 1893 (by the R.A.M.).

LJUBLJANA 3 October 1905 (in Slovenian).

ST. PETERSBURG Spring 1907 (in Russian) revived 5 February 1919.

TSINGTOU 1908 (in German).

OXFORD 25 November 1930 (new English version by S. Austin and W. A. Halpern).

SOFIA 4 October 1933 (in Bulgarian).

CAPE TOWN Autumn 1937 (in German; first opera sung there in that language).

VINC. FIORAVANTI: *Il Ritorno di Pulcinella dagli Studj di Padova*

27 December. Naples, T.N.

Text by A. Passaro. Two acts.

The most successful work of the younger Fioravanti. Given at Malta 1838 as *Il Ritorno di Stenterello da Padova*.

Very successful in an adaptation for Northern Italy, as *Il Ritorno di Columella ossia Il Pazzo per Amore* (libretto altered by C. Cambiaggio, recitatives and some new pieces by Eduardo Bauer): Milan, T. Rè 17 June 1842; Venice 14 September 1842, etc. Last revived Leghorn 27 August 1877 and Florence, T. Niccolini 11 April 1902.

In Italian also produced at: Cagliari, Sardinia Autumn 1843; Copenhagen December 1843; Odessa Summer 1844; Nice 31 December 1844; Madrid 26 March 1845; Constantinople February 1846; Lisbon 29 April 1847; Brussels 17 March 1849; Santiago, Chile 1855; London, St. J.'s 10 November 1857; Mexico 8 December 1858; Paris 11 April 1867.

In Portuguese (translated by L. V. de Simoni), Rio de Janeiro 24 November 1857.

In Spanish (adapted by M. del Palacio), Madrid, Z. 10 November 1859.

An English version by A. Baildon was announced for performance at the Academy of Music, New York October 1871. Produced by the Parepa Rosa Company, not in New York, but probably in other American towns about the same time. Libretto printed.

1838

ADAM: *Le fidèle Berger*

6 January. Paris, O.C.

Text by A. E. Scribe and J. H. Vernoy de Saint-Georges. Three acts.

In French also, Brussels 12 February 1846; revived with alterations, Paris, O.C. 14 July 1851.

In German (translated by C. A. L. von Lichtenstein), Berlin, Kgst. 15 September 1838; Prague 12 March 1839; Vienna, Jos. 25 June 1839 (Kä. 16 September 1848); Budapest 19 September 1839, etc.

Revived Prague 17 December 1869 and 18 March 1886 (in Czech, translated by E. Züngel).

SALDONI: *Ipermestra*

20 January. Madrid, T. de la Cruz

Metastasio's text (1744), altered and reduced to 2 acts by I. Pasini.

Saldoni's first opera; successful in Spain. Revived at Madrid 6 June 1843.

DONIZETTI: *Maria di Rudenz*

30 January. Venice, F.

Text by S. Cammarano. Three acts.

Outside Italy, produced at Madrid 26 April 1841; Corfu Autumn 1841; Lisbon 27 February 1842; Malta 1843; Alexandria 28 December 1844; Barcelona 22 November 1845; Rio de Janeiro 2 December 1851; Buenos Aires 25 October 1854.

MAZZUCATO: *Esmeralda*

10 February. Mantua

Text by F. de' Boni (founded on Victor Hugo's *Notre-Dame de Paris*). Four acts.

Mazzucato's most successful opera. Outside Italy, given at Lisbon 1 January 1840; Barcelona 14 November 1840.

MARSCHNER: *Der Bäbu*

19 February. Hanover

Text by W. A. Wohlbrück. Three acts.

Given also on some other German stages and,

in Danish (translated by T. Overskou), at Copenhagen on 11 April 1839.

HALÉVY: *Guido et Ginèvra* ou *La Peste de Florence*

5 March. Paris, O.

Text by A. E. Scribe. Five acts.

Given in a reduced 4-act version, Paris, O. 23 October 1840.

In French also, Amsterdam 1838; Hague January 1839; Antwerp 27 February 1839; Brussels 14 April 1845, etc.; London, C.G. 11 June 1845 (the first act only).

In German (translated by J. C. Grünbaum), Hamburg 16 January 1839; Berlin, Kgst. 6 March 1839; Budapest 25 November 1839; Prague 30 April 1841; Vienna, Jos. 4 May 1841 and Kä. 5 January 1844, etc.

Revived Paris, Th.I. 17 February 1870 (in Italian); O. Populaire 27 October 1879 (in French); Mannheim 3 April 1881 and Hamburg 20 March 1882 (in German).

CARNICER: *Ismalia* ossia *Morte ed Amore*

12 March. Madrid, T. de la Cruz

Text by F. Romani (first set to music by Mercadante in 1832). Two acts.

The last opera of the Spanish composer.

F. RICCI: *La Prigione d'Edimburg*

13 March. Trieste

Text by G. Rossi (founded on Scribe and Planard's French libretto, see 1833). Three acts.

In Italian also produced at Cagliari, Sardinia Carnival 1840; Vienna 2 April 1840; Barcelona 24 July 1840; Nice 22 November 1840; Malta 1841; Odessa Autumn 1841; Copenhagen November 1841; Lisbon 12 December 1841; Mexico 14 January 1842; Prague 5 April 1843; Warsaw October 1844; Buenos Aires 7 October 1853.

In German, Hamburg 27 April 1842; Budapest 15 October 1842.

In Spanish (as *Susana*, adapted by M. Pastorfido), Madrid 23 May 1867 (previously published in 1859 as *La Loca por Amor o Las Prisiones de Edimburgo*).

A. THOMAS: *Le Perruquier de la Régence*

30 March. Paris, O.C.

Text by F. A. E. de Planard and P. Duport. Three acts.

In French also Brussels 25 December 1838.

In German (translated by C. A. L. von Lichtenstein), Berlin, Kgst. 4 December 1838 (with additional music by Gläser); Prague 18 May 1839, etc.

In Danish (translated by T. Overskou), Copenhagen 2 September 1839.

BENEDICT: *The Gipsy's Warning*

19 April. London, D.L.

Text by G. Linley and R. B. Peake. Two acts.

Benedict's first English opera. New York 20 April 1841, etc.

In German, Lemberg 27 August 1839; Berlin, Kgst. 14 October 1840 (translated by T. Hell); Stuttgart 3 October 1841 (translation revised by C. Gollmick).

In Russian, St. Petersburg 1860.

DESSAUER: *Ein Besuch in Saint-Cyr*

6 May. Dresden

Text by E. von Bauernfeld. Three acts.

Dessauer's best work. Prague 31 January 1839; Vienna 23 October 1839, etc.

BALFE: *Diadeste;* or, *The Veiled Lady*

17 May. London, D.L.

Text by E. Fitzball (founded on a French libretto by L. Pillet and A. Villain de Saint-Hilaire, set to music by Godefroid in 1836). Two acts.

Balfe's first English comic opera. (Diadeste is the name of an Arabian game, not that of the "Veiled Lady") Cork 28 July 1838.

BALFE: *Falstaff*

19 July. London, H.M.'s

Text by S. M. Maggioni. Two acts.

The only Italian opera Balfe wrote for London.

CUYÁS: *La Fattuchiera*

23 July. Barcelona, T. Principal

(Italian) text by F. Romani (originally called *Ismalia*, first set to music by Mercadante in 1832). Two acts.

The only opera of the Spanish composer, who died in 1839 at the age of 23.

MACFARREN: *The Devil's Opera*

13 August. London, Ly.

Text by G. Macfarren (the father of the composer). Two acts.

Macfarren's first opera (a satire on the diabolic features in *Freischütz*, *Robert le Diable* and other works then in vogue). Revived Taunton 13 August 1888.

BERLIOZ: *Benvenuto Cellini*

10 September. Paris, O.

Text by L. de Wailly and A. Barbier. Two acts.

Berlioz's first opera; failure, 29 rehearsals—7 performances. Revived only 14 years later by Liszt, at:

WEIMAR 20 March 1852 (in German, translated by A. F. Riccius) and again 18 February 1856 (in a new German version by P. Cornelius).

LONDON, C.G. 25 June 1853 (in Italian, translated by J. Nicodemo; under Berlioz).

HANOVER 2 February 1879 (in German; under H. von Bülow).

PRAGUE 10 October 1894 (in Czech, translated by V. J. Novotný).

BERLIN 21 November 1896 (in German).

STRASBOURG 11 December 1903 (in German).

VIENNA 25 February 1911 (in German).

ZURICH November 1912 (in German).

ROTTERDAM December 1919 (concert performance).

GLASGOW 23 March 1936 (for the first time in English, translated by E. J. Dent).

Revived in Paris 3 April 1913 (at the inauguration of the Th. des Champs-Elysées); one of the latest revivals in Germany was at Dresden 12 June 1929.

ADAM: *Le Brasseur de Preston*

31 October. Paris, O.C.

Text by A. de Leuven and L. L. Brunswick. Three acts.

Not very successful in Paris (revived Opéra-National 22 January 1848), but popular in other countries.

In French, Antwerp 14 March 1839; Brussels 1 April 1839; Amsterdam 1839; New Orleans November 1842.

In German (translated by J. Cornet), Hamburg 21 March 1839; Berlin, Kgst. 20 April 1839; (translated by C. A. L. von Lichtenstein) Berlin, O. 28 April 1839.

In German also, Prague 23 August 1839; Riga 1839; St. Petersburg 25 February 1840 (under Adam's direction); Basle 23 March 1840; Vienna, Jos. 10 July 1844 and Kä. 25 February 1851; New York 20 March 1855. Revived Munich 2 March 1883; Berlin 31 December 1883; Gotha February 1904.

In Danish (translated by T. Overskou), Copenhagen 6 February 1840.

In Swedish (translated by N. E. W. af Wetterstedt), Stockholm 25 March 1840.

In Polish (translated by J. B. Wagner), Warsaw 6 March 1841.

In English, New York 23 March 1846; Philadelphia 27 April 1846.

In Czech (translated by J. Zelenka), Prague 22 March 1867 (revived 24 May 1890).

For an Italian version of the libretto, see 1847.

DORN: *Der Schöffe von Paris*

13 November. Riga

Text by W. A. Wohlbrück. Two acts.

Dorn's most successful opera.

In German also, Königsberg 3 April 1840; Budapest 28 January 1841; Cologne 22 November 1843; Leipzig 10 September 1844, etc.; Berlin 6 February 1852.

MERCADANTE: *Elena da Feltre*

26 December. Naples, S.C.

Text by S. Cammarano. Three acts.

Successful in Italy.

In Italian also, Lisbon 4 April 1840; Barcelona 9 May 1840; Vienna 20 May 1840; Malta Spring 1840; London, C.G. 15 January 1842 (in English, translated by H. F. Chorley, as *Elena Uberti*) and H.M.'s 31 May 1842 (in Italian); Corfu Autumn 1842; Amsterdam Autumn 1845.

1839

ADAM: *Régine* ou *Les deux Nuits*

17 January. Paris, O.C.

Text by A. E. Scribe. Two acts.

Brussels 14 April 1840; revived Paris, O.C. 16 June 1849.

In German (translated by C. A. L. von Lichtenstein), Berlin, Kgst. 24 August 1839.

GRISAR: *L'Eau merveilleuse*

30 January. Paris, Ren.

Text by T. Sauvage. Two acts.

Grisar's first greater success (Flotow contributed parts of the music).

Transferred to the O.C. on 18 November 1842 and given there until 1858.

In French also, Brussels 7 August 1839; Antwerp 24 January 1840; Amsterdam 1840, etc.

In English (as *The Wonderful Water Cure*, translated by B. N. Webster, music arranged by T. G. Reed), London, Hm. 15 July 1846.

In German (translated by Flotow under the pseudonym of F. Marckwordt), Lemberg 1851; Breslau 11 July 1859; Vienna, W. September 1862.

BARNETT: *Farinelli*

8 February. London, D.L.

Text by C. Z. Barnett (*A serio comic opera*). Two acts.

Barnett's third and last opera; the composer took his leave from the stage at the age of 37 and

lived on for 51 years without writing another opera (cf. col.360 and 719). Balfe sang the name-part in *Farinelli*.

LINDPAINTNER: *Die Genueserin*

8 February. Vienna, Kä.

Text by C. P. Berger. Two acts.

Given at Breslau 8 March 1840 and on a few other German stages.

KÜCKEN: *Die Flucht nach der Schweiz*

26 February. Berlin, O

Text by K. Blum. Two acts.

Successful Singspiel of the well-known *Lied* composer. Hamburg 10 October 1840 etc.

MERCADANTE: *Il Bravo*

9 March. Milan, Sc.

Text by G. Rossi and M. M. Marcello. Three acts.

Successful in Italy; given at Milan 40 nights running; last revived there at the T. Manzoni 27 April 1893.

In Italian also given at Trieste 20 February 1840; Vienna 12 April 1841; Lisbon 29 June 1841; Barcelona 2 October 1841; Malta 1842; Agram March 1843; Amsterdam 26 February 1845; Havana 1847; Paris 12 May 1853; Rio de Janeiro 1853; Constantinople Carnival 1854; Buenos Aires 13 May 1854; Corfu Autumn 1855; St. Petersburg Carnival 1856; Oporto 1858.

In German (translated by J. C. Grünbaum), Berlin 2 October 1840; revived Hanover 30 October 1851.

In Polish (translated by J. Checińsky), Warsaw 17 March 1853.

AUBER: *Le Lac des Fées*

1 April. Paris, O.

Text by A. E. Scribe and A. H. J. Mélesville. Five acts.

Unsuccessful in Paris (30 performances only).

In French also, Amsterdam 1839; Brussels 11 October 1846, etc.

In English (adapted by C. Selby, with additional music from Hérold, Marschner and Mercadante), London, Strand 13 May 1839 and (adapted by A. Lee), D.L. 26 October 1839.

In English also, New York 1 December 1845 (translated by W. K. Northall).

In German (translated by J. C. Grünbaum), Leipzig 31 December 1839; Berlin 14 October 1840, etc.; Graz 5 June 1841; Riga 16 April 1845; revived Carlsruhe 17 April 1865; Stuttgart 24 September 1871.

In Polish (translated by J. Jasiński), Warsaw 30 March 1843.

In Czech (translated by J. K. Tyl), Prague 9 May 1847.

BARTAY: *Csel*
(The Trick)

29 April. Budapest

Text by I. Jakab. Two acts.

The first original Hungarian comic opera; produced at the Nemzeti Szinház, the first regular Hungarian theatre at Budapest (opened 22 August 1837).

ROOKE: *Henrique; or, The Love Pilgrim*

2 May. London, C.G.

Text by J. T. Haines. Three acts.

Rooke's last performed opera (given for five nights only).

A. THOMAS: *Le Panier fleuri*

6 May. Paris, O.C.

Text by A. de Leuven and L. L. Brunswick. One act.

In French also, Brussels 28 September 1844; London, D.L. 23 July 1845; Buenos Aires 1852; revived Paris, Th.L. 26 March 1854.

In German (translated by J. Franke), Vienna 13 November 1841.

In English (as *The Fox and the Goose; or, The Widow's Husband*, adapted by B. N. Webster and D. Boucicault), London Adelphi 2 October 1844.

In Polish (translated by P. Krzemiński), Warsaw 21 October 1854.

I. LACHNER: *Die Regenbrüder*

20 May. Stuttgart

Text by E. Mörike (the famous German poet and novelist) and H. Kurz. Two acts.

Unsuccessful, not given on any other stage. The libretto was published in Mörike's *Iris*, 1839.

MONTFORT: *Polichinelle*

14 June. Paris, O.C.

Text by A. E. Scribe and C. Duveyrier. One act. Montfort's most successful opera.

In French also given at New York 19 May 1843; Philadelphia 14 October 1843; Brussels 7 January 1845; London, St. J.'s 22 January 1849.

NINI: *La Marescialla d'Ancre*

23 July. Padua

Text by G. Prati (founded on A. de Vigny's drama). Two acts.

Very successful in Italy.

In Italian also, Barcelona 5 August 1843; Cagliari, Sardinia Carnival 1844; Lisbon 4 April 1845; Buenos Aires 20 July 1855; Santiago, Chile 1860.

(Date of first performance according to the review in *A.M.Z.*)

HALÉVY: *Le Shérif*

2 September. Paris, O.C.

Text by A. E. Scribe. Three acts.

Never revived in Paris.

In Danish (translated by T. Overskou), Copenhagen 1 September 1840.

In German (translated by V. A. Swoboda), Prague 27 November 1840.

ADAM: *La Reine d'un Jour*

19 September. Paris, O.C.

Text by A. E. Scribe and J. H. Vernoy de Saint-Georges. Three acts.

In French also, Antwerp 13 February 1840; Brussels 21 April 1840, etc.; revived Paris, Th.L. 25 April 1854.

In German (translated by C. A. L. von Lichtenstein), Munich 23 March 1840; Berlin, Kgst. 14 April 1840; Hamburg 18 September 1840; Vienna 4 March 1842; Prague 1848, etc.

In Danish (translated by T. Overskou), Copenhagen 14 April 1841.

In English (adapted by J. T. Haines), London, Surrey 14 June 1841.

MARLIANI: *La Xacarilla*

28 October. Paris, O.

Text by A. E. Scribe. One act (2 scenes).

Marliani's most successful work; given in Paris 112 times until 1866 (100th performance 11 July 1862).

In French also, Brussels 9 April 1847.

In German (translated by J. Franke), Vienna 17 August 1841.

In Italian (as *Lazzarello*, translated by A. Berrettoni), Venice, S. Ben. 23 February 1842; Milan 28 July 1842; Lisbon 5 May 1852.

SPERANZA: *I due Figaro* ossia *Il Soggetto d'una Commedia*

30 October. Turin, T. Carignano

Text by F. Romani (first set to music by Carafa in 1820). Two acts.

Speranza's most popular work; given all over Italy and Lisbon 1841; Cagliari, Sardinia Autumn 1841; Barcelona 14 February 1844; Odessa 23 April 1844.

VERDI: *Oberto, Conte di S. Bonifacio*

17 November. Milan, Sc.

Text: according to Verdi's own account the libretto had been given to him by one "Masini" (*recte* Pietro Massini),conductor of a musical amateur society at Milan. The text, however, was not written by Massini, but by a Milan journalist, Antonio Piazza; it was, in 1839, revised and al-

tered by B. Merelli (then impresario of the Teatro della Scala) and by T. Solera, the composer and librettist. Two acts.

Verdi's first opera and, as such, fairly successful. Also given at Turin, Carnival 1840, Genoa January 1841, and Naples, S.C. Spring 1841; Barcelona 1 February 1842; Malta 1860.

Revived Milan 17 November 1889; Chicago October 1903 (in concert form); Parma 6 September 1913; Busseto (Verdi's native town) 30 July 1939 (celebrating the centenary of the opera).

The *Oberto* libretto was set to music once more by A. Graffigna; produced as *I Bonifazi ed i Salinguerra*, Venice, S. Ben. 28 March 1842 and as *Eleonora di San Bonifazio*, Verona 11 March 1843.

A French translation by L. Danglas was published in 1855.

1840

SALDONI: *Cleonice, Regina di Siria*

24 January. Madrid, T. de la Cruz

Librettist unknown (not even the composer himself in his *Diccionario . . . de Músicos Españoles* states whose text he used; probably it was a reduced version of Metastasio's *Demetrio*).Two acts.

Barcelona 29 September 1841.

DONIZETTI: *La Fille du Régiment*

11 February. Paris, O.C.

Text by J. H. Vernoy de Saint-Georges and J. F. A. Bayard. Two acts.

Donizetti's first French opera and one of his most popular works; equally successful in France, Italy and other countries. The 600th performance at the O.C. was on 29 September 1875; given there about 1,000 times until 1916.

Outside France:

COPENHAGEN 6 October 1840 (in Danish, translated by T. Overskou).

MILAN 30 October 1840 (in Italian), translated by C. Bassi)[1]

[1] Another contemporary Italian version was by A. Passaro.

GENEVA Autumn 1840 (in French).

LIÉGE 11 April 1841; Brussels 9 July 1841 (in French).

VIENNA 11 May 1841 (in Italian) and 23 September 1843 (in German).

CAGLIARI, SARDINIA Summer 1841 (in Italian).

MALTA 1841 (in Italian).

LISBON 6 October 1841 (in Italian) and 19 May 1878 (in French).

STUTTGART 21 November 1841 (in German, translated by C. Gollmick).

CHRISTIANIA 15 December 1841 (in Danish).

MADRID 31 January 1842 (in Italian); July 1859 (in French) and 11 September 1860 (in Spanish, translated by E. Álvarez as *La Hija del Regimiento*); an earlier Spanish version, by José Sánchez y Albarrán, *La Cantinera de los Alpes*, music adapted by Ventura Sánchez Lamadrid, was produced at Cádiz [8 July] 1858.

BERLIN, O. 29 July 1842 (in German) and KGST. 28 December 1842 (in Italian).

RIGA Autumn 1842 (in German).

PRAGUE 7 December 1842 (in German) and 29 October 1843 (in Czech, translated by J. Pečírca).

NEW ORLEANS 6 March 1843 (in French).

BUDAPEST 6 May 1843 (in German) and 14 March 1844 (in Hungarian, translated by B. Egressy).

NEW YORK 19 July 1843 (in French); 5 June 1844 (in English); and 15 May 1855 (in German).

BASLE 25 October 1843 (in German).

ODESSA Spring 1844 (in Italian).

STOCKHOLM 9 June 1845 (in Swedish, translated by N. E. W. af Wetterstedt).

BUCHAREST Carnival 1846 (in Italian).

WARSAW 9 May 1846 (in Polish, translated by J. Jasiński).

ST. PETERSBURG Carnival 1847 (in Italian) and 1855 (in Russian).

LONDON, H.M.'s 27 May 1847 (in Italian); Surrey 21 December 1847 (in English, translated by E. Fitzball); and O.C. 4 May 1872 (in French). An earlier adaptation by Fitzball, *Madelaine; or, The Daughter of the Regiment*, had been given at D.L. on 30 November 1843 as a play with incidental music. Another English version, *La*

Vivandière; or, The Daughter of the Regiment, was produced at the Princess's 26 June 1848.

DUBLIN 14 October 1848 (in Italian).

HELSINKI 1 July 1849 (in German) and 14 March 1876 (in Finnish, translated by A. Törneroos and K. Bergbom).

SYDNEY 1851 (in English).

ZAGREB January 1852 (in Italian) and 11 December 1901 (in Croatian, translated by F. Miler).

BUENOS AIRES 12 March 1852 (in French) and 20 April 1854 (in Italian).

MEXICO 11 October 1852 (in Italian).

SAN FRANCISCO April 1854 (in English).

BOGOTÁ, COLOMBIA 1858 (in Spanish).

BADEN-BADEN 29 August 1862 (in French).

SOERABAYA 19 December 1864 (in French).

CALCUTTA 1867 (in Italian).

CAIRO 1870 (in Italian).

LJUBLJANA 1878 (in Slovenian).

BRISTOL 13 October 1890 (new English version by O. Weil).

SHANGHAI 1898 (according to *Gazzetta Musicale di Milano*).

TALLINN 1915 (in Estonian).

QUEBEC January 1931 (in French).

NICOLAI: *Il Templario*

11 February. Turin, T.R.

Text by G. M. Marini (founded on Scott's *Ivanhoe*). Three acts.

The most successful of Nicolai's Italian operas; given at Naples, S.C. 1840 and Autumn 1843 as *Teodosia ossia Il Templario*. Last revived in Italy, Leghorn 13 February 1879.

In Italian also, Trieste 19 September 1840; Vienna 31 May 1841; Barcelona 8 June 1841 (and in many other Spanish towns); Mexico 15 April 1842; Lisbon 18 May 1842; Cagliari, Sardinia Carnival 1843; Budapest July 1843; Palma, Mallorca August 1844; Berlin, Kgst. 15 September 1844; St. Petersburg January 1846; Copenhagen Spring 1846; Bucharest 1847; Malta 1849; Buenos Aires 25 September 1851; Nice February 1854; Paris, Th.I. 28 January 1868; (and, according to G. R. Kruse, also at Constantinople and New

York; as far as New York is concerned, that statement is not correct).

In German (translated by S. Kapper), Vienna 20 December 1845.

In French (translated by L. Danglas), Antwerp 1 April 1861; Brussels 28 March 1862; Bordeaux April 1864.

In Hungarian (translated by F. Ney), Budapest 30 June 1842.

MERCADANTE: *La Vestale*

10 March. Naples, S.C.

Text by S. Cammarano. Three acts.

Very successful in Italy; given at Rome Autumn 1842 as *Emilia*. The latest revivals were at Milan, T.d.V. 18 April 1877; Siena 26 December 1880; Altamura (Mercadante's native town) 17 September 1895 and subsequently at Naples.

In Italian also given at Barcelona 8 May 1841; Malta 1841; Paris 23 December 1841; Vienna 2 April 1842; Lisbon 29 July 1842; Corfu and Cagliari Autumn 1842; Berlin, Kgst. 16 November 1844; Bucharest 1847; Rio de Janeiro June 1849; Agram January 1852; Havana 1855; Buenos Aires 1 September 1855; Mexico December 1855; Smyrna 1867; Santiago, Chile 1868.

French vocal score (translated by L. E. Crevel de Charlemagne) published.

DONIZETTI: *Les Martyrs*

10 April. Paris, O.

Text by A. E. Scribe (founded on Corneille's *Polyeucte*). Four acts.

The opera had originally been composed to an Italian libretto by S. Cammarano, *Poliuto* (3 acts). Written for the French singer, Adolphe Nourrit, and to be produced at Naples, but not passed there by the censor.

Not a great success in Paris (20 performances); but given in many other countries all the same.

In French also, Amsterdam 1840; Hague March 1841; Ghent 14 March 1843; Brussels 7 December 1843; New Orleans 1846; Buenos Aires 21 April 1854.

In German (translated by C. A. L. von Lichtenstein), Hamburg 1 February 1841; (as *Die Römer in Melitone*, Lichtenstein's version, altered by J. Kupelwieser) Vienna, Jos. 15 June 1841 and Kä. 13 October 1841; Budapest 11 September 1841; Prague 16 October 1841; Graz 19 February 1842.

In Italian (as *I Martiri*, re-translated by C. Bassi), Lisbon 15 February 1843; Madrid 20 February 1845; Barcelona 15 December 1849; London, C.G. 20 April 1852.

In Italy the opera was performed only after Donizetti's death, mostly in its original 3-act form as *Poliuto*: Naples, S.C. 30 November 1848; Rome 26 December 1849 (as *Paolina e Severo*), etc.

Poliuto, in Italian, was also given at Malta 1849; Boston 16 December 1849 (in concert form); Vienna 10 March 1853 (as *Paolina e Poliuto*); Bucharest 1853; Rio de Janeiro 1853; Buenos Aires 8 March 1854; St. Petersburg December 1854; Madrid 19 December 1854; Warsaw August 1857; Mexico October 1858; Paris, Th.I. 14 April 1859; New York 25 May 1859; Lisbon 17 October 1860; Sydney September 1873; Berlin, Skating Rink 8 April 1882; Santiago, Chile 1883; Alexandria 1 August 1895.

Revived in French, Paris, Château d'Eau 5 June 1884; in Italian, Bergamo 16 November 1907 (at the inauguration of the T. Rubini); Malta 1926.

CLAPISSON: *La Perruche*

28 April. Paris, O.C.

Text by J. H. Dupin and P. F. Pinel Dumanoir. One act.

Clapisson's first greater success.

In French also, Brussels 3 September 1841; Antwerp 11 November 1841, etc.; New York 24 May 1843; Philadelphia 17 October 1843.

Revived Paris, O.C. 23 April 1852 and 4 December 1860; Galerie Vivienne 15 October 1896.

In German (as *Der Papagei*), Vienna 13 February 1843.

AUBER: *Zanetta* ou *Jouer avec le Feu*

18 May. Paris, O.C.

Text by A. E. Scribe and J. H. Vernoy de Saint-Georges. Three acts.

In French also, Amsterdam 1840; Brussels 20 December 1845; London, St. J.'s 12 February 1849.

In German (translated by I. F. Castelli), Prague 27 August 1841.

In Danish (translated by T. Overskou), Copenhagen 13 September 1841.

LORTZING: *Hans Sachs*

23 June. Leipzig.

Text by the composer and P. Reger (founded on a play by J. L. F. Deinhardstein). Three acts.

Berlin 5 August 1841; Prague 8 October 1842, etc. Revived Mannheim 30 March 1883; Berlin 18 November 1889 (in concert form); Hamburg 21 November 1889; Strasbourg 23 October 1901.

Lately revived in two modern adaptations: Stuttgart 5 May 1934 (libretto revised by O. Kühn, music arranged by H. Rücklos); Rostock 23 October 1934 and Berlin, D.O. 4 March 1936 (new libretto by P. Hensel-Haerdrich, founded on A. von Kotzebue's comedy, *Die deutschen Kleinstädter*, under the title, *Die kleine Stadt*).

Lortzing's *Hans Sachs* is interesting as a forerunner of the *Meistersinger*. For a comparison of the two librettos see H. Laue, *Die Operndichtung Lortzings*, p.102, etc. Some years earlier yet another German composer, Gyrowetz, had treated the same subject. His *Hans Sachs* was never acted, but parts of it were heard at concerts in Vienna 26 December 1836 and again 26 December 1837. The librettist of Gyrowetz's opera is unknown; the music was recovered in 1903 (see K. Mey, in *Die Musik*, May 1903).

ERKEL: *Báthory Mária*

8 August. Budapest

Text by B. Egressy. Two acts.

The first opera of the famous Hungarian composer. Given at Clausenburg on 25 April 1846, etc.

VERDI: *Un Giorno di Regno*

5 September. Milan, Sc.

Text by F. Romani (first set to music by Gyrowetz, see 1818). Two acts.

Verdi's second opera and, except for *Falstaff* (1893), the only comic opera he ever wrote. Given at the Scala only once. Revived as *Il finto Stanislao*, Venice, S. Ben. 11 October 1845; Rome, Valle 9 February 1846; Naples, T.N. 11 June 1859.

PENTENRIEDER: *Die Nacht zu Paluzzi*

2 October. Munich

Text by J. von Forst. Three acts.

Fairly successful in Germany: Leipzig 31 December 1840; Brunswick 16 September 1841, etc. In German also, Budapest 31 July 1841.

COPPOLA: *Giovanna Prima, Regina di Napoli*

11 October. Lisbon, S.C.

Text by F. Romani (altered version of *Lucrezia Borgia*, see 1833). Prologue and 2 acts.

Successful at Lisbon, where Coppola had been appointed court conductor in 1839. Also given at Turin January 1844 and revived at Lisbon 3 February 1866.

PACINI: *Saffo*

29 November. Naples, S.C.

Text by S. Cammarano. Three parts.

Pacini's chief work. Very successful in Italy; some of the latest revivals were at Parma 28 September 1889; Rome 8 March 1900; Milan, Sc. 29 January 1911; Catania July 1939.

In Italian also given at:

PARIS 15 March 1842.
VIENNA 2 June 1842.
MALTA 1842.
MADRID 9 August 1842.
LISBON 23 March 1843.
CORFU Autumn 1843.
ODESSA Summer 1844.
COPENHAGEN 3 November 1844.
BERLIN, KGST. 22 March 1845.
CONSTANTINOPLE November 1845.
HAVANA 1846.

BOSTON May 1847.

NEW YORK 14 June 1847.

BUENOS AIRES 15 September 1854.

ST. PETERSBURG December 1854.

MEXICO December 1857.

WARSAW December 1869.

SYDNEY 1871.

BUCHAREST 1871.

In English (translated by T. J. Serle, music adapted by J. L. Hatton), London, D.L. 1 April 1843.

Spanish translation by Pío del Castillo published Barcelona 1863.

DONIZETTI: *La Favorite*

2 *December.* Paris, O.

Text by A. Royer, G. Vaëz (and A. E. Scribe). Four acts.

(The opera originally was in three acts and called *L'Ange de Niside* and had been written for the Th. de la Renaissance.) Richard Wagner arranged the vocal score. Given at the Paris Opéra more than 650 times until 1904; revived at the Th. Porte St. Martin 28 May 1934. Still on the boards in France and Italy.

Outside Paris, given at:

LIÉGE 26 March 1841; Brussels 13 August 1841, etc. (in French).

HAGUE 20 April 1841 (in French).

CASSEL 31 May 1841 (in German, translated by R. O. Spazier); Frankfort 27 September 1841, etc.

VIENNA 26 December 1841 (in German, as *Richard und Mathilde*; given there as *Leonore* 4 October 1853; and 11 May 1864 (in Italian).

PADUA June 1842 (for the first time in Italian, translated by F. Jannetti, as *Leonora di Guzman*; as *La Favorita*, translated by C. Bassi, Milan, Sc. 16 August 1843). Given at Venice 1847 as *La Favorita* with different characters, Louis VII of France being substituted for Alfonso XI of Castile and Elda (a Greek girl) for Leonora di Guzman. In Italy also given as *Daila* (Rome 29 September 1860, text altered by G. Cencetti) and as *Riccardo e Matilda*.

BUDAPEST 12 March 1842 (in German, translated by J. Kupelwieser, as *Die Templer in Sidon*) and 3 April 1869 (in Hungarian, translated by G. Böhm).

ST. PETERSBURG Autumn 1842 (in Russian) and Carnival 1846 (in Italian).

BERLIN, KGST. 15 October 1842 (in Italian) and O. 25 August 1852 (in German).

LISBON 11 December 1842 (in Italian).

GENEVA December 1842 (in French).

NEW ORLEANS 9 February 1843 (in French).

MILAN, SC. 16 August 1843 (in Italian).

MADRID 26 August 1843 (in Italian).

LONDON, D.L. 18 October 1843 (in English, translated by E. Fitzball); C.G. 9 June 1845 (in French); H.M.'s 16 February 1847 (in Italian); last revived at C.G. on 13 May 1896.

CAGLIARI, SARDINIA Autumn 1844 (in Italian).

NEW YORK 25 June 1845 (in French); 4 October 1847 (in English); 21 December 1855 (in Italian).

RIO DE JANEIRO Autumn 1846 (in French) and 1852 (in Italian).

BUCHAREST 1847 (in Italian).

ALGIERS Spring 1847 (in French).

HAVANA 1849 (in Italian).

STOCKHOLM 9 March 1850 (in Swedish, translated by A. F. Lindblad).

BASLE 15 March 1850 (in German).

WILNA 6 January 1851 (in Polish, translated by J. Checiński).

MALTA 1851 (in Italian).

BRÜNN 17 November 1851 (in German).

MEXICO 25 May 1852 (in Italian).

BUENOS AIRES 22 July 1852 (in French) and 19 October 1855 (in Italian).

DUBLIN 20 September 1856 (in Italian).

MELBOURNE 1858 (in English).

SOERABAYA 2 January 1865 (in French).

VALPARAISO 1865 (in Italian).

CAIRO November 1870 (in Italian).

ZAGREB 4 December 1875 (in Croatian, translated by I. Trnski).

PRAGUE 6 December 1889 (in Czech, translated by V. J. Novotný).

CAPE TOWN 1895 (in Italian).

HELSINKI 23 September 1896 (in Italian).

LJUBLJANA 1902 (in Slovenian).

PONIATOWSKY: *Don Desiderio*

26 December. Pisa

Text by C. Zaccagnini (founded on a comedy by G. Giraud); sub-title: *Il Disperato per Eccesso di buon Cuore.* Two acts.

Subsequently given at Venice 29 March 1841; Florence 22 June 1841; Naples, T.N. Summer 1844, etc.

In Italian also, Paris 16 March 1858.

In Polish, Lemberg 12 February 1878.

HOVEN: *Johanna d'Arc*

30 December. Vienna, Kä.

Text by O. Prechtler (founded on Schiller's *Die Jungfrau von Orleans*). Five acts.

The most successful of Hoven's operas. Dresden 16 February 1845, etc.

1841

HALÉVY: *Le Guitarréro*

21 January. Paris, O.C.

Text by A. E. Scribe. Three acts.

In French also, Brussels 21 December 1841; Hague August 1842, etc.

In German (translated by J. C. Grünbaum), Cassel 29 September 1841; Berlin 15 October 1841.

In Italian, Malta 1890.

DONIZETTI: *Adelia*, ossia *La Figlia dell'Arciere*

11 February. Rome, Valle

Text by F. Romani (first set to music by Coccia in 1834) and G. M. Marini (who added a new third act for Donizetti). Three acts.

Outside Italy, given at Lisbon 28 March 1842; Malta 1842; Madrid 23 September 1842; London 11 March 1843.

AUBER: *Les Diamants de la Couronne*

6 March. Paris, O.C.

Text by A. E. Scribe and J. H. Vernoy de Saint-Georges. Three acts.

Given at the O.C. 379 times until 1889; revived Marseilles 20 March 1896.

Outside France, given at:

BRUSSELS 25 November 1841 (in French).

MUNICH 15 July 1842 (in German, translated by V. A. Swoboda).

PRAGUE 13 August 1842 (in German) and 4 December 1865 (in Czech, translated by B. Peška).

HAMBURG 29 October 1842 (in German).

RIGA 1843 (in German).

AMSTERDAM 1843 (in French).

BERLIN, O. 11 February 1843 (in German) and Vict. Th. 30 May 1862 (in French).

COPENHAGEN 17 February 1843 (in Danish, translated by T. Overskou).

NEW YORK 14 July 1843 (in French).

LONDON, PRINCESS'S 2 May 1844 (in English, translated by T. H. Reynoldson); C.G. 11 June 1845 (in French); D.L. 16 April 1846 (new English version by E. Fitzball, additional music by H.B. Richards and J. H. Tully); C.G. 3 July 1873 (in Italian, translated by G. Zaffira, recitatives by A. Vianesi).

STOCKHOLM 17 September 1845 (in Swedish, translated by N. E. W. af Wetterstedt).

RIO DE JANEIRO September 1846 (in French).

LEMBERG 1848 (in German).

VIENNA 25 January 1849 (in German; revived 18 December 1884).

BUENOS AIRES 11 April 1852 (in French).

BOSTON 1854 (in English, Fitzball's version).

SAN FRANCISCO 1854 (in English, Fitzball's version).

TURIN 3 April 1858 (in French).

SYDNEY August 1863 (in English, the D.L. version).

BARCELONA 20 October 1866 (in French).

ST. PETERSBURG 15 January 1876 (in Italian).

LISBON 26 April 1878 (in French).

NAPLES, TH. BELLINI 30 April 1879 (in Italian, translated by M. M. Marcello, recitatives by E. Gelli).

MEXICO 8 May 1879 (in French).

BUDAPEST 1880 (in Hungarian, translated by K. Abrányi).

MALTA 1890 (in Italian).

BARCELONA 22 August 1891 (*Zarzuela buffa*, 2 acts, *El Collar de Perlas*, text by José María Nogués and Ricardo Revenga, music adapted by Tomás Fernández Grájal).

BALFE: *Keolanthe; or, The Unearthly Bride*

9 March. London, Ly.

Text by E. Fitzball. Two acts.

In English also, Melbourne May 1855.

In German (as *Keolanthe, oder: Das Traumbild*, translated by C. Gollmick), Vienna 3 December 1853 (enlarged 3-act version, with seven additional numbers).

NICOLAI: *Il Proscritto*

13 March. Milan, Sc.

Text by G. Rossi (originally written for Verdi). Three acts.

Nicolai's last Italian opera; given at Milan for one night only.

In German (translated by S. Kapper), Vienna 3 February 1844; Berlin 19 November 1849.

Revived Vienna 9 October 1857.

F. RICCI: *Luigi Rolla e Michelangelo*

30 March. Florence, P.

Text by S. Cammarano. Three acts.

Successful in Italy; last revived Florence 18 April 1876.

In Italian also, Dresden 24 August 1843; Madrid 25 January 1845; Copenhagen November 1848; Warsaw August 1851; Lisbon 13 May 1855; St. Petersburg 23 December 1864.

ESLAVA: *Il Solitario del Monte Selvaggio*

June. Cadiz

Text probably an Italian version, by C. Bassi, of Planard's *Solitaire* (see 1822), originally called *Il Solitario* and first set by Persiani (Milan 20 April 1829). Three acts.

The first of Eslava's (Italian) operas. Madrid 7 December 1841.

KASTNER: *La Maschera*

17 June. Paris, O.C.

Text by J. de Wailly and A. J. F. Arnould. Two acts.

The most successful opera of Kastner, who was a theoretician and writer on music of considerable importance.

B. BASILJ: *El Contrabandista* (The Smuggler)

20 June. Madrid, T. de la Cruz.

(Spanish) text by T. Rodríguez y Díaz Rubí. Three acts.

Has been called, if not quite correctly, the first Spanish opera of the 19th century.

F. RICCI: *Corrado d'Altamura*

16 November. Milan, Sc.

Text by G. Sacchéro. There is an edition of the libretto (Rome 1842) on the title-page of which the name of the author is printed "Sauliero." Two acts.

Successful in Italy.

In Italian also, Vienna 21 April 1842; Barcelona 20 May 1843; Paris 15 March 1844; London, H.M.'s 10 August 1844; Amsterdam Carnival 1845; Copenhagen December 1845; Lisbon 2 February 1846; Boston September 1847; Santiago, Chile 1850; Malta 1851; Buenos Aires 12 May 1860.

In German (translated by S. Schlesinger), Budapest 27 August 1844.

F. LACHNER: *Catharina Cornaro,*
Königin von Cypern

3 December. Munich

Text by A. Büssel (a German version of Saint-
Georges's French libretto which he had sold to
both Lachner and Halévy; the latter's setting was
produced in Paris three weeks later). Four acts.

Lachner's most important work. Successful on
German stages: Vienna 19 November 1842 (altered); Berlin 15 October 1845, etc. In German
also, Brussels 26 July 1846.

Revived Mannheim 14 April 1878; Munich 4
October 1891 and 5 May 1903.

(For an English version of the libretto, see
Balfe's *Daughter of St. Mark,* 1844.)

HALÉVY: *La Reine de Chypre*

22 December. Paris, O.

Text by J. H. Vernoy de Saint-Georges. Five acts.

Given at the Paris O. 118 times until 1878;
100th performance 19 May 1854; last revival 6
August 1877; the vocal score was arranged by
Richard Wagner.

In French also, Antwerp 2 February 1843;
Brussels 21 August 1844; New Orleans 25 March
1845; London, D.L. 7 July 1845; New York 10
September 1845; Buenos Aires 21 June 1854;
Soerabaya 10 February 1865.

In German (translated by J. C. Grünbaum),
Leipzig 19 September 1842, etc.; Vienna 20 February 1858.

In Italian, Florence 26 December 1842; revived
Parma 26 December 1882 (translated by A. Zanardini).

DONIZETTI: *Maria Padilla*

26 December. Milan, Sc.

Text by G. Rossi (founded on a play by F. Ancelot). Three acts.

In Italian also, Lisbon 26 December 1845;
Malta 1846; Barcelona 15 August 1846; Vienna
18 May 1847.

In French (translated by H. Lucas), Versailles
March 1845; Nantes 7 February 1850; Marseilles
5 May 1854.

LORTZING: *Casanova*

31 December. Leipzig

Text by the composer (founded on a French
vaudeville, *Casanova au Fort Saint-André,* by C. V.
Varin, E. Arago and Desvergers). Three acts.

In German also, given at Riga December 1846.

Revived Berlin 8 February 1888 (in concert
form); on the stage: Hamburg 4 December 1889;
Leipzig 6 January 1900; Pyrmont 29 June 1901;
Rostock 7 February 1904.

A modern revival was at Wiesbaden 12 September 1925 (as *Der Mazurka-Oberst oder Die
galante Festung,* text revised by W. Jacoby, music
arranged by H. Spangenberg from *Casanova* and
other works by Lortzing).

1842

AUBER: *Le Duc d'Olonne*

4 February. Paris, O.C.

Text by A. E. Scribe and X. B. Saintine. Three
acts.

In French also, Brussels 19 October 1842.

In German (translated by H. Börnstein), Berlin
13 November 1842; Prague 14 August 1843.

In Portuguese, Lisbon 26 February 1843.

In English (translated by T. H. Reynoldson),
London, Princess's Th. 14 April 1845.

In Norwegian (translated by A. Vibe), Christiania 1847.

EUGEN (DUKE OF WÜRTTEMBERG):
Die Geisterbraut

22 February. Breslau

Text by the composer (founded on the poem by
G. A. Bürger). Three acts.

Given at Breslau 26 times during the first season. Revived Stuttgart 26 December 1880.

The vocal score had been published already in
1838.

VERDI: *Nabucodonosor*

9 March. Milan, Sc.

Text by T. Solera (first offered to and refused by
Nicolai). Four acts.

Verdi's first great success and the first of his operas which made the composer's name known in other countries. Repeated at the Scala in the next season, 13 August, and given there 67 times until 4 December 1842.

Outside Italy, produced at:

VIENNA 4 April 1843 (in Italian; first Verdi opera in Vienna; in German 22 January 1848).

CAGLIARI, SARDINIA Autumn 1843 (in Italian).

LISBON 29 October 1843 (in Italian).

BARCELONA 2 May 1844 (in Italian).

BERLIN, KGST. 21 September 1844 (in Italian).

STUTTGART 27 September 1844 (for the first time in German, translated by H. Proch).

CORFU 28 September 1844 (in Italian).

MALTA Autumn 1844 (in Italian).

MARSEILLES July 1845 (in Italian).

ALGIERS Summer 1845 (in Italian).

PARIS 16 October 1845 (in Italian).

HAMBURG 29 October 1845 (in German).

COPENHAGEN Carnival 1846 (in Italian).

LONDON, H.M.'s 3 March 1846 (in Italian, as *Nino*) and C.G. 30 May 1850 (as *Anato*).

BUDAPEST 31 August 1846 (in German), 2 January 1847 (in Hungarian, translated by B. Egressy) and October 1847 (in Italian).

CONSTANTINOPLE Autumn 1846 (in Italian).

HAVANA 1847 (in Italian).

BUCHAREST November 1847 (in Italian; Rumanian translations published Jassy 1851 and Bucharest 1856).

NEW YORK 4 April 1848 (in Italian).

BRUSSELS 29 November 1848 (in French, translated by F. Gravrand and J. Guilliaume).

GRAZ 8 January 1849 (in German).

PRAGUE 5 March 1849 (in German) and 7 December 1868 (in Czech, translated by B. Peška).

LEMBERG 1850 (in German).

BUENOS AIRES 22 August 1850 (in Italian).

ZURICH 1851 (in German).

ST. PETERSBURG 27 December 1851 (in Italian).

MONTEVIDEO 1852 (in Italian).

RIO DE JANEIRO 1856 (in Italian).

MEXICO December 1856 (in Italian).

RIGA October 1858 (in German).

GOTHENBURG 1865 (in German).

ZAGREB 1 October 1878 (in Croatian, translated by J. E. Tomić).

Still given in Italy; some of the latest revivals were at Florence 22 April 1933 (opening of the first Maggio Musicale Fiorentino) and at Milan, Sc. 26 December 1933; revived at Amsterdam November 1936 (in Italian).

Revived in Germany (after a long period of oblivion) Mannheim 28 October 1928 (new translation by L. Schottlaender) and subsequently on many other German stages. Berlin, Berliner Th. 4 April 1935 (by the "Jüdischer Kulturbund"). Cassel 25 December 1939 (new translation by J. Kapp).

NETZER: *Mara*

16 March. Vienna, Kä.

Text by O. Prechtler. Three acts.

Netzer's most successful work. Prague 10 November 1843; Berlin 23 July 1844, etc.

DONIZETTI: *Linda di Chamounix*

19 May. Vienna, Kä.

Text by G. Rossi. Three acts.

The first of the two Italian operas Donizetti wrote for Vienna (first given there in German 28 March 1849).

TURIN, T. CARIGNANO 24 August 1842 and all over Italy.

BUDAPEST 10 September 1842 (in German, translated by H. Proch) and 1844 (in Hungarian, translated by B. Egressy).

PARIS, TH.I. 17 November 1842 (in Italian).

HAMBURG 10 December 1842 (in German).

BERLIN, O. 18 December 1842 (in German) and Kgst. 8 September 1845 (in Italian).

LONDON, H.M.'s 1 June 1843 (in Italian) and D.L. 12 January 1848 (in English, translated by M. D. Ryan).

SEVILLA November 1843 (in Italian); Madrid 9 December 1843, etc.

BRUSSELS 1 February 1844 (in French, translated by H. Lucas).

AGRAM March 1844 (in German).

PRAGUE 23 April 1844 (in German) and 5 January 1865 (in Czech, translated by F. Martinec).

CAGLIARI, SARDINIA 15 November 1844 (in Italian).

COPENHAGEN Carnival 1845 (in Italian).

MALTA Carnival 1845 (in Italian).

ST. PETERSBURG February 1845 (in Italian) and 10 March 1861 (in Russian).

CLAUSENBURG 29 March 1845 (in Hungarian, translated by B. Egressy).

CORFU Autumn 1845 (in Italian).

LISBON 19 October 1845 (in Italian).

ZANTE November 1845 (in Italian).

BUCHAREST Carnival 1846 (in Italian) and 18 May 1885 (in Rumanian).

NEW YORK 4 January 1847 (in Italian) and 4 August 1847 (in English; Ann Bishop's American début).

DUBLIN 28 April 1847 (in English) and 21 February 1850 (in Italian).

HAVANA 1847 (in Italian).

WARSAW 11 July 1847 (in Polish, translated by J. Jasiński).

BASLE 10 November 1847 (in German).

STOCKHOLM 1849 (in Italian; Swedish translation in libretto by N. E. W. af Wetterstedt) and 21 April 1855 (in Swedish, translated by C. W. A. Strandberg).

BUENOS AIRES 4 October 1849 (in Italian).

RIGA 1851 (in German).

MEXICO 1852 (in Italian).

MONTEVIDEO 1852 (in Italian).

CONSTANTINOPLE Carnival 1854 (in Italian).

SANTIAGO, CHILE 1854 (in Italian).

MARSEILLES 17 December 1855, Lille 28 February 1856, Lyons 6 April 1858 (in French).

HELSINKI 30 July 1857 (in German) and 21 November 1878 (in Finnish, translated by P. Cajander).

MELBOURNE 1861 (in English).

CALCUTTA 1867–68.

ATHENS 1874 (in Italian).

BATAVIA 1892 (in Italian).

Still given in Italy (Milan, Sc. 9 December 1939); outside Italy, some of the more recent revivals were at:

BERLIN, TH. D. W. 4 October 1899 (in German).

ST. PETERSBURG February 1906 (in Italian).

MONTE CARLO 21 March 1911 (in Italian).

LJUBLJANA 1932 (in Slovenian).

NEW YORK, M. 1 March 1934 (in Italian).

ADAM: *Le Roi d'Yvetot*

13 October. Paris, O.C.

Text by A. de Leuven and L. L. Brunswick (founded on a poem by Béranger). Three acts.

In French also, Brussels 10 April 1843; London, St. J.'s 11 February 1850; revived Paris, Th.L. 5 January 1853.

In German (translated by J. Franke), Leipzig 25 March 1843; Berlin 23 June 1844, etc.

R. WAGNER: *Cola Rienzi, der Letzte der Tribunen*

20 October. Dresden

Text by the composer (founded on Bulwer Lytton's novel). Five acts.

In the same year as Verdi, Wagner had his first greater success. Most stages, however, produced *Rienzi* only after *Holländer*, *Tannhäuser*, or even *Lohengrin*, and some other stages never at all.

Given at Dresden sometimes in two parts and on two subsequent nights (as *Rienzis Grösse* and *Rienzis Fall*, first on 23 and 24 January 1843). The 100th performance at Dresden was on 18 December 1873, the 200th on 30 August 1908.

After Dresden, given at Hamburg 21 March 1844; Königsberg 1845; Berlin 26 October 1847, etc. At Berlin, given 155 times up to 1935 (revived 11 March 1933).

Outside Germany:

PRAGUE 24 October 1859 (in German).

STOCKHOLM 5 June 1865 (in Swedish, translated by F. Arlberg).

GRAZ 13 November 1865 (in German).

ROTTERDAM 13 January 1868 (in German).

PARIS, TH.L. 6 April 1869 (in French, translated by C. Nuitter and J. Guilliaume).

VIENNA 30 May 1871 (in German).

GHENT 22 March 1872 (in French).

ANTWERP 27 March 1873 (in French).

VENICE 15 March 1874 (in Italian, translated by A. Boito); Bologna 14 November 1876; Rome 3 October 1880, etc.

BUDAPEST November 1874 (in Hungarian, translated by G. Böhm); revived March 1936.

MADRID 5 February 1876 (in Italian; first Wagner opera in Spain).

RIGA 9 February 1878 (in German).

NEW YORK 4 March 1878 (in German); Philadelphia 20 March 1878, etc.

LONDON, H.M.'s 27 January 1879 (in English, translated by J. P. Jackson); revived Lyric 27 August 1909.

ST. PETERSBURG 3 November 1879 (in Russian, translated by G. A. Lishin); revived 7 November 1923.

ZURICH 22 December 1880 (in German).

ZAGREB 15 January 1901 (in Croatian, translated by F. Miler).

REVAL 1902 (in German).

Catalan version by X. Viura and J. Pena published 1906.

DIETSCH: *Le Vaisseau-Fantôme*

9 November. Paris, O.

Text by P. H. Foucher and B. H. Révoil (founded on the scenario of *Der fliegende Holländer* which Wagner had been forced to sell for 500 francs). Two acts.

Dietsch's opera was a failure and given for 11 nights only (see G. Servières, in his *Episodes d'Histoire Musicale*, 1914).

Incidentally, the composer of *Le Vaisseau-Fantôme* was to conduct *Tannhäuser* in Paris 19 years later.

GLINKA: *Ruslan i Lyudmila*

Русланъ и Людмила

9 December. St. Petersburg

Text after Pushkin, partly drafted by K. A. Bakhturin, mainly by V. F. Shirkof, with additions by N. Kukolnik, M. A. Gedeonov, one Markevitch and Glinka himself. Five acts.

Glinka's second and last opera, equally important if not quite as popular as *A Life for the Czar* (see 1836). Full score not published until 1878.

First produced at Moscow in 1847. 300th performance at St. Petersburg 6 December 1893;

given there in Italian (translated by V. Narducci) 20 January 1899.

Outside Russia produced at:

PRAGUE 16 February 1867 (in Czech, translated by J. J. Kolár; revived 20 June 1886).

TIFLIS February 1881 (in Russian).

LJUBLJANA 3 November 1906 (in Slovenian).

HELSINKI 2 April 1907 (in Russian).

PARIS, CHÂTELET 4 June 1909 (the first act only); CH. É. 24 May 1930, (the whole work, in Russian).

SAN SEBASTIAN October 1930 (in Russian).

LONDON, LY. 4 June 1931 (in Russian).

RIGA 3 September 1931 (in Lettish).

Still given in U.S.S.R.; produced at Baku Spring 1937 (in Azerbaidzhan).

Ruslan i Lyudmila was the first opera founded on one of the works of A. S. Pushkin (1799–1837), the great animating spirit of Russian music in the 19th century. A list of operas taken from his plays and poems will be found in *Pamy A. S. Pushkina* (1900), pp. 124–131.

PACINI: *La Fidanzata Corsa*

10 December. Naples, S.C.

Text by S. Cammarano (founded on Mérimée's *Colomba*). Three acts.

In Italian also given at Paris 17 November 1846; Lisbon 12 March 1848; Barcelona 18 August 1848; Rio de Janeiro 1850; Buenos Aires 17 February 1854.

LORTZING: *Der Wildschütz* oder *Die Stimme der Natur*

31 December. Leipzig

Text by the composer (founded on a play by A. von Kotzebue *Der Rehbock*). Three acts.

Very popular in Germany: Vienna, Jos. 18 August 1843 (Kä. only 21 January 1860); Berlin 24 October 1843; Prague 3 February 1844; Graz 3 May 1845; Basle 18 February 1846, etc.

In German also, Helsinki 30 June 1850; Milwaukee 1853; Ghent 18 April 1855; New York 25 March 1859; Rotterdam Autumn 1861; Philadelphia 21 January 1863; London, D.L. 3 July 1895.

In Swedish (translated by G. L. Silverstolpe), Stockholm 31 October 1849.

In Czech (translated by E. Züngel), Prague 1882.

In Hungarian (translated by E. Abrányi), Budapest 10 February 1894.

In Croatian (translated by M. Pogačić), Zagreb 26 September 1899.

In Flemish, Antwerp 9 November 1907.

In English (translated by A. Houghton), Brooklyn, Little Th. 9 November 1931 and New York, Heckscher Th. 16 November 1931.

1843

WAGNER: *Der fliegende Holländer*

2 January. Dresden

Text by the composer (founded on an episode in Heine's *Memoiren des Herrn von Schnabelewopski*). Three acts.

Given at Dresden in 1843 four times only and not revived there until 1865; 100th performance 13 March 1884, 200th 2 January 1899, 300th 13 February 1910.

The next productions were at:

RIGA 3 June 1843 (in German, under H. Dorn); in Lettish much later, see below.

CASSEL 5 June 1843 (under Spohr).

BERLIN 7 January 1844 (500th performance 18 October 1936).

ZURICH 25 April 1852 (Basle only 29 November 1877).

PRAGUE 7 September 1856 (Brünn only 2 December 1871); in Czech much later, see below.

VIENNA 2 November 1860.

ROTTERDAM 30 October 1869.

LONDON, D.L. 23 July 1870 (in Italian, as *L'Olandese dannato*, translated by S. de Castrone, Marchese della Rajata; the printed English version in the libretto by L. H. F. du Terreaux). First Wagner opera ever produced in London (conductor: Arditi); Ly. 3 October 1876 (in English, translated by J. P. Jackson); D.L. 20 May 1882 (in German).

GRAZ 29 July 1870.

STOCKHOLM 24 January 1872 (in Swedish, translated by F. Arlberg).

BRUSSELS 6 April 1872 (in French, translated by C. Nuitter).

BUDAPEST 10 May 1873 (in Hungarian, translated by K. Abrányi).

PHILADELPHIA 8 November 1876 (for the first time in America, in Italian).

NEW YORK 26 January 1877 (in English); 12 March 1877 (in German); and 31 March 1892 (in Italian).

EDINBURGH February 1877 (in English).

DUBLIN 9 August 1877 (in Italian).

BOLOGNA 20 November 1877 (for the first time in Italy, as *Il Vascello Fantasma*, translated by A. Giovannini); Turin 2 November 1886; Rome, Ap. 3 April 1887; Florence 23 May 1887, etc.

NEW ORLEANS 29 November 1877 (in French).

GHENT 20 December 1880 (in German).

COPENHAGEN 7 September 1884 (in Danish, translated by A. Zinck).

BARCELONA 12 December 1885 (in Italian); Catalan version by X. Viura and A. Ribera published 1904.

BUENOS AIRES 9 August 1887 (in Italian).

MEXICO 3 April 1891 (in English).

REVAL (TALLINN) 9 December 1892 (in German) and 1925 (in Estonian, translated by H. Kompus).

LILLE 28 January 1893 (in French, for the first time in France); Rouen 12 February 1896, etc., Lyons as late as 25 March 1909.

LISBON March 1893 (in Italian).

GENEVA 27 December 1893 (in French).

MOSCOW 18 February 1894 (in Italian) and 2 December 1902 (in Russian).

ANTWERP 30 January 1895 (in Flemish).

MONTREAL 3 April 1895 (in English; concert performance).

ZAGREB 28 March 1896 (in Croatian, translated by F. Miler).

MADRID 27 October 1896 (in Italian).

PARIS, O.C. 17 May 1897 (in French).

ST. PETERSBURG 7 March 1898 (in German).

LJUBLJANA 27 January 1900 (in Slovenian, translated by A. Štritov).

HELSINKI 26 May 1900 (in German) and 2 December 1924 (in Finnish, translated by T. Muroma).

CHRISTIANIA (OSLO) 9 May 1901 (in Norwegian).

LEMBERG 7 February 1902 (in Polish, translated by T. Mianowski).

PRAGUE 17 December 1907 (in Czech, translated by V. J. Novotný).

RIGA September 1918 (in Lettish, translated by R. Egle).

BUCHAREST 2 October 1922 (in Rumanian).

BELGRADE 6 November 1923 (in Serbian).

SOFIA 10 February 1930 (in Bulgarian, translated by V. Bobchevsky).

Wagner was not the first to write a *Flying Dutchman* opera. Apart from Dietsch's *Le Vaisseau-Fantôme* (see 1842), there was an English melodrama *The Flying Dutchman; or, The Phantom Ship*, text by E. Fitzball, music by G. Rodwell, performed at the Adelphi Th., London 1 January 1827 and in New York 9 April 1827. On its possible connection with Wagner's opera, see the study by W. A. Ellis in *The Meister*, February 1892.

DONIZETTI: *Don Pasquale*

3 January. Paris, Th.I.

Text founded on Anelli's *Ser Marc'Antonio* (see 1810), re-written by Donizetti himself and "Michele Accursi", pseudonym of G. Ruffini, who is mentioned in later editions of the vocal score). Three acts.

There has always been some uncertainty as to the author of the text and different names occur in different books of reference. It is attributed to the Neapolitan Carlo Zanobi Cafferecci (1811–60) by C. Martorana (*Notizie biografiche*, 1874) and in Wotquenne's catalogue of the library of the Brussels Conservatoire, Vol.II, p.110.

Donizetti's last great success and of his 66 operas the one which is most popular at present.

A French parody *Don Pasquale*, *Opéra buffa, mêlé de couplets*, by P. A. Chapelle, was produced at the Gymnase-Dramatique, Paris 14 March 1843.

Outside Paris given at:

MILAN, SC. 17 April 1843, Turin, T. d'Angennes in the same stagione, Naples, T.N. Summer 1843 and all over Italy.

VIENNA 14 May 1843 (in Italian) and 4 October 1879 (in German).

LONDON, H.M.'s 29 June 1843 (in Italian) and Princess's 23 October 1843 (in English, translated by T. H. Reynoldson).

BRUSSELS 11 August 1843 (in French, translated by A. Royer and G. Vaëz).

LILLE 9 November 1843 (in French).

CORFU 2 December 1843 (in Italian).

ST. PETERSBURG 1844 (in Italian).

HANOVER 28 May 1844 (in German, translated by H. Proch).

DUBLIN 12 September 1844 (in Italian).

COPENHAGEN Carnival 1845 (in Italian).

MADRID 4 January 1845 (in Italian) and [21 May] 1863 (in Spanish, translated by M. Pastorfido).

BRÜNN 7 February 1845 (in German).

BERLIN, KGST. 24 February 1845 (in Italian); O. 19 April 1852 (in German); Vict. Th. 4 April 1886 (in French).

LISBON 30 November 1845 (in Italian).

NEW YORK 9 March 1846 (in English) and 29 November 1849 (in Italian).

CLAUSENBURG 20 March 1846 and Budapest 1 October 1846 (in Hungarian, translated by B. Egressy).

WARSAW 20 August 1846 (in Polish, translated by J. Jasiński).

MALTA 1847 (in Italian).

CONSTANTINOPLE May 1847 (in Italian).

SANTIAGO, CHILE 1848 (in Italian).

STOCKHOLM 1848 (in Italian) and 6 December 1869 (in Swedish, translated by E. A. Wallmark).

PRAGUE 1849 (in German) and 15 June 1869 (in Czech, translated by J. Böhm).

BUENOS AIRES 16 May 1851 (in Italian).

MEXICO 1852 (in Italian).

LIMA, PERU 1852 (in Italian).

AMSTERDAM 1853 (in Italian).

RIO DE JANEIRO 1853 (in Italian).

MELBOURNE 1856 (in English).

BUCHAREST 1857 (in Italian) and Autumn 1929 (in Rumanian).

PARIS, TH.L. 9 September 1864 (in Paris for the first time in French; O.C. 24 June 1896).

CALCUTTA 1866 (in Italian).

HELSINKI 22 May 1878 (in Finnish, translated by A. Törneroos).

RIGA 1906 (in German).

ZAGREB 19 October 1921 (in Croatian).

LJUBLJANA 1925 (in Slovenian).

SOFIA 8 April 1932 (in Bulgarian).

KAUNAS 23 October 1936 (in Lithuanian).

Still on the stage in many countries; a new German version by O. J. Bierbaum and W. Kleefeld was first produced at Frankfort 14 September 1902; at Vienna 14 September 1911. Revived (in English) Birmingham 4 July 1921; in Hungarian (new translation by V. Lányi) Budapest 26 March 1931; in Russian, Leningrad 29 June 1931; in Italian, last revived at New York, M. 23 February 1935; London, C.G. 21 April 1937; first given at Glyndebourne 28 June 1938.

AUBER: *La Part du Diable*

16 January. Paris, O.C.

Text by A. E. Scribe. Three acts.

Revived at the O.C. 4 September 1858 and 25 March 1868. Given there 263 times altogether.

Outside Paris, given at:

VIENNA, W. 8 July 1843 and Kä. 25 September 1847 (in German, translated by H. Börnstein and C. Gollmick).

COPENHAGEN 31 July 1843 (in French).

BRUSSELS 29 August 1843 (in French).

FRANKFORT 17 September 1843 (in German).

BERLIN 19 November 1843 (in German).

PRAGUE 17 February 1844 (in German) and 6 March 1853 (in Czech, translated by J. J. Litněnský); new translation by E.Züngel published 1881.

STOCKHOLM 18 December 1844 (in Swedish, translated by L. A. Weser).

BUDAPEST 21 December 1844 (in German) and 3 October 1846 (in Hungarian).

LONDON, C.G. 13 June 1845 (in French) and Grecian Th. 13 February 1849 (in English, translated by J. H. Horncastle).

BASLE 10 October 1845 (in German).

WARSAW 1 February 1846 (in Polish, translated by J. Jasiński).

CLAUSENBURG 28 February 1846 (in Hungarian, translated by B. Egressy).

RIO DE JANEIRO Autumn 1846 (in French).

LISBON 27 May 1849 (in French).

HELSINKI 25 June 1849 (in German).

NEW YORK 10 May 1852 (in English) and 25 January 1875 (in German).

BERGEN 4 November 1855 (in Danish, translated by E. Bøgh; pasticcio).

MADRID 1863 (in Spanish, translated by E. Álvarez).

Revived Plymouth 7 May 1870 (in English); Budapest 7 December 1889 (in Hungarian); Basle 19 March 1902 (in German); Oppeln, Silesia 21 January 1930 (in German).

(The hero of the opera is the famous castrato Carlo Broschi, called Farinelli. The story has nothing to do with the *Devil to pay* subject as sometimes stated).

VERDI: *I Lombardi alla prima Crociata*

11 February. Milan, Sc.

Text by T. Solera (founded on T. Grossi's poem). Four acts.

This first version of the opera was outside Italy (in Italian), also produced at:

ODESSA March 1845.

BARCELONA 7 June 1845.

BERLIN, KGST. 25 August 1845.

CAGLIARI, SARDINIA 6 September 1845.

BUCHAREST Autumn 1845.

CORFU October 1845.

ST. PETERSBURG November 1845.

LONDON, H.M.'s 12 May 1846.

VIENNA 27 May 1846.

COPENHAGEN Carnival 1847.

NEW YORK 3 March 1847. (First Verdi opera in New York.)

LISBON 16 March 1847.
MALTA 1847.
PHILADELPHIA 17 July 1847.
HAVANA 1848.
STOCKHOLM 1849.
CONSTANTINOPLE 1850.
BUENOS AIRES 26 April 1851.
MEXICO July 1852.

New French version, *Jérusalem*, translated by A. Royer and G. Vaëz, with several additional numbers: Paris, O. 26 November 1847; in French also, Brussels 15 July 1848; New Orleans January 1850; Soerabaya 24 October 1864.

In Polish (translated by J. Jasiński), Warsaw 25 March 1848.

In German (translated by J. von Seyfried), Hamburg 10 July 1849; Darmstadt 16 December 1849; Graz 28 December 1861, etc.

In Italian (re-translated by C. Bassi, as *Gerusalemme*): Milan, Sc. 26 December 1850; Constantinople January 1851 (as *Giselda*, libretto altered by Tondi); Vienna 16 May 1853; Alexandria Spring 1855; Algiers Spring 1857; Oporto and Seville 1858; Buenos Aires 20 November 1858; Paris, Th.I. 10 January 1863 (in Paris for the first time in Italian); Sydney Summer 1874.

In Portuguese (translated by L. V. de Simoni), Rio de Janeiro 1859.

In Russian (translated by P. I. Kalashnikov), Kiev 1872.

In Dutch, Amsterdam 24 September 1895.

Some of the latest revivals in Italy were at Turin, T.R. 16 December 1926; Milan, Sc. 7 December 1931.

HALÉVY: *Charles VI*

15 March. Paris, O.

Text by C. and G. Delavigne. Five acts.

Revived, with some alterations, Paris, O. 4 October 1847; Th.L. 5 April 1870.

In French also, Brussels 2 October 1845; Hague 25 April 1846; New Orleans 22 April 1847; Buenos Aires 4 May 1854; Batavia 27 April 1866; Barcelona 29 April 1871; Mexico 19 January 1882; last revived Marseilles 8 April 1901.

In German, Hamburg 13 February 1851.

In Italian, Milan 16 March 1876.

Dutch version by J. Schmier published Amsterdam 1895.

BALFE: *Le Puits d'Amour*

20 April. Paris, O.C.

Text by A. E. Scribe and A. de Leuven. Three acts.

The first opera Balfe wrote to French words.

In French also, Lyons 26 August 1843, etc.; Brussels 28 December 1843.

In English (as *Geraldine; or, The Lover's Well*, translated by G. A. A'Beckett), London, Princess's 14 August 1843.

In Norwegian (translated by A. Vibe), Christiania 1845.

In German (as *Der Liebesbrunnen*, translated by J. Kupelwieser), Vienna, W. 4 November 1845; Hermannstadt 1850.

BUZZI: *Saul*

31 May. Ferrara

Text by C. Giuliani. Four acts.

Successful in Italy: Rome 29 April 1845, etc.

In Italian also, Buenos Aires 16 November 1854; Barcelona 31 October 1857.

DONIZETTI: *Maria di Rohan*

5 June. Vienna, Kä.

Text by S. Cammarano (originally called *Il Conte di Chalais* and set to music by Lillo in 1839). Three acts.

In Italian also given at Paris 20 November 1843; Parma 1 May 1844, etc. (Naples Autumn 1844 and Rome 26 December 1846 as *Il Conte di Chalais*); Malta 1845; St. Petersburg Carnival 1846; Corfu 5 January 1846; Barcelona 2 May 1846; London, C.G. 8 May [not 8 April] 1847; Berlin, Kgst. 4 September 1847; New York 10 December 1849; Lisbon 2 February 1850; Constantinople 15 February 1850; Agram January 1852; Mexico 5 June 1852; Lima, Peru 12 June 1853; Buenos Aires 11 December 1853; Bucharest 1858.

In French (translated by J. P. Lockroy and E. Badon), Brussels 7 January 1845.

In German (translated by J. Kupelwieser), Budapest 4 January 1845; Vienna 11 August 1849; Lemberg 1850; Prague 1851; Graz 20 October 1853.

In Czech (translated by V. Zabranský), Prague 14 May 1865.

In Polish, Lemberg 30 November 1876.

In Rumanian, Bucharest 1903.

Revived Florence 8 October 1885 and 11 January 1910; Vienna 1 April 1880 (in German) and 12 June 1910 (in Italian); Barcelona 27 November 1906 (in Italian); Paris, O. 22 March 1917 (in French).

A. THOMAS: *Mina* ou *Le Ménage à trois*

10 October. Paris, O.C.

Text by F. A. E. de Planard. Three acts.

In French also, Antwerp 17 November 1844; Brussels 20 January 1847, etc.

In German (translated by C. Gollmick), Lemberg August 1847.

DONIZETTI: *Don Sébastien, Roi de Portugal*

13 November. Paris, O.

Text by A. E. Scribe. Five acts.

The last opera of Donizetti which was produced in his lifetime. Donizetti himself thought *Don Sébastien* to be his masterpiece; the disappointment caused by the failure accelerated the paralysis which finished his activity in 1844.

Given at Paris 32 times until 1845.

In French also, Antwerp 16 January 1848; Brussels 5 April 1848, etc.

In Italian (translated by G. Ruffini), Lisbon 4 May 1845; Milan 14 August 1847; Barcelona 21 September 1848; Rio de Janeiro 1856; Buenos Aires 13 December 1856; Malta 1860; New York 25 November 1864; Mexico 6 December 1866.

In German (translated by L. Herz), Vienna 6 February 1845; Budapest 3 June 1846; Prague 10 October 1846; Dresden 6 January 1848; Hamburg

15 January 1848; Graz 9 October 1852, etc.; Riga Autumn 1856 and Helsinki 16 August 1857 (as *Dom Vincente*).

In Czech (translated by J. A. Zabranský), Prague 8 November 1867.

The opera was revived in German at Carlsruhe on 10 March 1901; in Italian, Bergamo May 1909 and Rome April 1911.

Never given in London (although a production was planned in the 'sixties and an Italian-English libretto was printed).

BALFE: *The Bohemian Girl*

27 November. London, D.L.

Text by A. Bunn (founded on *La Gipsy*, a ballet-pantomime by J. H. Vernoy de Saint-Georges, produced at the Paris Opéra 28 January 1839, with music by F. Benoist, A. Thomas and M. A. Marliani, itself based on Cervantes's story *La Gitanella*). Three acts.

Balfe's most popular work; in fact, the most successful English opera of the early 19th century and about the only one which made headway in other countries as well. The 100th performance at D.L. was as early as 13 November 1844; subsequently given at Dublin 24 June 1844; New York 25 November 1844; Philadelphia 16 December 1844; Sydney 15 July 1846; and in all English-speaking countries.

In English also, Toronto June 1874; New Orleans December 1876; Mexico 18 February 1884; Cape Town 1887.

In Italian (as *La Zingara*), London, H.M.'s 6 February 1858; Dublin 16 August 1858; New York 10 January 1859, etc.

In German (first translated by J. P. T. Lyser), Vienna, W. 24 July 1846 (Kä. 1 October 1849, translated by J. Staudigl, with recitatives by H. Proch); Hamburg 17 December 1846; Brünn 15 May 1847; Prague 19 November 1847; Frankfort 22 October 1849; Munich 11 April 1850; Berlin 15 October 1850; Zurich October 1854; Amsterdam 9 October 1855; Basle 11 October 1861; Gothenburg 1865; New York 19 September 1873.

The latest revivals in German were at Chemnitz 4 March 1879; Berlin, Louisenstadt 20 July 1881; Teplitz 10 February 1886; Darmstadt 25 November 1888; Coburg 17 May 1892; Posen 30 April 1902.

In Italian (translated by R. Paderni), Madrid 9 April 1845; Trieste 12 February 1854; Brescia Summer 1854; Bologna Autumn 1854, etc.

In Swedish (translated by A. T. Blanche), Stockholm 28 March 1849.

In French (translated by J. H. Vernoy de Saint-Georges, recitatives and two new arias by Duprato), Rouen 23 April 1862; Liége 9 February 1863; Paris, Th.L. 30 December 1869.

In Croatian (translated by A. Šenoa), Zagreb 5 October 1872.

According to Morkov also given at St. Petersburg between 1855–62, in Russian.

A 50th anniversary performance took place at D.L. on 27 November 1893; a 75th anniversary performance at the Shaftesbury Th. on 8 June 1918.

Still given on English provincial and amateur stages; one of the latest productions was at Dublin on 6 November 1920; there was an open-air revival at Scarborough on 24 July 1939.

Revived New York, Majestic 27 July 1933; and, as a musical comedy, *Gypsy Blonde*, rewritten by K. Jones, lyrics by F. Gabrielson, Lyric Th. 25 June 1934.

PACINI: *Medea*

28 November. Palermo

Text by B. Castiglia. Three acts.

Outside Italy, given at Barcelona 15 October 1845; Malta 1858; Mexico 10 October 1858; New York 27 September 1860; Buenos Aires 7 June 1865; Rio de Janeiro Autumn 1865.

FLOTOW: *L'Esclave de Camoëns*

1 December. Paris, O.C.

Text by J. H. Vernoy de Saint-Georges.

This opera, originally in one act, went through several different versions; translated into German by G. zu Putlitz it was given as *Indra, das Schlan-*

genmädchen (enlarged to three acts) at Vienna 18 December 1852; Frankfort 16 February 1853; Berlin 22 March 1853; Budapest 21 January 1854; Prague 22 February 1854; Riga 25 October 1855; Amsterdam 11 December 1855; Helsinki 9 August 1857, etc.

In Russian, St. Petersburg 8 May 1857; Moscow 19 October 1866.

Translated into Italian by A. de Lauzières (as *Alma l'Incantatrice*, 4 acts), given at Paris, Th.I. 9 April 1878 and London, C.G. 9 July 1878. This Italian version was again translated into German (by A. von Wolzogen) and given as *Alma* at Schwerin 28 February 1879.

The German *Indra* was revived at Posen 24 November 1882; Cassel 21 November 1883; Berlin, Louisenstadt Th. 12 July 1884; Basle 6 November 1889; Leipzig 18 September 1892; Reval 1896; Coburg 22 November 1901; Elberfeld October 1902.

1844

ERKEL: *Hunyady László*

27 January. Budapest

Text by B. Egressy. Four acts.

Erkel's most famous work; in the history of Hungarian music this opera holds the same position as *A Life for the Czar* (see 1836) in Russia, *Halka* (1854) in Poland, or *The Bartered Bride* (1866) in Czechoslovakia. Very successful in Hungary; the 200th performance at Budapest was on 24 February 1874; the 300th on 24 November 1898; last revived there in September 1933.

In Hungarian also, Clausenburg 26 April 1846; Temesvar 1852; Pressburg 1856; Vienna, W. 14 August 1856 (by a company from Arad); Zagreb July 1860.

In German (translated by A. Prasch), Prague 27 October 1895.

HATTON: *Pasqual Bruno*

2 March. Vienna, Kä.

(Original English) text by E. Fitzball, German version by J. von Seyfried. Three acts.

Unsuccessful in Vienna and never performed in England.

"Hatton . . . who, not being able to get it represented, and not having the patience of Rooke, to wait 20 years, took it over to Germany, had it translated into that language, and, on returning brought me a play-bill, thinking that I should be sufficiently delighted, and perfectly satisfied (as I was forced to be) at seeing my name Herr Fixball inserted as the English author of the libretto" (E. Fitzball, *Thirty-five Years*, Vol. II, p.158).

Hatton's second and last, equally unsuccessful, opera, *Rose; or, Love's Ransom*, text by H. S. Edwards, was produced 20 years later, London, C.G. 26 November 1864.

VERDI: *Ernani*

9 *March.* Venice, F.

Text by F. M. Piave (founded on Victor Hugo's drama *Hernani*). Four acts.

Even more successful than *Nabucodonosor* (1842) and *I Lombardi* (1843).

Performed on every Italian stage in Europe and oversea. The *Gazzetta Musicale Italiana* even records a performance at Manila (Philippines) on 8 December 1888. Sometimes performed as *Il Proscritto* (see Paris), *Elvira d'Aragona* (Palermo Carnival 1845), *Il Corsaro di Venezia* (Naples, T. Fondo 1847). Still given in Italy and other countries.

VIENNA 30 May 1844 (in Italian) and 3 March 1849 (in German).

LISBON 1 January 1845 (in Italian) and 15 January 1881 (in Portuguese).

MADRID 4 March 1845 (in Italian).

LONDON, H.M.'s 8 March 1845 (in Italian) and Surrey Th. 1 November 1851 (in English, translated by J. W. Mould); last revived Dalston Th. 6 March 1914.

ALGIERS 31 May 1845 (in Italian).

AMSTERDAM Autumn 1845 (in Italian).

PALMA, MALLORCA 27 November 1845 (in Italian).

BRUSSELS 17 December 1845 (in French, translated by M. and L. Escudier).

BERLIN, KGST. 27 December 1845 (in Italian) and O. 16 May 1859 (in German); revived 12 December 1934 (new German version by J. Kapp).

PARIS, TH.I. 6 January 1846 (in Italian, as *Il Proscritto ossia Il Corsaro di Venezia*, Victor Hugo protesting against the use of the title *Ernani*).

LILLE 8 January 1846 (in French).

CAGLIARI, SARDINIA Carnival 1846 (in Italian).

CONSTANTINOPLE Carnival 1846 (in Italian).

COPENHAGEN Carnival 1846 (in Italian).

MALTA 1846 (in Italian).

BUDAPEST 6 August 1846 (for the first time in German, translated by J. von Seyfried) and 3 February 1847 (in Hungarian, translated by B. Egressy).

LUGANO 10 October 1846 (in Italian).

ST. PETERSBURG October 1846 (in Italian).

HAVANA Carnival 1847 (in Italian).

HAMBURG 20 January 1847 (in German).

NEW YORK 15 April 1847 (in Italian).

BOSTON 23 April 1847 (in Italian).

SANTIAGO, CHILE 1847 (in Italian).

GRAZ 7 September 1847 (in German).

STOCKHOLM 1848 (in Italian) and 25 May 1853 (in Swedish, translated by G. L. Silverstolpe).

BUENOS AIRES 26 July 1849 (in Italian).

CHRISTIANIA August 1849 (in Italian) and January 1876 (in Norwegian).

PRAGUE 15 December 1849 (in German) and 7 September 1865 (in Czech, translated by B. Peška).

MEXICO 15 May 1850 (in Italian; partly orchestrated by J. Bustamente).

LEMBERG 1850 (in German).

WARSAW 25 January 1851 (in Polish, translated by J. Checiński); Wilna 2 February 1860.

DUBLIN 24 February 1851 (in Italian).

SAN FRANCISCO February 1851 (in Italian).

ZAGREB 19 March 1852 (in Italian); April 1856 (in German); and 18 November 1871 (in Croatian, translated by L. Vukotinović).

ZURICH January 1853 (in German); Geneva 10 January 1865 (in French); but see above, Lugano, for the first performance in Switzerland.

TIFLIS February 1854 (in Italian).

CARACAS, VENEZUELA October 1854 (in Italian).

RIO DE JANEIRO 11 November 1854 (in Italian).

SYDNEY April 1857 (in English).

BUCHAREST 1857 (in Italian) and October 1932 (in Rumanian).

HELSINKI 19 July 1857 (in German) and 4 January 1876 (in Finnish, translated by A. Törneroos).

BOGOTÁ, COLOMBIA 1865 (in Spanish).

SOERABAYA 7 December 1866 (in French).

CAIRO December 1869 (in Italian).

LJUBLJANA 1893 (in Slovenian).

CAPE TOWN 1895 (in Italian).

RIGA 30 January 1931 (in Lettish); earlier given there in German.

A Bulgarian translation was published at Shumen in 1905.

AUBER: *La Sirène*

26 March. Paris, O.C.

Text by A. E. Scribe. Three acts.

Successful in Paris; revived at the Th.L. 19 June 1855, at the O.C. 4 November 1861 and 26 January 1887 (164 performances).

In French also, Antwerp 2 November 1844; Brussels 18 November 1844, etc; New Orleans 1845; Buenos Aires 11 May 1854; London, St. J.'s 1 July 1854.

In German (translated by J. Franke), Frankfort 1 September 1844; Vienna, Jos. 21 September 1844; Berlin 15 October 1844; Würzburg 6 December 1844 (here, translated by H. Mainhardt); Graz 11 October 1845; Prague 7 January 1846, etc.

In English (translated by G. Soane), London, Princess's 14 October 1844; three days later another English version, by A. Bunn, was produced at D.L. (music adapted by J. H. Tully). In English also, New York 20 November 1854.

In Polish (translated by J. Jasiński), Warsaw 1 January 1845.

In Swedish (translated by J. M. Rosén), Stockholm 30 October 1846.

In Russian, St. Petersburg October 1851.

BENEDICT: *The Brides of Venice*

22 April. London, D.L.

Text by A. Bunn and the composer. Two acts.

In German (translated by K. Klingemann), Cassel 20 August 1845.

Revived Manchester 27 September 1877.

BOOM: *Necken,* eller *Elfspelet*
(The Sprite; or, Elves' Play)

11 May. Stockholm

Text by J. H. Meyersson. Three acts.

The only (*romantisk*) opera of the Dutch-Swedish composer.

SALOMAN: *Tordenskjold i Dynekilen*

23 May. Copenhagen

Text by H. Hertz (partly translated from a German libretto by J. P. T. Lyser). Three acts.

The first opera of the Danish composer; the overture had been heard at a concert at Dresden on 14 February 1842.

COSTA: *Don Carlos*

20 June. London, H.M.'s

(Italian) text by L. Tarantini. Three acts.

Costa's last opera; unsuccessful.

BALFE: *Les quatre Fils Aymon*

15 July. Paris, O.C.

Text by A. de Leuven and L. L. Brunswick. Three acts.

Given in Paris 17 times only; not very successful in England either; but very popular on German stages, where its success even surpassed that of *The Bohemian Girl* (see 1843).

In French also produced at Count Farrobo's private theatre, Lisbon 10 May 1846.

In English (as *The Castle of Aymon; or, The Four Brothers,* translated by G. A. A'Beckett ?), London, Princess's 20 November 1844.

In German (translated by J. Kupelwieser), Vienna, Jos. 14 December 1844 and (translated by J. von Seyfried) Kä. 27 September 1845; Prague 14 March 1845 (revived 22 January 1870); Frankfort 21 July 1845; Leipzig 29 August 1845; Hamburg 12 September 1845; Basle 11 February 1846;

Amsterdam March 1846; Berlin Kroll's 6 June 1852 (revived Woltersdorf Th. 18 December 1877), etc.; on German stages until about 1880.

In Hungarian (translated by B. Egressy), Budapest 1845; Clausenburg 3 November 1845.

In Italian (translated by S. M. Maggioni), London, H.M.'s 11 August 1851.

LVOV: *Bianca und Gualtiero*

13 October. Dresden

(Original French) text by J. Guillou, German version by J. C. Grünbaum. Three acts.

The first opera of the Russian composer. Given at St. Petersburg 9 February 1845 (in Italian).

VERDI: *I due Foscari*

3 November. Rome, Arg.

Text by F. M. Piave (founded on Byron's drama). Three acts.

In Italian also given at:
VIENNA 1 April 1845.
BARCELONA 8 July 1845.
HAVANA 1846.
CAGLIARI, SARDINIA 20 September 1846.
CONSTANTINOPLE 12 October 1846.
COPENHAGEN November 1846.
PARIS 17 December 1846.
ST. PETERSBURG Carnival 1847.
LONDON, C.G. 10 April 1847.
BOSTON May 1847.
NEW YORK 9 June 1847.
LUGANO 1848.
SANTIAGO, CHILE 1848.
MALTA 1849.
RIO DE JANEIRO 4 September 1849.
BUCHAREST 14 January 1850.
BUENOS AIRES 25 May 1850.
BRUSSELS September 1850.
MEXICO December 1852.
GRAZ 6 June 1853.
OPORTO Carnival 1855.
SYDNEY May 1868.

In Polish (translated by J. Jasiński), Warsaw 24 May 1849; Lemberg 3 August 1876.

In French (translated by M. and L. Escudier), Antwerp 18 December 1849; Brest November 1850.

In Hungarian, Budapest 9 December 1850 (translated by B. Egressy).

In German, Weimar 8 April 1856; Lemberg April 1857.

Rumanian translation published Jassy 1851.

Revived New York 27 October 1886.

Revived in Italy, Siena 10 January 1892; Milan, T. Fossati 4 September 1903, etc.

Revived in a new German version by R. Franz, Halle 12 February 1929.

(From a note in a copy of the score it would seem that *I due Foscari* was performed at Hongkong in Autumn 1870; see R. Franz in *Zeitschrift für Musik*, 1929, p.71.)

SECHTER: *Ali Hitsch-Hatsch*

12 November. Vienna, Jos.

Text by "Theodor Heiter" (pseudonym). Three acts.

The only opera of Sechter, who was the teacher of Bruckner, and one of the most important German theoreticians of the 19th century. Previously performed at Matzleinsdorf (near Vienna) at the private theatre of Baron Dietrich. A record of this curious work will be found in *Allgemeine Musikalische Zeitung*, 20 September 1871.

BALFE: *The Daughter of St. Mark*

27 November. London, D.L.

Text by A. Bunn (founded on J. H. Vernoy de Saint-Georges's *La Reine de Chypre*, see 1841). Three acts.

Sydney 22 June 1852; New York 18 June 1855, etc.

A German translation by J. P. T. Lyser was published in 1849; produced probably Lemberg 1850.

MERCADANTE: *Leonora*

5 December. Naples, T.N.

Text by M. d'Arienzo. Four acts.

Given in Italy until 1876.

Outside Italy, Lisbon 13 April 1846; Madrid 5 June 1847; Berlin, Kgst. 13 November 1847; Copenhagen Carnival 1848; Rio de Janeiro 1853; Buenos Aires 6 July 1855; Paris 8 January 1866.

NIEDERMEYER: *Marie Stuart*

6 December. Paris, O.

Text by T. Anne. Five acts.

Niedermeyer's best work (containing the famous romance *Adieux donc, belle France*).

In German (translated by F. Gumbert), Stuttgart 18 November 1877 and 20 April 1887.

MEYERBEER: *Ein Feldlager in Schlesien*

7 December. Berlin, O.

Text by L. Rellstab (*Singspiel in Lebensbildern aus der Zeit Friedrich's des Grossen*). Three acts.

Written for the re-opening of the Berlin Opernhaus (after the fire of 18 August 1843). Given in Berlin 64 times until 17 October 1894.

In German also, Vienna, W. 18 February 1847 (as *Vielka*, with Jenny Lind). Meyerbeer afterwards introduced parts of the music into his *L'Etoile du Nord* (see 1854).

FLOTOW: *Alessandro Stradella*

30 December. Hamburg

Text by W. Friedrich. Three acts.

This opera is developed from a French *comédie mêlée de chant* by P. A. A. Pittaud de Forges and P. Duport, originally produced, with some new airs by Flotow, at the Palais Royal, Paris 4 February 1837.[1] Apart from *Martha* (see 1847), Flotow's most successful work.

Given at:

BERLIN 29 August 1845, etc. (in German).

VIENNA, W. 30 August 1845 and Kä. 9 September 1845 (in German).

BUDAPEST 27 September 1845 (in German).

[1] An English version *The Musician of Venice* was produced at St. J.'s, London, 17 January 1838, according to the play-bill with music by Pilati. The original French vaudeville was given at the same theatre 2 February 1844.

PRAGUE 21 November 1845 (in German) and 29 March 1846 (in Czech, translated by V. A. Swoboda).

BASLE 2 January 1846 (in German).

LONDON, D.L. 6 June 1846 (in English, translated by A. Bunn, music arranged by Benedict); D.L. 21 May 1849 (in German); and C.G. 4 June 1864 (in Italian).

WARSAW 20 June 1846 (in Polish, translated by J. Jasiński).

LYONS 21 July 1846 (in German).

STOCKHOLM 22 January 1847 (in Swedish, translated by G. L. Silverstolpe).

REVAL October 1848 (in German).

HELSINKI 13 June 1849 (in German) and 21 October 1875 (in Finnish, translated by A. Törneroos).

ST. PETERSBURG 13 November 1851 (in Russian) and 11 January 1862 (in Italian).

NEW YORK 29 November 1853 (in German) and 20 April 1860 (in Italian); English version by D. Buck published at Hartford, Connecticut 1868.

COPENHAGEN June 1858 (in German).

CLEVELAND 1859 (in German).

BRUSSELS 7 March 1859 (in French, translated by G. Oppelt and A. Royer).

HAGUE 15 January 1860 (in French, translated by G. Oppelt and A. Royer).

STRASBOURG 19 January 1860 (in French, translated by G. Oppelt and A. Royer).

ROTTERDAM Autumn 1860 (in German).

MEXICO Spring 1861 (in Italian).

MADRID, Z. 23 October 1861 (in Spanish, translated by L. Rivera and M. del Palacio).

PARIS, TH.I. 19 February 1863 (in Italian, translated by C. Bassi).

GENOA Autumn 1863 (in Italian, Bassi's translation).

SANTIAGO, CHILE 1869 (in Italian, Bassi's translation).

BUENOS AIRES 20 August 1872 (in Italian, Bassi's translation).

CHRISTIANIA 23 March 1875 (in Norwegian).

ZAGREB 9 October 1875 (in Croatian, translated by I. Trnski).

SARAJEVO 22 October 1881 (in German).
RIO DE JANEIRO 1889 (in concert form; in Italian).
LJUBLJANA 1901 (in Slovenian).

1845

SPOHR: *Die Kreuzfahrer*

1 January. Cassel

Text by the composer (founded on a play by A. von Kotzebue). Three acts.

Spohr's last opera. Berlin 26 July 1845, etc.

Revived Cassel 7 April 1899 and Leipzig 8 August 1902 (revised by F. Beier and M. Paar).

MARSCHNER: *Kaiser Adolph von Nassau*

5 January. Dresden

Text by H. Rau. Four acts.

(Wagner conducted the first performance.) Hamburg 15 February 1845, etc.

Revived Berlin 13 April 1886 (in concert form, by the Bloch'scher Opernverein).

H. RUNG: *Stormen paa København* (Storm over Copenhagen)

21 January. Copenhagen

Text by T. Overskou. Five acts.

The most successful of Rung's works; early attempt at Danish historical opera.

VERDI: *Giovanna d'Arco*

15 February. Milan, Sc.

Text by T. Solera (founded on Schiller's drama). Four acts.

One of Verdi's less successful works. Given at Rome, Arg. 3 May 1845 and Naples, T. S. Ferdinando Carnival 1855 as *Orietta di Lesbo*. Last (?) revived Milan, T. Castelli April 1876.

In Italian also, Madrid 30 October 1846; Lisbon 10 November 1847; St. Petersburg December 1849; Malta 1852; Buenos Aires 19 August 1854; Santiago, Chile 1855; Vienna 2 May 1857; Mexico December 1857; Paris 28 March 1868.

A French translation by L. Danglas was published in 1855.

ARRIETA: *Ildegonda*

28 February. Milan, Conservatorio

Text by T. Solera (first set to music by Solera himself, produced Milan 20 March 1840). Two acts.

The first opera of the Spanish composer.

In Italian also, Madrid, Palacio Real 10 October 1849; Lisbon 6 February 1852.

PACINI: *Lorenzino de' Medici*

4 March. Venice, F.

Text by F. M. Piave. Three acts.

Successful in Italy; revived Rome 3 January 1854 (as *Elisa Valasco*); Naples March 1858 (as *Torrismondo*, text altered by D. Bolognese).

In Italian also, Barcelona 24 February 1858; Vienna 18 May 1859.

ESSER: *Die zwei Prinzen*

11 April. Munich

Text by M. G. Friedrich (founded on a French play by Scribe and Mélesville). Three acts.

Esser's last and best opera. Berlin 15 October 1846; Frankfort 5 April 1847; Brünn August 1847, etc.

LORTZING: *Undine*

21 April. Magdeburg

Text by the composer (founded on La Motte Fouqué's story). Four acts.

Successful in Germany: Hamburg 24 April 1845; Vienna, W. 20 November 1847 (O. not until 4 December 1881); Berlin 28 September 1850, etc.

In German also, Helsinki 14 July 1849; Zurich 1853; New York 9 October 1856; Prague 18 August 1864; Riga April 1865; Laibach 1870; Ghent 21 February 1881; St. Petersburg 16 November 1887.

In Flemish (translated by J. Ferguut), Brussels 19 December 1867.

In Lettish, Riga 1893.

In Croatian (translated by F. Miler), Zagreb 10 December 1898.

Still given in Germany. Revived Berlin, D.O. 16 August 1932. Lately (*c.*1934) revived at Strasbourg in a French version by L. Mancini.

AUBER: *La Barcarolle* ou *L'Amour et la Musique*

22 April. Paris, O.C.

Text by A. E. Scribe. Three acts.

In German (translated by G. Ball), Vienna, W. 5 September 1846 and Kä. 9 August 1849.

In English, London, Princess's 5 April 1847.

Given at Lisbon 1847 (in French) and July 1850 (in Portuguese, translated by J. J. da Silva Mendes Leal).

DADDI: *O Salteador*
(The Highwayman)

11 May. Lisbon

Librettist unknown. One act.

Early Portuguese comic opera, performed at the private theatre of Count de Farrobo das Larangeiras.

BALFE: *The Enchantress*

14 May. London, D.L.

Text by A. Bunn (translated from a French libretto by Vernoy de Saint-Georges). Three acts.

In English also, Philadelphia 31 January 1846; New York 26 March 1849; Sydney 1851; San Francisco 1854.

(This is not the English version of Balfe's *L'Étoile de Séville* as stated in Riemann's *Opernhandbuch*).

FRY: *Leonora*

4 June. Philadelphia

Text by J. R. Fry (the brother of the composer), founded on E. Bulwer Lytton's *The Lady of Lyons*). Three acts.

The "first publicly performed grand opera written by a native American" (*Dict. American Biography*).

Given at Philadelphia 16 times in 1845–46; revived (in Italian, in an enlarged 4-act version) New York 29 March 1858. Fragments revived in a concert version by O. Kinkeldey New York May 1929, at a Pro Musica concert.

PACINI: *Bondelmonte*

18 June. Florence, P.

Text by S. Cammarano. Three acts.

Successful in Italy. Revived Milan, T. Carcano Autumn 1885.

In Italian also given at Malta 1847; Rio de Janeiro January 1851; Trieste 24 September 1853; Odessa Carnival 1855; Barcelona 8 April 1855; Buenos Aires 7 October 1860; Mexico 12 August 1865.

ESPÍN Y GUILLÉN: *Padilla* o *El Asedio di Medina*
(Padilla or the Siege of Medina)

9 July. Madrid, T. del Circo

Text by G. Romero Larrañaga. Three acts.

Spanish opera, of which only one act was performed.

VERDI: *Alzira*

12 August. Naples, S.C.

Text by S. Cammarano (after Voltaire). Two acts.

Unsuccessful, even in Italy.

In Italian also, Lisbon, Acc. Filarmonica 1847 and S.C. 29 October 1849; Barcelona 3 February 1849; Malta 1858.

In a German translation by L. Riedinger, *Alzira* was broadcast from Vienna 18 September 1936—otherwise it does not seem to have been revived anywhere.

FORBES: *The Fairy Oak*

18 October. London, D.L.

Text by H. C. Coape (according to the printed libretto; A. Nicoll attributes the text to Fitzball). Three acts. Forbes's only opera.

R. WAGNER: *Tannhäuser und der Sängerkrieg auf Wartburg*

19 October. Dresden

Text by the composer (*Handlung*). Three acts.

Very successful at Dresden; given there with slightly altered endings 4 September 1846 and 1 August 1847. 100th performance 12 December 1872; 500th performance 16 November 1913 (500th Berlin performance 26 August 1907).

The next productions were at Weimar 16 February 1849 (under Liszt); Schwerin 26 January 1852; Breslau 6 October 1852; Freiburg 7 November 1852; Wiesbaden 13 November 1852; Frankfort 15 January (not February) 1853; Riga 18 January 1853; Leipzig 31 January 1853; Posen 22 May 1853; Darmstadt 23 October 1853; Hamburg 11 November 1853; Königsberg 18 November 1853; Cologne 25 November 1853, etc.; given in 1853 and in 1854 on about 15 new stages each.

Outside Germany produced at:

RIGA 18 January 1853 (in German) and 2 December 1919 (in Lettish, on the opening night of the Latvian State Opera House).

REVAL (TALLINN) January 1854 (in German) and 1930 (in Estonian).

GRAZ 20 January 1854 (not 20 June 1854); for the first time in Austria and as the first Wagner opera in Austria.

PRAGUE 25 November 1854 (in German) and 28 January 1891 (in Czech, translated by V. J. Novotný).

ZURICH 16 February 1855 (for the first time in Switzerland; Basle 30 March 1857, etc.).

ANTWERP 13 March 1855 (in German); 26 January 1894 (in Flemish); and 2 December 1897 (in French).

STRASBOURG 12 July 1855 (in German).

BERLIN 7 January 1856 (in German).

GENEVA 23 May 1857 (in German) and 29 January 1895 (in French).

HELSINKI 5 August 1857 (in German) and 17 October 1919 (in Finnish, translated by T. Muroma).

VIENNA, THALIA TH. 28 August 1857 and Kä. 19 November 1859 (in German); the Paris version 22 November 1875.

AMSTERDAM 24 March 1858 (in German) and 17 December 1895 (in Dutch); Rotterdam 28 December 1860 and Hague 26 October 1870 (in German).

NEW YORK 4 April 1859 (in German; first Wagner opera in America); 4 April 1888 (in English); 10 December 1909 (in French); Philadelphia 12 February 1864; Chicago January 1865; Boston 20 January 1871; Cincinnati 22 January 1875 (in German).

PARIS, O. 13 March 1861 (in French, translated by E. Roche, R. Lindau and C. Nuitter), with alterations and additions; withdrawn by the composer after the third night. Revived there only 34 years later, on 13 May 1895; 100th performance 26 November 1900; 200th 26 July 1909.

BUDAPEST 6 March 1862 (in German) and 11 March 1871 (in Hungarian, translated by K. Abrányi).

HERMANNSTADT 11 August 1866 (in German).

MUNICH 1 August 1867 (first German production of the Paris version).

BOLOGNA 7 November 1872 (in Italian, translated by S. de Castrone, Marchese della Rajata); Trieste 16 November 1878; Rome, Ap. 18 April 1886; Venice 21 January 1887; Turin 26 December 1888; Naples 20 April 1889; Milan 26 December 1891; Genoa 19 January 1895, etc.

BRUSSELS 20 February 1873 (in French).

LAIBACH (LJUBLJANA) March 1874 (in German) and 10 December 1901 (in Slovenian, translated by A. Štritov).

ST. PETERSBURG 25 February 1873 (in Russian, translated by K. Svantsov; another Russian version, by G. A. Lishin, was published in 1875) and 8 January 1879 (in Italian).

COPENHAGEN 17 March 1875 (in Danish, translated by A. Hertz).

CHRISTIANIA 18 November 1876 (in Danish, translated by A. Hertz).

LONDON, C.G. 6 May 1876 (in Italian); H.M.'s 14 February 1882 (in English, translated by J. P. Jackson); D.L. 23 May 1882 (in German); C.G. 27 May 1896 (in French, the Paris version); 100th C.G. performance 28 May 1906.

STOCKHOLM 16 August 1876 (in Swedish, translated by F. T. Hedberg).

MOSCOW 8 February 1877 (in Italian) and 28 January 1882 (in Russian).

NEW ORLEANS 12 December 1877 (in Italian).

WARSAW 29 April 1883 (in Polish, translated by M. Radzikowski).

BARCELONA 11 February 1887 (in Italian); Catalan version by J. Lleonart and A. Ribera published 1904; another by J. Zanné and J. Pena published 1907.

MADRID 14 March 1890 (in Italian).

MEXICO 29 March 1891 (in English!).

LYONS 4 April 1892 (in French); Nantes 27 March 1894; Marseilles 11 March 1896; Rouen 22 January 1897; Lille 18 March 1897, etc.).

RIO DE JANEIRO 30 September 1892 (in Italian).

LISBON 23 December 1893 (in Italian).

BUENOS AIRES 21 July 1894 (in Italian).

ZAGREB 5 June 1895 (in Croatian, translated by A. Harambašić).

MONTREAL 29 April 1896 (in English; concert performance).

ALGIERS 25 March 1897 (in Italian).

SANTIAGO, CHILE 24 July 1897 (in Italian).

ALEXANDRIA 20 February 1898 (in Italian).

CAIRO Carnival 1901 (in French).

JOHANNESBURG 1905 (in English).

BUCHAREST 16 October 1929 (in Rumanian).

KAUNAS 26 October 1930 (in Lithuanian).

SOFIA 30 January 1931 (in Bulgarian).

Of several parodies, the following three may be mentioned:

Tannhäuser, Zukunftsposse in 3 Acten mit vergangener Musik und gegenwärtigen Gruppirungen, text by J. Nestroy (founded on a parody by H. Wollheim, Breslau 1854) music by C. Binder, Vienna Leop. 31 October 1857.

Panne-aux-Airs, in 2 acts, text by Clairville, music by F. E. Barbier, Paris, Th. Déjazet 30 March 1861.

Ya-Mein-Herr, Cacophonie de l'Avenir, en 3 actes entr'acte mêlée de chants, de harpes et de chiens savants, text by Clairville, A. Delacour, and L. Thiboust, with some new airs by V. Chéri, Paris, Variétés 6 April 1861.

WALLACE: *Maritana*

15 November. London, D.L.

Text by E. Fitzball (founded on the French play, *Don César de Bazan*, by d'Ennery and Pinel Dumanoir). Three acts.

Wallace's first and most famous opera. Dublin 1 July 1846; Philadelphia 9 November 1846; Edinburgh 15 December 1847; New York 4 May 1848; Sydney 19 April 1849, etc. In English also, New Orleans December 1876; Mexico 20 February 1884; Cape Town 1887.

In German (translated by A. J. Becher), Vienna, W. 8 January 1848; Hamburg 16 February 1849; Prague 1851, etc.

In Italian (recitatives by T. Mattei), Dublin 4 March 1877; London, H.M.'s 9 December 1880; New York 20 December 1885.

Frequently revived on English stages and still given in the provinces. The so far latest revivals in London were at the Ly. 22 May 1925; Old Vic 30 March 1931.

BALFE: *L'Étoile de Séville*

17 December. Paris, O.

Text by H. Lucas. Three acts.

The only opera Balfe wrote for the "Académie Royale de Musique." Not very successful there (15 performances) and never given in England.

In French also, Antwerp 13 March 1849.

German translation by C. Gollmick published 1847.

FLOTOW: *Die Matrosen*

23 December. Hamburg

Text by W. Friedrich. Four acts.

Berlin 17 July 1853; Vienna 11 March 1854, etc.

In Polish (translated by J. Jasiński), Warsaw 17 June 1848.

(This was a new version of *Le Naufrage de la Méduse*, text by H. and T. Cogniard, music by Flotow, Grisar, and Pilati: Paris, Ren. 31 May 1839; Brussels 4 November 1839; Antwerp 6 November 1839. The score was burnt and rewritten by Flotow for the German stage).

1846

HALÉVY: *Les Mousquetaires de la Reine*

3 February. Paris, O.C.

Text by J. H. Vernoy de Saint-Georges. Three acts.

Given at the O.C. until 1865 and revived 10 January 1878; revived at Marseilles 8 March 1900.

In French also, Brussels 15 April 1846; Hague 7 May 1846; London, D.L. 3 August 1846; New Orleans November 1846; Madrid 1 October 1853; Buenos Aires 4 May 1854; Turin April 1858; Rio de Janeiro October 1861; Berlin, Victoria Th. 15 May 1862; Batavia 12 February 1866; Barcelona 7 July 1866; New York 9 October 1866; Lisbon 27 April 1878; Mexico 25 February 1879.

In German (translated by J. C. Grünbaum), Berlin 22 July 1846; (translated by J. Kupelwieser), Vienna, W. 20 August 1846 and Kä. 5 September 1846 (with additional music by Reuling); Lemberg April 1847; Prague 1850, etc. Revived Leipzig 23 June 1895.

In Danish (translated by C. Hvid), Copenhagen 7 October 1848.

In Swedish (translated by N. E. W. af Wetterstedt), Stockholm 8 November 1848.

In Russian, St. Petersburg 1855.

In English, Boston March 1882; New York 15 February 1883.

MACFARREN: *An Adventure of Don Quixote*

3 February. London, D.L.

Text by G. Macfarren (the father of the composer). Two acts.

Macfarren's second opera. Unsuccessful.

PACINI: *La Regina di Cipro*

7 February. Turin, T.R.

Text by F. Guidi. Four acts.

In Italian also, Lisbon 22 January 1848; Rio de Janeiro 1852; Buenos Aires 26 July 1854.

BENEDICT: *The Crusaders*

26 February. London, D.L.

Text by A. Bunn. Three acts.

One of Benedict's best works; more popular in Germany than in England.

In German (as *Der Alte vom Berge*, translated by G. Schilling), Prague May 1847; Stuttgart 23 January 1848; Frankfort 6 September 1850; Munich 6 January 1854; Königsberg 10 March 1854, etc. Revived Hamburg 23 April 1868.

B. BASILJ: *El Diablo Predicador* (The Devil a Preacher)

4 March. Madrid, T. de la Cruz

Text by V. de la Vega (*Drama lírico, imitación de la comedia antigua española*). Three acts.

Successful Spanish comic opera; repeated Madrid 26 May 1847 and Barcelona 12 September 1849.

VERDI: *Attila*

17 March. Venice, F.

Text by T. Solera. Prologue and 3 acts.

"Cet opéra, un des plus faibles du maître, n'a pas eu de succès" (Clément-Larousse). "None, perhaps, of Verdi's works had kindled more enthusiasm in Italy or crowned the fortunate composer with more abundant laurels than his *Attila*" (B. Lumley, 1864).

Given at Palermo Carnival 1854 as *Gli Unni ed i Romani*.

Outside Italy:

COPENHAGEN Carnival 1847.

MADRID 5 January 1847.

LISBON 5 April 1847.

LONDON, H.M.'s 14 March 1848.

MALTA 1848.

HAVANA 1848.

CONSTANTINOPLE 1849.

CHRISTIANIA August 1849.

BUCHAREST 2 October 1849.

NEW YORK 15 April 1850.

VIENNA 11 June 1851.

BUDAPEST Summer 1852.

RIO DE JANEIRO 1853.

BUENOS AIRES 23 September 1853.

MEXICO 31 August 1854.

CARACAS 20 October 1854.

NICE 10 October 1863.

SYDNEY October 1870.

In French (translated by L. Danglas), Brussels 13 December 1850.

In German (translated by W. Haeser), Stuttgart 12 February 1854.

In Spanish, Bogotá 1865.

The latest revivals in Italy were at Genoa 26 May 1880; Pisa 1 September 1889; Trieste 10 March 1894; Lodi, Collegio S. Francesco Carnival 1911.

LUX: *Das Käthchen von Heilbronn*

23 March. Dessau

Text by F. Meck (founded on H. von Kleist's drama). Five acts.

New version (prologue and 3 acts), Wiesbaden 9 January 1847; Mayence 15 November 1852.

Revived Dessau 11 December 1881 and Mayence 16 February 1900.

LISINSKI: *Ljubav i Zloba*
(Love and Malice)

28 March. Zagreb

Text by D. Demeter. Two acts.

The first Croatian opera; produced by amateurs. Revived at Zagreb 21 October 1871 and 19 October 1895.

According to contemporary journals, the opera was orchestrated by F. Wiesner von Morgenstern. Libretto printed in 1846 (copy British Museum) and 1872. Cf. P. Loewe, in *Der Merker* (Vienna), 1917, p.232; and A. Dobronić, *A Study of Jugoslav Music*, in *The Musical Quarterly*, Vol. XII (1926).

Lisinski's second and last opera was produced 51 years after *Ljubav i Zloba* (43 years after the composer's death, see 1897).

FÜCHS: *Guttenberg*

1 April. Graz

Text by O. Prechtler. Four acts.

Füchs's most successful work: Brünn 18 October 1846; Vienna, W. 19 November 1846 and Kä. 3 January 1852; Prague January 1847; Hamburg 7 October 1847; Dresden 14 June 1848, etc. In German also, Riga November 1857.

SCHINDELMEISSER: *Der Rächer*

4 April. Budapest

Text by O. Prechtler (founded on Corneille's *Cid*). Three acts.

The most successful opera of Schindelmeisser (then conductor of the German opera at Budapest). Given also at Frankfort 23 December 1849; Mayence 8 December 1850; Darmstadt 21 November 1852, etc.

J. P. E. HARTMANN: *Liden Kirsten*
(Little Christina)

12 May. Copenhagen

Text by H. C. Andersen. One act.

Very successful at Copenhagen; given since 29 October 1858 in an enlarged 2-act version; last revived there 27 February 1910 and 24 September 1922. The 200th performance was on 15 December 1912.

In Danish also, Stockholm 3 February 1928 (by the Copenhagen company).

In German, Weimar 17 January 1856.

BAZIN: *Le Trompette de M. le Prince*

15 May. Paris, O.C.

Text by A. H. J. Mélesville. One act.

Given at the O.C. until 1856.

In French also, Brussels 10 November 1846; Buenos Aires 14 July 1854.

In German (translated by J. C. Grünbaum), Berlin 6 December 1849.

In Swedish (translated by E. A. Wallmark), Stockholm 19 September 1861.

MANGOLD: *Tanhäuser*

17 May. Darmstadt

Text by E. Duller. Three acts.

Independent of Wagner. (Tannhäuser gets married in the end!) Revived Darmstadt 17 January 1892 (as *Der getreue Eckart*, libretto revised by E. Pasqué).

LORTZING: *Der Waffenschmied*

31 May. Vienna, W.

Text by the composer (founded on F. W. Ziegler's comedy, *Liebhaber und Nebenbuhler in einer Person*, 1790; the same play on which Weigl's *Il Rivale di se stesso*, see 1808, was based). Three acts.

One of Lortzing's most successful works. Dresden 29 November 1846; Basle 27 October 1847; Prague 1848; Graz 23 February 1850; Berlin, Kroll's 12 August 1850 (O. only 31 December 1887); Vienna, Kä. 24 August 1865, etc.

In German also, Helsinki 6 July 1849; Gothenburg 9 October 1864; New York 4 February 1867 (revived 26 September 1925); Ghent 13 October 1880; St. Petersburg 11 September 1887.

In Czech (translated by J. Pražský), Prague 21 January 1849; revived 25 August 1894 (new Czech version by V. J. Novotný).

In Swedish, Stockholm 11 December 1885.

In Hungarian (translated by A. Radó), Budapest 17 January 1891.

In Croatian (translated by M. Pogačić), Zagreb 23 March 1899.

GORDIGIANI: *Consuelo*

6 June. Prague

(Italian) text by the composer (founded on G. Sand's novel). Four parts.

An isolated instance of an Italian opera produced at Prague in the 19th century. The composer was a teacher at the Prague Conservatoire. A German version, by C. Gordigiani, was published at Vienna.

(See on this production O. Teuber, *Geschichte des Prager Theaters*, II, p.357.)

FLOTOW: *L'Âme en Peine*

29 June. Paris, O.

Text by J. H. Vernoy de Saint-Georges. Two acts.

In French also, Liége 8 February 1847; Antwerp 2 December 1847; revived Paris, O. 4 November 1859.

Like most operas of Flotow, *L'Âme en Peine* was given under many different titles. In German (as *Der Förster*, translated by G. N. Bärmann), Vienna 9 January 1847; Hamburg 15 March 1847, etc.

In English (as *Leoline*), London, Princess's Th. 16 October 1848.

In Polish (as *Paola*, translated by L. Matuszyński), Warsaw 3 June 1852.

In Italian (translated by C. Bassi), Lisbon 29 October 1852 (as *Paula, l'Orfana tradita*); Turin 30 November 1872 (as *Il Boscaiuolo ossia L'Anima tradita*).

LINDPAINTNER: *Lichtenstein*

26 August. Stuttgart

Text by F. von Dingelstedt (founded on a novel by W. Hauff). Five acts.

Written for the inauguration of the new court theatre, Stuttgart.

LODER: *The Night Dancers*

28 October. London, Princess's

Text by G. Soane. Two acts.

Loder's best work. New York 6 October 1847; Sydney November 1847, etc.

Revived London, C.G. 10 October 1860. "The Princess's Theatre in Oxford Street was opened for English opera in 1842 [1] under the management of Mr. Maddox, who carried it on till last season, 1850. The pieces performed by him were chiefly versions of popular foreign operas. He produced, however, two original English operas of the highest merit, *The Night Dancers* (1846) and *King Charles the Second* (1849): the one wild,

[1] Viz. 26 December, with Bellini's *La Sonnambula*, in English, under Schira.

romantic, and imaginative; the other gay, genial, and full of English character; and both worthy to be classed among the most remarkable works of the present century" (G. Hogarth, *Memoirs*, Vol. II, p.375).

LAVENU: *Loretta, a Tale of Seville*

9 November. London, D.L.

Text by A. Bunn. Three acts.

Written for Ann Bishop.

MERCADANTE: *Gli Orazi ed i Curiazi*

10 November. Naples, S.C.

Text by S. Cammarano. Three acts.

Successful in Italy. Last revived Naples 21 March 1882.

In Italian also, Barcelona 24 August 1848; Lisbon 9 April 1849; St. Petersburg December 1849; Malta 1853; Rio de Janeiro 1856.

In Hungarian, Budapest 13 May 1848 (translated by B. Egressy).

BALFE: *The Bondman*

11 December. London, DL.

Text by A. Bunn (from Mélesville's *Le Chevalier de Saint-George*). Three acts.

In German (as *Der Mulatte*, translated by J. C. Grünbaum), Berlin 25 January 1850.

F. MALIPIERO: *Alberigo da Romano*

26 December. Venice, F

Text by C. Berti. Three acts.

The most successful opera of Malipiero (the father of G. F. Malipiero).

Revived at Venice, T. Apollo 27 November 1869 and once more at the T. Goldoni 14 April 1886.

1847

BOISSELOT: *Ne touchez pas à la Reine*

16 January. Paris, O.C.

Text by A. E. Scribe and G. Vaëz. Three acts.

Boisselot's best work.

In French also, Brussels 18 March 1847; London, St. J.'s 21 May 1849; Santiago, Chile 1851; New York 20 August 1852.

Revived Paris, Th.L. (Athénée) 12 September 1871.

In German (as *Die Königin von Leon*), Vienna, W. 15 July 1847; Leipzig 16 September 1847; Munich 3 October 1847, etc. In German also, Helsinki 14 July 1850. Last revived Munich 17 January 1879.

In English, London, Grecian Th. 14 February 1853.

In Spanish (translated by Luis Cortés y Suana, music adapted by Genovés), Valladolid [8 April] 1850.

L. RICCI: *Il Birraio di Preston*

4 February. Florence, P.

Text by F. Guidi (founded on De Leuven and Brunswick's French libretto, see 1838). Three acts.

Successful in Italy; in Italian also, Corfu 1854; Barcelona 8 April 1855; Mexico February 1857 (as *Il Eroe per Forza*); London, St. J.'s 24 November 1857.

Revived Madrid 2 July 1868; Genoa 16 March 1886; Lodi Carnival 1890 (at the Collegio S. Francesco).

WALLACE: *Matilda of Hungary*

22 February. London, D.L.

Text by A. Bunn (his last libretto and "one of the worst librettos in existence", according to the *Dict. Nat. Biogr.*). Three acts. Unsuccessful.

C. L. A. VOGEL: *Le Siège de Leyde, 1574*

4 March. Hague

Text by H. Lucas. Four acts.

One of the first original works produced at the Royal French Opera at The Hague. The subject had been suggested by King William II of Holland.

Revived at the Hague in 1854 and as late as February 1870.

VERDI: *Macbeth*

14 March. Florence, P.

Text by F. M. Piave (after Shakespeare). Four acts.

One of the best of Verdi's earlier operas.

Given all over Italy and at:

MADRID 20 February 1848 (in Italian).

WARSAW I January 1849 (in Polish, translated by J. Jasiński).

LISBON 13 January 1849 (in Italian).

MALTA 1849 (in Italian).

HAVANA 1849 (in Italian).

VIENNA II December 1849 (in German) and 21 April 1851 (in Italian).

NEW YORK 24 April 1850 (in Italian).

CONSTANTINOPLE 1850 (in Italian).

BUDAPEST 1850 (in Hungarian, translated by B. Egressy).

HANOVER 23 December 1850 (in German).

RIO DE JANEIRO 25 March 1852 (in Italian).

STOCKHOLM 29 April 1852 (in Swedish, translated by C. W. A. Strandberg).

BUENOS AIRES 21 March 1854 (in Italian).

ST. PETERSBURG December 1854 (in Italian, as *Sivardo il Sassone*).

SANTIAGO, CHILE 1855 (in Italian).

ATHENS 1856.

PRESSBURG 1856 (in German).

GRAZ 22 September 1856.

MEXICO December 1857 (in Italian).

BUCHAREST 1858 (in Italian).

DUBLIN 30 March 1859 (in Italian).

AMSTERDAM 1860 (in Italian).

PARIS, TH.L. 21 April 1865 (in French, translated by C. Nuitter and A. Beaumont, with many alterations and additions); an earlier translation, by L. Danglas, had been published in 1853.

SYDNEY 1872 (in Italian).

ZAGREB 13 May 1886 (in Croatian, translated by I. Trnski).

Macbeth was to be produced in London in 1861 and again in 1870; both times the production did not take place. A libretto, in English and Italian, was printed *c.*1850.

Still given in many countries, frequently revived in Italy (Milan, Sc. 26 December 1938); outside Italy, some of the more recent revivals were at:

STOCKHOLM 15 October 1921 (new Swedish version by H. Key).

DRESDEN 21 April 1928 (new German version by G. Göhler).

ZURICH 1928 (Göhler's version).

BERLIN I October 1931 (Göhler's version).

VIENNA 28 April 1933 (Göhler's version).

PRAGUE December 1935 (Göhler's version.)

GLYNDEBOURNE 21 May 1938 (in Italian; for the first time in England).

BUENOS AIRES June 1939 (in Italian).

SALOMAN: *Diamantkorset*

(The Diamond Cross)

20 March. Copenhagen

Text by T. Overskou. Three acts.

Saloman's best work. In German, Berlin 19 September 1848. In Swedish, Stockholm 18 April 1886.

OFFENBACH: *L'Alcôve*

24 April. Paris

Text by P. A. A. Pittaud de Forges and A. de Leuven. One act.

Offenbach's first operetta; score preserved.

Produced at a concert at the Salle de la Tour d'Auvergne for Offenbach's benefit, with orchestra and scenery.

Also given at Cologne 9 January 1849 (in German, as *Marielle oder Sergeant und Commandant*, translated by C. O. Sternau).

CAGNONI: *Don Bucefalo*

28 June. Milan, Conservatorio

Text by C. Bassi. Three acts.

Cagnoni's first opera; very successful in Italy, given there until 1888.

In Italian also, Lisbon I January 1850; Warsaw 1853; Buenos Aires 17 June 1854; Malta 1854; Barcelona 22 January 1856; Constantinople 1857;

Dublin 21 September 1860; Marseilles April 1865; Paris 9 November 1865; New York 18 October 1867; Santiago, Chile 1868; St. Petersburg 17 December 1868; London, C.G. 29 May 1869; Vienna 16 April 1876 and 7 May 1881 (parts only).

In Spanish (translated by M. del Palacio), Madrid 18 October 1860.

In German (name-part sung in Italian), Berlin 19 May 1867.

VERDI: *I Masnadieri*

22 July. London, H.M.'s

Text by A. Maffei (founded on Schiller's *Die Räuber*). Four acts.

The only opera Verdi wrote for London.

Subsequently given at Rome, Ap. 12 February 1848; Florence March 1848; Venice 10 May 1851; Milan 20 September 1853, etc.; Barcelona 3 June 1848; Madrid 10 February 1849 (orchestrated by J. D. Skoczdopole); Lisbon 8 March 1849; Malta 1849; Rio de Janeiro 1849; Havana 1849; Lugano 1850; Brussels 3 October 1850; Smyrna 1851; Budapest Summer 1852; Athens 18 November 1852; Bucharest 1853; Odessa Carnival 1853 as *Adele di Cosenza;* Buenos Aires 11 September 1853; Vienna 3 June 1854; Mexico December 1856; New York 2 June 1860.

In Hungarian (translated by L. Nádaskay) Budapest 12 May 1853.

In French (translated by J. Ruelle), Paris, Athénée 3 February 1870; (translated by L.Danglas and M. and L. Escudier) Lille 24 March 1870.

The latest revivals in Italy seem to have been at Bergamo 26 December 1891 and Milan, T. Fossati 29 August 1903.

Revived at Barmen 29 March 1928 (for the first time in German, translated by R. Franz).

A. E. FESCA: *Der Troubadour*

25 July. Brunswick

Text by F. Schmezer. Five acts.

The composer of this *Troubadour* opera six years before Verdi was the son of F. E. Fesca (see 1820).

G. SCHMIDT: *Prinz Eugen, der edle Ritter*

26 July. Frankfort

Text by A. Rost. Three acts.

Very successful, given on German stages until 1884.

In German also, Prague 1848; Riga 1849; Berlin, Kroll's 17 July 1850; Zurich 1850, etc.; New York 26 May 1871 (as *Prinz Eugen; oder, Der Uhrenhändler aus dem Schwarzwald*); revived Brooklyn 21 February 1881.

DOPPLER: *Grof Benjowsky* (Count Benyowsky)

29 September. Budapest

(Hungarian) text by R. Köffinger (founded on a play by A. von Kotzebue). Three acts.

The first opera of the Hungarian composer.

Revived in a new version, as *Afanasia*, Budapest, *c.* 30 January 1854.

In German, Würzburg 27 March 1852; Lemberg 26 December 1857.

MAILLART: *Gastibelza, ou Le Fou de Tolède*

15 November. Paris, Opéra-National

Text by A. P. d'Ennery and E. Cormon (founded on a French ballad *Le Fou de Tolède*). Three acts.

In French also, Antwerp 26 October 1848; New Orleans November 1848; Brussels 30 August 1849; Buenos Aires 27 August 1854.

There is a printed Italian version by C. Bassi; but the opera does not seem to have been given in Italy.

Gastibelza was the opening opera of the third Paris opera-house, the Opéra-National, better known under its later name of Théâtre-Lyrique (which it adopted 12 April 1852).

FLOTOW: *Martha* oder *Der Markt von Richmond*

25 November. Vienna, Kä.

Text by W. Friedrich (operatic version of a ballet-pantomime, *Lady Henriette ou La Servante de*

Greenwich, scenario by Vernoy de Saint-Georges, music by Flotow, Burgmüller and Deldevez, first produced Paris, O. 21 February 1844). Four acts.

Flotow's most popular work. Subsequently given at:

WEIMAR 16 February 1848.

DRESDEN and LEIPZIG 1 March 1848.

BERLIN 7 March 1848, and all over Germany.

BUDAPEST 11 July 1848 (in Hungarian, translated by J. Szerdahelyi).

PRAGUE 24 March 1849 (in German) and 17 February 1850 (in Czech, translated by F. Ćenský).

RIGA 1849 (in German) and 1893 (in Lettish).

LONDON, D.L. 4 June 1849 (in German); C.G. 1 July 1858 (in Italian); D.L. 11 October 1858 (in English, translated by T. H. Reynoldson). New English version by E. J. Dent, published 1941.

HELSINKI 26 June 1849 (in German) and 27 April 1876 (in Finnish).

WARSAW 20 January 1850 (in Polish, translated by J. Jasiński).

BASLE 8 February 1850 (in German).

STOCKHOLM 27 November 1850 (in Swedish, translated by C. W. A. Strandberg).

NEW YORK 1 November 1852 (in English); 13 March 1855 (in German); 7 January 1859 (in Italian).

COPENHAGEN 23 December 1852 (in Danish, translated by C. Hvid and A. Zinck).

SAN FRANCISCO 1853 (in English).

ANTWERP 20 November 1854 (in German).

SYDNEY 1855 (in English).

ZAGREB April 1856 (in German) and 1 January 1872 (in Croatian, translated by A. Šenoa).

ST. PETERSBURG 1856 (in Russian, translated by N. I. Kulikov) and Carnival 1859 (in Italian).

PARIS, TH.I. 11 February 1858 (in Italian, translated by A. de Lauzières) and Th.L. 16 December 1865 (in French, translated by J. H. Vernoy de Saint-Georges).

BRUSSELS 13 February 1858 (for the first time in French, translated by L. Danglas).

STRASBOURG May 1858 (in another French version, by L. E. Crevel de Charlemagne).

ALGIERS Spring 1858 (in Italian) and Carnival 1861 (in French).

MARSEILLES 15 December 1858 (in French).

GENEVA 5 April 1859 (in French).

DUBLIN 9 April 1859 (in Italian).

MILAN, CANOBBIANA 25 April 1859 (in Italian).

BARCELONA 9 February 1860 (in Italian).

ROTTERDAM September 1860 (in German).

LISBON 27 February 1861 (in Italian).

MADRID, Z. 13 March 1861 (in Spanish, translated by E. Álvarez and M. del Palacio) and T.R. 21 December 1861 (in Italian).

MEXICO Spring 1861 (in Italian) and 18 June 1869 (in Spanish).

PALMA, MALLORCA Autumn 1861 (in Italian).

MALTA 1863 (in Italian).

BATAVIA 15 January 1864 (in French).

BUENOS AIRES 1 June 1864 (in Italian).

SANTIAGO, CHILE 1865 (in Italian).

NAPLES, S.C. 24 January 1865 (in Italian).

RIO DE JANEIRO Autumn 1865 (in Italian).

CAIRO January 1872 (in Italian).

TORONTO 15 June 1874 (in English).

CHRISTIANIA Autumn 1875 (in Norwegian).

SARAJEVO 1882 (in German).

LJUBLJANA 1894 (in Slovenian, translated by A. Funtek).

KAUNAS 15 September 1935 (in Lithuanian).

KALLIWODA: *Blanda* oder *Die silberne Birke*

29 November. Prague

Text by F. Kind (posthumous libretto of the *Freischütz* author). Three acts.

The only opera of the well-known violinist and instrumental composer.

LORTZING: *Zum Grossadmiral*

13 December. Leipzig

Text by the composer (founded on A. Duval's comedy, *La Jeunesse de Henri V*). Three acts.

Vianna, Jos. February 1849, etc. Revived Schwerin 26 April 1936 (revised by A. Treumann-Mette).

DARGOMUIZHSKY: *Esmeralda*
Эсмеральда

17 December. Moscow

Text by the composer (translated from Victor Hugo's French libretto, see 1836). Four acts.

Dargomuizhsky's first opera. St. Petersburg 11 December 1851, etc. Given in Russia until about 1876.

BALFE: *The Maid of Honour*

20 December. London, D.L.

Text by E. Fitzball (the same subject as Flotow's *Martha*, see above). Three acts.

Balfe himself considered this opera his most finished production—but it was unsuccessful.

AUBER: *Haydée ou Le Secret*

28 December. Paris, O.C.

Text by A. E. Scribe. Three acts.

Auber's greatest success after *Le Domino noir* (1837). Given at the O.C. 498 times until 1898.

In French also, Antwerp 2 April 1848; Brussels 9 August 1848, etc.; New Orleans 1849; Buenos Aires 11 June 1854; Turin April 1858; Soerabaya 11 November 1867; Barcelona 6 September 1868; Lisbon 4 May 1878; New York 25 January 1879; Mexico 20 February 1879.

In English (translated by G. Soane), London, Strand 3 April 1848; another English version by H. F. Chorley was given at C.G. on 4 November 1848 (music adapted by L. H. Lavenu).

In German, Cassel 20 August 1848; Munich 8 October 1848; Vienna, Jos. 28 December 1848 and Kä. 10 November 1849; Prague and Riga 1849; Berlin, Kroll's 8 May 1854.

In Polish (translated by J. Jasiński), Warsaw 28 July 1849.

In Spanish (translated by R. Puente y Brañas, music adapted by F. A. Barbieri), Madrid, Circo 22 June 1871.

Last revived, Nice January 1934.

1848

KITTL: *Bianca und Giuseppe oder Die Franzosen vor Nizza*

19 February. Prague

Text by Richard Wagner. Four acts.

Also given at Frankfort 11 April 1853; Graz 5 December 1854. Revived Prague 7 March 1857; 5 May 1868; and 1 August 1886; Hamburg 2 January 1886 (as *Die hohe Braut*, revised by H. Zumpe).

In Prague also produced in a Czech version by B. Peška 20 September 1875.

(Wagner had written the scenario at Königsberg in 1836, originally intending to set the text himself; it is based upon a novel by one Heinrich König. Later on, in 1842, at Dresden, Wagner altered the libretto for Reissiger who, however, did not set it either. See E. Newman, *Richard Wagner*, Vol.1, pp.216–17.)

GRISAR: *Gilles Ravisseur*

21 February. Paris, O.C.

Text by T. M. F. Sauvage. One act.

Given at the O.C. until 1855. Liége 18 February 1849; Brussels 20 April 1849; Antwerp 7 February 1850, etc. Revived Paris, F.P. 21 December 1868; Brussels 10 April 1864 and 21 July 1880.

PIERSON: *Leila*

22 February. Hamburg

Text by C. Leonhardt-Lyser (the wife of the composer). Three acts.

The most important of Pierson's four German operas (none of which was ever performed in England).

HACKLÄNDER: *Soldatenleben*

4 June. Stuttgart

Text by the composer. Three acts.

The only operatic attempt of Hackländer, who was a popular novelist in his time. The opera was orchestrated by the singer Schlooz.

CSÁSZÁR: *A Kúnok*
(The Cumans)

16 September. Budapest

Text by Hegyalji. Four acts.

The most successful of Császár's Hungarian operas. Given at Budapest more than 100 times.

In Hungarian also, Temesvar 15 June 1852; Zagreb July 1860. Revived Budapest 15 May 1904.

LVOV: *Undina*
Ундина

20 September. St. Petersburg

Text by V. A. Sollogub (translated from a French libretto by Vernoy de Saint-Georges). Three acts.

In German (as *Die Tochter der Wellen*, translated by O. Prechtler), Vienna 30 October 1852.

MIRÓ: *A Marqueza*

4 October. Lisbon

Text by P. Midosi (founded on a French libretto *La Marquise*, by Vernoy de Saint-Georges, composed by Adam in 1835). One act.

The most successful of Miró's Portuguese operas.

VERDI: *Il Corsaro*

25 October. Trieste

Text by F. M. Piave (founded on Byron's poem). Four acts.

Of all Verdi operas *Il Corsaro* was the least fortunate one; it was repeated at Milan, T. Carcano 7 February 1852; Modena 26 December 1852; Turin Autumn 1852; Novara Carnival 1853; Venice, F. February 1853; Malta 1853 and Naples, S.C. 1854, but apparently nowhere else.

HALÉVY: *Le Val d'Andorre*

11 November. Paris, O.C.

Text by J. H. Vernoy de Saint-Georges. Three acts.

One of Halévy's greatest successes.

Antwerp 19 February 1849; Brussels 14 March 1849, etc.

In French also, New Orleans December 1849.

In German (translated by L. Rellstab), Berlin 8 April 1849, etc.; in German also, Riga 14 April 1852; Prague 20 November 1856.

London, St. J.'s 7 January 1850 (in French) and Princess's 28 January 1850 (in English); New York 15 March 1851 (in English); St. Petersburg Spring 1852 (in Russian, translated by P. S. Fedorov); Warsaw 9 October 1852 (in Polish, translated by J. Jasiński); Milan, T. d. V. 5 December 1876 (in Italian); Stockholm 1 April 1888 (in Swedish).

Revived in Paris: Th.L. 15 October 1860; O.C. 14 October 1875; Tr.L. 16 October 1915.

Revived in German: Cassel 1 September 1880; Hamburg 28 September 1885; Carlsruhe 3 December 1900.

1849

A. THOMAS: *Le Caïd*

3 January. Paris, O.C.

Text by T. M. F. Sauvage. Two acts.

Apart from *Mignon* and *Hamlet*, Thomas's most successful work.

In French also, Brussels 26 August 1849; New Orleans December 1850; London, St. J.'s 28 January 1850; New York 28 June 1852; Buenos Aires Spring 1852; Turin 4 April 1858; Madrid 7 July 1859; Batavia 18 March 1864.

In English (translated by B. N. Webster), London, Little Hm. 18 June 1851; revived Manchester 8 December 1880 (translated by A. Matthison).

In German (translated by C. Gollmick), Vienna 29 August 1856; Berlin 22 September 1857; Prague May 1860, etc.

In Italian (translated by M. M. Marcello, recitatives by P. Repetto), Milan February 1863; Barcelona 25 August 1865; Florence 7 December 1877; Naples 4 August 1889.

In Polish (translated by L. Matuszyński), Warsaw 1870.

Last revived Paris, O.C. 16 February 1911 and Gaîté Lyrique 18 May 1931.

VERDI: *La Battaglia di Legnano*

27 January. Rome, Arg.

Text by S. Cammarano. Three acts.

In Italy sometimes, and at Oporto 1858, given as *L'Assedio d'Arlem*. In Italian also, Malta 1861.

In a French 4-act version by M. Drack (*Patria*), Verdi's work was chosen as the opening opera of the new Théâtre du Château d'Eau in 1889; it was, however, not produced and has never been given in France.

Revived Milan, Sc. 19 January 1916 and Buenos Aires 28 May 1916 (in Italian); Augsburg 20 March 1932 (in German, as *Die Schlacht von Legnano*, translated by F. X. Bayerl); Bremen 6 March 1937 (as *Das heilige Feuer*, translated by J. Kapp).

GLÄSER: *Bryllupet vet Como-Søen*
(The Wedding on Lake Como)

29 January. Copenhagen

Text by H. C. Andersen (founded on Manzoni's *I promessi Sposi*). Three acts.

The most successful of Gläser's three Danish operas; he had been appointed court conductor at Copenhagen in 1842.

NICOLAI: *Die lustigen Weiber von Windsor*

9 March. Berlin, O.

Text by S. H. Mosenthal (from Shakespeare's *The Merry Wives of Windsor*). Three acts.

Nicolai's chief work and his last opera (d. 11 May 1849).

Written for Vienna but refused there and eventually produced at Berlin. Very popular on German stages, and successful also abroad; not even Verdi's *Falstaff* (1893) was able to displace it.

Given at the Berlin O. more than 300 times until 1926; the 250th performance was on 2 March 1908. Subsequently produced at:

RIGA 1 December 1851 (in German) and 27 March 1923 (in Lettish).

VIENNA 12 February 1852 (with recitatives by H. Proch).

ZURICH 26 November 1852 (in German).

PRAGUE November 1853 (in German) and 4 March 1865 (in Czech, translated by B. Peška).

AMSTERDAM March 1857 (in German).

STOCKHOLM 18 May 1857 (in Swedish, translated by G. A. Elkan); revived 15 February 1897.

TEMESVAR 2 February 1858 (in German).

BUDAPEST 19 October 1859 (in Hungarian, translated by L. Csepregi).

ANTWERP 9 January 1861 (in French, translated by L. Danglas).

PHILADELPHIA 16 March 1863 (in German).

NEW YORK 27 April 1863 (in German) and 5 February 1886 (in English, translated by H. E. Krehbiel).

LONDON, H.M.'S 3 May 1864 (in Italian, translated by S. M. Maggioni); Adelphi 11 February 1878 (in English); and C.G. 16 February 1907 (in German).

BORDEAUX 1864 (in French).

WARSAW 1865 (in Polish, translated by J. Matuszewski).

PARIS, TH.L. 25 May 1866 (in French, translated by J. Barbier).

COPENHAGEN 14 September 1867 (in Danish, translated by A. Zinck).

DUBLIN 24 September 1867 (in Italian) and 17 October 1877 (in English).

LAIBACH (LJUBLJANA) 27 February 1868 (in German) and 1920 (in Slovenian).

ZAGREB 12 February 1876 (in Croatian, translated by A. M. Bišćan).

ABERDEEN 10 October 1877 (for the first time in English, translated by H. Hersee).

SYDNEY October 1877 (in English).

NAPLES, T. BELLINI 1 March 1889 (for the first time in Italy; new Italian version by S. de Castrone, Marchese della Rajata; Milan, Sc. as late as 5 February 1912).

BARCELONA November 1895 (in Italian).

HELSINKI 20 May 1900 (in German) and 15 February 1922 (in Finnish).

BELGRADE 1922 (in Serbian).

KAUNAS 15 May 1928 (in Lithuanian).

SOFIA 13 December 1929 (in Bulgarian).

TALLINN 1930 (in Estonian).

BUCHAREST Spring 1934 (in Rumanian).

Last revived in New York 22 April 1936 (by the Juilliard School of Music, Krehbiel's translation); revived in London 6 July 1937 (by the R.C.M.).

HERNANDO: *Colegialas y Soldados*
(College Girls and Soldiers)

21 March. Madrid, Comedia

Text by M. Pina. Two acts.

Although this is not the "first zarzuela" as it has been called, not even the first zarzuela of the 19th century, it certainly is the work which stands at the beginning of a new school of Spanish musical drama which, in the following years, slowly secured victory over the hitherto unchallenged rule of Italian opera in Spain. After Hernando, the chief composers were Gaztambide, Barbieri, Arrieta, and Oudrid. The vocal score of *Colegialas y Soldados* was published in 1872.

LIMNANDER: *Les Monténégrins*

31 March. Paris, O.C.

Text by J. E. Alboize du Pujol and G. Labrunie de Nerval. Three acts.

The most successful work of the Belgian composer.

Antwerp 6 January 1850; Brussels 30 January 1850, etc.

Revived Paris, O.C. 14 August 1858 (reduced to two acts); last revived at Brussels 28 August 1880.

MEYERBEER: *Le Prophète*

16 April. Paris, O.

Text by A. E. Scribe. Five acts.

The 100th performance in Paris was on 14 July 1851; the 500th on 26 November 1898; last revived there 26 February 1912. Outside Paris given at:

LONDON, C.G. 24 July 1849 (in Italian, translated by S. M. Maggioni); Surrey Th. 7 August 1854 (in English); C. G. 23 June 1890 (in French); last revived at C.G. 15 May 1895 (150th performance there).

HAMBURG 24 January 1850 (in German, translated by L. Rellstab).

AMSTERDAM 29 January 1850 (in German, translated by L. Rellstab).

VIENNA 28 February 1850 (in German, translated by L. Rellstab).

LISBON 1 April 1850 (in Italian).

ANTWERP 2 April 1850 (in French).

NEW ORLEANS 2 April 1850 (in French).

BERLIN 28 April 1850 (in German).

BUDAPEST 11 June 1850 (in Hungarian, translated by B. Egressy and J. Szerdahelyi).

BRUSSELS 6 September 1850 (in French); a Flemish parody by H. van Peene was given at Ghent 10 March 1851.

GRAZ 10 October 1850.

PRAGUE 6 December 1850 (in German) and 5 December 1875 (in Czech, translated by B. Peška).

BASLE 13 December 1850 (in German).

CONSTANTINOPLE Autumn 1851 (in Italian).

ST. PETERSBURG 17 March 1852 (in Italian) and 24 December 1869 (in Russian, translated by P. I. Kalashnikov).

STOCKHOLM 8 November 1852 (in Swedish, translated by C. W. A. Strandberg).

FLORENCE 26 December 1852 (for the first time in Italy, in Italian).

NEW YORK 25 November 1853 (in Italian); 7 May 1872 (in German); and 1 January 1892 (in French).

DUBLIN 6 September 1855 (in Italian).

MILAN SC. 1855 (in Italian, translation revised by L. Fortis).

REVAL March 1856 (in German, as *Die Belagerung von Gent*).

HELSINKI 8 June 1856 (in German).

HAVANA 1857 (in Italian).

MEXICO 8 June 1861 (in Italian).

BARCELONA 21 January 1863 (in Italian).

ALGIERS Spring 1863 (in Italian).

MELBOURNE and SYDNEY Summer 1864 (in English).

NAPLES S.C. November 1865.

WARSAW 1867 (in Polish, translated by J. Checiński).

MALTA 1873 (in Italian).

BUENOS AIRES 22 August 1873 (in Italian).

CAIRO February 1875 (in Italian).

RIO DE JANEIRO Autumn 1876 (in Italian).

ZAGREB 20 March 1897 (in Croatian, translated by F. Miler).

Given at Brisbane, Queensland, in the universal language, "Volapük," on 1 July 1889 (according to contemporary journals).

Still on the stage in several countries; revived at Brussels 1 August 1926; Leningrad October 1934 (in Russian).

ADAM: *Le Toréador* ou *L'Accord parfait*

18 May. Paris, O.C.

Text by T. M. F. Sauvage. Two acts.

Adam says in his autobiographical notes that he wrote the score in six days. Very successful in Paris; the latest revivals at the O.C. were on 28 December 1881, 1 June 1893, and 2 February 1911.

In French also given at Brussels 13 November 1849; London, St. J.'s 18 February 1859; Madrid, Z. July 1859; New York 18 October 1866; Barcelona 30 June 1868; Lisbon 29 May 1878.

In Swedish (translated by C. W. A. Strandberg), Stockholm 23 November 1857.

In German (translated by R. Schickele and F. Rumpel, music revised by M. Morris), Berlin, K.O. 27 March 1909; Prague 18 August 1909.

Revived Duisburg, October 1929 (in German); Johannesburg, Winter 1929 (in English).

LORTZING: *Rolands Knappen* oder *Das ersehnte Glück*

25 May. Leipzig

Text by the composer, G. Meisinger, and C. Haffner (see H. Laue, *Die Operndichtung Lortzing's*, pp.180–186), founded on a tale by J. K. A. Musäus. Three acts.

Berlin, Fr. W. 9 August 1862. Revived Bremen 8 March 1906 (revised by G. R. Kruse and P. Nodermann); Berlin, Th.d.W. 27 October 1906, etc. As *Die Glücksnarren* (new libretto by P. Hensel-Haerdrich), Rostock and Cassel 26 October 1937.

HERNANDO: *El Duende* (The Ghost)

6 June. Madrid, Variedades

Text by L. de Olona. Two acts.

Very successful zarzuela, running for 120 nights. A second part, by the same authors, followed on 18 February 1851 at the Teatro Lírico Español; *El Duende* was given at Barcelona Autumn 1850; Mexico 15 December 1854; and Buenos Aires 1856 as the first zarzuela there.

LAURO ROSSI: *Il Domino nero*

1 September. Milan, Can.

Text by F. Rubino (founded on Scribe's French libretto, see 1837). Three acts.

Successful in Italy; last revived Turin 12 June 1873; Pistoia February 1878.

In Italian also, Vienna 17 May 1851; Barcelona 6 December 1851; Malta 1852.

HALÉVY: *La Fée aux Roses*

1 October. Paris, O.C.

Text by A. E. Scribe and J. H. Vernoy de Saint-Georges. Three acts.

In French also, Brussels 20 June 1850; New Orleans January 1851.

In German (translated by J. C. Grünbaum), Leipzig 19 September 1850.

In Polish (translated by J. Checiński), Warsaw 15 February 1855.

In Russian, St. Petersburg 1855.

Revived Paris, Galerie Vivienne 12 April 1897; Geneva 11 January 1898.

MACFARREN: *King Charles II*

27 October. London, Princess's

Text by M. D. Ryan (founded on the comedy by J. H. Payne). Two acts.

"The triumphant success achieved by Mr. Macfarren's new opera has been chronicled by the whole of the metropolitan press. We have not heard one dissentient voice, nor read one dissentient opinion as to the merits of *King Charles II*. That it is the finest and most complete operatic work of a native musician ever produced on the stage is no less universally allowed. The production of such a work and its reception must be regarded as an epoch in the history of the music of the country". (*Musical World*, 3 November 1849.)

FUERTES: *El Tío Caniyitas, o El Mundo Nuevo di Cádiz*
(Goodfellow Caniyitas, *or* The New World of Cádiz)
November. Sevilla

Text by J. Sanz Pérez. Two acts.

Fuertes's best zarzuela; popular in Spain; Madrid, Circo December 1850, etc.

Also given at Mexico Spring 1855, etc.

VERDI: *Luisa Miller*
8 December. Naples, S.C.

Text by S. Cammarano (from Schiller's drama, *Kabale und Liebe*). Three acts.

In Italian also given at:

MALTA 1850.
MADRID 27 April 1851.
LISBON 22 June 1851.
BARCELONA 25 October 1851.
VIENNA 20 April 1852.
PARIS 7 December 1852.
CONSTANTINOPLE Carnival 1853.
RIO DE JANEIRO 1853.
BUCHAREST 1853.
BUENOS AIRES 28 January 1854.
NEW YORK 20 July 1854.
ST. PETERSBURG 1857.
CORFU 1857.
BASTIA, CORSICA Carnival 1858.
LONDON, H.M.'s 8 June 1858.
WILNA 1873.

In German, Hanover 27 May 1851.

In Hungarian (translated by B. Egressy), Budapest 30 May 1851.

In French (translated by B. Alaffre and E. Pacini), Paris, O. 2 February 1853.

In English (translated by C. Jefferys), London, Sadler's Wells 3 June 1858; Melbourne 1860.

Still given in Italy; outside Italy, the latest revivals were at Berlin 10 December 1927 (in German, translated by G. Göhler); Budapest March 1929 (in Hungarian, translated by V. Lányi); New York, M. 21 December 1929 (in Italian); Vienna, Akademie Th. 14 March 1930 (in German); Leningrad May 1936 (in Russian); Zurich 1938 (in German).

GAZTAMBIDE: *La Mensajera*
(The Errand Girl)
24 December. Madrid

Text by L. de Olona. Two acts.

Gaztambide's first zarzuela; produced at the T. Español (formerly T. del Principe).

DOPPLER: *Ilka*, vagy: *A Huszártoborzó*
(Ilka; or, The Hussar Recruiting)
29 December. Budapest

Text by J. Janotyckh von Adlerstein. Three acts.

Successful Hungarian comic opera; revived at Budapest 29 December 1892 and given there until 1900.

In German, Pressburg November 1857; Hanover 26 November 1858; Vienna 23 March 1867.

1850

HOVEN: *Ein Abenteuer Carl des Zweiten*
12 January. Vienna, Kä.

Text by S. H. von Mosenthal. One act.

Hoven's most successful work; subsequently given at Weimar 7 April 1850; Berlin, Fr. W. 19 November 1851; Dresden 29 November 1851, etc.

Revived at the Vienna Conservatoire March 1879; and Lauchstedt 26 June 1938 (by the Leipzig University Collegium Musicum).

GRISAR: *Les Porcherons*
12 January. Paris, O.C.

Text by T. M. F. Sauvage and J. J. Gabriel. Three acts.

Brussels 13 August 1850; Antwerp 25 October 1850, etc.

Revived Paris, O.C. 26 August 1865.

German vocal score, translated by C. Gollmick, published 1851.

GADE: *Mariotta*

17 January. Copenhagen

Text by C. Borgaard (founded on a comedy by Scribe). Three acts.

The only (unsuccessful) opera of the famous Danish romantic composer.

L. and F. RICCI:
Crispino e la Comare ossia
Il Medico e la Morte

28 February. Venice, S. Ben.

Text by F. M. Piave (*melodramma fantastico-giocoso*, founded on a comedy by S. Fabbrichesi, 1835). Three acts.

The most popular work of the brothers Ricci, very successful in Italy and abroad:

CONSTANTINOPLE Carnival 1854 (in Italian).

BARCELONA 18 March 1854 (in Italian).

MALTA 1856 (in Italian).

LONDON, ST. J.'s 17 November 1857 (in Italian; last revived Shaftesbury 19 October 1891).

CÁDIZ [16 April] 1858 (in Spanish, translated by J. Sanz Pérez, music adapted by V. Lamadrid).

RIO DE JANEIRO March 1861 (in Portuguese) and 1875 (in Italian).

PARIS, TH. I. 4 April 1865 (in Italian) and Athénée 18 September 1869 (in French).

NEW YORK 24 October 1865 and Philadelphia 15 October 1866 (in Italian); New York 13 November 1882 (in English).

WARSAW 9 December 1865 (in Italian).

NEW ORLEANS 7 November 1866 (in Italian).

MEXICO 22 November 1866 (in Italian).

LIÉGE 17 December 1866 (in French, translated by C. Nuitter and A. Beaumont).

BRUSSELS 18 December 1866 (in French, translated by C. Nuitter and A. Beaumont).

LISBON 22 February 1867 (in Italian; revived 7 February 1891).

BUENOS AIRES 22 March 1867 (in Italian).

VIENNA 10 May 1867 (with additions) (in Italian).

SANTIAGO, CHILE 1867 (in Italian).

BADEN BADEN 12 August 1867 (in Italian).

BERLIN, VICT. TH. 15 October 1867 (in Italian).

ST. PETERSBURG 17 February 1868 (in Italian).

PRAGUE 20 June 1869 (in Czech, translated by J. Böhm).

BRESLAU 20 February 1870 (for the first time in German; revived Stuttgart 6 March 1887).

CAIRO March 1870 (in Italian).

ZAGREB 7 April 1874 (in Croatian, translated by A. M. Bišćan).

SYDNEY Summer 1874 (in Italian).

HELSINKI 1880 (in Swedish, translated by R. Hertzberg).

BUCHAREST 1903 (in Rumanian).

Revived New York 18 January 1919; one of the latest revivals in Italy was at Turin, T. Carignano 2 February 1937.

F. A. BARBIERI: *Gloria y Peluca*
(Glory and Wig)

9 March. Madrid, Variedades

Text by J. de la Villa del Valle. One act.

Barbieri's first zarzuela (of more than 70).

(THRANE): *Fjeldeventyret*
(Mountain Adventure)

9 April. Christiania

Text by H. A. Bjerregaerd. Two acts.

This first Norwegian opera had been printed as early as 1824 and given a concert performance at Christiania in March, 1827 (see note in *The Harmonicon*, 1826, p.208).

Bergen 2 October 1851; Copenhagen 26 May 1858.

In Swedish (translated by C. A. K. Almlöf and E. A. Wallmark), Stockholm 16 August 1861.

Revived Christiania 5 April 1908 and still given there as late as 1929 and 1933.

ŠKROUP: *Libušin Sňatek*

(The Marriage of Libussa)

11 April. Prague

Text by J. K. Chmelenský. Three acts.

Early Czech national opera (Smetana treated the same subject in 1881).

A. THOMAS: *Le Songe
d'une Nuit d'Eté*

20 April. Paris, O.C.

Text by J. B. Rosier and A. de Leuven (not founded on Shakespeare's *A Midsummer Night's Dream*, but dealing with an episode in Shakespeare's life, with the poet himself, Queen Elizabeth and Sir John Falstaff appearing in it). Three acts.

Very successful in France.

Revived at the O.C. 22 September 1859 and 17 April 1886 (with some new pieces); revived at the Tr.L. 12 November 1915; at Lille as late as 13 February 1936; at Brussels 25 September 1937.

Outside France:

LIÉGE 24 March 1851; Brussels 1 July 1851, etc. (in French).

NEW ORLEANS 1851 (in French).

FRANKFORT 22 April 1852 (in German, translated by C. Gollmick).

NEW YORK 21 June 1852 (in French) and 15 October 1877 (in English, translated by M. A. Cooney).

VIENNA 12 January 1854 (in German).

BERLIN, FR. W. 2 February 1854 (in German).

GENEVA March 1854 (in French).

BUENOS AIRES 7 October 1854 (in French).

BARCELONA 1 August 1868 (in French).

LISBON 10 April 1878 (in French).

MEXICO 24 April 1879 (in French).

PADUA 24 February 1897 (in Italian, translated by A. Zanardini).

GLASGOW 18 February 1898 (in English, as *A Poet's Dream*, translated by W. B. Kingston).

HALÉVY: *La Tempesta*

8 June. London, H. M.'s

(Original French) text by A. E. Scribe (from Shakespeare's *Tempest*), Italian version by P. Giannone. Three acts.

(Originally the libretto had been written for Mendelssohn). The only opera Halévy wrote for London; unsuccessful.

In Italian also, Paris 25 February 1851.

SCHUMANN: *Genoveva*

25 June. Leipzig

The original text, by R. Reinick, was altered by the composer himself, who based the libretto on L. Tieck's and F. Hebbel's *Genoveva* dramas. Four acts.

Schumann's only opera; it was never a success although produced on several stages:

WEIMAR 9 April 1855.

CARLSRUHE 3 December 1867.

MUNICH 12 October 1873.

VIENNA 8 January 1874.

WIESBADEN 7 February 1874.

HANOVER 14 November 1874.

MANNHEIM 14 March 1875.

BERLIN 1 March 1877.

CASSEL 18 March 1878.

HAMBURG 8 January 1879.

FRANKFORT 15 October 1880.

BASLE 18 February 1881.

COLOGNE 21 October 1881.

DRESDEN 24 January 1882.

AUGSBURG 14 March 1882.

ROTTERDAM 9 December 1882.

DARMSTADT 27 March 1887.

PRAGUE 27 August 1902.

Revived Rudolstadt February 1935.

Outside the German-speaking countries given at:

LONDON, D.L. 6 December 1893 (by the R.C.M., in English, translated by L. Vance; a concert selection had been given by the Bach Choir at St. James's Hall, on 8 March 1887); R.C.M., again, 1910.

PARIS 16 December 1894 (in concert form at the Concerts d'Harcourt; in French, translated by E. d'Harcourt and C. Grandmougin).

ST. PETERSBURG 20 April 1896 (in Russian; in German given there privately 24 February 1870 already).

F. A. BARBIERI: *Tramoya*
(The Trick)

27 June. Madrid, Comedia

Text by J. de Olona. One act.

This zarzuela was very successful in Spain and South America.

DE GIOSA: *Don Checco*

11 July. Naples, T.N.

Text by A. Spadetta. Two acts.

De Giosa's most popular work, according to Clément "un des plus grands succès de l'opéra bouffe".

One of the latest revivals was at Naples on 7 December 1902.

In Italian also given at Malta, Autumn 1854; Barcelona February 1859; Santiago, Chile 1870; Cairo November 1870; Sydney January 1885.

In Portuguese (translated by L. V. de Simoni), Rio de Janeiro 17 November 1860.

In Spanish (as *De Incógnito*, translated by C. Frontaura, music adapted by Luis Cepeda), Madrid, Circo 30 May 1861 and Mexico 29 November 1892.

ADAM: *Giralda* ou *La nouvelle Psyché*

20 July. Paris, O.C.

Text by A. E. Scribe. Three acts.

Successful in Paris; revived at the O.C. 28 March 1862 and 24 January 1883; Tr.L. 7 May 1915.

In French also, Brussels 20 December 1850; Hague September 1851.

In Portuguese, Lisbon December 1850.

In German (translated by W. Friedrich), Berlin 25 February 1851; Vienna 4 October 1851; Prague 25 October 1855, etc. Revived Berlin, Fr.

W. 1 July 1880; Hanover 9 December 1884; Leipzig 25 December 1888.

In Spanish (translated by M. Pina), Granada 27 May 1858 and Madrid, Z. 19 June 1858; (translated by C. Frontaura), Barcelona November 1862; Mexico July 1893.

In Russian, Moscow 1869.

In English (translated by A. Baildon), London, Ly. 21 September 1876; Boston 4 March 1885.

In Swedish, Stockholm 13 September 1893.

COSSOUL: *A Cisterna do Diabo*
(The Devil's Cistern)

17 August. Lisbon

Text by J. F. O. Romano. One act.

Early Portuguese comic opera, produced at the Theatro do Gymnasio.

R. WAGNER: *Lohengrin*

28 August. Weimar

Text by the composer. Three acts.

Written 1846–48. Originally intended to be produced at Dresden, but rejected there in 1848. Produced by Liszt at Weimar when Wagner was a political exile in Switzerland. He did not attend a performance of *Lohengrin* until after 11 years (at Vienna 15 May 1861). The next productions were at Königsberg 1853; Wiesbaden 2 July 1853; Leipzig 7 January 1854; Schwerin 15 January 1854; Frankfort 12 April 1854; Darmstadt 17 April 1854 (not 1855); Breslau 31 October 1854; Cologne 4 January 1855; Hamburg 19 January 1855, etc.

RIGA 5 February 1855 (in German) and 2 October 1920 (in Lettish, translated by A. Anderson).

PRAGUE 23 February 1856 (in German) and 12 January 1885 (in Czech, translated by V. J. Novotný; first Wagner opera sung in that language).

VIENNA, O. 19 August 1858 (688 performances until 1936).

BERLIN, O. 23 January 1859 (745 performances until 1935; 500th performance 23 March 1906).

ROTTERDAM 19 November 1862 (in German).

GRAZ 5 December 1863.

BUDAPEST 1 December 1866 (in Hungarian, translated by G. Böhm and F. Ormai).

ST. PETERSBURG 16 October 1868 (in Russian, translated by K. Svantsov); Moscow 31 December 1881.

BRUSSELS 23 March 1870 (for the first time in French, translated by C. Nuitter).

COPENHAGEN 30 April 1870 (in Danish, translated by A. Hertz).

HAGUE 30 November 1870 (in German) and 20 May 1871 (in French).

NEW YORK 3 April 1871 (in German); 23 March 1874 (in Italian); and 20 January 1886 (in English, translated by N. Macfarren).

BOLOGNA 1 November 1871 (in Italian, translated by S. de Castrone, Marchese della Rajata); first Wagner opera in Italy; conductor, A. Mariani. Subsequently produced at Florence, T. Pagliano 8 December 1871; Milan, Sc. 20 March 1873 (under Faccio); Trieste 4 October 1876 (under Mancinelli); Turin 14 March 1877 (under Pedrotti); Rome, Ap. 25 April 1878 (under Ponchielli); Genoa 15 June 1880 (under Mancinelli); Naples, S.C. 26 February 1881; Venice 2 January 1882 (under Usiglio), etc.

STOCKHOLM 22 January 1874 (in Swedish, translated by F. T. Hedberg).

LONDON, C.G. 8 May 1875 (in Italian); H.M.'s 7 February 1880 (in English, translated by J. P. Jackson); D.L. 18 May 1882 (in German). 100th performance at C.G. 8 May 1899.

DUBLIN 11 October 1875 (in Italian).

BASLE 8 December 1876 (in German); concert performances already Berne 1 March 1873 (first act) and Zurich 13 March 1874.

LEMBERG 21 April 1877 (in Polish, translated by A. Urbański).

NEW ORLEANS 3 December 1877 (in Italian) and 4 March 1889 (in French).

GHENT 22 October 1880 (in German) and 9 April 1888 (in French).

ANTWERP 12 March 1881 (in German); 21 March 1889 (in French); 15 December 1896 (in Flemish).

NICE 21 March 1881 (in Italian); for the first time in France.

MADRID 25 March 1881; Barcelona 17 May 1882; Bilbao 17 June 1890 (in Italian); a fragment of *Lohengrin* had been performed at a concert at Bilbao as early as 1872. Catalan version by X. Viura and J. Pena published 1905; Spanish (Castilian) version by A. Gil y Gordaliza published 1910.

LISBON 14 March 1883 (in Italian).

REVAL (TALLINN) 15 March 1883 (in German); August 1913 (in Italian!); and 1927 (in Estonian, translated by G. Tuksam).

BUENOS AIRES 17 July 1883 (in Italian).

RIO DE JANEIRO 19 September 1883 (in Italian).

CHRISTIANIA 2 December 1885 (in Norwegian).

PARIS, TH. EDEN 3 May 1887 (in French); then Rouen 7 February 1891; Angers and Nantes 21 February 1891; Lyons 26 February 1891; Bordeaux 31 March 1891; Paris, O. only 16 September 1891; Marseilles 26 February 1892; Monte Carlo 8 March 1902.

MONTREAL 7 January 1888 (in English).

SANTIAGO, CHILE December 1889 (in Italian).

GENEVA 27 December 1889 (in French).

MEXICO 8 November 1890 (in Italian) and 8 April 1891 (in English).

ZAGREB 28 June 1893 (in Croatian, translated by A. Harambašić).

BUCHAREST December 1893 (in Italian) and 8 December 1921 (in Rumanian, on the opening night of the Rumanian State Opera).

MALTA 1896 (in Italian).

ALEXANDRIA January 1897 (in Italian).

LJUBLJANA 19 January 1899 (in Slovenian, translated by M. Markič).

PERM 7 November 1899 (in Russian).

HELSINKI 2 May 1900 (in German) and 6 May 1920 (in Finnish, translated by P. J. Hannikainen).

CORFU 1902 (in Italian).

JOHANNESBURG 1905 (in English).

MELBOURNE 30 March 1907 (first opera in Australia sung in German).

KHARKOV 1925 (in Ukrainian).

KAUNAS 3 February 1926 (in Lithunian).

ATHENS November 1931 (in Italian).

TOKYO 1932 (the first act, in concert form).

SOFIA 5 September 1934 (in Bulgarian).

ARRIETA: *La Conquista di Granada*

10 October. Madrid, T. del Real Palacio
(Italian) text by T. Solera. Three acts.

Revived Madrid, T. de la Plaza de Oriente 18
December 1855.

VERDI: *Stiffelio*

16 November. Trieste

Text by F. M. Piave ("uno dei maggiori delitti
poetici del Piave", according to L. Miragoli),
founded on a French play by E. Souvestre and
E. Bourgeois. Three acts.

Unsuccessful; given on a few Italian stages; at
Rome 23 February 1851 and Florence 30 May
1851 as *Guglielmo Wellingrode*; outside Italy, only
Barcelona 20 October 1856.

Verdi revised this opera some years later for the
inauguration of the Teatro Nuovo, Rimini; it
was given there as *Aroldo* (4 acts) on 16 August
1857; this new version was somewhat more
successful; given at Rome 31 January 1858, etc.;
and, in Italian also, at Vienna 5 May 1858; Malta
1859; Buenos Aires 15 November 1860; Lisbon
25 November 1860; New York 4 May 1863;
Mexico 23 September 1864; Rio de Janeiro November 1864; Santiago, Chile 1865.

Given on Italian stages until 1883 (Crema).

French vocal score (translated by E. Duprez)
published *c*.1865.

FLOTOW: *Sophia Catharina* oder
Die Grossfürstin

19 November. Berlin, O.

Text by C. Birch-Pfeiffer. Four acts.

Given on many other German stages and, in
Swedish (translated by T. Knös), at Stockholm
20 March 1852. Revived Berlin 5 October 1858.

MASSÉ: *La Chanteuse Voilée*

26 November. Paris, O.C.

Text by A. E. Scribe and A. de Leuven. One act.

Massé's first greater success.

In French also, Brussels 7 March 1851; Lisbon
1855; revived at the O.C., Paris 27 April 1863.

In German (translated by A. Schirmer), Vienna,
Ca. 3 November 1860 (revived 31 March 1874).

In Swedish (translated by E. A. Wallmark),
Stockholm 7 November 1868.

AUBER: *L'Enfant prodigue*

6 December. Paris, O.

Text by A. E. Scribe. Five acts.

Auber's only opera on a biblical subject.

Given in Paris 44 times. In French also, Brussels
4 April 1851.

In English (as *Azael, the Prodigal*, translated by
E. Fitzball, music adapted by H. Laurent), London, D.L. 19 February 1851; New York 2 June
1851.

In Italian, London, H.M.'s 12 June 1851; revived Florence 12 September 1875.

In German (translated by J. C. Grünbaum),
Graz 22 October 1851; Vienna 21 November
1851; Munich 15 March 1852, etc.

1851

STRAKOSCH: *Giovanna Prima
di Napoli*

6 January. New York, Astor Place Opera House

Librettist not mentioned; perhaps an altered version of A. Pendola's libretto of this title (set by
Granara, Venice 1836). Three acts.

The only Italian opera of the well-known impresario, who was the brother-in-law of Adelina
Patti.

LORTZING: *Die vornehmen Dilettanten*
oder *Die Opernprobe*

20 January. Frankfort

Text by the composer (founded on a French play
by R. Poisson). One act.

The last of Lortzing's operas which was produced in his lifetime; he died at Berlin the day
after the first performance at Frankfort.

Popular on German stages; Berlin, Fr.W. 28
September 1851; Vienna, W. 7 October 1858,
etc. Revived Carlsruhe 16 October 1885; Dres-

den 29 January 1893; Vienna, O. 10 February 1899; Brünn 10 November 1901; Riga 10 December 1901; Graz 15 January 1902; Berlin, Kroll's 5 December 1903, D.O. 12 May 1926, Th. am Kurfürstendamm 27 November 1932.

In Czech, Prague 10 October 1915.

Heard in London at a concert of the Vienna Sängerknaben on 9 October 1934.

BATTISTA: *Ermelinda*

15 February. Naples, T.N.

Text by D. Bolognese (founded on Victor Hugo's *Notre-Dame de Paris*). Four acts.

Successful in Italy; given sometimes as *Esmeralda*. Revived Milan 28 April 1866; Parma 17 July 1883; Milan, T. Carcano August 1900.

In Italian also, Malta 1856; Lisbon 19 April 1857.

In English (translated by C. Jefferys), London, D.L. 30 June 1856.

GRISAR: *Bonsoir, M. Pantalon*

19 February. Paris, O.C.

Text by De Morvan and J. P. Lockroy (founded on J. Oxenford's play *Twice Killed*). One act.

The most successful of Grisar's works; given at the O.C. until 1874; frequently revived on French stages, at Brussels as late as 28 October 1933. After Paris it was given at Antwerp 22 April 1851; Brussels 25 April 1851, etc.

In French also, Naples 22 May 1869.

In English, London, Adelphi 29 May 1851 (running for 132 nights).

In German (translated by J. C. Grünbaum), Vienna, W. 2 December 1851 (Kä. 15 September 1855; O. 3 April 1882); Munich 21 December 1851; Dresden 9 February 1852; Berlin 13 June 1853, etc. Revived in German, Hanover 30 January 1911; Zurich 18 October 1907.

In Polish (translated by L. Matuszyński), Warsaw 17 January 1852.

In Danish (translated by H. P. Holst), Copenhagen 4 March 1867.

In Czech (translated by A. P.), Prague 28 April 1871 (in German only 28 March 1905).

In Hungarian (translated by E. Abrányi), Budapest 3 September 1887.

RAFF: *König Alfred*

9 March. Weimar

Text by G. Logau, altered by the composer. Four acts.

The first opera of the well-known instrumental composer and friend of Wagner and Liszt. Also given Wiesbaden 28 August 1856 (rectify Riemann's *Musiklexikon*).

VERDI: *Rigoletto*

11 March. Venice, F.

Text by F. M. Piave (founded on Victor Hugo's *Le Roi s'amuse* and originally called *La Maledizione*). Three acts.

Given on Italian stages also as *Viscardello* (Rome 27 September 1851; Bologna 26 December 1852); *Clara di Pert* (text altered by L. E. Bardare, Naples, T.N. December 1853); *Lionello* (Naples 1858).

Outside Italy:

VIENNA 12 May 1852 (in Italian) and 24 November 1860 (in German).

BUDAPEST 18 December 1852 (in Hungarian, translated by L. Nádaskay).

BRÜNN 8 January 1853 (in German, translated by J. C. Grünbaum).

GRAZ 18 January 1853 (in German, translated by J. C. Grünbaum).

STUTTGART 30 January 1853 (in German, translated by J. C. Grünbaum).

PRAGUE 5 February 1853 (in German) and 10 September 1864 (in Czech).

ST. PETERSBURG 12 February 1853 (in Italian) and 18 November 1878 (in Russian, translated by G. A. Lishin).

LONDON, C.G. 14 May 1853 (in Italian; 200th performance 3 June 1911); H.M.'s 25 November 1886 (in French); C.G. 20 October 1909 (in English, translated by N. Macfarren; People's 10 April 1912 (in Yiddish, translated by S. Alman). Revived Sadler's Wells 24 February 1937 (new English version by E. J. Dent).

WARSAW 1853 (in Polish, translated by J. Che-ciński).

MADRID 18 October 1853 (in Italian); Spanish version by M. Capdepón published 1903; Spanish parody by A. Piñadas published 1881.

ATHENS 28 October 1853 (in Italian).

LISBON 29 January 1854 (in Italian).

CONSTANTINOPLE Carnival 1854 (in Italian).

TIFLIS February 1854 (in Italian).

NEW YORK 19 February 1855 (in Italian); 14 December 1870 (in German); 27 January 1874 (in English); and 8 June 1922 (in Russian).

BUENOS AIRES 16 June 1855 (in Italian).

HAVANA 1855 (in Italian).

RIO DE JANEIRO 12 January 1856 (in Italian).

PARIS, TH.I. 19 January 1857 (in Italian) and Th.L. 24 December 1863 (in French).

SANTIAGO, CHILE 1857 (in Italian).

MEXICO 1857 (in Italian) and April 1893 (in Spanish, translated by J. Vigil y Robles).

BUCHAREST 1857 (in Italian).

DUBLIN 4 August 1857 (in Italian).

BASTIA, CORSICA Carnival 1858 (in Italian, as *Viscardello*).

RIGA January 1858 (in German) and 1915 (in Lettish).

BRUSSELS 22 November 1858 (for the first time in French, translated by E. Duprez).

AGRAM (ZAGREB) April 1859 (in Italian) and 13 December 1873 (in Croatian, translated by A. M. Bišćan).

BERLIN, VICT. TH. 4 February 1860 (in Italian); O. 5 November 1860 (in Italian) and 15 March 1865 (in German).

NEW ORLEANS 19 March 1860 (in Italian).

MARSEILLES 13 May 1860 (in French, for the first time in France).

BASLE 31 January 1861 (in German).

STOCKHOLM 3 June 1861 (in Swedish, translated by E. A. Wallmark).

SYDNEY November 1861 (in English).

MALTA 1863 (in Italian).

SMYRNA 1867 (in Italian).

SOERABAYA 27 January 1868 (in French).

CHRISTIANIA April 1868 (in Italian) and 20 September 1915 (in Norwegian).

CAIRO December 1869 (in Italian).

KIEV 1876 (in Russian, translated by P. I. Kalashnikov).

COPENHAGEN 18 September 1879 (in Danish, translated by A. Hertz).

LIVERPOOL August 1888 (in Russian).

CAPE TOWN 1895 (in Italian); Johannesburg March 1912 (in English).

LJUBLJANA 1896 (in Slovenian).

TUNIS 12 April 1903 (in Italian).

HELSINKI 24 April 1917 (in Finnish).

SHANGHAI 1918 (in Russian).

YOKOHAMA Autumn 1919 (in Italian).

SOFIA 13 December 1920 (in Bulgarian, translation published already at Shumen 1905); in German 16 November 1938.

TALLINN 1921 (in Estonian).

BELGRADE 1921 (in Serbian).

KAUNAS 3 November 1921 (in Lithuanian).

JERUSALEM 30 October 1923 (in Hebrew, translated by M. Freidmann).

ROSENHAIN: *Le Démon de la Nuit*

17 March. Paris, O.

Text by E. Arago and J. F. A. Bayard. Two acts.

The most successful opera of the Frankfort composer (a new version of his German opera *Liswenna*, written in 1836, never performed).

In French also, Brussels 8 January 1852.

In German (translated by C. Gollmick), Frankfort 10 December 1851.

ERNST II DUKE OF SAXE-COBURG-GOTHA: *Casilda*

23 March. Gotha

Text by "M. Tenelli" (pseudonym of J. H. Millenet). Four acts.

The Duke's first greater success as an opera composer; given also at Vienna 18 August 1851; Berlin 19 November 1851, etc. Revived Gotha 12 February 1888; Darmstadt and Leipzig 3 May 1892.

In French (translated by G. Oppelt), Brussels 14 April 1852 and Ghent 19 March 1856.

In Italian, London, H.M.'s 5 August 1852.

SANELLI: *Il Fornaretto*

24 March. Parma

Text by A. Codebò. Three acts.

Of Sanelli's eleven operas the most successful one. Also given as *Piero di Vasco.* Revived Parma 9 March 1870; Milan, T. Carcano 12 July 1873.

In Italian also, Trieste 26 December 1851; Valparaiso 1854; Buenos Aires 8 May 1858; Barcelona 27 November 1859; Malta 1866.

ALARY: *Le tre Nozze*

29 March. Paris, Th.I.

Text by A. Berrettoni. Three acts.

This opera was famous for a polka duet sung by Henriette Sontag and Lablache, both in Paris and London.

In Italian also, London, H.M.'s 8 May 1851 and Madrid 27 March 1860.

(MENDELSSOHN): *Die Heimkehr aus der Fremde*

10 April. Leipzig

Text by K. Klingemann. One act.

This "Liederspiel" had originally been written for the silver-wedding of the composer's parents and had been privately performed at their house at Berlin on 26 December 1829. The first public performance was at Leipzig on 10 April 1851 (not 20 April as most books of reference, following Lampadius, have it), three years after Mendelssohn's death. Subsequently given at Berlin, Fr.W. 4 December 1851 and O. 30 December 1851, etc.; Vienna, Jos. 18 August 1853 and Kä. 3 January 1862; Prague 16 November 1853; Lucerne 1867; revived Stuttgart 11 May 1879; Leipzig 4 November 1883; Frankfort 22 November 1883; Berlin 2 October 1890 (at the Architektenhaus, by the "Gesellschaft der Opernfreunde"); Breslau May 1900; Bremen 3 February 1909.

In English (as *Son and Stranger,* translated by H. F. Chorley), London, Little Hm. 7 July 1851; revived C.G. 11 March 1861; Guildhall School of Music 23 December 1896.

In French (as *Lisbeth ou La Cinquantaine,* translated by J. Barbier), Paris, Th.L. 9 June 1865.

In Swedish, Stockholm 27 November 1901. In Hungarian (translated by S. Várady), Budapest 14 February 1909.

GOUNOD: *Sapho*

16 April. Paris, O.

Text by E. Augier. Three acts.

Gounod's first opera.

In Italian (translated by S. M. Maggioni), London, C.G. 9 August 1851. Revived Paris, O. 26 July 1858 (in a reduced two-act version) and again 2 April 1884 (in an enlarged four-act version); revived also Antwerp 1 February 1894.

AUBER: *Zerline ou La Corbeille d'Oranges*

16 May. Paris, O.

Text by A. E. Scribe. Three acts.

In French also, Brussels 26 October 1851. In Italian, London, H.M.'s 22 July 1851.

PETRELLA: *Le Precauzioni* ossia *Il Carnevale di Venezia*

20 May. Naples, T.N.

Text by M. d'Arienzo. Three acts.

Petrella's first greater success. Given in a new version at Milan 16 February 1858. Frequently revived in Italy; at Rome, Arg. as late as 1924.

In Italian also given at Malta 1856; Barcelona 11 April 1863; New York 3 April 1867; Santiago, Chile 1869; London, Ly. 21 March 1871; St. Petersburg 18 January 1883.

In Spanish (translated by E. Noriega and V. d'Alessio), Mexico 13 July 1890.

A. THOMAS: *Raymond ou Le Secret de la Reine*

5 June. Paris, O.C.

Text by A. de Leuven and J. B. Rosier. Three acts.

Unsuccessful in Paris; Brussels 4 February 1852. Popular on German stages (translated by J. C. Grünbaum): Frankfort 4 March 1855; Vienna, Jos. April 1857; Graz 10 October 1857; Berlin,

Wallner Th. 2 June 1861; Prague 1862, etc. Revived Schwerin 28 January 1870; Frankfort 6 January 1878.

PAULLI: *Lodsen*
(The Pilot)

25 September. Copenhagen

Text by P. Chiewitz and A. F. von der Recke. One act.

The only opera of Paulli who, as a conductor, did much to popularize Wagner's music in Denmark.

BOISSELOT: *Mosquita la Sorcière*

27 September. Paris, Th.L.

Text by A. E. Scribe and G. Vaëz. Three acts.

Written for the re-opening of the third Paris opera-house, the "Théâtre-Lyrique", then called "Théâtre National" (see 1847). Given also at Brussels 24 December 1851.

F. A. BARBIERI: *Jugar con Fuego*
(Playing with Fire)

6 October. Madrid, Circo

Text by V. de la Vega (founded on the French play *La Comtesse d'Egmont* by J. Ancelot and A. Decomberousse). Three acts.

Very successful zarzuela, frequently revived in Spain, where it still holds the boards.

In Spanish also, Mexico 11 April 1855 (first zarzuela there); Havana March 1856; Buenos Aires 1856; Lisbon 1 July 1859.

In Portuguese (translated by J. F. de Castilhos), Rio de Janeiro 31 August 1857.

FORONI: *I Gladiatori*

7 October. Milan, Can.

Text by G. Peruzzini (the original title *Spartaco* had to be changed by order of the police). Prologue and 3 acts.

The most successful Italian opera of Foroni, who, in 1849, had become court conductor at Stockholm. Last revived Turin 20 October 1883.

DUPREZ: *L'Abîme de la Maladetta*

19 November. Brussels, M.

Text by E. Duprez and G. Oppelt. Three acts. Paris, Th.L. 11 March 1852 (as *Joanita*). (The composer was the famous tenor and singing teacher.)

PEDROTTI: *Fiorina* ossia *La Fanciulla di Glaris*

22 November. Verona

Text by L. Serenelli Honorati. Two acts. Pedrotti's first success.

In Italian also, Trieste 26 December 1852; Warsaw 1853; Paris 8 December 1855; Barcelona 13 June 1856; Rio de Janeiro 1857; Vienna 3 June 1859; Lisbon 11 March 1863; Malta 1863.

In Hungarian, Budapest 1859.

F. DAVID: *La Perle du Brésil*

22 November. Paris, Th.L.

Text by J. J. Gabriel and S. Saint-Etienne. Three acts.

The first opera of David, who then already was famous as the composer of *Le Désert* and other *Odes-Symphonies.*

In French also, Brussels 5 November 1852; revived Paris, O.C. 17 May 1883; Rouen 30 January 1889.

ŠKROUP: *Der Meergeuse*

29 November. Prague

Text by J. K. Hickel. Three acts.

The last opera of the Czech composer; given also at Rotterdam 17 April 1861 (where Škroup was the first conductor at the German opera-house founded there in 1860).

1852

GRISAR: *Le Carillonneur de Bruges*

20 February. Paris, O.C.

Text by J. H. Vernoy de Saint-Georges. Three acts.

In French also, Antwerp 2 December 1852; Brussels 9 March 1853, etc. Revived Antwerp 13 February 1897 (in Flemish).

ADAM: *La Poupée de Nuremberg*

21 February. Paris, Th.L.

Text by A. de Leuven and L. L. Brunswick. One act.

One of Adam's most long-lived operas.

In French also, Brussels 25 April 1852, etc.

In German (translated by Herrmann), Berlin, Fr.W. 26 November 1852, etc.; Vienna, Ca. December 1860.

In Swedish (translated by C. W. A. Strandberg), Stockholm 25 November 1853.

In English (as *Dolly*), Cork 26 December 1860; London, Gaiety 22 August 1870. Another version (*The Toy-Maker*, text and new music by G. Linley) was given at C.G. 19 November 1861; and an adaptation from the Swedish (!), by W. Wardroper, at Sheffield 12 July 1886 (as *The Miraculous Doll*, with Adam's original music).

In Russian, St. Petersburg 22 May 1854.

In Polish (translated by L. Matuszyński), Warsaw 30 September 1855.

In Danish (translated by A. F. von der Recke), Copenhagen 23 November 1861; Christiania 1868.

In Hungarian (translated by M. Havi), Budapest 16 May 1863.

In Croatian, Zagreb 1865.

In Finnish (translated by A. Törneroos), Helsinki 4 January 1880.

Still popular in France and frequently revived in many other countries, viz.:

FRANKFORT 18 September 1875 (new German version by E. Pasqué).

BERLIN, FR.W. 3 March 1880 (Pasqué's version).

VIENNA, W. 20 November 1880 and O. 23 December 1881 (Pasqué's version).

RIGA 1895 (Pasqué's version).

BASLE 28 March 1900 (Pasqué's version).

MONTE CARLO 17 November 1903 (in French).

BARMEN 28 February 1930 (in German).

ST. GALLEN 6 April 1931 (in German).

BRNO January 1936 (in Czech).

TEL-AVIV 12 January 1938 (in Hebrew, translated by E. Troche).

ADAM: *Le Farfadet*

19 March. Paris, O.C.

Text by F. A. E. de Planard. One act.

Antwerp 6 February 1853; Brussels 9 January 1857, etc. Frequently revived in Paris, F.P. 3 February 1868; O. Populaire 30 December 1879; O.C. 5 February 1899; revived at Grenoble 4 May 1931.

PACIUS: *Kung Carls Jakt*
(King Charles's Hunting Party)

24 March. Helsinki

Text by Z. Topelius. Three acts.

Generally regarded at the first Finnish opera; but as a matter of fact the composer was German and the opera was sung in Swedish. Performed by amateurs; previously given there in concert form 18 March 1851.

In Swedish also, Stockholm 1 December 1856 (produced at the coronation of King Charles xv).

Revived in Finnish (translated by J. Finne) Viipuri (Viborg) 17 March 1905 and Helsinki 19 April 1909.

MASSÉ: *Galatée*

14 April. Paris, O.C.

Text by J. Barbier and M. Carré. Two acts.

One of Massé's most successful works; given at the O.C. throughout the 19th century and revived there 23 January 1908; Tr.L. 10 October 1915.

In French also, Brussels 22 September 1852 (last revived 30 October 1904); Buenos Aires 5 September 1854; New Orleans 1858; Madrid, Z. 15 July 1859; Barcelona 28 October 1866; New York 30 November 1866; Soerabaya 13 February 1868; London, O.C. 23 May 1872; Orange 24 August 1874 (open-air performance); Berlin, Vict. Th. 7 April 1886 and Kroll's 22 April 1902.

In Danish (translated by A. F. von der Recke), Copenhagen 22 September 1866.

In Spanish (translated by F. Camprodón and E. Álvarez), Madrid 7 February 1868.

In German, Vienna 19 April 1869.

In Czech (translated by E. Züngel), Prague 17 December 1873.

In English (translated by F. A. Schwab), Philadelphia 20 November 1886; New York 30 December 1886; Bristol 8 October 1887.

In Dutch (translated by J. Schmier), Amsterdam 2 November 1889.

OUDRID: *Buenas Noches, Señor Don Simón*

16 April. Madrid, Circo

Text: a Spanish version, by L. de Olona, of *Bonosir, M. Pantalon* (see 1851). One act.

Successful zarzuela. Mexico 14 February 1854; Buenos Aires January 1858.

In Portuguese (translated by Q. Bocayuva), Rio de Janeiro 30 October 1857.

A sequel *Pablito*, by the same authors, was produced at Madrid on 24 December 1854.

RUBINSTEIN: *Dmitry Donskoy* ili *Kulikova Bitva*

Дмитрій Донской или Куликова Битва (Dmitry Donskoy; or, The Battle of Kulikov)

30 April. St. Petersburg

Text by V. A. Sollogub and V. R. Zotov. Three acts.

Rubinstein's first opera.

F. RICCI: *Il Marito e l'Amante*

9 June. Vienna, Kä.

Text by G. Rossi. Three acts.

In Italian also, St. Petersburg 2 December 1853.

In French (as *Une Fête à Venise*, translated by C. Nuitter and A. Beaumont), Paris, Th.L. 15 February 1872.

Never given in Italy.

BALFE: *The Devil's in it*

26 July. London, Surrey

Text by A. Bunn. Prologue and 3 acts.

Subsequently given at New York 17 December 1852 as *The Basket Maker's Wife*.

Revived London, Gaiety 14 June 1871 as *Letty the Basket Maker* (text re-written by J. P. Simpson).

Balfe himself, in a list of his operas (see C. L. Kenney, *A Memoir of M. W. Balfe*, p.256) erroneously gives 1847 as the year of the first production of *The Devil's in it*, and his authority, of course, has been followed by all biographers and books of reference. Nevertheless, no production took place before 1852.

Yet another error is to be found in all biographies of Balfe and elsewhere, namely that *The Devil's in it* is an English version of Scribe's *La Part du Diable* libretto (set by Auber, see 1843). Bunn's and subsequently Simpson's, text has nothing to do with it, but is a new version of the old English *The Devil to pay* subject (see 1731).

RAIMONDI: *Putifar-Giuseppe-Giacobbe*

7 August. Rome, Arg.

Text by G. Sapio (*tre drammi lirici in uno*).

Three opera oratorios in one; they were performed first one after the other and then simultaneously (the same night, not as often stated on four subsequent nights). An account of this curious contrapuntal experiment will be found in *Neue Berliner Musikzeitung*, 1852, p.292; see also C. Gray in *The Music Review*, February 1940.

JULLIEN: *Pietro il Grande*

17 August. London, C.G.

Text by S. M. Maggioni (translated from an English libretto by M. D. Ryan). Three acts.

The only opera of Jullien who was the founder of the London Promenade Concerts and played an important part in the musical life of London in those years. "The success of *Pietro il Grande* is beyond all dispute, and we have no doubt it will prove, for many years to come, one of the most attractive operas in the splendid repertory of the Royal Italian Opera" (*Musical World*, 28 August

1852). The opera was a complete failure; parts of it were given at a concert in New York on 22 September 1853.

ADAM: *Si j'étais Roi*

4 September. Paris, Th.L.

Text by A. P. d'Ennery and J. Brésil. Three acts.

The third successful opera by Adam produced in that year.

Frequently revived in Paris; Brussels 17 January 1853, etc.

In French also, Turin April 1858; New Orleans 1858; Soerabaya 21 October 1864; Barcelona 15 October 1866; Lisbon 24 April 1878; Buenos Aires 13 September 1881; New York 29 November 1881; Mexico 10 February 1882.

In Czech, Prague 15 January 1875.

In Swedish (translated by E. A. Wallmark), Stockholm 25 January 1882.

In English (translated by W. Castle and J. Rosewald), New York 14 December 1882; (translated by V. Smith), Newcastle 20 February 1893; London, Parkhurst Th. (Holloway) 23 May 1893.

In Norwegian, Christiania 1883.

In Danish (translated by S. Bauditz), Copenhagen 17 March 1889.

In German (translated by M. Schlesinger, music adapted by O. Nowack), Breslau 22 January 1904; (translated by P. Wolff), Berlin, Morwitz Oper 27 June 1908; Riga 1909; Prague 1909; Vienna, V.O. 4 October 1911.

Revived Schwerin 29 September 1918; Berlin, D.O. 13 December 1924; Graz December 1928; Vienna, V.O. 6 November 1937; Berlin, V.O. February 1939.

In Bulgarian, Sofia 15 December 1930; in Rumanian Bucharest Spring 1936.

Still popular in France as well as in other countries; last revived in Paris, Th. Porte St. Martin 7 May 1934.

GAZTAMBIDE: *El Valle de Andorra*

5 November. Madrid, Circo

Text by L. de Olona (from J. H. Vernoy de Saint-Georges's French libretto, see 1848; during the following years, very many Spanish zarzuela librettos were taken from French sources). Three acts.

Popular in Spain; given in Summer 1855 at Mexico and Havana; in 1856 at Lima (first zarzuela there) and Buenos Aires.

AUBER: *Marco Spada*

21 December. Paris, O.C.

Text by A. E. Scribe. Three acts.

Given at the O.C. 78 times.

Revived as a ballet, Paris, O. 1 April 1857 (as *Marco Spada ou La Fille du Bandit*, with additional music from *Fra Diavolo, Zerline*, and *La Fiancée*, choreography by Mazilier. The operatic version was also given at:

BRUSSELS 23 May 1853 (in French).

HANOVER 8 December 1853 (in German).

BERLIN, KROLL'S 12 March 1854 (in German).

WARSAW 23 April 1854 (in Polish, translated by J. Checiński).

VIENNA, THALIA TH. 6 June 1857 (in German, with recitatives and additional music by H. Proch).

STOCKHOLM 18 September 1867 (in Swedish, translated by A. E. Wallmark and C. O. Wijkander).

Last given Mannheim 21 December 1881 (in German).

Auber's opera was never given in London; a drama by J. P. Simpson, founded on Scribe's libretto, with Auber's overture and incidental music by R. Stöpel, was produced at the Princess's Th. on 28 March 1853.

1853

VERDI: *Il Trovatore*

19 January. Rome, Ap.

Text by S. Cammarano (founded on a Spanish play by A. García Gutiérrez, 1836).[1] Four acts.

The libretto was completed, after Cammarano's death, by L. E. Bardare.

---

[1] See C. A. Regensburger, *Über den Trovador des Garcia Gutiérrez*, etc., 1911.

One of Verdi's most popular works, given all over the world:

CORFU Autumn 1853 (in Italian).

MALTA 1 October 1853 (in Italian).

TRIESTE 22 October 1853 (in Italian).

CONSTANTINOPLE Carnival 1854 (in Italian).

MADRID 16 February 1854 (in Italian).

ATHENS Spring 1854 (in Italian).

ODESSA 1854 (in Italian).

VIENNA 11 May 1854 (in Italian); in German, Jos. 9 October 1857, Kä. 20 December 1859.

WARSAW 1854 (in Italian) and 1859 (in Polish, translated by J. Checiński).

RIO DE JANEIRO 7 September 1854 (in Italian) and 2 January 1856 (in Portuguese, translated by Q. Bocayuva).

BUDAPEST 31 October 1854 (in Hungarian, translated by L. Nádaskay).

LISBON 8 November 1854 (in Italian).

PARIS, TH.I. 23 December 1854 (in Italian) and O. 12 January 1857 (in French).

BUENOS AIRES 4 January 1855 (in Italian).

TEMESVAR 9 January 1855 (apparently for the first time in German).

ALEXANDRIA Spring 1855 (in Italian).

BRUNSWICK 20 April 1855 (in German).

NEW YORK 2 May 1855 (in Italian); 4 October 1858 (in English, translated by T. T. Barker); 9 January 1867 (in French); and 13 September 1870 (in German).

LONDON, C.G. 10 May 1855 (in Italian; 100th performance 26 September 1902) and D.L. 24 March 1856 (for the first time in English, as The Gipsy's Vengeance, translated by C. Jefferys). Revived Sadler's Wells 25 January 1937 (new English version by E. J. Dent).

BRÜNN 25 August 1855 (in German).

DUBLIN 3 September 1855 (in Italian).

GRAZ 29 September 1855 (in German).

DARMSTADT 1 December 1855 (in German, translated by H. Proch).

ST. PETERSBURG December 1855 (in Italian) and 22 December 1859 (in Russian, translated by T. M. Rudnev).

EDINBURGH 21 January 1856 (in Italian).

MEXICO 27 January 1856 (in Italian).

MARSEILLES 22 February 1856 (for the first time in French, translated by E. Pacini).

BRUSSELS 20 May 1856 (in French).

PRAGUE 19 July 1856 (in German) and 30 June 1861 (in Czech, translated by E. Züngel).

BERLIN 24 March 1857 (in German).

NEW ORLEANS 13 April 1857 (in French).

LEMBERG 23 January 1858 (in German).

AGRAM (ZAGREB) April 1858 (in Italian) and 14 February 1871 (in Croatian, translated by A. Šenoa).

MELBOURNE and SYDNEY 1859 (in English).

ZURICH 1859 (in German).

BASLE 20 January 1860 (in German).

STOCKHOLM 31 May 1860 (in Swedish, translated by C. W. A. Strandberg).

ROTTERDAM Autumn 1860 (in German).

CHRISTIANIA 8 July 1861 (in Danish).

HELSINKI 6 July 1862 (in Swedish) and 25 November 1870 (in Finnish, translated by A. Törneroos).

VALPARAISO 1864 (in Italian).

COPENHAGEN 10 September 1865 (in Danish, translated by H. P. Holst).

BATAVIA 3 March 1866 (in French).

SMYRNA 1867 (in Italian).

CAIRO Carnival 1870 (in Italian).

TORONTO 10 June 1874 (in English).

CAPE TOWN 1875 (in Italian).

TIFLIS 1875 (in Italian).

LJUBLJANA 1894 (in Slovenian, translated by A. Štritof).

RIGA 1902 (in Lettish; earlier given there in German).

JOHANNESBURG 1905 (in English).

SOFIA 17 January 1914 (in Bulgarian; translation published already Shumen 1905).

BELGRADE 1920 (in Serbian).

JERUSALEM 21 December 1924 (in Hebrew, translated by A. Aschmann).

TALLINN 1926 (in Estonian).

KAUNAS 14 November 1929 (in Lithuanian).

SINGAPORE c.March 1932 (in Italian).

ADAM: *Le Sourd* ou
L'Auberge Pleine

2 February. Paris, O.C.

Text by A. de Leuven and F. Langlé (founded on
a comedy by P. J. B. Choudard Desforges, 1790).
Three acts.

In French also, Brussels 22 December 1853;
New York 18 February 1870; Mexico 23 February 1879.

In Swedish (translated by C. H. Rydberg),
Stockholm 29 November 1854.

In Spanish (translated by M. Pina), Madrid, Z.
24 April 1859 (music adapted by M. Vázquez).

In German (as *Kein Platz im Gasthofe*, translated by C. Juin), Vienna, Ca. 2 December 1861.

In Russian, Moscow 1866.

In Norwegian, Christiania April 1873.

Frequently revived in Paris, at the O.C. as late
as 12 February 1893 and 23 October 1934.

MASSÉ: *Les Noces de Jeannette*

4 February. Paris, O.C.

Text by J. Barbier and M. Carré. One act.

Massé's most successful work; the 1,000th performance at the O.C. was on 10 May 1895. Still
given on French stages.

Outside France:

BRUSSELS 7 September 1853 (in French).

DRESDEN 9 January 1854 (in German, translated
by I. Schuselka-Brüning).

BUENOS AIRES 28 May 1854 (in French).

NEW ORLEANS November 1854 (in French).

NEW YORK 9 April 1855 (in English, as *Georgette's
Wedding*, translated by W. Harrison) and 28 October 1861 (in French); revived Boston 24 April
1886 (new English version by F. A. Schwab).

ST. PETERSBURG c.January 1855 (in Russian).

STOCKHOLM 9 October 1855 (in Swedish, translated by J. C. Stjernström); revived 25 May
1893.

BERLIN 30 October 1857 (in German).

LONDON, C.G. 26 November 1860 (in English,
Harrison's translation) and O.C. 16 May 1872
(in French).

RIO DE JANEIRO 1861 (in Portuguese, translated by
J. M. Machado de Assis).

VIENNA, QUAI TH. 18 October 1862 (in German);
revived O. 17 January 1884.

LEMBERG 10 November 1865 (in Polish, translated
by M. Radziszewski).

BARCELONA 25 July 1866 (in French); revived
March 1924 (in Spanish).

MILAN 16 September 1868 (in French).

HELSINKI 1 February 1876 (in Finnish, translated
by A. Rahkonen).

NAPLES 20 May 1877 (in Italian, translated by E.
Golisciani; a later Italian version, by A. Zanardini, was published in 1896).

BUDAPEST 4 February 1879 (in Hungarian, translated by G. Böhm).

COPENHAGEN 9 February 1879 (in Danish, translated by A. Zinck); revived 14 January 1928.

MEXICO 23 March 1879 (in French).

BELGRADE 1883 (in Serbian, translated by J. N.
Marinovič).

A Greek translation by G. Sklabos was published in 1912.

ARRIETA: *El Dominó azul*
(The Blue Domino)

19 February. Madrid, Circo

Text by F. Camprodón. Three acts.

The first of three successful zarzuelas by Arrieta
produced in that year.

In Spanish also, Mexico 16 June 1855; Havana
1855; Buenos Aires November 1869.

In Portuguese (translated by Q. Bocayuva),
Rio de Janeiro 8 May 1858.

VERDI: *La Traviata*

6 March. Venice, F.

Text by F. M. Piave (founded on A. Dumas's *La
Dame aux Camélias*). Three acts.

The opera was a complete failure at its first performance; on 7 March Verdi wrote to Emanuele
Muzio: "*La Traviata* ieri sera fiasco. La colpa è
mia o dei cantanti? Il tempo giudicherà". It was
triumphantly received in the same town, at the
Teatro S. Benedetto, on 6 May 1854; given at

Rome, T. Apollo 30 December 1854 as *Violetta*.
Outside Italy:

MADRID 1 February 1855 (in Italian) and 1918 (in Spanish, adapted by L. Pascual Frutos).

VIENNA 4 May 1855 (in Italian) and 5 February 1879 (in German).

MALTA 1 October 1855 (in Italian).

BARCELONA, L. 25 October 1855 (in Italian).

LISBON 29 October 1855 (in Italian) and 14 May 1878 (in French).

RIO DE JANEIRO 15 December 1855 (in Italian) and 19 March 1862 (in Portuguese).

LONDON, H.M.'s 24 May 1856 (in Italian) and Surrey Th. 8 June 1857 (in English, translated by T. H. Reynoldson); the 150th performance at C.G. was on 22 May 1912.

BUENOS AIRES 10 June 1856 (in Italian).

WARSAW Summer 1856 (in Italian) and 1865 (in Polish, translated by J. Checiński).

MOSCOW 24 September 1856 (in Italian).

DUBLIN 14 October 1856 (in Italian).

MEXICO November 1856 (in Italian).

NEW YORK 3 December 1856 (in Italian) and 4 March 1886 (in English).

PARIS, TH.I. 6 December 1856 (in Italian) and Th.L. 27 October 1864 and O.C. 12 June 1886 (in French, as *Violetta*).

SANTIAGO, CHILE 1857 (in Italian).

MONTEVIDEO 1857 (in Italian).

HAMBURG 10 November 1857 (in German, translated by N. Frassini).

BUDAPEST 10 November 1857 (in Hungarian, translated by J. Pataki).

BUCHAREST 1858 (in Italian) and 1903 (in Rumanian).

GRAZ 21 July 1858.

AGRAM (ZAGREB) April 1859 (in Italian) and 11 March 1879 (in Croatian, translated by J. E. Tomić).

BASTIA, CORSICA Autumn 1859 (in Italian).

AMSTERDAM 1860 (in Italian).

MELBOURNE 1860 (in English).

BERLIN, VICT. TH. 10 November 1860 (in Italian); O. 13 December 1860.

BRUSSELS 6 March 1861 (in Italian) and 20 October 1865 (in French).

MILWAUKEE 1861 (in German).

LILLE 26 November 1861 (for the first time in French, translated by E. Duprez).

PRAGUE June 1862 (in German) and 13 June 1868 (in Czech, translated by J. Böhm and E. Züngel).

ZURICH 1863 (in German).

STOCKHOLM 21 February 1868 (in Swedish, translated by E. A. Wallmark).

CHRISTIANIA April 1868 (in Italian) and 3 October 1888 (in Norwegian).

ST. PETERSBURG 8 May 1868 (in Russian, translated by P. I. Kalashnikov).

CAIRO December 1869 (in Italian).

LEMBERG 11 May 1872 (in Polish).

TIFLIS 1875 (in Italian).

HELSINKI 21 August 1876 in Finnish, translated by A. Törneroos).

HAVANA 1877 (in Italian).

COPENHAGEN 29 November 1887 (in Danish, translated by S. Bauditz).

LJUBLJANA 1898 (in Slovenian).

SOFIA 10 February 1910 (in Bulgarian; translation published already at Shumen 1905).

RIGA 1913 (in Lettish); earlier given there in German.

TALLINN 1915 (in Estonian).

YOKOHAMA Autumn 1919 (in Italian).

KAUNAS 31 December 1920 (in Lithuanian; first opera sung in that language).

BELGRADE 1921 (in Serbian).

TEL-AVIV 28 July 1923 (in Hebrew, translated by A. Aschmann; apparently first opera sung there in Hebrew).

TRIPOLIS March 1935 (in Italian).

GRISAR: *Les Amours du Diable*

11 March. Paris, Th.L.

Text by J. H. Vernoy de Saint-Georges. Four acts.

Brussels 5 November 1853; Geneva January 1854, etc.

In French also, New Orleans 1858; New version Paris, O.C. 24 August 1863; revived Th. du Châtelet 18 November 1874 (with ballet music by Salvayre added); also given at Buenos Aires 28 July 1876; Mexico 15 April 1879; revived at Brussels 18 March 1882 and 7 September 1898; revived at Lyons 31 December 1890.

In Spanish (translated by Ramon de Navarrete y Fernández y Landa) Madrid 1 May 1871.

MIGONI: *Sampiero*

4 April. Lisbon, S.C.

(Italian) text by L. Arceri. Three acts.
Successful at Lisbon.

BAY: *Lazarilla* eller *Sangerinden med Sløret*

(Lazarilla, or The veiled Songstress)

21 May. Copenhagen

Text by A. F. von der Recke (from Scribe's and De Leuven's *La Chanteuse voilée*, see 1850). One act.

Bay's only opera; also given at Bergen on 10 May 1857.

ARRIETA: *El Grumete*

(The Cabin Boy)

17 June. Madrid, Circo

Text by A. García Gutiérrez. One act.

In Spanish also, Mexico June 1855; Lisbon 1 June 1870. (A sequel by the same authors *La Vuelta del Corsario* was given at Madrid on 18 November 1863.)

POISE: *Bonsoir, Voisin*

18 September. Paris, Th.L.

Text by L. L. Brunswick and A. de Beauplan. One act.

Poise's first (very successful) opera.

Liége 13 December 1857; Antwerp 19 December 1858; Brussels 28 September 1863.

In French also, Baden-Baden 14 August 1861. New York 26 October 1870; London, Royalty 29 January 1873.

Revived Paris, F.P. 17 January 1866; O.C. 12 June 1872; revived Nice Spring 1931.

In Swedish (translated by F. Arlberg), Stockholm 30 December 1856.

In German (as *Jungfer Nachbarin*, translated by K. Treumann, orchestrated by K. Krottenthaler), Vienna, Ca. 3 March 1859; revived Vienna, K.O. 28 January 1874; Berlin, Fr. W. 23 October 1874 (new translation by J. Hopp); lately revived in a new German version by L. Andersen, Essen 26 November 1926.

ADAM: *Le Bijou perdu*

6 October. Paris, Th.L.

Text by A. de Leuven and P. A. A. Pittaud de Forges. Three acts.

Brussels 27 January 1854; Geneva, March 1854, etc.

In French also, London, St. J.'s 7 June 1854; Turin April 1858; New Orleans January 1861.

Revived Paris, Athénée 18 October 1873; Gal. Vivienne 13 November 1896; Ren. 10 March 1900.

(Adam introduced into this opera one air from Rameau's *Castor et Pollux*, see 1737.)

LIMNANDER: *Le Maître Chanteur*

17 October. Paris, O.

Text by H. Trianon. Originally in 2 acts.

Revived at the Paris Opéra 5 March 1856 as *Maximilien*; revived in a new 3-act version, Brussels 28 April 1874 (as *Maximilien à Francfort*, text altered by H. Leroy); revived in 4 acts, again as *Maximilien*, Ghent 10 March 1876.

OFFENBACH: *Pepito*

28 October. Paris, Variétés

Text by L. Battu and J. Moinaux. One act.

First given at the Bouffes-Parisiens 10 March 1856.

In French also, London, St. J.'s 24 June 1857; Berlin, Kroll's 17 June 1858.

This was one of the first successes of Offenbach in Germany and Austria where it was given as *Das Mädchen von Elizondo* (translated by J. C. Grünbaum and T. Gassmann): Vienna, Ca. 18 December 1858 (orchestrated by C. Binder);

Graz 31 March 1859; Prague 9 April 1859; Budapest May 1859; Berlin 8 November 1859, etc.

In Croatian, Zagreb 1863.

In Polish (translated by L. Matuszyński), Warsaw 1865.

Last revived Prague, May 1934 (in German) and Jerusalem 1934 (in Hebrew, translated by M. Freidmann).

FLOTOW: *Rübezahl*

26 November. Frankfort

Text by G. H. Gans zu Putlitz. Three acts.

Previously performed (in 2 acts) at Retzien, the estate of the librettist Putlitz, on 13 August 1852 (privately). Berlin 11 January 1854, etc.

Revived Brunswick 10 March 1934 (revised by O. Felix and R. Senger).

1854

PETRELLA: *Marco Visconti*

9 February. Naples, S.C.

Text by D. Bolognese. Three acts.

Milan 26 December 1854, etc. Very successful in Italy; last revived Rome 11 March 1900.

In Italian also given at Madrid 9 January 1855; Vienna 13 May 1855; Barcelona 27 November 1855; Lisbon 6 January 1856; Mexico 17 February 1859; Buenos Aires 27 April 1859; Rio de Janeiro 1860; Malta 1860.

MEYERBEER: *L'Étoile du Nord*

16 February. Paris, O.C.

Text by A. E. Scribe. Three acts.

Meyerbeer used parts of the music (6 numbers) of his *Feldlager in Schlesien* (see 1844).

Given in Paris until 1887. The 100th performance at the O.C. was as early as 16 February 1855. Outside France:

BRUSSELS 4 December 1854 (in French).

STUTTGART 27 September 1854 (in German, translated by L. Rellstab).

AMSTERDAM 20 February 1855 (in German, translated by L. Rellstab).

NEW ORLEANS 1 April 1855 (in French).

LONDON, C.G. 19 July 1855 (in Italian, translated by S. M. Maggioni); D.L. 17 April 1890 and Kennington Th. 25 September 1901 (in English).

VIENNA 29 December 1855 (in German).

BUDAPEST 31 January 1856 (in Hungarian, translated by M. Havi).

ST. PETERSBURG 26 January 1856 (in Italian).

ALGIERS Spring 1856 (in French).

MILAN 30 April 1856 (in Italian, translated by E. Picchi).

NEW YORK 24 September 1856 (in Italian) and 3 March 1876 (in English, translated by C. L. Kellogg).

GENEVA 9 February 1858 (in French).

PRAGUE 9 October 1858 (in German).

GRAZ 20 December 1866.

MEXICO 19 November 1872 (in Italian).

MADRID 24 February 1877 (in Italian).

NAPLES, S.C. December 1879 (in Italian).

STOCKHOLM 2 December 1881 (in Swedish, translated by E. A. Wallmark).

BARCELONA 22 October 1882 (in French).

ZURICH 15 December 1884 (in German).

LIVERPOOL 1 February 1889 (in English, translated by F. W. Pratt).

BUENOS AIRES 13 July 1889 (in Italian).

MONIUSZKO: *Halka*

16 February. Wilna

Text by W. Wolski (founded on a story by K. W. Wójcicki). Originally in 2 acts.

Previously the opera had been produced privately at Wilna (Sala Miller) 20 December 1847 by amateurs. Given in its final version, enlarged to 4 acts, at Warsaw 1 January 1858.

The most popular Polish opera ever written; the 500th performance at Warsaw was on 9 December 1900, the 1000th on 8 October 1935. The 4-act version was first produced at Wilna 26 November 1860; subsequently given at Grodno and Kovno (Kaunas) 1861; Cracow 1 December 1866; Lemberg 17 March 1867, etc. Given at Poznań (Posen) 8 March 1873 in Polish and 25 November 1898 in German, translated by M.

Morris. In German also, Bydgoszcz (Bromberg) 10 April 1899.

In Esperanto (translated by A. Grabowski) performed at Cracow August 1912. Outside Poland produced at

PRAGUE 28 February 1868 (in Czech, translated by V.Š.K.; revived 19 September 1886).

MOSCOW March 1869 (in Russian, translated by N. I. Kulikov; revived 20 September 1898 and 17 September 1904).

ST. PETERSBURG 16 February 1870 (in Russian).

RIGA 1888 (in German).

VIENNA, EXHIBITION TH. 10 September 1892 (in Polish) and V.O. 29 April 1926 (in German, translated by W. Klein).

LJUBLJANA 15 November 1898 (in Slovenian, translated by P. Podravsky-Miklavec).

NEW YORK June 1903 (in Russian); revived Mecca Temple 18 February 1940 (in Polish).

MILAN 5 November 1905 (in Italian, translated by G. A. Bonoldi).

SOFIA 3 May 1921 (in Bulgarian).

MILWAUKEE 13 May 1923 (in Polish).

BERNE January 1934 (in German).

ZAGREB 20 March 1934 (in Croatian).

HAMBURG 14 May 1935 (in German, translated by F. Greissle).

BERLIN 15 November 1936 (in German, translated by F. Greissle).

TALLINN 1937 (in Estonian).

CLAPISSON: *La Promise*

16 March. Paris, Th.L.

Text by A. de Leuven and L. L. Brunswick (*historiette provençale*). Three acts.

Apart from *Fanchonnette* (see 1856), this was Clapisson's most popular work. Liége 14 December 1854; Antwerp 4 January 1855; Brussels 28 March 1855, etc.

In French also, London, St. J.'s 12 June 1854.

DORN: *Die Nibelungen*

27 March. Berlin, O.

Text by E. Gerber. Five acts.

Fairly successful in Germany. Given at Weimar 22 January 1854; Königsberg 15 May 1855; Bres-

lau 28 November 1855; Vienna 20 February 1857; Stettin 6 March 1857; Sondershausen 22 March 1861. See on the origin of this *Nibelungen* opera H. Dorn's autobiographic sketches *Aus meinem Leben*, Vol. II, p.40, etc. The text (let alone the music) has hardly anything to do with Wagner whose *Ring des Nibelungen* text had been privately printed in January 1853.

It may be mentioned here that the suggestion of turning the *Nibelungen* subject into an opera occurs—for the first time as far as I can see—as early as in 1844 in F. T. Vischer's *Kritische Gänge* (Vol. II, p.399), where also a scenario is given. The idea was taken up by Louise Otto who, one year later, published in the *Neue Zeitschrift für Musik* (Vol. XXIII) a series of articles on this subject containing also the beginning of her—the first—*Nibelungen* libretto (which was to be set by N. W. Gade in 1846). It was published as a whole at Gera in 1852.

ERNST II DUKE OF SAXE-COBURG-GOTHA: *Santa Chiara*

2 April. Gotha

Text by C. Birch-Pfeiffer. Three acts.

The most important of the Duke's operas. Successful in Germany: Coburg 15 October 1854; Hamburg 21 February 1855, etc. Also Graz 21 December 1855; Vienna, Jos. 13 March 1858; Prague April 1866. Last revived Hamburg 5 February 1891; Berlin, Kroll's 5 August 1891; Coburg 24 September 1893.

In French (translated by G. Oppelt), Paris, O. 27 September 1855 and Brussels 19 April 1858. In Italian, London, C.G. 30 June 1877.

BOVY-LYSBERG: *La Fille du Carillonneur*

17 April. Geneva

Librettist unknown. One act.

Early example of a French opera originally produced in Switzerland. The score is lost. See P. Long des Clavières in *Schweizerisches Jahrbuch für Musikwissenschaft*, Vol. III (1928).

REYER: *Maître Wolfram*

20 May. Paris, Th.L.

Text by F. J. Méry. One act.

Reyer's first opera. Revived Baden-Baden 24 July 1863; Brussels 26 September 1868; Paris, O.C. 5 December 1873 and 7 February 1902; Rouen 1 February 1905.

(SCHUBERT): *Alfonso und Estrella*

24 June. Weimar

Text by F. von Schober. Three acts.

Written in 1821–22. Produced by Liszt (who published the first account of this opera in the *Neue Zeitschrift für Musik*). Revived (in a new version by J. N. Fuchs) Carlsruhe 22 March 1881; Cassel 8 December 1881; Mannheim 29 March 1882; Vienna 15 April 1882; Berlin 11 May 1882; Cologne 4 October 1882; Munich 26 November 1882; Hanover 10 December 1882, etc.

DUPRATO: *Les Trovatelles*

28 June. Paris, O.C.

Text by M. Carré and J. Lorin. One act.

Duprato's first and most successful opera; given at the O.C. 107 times until 1861. In French also, Liége 28 February 1858.

F. A. BARBIERI: *Los Diamantes de la Corona*

15 September. Madrid, T. del Circo

Text by F. Camprodón (founded on Scribe's libretto, see 1841). Three acts.

Successful zarzuela; also given at Havana 1855; Mexico Summer 1856; Buenos Aires September 1867.

In Portuguese (translated by Q. Bocayuva), Rio de Janeiro May 1858.

BOULANGER: *Les Sabots de la Marquise*

29 September. Paris, O.C.

Text by J. Barbier and M. Carré. One act.

Brussels 13 February 1857, etc. In French also

Baden-Baden 22 July 1864. Given at the O.C. until 1866; revived Paris, Ren. 8 November 1899.

GOUNOD: *La Nonne sanglante*

18 October. Paris, O.

Text by A. E. Scribe and G. Delavigne (founded on M. G. Lewis's novel *The Monk*). Five acts.

The libretto had been refused by Halévy, Meyerbeer, Berlioz, David, Grisar, Verdi and Clapisson before Gounod accepted it. Gounod's second opera; failure, never revived.

GAZTAMBIDE: *Catalina*

23 October. Madrid, Circo

Text by L. de Olona (founded on Scribe's *L'Étoile du Nord*, see above). Three acts.

This zarzuela was also given at Mexico Summer 1856; Lisbon 25 June 1859; Havana 1868; Buenos Aires December 1869.

BALFE: *Pittore e Duca*

21 November. Trieste

Text by F. M. Piave. Prologue and 3 acts.

Revived London, H.M.'s 28 January 1882 (in English, as *Moro, the Painter of Antwerp*, translated by W. A. Barrett).

The correct date of the first production will be found in *The Musical World*, 1854, no.49, p.809. Both the composer himself (see the facsimile list in C. L. Kenney's *Memoir of M. W. Balfe*) and the English translator (see W. A. Barrett, *Balfe: His Life and Work*, p.219) give the wrong date of 1856.

LØVENSKJOLD: *Turandot*

3 December. Copenhagen

Text by H. H. Nyegaard (founded on Gozzi's comedy). Two acts.

The only (unsuccessful) opera of the Danish composer.

1855

GRISAR: *Le Chien du Jardinier*

16 January. Paris, O.C.

Text by J. P. Lockroy and E. Cormon. One act.
Liége 7 October 1855, etc.

Revived Paris, O.C. 10 December 1866; given at Brussels until about 1890.

In Czech (translated by J. J. Stankovský), Prague 7 November 1872.

In German (translated by E. Mautner), Vienna 18 February 1884.

Revived Antwerp 24 October 1909 (in Flemish).

APOLLONI: *L'Ebreo*

23 January. Venice, F.

Text by A. Boni (founded on E. Bulwer Lytton's *Leila*). Prologue and three acts.

Very successful all over Italy: Rome 20 November 1855 (as *Lida di Granata*), Milan 26 December 1855, etc.

In Italian also, Barcelona 6 October 1855; Lisbon 26 March 1856; Rio de Janeiro Spring 1856; Malta 1857; Santiago, Chile 1864; Mexico 29 January 1884; Buenos Aires 6 February 1905.

The latest revivals in Italy were at Venice 4 May 1901; Trieste 8 July 1905 (inauguration of the new Politeama Minerva); Malta 14 February 1906; and Vicenza 8 April 1922 (celebrating Apolloni's 100th birthday).

HALÉVY: *Jaguarita l'Indienne*

14 May. Paris, Th.L.

Text by J. H. Vernoy de Saint-George and A. de Leuven. Three acts.

In French also, Brussels 6 February 1856; New Orleans 18 January 1859.

In German (translated by J. C. Grünbaum), Hamburg 27 November 1858; Amsterdam January 1859.

Revived Paris, O.C. 10 May 1869; O. Populaire 24 August 1886.

For an English version, see 1863.

VERDI: *Les Vêpres Siciliennes*

13 June. Paris, O.

Text by A. E. Scribe and C. Duveyrier. Five acts.

The first of Verdi's two French operas; given in Paris 62 times until 1865.

In French also, Brussels 18 November 1856.

In Italian (as *Giovanna de Guzman*, translated by A. Fusinato), Parma 26 December 1855; Milan, Sc. 4 February 1856 (translated by E. Caimi), etc.

Given at Naples, T.N. Spring 1857 as *Giovanni di Sicilia* and S.C. Autumn in the same year as *Batilde di Turenna*.

In Italian also: Barcelona 4 October 1856; Lisbon 12 March 1857; St. Petersburg 1857; Santiago, Chile 1857; London, D.L. 27 July 1859; New York 7 November 1859; Constantinople October 1860; Buenos Aires 23 May 1862; Havana 1862; Malta 1862; Mexico November 1864; Sydney May 1870; Rio de Janeiro 1871.

In Hungarian, Budapest 1856.

In German (translated by K. F. Dräxler-Manfred), Darmstadt 14 March 1857; Vienna 19 November 1857; Prague 1859; revived Darmstadt 12 September 1887; Hamburg 14 April 1901.

In Polish, Warsaw 1872.

Swedish translation by F. Arlberg published in 1872.

Still given in Italy; revived Milan 21 February 1909, etc.; Palermo 31 March 1937; also Malta December 1938.

Revived in a new German version by G. Bundi: Stuttgart 27 November 1929; Zurich December 1930; Basle 1 September 1932; revised by J. Kapp, Berlin 5 June 1932.

OFFENBACH: *Les deux Aveugles*

5 July. Paris, B.P.

Text by J. Moinaux (*bouffonnerie*). One act.

Written for the inauguration of the *Bouffes-Parisiens* and given there on the opening night on the same bill with a prologue *Entrez, Messieurs, Mesdames* and another one-act operetta *La Nuit blanche*, also composed by Offenbach.

Les deux Aveugles was also given (in French), by the B.P. on their first tour at Berlin, Kroll's 10 March 1856; Vienna, Ca. 19 April 1856; Antwerp 21 November 1856; London, St. J.'s 20 May 1857 (opening night of the first season of the B.P. in London, lasting until 14 July).

First given in:

LONDON, HANOVER SQUARE ROOMS 27 June 1856 (in French) and Gaiety 15 April 1871 (in English, translated by H. B. Farnie) and 31 August 1874 (translated by A. Clements).

NEW YORK 26 August 1858 (in French) and 31 October 1859 (in English, as *Going blind*, translated by M. G. Walcot).

STOCKHOLM October 1858 (in French) and 31 January 1859 (in Swedish, translated by A. Säfström).

BUENOS AIRES 13 October 1861 (in French).

VIENNA, QUAI TH. May 1863 (in German, translated by K. F. Wittmann).

SAIGON Autumn 1864 (in French; first opera there).

GRAZ 8 February 1866.

DRESDEN 19 November 1866 (in German).

COPENHAGEN 20 May 1868 (in Danish, translated by J. Petersen).

VALPARAISO 1869 (in French).

Revived: Monte Carlo 7 May 1902; Paris, O.C. 14 December 1910; London Ambassador's 11 May 1914 (in French).

BRISTOW: *Rip van Winkle*

27 September. New York, Niblo's Garden

Text by J. H. Wainwright (founded on Irving's story). Three acts.

This early American opera was revived at New York 9 November 1870, at Philadelphia 21 November 1870; and once more (in concert-form), New York 11 December 1898.

DE FERRARI: *Pipelè* ossia *Il Portinaio di Parigi*

25 November. Venice, S. Ben.

Text by R. Berninzone (founded on E. Sue's *Les Mystères de Paris*). Three acts.

Ferrari's most successful opera. Given in Italy until 1906.

In Italian also, Malta 1857; Barcelona 12 July 1864; Santiago, Chile 1866; New York 10 December 1869; Philadelphia 13 January 1870; Buenos Aires 11 November 1870; Sydney 1871; Oporto May 1890.

In Portuguese (translated by J. M. Machado de Assis) Rio de Janeiro 28 October 1859.

1856

BOTTESINI: *L'Assedio di Firenze*

21 February. Paris, Th.I.

Text by C. Corghi (founded on a libretto *Maria de' Ricci* by F. Manetta). Four acts.

The first opera of the famous double-bass virtuoso. Milan 5 September 1860, etc.

AUBER: *Manon Lescaut*

23 February. Paris, O.C.

Text by A. E. Scribe (founded on Prévost's novel). Three acts.

The first operatic version of A. F. Prévost's novel (for Massenet's and Puccini's operas, see 1884 and 1893).

Revived Liége 12 February 1875; Paris, O.C. 1 February 1882.

"La perle de la partition est la Mort de Manon, page unique dans l'œuvre d'Auber par sa simple grandeur et sa réelle émotion" (Malherbe).

CLAPISSON: *La Fanchonnette*

1 March. Paris, Th.L.

Text by J. H. Vernoy de Saint-Georges and A. de Leuven. Three acts.

Clapisson's best work. Ghent 13 December 1856; Brussels 3 May 1857, etc.

Revived Paris, Athénée 19 February 1873 and Château d'Eau 23 July 1880.

In German (translated by A. Schwarz), Frankfort April 1857; Vienna, W. 13 November 1858.

PETRELLA: *Elnava* ossia
L'Assedio di Leida

4 March. Milan, Sc.

Text by D. Bolognese. Prologue and 3 acts.

In Italian also given at Lisbon 16 September 1856; Malta 1857; Barcelona 1 October 1859.

ARDITI: *La Spia*

24 March. New York, Ac. of Music

Text by F. Manetta (founded on J. F. Cooper's *The Spy*). Three acts.

Arditi, the composer of this Italo-American opera, composer also of the famous waltz *Il Bacio*, played, from 1858 onwards, an important part in the musical life of London. (See his *Reminiscences*, 1896, pp.32–34.)

J. Mattfeld in *A Hundred Years of Grand Opera in New York*, pp.75 and 84, erroneously gives 1854 as the year of the production of *La Spia*).

ADAM: *Les Pantins de Violette*

29 April. Paris, B.P.

Text by L. Battu. One act.

Adam's last opera; he died 4 days after the first night.

In French also given at London, St. J.'s 22 May 1857; Berlin, Kroll's 18 June 1858; Brussels 8 December 1859; New York 15 December 1863; Naples 3 August 1868.

In German, Vienna, Quai Th. 7 September 1861.

In Croatian, Zagreb 1865.

In Czech (translated by J. Böhm), Prague 6 December 1867.

In Slovenian, Ljubljana 1 May 1870 (first opera sung in that language).

DARGOMUIZHSKY: *Rusalka*

Русалка

16 May. St. Petersburg

Text by the composer (from Pushkin's dramatic poem). Four acts.

Very successful in Russia; Moscow 1858, etc.

Given at St. Petersburg on 16 February 1899 in Italian (translated by V. Narducci). Last revived

Leningrad, Conservatory February 1936; Moscow 1937.

Outside Russia:

COPENHAGEN June 1888 (in Russian).

HELSINKI 27 January 1889 (in Russian) and 17 November 1937 (in Finnish).

PRAGUE 23 November 1889 (in Czech, translated by A. E. Mužík).

BERLIN, KROLL'S 6 June 1908 (in Russian).

MONTE CARLO 25 March 1909 (in Russian).

PARIS, TH S.B. 2 May 1911 (in Russian) and 3 May 1911 (!) (in French).

SAN FRANCISCO 10 January 1922 (in Russian).

NEW YORK 8 May 1922 (in Russian).

RIGA 23 October 1923 (in Lettish).

JERUSALEM 3 May 1926 (in Hebrew, translated by A. Aschmann).

LONDON, LY. 18 May 1931 (in Russian).

OUDRID: *El Postillón de la Rioja*

7 June. Madrid, Circo

Text by L. de Olona. Two acts.

Successful in Spain and South America. Revived Mexico July 1868; Buenos Aires March 1870.

PONCHIELLI: *I Promessi Sposi*

30 August. Cremona

Text founded on Manzoni's novel. Librettist unknown; in 1872 the text was revised by E. Praga. Four acts.

Ponchielli's first opera. Revived (in a new version) Milan, T.d.V. 5 December 1872 and Sc. 11 October 1874; Cremona 5 April 1891.

In Italian also, Barcelona 7 August 1875; Bucharest 1877; Malta 1877; Lisbon 8 June 1886.

In English (translated by H. Hersee), Edinburgh 23 March 1881; revived Glasgow Summer 1931.

SÖDERMAN: *Hin Ondes första
Lärospån*
(The Devil's First Lesson)

14 September. Stockholm

Text by F. Arlberg (founded on a French libretto by Scribe, *Le Diable à l'École*, set to music by langer in 1842). One act.

Popular Swedish operetta, revived at Stockholm in 1871, 1882, 12 May 1910 and 1931.

MAILLART: *Les Dragons de Villars*

19 September. Paris, Th.L.

Text by J. P. Lockroy and E. Cormon. Three acts.

Maillart's most popular work; very successful in Paris (where it was transferred to the O.C. on 6 June 1868) and in other countries:

GHENT 3 April 1857 (in French); Brussels 7 May 1857, etc.

GENEVA 14 April 1857 (in French).

HAGUE January 1858 (in French).

ALGIERS June 1859 (in French).

NEW ORLEANS 1859 (in French).

BERLIN, FR.W. 29 November 1860 (in German, as *Das Glöckchen des Eremiten*, translated by G. Ernst).

VIENNA 14 September 1861 (in German, as *Das Glöckchen des Eremiten*, translated by G. Ernst).

RIGA December 1861 (in German, as *Das Glöckchen des Eremiten*, translated by G. Ernst).

STOCKHOLM 4 May 1863 (in Swedish, translated by E. G. Kolthoff).

MADRID [29 September] 1864 (in Spanish, translated by M. Pastorfido) and Circo 28 August 1871 (translated by R. Puente y Brañas).

PRAGUE August 1866 (in German) and 4 February 1887 (in Czech, translated by J. J. Stankovský).

ZURICH November 1867 (in German).

BASLE 30 December 1867 (in German).

NEW YORK 22 April 1868 (in German); 10 May 1869 (in French); and 6 June 1878 (in English).

BARCELONA 20 June 1868 (in French).

COPENHAGEN 19 October 1870 (in Danish, translated by H. P. Holst).

ODESSA October 1871 (in French).

MILAN, S. RADEGONDA 1 March 1875 (in Italian); Naples 4 December 1875, etc.

LONDON, GAIETY 24 June 1875 (in French) and Folly 14 April 1879 (in English, as *The Dragoons*, translated by H. Hersee).

MEXICO 3 February 1878 (in French) and 24 June 1882 (in Spanish).

LISBON 9 May 1878 (in French).

LAIBACH 1880 (in German).

BUDAPEST 14 January 1881 (in Hungarian, translated by J. Rákosi and L. Evva).

ZAGREB 19 January 1884 (in Croatian, translated by J. E. Tomić).

LIVERPOOL 18 January 1886 (as *Fadette*, adapted by W. Grist).

ST. PETERSBURG 3 October 1887 (in German).

CHRISTIANIA 9 February 1893 (in Norwegian).

HELSINKI Summer 1899 (in German).

WARSAW 1902 (in Polish).

MOSCOW 1908 (in Russian).

Some of the more recent revivals were at:

BASLE 22 March 1925 (in German).

BERLIN, D.O. 13 January 1927 (in German).

BRUSSELS 27 October 1931 (in French).

PARIS, PORTE ST. MARTIN 3 June 1935 (in French). Still given on French and German stages.

PEDROTTI: *Tutti in Maschera*

4 November. Verona

Text by M. M. Marcello (founded on Goldoni's comedy, *L'Impresario delle Smirne*). Three acts.

Pedrotti's chief work. Frequently revived in Italy; some of the latest productions were at Trieste 5 December 1888; Novara November 1899; Verona May 1924; and Pesaro February 1930.

In Italian also, Malta 1862; Barcelona 22 April 1863; Vienna 18 May 1865.

Given at Budapest May 1859 (in German) and in the same year in Hungarian, translated by F. Ney.

In French (translated by C. Nuitter and A. Beaumont), Paris, Athénée 23 September 1869.

In Croatian (translated by J. E. Tomić), Zagreb 1 April 1880.

BAZIN: *Maître Pathelin*

12 December. Paris, O.C.

Text by A. de Leuven and J. A. F. Langlé. One act.

One of Bazin's most popular works; given at the O.C. until 1869 and revived at the O. Populaire 30 April 1887; revived at Marseilles 8 February 1919; at Verviers *c.* October 1929.

In French also, New York 4 December 1869.

In German, Berlin 21 January 1858.

In Danish (translated by O. Zinck), Copenhagen 10 March 1875 (revived 13 April 1912).

For a Swedish version, see 1858.

DOPPLER: *Wanda*

16 December. Budapest

Text by T. Bakody. Three acts.

The most successful of Doppler's Hungarian operas.

In German (translated by O. Prechtler), Vienna 27 September 1862; Stuttgart 6 March 1865; Dresden 4 June 1866; Riga 9 November 1867; Darmstadt 19 May 1872; Posnań (Posen) 16 November 1877.

In Polish, Lemberg December 1874.

MASSÉ: *La Reine Topaze*

27 December. Paris, Th.L.

Text by J. P. Lockroy and L. Battu. Three acts.

Given in Paris 170 times. Geneva 12 November 1857; Antwerp 13 April 1859; Brussels 17 October 1864, etc.

In German (translated by H. Proch), Vienna 19 November 1858.

In English (translated by J. Oxenford, music adapted by G. Linley), London, H.M.'s 26 December 1860; (translated by F. A. Schwab), Boston 8 January 1889.

1857

A. THOMAS: *Psyché*

26 January. Paris, O.C.

Text by J. Barbier and M. Carré. Three acts.

Revived Paris, O.C. 21 May 1878 (new version).

VERSTOVSKY: *Gromoboy*

Громобой

(Thunder)

5 February. Moscow

Text by D. T. Lensky (founded on a poem by V. A. Zhukovsky). Four acts.

Apart from *Askoldova Mogila* (see 1835), Verstovsky's most popular work; given in Russia until about 1900.

VERDI: *Simon Boccanegra*

12 March. Venice, F.

Text by F. M. Piave (founded on a Spanish drama by A. García Gutiérrez). Prologue and 3 acts.

Outside Italy also Malta 1860; Madrid 7 January 1861; Lisbon 29 October 1861; Buenos Aires 29 June 1862. Revived in a new version (libretto altered by A. Boito) Milan 24 March 1881, etc. This version was given outside Italy at Vienna 18 November 1882 (in German, translated by K. F. Niese); Paris 27 November 1883 and Buenos Aires 13 August 1889 (in Italian).

Again revived: Vienna 12 January 1930 (new German translation by F. Werfel); this version was also given at Berlin 8 February 1930; Prague 1931; Basle 3 September 1931, and on many other German stages.

Zagreb 14 May 1931 (in Croatian).

New York, M. 28 January 1932 (in Italian; for the first time in America); revived 13 January 1939. Revived at Buenos Aires 6 June 1935.

Budapest June 1937 (in Hungarian).

GAZTAMBIDE: *Los Magyares*

12 April. Madrid, Z.

Text by L. de Olona. Four acts.

The first great success at the new Teatro de la Zarzuela, Madrid, inaugurated 10 October 1856. *Los Magyares* was also given at Lisbon 8 July 1859; Mexico 8 October 1868; and Buenos Aires 3 June 1870.

A. PERI: *Vittore Pisani*

21 April. Reggio

Text by F. M. Piave. Three acts.

Successful in Italy. Milan, Sc. 4 October 1860, etc.

In Italian also, Barcelona 2 March 1859; Constantinople October 1860; Malta 1861; Buenos Aires Summer 1865.

GASTINEL: *L'Opéra aux Fenêtres*

5 May. Paris, B.P.

Text by Lud. Halévy (founded on a play by A. von Kotzebue). One act.

The most successful of Gastinel's operettas. Revived Nice April 1898.

London, St. J.'s 5 June 1857 (in French) and Gaiety 19 April 1869 (in English, as *An Eligible Villa*).

In German (translated by J. C. Grünbaum), Vienna, W. 4 February 1859; Breslau April 1859; Berlin, Fr.W. 19 January 1860, etc.

LASSEN: *Landgraf Ludwigs Brautfahrt*

10 May. Weimar

Text by E. Pasqué (translated from a French libretto, *Le Roi Edgar*). Five acts.

The first of the three (unsuccessful) operas of Lassen who, in 1861, succeeded Liszt as conductor at the Weimar Hoftheater.

VIVIER: *Spadillo le Tavernier*

22 May. Brussels, M.

Text by C. Michaels. One act.

The only opera of Vivier (who is better-known as the author of the famous *Traité complet d'Harmonie*).

GAUTIER: *Le Mariage extravagant*

20 June. Paris, O.C.

Text by E. Cormon (founded on a comédie-vaudeville by M. A. M. Desaugiers and J. J. C. Mourier, 1812). One act.

Gautier's best work.

In French also, Liége 1 January 1858; Brussels 1 February 1858. Revived Paris, O.C. 27 October 1871.

In Swedish (translated by L. E. Granberg), Stockholm 26 February 1859.

OFFENBACH: *Le Mariage aux Lanternes*

10 October. Paris, B.P.

Text by "Jules Dubois" (pseudonym of M. Carré and L. Battu). One act.

(An earlier version, called *Le Trésor à Mathurin*, had been given in concert form at the Salle Hertz, Paris in May 1853).

The most popular of Offenbach's numerous 1-act operettas produced before *Orphée aux Enfers* (1858).

Outside Paris, given at:

BERLIN, KROLL's 17 June 1858 (in French, by the Bouffes-Parisiens) and O. 13 December 1858 (in German).

VIENNA, CA. 16 October 1858 (in German, translated by K. Treumann, orchestrated by C. Binder).

LEMBERG 3 January 1859 and Warsaw 20 March 1859 (in Polish, translated by J. B. Wagner).

PRAGUE 8 January 1859 (in German) and 20 May 1865 (in Czech, translated by J. Böhm).

GRAZ 15 January 1859.

COPENHAGEN 5 March 1859 (in Danish, translated by A. F. von der Recke).

BUDAPEST May 1859 (in German) and 21 November 1860 (in Hungarian, translated by M. Feleki).

NEW YORK 18 March 1860 (in German); 6 February 1864 (in French); and 21 August 1868 (in English).

LONDON, LY. 11 May 1860 (in French) and New Royalty 18 January 1862 (in English, translator not mentioned; this seems to have been the first production of an Offenbach operetta in English; not recorded by R. Northcott. There were three later English versions, produced in 1869, 1871, and 1915).

BRUSSELS 9 June 1860 (in French).

STOCKHOLM 29 October 1860 (in Swedish, translated by E. A. Wallmark, orchestrated by J. A. Söderman).

BASLE 10 January 1862 (in German).

ZAGREB 8 November 1863 (in Croatian, translated by J. Freudenreich).

MOSCOW 1871 (in Russian).

MILAN 19 March 1875 (in Italian).

BELGRADE 1884 (in Serbian, translated by J. N. Marinović).

LJUBLJANA 1892 (in Slovenian).

TSINGTOU April 1908 (in German).

TEL AVIV 12 January 1938 (in Hebrew, translated by E. Troche).

Revived Paris, O.C. 4 December 1919; Stockholm 15 October 1927; Berlin, O. 31 December 1930.

BALFE: *The Rose of Castille*

29 October. London, Ly.

Text by A. G. Harris and E. Falconer (founded on a French libretto by d'Ennery and Clairville, *Le Muletier de Tolède*, composed by Adam in 1854). Three acts.

Successful in London; the 100th performance at the Lyceum was on 9 October 1858.

Revived London 30 September 1871 at the inauguration of the "Royal National Opera," St. James's Theatre; also Grand Th. Islington April 1907; Old Vic. October 1909 and April 1914. Given at New York on 27 July 1864.

In German (translated by H. Proch), Vienna 5 February 1859.

Frequently revived on English provincial stages. Given at Dublin as late as 26 June 1920, at Birmingham 28 September 1922.

TAUBERT: *Macbeth*

16 November. Berlin, O.

Text by F. Eggers (after Shakespeare). Five acts.

Given at Berlin until 1872; revived Magdeburg 10 April 1877.

FLOTOW: *Pianella*

27 December. Schwerin

Text by E. Pohl (a German version of the *Serva Padrona* subject, see 1733). One act.

In French (translated by O. Féré and Saint-Yves), Paris, Th. Déjazet 11 May 1860; New York 31 March 1864. Revived (in German) Bremen 26 March 1881.

1858

BRUCH: *Scherz, List und Rache*

14 January. Cologne

Text by L. Bischoff (reduced from Goethe's 4-act Singspiel, first set by P. C. Kayser in 1785–86). One act.

Bruch's first opera (it had been privately given at F. Hiller's, Cologne 14 December 1856).

GOUNOD: *Le Médecin malgré lui*

15 January. Paris, Th.L.

Text: Molière's comedy, with slight alterations by the composer, J. Barbier and M. Carré. Three acts.

Gounod's first opéra-comique and his first greater success. Revived Paris, O.C. 22 May 1872, 15 May 1886, 15 November 1902, and 24 March 1938.

Outside France, given at:

BRUSSELS 25 February 1859 (in French).

WARSAW October 1862 (in Polish).

HAMBURG 22 November 1862 (in German, translated by T. Gassmann).

STOCKHOLM 14 December 1863 (in Swedish, translated by E. A. Wallmark).

LONDON, C.G. 27 February 1865 (in English, as *The Mock Doctor*, translated by C. L. Kenney); revived Grand, Islington 24 November 1890 (translation revised by R. Temple); Avenue 26 February 1891 (by the R.A.M.), etc.

COPENHAGEN 5 April 1876 (in Danish, translated by A. Zinck); revived (in a new German version by E. N. von Reznicek), Berlin, K.O. 3 September 1910 and again, Kroll's 4 February 1928.

PRAGUE 22 June 1911 (in Czech, translated by V. J. Novotný) and 27 August 1931 (in German).

NEW YORK 10 May 1917 (in English, translated by A. Mattulath).

MONTE CARLO 5 January 1924 (produced by Diaghilev, recitatives by E. Satie); in French also, Cairo Spring 1938.

A new English adaptation, *The Frantic Physician; or, Three Drams of Matrimonium*, by A. Dean, music arranged by M. Bartholomew, was published at Newark, N.Y. in 1935 and produced at Juilliard School of Music New York 1936.

PETRELLA: *Jone*

26 January. Milan, Sc.

Text by G. Peruzzini (founded on E. Bulwer Lytton's *The Last Days of Pompeii*). Four acts.

Very successful in Italy, given there until about 1910.

Outside Italy (in Italian):

MALTA 1861.

HAVANA 1862.

NEW YORK 6 April 1863 (revived 18 October 1886).

BARCELONA 3 October 1863.

BUENOS AIRES 21 July 1864.

RIO DE JANEIRO Autumn 1865.

MEXICO 28 October 1865.

NEW ORLEANS 8 February 1867.

ATHENS 1868.

LISBON 15 December 1869.

SYDNEY Autumn 1870.

BUCHAREST 1871.

VIENNA, W. 28 July 1871.

LONDON, BIJOU TH. 28 June 1876 (by amateurs).

CAIRO January 1877.

ODESSA Carnival 1881.

SANTIAGO, CHILE 1883.

G. SCHMIDT: *Weibertreue* oder *Kaiser Konrad vor Weinsberg*

16 February. Weimar

Text by the composer. Three acts.

Berlin 30 March 1860, etc. Revived Zurich 22 November 1883.

OFFENBACH: *Mesdames de la Halle*

3 March. Paris, B.P.

Text by A. Lapointe. One act.

In French also given at Berlin, Kroll's 7 July 1858; Brussels 13 June 1860, etc.

In German (translated by A. Berla), Vienna, Quai Th. 22 February 1862; Berlin, Kroll's 6 August 1867.

In Polish, Lemberg 19 April 1868.

In Czech (translated by J. Hanuš), Prague 8 June 1871.

Revived (in French), Monte Carlo 18 December 1908; Paris, O.C. 4 May 1940.

HALÉVY: *La Magicienne*

17 March. Paris, O.

Text by J. H. Vernoy de Saint-Georges. Five acts.

The last opera of Halévy which was produced in his lifetime; performed 42 times within one year, but never revived.

GEVAERT: *Quentin Durward*

25 March. Paris, O.C.

Text by E. Cormon and M. Carré (founded on Scott's novel). Three acts.

Brussels 5 October 1858; Ghent 17 December 1858; Antwerp 25 December 1859, etc. Geneva 14 February 1890; Hague December 1891. Successful in Belgium; last revived at Brussels 13 October 1930.

In Swedish, Stockholm 7 December 1865.

In German (translated by O. Neitzel), Weimar 20 May 1888.

PACINI: *Il Saltimbanco*

24 May. Rome, Arg.

Text by G. Checchetelli (originally called *Pagliaccio*). Three acts.

In Italian also given at Madrid 21 March 1859 and Barcelona 24 March 1859; Malta 1860; Buenos Aires 7 November 1866.

MONIUSZKO: *Flis*
(The Raftsman)

24 September. Warsaw

Text by S. K. Boguslawski. One act.

Lemberg 14 March 1860, etc.

Frequently revived in Poland; Lemberg 9 May 1919; Poznań Summer 1931; Warsaw March 1932.

OFFENBACH: *Orphée aux Enfers*

21 October. Paris, B.P.

Text by H. Crémieux and Lud. Halévy (from a German scenario by Karl Cramer? See A. Henseler, *Offenbach*, p.275). Two acts.

Of Offenbach's more than 100 works for the stage, *Orphée* may be regarded as the most popular one; given at the B.P. 227 nights running; revived in a new 4-act version (as *opéra-féerique*), Paris, Gaîté 7 February 1874; the 400th Paris performance was on 18 December 1862, the 800th on 8 September 1874; the so far latest revival at the Th. Mogador in December 1931.

Outside Paris given at:

BRESLAU 17 November 1859 (for the first time in German, translated by L. Kalisch).

PRAGUE 31 December 1859 (in German) and 15 September 1869 (in Czech, translated by J. Böhm and E. Züngel).

VIENNA, CA. 17 March 1860 (new German version by J. Nestroy).

BERLIN, FR.W. 23 June 1860 (in German: 300th performance 26 December 1870).

BRUSSELS 28 June 1860 (in French).

GRAZ 4 September 1860.

STOCKHOLM 13 September 1860 (in Swedish, translated by E. A. Wallmark and C. A. K. Almlöf); there are several other Swedish versions.

COPENHAGEN 11 October 1860 (in Danish, translated by H. P. Holst).

NEW YORK March 1861 (in German); 17 January 1867 (in French); and 22 April 1874 (in English).

WARSAW 1861 (in Polish, translated by L. Matuszyński).

ST. PETERSBURG December 1861 (in German) and 1869 (in Russian).

BUDAPEST 28 December 1861 (in German) and 12 May 1882 (in Hungarian).

ZURICH May 1862 (in German).

AMSTERDAM 1862 (in German) and January 1865 (in Dutch).

MADRID, Z. 27 March 1864 (in Spanish, translated by M. Pina).

CHRISTIANIA 1864 (in Norwegian).

RIO DE JANEIRO 3 February 1865 (in French).

MOSCOW 12 December 1865 (in Russian, translated by V. A. Kruilov).

LONDON, HM. 26 December 1865 (in English, adapted by J. R. Planché) and St. J.'s 12 July 1869 (in French); Northcott records four later English versions.

BUENOS AIRES 30 November 1866 (in French) and October 1906 (in German).

MILAN May 1867 (in French).

NAPLES 23 September 1868 (in French) and 29 May 1869 (in Italian).

MEXICO 22 June 1869 (in Spanish).

VALPARAISO 1869 (in French).

SYDNEY 1872 (in English).

SOFIA Summer 1893 (in German; Bulgarian translation by T.N. Shishkov published Varna 1892).

ZAGREB 19 April 1897 (in Croatian, translated by P. Brani).

BELGRADE 1902 (in Serbian, translated by J. R. Odavić).

RIGA 5 March 1932 (in Lettish; earlier given there in German).

HELSINKI 15 March 1932 (in Finnish).

(FORONI): *Advokaten Patelin*

4 December. Stockholm

Text by E. G. Kolthoff (translated from De Leuven and Langlé's French libretto, see 1856), lyrics by D. Hwasser and J. Jolin. One act.

Produced at Stockholm three months after Foroni's death; very successful there; revived in 1875, 1879, 1894, 1908 and 1926.

ERNST II DUKE OF SAXE-COBURG-GOTHA: *Diana von Solange*

5 December. Coburg

Text by O. Prechtler. Five acts.

Gotha 16 January 1859; Dresden 25 January 1859; Vienna 19 March 1859; Berlin, Kroll's 15 July 1882.

In German also, Rotterdam April 1874; Prague March 1875; Brünn 20 November 1875; Riga 1876; Reval November 1876; New York 9 January 1891.

Last revived: Bremen 10 March 1892.

Polish translation by J. Jasiński published 1860 French translation by H. Lefebvre published 1863.

CORNELIUS: *Der Barbier von Bagdad*

15 December. Weimar

Text by the composer. Two acts.

Cornelius's first opera. At the first night, the theatre became the battlefield between Liszt's and Dingelstedt's adherents and as a result of the events connected with the production, Liszt resigned his post as court conductor at Weimar. The opera was never given again in Cornelius's lifetime.

When revived 19 years later at Hanover 24 May 1877 it was again a failure.

The score was then revised and re-orchestrated by F. Mottl and the new version was produced at Carlsruhe 1 February 1884. Only from that date onwards (and not even in its original form) *Der Barbier von Bagdad* was recognised, still very slowly and reluctantly, as one of the masterpieces of German comic opera.

The Mottl version, after Carlsruhe, was given at Munich 15 October 1885 (under H. Levi; with new alterations); further productions (in German):

HAMBURG 23 November 1886.
COBURG 28 October 1887.
LEIPZIG 11 November 1887.
WEIMAR 15 January 1888.
COLOGNE 3 January 1889.
BONN 16 April 1889.
VIENNA 4 October 1890.
DRESDEN 22 October 1890.
STUTTGART 8 May 1892.
DARMSTADT 16 May 1895.
DÜSSELDORF 23 October 1896.
HALLE 28 October 1899.
BASLE 23 February 1900.
FRANKFORT 18 March 1900.
ZURICH 2 November 1900.
ROSTOCK 4 November 1900.
BROMBERG 23 April 1901.
GRAZ 2 November 1901.

In German also, Prague 30 September 1888; New York 3 January 1890; Chicago 5 May 1890; Rotterdam 31 October 1900; Brünn 24 April 1901; Metz 28 November 1901; London, C.G. 11 May 1906.

First given at Berlin, Lessing Th. 28 June 1891 (by the Prague company); O. 6 November 1900 (revived 11 December 1907; 27 February 1922; 24 April 1929).

The original version in 1904 found a new advocate in M. Hasse[1] and was revived at Weimar on 6 June of that year.

In English (translated by M. E. Browne), London, Savoy 9 December 1891 (by the R.C.M.); revived C.G. 11 May 1906 (in German).

In Hungarian (translated by K. Abrányi), Budapest 30 December 1891.

In Flemish, Antwerp 8 October 1904.

In Danish (translated by J. Lehmann), Copenhagen 21 November 1904.

·In Russian, Moscow, Th. Zimin January 1905.

In Czech (translated by J. Vymětal), Prague 21 December 1906.

In Slovenian (translated by F. Bučar), Ljubljana 29 May 1925.

An open-air performance took place at Arnhem (Holland) 13 September 1925.

BALFE: *Satanella; or, The Power of Love*

20 December. London, C.G.

Text by A. G. Harris and E. Falconer (from Lesage's *Le Diable boiteux*). Four acts.

Sydney 6 July 1862; New York 23 February 1863; Philadelphia 28 October 1871. Revived London, Gaiety 14 August 1875 and C.G. 26 January 1884.

GAZTAMBIDE: *El Juramento* (The Oath)

20 December. Madrid, Z.

Text by L. de Olona (partly founded on a French libretto *La Rose de Péronne*). Three acts.

Successful in Spain.

Also given at Havana Autumn 1860; Buenos Aires December 1867; Mexico Summer 1868. Last revived at Madrid in October 1933.

---

[1] See his pamphlet *Peter Cornelius und sein Barbier von Bagdad, die Kritik zweier Partituren*, etc., 1904.

1859

VERDI: *Un Ballo in Maschera*

17 February. Rome, Ap.

Text by A. Somma (founded on Scribe's *Gustave III*, see 1833). Three acts.

Originally the opera was called *La Vendetta in Domino* and had been written for Naples; but it was not allowed to be acted for political reasons; the libretto had to be changed and a governor of Boston to be substituted for Gustav III, King of Sweden. In the original form the opera was revived at Copenhagen on 25 September 1935. Outside Italy given at:

LISBON 15 April 1860 (in Italian).

PARIS, TH.I. 13 January 1861 (in Italian with the scene transposed to Florence) and Th.L. 17 November 1869 (in French, translated by E. Duprez).

BARCELONA 31 January 1861 (in Italian).

NEW YORK 11 February 1861 (in Italian); 5 February 1871 (in English) and 11 December 1889 (in German).

LONDON, LY. 15 June 1861 (in Italian).

DUBLIN 25 September 1861 (in Italian).

BERLIN 23 November 1861 (in Italian) and 12 February 1873 (in German).

ST. PETERSBURG December 1861 (in Italian).

STUTTGART 6 March 1862 (for the first time in German, translated by J. C. Grünbaum).

BUENOS AIRES 4 October 1862 (in Italian).

LIMA, PERU 1863 (in Italian).

BUDAPEST December 1863 (in German) and 16 January 1864 (in Hungarian, translated by G. Böhm).

VIENNA 1 April 1864 (in Italian) and 19 November 1866 (in German).

BRUSSELS 9 April 1864 (in Italian) and 5 March 1872 (in French).

MEXICO August 1864 (in Italian).

VALPARAISO 1864 (in Italian).

WARSAW 22 October 1865 (in Italian).

PRAGUE August 1866 (in German) and 30 June 1869 (in Czech, translated by E. Züngel).

NEW ORLEANS 1 February 1867 (in Italian).

COPENHAGEN 18 May 1867 (in Italian); revived 25 September 1935 in the original *Gustav III* version (in Danish, translated by P. Biørn).

CHRISTIANIA April 1868 (in Italian).

SYDNEY 2 June 1868 (in Italian).

RIGA 1869 (in German) and 14 May 1927 (in Lettish).

CAIRO Carnival 1870 (in Italian).

RIO DE JANEIRO 1871 (in Italian).

HAVANA 1872 (in Italian).

WILNA 1873 (in Italian).

GENEVA 29 April 1873 (in French).

GRAZ 27 February 1874.

MALTA 1876 (in Italian).

ZAGREB 2 October 1877 (in Croatian, translated by I. Trnski).

LAIBACH (LJUBLJANA) 1880 (in German) and 1927 (in Slovenian).

HELSINKI 1879 (in Swedish, translated by R. Hertzberg); 25 October 1896 (in Italian) and 26 April 1922 (in Finnish).

BUCHAREST April 1923 (in Rumanian; translation published already Jassy 1864).

SOFIA 22 October 1926 (in Bulgarian; translation published already Varna 1905).

KAUNAS 30 October 1926 (in Lithuanian).

TALLINN 1928 (in Estonian).

Given at Stockholm for the first time on 12 February 1927 (the reasons for this very late production being obvious; a Swedish translation of the libretto, however, by E. A. Wallmark had been published at Stockholm in 1868 and another for Helsinki in 1879 (see above).

F. DAVID: *Herculanum*

4 March. Paris, O.

Text by F. J. Méry and T. Hadot. Four acts.

The work was originally called *Le dernier Amour* and had been written for the Théâtre-Lyrique. Given in Paris 74 times until 1868; in French also Brussels 29 November 1860.

In Italian (translated by M. M. Marcello), St. Petersburg 27 January 1865; Venice 17 February 1870.

(In 1867 *Herculanum* was awarded the prize of 20,000 francs, founded by Napoléon III for "l'œuvre ou la découverte la plus propre à honorer le pays".)

GOUNOD: *Faust*

19 March. Paris, Th.L.

Text by J. Barbier and M. Carré (founded on Goethe's tragedy). Five acts.

Gounod's chief work and one of the most successful French operas ever written. First produced at the Th.L. in the form of an "opéra-comique" with spoken dialogue; given there 57 times until 31 December 1859. The recitatives were added for a production at Strasbourg in April 1860; subsequently given at Rouen 16 April 1860 and all over France.

In Paris *Faust* was resumed at the Th.L. 18 December 1862 (150 more performances there and at its temporary branch, the Th. de la Renaissance, until 4 May 1868) and finally transferred to the Opéra (with the ballet music added) 3 March 1869.

> 500th Paris performance   4 November 1887.
> 1,000th   ,,   ,,   14 December 1894.
> 1,500th   ,,   ,,   1 January 1912.
> 2,000th   ,,   ,,   31 December 1934.

Outside France given at:

LIÉGE 5 March 1860 (in French).

GHENT 24 December 1860 (in French).

DARMSTADT 10 February 1861 (for the first time in German, translated by K. Gollmick; first given as *Faust*; Dresden 31 August 1861 as *Margarete*; Stuttgart 27 September 1861 as *Gretchen*). German parody *Margarethe* published Breslau 1862.

ANTWERP 15 February 1861 (in French) and 12 December 1918 (in Flemish).

BRUSSELS 25 February 1861 (1,000th performance 26 November 1924).

PRAGUE 24 October 1861 (in German) and 6 June 1867 (in Czech, translated by J. Böhm).

AMSTERDAM 14 January 1862 (in French) and 16 October 1886 (in Dutch).

GENEVA 23 January 1862 (in French).

VIENNA 8 February 1862 (in German); 4 March 1876 (in Italian); and 11 May 1928 (in French).

RIGA May 1862 (in German) and 1902 (in Lettish).

STOCKHOLM 5 June 1862 (in Swedish, translated by E. A. Wallmark).

MILAN, SC. 11 November 1862 (for the first time in Italian, translated by A. de Lauzières).

BERLIN 5 January 1863 (in German).

GRAZ 8 January 1863.

LONDON, H.M.'S 11 June 1863 (in Italian); 23 January 1864 (in English, translated by H. F. Chorley; see C. E. Pearce, *Sims Reeves*, p.241); 6 November 1886 (in French). First given at C.G. 2 July 1863; 200th performance there 6 June 1893, 300th 10 May 1906. *Faust* was included in every C.G. season from 1863 to 1911.

ZURICH 1863 (in German).

BUDAPEST 2 September 1863 (in Hungarian, translated by F. Ormai).

DUBLIN 1 October 1863 (in Italian).

PHILADELPHIA 18 November 1863 (in German).

NEW YORK 25 November 1863 (in Italian); 18 December 1863 (in German); 18 May 1868 (in English); 27 April 1881 (in French); the Metropolitan Opera House was inaugurated with a production of *Faust* (in Italian) 22 October 1883.

ST. PETERSBURG January 1864 (in Italian) and 27 September 1869 (in Russian); revived Leningrad 27 October 1922.

BARCELONA 17 February 1864 (in Italian).

SYDNEY Spring 1864 (in English).

MALTA 1864 (in Italian).

MEXICO 12 October 1864 (in Italian).

COPENHAGEN 12 December 1864 (in Danish, translated by A. Hertz).

WARSAW 1865 (in Polish, translated by L. Matuszyński).

LISBON 1 December 1865 (in Italian); 16 May 1878 (in French); and 8 January 1882 (in Portuguese).

BATAVIA 20 July 1866 and Soerabaya 14 December 1866 (in French).

HAVANA 1866 (in Italian).

BUENOS AIRES 22 August 1866 (in Italian).

NEW ORLEANS 20 November 1866 (in French).

MOSCOW 22 November 1866 (in Russian, translated by P. I. Kalashnikov).

NAPLES, S.C. Carnival 1867 (in Italian).

CONSTANTINOPLE 12 February 1868 (in Italian).

CHRISTIANIA May 1869 (in Italian) and December 1874 (in Norwegian).

CAIRO January 1870 (in Italian).

SMYRNA 1870 (in Italian).

RIO DE JANEIRO Carnival 1871 (in Italian).

LEMBERG 13 April 1872 (in Polish).

ZAGREB 19 March 1873 (in Croatian, translated by A. Šenoa).

HELSINKI 10 February 1876 (in Finnish, translated by A. Törneroos).

CARACAS, VENEZUELA Carnival 1881 (in Italian).

MANILA 20 October 1882 (in Italian).

LJUBLJANA 1896 (in Slovenian).

BUCHAREST 1903 (in Rumanian).

JOHANNESBURG 1905 (in English).

SOFIA 10 March 1910 (in Bulgarian; translation published already Shumen 1905).

CASABLANCA, MOROCCO April 1913 (in French).

REVAL (TALLINN) 1913 (in Estonian).

SHANGHAI 1918 (in Russian).

YOKOHAMA Autumn 1919 (in Italian).

KAUNAS 16 March 1922 (in Lithuanian).

BELGRADE 1922 (in Serbian).

JERUSALEM 19 February 1924 (in Hebrew, translated by A. Aschmann).

ATHENS Summer 1933 (in Greek).

MEYERBEER: *Le Pardon de Ploërmel*

4 April. Paris, O.C.

Text by J. Barbier and M. Carré. Three acts.

Very successful in Paris; revived at the O.C. 27 August 1874, 23 May 1881, 6 June 1896 and 16 March 1912. Last revived at Brussels on 11 January 1939.

Outside France (mostly given as *Dinorah*):

LONDON, C.G. 26 July 1859 (in Italian, translated by A. de Lauzières) and 3 October 1859 (in English, translated by H. F. Chorley).

COBURG 6 December 1859 (in German, translated by J. C. Grünbaum).

HAGUE 8 December 1859 (in French).

BRUSSELS 23 December 1859 (in French).

GENEVA 5 January 1860 (in French).

ST. PETERSBURG 4 February 1860 (in Italian).

PRAGUE 25 February 1860 (in German) and 12 October 1862 (in Czech, translated by J. Pražský).

BUDAPEST 17 November 1860 (in Hungarian, translated by L. Csepregi; revived December 1917).

LINZ 25 November 1860 (in German).

NEW ORLEANS 4 March 1861 (in French).

LEMBERG 12 November 1861 (in German) and 22 March 1873 (in Polish).

GRAZ 25 October 1862.

NEW YORK 24 November 1862 (in Italian; revived 22 January 1925).

BASLE 12 December 1862 (in German).

ALGIERS March 1864 (in French).

VIENNA 11 March 1865 (in German).

GOTHENBURG 1866 (in German).

FLORENCE 29 March 1867 (for the first time in Italy; revived Naples, T. Fondo July 1873 and Milan 26 March 1904).

BARCELONA 11 February 1868 (in Italian).

DUBLIN 14 September 1869 (in Italian).

CONSTANTINOPLE 22 January 1870 (in Italian).

WARSAW Spring 1870 (in Italian) and 3 December 1887 (in Polish).

STOCKHOLM 23 May 1870 (in Swedish, translated by E. A. Wallmark).

HAVANA 1872 (in Italian).

MEXICO 28 August 1872 (in Italian).

BUENOS AIRES 7 September 1872 (in Italian).

RIGA 10 December 1873 (in German).

MALTA 1874 (in Italian).

LISBON 28 April 1874 (in Italian) and 22 May 1878 (in French).

CAIRO March 1875 (in Italian).

HELSINKI 27 February 1878 (in Finnish, translated by A. Törneroos).

RIO DE JANEIRO 24 October 1878 (in Italian).

BERLIN, O. 31 October 1881 (in German) and Kroll's 13 October 1885 (in Italian).

SANTIAGO, CHILE 1883 (in Italian).

ROTTERDAM 11 February 1885 (in German).

COPENHAGEN 14 December 1892 (in Danish).

FLOTOW: *Veuve Grapin*

21 September. Paris, B.P.

Text by P. A. A. Pittaud de Forges. One-act operetta.

In French also, Brussels 1 January 1860.

In German (translated by the composer under the pseudonym of F. Marckwordt), Berlin, Fr. W. 31 January 1861; Vienna, Quai Th. 1 June 1861; Budapest 7 June 1885.

In Russian, St. Petersburg, February 1868.

In Finnish, Helsinki, 27 March 1879.

Revived Berlin, Th.d.W. 6 November 1898 and at the "Theater Die Rampe" as late as 18 November 1922.

SOBOLEWSKI: *Mohega*

11 October. Milwaukee

(German) text by the composer. Three acts.

One of the earliest German operas which had their original productions in the U.S.A. "*Mohega* was probably the first operatic treatment of an episode from the Revolutionary War, the libretto celebrating the love and tragic end of Count Pulaski and the Indian maid Mohega at the siege of Savannah in 1779" (*Dict. Americ. Biogr.*).

(Sobolewski was a native of Königsberg who settled in America in 1859. Liszt had produced his opera, *Komala* at Weimar on 30 October 1858.)

OFFENBACH: *Geneviève de Brabant*

19 November. Paris, B.P.

Text by A. Jaime and E. Tréfeu. The original 2-act version was enlarged to 3 acts at the Menus-Plaisirs 26 December 1867 (text revised by H. Crémieux) and to 5 acts at the Gaîté 25 February 1875. Last revived in Paris 21 February 1908 (Th. des Variétés).

Outside Paris given at:

VIENNA, CA. 3 April 1861 (in German, translated by E. Dohm, as *Die schöne Magellone*).

BERLIN, FR.W. 1 July 1861 (in German, translated by E. Dohm, as *Die schöne Magellone*).

PRAGUE February 1864 (in German) and 13 May 1871 (in Czech, translated by J. Hrubý).

NEW YORK 22 October 1868 (in French) and 2 November 1874 (in English).

BRUSSELS 4 March 1869 (in French; the second version).

MADRID 4 September 1869 (in Spanish, translated by F. Moreno Godino and F. Bardán).

LONDON, PHILHARMONIC 11 November 1871 (in English, translated by H. B. Farnie).

SYDNEY 1873 (in English, translated by G. Walch).

MEXICO 31 January 1874 (in French).

NAPLES 5 July 1879 (in Italian, translated by A. Scalvini).

KASHPEROV: *Maria Tudor*

7 December. Milan, T. Carcano

Text by A. Ghislanzoni. Four acts.

Since 1788 (see note on Sacchini's *Armida*, 1772), this was probably the first opera written by a Russian composer for Italy.

In Italian also, Nice March 1860.

MELLON: *Victorine*

19 December. London, C.G.

Text by E. Falconer. Three acts.

Successful in London. Dublin 2 May 1861, etc.

(Rectify A. Nicoll, *A History of Early 19th Century Drama*, Vol. II, p.300, where the name of the composer is mis-spelt and the year 1839 is given instead of 1859.)

1860

CASPERS: *Ma Tante Dort*

21 January. Paris, Th.L.

Text by H. Crémieux (and, according to Goizet, E. About). One act.

Caspers's most successful work; transferred to the O.C. on 17 September 1860. Brussels 12 January 1861, etc.

In German (translated by M. Oscar), Vienna, Quai Th. 1 November 1860; Berlin, Fr.W. 26 August 1861.

Revived (in German), Leipzig 17 February 1903; Prague 27 January 1904; Berlin, Th.d.W. 13 February 1904; Vienna, O. 7 March 1914.

MONIUSZKO: *Hrabina*

(The Countess)

7 February. Warsaw

Text by W. Wolski. Three acts.

Successful in Poland; given at Lemberg 22 March 1872 (in German) and 22 October 1874 (in Polish).

Frequently revived in Poland; Warsaw October 1929; Lemberg 1930.

GOUNOD: *Philémon et Baucis*

18 February. Paris, Th.L.

Text by J. Barbier and M. Carré. Three acts.

Brussels 21 February 1862; Antwerp 17 March 1863, etc. More successful in a reduced 2-act version (Paris, O.C. 16 May 1876) which was also given at:

BASLE 23 May 1878 (in French).

VIENNA 4 October 1878 (in German, translated by J. Hopp).

STOCKHOLM 26 March 1879 (in Swedish, translated by F. T. Hedberg).

PRAGUE 1 January 1880 (in German) and 28 November 1892 (in Czech, translated by V. J. Novotný).

BUDAPEST September 1880 (in Hungarian, translated by K. Abrányi).

MADRID 24 March 1883 (in Spanish).

ST. PETERSBURG 28 December 1883 (in Italian, translated by A. Zanardini).

DRESDEN 3 September 1884 (in German).

LIVERPOOL March 1888 (for the first time in English, by amateurs); Birmingham 19 November 1892 (in concert form).

LONDON, C.G. 24 October 1891 (in French) and D.L. 26 April 1894 (in English, translated by J. Bennett).

BERLIN, KROLL'S 28 October 1892 (in French).

NEW YORK 16 November 1893 (in English) and 29 November 1893 (in French).

Revivals:

LINZ 10 February 1900 (in German).

CARLSRUHE 7 January 1904 (in German).

BERLIN, KURF. O. 11 December 1911 (in German).

MONTE CARLO 10 January 1924 (in French).

AIX-LES-BAINS Summer 1930 (in French).

PARIS, TR.L. 13 November 1931 (in French).

WALLACE: *Lurline*

23 February. London, C.G.

Text by E. Fitzball. Three acts.

Apart from *Maritana*, Wallace's most popular work; it anticipates Wagner in having a scene at the bottom of the Rhine.

Given at Dublin 30 April 1861; Sydney September 1862; Cambridge, Mass. 1 June 1863 (in concert form); New York 13 May 1869 (in English and the very next night in Italian, translated by G. Vacotti).

In German (translated by J. Mielck), Königsberg February 1863.

Very successful on English stages; revived Liverpool 22 January 1890 and London, D.L. 12 April 1890; given in the provinces as late as 1917.

PONIATOWSKY: *Pierre de Médicis*

9 Mars. Paris, O.

Text by J. H. Vernoy de Saint-Georges and E. Pacini. Four acts.

Poniatowsky's first French opera and his most successful one.

Given in Paris 47 times.

In Italian (translated by A. Berrettoni), Madrid 5 April 1863; Milan, Sc. 26 December 1869.

(The composer was the nephew of the Napoleonic marshal and a friend of Napoléon III.)

A. PERI: *Giuditta*

26 March. Milan, Sc.

Text by M. M. Marcello. Three acts.

Peri's chief work.

Outside Italy also given at Madrid 20 November 1861; Barcelona 5 November 1862; and New York 11 November 1863 (in Italian).

OFFENBACH: *Daphnis et Chloé*

27 March. Paris, B.P.

Text by Clairville and J. Cordier. One act.

In German (translated by G. Ernst), Berlin, Fr. W. 23 December 1860; (translated by J. Nestroy),

Vienna, Ca. 2 March 1861, Graz 30 November 1861, etc. Budapest March 1862 (in German) and June 1862 (in Hungarian).

In Polish, Lemberg 24 November 1865.

In Czech (translated by Ć. Pilulka), Prague 11 May 1867; revived 14 March 1901 (new Czech version by V. J. Novotný).

In Croatian, Zagreb 1868.

In French, Brussels 3 June 1873.

In Swedish (translated by C. G. W. Michal), Stockholm 30 October 1886.

Revived Monte Carlo 7 February 1907; in German, Wiesbaden March 1911 and Prague December 1934.

ZAJC: *Amelia* ossia *Il Bandito*

14 April. Fiume

Text: an altered version of J. Crescini's *I Briganti* (see 1836). Four acts.

Revived Zagreb 28 December 1872 (in Croatian, translated by V. Gjorgjević).

Zajc became conductor of the Zagreb theatre in 1870 and was one of the first composers to write operas in the Croat language.

(DONIZETTI): *Rita* ou *Le Mari Battu*

7 May. Paris, O.C.

Text by G. Vaëz. One act.

The opera had been written in Summer 1840.

In French also, Brussels 27 December 1860; revived Paris, O. Populaire 22 November 1879.

In Italian, Naples 18 May 1876 (revived Verona 21 March 1924).

In Hungarian (translated by E. Kuliffay), Budapest 1879.

A Spanish version seems to be *El Propósito de Mujer* (text adapted by E. Álvarez), produced Madrid 1864.

GOUNOD: *La Colombe*

3 August. Baden-Baden

Text by J. Barbier and M. Carré (after Lafontaine). Two acts.

In French also, Paris, O.C. 7 June 1866; Brussels 5 December 1867.

In Swedish, Stockholm 11 February 1868.

In English (as *The Pet Dove*, translated by H. B. Farnie), London, Crystal Palace 20 September 1870.

In Danish (translated by A. Schwartz), Copenhagen 27 April 1873.

In Czech translated by E. Züngel), Prague 22 September 1873.

In Italian, Bologna 23 February 1912.

Revived Monte Carlo 1 January 1924 (produced by Diaghilev; recitatives by F. Poulenc).

GAUTIER: *Le Docteur Mirabolan*

28 August. Paris, O.C.

Text by E. Cormon and H. Trianon. One act.

Brussels 12 October 1864; revived Paris, O.C. 11 July 1868; Antwerp 5 February 1880.

In Russian, Moscow 1869.

MACFARREN: *Robin Hood*

11 October. London, H.M.'s

Text by J. Oxenford. Three acts.

Successful in London; revived Crystal Palace 11 June 1872; National Standard Th. 29 April 1889; Princess's 7 August 1889. Revived at Birmingham 18 February 1889.

MAILLART: *Les Pêcheurs de Catane*

19 December. Paris, Th.L.

Text by E. Cormon and M. Carré. Three acts.

In German (translated by J. C. Grünbaum), Hamburg 14 March 1862; Berlin, Fr.W. 4 February 1863.

DYUTSH: *Kroatka*

Кроатка

21 December. St. Petersburg

Text by N. I. Kulikov. Four acts.

In Polish, Warsaw January 1861; revived St. Petersburg 12 November 1892.

The alternative title in the vocal score is *Sopyernitsi* (*The Rivals*).

OFFENBACH: *Barkouf*

24 December. Paris, O.C.

Text by A. E. Scribe and H. Boisseaux. Three acts.

The first work of Offenbach which was given at the Opéra-Comique; failure, 7 performances only.

Offenbach used parts of the music for his operetta *Boule-de-Neige*, text by C. Nuitter and E. Tréfeu; Paris B.P. 14 December 1871. Also performed in German (translated by J. Hopp), Vienna, Ca. 3 February 1872, Berlin, Vict. Th. 23 March 1872, Graz 30 December 1872, and in Czech (translated by J. J. Kolár), Prague 19 June 1872.

1861

MONIUSZKO: *Verbum Nobile*

1 January. Warsaw

Text by J. Checiński. One act.

Successful in Poland; Lemberg 24 August 1872, etc.

Revived Lemberg 1926; Poznań Summer 1931.

OFFENBACH: *La Chanson de Fortunio*

5 January. Paris, B.P.

Text by H. Crémieux and Lud. Halévy (a sequel to A. de Musset's *Le Chandelier* for which Offenbach had written one song in 1850). One act.

Given also at:

BRUSSELS 7 March 1861 (in French).

VIENNA, QUAI TH. 25 April 1861 (in German, translated by G. Ernst).

BERLIN, FR.W. 21 July 1861 (in German, translated by G. Ernst).

BUDAPEST January 1862 (in Hungarian).

PRAGUE June 1862 (in German) and 6 October 1865 (in Czech, translated by J. Böhm).

GRAZ 3 September 1862.

STOCKHOLM 17 October 1862 (in Swedish, translated by E. A. Wallmark; revived 29 April 1922).

ST. PETERSBURG January 1864 (in German) and 4 March 1905 (in French).

WARSAW 1865 and Lemberg 23 November 1868 (in Polish, translated by J. B. Wagner).

ZAGREB 14 December 1865 (in Croatian, translated by S. Udbinski).

NEW YORK 14 September 1867 (in German); 21 December 1868 (in French); 23 April 1883 (in English).

BASLE 11 November 1867 (in German).

MILAN 16 September 1868 (in French).

LONDON, GAIETY 1 July 1871 (in French) and R.A.M. 11 December 1907 (in English, adapted by L. H. F. du Terreaux).

MOSCOW and ST. PETERSBURG 1874 (in Russian).

NAPLES 24 February 1875 (in Italian).

Revived Prague 18 December 1901 (new Czech version by V. J. Novotný). In French: Monte Carlo 24 November 1903; Paris, Tr. L. 28 January 1910.

AUBER: *La Circassienne*

2 February. Paris, O.C.

Text by A. E. Scribe. Three acts.

Given 49 times in 1861, but never revived. English vocal score (translated by T. Oliphant) published 1861. For a German adaptation of the libretto, see Suppé's *Fatinitza*, 1876.

RUBINSTEIN: *Die Kinder der Heide*

23 February. Vienna, Kä.

Text by S. H. Mosenthal (founded in K. Beck's *Janko*). Four acts.

Rubinstein's first greater success as an opera composer.

In German also given at Weimar 8 April 1862, etc.

In Russian, Moscow 22 February 1867.

Revived Danzig 4 October 1885; Cassel 28 October 1886; Prague 25 January 1891; Bremen 2 December 1892; Berlin, Kroll's 2 June 1893; Dresden 12 December 1893.

WALLACE: *The Amber Witch*

28 February. London, H.M.'s

Text by H. F. Chorley (founded on W. Meinhold's novel *Die Bernsteinhexe*, translated as *The Amber Witch* by Lady Duff Gordon). Four acts.

In Wallace's opinion his best work but not very successful.

Revived Southport 12 January 1899 and London (Clapham) 22 March 1899.

ERKEL: *Bánk-Bán*

9 March. Budapest

Text by B. Egressy (founded on a play by J. Katona). Three acts.

After *Hunyady László* (see 1844) Erkel's second great national opera.

Given at Budapest *c.*300 times until 5 March 1934.

OFFENBACH: *Le Pont des Soupirs*

23 March. Paris, B.P.

Text by H. Crémieux and Lud. Halévy. Two acts.
Enlarged to 4 acts: Variétés 8 May 1868.

In French also, Vienna June 1861; Brussels 20 August 1861; Buenos Aires 1870; New York 27 November 1871.

In German (translated by J. Lasker), Vienna, Quai Th. 12 May 1862 (with additional airs by Suppé); Berlin, Fr.W. 17 May 1862, Graz 20 September 1865, etc. In German also, Budapest June 1865.

London, St. J.'s 18 November 1872 (in English, translated by H. S. Leigh); another English version, by H. B. Farnie (*Venice*), Alhambra 5 May 1879. In English also, New York 20 April 1885.

Milan 1877 (in Italian).

Revived Basle 26 March 1933 (new German version by O. Maag).

REYER: *La Statue*

11 April. Paris, Th.L.

Text by J. Barbier and M. Carré. Three acts.

In German (translated by K. F. Dräxler-Manfred and E. Pasqué, with recitatives instead of spoken dialogue), Weimar 8 April 1864; Darmstadt 13 May 1864, etc.

In French, the new version was first given at Brussels 20 March 1865.

Revived Paris, O.C. 20 April 1878 and Antwerp 21 April 1881; in German, Weimar 30 December 1888. Again revived (in 5 acts), Paris, O. 27 February 1903 and, lately, Antwerp March 1931.

PEDROTTI: *Guerra in quattro*

25 May. Milan, Can.

Text by M. M. Marcello. Three acts.

Remodelled: Trieste 22 February 1862; Nice Carnival 1864.

DEFFÈS: *Le Café du Roi*

17 August. Ems

Text by H. Meilhac. One act.

Deffès's most successful operetta.

Paris, Th.L. 16 November 1861; revived O.C. 2 September 1868 and 29 September 1889; in French also Liége 1 March 1869.

(SCHUBERT): *Die Verschworenen* oder *Der häusliche Krieg*

29 August. Frankfort

Text by I. F. Castelli (the plot taken from Aristophanes's *Lysistrata*). One act.

Composed in 1823. Of Schubert's numerous operas which were produced after his death (see note on *Die Zwillingsbrüder*, 1820) this was the most successful one. It had been given in concert form at Vienna on 1 March 1861 already (by the "Singverein", under J. Herbeck).

After Frankfort produced at Vienna 19 October 1861 and on many other German stages. In German also, Budapest April 1862; Hoboken 21 March 1863; London, Crystal Palace 2 March 1872 (in concert form); New York 16 June 1877; Prague 14 March 1880.

In French (as *La Croisade des Dames*, translated by V. Wilder), Paris, F.P. 3 February 1868.

In Hungarian (translated by E. Kuliffay), Budapest 15 April 1884.

In Russian, St. Petersburg, Conservatoire December 1898.

Revivals in the 20th century include: Weimar 18 October 1903; Amsterdam 24 January 1911 (in German); Königsberg 20 October 1919 (revised by R. Hirschfeld); Stuttgart 2 July 1922 (new

German version by R. Lauckner, music arranged by F. Busch and D. F. Tovey); this version was also given at Basle 15 April 1923; Budapest November 1928 (new Hungarian version by Z. Harsányi); Vienna 22 November 1928; Berlin, Hochschule 27 November 1928; Monte Carlo Spring 1929 (the Paris 1868 version, as *Guerre et Amour*).

GOMES: *Noite do Castello*
(Night in the Castle)

4 September. Rio de Janeiro

Text by A. J. Fernandes dos Reis (founded on a poem by A. F. de Castilho). Three acts.

The first opera of the Brazilian composer. Performed at the Theatro Lyrico Fluminense which was the first theatre at Rio de Janeiro where operas were sung in the Portuguese language.

SIBONI: *Carl den Andens Flugt*

9 October. Copenhagen

Text by T. Overskou. Three acts.

The last opera of the Danish-Italian composer who was the son of the famous tenorist Giuseppe Siboni (The hero of this opera is King Charles II of England.)

GLOVER: *Ruy Blas*

24 October. London, C.G.

Text by the composer (founded on V. Hugo's drama). Three acts.

Glover's most successful opera. (Date of the first performance verified from the contemporary papers; in the dictionaries there also occur the dates 21 October, 28 October and 31 October.)

VILBOA: *Natasha ili Volzhskie Razboyniki*
Наташа или Волжскіе Разбойники
(Natasha, or The Volga Bandits)

31 October. Moscow

Text by N. I. Kulikov. Two acts.

St. Petersburg 30 January 1863. The only performed opera of the French-Russian composer. Vocal score published in 1861.

BALFE: *The Puritan's Daughter*

30 November. London, C.G.

Text by J. V. Bridgeman. Three acts.

New York 11 September 1869. Successful on English stages; last revived Birmingham 25 October 1915; Dublin 9 June 1920; Leeds 22 October 1920.

MOSONYI: *Szép Ilonka*
(Fair Ilonka)

16 December. Budapest

Text by M. Fekete (founded on Vörösmarty's poem of the same title). Five (produced in 4) acts.

Successful Hungarian comic opera. Mosonyi's first opera and the only one which was produced during his lifetime (see 1934).

ALARY: *La Voix humaine*

30 December. Paris, O.

Text by A. J. Mélesville. Two acts.

This (unsuccessful) opera was commissioned by the Paris Opéra in order to make use of the expensive settings and costumes of Wagner's *Tannhäuser* (hissed off the boards on 13 March of the same year). The action of *La Voix humaine* takes place at the Wartburg. The opera had 13 performances (10 more than *Tannhäuser*).

1862

OFFENBACH: *Monsieur et Madame Denis*

11 January. Paris, B.P.

Text by M. Laurencin and M. Delaporte. One act.

Particularly successful on German stages (translated by G. Ernst): Vienna, Quai Th. 31 March 1862 (Kä. 10 January 1870; last new work produced there before the opening of the Hof-oper); Hamburg 22 May 1862; Berlin, Fr.W. 22 June 1862, Graz 10 December 1862, etc.; Prague December 1862 (in German) and 15 January 1868 (in Czech, translated by J. Bučinský); Budapest

31 July 1862 (in Hungarian, translated by K. Szerdahelyi) and February 1863 (in German). Warsaw 1865 (in Polish, translated by L. Matuszyński). Zagreb 1865 (in Croatian); New York 16 July 1873 (in German).

Revived in German: Basle 23 December 1929; Munich 1932; Prague, May 1934.

BENEDICT: *The Lily of Killarney*

8 February. London, C.G.

Text by J. Oxenford and D. Boucicault (founded on the latter's play *Colleen Bawn*). Three acts.

Benedict's most successful work; given in all English-speaking countries, viz.: Dublin 21 April 1862; Edinburgh 19 April 1863; Melbourne 29 July 1864; New York 1 January 1868; Calcutta 27 November 1875, etc. Produced in a revised version, London, Ly. 12 September 1876.

Successful also in a German version by F. von Dingelstedt, as *Die Rose von Erin*: Brunswick 28 January 1863; Hamburg 22 February 1863; Berlin 9 February 1864, etc.

Still given on English provincial stages; last revived in London, C.G. 11 September 1902; Old Vic. 15 March 1928 and 14 March 1931.

F. HILLER: *Die Katakomben*

15 February. Wiesbaden

Text by M. Hartmann. Three acts.

Successful in Germany; in German also Rotterdam 19 December 1863.

GOUNOD: *La Reine de Saba*

28 February. Paris, O.

Text by J. Barbier and M. Carré. Four acts.

In Paris given 15 times only.

In French also, Brussels 5 December 1862; New Orleans 12 January 1889.

Revived Marseilles 21 November 1900; Paris 27 November 1900 (at the inauguration of the Opéra-Populaire).

In German (translated by E. Pasqué), Darmstadt 25 January 1863.

In English (adapted by H. B. Farnie, as *Irene*), London, Crystal Palace 12 August 1865 (in concert form); on the stage, Manchester 10 March 1880; revived by the Guildhall School of Music, London 11 November 1909.

EICHBERG: *The Doctor of Alcantara*

7 April. Boston

Text by B. E. Woolf. Two acts.

The most popular of Eichberg's four American "comic operettas".

New York 28 May 1866, etc. Libretto published Philadelphia 1870 and Boston 1879.

Outside the U.S.A. also given at Liverpool 21 October 1873 [1] (as *The Village Doctor*); London, Connaught Th. (late Amphitheatre, Holborn) 1 November 1879; revived London, O.C. 6 February 1897 (by amateurs).

BERWALD: *Estrella de Soria*

9 April. Stockholm

Text by E. A. Wallmark (translated from a German libretto by O. Prechtler). Four acts.

Successful at Stockholm; parts of the work were revived there on 19 September 1898 (at the inauguration of the new opera-house); the whole work on 15 November 1899.

F. DAVID: *Lalla-Roukh*

12 May. Paris, O.C.

Text by H. Lucas and M. Carré (from Moore's poem). Two acts.

The most important of David's operas. Given in Paris until 1897.

In French also, Liége 20 October 1862; Brussels 27 October 1862; Antwerp 29 October 1862; Geneva 19 January 1864, etc.

In German (translated by E. Pasqué), Coburg 25 December 1862; Mayence 26 December 1862; Munich 16 March 1863; Vienna 22 April 1863; etc. Berlin, Meysel's Th. 7 August 1865.

In Hungarian (translated by L. Csepregi), Budapest 31 January 1863.

---

[1] First novelty produced by Carl Rosa's English Opera Company (which had started with a performance of Wallace's *Maritana*, at Manchester 1 September 1873).

In Polish (translated by L. Matuszyński), Warsaw 8 March 1866.

In Swedish (translated by E. A. Wallmark), Stockholm 12 January 1870.

In Italian (translated by M. M. Marcello), Milan, T. Rè 7 September 1870.

In Russian, St. Petersburg 5 February 1884 and Moscow 10 February 1896.

OFFENBACH: *Bavard et Bavarde*

11 June. Ems

Text by C. Nuitter (founded on Cervantes's intermezzo *Los Habladores*). Two acts.

Given in an enlarged version, as *Les Bavards*, Paris, B.P. 20 February 1863; Brussels 28 December 1867, etc.

In French also, New York 9 December 1868; London, Gaiety 1 July 1871; Rio de Janeiro Summer 1871.

In German (as *Die Schwätzerin von Saragossa*, translated by K. Treumann), Vienna, Quai Th. November 1862; Frankfort 30 September 1863; Berlin, Fr.W. 9 November 1863; Graz 14 October 1865, etc.; New York 28 October 1867.

In Russian, Moscow 23 January 1867.

In Croatian (translated by D. Demeter), Zagreb 30 November 1867.

In Spanish (translated by S. M. Granés), Madrid 15 April 1872.

In Swedish (translated by E. A. Wallmark), Stockholm 21 June 1873.

In Italian, Rome 7 March 1875.

In Norwegian, Christiania 6 October 1910.

Revived Milan, T.L. 21 December 1915 (new Italian version by C. Clausetti); Berlin, D.O. 4 June 1919 (in German); Paris, O.C. 3 May 1924 (in French).

ERKEL: *Sarolta*

26 June. Budapest

Text by J. Czanyuga. Three acts.

Erkel's first comic opera. Revived Budapest 24 January 1901.

BERLIOZ: *Béatrice et Bénédict*

9 August. Baden-Baden

Text by the composer (founded on Shakespeare's *Much Ado about Nothing*). Two acts.

The Baden-Baden production was in French; given at the Paris O.C. as late as 4 June 1890.

In German (translated by R. Pohl), Weimar 8 April 1863; Carlsruhe 6 April 1888 (with recitatives by F. Mottl); Vienna 20 March 1890; Leipzig 27 March 1913 (re-modelled by J. Stransky and W. Kleefeld); Plauen (Saxony) 25 September 1929.

Given for the first time in English (translated by G. F. MacCrone) at Glasgow 24 March 1936.

REYER: *Érostrate*

22 August. Baden-Baden

Text by F. J. Méry and E. Pacini. Two acts.

Produced at Baden-Baden by artists of the Paris Opéra. Paris, O. 16 October 1871 (performed there only twice). Revived Marseilles 17 October 1899.

SUPPÉ: *Zehn Mädchen und kein Mann*

25 October. Vienna, Quai Th.

Text by K. Treumann (from a French libretto by A. Jaime and A. Choler, *Six Demoiselles à marier*, composed by Delibes in 1856). One act.

One of Suppé's first great successes. (Oddly enough, Suppé, a native of Spalato and descendent from a Belgian family, was proclaimed the German Offenbach—the real Offenbach being a native of Cologne!) Berlin, Fr.W. 3 May 1863 and all over Germany; Basle 24 November 1865.

In German also, New York 24 April 1867. Given at the Vienna O. 15 April 1873 in an "enlarged" version as *25 Mädchen und kein Mann*.

In Polish (translated by W. L. Anczyc), Warsaw 1865 and Lemberg 11 April 1866.

In Croatian (translated by J. Freudenreich), Zagreb 17 November 1866.

In Czech (translated by J. Böhm), Prague 27 June 1867.

In Italian (as *Le Amazzoni*, translated by A. Scalvini), Milan, S. Rad. Carnival 1872; Modena, T. Aliprandi April 1873 (as *Le Donne guerriere*, additional music by P. Piacenza).

In English (as *Ten of 'em*, translated by A. Matthison), London, D.L. 2 December 1874.

In Yiddish, New York 14 January 1887.

In Hungarian (translated by E. Latabár), Budapest 18 Jannary 1897,

In Finnish, Helsinki 20 March 1901.

Still occasionally revived on minor German stages.

VERDI: *La Forza del Destino*

10 November. St. Petersburg

Text by F. M. Piave (founded on a Spanish drama by Angelo Pérez di Saavedra, Duke of Rivas, *Don Alvaro, o La Fuerza de Sino*, 1835). Four acts.

First given in Italy: Rome, T. Apollo 7 February 1863 (as *Don Alvaro*).

In Italian also, Madrid 21 February 1863; New York 24 February 1865; Vienna 2 May 1865; Buenos Aires 9 July 1866; London, H.M.'s 22 June 1867.

New version (libretto altered by A. Ghislanzoni): Milan 27 February 1869, etc. Also, Rio de Janeiro 1871; Lisbon 15 March 1872; Cairo March 1873; Malta 1873; Paris 31 October 1876; Berlin, Kroll's 12 October 1878; Corfu Autumn 1881; Santiago, Chile 1883; St. Petersburg 7 February 1901.

In Hungarian, Budapest 9 November 1875.

In Croatian (translated by J. E. Tomić), Zagreb 11 February 1882.

In French (translated by C. Nuitter and C. Du Locle); Antwerp 14 March 1883; Geneva 24 March 1884.

In English (translated by P. E. Pinkerton), Manchester 25 November 1909; London, Kennington Th. 2 September 1910.

In German (translated by J. C. Grünbaum), Hamburg 20 September 1913 (revised by G. Göhler; this production was the beginning of the Verdi "Renaissance" movement in Germany). Grünbaum's translation had been published in 1863.

Revived in a new German version by F. Werfel: Altenburg 8 November 1925; Dresden 20 March 1926; Vienna 27 November 1926; Berlin 30 April 1927; Basle 2 September 1927; Prague 1927.

Translated from Werfel's version:

STOCKHOLM 21 January 1928 (in Swedish).

BUDAPEST 23 March 1929 (in Hungarian, translated by V. Lányi).

LEMBERG 1929 (in Polish).

LJUBLJANA 2 November 1930 (in Slovenian, translated by N. Štritov).

RIGA 13 December 1931 (in Lettish).

SOFIA 21 February 1934 (in Bulgarian).

LENINGRAD January 1935 (in Russian, translated by S. Levik; concert performance).

PRAGUE 13 April 1937 (in Czech).

Danish translation by T. Thygesen published 1937.

Revived in French: Brussels 15 October 1931.

Revived in London: Old Vic. 10 April 1930 (in English, translated by J. B. Gordon) and C.G. 1 June 1931 (in Italian).

Revived in Italian: Buenos Aires July 1933; Tripolis November 1934.

Still very popular in Italy and in many other countries.

1863

DOBRZYŃSKI: *Monbar czyli Flibusterowie*

(Monbar; or, The Filibusters)

January ? Warsaw

Text by S. Pruszakowa and L. Paprocki (based on a story by C. J. van der Velde). Three acts.

A concert performance had been given at Warsaw 1839.

Parts of this Polish opera were also given in concert form at Berlin 1845 and 20 June 1846; Dresden 20 January 1846; German translation by Elkan.

The overture was heard at a Leipzig concert on 6 November 1845.

G. SCHMIDT: *La Réole*

24 January. Breslau

Text by C. Birch-Pfeiffer (originally written for Flotow). Three acts.

Successful in Germany: Dresden 16 September 1863; Berlin 24 October 1863, etc. Last revived Darmstadt 17 September 1874.

BALFE: *The Armourer of Nantes*

12 February. London, C.G.

Text by J. V. Bridgeman (founded on Victor Hugo's *Marie Tudor*). The acts.

Successful in London.

RUBINSTEIN: *Feramors*

24 February. Dresden

Text by J. Rodenberg (founded on Moore's poem). Two acts.

(Originally the opera was called *Lalla Rookh*, but the title was changed because of David's opera on the same subject, see 1862.)

New enlarged 3-act version: Vienna 24 April 1872; Berlin 4 March 1879. Revived Riga *c.* January 1909 (in German).

In Russian (translated by E. A. Tr.), St. Petersburg 6 May 1884 and revived 27 September 1898, etc.

Italian version by A. Zanardini published 1874.

NORONHA: *Beatrice di Portogallo*

7 March. Oporto

(Original Portuguese) text by C. Monthoro (founded on Almeida Garrett's *Auto de Gil-Vicente*), Italian version by L. Bianchi. Four acts.

The first opera of the Portuguese composer.

SUPPÉ: *Flotte Bursche*

18 April. Vienna, Quai Th.

Text by J. Braun. One act.

Berlin, Fr.W. 3 December 1863 and all over Germany where it is still occasionally revived.

In German also given at Budapest July 1863; Basle 17 November 1865; New York 25 October

1867; Helsinki June 1899; Buenos Aires October 1906.

In Croatian (translated by J. Freudenreich), Zagreb 2 February 1866.

In Russian, Moscow 1867.

In Polish (translated by W. L. Anczyc), Warsaw 24 November 1867.

In Czech (translated by E. Züngel), Prague 13 April 1872.

In Swedish (translated by A. Jonason), Stockholm 1875.

In Italian (as *Le Collegiali*), Venice, T. Malibran 30 December 1880.

In Rumanian, Bucharest 6 March 1908.

Revived Vienna, Redoutensaal 26 December 1931.

SEROV: *Judith*

Юдиѳъ

28 May. St. Petersburg

Text by the composer and A. N. Maikov (founded on P. Giacometti's drama, *Giuditta*). Five acts.

Serov's first opera, very successful in Russia. Revived St. Petersburg 20 November 1874 and given there until *c.*1915.

In Russian also, Paris, Châtelet 7 June 1909 (parts only).

BRUCH: *Die Loreley*

14 June. Mannheim

Text by E. Geibel (originally written for Mendelssohn, of whose setting there exist only the finale of the first act, an "Ave Maria," and the chorus of the vintagers). Four acts.

Successful in Germany; revived (text altered by O. Walther), Leipzig 9 September 1887; Breslau 4 March 1888; Cologne 5 January 1896; Strasbourg 26 March 1916 (first version). In German also, Prague 8 December 1866; Rotterdam 14 November 1868; Amsterdam 22 February 1869.

The fragments of Mendelssohn's setting had been given first at a concert at Leipzig on 27 March 1851; on the stage, Leipzig 19 January 1852; Frankfort 16 February 1852, etc.; Prague 16 November 1853; Basle 5 January 1854; Vienna, Jos.

November 1857 (Kä. 15 November 1860, in concert form); Berlin, O. 14 March 1875; Cassel 17 January 1884; Wiesbaden 30 September 1884. In concert form also Birmingham 8 September 1852 (in English, translated by W. Bartholomew); revived London, Twentieth Century Th. 1 June 1940. In Hungarian (translated by E. Abrányi), Budapest 1 March 1891.

Geibel's libretto was written in 1846–47, published in 1861 and dedicated to the memory of Mendelssohn.

OFFENBACH: *Lischen et Fritzchen*

21 July. Ems

Text by "Paul Dubois" (pseudonym of P. Boisse-lot and C. Nuitter?; see A. Henseler, *Offenbach*, p.468). One act.

Paris, B.P. 5 January 1864; Brussels 5 September 1864, etc.

In French also, Mexico 12 September 1875; Naples, T. Sannazaro 1878.

In German (first given as *Französische Schwaben*, translated by P. Henrion), Vienna, Ca. 16 April 1864; Berlin, Fr.W. 23 June 1864, etc.; Basle 11 March 1868; Graz 14 August 1869.

London, St. J.'s 2 June 1868 (in French) and Gaiety 9 August 1869 (in English, translated by W. Guernsey).

New York 25 June 1868 (in French), 8 October 1868 (in English), and 26 May 1872 (in German).

In Russian, Moscow 1868; in English, Sydney 1871; in Dutch, Hague 1872; in Finnish, Helsinki 1 October 1897.

(MARSCHNER): *Sangeskönig Hiarne und das Tyrfingschwert*

13 September. Frankfort

Text by W. Grothe. Four acts.

Marschner's last opera, produced two years after his death. Revived Munich 7 March 1883 (revised by H. Levi) and Hamburg 2 January 1884.

SKUHERSKÝ: *Vladimír, Bohův Zvolenec*

27 September. Prague, Cz.

Text by H. Mostecký (after J. V. Frič). Four acts.

The first original Czech opera which was given at the "Královské Zemské České Prozatimní Divadlo", the first theatre at Prague exclusively reserved for Czech plays and operas; this theatre was replaced by the "Narodni Divadlo" in 1881.

BIZET: *Les Pêcheurs de Perles*

30 September. Paris, Th.L.

Text by E. Cormon and M. Carré. Three acts.

In 1863 given for 18 nights only; the great success of the opera came many years after the composer's death:

MILAN 20 March 1886 (in Italian, translated by A. Zanardini).

AIX-LES-BAINS 8 August 1886 (first production in France since 1863).

COBURG 14 November 1886 (in German, translated by F. Fremery).

LISBON 1886 (in Italian).

GENEVA 3 March 1887 (in French).

LONDON, C.G. 22 April 1887 (in Italian, as *Leila*) and 18 May 1889 (as *I Pescatori di Perle*).

BARCELONA 29 October 1887 (in Italian).

BRUSSELS 25 November 1887 (in French).

MEXICO 26 November 1887 (in Italian).

BUENOS AIRES 24 June 1888 (in Italian).

BUDAPEST 25 October 1888 (in Hungarian, translated by E. Abrányi).

ST. PETERSBURG 15 January 1889 (in Italian).

PRAGUE 17 January 1889 (in Czech).

PARIS, GAÎTÉ 20 April 1889 (in Italian; in French, revived at the O.C. as late as 24 April 1893).

BERLIN, KROLL'S 10 June 1893 (in German).

PHILADELPHIA 25 August 1893 (in Italian); revived 16 May 1928.

KHARKOV January 1898 (in Russian).

COPENHAGEN 25 February 1900 (in Danish, translated by J. Lehmann).

ZAGREB 24 March 1900 (in Croatian, translated by V. Badalič).

MALTA 1900 (in Italian).

RIO DE JANEIRO 30 August 1902 (in Italian).

GRAZ January 1903 (in German).

MOSCOW 16 December 1903 (in Russian).

WARSAW January 1904 (in Polish).

LJUBLJANA 1906 (in Slovenian).

STOCKHOLM 5 November 1913 (in Swedish, translated by E. Grandinson).

NEW YORK 13 November 1916 (in French; the first two acts already 11 January 1896).

SOFIA 12 September 1927 (in Bulgarian).

AMSTERDAM January 1929 (in Italian).

RIGA 25 May 1933 (in Lettish).

SYDNEY 1935 (in English, translated by C. Prerauer).

Still given on French and Italian stages; revived at the O.C., Paris 17 March 1932 and 27 October 1938; Berlin, O. 21 June 1934; at the Scala, Milan 23 February 1938. So far never produced at Vienna.

WALLACE: *The Desert Flower*

12 October. London, C.G.

Text by A. G. Harris and T. J. Williams (founded on Vernoy de Saint-Georges's and De Leuven's *Jaguarita l'Indienne*, see 1855). Three acts.

Wallace's last opera. Also given at New York 15 January 1868.

MACFARREN: *Jessy Lea*

2 November. London, Gallery of Illustration

Text by J. Oxenford (founded on Scribe's *Le Philtre*, see 1831). *An opera di camera.* Two acts.

Also given at New York 8 October 1868. Revived London, Hm. 11 February 1886 (by the R.A.M.); Kilburn Town Hall 9 May 1890.

BERLIOZ: *Les Troyens à Carthage*

4 November. Paris, Th.L.

Text by the composer (after Virgil). Prologue and 5 acts.

The second part of Berlioz's *Les Troyens* (written 1856–58), consisting of 8 acts (11 scenes) altogether and published in 1864. The whole work was not produced until 21 years after the composer's death (see 1890).

For the production at the Th.L., Berlioz divided the original 3 acts of the second part into 5 acts and added a prologue which served to replace the first part. The work was produced under the somewhat misleading title of *Les Troyens* (which, in reality, is the title of the whole). Given at the Th.L. 21 times until 20 December 1863.

Revived in Paris, O.C. 9 June 1892 (for further revivals see 1890).

Outside Paris, the second part was produced at New York 26 February 1887 (in a concert version by F. van der Stucken, English translation by H. E. Krehbiel and J. S. Tunison); Carlsruhe 7 December 1890 (in German, translated by O. Neitzel, music arranged by F. Mottl); also given at Leipzig 27 June 1900.

Liverpool 30 March 1897 (concert performance in English, translated by F. Corder); revived in concert form Manchester 1 November 1928.

Moscow 26 December 1899 (in Russian, translated by E. N. Kletkova).

An open-air performance took place at the Roman Theatre, Orange on 5 August 1905.

GAZTAMBIDE: *La Conquista de Madrid*

23 December. Madrid, Z.

Text by M. J. de Larra. Three acts.

Also given at Havana 1868. The first and only Spanish zarzuela which was performed in Germany: Coburg 25 December 1878 (translated by A. Eilers).

1864

MIRY: *Bouchard d'Avesnes*

5 February. Ghent

Text by H. van Peene. Five acts.

The most successful work of the Belgian composer. Liége 8 April 1864; Brussels 16 December 1864, etc.; revived Brussels 24 August 1871.

A parody, by E. Humbert, called *Bouchard pas d'Veine, Opéra faite avec Peine*, was published at Brussels in 1864.

(Date of first performance wrongly given by Claeys and Wotquenne as 6 March 1862; by Dupont as 6 February 1863.)

PETRELLA: *La Contessa d'Amalfi*

8 March. Turin, T.R.

Text by G. Peruzzini (founded on O. Feuillet's *Dalila*). Four acts.

Successful in Italy: last revived Milan 12 October 1888; Foligno 13 February 1892; Florence 5 October 1897.

In Italian also, Malta 1865; Buenos Aires 29 June 1872; Mexico 3 October 1872; Barcelona 21 March 1874.

GOUNOD: *Mireille*

19 March. Paris, Th.L.

Text by M. Carré (founded on a poem by F. Mistral). Originally in 5 acts.

The opera was given in a reduced 3-act version at the same theatre on 15 December 1864; revived at the O.C. on 10 November 1874, 29 November 1889, 13 March 1901 (in 4 acts), etc. Gaîté-Lyrique 11 May 1930; O.C. 6 June 1939. Outside Paris:

LONDON, H.M.'s 5 July 1864 (in Italian, translated by G. Zaffira); C.G. 10 June 1891 (in French); and Guildhall School of Music 4 December 1899 (in English, translated by H. F. Chorley).

DUBLIN 29 September 1864 (in Italian).

PHILADELPHIA 17 November 1864 (in German; the first two acts only).

ANTWERP 10 March 1865; Brussels 12 May 1865, etc. (in French).

ST. PETERSBURG 9 February 1874 (in Italian).

VIENNA 26 April 1876 (in Italian).

GENEVA 12 April 1877 (in French); revived 19 January 1938.

ROME 31 May 1880 (in Italian, by the Circolo Filodrammatico).

CHICAGO 13 September 1880 (in English).

NEW YORK 18 December 1884 (in Italian).

NEW ORLEANS 29 December 1884 (in Italian).

TURIN 20 October 1885 (in Italian).

BERLIN, KROLL's 5 February 1893 and 18 April 1902 (in French).

GLASGOW March 1894 (in English).

BARCELONA September 1900 (in Spanish).

ALGIERS Spring 1902 (in French).

BREMEN 19 March 1903 (in German, translated by A. Bertuch).

BUENOS AIRES 8 July 1911 (in French).

CAIRO Spring 1938 (in French).

Still given on French stages; an open-air performance at St. Rémy-de-Provence (where the opera had been written) took place on 7 September 1913.

MAILLART: *Lara*

21 March. Paris, O.C.

Text by E. Cormon and M. Carré (after Byron). Three acts.

Brussels 4 March 1865; in French also, Barcelona 7 July 1881.

In Polish (translated by L. Matuszyński), Warsaw 1864.

In German (translated by E. Pasqué), Prague 26 October 1864; Leipzig 29 October 1864; Cologne 3 November 1864, etc. Revived Stuttgart 26 September 1879.

In English (translated by J. Oxenford), London, H.M.'s 31 January 1865.

FRY: *Notre-Dame of Paris*

4 May. Philadelphia

Text by J. R. Fry (the brother of the composer), founded on V. Hugo's novel. Four acts.

Fry's second and last opera, produced at the American Academy of Music, Philadelphia on the above date (not in 1863 as many books of reference have it).

MERMET: *Roland à Roncevaux*

3 October. Paris, O.

Text by the composer. Four acts.

Mermet's best work. Given at the Paris Opéra 65 times until 1867.

In French also, Antwerp 22 March 1865; Ghent 28 March 1865; Brussels 11 May 1865, New Orleans 1869; etc.

Revived Paris, O. Populaire 13 October 1883; Amsterdam Spring 1887; Ghent 1888–89.

MACFARREN: *Helvellyn*

3 November. London, C.G.

Text by J. Oxenford (founded on Mosenthal's novel, *Der Sonnenwendhof*). Four acts.

Macfarren's last opera.

BENEDICT: *The Bride of Song*

3 December. London, C.G.

Text by H. B. Farnie. One act.

Benedict's last opera. (Previously given in concert form at Hanover Square Rooms, London 23 May 1864.)

OFFENBACH: *La belle Hélène*

17 December. Paris, Variétés

Text by H. Meilhac and Lud. Halévy. Three acts.

One of Offenbach's greatest successes, in Paris as well as elsewhere.

VIENNA, W. 17 March 1865 (in German).

PRAGUE 17 April 1865 (in German) and 6 August 1875 (in Czech, translated by S. Jiný).

STOCKHOLM 11 May 1865 (in Swedish, translated by E. A. Wallmark).

BERLIN, FR.W. 13 May 1865 (in German).

GRAZ 31 May 1865 (in German).

BRUSSELS 3 June 1865 (in French).

HELSINKI 1865 (in Swedish) and 4 May 1927 (in Finnish).

PRESSBURG 28 October 1865 (in German).

COPENHAGEN 24 November 1865 (in Danish, translated by A. F. von der Recke).

CHRISTIANIA 13 May 1866 (in Danish, translated by A. F. von der Recke).

LONDON, ADELPHI 30 June 1866 (in English, as *Helen; or, Taken from the Greek*, adapted by F. C. Burnand) and St. J.'s 13 July 1868 (in French).

CONSTANTINOPLE April 1867 (in French).

MILAN, T. RÈ 27 April 1867 (in French).

ST. PETERSBURG 14 October 1867 (in German) and October 1868 (in Russian, translated by K. I. Babikov); revived 19 June 1931 (new translation by H. Erdman and V. Mass).

NEW YORK 3 December 1867 (in German); 26 March 1868 (in French); and 13 April 1868 (in English, translated by M. St. John); revived Boston 20 October 1919 (new English version by A. Strong and C. H. Towne).

BASLE 24 February 1868 (in German).

NAPLES, T.N. 18 September 1868 (in Italian, translated by F. Mastriani).

CAIRO 4 January 1869 (in French).

WARSAW 1869 (in Polish, translated by J. Checiń-ski).

MADRID 1869 (in Spanish, translated by M. Pastorfido and T. Fortun) and Circo 31 December 1870 (translated by R. Puente y Brañas).

LISBON 1869 (in Portuguese, translated by J. da Silva Mendes Leal).

BUDAPEST 14 September 1870 (in German) and 7 October 1882 (in Hungarian).

MEXICO 6 January 1874 (in French).

BUENOS AIRES October 1876 (in Spanish).

ZAGREB 14 February 1897 (in Croatian, translated by P. Brani).

SOFIA 4 November 1935 (in Bulgarian).

New German translation by L. Fulda 1931. Another by E. Friedell and H. Sassmann, music arranged by E. W. Korngold, Berlin, Th. am Kurfürstendamm 15 June 1931.

The latest revival in London so far was at the Adelphi 30 January 1932 (new adaptation by A. P. Herbert).

F. A. BARBIERI: *Pan y Toros*
(Bread and Bulls)

22 December. Madrid, Z.

Text by J. Picón. Three acts.

Barbieri's most successful zarzuela, very popular in Spain and South America. Mexico 2 July 1869, etc.

Frequently revived at Madrid up to the present. (The hero of the work is the painter Goya.)

1865

C. E. DI BARBIERI: *Perdita* oder *Ein Wintermärchen*

11 January. Prague, G.

Text by K. Gross (founded on F. von Dingel-stedt's German version of Shakespeare's *A Winter's Tale*). Four acts.

The most successful work of Barbieri, who was a pupil of Mercadante and a conductor in Hungary, Germany, and Rio de Janeiro.

In German also, Budapest 11 February 1865; Leipzig 9 May 1865; Graz 18 August 1867, etc. Berlin 11 January 1870 (at Nowack's Th.).

LASSEN: *Le Captif*

24 April. Brussels, M.

Text by E. Cormon (dealing with an incident in the life of Cervantes). One act.

In German (translated bv P. Cornelius), Weimar 8 April 1869.

(MEYERBEER): *L'Africaine*

28 April. Paris, O.

Text by A. E. Scribe. Five acts.

Meyerbeer's last opera; he had begun working at it as early as 1838, but it was not performed until a year after his death (original title, *Vasco da Gama*; several different versions before the final one which was revised by Fétis).

The 100th performance at the Paris O. took place within less than one year, on 9 March 1866; given there 485 times until 1893.

Outside Paris, produced at:

LONDON, C.G. 22 July 1865 (in Italian, translated by J. Nicodemo) and 21 October 1865 (in English, translated by C. L. Kenney).

MADRID 14 October 1865 (in Italian, translated by M. M. Marcello).

BOLOGNA 4 November 1865 (in Italian, translated by M. M. Marcello).

BERLIN 18 November 1865 (in German, translated by F. Gumbert; given there until 1917).

ANTWERP 25 November 1865; Brussels 30 November 1865 (in French).

NEW YORK 1 December 1865 (in Italian) and 2 May 1871 (in German).

HAGUE 25 December 1865 (in French).

ST. PETERSBURG 19 January 1866 (in Italian) and 11 November 1890 (in Russian, translated by G. A. Lishin).

BUDAPEST 15 February 1866 (in Hungarian, translated by G. Böhm and F. Ormai).

VIENNA 27 February 1866 (in German) and 28 March 1876 (in Italian).

SYDNEY April 1866 (in English).

LEMBERG 27 December 1866 (in German) and 10 March 1874 (in Polish).

HAVANA 1866 (in Italian).

GENEVA 19 February 1867 (in French).

RIGA 13 March 1867 (in German).

STOCKHOLM 28 April 1867 (in Swedish, translated by E. A. Wallmark).

BRÜNN 30 April 1867 (in German).

PRAGUE 8 May 1867 (in German) and 6 June 1884 (in Czech, translated by E. Züngel).

NAPLES, S.C. November 1867 (in Italian).

ALGIERS March 1869 (in Italian).

CONSTANTINOPLE Spring 1869 (in Italian).

MONTEVIDEO Summer 1869 (in Italian).

ALEXANDRIA 21 October 1869 (in Italian).

GRAZ 23 November 1867 (in German).

NEW ORLEANS 18 December 1869 (in French).

LISBON 8 January 1870 (in Italian).

BUENOS AIRES 2 June 1870 (in Italian).

MALTA 1870 (in Italian).

RIO DE JANEIRO 1870 (in Italian).

WARSAW 1870 (in Polish, translated by L. Sygietyński).

TIFLIS March 1872 (in Italian).

MEXICO 8 December 1873 (in Italian).

CAIRO 18 January 1876 (in Italian).

SANTIAGO, CHILE 1876 (in Italian).

ZAGREB 8 November 1879 (in Croatian, translated by J. E. Tomić).

LAIBACH (LJUBLJANA) 1880 (in German) and 1895 (in Slovenian, translated by F. Gangl).

REVAL 1890 (in German).

HELSINKI 29 November 1896 (in Italian).

Still given on French and Italian stages; revived in German, Vienna 30 October 1935; in French, Brussels 4 January 1938; in Swedish, Stockholm 4 October 1938.

CORNELIUS: *Der Cid*

21 May. Weimar

Text by the composer. Three acts.

Cornelius's second opera, the last which was performed in his lifetime. Revived in a revised version by H. Levi, Munich 21 April 1891; Mayence 8 January 1893; Dresden 17 January 1899; Mannheim 26 February 1899; Prague 22 September 1900. Revived in its original form (re-constructed by M. Hasse), Weimar 9 June 1904; Dessau 25 December 1913; Stuttgart 15 May 1938.

FACCIO: *Amleto*

30 May. Genoa, C.F.

Text by A. Boito (after Shakespeare). Four acts.

The second and last opera of the famous conductor. Milan, Sc. 9 February 1871, etc. Never produced outside Italy and, so far, never revived.

R. WAGNER: *Tristan und Isolde*

10 June. Munich

Text by the composer. Three acts.

Libretto finished 18 September 1857, published 1858. Music written 1 October 1857–9 August 1859; full score and vocal score (by H. von Bülow) published 1860. Wagner first thought of producing *Tristan* at Rio de Janeiro (see his letter of 5 May 1857); further projects included Strasbourg, Paris, Prague, Carlsruhe, Vienna (first rehearsed there 26 October 1862), Weimar; in 1864 Munich was decided upon.

A parody, *Tristanderl und Süssholde*, music by Rauchenecker, was produced at the Isar-Vorstadt Th., Munich 29 May 1865, earlier than the opera itself, the performance of which was postponed from week to week (after the dress rehearsal on 11 May).

In order to show how very slowly *Tristan und Isolde* conquered town after town and country after country, the following list contains all pro-

ductions up to 1900 (and the more important ones after 1900).

Productions in German:

MUNICH 10 June 1865 (under H. von Bülow; repeated 13 June, 19 June and 1 July 1865; 20 June and 23 June 1869; and again three times in October 1872).

WEIMAR 14 June 1874 (under E. Lassen).

BERLIN 20 March 1876 (under K. Eckert; 100th performance 1 September 1907; 250th performance 9 October 1932).

KÖNIGSBERG 10 December 1881 (under H. Seidel).

LEIPZIG 2 January 1882 (under A. Seidl).

LONDON, D.L. 20 June 1882 (under H. Richter).

HAMBURG 23 November 1882 (under J. Sucher).

VIENNA 4 October 1883 (under H. Richter; had been rehearsed there 77 times in 1862–63!).

BREMEN 26 December 1883.

DRESDEN 21 May 1884.

FRANKFORT 15 October 1884.

CARLSRUHE 3 December 1884.

SONDERSHAUSEN 9 July 1885.

PRAGUE 29 April 1886.

BAYREUTH 23 July 1886.

NEW YORK 1 December 1886.

BRESLAU 3 February 1888.

MANNHEIM 23 December 1888.

NUREMBERG 27 January 1889.

COLOGNE 18 February 1889.

BERNE 18 March 1889.

STRASBOURG 6 February 1890.

ROTTERDAM 22 March 1890.

MAGDEBURG 27 March 1890.

DÜSSELDORF 26 January 1891.

HALLE 28 January 1891.

DARMSTADT 5 April 1891.

ZURICH 29 January 1892.

BASLE 14 March 1892.

EISENACH 23 March 1892.

BRÜNN 18 February 1893.

HANOVER 3 April 1893.

GRAZ 12 February 1894.

BRUNSWICK 13 February 1894.

ELBERFELD 8 March 1894.

MAYENCE 15 February 1895.

BOSTON 1 April 1895.

CHICAGO 17 April 1895.

LÜBECK 22 January 1896.

AMSTERDAM 8 May 1896.

STUTTGART 12 May 1897.

WIESBADEN 25 May 1897.

FREIBURG 16 March 1898.

AACHEN 20 March 1898.

ST. PETERSBURG 25 March 1898.

STETTIN 10 April 1898.

COBURG 5 November 1899.

ULM 28 March 1900.

DESSAU 5 April 1900.

POSEN 1 October 1900.

GOTHA 25 January 1901.

AUGSBURG 17 March 1901.

BRUSSELS 6 May 1901.

CASSEL 16 June 1901.

HAGEN 27 November 1901.

METZ 6 February 1902.

REGENSBURG December 1902.

ERFURT 7 January 1903.

ESSEN 24 January 1904.

RIGA 4 November 1904.

KIEL 5 April 1905.

DORTMUND 24 February 1906.

WÜRZBURG 6 April 1906.

HALBERSTADT 13 September 1906.

ROSTOCK 1907.

GERA 1908.

SCHWERIN 21 November 1909.

ALTENBURG 23 March 1913.

PARIS, CH.É. 20 May 1914.

SALZBURG 5 August 1933(!).

In Italian (translated by A. Boito), Bologna 2 June 1888 (under G. Martucci); Turin 14 February 1897; Barcelona 8 November 1899; Trieste 25 December 1899; Milan, Sc. 29 December 1900 (new translation by P. Floridia); Buenos Aires 1 August 1901; Ravenna 11 May 1902; Rome 26 December 1903; Alexandria February 1905; Rovereto 1905; Brescia 1906; Genoa 12 February 1908; Naples, Parma, Lisbon 1908; Venice February 1909; Palermo, Cesena 1909; Rio de Janeiro 27 May 1910; Madrid March 1911; Padua 1913; Montevideo Summer 1920. New Italian translation by F. Gozo published 1934.

In French (translated by V. Wilder), Monte Carlo 22 March 1893; Brussels 21 March 1894 (not 1893); Aix-les-Bains September 1897; Nice February 1899; Paris, Nouveau Th. 28 October 1899 (under Lamoureux who had conducted the first act in concert form on 16 March 1884 already); Lyons 6 March 1900; Cairo 1901; Paris, Château d'Eau 1 June 1902 (under Cortot); Paris, O. 14 December 1904 (under Taffanel; new French version by A. Ernst, L. de Fourcaud and P. Bruck); Geneva 25 February 1909; Paris, O.C. 26 May 1925 (new translation by M. Léna and J. Chantavoine); Marseilles March 1928; Brussels 19 February 1930 and Paris, O. 28 February 1936 (new translation by G. Samazeuilh; 100th Paris performance 22 June 1938).

In English (translator not mentioned; there were printed versions by H. and F. Corder, 1882; F. Jameson, 1886; and A. Forman 1891): Liverpool 15 April 1898; London, Ly. 3 February 1899; Hull, Leeds, Manchester, Glasgow, Edinburgh March and April 1912; Johannesburg March 1912; Cape Town 1912; Middlesborough 6 March 1914; New York 20 November 1920.

In Russian (translated by V. E. Cheshikhin), St. Petersburg 17 April 1899; Moscow 12 November 1909 (new translation by V. Kolomiitsov).

In Hungarian (translated by E. Abrányi), Budapest 28 November 1901.

Catalan version by J. Maragall and A. Ribera published 1904; another by J. Zanné and J. Pena 1906. Probably never produced in that language.

In Swedish (translated by O. W. Peterson-Berger), Stockholm 11 February 1909; Helsinki 23 April 1921.

In Czech (translated by V. J. Novotný), Prague 10 February 1913; Brno 26 January 1922 and Prague 18 December 1924 (new translation by K. Burian).

In Danish (translated by K. Gjellerup), Copenhagen 14 February 1914.

In Croatian (translated by M. Nehajev), Zagreb 29 June 1917.

In Lettish (translated by A. Anderson), Riga 23 April 1921.

In Flemish, Antwerp 3 February 1924.

In Dutch, Amsterdam Spring 1929.
In Norwegian, Oslo Autumn 1932.
In Rumanian, Bucharest January 1934.

SUPPÉ: *Die schöne Galatea*

30 June. Berlin, Meysel's Th.

Text by "Poly Henrion" (pseudonym of L. Kohl von Kohlenegg). One act.

The most successful of Suppé's early operettas; Vienna, Ca. 9 September 1865, etc.; Basle 23 October 1867; in German also, New York 6 September 1867; St. Petersburg October 1867; Riga 16 December 1867.

In Polish (translated by F. Szober), Lemberg 9 December 1867.

In Croatian (translated by D. Demeter), Zagreb 4 August 1868.

In Swedish (translated by J. Philipsson), Stockholm 8 August 1868.

In English (as *Ganymede and Galatea*), London, Gaiety 20 January 1872 (translator not mentioned; certainly not W. S. Gilbert as stated in *The Stage Cyclopaedia*); New York 14 September 1882 (pasticcio from Suppé's operetta and from Massé's *Galatée*, see 1852, arranged by I. W. Norcross).

In Italian, Turin Summer 1875.

In Hungarian, Budapest 26 April 1876.

In Russian, Moscow 1894.

In Czech, Prague 18 September 1894.

Frequently revived in many countries. Last revived in London, Victoria Palace 28 September 1936.

(The operetta was originally produced at Berlin, not at Vienna as usually stated.)

MONIUSZKO: *Straszny Dwór*
(The Haunted Castle)

28 September. Warsaw

Text by J. Checiński. Four acts.

Apart from *Halka* (see 1854) Moniuszko's chief work. Very successful in Poland: Lemberg 18 January 1877, etc. Frequently revived on Polish stages.

In Polish also, Vienna 11 September 1892 (at the Exhibition Th.).

In Czech (translated by J. Böhm), Prague 29 October 1891.

Given for the first time in German (translated by J. Sliwinski), Basle 20 September 1939.

ŠEBOR: *Templáři na Moravě*
(The Templars in Moravia)

19 October. Prague, Cz.

Text by K. Sabina. Three acts.

The first of Šebor's five Czech operas.

MARCHETTI: *Romeo e Giulietta*

25 October. Trieste

Text by M. M. Marcello (after Shakespeare). Four acts.

Marchetti's first success. Revived Rome 10 April 1876.

SEROV: *Rognyeda*
Рогнѣда

8 November. St. Petersburg

Text by D. V. Averkiev. Five acts.

Moscow 15 December 1868; Kiev 1873, etc.

Very successful in Russia; revived Moscow 11 October 1897; St. Petersburg 11 October 1904.

BAZIN: *Le Voyage en Chine*

9 December. Paris, O.C.

Text by E. M. Labiche and A. Delacour. Three acts.

Bazin's most successful work. Last revived in Paris, Ren. 31 December 1899; Th.Trianon 6 September 1906; and Tr.L. 23 February 1915.

Outside France:

LIÉGE 9 April 1866; Brussels 3 September 1866, etc.

VIENNA, W. 12 May 1866 (in German, translated by J. C. Grünbaum) and 27 May 1872 (in French).

STOCKHOLM 14 November 1866 (in Swedish, translated by E. A.Wallmark).

PRAGUE January 1867 (in German).

BERLIN, WALLNER TH. 2 July 1867 (in German); revived Th.d.W. 15 September 1899.

COPENHAGEN 10 January 1868 (in Danish, translated by A. F. von der Recke; as pasticcio? Offenbach is mentioned as the composer).

CHRISTIANIA 22 January 1869 (in Danish, translated by A. F. von der Recke; as pasticcio? Offenbach is mentioned as the composer).

LISBON 17 April 1869 (in Portuguese, translated by A. Mendes Leal) and 25 May 1878 (in French).

HAGUE 1873 (in Dutch, translated by C. P. T. Bigot).

LONDON, ROYALTY 13 February 1873 (in French) and Garrick Th. 5 June 1879 (in English; translator not mentioned).

BUENOS AIRES 1873 (in French).

NEW YORK 11 January 1875 (in French).

MEXICO January 1876 (in French).

BUCHAREST 1903 (in Rumanian).

Still given on French stages; revived Montreal January 1920; Geneva 9 April 1923; Antwerp 17 April 1931, etc.

FLOTOW: *Naida*
Наида

11 December. St. Petersburg

(Original French) text by J. H. Vernoy de Saint-Georges and Léon Halevy, first called *Le Vannier* and written for Paris in 1856; then translated into German by F. von Dingelstedt, but not performed in Germany either. From Dingelstedt's version it was translated into Russian. Three acts.

Revived Milan, T. Manzoni 7 June 1873 (in Italian, translated by G. Eisner); also Genoa 12 November 1873, etc.

In 1873 the opera was announced as new and the fact of its having been produced in Russia eight years earlier was forgotten; accordingly, no book of reference mentions the St. Petersburg performance.

1866

SMETANA: *Braniboři v Čechách*
(The Brandenburgers in Bohemia)

5 January. Prague, Cz.

Text by K. Sabina. Three acts.

Smetana's first opera. Revived Prague 9 April

1885 (libretto revised by V. J. Novotný); 12 May 1903; 12 May 1916; 2 March 1924.

In Czech also, Vienna 28 May 1924 (by the Olomouc opera company).

MORALES: *Ildegonda*

27 January. Mexico

(Italian) text by T. Solera (see 1845). Three acts.

Morale's setting was also given at Florence, T. Pagliano on 6 March 1869.

(An account of *Ildegonda*—which was the first and probably still is the only opera by a Mexican composer ever performed in Europe—will be found in *The Musical World*, 2 June 1866.)

(MOZART): *Zaide*

27 January. Frankfort

Original text by J. A. Schachtner, re-written by K. Gollmick. Two acts.

This German Singspiel had been written probably in 1779, for J. Böhm's troupe; Mozart left it unfinished and without title (which was supplied by André when he published the score in 1838).

Of Schachtner's libretto (on its source, see A. Einstein, in *Acta Musicologica*, Vol. VIII, 1936) only the lyrics were extant. For the Frankfort 1866 production the lost dialogue was re-written by K. Gollmick; overture and finale were added by Anton André. *Zaide* was revived at Vienna 4 October 1902 (revised by R. Hirschfeld, who altered the libretto again and replaced André's additions by substituting parts from Mozart's *König Thamos* music); this version was also given at Carlsruhe 27 January 1903.

Further revivals: Carlsruhe 5 May 1917 (revised by A. Rudolph); Zurich 22 June 1918 (by puppets); Oldenburg January 1927 (in the original form); Berlin, Th. in der Klosterstrasse 10 April 1928; Würzburg, July 1933 and Potsdam, Neues Palais 7 June 1939 (revised by W. Meckbach).

A French version by J. Chantavoine was produced at Monte Carlo 7 January 1930.

OFFENBACH: *Barbe-Bleue*

5 February. Paris, Variétés

Text by H. Meilhac and Lud. Halévy. Three acts.
Like most Offenbach operettas of the 'sixties
produced in every country, viz.:

LONDON, OLYMPIC 2 June 1866 (in English, as
Bluebeard repaired, adapted by H. Bellingham,
music arranged by J. H. Tully); St. J.'s 28 June
1869 (in French); Gaiety 29 August 1870 (in
English, translated by C. L. Kenney).

VIENNA, W. 21 September 1866 (in German, translated by J. Hopp).

BRUSSELS 13 October 1866 (in French).

STOCKHOLM 23 February 1867 (in Swedish, translated by E. A. Wallmark).

BERLIN, FR.W. 13 March 1867 (in German, Hopp's
translation altered by E. Pohl).

BUDAPEST 5 April 1867 (in Hungarian, translated
by E. Latabár).

MILAN, T.RÈ 3 May 1867 (in French).

COPENHAGEN October 1867 (in Danish).

LISBON 14 June 1868 (in Portuguese, translated by
F. Palha) and 28 May 1870 (in Spanish). Another Portuguese translation by A. Mendes Leal
published 1868.

GRAZ 1 June 1868 (in German.)

AMSTERDAM 1868 (in Dutch).

NEW YORK 13 July 1868 (in French) and 15 February 1870 (in German); 30 October 1886 (in
Yiddish).

NAPLES 27 July 1868 (in French) and 1869 (in
Italian, translated by F. Mastriani).

MADRID 1869 (in Spanish, translated by A. Pove-
dano y Vidal).

LAIBACH 1870 (in German).

VALPARAISO 1870 (in French).

ODESSA 1870 (in Russian, translated by G. A.
Lishin).

MEXICO 4 May 1871 (in Spanish).

SYDNEY 1872 (in English).

LEMBERG 13 December 1873 (in Polish, translated
by L. Matuszyński).

PRAGUE 8 August 1874 (in Czech, translated by
E. Züngel and J. J. Stankovský).

MALTA 1875 (in Italian).

RIGA 1875 (in German).

SARAJEVO 1882 (in German).

HELSINKI Summer 1899 (in German).

ZAGREB 5 October 1904 (in Croatian, translated
by F. Miler).

THOOFT: *Aleida von Holland*

10 March. Rotterdam

(German) text by E. Pasqué. Three acts.
Thooft's only opera and the first opera by a
Dutch composer which was produced at the Ger-
man Opera, Rotterdam (founded in 1860). Also
given at The Hague on 29 March 1871; revived
Rotterdam 28 March 1889.

J. T. RADOUX: *Le Béarnais*

14 March. Liége

Text by A. Pellier-Quengsy. Three acts.
Brussels 30 January 1868 (libretto altered by H.
Kirsch). Revived Lille 30 October 1879.

MERCADANTE: *Virginia*

7 April. Naples, S.C.

Text by S. Cammarano (founded on Alfieri's tragedy). Three acts.
Mercadante's last opera, written in 1851, but
not allowed to be acted then. Revived Turin 30
September 1877; Naples 7 February 1901. According to Clément, ". . . aux yeux des connaisseurs
un des grands opéras modernes soumis au jugement du public . . . ."

ABERT: *Astorga*

27 May. Stuttgart

Text by E. Pasqué (dealing with incidents of the
life of the composer Astorga, see 1709). Three
acts.
Successful on German stages: Leipzig 29 October 1866; Prague 4 December 1866, etc.; Vienna,
Ca. 30 July 1870; Basle 17 February 1876; Graz
16 January 1880; Posen 1888. In Czech (translated
by J. Böhm), Prague 1876. French vocal score
(translated by V. Wilder), published c.1870; an
intended production in Paris was frustrated by the
Franco-Prussian War.

FLOTOW: *Zilda*

28 May. Paris, O.C.

Text by J. H. Vernoy de Saint-Georges and H. C. Chivot. Two acts.

In German (translated by M. A. Grandjean and R. Genée), Prague 21 February 1867; Berlin, Fr.W. 9 August 1867; Vienna, W. November 1869, etc.

In Spanish (translated by A. Mondejar y Mendoza and L. Pacheco), Madrid 1873.

Some of the music of Flotow's *Zilda* was used in *Fatme,* by B. Bardi. Berlin, Th. d. W. 8 March 1925, etc.; Prague 1933.

SMETANA: *Prodaná Nevěsta*
(The Bartered Bride)

30 May. Prague, Cz

Text by K. Sabina. Three acts.

Smetana's chief work; the most popular Czech opera ever written. Very successful at Prague where it was repeated with some alterations on 29 January 1869, in a third version 1 June 1869 and in its final version 25 September 1870, and where the 100th performance was on 5 May 1882; 500th performance 8 August 1909; 1,000th performance 30 May 1927; 1,400th performance 16 October 1938. The success of *The Bartered Bride* was limited to Slavonic stages until 25 years later when it was first given, in Czech, at the Vienna Exhibition Theatre 1 June 1892 and, translated into German by M. Kalbeck, at the Th. an der Wien 2 April 1893.

The first performances were at:

ST. PETERSBURG 11 January 1871 (in Russian, translated by P. I. Kalashnikov). Revived Leningrad 25 May 1937 (new translation by Aleksyei Nikolaevich Tolstoy and V. Rozhdestvensky, founded on earlier translation by F. Kub).

ZAGREB 18 October 1873 (in Croatian, translated by A. Šenoa).

VIENNA 1 June 1892 (in Czech) and 2 April 1893 (in German, see above); O. 4 October 1896.

BERLIN 1 July 1893 (in German, at the Th. Unter den Linden; O. 24 May 1894).

CHICAGO 20 August 1893 (in Czech).

BUDAPEST 21 September 1893 (in Hungarian, translated by K. Abrányi).

LJUBLJANA 15 February 1894 (in Slovenian, translated by A. Funtek).

STOCKHOLM 6 October 1894 (in Swedish).

STRASBOURG 27 January 1895 (in German).

LONDON, D.L. 26 June 1895 (in German) and S.'s W. 21 November 1935 (in English, translated by R. Newmarch).

RIGA 1895 (in German) and 28 October 1934 (in Lettish).

AMSTERDAM 4 October 1896 (in German), December 1902 (in Dutch) and January 1937 (in Czech).

BASLE 31 March 1897 (in German).

WARSAW September 1903 (in Polish).

BUCHAREST 1903 (in Czech, by the Prague company) and 30 March 1908 (in Rumanian).

MILAN, T.L. 9 October 1905 (in Italian, translated by F. Ghione); revived Sc. 27 February 1935 (translation revised by L. Mandaus).

BRUSSELS 23 February 1907 (in French, translated by R. Brunel).

BUENOS AIRES 1 August 1907 (in Italian) and 9 August 1934 (in German).

NEW YORK 19 February 1909 (in German) and 15 May 1936 (in English, translated by G. Jones).

HELSINKI 29 March 1910 (in Finnish, translated by T. Wallenius).

SOFIA 7 September 1912 (in Bulgarian).

BELGRADE 1922 (in Serbian).

BARCELONA 12 February 1924 (in Czech); Catalan translation by J. Pena and R. J. Slaby published in that year.

TALLIN 1924 (in Estonian, translated by A. Trilljärv).

PARIS, O.C. 26 October 1928 (in French, translated by R. Brunel and D. Muller).

OXFORD 26 November 1929 (for the first time in English, translated by A. Raleigh).

COPENHAGEN 15 May 1930 (in Danish, translated by H. H. Seedorff Pedersen).

CHICAGO June 1933 (in Czech) and December 1933 (in English, translated by L. Bartusek).

KAUNAS 7 March 1934 (in Lithuanian).

OFFENBACH: *La Vie Parisienne*

31 October. Paris, Palais Royal

Text by H. Meilhac and Lud. Halévy. Five acts. Even more successful than *Barbe-Bleue* earlier in the same year. Still given in many countries; the latest revival in Paris was on 26 September 1934 at the Th. Mogador. Outside Paris given at:

BRUSSELS 30 January 1867 (in French).

VIENNA, CA. 31 January 1867 (in German, translated by K.Treumann)and 5July1871(in French).

BERLIN, FR.W. 22 May 1867 (in German). Revived in a new German version by P. Scher, Munich 2 February 1929 and Berlin, Renaissance Th. 6 December 1929.

BUDAPEST 25 May 1867 (in German).

STOCKHOLM 6 June 1868 (in Swedish, translated by R. A. Gustafson).

GRAZ 26 August 1868 (in German).

NEW YORK 29 March 1869 (in French); 15 November 1869 (in German); 18 March 1884 (in English, translated by H. B. Farnie).

MADRID, Z. 26 July 1869 (in Spanish, translated by L. Rivera. An adaptation *La Vida Madrileña*, by M. Pina, music adapted by Sedó, T. Eslava, April 1886).

BASLE 30 March 1870 (in German).

LISBON 29 May 1870 (in Spanish).

WARSAW 1871 and Lemberg 10 July 1873 (in Polish, translated by J. Checiński).

LONDON, HOLBORN TH. 30 March 1872 (in English, translated by F. C. Burnand; last revived Lyric, Hammersmith 18 April 1929 in a new adaptation by A. P. Herbert and A. D. Adams).

ST. PETERSBURG 9 October 1873 (in Russian).

MEXICO 10 February 1874 (in French).

NAPLES 1874 (in French).

RIGA 1874 (in German).

COPENHAGEN 15 November 1876 (in Danish, translated by K. Møller and W. Faber).

PRAGUE 1876 (in Czech, translated by J. J. Stankovský).

A. THOMAS: *Mignon*

17 November. Paris, O.C.

Text by J. Barbier and M. Carré (founded on Goethe's *Wilhelm Meisters Lehrjahre*). Three acts.

Thomas's most successful work; the 500th performance at the O.C. was on 22 Octobre 1878, the 1,000th on 13 May 1894, the 1,600th on 22 May 1927.

Outside Paris, given at:

ANTWERP 7 March 1867 (in French).

BRUSSELS 29 March 1867 (in French).

GENEVA 28 January 1868 (in French).

WEIMAR 13 April 1868 (in German, translated by F. Gumbert).

VIENNA 24 October 1868 (in German) and 9 March 1876 (in Italian).

PRAGUE 19 January 1869 (in German) and 15 November 1884 (in Czech, translated by J. Böhm).

BADEN-BADEN 4 September 1869 (new version with recitatives instead of spoken dialogue).

BERLIN 10 December 1869 (in German).

TRIESTE 10 March 1870 (in Italian, translated by G. Zaffira).

LONDON, D.L. 5 July 1870 (in Italian) and H.M.'s 13 January 1880 (in English, translated by A. Matthison).

GRAZ 17 August 1871 (in German).

NEW YORK 22 November 1871 (in Italian); 11 October 1875 (in English, translated by C. L. Kellogg); 1 December 1879 (in French).

ST. PETERSBURG 26 December 1871 (in Italian); in Russian Leningrad 27 November 1918 (if not earlier).

RIGA February 1873 (in German) and 28 February 1926 (in Lettish).

STOCKHOLM 10 March 1873 (in Swedish, translated by F. T. Hedberg).

WARSAW 1873 (in Polish, translated by F. Szober).

BUDAPEST 20 September 1873 (in Hungarian, translated by F. Ormai).

BARCELONA 13 February 1875 (in Italian).

MILAN 6 May 1875 (in Italian).

LISBON 22 March 1877 (in Italian) and 1 May 1878 (in French).

NAPLES, T. BELLINI 15 February 1879.

MEXICO 28 February 1879 (in French).

DUBLIN 18 August 1879 (in English, translated by A. Matthison).

EDINBURGH 1 September 1879 (in English, translated by A. Matthison).

COPENHAGEN 6 January 1880 (in Danish, translated by A. Hertz).

CHRISTIANIA June 1880 (in Norwegian).

BUENOS AIRES 1881 (in French) and 8 May 1883 (in Italian).

MELBOURNE 22 May 1882 (in English).

ZURICH 14 December 1882 (in German).

MALTA 1883 (in Italian).

AMSTERDAM 1 October 1887 (in Dutch).

ATHENS 27 October 1888 (in French; at the opening of the new opera-house there).

ZAGREB 20 May 1894 (in Croatian, translated by M. Pogačić).

REVAL (TALLINN) 1896 (in German) and 1927 (in Estonian).

HELSINKI 19 November 1896 (in Italian); 2 September 1900 (in Swedish); 6 November 1929 (in Finnish).

LJUBLJANA 1905 (in Slovenian).

BELGRADE 1921 (in Serbian).

SOFIA 23 December 1921 (in Bulgarian).

KAUNAS 1 October 1926 (in Lithuanian).

BUCHAREST March 1929 (in Rumanian).

1867

BAZZINI: *Turanda*

13 January. Milan, Sc.

Text by A. Gazzoletti (after Gozzi). Four acts.

Bazzini's only opera; like Faccio's *Amleto* (see 1865), written in a more serious style than the average Italian operas of those years; unsuccessful.

BENOÎT: *Isa*

24 February. Brussels

Text by E. Hiel. Three acts.

Early Flemish opera, produced at the Théâtre du Cirque.

VERDI: *Don Carlos*

11 March. Paris, O.

Text by F. J. Méry and C. Du Locle (founded on Schiller's drama). Five acts.

Verdi's second (and last) French opera. Performed in Paris 43 times in 1867, but never revived there in French.

Outside Paris, given at:

LONDON, C.G. 4 June 1867 (in Italian, translated by A. de Lauzières).

BOLOGNA 27 October 1867 (in Italian, translated by A. de Lauzières).

BRUSSELS 11 March 1868 (in French).

BUDAPEST 14 March 1868 (in Hungarian).

DARMSTADT 29 March 1868 (in German, translated by M. R. Behr).

MALTA Carnival 1869 (in Italian).

ST. PETERSBURG 1 January 1869 (in Italian).

BARCELONA 27 January 1870 (in Italian).

PRAGUE 13 October 1870 (in German).

LISBON 21 December 1871 (in Italian).

MADRID 15 June 1872 (in Italian).

BUENOS AIRES 17 June 1873 (in Italian).

NEW YORK 12 April 1877 (in Italian).

LEMBERG 8 January 1878 (in Polish); revived 1933; Warsaw 1935.

SANTIAGO, CHILE 1883 (in Italian).

New version, reduced to 4 acts:

MILAN 10 January 1884, etc.

DRESDEN 31 January 1885 (German version by K. F. Niese).

MEXICO 13 November 1886 (in Italian).

Revivals:

MONTE CARLO 15 March 1906 (in French).

BERLIN 9 April 1907 (in French, by the Monte Carlo Opera) and 11 October 1913 (in German).

ZURICH Spring 1911 (in German).

PARIS, GAÎTÉ 2 June 1911 (in Italian).

MILAN 26 October 1912 (in Italian).

GRAZ 10 October 1913 (in German).

NEW YORK 23 December 1920 (in Italian).

PRAGUE April 1921 (in German) and 21 January 1931 (for the first time in Czech, translated by K. Kügler).

HELSINKI 14 January 1932 (in Finnish).

VIENNA 10 May 1932 (new German version by F. Werfel and L. Wallerstein).

LONDON, C.G. 1 June 1933 (in Italian) and S.'s W. 6 December 1938 (for the first time in English, translated by S. Austin).

STOCKHOLM 2 November 1933 (for the first time in Swedish).

BASLE 16 March 1934 (in German).

BUDAPEST 29 March 1934 (new Hungarian version by V. Lányi).

BRUSSELS 10 January 1936 (in French).

BERLIN 21 October 1936 (in German).

SOFIA 28 December 1936 (in Bulgarian).

MASSENET: *La Grand' Tante*

3 April. Paris, O.C.

Text by J. Adenis and C. Grandvallet. One act. Massenet's first opera; it had 17 performances in 1867, but was never revived.

OFFENBACH: *La Grande-Duchesse de Gérolstein*

12 April. Paris, Variétés

Text by H. Meilhac and Lud. Halévy. Three acts. One of Offenbach's greatest successes; by July, 1873 it was stated to have been given on 65 French and 117 foreign stages. Produced at:

VIENNA, W. 13 May 1867 (in German, translated by J. Hopp) and 25 May 1872 (in French). Graz 14 August 1867 (in German).

BRUSSELS 1 June 1867 (in French).

STOCKHOLM 4 September 1867 (in Swedish, translated by E. A. Wallmark).

NEW YORK 24 September 1867 (in French); 23 April 1868 (in English); and 12 January 1870 (in German). Offenbach's first great success in America. Salt Lake City 1 June 1869 (first opera there).

LONDON, C.G. 18 November 1867 (in English, translated by C. L. Kenney); in French St. J'.s 22 June 1868; last revived Daly's 29 April 1937, new English version by G. P. Robinson.

BERLIN, FR.W. 10 January 1868 (in German).

RIO DE JANEIRO 29 February 1868 (in Portuguese).

MILAN 4 September 1868 and Naples, T. Grégoire 1872 (in French).

CHRISTIANIA Autumn 1868 (in Norwegian).

MADRID 7 November 1868 (in Spanish, translated by R. Puente y Bragas).

DUBLIN 10 May 1869 (in English).

VALPARAISO 1869 (in French).

CAIRO December 1869 (in French).

CONSTANTINOPLE January 1870 (in French).

BARCELONA 21 May 1870 (in Catalan, adapted by I. Llaurador).

BUDAPEST 1 October 1870 (in German).

SYDNEY 29 January 1871 (in English).

MEXICO 16 March 1871 (in Spanish).

BASLE 20 November 1872 (in German).

LEMBERG 30 December 1872 (in Polish).

BUENOS AIRES 1873 (in French).

PRAGUE 11 June 1873 (in Czech, translated by E. Züngel).

Revived Leningrad 29 December 1922 (in Russian) new German translation by W. Mehring 1931.

GOUNOD: *Roméo et Juliette*

27 April. Paris, Th.L.

Text by J. Barbier and M. Carré (after Shakespeare). Five acts.

Apart from *Faust* Gounod's greatest success; given in Paris 322 times at the Th. L., since 20 January 1873 at the O.C., since 28 November 1888 at the O; the 500th performance was on 7 January 1898. Outside Paris given at:

LONDON, C.G. 11 July 1867 (in Italian, translated by G. Zaffira); C.G. 15 June 1889 (in French); and D.L. 5 April 1890 (in English); 100th performance at C.G. 29 July 1901.

DRESDEN 30 November 1867 (in German, translated by T. Gassmann).

NEW YORK 15 November 1867 (in Italian); 14 January 1881 (in English); and 8 December 1893 (in French).

BRUSSELS 18 November 1867 (in French).

MILAN 14 December 1867 (in Italian).

VIENNA 5 February 1868 (in German) and 23 March 1876 (in Italian).

STOCKHOLM 11 June 1868 (in Swedish, translated by E. A. Wallmark).

WARSAW April 1869 (in Italian).

PRAGUE 29 August 1869 (in Czech, translated by E. Züngel) and 11 September 1873 (in German)

BERLIN 25 November 1869 (in German).

MOSCOW 21 February 1870 (in Italian).

BUDAPEST 27 January 1872 (in Hungarian, translated by F. Ormai).

ST. PETERSBURG 8 February 1872 (in Italian) and 23 January 1891 (in Russian, translated by N. M. Spassky). Revived Leningrad 25 April 1920 and 16 March 1936 (in Russian).

MADRID 19 November 1873 (in Italian).

HELSINKI 31 January 1879 (in Finnish) and 23 January 1899 (in Italian).

MEXICO 19 December 1882 (in French) and 20 September 1890 (in Italian).

BUENOS AIRES 20 August 1887 (in Italian).

LISBON 18 December 1887 (in Italian).

COPENHAGEN 20 March 1888 (in Danish, translated by H. Drachmann).

LIVERPOOL 15 January 1890 (in English, translated by H. B. Farnie).

BUCHAREST 23 April 1891 (in Italian).

ZAGREB 5 May 1894 (in Croatian, translated by M. Pogačić).

HONOLULU 1895 (in Italian).

LJUBLJANA 1907 (in Slovenian).

JERUSALEM 14 April 1924 (in Hebrew, translated by A. Aschmann).

KAUNAS 11 February 1925 (in Lithuanian).

RIGA 26 April 1928 (in Lettish).

TALLINN 1928 (in Estonian, translated by S. Mamontov).

SOFIA 17 March 1933 (in Bulgarian).

Still given in France, Italy and other countries. The so far latest revival in London was at D.L. on 26 June 1918.

SULLIVAN: *Cox and Box*

11 May. London, Adelphi

Text by F. C. Burnand (from J. M. Morton's farce *Box and Cox*). One act.

The first performance was given by amateurs for the benefit of the widow and children of the late C. H. Bennett; the first public performance took place at the "Royal Gallery of Illustration", London, on 29 March 1869 on the same bill with *No Cards*, a piece by W. S. Gilbert(!). First given in New York on 13 August 1875, etc.

Revived London, Prince's 28 November 1921 and still in the "Gilbert-Sullivan" repertory (as

the only operetta the text of which is not by Gilbert).

(MOZART): *L'Oie du Caire*

6 June. Paris, F.P.

Original Italian text (*L'Oca del Cairo*) by G. B. Varesco, French version by V. Wilder. Two acts.

Mozart wrote this opera in 1783, but never finished it; the fragments (8 numbers of the first act) were published by André in 1855. For the Paris production they were, together with parts from another unfinished Mozart opera, *Lo Sposo deluso*, and from Mozart's additions to Bianchi's *La Villanella rapita* (see 1783), arranged by T. C. Constantin and adapted to a new French libretto by V. Wilder.

Previously, the fragments had been given in concert form at Frankfort in April 1860 (by the "Operngesangverein"), and subsequently at Magdeburg 3 February 1861, Leipzig 5 December 1861, Jena 5 February 1862, etc.

Wilder's French version was translated into German (by?) and produced at Berlin, Fr.W. 4 October 1867; Vienna, Ca. 15 April 1868; Leipzig 17 April 1868; and Königsberg 25 October 1872.

The Paris version was also given in London, D.L. 12 May 1870 (in Italian, translated by G. Zaffira, recitatives by Bottesini; the English version in the printed libretto by L. H. F. du Terreaux); Copenhagen January 1882 (in Danish).

In the 20th century the following revivals and arrangements are to be recorded:

L'Oie du Caire, in Wilder's French version, Paris, Tr. Lyr. 1 March 1918. *L'Oca del Cairo*, in a concert arrangement by R. Schulze-Reudnitz, Lucerne 1935; in a new stage version by V.Mortari, Salzburg 22 August 1936 (text revised by L. Cavicchioli) and Milan, Sc. 5 March 1940 (text revised by D. Valeri); finally, in a new adaptation by H. F. Redlich, London, Sadler's Wells 30 May 1940 (in Italian).

An attempt has also been made to adapt the musical fragments of both *L'Oca del Cairo* and *Lo Sposo deluso* to a German version of the libretto of the latter opera (which has been preserved: *Lo Sposo* deluso ossia *La Rivalità di tre Donne per un solo Amante*), text perhaps by L. da Ponte (see E. Anderson in *Music and Letters*, April 1937); Mozart's music, written in the same year as *L'Oca del Cairo*, consists of the overture, two airs, one quartet and one terzet. Produced as *Der betrogene Bräutigam*, text by A. Schremmer, music arranged by L. Kusche, Gotha 28 February 1929.

REINECKE: *König Manfred*

26 July. Wiesbaden

Text by F. Roeber. Five acts.

The most important of Reinecke's five operas. Leipzig 25 May 1868, etc.

Revived Leipzig 23 April 1885; also St. Petersburg 26 April 1887 (in Russian, at the Musical Dramatic Club).

LESCHETIZKY: *Die erste Falte*

9 October. Prague, G.

Text by S. H. Mosenthal. One act.

The only opera of the famous pianist.

Successful on German stages: Wiesbaden 14 December 1880; Mannheim 19 April 1882; Vienna 4 January 1883.

HERVÉ: *L'Œil crevé*

12 October. Paris, F.Dr.

Text by the composer (*folie musicale*). Three acts. Hervé's first great success.

Revived Paris, Ren. 24 September 1881 (H. Crémieux is mentioned as co-author in the 1881 edition); Variétés 18 April 1896.

In French also, New York 11 January 1869; Naples 15 June 1869; London, Globe 15 June 1872; Mexico 25 January 1874.

In German, Vienna, W. March 1868 (as *Der Pfeil im Auge*, translated by J. Hopp); Berlin, Fr. W. 22 May 1868 (as *Fleur de Noblesse*, translated by J. Stettenheim).

In English, London, Olympic 13 April 1868 (as *Hit or Miss*, translated by F. C. Burnand); another adaptation, by H. B. Farnie, was given at the O.C., London 21 October 1872.

COHEN: *Les Bleuets*

23 October. Paris, Th.L.

Text by E. Cormon and H. Trianon. Four acts.

Revived London, C.G. 3 July 1880 (in Italian, as *Estella*, translated by A. de Lauzières); Adelina Patti sung the name-part.

KASHPEROV: *Groza*

Гроза

(The Tempest)

11 November. St. Petersburg and Moscow

Text by A. N. Ostrovsky (founded on his play of the same title). Four acts.

The first performance took place both at St. Petersburg and Moscow the same night.

BLODEK: *V Studni*

(In the Well)

17 November. Prague, Cz.

Text by K. Sabina. One act.

Successful Czech comic opera. Revived at Prague 2 December 1883, 7 December 1924, and 3 October 1934.

In Croatian (translated by J. E. Tomić), Zagreb 31 October 1885.

In Slovenian, Ljubljana 1889.

In German (translated by F. Binder), Leipzig 29 October 1893; Vienna, W. September 1894 (previously given there in Czech at the Jos. Th. 14 April 1893); Berlin, Th.d.W. 4 March 1902.

In Bulgarian, Sofia 20 April 1912.

In Czech also New York 6 March 1920 (at the Jan Huss Neighborhood House).

(In this opera occurs an *Intermezzo sinfonico* 23 years before *Cavalleria rusticana*.)

BORODIN: *Bogatyri*

Богатыри

(Heroes)

18 November. Moscow

Text by V. A. Kruilov. *Opera-farce*. Five acts.

Borodin partly composed the music, partly compiled it from operas by Meyerbeer, Rossini,

Offenbach, Cavos, Serov, Verdi, etc. (22 numbers altogether); the score was arranged and orchestrated by I. N. Merten and F. F. Buechner. Apart from *Prince Igor* (see 1890), Borodin's only work for the stage, a musical satire on Serov's *Rogneda* (see 1865), and soon forgotten until 1922 when I. Glyebov discovered the score at a Leningrad library. It was revived at the Kamerny Theatre, Moscow 12 November 1936 with a new libretto by D. Byednuy, but after a few nights banned by the Soviet authorities. See I. Glyebov in *Revue Musicale* (December 1929 and February 1930) and P. Lamm and S. Popov in *Sovietskaya Muzyka* (January 1934.)

OFFENBACH: *Robinson Crusoé*

23 November. Paris, O.C.

Text by E. Cormon and H. Crémieux. Three acts.

Offenbach's second attempt at the O.C., like *Barkouf* (see 1860), a comparative failure (32 nights only).

In French also, Brussels 17 February 1868; New York 6 September 1875. The opera was (in a German version by E. Pasqué) to be produced at Darmstadt, but the performance was frustrated by the Franco-Prussian war. *Robinson Crusoé* was revived in German only about 60 years later: Leipzig 21 September 1930; Zurich 31 December 1930; Prague Spring 1931, etc. (as *Robinsonade*, new libretto by E. Walther, music arranged by G. Winkler). Also given at Ljubljana 1932 (in Slovenian). An English version by A. Sterne was broadcast from London on 29 April 1937.

BIZET: *La jolie Fille de Perth*

26 December. Paris, Th.L.

Text by J. H. Vernoy de Saint-Georges and J. Adenis (founded on Scott's novel). Four acts.

Brussels 14 April 1868, etc. Geneva 23 November 1885. Revived Paris, O.C. 3 November 1890.

In German (translated by J. Hopp), Weimar 8 April 1883; Vienna 5 May 1883, etc.

In Italian (translated by A. Zanardini), Parma 14 January 1885, etc.; Barcelona September 1890.

In Russian, Kiev 2 January 1887.

In English (translator not mentioned), Manchester 4 May 1917; London, D.L. 8 June 1917.

1868

BENDL: *Leila*

4 January. Prague, Cz.

Text by E. Krásnohorská (founded on E. Bulwer Lytton's novel). Five acts.

Bendl's first opera. Revived Prague 2 May 1891.

SALOMAN: *Karpatskaya Roza*
Карпатская Роза
(The Rose of the Carpathian Mountains)

7 January. Moscow

Original German text by W. Müller von Königswinter, translated into Russian by ? Five acts.

Also given at Stockholm on 23 May 1881 (in Swedish, as *Karpathernas Ros*, translated by F. Hedberg). (An opera, written by a Danish composer to German words, produced in Russian and in Swedish!)

AUBER: *Le premier Jour de Bonheur*

15 February. Paris, O.C.

Text by A. P. d'Ennery and E. Cormon. Three acts.

The last great success of the then 86 years old composer. Given at the O.C. 175 times until 1873.

In French also, Brussels 4 November 1868; Geneva 26 January 1869.

In Czech (translated by E. Züngel), Prague 11 September 1868.

In German (translated by E. Pasqué), Munich 27 September 1868; Leipzig 11 November 1868, etc.; Vienna, K.O. 7 November 1874; Brünn 14 November 1876; Berlin, Fr.W. 15 January 1881.

In Hungarian, Budapest 17 December 1868.

In Spanish (translated by L. Rodríguez), Madrid 1870.

BOITO: *Mefistofele*

5 March. Milan, Sc.

Text by the composer (after Gœthe's *Faust*). Prologue, 4 acts, and epilogue.

At its first appearance this famous opera was a
complete failure; given at the Scala three nights
only. The great success came eight years later,
when *Mefistofele* was revived, in an altered version, at Bologna 4 October 1875 and, with new
alterations, at Venice 13 May 1876. Subsequently
given at Turin 26 December 1876; Rome 4 April
1877, etc.

Outside Italy, produced at:

LONDON, H.M.'s 6 July 1880 (in Italian) and Marl-
borough Th. (Holloway) 7 September 1912 (in
English); last revived at C.G. 25 May 1926 (in
Italian).

BOSTON 16 November 1880 (in English, translated
by T. T. Barker).

NEW YORK 24 November 1880 (in Italian) and 28
February 1881 (in English).

PHILADELPHIA 27 November 1880; Chicago 10
December 1880, etc.

BARCELONA 1 December 1880 (in Italian).

WARSAW 19 December 1880 (in Italian) and 1882
(in Polish, translated by M. Radziszewski).

ST. PETERSBURG 24 January 1881 (in Italian) and 17
December 1886 (in Russian, translated by G. A.
Lishin).

PRAGUE 19 February 1881 (in German, translated
by K. F. Niese) and 9 December 1885 (in Czech,
translated by V. J. Novotný; revived 5 May
1936).

COLOGNE 24 February 1881; Hamburg 26 February 1881, etc. (in German).

LISBON 24 February 1881 (in Italian).

BUENOS AIRES 22 July 1881 (in Italian).

RIO DE JANEIRO 26 September 1881 (in Italian).

VIENNA 18 March 1882 (in German) and 5 May
1884 (in Italian).

BUDAPEST 24 April 1882 (in Hungarian, translated
by A. Radó).

BRUSSELS 19 January 1883 (in French, translated
by P. Milliet) and 10 May 1910 (in Italian).

MADRID 27 January 1883 (in Italian).

STOCKHOLM 26 February 1883 (in Swedish, translated by E. A. Wallmark).

DUBLIN 21 August 1884 (in English, translated by
T. Marzials).

COPENHAGEN 20 January 1885 (in Danish, translated by S. Bauditz).

MALTA 25 March 1886 (in Italian).

NANTES 23 April 1887 (in French, for the first time
in France).

MEXICO 14 November 1888 (in Italian).

BUCHAREST 17 November 1891 (in Italian) and
December 1921 (in Rumanian).

CHRISTIANIA 14 May 1893 (in Norwegian).

VALPARAISO August 1895 (in Italian).

HELSINKI 28 November 1898 (in Italian) and 2
February 1933 (in Finnish).

ZAGREB 13 April 1901 (in Croatian, translated by
F. Miler).

HAGUE January 1905 (in Italian).

BERLIN 5 April 1907 (in French, by the Monte
Carlo company).

PARIS, O. 9 May 1912 (in Italian) and Th.L. 25 December 1919 (in French).

LJUBLJANA 1922 (in Slovenian).

ZURICH June 1926 (for the first time in Switzerland).

RIGA 27 September 1929 (in Lettish).

An open-air performance at the Roman Theatre,
Orange, took place on 6 August 1905 (in Italian).

A. THOMAS: *Hamlet*

9 March. Paris, O.

Text by J. Barbier and M. Carré (after Shakespeare). Five acts.

Very successful in Paris; 100th performance 20
March 1874; 200th 21 February 1883; 300th 5
June 1899; latest revival 1 December 1933.

Outside Paris, given at:

LEIPZIG 1 April 1869 (in German, translated by
W. Langhans).

LONDON, C.G. 19 June 1870 (in Italian, translated
by A. de Lauzières) and 22 June 1898 (in
French); last revived there 3 October 1910.

BUDAPEST 19 March 1870 (in Hungarian, translated by G. Böhm).

BRUSSELS 26 December 1871 (in French).

PRAGUE 4 January 1872 (in German).

NEW YORK 22 March 1872 (in Italian) and 10 February 1892 (in French).

ALGIERS 8 October 1872 (in French).

ST. PETERSBURG 26 October 1872 (in Italian).

BERLIN 14 April 1873 (in German).

VIENNA 14 July 1873 (in German) and 24 March 1878 (in Italian).

GENEVA 2 March 1875 (in French).

VENICE, F. 26 February 1876 (in Italian).

BUENOS AIRES 6 September 1876 (in French) and 1 September 1887 (in Italian); revived 25 June 1937.

LAIBACH 1877 (in German).

LISBON 17 March 1881 (in Italian).

COPENHAGEN 20 November 1881 (in Danish, translated by H. P. Holst).

BARCELONA 9 April 1882 (in Italian).

MEXICO 1 April 1883 (in French).

RIO DE JANEIRO Summer 1886 (in Italian).

LEMBERG May 1904 (in Polish, translated by L. German).

AMSTERDAM January 1933 (in Italian).

This opera seems to be the first in which a saxophone was used in the orchestra.

LECOCQ: *Fleur-de-Thé*

11 April. Paris, Athénée

Text by H. C. Chivot and A. Duru. Three acts. Lecocq's first great success.

In French also, Brussels 1 July 1868; Rio de Janeiro 16 January 1869; New York 1 February 1869; Geneva 14 February 1869; Naples 30 March 1869; London, Ly. 12 June 1871; Mexico 4 February 1874; Santiago, Chile 1875.

In Spanish (translated by M. Pastorfido and F. Moreno Godino), Madrid 14 November 1868.

In German (translated by E. Dohm), Berlin, Fr.W. 13 January 1869; Vienna, W. 1 February 1869; Graz 28 January 1873, etc.

In Swedish (translated by E. A. Wallmark), Stockholm 17 May 1869.

In Norwegian, Christiania 1869.

In Danish (translated by A. L. C. de Coninck

and S. Neumann), Copenhagen 20 October 1870.

In Russian, Moscow 1872.

In English (translated by J. H. Jarvis), Newcastle 15 March 1875 and London, Criterion 9 October 1875; (as *The Pearl of Pekin*) New York 19 March 1888.

In Czech (translated by B. Peška), Prague 30 December 1875.

USIGLIO: *Le Educande di Sorrento*

1 May. Florence, T. Alfieri

Text by R. Berninzone. Three acts.

One of the few successful Italian comic operas of those years. Given in Italy sometimes as *La Figlia del Generale*.

In Italian also, Vienna, Ca. 7 August 1872; Malta 1875; Buenos Aires 25 November 1876; Barcelona 28 October 1882.

In Spanish (translated by Francisco Luis de Retes and Francisco Pérez Echevarría) Madrid, Z. 4 January 1872; Mexico August 1890.

In German (as *Das Pensionat von Sorrent*, translated by F. Falzari), Berlin, V.O. 18 February 1911.

SMETANA: *Dalibor*

16 May. Prague, Cz.

(Original German) text by J. Wenzig, translated into Czech by E. Špindler. Three acts.

Very successful in Bohemia; the 200th performance at Prague was on 12 May 1914, the 300th on 10 March 1924.

In Czech also, Vienna, Exhibition Th. 5 June 1892.

In German (translated by M. Kalbeck), Munich 28 November 1894; Vienna 4 October 1897; Berlin, Th.d.W. 12 September 1903, etc. Revived in German, Vienna 2 March 1924; Prague May 1930; Zurich October 1930; Vienna 26 February 1938 (new translation by L. Wallerstein); Coburg February 1940 and Berlin, O. 5 October 1940 (new translation by J. Kapp).

In Croatian (translated by A. Harambašić), Zagreb 16 November 1895.

In Slovenian, Ljubljana 1899.

In Russian, St. Petersburg 11 January 1900.

In Polish, Warsaw March 1902.

In Flemish, Antwerp 4 November 1902.

In Hungarian (translated by D. Vidor), Budapest 23 October 1909.

In Bulgarian, Sofia 15 September 1924.

WAGNER: *Die Meistersinger von Nürnberg*

21 June. Munich

Text by the composer. Three acts.

Libretto first published 1863; full score and vocal score (by K. Tausig) 1868. On Wagner's sources and for a *Meistersinger* bibliography, see H. Laue, *Die Operndichtung Lortzings* (1932), p.83. For earlier operas on the same subject, see 1840 (Lortzing's *Hans Sachs*).

Of all Wagner operas *Die Meistersinger* was the one which made its way most quietly and steadily, and without that note of sensation and hostility so characteristic of the earlier (and later) operas.

Produced at:

DRESDEN 21 January 1869; Dessau 29 January 1869; Carlsruhe 5 February 1869; Mannheim 5 March 1869; Weimar 28 November 1869; Hanover 26 February 1870; first given at Nuremberg 24 March 1874.

VIENNA 27 February 1870 (first new work at the Hof-Oper, opened 26 May 1869); Graz 7 March 1878.

BERLIN 1 April 1870 (400th performance 22 May 1928).

PRAGUE 26 April 1871 (in German) and 7 February 1894 (in Czech, translated by V. J. Novotný).

RIGA 4 January 1872 (in German) and 25 March 1925 (in Lettish, translated by R. Egle).

COPENHAGEN 23 March 1872 (in Danish, translated by A. Hertz).

ROTTERDAM 12 March 1879 (in German).

LONDON, D.L. 30 May 1882 (in German); C.G. 13 July 1889 (in Italian, translated by G. A. Mazzucato); and Garrick Th. 22 January 1897 (in English).

AMSTERDAM 16 March 1883 (in German) and 12 October 1900 (in Dutch).

BUDAPEST 8 September 1883 (in Hungarian, translated by A. Váradi).

BASLE 20 February 1885 (in German).

BRUSSELS 7 March 1885 (in French, translated by V. Wilder).

NEW YORK 4 January 1886 (in German) and 2 March 1892 (in Italian).

STOCKHOLM 2 April 1887 (in Swedish, translated by F. T. Hedberg).

MILAN 26 December 1889 (in Italian, translated by A. Zanardini); Turin 28 December 1892; Venice 26 December 1899; Rome 26 December 1901.

MADRID 3 March 1894 (in Italian).

POSEN 3 March 1896 (in German).

MANCHESTER 16 April 1896 (for the first time in English, translator not mentioned).

LYONS 30 December 1896 (in French, translated by A. Ernst); Marseilles 23 February 1904, etc.

PARIS, O. 10 November 1897 (in French) and Ch. É. 27 May 1914 (in German).

ST. PETERSBURG 15 March 1898 (in German) and December 1912 (in Russian); revived Leningrad 4 May 1932.

BUENOS AIRES 6 August 1898 (in Italian).

LISBON January 1902 (in Italian).

ANTWERP 16 January 1904 (in Flemish).

BARCELONA January 1905 (in Italian) and 8 November 1928 (in German); Catalan translation by J. Lleonart and A. Ribera published 1904; another by X. Viura and J. Pena published 1905.

RIO DE JANEIRO 3 August 1905 (in Italian).

WARSAW 22 October 1908 (in Polish, translated by A. Bandrowski).

MOSCOW 12 September 1909 (in Russian, translated by V. Kolomiitsev).

JOHANNESBURG 1913 (in English).

HELSINKI 17 November 1921 (in Finnish, translated by J. Finne).

MONTE CARLO February 1928 (in French).

ZAGREB 15 June 1929 (in Croatian).

MELBOURNE March 1933 (for the first time in Australia?).

BUCHAREST December 1934 (in Rumanian).

CINCINNATI 20 March 1936 (in America for the first time in English).

ADELBURG: *Zrinyi*

23 June. Budapest

Text by the composer (founded on T. Körner's drama). Five acts.

The first opera of the well-known violinist; mportant Hungarian national opera.

ŠEBOR: *Husitská Nevěsta*

(The Hussite Bride)

28 September. Prague, Cz.

Text by E. Rüffer. Five acts.

Šebor's most successful opera. Revived at Prague 30 April 1884 and 2 August 1891.

OFFENBACH: *L'Ile de Tulipatan*

30 September. Paris, B.P.

Text by H. C. Chivot and A. Duru. One act.

Brussels 20 December 1868, etc.

In German (translated by E. Pohl), Vienna, Ca. 5 May 1869; Berlin, Fr.W. 21 July 1869; Graz 25 August 1869.

In Swedish (translated by B. F. Schöldström), Stockholm 1871.

In Russian, Moscow 1871.

In English (adapted by F. C. Burnand), London, O.C. 12 July 1873.

In Italian, Modena, T. Aliprandi May 1873 (as *Kakatoa XXII, Duca dell'Isole di Tulipatan.*)

Revived Monte Carlo 26 November 1909 (in French). In German (as *Die glückliche Insel,* text by O. Blumenthal, music arranged by L. Schmidt), Berlin, D.O. 26 April 1917; Vienna, V.O. 8 June 1918.

OFFENBACH: *La Périchole*

6 October. Paris, Variétés

Text by H. Meilhac and Lud. Halévy. Two acts.

Brussels 5 December 1868, etc. In an enlarged 3-act version, Paris, Variétés 25 April 1874.

In French also, New York 4 January 1869; Rio de Janeiro Summer 1869; Algiers 1869; Buenos Aires 1870; London, Princess's 27 June 1870;

Naples 3 March 1871; Mexico 1 January 1874; Zagreb 2 April 1891.

In German (translated by R. Genée), Vienna, W. 9 January 1869 (the second version 25 April 1878); Prague 12 August 1869; (translated by L. Kalisch), Berlin, Fr.W. 6 April 1870; Graz 25 May 1871; New York 11 March 1874.

In Swedish (translated by R. A. Gustafson), Stockholm 6 February 1869.

In Russian, St. Petersburg 1870; Leningrad 13 October 1918 (translated by V. Kruilov) and 25 December 1933 (translated by P. K. Veisbrem and J. J. Sollertimsky); Moscow 14 July 1922 (translated by M. Galperin).

In Spanish (translated by M. Pastorfido), Madrid 4 September 1870.

In Polish (translated by J. Checiński), Warsaw 1874; Lemberg 29 December 1875.

In English (translated by F. Desprez), London, Royalty 30 January 1875; (translated by A. Murray) Alhambra 9 November 1878; Cape Town 1887.

In Italian, Milan 1876.

In Yiddish, New York 1 February 1887.

Frequently revived in many countries; London, King's Hall 17 January 1919 (in English); New York 21 December 1925 (in Russian, by the Moscow Art Theatre); Berlin, Kroll's 27 March 1931 (new German version by K. Kraus); Kaunas 9 April 1931 (in Lithuanian).

HOLSTEIN: *Der Haideschacht*

22 October. Dresden

Text by the composer (founded on a story by E. T. A. Hoffmann). Three acts.

Holstein's first and most successful opera. Munich 1 December 1871, etc.

In German also, Rotterdam 31 January 1874; Riga September 1875; Berlin, Louisenstadt Th. 2 August 1883; Zurich 30 November 1885.

Last revived Brunswick 29 May 1899; Elberfeld 25 March 1901; Berlin, Morwitz-Oper 19 June 1903.

(The opera had already been given privately, in concert form, at Leipzig in April 1867.)

HERVÉ: *Chilpéric*

24 October. Paris, F.Dr.

Text by the composer. Three acts.

In French also, New York 1 June 1869; London, Globe 3 June 1872; Buenos Aires 1873. Revived Paris, Variétés 1 February 1895 (in a new version, libretto altered by P. Ferrier).

In English (translated by R. Reece), London, Ly. 22 January 1870; New York 9 December 1874; Sydney 6 February 1875. Revived London, Coronet 9 March 1903 (new English version by A. M. Thompson and R. Mansell).

In German (translated by E. Jacobson and W. Mannstaedt), Berlin, Th. Unter den Linden 21 December 1895; Vienna, Ca. 28 November 1896, etc.

(At the beginning of 1869, during the successful run of *La Périchole* at the Variétés and of *Chilpéric* at the Folies-Dramatiques, a parody, called *Chilpérichole*, was produced at the Alcazar, Paris.)

1869

NAPRAVNIK: *Nizhegorodcy*
Нижегородцы
(The People of Nizhegorod)

8 January. St. Petersburg

Text by P. I. Kalashnikov. Five acts.

The first opera of Napravnik, who, from 1869 to 1915, was chief conductor at the Maryinski Theatre, St. Petersburg. Revived Moscow December 1884 and St. Petersburg 7 December 1888.

Also given in Czech (translated by J. Hrubý), Prague 5 November 1875.

STAUFFER: *Die Touristen* oder *Das romantische Abenteuer*

January. Lucerne

Text by the composer. Three acts.

One of the few early German-Swiss operas; revived on several stages; last given at St. Gall in 1887.

F. RICCI: *Une Folie à Rome*

30 January. Paris, F.P.

(Original Italian) text by the composer, French version by V. Wilder. Three acts.

Successful in Paris, running for 77 nights.

In French also, Antwerp 10 February 1870; Brussels 11 February 1870; Geneva 1870, etc.

In the original Italian, Florence, P. 2 February 1871.

(A. Heulhard, in 1870, devoted a special book to this opera.)

CHAIKOVSKY: *Voyevoda*
Воевода

11 February. Moscow

Text by the composer and A. N. Ostrovsky (founded on a play by Ostrovsky). Four acts.

Chaikovsky's first opera; given for five nights only. The composer destroyed the greater part of the music; only some fragments were extant until 1935, when a copy of the score was reported to have been discovered at a Moscow library.

KYUI: *William Ratcliff*
Вильям Ратклифъ

26 February. St. Petersburg

Text by A. N. Pleshcheev (founded on Heine's drama). Three acts.

Revived Moscow 28 December 1900.

OFFENBACH: *Vert-Vert*

10 March. Paris, O.C.

Text by H. Meilhac and C. Nuitter. Three acts.

Given at the O.C. 58 times.

In German, as *Kakadu* (translated by J. Hopp), Vienna, Ca. 3 February 1870; Berlin, Fr. W. 4 June 1870; Prague 6 June 1870; Graz 12 October 1871, etc.; New York 31 October 1870.

Revived Berlin, Fr. W. 9 November 1888.

In English (translated by H. Herman and R. Mansell), London, St. J.'s 2 May 1874.

New German version by K. Krauss published 1932.

MARCHETTI: *Ruy Blas*

3 April. Milan, Sc.

Text by C. d'Ormeville (from Victor Hugo's drama). Four acts.

Marchetti's chief work; given in Italy until after 1930.

Outside Italy, in Italian also, given at:

MALTA 1871.

LISBON 24 February 1872.

BUENOS AIRES 10 June 1872.

BARCELONA 28 August 1872.

MEXICO 23 October 1872.

CAIRO 11 February 1873.

SANTIAGO, CHILE 1873.

HAVANA 1873.

RIO DE JANEIRO 9 August 1873.

NEW YORK 14 October 1874.

SYDNEY November 1876.

ST. PETERSBURG 12 November 1877.

LONDON, H.M.'s 24 November 1877 (by amateurs at Albert Hall already 23 July 1875).

BERLIN, VICT. TH. 8 March 1882.

HELSINKI 30 December 1896.

MONTE CARLO 27 March 1919.

In Croatian (translated by J. E. Tomić), Zagreb 20 May 1875.

In Polish (translated by M. Radziszewski), Lemberg 14 December 1878.

In German (translated by K. F. Niese), Dresden 6 September 1879.

In Czech (translated by E. Züngel), Prague 1881.

In English (translated by W. Grist), Liverpool 4 February 1886.

VIARDOT: *Der letzte Zauberer*

8 April. Weimar

(Original French) text by I. S. Turgenev, German version by R. Pohl. Two acts.

Also given at Carlsruhe 28 January 1870; Riga 1871.

The only opera of the famous contralto which was performed in public. Previously it had been heard at Turgenev's villa at Baden-Baden, with piano accompaniment, in Spring 1868.

HERVÉ: *Le petit Faust*

29 April. Paris, F.Dr.

Text by H. Crémieux and A. Jaime. Three acts.

Hervé's most successful operetta, still given on French stages; the so far latest revival in Paris was at the Th. Porte St. Martin 19 December 1934.

In French also, Brussels 14 August 1869, etc.; New York 26 September 1870; Naples 2 April 1871; Mexico 8 January 1874; Buenos Aires 1884.

In Russian (translated by V. S. Kurochkin), St. Petersburg 1869.

In English (translated by H. B. Farnie), London, Ly. 18 April 1870; New York 29 August 1870.

In German (translated by R. Genée), Vienna, W. May 1870; Berlin, Woltersdorf Th. 10 July 1872, etc.

In Italian, Naples 6 May 1871.

In Swedish (translated by A. E. Hellgren), Stockholm 29 October 1883.

Spanish version by Antonio Carralón de Larrúa published 1869.

OFFENBACH: *La Princesse de Trébizonde*

31 July. Baden-Baden

Text by C. Nuitter and E. Tréfeu. Two acts.

Enlarged to 3 acts, Paris, B.P. 7 December 1869; Brussels 9 February 1870.

In French also, Hague March 1870; Naples 4 March 1871; Rio de Janeiro Summer 1871; Vienna, Ca. 1 July 1871; New York 10 September 1874; Mexico January 1876.

In English (translated by C. L. Kenney), London, Gaiety 16 April 1870; New York 11 September 1871.

In Spanish, Madrid Spring 1870.

In Danish (translated by E. Bøgh), Copenhagen 26 December 1870.

In Swedish (translated by C. G. W. Michal and A. Bosin), Stockholm 21 January 1871.

In German (translated by J. Hopp), Vienna, Ca. 18 March 1871; Prague 15 May 1871; Berlin, Fr.W. 30 June 1871; Graz 20 July 1871, etc. New

York 14 December 1882. Revived Berlin, D.O. 31 December 1932.

In Czech (translated by E. Züngel), Prague 9 June 1871.

In Rumanian (translated by G. Bengescu), Bucharest 1875.

In Portuguese, Rio de Janeiro 1883.

In Croatian (translated by G. Prejac), Zagreb 6 January 1907.

SEMET: *La petite Fadette*

11 September. Paris, O.C.

Text by M. Carré and G. Sand (founded on the latter's novel of the same title). Three acts.

Semet's best-known work; he had treated the same subject before, as a 2-act vaudeville, text by A. Bourgeois and C. Lafont, produced Paris, Variétés 20 April 1850.

In German (translated by N. Roda), Cologne 31 March 1882.

R. WAGNER: *Das Rheingold*

22 September. Munich

Text by the composer; the first part ("Vorabend") of Wagner's *Der Ring des Nibelungen*. One act (4 scenes).

The unsatisfactory dress rehearsal took place on 27 August.

For dates concerning the origin of the *Ring* and for productions of the whole cycle, see 1876.

Separately, *Das Rheingold* was performed at:

VIENNA 24 January 1878 (in German).

PRAGUE 19 December 1885 (in German) and 19 March 1915 (in Czech).

NEW YORK 4 January 1889 (in German) and 10 November 1924 (in English).

BUDAPEST 26 January 1889 (in Hungarian, translated by A. Radó).

RIGA 26 October 1890 (in German).

ROTTERDAM 27 October 1890 (in German).

POSEN 10 March 1893 (in German).

ZURICH 20 March 1894 (in German).

BRUSSELS 31 October 1898 (in French, translated by A. Ernst; in German earlier; see the *Ring*, 1876).

STOCKHOLM 26 October 1901 (in Swedish, translated by S. Elmblad).

NICE 19 March 1902 (for the first time in France; in French).

LYONS 1 April 1903 (in French).

MILAN, SC. 10 December 1903 (in Italian, translated by A. Zanardini).

ST. PETERSBURG 9 January 1906 (in Russian; in German earlier; see the *Ring*, 1876).

LEMBERG 13 February 1908 (in Polish, translated by A. Bandrowski).

COPENHAGEN 2 May 1908 (in Danish, translated by J. Lehmann).

PARIS, O. 17 November 1909 (in French; fragments had been given there on 6 May 1893 already, and the opera had been heard in full at a Lamoureux concert on 13 January 1901).

ANTWERP 19 February 1910 (in Flemish, translated by W. Kloos).

MADRID March 1910 (in Italian).

BUENOS AIRES 11 August 1910 (in Italian).

JOHANNESBURG 1913 (in English).

RIO DE JANEIRO September 1922 (in German).

HELSINKI 13 March 1930 (in Finnish).

ZAGREB 11 March 1935 (in Croatian).

Catalan translation by S. Vilaregut published 1902; another by J. Zanné and J. Pena published 1910.

HEISE: *Paschaens Datter*
(The Pasha's Daughter)

30 September. Copenhagen

Text by H. Hertz. Four acts.

The first opera of the Danish composer.

PETRELLA: *I Promessi Sposi*

2 October. Lecco

Text by A. Ghislanzoni (founded on Manzoni's novel). Four acts.

First performed at Lecco, the small town where the action of Manzoni's novel takes place. Milan October 1872; Naples, S.C. April 1873, etc.; Buenos Aires 25 December 1878. Successful in Italy; last revived Genoa 8 March 1913.

OFFENBACH: *Les Brigands*
10 December. Paris, Variétés

Text by H. Meilhac and Lud. Halévy. Three acts.
Successful in Paris; outside France given at:

VIENNA, W. 13 March 1870 (in German, translated by E. Dohm).

ANTWERP 29 March 1870 (in French).

PRAGUE 30 June 1870 (in Czech, translated by E. Züngel).

STOCKHOLM 27 August 1870 (in Swedish, translated by E. A. Wallmark).

BERLIN, FR.W. 24 September 1870 (in German).

MADRID October 1870 (in Spanish, translated by M. Pina).

BUDAPEST 13 October 1870 (in German).

NEW YORK 14 November 1870 (in French); 2 October 1873 (in German); and 9 May 1889 (in English, as *The Brigands*, translated by W. S. Gilbert; this version was given at Plymouth 2 September 1889 and at the Avenue Th., London 16 September 1889).

GRAZ 26 November 1870 (in German).

LONDON, GLOBE TH. 22 April 1871 (in English, as *Falsacappa*, translated by H. S. Leigh) and Ly. 1 July 1871 (in French).

MILAN 11 March 1872 (in Italian, translated by E. Golisciani).

BUENOS AIRES 1873 (in French).

WARSAW 1873 (in Polish, translated by J. Checiński).

NAPLES, T. FILARMONICO 6 January 1874.

MEXICO 21 January 1874 (in French).

RIO DE JANEIRO 1875 (in French).

CHRISTIANIA 2 December 1902 (in Norwegian).

Another Italian translation by L. E. Tettoni and G. Gargano performed at Ancona 1874 and Genoa 1875.

Still given in many countries; some of the latest revivals were at Paris, Gaîté Lyrique 10 December 1921; O.C. 15 June 1931; Montreal December 1923 (in French); Stockholm 30 August 1928 (in Swedish); Carlsruhe 9 February 1930 (new German version by E. Noether and O. F. Schuh); Stendal 2 April 1930 and Berlin, D.O. 29 May 1932 (new German version by K. Kraus); Budapest 1 April 1933 (in Hungarian, translated by Z.

Harsányi); Helsinki 22 November 1933 (in Finnish); Monte Carlo 27 December 1934 (in French).

MONIUSZKO: *Paria*
11 December. Warsaw

Text by J. Checiński (founded on C. Delavigne's tragedy). Three acts.

Successful in Poland; given at Warsaw until 1887.

AUBER: *Rêve d'Amour*
20 December. Paris, O.C.

Text by A. P. d'Ennery and E. Cormon. Three acts.

Auber's 46th and last (unsuccessful) opera. (Auber was then 88 years old; his first opera had been produced in 1805.)

CAMPANA: *Esmeralda*
30 December. St. Petersburg

Text by G. T. Cimino (founded on Victor Hugo's *Notre-Dame de Paris*). Four acts.

Written for Adelina Patti.

In Italian also, London, C.G. 14 June 1870; Homburg (near Frankfort) 29 August 1871; Trieste January 1874; Mexico 24 September 1879. Revived Florence 10 November 1890.

1870

UDBYE: *Junkeren og Flubergvaesen*
7 January. Christiania

Text by H. Ø. Blom. One act.

This operetta was the first Norwegian musical work for the stage since Thrane's *Fjeldeventyret* (see 1850).

PEREIRA: *Eurico*
23 February. Lisbon, S.C.

(Italian) text by P. de Lima (founded on the Portuguese novel *Eurico o Presbytero*, by A. Herculano). Four acts.

Oporto 17 January 1874 (reduced to 3 acts); Rio de Janeiro 1878.

GOMES: *Il Guarany*

19 March. Milan, Sc.

Text by A. Scalvini (founded on a novel by José de Alencar), revised by C. d'Ormeville. Four acts.

Gomes's most successful work and the most outstanding opera ever written by a Brazilian composer. Very popular and still being given in Brazil and Italy (Milan, T.L. 21 October 1936; Naples, S.C. January 1937).

First produced at:

RIO DE JANEIRO 2 December 1870.
LONDON, C.G. 13 July 1872.
BUENOS AIRES 27 June 1874.
BARCELONA 7 March 1876.
MONTEVIDEO 1876.
HAVANA 1878.
ST. PETERSBURG 12 February 1879.
MALTA 21 October 1879.
NICE 1 March 1880.
LISBON 31 March 1880.
MEXICO December 1883.
SAN FRANCISCO 1884.
NEW YORK 3 November 1884.

In Croatian (translated by J. E. Tomić), Zagreb 21 April 1883.

R. WAGNER: *Die Walküre*

26 June. Munich

Text by the composer. The second part ("Erster Tag") of Wagner's *Ring des Nibelungen*. Three acts.

As a single opera, *Die Walküre* may be called the most popular part of the whole cycle; in most towns and countries it was produced much earlier than the other parts. Apart from the cyclic performances (see 1876), given at:

VIENNA 5 March 1877 (in German); Schwerin 7 January 1878; Hamburg 30 March 1878, etc.
NEW YORK 2 April 1877 (in German).
ROTTERDAM 17 April 1878 (in German).
STRASBOURG 23 December 1883 (in German).
BERLIN 7 April 1884 (in German).
PRAGUE 20 December 1885 (in German) and 14 February 1916 (in Czech).
ZURICH 27 January 1886 (in German).

BRUSSELS 9 March 1887 (in French, translated by V. Wilder).
BUDAPEST 27 January 1889 (in Hungarian, translated by G. Csiky).
RIGA 25 October 1889 (in German) and 13 October 1926 (in Lettish, translated by A. Anderson).
GHENT 23 March 1890 (in German).
COPENHAGEN 7 March 1891 (in Danish, translated by K. Gjellerup).
MEXICO 14 April 1891 (in English!).
TURIN 22 December 1891 (in Italian, translated by A. Zanardini); Milan 27 December 1893, etc.
GENEVA 10 March 1893 (in French).
PARIS, O. 12 May 1893 (in French); Lyons 4 January 1894; Marseilles 9 April 1897, etc.
AMSTERDAM 24 November 1894 (in German) and 13 April 1897 (in Dutch).
LONDON, C.G. 16 October 1895 (in English, translated by H. and F. Corder) and 13 June 1896 (in French!).
STOCKHOLM 7 November 1895 (in Swedish, translated by O. Bensow).
ZAGREB 16 April 1898 (in Croatian, translated by F. Miler).
BARCELONA 25 January 1899 (in Italian); Catalan translation by X. Viura and A. Ribera published 1903; another by J. Pena and J. Zanné published 1910; produced in Catalan, Barcelona January 1912.
MADRID 29 January 1899 (in Italian).
BUENOS AIRES 10 May 1899 (in Italian).
ST. PETERSBURG 7 December 1900 (in Russian, translated by G. Tyumenev).
CAIRO 1901 (in French).
WARSAW 31 December 1901 (the first act only, in concert form; Polish version by T. Mianowski); stage production of the whole opera, Cracow August 1903 (Polish version by A. Bandrowski); there are two more printed Polish translations, by M. Radziszewski and by A. Bednarski, both 1903).
MOSCOW 24 February 1902 (in Russian, translated by A. K. Abramova) and 20 March 1902 (in German); revived Moscow, Bolshoi Th. 21 November 1940.
REVAL (TALLINN) 1902 (in German).

ANTWERP 11 February 1905 (in Flemish).

HELSINKI 3 April 1905 (in German) and 30 September 1920 (in Finnish, translated by J. Finne).

MELBOURNE 1907 (in German).

LISBON 1909 (in Italian).

JOHANNESBURG March 1912 (in English).

RIO DE JANEIRO September 1913 (in Italian) and September 1922 (in German).

OSLO 24 August 1920 (in German).

BUCHAREST 8 November 1923 (in Rumanian).

LJUBLJANA 17 November 1929 (in Slovenian).

BELGRADE 17 May 1938 (in German, by the Frankfurt Opera Company).

FLOTOW: *L'Ombre*

7 July. Paris, O.C.

Text by J. H. Vernoy de Saint Georges. Three acts.

Flotow's last great success; revived in Paris, O. Populaire 30 April 1887 and 20 April 1900; O.C. 4 June 1888; and Galerie Vivienne 25 October 1898.

Outside Paris, given at:

BRUSSELS 19 October 1870 (in French).

GENEVA 31 March 1871 (in French).

ALGIERS 1871 (in French).

VIENNA, W. 10 November 1871 (in German, translated by R. Genée).

BUDAPEST 18 November 1871 (in Hungarian, translated by F. Ormai).

GENOA November 1871 (in Italian, translated by A. de Lauzières); Turin 6 April 1872; Naples, T. Sannazaro 8 December 1815, etc.

CASSEL 7 February 1872 (in German).

HAGUE March 1872 (in French).

BERLIN 22 March ·1873 (in Italian, privately at court); publicly Sch. 27 February 1875 (in German).

MADRID October 1873 (in Spanish).

NEW YORK 9 April 1875 (in Italian).

LONDON, H.M.'s 12 January 1878 (in English, translated by G. A. A'Beckett).

BASLE 16 July 1883 (in French).

Revived in Italy, Rome 7 September 1892; Pavia 10 June 1898; Milan 16 April 1900 and 26

December 1933; revived in Germany both at Hamburg and Schwerin on 15 October 1933 (new German version by H. and S. Scheffer).

DOPPLER: *Judith*

30 December. Vienna, O.

Text by S. H. Mosenthal. Four acts.

The only German opera of the Hungarian composer.

First original production of a new work at the Vienna Hof-Oper (inaugurated 25 May 1869, with a performance of *Don Giovanni*). The old Kärntnertor Theatre was officially closed 17 April 1870, but used for another five years as a house for lighter operas (finally closed 1 September 1875, and then pulled down).

1871

BOTTESINI: *Ali Baba*

18 January. London, Ly.

Text by E. Taddei. Four acts.

The famous double-bass virtuoso wrote this opera for the "Opera Buffa", newly established at the Lyceum on 3 May 1869. Revived in London, Garrick Th. 26 July 1924 (as a puppet opera, by the Teatro dei Piccoli).

J. STRAUSS: *Indigo und die vierzig Räuber*

10 February. Vienna, W.

Text by M. Steiner. Three acts.

Strauss's first operetta; popular on German stages. Graz 11 May 1871; Berlin, Vict. Th. 1 September 1871 (text altered by E. Dohm), etc.

In German also, New York 7 April 1875; Laibach 1877; Brünn 18 February 1878; Prague 13 October 1878; Zurich 15 February 1881, etc.

In French (as *Reine Indigo*, adapted by A. Jaime and V. Wilder), Paris, Ren. 27 April 1875; Brussels 24 June 1876; New York 14 December 1877; Mexico 5 February 1878.

In Russian, St. Petersburg 1875.

In Italian, Naples 20 October 1875; Malta 1890.

In Polish, Lemberg 21 March 1876.

In Spanish (translated by M. Pina), Madrid 1877; (translated by A. Chavero) Mexico 20 December 1878 (as *Fantasca*).

In English (translated by F. C. Burnand), London, Alhambra 24 September 1877; (translated by M. Freeman and E. Smith) New York 25 August 1891.

The operetta was revived in several different versions: Vienna 9 October 1877 (as *Königin Indigo*, re-adapted from the French by J. Braun); Vienna 15 June 1906 (as *Tausend und eine Nacht*, music revised by E. Reiter, text re-written by O. Stein and C. Lindau; this version was also given at Graz 29 October 1906; Prague December 1907 and (in Rumanian) Bucharest 25 February 1908; Breslau 25 October 1925 (in the original form); London, Rudolf Steiner Hall 30 January 1936 (as *1001 Nights*, translated by A. Turner); Nuremberg 30 August 1936 (as *Eine Nacht am Bosporus*, new libretto, by G. Heidrich, music arranged by E. Schliepe).

CAGNONI: *Papà Martin*

4 March. Genoa, T. Nazionale

Text by A. Ghislanzoni. Three acts.

Very successful in Italy; frequently revived, last at Novara in November 1933.

In Italian also, Barcelona 22 October 1882; Buenos Aires November 1883; Malta 1887.

In English (as *The Porter of Havre*, translated by J. Oxenford), London, Princess's 15 September 1875.

ARRIETA: *Marina*

16 March. Madrid, T.R.

Text by M. Ramos Carrión (originally a 2-act zarzuela, text by F. Camprodón, produced at the T. del Circo on 21 September 1855, now transformed into a grand opera and enlarged to 3 acts).

First opera ever sung in Spanish at the Madrid Court Theatre. Given at Havana Carnival 1872; Mexico 4 January 1879 and revived 7 September 1919.

In Spanish also, New York 20 December 1916; revived at Buenos Aires 10 November 1934.

In Italian (as *L'Orfana di Lloret*), Naples 31 July 1879.

(SEROV): *Vrazhya Sila*
Вражья Сила
(The Power of Evil)

1 May. St. Petersburg

Text by A. N. Ostrovsky, P. I. Kalashnikov and N. F. Zhokhov (founded on Ostrovsky's play, *Don't live as you'd like to*). Five acts.

The opera was completed by N. T. Solovyev and produced three months after Serov's death (d. 1 February 1871). Moscow 15 December 1872, etc. Very successful in Russia; revived St. Petersburg 26 September 1893; Moscow 7 October 1902; Petrograd December 1915.

BRAGA: *Reginella*

16 September. Lecco

Text by A. Ghislanzoni. Prologue and 3 acts.

The most successful of Braga's operas. Milan 31 October 1872, etc.

VERDI: *Aida*

24 December. Cairo

Text by A. Ghislanzoni (founded on a scenario by the egyptologist, F. A. F. Mariette, which was finished by C. Du Locle. Verdi himself had a rather important share in the libretto; see E. Istel in *The Musical Quarterly*, Vol. III [1917], p. 34). Four acts.

Written for the celebration of the opening of the Suez Canal. Most successful in Italy and all over the world. There was an open-air production at the Pyramids on 3 March 1912.

Given at:

MILAN, SC. 8 February 1872, etc.; Naples, Sc. 31 March 1873, Trieste 4 October 1873 (in Italian).

BUENOS AIRES 4 October 1873 (in Italian).

NEW YORK 26 November 1873 (in Italian); 9 March 1881 (in English); 29 April 1881 (in French); and 12 November 1886 (in German).

BERLIN 20 April 1874 (in German, translated by J. A. Schanz).

VIENNA 29 April 1874 (in German) and 19 June 1875 (in Italian).

MADRID 12 December 1874 (in Italian).

BUDAPEST 10 April 1875 (in Hungarian, translated by F. Ormai).

WARSAW 23 November 1875 (in Polish, translated by M. Radziszewski).

ST. PETERSBURG 1 December 1875 (in Italian) and 13 April 1877 (in Russian).

PRAGUE 11 December 1875 (in German) and 15 February 1884 (in Czech, translated by V. J. Novotný).

PARIS, TH.I. 22 April 1876 (in Italian); in French, Th.I. 1 August 1878 and O. 22 March 1880.

LONDON, C.G. 22 June 1876 (in Italian) and H.M.'s 19 February 1880 (in English, translated by H. Hersee); 100th performance at C.G. 29 July 1912.

KIEV 1876; Khasan Spring 1878; Moscow 31 August 1879, etc. (in Russian, translated by G. A. Lishin).

RIO DE JANEIRO 2 October 1876 (in Italian).

LEMBERG 26 October 1876 (in Polish).

BUCHAREST November 1876 (in Italian) and September 1920 (in Rumanian).

BRUSSELS 15 January 1877 (for the first time in French, translated by C. Nuitter and C. Du Locle).

TIFLIS 18 January 1877 (in Italian).

MARSEILLES 31 January 1877 (in French).

HAVANA 1877 (in Italian).

MEXICO 1 September 1877 (in Italian).

MALTA 15 October 1877 (in Italian).

LISBON 6 February 1878 (in Italian).

MONTEVIDEO 1879 (in Italian).

STOCKHOLM 16 February 1880 (in Swedish, translated by H. Sandberg).

LAIBACH (LJUBLJANA) 1880 (in German) and 1898 (in Slovenian).

ZAGREB 1 October 1881 (in Croatian, translated by J. E. Tomić).

SANTIAGO, CHILE October 1881 (in Italian).

GENEVA 15 December 1881 (in French).

RIGA 21 January 1882 (in German) and 9 September 1922 (in Lettish).

ATHENS June 1882 (in Italian).

ZURICH 5 March 1883 (in German).

COPENHAGEN 4 October 1885 (in Danish, translated by A. Zinck).

CONSTANTINOPLE 1 December 1885 (in Italian).

ROTTERDAM 1886 (in German).

REVAL (TALLINN) 1890 (in German) and 1922 (in Estonian).

HELSINKI 17 September 1896 (in Italian) and 17 April 1916 (in Finnish, translated by T. Muroma).

MELBOURNE 1 June 1901 (in English).

AMSTERDAM 19 December 1903 (in Dutch).

CHRISTIANIA 6 November 1909 (in Norwegian).

JOHANNESBURG March 1912 (in English).

SOFIA 19 May 1914 (in Bulgarian; translated by V. Shak; already published 1896).

SHANGHAI 1918 (in Russian).

YOKOHAMA Autumn 1919 (in Italian).

TEL-AVIV 20 November 1924 (in Hebrew, translated by A. Schlonsky).

KAUNAS 10 November 1927 (in Lithuanian).

SULLIVAN: *Thespis;* or, *The Gods Grown Old*

26 December. London, Gaiety

Text by W. S. Gilbert (*An entirely original grotesque opera*). Two acts.

First association between Gilbert and Sullivan. Of the music only one song was published in 1872.

1872

OFFENBACH: *Fantasio*

18 January. Paris, O.C.

Text by P. de Musset (founded on his brother Alfred de Musset's comedy of the same title). Three acts.

In German (translated by E. Mautner and R. Genée), Vienna, W. 21 February 1872; Graz 17 October 1872; Prague 24 October 1872; Berlin Fr.W. 19 August 1873, etc.

Revived Magdeburg June 1927 (as *Der Narr der Prinzessin*, new version by F. Gessner and E. Fischer).

HOLSTEIN: *Der Erbe von Morley*

23 January. Leipzig

Text by the composer (originally *Des Bruders Heimkehr* oder *Der Erbe von Morley*). Three acts.

Successful in Germany; Weimar 8 April 1874, etc. In German also, Rotterdam 1875.

Revived Frankfort 25 January 1895; Brunswick 15 October 1899.

MONIUSZKO: *Beata*

2 February. Warsaw

Text by J. Checiński. One act.

The last opera of the Polish composer.

(DARGOMUIZHSKY): *Kamyeny Gost*
Каменный Гость
(The Stone Guest)

28 February. St. Petersburg

Text: Pushkin's dramatic poem (1830) without alterations. Three acts.

This Russian opera on the *Don Juan* subject was performed three years after Dargomuizhsky's death; the work was orchestrated by Rimsky-Korsakov, the overture was written by Kyui.

Revived Moscow 1 January 1907; Petrograd 14 December 1915, etc.

In Russian also, Salzburg 7 August 1928.

In Czech, Prague February 1935, by the Czech Artists' Club (Umelecká Beseda).

LECOCQ: *Les cent Vierges*

16 March. Brussels, F.P.

Text by H. C. Chivot, A. Duru, and Clairville. Three acts.

The first of a series of very successful operettas written by Lecocq for Brussels. Produced there at the Th. des Fantaisies-Parisiennes; subsequently given at Paris, Variétés 13 May 1872, and in many other countries, viz.:

ST. PETERSBURG October 1872 (in French) and 1873 (in Russian, translated by G. Valyano).

MADRID November 1872 (in Spanish, translated by M. Pastorfido and A. Opiso).

BERLIN, FR. W. 5 December 1872 (in German).

NEW YORK 23 December 1872 (in French); 17 July 1876 (in English); 29 October 1886 (in German).

VIENNA, CA. 15 March 1873 (in German).

LONDON, ST. J.'s 21 June 1873 (in French) and Gaiety 14 September 1874 (in English, as *The Island of Bachelors*, adapted by R. Reece).

STOCKHOLM 1873 (in Swedish, translated by C. G. W. Michal).

BUENOS AIRES 1873 (in French).

MEXICO 7 January 1874 (in French).

MILAN 11 April 1874 (in French).

BRIGHTON 17 October 1874 (in English, translated by J. Grantham).

LEMBERG 15 July 1880 (in Polish).

BUDAPEST 5 January 1884 (in German).

Czech translation by J. J. Stankovský published 1874; Italian translation by A. Boito published 1877.

BRUCH: *Hermione*

21 March. Berlin, O.

Text by E. Hopffer (founded on Shakespeare's *A Winter's Tale*). Four acts.

Cologne 12 December 1872; Dresden 24 January 1873, etc. Given on German stages until about 1900.

VASSEUR: *La Timbale d'Argent*

9 April. Paris, B.P.

Text by A. Jaime and J. Noriac. Three acts.

The first and most successful of Vasseur's 30 operettas. The 300th performance in Paris was on 11 January 1874.

In French also given at Brussels 1 August 1872, etc. Buenos Aires 1873; New York 24 August 1874; Naples, T. Filarmonico 1875; Mexico January 1876.

In German, Vienna, W. 16 November 1872.

In Russian, St. Petersburg 1874.

In Italian, Bergamo 1874, etc.

Revived Paris, F. Dr. 11 January 1897.

PIERSON: *Contarini* oder *Die Verschwörung zu Padua*

16 April. Hamburg

Text by M. E. Lindau. Five acts.

Pierson's last opera (written as early as 1853).

Revived Dessau 24 April 1883 (as *Fenice*; this is not a different work as stated in Riemann's dictionary).

PALADILHE: *Le Passant*

24 April. Paris, O.C.

Text by F. Coppée. One act.

Paladilhe's first opera; unsuccessful, given in Paris for three nights only.

In French also, Brussels 12 March 1874.

In Hungarian, Budapest 17 February 1873.

Revived St. Petersburg, March 1895 (privately); Toulouse December 1905; Weimer 20 October 1907 (in German).

A. FOERSTER: *Gorenjski Slavček* (Nightingale of Carniola)

27 April. Ljubljana

Text by L. Pesjakova. (*Lirična Opereta*). Two acts.

One of the earliest Slovenian operas. Very successful at Ljubljana where it was revived in a new version (text revised by E. Züngel) in 1896 and again 30 November 1922 and (with a new libretto by J. Vidmar) 23 November 1937 (music altered and enlarged by M. Polič, *quasi* as a new opera based on the tunes of the original work).

HŘIMALY: *Zakletý Princ* (The Enchanted Prince)

13 May. Prague, Cz.

Text by J. Böhm. Three acts.

Popular on Czech stages.

In Croatian (translated by J. E. Tomić), Zagreb 17 January 1885.

Last revived at Prague 6 December 1933.

BIZET: *Djamileh*

22 May. Paris, O.C.

Text by L. Gallet (founded on A. de Musset's *Namouna*). One act.

When first produced in Paris given for 11 nights only, and revived there as late as 27 October 1938. Outside France given at:

STOCKHOLM 25 February 1889 (in Swedish, translated by E. G. Lundquist).

ROME 28 October 1890 (in Italian, translated by V. Valle).

DUBLIN 10 September 1892 (in English, translated by J. Bennett).

PRAGUE 17 September 1892 (in Czech, translated by V. J. Novotný) and 1915 (in German).

MANCHESTER 22 September 1892 (in English, translated by J. Bennett).

BERLIN 1 October 1892 (in German, translated by L. Hartmann).

LONDON, C.G. 13 June 1893 (in French).

ST. PETERSBURG 11 December 1893 (in Russian, translated by N. M. Spassky).

BUDAPEST 6 April 1895 (in Hungarian, translated by E. Abrányi).

RIGA 2 April 1897 (in German).

VIENNA 22 January 1898 (in German).

ZAGREB 13 May 1902 (in Croatian, translated by M. Nehajev).

BASLE 13 March 1904 (in German).

BARCELONA April 1905 (in Spanish).

COPENHAGEN 9 September 1905 (in Danish, translated by N. Lützhøft).

BELGRADE 1919 (in Serbian).

Revived London, C.G. 18 December 1919 (in English); Berlin, D.O. 15 September 1927 (in German); Brussels, 15 March 1933 (in French); Vienna 9 February 1938 (in German); Paris, O.C. 27 October 1938 (for the first time there since 1872). Apparently not yet produced in America.

PONIATOWSKI: *Gelmina*

4 June. London, C.G.

(Italian) text by F. Rizzelli. Three acts.

Poniatowski's last opera; written for Adelina Patti.

SAINT-SAËNS: *La Princesse Jaune*

12 June. Paris, O.C.

Text by L. Gallet. One act.

Saint-Saëns's first opera.

Revived Angers 7 February 1885; Paris, O.C. 9 November 1906 and 11 October 1935.

In German (translated by A. von Loën), Stuttgart January 1880 (private performance at court).

This little work set the fashion for Japanese subjects in opera.

MASSENET: *Don César de Bazan*

30 November. Paris, O.C.

Text by A. P. d'Ennery and J. Chantepie (founded on the play of the same title by A. P. d'Ennery and P. E. Pinel Dumanoir, 1844). Three acts.

Massenet's second opera.

In German, Vienna, K.O. 4 October 1874.

In Swedish (translated by E. A. Wallmark), Stockholm 1879.

In Portuguese, Lisbon April 1907.

Revived in a new version: Geneva 20 January 1888; Antwerp 15 January 1889; Lyons 22 March 1890; Nice 15 March 1895; Brussels 16 November 1896; Paris, Tr. L. 3 May 1912; Hague February 1925.

LECOCQ: *La Fille de Madame Angot*

4 December. Brussels, Alcazar

Text by Clairville, P. Siraudin, and V. Koning (founded on a vaudeville by A. F. Eve Maillot, *Madame Angot, ou La Poissarde parvenue*, 1796). Three acts.

Lecocq's most popular work and one of the most successful operettas of the post-Offenbach period; given at Brussels *c.*500 nights running.

Outside Brussels given at:

PARIS, F.DR. 21 February 1873 (500th performance 27 December 1874).

LONDON, ST. J.'s 17 May 1873 (in French) and Philharmonic 4 October 1873 (in English, translated by H. J. Byron); there are numerous other English versions[1]; Edinburgh 22 June 1874 (in English).

STOCKHOLM 1873 (in Swedish, translated by L. Strindberg).

ALEXANDRIA 1873 (in French).

AMSTERDAM 1873 (in French).

NEW YORK 25 August 1873 (in French); 29 September 1873 (in English); and 17 April 1874 (in German).

TURIN 1 October 1873 (in French).

GENEVA 30 October 1873 (in French).

BERLIN, FR.W. 20 November 1873 (in German, translated by E. Dohm).

MADRID, Z. 6 December 1873 (in Spanish, translated by R. Puente y Brañas).

VIENNA, CA. 2 January 1874 (in German).

MEXICO 4 January 1874 (in French).

ALGIERS February 1874 (in French).

PRAGUE 21 February 1874 (in German) and 4 February 1875 (in Czech, translated by J. Böhm).

RIGA 3 April 1874 (in German) and 20 December 1927 (in Lettish).

MOSCOW 1874 (in Russian, translated by V. S. Kurochkin).

MILAN, T.D.V. 25 July 1874 (in Italian, translated by G. B.); Naples T.N. 1874.

COPENHAGEN 18 September 1874 (in Danish, adapted by R. Schrøder).

LEMBERG 18 September 1874 (in Polish, translated by J. Checiński and F. Szober).

BUDAPEST 2 December 1875 (in Hungarian, translated by L. Evva).

SYDNEY Autumn 1877 (in English).

MALTA 1879 (in Italian).

ZAGREB 5 November 1881 (in Croatian, translated by I. Orešković).

SARAJEVO 1883 (in German).

CAPE TOWN 1887 (in English).

HELSINKI Summer 1899 (in German).

Some notable revivals:

PARIS, O.C. 16 February 1919 (for the first time at that theatre).

[1] See W. D. Adams, *A Dictionary of the Drama*, p.515. For other French works on the same subject see A. Dupont, *Répertoire Dramatique Belge*, Vol. I, p.147.

LONDON, D.L. 2 July 1919 (new English version by D. C. Calthrop and G. Marsden).

MOSCOW, ART TH. 16 May 1920 (in Russian, translated by M. Galperin; Nemirovich-Danchenko's production, which was also given at Berlin, Berliner Th. 22 October 1925 and New York 28 December 1925).

VENICE, T. MALIBRAN 23 September 1920 (in Italian).

BRUSSELS, M. 13 April 1921 (for the first time at that theatre).

The latest revival in Paris so far was at the Th. Porte St. Martin 21 May 1934; revived at Cairo Spring 1938; at Stockholm 28 October 1939.

1873

DIAZ: *La Coupe du Roi de Thulé*

10 January. Paris, O.

Text by L. Gallet and E. Blau. Three acts.

The best of the three operas of Diaz (who was the son of the well-known painter). The opera was awarded the first prize in a competition arranged by the Ministère des Beaux-Arts; it had 21 performances. The libretto was also used by Bizet.

RIMSKY-KORSAKOV: *Pskovityanka*
Псковитянка
(The Maid of Pskov)

13 January. St. Petersburg

Text by the composer (founded on a play by L. A. Mei). Four acts.

Rimsky-Korsakov's first opera.

Revived St. Petersburg 18 April 1895 and (with a new prologue *Boyarynya Vera Sheloga*), Moscow 27 December 1898 and St. Petersburg 10 November 1903.

Outside Russia given at:

PARIS, CHÂTELET 26 May 1909 (in Russian).

MILAN 11 April 1912 (in Italian, translated by M. Delines and G. Macchi).

LONDON, D.L. 8 July 1913 (in Russian).

LONDON, D.L. 22 September 1917 (in English, translated by R. Newmarch).

MANCHESTER, 16 January 1918 (in English, translated by R. Newmarch).

CREFELD 19 December 1924 (in German, translated by H. Möller).

BARCELONA 13 December 1927 (in Russian).

In Western Europe the opera is known as *Ivan the Terrible* (baptized thus by Diaghilev at the Paris 1909 production).

GOMES: *Fosca*

16 February. Milan, Sc.

Text by A. Ghislanzoni. Four acts.

Buenos Aires 7 July 1877; Rio de Janeiro 15 July 1877, etc.

Revived Milan 26 October 1890, etc.; Malta 1900.

Still given in Brazil where the opera was last revived at Rio de Janeiro in August 1935.

J. STRAUSS: *Der Karneval in Rom*

1 March. Vienna, W.

Text by J. Braun, F. Zell, and R. Genée (founded on V. Sardou's *Piccolino*). Three acts.

Berlin, Fr.W. 25 April 1874, etc.

In German also, Graz 23 October 1873; Amsterdam and Laibach 1876; Basle 19 November 1877; New York 1 April 1881; Posen 24 May 1881; Riga 18 August 1881.

In Italian (translated by E. Golisciani), Naples T.N. 1877.

In Czech (translated by E. Züngel), Prague 1882.

Revived (as *Der blaue Held*, new libretto by F. Stollberg), Vienna, W. 18 October 1912; in its original form, Vienna, V.O. 20 June 1921; in a new version by E. Rex (music revised by F. Marszalek), Dortmund 30 November 1937.

SKUHERSKY: *Rektor a General*

28 March. Prague, Cz.

Text by E. Züngel. Three acts.

The last and best opera of the Czech composer.

DUPRAT: *Pétrarque*

19 April. Marseilles

Text by the composer and F. Dharmenon. Four acts.

Duprat's most successful work.

Lyons 21 March 1874; Toulouse 10 May 1875; Paris, O. Populaire 11 February 1880.

In Italian (translated by V. Meini), Milan 22 November 1876.

Revived Toulon 16 October 1924.

For a detailed account see A. Rostand, *La Musique à Marseille* (1874), pp.163-179.

DELIBES: *Le Roi l'a dit*

24 May. Paris, O.C.

Text by E. Gondinet. Three acts.

After some 12 operettas, this was Delibes's first attempt at comic opera on a more ambitious scale. Very successful in Paris and abroad. Given at:

ANTWERP 18 August 1873 (in French).

VIENNA, K.O. 20 April 1874 (in German, translated by A. Schirmer); O. 20 September 1882.

CARLSRUHE 9 September 1874 (in German).

PRAGUE September 1874 (in German) and 9 October 1874 (in Czech, translated by E. Züngel).

RIGA 1876 (in German).

BUDAPEST February 1877 (in German) and 22 March 1879 (in Hungarian, translated by I. Huszár).

STOCKHOLM 21 March 1877 (in Swedish, translated by F. T. Hedberg).

BERLIN, 19 April 1877 (Schirmer's translation revised by F. Gumbert).

LAIBACH 1877 (Schirmer's translation revised by F. Gumbert).

COPENHAGEN 2 December 1877 (in Danish, translated by H. P. Holst).

TEMESVAR 1883 (in German).

ZAGREB 3 October 1885 (in Croatian, translated by I. Trnski).

BRUSSELS 9 April 1888 (in French).

WARSAW 1888 (in Polish, translated by R. Morozowicz).

GENEVA 17 March 1890 (in French).

LONDON, P. OF W.'S. 13 December 1894 (in English translated by R. Temple; R.C.M. performance).

The opera was revived at the O.C. 23 March 1898, in a reduced 2-act version by P. Gille. Still given in France and sometimes revived in other countries; Stuttgart 3 April 1930 (in German); London 20 June 1939 (by the Webber-Douglas School, new English version by A. Webber).

G. CORONARO: *Un Tramonto*

8 August. Milan, Conservatorio

Text by A. Boito. One act.

Successful in Italy. In Italian also, Chicago 25 May 1893.

In German (translated by S. Arkel), Hamburg 18 April 1891.

GROSSMANN: *Duch Wojewody*
(The Ghost of the Voyvod)

25 October. Warsaw

Text by W. L. Anczyc. Three acts.

Successful Polish comic opera; Lemberg 22 January 1878, etc.

In German (translated by A. Langer), Vienna, K.O. 28 January 1877 and Berlin, Walhalla Th. 9 February 1884.

In Russian, St. Petersburg 26 December 1877.

(PACINI): *Niccolo dei Lapi*

29 October. Florence, T. Pagliano

Text (according to the printed libretto) by Pacini himself; but it is chiefly taken from an earlier opera of his, *La Punizione* (text by G. Cencetti, produced Venice 8 March 1854). Three acts.

Pacini's last performed opera; it had been written for Rio de Janeiro as early as 1857; but the production announced there in September of that year did not take place.

Revived Florence 8 July 1879, Leghorn 9 November 1879.

PINSUTI: *Il Mercante di Venezia*

9 November. Bologna, T.C.

Text by G. T. Cimino (after Shakespeare). Four acts.

Successful in Italy. The first and best of the operas of Pinsuti who, since 1856, had been R.A.M. professor in London.

OFFENBACH: *La jolie Parfumeuse*

29 November. Paris, Ren.

Text by H. Crémieux and E. Blum. Three acts.

In French also, Brussels 29 November 1872; Antwerp 20 November 1874; New York 31 March 1875; Milan 11 May 1875; Mexico 6 January 1876; Naples, T. Sannazaro 1878.

In German (as *Schön Röschen*, translated by K. Treumann, additional music by J. Brandl), Vienna, Ca. 6 November 1874; Berlin, Wallner Th. 16 January 1875; Graz 4 September 1875; Laibach 1878; Berne 9 December 1878; Brünn 19 February 1879, etc.

In English (translated by H. J. Byron), London, Alhambra 18 May 1874; (translated by C. L. Kenney), Birmingham 8 July 1875.

In English also, New York 5 October 1876.

In Swedish (translated by E. G. Lundquist), Stockholm 13 January 1891.

In Spanish (translated by G. Jover and J. M. Pous), Barcelona 31 January 1908.

Revived Munich 19 December 1899 (in German); Monte Carlo December 1932 (in French).

GOBATTI: *I Goti*

30 November. Bologna, T.C.

Text by S. Interdonato. Four acts.

Gobatti's first opera. Very successful in Italy; revived in a new version, Bologna 27 August 1898 and Messina 11 February 1899.

Some Italian critics, during the seventies, called Gobatti "the Italian Wagner" and set the boldest hopes in his further development; his following two works, however (*Lux*, 1875, and *Cordelia*, 1881), were failures; and Verdi called even *I Goti* "il più mostruoso aborto musicale che sia stato mai composto".

1874

LAURO ROSSI: *La Contessa di Mons*

31 January. Turin, T.R.

Text by M. d'Arienzo (founded on V. Sardou's *Patrie*). Four acts.

Successful in Italy; Milan, Sc. 9 January 1877, etc.

MUSORGSKY: *Boris Godunov*
Борис Годунов

8 February. St. Petersburg

Text by the composer "after Pushkin and Karamzin", meaning Pushkin's drama of the same title (1830) and N. M. Karamzin's *History of the Russian Empire* (1816–29). Prologue and 4 acts (9 scenes).

The original version of this most famous of all Russian operas, written in 1868–69, was rejected by the St. Petersburg Imperial Opera in 1870. The composer then partly re-wrote it in 1871–72 and succeeded in getting this second version produced. Three scenes were given on 17 February 1873, and the whole opera one year later, 8 February (27 January, Russian style), 1874. Cheshikhin (followed by Riesemann and many others) gives the incorrect date 5 February (24 January) 1874. The vocal score of the 1874 version was published in that year and re-issued in 1926. After 26 performances the opera was withdrawn from the repertoire in St. Petersburg. It was first performed in Moscow (Bolshoy Theatre) on 28 December 1888 and from that date till 24 January 1890 had 10 performances in Moscow. The opera was first revived in the earliest of Rimsky-Korsakov's very much altered versions at St. Petersburg 10 December 1896 (Great Hall of the Conservatoire), at Moscow by the Mamontov Opera Company, with Shalyapin, on 19 December 1898 and at the Bolshoy Theatre 26 April 1901, and again at St. Petersburg by the Mamontov Company on 19 March 1899 (Great Hall of the Conservatoire) and at the Maryinsky Theatre on 22 November 1904. It was in the Rimsky-Korsakov version (which has been called a falsification) that

Boris Godunov became known outside Russia and this version is still given in many countries.

The first performances outside Russia were at:

PARIS, O. 19 May 1908 (in Russian, with additional music by Rimsky-Korsakov)[1] and 7 March 1922 (in French).

MILAN, SC. 14 January 1909 (in Italian, translated by M. Delines and E. Palermi).

BUENOS AIRES 13 September 1909 (in Italian, translated by M. Delines and E. Palermi).

RIO DE JANEIRO 18 June 1910 (in Italian, translated by M. Delines and E. Palermi).

PRAGUE 25 November 1910 (in Czech, translated by R. Zamrzla) and 1934 (in German).

STOCKHOLM 5 November 1911 (in Swedish, translated by S. Nyblom).

LEMBERG January 1912 (in Polish).

MONTE CARLO 23 January 1912 (in Russian).

LYONS 28 January 1913 (for the first time in French, translated by M. Delines and L. Laloy).

NEW YORK 29 March 1913 (in Italian) and 11 May 1922 (in Russian).

LONDON, D.L. 24 June 1913 (in Russian); Aldwych 5 July 1916 (in French); and D.L. 2 June 1917 (in English).

BRESLAU 29 October 1913 (for the first time in German, translated by M. Lippold); Stuttgart May 1921, Frankfort 25 September 1921, etc.

BUDAPEST 20 December 1913 (in Hungarian, translated by S. Hevesi).

BARCELONA 20 November 1915 (in Italian) and 16 November 1922 (in Russian); Catalan translation by J. Pena published 1915.

BIRMINGHAM 23 February 1917 (for the first time in English, translated by R. Newmarch).

SHANGHAI 1918 (in Russian).

ZAGREB 23 December 1918 (in Croatian, translated by A. Schneider).

ROTTERDAM April 1921 (concert performance).

LJUBLJANA 1 October 1921 (in Slovenian, translated by C. Golar).

BRUSSELS 12 December 1921 (in French).

SAN FRANCISCO 15 January 1922 (in Russian).

---

[1] For an account of the famous Diaghilev production of 1908, see Chapter XXI of M. D. Calvocoressi's *Musicians Gallery* (1933).

VIENNA, V.O. 4 November 1922 and O. 24 October 1925 (in German).

LISBON February 1923 (in Italian).

BASLE 2 September 1923 (in German).

COPENHAGEN 24 January 1924 (in Danish, translated by J. Lehmann).

BERLIN, V.O. 21 February 1924 and O. 18 February 1926 (in German) and 12 May 1928 (in Russian).

RIGA 3 May 1924 (in Lettish; re-orchestrated from the 1874 vocal score by E. Melngailis).

MONTEVIDEO August 1924 (in Italian).

HELSINKI 1 February 1925 (in Finnish, translated by M. A. Bergh-Wuori).

BUCHAREST October 1925 (in Rumanian).

SOFIA 14 June 1929 (in Bulgarian).

KAUNAS 27 February 1930 (in Lithuanian).

TALLINN 1930 (in Estonian, translated by S. Lipp).

VERONA 2 August 1930 (in Italian; first open-air performance).

TURIN November 1931 (in Russian).

ANTWERP 14 October 1933 (in Flemish).

ATHENS March 1936 (concert performance).

The original *Boris* as written in 1868–69 was published for the first time in 1928 (edited by P. Lamm) and revived at:

LENINGRAD 16 February 1928 and Moscow 21 October 1928 (in Russian).

LONDON, S's WELLS 30 September 1935 (English version by M. D. Calvocoressi).

PARIS, SALLE GAVEAU 31 December 1935 (concert performance; French version also by M. D. Calvocoressi).

HAMBURG 22 January 1936 (in German, Lippold's translation revised by H. Möller).

PONCHIELLI: *I Lituani*

7 *March*. Milan, Sc.

Text by A. Ghislanzoni (founded on A. Mickiewicz's *Konrad Wallenrod*). Prologue and 3 acts.

Given at Milan in a new version on 6 March 1875 and revived there 4 April 1903.

In Italian also, St. Petersburg 20 November 1884 (as *Aldona*); Buenos Aires 26 June 1889.

GOMES: *Salvator Rosa*

21 March. Genoa, C.F.

Text by A. Ghislanzoni. Four acts.

Milan 10 September 1874, etc. Revived Rome 27 October 1903.

Outside Italy, given at Malta 1879; Athens April 1880; Rio de Janeiro 17 August 1880 (revived 7 September 1905); Buenos Aires 30 March 1897.

KRETSCHMER: *Die Folkunger*

21 March. Dresden

Text by S. H. Mosenthal. Five acts.

Kretschmer's first and best work. Successful on German stages.

Given at Graz 5 February 1876; Riga 2 May 1876; Vienna 23 September 1876; Berlin 27 October 1876; Prague 21 December 1876; Rotterdam Spring 1880; St. Gall April 1883; Posen 23 December 1883.

Revived Brünn 4 October 1892; Bremen 5 November 1893, etc.; Erfurt 23 January 1900; Reval 1900.

LECOCQ: *Giroflé-Girofla*

21 March. Brussels, Alcazar

Text by A. Vanloo and E. Leterrier. Three acts. Very successful all over the world. Given at:

LONDON, O.C. 6 June 1874 (in French) and Philharmonic 3 October 1874 (in English, translated by C. O'Neil and C. Clarke); Edinburgh 14 June 1875 (in English).

PARIS, REN. 11 November 1874 (in French) and Vaudeville 3 June 1911 (in German).

BERLIN, FR.W. 22 December 1874 (in German).

VIENNA, CA. 2 January 1875 (in German).

BUDAPEST 1875 (in German).

MILAN 13 January 1875 (in Italian); Naples, T.N. 1876 (in French).

NEW YORK 4 February 1875 (in French); 10 March 1875 (in German); and 19 May 1875 (in English); revived Jolson's 22 November 1926 (in French).

PRAGUE 31 March 1875 (in Czech, translated by B. Peška).

BUENOS AIRES 1875 (in French).

SYDNEY 23 August 1875 (in English).

LEMBERG 29 September 1875 (in Polish).

ST. PETERSBURG 10 October 1875 (in Russian).

In French also, Mexico and Cairo December 1875.

In Spanish (translated by J. Coll y Britipaja), Madrid 1875; Havana 1876.

In Swedish, Stockholm 1876.

In German, Laibach 1876; Czernowitz 1878; Reval 24 February 1879; Riga 3 December 1879; Sarajevo 1882.

In English, Cape Town 1887.

In Croatian (translated by A. Schneider), Zagreb 23 April 1899.

SMETANA: *Dvě Vdovy*
(Two Widows)

27 March. Prague, Cz.

Text by E. Züngel (founded on a comedy by P. J. F. Mallefille). Two acts.

New version (with recitatives instead of dialogue), Prague 15 March 1878 and frequently revived there since (175 performances until 1924).

In German (translated by R. Fels), Hamburg 28 December 1881 (first Smetana opera in Germany). Revived in German, Prague October 1934. Given at Vienna 6 June 1924 (in Czech, by the Olomouc Opera Company).

In Croatian, Zagreb 16 March 1924.

J. STRAUSS: *Die Fledermaus*

5 April. Vienna, W.

Text by C. Haffner and R. Genée (from a French vaudeville, *Le Réveillon*, by H. Meilhac and Lud. Halévy which, itself, was taken from a German comedy, *Das Gefängnis*, by R. Benedix). Three acts.

Strauss's most famous operetta. Given at:

BERLIN, FR.W. 8 July 1874 (500th performance 18 June 1892).

BUDAPEST 14 November 1874 (in German) and 25 August 1882 (in Hungarian).

NEW YORK 21 November 1874 (in German) and 16 March 1885 (in English).

NAPLES, T.N. 26 June 1875 (in Italian, translated by E. Golisciani).

PRAGUE 7 September 1875 (in Czech, translated by E. Züngel) and 21 November 1875 (in German); revived 20 November 1888 (new Czech translation by A. Wenig).

BRÜNN 2 October 1875 (in German).

STOCKHOLM 2 December 1875 (in Swedish, translated by E. A. Wallmark).

AMSTERDAM 1876 (in German).

LAIBACH (LJUBLJANA) 1876 (in German) and 1899 (in Slovenian).

BASLE 12 November 1876 (in German).

LONDON, ALHAMBRA 18 December 1876 (in English, translated by H. Aïdé) and Royalty 1 January (1895 in German).

RIGA 1877 (in German) and 15 April 1931 (in Lettish).

PARIS, REN. 30 October 1877 (in French, as *La Tzigane*, adapted to a new libretto by A. Delacour and V. Wilder); Variétés 22 April 1904 (translated by P. Ferrier).

LEMBERG 29 March 1879 (in Polish); revived Warsaw 16 November 1932 (new Polish translation by J. Tuwim).

COPENHAGEN 9 May 1880 (in Danish, translated by R. Schrøder).

ST. PETERSBURG Summer 1881 (in Russian).

SARAJEVO 1882 (in German).

ZAGREB 20 October 1883 (in Croatian, translated by L. Varjačić).

BRUSSELS 17 January 1886 (in German) and 1 February 1906 (in French).

MADRID 1887 (in Spanish, translated by F. J. Osorno, J. Nombelá, and A. Vidal y Llimona) and 24 February 1888 (translated by C. Navarro).

BUCHAREST April 1894 (in German) and Autumn 1929 (in Rumanian).

CONSTANTINOPLE 14 November 1903 (in German).

BUENOS AIRES October 1906 (in German).

HELSINKI 8 September 1921 (in Finnish).

SOFIA 18 February 1927 (in Bulgarian).

By 1880 the operetta had been produced on 171 German stages. First given at the Vienna O. 28

October 1894; at the Berlin O. 8 May 1899; at the Metropolitan Opera House, New York 16 February 1905 (in German).

Revived London, H.M.'s 4 July 1910 (new English version by A. Kalisch).

New Italian version, *Il Principe si diverte*, Rome 22 March 1934. New French version, *La Chauve-Souris*, Paris, Th. Pigalle 28 November 1933.

Recent English and American adaptations are *Night Birds*, by G. Unger and A. Anderson, London, Lyric 30 December 1911 and (as *The Merry Countess*), New York, Casino 20 August 1912. *A Wonderful Night*, by F. Todd Mitchell, New York, Majestic 31 October 1929. *Champagne, Sec*, by A. Child and R. A. Simon, New York, Morosco 14 October 1933.

PEDRELL: *L'ultimo Abenzerraggio*

14 April. Barcelona, L.

(Original Catalan) text by the composer (after Chateaubriand), versification by J. B. Altés y Alabert, Italian version by F. de Paula Fors de Casamayor. Four acts.

Pedrell's first opera. Revived Barcelona, T.L. 8 October 1889.

FIBICH: *Bukovín*

16 April. Prague, Cz.

Text by E. Krásnohorská. Three acts.
Fibich's first opera.

CHAIKOVSKY: *Oprichnik*
Опричникъ
(The Life-Guardsman)

24 April. St. Petersburg

Text by the composer (founded on a drama by I. I. Lazheshnikov). Four acts.

Kiev 21 December 1874; Moscow 16 May 1875, etc.

Revived St. Petersburg 30 December 1888 (at the Conservatoire) and 23 November 1893 (publicly); Moscow September 1911.

In Russian also, Helsinki 24 March 1908.

ERKEL: *Brankovich György*

20 May. Budapest

Text by L. Ódry and F. Ormai (founded on a play by K. Obernyik). Four acts.

Given at Budapest until 1910. (The opera contains Turkish and Serbian folk-tunes.)

HALLSTRÖM: *Den Bergtagna*
(The Mountain Ghost)

24 May. Stockholm

Text by F. T. Hedberg (*Sagaopera*). Five acts.

Successful Swedish opera, given at Stockholm 85 times until 1910.

In German (translated by E. Peschier, revised by F. Grandaur), Munich 23 April 1876; Hamburg 25 December 1876, etc.

In Danish (translated by A. Hertz), Copenhagen 10 May 1876.

(BALFE): *Il Talismano*

11 June. London, D.L.

Original English text (*The Knight of the Leopard*) by A. Matthison (after Scott), Italian version by G. Zaffira. Three acts.

Balfe's last opera, posthumously produced.

In Italian also, Dublin 23 September 1874; in the original English (as *The Talisman*), New York 10 February 1875. Revived (in English), Liverpool 15 January 1891; and Monte Carlo 26 March 1918 (as *King Richard in Palestine*).

(Date of first performance 11 June, not 11 January, as stated in several books of reference.)

GOETZ: *Der Widerspänstigen Zähmung*

11 October. Mannheim

Text by J. V. Widmann (after Shakespeare). Four acts.

Goetz's first opera; rather successful in Germany (though never a very popular work). Given at:

VIENNA 2 February 1875 (in German).
BERLIN 11 December 1876 (in German).
RIGA 4 December 1877 (in German).

LONDON, D.L. 12 October 1878 and H.M.'s 20 January 1880 (in English, translated by J. Troutbeck); P. of W.'s 10 July 1889 (by the R.C.M.).
ROTTERDAM March 1881 (in German).
PRAGUE 29 June 1883 (in German) and 4 November 1909 (in Czech, translated by A. Wenig).
ZURICH 29 February 1884 (in German).
NEW YORK 4 January 1886 (in English) and 15 March 1916 (in German).
STOCKHOLM 30 April 1888 (in Swedish, translated by F. Arlberg).
COPENHAGEN 10 May 1890 (in Danish, translated by E. Bøgh).
ANTWERP 16 February 1903 (in Flemish).
BUDAPEST 20 May 1909 (in Hungarian, translated by D. Vidor).

French adaptation by G. T. Antheunis, *Le Diable à la Maison*, made for Brussels 1889, printed but not performed; vocal score published.

OFFENBACH: *Madame l'Archiduc*

31 October. Paris, B.P.

Text by A. Millaud (the first act by H. Meilhac and Lud. Halévy). Three acts.

In French also given at Milan 19 May 1875; New York 6 September 1875; Mexico 25 December 1875; Buenos Aires 1877, etc.

In English (translated by ?), New York 29 December 1874; (adapted by H. B. Farnie) London, O.C. 13 January 1876; Sydney 15 September 1877.

In German (translated by J. Hopp), Vienna, W. 16 January 1875; Berlin, Fr.W. 3 July 1875; Graz 24 August 1875; Prague and Laibach 1876, etc.

In Italian (translated by E. Golisciani), Naples 8 May 1875.

In Czech (translated by B. Peška), Prague 30 May 1875.

In Swedish, Stockholm 1875.

In Russian (translated by A. Y. von Asheberg), St. Petersburg 1876.

Revived Paris, Variétés 10 October 1924; in a new German version by K. Kraus, Stendal 15 January 1929; Basle 5 October 1930; Prague February 1932.

DVOŘÁK: *Král a Uhlíř*
(King and Collier)

24 November. Prague, Cz.

Text by B. Guldener. Three acts.

Dvořák's first performed opera. Revived Prague 15 June 1887 (text altered by V. J. Novotný) and 1 November 1914 (revised by K. Kovařovič); and, in an earlier completely different version (1871) which had never been produced before and was recovered in 1916, Prague 28 May 1929.

BONAWITZ: *Ostrolenka*

3 December. Philadelphia

(Original German) text by P. Haimbach, English version by H. M. Wetherill and G. W. Tryon. Four acts.

Revived London, St. George's Hall 2 April 1884.

BARBIERI: *El Barberillo de Lavapiés*
(The Barber of Lavapiés)

18 December. Madrid, Z.

Text by M. J. de Larra. Three acts.

Successful zarzuela. Frequently revived on Spanish stages, at Buenos Aires as late as January 1936.

1875

RUBINSTEIN: *Dyemon*
Демонъ
(The Demon)

25 January. St. Petersburg

Text by P. A. Viskovatov (founded on Lermontov's poem). Three acts.

Rubinstein's most successful opera.

Moscow 3 November 1879 (in Italian 11 February 1894); Odessa 25 January 1892, and all over Russia; the 100th performance at St. Petersburg was on 13 October 1884.

Outside Russia, given at:

HAMBURG 3 November 1880 (in German, translated by A. Offermann).

LONDON, C.G. 21 June 1881 (in Italian, translated by G. Vacotti) and 22 October 1888 (in Russian), at the Novelty (Great Queen Street) Th.; first opera in London ever sung in Russian; revived in Russian, Coliseum 19 February 1912 and Wigmore Hall 24 November 1934 (in concert form).

PRAGUE 18 October 1885 (in Czech).

BERLIN, VICT. TH. 15 May 1888 (in Russian; revised Kroll's 23 May 1908, in Russian).

COPENHAGEN June 1888 (in Russian).

MANCHESTER 2 July 1888 (in Russian, by the same touring company as in Berlin and Copenhagen; produced in other English towns and eventually in London, see above).

RIGA 1893 (in German) and 1912 (in Lettish).

HELSINKI 10 November 1896 (in Italian) and 2 November 1932 (in Finnish).

WARSAW Autumn 1897 (in Italian).

VIENNA 23 October 1899 (in German).

LISBON 1904 (in Italian).

BARCELONA Autumn 1905 (in Italian).

MONTE CARLO 24 March 1906 (in Italian) and 26 February 1916 (in Russian); revived 3 March 1925.

LEMBERG Spring 1909 (in Polish, translated by T. Mianowski).

BUENOS AIRES 31 August 1909 (in Italian).

SOFIA 2 January 1910 (in Bulgarian).

PARIS, TH.S.B. 6 May 1911 (in Russian) and 9 May 1911 (in French).

SHANGHAI 1918 (in Russian).

SAN FRANCISCO 17 January 1922 (in Russian).

KAUNAS 16 June 1921 (in Lithuanian).

NEW YORK 13 May 1922 (in Russian).

TALLINN 1924 (in Estonian).

PHILADELPHIA 7 November 1928 (in Russian).

TEL AVIV 2 June 1932 (in Hebrew, translated by A. Aschmann).

Still revived in Russia now and then (Leningrad Conservatory Summer 1938).

SCHIRA: *Selvaggia*

20 February. Venice, F.

Text by G. T. Cimino. Prologue and 3 acts.

Schira's most important opera; successful in Italy; also given at Barcelona on 25 November 1877.

J. STRAUSS: *Cagliostro in Wien*

27 February. Vienna, W.

Text by F. Zell and R. Genée. Three acts.

Berlin, Fr.W. 18 September 1875 (revived 14 May 1887), etc.

In German also, Budapest 1875; Graz 29 September 1875; Prague 13 October 1877; Czernowitz 1878, etc.

In Czech (translated by E. Züngel), Prague 19 June 1875.

English version by E. J. Austen published (and produced?) Chicago 1886.

BIZET: *Carmen*

3 March. Paris, O.C.

Text by H. Meilhac and Lud. Halévy (founded on Mérimée's story). Four acts.

Bizet's chief work; his last opera; he died the night of its 23rd performance, on 3 June 1875. When first produced in Paris, given for 50 nights only, during the season 1875–76; the great run began after a revival on 21 April 1883 (when *Carmen* had already been performed in several other countries, see below).

The 500th performance at the O.C. was on 23 October 1891, the 1,000th on 23 December 1904, the 1,200th on 1 January 1910; given there more than 2,200 times to date. Outside Paris, produced at:

VIENNA 23 October 1875 (in German, translated by J. Hopp); here the opera was performed not, as in Paris, with spoken dialogue, but for the first time with the recitatives by E. Guiraud. There was also introduced the Gipsy dance from Bizet's *La jolie Fille de Perth* (later on mostly replaced by dances from *L'Arlésienne*). The dialogue form was restored at Essen 1928, Vienna October 1937, Munich November 1938 (new German version by C. Studer-Weingartner). Another new German version by G. Brecher printed 1937.

BRUSSELS 3 (not 1, 8, or 9) February 1876 (in French; 500th performance 11 October 1913).

ANTWERP 1 April 1876 (in French) and 6 February 1919 (in Flemish).

BUDAPEST 28 October 1876 (in Hungarian, translated by K. Abrányi).

ST. PETERSBURG 28 February 1878 (in Italian, translated by A. de Lauzières) and 12 October 1885 (in Russian, translated by A. A. Gorchakova); revived Leningrad 16 January 1933 (new translated by V. I. Epaneshnikov).

STOCKHOLM 22 March 1878 (in Swedish, translated by F. T. Hedberg).

LONDON, H.M.'s 22 June 1878 (in Italian); 5 February 1879 (in English, translated by H. Hersee); and 8 November 1886 (in French); first produced at C.G. 27 May 1882; 150th performance there 9 November 1909. A new English version by J. and A. Galsworthy was published in 1932.

DUBLIN 9 September 1878 (in Italian).

NEW YORK 23 October 1878 (in Italian); 2 March 1881 (in English); 2 May 1882 (in French); and 25 November 1885 (in German).

PHILADELPHIA 25 October 1878, etc. (in Italian).

MELBOURNE Summer 1879 and Sydney 13 December 1884 (in English).

NAPLES, T. BELLINI 15 November 1879 (in Italian).

HAMBURG 31 January 1880 (for the first time in Germany).

BERLIN 12 March 1880 (in German; given at the O. 850 times until 1935).

PRAGUE 29 March 1880 (in German) and 3 January 1884 (in Czech, translated by E. Krásnohorská).

GENEVA 24 December 1880 (in French).

ZURICH 19 January 1881 (in German).

MEXICO 11 February 1881 (in French) and 7 June 1883 (in Spanish, translated by A. Chavero).

RIO DE JANEIRO 23 May 1881 (in French).

MALTA 1881 (in Italian).

BARCELONA 2 August 1881 (in French).

BUENOS AIRES 9 August 1881 (in French) and 16 June 1883 (in Italian).

RIGA 13 May 1883 (in German) and 1902 (in Lettish).

SANTIAGO, CHILE 1883 (in Italian).

TEMESVAR 15 December 1884 (in German).

REVAL (TALLINN) 12 March 1885 (in German) and 1920 (in Estonian).

LISBON November 1885 (in Italian).

AMSTERDAM 22 January 1887 (in Dutch).

COPENHAGEN 24 April 1887 (in Danish, translated by E. Bøgh and H. P. Holst).

HELSINKI 10 February 1889 (in Russian); 14 March 1889 (in Swedish); and 3 December 1912 (in Finnish).

ZAGREB 18 June 1893 (in Croatian, translated by A. Harambašič).

LAIBACH (LJUBLJANA) 1894 (in German) and 1896 (in Slovenian).

CAPE TOWN 1895 (in Italian) and Johannesburg 1905 (in English).

CHRISTIANIA (OSLO) 7 May 1900 (in Norwegian, at the opening of the Norwegian State Opera-House); previously given there in 1880.

SOFIA 9 March 1912 (in Bulgarian).

SHANGHAI 1918 (in Russian).

YOKOHAMA Autumn 1919 (in Italian).

BUCHAREST Spring 1920 (in Rumanian).

SEATTLE 4 January 1922 (in Russian).

BELGRADE 1922 (in Serbian).

KAUNAS 7 February 1924 (in Lithuanian).

MOSCOW 4 June 1924 (as *Karmencita i Soldat*, Russian adaptation from Mérimée by K. A. Lipskerov).

KHARKOV 1925 (in Ukrainian).

TEL AVIV 10 November 1925 (in Hebrew, translated by A. Aschmann).

ATHENS November 1931 (in Italian).

TOKYO 24 March 1935 (in Japanese).

GOLDMARK: *Die Königin von Saba*

10 March. Vienna, O.

Text by S. H. Mosenthal. Four acts.

Goldmark's first and best opera.

Very successful on German stages and abroad. The 100th performance at Vienna was on 21 March 1897; at Budapest already on 22 February 1897.

Produced at:

BUDAPEST 18 March 1876 (in Hungarian, translated by L. Dóczy).

HAMBURG 17 March 1877 (in German).

PRAGUE 24 January 1878 (in German) and 2 April 1886 (in Czech, translated by V. J. Novotný).

TURIN 1 March 1879 (in Italian, translated by A. Zanardini).

BERLIN 1 December 1879 (in German).

ST. PETERSBURG 6 March 1880 (in Italian).

ROTTERDAM May 1881 (in German).

NEW YORK 2 December 1885 (in German) and 3 April 1888 (in English).

MADRID January 1887 (in Italian).

BOSTON 10 January 1888 (in English, translated by J. H. Cornell).

WARSAW 15 September 1891 (in Polish).

RIGA 1892 (in German) and 20 March 1935 (in Lettish).

ZURICH 15 March 1897 (in German).

ANTWERP 8 February 1898 (in Flemish).

BUENOS AIRES 4 July 1899 (in Italian).

AMSTERDAM 1 September 1899 (in Dutch).

ZAGREB 17 January 1900 (in Croatian, translated by M. Pogačić).

MANCHESTER 12 April 1910 (in English).

LONDON, KENNINGTON TH. 29 August 1910 (in English).

LJUBLJANA 1910 (in Slovenian).

SOFIA 23 September 1935 (in Bulgarian).

BRUSSELS 5 October 1937 (for the first time in French, translated by P. Solanges).

HELSINKI 31 October 1938 (in Finnish).

SULLIVAN: *Trial by Jury*

25 March. London, Royalty

Text by W. S. Gilbert (*A novel and original cantata*). One act.

The only Gilbert-Sullivan operetta without spoken dialogue.

Revived London, Savoy 11 October 1884 and 22 September 1898; Prince's 6 January 1920, etc. First given at New York, Eagle Th. 15 November 1875; Edinburgh 21 August 1876; Georgetown, British Guiana 15 April 1884. Given at Berlin, Wallner Th. 14 June 1886 and Leipzig 1 August 1886 (in English) and Alexander-Platz Th. 1 October 1892 (in German, translated by C. Carlotta).

SCHOLZ: *Golo*

4 April. Nuremberg

Text by the composer (founded on L. Tieck's *Genoveva*). Prologue and 3 acts. Weimar 9 May 1875, etc. Revived Frankfort 1 November 1891.

RUBINSTEIN: *Die Maccabäer*

17 April. Berlin, O.

Text by S. H. Mosenthal. Three acts.

The second successful opera by Rubinstein produced in 1875.

In German also given at Prague 10 October 1875; Vienna 24 February 1878, etc.; Riga 26 March 1899. Revived Dresden 26 October 1904.

In Russian, St. Petersburg 3 February 1877; Moscow 7 March 1883; Saratov 7 February 1893; revived Moscow 17 October 1899.

Produced in a Hebrew translation by M. Freidmann at Jerusalem 15 December 1925.

MERTENS: *Liederik, de Rentmeester*
(Liederik the Treasurer)

August. Antwerp

Text by P. Billiet. Three acts.

In Flemish also, Amsterdam 9 May 1876; Brussels 4 February 1879.

Revived Antwerp 24 February 1888 (in French, translated by G. Lagye); Amsterdam 15 March 1892 and Antwerp 26 December 1893 (in Flemish).

SARRIA: *La Campana dell' Eremitaggio*

25 September. Naples, T. Mercadante

Text by E. Cofino (founded on *Les Dragons de Villars*, by Lockroy and Cormon, see 1856). Three acts.

The most successful of Sarria's eight operas. Given in Italy until 1896.

In Italian also, Malta 1881 and Buenos Aires 6 February 1891.

GRAMMANN: *Melusine*

25 September. Wiesbaden

Text by the composer. Three acts.

Successful in Germany; in German also, Rotterdam 6 February 1878.

In Italian (translated by V. Betteloni), Turin 15 March 1881.

Revived (in a new version) Dresden 23 May 1891.

OFFENBACH: *La Créole*

3 November. Paris, B.P.

Text by A. Millaud, H. Meilhac and Lud. Halévy. Three acts.

In German (translated by J. Hopp), Vienna, W. 8 January 1876; Berlin, Wallner Th. 4 June 1876, etc.

In Polish, Lemberg 30 September 1876.

In English (translated by R. Reece and H. B. Farnie), Brighton 3 September 1877 and London, Folly 15 September 1877; revived (as *The Commodore*) London, Avenue Th. 10 May 1886 and New York 4 October 1886.

In French, Brussels 6 November 1877, etc.

In Spanish, Mexico 21 June 1885.

Revived (libretto re-written by A. Willemetz and G. Delance) Paris, Th. Marigny 15 December 1934.

LECOCQ: *La petite Mariée*

21 December. Paris, Ren.

Text by A. Vanloo and E. Leterrier. Three acts.

Successful on French stages: Brussels 24 February 1876; Antwerp 6 March 1876, etc.

In French also, London, O.C. 6 May 1876; Algiers July 1876; Lisbon, Madrid, Cairo December 1876; New York 6 February 1877. Revived Paris, Th. Moncey 6 August 1915; Th. Mogador 16 February 1921; Tr.L. 6 November 1931.

In Hungarian, Budapest 21 September 1876.

In Russian, St. Petersburg 17 October 1876.

In Italian, Naples, T.N. 11 November 1876.

In German (as *Graziella*, translated by K. Treumann), Vienna, Ca. 11 November 1876; Berlin, Fr.W. 23 August 1877; Zurich 18 December 1880, etc.

In Spanish, Mexico 18 November 1876.

In Swedish (translated by C. G. W. Michal), Stockholm 26 May 1877.

In Czech (translated by E. Züngel), Prague 1877.

In English (as *The Scarlet Feather*, adapted by H. Greenbank), London, Shaftesbury Th. 17 November 1897.

BRÜLL: *Das goldene Kreuz*

22 December. Berlin, O.

Text by S. H. Mosenthal (founded on a French play, *Cathérine*, by A. H. J. Mélesville and N. Brazier). Two acts.

Brüll's most successful work, very popular in Germany. The 100th performance at Berlin was on 20 August 1895.

In German also given at Prague 1 July 1876; Vienna 4 October 1876; Riga 1877; Rotterdam 2 November 1878; Basle 3 February 1879; New York 19 July 1879 (produced by a German Gesangverein) and 19 November 1886 (at the Metropolitan); Laibach 1880; Temesvar 1883.

In Czech (translated by J. Klíma), Prague 12 December 1876.

In English (translated by J. P. Jackson), London, Adelphi 2 March 1878.

In Swedish (translated by F. T. Hedberg), Stockholm 8 September 1879.

In Croatian (translated by M. Pogačić), Zagreb 11 March 1899.

Bulgarian translation by V. Shak published 1892.

Dutch translation by C. L. Schenk published 1910.

1876

SUPPÉ: *Fatinitza*

5 January. Vienna, Ca.

Text by F. Zell and R. Genée (founded on Scribe's *Circassienne*, see 1861). Three acts.

Suppé's first world success. Given at:

PRAGUE 12 August 1876 (in German) and 1876 (in Czech, translated by E. Züngel).

LAIBACH, AMSTERDAM, BUDAPEST 1876 (in German).

BERLIN, FR.W. 16 September 1876 (in German).

STOCKHOLM 15 and 16 November 1876 (in different Swedish versions by A. Lindgren and E. A. Wallmark).

NAPLES, T.N. 25 November 1877 (in Italian, translated by V. A. Bacichi) and T. Sannazaro 14 February 1881 (in German).

BERNE 3 December 1877 (in German).

RIGA 14 December 1877 (in German).

LONDON, ALHAMBRA 20 June 1878 (in English, translated by H. S. Leigh).

REVAL 30 October 1878 (in German).

BRUSSELS 28 December 1878 (in French, translated by F. Coveliers).

PARIS, NOUVEAUTÉS 15 March 1879 (in French, translated by A. Delacour and V. Wilder).

NEW YORK 14 April 1879 (in German); 22 April 1879 (in English, translated by J. B. Polk); and 14 October 1887 (in French).

LEMBERG 21 October 1879 (in Polish).

BUENOS AIRES 1881 (in French).

RIO DE JANEIRO 6 December 1881 (in Portuguese, translated by Ed. Garrido and A. Azevedo).

SYDNEY October 1882 (in English).

MEXICO 9 March 1884 (in English).

TARTU (DORPAT) 1887 (in Estonian).

ZAGREB 25 February 1899 (in Croatian, translated by V. Badalić).

HOLSTEIN: *Die Hochländer*

16 January. Mannheim

Text by the composer. Four acts.

Holstein's last opera. In German also given at Rotterdam 21 November 1877. Last revived Altenburg 14 December 1900.

KYUI: *Angelo*

Анжело

13 February. St. Petersburg

Text by V. P. Burenin (founded on V. Hugo's drama). Four acts.

Revived Moscow 17 January 1901; St. Petersburg 24 January 1910.

d'ARNEIRO: *L'Elisire di Giovinezza*

31 March. Lisbon, S.C.

(Italian) text by J. J. Magne. Four acts.

The first opera of the Portuguese composer.

Given also at Milan on 2 June 1877.

According to Riemann's *Musiklexikon* (Vol.I, p.62) this opera was revived in 1885 (as *La Derelitta*). An opera of that title was produced at Lisbon on 14 March 1885, text by R. Paravicini, founded on a novel by Ann Radcliffe. Perhaps the composer used parts of the *L'Elisire di Giovinezza* music for *La Derelitta*.

MERMET: *Jeanne d'Arc*

5 April. Paris, O.

Text by the composer. Four acts.

First new work produced in the new building of the Paris Opéra, Boulevard des Capucines ("Salle Garnier") inaugurated 5 January 1875 (opening programme: overtures *La Muette de Portici* and *Guillaume Tell*; scenes from *Les Huguenots* and from Delibes's ballet, *La Source*; and the first two acts of *La Juive*).

Jeanne d'Arc was performed 15 times.

PONCHIELLI: *Gioconda*

8 April. Milan, Sc.

Text by A. Boito (pseudonym "Tobia Gorrio"), founded on V. Hugo's *Angelo.* Four acts.

Ponchielli's most famous work; still very successful in Italy.

Outside Italy given at:

SANTIAGO, CHILE November 1882 (in Italian).

ST. PETERSBURG 30 January 1883 (in Italian) and February 1888 (in Russian, translated by G. A. Lishin).

BARCELONA 26 February 1883 (in Italian).

LONDON, C.G. 31 May 1883 (in Italian) and Kennington Th. 6 May 1903 (in English, translated by H. Hersee).

BUDAPEST 8 December 1883 (in Hungarian, translated by V. Radó); revived 22 February 1930 (new translation by V. Lányi).

NEW YORK 20 December 1883 (in Italian) and 23 September 1913 (in English).

VIENNA 29 April 1884 (in Italian) and 17 February 1885 (in German).

WIESBADEN 5 May 1884 (in German, translated by K. F. Niese).

ZAGREB 18 May 1884 (in Croatian, translated by J. E. Tomić).

BUENOS AIRES 28 June 1884 (in Italian).

PRAGUE 1884 (in German; revived 1937).

WARSAW December 1884 (in Polish, translated by M. Radziszeski).

RIO DE JANEIRO 10 August 1885 (in Italian).

MEXICO 14 October 1885 (in Italian).

LISBON February 1886 (in Italian).

NICE 29 December 1886 (in Italian).

MALTA 1887 (in Italian).

BRUSSELS 28 December 1887 (in French, translated by P. Solanges); revived 14 February 1939.

BERLIN 23 October 1889 (in German).

BUCHAREST 30 November 1889 (in Italian) and January 1921 (in Rumanian).

STOCKHOLM 10 March 1892 (in Swedish, translated by E. G. Lundquist).

RIGA 1893 (in German) and 15 November 1928 (in Lettish).

ROUEN 14 March 1895 (in French).

CAPE TOWN 1895 (in Italian).

HELSINKI 24 January 1897 (in Italian) and 23 November 1927 (in Finnish).

GENEVA 3 April 1902 (in French).

HAGUE January 1905 (in Italian).

MONTE CARLO 4 February 1908 (in French).

MONTREAL 1914 (in French).

TRIPOLIS April 1928 (in Italian).

KAUNAS 2 May 1929 (in Lithuanian).

SOFIA 9 November 1934 (in Bulgarian).

LJUBLJANA 4 June 1938 (in Slovenian, translated by R. Petelinova).

Apparently never produced in Paris.

GUIRAUD: *Piccolino*

11 April. Paris, O.C.

Text by V. Sardou and C. Nuitter. Three acts. Guiraud's most successful work.

In French also, Brussels 4 November 1876 (revived 7 April 1902); Hague December 1876; Buenos Aires Autumn 1881; Mexico 28 January 1882; Geneva 24 April 1883.

In Hungarian (translated by G. Böhm), Budapest 1878.

In English (translated by S. Samuel), Dublin 4 January 1879; London, H.M.'s 29 January 1879; Edinburgh 3 September 1879, etc.

In Swedish (translated by E. G. Lundquist), Stockholm 1882.

DVOŘÁK: *Vanda*

17 April. Prague, Cz.

Text by V. Beneš-Šumavský (translated from a Polish libretto by J. Surzycki). Five acts.

Failure; only the overture was printed. Revived Prague 3 May 1929.

JONCIÈRES: *Dimitri*

5 May. Paris, O.N.L.

Text by H. de Bornier and P. A. Silvestre (founded on Schiller's *Demetrius*). Five acts.

Written for the opening of the "Opéra National Lyrique" (late Gaîté).

Joncières's first success; revived Lille 17 March 1888; Paris, O.C. 5 February 1890; Ghent 7 November 1894.

MARÉCHAL: *Les Amoureux de Catherine*

8 May. Paris, O.C.

Text by J. Barbier (founded on a story by Erckmann-Chatrian). One act.

Maréchal's first and best opera; Brussels 12 September 1877, etc. Revived at the O.C. 20 February 1888 and 30 January 1915.

CHAPI: *La Hija de Jefté*
(Jephthah's Daughter)

11 May. Madrid, T.R.

(Spanish) text by A. Arnao. One act.

Chapi's first opera.

DENZA: *Wallenstein*

13 May. Naples, T. Mercadante

Text by A. Bruner (founded on Schiller's tragedy). Four acts.

The only opera of Denza, who was the composer of the famous Neapolitan song, *Funiculì, Funiculà,* and spent the greater part of his life, from 1879 until his death in 1922, in London.

R. WAGNER: *Siegfried*

16 August. Bayreuth

R. WAGNER: *Götterdämmerung*

17 August. Bayreuth

Text by the composer. *Siegfried*: Three acts. *Götterdämmerung*: Prologue and 3 acts.

The last two parts of the tetralogy, *Der Ring des Nibelungen.* The first two parts had been produced separately at Munich in 1869 and 1870. The first cyclic performance of the whole work, under the direction of Hans Richter and under Wagner's personal supervision, took place at the Festspielhaus, Bayreuth, on 13, 14, 16 and 17 August 1876.

The text of *Götterdämmerung*, originally called *Siegfrieds Tod,* was written as early as in 1848 (finished 28 November 1848). The other parts followed in reverse order: *Siegfried* text finished 24 June 1851, *Walküre* 1 July 1852, *Rheingold* November 1852; then *Siegfried* and *Götterdämmerung* were revised. The whole tetralogy was printed privately in January 1853.

Rheingold score finished 28 May 1854; *Walküre* score finished March 1856; *Siegfried* music started 22 September 1856; second act 30 July 1857. Interval of eight years. Scoring of *Siegfried* resumed July 1865; third act 1868; score finished 5 February 1871. *Götterdämmerung* score from 3 May 1873 to 21 November 1874.

It was Wagner's wish that the cycle should be given everywhere as a whole or at least in the proper order. Yet most stages produced *Die Walküre* first.

First performances of *Siegfried*:

VIENNA 9 November 1878.

BERLIN, O. 8 December 1885 (at the Victoria Th. earlier, see below).

PRAGUE 9 January 1887 (in German) and 23 March 1932 (in Czech, translated by V. Kühnel).

NEW YORK 9 November 1887 (in German).

BRUSSELS 12 January 1891 (in French, translated by V. Wilder).

BUDAPEST 9 April 1892 (in Hungarian, translated by A. Radó).

MOSCOW 8 February 1894 (in Russian, translated by Levental and A. K. Abramova).

ZURICH 29 November 1894 (in German).

AMSTERDAM 1 February 1895 (in German).

RIGA 28 March 1898 (in German).

MILAN 26 December 1899 (in Italian, translated by A. Zanardini).

ROUEN 17 February 1900 (in French; for the first time in France).

BARCELONA 15 November 1900 (in Italian); Catalan translation by X. Viura and J. Pena published 1904.

MADRID 8 March 1901 (in Italian).

MANCHESTER 18 October 1901 (in English, translated by H. and F. Corder).

LONDON, CORONET 31 October 1901 (in English, translated by H. and F. Corder).

PARIS, O. 3 January 1902 (in French, translated by A. Ernst).

ST. PETERSBURG 17 February 1902 (in Russian, translated by G. Tyumenev).

COPENHAGEN 22 April 1903 (in Danish, translated by E. Christiansen).

HELSINKI 15 October 1905 (in German) and 2 January 1934 (in Finnish).

STOCKHOLM 11 December 1905 (in Swedish, translated by S. Elmblad).

LEMBERG 21 February 1907 (in Polish, translated by A. Bandrowski).

BUENOS AIRES 29 August 1908 (in Italian).

ANTWERP 22 December 1908 (in Flemish).

JOHANNESBURG 1913 (in English).

RIO DE JANEIRO 21 September 1922 (in German).

ZAGREB 26 May 1938 (in Croatian).

First performances of *Götterdämmerung*:

VIENNA 14 February 1879 (in German).

PRAGUE 10 January 1887 (in German).

NEW YORK 25 January 1888 (in German).

BERLIN, O. 27 September 1888 (in German).

BUDAPEST 10 December 1892 (in Hungarian, translated by A. Radó).

STRASBOURG 25 December 1894 (in German).

TURIN 22 December 1895 (in Italian, translated by A. Zanardini).

ZURICH 4 February 1897 (in German).

AMSTERDAM 15 May 1897 (in German).

BARCELONA 16 November 1901 (in Italian). Catalan version by J. Zanné and A. Ribera published 1901; another by X. Viura and J. Pena 1906; Spanish (Castilian) version by E. López Marín published 1909.

BRUSSELS 24 December 1901 (in French, translated by V. Wilder and A. Ernst).

RIGA 25 February 1902 (in German).

PARIS, CHÂTEAU D'EAU 17 May 1902 and O. 23 October 1908 (in French).

ST. PETERSBURG 2 February 1903 (in Russian).

COPENHAGEN 23 February 1905 (in Danish, translated by J. Lehmann).

STOCKHOLM 28 February 1907 (in Swedish, translated by S. Elmblad).

ANTWERP 19 March 1910 (in Flemish).

BUENOS AIRES 14 July 1910 (in Italian).

MARSEILLES 7 November 1913 (in French).

RIO DE JANEIRO 6 October 1922 (in German).

HELSINKI 7 April 1935 (in Finnish).

Apparently there were no separate productions of *Götterdämmerung* in London.

First cyclic performances of the complete "Ring" tetralogy:

BAYREUTH 13-17 August 1876.

MUNICH 17-23 November 1878.

LEIPZIG 3-7 January 1879.

VIENNA 26-30 May 1879.

HAMBURG 1880.

BERLIN, VICT. TH. 5-9 May 1881; Berlin, O. 8-17 December 1888.

Angelo Neumann's touring "Richard Wagner-Theater" performed the "Ring" (in German) at:

LONDON, H.M.'S 5-9 May 1882.

BRESLAU September 1882.

AMSTERDAM 2-6 January 1883.

BRUSSELS 23-27 January 1883.

BASLE 26-30 March 1883.

VENICE 14-18 April 1883.

BOLOGNA 21-26 April 1883.

ROME 28 April-3 May 1883.

TURIN 8-12 May 1883.

TRIESTE 18-21 May 1883.

BUDAPEST 23-27 May 1883.

GRAZ 1-5 June 1883.

PRAGUE 9-13 February 1887 (in German).

NEW YORK 4-11 March 1889 (in German).

ST. PETERSBURG 11-16 March 1889; Moscow 6-10 April 1889 (in German, by Angelo Neumann's company).

BUDAPEST 20 January-4 February 1893 (in Hungarian; for the first time in a language other than German).

RIGA November 1902 (in German).

BRUSSELS 15-27 April 1903 (in French).

STOCKHOLM 14-20 March 1907 (in Swedish).

LONDON, C.G. 27 January-1 February 1908 (in English, translated by F. Jameson).

MONTE CARLO 26-31 January 1909 (in French).

LISBON Spring 1909 (in Italian).

COPENHAGEN 30 April-5 May 1909 (in Danish).

EDINBURGH 28 February-5 March 1910 (in English).

ANTWERP April 1910 (in Flemish).

BARCELONA April 1910 (in Italian).

LEMBERG February 1911 (in Polish, translated by A. Bandrowski).

LEEDS 28 March-1 April 1911 (in English).

MANCHESTER 3-9 April 1911 (in English).

GLASGOW 11-15 April 1911 (in English).

PARIS, O. 10-14 June 1911 (in French) and Ch.É. June 1929 (in German).

BUENOS AIRES Summer 1922 (in German).

BUCHAREST 27 April-3 May 1938 (in German, by the Frankfort opera company).

SOFIA 10-15 November 1938 (in German, by the Frankfort opera company).

ATHENS 26 November-2 December 1938 (in German, by the Frankfort opera company).

LACOME: *Jeanne, Jeannette et Jeanneton*

10 October. Paris, F.Dr.

Text by Clairville and A. Delacour. Three acts.
The most successful of Lacome's 23 operettas.
In French also, Liége 19 February 1877, etc.;
New York 28 October 1878.

In Spanish (translated by E. Álvarez), Madrid 1877.

In German (translated by G. F. Reiss), Hamburg 30 September 1877; Berlin, Fr.W. 9 October 1877; Vienna, Ca. 23 February 1878; Brünn 22 November 1881, etc.

In Italian, Naples Circo Nazionale 13 June 1878 (as *Le tre Giovanne*).

In English (translated by R. Reece), London, Alhambra 28 March 1881; New York 19 September 1887 (as *The Marquis*).

Revived Monte Carlo 16 April 1904 (in French).

RENTE: *Verde Gaio*
(Light Green)

15 October. Oporto

Text by M. M. Rodrigues. Three acts.
The most successful of Rente's numerous Portuguese operettas.

GENÉE: *Der Seekadett*

24 October. Vienna, W

Text by F. Zell. Three acts.
Genée's most successful operetta.

In German also given at Berlin, Fr.W. 3 March 1877; Laibach 1877; Brünn 3 May 1878; Czernowitz 1878; Riga 13 December 1878; Basle 21 April 1879; Posen 16 July 1879; Reval 16 July 1879; New York 27 October 1879; Rome 9 March 1882; Sofia Summer 1893; Helsinki Summer 1899.

In Hungarian, Budapest February 1877.

In Swedish (translated by E. A. Wallmark), Stockholm 31 January 1879.

In Italian (as *Lo Scacchiere della Regina*, adapted by A. Scalvini), Naples, Circo Nazionale 5 August 1879.

In French (translated by G. Lagye), Brussels 28 January 1880; Rouen 19 April 1881.

In English (translated by H. B. Farnie), London, Globe 27 March 1880; New York 7 June 1880.

In Polish, Lemberg 20 June 1880.

In Danish, Copenhagen 1883.

In Croatian (translated by G. Prejac), Zagreb 2 May 1909.

Still occasionally revived on minor German stages.

ZAJC: *Nikola Šubic Zrinski*

4 November Zagreb

Text by H. Badalić (founded on the play by T. Körner). Three acts.

The first Croatian national opera. Revived at the inauguration of the new building of the National Theatre, Zagreb 14 October 1895; and at Ljubljana 2 October 1900, in Slovenian. Still given in Yugoslavia.

Vocal score published in 1889; libretto in 1876, 1885, and 1901.

SMETANA: *Hubička*
(The Kiss)

7 November. Prague, Cz.

Text by E. Krásnohorská (founded on a story by K. Světlá). Two acts.

Successful in Czechoslovakia. Revived at Prague 22 September 1900; 19 May 1909; 9 February 1923.

In German (translated by L. Hartmann), Leipzig 6 October 1893; Vienna 27 February 1894; Berlin, Th.d.W. 4 March 1902, etc. Revived (in a new German version by L. Schottländer) Prague 30 March 1924; Aachen 30 November 1926; Berne October 1941.

In Slovenian (translated by A. Funtek), Ljubljana 1894.

In Croatian (translated by E. Kristan), Zagreb 18 April 1895.

In Polish, Lemberg October 1901.

In Flemish, Antwerp 7 January 1905.

In English, Liverpool 8 December 1938 (by amateurs).

MASSÉ: *Paul et Virginie*

15 November. Paris, O.N.L.

Text by J. Barbier and M. Carré (founded on Saint-Pierre's story). Three acts.

Successful in Paris; revived at the O.C. 18 December 1894; at the Gaîté-Lyrique 15 September 1908.

Outside Paris, given at:

BUDAPEST 16 June 1877 (in Hungarian, translated by K. Abrányi).

BRUSSELS 10 November 1877 (in French).

GENEVA 7 March 1878 (in French).

LONDON, C.G. 1 June 1878 (in Italian, translated by A. de Lauzières).

NEW ORLEANS 7 February 1879 (in English, translated by C. Florio).

NEW YORK 8 September 1879 (in English, translated by M. X. Hayes) and 4 May 1882 (in French).

VIENNA 5 January 1880 (in German, translated by F. Gumbert).

BUENOS AIRES September 1881 (in French).

MEXICO 23 December 1882 (in French).

STOCKHOLM 3 March 1886 (in Swedish, translated by E. A. Wallmark).

NAPLES 29 January 1889 (in Italian).

COWEN: *Pauline*

22 November. London, Ly.

Text by H. Hersee (founded on E. Bulwer Lytton's *The Lady of Lyons*). Four acts.

Cowen's first opera.

CHAIKOVSKY: *Vakula Kuznyets*
Вакула Кузнецъ
(Vakula the Smith)

6 December. St. Petersburg

Text by Y. P. Polonsky (founded on Gogol's *Christmas Eve*). Four acts.

(Originally the libretto had been written for Serov.)

Revived in a new version as *Cherevichki* (*The Little Shoes*) Moscow 31 January 1887; this version was very popular and has been frequently revived since (Petrograd 1 December 1915, etc.).

Outside Russia, given at:

NEW YORK 26 May 1922 (in Russian).

BARCELONA 17 December 1929 (in Russian).

MANNHEIM 2 December 1932 (in German, translated by H. Burkard, as *Die goldenen Schuhe*).

COLOGNE 29 December 1932 (in German, translated by M. Hofmüller, as *Der Pantoffelheld*).

(There is a third title of this opera, *Le Caprice d'Oxane*, under which it was published in 1885.)

DE GIOSA: *Napoli di Carnovale*

28 December. Naples, T.N.

Text by M. d'Arienzo. Three acts.

One of De Giosa's most popular works, very successful in Italy.

In Italian also, Buenos Aires 2 September 1884.

The latest revivals seem to have been at Malta in Carnival 1903 and at Bari 5 May 1923.

1877

J. STRAUSS: *Prinz Methusalem*

3 January. Vienna, Ca.

Text by K. Treumann (translated from a French libretto by V. Wilder and A. Delacour). Three acts.

Successful on German stages; Berlin, Fr.W. 24 January 1878, etc.

In German also, Czernowitz 1878; Prague 1878; Graz 15 March 1879; Zurich 2 May 1880; New York 29 October 1880; Posen 7 May 1881; Naples 2 January 1882; Moscow 1884.

Revived Berlin, Th.d.W. 9 February 1932 (text revised by B. Jenbach and P. Herz, music arranged by K. Panspertl).

In English (translated by H. S. Leigh), London, Novelty 19 May 1883; New York 25 June 1883.

In Croatian (translated by F. Miler), Zagreb 30 January 1904.

LAURO ROSSI: *Biorn*

17 January. London, Queen's

(English) text by F. Marshall (founded on Shakespeare's *Macbeth*). Five acts.

See on this rather strange *Macbeth* opera (the action of which was moved to Norway) J. Bennett's amusing report in his *Forty Years of Music* (1908), p.264. The opera was a failure and neither text nor music seem to have been preserved; it was Rossi's last opera and the only one he wrote to English words. Produced at the short-lived Queen's Theatre in Long Acre.

SAINT-SAËNS: *Le Timbre d'Argent*

23 February. Paris, Th.L.

Text by J. Barbier and M. Carré. Four acts.

Brussels 10 February 1879, etc.

In German (translated by H. Marion), Elberfeld 5 February 1904; Berlin, National Th. 17 January 1905.

Revived Monte Carlo 26 February 1907; and, in a new version, Brussels 2 March 1914 (with recitatives, instead of the original spoken dialogue).

AUDRAN: *Le Grand Mogol*

24 February. Marseilles

Text by H. C. Chivot and A. Duru. Three acts.

Audran's first great success.

In French also given at Milan, T. Manzoni 20 May 1879; Paris, Gaîté 19 September 1884 (enlarged to 4 acts); Antwerp 19 November 1886; New York 26 September 1887; Mexico 28 December 1887; Zagreb 1 April 1891.

In English (as *The Snake Charmer*), New York 29 October 1881; (translated by H. B. Farnie), London, Comedy 17 November 1884.

In German (translated by E. Jacobson), Berlin, Fr.W. 18 April 1885.

Italian version by V. Valle published Milan 1886; Polish version by A. Kiczman published Lemberg 1891; Greek version published Athens 1909.

Revived Paris, G.L. 4 March 1915 (in French); London, King's Hall 16 June 1917 (in English).

GENÉE: *Nanon, die Wirtin vom Goldenen Lamm*

10 March. Vienna, W.

Text by F. Zell (founded on a comedy by E. G. M. Théaulon and F. V. A. d'Artois). Three acts.

Genée's most popular operetta. Given at Berlin, Walhalla Th. 30 October 1883 (300th performance 11 September 1884), etc.

In German also, Budapest 29 January 1884; St. Petersburg 16 February 1884; Brünn 30 September 1884; Riga 20 December 1884; New York 2 January 1885; Basle 23 January 1885; Reval 14

February 1885; Prague 23 August 1885; Strasbourg 8 November 1885; Brussels 5 January 1886; Copenhagen May 1897.

In English (translated by L. C. Elson), New York 29 June 1885; Birmingham 16 September 1889.

In Croatian (translated by I. Trnski), Zagreb 16 March 1886.

In Swedish (translated by E. A. Wallmark), Stockholm 24 March 1886.

In Polish, Warsaw 26 March 1886.

In Italian, Rome 23 October 1888.

Frequently revived on German stages; in a new arrangement by A. Treumann-Mette Lübeck 6 February 1938.

GOUNOD: *Cinq-Mars*

5 April. Paris, O.C.

Text by L. Gallet and P. Poirson (*opéra dialogué*, founded on A. de Vigny's novel). Four acts.

Transformed into a grand opera in 5 acts: Lyons 1 December 1877.

Outside France, given at:

LIÉGE 10 January 1878 (in French).

BRUSSELS 11 January 1878 (in French).

MILAN 19 January 1878 (in Italian, translated by A. de Lauzières).

BARCELONA 29 January 1878 (in Italian, translated by A. de Lauzières).

ST. PETERSBURG 16 February 1878 (in Italian, translated by A. de Lauzières).

BUDAPEST March 1878 (in Hungarian, translated by K. Abrányi).

NAPLES, S.C. April 1878 (in Italian).

MOSCOW 20 December 1885 (in Russian).

LEEDS 26 October 1900 (in English, translated by W. Van Noorden and S. J. A. Fitz-Gerald).

LONDON, CORONET 17 November 1900 (in English, translated by W. Van Noorden and S. J. A. Fitz-Gerald).

PLANQUETTE: *Les Cloches de Corneville*

19 April. Paris, F.Dr.

Text by Clairville and C. Gabet. Three acts.

Planquette's most popular work and one of the most successful operettas of the 'seventies. The

1000th performance at the F.Dr. was on 18 October 1886; frequently revived in Paris and still given in France and in other countries.

First produced at:

BRUSSELS 29 September 1877 (in French).

NEW YORK 22 October 1877 (in English); 13 May 1878 (in French); and 1 October 1881 (in German).

MADRID 22 December 1877 (in Spanish, translated by L. M. de Larra).

MEXICO 8 February 1878 (in French) and 14 July 1878 (in Spanish).

LONDON, FOLLY 23 February 1878 (in English, translated by H. B. Farnie and R. Reece; this production had a run of 705 nights).

BUDAPEST 23 March 1878 (in Hungarian).

BERLIN, FR.W. 27 March 1878 (in German, translated by E. Dohm).

EDINBURGH 17 June 1878 (in English).

NAPLES 3 November 1878 (in French) and 31 May 1879 (in Italian, adapted by A. Scalvini).

LAIBACH (LJUBLJANA) 1878 (in German) and 1905 (in Slovenian).

STOCKHOLM 3 September 1878 (in Swedish, translated by C. G. W. Michal).

VIENNA, W. 28 September 1878 (in German).

BRÜNN 12 March 1879 (in German).

PRAGUE 13 January 1880 (in German) and 1 July 1888 (in Czech, translated by E. Züngel).

LEMBERG 18 February 1880 (in Polish).

BASLE 30 November 1880 (in French).

BUENOS AIRES 1881 (in French).

PORT ELIZABETH 1881 (in English).

RIGA 24 November 1881 (in German) and 1886 (in Lettish).

ZAGREB 10 January 1882 (in Croatian, translated by J. E. Tomić).

SARAJEVO 1882 (in German).

DORPAT (TARTU) 1885 (in Estonian).

CHRISTIANIA (OSLO) 12 September 1914 (in Norwegian).

HELSINKI 11 September 1928 (in Finnish).

KAUNAS 29 April 1932 (in Lithuanian).

CAIRO Spring 1938 (in French).

The so far latest revival in London was at the Prince Edward Th. 16 March 1931; in New York at Erlanger's 2 November 1931; in Paris at the Th. Mogador 9 March 1940.

MASSENET: *Le Roi de Lahore*

27 April. Paris, O.

Text by L. Gallet. Five acts.

Given at the Paris O. 57 times until 1879; revived Marseilles 4 April 1905; Monte Carlo 13 February 1906; New York 29 February 1924 (in French).

First produced at:

TURIN 13 February 1878 (in Italian, translated by A. Zanardini).

BUDAPEST 25 January 1879 (in Hungarian, translated by K. Abrányi).

MUNICH 13 May 1879 (in German, translated by F. Gumbert).

LONDON, C.G. 28 June 1879 (in Italian).

BUENOS AIRES 26 July 1879 (in Italian).

RIO DE JANEIRO 13 October 1879 (in Italian).

PRAGUE 29 October 1879 (in Czech) and 29 October 1882 (in German).

MADRID 14 February 1880 (in Italian).

ST. PETERSBURG 10 February 1882 (in Italian).

NEW ORLEANS 1883 (in French).

LISBON 3 April 1884 (in Italian).

ANTWERP 27 December 1894 (in French).

SANTIAGO, CHILE Autumn 1895 (in Italian).

ZAGREB 3 October 1900 (in Croatian, translated by F. Miler).

MERTENS: *Die zwarte Kapitein*
(The Black Captain)

12 May. Hague

(Dutch) text by R. Faassen. Four acts.

Mertens's best work. In Dutch also, Antwerp August 1877.

In French (translated by G. Lagye), Hague 13 February 1882.

In German (translated by H. Flemmich), Hamburg 21 February 1885.

Revived Amsterdam March 1893 (in French) and Antwerp 15 March 1919 (in Flemish).

(GOETZ): *Francesca da Rimini*

30 September. Mannheim

Text by the composer. Three acts.

The opera was completed by E. Frank and produced one year after Goetz's death. Also given at Leipzig 11 August 1881; Schwerin 25 January 1882; Hanover 1 May 1882, etc. Revived Baden-Baden 27 September 1891 and Zurich 4 December 1901 (revised by R. Gound); once more Aachen January 1925.

Given in London. H.M.'s (by the R.C.M.) 3 December 1908 (in English, translated by M. E. Browne).

BRÜLL: *Der Landfriede*

4 October. Vienna, O.

Text by S. H. Mosenthal (founded on a comedy by E. von Bauernfeld). Three acts.

Successful on German stages; Berlin 18 October 1877, etc.

In German also, Prague 19 June 1879.

POISE: *La Surprise de l'Amour*

31 October. Paris, O.C.

Text by C. P. Monselet (founded on a play by C. C. de Marivaux). Two acts.

Liége 22 March 1880; Antwerp 23 December 1880, etc. Revived Brussels 15 April 1902.

SULLIVAN: *The Sorcerer*

17 November. London, O.C.

Text by W. S. Gilbert. Two acts.

At its first production ran for 175 nights; revived (with alterations and additions), Savoy 11 October 1884; Prince's 13 January 1920, etc. First given in New York, Broadway Th. 21 February 1879.

CHABRIER: *L'Étoile*

28 November. Paris, B.P.

Text by E. Leterrier and A. Vanloo. Three acts. Chabrier's first work for the stage.

In German (as *Sein Stern*), Berlin, Fr.W. 4 October 1878; (as *Lazuli*), K.O. 4 February 1909.

In Hungarian, Budapest 29 November 1878.

In English (as *The Merry Monarch*, adapted by J. C. Goodwin and W. Morse, music arranged by J. P. Sousa), New York, Broadway Th. 18 August 1890; Boston 17 November 1890, etc. This version was given in London as *The Lucky Star* at the Savoy 7 January 1899 ("founded on and adapted from the French original . . . and an American version thereof. . . . Some new dialogue by C. H. E. Brookfield, new lyrics by A. Ross and A. Hopwood, the whole revised and put together by H. Lenoir") with new music by I. Caryll (only small parts of Chabrier's original music were retained).

Revived in French, Brussels 16 January 1909; Paris, Th. de l'Exposition 12 June 1925; Monte Carlo January 1934 (new libretto by R. Bergeret and G. de Saix).

SAINT-SAËNS: *Simson und Delila*

2 December. Weimar

(Original French) text (*Samson et Dalila*) by F. Lemaire, German version by R. Pohl. Three acts.

Saint-Saëns's most famous opera; it came to France only many years after its first production: Rouen 3 March 1890; Paris, Th. Eden 31 October 1890; Paris, O. 23 November 1892 (200th performance 19 June 1903; 500th performance 28 June 1922). An open-air production at Orange took place on 16 June 1902. Given at:

BRUSSELS 5 May 1878 (in French, in concert form); M. 25 October 1894.

GENEVA 11 December 1891 (in French, on the stage).

NEW YORK 25 March 1892 (in concert form); on the stage 8 February 1895 (in French) and 11 November 1913 (in English).

FLORENCE, T. PAGLIANO 26 March 1892 (for the first time in Italian, translated by A. Zanardini).

ALGIERS Spring 1892 (in French).

NEW ORLEANS 4 January 1893 (in French).

MILAN, SC. 27 January 1893 (in Italian) and 25 February 1910 (in French).

CAIRO February 1893 (in Italian).

LONDON, C.G. 25 September 1893 (in English, translated by E. Oudin; concert performance);

on the stage C.G. 26 April 1909 (in French) and Aldwych 14 October 1916 (in English).

ANTWERP 7 December 1893 (in French) and 30 September 1934 (in Flemish).

MOSCOW 8 January 1894 (in Italian).

ST. PETERSBURG 18 March 1894 (in French) and 1 December 1896 (in Russian).

SARATOV 29 January 1895 (in Russian, translated by A. A. Gorchakova).

MONTREAL 4 April 1895 (in concert form; in English).

BUENOS AIRES 2 July 1896 (in Italian).

BARCELONA 8 January 1897 (in Italian).

LISBON 1898 (in Italian).

RIO DE JANEIRO 25 August 1898 (in Italian).

AMSTERDAM 18 January 1901 (in Dutch; Dutch translation by J. Schmier already published in 1897).

BERLIN 28 March 1901 (in German).

RIGA 17 October 1901 (in German) and 8 September 1924 (in Lettish).

BRÜNN 30 December 1901 (in German).

BASLE 5 January 1902 (in German).

WARSAW 1902 (in Italian).

PRAGUE 6 January 1903 (in German) and 11 November 1933 (in Czech).

STOCKHOLM 11 February 1903 (in Swedish, translated by K. Valentin).

MALTA 1904 (in Italian).

BUDAPEST 22 October 1904 (in Hungarian, translated by A. Radó).

GRAZ 9 October 1905 (in German).

COPENHAGEN 18 March 1906 (in Danish, translated by E. Christiansen).

LEMBERG April 1906 (in Polish, translated by A. Bandrowski).

VIENNA 11 May 1907 (in German).

LJUBLJANA 1908 (in Slovenian).

DUBLIN 11 January 1910 (in English).

SOFIA 20 April 1912 (parts) and 2 February 1924 (complete, in Bulgarian).

JOHANNESBURG 1913 (in English).

ZAGREB 20 February 1914 (in Croatian, translated by J. Dević).

BUCHAREST Autumn 1920 (in Rumanian, translated by D. Cuclin).

HELSINKI 1 February 1924 (in Finnish).

TEL AVIV 12 March 1925 (in Hebrew, translated by A. Aschmann; an earlier Hebrew version, by Ravreb, was produced at the St. Petersburg Conservatoire in Spring 1912).

KAUNAS 8 May 1931 (in Lithuanian).

TALLINN 1933 (in Estonian).

ATHENS October 1935 (in concert form).

KRETSCHMER: *Heinrich der Löwe*

8 December. Leipzig

Text by the composer. Four acts.

Cologne 21 April 1878; Dresden 19 October 1880, etc. Revived Leipzig 19 January 1886 and 1 February 1894.

1878

LANGE-MÜLLER: *Tove*

19 January. Copenhagen

Text by the composer. Three acts.

Lange-Müller's first opera. The second act was, under the title of *Der gaar Dans i Borgegaard*, revived at Copenhagen on 10 January 1912.

LECOCQ: *Le petit Duc*

25 January. Paris, Ren.

Text by H. Meilhac and Lud. Halévy. Three acts.

Frequently revived in France; the so far latest revival in Paris was at the Th. Mogador on 25 March 1921.

In French also given at Brussels 4 April 1878; Amsterdam 1 October 1878; New York 12 April 1879; Mexico 13 April 1879; Basle 14 December 1880; Rio de Janeiro 14 May 1881; Buenos Aires September 1881, etc.; London, Coronet 8 April 1907.

In English (translated by S. and B. Rowe), London, Philharmonic 27 April 1878; (translated by F. Williams and T. R. Sullivan), New York 17 March 1879 and (adapted by H. C. Bunner and W. J. Henderson) 4 August 1884. Revived London, King's Hall 19 May 1916; Brighton 7 July 1916.

In Swedish, Stockholm 17 August and 16 November 1878 (in different versions by E. A. Wallmark and by E. G. Lundquist respectively).

In Italian, Madrid September 1878; Turin Autumn 1878; Naples, T.N. 1879.

In Hungarian (translated by J. Rákosi), Budapest October 1878.

In German (translated by H. Wittmann), Vienna, Ca. 9 November 1878; Berlin, Fr.W. 24 November 1878; Prague 14 December 1878; Laibach December 1878; Riga 19 March 1880; Zurich 4 July 1880.

In Polish, Lemberg 23 October 1880.

In Czech (translated by E. Züngel), Prague 14 July 1888.

In Croatian (translated by J. E. Tomić), Zagreb 2 April 1889.

DVOŘÁK: *Šelma Sedlák*

(The Cunning Peasant)

27 January. Prague, Cz.

Text by J. O. Veselý. Two acts.

Very successful on Czech stages. The latest revival at Prague was on 11 October 1938.

In German (translated by E. Züngel), Dresden 24 October 1882; Hamburg 3 January 1883; Vienna 19 November 1885, etc.

CABALLERO: *El Salto del Pasiego*

(The Leap of the Highlander)

17 March. Madrid, Z.

Text by L. de Eguílaz. Three acts.

Caballero's first success as a composer of zarzuela Mexico 25 December 1881; Buenos Aires 13 October 1886.

SULLIVAN: *H.M.S. Pinafore*

25 May. London, O.C.

Text by W. S. Gilbert. (Sub-title, *The Lass that loved a Sailor.*) Two acts.

Sullivan's first world success. Boston 25 November 1878; S. Francisco 23 December 1878; Philadelphia 6 January 1879; New York 15 January 1879; Calcutta 1879; Cape Town 1880;

Sydney 21 August 1880; Suva, Fiji Islands 12 January 1893.

In English also, Mexico 23 February 1884; Berlin, Kroll's 27 November 1887.

In London ran for 700 nights. The 1,000th London performance was at the Savoy on 16 September 1899.

In German (translated by E. Dohm?), New York 22 March 1879.

In Spanish, Madrid 1885? (anonymous Spanish adaptation published in that year).

A travesty by C. F. Pidgin, *M.S.S. Pinback; or, The white Lass that loved a colored Sailor*, was copyrighted (and produced?) at Boston in 1878.

Dutch Pinafore, a translation into Pennsylvania German by A. C. Moss, was copyrighted in 1901.

A sequel, *The Wreck of the Pinafore*, by H. Lingard, music by L. Searelle, was produced at the O.C., London 27 May 1882.

The following dates (taken from Vol. x of G. C. D. Odell's *Annals of the New York Stage*) may serve to illustrate the unprecedented vogue *H.M.S. Pinafore* had in New York.

It was first produced there at the Standard Th. 15 January 1879 (212 performances until 15 November). Rival productions followed at the Lyceum 23 January; Park Th., Brooklyn 3 February; Fifth Avenue Th., Niblo's Garden, and Novelty, Williamsburgh, all three 10 February; next came a parody, *T.P.S. Canal Boat Pinafore*, at Tony Pastor's Th. 17 February, and another burlesque at the Olympic, Brooklyn 24 February; the same night the original again at the Windsor Th. and 10 March at the Broadway Th., produced by Gorman's Philadelphia Church Choir Company[1] 17 March, Olympic Th., New York 20 March, Brooklyn Athenäum, produced by the Young Apollo Club 22 March followed the German production at the Germania Th., 25 March produced by amateurs at the Brooklyn Academy of Music (and 25 April at the New York Academy of Music); Globe Th. 21 April, by a Church Choir, and one week later by a negro company;

[1] This version was orchestrated by J. P. Sousa. See his recollections *Marching along* (1928), pp.62–64.

the same night, 28 April, given at the Union League Th. by Columbia College students; 5 May at Wallack's Th. by Ford's Miniature Pinafore Company, and by another children's company at Haverley's Lyceum 12 May (matinée), and at the same theatre the following night by adults. 2 June Madison Square Th.; June, by amateurs at Staten Island; 9 July, a burlesque by Joe Burgess at Bovery Garten; 11 August Aquarium; 25 August Gilmore's Garden.

As no appropriate copyright then protected a play originally produced in Europe, all those versions were pirated and more or less mutilated. The original operetta as produced in London was, under Sullivan's own direction, performed at the Fifth Avenue Th. 1 December, of the same year 1879; it ran until the end of the month, when *The Pirates of Penzance* had its first American production there (see 1879).

PARRY: *Blodwen*

20 June. Swansea

Text by W. Rowlands. Three acts.

The first Welsh opera. Vocal score (Welsh version by "Mynydogg", Richard Davies) published 1915. Given in concert form at Aberdare 25 December 1886; Liverpool 1 August 1887; Merthyr 26 December 1887; Cardiff 2 June 1890, etc. Revived Colwyn Bay 29 April 1919 (by the Colwyn Bay Musical Society; first stage performance); Liverpool 5 May 1921 (by the Welsh Operatic Society).

SMETANA: *Tajemství*
(The Secret)

18 September. Prague, Cz.

Text by E. Krásnohorská. Three acts.

Successful in Czechoslovakia. Revived at Prague 2 May 1901; 8 April 1913; 12 May 1922; November 1938.

In German (translated by M. Kalbeck), Vienna 27 March 1895.

In Slovenian, Ljubljana 1922.

COTTRAU: *Griselda*

25 September. Turin, T. Alfieri

Text by E. Golisciani. Four acts.

The most successful of Cottrau's operas; Malta May 1880; revived in a new version (reduced to 3 acts), Florence 18 October 1890; Rome 15 March 1902.

In German (translated by L. Hartmann), Pressburg 29 December 1898; Sondershausen 21 March 1899.

HEISE: *Drot og Marsk*
(King and Marshal)

25 September. Copenhagen

Text by C. Richardt (*tragisk sangdrama*). Four acts.

Very successful in Denmark; revived at Copenhagen 10 September 1909 and 15 September 1922.

In German (translated by A. Harlacher), Stuttgart 2 May 1906.

DESWERT: *Die Albigenser*

1 October. Wiesbaden

Text by W. Rullmann. Three acts.

Frankfort 5 March 1880; Breslau 20 January 1884, etc.

In German also, Strasbourg 27 January 1881 and Ghent 30 March 1881.

In French (translated by G. Lagye), Antwerp 15 March 1882.

GOUNOD: *Polyeucte*

7 October. Paris, O.

Text by J. Barbier and M. Carré. Five acts.

Unsuccessful (29 performances); outside France, only given at Antwerp 17 April 1879 and Geneva 28 April 1882.

ABERT: *Ekkehard*

11 October. Berlin, O.

Text by the composer (founded on J. V. von Scheffel's novel). Five acts.

Successful in Germany.

In German also, St. Gall 1 January 1882. Revived at Stuttgart (where Abert was court conductor) 9 October 1887; 10 October 1892; and 5 November 1899.

d'IVRY: *Les Amants de Vérone*

12 October. Paris, Th. Ventadour

Text by the composer (founded on Shakespeare's *Romeo and Juliet*). Five acts.

Privately performed in Paris as early as in May 1867. Revived in Italian (translated by A. de Lauzières), London, C.G. 24 May 1879.

HOFMANN: *Aennchen von Tharau*

6 November. Hamburg

Text by R. Fels. Three acts.

Successful in Germany; Berlin, Kroll's 2 July 1886 and O. 5 December 1889.

In German also, Riga 1879; Brünn 23 September 1879; Graz 7 November 1879; Rotterdam 22 December 1879; Basle 14 March 1884. Revived Altenburg 28 February 1897.

In English (translated by Mme Zoblinsky), Edinburgh 12 April 1880.

J. STRAUSS: *Blindekuh*

18 December. Vienna, W.

Text by R. Kneisel. Three acts.

Berlin, Fr.W. 3 April 1879; Brünn 20 November 1879, etc. Revived Bremen 21 April 1937 (text re-written by G. Quedenfeldt, music revised and re-orchestrated from the vocal score by F. Werther).

OFFENBACH: *Madame Favart*

28 December. Paris, F.Dr.

Text by A. Duru and H. C. Chivot. Three acts.

Successful in Paris; revived there Th. Apollo 18 October 1911 and Tr.L. 3 November 1934.

Outside Paris, given at:

VIENNA, W. 7 February 1879 (in German, translated by J. Hopp).

LONDON, STRAND 12 April 1879 (in English, translated by H. B. Farnie; running for 502 nights); revived King's Hall 21 January 1916.

NEW YORK 12 May 1879 (in French); 10 January 1881 (in German); and 19 September 1881 (in English).

STOCKHOLM 1879 (in Swedish).

LEIPZIG 1 June 1879 (in German).

BERLIN, FR.W. 15 August 1879 (in German).

BRUSSELS 15 October 1879 (in French).

NAPLES, T. SANNAZARO 1879 (in French).

BUDAPEST 13 November 1879 (in Hungarian).

MEXICO 11 January 1881 (in French) and 19 July 1885 (in Spanish).

LEMBERG 21 January 1881 (in Polish).

MILAN 21 August 1902 (in Italian).

Revived in a new German version by A. Hanemann: Reichenberg 19 March 1920; in a new German version by S. Anheisser: Cologne September 1930; Berlin, Lessing Th. 25 December 1932.

1879

BOTTESINI: *Ero e Leandro*

11 January. Turin, T.R.

Text by A. Boito (who originally wrote the libretto for himself; it was also set to music by Mancinelli, see 1897). Three acts.

The most successful opera of the famous double-bass virtuoso.

Outside Italy, given at Buenos Aires 1 August 1879 and Aix-les-Bains September 1883.

SUPPÉ: *Boccaccio*

1 February. Vienna, Ca.

Text by F. Zell and R. Genée. Three acts.

Suppé's most popular operetta. Subsequently given at Frankfort 13 March 1879; Prague 23 March 1879; Berne 14 June 1879; Berlin, Fr.W. 20 September 1879; Budapest November 1879; Strasbourg 27 January 1880; New York 23 April 1880; Riga 23 April 1880; Reval 12 November 1880; Venice 6 December 1880; Naples, T. San-

nazaro 1881; St. Petersburg 12 November 1882; Sarajevo 1883; Amsterdam 8 January 1884.

In Hungarian, Budapest Spring 1879; revived 26 October 1913 (new Hungarian version by Z. Harsányi).

In Swedish (translated by C. G. W. Michal), Stockholm 11 December 1879.

In Italian, Venice February 1880; Naples, Circo Nazionale 23 June 1880, etc.; Rio de Janeiro 9 May 1883; Malta 11 January 1886 (as *Fiammetta*); new Italian version by A. Novelli published 1905. Revived Milan, T.d.V. September 1931 (with recitatives by A. Bettinelli and G. Pavan).

In English (translated by D. Smith), Boston 10 May 1880; New York 17 May 1880; (translated by H. B. Farnie and R. Reece), London, Comedy 22 April 1882; Sydney 7 April 1883; Johannesburg 1907.

In Polish, Lemberg 30 April 1880.

In Russian, St. Petersburg Summer 1881; revived 24 May 1930.

In French (translated by H. C. Chivot, A. Duru and G. Lagye), Brussels 3 February 1882; Paris, F.Dr. 29 March 1882; Mexico April 1883; New York 16 May 1883; Lisbon April 1901.

In Spanish (translated by L. M. de Larra), Madrid 12 December 1882.

In Portuguese (adapted by E. Garrido) Lisbon 23 May 1884; Rio de Janeiro 1885.

In Czech, Prague 6 September 1888.

In Croatian (translated by A. Harambašić and F. Miler), Zagreb 26 May 1895.

First given at the Metropolitan New York 2 January 1931 (with recitatives by A. Bodanzky); first given at the Vienna O. 2 June 1932.

SKIBINSKI: *Verful cu Dor*
(The Summit of Desire)

6 February. Bucharest

Original German text by Queen Elizabeth of Rumania ("Carmen Sylva"), from a tale of the same title, which was later published in the Queen's *Pelesch-Märchen*; Rumanian version by M. Eminescu. One of the earliest Rumanian operas (sung by Italian artists).

SAINT-SAËNS: *Etienne Marcel*

8 February. Lyons

Text by L. Gallet. Four acts.

Paris, O. Populaire 24 October 1884. In French also, Algiers March 1895.

In Czech, Prague 19 March 1887.

Revived Monte Carlo 7 March 1918 (in French).

USIGLIO: *Le Donne curiose*

11 February. Madrid, T.R.

Text by A. Zanardini (founded on Goldoni's comedy, 1753). Three acts.

In Italian also, Milan 2 August 1879; Naples, T. Bellini 8 January 1880, etc.; Malta 1882. Successful on Italian stages; last given at Pisa 18 May 1889 and Faenza 5 January 1895.

NESSLER: *Der Rattenfänger von Hameln*

19 March. Leipzig

Text by F. Hofmann (founded on a novel by J. Wolff). Five acts.

Successful in Germany, given until about 1914. Berlin 21 February 1880, etc.

In German also, Strasbourg 15 January 1880; Riga 30 November 1880; Graz 21 December 1880; Basle 20 November 1881; Prague 21 June 1882; Rotterdam 1 December 1883; Moscow 1884; Ghent 18 December 1889; Reval 1896; Vienna, W. 30 April 1897.

In English (translated by H. Hersee), Manchester 16 November 1882; London, C.G. 7 January 1884.

CHAIKOVSKY: *Yevgeny Onyegin*

Евгеній Онѣгинъ

29 March. Moscow

Text by the composer and K. S. Shilovsky (founded on Pushkin's poem). Three acts.

First performed by the Imperial College of Music at the Little Theatre, Moscow; publicly, Moscow 23 January 1881; St. Petersburg April 1883 (by the Musical Dramatic Club) and 31 October 1884 (at the Imperial Theatre).

Very successful in Russia; given at St. Petersburg on 6 February 1898 in Italian (translated by V. Narducci). Outside Russia:

PRAGUE 6 December 1888 (in Czech, translated by M. Červinková-Riegrová).

HAMBURG 19 January 1892 (in German, translated by A. Bernhard).

LONDON, OLYMPIC 17 October 1892 (in English, translated by H. S. Edwards) and C.G. 29 June 1906 (in Italian).

NICE 7 March 1895 (in French, translated by M. Delines).

RIGA 1896 (in German) and 1912 (in Lettish).

ZAGREB 30 October 1897 (in Croatian, translated by J. Dević).

VIENNA 19 November 1897 (in German).

BERLIN 22 September 1898 (in German) and Kroll's Th. 25 May 1908 (in Russian).

MADRID 1898 (in Spanish, translated by A. Vidal y Llimona).

REVAL 1899 (in German).

WARSAW 4 May 1899 (in Italian).

MILAN, SC. 7 April 1900 (in Italian).

STRASBOURG 29 September 1901 (in German) and 1913 (in Estonian).

BUDAPEST 30 January 1902 (in Hungarian, translated by S. Várady).

LJUBLJANA 1903 (in Slovenian).

CONSTANTINOPLE July 1903 (in Italian).

STOCKHOLM 12 October 1903 (in Swedish, translated by E. A. Wallmark).

AMSTERDAM January 1906 (in Italian).

HELSINKI 18 March 1906 (in Russian) and 26 April 1909 (in Finnish).

LEMBERG 30 October 1906 (in Polish, translated by L. German).

PARIS, TH.S.B. 23 May 1911 (in Russian) and O. 9 December 1915 (in French; two scenes only).

BUENOS AIRES 20 August 1911 (in Italian).

ANTWERP 8 November 1913 (in Flemish).

COPENHAGEN 28 November 1915 (in Danish, translated by O. Rode and G. Hetsch).

MONTE CARLO 7 March 1916 (in Russian).

OSLO 29 December 1917 (in Norwegian).

SOFIA 10 December 1919 (in Bulgarian).

NEW YORK 24 March 1920 (in Italian; previously given there in concert form 1 February 1908, in English).

BELGRADE 1921 (in Serbian).

SEATTLE 7 January 1922 (in Russian).

BASLE 4 March 1923 (in German).

KAUNAS 24 April 1923 (in Lithuanian).

BUCHAREST Spring 1938 (in Rumanian).

WEISSHEIMER: *Meister Martin und seine Gesellen*

14 April. Carlsruhe

Text by A. Schricker (founded on a story by E. T. A. Hoffmann). Three acts.

Leipzig 6 March 1880, etc; Berne 24 November 1882. Revived Darmstadt 1 December 1901.

(The date of the first performance is incorrectly given as 22 February 1879 or 22 March 1879 in several books of reference.)

CHABRIER: *Une Education manquée*

1 May. Paris

Text by E. Leterrier and A. Vanloo. One act.

Privately produced at the "Cercle de la Presse" with piano accompaniment.

Revived with orchestra, Paris, Th. des Arts 9 January 1913; Monte Carlo 17 January 1924 (produced by Diaghilev, recitatives by D. Milhaud); Paris, O.C. 24 March 1938; Brussels 3 February 1940.

ŠEBOR: *Zmařená Svatba* (The frustrated Wedding)

25 October. Prague, Cz.

Text by M. Červinková-Riegrová. Three acts.

Sebor's last opera. Revived Prague May 1914.

RUBINSTEIN: *Nero*

1 November Hamburg

(Original French) text by J. Barbier, German version by R. Pohl. Four acts.

In German also, Berlin 3 December 1880, etc.

Outside Germany, given at:

ST. PETERSBURG 10 February 1884 and Moscow 19 March 1884 (in Italian, translated by A. de

Lauzières); in Russian, St. Petersburg December 1902 (at the Conservatoire) and 6 November 1906 (at the Maryinski Th.).

ANTWERP 30 December 1884 (in the original French); Ghent 19 January 1885.

VIENNA 20 April 1885 (in German).

NEW YORK 14 March 1887 (in English, translated by J. P. Jackson).

ROUEN 14 February 1894 (in French).

BARCELONA 27 January 1898 (in Italian).

AUDRAN: *Les Noces d'Olivette*

13 November. Paris, B.P.

Text by H. C. Chivot and A. Duru. Three acts.

In French also, Brussels 21 September 1880; Naples 20 November 1880; New York 6 December 1881; Mexico 5 February 1882.

In Hungarian, Budapest 8 September 1881

In English (translated by H. B. Farnie), London, Strand 18 September 1880 (running for 466 nights); New York 25 December 1880.

In German, Vienna, Ca. 29 October 1881; Munich 4 November 1883; Berlin, Th. U. d. Linden 23 February 1895 (as *Kapitän Caricciolo*).

OFFENBACH: *La Fille du Tambour-Major*

13 December. Paris, F.Dr.

Text by H. C. Chivot and A. Duru. Three acts.

The last of Offenbach's works which was produced in his lifetime (d. 4 October 1880). Successful in Paris and abroad.

In French also given at Liége 23 February 1880; Brussels 2 March 1880; Buenos Aires 1880; New York 13 September 1880; Naples 1 December 1880; Mexico 18 January 1881.

In German (translated by J. Hopp), Vienna, W. 10 April 1880; Aachen 12 February 1881; Berlin, Walhalla Th. 11 September 1883 (Hopp's translation revised by A. Rheinisch).

In English (translated by H. B. Farnie), London, Alhambra 19 April 1880; New York 4 October 1880. In other English versions by M. Freeman and E. Smith, New York, Casino 16 September 1889; by F. Bowyer and W. E. Sprange, London, Coronet 1 October 1900.

In Swedish (translated by E. A. Wallmark), Gothenburg 16 October 1880.

In Hungarian (translated by L. Evva and J. B. Fáy), Budapest 1880.

In Flemish, Brussels 9 October 1885.

Revived Paris, Gaîté 27 March 1907 and 7 October 1920; Milan 1907 (in Italian); London, Shaftesbury 1 June 1908 (in French). Still given on French stages. Revived at Amsterdam February 1940.

SULLIVAN: *The Pirates of Penzance*

30 December. Paignton

Text by W. S. Gilbert. Two acts.

The production at the Bijou Theatre, Paignton (Devonshire), was a copyright performance; the next night, 31 December 1879, the work was produced at the New Fifth Avenue Th., New York (as at Paignton with the sub-title, *Love and Duty*). First given in London, O.C. 3 April 1880 (with the new sub-title, *The Slave of Duty*; running for 363 nights); Edinburgh 17 January 1881; Cape Town 1881, etc.

In English also, Mexico 1 March 1884.

In German (translated by F. Zell and R. Genée), Vienna, W. 1 March 1889.

Revived Düsseldorf 1 December 1936 (new German version by F. A. Beyerlein).

1880

ZENGER: *Wieland der Schmied*

18 January. Munich

Text by P. Allfeld. Four acts.

The best of Zenger's four operas. Revived in a new version, Munich 5 April 1894.

RIMSKY-KORSAKOV: *Maiskaya Noch*

Майская Ночь

(May Night)

21 January. St. Petersburg

Text by the composer (founded on a story by Gogol). Three acts.

Successful in Russia; Moscow Autumn 1892, etc.; revived St. Petersburg 10 October 1894; 24 March 1902; Moscow 9 May 1909; Petrograd 12 March 1917, on the opening night of the Russian State Opera-House, later Maryinsky Th., after the revolution of February, 1917[1]; Leningrad 1 October 1921. Outside Russia, given at:

PRAGUE 31 August 1896 (in Czech, translated by V. J. Novotný).

FRANKFORT 3 May 1900 (in German, translated by A. Bernhard).

LONDON, D.L. 26 June 1914 (in Russian).

RIGA 4 April 1922 (in Lettish).

LJUBLJANA 4 October 1924 (in Slovenian).

SOFIA 30 January 1925 (in Bulgarian).

BARCELONA 15 December 1926 (in Russian); Catalan version by J. Pena and R. J. Slaby published in that year.

OXFORD 24 November 1931 (in English, translated by E. Agate?).

CATALANI: *Elda*

31 January. Turin, T.R.

Text by C. d'Ormeville (*dramma fantastico*). Four acts.

Catalani's first opera; it became a great success only 10 years later when the composer revised it under the new title of *Loreley* (text altered and reduced to 3 acts by A. Zanardini: *azione drammatica*). It was produced at the same theatre on 16 February 1890 and still holds the boards in Italy.

In Italian also given at:

ODESSA Carnival 1901.

BUENOS AIRES 23 July 1905.

ALEXANDRIA Carnival 1907.

LONDON, C.G. 12 July 1907.

RIO DE JANEIRO 4 June 1910.

MADRID April 1916.

CHICAGO 17 January 1919.

NEW YORK 13 February 1919.

MALTA 1919.

MONTEVIDEO 25 August 1920.

[1] At Moscow, the opening bill (April 8), consisted of one act each from Glinka's *Ruslan i Lyudmila* (see 1842) and from Rimsky-Korsakov's *Sadko* (see 1898).

SUPPÉ: *Donna Juanita*

21 February. Vienna, Ca.

Text by F. Zell and R. Genée. Three acts.

Suppé's last great success.

In German, Nuremberg 25 April 1880; Prague 12 June 1880; Berlin, Fr.W. 2 October 1880; Budapest 9 October 1880; Trieste 20 October 1880; Venice 30 November 1880; Laibach, Bucharest and Czernowitz 1880; Naples February 1881; New York 27 September 1881; Basle 17 January 1883; St. Petersburg 11 April 1883; Sarajevo 1883; Lodz 8 December 1883; Amsterdam 15 December 1883; Reval 12 March 1885; Sofia Summer 1893.

In Czech (translated by B. Peška and E. Züngel), Prague 1880.

In Swedish (translated by C. G. W. Michal), Stockholm 23 November 1880.

In Hungarian, Budapest 25 December 1880.

In English (translated by?), New York 16 May 1881.

In Russian, St. Petersburg Summer 1881.

In Italian (translated by P. Morelli), Malta 1886.

In French (translated by E. Leterrier and A. Vanloo), Brussels 22 October 1883; Paris, F.Dr. 4 April 1891.

In Danish (translated by C. Kjerulf), Copenhagen 1884.

In Spanish (translated by J. Molas y Casas), Barcelona 20 September 1884; Mexico 14 May 1885.

In Croatian (translated by M. Pogačić), Zagreb 28 November 1905.

Revived Berlin, Th.d.W. 12 June 1926 (as *Die grosse Unbekannte*); New York, M. 2 January 1932 (in English, translated by A. Mattulath, with recitatives by A. Bodanzky); Coblentz 6 November 1937 (revised by A. Treumann-Mette).

RUBINSTEIN: *Kupyets Kalashnikov*
Купецъ Калашниковъ
(The Merchant Kalashnikov)

5 March. St. Petersburg

Text by N. I. Kulikov (founded on Lermontov's poem). Three acts.

One of Rubinstein's best works; after the second performance it was banned by the police for political reasons. Revived only eight years later: St. Petersburg 22 January 1888, then Moscow 25 March 1901, etc.

DELIBES: *Jean de Nivelle*

8 March. Paris, O.C.

Text by E. Gondinet and P. Gille. Three acts.

Given at the O.C. 100 times until 6 January 1881 and revived at the Gaîté-Lyrique 5 October 1908. Outside Paris, given at:

STOCKHOLM 1 December 1880 (in Swedish, translated by F. T. Hedberg).

BUDAPEST 17 March 1881 (in Hungarian, translated by A. Váradi).

COPENHAGEN 17 March 1881 (in Danish, translated by A. Zinck).

VIENNA 29 March 1881 (in German, translated by F. Zell).

GENEVA 19 April 1881 (in French).

ST. PETERSBURG 14 December 1881 (in Italian, translated by A. Zanardini).

BRUSSELS 28 November 1882 (in French).

CAUDELLA and OTREMBA: *Oltenca*

March. Jassy

Text by G. Bengescu. Three acts.

Early Rumanian comic opera; libretto printed 1880.

VARNEY: *Les Mousquetaires au Couvent*

16 March. Paris, B.P.

Text by P. Ferrier and J. Prével. Three acts.

The most successful of Varney's more than 30 operettas; still popular in France; the so far latest revival in Paris was at the G.L. on 15 April 1924.

In French also given at Brussels 3 June 1880; Geneva 24 September 1880; Cairo 4 November 1880; Mexico 7 January 1882; New York 25 April 1882; Buenos Aires 1882; Berlin, Apollo Th. 13 February 1893; London, Coronet 10 April 1907.

In English (translated by H. B. Farnie), London, Globe 31 October 1880; Boston March 1882.

In Spanish (translated by F. Serrat y Weiler and J. M. Casademunt), Barcelona 24 August 1881.

In Russian, St. Petersburg Summer 1881.

In German (translated by J. Hopp and E. Mautner), Vienna, W. 30 September 1881; Berlin, Alexanderplatz Th. 21 March 1896.

In Italian (as *Amore ed Armi*), Rome 15 January 1883.

MATHIEU: *La Bernoise*

1 April. Brussels, M.

Text by L. Solvay. One act.

Revived Antwerp 11 March 1897 (in French) and 5 October 1912 (in Flemish).

J. STRAUSS: *Das Spitzentuch der Königin*

1 October. Vienna, W.

Text by H. Bohrmann-Riegen and R. Genée (originally written for Suppé; a *Cervantes* operetta). Three acts.

In German also, Berlin, Fr.W. 24 November 1880 (text revised by J. Rosen; last revived in Berlin, D.O. 22 May 1931); Czernowitz 20 January 1881; Budapest 21 February 1881; Strasbourg 24 February 1881; Brünn 5 March 1881; Graz 20 March 1881; Zurich 12 August 1881; Prague 6 January 1883; New York 1 October 1883; Amsterdam 1 February 1884; Reval 1887.

In Swedish (translated by E. A. Wallmark), Stockholm 1881.

In English (translated by L. C. Elson), New York 21 October 1882.

In Hungarian, Budapest 29 December 1885.

In Croatian (translated by F. Miler), Zagreb 2 December 1910.

(The famous waltz, *Rosen aus dem Süden*, consists of tunes from this operetta.)

BUCK: *Deseret;* or, *A Saint's Affliction*

11 October. New York, Haverley's

Text by W. A. Croffut. Three acts.

American comic opera, successful in the U.S.A.

ERKEL: *Névtelen Hösök* (Nameless Heroes)

30 November. Budapest

Text by E. Tóth. Four acts.

Revived Budapest 15 January 1916 (new libretto by A. Kern and F. Martos, music revised by N. Rékai).

MILLÖCKER: *Apajune der Wassermann*

18 December. Vienna W.

Text by F. Zell and R. Genée. Three acts.

Very successful on German stages for about 30 years. Given at Pressburg 21 February 1881; Hamburg 6 May 1881; Brünn 8 October 1881; Berlin, Fr.W. 10 December 1881; New York 13 January 1882; Temesvar 1882; Budapest 2 October 1882; Prague 26 April 1883.

In Hungarian, Budapest 4 March 1881.

In English (translated by ?), New York 25 February 1882.

In Croatian (translated by A. Harambašić) Zagreb 11 November 1885.

POISE: *L'Amour Médecin*

20 December. Paris, O.C.

Text by C. P. Monselet (founded on Molière's comedy). Three acts.

Successful in Paris; given at the O.C. until 1898.

In French also, Brussels 19 January 1887.

PONCHIELLI: *Il Figliuol prodigo*

26 December. Milan, Sc.

Text by A. Zanardini. Four acts.

Successful in Italy; the latest revivals were at Cremona 1 July 1934 (open-air performance) and Milan, Sc. 26 December 1934. Outside Italy, only given at Buenos Aires 22 May 1897.

AUDRAN: *La Mascotte*

28 December. Paris, B.P.

Text by A. Duru and H. C. Chivot. Three acts.

Audran's most popular operetta; the 1,000th Paris performance was in December 1885, the

1,700th on 29 August 1897; the so far latest revival at the Th. Porte St. Martin 13 May 1935.
Given at:

VIENNA, W. 12 February 1881 (in German).

ANTWERP 24 March 1881 (in French).

BUDAPEST 10 April 1881 (in Hungarian).

STOCKHOLM 28 April 1881 (in Swedish, translated
by E. G. Lundquist).

NEW YORK 5 May 1881 (in English); 30 November 1881 (in French); and 5 December 1881 (in
German); revived Jolson's 1 December 1926
(in French).

BUENOS AIRES September 1881 (in French).

BRIGHTON 19 September 1881 (in English, translated by H. B. Farnie and R. Reece).

LONDON, COMEDY 15 October 1881 (in English)
and Royalty 23 January 1888 (in French).

BERLIN, Fr.W. 25 October 1881 (in German) and
Walhalla Th. 25 January 1888 (in French).

PRAGUE 8 November 1881 (in German).

MEXICO 4 January 1882 (in French) and 13 May
1883 (in Spanish).

BARCELONA Summer 1882 (in French).

COPENHAGEN 1882 (in Danish, translated by P.
Sørensen).

MILAN 30 November 1886 (in French) and 6 October 1889 (in Italian).

CAPE TOWN 1887 (in English).

ZAGREB 30 March 1891 (in French) and 9 December 1897 (in Croatian, translated by S. Albini).

RIGA and REVAL 1891 (in German).

BASLE 31 October 1894 (in German).

LISBON May 1901 (in French).

1881

STANFORD: *Der verschleierte Profet*

6 February. Hanover

Original English text by W. B. Squire (*The Veiled
Prophet of Khorassan*, founded on Moore's *Lalla
Rookh*), German version by E. Frank. Three acts.

The first opera of the Irish composer.

Revived (with alterations), London, C.G. 26
July 1893 (in Italian, translated by G. A. Mazzucato).

(OFFENBACH): *Les Contes d'Hoffmann*

10 February. Paris, O.C.

Text by J. Barbier and M. Carré (founded on a
play by the same authors, first produced at the
Odéon, Paris, 31 March 1851). Prologue, three
acts and epilogue.

Carré's name as joint librettist appears only in
the first edition of the vocal score. In all later editions Barbier alone is mentioned. The libretto was
originally written to be set to music by Hector Salomon. Offenbach did not live to finish the work,
which was orchestrated by E. Guiraud. The
drinking song and the famous barcarole were
taken from Offenbach's German opera, *Die
Rheinnixen* (Vienna 1864).

Very successful in Paris; given at the O.C. 101
times in 1881. Revived Th.L. (Renaissance) 7
February 1893 and O.C. 13 November 1911
(given there over 600 times to date).

Outside Paris, given at:

VIENNA 7 December 1881 (in German, translated
by J. Hopp; produced at the "Ringtheater",
which was burnt down the night of the second
performance; this disaster always being associated with Offenbach's work, the opera did
not become popular in Germany until about
25 years later. Given at Vienna, W. 8 June 1883
(in Hungarian, by the Budapest company); O.
11 November 1901 (in German).

GENEVA 8 April 1882 (in French).

BUDAPEST 15 April 1882 (in Hungarian, translated
by A. Váradi).

HAMBURG 20 September 1882 (in German).

NEW YORK 16 October 1882 (in French) and 30
September 1913 (in English, translated by C. H.
Meltzer).

MEXICO 15 December 1882 (in French).

PRAGUE Summer 1883 (in German) and 18 October 1888 (in Czech, translated by V. J. Novotný).

ANTWERP 30 November 1883 (in French) and 25
January 1912 (in Flemish).

BERLIN, FR. W. 22 March 1884 (in German); revived K.O. 17 November 1905 (new German

version by M. Morris; prologue, 3 acts and epilogue; with some new numbers from Offenbach's original score and with recitatives instead of spoken dialogue). This production (by H. Gregor) reached its 500th night on 24 September 1909 and served as a model for many later revivals in Germany and elsewhere. First produced at the Berlin O. 23 September 1915.

LEMBERG 1884 (in Polish, translated by A. Urbański).

WARSAW 1905 (in Polish, translated by A. Urbański).

BRUSSELS 28 January 1887 (in French).

STOCKHOLM 17 May 1889 (in Swedish, translated by E. A. Wallmark).

COPENHAGEN 1 January 1890 (in Danish, translated by E. Bøgh).

BUENOS AIRES 1894 (in French) and 25 August 1921 (in Italian).

BASLE 27 November 1895 (in German).

RIGA 3 December 1897 (in German) and 9 January 1923 (in Lettish).

ST. PETERSBURG 17 February 1899 (in Russian); revived 31 January 1924.

ZAGREB 19 April 1902 (in Croatian, translated by F. Miler).

LJUBLJANA 1902 (in Slovenian).

AMSTERDAM September 1902 (in Dutch).

BOLOGNA 28 November 1903 (in Italian, translated by A. Zanardini).

BARCELONA April 1905 (in Spanish) and 5 February 1924 (in Italian).

REVAL (TALLINN) Spring 1905 (in German) and 1923 (in Estonian).

LONDON, ADELPHI 17 April 1907 (in German) and H.M.'s 12 May 1910 and C.G. 5 October 1910 (in English, translated by E. Agate).

BUCHAREST Spring 1907 (in German) and February 1926 (in Rumanian).

JOHANNESBURG 5 March 1912 (in English).

HELSINKI 14 April 1912 (in Swedish) and 22 April 1925 (in Finnish).

OSLO 14 December 1916 (in Norwegian).

MALTA 1917 (in Italian).

BELGRADE 1921 (in Serbian).

SOFIA 9 March 1922 (in Bulgarian).

KHARKOV 1925 (in Ukrainian).

KAUNAS 12 November 1925 (in Lithuanian).

TEL-AVIV 27 March 1939 (in Hebrew, translated by A. Aschmann).

CHAIKOVSKY: *Orleanskaya Dyeva*
Орлеанская Дѣва
(The Maid of Orleans)

25 February. St. Petersburg

Text by the composer (founded on V. A. Zhukovsky's Russian version of Schiller's tragedy). Four acts.

Revived Moscow 1899 and September 1907.

In Czech, Prague July 1882 (first opera of Chaikovsky that was heard outside Russia).

WAELPUT: *Stella*

14 March. Brussels, Alhambra

(Flemish) text by I. Teirlinck and R. Stijns. Revived Antwerp November 1890.

PERFALL: *Raimondin*

27 March. Munich

Text by H. T. von Schmid. Five acts.

Leipzig 3 April 1882; Berlin 21 November 1882, etc. Given in a reduced 3-act version as *Melusine* at Munich 30 September 1885.

GOUNOD: *Le Tribut de Zamora*

1 April. Paris, O.

Text by A. P. d'Ennery and J. Brésil. Four acts.

Given in Paris 50 times until 1885.

In French also, Antwerp 16 November 1882; Geneva 19 March 1885.

In Italian (translated by A. Zanardini), Turin 5 March 1882.

In German, Vienna 30 January 1883; Hamburg 25 February 1884; Prague 1892.

The first act was revived at Monte Carlo 2 April 1918.

SULLIVAN: *Patience; or, Bunthorne's Bride*

25 April. London, O.C.

Text by W. S. Gilbert. Two acts.

In London ran for 578 nights. St. Louis 28 July 1881; New York, Standard Th. 22 September 1881, etc.

In English also, Berlin, Kroll's 30 April 1887; Vienna, Ca. 28 May 1887; Leipzig 2 July 1887; Budapest *c.*1887; Amsterdam 1 February 1888.

The Savoy Theatre, London, was inaugurated with *Patience* on 10 October 1881.

A parody, *Im-Patience*, text by W. Browne, music by F. Stanislaus, was produced at Liverpool 25 August 1884.

J. HUBER: *Irene*

3 June. Stuttgart

Text by P. Lohmann (published as early as 1865). Symphonic 1-act drama, in some respect anticipating operas like R. Strauss's *Salome*, etc.

SMETANA: *Libuše*

11 June. Prague, Cz.

(Original German) text by J. Wenzig, translated into Czech by E. Špindler. Three acts.

The opera had been written in 1871–72; produced only nine years later, at the inauguration of the Czech National Theatre ("Národní Divadlo"), Prague; the theatre burnt down two months later (12 August) and the new building, on 18 November 1883, again was inaugurated with *Libuše*.

Along with *Dalibor* (see 1868) Smetana's most important serious Czech national opera. Revived at Prague 18 November 1902; 24 May 1915; 25 June 1920; 12 May 1924; and 18 May 1938 (*c.*200 performances altogether). The 1,000th Smetana performance at Prague (counting all his operas) was celebrated with *Libuše*, 27 August 1905.

Given all over Czechoslovakia; also produced at:

VIENNA 4 June 1924 (in Czech, by the Olomouc Opera Company).

ZAGREB 27 October 1933 (in Croatian).
LJUBLJANA 11 April 1934 (in Slovenian).

GOULA: *A la Voreta del Mar* (On the Seashore)

July. Barcelona, T. Principal

Text by D. Calvet. One act.

The first opera (or rather operetta) ever written and sung in the Catalan language.

DVOŘÁK: *Tvrdé Palice* (The Pigheaded Peasants)

2 October. Prague, Cz.

Text by J. Štolba. One act.

Revived Prague 8 September 1901; 25 September 1910; 24 October 1913; and 31 August 1928.

In German, Zurich Spring 1907.

HALLÉN: *Harald der Wiking*

16 October. Leipzig

Text by H. Herrig. Three acts.

In Swedish (translated by A. Lindgren), Stockholm 18 February 1884 (given there until 1912). Parts of the opera were heard in concert form at Berlin on 4 April 1892.

LISZT: *Die Legende von der heiligen Elisabeth*

23 October. Weimar

Text by O. Roquette. Prologue and 4 scenes.

First stage production of Liszt's oratorio (first given at Budapest 15 August 1865, in Hungarian [*Szent Erzsébet Legendája*] and Munich 24 February 1866, in German). Further operatic performances took place only after Liszt's death:

VIENNA 25 December 1889 (in German).
PRAGUE 16 December 1890 (in Czech).
BUDAPEST 15 September 1891 (in Hungarian, translated by K. Abrányi; given there until 1933).
GRAZ 19 November 1892 (in German).
BRÜNN 18 November 1893 (in German).

MANNHEIM 22 December 1897 (in German).
GOTHA 6 March 1898 (in German).
RIGA December 1907 (in German).
NEW YORK 3 January 1918 (in German).
BERLIN 27 January 1918 (in German).

GURJÃO: *Idalia*

3 November. Belem do Pará

(Italian) text by the composer (who was a pupil of Pacini). Three acts.

The vocal score of this early opera by a Brazilian composer was published at Belem do Pará in 1882.

J. STRAUSS: *Der lustige Krieg*

25 November. Vienna. W.

Text by F. Zell and R. Genée. Three acts.

In German also, given at Berlin, Fr.W. 19 January 1882 (300th performance 15 September 1885); Brünn and Graz 11 February 1882; Prague 12 February 1882; Naples 13 February 1882; Posen 22 February 1882; New York 15 March 1882; Basle 17 March 1882; Strasbourg 10 April 1882; Sarajevo 1882; St. Petersburg 20 January 1883; Riga 25 February 1883; Dorpat 8 July 1883; Czernowitz 1883; Moscow 23 December 1884; Helsinki Summer 1900.

In Hungarian, Budapest 31 January 1882.

In Czech (translated by E. Züngel), Prague 1882.

In English (translated by L. C. Elson), New York 27 June 1882; (translated by R. Reece), London, Alhambra 15 October 1882.

In Swedish (translated by E. A. Wallmark), Stockholm 1882.

In French (translated by A. and M. Hennequin), Brussels 19 November 1885 (music adapted by M. Kufferath).

In Croatian, Zagreb 1 May 1900.

In Flemish, Ghent November 1901.

Frequently revived on German stages; revived in English, London, New St. Pancras Th. 2 February 1939.

FIBICH: *Blaník*

25 November. Prague, Cz.

Text by E. Krásnohorská. Three acts.

Fibich's second opera. Revived at Prague 4 April 1894 and 17 April 1925.

REINTHALER: *Das Käthchen von Heilbronn*

7 December. Frankfort

Text by H. Bulthaupt (founded on H. von Kleist's drama). Four acts.

After a competition this opera had been chosen for the opening night of the new Frankfort opera house. Berlin 23 March 1889.

MASSENET: *Hérodiade*

19 December. Brussels, M.

Text by P. Milliet and "H. Grémont" (G. Hartmann), founded on a story by Flaubert. Four acts.

One of Massenet's most successful works; still given on French stages.

Produced at:

MILAN, SC. 23 February 1882 (in Italian, translated by A. Zanardini, with some additions).

BUDAPEST 23 December 1882 (in Hungarian, translated by E. Abrányi).

HAMBURG 20 January 1883 (in German, translated by G. F. Reiss).

NANTES 29 March 1883 (for the first time in France, in French).

PRAGUE 3 November 1883 (in German).

PARIS, TH.I. 1 February 1884 (in Italian; in French only 21 October 1903 at the opening of the new "Théâtre-Lyrique de la Gaîté").

GENEVA 10 December 1884 (in French).

LISBON 1886 (in Italian).

RIO DE JANEIRO 1889 (in Italian).

NEW ORLEANS 13 February 1892 (in French).

CAIRO December 1894 (in French).

ALGIERS Spring 1896 (in French).

HAGUE December 1896 (in French).

AMSTERDAM March 1900 (in Dutch).

LONDON, C.G. 6 July 1904 (in French, as *Salomé*) and L.O.H. 15 December 1911 (as *Hérodiade*).

BUENOS AIRES 6 July 1907 (in Italian).

NEW YORK 8 November 1909 (in French).

BARCELONA 13 December 1924 (in Italian).

CASABLANCA, MOROCCO 14 April 1934 (in French).

An open-air performance at the Roman Theatre, Orange, took place on 15 June 1902. First given at the Paris O. 22 December 1921 and revived there 31 December 1928 and 12 April 1935.

1882

RIMSKY-KORSAKOV: *Snyegurochka*
Снѣгурочка
(The Snow Maiden)
10 February. St. Petersburg

Text by the composer (founded on a play by A. N. Ostrovsky). Prologue and 4 acts.

Moscow 7 February 1893; Kiev 16 January 1896, etc. Revived Leningrad 28 April 1928 and 23 September 1934. Outside Russia, given at:

PRAGUE 29 March 1905 (in Czech).

PARIS, O.C. 22 May 1908 (in French, translated by P. Halperine and P. Lalo) and Ch.É. 9 February 1929 (in Russian).

ZAGREB 28 June 1921 (in Croatian).

SEATTLE 5 January 1922 (in Russian).

NEW YORK 23 January 1922 (in French) and 9 March 1935 (in English).

BARCELONA 24 January 1922 (in Russian).

BERLIN, V.O. 27 September 1923 (in German, translated by A. Bernhard).

ANTWERP 8 November 1927 (in Flemish).

BUDAPEST February 1928 (in Hungarian).

SOFIA 8 September 1929 (in Bulgarian).

BUENOS AIRES 21 September 1929 (in Russian).

LONDON, SADLER'S WELLS 12 April 1933 (in English, translated by E. Agate).

TURIN November 1931 (in Russian).

CHAPI: *La Tempestad*
(The Storm)
11 March. Madrid, T. de Jovellanos

Text by M. Ramos Carrión (founded on Erckmann-Chatrian's *Le Juif Polonais*). Three acts.

Chapi's first successful zarzuela; very popular in Spain, "causando un verdadero delirio de entusiasmo".

In Spanish also, New York 27 April 1917. Revived Madrid, T. Price March 1934.

MIHALOVICH: *Hagbarth und Signe*
12 March. Dresden

Text by A. Stern (founded on a play by A. G. Oehlenschläger). Three acts.

Mihalovich's first opera; in Hungarian (translated by A. Váradi), Budapest 17 January 1886.

(DONIZETTI): *Il Duca d'Alba*
22 March. Rome, Ap.

(Original French) text by A. E. Scribe, Italian version by A. Zanardini. Four acts.

The opera had been written for the Paris Opéra in 1840, but was not produced then. Scribe afterwards altered the libretto for Verdi; it became *Les Vêpres siciliennes* (see 1855). Donizetti's score was recovered at Bergamo in 1875 and completed by Matteo Salvi. After Rome it was given at Naples, Bergamo, Turin and at Barcelona 19 December 1882 and Malta 1884.

LUX: *Der Schmied von Ruhla*
29 March. Mayence

Text by L. Bauer. Three acts.

Popular on German stages during the 'eighties; also given at Strasbourg 21 March 1886; Basle 21 November 1886; Graz 23 March 1887.

A. THOMAS: *Françoise de Rimini*
14 April. Paris, O.

Text by J. Barbier and M. Carré. Prologue, 4 acts and epilogue.

Thomas's last opera. Given in Paris 42 times until 1885.

Outside Paris only given at Antwerp 11 December 1883 (in French).

LENEPVEU: *Velleda*

4 July. London, C.G.

(Original French) text by A. Challamel and J. Chantepie (founded on Chateaubriand's *Les Martyrs*), Italian version by G. Vacotti. Four acts.

Written for Adelina Patti. Revived (in the original French) Rouen 18 April 1891.

R. WAGNER: *Parsifal*

26 July. Bayreuth

Text by the composer (*Ein Bühnenweihfestspiel*). Three acts.

Wagner's last opera. Written 1877–79; score finished January 1882. Text published 1877 (first English translation by H. and F. Corder 1879). Vocal score (by J. Rubinstein) 1882, full score 1885.

The production of *Parsifal* was limited to Bayreuth until 30 years after the composer's death (100th performance 19 August 1897). The copyright ran out on 31 December 1913. There are, however, several performances before that date to be recorded.

Private performances for King Ludwig of Bavaria took place at Munich on 3, 5 and 7 May, and 5 and 7 November 1884; and on 26, 27 and 29 April 1885.

Concert performances, more or less complete, were at:

LONDON, ALBERT HALL 10 November 1884 (under J. Barnby).

NEW YORK 3 March 1886 (under W. Damrosch).

BOSTON 15 April 1891 (in English, under B. Lang).

AMSTERDAM 3 December 1896 (under H. Viotta), and in many other towns.

Stage productions, against the privilege of Bayreuth and much discussed then, were at:

NEW YORK, M. 24 December 1903 (in German, under A. Hertz, produced by H. Conried).

BOSTON 17 October 1904 (in English, translated by J. P. Jackson; under W. H. Rothwell, produced by H. Savage); subsequently given at New York 31 October 1904 and in other American towns; at New Orleans 24 April 1905; Montreal April 1905.

AMSTERDAM 20 June 1905 (in German, under H. Viotta).

MONTE CARLO February 1913 (privately).

ZURICH 13 April 1913 (in German, under L. Kempter; the Swiss copyright had expired by that time).

BUENOS AIRES 20 June 1913 (in Italian, translated by A. Zanardini[1]; under G. Marinuzzi).

RIO DE JANEIRO 8 September 1913 (in Italian, translated by A. Zanardini; under G. Marinuzzi).

After 31 December 1913, *Parsifal* was first given at Barcelona (in Italian; the performance began at midnight!); a Catalan version by J. Zanné and J. Pena had been published in 1907).

On 1 January 1914 also, Berlin, D.O.; Bremen, Breslau, Kiel; Prague (both in German and in Czech, translated by J. Vymětal); Budapest (in German, at the People's Opera); Bologna, Rome, and Madrid (in Italian).

FRANKFORT and MAYENCE 2 January 1914.

ST. PETERSBURG 3 January 1914 (in Russian).

FREIBURG and PARIS, O. 4 January 1914 (in French, translated by A. Ernst).

BERLIN, O. 5 January 1914 (100th performance 31 March 1923).

BRUSSELS 5 January 1914 (in French, translated by M. Kufferath and J. Gautier).

MILAN, SC. 9 January 1914 (in Italian, translated by G. Pozza[1]).

COLOGNE 11 January 1914.

VIENNA, O. 14 January 1914.

MARSEILLES and MONTE CARLO 20 January 1914 (in French).

VIENNA, V.O. 25 January 1914.

LONDON, C.G. 2 February 1914 (in German).

LYONS 13 February 1914 (in French).

ANTWERP 17 March 1914 (in Flemish, translated by L. van Riel).

DRESDEN 24 March 1914.

GENOA 2 May 1914 (in Italian).

PARIS, CH.É. 3 June 1914 (for the first time there in German).

[1] Besides Zanardini's and Pozza's, there are three more printed Italian versions of *Parsifal*, by F. Verdinois, 1909; by G. Vaccaro, 1914; and by F. Spetrino, n.d.

Up to 1 August 1914 also produced at Hamburg, Königsberg, Barmen, Elberfeld, Strasbourg, Halle, Chemnitz, Wiesbaden, Leipzig, Nuremberg, Hanover, Stuttgart, Stettin, Cassel, Weimar, Augsburg, Posen, Munich, Brünn, Pisa, Venice, Florence, etc.

Some later productions:

COPENHAGEN 9 April 1915 (in Danish, translated by J. Lehmann).

STOCKHOLM 21 April 1917 (in Swedish, translated by S. Elmblad).

LONDON, C.G. 17 November 1919 (in English).

MANCHESTER 12 January 1920 (in English).

NAPLES, S.C. 19 February 1921 (in Italian).

LISBON September 1921 (in Italian).

HAVANA 1921 (in Italian).

ZAGREB 28 April 1922 (in Croatian).

BASLE 20 September 1922 (in German).

AMSTERDAM 10 April 1923 (in Dutch, translated by L. van Riel).

BUDAPEST 1 June 1924 (in Hungarian, translated by I. Kereszty and V. Lányi).

BUCHAREST December 1932 (in Rumanian).

HELSINKI 1 March 1933 (in Finnish).

LJUBLJANA 14 April 1933 (in Slovenian, translated by M. Polič).

RIGA 14 March 1934 (in Lettish).

BELGRADE June 1938 (in Serbian).

A Polish version by L. Poplawski had been published in 1906.

DVOŘÁK: *Dimitrij*

8 October. Prague, Cz.

Text by M. Červinková-Riegrová. Four acts.

The second new opera at the new Czech National Theatre (see 11 June 1881). New version, Prague 20 November 1883 and frequently revived there since (latest revival 27 April 1928).

In Czech also, Vienna 2 June 1892 (at the Exhibition Theatre) and 14 May 1929 (at the Stadt Th. by a company from Bratislava).

In Rumanian, Bucharest 1932.

PLANQUETTE: *Rip van Winkle*

14 October. London, Comedy

(Original French) text by H. Meilhac and P. Gille, English version by H. B. Farnie. Sub-title: *A Romance of Sleepy Hollow.* Three acts.

Apart from *Les Cloches de Corneville* (see 1877) the most successful of Planquette's more than 20 operettas. In London it ran for 328 nights: subsequently given at:

NEW YORK 28 October 1882 (in English).

VIENNA, W. 22 December 1883 (in German, translated by F. Gumbert and E. Jacobson).

BUDAPEST 28 December 1883 (in Hungarian).

PRAGUE 14 April 1884 (in German).

DRESDEN 3 May 1884 (in German).

STOCKHOLM 1884 (in Swedish).

PARIS, F.DR. 11 November 1884 (in French).

BRUSSELS 19 February 1885 (in French).

MEXICO 7 June 1885 (in Spanish, translated by J. Nombelá).

BERLIN, WALHALLA 13 November 1886 (in German).

MADRID 1909 (in Spanish, translated by R. Fernández y Gonzalez).

Still given on French stages. Revived Paris, G.L. 3 November 1924; Monte Carlo December 1929; Geneva February 1939.

GRANDJEAN: *Colomba*

15 October. Copenhagen

Text by H. P. Holst (founded on Mérimée's story). Three acts.

The most successful of Grandjean's operas.

SMETANA: *Čertova Stěna*
(The Devil's Wall)

29 October. Prague, Cz.

Text by E. Krásnohorská. Three acts.

Smetana's last performed opera (apart from the fragments of his unfinished *Viola*). Revived at Prague 12 May 1904; 26 May 1909; 20 May 1917; and 2 February 1924.

In Czech also, Vienna 30 May 1924 (by the Olomouc Opera Company).

AUDRAN: *Gillette de Narbonne*

11 November. Paris, B.P.

Text by H. C. Chivot and A. Duru (partly founded on Shakespeare's *All's Well That Ends Well*). Three acts.

Successful in Paris; the so far latest revival there was at the Th. Porte St. Martin on 24 June 1935.

In French also given at Brussels 9 January 1883; Geneva 19 January 1883; Rio de Janeiro 28 June 1883.

In English (translated by H. S. Clarke), London, Royalty 19 November 1883.

In German (translated by F. Colberg), Berlin, Walhalla Th. 24 October 1884; Vienna, W. 27 March 1885; Prague 20 June 1885; New York 22 May 1887.

In Croatian (translated by F. Miler), Zagreb 1 January 1901.

SULLIVAN: *Iolanthe;* or,
The Peer and the Peri

25 November. London and New York

Text by W. S. Gilbert. Two acts.

Produced the same night both at the Savoy Th., London, and at the Standard Th., New York. In London ran for 398 nights.

In English also, Mexico 29 February 1884.

MILLÖCKER: *Der Bettelstudent*

6 December. Vienna, W.

Text by F. Zell and R. Genée. Three acts.

Millöcker's most famous operetta.

In German also given at Berlin, Fr.W. 24 January 1883 (300th performance 1 June 1884); Graz 11 February 1883; Prague 17 February 1883; Amsterdam 8 September 1883; Basle 26 September 1883; New York 19 October 1883; Bucharest, October 1883; Riga 1 November 1883; Strasbourg 8 November 1883; St. Petersburg 19 December 1883; Czernowitz and Temesvar 1883; Reval 19 February 1884; Moscow 29 April 1884; London, Royalty 12 January 1895; Paris, Vaudeville 30 June 1911.

In Hungarian, Budapest 23 February 1883.

In Swedish (translated by E. A. Wallmark), Stockholm 2 May 1883.

In Italian (as *Il Guitarrero*), Leghorn October 1883.

In English (translated by F. A. Schwab), New York 29 October 1883 (revived 22 March 1913); (translated by W. B. Kingston), London, Alhambra 12 April 1884.

In Croatian (translated by A. Harambašić), Zagreb 15 March 1884.

In French (translated by A. Hennequin and A. Vallabrègue), Brussels 10 January 1885 (music adapted by M. Kufferath); (translated by E. Hermil and A. J. Numès) Paris, Menus-Plaisirs 18 January 1889.

In Spanish (translated by F. J. Osorno), Mexico 22 July 1887.

In Russian, Leningrad 26 May 1920. Russian translation by M. G. Yaron published 1930.

In Finnish, Helsinki 23 April 1926.

Frequently revived on German stages; first produced at the Berlin O. 30 December 1934 (revised by R. Hagemann); at the Vienna O. 17 June 1936.

1883

MACHADO: *Lauriane*

9 January. Marseilles

(French) text by A. Guiou and J. J. Magne (founded on the play *Les beaux Messieurs de Bois-Doré*, by G. Sand and P. Meurice). Four acts.

The first opera of the Portuguese composer.

In Italian (translated by C. Fereal), Lisbon 2 February 1884 and Rio de Janeiro 13 August 1886.

KYUI: *Kavkasky Plennik*
Кавказскій Плѣнникъ
(The Captive in the Caucasus)

16 February. St. Petersburg

Text by V. A. Kruilov (founded on Pushkin's poem). Three acts.

Revived St. Petersburg 8 November 1907; Moscow 29 December 1909.

In French (translated by L. de Mercy-Argen-teau), Liége 13 January 1886.

(The opera, originally in 2 acts, had been written as early as 1857.)

SAINT-SAËNS: *Henri VIII*

5 March. Paris, O.

Text by L. Détroyat and P. A. Silvestre. Four acts.

Successful on French stages; given at the Paris Opéra since 19 July 1889 in a reduced 3-act version; last revived there 1 December 1917; revived at Brussels 14 October 1935. Given at:

FRANKFORT 16 February 1887 (in German, translated by H. Wolff).

MILAN 26 December 1895 (in Italian, translated by A. de Lauzières).

MOSCOW 9 February 1897 (in Russian, translated by S. E. Pavlovsky).

LONDON, C.G. 14 July 1898 (in French).

ANTWERP 22 February 1900 (in French).

PRAGUE 6 April 1900 (in German).

MONTE CARLO 24 March 1908 (in French).

DOSS: *Percifal*

8 March. Liége

Text by L. Bailly. Four acts.

Produced at the Collège St. Servais; revived publicly at Trèves in January 1909. Doss claimed to have written this *opéra dialogué*, unlike Wagner, in a "true Christian spirit". Vocal score published.

CATALANI: *Dejanice*

17 March. Milan, Sc.

Text by A. Zanardini. Four acts.

Successful in Italy; revived at Turin 11 February 1920; Genoa 30 October 1920; Milan, T.d. V. 1 March 1931, etc.

In Italian also, Nice 28 February 1886; Malta 1924.

In German (translated by S. Heller), Prague 26 November 1886.

A. G. THOMAS: *Esmeralda*

26 March. London, D.L.

Text by T. J. H. Marzials and A. Randegger (after Victor Hugo). Four acts.

Thomas's first opera. Revived London, C.G. 12 July 1890 (in French, translated by P. Milliet) and 3 January 1908 (in the original English).

In German (translated by E. Frank), Cologne 14 November 1883; Hamburg 27 September 1884; Berlin, Kroll's 26 August 1891.

In English, New York 19 November 1900.

MACKENZIE: *Colomba*

9 April. London, D.L.

Text by F. Hueffer (founded on Mérimée's story). Four acts.

Mackenzie's first opera.

In German (translated by E. Frank), Hamburg 27 January 1884; Darmstadt 29 April 1884.

Revived London, H.M.'s 11 December 1909 and 9 December 1912 (by the R.C.M., in a new version, text altered and reduced to 3 acts by C. Aveling).

(Date of first performance 9 April, not 5 April as sometimes stated.)

DELIBES: *Lakmé*

14 April. Paris, O.C.

Text by E. Gondinet and P. Gille. Three acts.

Delibes's most famous work; the 200th performance at the O.C. was on 30 April 1895; the 1,000th on 13 May 1931.

Outside Paris, given at:

FRANKFORT 3 December 1883 (in German, translated by F. Gumbert).

GENEVA 4 March 1884 (in French).

ROME, ARG. 31 March 1884 (in Italian, translated by A. Zanardini).

PRAGUE 30 November 1884 (in Czech).

ST. PETERSBURG 18 December 1884 (in Italian).

LONDON, GAIETY 6 June 1885 (in French).

ANTWERP 25 December 1885; Brussels 29 November 1886 (in French).

NEW YORK 1 March 1886 (in English); 2 April 1890 (in Italian); and 22 February 1892 (in French).

BUDAPEST 12 November 1887 (in Hungarian, translated by E. Abrányi).

BUENOS AIRES 20 June 1888 (in Italian).

LISBON January 1889 (in Italian).

BERLIN, KROLL's 20 March 1889 (in Italian) and 18 July 1891 (in German).

STOCKHOLM 15 January 1890 (in Swedish, translated by E. A. Wallmark).

AMSTERDAM 20 September 1890 (in Dutch, translated by E. van S.).

MOSCOW 15 November 1892 (in Russian, translated by E. N. Kletkova).

NEW ORLEANS 1 February 1893 (in French).

COPENHAGEN 1 January 1896 (in Danish, translated by E. Christiansen).

WARSAW October 1896 (in Italian).

RIO DE JANEIRO 11 August 1902 (in Italian).

VIENNA 14 November 1904 (in German).

ZAGREB 20 March 1912 (in Croatian, translated by A. Kassowitz-Cvijić).

HELSINKI 28 April 1915 (in Finnish).

LIVERPOOL 8 March 1918 (in English, translated by C. Aveling).

OSLO 30 December 1918 (in Norwegian).

YOKOHAMA Autumn 1919 (in Italian).

BUCHAREST February 1922 (in Rumanian).

BELGRADE October 1923 (in Serbian).

SOFIA 13 September 1926 (in Bulgarian).

RIGA 30 April 1927 (in Lettish).

MALTA 1927 (in Italian).

TALLINN 1930 (in Estonian).

ATHENS December 1932 (in Greek).

KAUNAS 14 April 1934 (in Lithuanian).

J. STRAUSS: *Eine Nacht in Venedig*

3 October. Berlin, Fr.W.

Text by F. Zell and R. Genée. Three acts.

Written for the opening of the new Friedrich-Wilhelmstädtisches Theater (late Woltersdorff-Theater), Berlin. Subsequently given at Vienna, W. 9 October 1883 and all over Germany and Austria.

In German also, Budapest 10 November 1883; Prague 19 December 1883; Brünn 28 February 1884; Graz 13 September 1884; Amsterdam 1885; Strasbourg 16 November 1886; Basle 24 February 1889; New York 8 January 1890 (as *Venetianische Nächte*); Reval 1890; Riga 1892; Sofia Autumn 1892; Helsinki Summer 1899.

In English (translated by ?), New York 24 April 1884.

In Italian, Venice October 1888; Milan 9 April 1889, etc.

In Spanish, Buenos Aires 14 March 1890.

In Croatian (translated by F. Miler), Zagreb 19 May 1896.

Frequently revived in several countries: Budapest 1924 (in Hungarian); Vienna, O. 23 June 1929 and Berlin, O. 20 February 1931 (new arrangement by E. W. Korngold and E. Marischka); Monte Carlo 19 March 1930 (for the first time in French); Helsinki 13 May 1930 (in Finnish).

New arrangement by C. Hagemann 1934. New arrangement by G. Quedenfeldt and E. Rex (text) and K. Tutein (music) 1936.

LANGE-MÜLLER: *Spanske Studenter*

21 October. Copenhagen

Text by W. Faber. Two acts.

Lange-Müller's best opera, successful at Copenhagen.

In German (translated by J. Christensen), Hamburg 10 March 1884.

In Swedish (translated by H. Christiernsson), Stockholm 4 May 1884.

RUBINSTEIN:
Sulamith and *Unter Räubern*

8 November. Hamburg

Two short operas, produced on the same bill. *Sulamith* (text by J. Rodenberg, 5 scenes) was also given at Berlin 4 May 1888 and Amsterdam January 1889 (both in concert form) and, in Russian, St. Petersburg 16 January 1901. *Unter Räubern* (text by E. Wichert, 1 act) also Berlin 24 April 1893.

SALVAYRE: *Riccardo III*

21 December. St. Petersburg

Original French text by E. R. Blavet (after Shakespeare), Italian version by?. Four acts.

One of the last Italian operas originally produced in Russia.

In French, Nice 29 January 1891; Rouen 22 December 1893, etc. Revived Toulouse 26 November 1910.

1884

SULLIVAN: *Princess Ida;* or, *Castle Adamant*

5 January. London, Savoy

Text by W. S. Gilbert. *A respectful operatic perversion of Tennyson's Princess*. Three acts.

In London ran for 246 nights. New York and Boston 11 February 1884, etc. Revived London, Prince's Th. 23 January 1922, etc.

In German, Meran 20 April 1901 (by amateurs).

REYER: *Sigurd*

7 January. Brussels, M.

Text by C. Du Locle and A. Blau. Four acts.

Reyer's most important work (produced after an interval of more than 20 years since *Érostrate*). First given in France at Lyons 15 January 1885. First given at the Paris O. 12 June 1885; the 300th performance there was in June 1925, the latest revival 17 October 1934. Still given on French stages.

Further productions in French: New Orleans 25 December 1891; St. Petersburg April 1894; Geneva 17 January 1896; Mexico May 1897; Alexandria 3 February 1901.

In Italian (translated by G. A. Mazzucato), London, C.G. 15 July 1884; Milan, Sc. 26 December 1894.

MASSENET: *Manon*

19 January. Paris, O.C.

Text by H. Meilhac and P. Gille (founded on Prévost's novel). Five acts.

Massenet's greatest success. The 500th performance at the O.C. was on 13 January 1905, the 800th on 26 April 1913; given there more than 1,700 times to date. Outside France, given at:

BRUSSELS 18 March 1884 (in French; 500th performance 22 May 1934).

AMSTERDAM Spring 1884 (in French).

LIVERPOOL 17 January 1885 (in English, translated by J. Bennett).

GENEVA 7 March 1885 (in French).

LONDON, D.L. 7 May 1885 (in English) and C.G. 19 May 1891 (in French).

PRAGUE 19 September 1885 (in Czech) and 26 December 1904 (in German).

ST. PETERSBURG December 1885 (in Russian, translated by N. M. Spassky) and October 1896 (in Italian).

NEW YORK 23 December 1885 (in Italian) and 16 January 1895 (in French).

BUENOS AIRES 19 September 1890 (in French) and 27 September 1895 (in Italian).

VIENNA 19 November 1890 (in German, translated by F. Gumbert).

HAMBURG 31 October 1892 (in German, translated by F. Gumbert).

MILAN, T. CARCANO 19 October 1893 (in Italian, translated by A. Zanardini).

NEW ORLEANS 4 January 1894 (in French).

BARCELONA 29 December 1894 (in Italian).

MADRID 28 February 1895 (in Italian).

LISBON 13 March 1895 (in Italian).

STOCKHOLM 18 January 1896 (in Swedish, translated by F. Arlberg).

BATAVIA Autumn 1896 (in French).

ZAGREB 23 January 1897 (in Croatian, translated by P. Brani).

MALTA 1898 (in Italian).

RIGA 1898 (in German) and 29 September 1931 (in Lettish).

CORFU April 1900 (in Italian).

CONSTANTINOPLE July 1900 (in Italian).

BERLIN, KROLL'S 24 April 1902 (in French) and O. 1 December 1903 (in German).

CRACOW July 1901 (in Polish).

WARSAW September 1902 (in Polish).

BASLE 18 January 1903 (in German).

BUDAPEST 22 December 1905 (in Hungarian, translated by S. Várady).

LJUBLJANA 1907 (in Slovenian).

RIO DE JANEIRO Summer 1920 (in Italian).

BUCHAREST February 1921 (in Rumanian).

SOFIA 3 December 1926 (in Bulgarian).

TALLINN 1928 (in Estonian, translated by G. Tuksam).

MILLÖCKER: *Gasparone*

26 January. Vienna, W.

Text by F. Zell and R. Genée. Three acts.

Successful on German stages; Prague 23 March 1884; Dresden 13 April 1884; Berlin, Fr.W. 26 September 1884 (200th performance 16 April 1885).

In German also, Moscow 1 January 1885; New York 21 February 1885; Dorpat 29 May 1885; Riga 2 October 1885; Basle 8 December 1885; Strasbourg 21 February 1886; Rotterdam 4 February 1888; St. Petersburg 1889; Sofia Summer 1893; Copenhagen May 1897. New version by E. Steffan and P. Knepler, Berlin 20 November 1931.

In Hungarian, Budapest 25 April 1884.

In English (translated by ?), New York 21 February 1885 (at the Standard Th., the same day as in German at the Thalia Th.).

In Swedish (translated by E. A. Wallmark), Stockholm 1885.

In Polish (translated by A. Kiczman), Warsaw 11 October 1886.

In Croatian (translated by J. E. Tomić), Zagreb 27 October 1888.

In Italian, Milan 30 November 1889.

In Spanish (translated by F. J. Osorno), Mexico 17 June 1893.

GODARD: *Pédro de Zalaméa*

31 January. Antwerp

Text by L. Détroyat and P. A. Silvestre (after Calderón). Four acts.

Godard's first opera.

CHAIKOVSKY: *Mazeppa*

Мазепа

15 February. Moscow

Text by the composer and V. P. Burenin (founded on Pushkin's *Poltava*). Three acts.

St. Petersburg 19 February 1884; Tiflis Autumn 1885, etc. Still given in Russia; revived Moscow 1917; Kiev 9 March 1925, etc.

Outside Russia, given at:

LIVERPOOL 6 August 1888 (in Russian, by a touring company).

WARSAW March 1912 (in Polish).

WIESBADEN 23 May 1931 (in German, translated by A. Simon).

NEW YORK 4 February 1933 (in Russian, by a Ukrainian company, at the Mecca Temple).

VIENNA 21 April 1933 (in German, in concert form).

PRAGUE 15 September 1934 (in Czech).

SOFIA 8 October 1937 (in Bulgarian).

KISTLER: *Kunihild*

20 March. Sondershausen

Text by F. von Sporck. Three acts.

Revived Würzburg 30 July 1893 (special festival performances); Stuttgart 24 May 1894; Munich 18 April 1896, etc. English translation by W. A. Ellis, published 1893.

Kistler at that time was claimed by his adherents to be Wagner's legitimate successor, chiefly on the strength of *Kunihild*.

WEINGARTNER: *Sakuntala*

23 March. Weimar

Text by the composer (founded on Kalidasa's Indian drama). Three acts.

Weingartner's first opera. Also given at Danzig 17 February 1886.

A. VON GOLDSCHMIDT: *Heliantus*

26 March. Leipzig

Text by the composer. Three acts.

Goldschmidt's first and best opera; unsuccessful.

FIBICH: *Nevěsta Messinská*
(The Bride of Messina)

28 March. Prague, Cz.

Text by O. Hostinský (founded on Schiller's drama). Three acts.

Revived at Prague 1 May 1909; 26 October 1920; and Autumn 1938.

STANFORD: *Savonarola*

18 April. Hamburg

Original English text by G. A. A'Beckett, German version by E. Frank. Prologue and 3 acts.

In German also, London, C.G. 9 July 1884.

STANFORD: *The Canterbury Pilgrims*

23 April. London, D.L.

Text by G. A. A'Beckett. Three acts.

Unsuccessful like *Savonarola*; Birmingham 20 May 1884, etc.

NESSLER: *Der Trompeter von Säckingen*

4 May. Leipzig

Text by R. Bunge (founded on J. V. von Scheffel's poem). Four acts.

Very popular on German stages.

In German also, Basle 26 November 1884; Strasbourg 11 December 1884; Berlin 10 January 1885; Riga 18 April 1885; Prague 12 September 1885; Rotterdam 26 September 1885; Posen 20 December 1885; Vienna 30 January 1886; Reval 18 April 1886; New York 23 November 1887; St. Petersburg 1889; Ghent 18 October 1889; Brussels 12 November 1889; London, D.L. 8 July 1892; Helsinki 8 May 1900.

In Swedish (translated by E. A. Wallmark), Stockholm 21 September 1886.

In Hungarian (translated by E. Abrányi), Budapest 6 November 1886.

In English (translated by ?), New York 5 November 1889.

In Polish, Lemberg April 1898.

In Croatian (translated by F. Miler), Zagreb 7 January 1899.

Still occasionally revived on minor German stages (Berlin Plaza 1 February 1935).

KOVAŘOVIC: *Ženichové*
(The Bridegrooms)

13 May. Prague, Cz.

Text by A. Koukl (from S. K. Machaček's comedy of the same title, 1826). Three acts.

The first opera of Kovařovic, who from 1889 until his death in 1920 was the chief conductor of the Prague Národní Divadlo.

PUCCINI: *Le Villi*

31 May. Milan, T.d.V.

Text by F. Fontana. One act.

Puccini's first opera. New enlarged 2-act version, Turin 26 December 1884 and Milan, Sc. 24 January 1885. Successful in Italy; revived Rome 20 January 1925, etc.

Outside Italy, given at:

BUENOS AIRES 10 June 1886 (in Italian).

HAMBURG 29 November 1892 (in German, translated by L. Hartmann); Frankfort 19 November 1893, etc.

WARSAW 17 March 1893 (in Polish).

MANCHESTER 24 September 1897 (in English, translated by P. E. Pinkerton).

NEW YORK 17 December 1908 (in Italian).

BUCHAREST *c.* December 1925 (in Rumanian).

VIENNA Spring 1938 (in German).

MANNHEIM 7 February 1940 (in German).

MANCINELLI: *Isora di Provenza*

2 October. Bologna, T.C.

Text by A. Zanardini (founded on Victor Hugo's *La Légende des Siècles*). Three acts.

Mancinelli's first opera.

In German (translated by S. Arkel), Hamburg 21 April 1892.

POISE: *Joli Gilles*

10 October. Paris, O.C.

Text by C. P. Monselet (founded on Soulas d'Allainval's comedy, *L'Embarras des Richesses*, 1725) Two acts.

Poise's last performed opera. Brussels 7 February 1885; Geneva 21 December 1888, etc. In German (as *Toni's Schatz*, translated by F. Fremery), Berlin 31 December 1885.

In Flemish, revived Ghent December 1910.

MILLÖCKER: *Der Feldprediger*

31 October. Vienna, W.

Text by H. Wittmann and A. Wohlmuth. Three acts.

Berlin, Walhalla Th. 10 January 1885, etc.

In German also, Budapest 20 December 1884; Brünn 31 January 1885; Prague 9 April 1885; New York 1 May 1885; Amsterdam 1885; Sarajevo 1889.

In English (as *The Black Hussar*, adapted by S. Rosenfeld), New York 4 May 1885, etc.

In Polish (translated by M. Turczyński), Warsaw 1887.

In Spanish (as *El Alcalde di Strassberg*, translated by F. Jaques y Aguado, music adapted by M. Taberner), Madrid 16 November 1888.

T. DUBOIS: *Aben Hamet*

16 December. Paris, Th.I.

Original French text by L. Détroyat, Italian version by A. de Lauzières. Prologue and 4 acts.

This was the last original production of an Italian opera at Paris. (Previously heard privately at Détroyat's on 25 May 1882.) The French version was produced at Liége 12 March 1885; Paris 11 December 1889 (privately); Antwerp 1 April 1892; Rennes 9 February 1897.

1885

VERHEIJ: *Imilda*

28 January. Rotterdam

(German) text by W. W. Smalt. Four acts.

In German also, Amsterdam January 1886.

DE HAAN: *Die Kaiserstochter*

1 February. Darmstadt

Text by W. Jacoby. Three acts.

The most successful work of the Dutch composer.

In German also, Rotterdam 16 January 1886; Amsterdam 26 January 1886. Revived Darmstadt 22 October 1903.

ZELEŃSKI: *Konrad Wallenrod*

February. Lemberg

Text by Z. Sarnecki and W. Noskowski (founded on Mickiewicz's poem). Four acts.

The first opera of the Polish composer. Revived Pozńan May 1923.

HALLSTRÖM: *Neaga*

24 February. Stockholm

(Original German) text by "Carmen Sylva" (Queen Elizabeth of Rumania), Swedish version by F. T. Hedberg. Four acts.

JONCIÈRES: *Le Chevalier Jean*

11 March. Paris, O.C.

Text by L. Gallet and E. Blau. Four acts.

A failure in Paris. In French also, Geneva 19 January 1886; Liége 31 January 1887.

Successful on German stages (as *Johann von Lothringen*, translated by F. Gumbert; Cologne 26 November 1885; Berlin 17 April 1886; Frankfort 7 October 1886, etc.; Basle 31 December 1886; Riga 16 January 1887. Revived Berlin, Th.d.W. 22 March 1901.

In Czech, Prague 17 March 1889.

Italian version by A. Zanardini published 1887.

SULLIVAN: *The Mikado;* or, *The Town of Titipu*

14 March. London, Savoy

Text by W. S. Gilbert. Two acts.

Sullivan's most successful operetta. In London ran for 672 nights; the 1,000th London performance was on 31 October 1896. Given at Chicago 6 July 1885; New York, People's Th., Bowery 10 July 1885 and Union Square Th. 20 July 1885 (both pirated); Fifth Avenue Th. 19 August 1885 (legitimate) and Standard Th. 24 August 1885 (pirated), etc.; Sydney 14 October 1885; Cape Town 1889.

In English also, Berlin, Wallner Th. 2 June 1886; Vienna, Ca. 1 September 1886; and in many other German and Austrian towns as well as at Amsterdam 1 November 1887 and Copenhagen 1887 (Danish version in the printed libretto by E. A. Nyegaard); Rio de Janeiro 1890.

First given in German (translated by E. F. L. Gauss) at New York 13 February 1886; Chicago 16 January 1887. Revived Cincinnati 7 January 1912.

The Mikado was the only one of Sullivan's operettas which had a great and lasting success outside the Anglo-Saxon countries. Following the continental tours of the D'Oyly Carte Company, it was translated into German by F. Zell and R. Genée and produced at Vienna, W. 2 March 1888.

In German also given at Berlin, Fr.W. 6 December 1888 (200th performance 30 December 1891); St. Petersburg 23 December 1888; Prague 10 March 1889; Trieste 16 March 1889; Reval 1889; Bucharest Summer 1890; Riga 1890; Basle 1 December 1892; Helsinki Summer 1899; Buenos Aires October 1906. Produced at Vienna, Jos. 29 January 1899 by a troupe of 38 children. First given at the Berlin O. 10 June 1900. A German parody, *Der Miezekado*, text by O. Ewald, music by F. Beier, was first given at Cassel 26 December 1886; Berlin, Wallner Th. 21 December 1887, etc.

In Hungarian, Budapest 10 December 1886 (probably pirated and orchestrated from the vocal score); revived 25 February 1924.

In Russian, Moscow 30 April 1887 (by Stanislavsky's "Alekseev" Circle).

In French (translated by M. Kufferath), Brussels 23 December 1889; apparently never given in Paris (perhaps on account of Lecocq's "Japanese" operetta *Kosiki* produced there in 1876).

In Swedish (translated by E. A. Wallmark), Stockholm 22 January 1890; also given at Christiania 17 July 1890 and Gothenburg 18 September 1890. An earlier Swedish adaptation, also by Wallmark, had been produced at Stockholm on 24 November 1888 (music arranged by F. Ringvall, from *The Mikado* and from Lecocq's *Kosiki*).

In Croatian (translated by A. Harambašić), Zagreb 24 February 1892.

In Danish (translated by E. Bøgh), Copenhagen 13 March 1892.

In Italian (translated by G. Macchi), Florence, P. 5 December 1898.

In Czech (translated by B. K. = Boleslav Kalensky?), Prague 20 September 1903.

ERKEL: *István Király*
(King Stephen)

14 March. Budapest [1]

Text by A. Váradi (founded on a play by L. Dobsa). Four acts.

Erkel's last opera; given at Budapest until 1930.

PONCHIELLI: *Marion Delorme*

17 March. Milan, Sc.

Text by E. Golisciani (founded on V. Hugo's play). Four acts.

Successful in Italy; given in a new version at Brescia 9 August 1885.

In Italian also, São Paulo 13 May 1886 and Rio de Janeiro August 1886.

Revived Milan 15 April 1919.

DELLINGER: *Don Cesar*

28 March. Hamburg

Text by O. Walther (founded on the French play, *Don César de Bazan*, by d'Ennery and Pinel Dumanoir). Three acts.

Dellinger's best work and one of the most popular German operettas of the 'eighties. Budapest 21 September 1885; Berlin, Walhalla 23 September 1885; Vienna, Ca. 20 November 1885; Brünn 7 February 1886; Posen 13 February 1886; Temesvar 11 May 1886; New York 6 October 1886; Zurich and Riga 14 October 1886; St. Petersburg 16 October 1886; Strasbourg 24 October 1886; Prague 7 November 1886; Reval 1887; Sofia Autumn 1892.

[1] First new opera produced at the Magyar Királyi Operaház (inaugurated 27 September 1884 with the first act of Erkel's *Bánk Bán* and with the first act of *Lohengrin*).

In English (translated by W. von Sachs), Philadelphia 29 March 1886; New York 3 May 1886, etc.

In Swedish (translated by H. L. Westin), Gothenburg 18 February 1887 and (translated by E. A. Wallmark), Stockholm 12 December 1887.

In Spanish (translated by F. J. Osorno), Mexico 12 August 1893.

In Croatian (translated by F. Miler), Zagreb 1 February 1896.

In Lettish, Riga 18 December 1931.

New arrangement by Hans Weissbach published 1935.

(HALÉVY): *Noah*

5 April. Carlsruhe

(Original French) text (*Noé*) by J. H. Vernoy de Saint-Georges, German version by G. H. Gans zu Putlitz. Three acts.

Halévy's last opera, completed by Bizet, his son-in-law. Also given on some other German stages and, in Polish, Warsaw 2 February 1887. Never produced in France, but French vocal score published.

A. G. THOMAS: *Nadeshda*

16 April. London, D.L.

Text by J. R. Sturgis. Four acts.

Successful on English stages; Dublin 27 August 1885, etc.

Revived London, Duke's Hall 11 March 1921 (by the R.A.M.); Glasgow 21 February 1927.

In German (translated by F. Fremery), Breslau 20 April 1890.

(MASSÉ): *Une Nuit de Cléopâtre*

25 April. Paris, O.C.

Text by J. Barbier (founded on a story by T. Gautier). Three acts.

Massé's last opera. Geneva 14 April 1886, etc.

In German (translated by F. Fremery), Hamburg 9 February 1886.

Italian version by A. Zanardini published 1887.

ROZKOŠNÝ: *Popelka*

31 May. Prague, Cz.

Text by O. Hostinský. Three acts.

Rozkošný's most popular work (a Czech *Cinderella* opera).

Revived Prague 14 June 1902 and 22 September 1908.

A. RITTER: *Der faule Hans*

15 October. Munich

Text by the composer (founded on a story by F. Dahn). One act.

Successful in Germany; in German also, Riga 1890; Prague 3 December 1901.

Revived Hamburg 28 February 1907; Berlin 8 March 1907; Dresden 13 February 1915; Munich December 1933.

J. STRAUSS: *Der Zigeunerbaron*

24 October. Vienna, W.

Text by I. Schnitzer (founded on M. Jókai's story, *Saffi*). Three acts.

Apart from *Die Fledermaus* (see 1874) Strauss's most popular operetta; the 300th night was on 23 October 1903, the 1,000th Vienna performance on 19 April 1909. First given at the Vienna O. on 26 December 1910 (produced by F. Weingartner).

Outside Vienna, given at:

BUDAPEST 27 November 1885 (in German) and 26 March 1886 (in Hungarian, translated by K. Gerö and A. Radó).

BRESLAU 25 December 1885 (in German).

BERLIN, FR.W. 5 February 1886 (in German; 200th performance 2 January 1887).

NEW YORK 15 February 1886 (in English, translated by S. Rosenfeld) and 1 April 1886 (in German).

RIGA 11 March 1886 (in German) and 1893 (in Lettish).

ST. PETERSBURG 21 March 1886 (in German).

WARSAW 1886 (in Polish, translated by M. Turczyński).

REVAL 16 October 1886 (in German).

ROTTERDAM 10 November 1886 (in German).

AMSTERDAM 18 December 1886 (in Dutch, translated by B. Duplex).

STRASBOURG 25 December 1886 (in German).

ZURICH 30 December 1886 (in German).

GENOA October 1888; Milan 13 March 1890 (in Italian, translated by R. Nigri and P. Ceresa).

TARTU (DORPAT) 1889 (in Estonian).

ZAGREB 30 March 1895 (in Croatian, translated by P. Brani).

PARIS, F.DR. 20 December 1895 (in French, translated by A. Lafrique).

COPENHAGEN May 1897 (in German).

BRUSSELS 28 February 1902 (in French).

LJUBLJANA 1904 (in Slovenian).

BUENOS AIRES October 1906 (in German).

BUCHAREST Spring 1907 (in German) and September 1931 (in Rumanian).

MOSCOW 1913; Leningrad 10 March 1922 (in Russian).

HELSINKI 12 October 1927 (in Finnish).

JERUSALEM 16 June 1932 (in Hebrew, translated by H. Bregmann).

KAUNAS 16 October 1934 (in Lithuanian).

LONDON 12 February 1935 (in English, by amateurs, at Rudolf Steiner Hall).

STOCKHOLM 21 March 1938 (in Swedish).

SOFIA 12 October 1938 (in Bulgarian).

SOLOVYEV: *Kordeliya*
Корделія

24 November. St. Petersburg

Text by P. K. Bronnikov (founded on V. Sardou's *La Haine*). Four acts.

Moscow 25 November 1888, etc. Revived St. Petersburg 25 October 1898; 19 December 1902; 26 November 1909.

In German, Prague 18 August 1890 (revived 3 September 1901).

The opera was first performed under the title of *Mest* (*Vengeance*); the subject has nothing to do with *King Lear*.

MASSENET: *Le Cid*

30 November. Paris, O.

Text by A. P. d'Ennery, L. Gallet, and E. Blau (founded on Corneille's tragedy). Four acts.

The 100th performance at the Paris O. was on 1 October 1900; given there until 1912; frequently revived in France. Also given at:

ANTWERP 20 January 1887 (in French).

FRANKFORT 1 October 1887 (in German, translated by M. Kalbeck).

VIENNA 22 November 1887 (in German, translated by M. Kalbeck).

ROME C. 7 April 1889 (in Italian, translated by A. Zanardini).

NEW ORLEANS 23 February 1890 (in French).

GENEVA 23 December 1890 (in French).

NEW YORK 12 February 1897 (in French).

CHAUMET: *Hérode*

6 December. Paris, Conservatoire

Text by G. Boyer (*poème dramatique*). One act.

Chaumet's best work. Publicly performed at Bordeaux 30 January 1892.

MESSAGER: *La Béarnaise*

12 December. Paris, B.P.

Text by E. Leterrier and A. Vanloo. Three acts.

Messager's first great success. Revived Paris, Tr. L. 11 March 1925.

In Hungarian, Budapest 26 February 1886.

In English (translated by A. Murray), Birmingham 27 September 1886; London, Prince of Wales's 4 October 1886; revived King's Hall 19 January 1917. As *Jacquette*, New York 13 June 1887.

In Czech (translated by V. J. Novotný), Prague 15 July 1892.

1886

LITOLFF: *Les Templiers*

25 January. Brussels, M.

Text by J. Adenis, P. A. Silvestre and L. Bonnemère. Five acts.

In German (translated by F. Gumbert), Brunswick 17 March 1889; Prague 23 March 1890; Graz 6 February 1891. Revived Antwerp October 1912 (in Flemish).

KOVAŘOVIC: *Cesta Oknem*
(The Way through the Window)

11 February. Prague, Cz.

Text by E. Züngel (founded on a comedy by Scribe and Lemoine). One act.

Revived Prague 9 December 1921.

(MUSORGSKY): *Khovanshchina*
Хованщина

21 February. St. Petersburg

Text by the composer. Five acts.

The work was completed and orchestrated by Rimsky-Korsakov. The first performance was a private one and took place at the Kononov Theatre, produced by the "Musical Dramatic Club," under the direction of E. Goldstein. Given in public at Kiev 7 November 1892; Moscow, Th. Prenishkov November 1892; St. Petersburg, Th. Kononov 7 November 1893. First given at the Imperial Th., St.Petersburg, on 20 November 1911.

Outside Russia, produced at:

PARIS, CH.É. 5 June 1913 (in Russian; altered from Rimsky-Korsakov's version by Stravinsky and Ravel) and O. 13 April 1923 (in French, translated by R. and M. d'Harcourt).

LONDON, D.L. 1 July 1913 (in Russian) and D.L. 26 October 1917 and C.G. 25 November 1919 (in English, translated by R. Newmarch).

BARCELONA 12 December 1923 (in Russian).

FRANKFORT 19 February 1924 (in German, translated by E. Fritzheim).

MILAN 1 March 1926 (in Italian).

ZAGREB 19 June 1926 (in Croatian).

RIGA 26 February 1927 (in Lettish).

PHILADELPHIA 18 April 1928 (in English).

BUENOS AIRES 15 August 1929 (in Italian).

LYONS 2 December 1930 (in Russian).

NEW YORK 7 March 1931 (in Russian).

TURIN November 1931 (in Russian).

SOFIA 5 May 1933 (in Bulgarian).

LJUBLJANA 28 September 1934 (in Slovenian).

BUDAPEST Spring 1937 (in Hungarian).

Musorgsky's original version (without Rim-sky-Korsakov's additions) was not published until 1931.

CATALANI: *Edmea*

27 February. Milan, Sc.

Text by A. Ghislanzoni. Three acts.
Successful in Italy.

In Italian also, St. Petersburg 28 March 1888; Mexico 16 November 1895; Moscow 1 June 1901. Revived Turin December 1909.

PERFALL: *Junker Heinz*

9 April. Munich

Text by F. Grandaur (founded on W. Hertz's *Heinrich von Schwaben*). Three acts.

In German also, Brünn 12 December 1886; Prague 14 March 1887; Linz 31 March 1887. Revived Munich 8 February 1894; Wiesbaden 11 June 1901 and Munich 24 April 1902 (as *Jung Heinrich*).

CHABRIER: *Gwendoline*

10 April. Brussels, M.

Text by C. Mendès. Two acts.

In French also, Lyons 19 April 1893; Paris, O. 27 December 1893 and revived there in an enlarged 3-act version 3 May 1911 and 26 November 1926; Geneva 16 March 1911; revived at Brussels 11 February 1926. Still given on French stages.

In German (translated by F. Vogt), Carlsruhe 30 May 1889; Leipzig 14 February 1890; Dresden 5 July 1890; Munich 20 November 1890, etc.

SAMARA: *Flora Mirabilis*

16 May. Milan, T. Carcano

Text by F. Fontana. Three acts.

The first and best opera of the Greek composer. Given at the Sc., Milan 8 January 1887. In Italian also, Corfu February 1889; Vienna, W. 24 June 1893.

In German (translated by O. Berggruen), Cologne 7 November 1887.

CHUECA and VALVERDE:
La gran Via
(The great Road)

2 July. Madrid, T. Felipe

Text by F. Pérez y González. *Revista madrileña comica-lirica, fantástico-callejera*. One act (5 scenes).

One of the greatest successes of the "genero chico" of zarzuela (containing the famous march *Cádiz*). Very popular in Spain and South America; Mexico 9 May 1888; Buenos Aires July 1890, etc.

In Spanish also, Milan 1889, etc. Still given on Spanish stages.

In French (translated by M. Ordonneau), Paris, Th. Olympia 25 March 1896.

In English (as *Castles in Spain*, adapted by C. Hamilton, lyrics by E. Ponsonby, music arranged by H. Fragson), London, Royalty 18 April 1906.

In Italian, New York 1 July 1918.

CELLIER: *Dorothy*

25 September. London, Gaiety

Text by B. C. Stephenson. Three acts.

Cellier's most successful operetta.

In London ran for 931 nights (transferred 20 December 1886 to the Prince of Wales's and 17 December 1888 to the New Lyric) and was revived Trafalgar Square Th. 26 November 1892 and New Th. 21 December 1908.

New York 5 November 1887; Sydney 7 September 1889; Cape Town January 1890; Montreal February 1891, etc.

Still given on English stages. Also produced at Budapest, in Hungarian about 1890.

MILLÖCKER: *Der Vice-Admiral*

9 October. Vienna, W.

Text by F. Zell and R. Genée. Prologue and 3 acts.

Successful on German stages. Berlin, Fr.W. 29 October 1886, etc.

In German also, Budapest 29 November 1886; St. Petersburg 8 December 1886; Brünn 25 December 1886; Riga and Reval 1888; New York 24 October 1889; Basle 26 January 1890; Bucha-

rest Summer 1890; Sofia Autumn 1892; Helsinki Summer 1898.

In Swedish (translated by E. A. Wallmark), Stockholm 22 March 1888.

In Italian, Milan 17 September 1889; Barcelona July 1890.

In English (translated by ?), New York 18 June 1892.

In Spanish (translated by V. A. Galicia), Mexico 21 December 1895.

In Croatian (translated by F. Miler), Zagreb 1 May 1898.

Still given on German stages; revived as *Der Herzog von Mirenza* (text by F. Giblhauser, music arranged by F. Neupert), Fürth 4 January 1936; as *Das Heiratsnest* (text by A. Treumann-Mette), Regensburg 25 January 1936.

AUDRAN: *La Cigale et la Fourmi*

30 October. Paris, Gaîté

Text by H. C. Chivot and A. Duru. Three acts.

In French also, Geneva 15 May 1888; Algiers December 1905.

In English (translated by F. C. Burnand, additional music by I. Caryll), London, Lyric 9 October 1890 (given for 423 consecutive nights); New York 26 October 1891 (revived 30 April 1913).

In Italian, Turin 27 October 1898.

Revived Paris, Tr.L. 26 October 1915.

German translation by O. Neitzel published Cologne 1887.

KLUGHARDT: *Die Hochzeit des Mönchs*

10 November. Dessau

Text by E. Pasqué (founded on a story by C. F. Meyer). Four acts.

Given at Prague 19 April 1888 as *Astorre*; revived in a new version at Dessau 15 November 1889.

GOLDMARK: *Merlin*

19 November. Vienna, O.

Text by S. Lipiner. Three acts.

In German also, New York 3 January 1887; Hamburg 31 January 1887; Dresden 21 April 1887, etc.

In Hungarian (translated by L. Dóczy), Budapest 26 September 1887.

In Czech (translated by V. J. Novotný), Prague 23 January 1890.

Revived Frankfort 14 February 1904 (altered); Riga March 1907.

NAPRAVNIK: *Garold*
Гаролдъ

23 November. St. Petersburg

Text by P. P. Veinberg (founded on a German play by E. von Wildenbruch). Five acts.

In Czech, Prague 23 March 1888. German version by A. H. Petrick published.

PALADILHE: *Patrie*

20 December Paris, O.

Text by V. Sardou and L. Gallet (founded on Sardou's play of the same title). Five acts.

Paladilhe's best work; revived Paris, O. 9 April 1900 and 28 October 1907; given there until 1916.

In French also, Ghent 25 January 1888; Antwerp 6 March 1888; Geneva 19 February 1901. Revived Brussels 10 September 1931.

In Czech, Prague 28 April 1887.

In Italian (translated by A. Zanardini), Rome 23 November 1889.

In German (translated by O. Neitzel), Hamburg 1 January 1890.

In Dutch, Amsterdam 1 September 1898.

1887

SULLIVAN: *Ruddygore;* or, *The Witch's Curse*

22 January London, Savoy

Text by W. S. Gilbert (developed from his one-act operetta *Ages Ago*, produced with music by F. Clay at the Gallery of Illustration, London 22 November 1869). Two acts. (The name of Ruddygore was changed into Ruddigore later on.)

In London ran for 283 nights. New York 21 February 1887, etc. Wellington (New Zealand) 23 May 1895.

Revived Glasgow 6 December 1920; London, Prince's Th. 24 October 1921, etc.

A parody, *Ruddy George;* or, *Robin Red Breast*, by H. G. F. Taylor and P. Reeve was produced at Toole's Th., London 19 March 1887.

CORDER: *Nordisa*

26 January Liverpool

Text by the composer. Three acts.

Birmingham 22 February 1887; London, D.L. 4 May 1887, etc. Fairly successful on English stages.

VERDI: *Otello*

5 February Milan, Sc.

Text by A. Boito (after Shakespeare). Four acts.

After a long period of silence (his last opera, apart from the revised *Simon Boccanegra*, had been *Aida*, see 1871) this new work by the 74-years-old composer had been looked forward to with the utmost anticipation. *Otello* became one of Verdi's greatest successes and the first night at the Scala (with Francesco Tamagno as Otello, Victor Maurel as Jago, and Romilda Pantaleoni as Desdemona) may be called the culmination of his whole career.

Subsequently given at:

ROME 16 April 1887.
VENICE 18 May 1887.
BRESCIA 11 August 1887.
PARMA 14 September 1887.
TURIN 26 December 1887.
MODENA 11 January 1888.
NAPLES 4 February 1888.
FLORENCE 24 April 1888.
TRENTO 10 June 1888.
FERMO 13 August 1888.
TREVISO 19 October 1888.
BOLOGNA 30 October 1888.
GENOA 24 November 1888.
MESSINA 27 November 1888.
PALERMO December 1888.
TRIESTE 25 March 1889.
UDINE 10 August 1889.
LUCCA 2 September 1889, etc.

Outside Italy, produced at:

MEXICO 18 November 1887 (in Italian; pirated, orchestrated from the vocal score by P.Valline; the original was given there only on 18 January 1890).

ST. PETERSBURG 8 December 1887; Moscow 8 April 1889 (in Russian, translated by N. M. Spassky).

BUDAPEST 8 December 1887 (in Hungarian, translated by A. Radó).

PRAGUE 7 January 1888 (in Czech, translated by V. J. Novotný) and 1911 (in German).

HAMBURG 31 January 1888 (in German, translated by M. Kalbeck); Munich 5 February 1888; Cologne 3 April 1888; Bonn 23 April 1888; Frankfort 29 September 1888; Bremen 12 October 1888, etc.

BRÜNN 10 March 1888 (in German).

AMSTERDAM 10 March 1888 (in Dutch; pirated, orchestrated from the vocal score by J. Coenen); Rotterdam 1889 (in German).

VIENNA 14 March 1888 (in German) and 22 October 1909 (in Italian).

NEW YORK 16 April 1888 (in Italian) and 6 October 1903 (in English); Boston 30 April 1888; Philadelphia 4 May 1888; Chicago 2 January 1890; San Francisco 12 February, 1890.

BUENOS AIRES 12 June 1888 (in Italian).

CONSTANTINOPLE Autumn 1888 (in Italian; pirated).

HAVANA 10 January 1889 (in Italian).

LISBON 24 March 1889 (in Italian).

LONDON, LY. 5 July 1889 (in Italian) and Marlborough Th. (Holloway) 26 April 1907 (in English).

BERLIN 1 February 1890 (in German).

STOCKHOLM 27 May 1890 (in Swedish, translated by H. Key).

MADRID 9 October 1890 (in Italian).

RIGA January 1891 (in German) and 13 May 1926 (in Lettish).

NICE February 1891 (in Italian).

MANCHESTER 8 October 1892 (in English, translated by F. Hueffer); Dublin August 1893, etc.

WARSAW 3 October 1893 (in Polish, translated by Emes).

RIO DE JANEIRO Summer 1894 (in Italian).

PARIS, O. 12 October 1894 (in French, translated by A. Boito and C. Du Locle) and Th.I. 13 April 1897 (in Italian); Rouen 1 February 1895, etc.; Marseilles 9 March 1911; Lyons 11 July 1914 (in Italian).

ALEXANDRIA 9 January 1895 (in Italian).

MALTA 1897 (in Italian).

COPENHAGEN 20 April 1898 (in Danish, translated by S. Levysohn).

ZURICH 5 December 1898 (in German).

ZAGREB 10 October 1899 (in Croatian, translated by M. Pogačić).

GRAZ 6 November 1900 (in German).

MELBOURNE End of 1901 (in English).

BRUSSELS 22 February 1902 (in French).

LJUBLJANA 1903 (in Slovenian).

OSLO 1921 (in Norwegian).

SOFIA 17 May 1922 (in Bulgarian).

HELSINKI 2 February 1923 (in Finnish).

JERUSALEM 27 April 1925 (in Hebrew, translated by Dushmann).

TALLINN 1929 (in Estonian).

BUCHAREST December 1937 (in Rumanian).

KAUNAS 15 June 1938 (in Lithuanian).

RÜFER: *Merlin*

28 February. Berlin, O.

Text by L. Hoffmann (founded on C. L. Immermann's drama of the same title). Three acts.

The first opera of the German-Belgian composer.

SAINT-SAËNS: *Proserpine*

16 March. Paris, O.C.

Text by L. Gallet (founded on a play by A. Vacquerie). Four acts.

Revived Paris, O.C. 29 November 1899.

In French also, Alexandria 17 January 1903; Monte Carlo 5 March 1910; Brussels 7 April 1913. In Italian (translated by A. Galli), Lisbon June 1914.

CLÉRICE: *Le Meunier d'Alcala*

11 April. Lisbon, Th. Trinidad

(Original Portuguese) text by E. Garrido, French version by A. Lafrique. The best work of the

Argentine composer (produced in Portugal, in French). Three acts.

Revived London, Prince of Wales's 11 February 1899 (in English, as *The Coquette*, adapted by H. J. W. Dam and C. Bingham).

PACIUS: *Lorelei*

28 April. Helsinki

E. Geibel's text (first set to music by Mendelssohn and Bruch, see 1863). Four acts.

The last opera of the Finnish composer (produced in German, by amateurs).

CHABRIER: *Le Roi malgré lui*

18 May. Paris, O.C.

Text by E. de Najac and P. Burani (founded on a comedy by F. Ancelot). Three acts.

Chabrier's most successful opera and the last which was produced in his lifetime.

In German, Carlsruhe 2 March 1890, etc.

Revived Paris, O.C. 6 November 1929 (text revised by A. Carré) and 28 January 1937; Brussels 16 May 1931.

Revived in German (new translation by L. Sachse), Hamburg 17 April 1931; Prague 27 August 1931.

RADEGLIA: *Colomba*

15 June. Milan, T.d.V.

Text by F. Fontana (founded on Mérimée's story). Three acts.

The first opera of Radeglia (a native of Constantinople who was the composer of the Turkish national hymn).

ZÖLLNER: *Faust*

19 October. Munich

Text by the composer (after Goethe). Prologue and 4 acts.

In German also, Prague 2 September 1888.

Revived Leipzig 26 February 1905; Antwerp 10 October 1908 (in Flemish); Freiburg Summer 1929.

CHAIKOVSKY: *Charodyeka*

Чародѣйка

(The Enchantress)

1 November. St. Petersburg

Text by I. V. Shpazhinsky. Four acts.

Moscow 16 February 1890, etc. Revived St. Petersburg 20 June 1902; Moscow 1916.

CHAPI: *La Bruja*

(The Witch)

10 December. Madrid, Z.

Text by M. Ramos Carrión. Three acts.

As successful as his *La Tempestad* (see 1882). Mexico 16 February 1895, etc.

In Czech (translated by V. J. Novotný), Prague 13 November 1895.

J. STRAUSS: *Simplizius*

17 December. Vienna, W.

Text by V. Léon. Three acts.

Regarded by the composer as one of his best works; but not nearly as successful as his former operettas. Given at Prague 10 November 1888; Graz 25 December 1888 and Vienna, W. 19 September 1894 in a new version (libretto altered by L. Dóczy); also Budapest c.1890 (in Hungarian); revived at "Venedig in Wien", Vienna 5 July 1902 (as *Gräfin Pepi*, music arranged from *Simplizius* and *Blindekuh*, by J. Reiterer); this version was also given at Graz 22 November 1902, etc.; Berlin, Central Th. 27 February 1903.

1888

(C. M. VON WEBER): *Die drei Pintos*

20 January. Leipzig

Original text by T. Hell (founded on a story, *Der Brautkampf*, by C. L. Seidel). Three acts.

The opera had been left unfinished by Weber in 1821. After his death (1826) the fragments, seven pieces, were given to Meyerbeer who, however, never made use of them. In 1888 the opera was produced in a new arrangement of the text by K. von Weber, the composer's grandson. The music was arranged and completed by Gustav Mahler. Also given at Prague 18 August 1888; Vienna 18 January 1889; Berlin, Lessing Th. 4 July 1891 (by the Prague company).

Revived Weimar 5 November 1899; Prague 15 November 1900; Frankfort 6 October 1901; Hanover 29 August 1909; Riga 1911; Zurich 13 January 1915.

In Czech (translated by O. Zich), Prague January 1917.

F. RUNG: *Det hemmelige Selskab* (The Secret Party)

9 February. Copenhagen

Text by S. Bauditz. Two acts.
Rung's only opera.

FRANCHETTI: *Asrael*

11 February. Reggio

Text by F. Fontana (*Leggenda*). Four acts.
Franchetti's first opera. Outside Italy, given at:
HAMBURG 17 February 1890 (in German, translated by H. Wittmann).
PRAGUE 30 March 1890 (in Czech, translated by V. J. Novotný).
BUDAPEST 20 November 1890 (in Hungarian, translated by A. Radó).
NEW YORK 26 November 1890 (in Italian).
ALEXANDRIA 19 January 1897 (in Italian).
LISBON 1897 (in Italian).
BUENOS AIRES 15 June 1901 (in Italian).
LJUBLJANA 1903 (in Slovenian).

GODARD: *Jocelyn*

25 February. Brussels, M.

Text by P. A. Silvestre and V. Capoul (after Lamartine's poem). Four acts.

Also given at Paris, Château d'Eau 13 October 1888.

KEIL: *Donna Bianca*

10 March. Lisbon, S.C.

(Italian) text by C. Fereal (from Almeida Garrett's poem, *Dona Branca*). Prologue and 4 parts.

The first opera of Keil, who was the composer of the Portuguese national hymn. Also given at Rio de Janeiro 6 October 1891 (in Italian).

HIGNARD: *Hamlet*

21 April. Nantes

Text by P. de Garal (after Shakespeare). Five acts.

The vocal score of this *Hamlet* opera had been published as early as 1868 (dedication dated 2 February 1868); it was not produced on account of the great success obtained by Thomas's opera of the same title on 9 March 1868.

(See for an account of the work, Clément-Larousse's *Dictionnaire des Opéras*.)

LALO: *Le Roi d'Ys*

7 May. Paris, O.C.

Text by E. Blau. Three acts.

Lalo's most successful opera; still very popular in France. The 100th performance at the O.C. was on 5 June 1889, the 200th on 22 February 1906.
Outside Paris, given at:
GENEVA 23 November 1888 (in French).
AMSTERDAM December 1888 (in Dutch).
ANTWERP and BRUSSELS 7 February 1889 (in French).
NEW ORLEANS 23 January 1890 (in French).
ROME 12 March 1890 (in Italian, translated by A. Zanardini).
LONDON, C.G. 17 July 1901 (in French).
PRAGUE 17 May 1902 (in Czech, translated by O. Smrčka).
MOSCOW February 1906 (in Russian).
NEW YORK 5 January 1922 (in French).
BUCHAREST 1 October 1926 (in Rumanian).

(R. WAGNER): *Die Feen*

29 June. Munich

Text by the composer (founded on Gozzi's comedy, *La Donna Serpente*). Three acts.

Wagner's first opera, written at Würzburg in 1833. Vocal score published 1888.

Also given at Prague 8 February 1893 (in German); revived Munich 18 June 1910; Zurich Spring 1914; Stuttgart 19 November 1932.

An English translation by T. Reuss (lyrics by A. V. Sinclair) was published in New York 1894; there is also a printed Catalan translation by J. Zanné and J. Pena (1907).

SULLIVAN: *The Yeomen of the Guard; or, The Merryman and his Maid*

3 October. London, Savoy

Text by W. S. Gilbert. Two acts.

In London ran for 423 nights. First given at New York, Casino 17 October 1888, etc.

In German (as *Capitän Wilson*, translated by V. Léon and C. Lindau; pirated), Vienna, Ca. 2 February 1889; Budapest 1889; Prague 23 November 1890. Another German version, *Der Königsgardist* (translated by F. Zell and R. Genée), was produced at Berlin, Kroll's 25 December 1889.

HORNEMAN: *Aladdin*

19 November. Copenhagen

Text by B. Feddersen (founded on A. G. Oehlenschläger's play). Four acts.

Horneman's only opera. Written to celebrate the 25th jubilee of King Christian IX. Revived Copenhagen 4 April 1902.

VAN DER LINDEN: *Catharina en Lambert*

24 November. Amsterdam

(Anonymous Dutch) text by J. Van der W. (founded on A. de Leuven and L. L. Brunswick's vaudeville, *Le Mariage au Tambour*). Three acts.

The first new opera produced at the "Neederlandsche Oper", Amsterdam (founded 1886), of which Van der Linden was the first conductor.

1889

DVOŘÁK: *Jakobín*

12 February. Prague, Cz.

Text by M. Červinková-Riegrová. Three acts.

Successful in Czechoslovakia; frequently revived at Prague.

In Czech also, Vienna 5 May 1929 (by a company from Bratislava); Barcelona February 1936.

In German (translated by A. Heller and H. Grab), Teplitz-Schönau 12 December 1931; Prague May 1934.

In Croatian, Zagreb 19 March 1938.

In Slovenian (translated by V. Hreščakova), Ljubljana 28 March 1938.

BRETÓN: *Gli Amanti di Teruel*

12 February. Madrid, T.R.

(Original Spanish) text by the composer (founded on a play by J. E. Hartzenbusch), Italian version by A. Zanardini. Prologue and 4 acts.

In Italian also given at Barcelona 11 May 1889.

In German (translated by F. Adler), Prague 22 March 1891; Vienna 4 October 1891.

Buenos Aires 23 August 1892 (in Italian) and 1910 (in Spanish).

MANDL: *La Rencontre imprévue*

16 March. Rouen

Text by A. Larsonneur. One act.

In French also, Hague *c*.1890.

In German (translated by O. Berggruen), Prague 16 April 1890.

VAN MILLIGEN: *Brinio*

20 April. Amsterdam

(Dutch) text by M. G. L. van Loghem (founded on a novel by J. Van Lennep). Four acts.

In Dutch also given at Antwerp 1 October 1895.

(G. B. Shaw wrote a review of this opera; reprinted in his *London Music in 1888–89*, pp.100–103.)

PUCCINI: *Edgar*

21 April. Milan, Sc.

Text by F. Fontana (founded on Musset's *La Coupe et les Lèvres*). Four acts.

Revived in a new 3-act version, Ferrara 28 February 1892.

In Italian also, Madrid 19 March 1892 and Buenos Aires 8 July 1905; revived Malta April 1920.

MASSENET: *Esclarmonde*

15 May. Paris, O.C.

Text by E. Blau and L. de Gramont (*opéra romanesque*). Prologue, 4 acts and epilogue.

The 100th performance at the O.C. was as early as 6 February 1890.

In French also, Brussels 27 November 1889; Geneva 30 January 1897.

In Russian (translated by N. M. Spassky), St. Petersburg 18 January 1892.

Revived Paris, O. 24 December 1923 and 11 November 1931; Brussels 12 March 1934.

MUNCKTELL: *I Firenze*

29 May. Stockholm

Text by D. Fallström. One act.

Probably the first Swedish opera written by a women composer.

GOMES: *Lo Schiavo*

27 September. Rio de Janeiro

(Italian) text by R. Paravicini. Four acts.

Produced at the Teatro Lirico Dom Pedro II. Also given at São Paulo 11 November 1889. Last revived at Rio de Janeiro in April 1938.

SMAREGLIA: *Der Vasall von Szigeth*

4 October. Vienna, O.

(Original Italian) text by L. Illica and F. Pozza, produced in a German version by M. Kalbeck. Three acts.

In German also, New York, M. 12 December 1890.

Revived Pola September 1930 and Trieste October 1930 (in Italian).

PIZZI: *William Ratcliff*

31 October. Bologna, T.C.

Text by A. Zanardini (founded on Heine's tragedy). Prologue and 3 acts.

Awarded the Baruzzi prize in 1888.

In German (translated by O. Neitzel), Elberfeld 21 March 1905.

PHILPOT: *Dante and Beatrice*

25 November. London, Gresham Hall (Brixton)

Text by W. J. Miller. Three acts.

Revived London, Shaftesbury 7 June 1918; King's, Hammersmith 16 September 1920; C.G. 17 December 1920.

RUBINSTEIN: *Goriusha*

Горюша

(The Sorrowful)

3 December. St. Petersburg

Text by D. V. Averkiev. Four acts.

Rubinstein's last opera. Revived Moscow 1901.

SULLIVAN: *The Gondoliers;* or, *The King of Barataria*

7 December. London, Savoy

Text by W. S. Gilbert. Two acts.

In London ran for 554 nights. First given at New York, New Park Th. 7 January 1890; Cape Town 1890 and in all English-speaking countries.

In German (translated by F. Zell and R. Genée), Vienna, W. 20 September 1890; Berlin, Fr.W. 20 December 1890.

1890

MILLÖCKER: *Der arme Jonathan*

4 January. Vienna, W.

Text by H. Wittmann and J. Bauer. Three acts.

In German also, Berlin, Fr.W. 16 January 1890; Riga and Reval 1890; Bucharest Summer 1890; Prague 13 September 1890; Basle 10 October 1890; New York 2 January 1891.

In Hungarian, Budapest 14 March 1890.

In Russian, St. Petersburg 28 March 1890.

In Polish (translated by J. Kleczyński) Lemberg 1890.

In Swedish (translated by H. Molander), Stockholm 2 October 1890.

In English (translated by J. P. Jackson and R. A. Weill), New York 14 October 1890. In another English adaptation (by C. H. E. Brookfield and H. Greenbank), London, Prince of Wales's 15 June 1893 (with additional music by Albéniz).

In Croatian (translated by P. Brani), Zagreb 9 December 1894.

REYER: *Salammbô*

10 February. Brussels, M.

Text by C. Du Locle (founded on Flaubert's novel). Five acts.

Reyer's last opera. In France first given at Rouen 22 November 1890; Paris, O. 16 May 1892 (100th performance 17 June 1900).

In French also, New Orleans 25 January 1900; Cairo January 1901; New York 20 March 1901. Revived Brussels 15 October 1927; Paris, O. 3 June 1938.

FIBICH: *Námluvy Pelopovy* (The Wooing of Pelops)

21 February. Prague, Cz.

Text by J. Vrchlický. Four acts.

The first part of Fibich's melodramatic trilogy (1890–91). Revived Prague 18 August 1905 and 1 December 1923. Given at Vienna, Exhibition Th. 3 June 1892 (in Czech) and V.O. 9 April 1924 (in German, translated by E. Grün).

LOHSE: *Der Prinz wider Willen*

27 February. Riga

Text by R. Seuberlich. Three acts.

Given with alterations, Cologne 1 January 1898; Hamburg 30 September 1898; Strasbourg 27 October 1898; Berlin, Th.d.W. 12 November 1898. Revived Leipzig 27 January 1919; Basle 8 January 1920; Gera October 1925.

SAINT-SAËNS: *Ascanio*

21 March. Paris, O.

Text by L. Gallet (founded on A. Dumas's romance of the same title, 1843, and P. Meurice's play *Benvenuto Cellini*, 1852). Five acts.

Revived Paris, O. 9 November 1921.

GASTALDON: *Mala Pasqua!*

9 April. Rome, C.

Text by G. D. Bartocci-Fontana (after G. Verga; a 2-act version of the *Cavalleria rusticana* subject, see below).

In Italian also, Lisbon 2 February 1891.

COWEN: *Thorgrim*

22 April. London, D.L.

Text by J. Bennett (founded on the Icelandic romance, *Viglund the Fair*). Four acts.

Dublin September 1890; Birmingham 24 October 1890, etc.

SPINELLI: *Labilia*

7 May. Rome, C.

Text by V. Valle. One act.

This opera was awarded the second prize at the Concorso Sonzogno after *Cavalleria rusticana*, produced ten days later.

MASCAGNI: *Cavalleria rusticana*

17 May. Rome, C.

Text by G. Menasci and G. Targioni-Tozzetti (founded on G. Verga's play of the same title). One act (divided in two parts by the ever-popular intermezzo sinfonico).

Mascagni's first performed opera (his *Guglielmo Ratcliff*, produced in 1895, was written before *Cavalleria*, and *Pinotta*, produced as late as 1932, still earlier). Awarded the first prize in the (second) Concorso Sonzogno, 1888. The standard work of Italian *verismo* became an unprecedented world success at once. Given all over Italy and at: STOCKHOLM 11 December 1890 (in Swedish, translated by H. Key).

MADRID December 1890 and Barcelona 9 May 1891 (in Italian).

BUDAPEST 26 December 1890 (in Hungarian, translated by A. Radó).

HAMBURG 3 January 1891 (in German, translated by O. Berggruen; Dresden 16 January 1891, etc.; given at Munich 22 January 1891 as *Ritterlichkeit auf dem Dorfe*).

PRAGUE 4 January 1891 (in Czech, translated by V. J. Novotný) and 18 April 1891 (in German).

BUENOS AIRES 28 February 1891 (in Italian).

MOSCOW 17 March 1891 (in Italian) and 8 April 1892 (in Russian).

VIENNA, O. 20 March 1891 (in German) and Exhibition Th. 19 September 1892 (in Italian).

BUCHAREST April 1891 (in Italian) and 1903 (in Rumanian).

BERLIN, LESSING TH. 13 June 1891 and O. 21 October 1891 (in German); Th. U.d.L. 20 September 1895 (in Italian).

RIGA 1891 (in German) and 1913 (in Lettish).

LAIBACH (LJUBLJANA) 1891 (in German) and 1893 (in Slovenian).

PHILADELPHIA 9 September 1891; Chicago 30 September 1891; Boston 6 October 1891, etc. (in Italian).

RIO DE JANEIRO 10 September 1891 (in Italian).

BASLE 28 September 1891 (in German).

COPENHAGEN 30 September 1891 (in Danish, translated by E. Bøgh).

NEW YORK 1 October 1891 (the same day at two different theatres, matinée at the Casino Th. and evening at the Lennox Lyceum, in English [1]) and M. 30 December 1891 (in Italian).

AMSTERDAM 4 October 1891 (in German) and 3 February 1892 (in Dutch).

LONDON, SHAFTESBURY 19 October 1891 and C.G. 16 May 1892 (in Italian); 100th performance at C.G. 28 December 1907; Grand Th., Islington 9 April 1894 (in English).

MEXICO 27 October 1891 (in Italian) and July 1893 (in Spanish, translated by J. R. de la Portilla).

LISBON 12 November 1891 (in Italian).

MALTA Carnival 1892 (in Italian).

[1] The first English translations were by W. G. Day and J. C. Macy, both 1891.

NEW ORLEANS 3 January 1892 (in English) and 21 January 1897 (in French).

WARSAW 6 January 1892 (in Polish, translated by A. Strzelecki).

LIVERPOOL 14 January 1892 (in English, translated by F. E. Weatherly).

PARIS, O.C. 19 January 1892 (in French, translated by P. Milliet) and Châtelet 23 May 1910 (in Italian).

BRUSSELS 25 February 1892 (in French).

REVAL (TALLINN) 1892 (in German) and 1919 (in Estonian).

ST. PETERSBURG 30 January 1893 (in Russian, translated by M. M. Ivanov and N. M. Spassky).

ZAGREB 29 May 1893 (in Croatian, translated by A. Harambašić).

SOFIA Summer 1893 (in German) and 25 November 1910 (in Bulgarian).

CAPE TOWN 1895 (in Italian); Johannesburg 1905 (in English).

HELSINKI 5 May 1896 (in Italian) and 28 November 1917 (in Finnish, translated by W. Sola).

CHRISTIANIA (OSLO) 1896 (in Norwegian).

SIMLA, PUNJAB Autumn 1901 (in English?).

VIIPURI (VIBORG) 17 November 1908 (in Finnish).

SAIGON 1911 (in Italian).

TOKYO January 1912 (in Italian).

BELGRADE 1920 (in Serbian).

OSAKA 23 March 1924 (in Italian).

KAUNAS 21 January 1925 (in Lithuanian).

TEL-AVIV June 1925 (in Hebrew, translated by M. Freidmann).

Open-air performances of the opera took place at the Lewinsohn Stadium, New York 21 September 1916; at the Piazza S. Marco, Venice 19 July 1928. Festival performances to celebrate the 50th anniversary of the first production, conducted by the composer, took place at Venice, F. 19 February 1940; Rome, T.R. 5 March 1940; Milan, Sc. 12 April 1940.

FERRONI: *Rudello*

28 May. Rome, C.

Text by M. Zucchetti. One act.

The third prize opera of the Concorso Sonzogno.

LA NUX: *Zaïre*

28 May. Paris, O.

Text by E. Blau and L. Besson (founded on Voltaire's tragedy). Two acts.

Given in Paris 10 times only.

In German (translated by A. Harlacher), Stuttgart 10 October 1895; Prague 9 October 1903.

MESSAGER: *La Basoche*

30 May. Paris, O.C.

Text by A. Carré. Three acts.

One of Messager's most popular works; revived at the O.C. 16 November 1900, 20 December 1919, 19 December 1931 and 31 December 1939; revived at Brussels 27 October 1939.

Outside France, given at:

BRUSSELS 4 December 1890 (in French).

GENEVA 25 February 1891 (in French).

HAMBURG 19 October 1891 (in German, as *Die zwei Könige*, translated by L. Hartmann).

BERLIN, FR.W. 29 October 1891 (in German, as *Die Basoche*, translated by R. Genée).

LONDON, R.E.O. 3 November 1891 (in English, translated by A. H. G. Harris and E. Oudin); the second and last production at the "Royal English Opera", after Sullivan's *Ivanhoe* (see 1891).

PRAGUE 26 February 1892 (in Czech, translated by V. J. Novotný).

STOCKHOLM 21 May 1892 (in Swedish, translated by E. A. Wallmark).

CHICAGO January 1893 (in English, translated by M. L. Ryley).

NEW YORK 27 February 1893 (in English, translated by M. L. Ryley).

TURIN 5 March 1893 (in Italian, translated by R. Leoncavallo and E. Gentili).

E. M. BOSSI: *Il Veggente*

4 June. Milan, T.d.V.

Text by G. Macchi. One act.

In German (as *Der Wanderer*, translated by W. Weber), Mannheim 7 December 1906.

A. RITTER: *Wem die Krone?*

8 June. Weimar

Text by the composer. One act.

Ritter's second and last opera. Produced on the same bill with a revival of his *Der faule Hans* (see 1885). Berlin 1 October 1892.

DE KOVEN: *Robin Hood*

9 June. Chicago

Text by H. B. Smith. Three acts.

The most popular of De Koven's numerous operettas. Very successful in the U.S.A. Boston 22 September 1890; New York 28 September 1891, etc.

Given in London, Camden Town Park Hall 20 September 1890 and Prince of Wales's Th. 5 February 1891 as *Maid Marian*. (De Koven wrote a sequel to *Robin Hood*, actually called *Maid Marian*, and first performed at Philadelphia 4 November 1901.)

Frequently revived in New York; New Amsterdam Th. 6 May 1912; Jolson's 18 November 1929; Erlanger's 27 January 1932.

(BORODIN): *Knyaz Igor*
Князь Игорь
(Prince Igor)

4 November. St. Petersburg

Text by the composer (after a plan by V. V. Stasov). Prologue and 4 acts.

Borodin worked at this opera from 1871 until his death in 1887. It was completed and edited by Rimsky-Korsakov and Glazunov. First produced at Moscow 31 January 1898.

Outside Russia, given at:

PRAGUE 8 June 1899 (in Czech, translated by A. E. Mužík).

PARIS, CHÂTELET 19 May 1909 (parts only); the whole opera, Ch. É. 27 January 1929 (in Russian).

LONDON, D.L. 8 June 1914 (in Russian) and C.G. 26 July 1919 (in English, translated by E. Agate); another English version, by H. Procter-Gregg, was produced at Leicester on 16 October 1933.

MILAN, SC. 26 December 1915 (in Italian, translated by A. Lega; revived there 28 February 1940).

NEW YORK 30 December 1915 (in Italian).

BUENOS AIRES 5 August 1919 (in Italian).

SOFIA 29 September 1922 (in Bulgarian).

ZAGREB 16 December 1922 (in Croatian).

BARCELONA 20 December 1922 and Madrid April 1923 (in Italian).

MONTE CARLO 11 March 1924 (in French, translated by J. Ruelle).

BRUSSELS 14 November 1924 (in French, translated by J. Ruelle).

MANNHEIM 15 March 1925 (in German, translated by Mme. Aleksandrova).

LYONS 4 February 1926 (in French).

GENEVA 13 January 1928 (in Russian).

ZURICH 16 March 1928 (in German).

HELSINKI 18 September 1929 (in Finnish, translated by T. Muroma).

BUCHAREST December 1929 (in Rumanian).

LJUBLJANA 4 October 1930 (in Slovenian, translated by N. Štritof).

BERLIN 11 October 1930 (in German).

TALLINN 1932 (in Estonian).

SCHEVENINGEN September 1932 (in Russian).

ROME, ARG. 4 November 1932 (in Russian).

STOCKHOLM 11 March 1933 (in Swedish).

KAUNAS 9 February 1935 (in Lithuanian).

ANTWERP 29 February 1936 (in Flemish).

RIGA 6 November 1936 (in Lettish).

BUDAPEST Spring 1938 (in Hungarian).

AUDRAN: *Miss Hélyett*

12 November. Paris, B.P.

Text by M. Boucheron. Three acts.

Very successful in Paris. The 700th performance at the B.P. was on 21 August 1892; given there 816 nights running; revived Ren. 7 April 1900, etc.

Outside France:

BRUSSELS 26 December 1890 (in French).

BERLIN, WALLNER TH. 7 February 1891 (in German, translated by R. Genée).

LONDON, CRITERION 23 July 1891 (in English, as

Miss Decima, adapted by F. C. Burnand and P. Reeve).

NEW YORK 3 November 1891 (in English).

STOCKHOLM 21 November 1891 (in Swedish, translated by E. A. Wallmark).

VIENNA, W. 25 December 1891 (in German).

PRAGUE 3 January 1892 (in Czech, translated by V. J. Novotný).

MEXICO 27 November 1892 (in Spanish, translated by E. Labrada).

GENOA 11 September 1895 (in Italian).

LISBON April 1901 (in French).

MADRID 27 April 1905 (in Spanish, translated by S. M. Granés).

Spanish parody *Miss' Erere*, by Gabriel Merino y Pichilo, music by Luis Arnedo, Madrid 8 April 1893.

TRNEČEK: *Amaranta*

16 November. Prague, Cz.

(Original German) text by D. Hornicke (founded on a poem by O. von Redtwitz), Czech version by L. Dolanský. Prologue and 3 acts.

Trneček's first Czech opera.

(BERLIOZ): *Die Eroberung Trojas*

6 December. Carlsruhe

(Original French) text (*La Prise de Troie*) by the composer (after Virgil), German version by O. Neitzel. Three acts.

The first part of Berlioz's *Les Troyens* (published 1864). Together with the revival (5 December) of the second part (see 1863) this was the first production of the complete work (on two subsequent nights, under the direction of F. Mottl).

La Prise de Troie was first given in the original French at Nice February 1891 (according to Clément-Larousse, p. 905); Paris, O. 15 November 1899.

In Italian (translated by A. Galli), Milan, T.L. 23 November 1899.

Revived Geneva 22 November 1932 (in French).

Les Troyens (both parts) was revived at:

COLOGNE 30–31 March 1898 (in German).

BRUSSELS 26–27 December 1906 (in French).

STUTTGART 18 May 1913 (new German version by E. Gerhäuser, music arranged by M. von Schillings).

ROUEN February 1920 (in French); both parts in a reduced 5-act version (9 scenes).

PARIS, O. 10 June 1921 (in French); both parts in a reduced 5-act version (9 scenes); revived Paris, O. 5 June 1939.

BERLIN, O. 15 June 1930 (in German, translated and arranged by J. Kapp); 4 acts (6 scenes).

GLASGOW 18–19 March 1935 (in its entirety for the first time in English, translated by E. J. Dent).

CHAIKOVSKY: *Pikovaya Dama*
Пиковая Дама
(The Queen of Spades)

19 December. St. Petersburg

Text by M. I. Chaikovsky (the brother of the composer), founded on Pushkin's novel. Three acts.

Apart from *Yevgeny Onegin* (see 1879), Chaikovsky's most successful opera. Given at Kiev December 1890; Moscow 16 November 1891; Odessa 17 February 1892; Saratov 5 December 1892, etc. Outside Russia:

PRAGUE 11 October 1892 (in Czech, translated by V. J. Novotný).

ZAGREB 27 December 1898 (in Croatian, translated by F. Miler).

RIGA 19 April 1899 (in Russian); 2 February 1901 (in German); and 1915 (in Lettish).

DARMSTADT 11 March 1900 (in German, translated by A. Bernhard).

WARSAW 8 November 1900 (in Polish).

VIENNA 9 December 1902 (in German).

LJUBLJANA 1905 (in Slovenian).

MILAN, SC. 18 January 1906 (in Italian).

BERLIN, O. 20 March 1907 (in German) and Kroll's 22 May 1908 (in Russian).

STOCKHOLM 25 November 1909 (in Swedish, translated by E. Grandinson).

NEW YORK 5 March 1910 (in German) and 10 May 1922 (in Russian).

PARIS, TH.S.B. 8 June 1911 (in Russian).

LONDON, L.O.H. 29 May 1915 (in Russian).

SAN FRANCISCO 9 January 1922 (in Russian).

BARCELONA 1 December 1922 (in Russian).

HELSINKI 2 January 1923 (in Finnish, translated by M. A. Bergh-Wuori).

BUENOS AIRES 10 June 1924 (in Russian).

KAUNAS 22 May 1925 (in Lithuanian).

NUREMBERG January 1926 (new German version by R. Lauckner).

SOFIA 26 February 1926 (in Bulgarian).

TALLINN 1926 (in Estonian, translated by S. Lipp).

COPENHAGEN 14 December 1927 (in Danish, translated by W. van der Vliet and T. Krogh).

BUCHAREST October 1928 (in Rumanian).

BRUSSELS 28 November 1931 (for the first time in French; translator not mentioned).

ZURICH May 1940 (in German).

1891

ZELLER: *Der Vogelhändler*

10 January. Vienna, W.

Text by M. West and L. Held. Three acts.

The most successful of Zeller's operettas. Given at:

BERLIN, FR.W. 20 February 1891 (in German).

PRAGUE 1891 (in German).

NEW YORK 5 October 1891 (in English, as *The Tyrolean*) and 26 December 1892 (in German); revived 4 March 1910 (in English).

TRIESTE 1891 (in Italian).

REVAL 1892 (in German).

ZURICH 27 June 1892 (in German).

SOFIA Autumn 1892 (in German).

MEXICO June 1893 (in Italian) and 3 September 1893 (in Spanish).

STOCKHOLM 30 September 1893 (in Swedish, translated by E. Högman).

RIGA 1893 (in German).

MILAN 8 January 1894 (in Italian).

ST. PETERSBURG 1894 (in German).

ZAGREB 19 January 1895 (in Croatian, translated by A. Harambašić).

MADRID 20 April 1895 (in Spanish, translated by J. R. de la Portilla).

LONDON, D.L. 17 June 1895 (in German).

BRUSSELS 21 October 1896 (in French, translated by G. Garnir and G. Lagye).

COPENHAGEN May 1897 (in German).

STRASBOURG 25 December 1897 (in German).

GHENT December 1902 (in Flemish).

BUENOS AIRES October 1906 (in German).

JOHANNESBURG 1907 (in German; by amateurs).

POZNAŃ 1912 (in Polish, translated by A. Kiczman).

Frequently revived on German stages.

GAST: *Die heimliche Ehe*

23 January. Danzig

Text by the composer (founded on G. Bertati's *Matrimonio segreto*, see 1792). Three acts.

Gast's only opera; highly praised by Nietzsche. Vocal score printed in 1901 as *Der Löwe von Venedig*, under which title the opera was revived at Chemnitz 11 February 1933.

SULLIVAN: *Ivanhoe*

31 January. London, R.E.O.

Text by J. R. Sturgis (founded on Scott's novel). Five acts.

Written for the inauguration of the short-lived Royal English Opera House, Cambridge Circus. Sullivan's only grand opera, and probably the only grand opera which was ever produced for a continuous run (160 performances).

In German (translated by H. Wittmann), Berlin, O. 26 November 1895.

Revived London, C.G. 8 March 1910.

SERRANO Y RUIZ: *Irene de Otranto*

17 February. Madrid, T.R.

Text by J. Echegaray. Three acts.

The most successful of Serrano y Ruiz's Spanish operas.

MASSENET: *Le Mage*

16 March. Paris, O.

Text by J. Richepin. Five acts.

Given in Paris 31 times in 1891, but never revived.

In French also, Hague 25 January 1896.

FREITAS GAZUL: *Fra Luigi di Sousa*

19 March. Lisbon, S.C.

(Italian) text by J. Romano and P. Bottini (founded on a play by Almeida Garrett). Three acts.

The only opera of the Portuguese composer.

PLATANIA: *Spartaco*

29 March. Naples, S.C.

Text by A. Ghislanzoni. Four acts.

Successful in Italy; Rome 28 May 1891; Milan 13 May 1893, etc.

German version by E. Taubert published.

H. BRANDTS-BUYS: *Albrecht Beiling*

29 March. Amsterdam

(Dutch) text by M. A. Caspers. Four acts.

The opera had previously been performed as a concert drama at the 15th Dutch national "Zangersfeest", Amsterdam.

PESSARD: *Les Folies amoureuses*

15 April. Paris, O.C.

Text by A. Lénéka and E. Matrat (founded on J. F. Regnard's comedy, 1704). Three acts.

The most successful of Pessard's comic operas.

(CORNELIUS): *Gunlöd*

6 May. Weimar

Text by the composer. Three acts.

Cornelius's last opera, left unfinished at his death in 1874, completed by C. Hoffbauer. First produced under E. Lassen (who partly altered the orchestration). Also given at Strasbourg 20 March 1892; Carlsruhe 29 April 1892; Mannheim 23 March 1893.

Revived in a new version by W. von Baussnern, Cologne 15 December 1906; Magdeburg 28 November 1907; Halle Spring 1918. Baussnern's version was also given in concert form at Venlo, Holland 9 January 1910.

FIBICH: *Smír Tantalův*

(Tantalus's Atonement)

2 June. Prague, Cz.

Text by J. Vrchlický. Four acts.

The second part of Fibich's melodramatic trilogy (1890–91). Given at Antwerp 21 December 1893 (in Flemish). Revived Prague 11 June 1925 (in Czech).

BRUNEAU: *Le Rêve*

18 June. Paris, O.C.

Text by L. Gallet (founded on Zola's novel). Four acts.

In French also given at London, C.G. 29 October 1891; Brussels 12 November 1891.

In German (translated by L. Hartmann), Königsberg 19 January 1892; Hamburg 28 March 1892.

Revived Paris, O.C. 1 May 1914; 12 November 1925; 16 February 1939; Basle 30 May 1926 (in French); Brussels 12 October 1933.

CARDOSO: *O Burro do Senhor Alcaide*

(The Mayor's Donkey)

14 August. Lisbon, Th. da Avenida

Text by G. Lobato and J. da Camara. Three acts.

Successful Portuguese operetta, given at Lisbon 200 times until 1892 and subsequently produced at Oporto and Rio de Janeiro.

MASCAGNI: *L'Amico Fritz*

31 October. Rome, C.

Text by "P. Suardon" (pseudonym of N. Daspuro), founded on Erckmann-Chatrian's novel. Three acts.

After *Cavalleria rusticana*, Mascagni's greatest success. Still very popular on Italian stages. Outside Italy, given at:

BUDAPEST 23 January 1892 (in Hungarian, translated by K. Abrányi).

FRANKFORT 12 March 1892 (in German, translated by M. Kalbeck).

BERLIN 19 March 1892 (in German, translated by M. Kalbeck).

VIENNA, O. 30 March 1892 (in German) and Exhibition Th. 15 September 1892 (in Italian).

PRAGUE 18 April 1892 (in Czech, translated by V. J. Novotný).

LONDON, C.G. 23 May 1892 (in Italian).

PHILADELPHIA 8 June 1892 (in Italian).

BUENOS AIRES 24 June 1892 (in Italian).

DUBLIN August 1892 (in English, translated by F. E. Weatherly).

RIO DE JANEIRO 16 October 1892 (in Italian).

ZURICH 6 January 1893 (in German).

NEW YORK 31 January 1893 (in Italian).

MOSCOW 3 November 1893 (in Italian).

ANTWERP 17 February 1894 (in French, translator not mentioned).

LAIBACH 1894 (in German).

BARCELONA 8 December 1894 (in Italian).

STOCKHOLM 26 January 1895 (in Swedish, translated by E. A. Wallmark).

MALTA 1901 (in Italian).

PARIS, TH. S.B. 9 May 1905 (in Italian).

LEMBERG 15 November 1906 (in Polish, translated by A. Kiczman).

LISBON 1906 (in Italian).

MONTREAL 1911 (in Italian).

LYONS 17 July 1914 (in Italian).

FIBICH: *Smrt Hippodamie*

(Hippodamia's Death)

8 November. Prague, Cz.

Text by J. Vrchlický. Four acts.

The third and last part of Fibich's trilogy (see 21 February 1890 and 2 June 1891). The first cyclic performance at the Czech Opera House, Prague, was on 16–18 February 1893. *Smrt Hippodamie* was revived at Prague 28 October 1925 and 7 May 1932.

MORALES: *Cleopatra*

14 November. Mexico

(Italian) text by A. Ghislanzoni. Four acts.

The last opera of the Mexican composer (cf. 1865).

SPETRINO: *Celeste*

3 December. Bucharest

(Italian) text by A. Ghislanzoni (from L. Marenco's *idillio campestre*, 1868). Three acts.

One of the very few original Italian operas produced at Bucharest.

HUBAY: *Alienor*

5 December. Budapest

Text by A. Váradi (translated from a French libretto by E. Haraucourt). Four acts and epilogue.

The first opera of the famous violinist.

BOURGAULT-DUCOUDRAY: *Thamara*

28 December. Paris, O.

Text by L. Gallet. Two acts.

Revived Paris, O. 23 January 1907. The only opera of the "forgotten promoter of the modern renaissance of French music" (Calvocoressi) which was produced in his lifetime.

1892

J. STRAUSS: *Ritter Pázmán*

1 January. Vienna, O.

Text by L. Dóczy (founded on an Hungarian ballad by J. Arany). Three acts.

Strauss's only attempt at comic opera proper. Also given at Prague 24 April 1892 and Berlin 4 June 1892. Revived Budapest Autumn 1939 (in Hungarian, translated by V. Lányi).

WEIS: *Viola*

17 January. Prague, Cz.

Text by B. Adler, R. Šubert and V. Novohradský (from Shakespeare's *Twelfth Night*). Three acts.

Revived (in German, as *Die Zwillinge*), Frankfort 16 December 1902; Berlin 22 December 1908; revived in Czech, Prague 28 February 1917 (as *Blíženci*).

CATALANI: *La Wally*

20 January. Milan, Sc.

Text by L. Illica (founded on a German novel, *Die Geyer-Wally*, by Wilhelmine von Hillern). Four acts.

Catalani's last and best opera. Given at:

HAMBURG 16 February 1893 (in German, translated by W. von Hillern, the author of the original novel.)

BUENOS AIRES 28 July 1904 (in Italian).

RIO DE JANEIRO 7 October 1908 (in Italian).

NEW YORK 6 January 1909 (in Italian).

MALTA 1909 (in Italian).

LISBON 1910 (in Italian).

BARCELONA 3 January 1911 (in Italian).

WARSAW January 1914 (in Polish).

MANCHESTER 27 March 1919 (in English, translated by P. E. Pinkerton).

BUCHAREST January 1924 (in Rumanian).

LJUBLJANA 1926 (in Slovenian).

Revived Rome 10 October 1920, etc. Still given in Italy.

ENNA: *Heksen* (The Witch)

24 January. Copenhagen

Text by A. Ipsen (founded on a German play by A. Fitger). Four acts.

The most successful opera of the Danish composer. Also given at:

PRAGUE 1 June 1892 (in German, translated by M. von Borch).

MAGDEBURG 27 November 1892 (in German, translated by M. von Borch).

BERLIN 14 January 1893 (in German, translated by M. von Borch).

RIGA November 1893 (in German, translated by M. von Borch).

STOCKHOLM 9 January 1894 (in Swedish, translated by E. A. Wallmark).

MASSENET: *Werther*

16 February. Vienna, O.

(Original French) text by E. Blau, P. Milliet and G. Hartmann (after Goethe), first produced in a German version by M. Kalbeck. Four acts.

Apart from *Manon*, Massenet's most popular opera. Given at:

WEIMAR 13 November 1892 (in German).

GENEVA 27 December 1892 (for the first time in the original French).

PARIS, O.C. 16 January 1893 (in French).

BRUSSELS 24 January 1893 (in French).

CHICAGO 29 March 1894 (in French).

NEW YORK 19 April 1894 (in French).

ST. PETERSBURG April 1894 (in French); 29 January 1896 (in Russian); 16 January 1902 (in Italian)[1]. Revived in Russian, Leningrad 10 December 1920.

LONDON, C.G. 11 June 1894 (in French) and H.M.'s 27 May 1910 (in English, translated by H. G. Chapman).

NEW ORLEANS 3 November 1894 (in French).

MILAN, T.L. 1 December 1894 (in Italian, translated by G. Menasci and G. Targioni-Tozzetti).

KIEV January 1895 (for the first time in Russian, translated by N. M. Spassky).

BUENOS AIRES 17 July 1897 (in Italian).

LISBON 28 December 1898 (in Italian).

BARCELONA 29 April 1899 (in Italian).

RIGA 10 November 1899 (in German) and 16 November 1926 (in Lettish).

BRÜNN 26 December 1900 (in German).

ODESSA 13 January 1901 (in Italian).

PRAGUE 13 January 1901 (in Czech, translated by V. J. Novotný).

ZAGREB 29 October 1901 (in Croatian, translated by V. Badalić).

WARSAW November 1901 (in Polish, translated by L. German).

STOCKHOLM 1 December 1904 (in Swedish, translated by S. Nyblom).

RIO DE JANEIRO 12 August 1905 (in Italian).

ZURICH 20 October 1905 (in German)

BERLIN, K.O. 12 September 1907 (in German); revived Kroll's 7 March 1926.

COPENHAGEN 22 September 1907 (in Danish, translated by J. Lehmann).

LJUBLJANA 1909 (in Slovenian).

MONTREAL 1912 (in French).

[1] Name part (originally tenor) rewritten as baritone for Mattia Battistini.

SOFIA 6 May 1920 (in Bulgarian).

BELGRADE 1920 (in Serbian).

HELSINKI 28 January 1922 (in Swedish).

MALTA 1922 (in Italian).

BUCHAREST February 1923 (in Rumanian).

KAUNAS 2 January 1931 (in Lithuanian).

The 1,000th performance at the Paris, O.C. was on 11 October 1938. Still given on French and Italian stages.

(LACOMBE): *Winkelried*

17 February. Geneva

Text by Moreau-Sainti and L. Bonnemère. Four acts.

The first of three operas all produced after the composer's death.

In German (translated by H. Riemann), Coblenz 19 January 1896; Elberfeld 3 March 1900.

GIORDANO: *Mala Vita*

21 February. Rome, Arg.

Text by N. Daspuro. Three parts.

In Italian also, Berlin, Kroll's 13 February 1892; Vienna, Exhibition Th. 27 September 1892.

Revived in a new version (as *Il Voto*), Milan, T.L. 10 November 1897.

DRAESEKE: *Herrat*

10 March. Dresden

Text by the composer. Three acts.

Revived Dresden 7 October 1905; Coburg 13 November 1906.

BENDL: *Dítě Tábora*
(The Daughter of the Camp)

13 March. Prague, Cz.

Text by E. Krásnohorská. Three acts.

Revived Prague 11 October 1927.

BRÜLL: *Gringoire*

19 March. Munich

Text by V. Léon (after the French play by T. de Banville). One act.

Apart from *Das goldene Kreuz* (see 1875), Brüll's greatest success.

In German also given at Vienna 4 October 1892; Prague and Riga 1893; Colmar 27 November 1896 and Strasbourg 28 November 1897.

In Danish, Copenhagen 5 January 1902.

CILEA: *La Tilda*
7 April. Florence, T. Pagliano

Text by "A. Graziani" (pseudonym of A. Zanardini). Three acts.

In Italian also given at the Exhibition Th., Vienna 24 September 1892.

HOL: *Floris V*
9 April. Amsterdam

Text by M. Boddaert. Five acts.

Hol's first opera. Revived in a new version, Hague April 1902.

MOSZKOWSKI: *Boabdil, der letzte Maurenkönig*
21 April. Berlin, O.

Text by C. Wittkowsky. Three acts.

Moszkowski's only opera (containing the popular ballet music).

In German also given at Prague 5 September 1893.

In English (translated by C. F. Tretbar), New York 24 January 1893.

CHAPUIS: *Enguerrande*
9 May. Paris, O.C.

Text by V. Wilder (founded on a play by A. E. Bergerat). Four acts.

Chapuis's first opera.

BRETON: *Garin, l'Eremita di Montserrat*
14 May. Barcelona, L.

(Italian) text by C. Fereal. Four acts.

In Italian also given at Madrid 22 October 1892; Lisbon 10 February 1903; Oporto 1905.

In German (translated by F. Adler) Prague 8 March 1893.

LEONCAVALLO: *Pagliacci*
21 May. Milan, T.d.V.

Text by the composer. Prologue and 2 acts.

The first of Leoncavallo's operas which was performed, and his greatest success. Given at:

VIENNA 17 September 1892 (in Italian, at the Exhibition Th.) and O. 19 November 1893 (in German).

BERLIN, O. 5 December 1892 (in German, translated by L. Hartmann) and Th. U.d.L. 20 September 1895 (in Italian).

PRAGUE 10 February 1893 (in Czech, translated by V. J. Novotný) and 1893 (in German).

BUDAPEST 28 March 1893 (in Hungarian, translated by A. Radó).

LONDON, C.G. 19 May 1893 (in Italian) and 6 November 1895 (in English); 100th performance at C.G. 3 April 1920.

NEW YORK 15 June 1893 (in Italian); 18 December 1893 (in German); and 10 May 1895 (in English).

BUENOS AIRES 20 June 1893 (in Italian).

DUBLIN August 1893 (in English, translated by F. E. Weatherly).

STOCKHOLM 28 September 1893 (in Swedish, translated by E. A. Wallmark).

MEXICO 10 October 1893 (in Italian) and 3 February 1894 (in Spanish, translated by J. R. de la Portilla).

BASLE 29 October 1893 (in German).

MOSCOW 23 November 1893 (in Russian, translated by N. M. Spassky) and 22 January 1894 (in Italian); St. Petersburg 5 December 1893 (in Russian).

ZAGREB 22 April 1894 (in Croatian, translated by M. Pogačić).

MALTA 1894 (in Italian).

WARSAW 1894 (in Polish).

RIGA 1894 (in German), and 1913 (in Lettish).

BORDEAUX 26 November 1894 (in French, translated by E. Crosti).

BRUSSELS 11 February 1895 (in French, translated by E. Crosti).

COPENHAGEN 3 May 1895 (in Danish, translated by E. Bøgh).

CAPE TOWN 1895 (in Italian); Johannesburg 1905 (in English).

HELSINKI 24 April 1896 (in Italian); 2 October 1911 (in Swedish); 27 September 1919 (in Finnish).

LISBON 1897 (in Italian).

LJUBLJANA 1899 (in Slovenian).

PARIS, O. 17 December 1902 and O.C. 13 January 1910 (in French); Châtelet 23 May 1910 (in Italian.

CHRISTIANIA 14 May 1906 (in Norwegian).

MADRID 1908 (in Spanish, translated by A. Osete).

SOFIA 5 May 1909 (in Bulgarian; first opera which was sung in that language).

TALLINN 1912 (in Estonian).

YOKOHAMA Autumn 1919 (in Italian).

KAUNAS 23 September 1922 (in Lithuanian).

BELGRADE 1923 (in Serbian).

BUCHAREST December 1923 (in Rumanian); earlier given there in Italian.

TEL-AVIV 9 January 1924 (in Hebrew, translated by M. Freidmann).

ATHENS November 1931 (in Italian).

KELLEY: *Puritania; or, The Earl and the Maid of Salem*

9 June. Boston

Text by C. M. S. MacLellan. Two acts.

Subsequently given at New York 19 September 1892 and on several other American stages.

BEMBERG: *Elaine*

5 July. London, C.G.

(French) text by P. Ferrier (from Tennyson's *Idylls of the King*). Four acts.

Written for Nellie Melba. In French also, New York 17 December 1894. English version by E. Oudin published 1894.

MUGNONE: *Il Birichino*

11 August. Venice, T. Malibran

Text by E. Golisciani (*Bozzetto melodrammatico*). One act.

The most successful opera of Mugnone (who was the first conductor of *Cavalleria rusticana*).

In Italian also given at the Exhibition Th., Vienna 19 September 1892 and at Barcelona 1893.

FRANCHETTI: *Cristoforo Colombo*

6 October. Genoa, C.F.

Text by L. Illica. Four acts and epilogue.

Written to celebrate the 400th anniversary of the discovery of America.

Given in an altered version at Milan, Sc. 26 December 1892.

Outside Italy, produced at:

HAMBURG 5 October 1893 (in German, translated by L. Hartmann).

PRAGUE 10 June 1896 (in Czech, translated by V. J. Novotný).

BUENOS AIRES 17 July 1900 (in Italian).

BARCELONA 15 November 1902 (in Italian).

MONTE CARLO 9 February 1909 (in Italian).

PHILADELPHIA 20 November 1913 (in Italian).

Revived Milan 17 January 1923; Rome 7 February 1923 (altered); Treviso October 1937.

BANTOCK: *Caedmar*

18 October. London, Crystal Palace

Text by the composer. One act.

Bantock's first opera. Previously heard in concert form, at the R.A.M. 12 July 1892.

RIMSKY-KORSAKOV: *Mlada*
Млада

1 November. St. Petersburg

Text by the composer (founded on an earlier Russian libretto by S. A. Gedeonov). Four acts.

Originally, *Mlada* was commissioned by the Russian Imperial Theatres to be written by Kyui, Musorgsky, Rimsky-Korsakov, and Borodin collectively (one act to be set by each composer); this version was never finished. In 1889 Rimsky-Korsakov decided to re-write the whole work, both text and music. His setting was revived at Moscow September 1913; Leningrad October 1923.

KOVAŘOVIČ: *Noc Šimona a Judy*
(The Night of St. Simon and St. Jude)

5 November. Prague, Cz.

Text by K. Sípek (founded on P. A. de Alarćon's *El Sombrero de tres Picos* the same story from which Hugo Wolf's *Corregidor* and several other operas were taken). Three acts.

MASCAGNI: *I Rantzau*

10 November. Florence, P.

Text by G. Menasci and G. Targioni-Tozzetti (founded on the comedy by Erckmann-Chatrian). Four acts.

Also given at:

VIENNA 7 January 1893 (in German, translated by M. Kalbeck).

BERLIN 25 February 1893 (in German, translated by M. Kalbeck).

PRAGUE 2 May 1893 (in Czech, translated by V. J. Novotný).

LONDON, C.G. 7 July 1893 (in Italian).

BIRMINGHAM October 1893 (in English, translated by F. E. Weatherly).

WEINGARTNER: *Genesius*

15 November. Berlin, O.

Text by H. Herrig. Three acts.

Successful in Germany. In German also given at Prague 10 October 1899.

In Flemish, Antwerp 11 November 1905.

Revived Darmstadt 26 November 1917; Vienna, V.O. 8 October 1921.

TASCA: *A Santa Lucia*

16 November. Berlin, Kroll's

Text by E. Golisciani and G. Cognetti. Two acts.

Tasca's best opera. Produced at Berlin in Italian, and revived there at the Th.d.W. 10 November 1905, again in Italian. In Italian also Trieste 7 March 1893; Vienna 4 October 1893; Genoa 22 May 1897.

In German (translated by L. Hartmann), Prague 26 March 1893; Hamburg 29 May 1893.

In English (translated by W. Grist), Manchester 1 October 1894.

BLOCKX: *Maître Martin*

30 November. Brussels, M.

Text by E. Landoy (founded on a story by E. T. A. Hoffmann). Four acts.

CHAIKOVSKY: *Iolanta*
Іоланта

18 December. St. Petersburg

Text by M. I. Chaikovsky (the brother of the composer), founded on H. Hertz's Danish play, *Kong Renés Datter*. One act.

Chaikovsky's last opera, and one of his most successful works. Along with *Iolanta*, his famous ballet, *Casse-Noisette*, was produced for the first time.

First given at Moscow 23 November 1893. Revived at Leningrad 16 March 1922. Outside Russia, given at:

HAMBURG 3 January 1893 (in German, translated by H. Schmidt); Munich 20 May 1897.

COPENHAGEN 29 September 1893 (in Danish, translated by E. Bøgh).

STOCKHOLM 27 October 1893 (in Swedish, translated by E. G. Lundquist).

RIGA 1894 (in German) and 26 May 1930 (in Lettish).

VIENNA 22 March 1900 (in German).

BOLOGNA 23 November 1907 (in Italian, translated by A. Leawington).

HELSINKI 28 November 1917 (in Finnish, translated by T. Muroma).

OSLO March 1929 (in Norwegian, by students).

BUDAPEST Spring 1929 (in Hungarian).

SCARBOROUGH-ON-HUDSON 10 September 1933 (in Russian; open-air performance).

LJUBLJANA 14 December 1938 (in Slovenian, translated by M. Pugelj).

1893

J. STRAUSS: *Fürstin Ninetta*

10 January. Vienna, W.

Text by H. Wittmann and J. Bauer. Three acts.

In German also, Berlin, Fr.W. 18 January 1893; Prague 15 March 1893; Laibach 1894; Lodz 1902.

ALBÉNIZ: *The magic Opal*

19 January. London, Lyric

Text by A. Law. Two acts.

Transferred to the Prince of Wales's Th. 11 April 1893 (as *The magic Ring*).

In Spanish (as *La Sortija*, translated by E. Sierra), Madrid, Z. November 1893.

J. B. FOERSTER: *Debora*

27 January. Prague, Cz.

Text by J. Kvapil (founded on a play by S. H. von Mosenthal). Three acts.

Foerster's first opera. Revived Prague 5 January 1930.

MESSAGER: *Madame Chrysantème*

30 January. Paris, Ren.

Text by G. Hartmann and A. Alexandre (founded on P. Loti's novel of the same title). Prologue, 4 acts, and epilogue.

Written for the inauguration of L. Détroyat's short-lived "Théâtre-Lyrique de la Renaissance".

In French also given at Monte Carlo 20 December 1901; Brussels 9 November 1906; Montreal 1912; Chicago 19 January 1920; New York 28 January 1920; Quebec Summer 1929.

Italian version by F. Cirilli published.

PUCCINI: *Manon Lescaut*

1 February. Turin, T.R.

(Anonymous) text by M. Praga, D. Oliva, and L. Illica (founded on Prévost's novel). Four acts.

Puccini's first great international success; given all over Italy and at:

BUENOS AIRES 8 June 1893 (in Italian).

RIO DE JANEIRO 28 July 1893 (in Italian).

ST. PETERSBURG 31 October 1893 (in Italian).

MADRID 4 November 1893 (in Italian).

HAMBURG 7 November 1893 (in German, translated by L. Hartmann).

LISBON 2 February 1894 (in Italian).

BUDAPEST 17 March 1894 (in Hungarian, translated by A. Radó).

PRAGUE 24 April 1894 (in Czech, translated by V.

J. Novotný) and November 1923 (in German).

LONDON, C.G. 14 May 1894 (in Italian) and Shaftesbury 15 February 1916 (in English, translated by M. Marras).

MONTEVIDEO 15 August 1894 (in Italian).

PHILADELPHIA 29 August 1894 (in Italian).

MEXICO 11 October 1894 (in Italian).

MALTA Carnival 1895 (in Italian).

WARSAW 23 January 1895 (in Polish, translated by A. Kiczman).

ALEXANDRIA 20 February 1895 (in Italian).

SANTIAGO, CHILE July 1897 (in Italian).

NEW YORK 27 May 1898 (in Italian).

ATHENS 31 August 1898 (in Italian).

AMSTERDAM 22 October 1898 (in Italian).

TUNIS 1903 (in Italian).

NICE 19 March 1906 (in French, translated by M. Vaucaire).

MARSEILLES 12 February 1907 (in French, translated by M. Vaucaire).

ANTWERP 12 December 1907 (in French, translated by M. Vaucaire).

VIENNA, V.O. 22 January 1908 and O. 15 October 1923 (in German).

BERLIN, K.O. 16 October 1908 (in German) and O. 27 May 1929 (in Italian).

PARIS, CHÂTELET 9 June 1910 (in Italian).

BRUSSELS 10 February 1911 (in French).

MONTREAL 1912 (in Italian).

GENEVA 24 January 1913 (in French).

LJUBLJANA 1924 (in Slovenian).

ZAGREB 23 January 1926 (in Croatian).

GOTHENBURG 1926 (in Swedish).

STOCKHOLM 22 November 1929 (in Swedish).

COPENHAGEN 2 February 1930 (in Danish, translated by T. Krogh).

HELSINKI 27 February 1931 (in Finnish).

RIGA 25 March 1938 (in Lettish).

VERDI: *Falstaff*

9 February. Milan, Sc.

Text by A. Boito (founded on Shakespeare's *The Merry Wives of Windsor*). Three acts.

Verdi's last, and, apart from *Un Giorno di Regno*, produced 53 years earlier, his only comic opera.

Given all over Italy and at:

TRIESTE 11 May 1893 (in Italian).

VIENNA 21 May 1893 (in Italian) and 3 May 1904 (in German).

BERLIN 1 June 1893 (in Italian) and 6 March 1894 (in German).

BUENOS AIRES 8 July 1893 (in Italian).

RIO DE JANEIRO 29 July 1893 (in Italian; the same night at two different theatres).

STUTTGART 10 September 1893 (in German, translated by M. Kalbeck).

MEXICO 7 October 1893 (in Italian).

PRAGUE 16 November 1893 (in Czech, translated by V. J. Novotný) and 20 May 1894 (in German).

ST. PETERSBURG 29 January 1894 (in Russian, translated by N. M. Spassky); revived 6 October 1925.

MADRID 10 February 1894 and Barcelona 10 April 1896 (in Italian).

LISBON 27 February 1894 (in Italian).

PARIS, O.C. 18 April 1894 (in French, translated by A. Boito and P. Solanges) and Châtelet 3 June 1910 (in Italian).

LONDON, C.G. 19 May 1894 (in Italian) and Ly. 11 December 1896 (in English, translated by W. B. Kingston, revised by F. Hart; R.C.M. performance).

COPENHAGEN 16 January 1895 (in Danish, translated by E. Bøgh).

NEW YORK 4 February 1895 (in Italian).

ALEXANDRIA 23 February 1896 (in Italian).

STOCKHOLM 16 November 1896 (in Swedish, translated by E. A. Wallmark).

SANTIAGO, CHILE 12 August 1898 (in Italian).

STRASBOURG 7 February 1901 (in German).

ZURICH 8 April 1901 (in German).

RIGA 1902 (in Lettish).

LYONS 28 February 1919 (in French).

MONTE CARLO 1 April 1919 (in Italian).

BRUSSELS 17 December 1920 (in French).

CINCINNATI 22 August 1926 (in English).

BUDAPEST 12 May 1927 (in Hungarian, translated by V. Lányi).

MALTA November 1929 (in Italian).

ANTWERP 15 February 1930 (in Flemish).

LEMBERG December 1930 (in Polish).

AMSTERDAM November 1931 (in Italian).

ZAGREB 6 November 1937 (in Croatian).

BUCHAREST April 1939 (in Rumanian).

LJUBLJANA 22 April 1939 (in Slovenian, translated by J. Vidmar).

(A.G. THOMAS): *The golden Web*
15 February. Liverpool

Text by F. Corder and B. C. Stephenson. Three acts.

Thomas's last opera; produced one year after his death. The score was completed by S. P. Waddington. London, Lyric 11 March 1893; Glasgow 6 May 1893; Dublin August 1893, etc. Revived London, Duke's Hall 18 March 1920 (by the R.A.M.).

(BERLIOZ): *La Damnation de Faust*
18 February. Monte Carlo

Text by the composer and A. Gandonnière (from G. de Nerval's French version of Goethe's *Faust*). Five acts.

Originally a cantata (*Légende Dramatique* for soloists, chorus and orchestra); first performed as such Paris, O.C. 6 December 1846, and subsequently St. Petersburg 15 March 1847; Moscow 18 April 1847; Berlin 19 June 1847; London, D.L. 7 February 1848, etc. It was adapted for the stage by R. Gunsbourg (the director of the Monte Carlo Theatre), and the production there was the first notable achievement of that institute as one of the leading operatic centres in Europe[1].

La Damnation de Faust was, as an opera, also produced at:

MILAN, T.D.V. 21 April 1893 (in Italian, translated by E. Gentili).

STRASBOURG 25 April 1893 (in French).

LIVERPOOL 3 February 1894 (in English, translated by T. H. Friend).

MOSCOW 5 March 1894 (in Italian) and 19 March 1907 (in Russian).

NEW ORLEANS 1894 (in French).

[1] See Grove's *Dictionary*, 1940 edition, Vol.VI, p.258.

HAMBURG 30 October 1902 (in German, translated by Minslaff).

PARIS, TH. S.B. 7 May 1903 and O. 10 June 1910 (in French).

BUENOS AIRES 30 May 1903 (in Italian).

BARCELONA 18 November 1903 (in Italian).

BUDAPEST 29 March 1904 (in Hungarian, translated by A. Váradi).

RIO DE JANEIRO 17 September 1904 (in Italian).

LISBON 1906 (in Italian).

BRUSSELS 21 February 1906 (in French).

NEW YORK 7 December 1906 (in French).

ALEXANDRIA Carnival 1907 (in Italian).

BERLIN, K.O. 21 March 1907 (in German) and O. 4 April 1907 (in French, by the Monte Carlo company).

GENEVA 27 March 1908 (in French).

LONDON, C.G. 26 May 1933 (in Italian).

STOCKHOLM 1 February 1936 (in Swedish).

RIGA 26 February 1937 (in Lettish).

Still given on French and Italian stages.

The concert version was heard in many more countries; even at Tokyo 20 June 1936 (in French).

MIHALOVICH: *Toldi Szerelme*
(Toldi's Love)

18 March. Budapest

Text by G. Csiky and E. Abrányi (from J. Arany's poem). Three acts.

Given at Budapest until 1911.

G. B. CORONARO: *Festa a Marina*

21 March. Venice, F.

Text by V. Fontana (*Bozzetto lirico*). One act.

In Italian also, Vienna, W. 10 June 1893; Berlin, Neues Th. 30 September 1895.

This opera, together with Boezi's *Don Paez* (see below) was awarded the first prize in the (third) Concorso Sonzogno, 1892.

KEIL: *Irene*

22 March. Turin, T.R.

Text by C. Fereal (*Leggenda mistica*). Four parts.

In Italian also, Lisbon 20 February 1896 (revived November 1936).

(DELIBES): *Kassya*

24 March. Paris, O.C.

Text by H. Meilhac and P. Gille (founded on a story by L. von Sacher-Masoch). Four acts.

Delibes's last opera, produced two years after his death (orchestrated by Massenet). Unsuccessful; given 8 times only and never revived.

BOEZI: *Don Paez*

25 March. Venice, F.

Text by G. D. Bartocci-Fontana (founded on a story by A. de Musset). One act.

Boezi's only opera. Awarded the first prize in the Concorso Sonzogno, 1892, together with Coronaro's *Festa a Marina*, see above.

VAN DER LINDEN: *Leiden Ontzet*
(The Relief of Leyden)

1 April. Amsterdam

Text by E. van der Ven. Five acts.

The second and last opera of the Dutch composer. Also given at Antwerp 12 December 1893 (in Dutch).

RAKHMANINOV: *Aleko*
Алеко

9 May. Moscow

Text by V. I. Nemirovich-Danchenko (founded on Pushkin's poem, *The Gipsies*). One act.

Revived St. Petersburg 8 June 1899; Moscow 1 December 1903; Leningrad 10 April 1921; Moscow 11 January 1926.

In Russian also, London, L.O.H. 15 July 1915; revived Wigmore Hall 21 October 1941 (in concert form).

In Lettish, Riga 18 February 1932.

SCHJELDERUP: *Sonntagmorgen*

9 May. Munich

(Original Norwegian) text by the composer, German version by E. Klingenfeld. One act.

Schjelderup's first opera; produced at the Tonkünstlerfest of the Allgemeiner Deutscher Musikverein. Revived in Norwegian, Oslo 31 August 1915 (as *En Helligaften*).

BECHGAARD: *Frøde*

11 May. Copenhagen

Text by the composer. Three acts.

Bechgaard's only opera. In German (translated by M. von Borch), Prague 5 October 1894.

SMAREGLIA: *Cornill Schut*

20 May. Prague, Cz.

(Original Italian) text by L. Illica, Czech version by V. J. Novotný. Three acts.

In German (translated by L. Hartmann), Dresden 6 June 1893; Vienna 23 November 1894.

In Italian, Trieste 17 February 1900 and revived there 21 January 1928 (as *Pittori Fiamminghi*).

SAINT-SAËNS: *Phryné*

24 May. Paris, O.C.

Text by L. Augé de Lassus. Two acts.

One of Saint-Saëns's most successful works. Revived Paris, O.C. 13 January 1910; Tr.L. 11 December 1922; O.C. 11 October 1935. Outside France, given at:

STOCKHOLM 11 May 1894 (in Swedish).

GHENT 5 October 1894; Brussels 2 December 1896; Antwerp 18 December 1896 (in French).

GENEVA 28 March 1895 (in French).

MILAN 26 November 1896 (in Italian, translated by A. Galli).

ELBERFELD 11 October 1900 (in German).

MONTE CARLO 3 April 1919 (in French).

CAIRO Spring 1938 (in French).

DE LARA: *Amy Robsart*

20 July. London, C.G.

(Original English) text by A. H. G. Harris (founded on Scott's *Kenilworth*), produced in a French version by P. Milliet. Three acts.

In French also, Monte Carlo 30 March 1894; Boulogne 22 August 1894, etc.

In Italian, St. Petersburg 29 July 1894; Florence 26 March 1896.

Revived London, Grand (Croydon) 14 May 1920 (for the first time in English).

According to De Lara's autobiography also produced in German at Mayence, a statement I could not verify.

(VILLANUEVA): *Keofar*

29 July. Mexico

Text by G. Larrañaga. Three acts.

Successful Mexican comic opera; completed after the composer's death by Juan Hernandez Acevedo.

FORSTER: *Die Rose von Pontevedra*

30 July. Gotha

Text by J. J. Geiger (scenario by the composer). One act.

In German also given at Pressburg 24 January 1894 (libretto revised by M. Kalbeck); Vienna 10 April 1894; Hamburg 8 September 1894; Laibach 1894; Prague 9 December 1894; Riga 28 January 1898.

UMLAUFT: *Evanthia*

30 July. Gotha

Text by the composer. One act.

In German also given at Dresden 22 August 1893; Leipzig 24 October 1893; Riga 1895, etc.

These two operas were awarded the first prize in a competition for German one-act operas arranged by the Duke of Saxe-Coburg-Gotha (rather on the lines of the Concorso Sonzogno; there was, however, no German *Cavalleria rusticana* to be discovered).

F. d'ERLANGER: *Jehan de Saintré*

1 August. Aix-les-Bains

Text by J. and P. Barbier. Two acts.

d'Erlanger's first opera. In German (translated by L. Hartmann), Hamburg 26 February 1894.

SULLIVAN: *Utopia (Limited)*; or, *The Flowers of Progress*

7 October. London, Savoy

Text by W. S. Gilbert. Two acts.

In London ran for 245 nights. New York 26 March 1894, etc.

F. HUMMEL: *Mara*

11 October. Berlin, O.

Text by A. Delmar. One act.

Successful veristic opera of the *Cavalleria rusticana* school.

In German also, Prague 25 January 1894; Vienna 4 October 1894; Laibach 1894; Riga 1896; Basle 3 March 1897; Meran 20 March 1901, etc.

In Swedish, Stockholm 7 March 1894.

In Czech (translated by O. Kučera), Prague 28 November 1894.

In Italian, Florence 24 April 1895.

In Slovenian, Ljubljana 1906.

d'ALBERT: *Der Rubin*

12 October. Carlsruhe

Text by the composer (from F. Hebbel's comedy of the same title). Two acts.

d'Albert's first opera. Also given at Cassel 2 June 1897.

AZZALI: *Lhidiac*

October. Bogotá

Author of the (Italian?) text not mentioned. *Leggenda Indiana.* One act.

Probably the first original opera produced in Colombia. Also given at Caracas, Venezuela 23 February 1897.

LEONCAVALLO: *I Medici*

9 November. Milan, T.d.V.

Text by the composer. Four acts.

The first part of a trilogy, *Crepusculum*, the two other parts of which Leoncavallo never finished. Written before *Pagliacci*.

Outside Italy, given at:

BERLIN 17 February 1894 (in German, translated by E. Taubert); Nuremberg 28 February 1894; Frankfort 3 May 1894, etc.

MOSCOW 15 April 1894 (in Italian).

PRAGUE 5 January 1895 (in Czech, translated by V. J. Novotný).

BUENOS AIRES 29 June 1898 (in Italian).

COWEN: *Signa*

12 November. Milan, T.d.V.

(Original English) text by G. A. A'Beckett, H. A. Rudall, and F. E. Weatherly (founded on Ouida's novel of the same title), Italian version by G. A. Mazzucato. Three acts.

In Italian also, London, C.G. 30 June 1894 (reduced to two acts).

BRUNEAU: *L'Attaque du Moulin*

23 November. Paris, O.C.

Text by L. Gallet (founded on a story in Zola's *Soirées de Médan*). Four acts.

Successful in France; revived at the O.C. 25 March 1922.

Outside Paris, given at:

BRUSSELS 27 January 1894 (in French).

LONDON, C.G. 4 July 1894 (in French).

BRESLAU 5 November 1895 (in German, translated by H. B. Bolten-Bäckers).

GENEVA 11 December 1896 (in French).

MILAN, T.L. 8 January 1898 (in Italian, translated by A. Galli and A. Cortella).

HAGUE November 1903 (in French).

BARCELONA 7 January 1909 (in French).

NEW YORK 8 February 1910 (in French).

NEW ORLEANS 19 January 1911 (in French).

VIENNA, V.O. 13 March 1914 (in German).

BIRMINGHAM 15 October 1915 (in English, translated by F. E. Weatherly).

LONDON, GARRICK 18 May 1917 (in English, translated by F. E. Weatherly).

PIZZI: *Gabriella*

25 November. Boston

(Italian) text by C. A. Byrne and F. Fulgonio. Two acts.

Written for Adelina Patti. New York 16 March 1894, etc.

A copyright performance took place at St. George's Hall, London, the same day as in Boston (English version by M. Marras).

Publicly performed in London, Albert Hall 2 June 1894 (in concert form, in Italian).

HUMPERDINCK: *Hänsel und Gretel*

23 December. Weimar

Text by A. Wette (the sister of the composer), from a tale by the brothers Grimm. Three acts.
Humperdinck's first work for the stage.

This fairy opera became at once a great success not only for its own merits but because its simplicity offered a welcome change from the "blood and passion" standard of the *verismo* of those years.

First given at Berlin 13 October 1894 (more than 300 times until 1925) and all over Germany.
STRASBOURG 9 November 1894 (in German).
BASLE 16 November 1894 (in German).
GRAZ 11 December 1894 (in German).
VIENNA 18 December 1894 (in German).
LONDON, DALY'S 26 December 1894 (in English, translated by C. Bache; 100th performance 18 April 1895) and D.L. 24 June 1895 (in German).
PRAGUE 1 January 1895 (in German) and 3 December 1895 (in Czech, translated by A. E. Mužík).
BUDAPEST 2 February 1895 (in Hungarian, translated by E. Abrányi).
AMSTERDAM 30 March 1895 (in German) and 1 September 1895 (in Dutch).
STOCKHOLM 18 May 1895 (in Swedish, translated by E. A. Wallmark).
LJUBLJANA 1895 (in Slovenian, translated by M. Markič).
RIGA 1895 (in German) and 1914 (in Lettish).
NEW YORK 8 October 1895 (in English) and 25 November 1905 (in German).
ZAGREB 7 December 1895 (in Croatian, translated by F. Miler).
ST. PETERSBURG 14 January 1896 (in Russian, translated by E. N. Kletkova).

MOSCOW 9 February 1896 (in Russian, translated by E. N. Kletkova).
COPENHAGEN January 1897 (in Danish).
ANTWERP 23 February 1897 (in French, translated by C. Mendès) and 2 October 1902 (in Flemish).
MILAN, T. MANZONI 6 April 1897 (in Italian, translated by G. Macchi).
CHRISTIANIA November 1897 (in Norwegian).
BRUSSELS 17 December 1897 (in French).
ROUEN 11 January 1899 (in French).
PARIS, O.C. 30 May 1900 (in French).
BARCELONA 27 January 1901 (in Italian; Catalan translation by J. Maragall and A. Ribera published in that year).
CAIRO 1901 (in French).
MADRID 4 December 1901 (in Italian).
WARSAW January 1902 (in Polish).
RIO DE JANEIRO 1 October 1902 (in Italian).
SANTIAGO, CHILE 14 December 1902 (in Italian).
HELSINKI 28 January 1903 (in Finnish, translated by I. Mendelin).
BUENOS AIRES 11 June 1903 (in Italian).
TUNIS Spring 1909 (in French).
SHANGHAI November 1909 (in English).
NEW ORLEANS 25 December 1909 (in French).
LISBON 1910 (in Italian).
JOHANNESBURG March 1912 (in English).
TALLINN 1913 (in Estonian).
BUCHAREST March 1925 (in Rumanian).
SOFIA 11 March 1932 (in Bulgarian).

Broadcast from Covent Garden, London 6 January 1923 (first broadcast of an opera in Europe); 25 December 1931 first broadcast of an opera from the Metropolitan Opera House, New York.

1894

CHADWICK: *Tabasco*

29 January. Boston

Text by R. A. Barnet (*burlesque opera*). Two acts.
The most successful of Chadwick's operettas.
New York 14 May 1894, etc.

ENNA: *Cleopatra*

7 February. Copenhagen

Text by E. Christiansen (founded on the novel by H. R. Haggard). Three acts.

In Dutch, Amsterdam 30 November 1897; Antwerp 3 December 1898 (frequently revived).

In German (translated by E. Klingenfeld), Breslau 25 December 1898; revived Berlin, V.O. 27 January 1910; Zurich December 1910.

French translation by G. Sandré published *c.*1900.

BRETÓN: *La Verbena de la Paloma*
(The Festival of the Dove)

17 February. Madrid, T. Apolo

Text by R. de la Vega (*Sainete lirico*). One act.

Subtitle *El Boticario y las Chalupas y Celos mal reprimidos.*

Bretón's most successful zarzuela, very popular and still given in Spain and South America. Buenos Aires 1894; Mexico 1 December 1894, etc.

Revived Madrid 7 July 1921, etc.; Buenos Aires 28 November 1934.

(C. FRANCK): *Hulda*

8 March. Monte Carlo

Text by C. Grandmougin (founded on a play by B. Björnson). Four acts and epilogue.

The first of Franck's two operas, both of which were produced after his death.

Also given at The Hague, March 1895 and Toulouse 8 April 1895. The third act was heard at a Colonne concert, Paris 16 October 1904.

JAQUES-DALCROZE: *Janie*

13 March. Geneva

Text by P. Godet (founded on a story by G. de Peyrebrune). Three acts.

In German (translated by F. Vogt), Stuttgart 20 February 1895, etc.

MASSENET: *Thaïs*

16 March. Paris, O.

Text by L. Gallet (founded on A. France's novel). Three acts.

Very successful in Paris; given there with alterations 13 April 1898; 100th performance 28 May 1910; 300th 28 August 1924.

Outside France, given at:

BRUSSELS 7 March 1896 (in French; last revived 7 March 1938).

GENEVA 25 March 1898 (in French).

MILAN, T.L. 17 October 1903 (in Italian, translated by A. Galli).

LISBON December 1904 (in Italian, translated by A. Galli).

BARCELONA 22 February 1905 (in Italian, translated by A. Galli).

ST. PETERSBURG 27 March 1906 (in Italian) and 1911 (in Russian).

TUNIS February 1907 (in French).

NEW YORK 25 November 1907 (in French; revived 10 February 1939.

BUENOS AIRES 21 July 1908 (in Italian).

WARSAW March 1909 (in Italian).

HELSINKI 13 April 1910 (in French) and 9 November 1934 (in Finnish).

NEW ORLEANS 16 December 1910 (in French).

LONDON, C.G. 18 July 1911 (in French); revived 14 May 1919 and 10 June 1926.

LEMBERG May 1912 (in Polish).

STOCKHOLM 2 December 1912 (in Swedish).

RIO DE JANEIRO Summer 1920 (in Italian).

MONTREAL 16 November 1920 (in French).

LJUBLJANA 1921 (in Slovenian).

AMSTERDAM October 1921 (in Dutch) and November 1936 (in Italian).

BUDAPEST 1 May 1924 (in Hungarian, translated by K. Nádasdy).

MALTA 1929 (in Italian).

RIGA 7 November 1929 (in Lettish).

SOFIA 1 November 1937 (in Bulgarian).

CAIRO February 1939 (in French).

Still given on French and Italian stages.

H. HUBER: *Weltfrühling*

28 March. Basle

Text by R. Wackernagel. Three acts.
The first opera of the Swiss composer.

ASPESTRAND: *Die Seemansbraut*

29 March. Gotha

Text by the composer. Three acts.
Revived (in Norwegian) Christiania 8 May 1907 as the first opera by a native composer which was produced at the Norwegian Nationalteatret.

SPINELLI: *A basso Porto*

18 April. Cologne

(Original Italian) text by E. Checchi (founded on a play by G. Cognetti), first produced in a German version by L. Hartmann (with the Italian title). Three acts.

Spinelli's most successful work.

In German also given at Basle 6 November 1896; Berlin, Th.d.W. 2 July 1897; St. Petersburg 31 March 1898; Salzburg 23 April 1898; Prague 8 May 1898; Riga 6 December 1898; Posen 25 December 1898; Reval 1900.

In the original Italian, Rome, C. 11 March 1895, etc.

In Hungarian (translated by A. Radó), Budapest 25 April 1895.

In Dutch, Amsterdam 22 October 1897.

In English (translated by P. E. Pinkerton), St. Louis 8 January 1900; New York 22 January 1900; Brighton 17 March 1900; London, Coronet 14 November 1900.

Revived in German, Leipzig 18 February 1928; Wiesbaden 1934.

ARENSKY: *Rafael*

Рафаэлъ

6 May. Moscow

Text by A. Kryukov. One act.

Written for the first Congress of Russian Artists. St. Petersburg 25 December 1895, etc. Revived Moscow 4 October 1903; Leningrad 10 April 1921.

Also given at Barcelona, T. del Bosque, Summer 1907 (in Italian, translated by L. Egidi). London, Aeolian Hall 12 September 1942 (in concert form, in Russian).

RAIMANN: *Arden Énok*

8 May. Budapest

(Original German) text by K. Gross (after Tennyson's *Enoch Arden*), Hungarian version by A. Radó. One act.

In German, Breslau 18 December 1896; Graz 12 November 1897; Troppau 6 January 1898.

MASSENET: *Le Portrait de Manon*

8 May. Paris, O.C.

Text by G. Boyer. One act.

A sequel to *Manon* (see 1884), but not nearly as successful (given at the O.C. until 1904). Outside France, given at:

GENEVA 8 October 1894 (in French).

BRUSSELS 22 November 1894 (in French).

NAPLES 15 December 1894 (in Italian, translated by A. Galli).

ANTWERP 21 November 1895 (in French).

PRAGUE 28 December 1895 (in Czech, translated by V. J. Novotný).

NEW YORK 13 December 1897 (in French).

ZAGREB 16 May 1898 (in Croatian, translated by F. Miler).

Revived Monte Carlo 14 December 1909; Paris, Tr.L. 27 September 1922; New York 25 February 1933; still occasionally given in France.

R. STRAUSS: *Guntram*

10 May. Weimar

Text by the composer. Three acts.
Strauss's first opera. Also given at Munich 16 November 1895; Prague 9 October 1901.
Revived Frankfort 22 April 1910.

HAARKLOU: *Fra gamle Dage*
(Of Olden Days)

15 May. Christiania

Text by H. Wiers-Jenssen. Three acts.
Apart from Thrane's (see 1850) and Udbye's (see 1870) attempts, the first Norwegian opera.

SAMARA: *La Martire*

23 May. Naples, T. Mercadante

Text by L. Illica (*Novella sceneggiata*). Three acts.

Milan 22 September 1894 (opening of the new Teatro Lirico Internazionale, late Canobbiana), etc.

In Italian also, Berlin, Th.U.d.L. 14 September 1895.

In French (translated by E. Crosti), Antwerp 25 March 1897; Paris, Variétés 21 July 1898.

Revived in Italian, Malta 1913. In Greek, Athens Summer 1933.

MASSENET: *La Navarraise*

20 June. London, C.G.

Text by J. Claretie and H. Cain (*Episode lyrique*). Two acts.

Massenet's contribution to verism; of his three operas produced in that year, the most successful one. After London, given at:

BUDAPEST 4 October 1894 (in Hungarian, translated by E. Abrányi).

BRUSSELS 26 November 1894 (in French).

HAGUE 20 December 1894 (in French).

NUREMBERG 1 January 1895; Hamburg 2 January 1895, etc. (in German, translated by M. Kalbeck).

BORDEAUX 27 March 1895 (for the first time in France; in French).

STOCKHOLM 18 May 1895 (in Swedish, translated by E. A. Wallmark).

PARIS, O.C. 3 October 1895 (in French); revived 23 December 1928.

VIENNA 4 October 1895 (in German).

MOSCOW 4 November 1895 (in Russian).

NEW YORK 11 December 1895 (in French).

MILAN, SC. 6 February 1896 (in Italian, translated by A. Galli).

HELSINKI 28 October 1896 (in Italian) and 2 October 1911 (in Finnish, at the inauguration of the Finnish National Opera-House, the "Suomalainen Oopera").

ST. PETERSBURG 28 November 1896 (in Italian) and 18 January 1897 (in Russian).

NEW ORLEANS 5 January 1897 (in French).

MEXICO May 1897 (in French).

RIO DE JANEIRO 5 September 1898 (in Italian).

GENEVA 28 March 1899 (in French).

SAIGON Autumn 1900 (in French).

BERLIN, KROLL'S 22 April 1902 (in French) and 9 October 1902 (in German).

LISBON November 1909 (in French).

BUCHAREST March 1922 (in Rumanian).

L. E. BACH: *The Lady of Longford*

21 July. London, C.G.

(Original English) text by A. H. G. Harris and F. E. Weatherly, produced in an Italian version by G. A. Mazzucato. One act.

Repeated London, D.L. 20 April 1896 (in English).

In German, Breslau 15 December 1897; Prague 7 January 1900; Hamburg 23 November 1900.

FLORIDIA: *Maruzza*

23 August. Venice, T. Malibran

Text by the composer. Three acts.

In German (translated by L. Hartmann), Zurich 13 November 1896.

J. STRAUSS: *Jabuka* oder *Das Apfelfest*

12 October. Vienna, W.

Text by M. Kalbeck and G. Davis. Three acts.

Berlin, Fr.W. 7 November 1894; Laibach 1894; Prague 16 December 1895, etc.

In Polish, Lemberg September 1901.

AUDRAN: *L'Enlèvement de la Toledad*

17 October. Paris, B.P.

Text by F. Carré. Three acts.

In French also, Brussels 2 September 1895; Geneva 24 January 1900, etc.

In German (translated by V. Léon and H. von Waldberg), Vienna, Jos. 10 October 1896; Hamburg 3 April 1897; Berlin, Lessing Th. 17 April 1897; Prague 24 June 1900.

In Hungarian, Budapest 16 May 1899.

In English (adapted by A. Moore and H. Wood), Windsor 11 April 1903; London, Kennington 20 April 1903.

In Italian, Venice 11 May 1903.

ALBÉNIZ: *San Antonio de la Florida*

26 October. Madrid, T. Apolo

Text by E. Sierra. One act.

Barcelona 1894, etc. In French (as *L'Ermitage fleuri*, translated by L. Solvay and R. Sand), Brussels 3 January 1905.

HUBAY: *A Cremonai Hegedüs*

10 November. Budapest

(Original French) text by H. Beauclair (from F. Coppée's play, *Le Luthier de Crémone*, 1876), Hungarian version by E. Abrányi. One act (2 scenes).

Hubay's most successful opera.

In German (translated by M. Kalbeck), Leipzig 22 September 1895; Prague 13 October 1895; Strasbourg 7 January 1896; Basle 18 February 1898.

In the original French, New York 20 December 1897.

Still given in Hungary.

SCHILLINGS: *Ingwelde*

13 November. Carlsruhe

Text by F. von Sporck. Three acts.

Schillings's first opera. Wiesbaden 19 October 1896; Berlin 16 May 1899, etc.

Revived Stuttgart 6 November 1904; Breslau 21 January 1910; Dessau 5 February 1911; Berlin 3 May 1938 (text revised by the composer's widow, B. von Schillings).

MacCUNN: *Jeanie Deans*

15 November. Edinburgh

Text by J. Bennett (after Scott). Four acts.

Successful in England and Scotland. London, Daly's 22 January 1896.

Revived London, Shaftesbury Th. 10 May 1918; Edinburgh 10 April 1934.

REZNICEK: *Donna Diana*

16 December. Prague, G.

Text by the composer (founded on Moreto's comedy in C. A. West's German version). Three acts.

Successful on German stages: Carlsruhe 15 April 1895; Riga 7 October 1896; Zurich 5 November 1897; Vienna 9 December 1898; Berlin 30 April 1908.

Revived (text revised by J. Kapp) Wuppertal 15 November 1933; Berlin 31 December 1933.

1895

NAPRAVNIK: *Dubrovsky*
Дубровскій

15 January. St. Petersburg

Text by M. I. Chaikovsky (after Pushkin). Four acts.

Napravnik's best-known work. First given at Moscow 7 January 1896 and on many other Russian stages (until after 1918). Also given at:

PRAGUE 13 December 1896 (in Czech, translated by V. J. Novotný).

LEIPZIG 29 May 1897 (in German, translated by P. Bock).

BERLIN, KROLL'S 28 May 1908 (in Russian).

S. FRANCISCO 14 January 1922 (in Russian).

NEW YORK 13 June 1922 (in Russian).

KAUNAS 7 February 1929 (in Lithuanian).

RIGA 12 November 1933 (in Lettish; previously given there in Russian).

VAVRINECZ: *Rosmunda*

31 January. Frankfort

(Original Hungarian) text by A. Zigány, German version by L. Hartmann. One act.

In German also given at Prague 28 February 1895.

In Hungarian, Budapest 14 November 1900.

BLARAMBERG: *Tushintsi*

Тушинцы

5 February. Moscow

Text from the play by A. N. Ostrovsky. Four acts.

The best-known work of the Russian composer.

HOLMÈS: *La Montagne noire*

8 February. Paris, O.

Text by the composer. Four acts.

The last opera of the Irish-French woman composer and the only one which was performed. Unsuccessful (13 performances).

B. O. KLEIN: *Kenilworth*

13 February. Hamburg

Text by W. Müller (from Scott's novel). Prologue and 3 acts.

The only opera of the German-American composer.

MASCAGNI: *Guglielmo Ratcliff*

16 February. Milan, Sc.

Text: Heine's tragedy in A. Maffei's Italian version. Four acts.

The opera was written before *Cavalleria rusticana*. Also given at Buenos Aires 23 October 1895 (in Italian); Stuttgart 27 October 1895 (in German, translated by E. Taubert); Amsterdam 10 March 1898 (in Italian).

Revived Milan 18 June 1918; Barcelona 20 January 1919, etc. Still given in Italy.

FIBICH: *Bouře*

1 March. Prague, Cz.

Text by J. Vrchlický (from Shakespeare's *The Tempest*). Three acts.

Revived at Prague 19 December 1912; 23 September 1920; and 1 March 1935.

BRUCKEN-FOCK: *Seleneia*

5 March. Amsterdam

(Dutch) text by M. Constant. One act.

Revived Hague, June 1900; Rotterdam February 1904 (in concert form).

BERUTTI: *Tarass Bulba*

9 March. Turin, T.R.

Text by G. Godio (after Gogol). Four acts.

Buenos Aires 20 July 1895. The first opera of the Argentine composer which was given in his native country.

BRETÓN: *La Dolores*

16 March. Madrid, Z.

Text by the composer (founded on a play by J. Feliú y Codina). Three acts.

Very successful Spanish opera; given at Madrid 63 nights, at Barcelona 112 nights running. Frequently revived in Spain and South America, at Barcelona as late as in 1938.

First given at:

BARCELONA, TIVOLI August 1895 (in Spanish).

MEXICO 30 November 1895 (in Spanish).

BUENOS AIRES 18 January 1896 (in Spanish) and 1 October 1896 (in Italian).

RIO DE JANEIRO 1 August 1896 (in Italian, translated by E. Golisciani).

MILAN, T.D.V. 16 January 1906 (in Italian, translated by E. Golisciani).

PRAGUE 18 February 1906 (in German, translated by F. Adler).

English translation by C. A. Byrne published 1907.

A parody, *Dolores de Cabeza*, by Salvador María Granés, music by Luis Arnedo, was produced at Madrid on 13 April 1895.

MASCAGNI: *Silvano*

25 March. Milan, Sc.

Text by G. Targioni-Tozzetti (*Dramma marinaresco*). Two acts.

In Italian also, given at Berlin, Neues Th. 8 October 1895.

In German (translated by A. Harlacher), Stuttgart 28 March 1897.

Revived Malta 1926.

SMAREGLIA: *Nozze Istriane*

28 March. Trieste

Text by L. Illica. Three acts.

Smareglia's chief work. Given at Venice 9 May

1905, etc.; Malta 1911; Prague 14 October 1896 (in Czech, translated by V. J. Novotný); Vienna, V.O. 1 January 1908 (in German, translated by F. Falzari.

Revived Pola 2 March 1920; Trieste 23 April 1921, etc.

An open-air performance at Pola took place in July 1933.

(GODARD): *La Vivandière*
1 April. Paris, O.C.

Text by H. Cain. Three acts.

This posthumous opera (produced three months after his death) was Godard's most successful work; orchestration completed by P. Vidal. Given at:

DÜSSELDORF 15 November 1895 (in German, translated by H. B. Bolten-Bäckers).

LIVERPOOL 10 March 1896 (in English, translated by G. Whyte).

BRUSSELS 21 March 1896 (in French).

MILAN, T.L. 22 September 1896 (in Italian, translated by A. Galli).

LONDON, GARRICK 20 January 1897 (in English).

PRAGUE 25 February 1897 (in Czech, translated by V. J. Novotný).

MOSCOW November 1905 (in Russian).

GENEVA 19 March 1909 (in French).

MONTREAL 1913 (in French).

Revived Paris, O.C. 13 December 1914; Brussels 18 April 1932.

PFITZNER: *Der arme Heinrich*
2 April. Mayence

Text by J. Grun. Three acts.

Pfitzner's first opera.

In German also given at Darmstadt 1 April 1897; Frankfort 7 January 1897; Prague 23 September 1899; Berlin 19 December 1900 (revived 31 March 1927); Leipzig 5 December 1909; Stuttgart 6 December 1910; Strasbourg 8 January 1911; Munich 29 May 1911; Dortmund 15 November 1912; Cologne 28 February 1913; Brünn 8 May 1913; Mannheim 10 February 1915; Vienna 17 March 1915; Zurich 10 September 1924.

KIENZL: *Der Evangelimann*
4 May. Berlin, O.

Text by the composer (founded on a story by L. F. Meissner). Two acts.

Kienzl's best-known work, and one of the most successful German operas between Wagner and Strauss. The 100th performance at Berlin was on 28 February 1908; given there 172 times until 1927. The 100th performance at Vienna was on 5 June 1919.

Altogether, by 4 May 1935 (within 40 years), the opera had been produced more than 5,300 times. Jubilee performances took place at Graz 27 April, at Vienna 5 May 1935.

First performed at:

PRAGUE 29 September 1895 (in German) and 19 October 1904 (in Czech, translated by P. Nebeský).

STRASBOURG 20 October 1895 (in German).

BASLE 25 October 1895 (in German).

VIENNA 11 January 1896 (in German).

BUDAPEST 7 March 1896 (in Hungarian, translated by A. Radó).

LAIBACH (LJUBLJANA) 1896 (in German) and 1907 (in Slovenian).

AMSTERDAM 22 December 1896 (in Dutch).

ZAGREB 27 April 1897 (in Croatian, translated by F. Miler).

LONDON, C.G. 2 July 1897 (in German) and Prince of Wales's 20 July 1914 (in English).

RIGA 22 February 1899 (in German, as *Matthias Freudhofer*).

REVAL (TALLINN) 1899 (in German) and 1925 (in Estonian, translated by A. Trilljärv).

STOCKHOLM 6 February 1905 (in Swedish).

LEMBERG 20 December 1906 (in Polish).

LYONS 21 November 1908 (in French, as *Le Prêcheur de St. Othmar*, translated by L. Schneider).

ANTWERP 6 February 1909 (in Flemish).

COPENHAGEN 1911 (in Danish, translated by A. Tofft, at the Dagmar Th.; at the Royal Th. 6 December 1914).

HELSINKI 12 March 1914 (in Finnish).

LIVERPOOL 17 April 1914 (for the first time in English, as *The Pious Beggar*, translated by P. E. Pinkerton).

CONSTANTINOPLE February 1916 (in German; first opera ever sung in German there).
CHICAGO 3 November 1923 (in German).
NEW YORK 1 January 1924 (in German).
DUBLIN 15 February 1924 (in English, as *The Apostle of St. Otmar*).

ALBÉNIZ: *Enrico Clifford*

8 May. Barcelona, L.

(Italian) text by G. M. Arteaga y Pereira (translated from an English libretto by F. B. Money-Coutts). Three acts.

Of Albéniz grand operas on a larger scale, the only one which was performed.

JARNO: *Die schwarze Kaschka*

12 May. Breslau

Text by V. Blüthgen. Four acts.

Posen 5 February 1897; Berlin 5 June 1898, etc. For about five years very successful in Germany.

COWEN: *Harold; or, The Norman Conquest*

8 June. London, C.G.

Text by E. Malet (then British Ambassador to Berlin). Three acts.

Cowen's last opera.

BENDL: *Máti Míla*
(Mother Mila)

25 June. Prague, Cz.

Text by V. J. Novotný (translated from a German libretto by A. Delmar). One act.

Bendl's last opera.

PARRY: *Sylvia*

12 August. Cardiff

Text by M. Parry (*Legendary grand opera*). Three acts.

The last opera of the Welsh composer which was performed.

PIERNÉ: *La Coupe enchantée*

24 August. Royan

Text by E. Matrat (founded on a comedy by Lafontaine and Champmeslé, 1688). Two acts.

Revived, in a new one-act version, Paris, O.C. 26 December 1905 and 16 February 1919.

In German (translated by A. Harlacher), Stuttgart 25 February 1907; Zurich 18 October 1907; and in a new translation by W. Riedel (as *Liebeserwachen*), Nuremberg 3 May 1922.

ZÖLLNER: *Der Überfall*

7 September. Dresden

Text by the composer (founded on a story, *Die Danaide*, by E. von Wildenbruch). Two acts.

Also given at Berlin 18 July 1896, etc.; Graz 20 January 1903. Revived Vienna, V.O. 21 November 1914.

TANEEV: *Oresteya*
Орестея

29 October. St. Petersburg

Text by A. A. Venkstern (from Aeschylus's trilogy). Three parts.

Taneev's only opera. Revived Petrograd October 1915.

ZARATE: *La Fioraia di Lugano*

1 November. Santiago

(Italian) text by the composer.

Probably the first opera by a Chilean composer which was produced in his native country.

SCHARRER: *Die Erlösung*

21 November. Strasbourg

(Original Italian) text (*La Redenzione*) by G. Menasci, German version by R. Specht. Three acts.

Scharrer's only opera. Nuremberg 1 November 1896, etc. In German also, Riga 1897.

T. DUBOIS: *Xavière*

26 November. Paris, O.C.

Text by L. Gallet (founded on a novel by F. Fabre). *Idylle dramatique*. Three acts.

Revived Paris, O.C. 18 January 1905.

J. STRAUSS: *Waldmeister*

4 December. Vienna, W.

Text by G. Davis. Three acts.

In German also, Berlin, Lessing Th. 2 May 1896; Prague 1896; Brünn 20 September 1896; Graz 17 October 1896; Basle 4 November 1896; Posen 1 January 1897; Riga 11 February 1897; Reval 1897; New York 29 November 1897; Helsinki June 1899.

RIMSKY-KORSAKOV: *Noch Pyered Rozhdyestvom*

Ночь Передъ Рождествомъ

(The Night before Christmas)

10 December. St. Petersburg

Text by the composer (after Gogol, like Chaikovsky's *Vakula Kuznyets*, see 1876). Four acts.

Moscow 8 November 1898. Frequently revived on Russian stages, but never given outside Russia.

1896

ALBÉNIZ: *Pepita Jiménez*

5 January. Barcelona, L.

(Original English) text by F. B. Money-Coutts (from a story by Juan Valera), Italian version by M. A. Galateri. One act (2 scenes).

Albéniz's most successful opera. Given at:

PRAGUE 22 June 1897 (in German, translated by O. Berggruen).

BRUSSELS 3 January 1905 (in French, translated by M. Kufferath).

PARIS, O.C. 18 June 1923 (in French, new translation by J. de Marliave).

(The opera was never given in Germany, as incorrectly stated in Riemann's *Musiklexikon*, Vol. 1, p.23, in H. Klein's *Musicians and Mummers*, p.259, and in many other books.)

CURTI: *Lili-Tsee*

12 January. Mannheim

Text by W. Kirchbach. One act.

Curti's most successful work; Frankfort 4 June 1896, etc.

In German also, Metz 15 March 1898; Danzig 28 February 1900.

In English (translated by S. Rosenfeld), New York 17 February 1898; Boston 25 April 1898.

HŘIMALÝ: *Švanda Dudák*

(Shvanda the Bagpiper)

20 January. Pilsen

Text by K. Želenský. Prologue and 3 acts.

This seems to be the earliest opera written on the favourite Czech subject (taken from a folktale by J. K. Tyl). Apart from Weinberger's well-known opera of the same title (see 1927), there are at least two more works based on the same story, viz. a German opera by the Bohemian composer K. Weis, *Die Dorfmusikanten*, produced at Prague 1 January 1905, and a Czech opera ballet by K. Bendl, produced at Prague 29 April 1907.

PUCCINI: *La Bohème*

1 February. Turin, T.R.

Text by G. Giacosa and L. Illica (founded on the novel by H. Murger). Four parts.

After *Le Villi* (1884), *Edgar* (1889) and *Manon Lescaut* (1893), Puccini's fourth opera, and even more successful than *Manon Lescaut*, as the following records show:

BUENOS AIRES 16 June 1896 (in Italian).

ALEXANDRIA 6 January 1897 (in Italian).

MOSCOW 1 February 1897 (in Italian).

LISBON 11 February 1897 (in Italian).

MANCHESTER 22 April 1897 (in English, translated by W. Grist and P. E. Pinkerton).

BERLIN, KROLL'S 22 June 1897 (in German, translated by L. Hartmann).

RIO DE JANEIRO 2 July 1897 (in Italian).

MEXICO 22 August 1897 (in Italian).

LONDON, C.G. 2 October 1897 (in English) and 1 July 1899 (in Italian); 150th performance 1 June 1923.

VIENNA, W. 5 October 1897 and O. 25 November 1903 (in German).

LOS ANGELES 14 October 1897 (in Italian).

HAGUE 19 October 1897 (in Italian).

PRAGUE 27 February 1898 (in Czech, translated by V. J. Novotný) and 3 May 1908 (in German).

BARCELONA 10 April 1898 (in Italian) and April 1905 (in Spanish).

ATHENS May 1898 (in Italian).

NEW YORK 16 May 1898 (in Italian) and 28 November 1898 (in English).

PARIS, O.C. 13 June 1898 (in French, translated by P. Ferrier; 200th performance 30 November 1907).

MALTA 1898 (in Italian).

VALPARAISO 6 July 1898 (in Italian).

WARSAW 1 October 1898 (in Italian).

ZAGREB 11 October 1898 (in Croatian, translated by F. Miler).

SMYRNA December 1898 (in Italian).

HELSINKI 7 January 1899 (in Italian) and 25 November 1918 (in Finnish).

ST. PETERSBURG 30 January 1899 (in Italian) and 23 February 1900 (in Russian); revived 19 September 1924.

ALGIERS January 1899 (in Italian).

TUNIS Spring 1899 (in Italian).

BUCHAREST November 1899 (in Italian) and December 1921 (in Rumanian).

ANTWERP 11 January 1900 (in French).

BRUSSELS 25 October 1900 (in French).

RIGA 11 January 1901 (in German) and 21 November 1922 (in Lettish).

GENEVA 17 December 1901 (in French) and Zurich 18 November 1906 (in German).

PORT SAID April 1901 (in Italian).

STOCKHOLM 29 November 1901 (in Swedish, translated by S. Nyblom).

LEMBERG 28 December 1901 (in Polish, translated by L. German).

LJUBLJANA 1903 (in Slovenian).

BUDAPEST 27 April 1905 (in Hungarian, translated by A. Radó).

COPENHAGEN 22 October 1908 (in Danish, translated by S. Levyson).

REVAL (TALLINN) 1911 (in German) and 1926 (in Estonian, translated by H. Laur).

JOHANNESBURG March 1912 (in English).

BELGRADE 1920 (in Serbian).

SOFIA 23 June 1922 (in Bulgarian; translation published already Rustshuk 1905).

KAUNAS 26 May 1927 (in Lithuanian).

OSLO Summer 1933 (in Italian).

An open-air performance took place at Torre del Lago on 20 August 1930.

ENNA: *Aucassin og Nicolette*

2 February. Copenhagen

Text by S. Michaelis (founded on the French 13th-century story). Four acts.

In German (translated by E. von Enzberg), Hamburg 11 January 1897; Prague 20 February 1897.

DAMROSCH: *The scarlet Letter*

10 February. Boston

Text by G. P. Lathrop (founded on his father-in-law Hawthorne's famous romance). Three acts.

The first opera of the American composer. Subsequently given at New York 6 March 1896.

FIBICH: *Hedy*

12 February. Prague, Cz.

Text by A. Schulzová (founded on the episode from Byron's *Don Juan*). Four acts.

Revived at Prague 9 November 1905; 6 May 1915; 11 September 1925; and 10 March 1938.

STANFORD: *Shamus O'Brien*

2 March. London, O.C.

Text by G. H. Jessop (*A story of Ireland a hundred years ago*, founded on the poem by J. S. Le Fanu). Two acts.

Stanford's most popular opera; successful on English stages.

First given at New York 5 January 1897 (not 1896 as T. A. Brown, *A History of the New York Stage*, Vol.III, p.415, has it).

In German (translator not mentioned), Breslau 12 April 1907 (with recitatives instead of spoken dialogue).

Revived London, H.M.'s 24 May 1910; Dublin 11 August 1924; London, Guildhall School 26 March 1936; Capetown 1939.

MASCAGNI: *Zanetto*

2 March. Pesaro

Text by G. Targioni-Tozzetti and G. Menasci (founded on F. Coppée's *Le Passant*). One act. Given at:

LONDON 23 June 1896 (privately, in Italian); revived St. J.'s 8 December 1908 (in English, by students).

VIENNA, W. 1 September 1896 (in Italian).

BRÜNN 1 January 1897 (in German).

STUTTGART 28 March 1897 (in German).

LEIPZIG 14 June 1897 (in German).

NEW YORK 4 January 1898 (in Italian).

MADRID August 1898 (in Italian).

BUENOS AIRES 22 December 1931 (in Italian).

Still occasionally revived in Italy.

SULLIVAN: *The Grand Duke; or, The Statutory Duel*

7 March. London, Savoy

Text by W. S. Gilbert (the last libretto he wrote for Sullivan). Two acts.

In London ran for 123 nights.

In German, Berlin, Th. U.d.L. 20 May 1896.

Revived London, King George's Hall 20 December 1924 (by the Sterling Mackinlay Operatic Society). Given at New York for the first time as late as 7 April 1937.

LEONCAVALLO: *Chatterton*

10 March. Rome, Arg.

Text by the composer (from the play by A. de Vigny). Three acts.

This was Leoncavallo's first opera; the libretto had been published as early as 1877 (in 4 acts).

Revived in a new version Nice 7 April 1905.

In Italian also, Rouen 11 May 1906 and in some other French towns; Malta 1910.

HALLÉN: *Häxfällan*
(Catching a Witch)

16 March. Stockholm

Text by F. T. Hedberg (from a German play, *Hexenfang*, by H. Hopfen). Two acts.

Revived at Stockholm in an enlarged 3-act version 15 March 1902 (as *Valborgsmässa*, new libretto by E. von Enzberg, translated into Swedish by A. Klinkowström).

HUBAY: *A Falu Rossza*
(The Village Vagabond)

20 March. Budapest

Text by A. Váradi (founded on a play by E. Tóth). Three acts.

In German (translated by L. von Neugebauer), Vienna, W. 29 October 1896; Berlin, Th.d.W. 8 October 1902.

GOLDMARK: *Das Heimchen am Herd*

21 March. Vienna, O.

Text by A. M. Willner (from Dickens's *The Cricket on the Hearth*). Three acts.

One of Goldmark's more successful operas; given at:

BERLIN 27 June 1896 (in German).

BRÜNN 3 October 1896 (in German).

BUDAPEST 4 October 1896 (in Hungarian, translated by E. Abrányi).

PRAGUE 18 October 1896 (in German) and 13 March 1897 (in Czech, translated by V. J. Novotný).

RIGA 6 November 1896 (in German).

BASLE 13 November 1896 (in German).

POSEN 4 December 1896 (in German).

STRASBOURG 25 December 1896 (in German).

ZAGREB 30 March 1897 (in Croatian, translated by F. Miler).

STOCKHOLM 10 November 1897 (in Swedish, translated by E. Högman).

ST. PETERSBURG 22 March 1898 (in German).

LONDON, BRIXTON 23 November 1900 (in English, translated by P. E. Pinkerton).

PHILADELPHIA 7 November 1912 (in English, translated by C. H. Meltzer).

CHICAGO 7 December 1912 (in English, translated by C. H. Meltzer).

REVAL 1912 (in German).

GIORDANO: *Andrea Chenier*
28 March. Milan, Sc.

Text by L. Illica. Four acts.

Giordano's most successful work. Still given in Italy every season, and lately revived in many other countries.

First productions were at:

NEW YORK 13 November 1896 (in Italian).

BRESLAU 28 January 1897 (in German, translated by M. Kalbeck); Hamburg 5 February 1897, etc.

BUDAPEST 30 January 1897 (in Hungarian, translated by A. Radó).

MOSCOW 8 April 1897 (in Italian).

PRAGUE 5 May 1897 (in Czech, translated by V. J. Novotný) and 24 October 1897 (in German).

BUENOS AIRES 3 July 1897 (in Italian).

LYONS 29 December 1897 (in French, translated by P. Milliet).

LISBON January 1898 (in Italian).

ALEXANDRIA February 1898 (in Italian).

ANTWERP 17 March 1898 (in French) and Autumn 1938 (in Flemish).

RIO DE JANEIRO 12 August 1898 (in Italian).

BARCELONA 13 November 1898 (in Italian).

BERLIN, TH.D.W. 21 December 1898 (in German); revived O. 15 June 1929.

HAVANA Carnival 1900 (in Italian).

MALTA 1901 (in Italian).

MANCHESTER 2 April 1903 (in English, translated by P. E. Pinkerton).

LONDON, CAMDEN TOWN 16 April 1903 (in English) and C.G. 11 November 1905 (in Italian).

WARSAW January 1905 (in Italian).

HAGUE February 1905 (in Italian).

PARIS, TH.S.B. 3 June 1905 (in Italian).

LEMBERG October 1907 (in Polish, translated by W. Brzeziński).

VIENNA, V.O. 14 January 1909 (in German); revived O. 28 January 1926 (in German) and 15 March 1935 (in Italian).

STOCKHOLM 17 April 1909 (in Swedish).

MONTE CARLO 17 February 1923 (in Italian).

HELSINKI 26 March 1926 (in Finnish).

BASLE 17 June 1927 (in Italian).

ZAGREB 10 October 1927 (in Croatian).

RIGA 21 January 1928 (in Lettish).

KAUNAS 21 September 1930 (in Lithuanian).

TALLINN October 1931 (in Estonian).

ATHENS November 1931 (in Italian).

SOFIA 15 January 1932 (in Bulgarian).

BUCHAREST October 1932 (in Rumanian).

LJUBLJANA 17 May 1933 (in Slovenian, translated by N. Štritov).

TRIPOLIS 10 February 1934 (in Italian).

ALGIERS January 1935 (in Italian).

(C. FRANCK): *Ghiselle*
6 April. Monte Carlo

Text by G. Augustin-Thierry. Four acts.

The second of Franck's two operas which were both produced after his death. The orchestration of *Ghiselle* was finished by several of Franck's pupils.

ZICHY: *Alár*
11 April. Budapest

Text by the composer. Prologue and 3 acts.

Zichy's first opera.

In German (translated by V. Léon), Carlsruhe 3 December 1897; Berlin 3 May 1898.

SOUSA: *El Capitan*
13 April. Boston

Text by C. Klein, lyrics by T. Frost. Three acts.

The most successful operetta of the famous American band leader.

First given at New York, Broadway Th. 20 April 1896 (not 1895 as T. A. Brown, *A History of the New York Stage*, Vol.III, p.414, has it).

Given in London, Lyric Th. 10 July 1899. Frequently revived in U.S.A., at Philadelphia as late as in March 1921.

JONES: *The Geisha*
25 April. London, Daly's

Text by O. Hall, lyrics by H. Greenbank. Two acts.

The most popular of Jones's numerous operettas; given at:

NEW YORK, DALY'S 9 September 1896, and in all English-speaking countries.

BERLIN, LESSING TH. 1 May 1897 (in German, translated by E. M. Roehr and J. Freund).

VIENNA, CA. 16 October 1897 (in German, translated by E. M. Roehr and J. Freund).

BUDAPEST 16 October 1897 (in Hungarian, translated by J. B. Fáy and E. Makai).

POSEN 6 November 1897 (in German).

BRÜNN 15 December 1897 (in German).

LAIBACH (LJUBLJANA) 1897 (in German) and 1908 (in Slovenian).

PARIS, ATHÉNÉE COMIQUE 8 March 1898 (in French, translated by C. Clairville, J. Lemaire, and A. Mars).

HELSINKI Summer 1898 (in German).

PRAGUE 23 October 1898 (in German) and 11 May 1899 (in Czech, translated by V. J. Novotný).

STOCKHOLM 24 October 1898 (in Swedish).

RIGA 3 February 1899 (in German) and 20 March 1929 (in Lettish).

ZAGREB 16 May 1899 (in Croatian, translated by M. Pogačić).

REVAL 1900 (in German).

BASLE 22 October 1900 (in German).

GENOA 5 December 1900 (in Italian).

BUENOS AIRES July 1901 (in Italian).

MONTE CARLO 2 December 1904 (in French).

When first produced in London *The Geisha* had a run of 760 nights.

So far, the latest revival in New York was on 5 October 1931 (at Erlanger's); in London 24 April 1934 (at the Garrick). At Berlin, the 500th performance was on 6 September 1900, the 1,000th 6 July 1904; it was revived there at the Staatsoper 30 December 1931.

SETACCIOLI: *La Sorella di Mark*

7 May. Rome, C.

Text by E. Golisciani. Three acts.

The most important of Setaccioli's operas; written for Gemma Bellincioni.

H. WOLF: *Der Corregidor*

7 June. Mannheim

Text by R. Mayreder (founded on P. A. de Alarcón's story, *El Sombrero de tres Picos*). Four acts.

Wolf's only completed opera; very celebrated, but given only on rare occasions.

The first performances were at Strasbourg 29 April 1898 (in a revised version); Prague 8 April 1899; Graz 24 May 1902; Munich 4 November 1903; Vienna 18 February 1904; Hamburg 4 March 1904; Stuttgart 10 April 1904; Carlsruhe 17 December 1905; Berlin, K.O. 15 January 1906, etc.

Given in London, R.A.M. 13 July 1934 (in English, translated by G. Dunn).

Fragments from Hugo Wolf's unfinished second opera, *Manuel Venegas* (text by M. Hoernes, after a novel by Alarcón, published 1902), were given in concert form at Mannheim 1 March 1903; Munich May 1932.

ZELENSKI: *Goplana*

23 July. Cracow

Text by L. German (founded on J. Slowacki's play, *Balladyna*). Three acts.

Zelenski's chief work; very successful and frequently revived in Poland.

First given at Lemberg 26 January 1897; Warsaw 8 January 1898. Revived Lemberg 10 September 1918; Warsaw 1921 and December 1935.

Czech translation by A. E. Mužík published 1899.

(SCHUBERT): *Der vierjährige Posten*

23 September. Dresden

Text by T. Körner. One act.

This Singspiel was composed in 1815; it was never produced in Schubert's lifetime. In 1896 it was given in an arrangement by R. Hirschfeld. Subsequently produced at Vienna 30 January 1897; Prague 30 January 1897; Frankfort 31 January 1897, etc.

Revived in a new version by R. Lauckner (2 acts), music arranged by F. Busch and D. F

Tovey, as *Der treue Soldat*, Stuttgart 2 July 1922; Basle 18 May 1924.

In English (as *The faithful Sentinel*, translated by S. Wilson), London, Court 12 June 1928; Glasgow 24 March 1936.

In Danish, Copenhagen 19 November 1928.

ELLING: *Kosakkerne*
(The Cossacks)

26 September. Christiania

Text by E. H. Bull. Three acts.

The only opera of the Norwegian composer.

SCHARWENKA: *Mataswintha*

4 October. Weimar

Text by E. Koppel (from F. Dahn's novel, *Ein Kampf um Rom*). Four acts.

The opera had previously been performed in concert form at Berlin 22 September 1894 and New York 13 February 1896. On the stage, it was revived at the Metropolitan, New York 1 April 1907 (one night only). Scharwenka's only opera.

BLOCKX: *De Herbergprinses*

10 October. Antwerp

(Flemish) text by N. de Tière. Three acts.

Blockx's most successful work, and one of the masterpieces of Flemish opera. It was mostly given in a French version by G. Lagye, as *Princesse d'Auberge*.

In French given at Ghent 9 March 1898; Brussels 14 December 1898; Antwerp 22 December 1898; Lille 5 January 1899; Hague 18 February 1899; Algiers December 1899; Marseilles 19 December 1899; Cairo 25 December 1899; Geneva 6 February 1900; New York 10 March 1909.

In the original Flemish, Amsterdam *c.*28 November 1903.

In German (translated by C. Hebbel), Hamburg 30 March 1905.

Frequently revived in Belgium; the latest revival at Brussels was on 15 November 1935 (in French); at Antwerp October 1939 (in Flemish).

E. HARTMANN: *Runenzauber*

15 October. Hamburg

(Original Danish) text by J. Lehmann (founded on H. Hertz's play, *Svend Dyrings Hus*), German version by E. Klingenfeld. One act.

Dresden 2 November 1896, etc.

In Danish (as *Ragnhild*), Copenhagen 27 December 1896.

AUDRAN: *La Poupée*

21 October. Paris, Gaîté

Text by M. Ordonneau. Four acts.

Audran's most popular operetta, still given in France as well as in other countries.

In French also, Brussels 13 September 1897, etc.; Madrid and Lisbon Spring 1901.

In English (translated by A. Sturgess), London, Prince of Wales's 24 February 1897 (running for 576 nights; revived Daly's 24 December 1931; H.M.'s 21 December 1935); New York 21 October 1897, etc.

In German (translated by A. M. Willner), Berlin, Central Th. 7 January 1899; Vienna 10 October 1899; Riga 6 December 1899; Brünn 25 December 1899; Laibach 1899; Prague 16 September 1900; Reval 1900; Zurich 1 February 1901; New York 13 April 1903.

In Hungarian (translated by F. Reiner), Budapest 1899.

In Croatian (translated by F. Miler), Zagreb 23 October 1900.

In Spanish (translated by E. Gomez Gereda and A. Soler, music adapted by R. G. Calleja), Madrid 18 April 1908.

In Polish (translated by A. Kiczman), Poznań 1910.

Italian version by C. Bertolazzi published Turin 1899.

SIBELIUS: *Jungfruburen*
(Maiden's Bower)

7 November. Helsinki

(Swedish) text by R. Hertzberg. One act.

This early work, produced by amateurs at the City Hall, Helsinki, has remained the only opera of the famous Finnish composer.

P. and L. HILLEMACHER: *Der Fluthgeist*

14 November. Carlsruhe

(Original French) text (*Le Drac*, founded on a play by G. Sand and P. Meurice) by L. Gallet, produced in a German version by E. Klingenfeld. Three acts.

The only opera of the two French composers (who always wrote in collaboration) which was produced in Germany (under F. Mottl), and the only one which was apparently never given in France or Belgium.

LEHÁR: *Kukuška*

27 November. Leipzig

Text by F. Falzari. Three acts.

Successful early folk-opera by the afterwards celebrated composer of operettas.

In German also given at Königsberg 4 April 1897, etc.

In Hungarian (translated by S. Várady), Budapest 2 May 1899.

Revived in a new version, as *Tatjana* (text rewritten by M. Kalbeck), Brünn 24 February 1905; Vienna, V.O. 10 February 1906; in Hungarian, Budapest 28 April 1907.

BUNGERT: *Odysseus' Heimkehr*

12 December. Dresden

Text by the composer. Prologue and 3 acts.

The third part of Bungert's tetralogy, *Homerische Welt* (see 1898, 1901, 1903). The third part was produced first.

Also given at Hamburg 16 November 1897 and Berlin 31 March 1898.

1897

NEŠVERA: *Lesní Vzduch* (Woodland Air)

23 January. Brno

Text by the composer. One act.

The most successful of Nešvera's five Czech operas.

Given in the same year at Olmütz 2 April 1897 (in German) and at Zagreb 5 November 1897 (in Croatian, translated by J. Dević).

VILHAR: *Smiljana*

31 January. Zagreb

Text by M. Kreković. Two acts.

The best of Vilhar's Croatian operas. In Slovenian, Ljubljana 1901.

(SCHUBERT): *Fierrabras*

9 February. Carlsruhe

Text by J. Kupelwieser after Calderón's *La Puente de Mantabile*, from A. W. von Schlegel's *Spanisches Theater*. Three acts.

Written in 1823, but not produced in Schubert's lifetime. Nor was it performed at Vienna as early as 1861 (a statement which is to be found in Riemann's dictionary and in many other books). Parts of the opera had been given, in concert form, at the Theater in der Josefstadt, Vienna 7 May 1835 (under Konradin Kreutzer), and again at the Redoutensaal, 28 February 1858 (under J. Herbeck; see E. Hanslick, *Aus dem Concertsaal*, p.148).

At Carlsruhe, 1897, the opera was produced in a revised version by O. Neitzel (text) and F. Mottl (music). Apparently not given on any other German stage.

Revived at Brussels 14 January 1926 (in French, translated by P. Spaak).

Parts of the opera were given in concert form by the "Opera Circle," London 6 November 1938 (in German).

BEER: *Der Strike der Schmiede*

18 February. Augsburg

Text by V. Léon (founded on a play by F. Coppée). One act.

Successful on German stages; given at Nuremberg 29 May 1897; Cologne 22 October 1897; Hamburg 11 January 1898; Berlin, Th.d.W. 29 September 1898, etc.

In German also, Brünn 23 September 1898; Strasbourg 11 November 1898; Zurich 13 January 1899.

In Hungarian (translated by S. Várady), Budapest 4 October 1899.

Revived Vienna, V.O. 4 June 1919.

BRUNEAU: *Messidor*

19 February. Paris, O.

Text by E. Zola. Prologue and 3 acts.

One of Bruneau's most important works. Given in Paris until 1917. In French also, Brussels 10 February 1898.

In German (translated by A. Brüggemann), Munich 15 January 1903.

(LACOMBE): *Meister Martin und seine Gesellen*

7 March. Coblenz

(Original French) text (*Le Tonnelier de Nuremberg*) by C. Nuitter (founded on E. T. A. Hoffmann's story), produced in a German version by H. Riemann. Two acts.

Like *Winkelried* (see 1892), this opera was not produced until some years after the composer's death.

d'INDY: *Fervaal*

12 March. Brussels, M.

Text by the composer (*Action dramatique*). Prologue and 3 acts.

First given at the O.C., Paris 10 May 1898; revived Paris, O. 8 January 1913.

German vocal score (translated by E. Klingenfeld) published 1897.

J. STRAUSS: *Die Göttin der Vernunft*

13 March. Vienna, W.

Text by A. M. Willner and B. Buchbinder. Three acts.

Strauss's last operetta. Stettin 15 July 1897; Berlin, Th. U.d.L. 20 January 1898.

Revived in a new version as *Reiche Mädchen* (libretto re-written by F. Stollberg), Vienna, Rai-

mund Th. 30 December 1909; Graz 5 March 1910; Munich 28 August 1910; Berlin Lessing Th. 21 May 1912.

In Italian, Turin 4 February 1911.

DE LARA: *Moina*

14 March. Monte Carlo

Text by L. Gallet. Two acts.

Successful on French stages. In French also, Lille 18 November 1897; Ghent December 1899.

Also given at Trieste 4 April 1898 (in Italian) and Düsseldorf 13 November 1906 (in German).

(Date of the first performance 14 March according to the play-bill; it is given as 11 March in the vocal score and in the composer's autobiography.)

FRANCHETTI: *Il Signor di Pourceaugnac*

10 April. Milan, Sc.

Text by F. Fontana (from Molière's comedy). Three acts.

Given in a revised version at Genoa 24 November 1897.

CABALLERO: *La Viejecita* (The Old Woman)

30 April. Madrid, Z.

Text by M. Echegaray.

Successful one-act zarzuela. Given at Mexico 4 November 1897; Barcelona December 1897, etc.

LEONCAVALLO: *La Bohème*

6 May. Venice, F.

Text by the composer (from H. Murger's novel). *Commedia lirica.* Four acts.

Written at the same time as Puccini's opera of the same title, and produced 15 months later; Leoncavallo's opera was much less successful. Still, it was given on many Italian stages, and at:
HAMBURG 24 September 1897 (in German, translated by L. Hartmann).
RIGA 1897 (in German, translated by L. Hartmann).

BUDAPEST 27 November 1897 (in Hungarian, translated by A. Radó).

VIENNA 23 February 1898 (in German) and 6 October 1907 (in Italian).

PRAGUE 30 May 1898 (in German).

NICE 23 February 1889 (in French, translated by E. Crosti).

PARIS, REN. 10 October 1899 (in French, translated by E. Crosti).

LISBON 1900 (in Italian).

ANTWERP 5 February 1901 (in French).

GENEVA 21 March 1901 (in French).

BERLIN, K.O. 11 December 1905 (in German).

MALTA 1920 (in Italian).

In 1913 the libretto was re-issued under the title *Mimi Pinson*.

NEŠVERA: *Perdita*
21 May. Prague, Cz.

Text by J. Kvapil (from Shakespeare's *A Winter's Tale*). Prologue and 3 acts.

F. d'ERLANGER: *Inès Mendo*
10 July. London, C.G.

Text by P. Decourcelle and A. Liorat (after P. Mérimée's play). Three acts.

In London produced in French (under the composer's pseudonym Frédéric Régnal); in German (as *Das Erbe*), Hamburg 8 February 1898; Frankfort 5 June 1898.

In Russian, Moscow January 1905.

BERUTTI: *Pampa*
27 July. Buenos Aires

Text by G. Borra. Three acts.

The Argentine composer's first opera on a national subject.

PANIZZA: *Il Fidanzato del Mare*
15 August. Buenos Aires

Text by R. Carugatti. One act.

Panizza's first opera; successful in South America. First given in Italy at Savona 28 June 1899.

(LISINSKI): *Porin*
2 October. Zagreb

Text by D. Demeter. Five acts.

Written about 1848–49. After *Lyubav i Zloba* (see 1846) this was the second and last opera of the Croatian composer. It was produced 43 years after Lisinski's death. Successful at Zagreb where it was last revived on 4 October 1934.

ZEMLINSKY: *Sarema*
10 October. Munich

Text by A. Schönberg (founded on a play by R. von Gottschall, *Die Rose vom Kaukasus*). Three acts.

Zemlinsky's first opera; awarded a prize in a competition instituted by Prince Luitpold of Bavaria. Also given at Leipzig 15 May 1899.

Schönberg is mentioned as the author of the text in contemporary reviews; he also arranged the vocal score of this opera written by his teacher and future brother-in-law.

MacCUNN: *Diarmid*
23 October. London, C.G.

Text by the Marquis of Lorne (J. G. Campbell), founded on "heroic Celtic legends". Four acts.

The second and last opera of the Scottish composer. Edinburgh 6 November 1897, etc.

URSPRUCH: *Das Unmöglichste von Allem*
5 November. Carlsruhe

Text by the composer (from Lope de Vega's comedy, *El major imposible*). Prologue and 3 acts.

Successful in Germany; given at Darmstadt 25 November 1897; Weimar 20 February 1898; Leipzig 27 March 1898; Cologne 20 October 1898; Elberfeld 10 January 1899; Frankfort 31 January 1899, etc. In German also, Prague 1 December 1899.

ENNA: *Pigen med Svovlstikkerne* (The Match Girl)
13 November. Copenhagen

Text by the composer and O. Rode (from Andersen's fairy tale). One act.

Successful in Denmark; also given at:

AMSTERDAM January 1900 (in Dutch).

BREMEN 2 November 1900 (in German, translated by E. von Enzberg and T. Rehbaum).

GRAZ 29 November 1900 (in German, translated by E. von Enzberg and T. Rehbaum).

PRAGUE 25 December 1900 (in German) and 14 July 1901 (in Czech).

STRASBOURG 28 December 1900 (in German).

VIENNA, JOS. 23 February 1901 (in German).

ZURICH 22 December 1902 (in German).

WARSAW 1933 (in Polish).

MESSAGER: *Les p'tites Michu*
16 November. Paris, B.P.

Text by A. Vanloo and G. Duval. Three acts.

One of Messager's most successful operettas. Frequently revived in Paris and still given in France. Also produced at:

ROME 23 March 1898 (in Italian, translated by A. Signorelli).

BERLIN, METROPOL 25 December 1898 (in German, translated by B. H. Bolten-Bäckers).

BRUSSELS 13 January 1899 (in French).

VIENNA 16 September 1899 (in German).

REVAL 1900 (in German).

LISBON Spring 1901 (in French).

PRAGUE 14 July 1901 (in Czech, translated by V. J. Novotný).

ALGIERS March 1904 (in French).

LONDON, DALY'S 29 April 1905 (in English, adapted by H. Hamilton, lyrics by P. Greenbank; ran for 401 nights).

NEW YORK, GARDEN TH. 31 January 1907 (in English).

ZURICH January 1908 (in German).

CHAPI: *La Revoltosa*
(The Revolutionary Girl)
25 November. Madrid, T. Apolo

Text by C. Fernández Shaw and J. López Silva. One act (3 scenes).

Successful zarzuela of the *genero chico*; given at Mexico 26 February 1898, Buenos Aires 1898, and on many other Spanish stages. Revived at Buenos Aires January 1936; Barcelona 1938.

MASSENET: *Sapho*
27 November Paris, O.C.

Text by H. Cain and A. Bernède (founded on the novel by A. Daudet). Five acts.

Outside France, given at:

MILAN, T.L. 14 April 1898 (in Italian, translated by A. Galli).

GENEVA 25 November 1898 (in French).

LISBON January 1899 (in Italian).

ALEXANDRIA 13 January 1899 (in Italian).

ALGIERS March 1899 (in French).

BUENOS AIRES 4 June 1899 (in Italian).

RIO DE JANEIRO 15 August 1899 (in Italian).

BUCHAREST 21 December 1899 (in Italian).

ANTWERP 12 November 1901 (in French).

HAGUE February 1903 (in French).

BRUSSELS 3 November 1903 (in French).

Revived in a new version at:

PARIS, O.C. 22 January 1909 (in French).

NEW YORK 17 November 1909 (in French).

MOSCOW December 1909 (in Russian).

NEW ORLEANS 27 December 1913 (in French).

BARCELONA 22 February 1919 (in French).

The latest revival at the O.C., Paris, was on 23 February 1935.

CILEA: *L'Arlesiana*
27 November Milan, T.L.

Text by L. Marenco (founded on A. Daudet's play). Four acts.

Given at the same theatre in a reduced 3-act version on 22 October 1898.

Revived Naples, S.C. 28 March 1912 and again Como 16 January 1937, S. Remo 22 February 1937, etc.

Enrico Caruso had his first great success in this opera.

MANCINELLI: *Ero e Leandro*
30 November. Madrid, T.R.

Text by A. Boito (first set to music by Bottesini, see 1879). Three acts.

Mancinelli's setting was written for the Norwich Festival, where it was performed as a concert cantata on 8 October 1896 (in an English ver-

sion by M. Marras). Produced on the stage at Madrid at the above date and at:
TURIN 1 January 1898 (in Italian).
LONDON, C.G. 11 July 1898 (in Italian).
NEW YORK 10 March 1899 (in Italian).
LISBON 1902 (in Italian).
WARSAW 23 November 1902 (in Polish).
RIO DE JANEIRO 12 September 1905 (in Italian).

RESTANO: *Margherita d'Orleans*
5 December. Turin, T.V.E.

Text by A. G. Lagomaggiore. Three acts.

Restano was one of the first Argentine composers whose operas were produced in Europe.

JAQUES-DALCROZE: *Sancho Panza*
13 December. Geneva

Text by R. Yve-Plessis (after Cervantes). Four acts.

In German (translated by F. Vogt), Strasbourg 28 November 1902.

FIBICH: *Šárka*
28 December. Prague, Cz.

Text by A. Schulzová. Three acts.

One of the best works of the Czech composer; according to the writer in Grove's *Dictionary* (3rd ed. 1927), "his finest achievement in dramatic lyricism".

Very successful in Czechoslovakia; revived at Prague 15 October 1903; 15 December 1910; 18 February 1917; 6 November 1925; and October 1938.

1898

TOFFT: *Vifandaka*
1 January. Copenhagen

Text by E. Christiansen. Three acts.

Tofft's first opera. Revived Copenhagen 1917.

HEUBERGER: *Der Opernball*
5 January. Vienna, W.

Text by V. Léon and H. von Waldberg. Three acts.

Heuberger's most successful work. Given at:
BERLIN, TH. U.D.L. 11 March 1898 (in German).
BRÜNN 10 April 1898 (in German).
PRAGUE 19 June 1898 (in German) and 19 January 1899 (in Czech).
HELSINKI Summer 1898 (in German).
BASLE 30 November 1898 (in German).
ZAGREB 10 March 1900 (in Croatian, translated by A. Schneider).
REVAL 1900 (in German).
RIGA 21 November 1900 (in German).
NEW YORK 24 May 1909 (in German) and 12 February 1912 (in English, translated by S. Rosenfeld and C. Kummer).

Frequently revived in Austria and Germany. First given at the Vienna O. 24 January 1931 and revived V.O. 31 December 1938.

RIMSKY-KORSAKOV: *Sadko*
Садко
7 January. Moscow

Text by the composer and V. I. Byelsky. Seven scenes (to be divided into 3 or 5 acts.)

Given at St. Petersburg Spring 1898 by the Moscow company and 8 February 1901 at the Maryinski Th. Successful in Russia; given in other countries only many years later, viz.:
PARIS, CHÂTELET 6 June 1911 (parts only; in Russian); the whole opera at the Ch.É. 7 June 1930 (in Russian).
MONTE CARLO 19 February 1921 (in Russian).
ANTWERP 14 February 1925 (in Flemish).
RIGA 15 October 1927 (in Lettish).
PRAGUE 31 January 1928 (in Czech, translated by R. Medek and F. Pujman).
BARCELONA 1928 (in Russian).
NEW YORK, M. 25 January 1930 (in French, translated by M. Delines).
ZAGREB 28 June 1930 (in Croatian).
BUENOS AIRES 1 August 1930 (in Italian, translated by R. Küfferle).
ROME, T.R. 4 April 1931 (in Italian, translated by R. Küfferle).
LONDON, LY. 9 June 1931 (in Russian).
SCHEVENINGEN September 1932 (in Russian).
STOCKHOLM 17 November 1934 (in Swedish).

SOFIA 17 May 1935 (in Bulgarian).
MILAN, SC. 2 February 1938 (in Italian).

BUNGERT: *Kirke*

29 January. Dresden

Text by the composer. Prologue and 3 acts.

The first part of the tetralogy, *Homerische Welt*, of which the third part had been produced in 1896 already. *Kirke* was also given at Hamburg 29 September 1899.

VAN DEN EEDEN: *Numance*

2 February. Antwerp

Text by M. Carré fils and C. Narrey. Four acts.
The first opera of the Belgian composer.

THUILLE: *Lobetanz*

6 February. Carlsruhe

Text by O. J. Bierbaum. Three acts.
Thuille's most successful opera.

In German also given at: Berlin 10 February 1898 (revived 25 September 1913); Zurich 26 October 1899; Vienna 18 March 1901; Strasbourg 4 November 1905; Zoppot 30 July 1911 (open-air performance); New York 18 November 1911; Philadelphia 12 December 1911; Riga 1914.

MACHADO: *Mario Wetter*

7 February. Lisbon, S.C.

Text by R. Leoncavallo (the composer). Three acts.

Successful (Italian) opera of the Portuguese composer who was the director of the Lisbon Conservatoire.

NOSKOWSKI: *Livia Quintilla*

16 February. Lemberg

Text by L. German. Three acts.

Noskowski's first and best opera. Warsaw 19 April 1902.

DE LEVA: *La Camargo*

2 March. Turin, T.R.

Text by G. Pessina. Four acts.

De Leva's only opera. Given in a new version at Naples, S.C. 23 April 1898.

BORCH: *Silvio*

7 March. Christiania

Text by the composer and O. A. Smith. One act.

The only opera of the Norwegian composer; a sequel to *Cavalleria rusticana*.

DEFFÈS: *Jessica*

25 March. Toulouse

Text by J. Adenis and H. Boisseaux (from Shakespeare's *The Merchant of Venice*). Four acts.

The best work of Deffès, who was a pupil of Halévy.

SZTOJANOVITS: *Ninon*

27 March. Budapest

Text by E. Abrányi (from a play by Z. Thury). Two acts.

The first opera of the Hungarian composer.

KOVAŘOVIČ: *Psohlavci* (The Dog Heads)

24 April. Prague, Cz.

Text by K. Šipek (founded on a novel by A. Jirásek). Three acts.

One of Kovařovič's most important works; revived at Prague 28 October 1910 and 22 September 1937.

In Czech also given at Cicero, Illinois 8 November 1936 (by the Sterling Morton High School). German version by R. Batka published 1900.

In Slovenian, Ljubljana 1902 (revived 1923).

SMYTH: *Fantasio*

24 May. Weimar

(German) text by the composer (from A. de Musset's play). Two acts.

Smyth's first opera; also given at Carlsruhe 10 February 1901.

S.A. ROUSSEAU: *La Cloche du Rhin*

8 June. Paris, O.

Text by G. Montorgueil and P. B. Gheusi. Three acts.

The best of Rousseau's five operas; given 9 times only.

HAUSEGGER: *Zinnober*

19 June. Munich

Text by the composer (founded on E. T. A. Hoffmann's *Klein Zaches*). Three acts.

Hausegger's second and last opera.

SCHYTTE: *Hero*

25 September. Copenhagen

Text by P. Levin. One act.

A modern attempt at monodrama of the 18th-century type.

NODERMANN: *König Magnus*

8 October. Hamburg

(Original Swedish) text by B. Moerner, German version by the composer. One act.

The first opera of the Swedish composer; in Sweden only fragments were given in concert form, at Malmö and Lund in December 1907.

d'ALBERT: *Die Abreise*

20 October. Frankfort

Text by F. von Sporck (founded on a play by A. von Steigentesch, 1813). One act.

One of d'Albert's most successful works and the best of his comic operas; given at:

BERLIN 24 February 1899 (revived 11 February 1922).
STRASBOURG 4 January 1900 (in German).
PRAGUE 30 September 1900 (in German).
AMSTERDAM February 1902 (in Dutch).
BASLE 13 March 1904 (in German).
VIENNA 28 February 1905 (in German).
ZAGREB 29 October 1915 (in Croatian, translated by K. Baranović).
LONDON, KING'S (HAMMERSMITH) 3 September 1925 (in English, translated by M. Bond and A. Skalski).
BRUSSELS 7 November 1932 (in French, translated by J. Bénédict).

LAZZARI: *Armor*

7 November. Prague, G.

(Original French) text by E. F. Jaubert, German version by the composer. Three acts.

Lazzari's first opera. In German also, Hamburg 24 October 1900.

In the original French, Lyons 22 November 1905.

GRANADOS: *María del Carmen*

12 November. Madrid, T. Parish

Text by J. Feliú y Codina. Three acts.

Granados's first opera; successful on Spanish stages. First given at Barcelona 26 August 1899 and revived there in January 1934 and January 1936.

GIORDANO: *Fedora*

17 November. Milan, T.L.

Text by A. Colautti (from V. Sardou's play). Three acts.

One of Giordano's most successful works; still given in Italy every season.

Outside Italy, given at:

BUENOS AIRES 14 May 1899 (in Italian).
RIO DE JANEIRO 8 July 1899 (in Italian).
MAYENCE 10 October 1899 (in German, translated by L. Hartmann).
ALEXANDRIA January 1900 (in Italian).
BARCELONA April 1900 (in Italian).
BRÜNN 21 April 1900 (in German).
VIENNA 16 May 1900 (in Italian).
LISBON 1900 (in Italian).
CAIRO Carnival 1902 (in Italian).
ANTWERP 2 January 1902 (in French).
BUDAPEST 27 May 1902 (in Hungarian, translated by S. Várady).
MALTA 1902 (in Italian).
ZAGREB 4 March 1903 (in Croatian, translated by F. Miler).
GENEVA 3 April 1903 (in French).
BERLIN, BERLINER TH. 1 August 1903 (in German) and Th.d.W. 15 November 1905 (in Italian); revived in German 22 January 1930.
PARIS, TH. S.B. 13 May 1905 (in Italian).

AMSTERDAM March 1906 (in Italian).
LONDON, C.G. 5 November 1906 (in Italian).
NEW YORK 5 December 1906 (in Italian).
MARSEILLES 5 March 1907 (in French).
NEW ORLEANS 29 January 1908 (in Italian).
RIGA 1909 (in German).
WARSAW January 1910 (in Italian).
MONTE CARLO 15 March 1910 (in Italian).
MONTREAL 1911 (in Italian).
BUCHAREST March 1925 (in Rumanian).
LEMBERG 1927 (in Polish).
SOFIA 22 March 1929 (in Bulgarian).
TRIPOLIS November 1934 (in Italian).
BRUSSELS 1 April 1935 (in French).

KIENZL: *Don Quixote*

18 November. Berlin, O.

Text by the composer (after Cervantes). Three acts.

In German also, Prague 25 December 1898; Graz 11 February 1905.

In Russian, Moscow 1911.

Revived in a new version at Graz 1 May 1934 and Vienna 22 November 1936.

MASCAGNI: *Iris*

22 November. Rome, C.

Text by L. Illica. Three acts.

Given with some alterations at Milan, Sc. 19 January 1899.

In Italian also:
BUENOS AIRES 22 June 1899.
BARCELONA 30 December 1900.
CAIRO January 1901.
LISBON 1901.
MONTEVIDEO 10 August 1901.
PHILADELPHIA 14 October 1902.
NEW YORK 16 October 1902.
RIO DE JANEIRO 23 September 1903.
HAGUE April 1905.
MALTA 1907.
ODESSA March 1908.
MONTE CARLO 27 March 1909.
LONDON, C.G. 8 July 1919.
CHICAGO 5 November 1929.

In German (translated by M. Kalbeck), Frankfort 26 September 1899, etc. Revived Wuppertal 18 April 1934.

In French (translated by M. Vaucaire), Marseilles 15 November 1911.

In Russian, Moscow 1913.

In Polish, Poznań 1931.

In Bulgarian, Sofia 27 December 1937.

CABALLERO: *Gigantes y Cabezudos*
(Giants and Big-Heads)

29 November. Madrid, Z.

Text by M. Echegaray. One act (3 scenes).

Successful in Spain; see Grove's *Dictionary*, Vol.v, p.779 (4th ed. 1940) where the little work is described.

In Spanish also given at Milan 2 October 1901.

SERRANO: *Gonzalo de Córdoba*

6 December. Madrid, T.R.

Text by the composer. Prologue and three acts. Successful Spanish opera on a national subject.

RIMSKY-KORSAKOV:
Mozart i Salieri
Моцартъ и Сальери

7 December. Moscow

Text: Pushkin's dramatic poem (1830). Two acts.

First given at St. Petersburg March 1899. Outside Russia, produced only many years later, viz.:
LJUBLJANA 9 January 1924 (in Slovenian).
LONDON, ALBERT HALL 11 October 1927 (in Russian); R.A.M. 10 December 1934 (in English, translated by G. Dunn).
WARSAW Spring 1929 (in Polish).
WÜRZBURG 26 April 1932 (in German, translated by A. Bernhard).
PARIS, O.C. 3 June 1932 (in Russian).
FOREST PARK, PA., UNITY HOUSE 6 August 1933 (for the first time in U.S.A.).

Date of first production according to Glyebov; in the Russian edition of Rimsky-Korsakov's *Autobiography* (1926) the date is given as 6–19 November 1898.

STENHAMMAR: *Tirfing*

9 December. Stockholm

Text by A. Boberg. Prologue, 2 acts, and epilogue.

Stenhammar's first opera.

CHAPI: *Curro Vargas*

10 December. Madrid, T. Parish

Text by J. Dicenta and M. Paso. Three acts.

One of Chapi's most important zarzuelas.

Also given at Barcelona July 1899, etc.

A parody, *Curro Bragas*, by Enrique García Alvarez and Antonio Paso, music by Ramón Estelles, was produced at the T. Apolo, Ma̕ id on 1 February 1899.

MESSAGER: *Véronique*

10 December. Paris, B.P.

Text by A. Vanloo and G. Duval. Three acts.

Very successful in and outside France.

In French also given at Brussels 19 January 1900; Lisbon Spring 1901; Geneva 11 February 1902; Bucharest February 1907; Cairo Spring 1938.

In German (as *Brigitte*, translated by B. H. Bolten-Bäckers), Vienna, W. 10 March 1900; Cologne 28 October 1900; Riga 23 November 1901; Berlin, Kroll's 13 September 1902.

In Italian, Milan 10 November 1904.

In Greek, Athens Spring 1935.

Given in London, Coronet 5 May 1903 (in French); in English (translated by H. Hamilton, lyrics by L. Eldée and P. Greenbank), Apollo 18 May 1904; this version ran for 495 nights. New York November 1905. Revived Adelphi 3 April 1915.

SZÁBADOS: *A Bolond*

(The Simpleton)

29 December. Budapest

Text by J. Rákosi (founded on a story by D. Malonyay). Three acts.

Szábados's most successful opera.

Revived at Budapest 14 March 1911 and given there until 1920.

1899

J. B. FOERSTER: *Eva*

1 January. Prague, Cz.

Text by the composer (from G. Preissová's drama, *Gazdina Roba*). Three acts.

Successful in Czechoslovakia; the latest revival at Prague so far was on 2 October 1926.

In German (as *Marja*, translated by J. Brandt), Vienna, V.O. 21 December 1915; Freiburg May 1923.

In Slovenian, Ljubljana 1925.

ZICHY: *Roland Mester*

(Master Roland)

10 January. Budapest

Text by the composer. Three acts.

In German (translated by M. Kalbeck), Prague 21 January 1900; Hamburg 26 April 1900 and Brunswick 29 April 1900.

In Flemish, Antwerp 20 October 1900.

(CHABRIER): *Briseis*

14 January. Berlin, O.

(Original French) text (*Briséis ou Les Amants de Corinthe*) by E. Mikhaël and C. Mendès (founded on Goethe's ballad, *Die Braut von Corinth*), German version by E. Klingenfeld.

Chabrier's last opera; unfinished, only one of the three acts was completed.

Before the production at Berlin, the fragment had been heard at a Lamoureux concert in Paris on 31 January 1897. Produced Paris, O. 8 May 1899 and revived there 4 November 1916 (in French). In concert form also, New York 3 March 1911 (in French).

GOLDMARK: *Die Kriegsgefangene*

17 January. Vienna, O.

Text by "E. Schlicht" (pseudonym of A. Formey). Two acts.

(Originally, the opera was called *Briseis*, like Chabrier's work produced three days earlier, although the subjects are quite different.)

In German also, Cologne 29 January 1899; Prague 3 March 1899, etc.

In Hungarian (translated by A. Radó), Budapest 6 April 1899.

S. WAGNER: *Der Bärenhäuter*

22 January. Munich

Text by the composer. Three acts.

The first and most successful opera of Richard Wagner's son. Leipzig 29 January 1899; Vienna 27 March 1899; Berlin 16 March 1900, etc.

In German also, Prague 31 May 1899; Riga 1 February 1900; Berne 7 February 1900; Strasbourg 27 January 1905. Still given in Germany.

In Hungarian (translated by S. Várady), Budapest 3 February 1900.

FALCHI: *Il Trillo del Diavolo*

29 January. Rome, Arg.

Text by U. Fleres. Three acts.

Falchi's last and most successful opera. Given in many Italian towns; in Italian also, Alexandria 22 February 1900.

(The hero of the opera is, of course, the famous violinist, Giuseppe Tartini, and its subject the well-known anecdote of the origin of his *Sonata del Diavolo*.)

NEUVILLE: *Tipheene*

11 February. Antwerp

(Original French) text by L. Payen, Flemish version by E. Keurvels. Two parts.

In Swedish, Stockholm 17 April 1901.

Revived Lyons 23 January 1906 (for the first time in French).

VIVES: *Don Lucas del Cigarral*

18 February. Madrid, T. Parish

Text by C. Fernández Shaw and T. Luceño (founded on F. de Rojas's comedy, *Entre Bobos anda el Juego*). Three acts.

Vives's first important work. Barcelona June 1899, etc.

KEIL: *Serrana*

13 March. Lisbon, S.C.

(Original Portuguese) text by H. Lopes de Mendonça, produced in an Italian version by C. Fereal.

Very successful at Lisbon, where it was revived in March 1923, in November 1936, and once more in 1938.

(LORTZING): *Regina*, oder *Die Marodeure*

21 March. Berlin, O.

Text by the composer, revised by A. L'Arronge. Three acts.

The work had been written in 1848, but was not performed then because of its "revolutionary tendencies." The score was recovered at Wiesbaden in 1872 and revised for the 1899 production by R. Kleinmichel.

Given on several other German stages; Hamburg 4 October 1900, etc.

In German also, Strasbourg 1 January 1901; Riga November 1909.

DE LARA: *Messaline*

21 March. Monte Carlo

Text by P. A. Silvestre and E. Morand. Four acts.

De Lara's most successful opera.

In French also given at London, C.G. 13 July 1899; Bordeaux February 1901; Algiers January 1902; New York 22 January 1902; Antwerp 2 December 1902; Hague 15 January 1903; Paris, Gaîté-Lyrique 24 December 1903; Geneva 2 February 1904; Cairo Carnival 1907; Tunis March 1920.

In Italian (translated by C. d'Ormeville), Milan, Sc. 7 April 1901.

In German (translated by O. Rupertus), Cologne 2 December 1905; Leipzig 25 October 1907.

In English (translated by V. Blackburn), London, King's (Hammersmith) 22 January 1930.

Still given on French stages. First produced at Monte Carlo on Tuesday 21 March 1899 (not 24 March as the composer himself says in his autobiography).

HALLÉN: *Waldemarsskatten*
(Valdemar's Treasure)

8 April. Stockholm

Text by A. Klinkowström. Four acts.

Written for the opening of the new building of the Stockholm opera-house.

In German (translated by E. von Enzberg), Carlsruhe 29 March 1903.

English translation by T. Stevens published 1905.

STENHAMMAR: *Das Fest auf Solhaug*

12 April. Stuttgart

Text from Ibsen's drama in M. von Borch's German version. Three acts.

In German also, Berlin 20 September 1905; revived Dortmund 8 June 1912.

In Swedish (translated by S. Elmblad), Stockholm 31 October 1902.

LE BORNE: *Mudarra*

18 April. Berlin, O.

(Original French) text by L. Tiercelin and L. Bonnemère, German version by A. Brunnemann. Four acts.

Revived in a new version Elberfeld 4 March 1904. Never given in France.

VANBIANCHI: *La Nave*

2 May. Genoa, Politeama

Text by G. Macchi (*Dramma simbolico*). Two acts.

The opera was awarded the first prize in the Concorso Steiner, Vienna 1896.

VOGL: *Der Fremdling*

7 May. Munich

Text by F. Dahn (originally written for Goldmark). Three acts.

In German also, Groningen, Holland 13 April 1901.

(The composer was the well-known *Tristan* singer.)

MASSENET: *Cendrillon*

24 May. Paris, O.C.

Text by H. Cain (after Perrault). Four acts.

The most important French opera of the *Hänsel und Gretel* school.

In French also given at Brussels 3 November 1899; Geneva 15 December 1899; Algiers January 1900; Hague April 1900; New Orleans 23 December 1902; Cairo Carnival 1907; Buenos Aires 10 September 1907; Philadelphia 6 November 1911; New York 26 February 1912; Montreal 24 December 1912.

In Italian (translated by A. Galli), Milan, T.L. 28 December 1899; Buenos Aires 13 August 1908.

In English, London, Little Th. 24 December 1928 (by puppets); revived Swindon (Wiltshire) 20 February 1939.

In Spanish, Bogotá, Colombia March 1933. Still given on French stages.

PIZZI: *La Rosalba*

31 May. Turin, T. Carignano

Text by L. Illica (*Novella scenica*). One act.

In English (translated by P. E. Pinkerton), London, C.G. 26 September 1902.

In German (translated by L. Hartmann), Cassel 21 October 1904; Berlin, K.O. 8 May 1908.

ZÖLLNER: *Die versunkene Glocke*

8 July. Berlin, Th.d.W.

Text by the composer (founded on G. Hauptmann's drama). Five acts.

Zöllner's best opera.

In German also given at Metz 15 November 1900; Graz 18 December 1901; Vienna, V.O. 16 January 1906; Riga 5 May 1906; Zurich March 1908; Amsterdam December 1908.

In Flemish, Antwerp 10 November 1906 (revived 1926).

Revived at Freiburg (the composer's home town), 16 April 1920; 5 July 1934; 4 July 1939.

BERUTTI: *Yupanky*

25 July. Buenos Aires

(Original Spanish) text by E. Rodríguez Larreta, Italian version by G. Tarnassi. Three acts.

An *Inca* opera; successful at Buenos Aires; name-part created by Caruso.

ENNA: *Lamia*

3 October. Antwerp

(Original Danish) text by H. Rode (founded on a story by P. Mariager), Flemish version by? Prologue and 2 acts.

In Danish, Copenhagen 24 March 1901. Parts of the music were afterwards used for *Ung Elskov* (new libretto by P. A. Rosenberg, 2 acts, from a story by K. Mikszath); first produced as *Heisse Liebe* (German version by W. Henzen), Weimar 2 December 1904; in Danish, Copenhagen March 1912.

RIMSKY–KORSAKOV:
Tsarskaya Nyevesta
Царская Невѣста
(The Tsar's Bride)

3 November. Moscow

Text by L. A. Mei. Three acts.

First given at St. Petersburg 12 November 1901 revived there 21 April 1922; 14 April 1931; 2 December 1936.

Outside Russia produced at:

PRAGUE 4 December 1902 (in Czech) and 1937 (in German).

HELSINKI 10 March 1906 (in Russian) and 21 January 1927 (in Finnish).

PARIS, TH. S.B. 16 May 1911 (in Russian).

SEATTLE 6 January 1922 (in Russian).

NEW YORK 9 May 1922 (in Russian).

BERLIN, TH.D.W. 24 March 1923 (in German, translated by A. Bernhard).

SOFIA 3 September 1923 (in Bulgarian).

LJUBLJANA 1 May 1924 (in Slovenian).

ZAGREB 24 October 1924 (in Croatian).

LONDON, LY. 19 May 1931 (in Russian).

TALLINN 1932 (in Estonian).

DVOŘÁK: *Čert a Káča*
(The Devil and Kate)

23 November. Prague, Cz.

Text by A. Wenig. Three acts.

Revived Prague 7 June 1918 and 29 June 1927.

In German (translated by R. Batka), Bremen 27 April 1909; Brünn 22 September 1931; Vienna, V.O. 19 February 1932 (previously given there in Czech by the Olomouc company on 11 June 1924).

In Slovenian (translated by Peterlin-Petruška), Ljubljana 15 February 1923.

In English (translated by N. Lindsay), Oxford 22 November 1932.

SCHILLINGS: *Der Pfeifertag*

26 November. Schwerin

Text by F. von Sporck. Three acts.

Carlsruhe 17 December 1899; Strasbourg 23 October 1900; Hamburg 31 January 1901; Berlin 17 September 1902, etc. In German also, Riga 1913. Revived Berlin 12 September 1931 (libretto revised by the composer).

SULLIVAN: *The Rose of Persia; or, The Story-Teller and the Slave*

29 November. London, Savoy

Text by B. Hood. Two acts.

Sullivan's last success. In London ran for 213 nights. New York 6 September 1901, etc. Revived London, Prince's Th. 28 February 1935.

German version by G. Okonkowski published.

1900

PUCCINI: *Tosca*

14 January. Rome, C.

Text by G. Giacosa and L. Illica (founded on the play by V. Sardou). Three acts.

Equally or even more successful than *La Bohème*, 1896. Given at:

BUENOS AIRES 16 June 1900 (in Italian).

LONDON, C.G. 12 July 1900 (in Italian) and Shaftesbury 20 October 1915 (in English).

CONSTANTINOPLE 8 September 1900 (in Italian).

RIO DE JANEIRO 13 September 1900 (in Italian).

MADRID 15 December 1900 (in Italian).

ODESSA 1 January 1901 (in Italian).

LISBON 29 January 1901 (in Italian).

NEW YORK 4 February 1901 (in Italian) and 28 September 1903 (in English).

MEXICO 27 July 1901 (in Italian).

SANTIAGO, CHILE 29 July 1901 (in Italian).

CAIRO 26 November 1901 (in Italian).

BUCHAREST 11 February 1902 (in Italian) and January 1920 (in Rumanian).

LEMBERG January 1902 (in Polish, translated by L. German).

DRESDEN 21 October 1902 (in German, translated by M. Kalbeck).

BUFFALO 17 November 1902 (for the first time in English, translated by W. B. Kingston).

MALTA 4 March 1903 (in Italian).

MONTE CARLO 28 March 1903 (in Italian).

TUNIS 1903 (in French, translated by P. Ferrier).

PARIS, O.C. 13 October 1903 (in French, translated by P. Ferrier).

WARSAW 6 November 1903 (in Italian).

PRAGUE 21 November 1903 (in Czech, translated by O. Smrčka) and 8 September 1904 (in German).

BUDAPEST 1 December 1903 (in Hungarian, translated by S. Várady).

STOCKHOLM 15 February 1904 (in Swedish, translated by S. Nyblom).

BRUSSELS 2 April 1904 (in French).

GRAZ 10 June 1904 (in German).

ANTWERP 29 November 1904 (in French).

HAGUE December 1904 (in Italian) and February 1905 (in French).

NEW ORLEANS 25 January 1905 (in English); 26 December 1907 (in Italian); 28 December 1911 (in French).

MOSCOW 1905 and St. Petersburg December 1905 (in Italian); Leningrad 19 September 1924 as *V Borbe za Kommunu*, new libretto by N. G. Vinogradov and S. D. Spassky; as *Tosca* 25 May 1929 and 5 November 1934 (in Russian, new translation by V. I. Epaneshnikov).

HELSINKI 20 September 1905 (in Italian) and 15 November 1919 (in Finnish).

LJUBLJANA 1906 (in Slovenian).

GENEVA 7 December 1906 (in French).

BERLIN, K.O. 23 January 1907 and O. 4 October 1921 (in German).

VIENNA, V.O. 20 February 1907 and O. 26 January 1910 (in German) and 7 October 1921 (in Italian).

LIVERPOOL 29 October 1909 (in English).

COPENHAGEN 5 May 1910 (in Danish, translated by K. Lindemann).

RIGA 1911 (in German) and 18 September 1923 (in Lettish, translated by B. Valle).

REVAL (TALLINN) 1911 (in German) and 1925 (in Estonian).

ZAGREB 6 October 1911 (in Croatian, translated by M. Ibler).

SHANGHAI 1918 (in Russian).

YOKOHAMA Autumn 1919 (in Italian).

OSLO 1921 (in Norwegian).

BELGRADE 1923 (in Serbian).

KAUNAS 28 October 1924 (in Lithuanian).

TEL-AVIV 22 January 1925 (in Hebrew, translated by M. Freidmann).

SOFIA 10 June 1925 (in Bulgarian).

BLOCKX: *Thyl Uylenspiegel*

18 January. Brussels, M.

Text by H. Cain and L. Solvay. Three acts.

    In Flemish, Antwerp 20 January 1900.

    Revived in a new version, Brussels 12 November 1920 (score revised by A. de Boeck).

BRETÓN: *Raquel*

20 January. Madrid, T.R.

Text by the composer (founded on F. Grillparzer's *Die Jüdin von Toledo*). Four acts.

ZEMLINSKY: *Es war einmal*

22 January. Vienna, O.

Text by M. Singer (founded on a Danish play by H. Drachmann). Prologue and 3 acts.

    Revived Mannheim May 1912; in German also, Prague October 1912.

G. CHARPENTIER: *Louise*

2 February. Paris, O.C.

Text by the composer (*Roman musical*). Four acts.
Charpentier's first opera. Very successful in
Paris right from the beginning.

The 300th performance at the O.C. was on 19
March 1911; 500th 17 January 1921; 800th 26
November 1931. Given all over France and at:

ALGIERS January 1901 (in French).

BRUSSELS 8 February 1901 (in French).

BUDAPEST 28 March 1901 (in Hungarian, translated by S. Várady).

MILAN, T.L. 14 April 1901 (in Italian, translated by A. Galli).

ELBERFELD 1 January 1902; Hamburg 3 January 1902; Leipzig 5 January 1902, etc. (in German, translated by O. Neitzel).

GENEVA 3 February 1903 (in French).

PRAGUE 13 February 1903 (in Czech, translated by V. J. Novotný); in German not before Autumn 1938.

BERLIN 4 March 1903 (in German).

VIENNA 24 March 1903 (in German).

STOCKHOLM 4 May 1903 (in Swedish, translated by E. A. Wallmark).

RIGA 30 October 1903 (in German).

HAGUE January 1904 (in French).

LEMBERG February 1904 (in Polish, translated by L. German).

BARCELONA 3 April 1904 (in Italian) and 13 February 1919 (in French); Catalan translation by J. Pena published 1904.

CAIRO Carnival 1907 (in French).

LISBON March 1907 (in Italian).

BRÜNN May 1907 (in German).

NEW YORK 3 January 1908 (in French) and 30 December 1913 (in English, translated by C. A. Byrne).

SAIGON February 1908 (in French).

LONDON, C.G. 18 June 1909 (in French) and Aldwych Th. 22 January 1917 (in English).

BUENOS AIRES 2 August 1910 (in Italian).

MOSCOW October 1911; Leningrad 7 November 1920 (in Russian).

MONTREAL January 1912 (in French).

MANCHESTER 17 October 1912 (in English, translated by H. G. Chapman).

JOHANNESBURG 1913 (in English, translated by H. G. Chapman).

ZAGREB 28 April 1919 (in Croatian, translated by M. Ibler).

LJUBLJANA 24 March 1922 (in Slovenian, translated by I. Šorli).

COPENHAGEN 7 January 1923 (in Danish, translated by F. Bendix).

RIO DE JANEIRO Summer 1926 (in Italian).

ATHENS June 1932 (in Greek?).

KAUNAS 9 November 1932 (in Lithuanian).

SOFIA 6 March 1935 (in Bulgarian).

BUCHAREST January 1940 (in Rumanian).

TRNEČEK: *Andrea Crini*

2 February. Prague, Cz.

Text by B. Beneš. Three acts.
Trneček's last opera.

SUK: *Lesnoy Tsar*
ЛѢсной Царь
(The Forest King)

16 February. Kharkov

(Czech) text by J. V. Frič (founded on a poem by
K. H. Mácha), Russian version by ? Four acts.

Suk's only opera. Also given at Prague 5 April
1903 (in Czech).

d'ALBERT: *Kain*

17 February. Berlin, O.

Text by H. Bulthaupt. One act.

In German also given at Prague 30 September
1900.

In Danish (translated by S. Levysohn), Copenhagen 8 April 1904.

GALEOTTI: *Anton*

17 February. Milan, Sc.

Text by L. Illica. Prologue, 2 acts, and epilogue.

Revived Monte Carlo 30 March 1924; Ghent
March 1925 (in French, translated by L. Laloy).

For an account of this opera see *Revue Musicale*,
February 1930.

WOLF-FERRARI: *Cenerentola*

22 February. Venice, F.

Text by M. Pezzè-Pascolato. Three acts.
Wolf-Ferrari's first opera.
In German (translated by J. Schweitzer), Bremen 31 January 1902; Brünn January 1903.
Revived (in a new German version by F. Rau), Bremen 18 December 1937.

HORÁK: *Babička*

(Grandmother)

3 March. Prague, Cz.

Text by A. Wenig (founded on a story by Božena Němcová). Three acts and epilogue.
The most successful opera of the Czech composer.

CATTELANI: *Atahualpa*

10 March. Buenos Aires

(Italian) text by C. F. Scotti. Four acts.
The only opera of Cattelani, who was a native of Parma and went to South America in 1886.

SCHJELDERUP: *Norwegische Hochzeit*

17 March. Prague, G.

Text by the composer. Two acts.
Revived in Norwegian (as *Bruderovet*), Oslo 1920.

C. ERLANGER: *Le Juif Polonais*

11 April. Paris, O.C.

Text by H. Cain and P. B. Gheusi (founded on Erckmann-Chatrian's novel *Conte d'Alsace*). Three acts.
Successful in France; revived at the O.C. 15 January 1916 and 21 November 1933.
In German (translated by F. Vogt), Elberfeld 29 November 1900; Vienna 4 October 1906. (In Germany, however, the opera by K. Weis on the same subject, see 1901, was much more successful.)
In Russian, St. Petersburg 25 December 1904.

LANGE-MÜLLER: *Vikingeblod*

(Vikings' Blood)

29 April. Copenhagen

Text by E. Christiansen. Four acts.
Lange-Müller's last opera. Also given at Stockholm 11 March 1904 (in Swedish).

MINHEJMER: *Mazeppa*

1 May. Warsaw

Text by M. Radziszewski (founded on J. Slowacki's tragedy). Four acts.
Minhejmer's best-known work; the opera had been written as early as about 1875. Successful in Poland; revived at Lemberg February 1910.
Also given at Turin 1 November 1902 (in Italian, translated by L. Miller).

FAURÉ: *Prométhée*

27 August. Béziers

Text by J. Lorrain and A. F. Hérold. Three acts.
Fauré's first opera. Produced at the Arènes, Béziers, in the open air. First given in Paris at the Hippodrome 5 December 1907; at the O. 17 May 1917; revived Ch.É. 3 May 1924.

ENNA: *Prinsessen paa Aerten*

(The Princess on the Pea)

15 September. Aarhus

Text by P. A. Rosenberg (from H. C. Andersen's tale). One act.
Written for the opening of the new theatre at Aarhus. Given at Copenhagen 5 January 1902 (at the inauguration of the Folke Oper).
In German (translated by W. Henzen), Crefeld 29 November 1918.

ZELENSKI: *Janek*

4 October. Lemberg

Text by L. German. Two acts.
Written for the inauguration of the Polish opera-house at Lemberg (Lwów). Successful in Poland; Cracow 12 July 1901; Warsaw 27 April 1903.

In Polish also, Kiev 1909. Revived Lemberg 1926; Warsaw Spring 1932.

VIVES: *Euda d'Uriach*

24 October. Barcelona, Novedades

(Original Catalan) text by A. Guimerá (from his tragedy, *Les Monjes de Sant Aymant*), produced in an Italian version by A. Bignotti. Four acts.

Revived at Barcelona January 1934.

RIMSKY-KORSAKOV: *Skazka o Tsarye Saltanye*

Сказка о Царѣ Салтанѣ

(The Tale of Tsar Saltan)

3 November. Moscow

Text by V. I. Byelsky (after Pushkin). Prologue and 4 acts.

First given at St. Petersburg 4 January 1904. Very successful in Russia.

Outside Russia, given only many years later, viz.:

BARCELONA 4 December 1924 (in Russian); Catalan translation by J. Pena and K. Gonsseff published 1935.

RIGA 16 December 1925 (in Lettish).

BRUSSELS 15 April 1926 (in French, translated by L. Laloy).

BUENOS AIRES 15 July 1927 (in Italian, translated by R. Küfferle).

AACHEN 2 March 1928 (in German, translated by A. Bernhard).

PARIS, CH.É. 29 January 1929 (in Russian).

MILAN, SC. 19 March 1929 (in Italian).

KAUNAS 12 March 1932 (in Lithuanian).

LONDON, S.'s WELLS 11 October 1933 (in English, translated by E. Agate).

SOFIA 6 December 1933 (in Bulgarian).

PRAGUE 18 June 1935 (in Czech).

(Date of first production, 21 October/2 November, according to Rimsky-Korsakov's autobiography; according to Central European periodicals, the production was one week later, 9 November 1900.)

(FIBICH): *Pád Arkuna*

(The Fall of Arcona)

9 November. Prague, Cz.

Text by A. Schulzová. Consists of a prologue (*Helga*) and 3 acts (called *Dargun*).

Fibich's last opera, produced 25 days after his death. Revived Prague 24 January 1925.

LEONCAVALLO: *Zazà*

10 November. Milan, T.L.

Text by the composer (founded on the French play by C. Simon and P. Berton). Four acts.

Very successful in Italy and abroad. Given at:

ANTWERP 6 February 1902 (in French).

HAGUE 1 March 1902 (in French).

BUENOS AIRES 9 August 1902 (in Italian).

LILLE 22 January 1903 (in French).

S. FRANCISCO 27 November 1903 (in Italian).

MOSCOW Spring 1905 (in Russian).

PARIS, TH.S.B. 22 May 1905 (in Italian) and Tr. L. 16 February 1911 (in French).

BARCELONA 29 September 1905 (in Italian).

CASSEL 22 April 1906 (in German, translated by F. Werner).

MALTA 1906 (in Italian).

GENEVA 22 February 1907 (in French).

ALEXANDRIA Carnival 1907 (in Italian).

BUCHAREST Spring 1907 (in Italian).

RIO DE JANEIRO 28 May 1907 (in Italian).

LISBON 1907 (in Italian).

BERLIN, K.O. 27 November 1908 (in German).

VIENNA, V.O. 5 April 1909 (in German).

LONDON, CORONET 30 April 1909 (in Italian).

RIGA 1909 (in German).

PRAGUE 15 November 1909 (in Czech, translated by A. Wenig).

MONTREAL 10 January 1913 (in French).

LEMBERG 1913 (in Polish, translated by A. Kiczman).

NEW YORK, M. 16 January 1920 (in Italian).

BUDAPEST 18 May 1923 (in Hungarian, translated by D. Vidor).

Still given in Italy. One of the latest revivals was at Milan, Sc. 10 April 1940.

CAUDELLA: *Petru Rareş*

14 November. Bucharest

(Original German) text by T. Rehbaum (founded on a story by N. Gane), Rumanian version by? Three acts.

The most important work of Caudella, who was director of the Jassy Conservatoire and one of the earliest composers of Rumanian operas. For a detailed account, see *Neue Zeitschrift für Musik*, 1899, Nos. 49 and 50.

PANIZZA: *Medio evo Latino*

17 November. Genoa, Politeama

Text by L. Illica. Three acts.

Buenos Aires 21 July 1901.

(The work consists of three one-act operas, the action of which is laid in different Latin countries and in different medieval centuries.)

1901

MASCAGNI: *Le Maschere*

17 January. Milan, Sc.; Rome, C.; Venice, F.; Turin, T.R.; Genoa, C.F.; Verona, T. Filarm.

Text by L. Illica (*Commedia lirica e giocosa*). Prologue and 3 acts.

The opera had his first production at six Italian towns the same night; in a seventh town, Naples, the first production was two nights later (without the prologue). Unsuccessful; at Rome (under the composer's own direction) the success was slightly better than elsewhere. Also given at Buenos Aires 2 July 1901. Revived (with alterations) Turin 7 June 1916; Milan, Sc. 8 March 1931, etc.

LEROUX: *Astarté*

15 February. Paris, O.

Text by L. de Gramont. Four acts.

The first of Leroux's operas which was given in Paris (19 performances).

BUONGIORNO: *Das Mädchenherz*

16 February. Cassel

(Original Italian) text by L. Illica (*Il Cuore delle Fanciulle*), German version by L. Hartmann. Four acts.

In German also, Dresden 5 October 1901, etc.; Brünn 13 October 1901; Graz 7 March 1902; Metz 14 March 1902.

In the original Italian, Piacenza 22 January 1903.

PIERNÉ: *La Fille de Tabarin*

20 February. Paris, O.C.

Text by V. Sardou and P. Ferrier. Three acts.

Given at the O.C. 14 times in 1901; not revived so far.

(The date of first performance is incorrectly given as 20 January, 8 February and 13 February in different books of reference.)

WEIS: *Der polnische Jude*

3 March. Prague, G.

Text by V. Léon and R. Batka (founded on Erckmann-Chatrian's novel). Two acts.

Weis's most successful work. Given on German stages until 1930.

Produced at:

DRESDEN 7 September 1901 (in German).

ZURICH 4 October 1901 (in German).

AMSTERDAM 10 March 1902 (in Dutch).

BERLIN, KROLL'S 7 June 1902 (in German).

BUDAPEST 25 October 1902 (in Hungarian, translated by D. Vidor).

VIENNA, W. 10 December 1902 (in German) and Stadt Th. 19 May 1929 (in Czech).

WARSAW 26 April 1906 (in Polish, translated by W. Rapacki).

LJUBLJANA 1906 (in Slovenian).

RIGA March 1907 (in German).

PRAGUE 25 November 1907 (for the first time there in Czech, translated by P. Nebeský).

ZAGREB 27 November 1916 (in Croatian, translated by M. Nehajev).

NEW YORK, M. 9 March 1921 (in English, translated by S. Spaeth and C. Cowdrey).

THUILLE: *Gugeline*

4 March. Bremen

Text by O. J. Bierbaum. Five acts.

Thuille's last opera. Also given at Darmstadt 5 May 1901.

BUNGERT: *Nausikaa*

20 March. Dresden

Text by the composer. Prologue and 3 acts.

The second part of his tetralogy *Homerische Welt* (see 1896, 1898, 1903).

Also given at Hamburg 20 February 1902.

DIBBERN: *Odja*

29 March. Amsterdam

Text by the composer. Three acts.

(For an account of this Dutch opera, see *Neue Zeitschrift für Musik*, 1901, No.21–22.)

DVOŘÁK: *Rusalka*

31 March. Prague, Cz.

Text by J. Kvapil. Three acts.

Of Dvořák's 9 operas perhaps the most popular one. Very successful on Czech stages; revived at Prague 1 March 1915; 11 October 1924; 19 June 1936. Given at:

LJUBLJANA 4 February 1908 (in Slovenian, translated by F. Juvančič); revived in 1919 and 1940.

VIENNA 1910 (in Czech, by a company from Brno), and 7 June 1924 (again in Czech, by a company from Olomouc).

ZAGREB 18 April 1912 (in Croatian, translated by A. Mitrović).

BARCELONA 21 February 1924 (in Czech).

LEMBERG 1929 (in Polish).

STUTTGART 5 October 1929 (in German, translated by J. Will).

BRÜNN 1930 (in German, translated by J. Will).

KAUNAS 12 November 1937 (in Lithuanian).

The opera was announced for production at C.G., London in the season of 1939. The production did not take place.

MASCHERONI: *Lorenza*

13 April. Rome, C.

Text by L. Illica. Three acts.

Written for Gemma Bellincioni. The first and most successful opera of the famous conductor. Given in a revised version at Brescia 3 September 1901.

Also produced at:

COLOGNE 14 November 1901 (in German, translated by T. Rehbaum).

BUENOS AIRES 19 June 1903 (in Italian).

BARCELONA 23 December 1903 (in Italian).

GHENT 19 November 1920 (in French, translated by H. Balieus).

Revived in Italian at Bari 12 February 1921.

BRUNEAU: *L'Ouragan*

29 April. Paris, O.C.

Text by E. Zola. Four acts.

In Russian, Moscow Spring 1905.

The third act was revived at the Opéra, Paris 17 February 1916.

FLONDOR: *Mosul Ciokârlan*
(Old Man Lark)

4 May. Czernowitz

Text by the composer. One act.

Early Rumanian comic opera, produced at Czernowitz (Cernauti) by the singing club "Armonia".

Also given at Bucharest, October 1906 (by a company from Hermannstadt).

PADEREWSKI: *Manru*

29 May. Dresden

(German) text by A. Nossig (founded on a novel by J. I. Kraszewski). Three acts.

The only opera of the famous pianist (who was Prime Minister of Poland in 1919) which was performed.

In Polish (translated by S. Rossowski), Lemberg 8 June 1901; Warsaw May 1902; Kiev 1902.

In German, Prague 24 November 1901; Zurich 30 January 1902; New York 14 February 1902 and on other American stages.

Revived (in Polish), Poznań October 1930.

STANFORD: *Much Ado About Nothing*

30 May. London, C.G.

Text by J. R. Sturgis (after Shakespeare). Four acts.

In German (translated by J. Bernhoff), Leipzig 25 April 1902.

Revived London, R.C.M. 9 July 1935.

PFEIFFER: *Le Légataire universel*

6 July. Paris, O.C.

Text by J. Adenis and L. Bonnemère (founded on the comedy by J. F. Regnard, 1708). Three acts.

Pfeiffer's most successful opera. In French also, Brussels 3 November 1902.

MAJOR: *Erzsike*

(Eliza)

24 September. Budapest

Text by A. Radó. One act.

In German (translated by I. Major) given at Pressburg November 1906.

SAINT-SAËNS: *Les Barbares*

23 October. Paris, O.

Text by V. Sardou and P. B. Gheusi. Prologue and three acts.

In French also, Algiers February 1902; Barcelona 5 December 1908.

In Paris given until 1913; revived Monte Carlo 26 March 1914.

PFITZNER: *Die Rose vom Liebesgarten*

9 November. Elberfeld

Text by J. Grun. Prologue, 2 acts, and epilogue.

In German also given at Mannheim 24 January 1904; Munich 21 February 1904; Bremen 28 February 1904; Hamburg 12 January 1905; Vienna

6 April 1905; Prague 12 February 1909; Leipzig 15 October 1912; Strasbourg 9 February 1913; Berlin 14 December 1924..

Revived Vienna 25 March 1926; Frankfort 5 May 1939 (in a revised version).

LEONI: *Ib and Little Christina*

14 November. London, Savoy

Text by B. Hood (founded on the story by H. C. Andersen). *A Picture in 3 Panels.*

Revived London, Daly's 11 January 1904.

In German given at Prague 12 March 1905.

MASSENET: *Grisélidis*

20 November. Paris, O.C.

Text by P. A. Silvestre and E. Morand (*conte lyrique*). Prologue and 3 acts.

Given at:

NICE 20 January 1902 (in French).

ALGIERS March 1902 (in French).

BRUSSELS 18 March 1902 (in French).

MILAN, T.L. 25 November 1902 (in Italian, translated by A. Galli).

ZURICH 6 February 1903 (in German, translated by A. Ehrenfeld).

TUNIS April 1903 (in French).

BUENOS AIRES 14 July 1903 (in Italian).

CAIRO Carnival 1904 (in Italian).

GENEVA 23 December 1904 (in French).

LISBON February 1905 (in Italian).

NEW YORK 19 January 1910 (in French).

CHICAGO 12 January 1917 (in French).

Revived Paris, O. 29 November 1922; Brussels 14 March 1932; Toulouse March 1939.

R. STRAUSS: *Feuersnot*

21 November. Dresden

Text by E. von Wolzogen (*Ein Singgedicht*). One act.

After *Guntram* (see 1894) this was Strauss's first greater success as an opera composer. Subsequently given at Frankfort 3 December 1901; Bremen 30 April 1902, etc. Also given at:

VIENNA 29 January 1902 (in German).

BERLIN 28 October 1902 (in German).

LONDON, H.M.'s 9 July 1910 (in English, translated by W. Wallace).

BRUSSELS, M. 16 March 1911 (in French, translated by J. Marnold).

PRAGUE 12 November 1912 (in Czech, translated by K. Šipek).

MILAN, SC. 16 November 1912 (in Italian, translated by O. Schanzer).

BUENOS AIRES 9 August 1913 (in Italian, translated by O. Schanzer).

Outside Germany, some of the latest revivals were at Philadelphia 1 December 1927 (in German); Genoa 1 March 1938 (in Italian).

KOVAŘOVIČ: *Na Starém Bělidle*
(At the old Bleaching Ground)

22 November. Prague, Cz.

Text by K. Šipek (founded on Božena Němcová's novel *Babička*, the same on which Horák's opera, see 1900, is based). Four acts.

Kovařovič's most successful work; frequently revived on Czech stages. The latest revival at Prague was on 5 September 1935.

G. OREFICE: *Chopin*

25 November. Milan, T.L.

Text by A. Orvieto. Four acts.

Orefice's most successful opera (no doubt, owing to the fact that the greater part of the music is founded upon melodies of Chopin himself).

Outside Italy given at:

WARSAW 11 April 1904 (in Polish, translated by M. Gawalewicz).

BUENOS AIRES 5 May 1904 (in Italian).

PRAGUE 17 March 1905 (in German, translated by F. Werner).

PARIS, TH.S.B. 13 June 1905 (in Italian).

MONTREAL 1912 (in Italian).

ZAGREB 13 March 1915 (in Croatian, translated by A. Mitrović).

Revived in Polish at Warsaw Spring 1933. In Italian Malta 1935–36.

BLOCKX: *De Bruid der Zee*
(The Bride of the Sea)

30 November. Antwerp

(Flemish) text by N. de Tière. Three acts.

After *Herbergprinses* (see 1896), Blockx's second great success as a composer of Flemish folk opera. Frequently revived in Belgium. Given at:

BRUSSELS 18 October 1902 (in French, translated by G. Lagye).

ROUEN 14 January 1903, Lille 2 April 1903, etc. (in French).

FRANKFORT 20 October 1903 (in German, translated by H. Marion).

AMSTERDAM February 1904 (in Dutch).

HAGUE March 1904 (in French).

ALGIERS February 1905 (in French).

GENEVA 20 March 1906 (in French).

The latest revival at Brussels was on 8 October 1925.

1902

PEDRELL: *I Pirenei*

4 January. Barcelona

(Original Catalan) text by V. Balaguer, produced in an Italian version by C. M. Arteaga Pereira. Prologue and 3 acts.

The first part of a trilogy, the two other parts of which, *La Celestina*, and *Raimundo Lulio* were never performed. Pedrell's chief work.

Also given at Buenos Aires 10 September 1910 (in Spanish, translated by G. Hermes).

The prologue had been heard at the Liceo Benedetto Marcello, Venice on 12 March 1897 already.

REZNICEK: *Till Eulenspiegel*

12 January. Carlsruhe

Text by the composer. Two parts and epilogue.

Berlin 5 May 1903, etc. Revived in a revised version Cologne 17 June 1937.

WEINGARTNER: *Orestes*

15 February. Leipzig

Text by the composer (founded on Aeschylus's trilogy). Three parts.

Given at Nuremberg 27 April 1902; Berlin 14 June 1902; Hamburg 19 March 1903; Frankfort 19 April 1903, etc. In German also, Prague 6 May 1909.

DLUSKI: *Urvasi*

February. Lemberg

(Polish) text by the composer. Two acts.

Also given at St. Petersburg 25 March 1902 (in Russian); a private performance in concert form had taken place at St. Petersburg in June 1901 already.

MASSENET: *Le Jongleur de Notre-Dame*

18 February. Monte Carlo

Text by M. Léna (*miracle*). Three acts.

One of Massenet's best and most successful works. Subsequently given at:

HAMBURG 24 September 1902 (in German, translated by H. Marion).

PARIS, O.C. 10 May 1904 (in French).

BRUSSELS 25 November 1904 (in French).

GENEVA 29 November 1904 (in French).

ALGIERS January 1905 (in French).

HAGUE 30 January 1905 (in French).

MILAN, T.L. 18 October 1905 (in Italian, translated by B. Montelioi).

BERLIN, K.O. 23 November 1905 (in German).

LISBON March 1906 (in Italian).

LONDON, C.G. 15 June 1906 (in French).

NEW YORK 27 November 1908 (in French).

BUENOS AIRES 2 July 1911 (in French) and 15 July 1915 (in Italian).

GRAZ November 1911 (in German).

VIENNA 23 December 1911 (in German).

MONTREAL 1912 (in French).

ZAGREB 21 December 1912 (in Croatian, translated by A. Kassowitz-Cvijić).

LEMBERG 1912 and Warsaw April 1923 (in Polish, translated by A. Kiczman).

PRAGUE Spring 1914 (in Czech).

RIO DE JANEIRO 15 September 1915 (in Italian).

BARCELONA 14 February 1919 (in French).

LJUBLJANA 1920 (in Slovenian).

The 100th performance at the O.C., Paris, was on 1 February 1909; last revived there 12 December 1933. Revived at the Scala, Milan 9 March 1938.

E. MOÓR: *La Pompadour*

22 February. Cologne

(German) text by L. von Ferro and A. L. Moór (the composer's wife), after Musset. Two acts.

The first opera of the Hungarian composer.

Revived London, Savoy 26 January 1911 (in English, translated by A. Grein).

FRANCHETTI: *Germania*

11 March. Milan, Sc.

Text by L. Illica. Prologue, 2 acts, and epilogue.

Successful in Italy where it was frequently revived until 1930.

Outside Italy given at:

BUENOS AIRES 13 July 1902 (in Italian).

MONTEVIDEO 21 August 1902 (in Italian).

LISBON 18 February 1903 (in Italian).

ODESSA 5 January 1904 (in Italian).

ST. PETERSBURG September 1905 (in Russian).

LONDON, C.G. 13 November 1907 (in Italian).

CARLSRUHE 10 November 1908 (in German, translated by A. Brüggemann).

MALTA 1909 (in Italian).

NEW YORK, M. 22 January 1910 (in Italian).

RIO DE JANEIRO 2 June 1910 (in Italian).

GERMAN: *Merrie England*

2 April. London, Savoy

Text by B. Hood. Two acts.

The most popular of German's operettas. Frequently revived on English stages; the latest revival on a professional stage in London was at the Prince's 6 September 1934.

SMYTH: *Der Wald*

9 April. Berlin, O.

(German) text by the composer. Prologue, 1 act, and epilogue.

In German also given at London, C.G. 18 July 1902; New York, M. 11 March 1903; Strasbourg 21 February 1904.

(It is incorrectly stated in some books of reference that this opera had its first production at Dresden in September 1901. See the chapter *A Winter of Storm* in the composer's autobiographical *Streaks of Life*, 1921.)

BUSTINI: *Maria Dulcis*

15 April. Rome, C.

Text by E. Checchi (founded upon Berlioz's story *Vicenza* published in his *Les Soirées de l'Orchestre*, 1853). Three acts.

Bustini's only performed opera.

DEBUSSY: *Pelléas et Mélisande*

30 April. Paris, O.C.

Text: M. Maeterlinck's play (1892), with slight alterations. Five acts.

Debussy's chief work and one of the most important modern operas in general. It was not given on any other stage until 1907.

In Paris, the opera had 103 performances until 1914 (100th: 28 January 1913); it was revived after the war (and after the composer's death) on 9 May 1919, reached the 200th performance on 26 August 1929 and has been given at the O.C. more than 250 times to date.

Maeterlinck, who had protested against the production of the opera in 1902, did not hear the work until 27 January 1920 (in New York).

Outside France, given at:

BRUSSELS 9 January 1907 (in French); Lyons 1 April 1908, etc.

FRANKFORT 19 April 1907 (in German, translated by O. Neitzel); Munich 9 October 1908, etc.

NEW YORK 19 February 1908 (in French); Boston 1 April 1909; Chicago 5 November 1910, etc.

MILAN, SC. 2 April 1908 (in Italian, translated by C. Zangarini) and 17 May 1925 (in French); Rome 28 March 1909, etc.

PRAGUE 28 September 1908 (in German) and 1 November 1921 (in Czech).

BERLIN, K.O. 6 November 1908 (in German).

LONDON, C.G. 21 May 1909 (in French) and H.M.'s 6 June 1924 (in English).

VIENNA 23 May 1911 (in German).

BUENOS AIRES 12 August 1911 (in French) and 4 September 1920 (in Italian).

GENEVA 8 March 1912 (in French).

BIRMINGHAM 19 September 1913 (in English, translated by E. Evans).

ST. PETERSBURG 1 November 1915 (in Russian).

BARCELONA, TIVOLI 1919 (in French); Catalan version by J. Pena published 1931.

ANTWERP 11 February 1920 (in Flemish).

RIO DE JANEIRO Summer 1920 (in Italian).

ZAGREB 12 December 1923 (in Croatian).

MONTE CARLO 6 March 1924 (in French).

LISBON Carnival 1925 (in Italian?).

COPENHAGEN 9 October 1925 (in Danish, translated by K. Friis Møller and P. Wiedemann).

BUDAPEST 26 November 1925 (in Hungarian, translated by S. Várady).

STOCKHOLM 18 January 1926 (in Swedish).

AMSTERDAM 10 November 1927 (in French).

WARSAW 25 March 1928 (parts only, in concert form).

CHAPÍ: *Circe*

7 May. Madrid, T.L.

Text by M. Ramos Carrión. Three acts.

This Spanish opera was written for the inauguration of the new Teatro Lirico, Madrid.

In Spanish also given at Buenos Aires 25 October 1910.

P. and L. HILLEMACHER: *Orsola*

21 May. Paris, O.

Text by P. B. Gheusi. Three acts.

The only work of the two brothers which was produced at the Paris Opéra. Unsuccessful; five performances only.

RENDANO: *Consuelo*

24 May. Turin, T.V.E.

Text by F. Cimmino (founded on the novel by G. Sand). Prologue and 3 acts.

Rendano's only opera. Given at Stuttgart 27 March 1903 (in German, translated by A. Harlacher); revived in German, Nuremberg 1924.

COQUARD: *La Troupe Jolicœur*

30 May. Paris, O.C.

Text by the composer (founded on a story by H. Cain). *Comédie musicale*, prologue and 3 acts.

Coquard's last opera; given 10 times only and never revived.

BUNNING: *Princesse Osra*

14 July. London, C.G.

(French) text by M. Bérenger (founded on a story by A. Hope). Three acts.

Bunning's only opera. English translation by R. H. Elkin published 1902.

BLECH: *Das war ich*

6 October. Dresden

Text by R. Batka (founded on a play by J. Hutt, 1805). One act.

Blech's first success as an opera composer.

In German also given at Prague 15 October 1902; Zurich 22 December 1902; Berlin 28 March 1903; Vienna 28 February 1905; Strasbourg 1906.

In Hungarian (translated by D. Vidor), Budapest 22 December 1903.

RIMSKY-KORSAKOV: *Servilia*
Сервилія

14 October. St. Petersburg

Text by the composer (founded on a play by L. A. Mei). Five acts.

First given at Moscow 15 November 1904. Never produced outside Russia.

ABBATE: *Matelda*

6 November. Kharkov

Text by V. Soldani. One act.

In Italian also given at Modena 23 November 1904; Malta 1907.

The only performed opera of Abbate, one of the last representatives of the 19th-century type of wandering maestro; he was a conductor in South America, Egypt, Holland, Russia, etc.

CILEA: *Adriana Lecouvreur*

6 November. Milan, T.L.

Text by A. Colautti (founded on the play by Scribe and Legouvé). Four acts.

Cilea's most successful work. Still given in Italy.

Outside Italy, produced at:

LISBON 1903 (in Italian).
BARCELONA 1903 (in Italian).
BUENOS AIRES 7 July 1903 (in Italian).
HAMBURG 15 November 1903 (in German, translated by F. Werner).
WARSAW November 1903 (in Italian).
GENEVA 4 December 1903 (in French).
CAIRO Carnival 1904 (in Italian).
ANTWERP 12 January 1904 (in French).
ODESSA Spring 1904 (in Italian).
LONDON, C.G. 8 November 1904 (in Italian).
PARIS, TH.S.B. 2 May 1905 (in Italian).
MALTA 1905 (in Italian).
ST. PETERSBURG February 1906 (in Russian).
NEW ORLEANS 5 January 1907 (in French).
NEW YORK, M. 18 November 1907 (in Italian).
HAGUE January 1925 (in Italian).
SOFIA 13 January 1933 (in Bulgarian).
BUDAPEST 2 January 1934 (in Hungarian, translated by K. Nádasdy).
MONTE CARLO March 1934 (in Italian).
BORDEAUX 30 January 1935 (in French).
TRIPOLIS March 1935 (in Italian).
BUCHAREST Spring 1936 (in Rumanian).
RIGA 3 September 1936 (in Lettish).
BERLIN, D.O. 24 March 1938 (in German).
LJUBLJANA 16 March 1940 (in Slovenian).

C. A. NIELSEN: *Saul og David*

28 November. Copenhagen

Text by E. Christiansen. Four acts.

Nielsen's first opera; successful on Danish stages, revived at Copenhagen 6 December 1912 and 27 February 1929. Also given in Swedish at Gothenburg 1929 and Stockholm 13 January 1931.

NAPRAVNIK: *Francesca da Rimini*

Франческа да Римини

9 December. St. Petersburg

Text by O. O. Paleček and E. P. Ponomarev (founded on the play by Stephen Phillips). Four acts.

Napravnik's last opera. (Date of first performance according to the yearbook of the Russian Imperial Theatres.)

HAHN: *La Carmélite*

16 December. Paris, O.C.

Text by C. Mendès. Four acts.

The first opera of the French-Venezuelan composer. Performed 17 times.

GOLDMARK: *Berlichingen Götz*

16 December. Budapest

(Original German) text by A. M. Willner (from Goethe's play), Hungarian version by S. Várady. Five acts.

In German (with some alterations), Frankfort 1 February 1903; Linz 17 November 1904; Brünn 18 March 1905. Revived (in a revised version), Vienna 18 May 1910.

DE BOECK: *En Winternachtsdroom*

(A Winter Night's Dream)

20 December. Antwerp

(Flemish) text by L. Du Catill. One act (2 scenes.)

Revived in French (translated by B. Lagye), Nantes 30 March 1913; Brussels 21 December 1923.

RIMSKY-KORSAKOV:

Kashchey Bessmyertny

Кащей Безсмертный

(The Immortal Kashchey)

25 December. Moscow

Text by the composer. One act (3 scenes).

First given at St. Petersburg 9 April 1905. Outside Russia:

BARCELONA 23 December 1924 (in Russian).

SALZBURG 7 August 1928 (in Russian; concert performance, by a company from Leningrad).

DORTMUND 15 October 1929 (in German, as *Unhold Ohneseele*, translated by A. Bernhard).

STOCKHOLM 25 April 1930 (in Swedish).

RIGA 21 May 1931 (in Lettish).

1903

d'INDY: *L'Étranger*

7 January. Brussels, M.

Text by the composer (*action musicale*). Two acts.

d'Indy's most important work for the stage. Given at the Opéra, Paris 4 December 1903 and revived there 31 October 1934.

In French also, Geneva 14 November 1913; Hague 5 February 1920; Barcelona 4 February 1921.

In Italian, Buenos Aires 14 June 1917 and Rio de Janeiro 3 September 1917.

A Catalan version by J. Pena was published in 1908.

DOPPER: *Het Eerekruis*

(The Cross of Honour)

19 January. Amsterdam

Text by H. Engelen. One act.

Revived Amsterdam 1910.

MASSENET: *Marie-Magdeleine*

9 February. Nice

Text by L. Gallet. Three acts.

Originally performed as an oratorio at the Odéon, Paris 11 April 1873 and elsewhere. On the stage, it was first given at Nice, and subsequently, in French, at The Hague April 1903; Paris, O.C. 12 April 1906; Brussels 16 April 1908; Algiers March 1910.

d'HARCOURT: *Le Tasse*

14 February. Monte Carlo

Text by J. and P. Barbier. Three acts.

In French also, Bordeaux 7 April 1905; Antwerp 22 March 1906; Geneva 2 February 1912.

HUBAY: *Moharózsa*

(Moss-Rose)

21 February. Budapest

(Original German) text by M. Rothauser (founded on Ouida's *Two Little Wooden Shoes*), Hungarian version by B. Cziglányi. Four acts.

DUPUIS: *Jean Michel*

4 March. Brussels, M.

Text by H. Vallier and G. Garnir. Four acts.

Dupuis's first opera. Successful in Belgium; Antwerp 3 February 1905; Liége 17 February 1906, etc.

MISSA: *Muguette*

18 March. Paris, O.C.

Text by M. Carré fils and G. Hartmann (like Hubay's Hungarian opera, produced 4 weeks earlier, founded on Ouida's *Two Little Wooden Shoes*). Four acts.

Missa's most successful work; given at the O.C. 18 times. Outside France:

GENEVA 10 November 1903 (in French).

HAMBURG 28 April 1904 (in German, translated by L. Hartmann).

MOSCOW January 1905 (in Russian).

LONDON, H.M.'s 25 May 1910 (in English, translated by W. Wallace).

HAESER: *Hadlaub*

19 March. Zurich

Text by the composer (founded on a story by G. Keller). Three acts.

TERRASSE: *Le Sire de Vergy*

16 April. Paris, Variétés

Text by R. de Flers and G. A. de Caillavet. Three acts.

Terrasse's first successful operetta. Given at:

ALGIERS January 1904 (in French).

MILAN 15 December 1904 (in Italian).

LONDON, APOLLO 30 September 1905 (in English, translated by A. Sturgess, additional music by T. Wendt).

BRUSSELS 5 January 1907 (in French).

Frequently revived in France; one of the latest revivals was at Monte Carlo December 1931.

C. ROSSI: *Nadeya*

5 May. Prague, G.

(Original Italian) text by L. Illica, German version by R. Batka. Prologue and 3 acts.

In the original Italian: Mantua 16 January 1904; revived Spezia 21 August 1920; Carpi Summer 1925.

PETERSON–BERGER: *Ran*

20 May. Stockholm

Text by the composer. Three acts.

Peterson-Berger's first opera; the text had been published in 1898.

KLOSE: *Ilsebill*

7 June. Carlsruhe

Text by H. Hoffmann (*Dramatische Symphonie*), founded on a tale by the brothers Grimm. Five scenes.

Munich 29 October 1905, etc. Revived Basle 3 January 1923, etc.

MISSA: *Maguelone*

20 July. London, C.G.

(French) text by M. Carré fils. One act.

In French also given at Besançon 28 July 1904; Geneva 15 March 1905; Paris, Gaîté 31 March 1909.

HOWLAND: *Sarrona*

3 August. Bruges

(English) text by the composer. Prologue and 1 act.

In Italian (translated by R.P.G.), Florence, T. Alfieri 3 February 1906 and subsequently on other Italian stages.

In English, New York, Amsterdam Th. 8 February 1910.

In German, Philadelphia 23 March 1911.

MACALPIN: *The Cross and the Crescent*

22 November. London, C.G.

(Anonymous) text founded on J. Davidson's English version of F. Coppée's play *Pour la Couronne.* Four acts.

Awarded the Charles Manners prize of £250 for the best English opera.

BLECH: *Alpenkönig und Menschenfeind*

1 October. Dresden

Text by R. Batka (founded on F. Raimund's play of the same title). Three acts.

Successful on German stages. Given at Zurich 11 December 1903; Prague 26 December 1903; Graz 14 April 1904; Riga 30 December 1904; Berlin, Kroll's 12 May 1906; Vienna, V.O. 2 March 1911.

Revived in a new version (as *Rappelkopf*), Berlin, O. 2 October 1917.

GILSON: *Prinses Zonneschijn* (Princess Sunshine)

10 October. Antwerp

(Flemish) text by P. de Mont. Four acts.

In French (translated by M. Lefèvre), Brussels 9 September 1905.

GRECHANINOV: *Dobrinya Nikitich* Добрыня Никитичъ

27 October. Moscow

Text by the composer. Three acts.

Grechaninov's first opera. Previously performed in concert form at Count Sheremetiev's. Revived Petrograd 30 September 1916.

CARYLL: *The Duchess of Dantzic*

17 October. London, Ly.

Text by H. Hamilton (from V. Sardou's *Madame Sans-Gêne*). Three acts.

The best of Caryll's numerous operettas. When first produced, ran for 236 nights. Frequently

revived on English stages; the latest professional revival in London was at Daly's 26 April 1932.

POLDINI: *A Csavargó és Királylány* (The Vagabond and the Princess)

17 October. Budapest

(Original German) text by A. F. Seligmann (from H. C. Andersen's story), Hungarian version by S. Várady. One act.

Poldini's first and most successful opera.

In the original German given at Prague 29 March 1906; London, C.G. 11 May 1906; Breslau 31 March 1907 Strasbourg January 1909; Vienna, V.O. 11 October 1917.

BUNGERT: *Odysseus' Tod*

30 October. Dresden

Text by the composer. Prologue and 3 acts.

The last part of his tetralogy, *Homerische Welt* (see 1896, 1898, 1901).

REBIKOV: *Yelka* Елка (The Christmas Tree)

30 October. Moscow

Text by S. I. Plaksin. One act (4 scenes).

Rebikov's most successful work for the stage; given in many Russian towns; also at Prague 27 November 1906 (in Czech, translated by B. Kalenský); Ljubljana 1907 (in Slovenian).

Revived Leningrad 15 January 1921; London, Fortune Th. 17 February 1934 (in Russian).

GERLACH: *Liebeswogen*

7 November. Bremen

Text by the composer (after H. Heine). *Gesprochene Oper.* One act.

Revived in a new version as *Das Seegespenst*, Altenburg 24 April 1914.

d'ALBERT: *Tiefland*

15 November. Prague, G.

Text by R. Lothar (founded on a Catalan play, *Terra Baixa*, by A. Guimerá, 1896). Prologue and 3 acts.

d'Albert's most popular work and the most successful opera of the German veristic school. Given with some alterations at Leipzig 17 February 1904 and all over Germany. First performed at:

STRASBOURG 18 April 1906 (in German).

ANTWERP 1 December 1906 (in Flemish).

BERLIN, K.O. 9 October 1907 (in German; given there more than 400 times; first produced at the O. 8 February 1916).

ZURICH 9 October 1907 (in German).

RIGA November 1907 (in German) and 2 November 1920 (in Lettish).

VIENNA 25 February 1908 (in German).

LAIBACH (LJUBLJANA) 1908 (in German) and 1909 (in Slovenian).

STOCKHOLM 9 October 1908 (in Swedish, translated by S. Nyblom).

AMSTERDAM 23 October 1908 (in German) and January 1931 (in Italian).

BUDAPEST 17 November 1908 (in Hungarian, translated by S. Várady).

NEW YORK, M. 23 November 1908 (in German) and Century O.H. 17 March 1914 (in English).

COPENHAGEN 21 October 1909 (in Danish, translated by J. Lehmann).

BARCELONA 18 January 1910 (in Italian, translated by F. Fontana).

LONDON, C.G. 5 October 1910 (in English, translated by R. H. Elkin).

ZAGREB 18 November 1910 (in Croatian, translated by F. Miler).

WARSAW March 1911 (in Polish, translated by I. Ziolkowski).

NICE 21 March 1911 (in French, translated by J. Bénédict).

GENEVA 21 November 1911 (in French, translated by J. Bénédict).

ROUEN 13 December 1911 (in French, translated by J. Bénédict).

REVAL (TALLINN) 1912 (in German) and 1923 (in Estonian).

OSLO 12 December 1913 (in Norwegian).

PETROGRAD 14 December 1915 (in Russian); revived 18 April 1926.

HELSINKI 8 January 1921 (in Swedish) and 9 January 1931 (in Finnish).

CLUS (CLAUSENBURG) 1924 and Bucharest Spring 1933 (in Rumanian).

SOFIA 13 January 1928 (in Bulgarian).

KAUNAS 21 February 1928 (in Lithuanian).

MONTE CARLO March 1931 (in French).

BRUSSELS 7 November 1932 (in French).

CAIRO 1937 (in German).

Successful as the opera was all over the world, it does not appear to have ever been produced either in Italy or in Paris.

WOLF-FERRARI:
Die neugierigen Frauen
27 November. Munich

(Original Italian) text by L. Sugano (founded on Goldoni's *Le Donne curiose*), German version by H. Teibler. Three acts.

Wolf-Ferrari's first great success; given at:

BERLIN, TH.D.W. 14 January 1905 (in German).

STRASBOURG 1905 (in German).

VIENNA 4 October 1905 (in German).

PRAGUE 8 October 1905 (in German).

ANTWERP 28 October 1905 (in Flemish).

RIGA November 1905 (in German).

WARSAW December 1905 (in Polish).

BUDAPEST 24 April 1906 (in Hungarian, translated by D. Vidor).

STOCKHOLM 15 May 1907 (in Swedish, translated by E. Grandinson).

NEW YORK, M. 3 January 1912 (for the first time in the original Italian).

MILAN, SC. 16 January 1913 (for the first time in Italy).

LJUBLJANA 1926 (in Slovenian).

Revived at Berlin 20 June 1928 and still given on German and other stages.

DAVIDOV: *Potonuvshy Kolokol*
Потонувши Колоколъ
(The Sunken Bell)
29 November. St. Petersburg

Text by V. P. Burenin (founded on the play by G. Hauptmann). Four acts.

The only opera of A. Davidov (who was a nephew of the famous 'cellist Karl Davidov). Also given in German at Mayence 30 September 1908.

(CHAUSSON): *Le Roi Arthus*

30 November. Brussels, M.

Text by the composer. Three acts.

The only opera of Chausson which was produced (four years after his death). The third act was revived at the Opéra, Paris 30 March 1916.

The statement that *Le Roi Arthus* was first produced at Carlsruhe in 1900, to be found in Riemann's *Musiklexikon*, Vol.I, p.301, and in many other books of reference, is not correct. Mottl intended a production of the opera; but it did not take place.

MANÉN: *Acté*

3 December. Barcelona, L.

(Catalan) text by the composer. Four acts.

The most successful opera of the famous violinist.

In German (translated by E. Schultz-Henke), Dresden 22 January 1908; Riga 1910.

Revived in a new version (as *Nero und Akte*), Carlsruhe 28 January 1928; Barcelona April 1933.

In Finnish, Helsinki 1 October 1938.

KYUI: *Mademoiselle Fifi*
Мадемуазель Фифи

15 December. Moscow

Anonymous text (founded on Maupassant's story). One act.

St. Petersburg January 1905, etc.

Kyui's opera was announced for performance in London in 1915; owing to lack of public support the season at the London Opera-House (under V. Rosing) came to a premature close and the performance did not take place.

GIORDANO: *Siberia*

19 December. Milan, Sc.

Text by L. Illica. Three acts.

Very successful in Italy, and also given at:

TRIESTE 20 March 1904 (in Italian).

LISBON 1904 (in Italian).

BUENOS AIRES 21 June 1904 (in Italian).

CAIRO Carnival 1905 (in Italian).

PARIS, TH.S.B. 4 May 1905 (in Italian) and O. 9 June 1911 (in French).

GENEVA 8 December 1905 (in French, translated by P. Milliet).

NICE 18 December 1905 (in French, translated by P. Milliet).

NEW ORLEANS 13 January 1906 (in French, translated by P. Milliet).

ANTWERP 8 February 1906 (in French, translated by P. Milliet).

MARSEILLES 29 March 1906 (in French, translated by P. Milliet).

STUTTGART 4 November 1906 (in German, translated by O. Neitzel).

ZURICH November 1907 (in German, translated by O. Neitzel).

NEW YORK 5 February 1908 (in Italian).

VIENNA, V.O. 18 October 1911 (in German).

BERLIN, K.O. 1 November 1911 (in German).

BUDAPEST 2 February 1912 (in Hungarian, translated by Z. Harsányi).

MALTA 1920 (in Italian).

Still given in Italy; revived Milan, Sc. 5 December 1927 (with alterations) and, lately, Milan, Castello 25 July 1939.

LEROUX: *La Reine Fiammette*

23 December. Paris, O.C.

Text by C. Mendès. Four acts.

One of Leroux's most successful operas.

In French also produced at Geneva 6 February 1906; Hague March 1906; Antwerp 8 November 1906; Cairo, Carnival 1907; Lisbon December 1909; Buenos Aires 24 April 1911; New York 24 January 1919.

In Czech (translated by O. Smrčka), Prague 13 October 1907.

Revived at the O.C., Paris 4 February 1910; 27 March 1919; and 21 May 1935.

First given at Brussels 30 September 1939.

1904

JANÁČEK: *Její Pastorkyňa*
(Her Foster-Daughter)

21 January. Brno

Text by the composer (founded on a story by G. Preissová). Three acts.

The first opera of the Moravian composer which was produced. The performance passed almost unnoticed at that time, and it was only many years later that the opera became famous under the new title of *Jenufa*. First given at the Czech opera-house, Prague 26 May 1916, and subsequently translated into German by M. Brod (from whose version most other translations were taken).

Given at:

VIENNA 16 February 1918 (in German) and 4 May 1929 (in Czech, by a company from Bratislava).

COLOGNE December 1918 (in German).

ZAGREB 29 June 1920 (in Croatian, translated by M. Nehajev).

LJUBLJANA 28 October 1922 (in Slovenian, translated by N. Štritov).

BERLIN 17 March 1924 (in German).

NEW YORK, M. 6 December 1924 (in German).

BASLE 30 October 1925 (in German).

PRAGUE September 1926 (for the first time there in German).

LEMBERG 1926 (in Polish).

BUCHAREST 1926 (in Rumanian).

ANTWERP 8 January 1927 (in Flemish).

HELSINKI 21 March 1928 (in Finnish).

S. WAGNER: *Der Kobold*

29 January. Hamburg

Text by the composer. Three acts.

One of the composer's most successful works; in German also given at Prague 27 November 1904; Graz 3 December 1904; Vienna, V.O. 18 January 1905; Riga February 1906; Berlin, Kroll's 6 July 1910 (revived O. 6 June 1939).

MELCER: *Marya*

16 February. Warsaw

Text founded on A. Malczewski's poem (like many other Polish operas of the same title). Three acts.

Melcer's first opera and the only one which was produced.

PUCCINI: *Madama Butterfly*

17 February. Milan, Sc.

Text by G. Giacosa and L. Illica (from D. Belasco's dramatization of a story by J. L. Long). Originally in 2 acts.

Given at the Scala one night only.

Produced in the final 3-act version at Brescia 28 May 1904 and all over Italy.

Outside Italy given at:

BUENOS AIRES 2 July 1904 (in Italian).

MONTEVIDEO 27 August 1904 (in Italian).

ALEXANDRIA 19 December 1904 (in Italian).

CAIRO February 1905 (in Italian).

LONDON, C.G. 10 July 1905 (in Italian) and Lyric 16 August 1907 (in English); 100th performance at C.G. 29 November 1919.

BUDAPEST 12 May 1906 (in Hungarian, translated by S. Várady).

WASHINGTON 15 October 1906 (in English, translated by R. H. Elkin).

NEW YORK 12 November 1906 (in English) and 11 February 1907 (in Italian).

PARIS, O.C. 28 December 1906 (in French, translated by P. Ferrier); 100th performance 10 April 1912.

SAN FRANCISCO 11 March 1907 (in English).

BARCELONA 4 August 1907 (in Spanish).

RIO DE JANEIRO 6 September 1907 (in Italian).

BERLIN 27 September 1907 (in German, translated by A. Brüggemann).

PRAGUE 30 September 1907 (in German) and 14 February 1908 (in Czech, translated by V. J. Novotný).

VIENNA 31 October 1907 (in German).

MADRID 20 November 1907 (in Italian).

LISBON March 1908 (in Italian).

ODESSA March 1908 (in Italian).

MALTA 1908 (in Italian).

WARSAW 1908 (in Polish, translated by A. Kiczman).

LJUBLJANA 1908 (in Slovenian).

RIGA October 1908 (in German) and 1924 (in Lettish).

STOCKHOLM 21 August 1909 (in Swedish, translated by S. Nyblom).

AMSTERDAM Spring 1909 (in French).

CHRISTIANIA 22 April 1909 (in Norwegian).

BRUSSELS 29 October 1909 (in French).

ZURICH November 1909 (in German).

GENEVA 30 November 1909 (in French).

SAIGON Spring 1910 (in French).

SYDNEY April 1910 (in English).

ZAGREB 7 October 1910 (in Croatian, translated by F. Miler).

CONSTANTINOPLE January 1911 (in Italian).

COPENHAGEN 15 October 1911 (in Danish, translated by E. Christiansen).

JOHANNESBURG March 1912 (in English).

REVAL (TALLINN) 1912 (in German) and 1927 (in Estonian, translated by A. Simm and J. Zeiger).

PETROGRAD November 1915 (in Russian).

SHANGHAI 1918 (in Russian).

HELSINKI 14 January 1920 (in Swedish) and 31 March 1927 (in Finnish).

BUCHAREST Spring 1920 (in Rumanian).

BELGRADE 1922 (in Serbian).

SOFIA 2 June 1924 (in Bulgarian).

KAUNAS 25 September 1924 (in Lithuanian).

TUNIS Carnival 1927 (in Italian).

TOKYO 1930 (in Italian).

ATHENS November 1931 (in Italian).

TRIPOLIS November 1934 (in Italian).

SAINT-SAËNS: *Hélène*

18 February. Monte Carlo

Text by the composer. Four acts.

Written for Nellie Melba.

In French also given at London, C.G. 20 June 1904.

In Italian (translated by A. Galli), Milan, T.L. 26 November 1904.

In German, Frankfort 14 January 1905.

First given in Paris, O.C. 18 January 1905 and revived at the Opéra 20 June 1919.

RABAUD: *La Fille de Roland*

16 March. Paris, O.C.

Text by P. Ferrier (founded on a play by H. de Bornier). Four acts.

Revived Brussels 7 October 1921; Paris, O. 27 October 1922.

DVOŘÁK: *Armida*

25 March. Prague, Cz.

Text by J. Vrchlický (founded on his Czech translation of Tasso's *La Gerusalemme liberata*). Four acts.

Dvořák's last opera. Revived Prague 30 December 1928; Brno February 1935.

DELIUS: *Koanga*

30 March. Elberfeld

(Original English) text by C. F. Keary (from G. W. Cable's novel *The Grandissimes*), German version probably by the composer or his wife. Prologue, 3 acts and epilogue.

Given in London, C.G. as late as 23 September 1935 (in the original English, text revised by T. Beecham and E. Agate).

KOSMOVICI and SCHMEIDLER: *Marioara*

8 May. Bucharest

Text from Carmen Sylva's play of the same title. Three acts.

Successful Rumanian opera.

Given in German at Prague 6 May 1905; Nuremberg April 1906; Czernowitz 28 December 1912; Vienna, V.O. 7 June 1914.

SOMMER: *Rübezahl und der Sackpfeifer von Neisse*

15 May. Brunswick

Text by E. König. Four acts.

Sommer's most popular work.

Given at Berlin 15 February 1905 and on many other German stages.

FILIASI: *Manuel Menendez*

15 May. Milan, T.L.

Text by V. Bianchi and A. Anile. One act.

Along with Dupont's *La Cabrera* (see next entry), awarded the first prize in the fourth (and last) Concorso Sonzogno, 1902.

Successful in Italy; also given at:

ZURICH 30 November 1904 (in German, translated by G. Droescher).

WARSAW December 1904 (in Italian).

CAIRO Carnival 1905 (in Italian).

BRESLAU April 1905 (in German).

LISBON 1905 (in Italian).

BUENOS AIRES 6 July 1905 (in Italian).

PRAGUE 2 November 1905 (in German).

DUPONT: *La Cabrera*

16 May. Milan, T.L.

(Original French) text by H. Cain, Italian version by A. Galli. One act.

The second prize-opera in the Concorso Sonzogno (see preceding entry); more successful than *Manuel Menendez*. Given at:

ZURICH 30 November 1904 (in German, translated by F. M. La Violette).

BUDAPEST 15 December 1904 (in Hungarian, translated by S. Várady).

WARSAW December 1904 (in Italian).

CAIRO Carnival 1905 (in Italian).

FRANKFORT 14 January 1905 (in German).

PARIS, O.C. 5 May 1905 (in the original French).

LISBON 1905 (in Italian).

PRAGUE 2 November 1905 (in German).

MOSCOW 1908 (in Russian).

Given in France until about 1930.

STATKOWSKI: *Philaenis*

14 September. Warsaw

(Original German) text by H. Erler, Polish version by the composer.

Awarded the first prize in the Moody-Manners Competition, London 1903.

Successful in Poland; revived at Warsaw as late as 1925.

GILSON: *Zeevolk*

15 October. Antwerp

(Original French) text by G. Garnir (founded on Victor Hugo's poem *Les pauvres Gens*), Flemish version by ? Two acts.

In French (as *Gens de Mer*), revived at Brussels 16 December 1929.

RIMSKY-KORSAKOV: *Pan Voyevoda*

Панъ Воевода

16 October. St. Petersburg

Text by I. F. Tyumenev. Four acts.

First produced at the inauguration of Prince Tsereteli's private opera.

First given at Moscow 17 September 1905.

In Polish, Warsaw Autumn 1905.

Revived at Leningrad, Conservatoire June 1935.

TERRASSE: *Monsieur de la Palisse*

2 November. Paris, Variétés

Text by R. de Flers and G. A. de Caillavet. Three acts.

Successful operetta. Given at:

BRUSSELS 4 November 1905 (in French).

MUNICH 21 April 1906 (in German, as *Der Kongress von Sevilla*).

BUDAPEST 12 January 1907 (in Hungarian).

ZAGREB 10 October 1907 (in Croatian, translated by F. Miler).

BOLOGNA 24 November 1909 (in Italian).

BERLIN, NEUES OPERETTENTH. 11 May 1912 (in German).

Revived Paris, Tr.L. 24 December 1924 and Gaîté-Lyrique 7 October 1930.

ALFANO: *Risurrezione*

30 November. Turin, T.V.E.

Text by C. Hanau (from Tolstoi's novel). Four acts.

Alfano's most successful work. Given at:

BRUSSELS 18 April 1906 (in French, translated by P. Ferrier).

BERLIN, K.O. 5 October 1909 (in German, translated by A. Brüggemann).

MODENA 18 February 1911 (in Italian, with alterations).

NOVARA 18 February 1911 (in Italian, with alterations).

MADRID 21 December 1911 (in Italian, with alterations).

Revived:

NICE 8 March 1925 (in French).

CHICAGO 31 December 1925 (in French).

PARIS, O.C. 14 April 1927 and 10 April 1934 (in French).

SANTIAGO, CHILE Summer 1928 (in Italian).

TURIN, T.R. 6 January 1936 (in Italian).

BERLIN, V.O. 4 October 1938 (as *Katjuscha*, new German version by E. Orthmann and H. Hartleb).

LEONCAVALLO: *Der Roland von Berlin*

13 December. Berlin, O.

(Original Italian) text by the composer (founded on W. Alexis's novel of the same title, 1840, which was dramatized for Leoncavallo by E. Taubert), German version by G. Droescher. Four acts.

The opera was commissioned by the Emperor William II. Successful at Berlin, given there 37 times until 1908.

In the original Italian produced at Naples, S.C. 19 January 1905.

OSTRČIL: *Vlasty Skon* (Vlasta's Death)

14 December. Prague, Cz.

Text by K. Pippich. Three acts.

Ostrčil's first opera. The text had originally been written for Fibich.

GIANNETTI: *Cristo alla Festa di Purim*

19 December. Rio de Janeiro

Text founded on G. Bovio's play of the same title. One act.

The most important opera of the Neapolitan composer (who died at Rio de Janeiro in 1934).

In Italian also given at Turin 5 December 1905 and Madrid 26 February 1911.

1905

CHELIUS: *Die vernarrte Prinzess*

15 January. Schwerin

Text by O. J. Bierbaum. Three acts.

The best of Chelius's three operas. Revived Brunswick 8 March 1913; Cologne 12 May 1918.

MARTY: *Daria*

27 January. Paris, O.

Text by A. Aderer and A. Ephraïm (founded on a story by V. G. Korolenko). Two acts.

Marty's second and last opera. Also given in Swedish at Stockholm 7 October 1907.

MONTEMEZZI: *Giovanni Gallurese*

28 January. Turin, T.V.E.

Text by F. d'Angelantonio. Three acts.

Montemezzi's first opera. Milan 11 November 1905, etc.

Revived New York, M. 19 February 1925 (in Italian).

MASSENET: *Chérubin*

14 February. Monte Carlo

Text by F. de Croisset and H. Cain (*comédie chantée*). Three acts.

In French also given at Paris, O.C. 23 May 1905; Antwerp 23 November 1905; Brussels 16 December 1905; Geneva 20 November 1908.

In German (translated by O. Neitzel), Magdeburg 10 April 1908.

ESPOSITO: *Il Borghese Gentiluomo*

February. Moscow

Text by P. de Luca (after Molière). Three acts.

One of the latest Italian operas which had its original production in Russia.

In Italian also given at Milan, T. Fossati 22 May 1906.

By Eugenio, not Michele Esposito, to whom the opera is ascribed in Riemann's *Musiklexikon*.

BRUNEAU: *L'Enfant Roi*

3 March. Paris, O.C.

Text by E. Zola. Five acts.

This was the last of three original librettos Zola wrote for Bruneau (see *Messidor*, 1897; *L'Ouragan* 1901; nearly all other operas of Bruneau are founded upon Zola's works). Given in Paris 12 times in 1905; never revived.

RESPIGHI: *Re Enzo*

12 March. Bologna, T. del Corso

Text by A. Donini (from Tassoni's poem *La Secchia rapita*, 1622). Three acts.

Respighi's first opera.

MASCAGNI: *Amica*

16 March. Monte Carlo

(French) text by "P. Bérel" (pseudonym of P. de Choudens), adapted for the stage by P. Collin. Two acts.

The only opera Mascagni wrote to French words. Given at:

ROME 13 May 1905 (in Italian, translated by G. Targioni-Tozzetti).

BUENOS AIRES 8 August 1905 (in Italian, translated by G. Targioni-Tozzetti).

NÎMES 17 August 1905 (in French; open-air performance).

RIO DE JANEIRO 28 September 1905 (in Italian).

MOSCOW November 1905 (in Russian).

ROUEN 6 December 1905 (in French).

STETTIN 11 February 1906 (in German, translated by O. Neitzel).

BARCELONA 1 January 1907 (in Italian).

ODESSA March 1908 (in Italian).

MALTA 1912 (in Italian).

Still occasionally revived in Italy; Milan, Castello 15 July 1939, etc.

LE BORNE: *Les Girondins*

25 March. Lyons

Text by "Delormeil and P. Bérel" (pseudonyms of A. Lénéka and P. de Choudens). Four acts.

In German (translated by O. Neitzel), Cologne 18 December 1910. First given at Paris, Gaîté 12 January 1912.

ZICHY: *Nemo*

30 March. Budapest

Text by the composer. Prologue and 3 acts.

The second part of a *Rákóczi* trilogy (see 1909 and 1912); this second part was produced first. Successful in Hungary; given at Budapest until 1918.

In German (translated by M. R. Abele), Pressburg 15 February 1906; Breslau 4 December 1906.

HUMPERDINCK: *Die Heirat wider Willen*

14 April. Berlin, O.

Text by H. Humperdinck (the composer's wife), from A. Dumas's *Les Demoiselles de Saint-Cyr*. Three acts.

In German also given at Brünn 14 November 1905; Strasbourg 3 May 1906.

Revived Leipzig 7 April 1935 (revised by W. Humperdinck and A. Vogl).

J. B. FOERSTER: *Jessika*

16 April. Prague, Cz.

Text by J. Vrchlický (founded on Shakespeare's *The Merchant of Venice*). Three acts.

Successful on Czech stages; revived at Prague 19 October 1911; 16 January 1920; 17 September 1928; and 29 December 1934. German version by R. Batka published 1910.

JAQUES-DALCROZE: *Onkel Dazumal*

25 May. Cologne

(Original French) text by Franc-Nohain (*Le Bonhomme Jadis*, after H. Murger), first produced in a German version by F. Karmin. One act.

Jaques-Dalcroze's most successful work.

In German also given at Berlin, K.O. 1 November 1906.

In the original French at Paris, O.C. 9 November 1906; Tunis March 1908; Marseilles 10 February 1909; Antwerp 25 March 1909; Monte Carlo 7 December 1909.

Revived Geneva 9 January 1919; Nice December 1922; Paris, Tr.L. 25 March 1925.

WEBBER: *Fiorella*

7 June. London, Waldorf Th.

(Original French) text by V. Sardou and B. P. Gheusi, Italian version by G. Macchi. One act.

Webber's only opera. Revived in English by the R.C.M., London 12 March 1928.

LEONI: *L'Oracolo*

28 June. London, C.G.

Text by C. Zanoni (from C. B. Fernald's story *The Cat and the Cherub*). One act.

Leoni's most successful work; in Italian also given at New York 4 February 1915; Philadelphia 10 April 1917; Chicago 28 June 1919; Rio de Janeiro 18 July 1921; Buenos Aires 21 September 1921.

Revived New York, M. 26 March 1926 and 23 November 1931.

K. MOOR: *Hjoerdis*

22 October. Prague, Cz.

Text by F. Khol (from Ibsen's play *Haermaendene paa Helgeland*). Four acts.

The most important work of the Czech composer.

GEORGES: *Miarka*

7 November. Paris, O.C.

Text by J. Richepin (founded on his novel *Miarka la Fille à l'Ourse*, 1883). Prologue and 4 acts.

Georges's best-known work. Revived Paris, O. 16 January 1925.

SAMARA: *Mademoiselle de Belle-Isle*

9 November. Genoa, Politeama

(Original French) text by P. Milliet (after Dumas), Italian version by A. Galli. Four acts.

In Italian also given at Monte Carlo 6 February 1906; Milan 30 September 1906, etc.; Constantinople Spring 1907.

In German, Berlin, K.O. 28 April 1909.

d'ALBERT: *Flauto Solo*

12 November. Prague, G.

Text by H. von Wolzogen. One act.

Successful comic opera.

In German also given at Stuttgart 25 January 1906; Zurich 30 April 1906; Strasbourg 1906; Riga September 1906; Vienna 28 November 1906.

In Flemish, Antwerp March 1909.

Revived Berlin, D.O. 29 December 1922.

STOJANOVITS: *A Tigris*
(The Tiger)

14 November. Budapest.

Text by S. Várady (translated from a German libretto by R. von Perger). One act.

Stojanovits's first opera.

GOETZL: *Zierpuppen*

15 November. Prague, G.

Text by R. Batka (founded on Molière's *Les Précieuses ridicules*). One act.

Goetzl's most successful opera.

Berlin, K.O. 1 November 1906; Graz 8 November 1906; Zurich February 1909.

Given on German stages until 1930.

COERNE: *Zenobia*

1 December. Bremen

Text by O. Stein. Three acts.

The only opera of the American composer which was performed.

GNECCHI: *Cassandra*

5 December. Bologna, T.C.

Text by L. Illica. Prologue and 2 parts.

Revived in a new version, Ferrara 29 February 1908.

In German (translated by L. Hartmann), Vienna, V.O. 29 March 1911.

In Italian, Philadelphia 26 February 1914.

Gnecchi's first opera; it was the subject of a musical sensation in 1909, when the Italian critic, G. Tebaldini, pointed out striking similarities between the *Elektra* of R. Strauss and Gnecchi's *Cassandra* (see *R.M.I.*, March 1909: *Telepatia Musicale*).

R. STRAUSS: *Salome*

9 December. Dresden

Text: Oscar Wilde's drama, as translated into German by H. Lachmann. One act.

The work which established Strauss's fame as one of the leaders of modern opera.

Salome (at Dresden conducted by Ernst von Schuch) was next given in Germany at Breslau 28 February 1906 (under Prüwer); Nuremberg 18 May 1906 (under Ottenheimer); Leipzig 25 May 1906 (under Hagel); Cologne 2 July 1906 (under Strauss himself).

Subsequently given at:

PRAGUE 5 May 1906 (in German) and 17 January 1923 (in Czech, translated by K. Kovařovič).

GRAZ 16 May 1906 (in German; for the first time under the composer's direction).

BERLIN 5 December 1906 (in German; given there 285 times until 1933).

TURIN 22 December 1906, Milan, Sc. 26 December 1906. Naples 1 February 1908, etc. (in Italian, translated by A. Leawington).

NEW YORK 22 January 1907 (in German) and 28 January 1909 (in French).

BRUSSELS 25 March 1907 (for the first time in French, translated by J. de Marliave and P. Gailhard) and 20 February 1914 (in German).

ZURICH 26 April 1907 (in German).

PARIS, CHÂTELET 8 May 1907 (in German) and O. 6 May 1910 (in French).

VIENNA 25 May 1907 (in German; at the Deutsches Volks Th. by the Breslau company); at the O. only 14 October 1918.

AMSTERDAM September 1907 (in German) and November 1907 (in Italian).

WARSAW 15 October 1907 (in Polish).

STOCKHOLM 14 April 1908 (in Swedish).

LISBON 1909 (in Italian).

BARCELONA 29 January 1910 (in Italian).

MADRID 16 February 1910 (in Italian).

BUENOS AIRES 13 June 1910 (in Italian).

RIO DE JANEIRO 15 July 1910 (in Italian).

LONDON, C.G. 8 December 1910 (in German).

CAIRO February 1911 (in Italian).

BUDAPEST 19 December 1912 (in Hungarian, translated by A. Pásztor).

COPENHAGEN Spring 1913 (in German, by the Kiel company) and 26 April 1919 (in Danish, translated by J. Lehmann).

ZAGREB 15 May 1915 (in Croatian, translated by A. Mitrović).

RIGA 24 February 1923 (in Lettish, translated by R. Egle).

MOSCOW Spring 1925 (in Russian, translated by S. Levik and R. Serken).

BUCHAREST Spring 1926 (in Rumanian, translated by Cocorescu).

ANTWERP 6 December 1927 (in Flemish).

LJUBLJANA 18 June 1828 (in Slovenian, translated by N. Štritov).

HELSINKI 9 April 1930 (in Finnish).

BELGRADE 1932 (in Serbian).

ALGIERS December 1933 (in French).

Spanish version by L. París y Cadenas published 1910; another by Eugenio Orrego Vicuna published Buenos Aires 1935.

WIDOR: *Les Pêcheurs de Saint-Jean*

26 December. Paris, O.C.

Text by H. Cain. Four acts.

Widor's most successful opera.

In French also, Geneva 2 April 1907; Antwerp 24 March 1908; Algiers November 1910; Hague March 1912. Revived Marseilles 18 January 1917.

In German (translated by O. Neitzel), Frankfort 15 April 1906.

LEHÁR: *Die lustige Witwe*

30 December. Vienna, W.

Text by V. Léon and L. Stein. Three acts.

The most successful of Lehár's operettas; given all over the world; the following records are only a very limited selection.

In German, Hamburg 3 March 1906; Brünn 25 March 1906; Prague 15 April 1906; Berlin, Berliner Th. 1 May 1906; Riga December 1906; Trieste 27 February 1907; Bucharest Spring 1907; Constantinople 26 February 1909; New York 15 November 1911.

In Czech (translated by P. Nebeský and J. Foman), Prague 1906.

In Norwegian, Christiania 26 December 1906.

In Russian, St. Petersburg 29 December 1906.

In Swedish, Stockholm 22 January 1907.

In Croatian (translated by G. Prejac), Zagreb 20 February 1907.

In Italian (translated by F. Fontana), Milan 27 April 1907.

In English (translated by E. Morton, lyrics by A. Ross), London, Daly's 8 June 1907 (running for 778 nights; revived Daly's 19 May 1923, for 222 nights; Ly. 28 May 1924 for 223 nights; Hippodrome 29 September 1932); New York, New Amsterdam Th. 21 October 1907 (in German, Weber's 15 November 1911; revived Knickerbocker's 5 September 1921; Jolson's 2 December 1929; Erlanger's 7 September 1931); Johannesburg 30 March 1908; Melbourne 16 May 1908.

In Spanish (translated by Manuel Linares Rivas y Astray and Federico Reparaz) Madrid 8 February 1909. Two other Spanish versions were published, by Bruno Güell 1910, and by A. Roger Junoi, Barcelona 1913.

In French (translated by R. de Flers and G. de Caillavet), Paris, Th. Apollo 28 April 1909 (1,000th performance 16 January 1914; revived Th. Apollo 17 April 1925; Gaîté Lyrique 1 September 1934); Brussels 6 January 1910.

In Polish (translated by A. Kiczman), Poznań 1909.

In Portuguese, Lisbon 1916.

In Lettish (translated by V. Zibelis), Jelgava (Mitau) 1929; Riga 11 March 1933.

In Finnish (translated by J. Finne), Helsinki 30 January 1934.

1906

MORERA: *Emporium*

20 January. Barcelona

(Original Catalan) text by E. Marquina, produced in an Italian version by A. Bignotti. Three acts.

The most important opera of Morera, who was a pupil of Pedrell.

Revived at Barcelona February 1929.

RAKHMANINOV: *Skupoy Ritsar*
Скупой Рыцарь
(The Miserly Knight)

RAKHMANINOV: *Francesca da Rimini*
Франческа да Римини

24 January. Moscow

Skupoy Ritsar: 3 scenes, text from Pushkin's dramatic scene; *Francesca da Rimini*: prologue, 2 scenes, and epilogue, text by M. I. Chaikovsky.

Two short operas, produced on the same bill. *The Miserly Knight* was also given at Boston 2 December 1910 (apparently in German, translated by F. Fiedler; Baklanov sang the name part); Leningrad 20 May 1921.

CONVERSE: *The Pipe of Desire*

31 January. Boston

Text by G. E. Barton. One act.

New York 18 March 1910 (first work by an American composer produced at the Metropolitan Opera House). Revived Boston 6 January 1911.

STATKOWSKI: *Marya*

February. Warsaw

Text founded on A. Malczewski's poem (cf. 16 February 1904; there are other operas on the same subject by M. Soltys, Lemberg 8 March 1910; by W. Gawroński, not performed; and by H. Opieński, Poznań 1924). Three acts.

Revived Warsaw February 1921.

DE LARA: *Sanga*

21 February. Nice

Text by E. Morand and P. de Choudens. Three acts. Paris, O.C. 9 December 1908.

SAINT-SAËNS: *L'Ancêtre*

24 February. Monte Carlo

Text by L. Augé de Lassus. Three acts.

In French also, Toulouse 5 January 1907; Paris, O.C. 23 January 1911; Montreal 1912; Antwerp 12 December 1912.

In German (translated by R. Batka), Prague 1 April 1908.

GATTY: *Greysteel; or, The Bearsarks come to Surnadale*

1 March. Sheffield

Text by R. Gatty (the composer's brother), founded on G. W. Dasent's translation of the Icelandic saga of *Gisli, the Soursop*. One act.

Gatty's first opera. London, Crystal Pal. 24 May 1906 and Lyric 6 September 1907.

Revived in an enlarged two-act version London, Sadler's Wells 23 March 1938.

(BIZET): *Don Procopio*

10 March. Monte Carlo

(Original Italian) text[1] by C. Cambiaggio (first set by Vincenzo Fioravanti and others in 1844), produced in a French version by P. de Choudens and P. Collin. Two acts.

The opera was written in 1858 and recovered from among Auber's possessions after his death. Produced in 1906 with French recitatives by C. Malherbe.

In French also given at Barcelona, T. del Bosque Summer 1907; in Italian, Rome 19 April 1908.

WOLF-FERRARI: *Die vier Grobiane*

19 March. Munich

(Original Italian) text by G. Pizzolato (from Goldoni's *I quattro Rusteghi*), German version by H. Teibler. Four acts.

[1] The original text is a reduced version of Prividali's *I Pretendenti delusi*, see 1811.

A typical example of an opera which had only a short vogue after its first production, and was "discovered" again many years later.

Given at:

BERLIN, TH.D.W. 21 March 1906 (in German); revived O. 23 April 1937.

MILAN, T.L. 2 June 1914 (in Italian); revived Rome 5 January 1940.

ZURICH November 1923 (in German).

BUENOS AIRES 21 June 1927 (in Italian).

BUDAPEST 12 February 1928 (in Hungarian, translated by V. Lányi).

BRÜNN 1928 (in German).

MOSCOW March 1933 (in Russian).

VIENNA 25 February 1934 (in German).

DRESDEN 1 September 1934 (in German).

ZAGREB 18 December 1934 (in Croatian).

LJUBLJANA 25 December 1934 (in Slovenian, translated by M. Polič).

KAUNAS 26 April 1935 (in Lithuanian).

BRUSSELS 18 March 1938 (in French, translated by G. Dalman).

BUCHAREST 5 November 1938 (in Rumanian).

C. ERLANGER: *Aphrodite*

27 March. Paris, O.C.

Text by L. de Gramont (founded on the novel by P. Louÿs). Five acts.

Very successful in Paris; the 100th performance at the O.C. was on 15 October 1913; given there about 180 times until 1927.

In French also, Brussels 4 December 1919; New York 27 February 1920.

FRANCHETTI: *La Figlia di Jorio*

29 March. Milan, Sc.

Text from G. d'Annunzio's *tragedia pastorale* of the same title (1904). Three acts.

In Italian also given at Buenos Aires 9 August 1906.

RASSE: *Deidamia*

3 April. Brussels, M.

Text by the composer and L. Solvay (from A. de Musset's *La Coupe et les Lèvres*). Four acts.

The first opera of the Belgian composer.

In French also given at Amsterdam Spring 1909; Antwerp 28 January 1913.

F. d'ERLANGER: *Tess*

10 April. Naples, S.C.

Text by L. Illica (founded on Thomas Hardy's *Tess of the d'Urbervilles*). Four acts.

In Italian also given at London, C.G. 14 July 1909.

In German (translated by P. Somogyi), Chemnitz 15 January 1911.

In Hungarian (translated by D. Vidor), Budapest 9 April 1911.

PAHISSA: *La Presó de Lleida*
(The Prison of Leyden)

14 April. Barcelona, T. Principal

Text by A. Gual. Five scenes.

Successful Catalan opera; Pahissa's first work for the stage.

Afterwards expanded to three acts as *La Princesa Margarida*, Barcelona, L. 8 February 1928. Revived Barcelona February 1936.

GANNE: *Hans, le Joueur de Flûte*

14 April. Monte Carlo

Text by M. Vaucaire and G. Mitchell. Three acts.

The most successful of Ganne's light operas. Still popular on French stages.

Given at:

MILAN 5 December 1907 (in Italian, translated by C. Zangarini).

BUENOS AIRES 10 May 1910 (in Italian, translated by C. Zangarini).

PARIS, TH. APOLLO 31 May 1910 (in French).

NEW YORK 20 September 1910 (in English, translated by A. S. Brennan).

BRUSSELS 15 December 1910 (in French).

BRESLAU 17 December 1910 (in German, translated by F. Falzari).

Last revived in Paris, Gaîté Lyrique 17 February 1937.

MASSENET: *Ariane*

31 October. Paris, O.

Text by C. Mendès. Five acts.

In French also, Brussels 23 November 1907, etc.; Algiers April 1909.

In Italian (translated by A. Leawington), Turin 19 December 1907; Buenos Aires 6 August 1908.

Revived Bordeaux 1924; Paris 21 February 1937 (at the re-opening of the Opéra after the fire of 1936).

DORET: *Les Armaillis*

9 November. Paris, O.C.

Text by H. Cain and D. Baud-Bovy. Two acts.

The most successful opera of the Swiss composer.

In French also given at Geneva 20 December 1907; Liége June 1908; Antwerp 9 November 1909.

In German (translated by H. Marion), Zurich 9 November 1910.

Revived (in an enlarged 3-act version), Paris, O.C. 5 May 1930; Strasbourg October 1933.

SMYTH: *Strandrecht*

11 November. Leipzig

(Original French) text adapted from a Cornish drama, *Les Naufrageurs*, by H. Brewster, produced in a German version by H. Decker and J. Bernhoff. Three acts.

Smyth's most successful opera. In German also, Prague 12 December 1906.

In London first produced in concert form at Queen's Hall 30 May 1908 (under Nikisch); on the stage, H.M.'s 22 June 1909 (as *The Wreckers*, translated into English by the composer and A. Strettell).

Revived in a revised version, London, Sadler's Wells 19 April 1939.

C. A. NIELSEN: *Maskarade*

11 November. Copenhagen

Text by V. Andersen (after Holberg). Three acts.

Regarded as the best Danish comic opera of

modern times; revived at Copenhagen 17 February 1918 and 21 February 1928.

FINO: *Il Battista*

13 November. Turin, T.V.E.

Text by S. Fino, the brother of the composer. *Azione sacra.* Three acts.

In Italian also, Amsterdam 11 December 1907; Buenos Aires 20 August 1910.

In Croatian (translated by I. Vojnović), Zagreb 22 May 1909.

PIZZI: *Vendetta*

1 December. Cologne

Text by A. Kaiser. Prologue and 3 acts.

Revived Bergamo 14 September 1926 (in Italian, as *Ivania*, translated by A. Lega).

SCHILLINGS: *Moloch*

8 December. Dresden

Text by E. Gerhäuser (founded on F. Hebbel's tragedy). Three acts.

Schwerin 10 March 1907, etc.

In German also, Prague 1909. Revived Berlin, D.O. 7 November 1934.

1907

LAMOTE DE GRIGNON: *Hesperia*

25 January. Barcelona, L.

Text by J. O. Bridgman. One act.

The first opera of the Spanish composer. Given at Madrid in 1909.

BRUNEAU: *Naïs Micoulin*

2 February. Monte Carlo

Text by the composer (from E. Zola's story, *La Douleur de Toine*). Two acts.

Never given in Paris.

MONLEONE: *Cavalleria rusticana*

5 February. Amsterdam

(Italian) text by G. Monleone (the brother of the composer), founded on the play by G. Verga. One act.

In Italian also, London, Coronet 10 May 1909 and (according to reports in contemporary papers) also at Athens, Marseilles, Vienna and Breslau (these performances I could not verify).

In Hungarian, Budapest 17 January 1908.

The opera was also produced in Italy, at the T. Vittorio Emanuele, Turin 10 July 1907. After that performance Mascagni and his publishers took action, and as a result of the proceedings the new *Cavalleria rusticana* had to be withdrawn. The music was then adapted to a new libretto, written expressly for that purpose by the composer's brother, and the new opera *La Giostra dei Falchi* was produced at Florence 18 February 1914 and Milan 5 September 1917.

MASSENET: *Thérèse*

7 February. Monte Carlo

Text by J. Claretie. Two acts.

One of the more successful of Massenet's later works. It was also given at:

BERLIN 11 December 1907 (in German, translated by O. Neitzel).

ALGIERS February 1908 (in French).

GENEVA 18 February 1908 (in French).

TUNIS March 1908 (in French).

ANTWERP 1 April 1909 (in French).

LISBON November 1909 (in French).

PARIS, O.C. 19 May 1911 (in French).

BRUSSELS 28 October 1911 (in French).

NAPLES, T. BELLINI 28 November 1911 (in Italian, translated by A. Leawington).

COPENHAGEN 22 September 1918 (in Danish, translated by J. Lehmann).

LONDON, C.G. 22 May 1919 (in French).

Revived Paris, O.C. 6 February 1930; Brussels 17 November 1930.

RIMSKY-KORSAKOV: *Kitezh*

20 February. St. Petersburg

Text by V. I. Byelsky. Four acts.

The full title reads: *Skazanye o nevidimom gradye Kitezh i dyeve Fevronye* (Сказаніе о невидимомъ градѣ Китежь и дѣвѣ Февроніе; *The Legend of the invisible City of Kitezh and the Maiden Fevronia*).

One of Rimsky-Korsakov's most successful works. Given at Moscow 28 February 1908 and frequently revived in Russia. Outside Russia given at:

BARCELONA 2 January 1926 (in Russian); Catalan version by J. Pena and R. J. Slaby published in that year.

LONDON, C.G. 30 March 1926 (in Russian, in concert form).

PARIS, O. 7 July 1926 (in Russian, in concert form) and Ch.É. 19 February 1929 (in Russian, on the stage); French vocal score (translated by A. Komarov) published.

RIGA 7 September 1926 (in Lettish).

BUENOS AIRES 14 September 1929 (in Russian).

ANN ARBOR, MICH. 21 May 1932 (in concert form; in English, translated by L. Pargment).

MILAN, SC. 30 December 1933 (in Italian, translated by R. Küfferle).

BRNO 8 November 1934 (in Czech).

DUISBURG 14 May 1935 (in German, translated by E. Brockmann-Neubauer).

ZAGREB 21 September 1935 (in Croatian).

PHILADELPHIA 4 February 1936 (in Russian).

NEW YORK 3 March 1936 (in Russian).

KAUNAS 22 November 1936 (in Lithuanian).

BERLIN 29 May 1937 (in German).

PRAGUE 22 April 1938 (in Czech).

BRUSSELS 30 April 1939 (in concert form; in Russian).

DELIUS: *Romeo und Julia auf dem Dorfe*

21 February. Berlin, K.O.

(German) text by the composer (founded on a story by G. Keller). Prologue and 3 acts.

Delius's most important opera.

In English (as *A Village Romeo and Juliet*), London, C.G. 22 February 1910; revived there 19 March 1920 and once more at the R.C.M. 27 June 1934.

STRAUS: *Ein Walzertraum*

2 March. Vienna, Ca.

Text by F. Dörmann and L. Jacobson. Three acts.

Straus's most successful operetta. Given at Ber-lin, Th.d.W. 21 December 1907 and all over Germany, Austria, etc.

In German also, Riga 1907; Laibach 1907, etc.

In Croatian (translated by J. Dević), Zagreb 23 November 1907.

In Rumanian, Bucharest 17 March 1908.

In English (translated by J. W. Herbert), Philadelphia 6 January 1908; New York, Broadway Th. 27 January 1908; London, Daly's 7 March 1908 (lyrics by A. Ross). Given in German at Weber's, New York 25 December 1911. Revived in English, London, Winter Garden 20 December 1934.

In Italian (translated by R. Nigri), Milan 19 November 1908.

In French (translated by L. Xanrof and J. Chancel), Brussels 30 January 1910; Paris, Th. Apollo 3 March 1910; revived Paris, Porte St. Martin 11 June 1934.

In Spanish (translated by Felipe Pérez Capo, music adapted by Manuel Peris) Granada 24 May 1910.

ABRÁNYI: *Monna Vanna*

2 March. Budapest.

Text by E. Abrányi, the father of the composer, founded on the play by M. Maeterlinck. Three acts.

The best opera of the Hungarian composer.

ARROYO: *Amore e Perdizione*

March. Lisbon, S.C.

(Italian) text by F. Braga (from a Portuguese novel, *Amor de Perdição*, by C. C. Branco). Three acts.

The only opera by a Portuguese composer which was also produced in Germany (as *Liebe und Verderben*, translated by L. Hartmann), Hamburg 25 January 1910.

ZELENSKI: *Stara Baśń* (The Old Tale)

14 March. Lemberg

Text by A. Bandrowski (founded on a story by J. I. Kraszewski). Four acts.

The last opera of the Polish composer.

GRELINGER: *Op Hoop van Zegen*
(On Board the "Hope of Blessing")

March. Amsterdam

(Dutch) text founded on H. Heijermans's play of the same title). Four acts.

Successful in Holland. Revived at The Hague October 1929.

In German (translated by W. Ehrenberg), Berlin, Morwitz Oper 11 July 1908.

WETZ: *Das ewige Feuer*

19 March. Düsseldorf

Text by the composer. One act.

Wetz's only performed opera. Hamburg 26 February 1908, etc.

LEROUX: *Théodora*

19 March. Monte Carlo

Text by V. Sardou and P. Ferrier. Five acts.
Also given at:
BERLIN 11 April 1907 (in French, by the Monte Carlo company).
BUENOS AIRES 10 August 1907 (in Italian, translated by A. Leawington).
MARSEILLES 11 March 1909 (in French).
MILAN, SC. 18 April 1909 (in Italian).

CILEA: *Gloria*

15 April. Milan, Sc.

Text by A. Colautti. Three acts.

Revived in a new version, Naples 20 April 1932 (text revised by E. Moschino).

In German (translated by A. Neisser), Dortmund October 1938.

FOURDRAIN: *La Légende du Pont d'Argentan*

17 April. Paris, O.C.

Text by H. Cain and A. Bernède. One act.

Successful in France. In French also, Lisbon December 1909. Revived Paris, O.C. 17 October 1922.

In Flemish, Antwerp 9 November 1909.

DUKAS: *Ariane et Barbe-Bleue*

10 May. Paris, O.C.

Text: M. Maeterlinck's play (1902), with slight alterations. Three acts.

Dukas's only opera. Successful in Paris. Also given at:
VIENNA, V.O. 2 April 1908 (in German, translated by H. La Violette).
BRUSSELS 2 January 1909 (in French).
NEW YORK 29 March 1911 (in French).
MILAN, SC. 17 April 1911 (in Italian, translated by G. Pozza).
BUENOS AIRES 7 July 1912 (in Italian) and 22 May 1934 (in French).
MADRID 15 February 1913 (in Italian).
BASLE 16 October 1923 (in French).
PRAGUE 20 May 1925 (in German).
AMSTERDAM 20 November 1935 (in French).
LONDON, C.G. 20 April 1937 (in French).
ANTWERP November 1938 (in Flemish).

Revived in Paris, O.C. 3 May 1921 and O. 26 December 1934.

LE BORNE: *La Catalane*

24 May. Paris, O.

Text by P. Ferrier and L. Tiercelin (founded, like d'Albert's *Tiefland*, see 1903, on A. Guimerá's *Terra Baixa*). Prologue and 3 acts.

Unsuccessful; given 9 times only and never revived.

(GLEASON): *Otho Visconti*

4 June. Chicago

Text by the composer. Three acts.

The only opera by the American composer which was performed (if only some years after his death).

MESSAGER: *Fortunio*

5 June. Paris, O.C.

Text by R. de Flers and G. A. de Caillavet (from A. de Musset's *Le Chandelier*). Five acts.

Successful in France; reduced to 4 acts, Paris, O.C. 12 November 1910; revived there 12 June

1915 and still occasionally given on French provincial stages.

Outside France given at:

ANTWERP 12 November 1907 and Brussels 4 January 1908 (in French).

BUDAPEST 22 December 1907 (in Hungarian, translated by S. Várady).

PRAGUE 25 September 1909 (in Czech, translated by J. Vymětal).

LISBON December 1909 (in French).

BUENOS AIRES 11 July 1911 (in French).

BITTNER: *Die rote Gret*

26 October. Frankfort

Text by the composer. Three acts.

Bittner's first opera. Also given at Vienna 10 April 1908; Brünn May 1909 (in German).

FALL: *Die Dollarprinzessin*

2 November. Vienna, W.

Text by A. M. Willner and F. Grünbaum. Three acts.

The most successful of Fall's numerous operettas. Given at:

BERLIN, N. SCHSPH. 6 June 1908; in German also, Riga 1908, etc.

MANCHESTER 24 December 1908 (in English, translated by B. Hood, lyrics by A. Ross).

LONDON, DALY'S 25 September 1909 (in English, translated by B. Hood, lyrics by A. Ross).

ATLANTIC CITY, N.Y. 30 August 1909 (in English, translated by G. Grossmith).

NEW YORK 6 September 1909 (in English, translated by G. Grossmith).

VENICE 13 February 1909 (in Italian).

MADRID 16 October 1909 (in Spanish, translated by Felipe Pérez Capo, music adapted by Manuel Peris and Enrique Brú).

ZAGREB 21 January 1910 (in Croátian, translated by M. Pogačić).

PRAGUE 1910 (in Czech, translated by V. Mára).

POZNAŃ 1910 (in Polish, translated by A. Kiczman).

NICE 11 March 1911 (in French, translated by H. Gauthier-Villars and others).

PARIS, VAUDEVILLE 16 June 1911 (in German) and Scala 6 December 1911 (in French).

HELSINKI 14 April 1937 (in Finnish).

Like *Die lustige Witwe*, see 1905, and *Ein Walzertraum*, see above, 1907, and many other Viennese dance operettas of those years, *Die Dollarprinzessin* was produced sooner or later in most countries all over the world. The above dates are only a limited selection. When first produced in London, the operetta had a run of 428 nights; it was revived at Daly's 4 February 1925.

LEROUX: *Le Chemineau*

6 November. Paris, O.C.

Text by J. Richepin. Four acts.

Leroux's most successful work. Given at:

BRUSSELS 14 February 1908 (in French).

GENEVA 3 March 1908 (in French).

HAGUE April 1908 (in French).

BUDAPEST 23 May 1908 (in Hungarian, translated J. Heltai; revived 1933).

LISBON 1908 (in French).

DÜSSELDORF 20 December 1908 (in German, translated by O. Neitzel).

VIENNA 14 January 1909 (in German, translated by O. Neitzel).

PRAGUE 2 February 1909 (in Czech, translated by J. Vymětal).

LONDON, C.G. 12 October 1910 (in English, translated by W. Wallace).

NEW ORLEANS 11 February 1911 (in French).

MONTREAL 1912 (in French).

CHICAGO 25 January 1919 (in French).

NEW YORK 31 January 1919 (in French).

ANTWERP 2 October 1932 (in Flemish).

Still given in France and Belgium; last revived at the O.C., Paris 9 January 1936 and 10 February 1940; at Brussels 21 March 1939.

GIORDANO: *Marcella*

9 November. Milan, T.L.

(Original French) text by H. Cain and J. Adenis Italian version by L. Stecchetti. Three acts.

In French (re-translated by J. Nouguès) given at Nice April 1909.

In Italian, revived Milan, Sc. 23 April 1938.
German version by F. Wahl published 1913.

MANCINELLI: *Paolo e Francesca*

11 November. Bologna, T.C.

Text by A. Colautti. One act.

In Italian also, Lisbon March 1908; Buenos
Aires 4 July 1908; Barcelona 26 January 1911.
Revived Rome, T.R. 24 January 1931.

DE LARA: *Solea*

19 December. Cologne

(Original French) text by J. Richepin, German
version by O. Neitzel. Four acts.

In French, Rouen 25 February 1911.

1908

GOLDMARK: *Ein Wintermärchen*

2 January. Vienna, O.

Text by A. M. Willner (from Shakespeare's *A
Winter's Tale*). Four acts.

Goldmark's last opera. Also given at:
BUDAPEST 30 April 1908 (in Hungarian, translated
by L. Dóczy).
FRANKFORT 29 October 1908 (in German).
TURIN 27 January 1909 (in Italian, translated by O.
Schanzer).
MOSCOW 5 March 1909 (in Russian, translated by
Melnikov).
BERLIN 17 May 1909 (in German).
BRÜNN May 1909 (in German).

BLOCKX: *Baldie*

25 January. Antwerp

(Flemish) text by N. de Tière. Three acts.

Revived in a new version (as *Liefdelied*), Antwerp 6 January 1912.

MIHALOVICH: *Eliána*

16 February. Budapest

(Original German) text by H. Herrig (from
Tennyson's *Idylls of the King*), Hungarian version
by E. Abrányi. Three acts.

Mihalovich's last opera. In German, Vienna,
V.O. 17 April 1909.

LAPARRA: *La Habanera*

26 February. Paris, O.C.

Text by the composer. Three acts.

Laparra's most successful opera. Given at:
FRANKFORT 29 November 1908 (in German, trans-
lated by G. Droescher).
BERLIN 2 December 1908 (in German, translated
by G. Droescher).
BRUSSELS 25 March 1909 (in French).
LONDON, C.G. 18 July 1910 (in French).
BOSTON 14 December 1910 (in French).
MILAN, SC. 12 December 1912 (in Italian, trans-
lated by R. Barabandy and C. Vizzotto).
NEW YORK, M. 2 January 1924 (in French).

Revived Paris, O.C. 14 October 1922; 7 October 1930; 12 March 1935.

PACCHIEROTTI: *Eidelberga Mia!*

27 February. Genoa, C.F.

Text by A. Colantuoni (founded on W. Meyer-
Förster's play *Alt-Heidelberg*). Three acts.

In German (translated by O. Piltz), Vienna,
V.O. 12 February 1909; Breslau 11 February
1911.

In Italian, Buenos Aires 12 August 1909.

JAQUES-DALCROZE: *Les Jumeaux de Bergame*

30 March. Brussels, M.

Text by M. Léna (after Florian). Two acts.

Jaques-Dalcroze's last opera. Revived (in
French), Nice April 1913; Geneva 9 January 1919.

SAMARA: *Rhea*

11 April. Florence, T. Verdi

(Original French) text by P. Milliet, Italian version by A. Galli(?). Three acts.

Milan, Sc. 28 March 1910, etc. In Italian also,
Cairo 27 February 1911.

SCHJELDERUP: *Frühlingsnacht*

1 May. Dresden

Text by the composer. One act.

In Norwegian (as *Vaarnat*), Oslo 31 August 1915.

Revived in an enlarged 3-act version (as *Liebesnächte*), Lübeck 18 October 1934; in Norwegian, Oslo 21 May 1935.

MERIKANTO: *Pohjan Neito*
(The Maid of Bothnia)

18 June. Viipuri

Text by A. Rytkönen (from the *Kalevala*). Three acts.

This was the first opera ever composed to Finnish words; written in 1898. Produced at Viipuri (Viborg) in the open air. First given at Helsinki 17 November 1908.

PANIZZA: *Aurora*

5 September. Buenos Aires

(Original Spanish) text by E. Quesada, Italian version by L. Illica. Four acts.

The opera was commissioned by the Argentine Government for the opening season of the new Teatro Colón, Buenos Aires.

(GRIEG): *Olav Trygvason*

8 October. Christiania

Text by B. Björnson.

Grieg's only opera; he left it unfinished after his death in 1907. Three scenes only are complete which were first heard in concert form at Christiania 19 October 1889.

In 1908 they were given on the stage, on the same bill with Olson's Norwegian two-act opera *Lajla*. Grieg's scenes were revived at Los Angeles June 1934.

MARIOTTE: *Salomé*

30 October. Lyons

Text: Oscar Wilde's play in its original French version. One act.

In French also given at Paris, Gaîté 22 April 1910; Geneva 12 November 1910; Marseilles 29 November 1910. Revived Paris, O. 2 July 1919.

In Czech, Prague May 1911.

(Mariotte's opera, although produced 3 years after Strauss's *Salome*, was written earlier than its more successful rival).

BLECH: *Versiegelt*

4 November. Hamburg

Text by R. Batka and A. S. Pordes-Milo (from a play by S. Raupach, 1828). One act.

Blech's most popular work.

In German also, Berlin 2 December 1908; Strasbourg and Zurich February 1909; Vienna 4 October 1909; Prague 1911; Riga 1911; New York 20 January 1912; Philadelphia 30 January 1912, etc.

In Swedish, Stockholm 12 May 1910.

In Danish (translated by S. Levyson), Copenhagen 25 September 1910.

In Croatian (translated by G. Prejac), Zagreb 17 March 1916.

In Slovenian, Ljubljana Autumn 1923.

STRAUS: *Der tapfere Soldat*

14 November. Vienna, W.

Text by L. Jacobson and R. Bernauer (from G. B. Shaw's *Arms and the Man*). Three acts.

Compared with other Viennese operettas of those years *Der tapfere Soldat* was not so very successful in Austria and Germany; Berlin, Th. d. W. 23 December 1908, etc. In German also, Laibach 1910; Reval 1911, etc.

In England and America, however, it was the most popular of Straus's works. First given in English as *The Chocolate Soldier*, (translated by S. Stangé), New York, Lyric 13 September 1909; London, Ly. 10 September 1910 (running for 500 nights).

In Italian, Genoa 26 January 1910. In Spanish (translated by José Zaldívar) Barcelona 19 January 1911; (translated by José María Martín de Eugenio) Madrid 22 April 1911. In French (translated by P. Veber), Brussels 8 September 1911; Paris, Th. Apollo 7 November 1912.

Revived Monte Carlo December 1931 (in French). The so far latest revival in London was at the Golders Green Hippodrome 18 February 1941; in New York at St. J's 2 May 1934.

OSTRČIL: *Kunálovy Oči*
(Kunala's Eyes)
25 November. Prague, Cz.

Text by K. Mašek (from a novel by J. Zeyer). Three acts.
Revived Prague 24 February 1929.

ZANDONAI: *Il Grillo del Focolare*
28 November. Turin, Politeama

Text by C. Hanau (founded on Dickens's *The Cricket on the Hearth*). Three acts.
Zandonai's first opera. In French (translated by M. Vaucaire), Nice 20 February 1911.
Revived Faenza 11 October 1919 (in Italian).

1909

FÉVRIER: *Monna Vanna*
13 January. Paris, O.

Text by M. Maeterlinck (altered from his play of the same title, 1902). Four acts.
Février's most important work. Successful in France where it still holds the boards. Produced at:
BRUSSELS 27 January 1909 (in French).
GENEVA 18 January 1910 (in French).
SCHWERIN 13 October 1912 (in German, translated by H. Liebstöckl).
BERLIN, SCHILLER TH. 26 July 1913 (in German, translated by H. Liebstöckl).
BOSTON 5 December 1913 (in French).
NEW YORK 17 February 1914 (in French).
BUENOS AIRES 4 September 1919 (in Italian).
BARCELONA 5 January 1920 (in French).
MONTEVIDEO Autumn 1925 (in Italian).
RIO DE JANEIRO Summer 1926 (in Italian).
Revived at the Paris Opéra 2 February 1918 and 25 January 1937.

R. STRAUSS: *Elektra*
25 January. Dresden

Text by H. von Hofmannsthal (after Sophocles). One act.
The first libretto Hofmannsthal wrote for Strauss. The opera had not quite the same success as *Salome* four years earlier. Still, it was produced at:
BERLIN 15 February 1909 (in German).
VIENNA 24 March 1909 (in German).
MILAN, SC. 6 April 1909 (in Italian, translated by O. Schanzer).
NEW YORK 1 February 1910 (in French, translated by H. Gauthier-Villars) and 3 December 1932 (in German).
HAGUE 12 February 1910 (in German).
LONDON, C.G. 19 February 1910 (in German).
BUDAPEST 11 March 1910 (in Hungarian, translated by S. Várady).
PRAGUE 25 April 1910 (in Czech, translated by K. Kovařovič) and 4 May 1910 (in German).
BRUSSELS 26 May 1910 (in French) and 18 February 1914 (in German).
HULL 28 February 1912 (in English, translated by A. Kalisch).
ST. PETERSBURG 3 March 1913 (in Russian, translated by M. A. Kuzmin).
BASLE 23 January 1917 (in German).
BUENOS AIRES 6 July 1923 (in German).
MONTEVIDEO August 1923 (in German).
ANTWERP 26 February 1929 (in Flemish).
PHILADELPHIA 29 October 1931 (in German).
PARIS, O. 29 February 1932 (in French).
A Catalan version by J. Pena was published in 1912; a Bulgarian version by V. Boyadyieva in 1932.

NAYLOR: *The Angelus*
27 January. London, C.G.

Text by W. Thornely. Prologue and 4 acts.
Naylor's only performed opera. Awarded the Ricordi prize for the best English opera. Revived Cambridge 5 March 1914 (in concert form); London, C.G. 1 December 1921.

ZICHY: *Rákóczy Ferenc II*

30 January. Budapest

Text by the composer. Prologue and 3 acts.

The second part of Zichy's *Rákóczy* trilogy (see 1905 and 1913). This second part was never given outside Hungary.

ALFANO: *Il Principe Zilah*

3 February. Genoa, C.F.

Text by L. Illica (from a French novel by J. Claretie). Prologue, 3 acts, and epilogue.

Given with alterations at Milan, T.d.V. 6 October 1909.

NOUGUÈS: *Quo Vadis*

9 February. Nice

Text by H. Cain (founded on H. Sienkiewicz's novel). Five acts.

Nouguès most successful opera. Given at:

PARIS, GAÎTÉ 26 November 1909 (in French).

ANTWERP 18 January 1910 (in French).

PRAGUE 19 April 1910 (in German, translated by H. Liebstöckl).

VIENNA, V.O. 12 October 1919 (in German, translated by H. Liebstöckl).

WARSAW October 1910 (in Polish).

MOSCOW October 1910 (in Russian).

BRUSSELS 26 November 1910 (in French).

GENEVA 13 December 1910 (in French).

PHILADELPHIA 25 March 1911 (in French).

NEW YORK 4 April 1911 (in French).

MILAN, T.D.V. 3 May 1911 (in Italian).

LONDON, L.O.H. 13 November 1911 (in French; at the opening of the new London Opera House, Kingsway).

BUDAPEST 7 December 1911 (in Hungarian; at the opening of the new People's Opera).

RIGA 1912 (in German).

BERLIN 17 February 1912 (in German; at the new Kurfürsten-Oper).

NEW ORLEANS 4 January 1913 (in French).

BARCELONA 28 November 1920 (in French).

Quo Vadis was a transitory success in other countries; but it is still given on French stages; revived in Paris, Ch. É. 27 February 1920; G.L. 24

April 1923. Open-air performance: Orange 22 April 1931.

RÓZYCKI: *Boleslaw Smialy*
(Boleslav the Bold)

11 February. Lemberg

Text by A. Bandrowski. Three acts.

Rózycki's first opera.

GUNSBOURG: *Le vieil Aigle*

13 February. Monte Carlo

Text by the composer (founded on a story by M. Gorky). One act.

Gunsbourg's first opera; orchestrated by L. Jehin. Also given at:

PARIS, O. 26 June 1909 (in French).

COLOGNE 26 December 1909 (in German).

BRUSSELS 19 May 1910 (in French).

MOSCOW October 1912 (in Russian).

CHICAGO 19 January 1917 (in French).

NEW YORK 28 February 1919 (in French).

BARCELONA 27 November 1919 (in French).

Revived at Monte Carlo, February 1935.

G. FERRARI: *Le Cobzar*

16 February. Monte Carlo

Text by P. Milliet (from a Rumanian libretto by H. Vacarescu). Two acts.

In French also, Aix-les-Bains 7 September 1909, etc. Paris, O. 30 March 1912.

In German (translated by O. Neitzel), Cassel 26 November 1913.

(Like *Cavalleria rusticana*, this opera contains an Intermezzo sinfonico.)

REUSS: *Herzog Philipps Brautfahrt*

22 February. Graz

Text by H. von Gumppenberg. Three acts.

The only opera of Reuss, who is better-known as a composer of songs and instrumental music.

CHAPI: *Margarita la Tornera*

24 February. Madrid, T.R.

Text by C. Fernández Shaw. Three acts.

Chapi's last opera (produced some weeks

before his death) and one of his most important works.

In Spanish also, Buenos Aires 12 November 1910.

MRACZEK: *Der Traum*

26 February. Brünn

Text by the composer (from F. Grillparzer's *Der Traum ein Leben*). Three acts.

Berlin 29 March 1912.

TINEL: *Katharina*

27 February. Brussels, M.

(Original German) text by L. van Heemstede, French version by F. van Duyse. Three acts.

In German, Coblenz 3 March 1910. Revived Brussels 12 April 1930 (in French).

(*Katharina* was frequently performed as an oratorio, in concert form.)

HÖEBERG: *Et Bryllup i Katakomberne*
(The Wedding in the Catacombs)

6 March. Copenhagen

Text by S. Michaelis. Three acts.

The only opera of the Danish composer.

MONTEMEZZI: *Hellera*

17 March. Turin, T.R.

Text by L. Illica (founded on B. Constant's *Adolphe*). Three acts.

Revived only 12 December 1937 (broadcast from Rome).

BRAUNFELS: *Prinzessin Brambilla*

25 March. Stuttgart

Text by the composer (founded on E. T. A. Hoffmann's story). Two acts.

The first of Braunfels's operas which was performed. Revived in a new version, Hanover 15 September 1931.

(MUSORGSKY): *Zhenitba*
Женитьба
(The Marriage)

1 April. St. Petersburg

Text from Gogol's comedy, called an *Attempt at Dramatic Music in Prose.*

Written in 1868; only the first act, consisting of 4 scenes, is finished. First heard in concert form at Kyui's on 6 October 1868 and in 1909 on the stage of the Suvorin Theatre School, but with piano accompaniment. First produced with orchestra at Petrograd 26 October 1917 along with the first production of *The Fair of Sorochintsy* (*q.v.*).

Also given in Paris April 1923 (privately; in French, translated by R. d'Harcourt, music arranged by Ravel); Monte Carlo 7 January 1930 (orchestrated by M. Béclart d'Harcourt).

In German, Essen 14 November 1937.

(See on *The Marriage*, C. Koechlin in *Revue Musicale*, May 1923, and A. Sandulenko in *The Chesterian*, 1934, No. 116.)

HADLEY: *Safié*

4 April. Mayence

(Original English) text by E. Oxenford, German version by O. Neitzel. One act.

The first opera of the American composer which was produced. Never given in America.

MASCHERONI: *La Perugina*

24 April. Naples, S.C.

Text by L. Illica. Four acts.

Mascheroni's last opera.

MASSENET: *Bacchus*

5 May. Paris, O.

Text by C. Mendès. Four acts.

Unsuccessful and never revived.

KÜNNECKE: *Robin's Ende*

5 May. Mannheim

Text by M. Morris. Two acts.

The first opera of Künnecke, who later made a name as a composer of successful operettas. Given at Berlin, K.O. 23 March 1910; Hamburg 30 November 1910; Riga 1911; Basle 29 October 1911, etc.

COLIN: *Maitena*

June. Bilbao

Text by E. Decrept. Two acts.

The first Basque opera, produced at the Teatro dos Campos-Elyseos, Bilbao, and repeated there 19 May 1910.

Revived Madrid, Z., May 1928; in Spanish also, St. Jean Pied-de-Port (Basses-Pyrénées, France), September 1931.

The work is frequently referred to as the first Basque opera. It seems, however, to have been produced not in the Basque language, but in Spanish; see *Bulletin Français of the I.M.S.*, 15 October 1910.

(RIMSKY-KORSAKOV): *Zolotoy Pyetushok*
Золотой Пѣтушокъ
(The Golden Cockerel)

7 October. Moscow

Text by V. I. Byelsky (founded on a satirical fairy tale by Pushkin). Three acts.

Rimsky-Korsakov's last opera, produced the year after his death (and not in 1910 as many books of reference have it). One of his best and most popular works. Outside Russia, given at:

PARIS, O. 24 May 1914 (in Russian, as opera ballet, choreography by M. Fokine) and 16 May 1927 (in French, translated by M. D. Calvocoressi).

LONDON, D.L. 15 June 1914 (in Russian) and 19 July 1918 (in English, translated by E. Agate).

NEW YORK 6 March 1918 (in French) and 28 March 1932 (in Russian).

BERLIN 18 June 1923 (in German, translated by H. Möller).

ANTWERP 24 November 1923 (in Flemish).

TURIN, T.R. 17 February 1925 (in Italian).

BUENOS AIRES 21 July 1925 (in Italian; revived 18 June 1937).

WARSAW December 1926 (in Polish).

RIGA 13 September 1928 (in Lettish).

VIENNA 8 May 1929 (in Czech, by a company from Bratislava).

SAN FRANCISCO 6 November 1933 (in English, translated by P. Kerby).

CHICAGO 1934 (in English, translated by P. Kerby).

BRUSSELS 20 November 1937 (in French).

HAGUE November 1938 (in Russian).

DOPPER: *William Ratcliff*

19 October. Weimar

Text from Heine's dramatic poem. Two acts.

The last opera of the Dutch composer. Revived (in Flemish), Antwerp 11 March 1913.

d'ALBERT: *Izeyl*

6 November. Hamburg

Text by R. Lothar (translated from a French play by P. A. Silvestre and E. Morand). Three acts.

In German also, Brünn, May 1910.

In Swedish (translated by E. Grandinson), Stockholm 2 November 1910.

HOLBROOKE: *Pierrot and Pierrette*

11 November. London, H.M.'s

Text by W. E. Grogan (*A lyrical music drama*). Two scenes.

Holbrooke's first performed opera.

PRATELLA: *La Sina d'Vargöun*

4 December. Bologna, T.C.

Text by the composer (*Scene della Romagna bassa per la Musica*). Three acts.

Awarded the Baruzzi prize in 1909. The curious title is the name of the heroine, Rossellina dei Vergoni, in the Romagnese dialect.

Revived Milan, T.d.V. 7 October 1924.

See on this opera, A. Toni in *R.M.I.*, 1910.

WOLF-FERRARI: *Susannens Geheimnis*

4 December. Munich

(Original Italian) text by E. Golisciani, German version by M. Kalbeck. One act.

This intermezzo turned out to be Wolf-Ferrari's most successful work. It was given at:

STRASBOURG 27 January 1910 (in German).

PRAGUE 18 August 1910 (in German) and 13 September 1910 (in Czech).

VIENNA 4 October 1910 (in German).

STOCKHOLM 11 January 1911 (in Swedish, translated by S. Nyblom).

NEW YORK 14 March 1911 (for the first time in the original Italian).

ZAGREB 21 March 1911 (in Croatian, translated by G. Prejac).

BASLE 21 April 1911 (in German).

LONDON, C.G. 11 July 1911 (in Italian) and 12 November 1919 (in English).

BRUSSELS 28 October 1911 (in French, translated by M. Kufferath).

BUDAPEST 18 November 1911 (in Hungarian, translated by S. Várady).

ROME 27 November 1911 (in Italian); Milan, T. d.V. 23 September 1915, etc.

MANCHESTER 19 February 1912 (in English, translated by C. Aveling).

BERLIN, KURF.O. 23 September 1912 (in German).

BUENOS AIRES 26 June 1913 (in Italian).

TOULOUSE December 1913 (in French).

LEMBERG 1913 (in Polish).

COPENHAGEN 15 March 1914 (in Danish, translated by J. Lehmann).

MONTREAL 1914 (in French).

MALTA 1916 (in Italian).

BARCELONA 2 December 1916 (in Italian).

PARIS, O.C. 28 June 1921 (in French).

LJUBLJANA Spring 1924 (in Slovenian).

CAPE TOWN 1924 (in English).

SÉVERAC: *Le Cœur du Moulin*

8 December. Paris, O.C.

Text by M. Magre. Two acts.

Séverac's only opera. Given at the O.C. 14 times in 1909-10; not revived so far.

MELARTIN: *Aino*

10 December. Helsinki

Text by J. Finne (from the *Kalevala*).

Melartin's only opera. An open-air performance took place at Nyslott (Olofsborg) 3 July

1912. Revived Helsinki 28 February 1923 and 23 February 1935.

GATTY: *Duke or Devil*

16 December. Manchester

Text by I. Gatty (the brother of the composer). *A farcical Opera.* One act.

Also given in London, Crystal Palace, 21 November 1911.

A revised edition was published in 1924.

1910

LEONCAVALLO: *Maia*

15 January. Rome, C.

(Original French) text by P. de Choudens, Italian version by A. Nessi. Three acts.

In German (translated by G. Droescher), Berlin 18 March 1911.

S. WAGNER: *Banadietrich*

23 January. Carlsruhe

Text by the composer. Three acts.

In German also, Prague 20 November 1910; Vienna 15 May 1912, etc.

DUPONT: *La Glu*

26 January. Nice

Text by J. Richepin and H. Cain (*drame musical populaire*), founded on Richepin's novel (1881) and play (1883) of the same title. Four acts.

In French also given at Rouen 4 January 1911; Brussels 11 January 1911; Antwerp 9 November 1911; Algiers January 1913; Geneva 14 February 1913; Lyons 14 November 1914.

MASSENET: *Don Quichotte*

19 February. Monte Carlo

Text by H. Cain (after Cervantes and J. Le Lorrain's comedy, *Le Chevalier de la Longue Figure*, 1906). Five acts.

Massenet's last great success. Given at: BRUSSELS 14 May 1910 (in French).

MOSCOW 25 November 1910 (in Russian, translated by M. A. Kuzmin).

MARSEILLES 17 December 1910 (in French).

PARIS, GAÎTÉ 29 December 1910 (in French).

NUREMBERG 31 March 1911 (in German, translated by E. Huldschinsky).

NEW ORLEANS 27 January 1912 (in French).

LONDON, L.O.H. 18 May 1912 (in French).

GENEVA 8 November 1912 (in French).

PHILADELPHIA 15 November 1913 (in French).

NEW YORK 3 February 1914 (in French).

RIO DE JANEIRO Summer 1926 (in Italian, translated by Cipriano di Rora).

CATANIA 5 January 1928 (in Italian, translated by Cipriano di Rora).

TRIESTE 7 January 1928 (in Italian, translated by Cipriano di Rora).

BERLIN, KROLL'S 25 May 1928 (in Russian!).

BARCELONA 21 December 1929 (in French).

First given at the O.C., Paris 7 October 1924 and revived there 10 January 1931.

Still given on French and Italian stages; revived at Brussels 10 November 1939.

NOUGUÈS: *L'Auberge rouge*

21 February. Nice

Text by S. Basset (after Balzac's story). Two acts. Paris, Tr. L. 21 December 1911.

DEBUSSY: *L'Enfant prodigue*

28 February. London, C.G.

Text by E. Guinand. One act.

Originally a *scène lyrique* for soloists, chorus and orchestra (the composer's Prix de Rome cantata, published 1884). As a concert cantata it was sung at the Sheffield Festival, 8 October 1908. In operatic form first produced in London 1910, in French, and subsequently given at:

ZURICH 9 November 1910 (in German, translated by E. Huldschinsky).

BOSTON 16 November 1910 (in French).

MAGDEBURG December 1910 (in German).

BARCELONA 26 January 1911 (in Catalan, translated by J. Pena).

JOHANNESBURG March 1912 (in English).

ANTWERP 12 November 1912 (in French).

NANTES 8 February 1913 (in French).

BUDAPEST 3 May 1913 (in Hungarian, translated by S. Hevesi).

BRUSSELS 9 December 1913 (in French).

MARSEILLES 24 March 1914 (in French).

LONDON, SHAFTESBURY 28 December 1915 and C.G. 30 May 1923 (in English, translated by N. Cox). R.C.M. 1930 (in French).

PARIS, TH.L. 10 December 1919 (in French).

BERGAMO March 1920 (in Italian, translated by F. Casanova).

AMSTERDAM 20 May 1921 (in French).

LYONS 19 January 1923 (in French).

SANTIAGO, CHILE Autumn 1934 (in French).

BRÉVILLE: *Eros Vainqueur*

7 March. Brussels, M.

Text by J. Lorrain. Three acts.

Bréville's only opera. First given at Paris, Salle Gaveau, in concert form, by the "Schola Cantorum," 4 February 1922; revived on the stage O.C. 8 February 1932.

ZICH: *Malířský Nápad*
(An Artist's Whim)

11 March. Prague, Cz.

Text by the composer (founded on a story by S. Čech). One act.

Zich's first opera. Revived Prague 27 January 1933.

GIORDANO: *Mese Mariano*

17 March. Palermo

Text by S. di Giacomo. One act.

Successful in Italy; in Italian also given at Buenos Aires 23 July 1910.

In German (translated by M. Kalbeck), Lucerne 8 January 1933.

The latest revivals in Italy were at Genoa 1 March 1938; Milan, Sc. 9 March 1940.

BITTNER: *Der Musikant*

12 April. Vienna, O.

Text by the composer. Two acts.

Successful on German stages; given at Frankfort 29 October 1910; Berlin, Kroll's 30 July 1911, etc.

In German also, Prague 1911; Strasbourg 1911; Riga January 1913.

Revived Vienna 21 November 1931.

PETERSON-BERGER: *Arnjlot*

13 April. Stockholm

Text by the composer. Three acts.

One of Peterson-Berger's most important works; revived at Stockholm 24 February 1922.

(The first act had been produced in the open air at Frösön, Jämtland, 21 June 1908.)

PALMGREN: *Daniel Hjort*

15 April. Åbo (Turku)

(Original Swedish) text by the composer (founded on a tragedy by J. J. Wecksell). Five acts.

Revived Helsinki 20 February 1929 (in Finnish, translated by K. Vesala and W. Sola).

BRÜGGEMANN: *Margherita*

18 April. Milan, Sc.

(Italian) text by the composer (from Goethe's *Faust*). Four acts.

Second part of an Italian *Faust* trilogy; the two other parts have not yet been performed.

SÁNCHEZ DE FUENTES: *Dolorosa*

23 April. Havana

(Spanish) text by F. Uhrbach. Prologue and 2 acts.

Probably the first opera of a Cuban composer which was also produced in Europe: Turin 8 August 1911 (Italian version by G. Macchi).

NEVIN: *Poia*

23 April. Berlin, O.

(Original English) text by R. Hartley (founded on Indian legends collected by W. MacClintock), German version by E. von Huhn. Three acts.

The first opera of the American composer; previously given in concert form at Pittsburgh, Pa., January 1907.

VAN OOSTERZEE: *Das Gelöbnis*

1 May. Weimar

(German) text by G. Klett and L. Wittich (founded on a story by R. Voss). Two acts.

The only opera of the Dutch woman composer, who was a native of Batavia.

TERRASSE: *Le Mariage de Télémaque*

4 May. Paris, O.C.

Text by J. Lemaître and M. Donnay. Five acts.

Successful on French stages; outside France given at Stockholm 8 March 1911 (in Swedish) and Buenos Aires 25 June 1911 (in French).

Revived Paris, O.C. 13 November 1913 (reduced to 3 acts) and 29 October 1921.

O'DWYER: *Eithne*

16 May. Dublin

Text by T. O'Ceallaigh (O'Kelly), founded on the Irish folk story *Ean an cheoil bhinn*. Two acts.

Apparently the first opera ever produced in Erse. Vocal score and libretto (both in Erse and in English) printed.

USANDIZAGA: *Mendi-Mendyian*

21 May. Bilbao

(Spanish) text by J. Power. Usandizaga's first opera.

PIERNÉ: *On ne badine pas avec l'Amour*

30 May. Paris, O.C.

Text by L. Leloir and G. Nigond (founded on the play by A. de Musset). Three acts.

Unsuccessful; performed 8 times only.

GURIDI: *Mirentxu*

June. Bilbao

Text by the composer and A. de Echave y Nazabal. Two acts.

The first opera of the Basque composer.
In Spanish also given at Barcelona 23 January 1913 and Madrid, Z. 1914.

CLUTSAM: *A Summer Night*

23 July. London, H.M.'s

Text by the composer (founded on a story from the *Heptameron*). One act.

Given at C.G. later in the same year, 24 November 1910.

HAARKLOU: *Marisagnet*
(St. Mary's Legend)

17 August. Christiania

Text by A. Winge. Seven scenes.
The last opera of the Norwegian composer.

ZANELLA: *Aura*

27 August. Pesaro

Text by I. Finzi. Three acts.
The first opera of Zanella, who had become Mascagni's successor as director of the Liceo Rossini, Pesaro, in 1905.

FLORIDIA: *Paoletta*

29 August. Cincinnati

(English) text by P. Jones (founded on his story, *The Sacred Mirror*). Four acts.

First produced at the Ohio Valley Exhibition; revived New York 21 March 1920 (in abridged form).

NEUMANN: *Liebelei*

18 September. Frankfort

Text from A. Schnitzler's play (without alterations). Three acts.
The most successful opera of the Moravian composer. Also given at:
BERLIN, K.O. 20 January 1911 (in German).
HELSINKI 18 October 1911 (in Finnish).
PRAGUE 14 November 1911 (in Czech).
VIENNA, V.O. 14 October 1913 (in German).
Revived Brno 1930.

GUNSBOURG: *Ivan le Terrible*

20 October. Brussels, M.

Text by the composer. Three acts.
Gunsbourg's chief work (orchestrated by L. Jehin).
In French also, Monte Carlo 2 March 1911; Paris, Gaîté 31 October 1911; Barcelona 27 November 1919; Rio de Janeiro 7 October 1922.

MERIKANTO: *Elinan Surma*
(Elina's Death)

17 November. Helsinki

Text by J. Finne (founded on a play by G. A. von Numers). Five acts.
Revived Helsinki 12 December 1917 and 23 March 1933.
Also given in Estonian, at Tallinn (Reval) 1932.

RESPIGHI: *Semirama*

20 November. Bologna, T.C.

Text by A. Cerè. Three acts. Respighi's second opera; unsuccessful.

KAISER: *Stella Maris*

25 November. Düsseldorf

(Original French) text by H. Revers, German version by the composer. Three acts.
Successful on German stages; given at Graz November 1912; Lucerne 1913; Berlin, Kurfürsten Oper 16 January 1913, etc.
In English, Liverpool 15 April 1919; London, King's, Hammersmith 23 May 1919 and Ly. 20 August 1919.
Produced in England after the composer's death in 1917; see *The Monthly Musical Record*, January 1918 (account by the composer's widow).

BLOCH: *Macbeth*

30 November. Paris, O.C.

Text by E. Fleg (after Shakespeare). Prologue and 3 acts.
Bloch's only opera, so far. Regarded by many critics as a most important work; unsuccessful

(13 performances). Revived only after 28 years, at Naples, S.C. 5 March 1938 (in Italian, translated by M. Tibaldi Chiesa).

ZEMLINSKY: *Kleider machen Leute*

2 December. Vienna, V.O.

Text by L. Feld (from a story by G. Keller). Prologue and 3 acts.

Revived in a new version at Prague March 1922; Düsseldorf November 1924; and again Cologne 12 October 1934; Zurich 1935.

PUCCINI: *La Fanciulla del West*

10 December. New York, M.

Text by G. Civinini and C. Zangarini (founded on D. Belasco's play, *The Girl of the Golden West*). Three acts.

Given at:

LONDON, C.G. 29 May 1911 (in Italian) and D.L. 31 May 1917 (in English).

ROME, C. 12 June 1911; Milan, Sc. 29 December 1912, etc. (in Italian).

BUENOS AIRES 25 July 1911 (in Italian).

WARSAW 5 October 1911 (in Polish).

LIVERPOOL 6 October 1911 (in English, translated by R. H. Elkin).

ALEXANDRIA 19 February 1912 (in Italian).

BUDAPEST 29 February 1912 (in Hungarian, translated by S. Várady).

MONTE CARLO 2 April 1912 (in Italian).

PARIS, O. 16 May 1912 (in Italian).

JOHANNESBURG April 1912 (in English).

MARSEILLES 8 November 1912 (in French, translated by M. Vaucaire).

BRUSSELS 17 March 1913 (in French) and 6 October 1913 (in Italian).

BERLIN, D.O. 28 March 1913 (in German, translated by A. Brüggemann).

RIGA 1913 (in German) and 16 December 1926 (in Lettish).

PRAGUE 1913 (in German).

MALTA 1913 (in Italian).

MOSCOW October 1913 (in Russian).

VIENNA 24 October 1913 (in German); revived 18 May 1936.

BARCELONA 24 April 1915 (in Italian).

ZAGREB 28 October 1916 (in Croatian, translated by M. Nehajev).

LJUBLJANA 9 May 1928 (in Slovenian).

BUCHAREST October 1931 (in Rumanian).

TRIPOLIS November 1934 (in Italian).

STOCKHOLM 29 December 1935 (in Swedish).

HELSINKI 21 October 1937 (in Finnish).

HUMPERDINCK: *Königskinder*

28 December. New York, M.

Text by E. Rosmer. Three acts.

Apart from *Hänsel und Gretel* (see 1893) Humperdinck's most successful opera. *Königskinder* originally was a play by E. Rosmer with melodramatic music by Humperdinck. In that form it was first produced at Munich 23 January 1897 and subsequently at Vienna, W. 10 May 1897; Prague 22 August 1897; Berlin 11 March 1898; Riga 25 October 1898, etc. In German also, New York 29 April 1898.

In English (translated by C. Armbruster), London, Court Th. 13 October 1897; in another English version (by F. Langbridge and A. H. Ferro), Dublin 4 September 1902 and New York 3 November 1902.

Parts of Humperdinck's music were first heard at a concert at Heidelberg 3 June 1896.

The operatic version was first produced at the Metropolitan, New York, in German, and subsequently at:

BERLIN 14 January 1911 (in German).

PRAGUE 15 January 1911 (in German).

STRASBOURG 30 April 1911 (in German).

RIGA 1911 (in German).

LONDON, C.G. 27 November 1911 (in German).

MILAN, SC. 26 December 1911 (in Italian, translated by G. Pozza and A. Lega).

BOSTON 16 April 1912 (in German).

BUENOS AIRES 20 August 1912 (in Italian).

AMSTERDAM 1912 (in German).

BUDAPEST 8 October 1912 (in Hungarian, translated by S. Várady).

BRUSSELS 25 October 1912 (in French, translated by R. Brussel).

VIENNA, V.O. 21 December 1912 (in German); O. only 19 October 1938.

MOSCOW October 1913 (in Russian).

ZAGREB 18 December 1915 (in Croatian, translated by A. Mitrović).

STOCKHOLM 30 December 1926 (in Swedish).

F. d'ERLANGER: *Noël*

28 December. Paris, O.C.

Text by J. and P. Ferrier. Three acts.

d'Erlanger's last opera.

In French also, Chicago 8 January 1913; Philadelphia 10 February 1913; Montreal 1913.

In Swedish, Stockholm 29 September 1924.

HÜE: *Le Miracle*

30 December. Paris, O.

Text by P. B. Gheusi and A. Mérane. Five acts.

Revived Paris, O. 18 November 1927.

1911

OSTRČIL: *Poupě*
(The Bud)

25 January. Prague, Cz.

Text by F. X. Svoboda. One act.

Successful in Czechoslovakia; revived Prague 6 October 1919 and 22 October 1935.

In German (translated by A. Heller), Teplitz-Schönau 25 February 1932.

R. STRAUSS: *Der Rosenkavalier*

26 January. Dresden

Text by H. von Hofmannsthal (*Komödie für Musik*). Three acts.

Strauss's most popular opera; given at Nuremberg the next night, 27 January 1911; Munich 1 February 1911; Bremen 28 February 1911; Frankfort 1 March 1911, etc.

First given at Berlin 4 April 1911 (300th performance 28 June 1933).

Outside Germany, given at:

BASLE 15 February 1911 (in German).

MILAN, SC. 1 March 1911 (in Italian, translated by O. Schanzer).

PRAGUE 4 March 1911 (in Czech, translated by K. Šipek) and May 1914 (in German).

VIENNA 8 April 1911 (in German).

BUDAPEST 21 May 1911 (in Hungarian, translated by S. Várady).

HAGUE 28 November 1911 and Amsterdam 10 January 1917 (in German).

STRASBOURG 28 March 1912 (in German).

LONDON, C.G. 29 January 1913 (in German) and Sadler's Wells 8 March 1939 (in English).

LAIBACH (LJUBLJANA) 1913 (in German) and 25 March 1936 (in Slovenian, translated by N. Štritov).

BIRMINGHAM 29 September 1913 (in English, translated by A. Kalisch).

NEW YORK 9 December 1913 (in German).

BUENOS AIRES 24 July 1915 (in Italian).

RIO DE JANEIRO 10 September 1915 (in Italian).

ZAGREB 29 April 1916 (in Croatian, translated by M. Nehajev) and 29 May 1938 (in German), by the Frankfort opera company.

COPENHAGEN 4 November 1916 (in Danish, translated by J. Lehmann).

AMSTERDAM 10 January 1917 (in German).

STOCKHOLM 20 April 1920 (in Swedish, translated by S. Nyblom).

BARCELONA 2 April 1921 (in German) and November 1934 (in Catalan, translated by J. Pena).

WARSAW April 1922 (in Polish, translated by P. Maszyński).

HELSINKI 12 October 1923 (in Swedish).

ANTWERP 6 March 1926 (in Flemish, translated by A. M. Pols).

MONTE CARLO March 1926 (in French, translated by J. Chantavoine).

PARIS, O. 11 February 1927 (in French, translated by J. Chantavoine).

LYONS 22 February 1928 (in French, translated by J. Chantavoine).

BUCHAREST October 1929 (in Rumanian, translated by R. Steiner) and 4 May 1938 (in German).

RIGA 16 May 1930 (in Lettish).

SOFIA 10 May 1938 (in German).

ATHENS 16 May 1938 (in German).

HERBERT: *Natoma*

25 February. Philadelphia

Text by J. D. Redding. Three acts.

Successful in the U.S.A. Given at New York, M. 28 February 1911; Baltimore 9 March 1911; Chicago 13 December 1911; Los Angeles 8 March 1913; San Francisco 15 March 1913; revived at the Century Th., New York 13 April 1914.

(A copyright performance of *Natoma* took place at Ladbroke Hall, London, the same night as at Philadelphia.)

CONVERSE: *The Sacrifice*

3 March. Boston

Text by the composer (lyrics by J. A. Macy). Three acts.

Converse's second and last opera.

(The date of the first production is incorrectly reported as 16 November 1910 in H. C. Lahee's *Annals of Music in America*, and, consequently, in many other books of reference.)

ATANASOV: *Borislav*

Бориславъ

4 March. Sofia

Text by N. P. Popov. Four acts.

One of the earliest original Bulgarian operas. Libretto published at Plovdiv.

SAINT-SAËNS: *Déjanire*

14 March. Monte Carlo

Text by L. Gallet. Four acts.

(Originally incidental music to Gallet's tragedy, performed at the Arènes, Béziers, 25 August 1898 and Paris, Odéon 11 November 1898). Operatic version first produced at Monte Carlo and subsequently at Paris, O. 22 November 1911 (in French); Brussels 6 December 1911 (in French); Dessau 1 January 1912 (in German, translated by P. Hiller); Chicago 9 December 1915 (in Italian).

HALVORSEN: *Mot Nordpolen*
(To the North Pole)

6 April. Christiania

Text by V. Dybwad. Three acts.

The only operetta of the well-known Norwegian composer and conductor.

LAPARRA: *La Jota*

26 April. Paris, O.C.

Text by the composer (*Conte lyrique*). Two acts.

Much less successful than his *Habanera*, three years earlier; given 8 times only and not revived so far.

RAVEL: *L'Heure espagnole*

19 May. Paris, O.C.

Text by Franc-Nohain (from his comedy of the same title, 1904). One act.

Ravel's first and most successful opera. Given at the O.C. 10 times in 1911 and transferred to the repertory of the Opéra on 5 December 1921.

Given on many French stages; the opera did not make its way into other countries until after the war:

LONDON, C.G. 24 July 1919 (in French).

CHICAGO 5 January 1920 (in French).

NEW YORK 28 January 1920 (in French) and Juilliard School 9 March 1936 (in English, translated by R. A. Simon).

BRUSSELS 27 January 1921 (in French).

BASLE 15 May 1923 (in French).

ROTTERDAM 13 October 1923 (in Dutch, translated by B. Verhagen).

PRAGUE 6 June 1924 (in German, translated by Leonhard and Strasser).

HAMBURG 5 February 1925 (in German, translated by Leonhard and Strasser).

STOCKHOLM 24 September 1925 (in Swedish).

TURIN, T.D.T. 18 May 1926 (in French).

BUDAPEST 29 March 1928 (in Hungarian, translated by V. Lányi).

WARSAW 1928 (in Polish).

LIVERPOOL 19 October 1928 (in English, translated by A. K. Holland; by amateurs, with piano accompaniment).

MILAN, SC. 9 February 1929 (in Italian, translated by P. Clausetti).

BERLIN 27 September 1929 (in German).

BUENOS AIRES 20 September 1932 (in French).

BUCHAREST November 1932 (in Rumanian).

AMSTERDAM 23 November 1933 (in French) and 26 March 1938 (in Dutch).

CAIRO March 1934 (in French).

VIENNA 13 February 1935 (in German).

COPENHAGEN 25 January 1940 (in Danish, translated by G. Hansen).

MASCAGNI: *Isabeau*

2 June. Buenos Aires

Text by L. Illica. Three acts.

Very successful in many countries. Given (in Italian) at Rio de Janeiro 21 July 1911; Milan, Sc. and Venice, F. 20 January 1912; Madrid 17 December 1912; Malta 1914; Chicago 12 November 1917; New York 13 February 1918; Barcelona 15 April 1920.

In German (translated by R. Cahn-Speyer), Vienna, V.O. 1 March 1913.

ZANDONAI: *Conchita*

14 October. Milan, T.d.V.

(Original French) text by M. Vaucaire (founded on P. Louÿs's novel, *La Femme et le Pantin*), Italian version by C. Zangarini.[1] Four acts.

Zandonai's first great success; outside Italy (in Italian) also given at Buenos Aires 14 June 1912; London, C.G. 3 July 1912; Rio de Janeiro 22 July 1912; San Francisco 28 September 1912; New York, M. 11 February 1913; Nice May 1914; Malta 1915.

In the original French (as *La Femme et le Pantin*), Paris, O.C. 11 March 1929.

Still given in Italy; revived Buenos Aires 30 June 1939; Milan, Sc. 8 December 1939.

BITTNER: *Der Bergsee*

9 November. Vienna, O.

Text by the composer. Prologue and 2 acts.

[1] The libretto originally was written for Puccini.

Munich 10 December 1911, etc. Revived Vienna April 1939.

KIENZL: *Der Kuhreigen*

23 November. Vienna, V.O.

Text by R. Batka (founded on a story by R. H. Bartsch). Three acts.

Apart from *Der Evangelimann* (see 1895), Kienzl's most successful opera; given at:

MAGDEBURG January 1912 (in German).

PRAGUE January 1912 (in German).

LAIBACH 1912 (in German).

BERLIN, KURF. O. 7 September 1912 (in German).

PHILADELPHIA 21 February 1913 (in French, translated by R. Brussel).

NEW YORK 25 February 1913 (in French, translated by R. Brussel).

BASLE 24 March 1913 (in German).

LIVERPOOL 23 January 1914 (in English, as *The Dance of Death*, translated by R. Sapio).

LONDON, BOROUGH 13 July 1914 (in English, as *The Dance of Death*, translated by R. Sapio).

ANTWERP 11 December 1914 (in Flemish).

Revived Vienna, O. 18 October 1921; 28 February 1932; and 12 January 1938.

MAGNARD: *Bérénice*

15 December. Paris, O.C.

Text by the composer (founded on Racine's tragedy). Three acts.

The first of Magnard's operas which was performed; his *Guercoeur*, written as early as 1900, was not produced until 1931 (*q.v.*). Performed 14 times in 1911–12, not revived so far.

WOLF-FERRARI: *Der Schmuck der Madonna*

23 December. Berlin, Kurfürsten-Oper

(Original Italian) text by E. Golisciani and C. Zangarini (*I Gioielli della Madonna*), German version by H. Liebstöckl. Three acts.

Wolf-Ferrari's first and only attempt at tragic opera in the veristic style. Very successful, given at:

CHICAGO 16 January 1912 (for the first time in Italian).

NEW YORK, M. 5 March 1912 (in Italian) and Century Th. 14 October 1913 (in English).

LONDON, C.G. 30 May 1912 (in Italian) and 3 December 1920 (in English).

PRAGUE May 1912 (in German).

VIENNA, V.O. 2 October 1912 (in German).

ANTWERP 15 February 1913 (in Flemish).

GLASGOW 28 February 1913 (not 1912; for the first time in English, translated by C. Aveling).

COPENHAGEN Spring 1913 (in German, by the Kiel company).

LAIBACH 1913 (in German).

PARIS, O. 12 September 1913 (in French, translated by R. Lara).

BRUSSELS 17 October 1913 (in French, translated by R. Lara).

ZAGREB 17 October 1913 (in Croatian, translated by A. Mitrović).

STOCKHOLM 4 December 1913 (in Swedish, translated by S. Nyblom).

BASLE 26 December 1913 (in German).

GENEVA 17 February 1914 (in French).

MALTA 1916 (in Italian).

AMSTERDAM October 1916 (in Dutch).

MONTREAL 6 October 1917 (in English?).

KAUNAS 17 November 1928 (in Lithuanian).

LEMBERG 1929 (in Polish).

RIGA 14 March 1931 (in Lettish).

BUCHAREST March 1933 (in Rumanian).

MONTE CARLO March 1933 (in Italian).

Revived with some alterations at Hanover 23 December 1933 (in German).

1912

WALTERSHAUSEN: *Oberst Chabert*

18 January. Frankfort

Text by the composer (founded on Balzac's story, *Le Colonel Chabert*). Three acts.

Waltershausen's most successful work. Given at:

BERLIN, KURF. O. 20 April 1912 (in German).

LAIBACH 1912 (in German).

STRASBOURG October 1912 (in German).

STOCKHOLM 21 October 1912 (in Swedish).

VIENNA 25 November 1912 (in German).

BASLE 8 December 1912 (in German).

BRÜNN January 1913 (in German).

BUDAPEST 2 March 1913 (in Hungarian, translated by V. Lányi).

LONDON, C.G. 24 April 1913 (in German).

PRAGUE 1913 (in German).

RIGA 1913 (in German).

ANTWERP January 1914 (in Flemish).

Revived Berlin, D.O. 4 February 1933.

ROPARTZ: *Le Pays*

1 February. Nancy

Text by C. Le Goffic. Three acts.

Ropartz's most important opera; given at Paris, O.C. 16 April 1913 and revived there 2 February 1924. In French also, Geneva 8 February 1918.

In German (translated by P. Magnette), Altenburg 24 April 1914.

NOUGUÈS: *L'Aigle*

2 February. Rouen

Text by H. Cain and L. Payen (*épopée lyrique*). Three acts.

Given at Paris, Gaîté 18 November 1912 and revived there at the Vaudeville 3 April 1915.

In Russian, Moscow October 1912.

LAZZARI: *La Lépreuse*

7 February. Paris, O.C.

Text by H. Bataille (*tragédie légendaire*). Three acts. Lazzari's most important opera.

In German (translated by the composer and E. Klingenfeld), Mayence 4 March 1913.

Revived Paris, O.C. 25 November 1922.

VAN DEN EEDEN: *Rhéna*

15 February. Brussels, M.

Text by M. Carré fils (founded on Ouida's story *Don Gesualdo*). Four acts.

Van den Eeden's most successful opera; revived at Brussels 7 February 1925 (in French); Amsterdam 15 October 1927 (in Dutch).

MASSENET: *Roma*

17 February. Monte Carlo

Text by H. Cain (founded on D. A. Parodi's tragedy, *Rome vaincue*). Five acts.

The last of Massenet's operas which was produced in his lifetime (d. 13 August 1912). Given at Paris, O. 24 April 1912 and revived there 29 December 1917.

In French also, Cairo January 1913; Brussels 15 January 1913; revived Antwerp December 1924.

H. HUBER: *Der Simplicius*

22 February. Basle

Text by A. Mendelssohn-Bartholdy. Three acts. Revived Basle 21 January 1926.

DE LARA: *Les trois Masques*

24 February. Marseilles

Text by C. Méré. Four acts.

Paris, Ch.É. 23 October 1913.

In German (translated by O. Neitzel) 5 March 1913.

In English, Greenock (near Glasgow) 27 June 1919.

N. BERG: *Leila*

29 February. Stockholm

Text by the composer (from Byron's *Giaour*). Four acts.

The first opera of the Swedish composer.

PARELLI: *I dispettosi Amanti*

6 March. Philadelphia

Text by E. Comitti. One act.

Subsequently given at Chicago 1 February 1913 (in Italian).

In Italian also, Milan, T. Carc. 22 May 1919; London, C.G. 10 March 1924. Given in Italy until 1930.

In English (as *A Lover's Quarrel*, translated by A. Strettell), New York 9 March 1913.

(28 February is wrongly given in the printed score as the date of the first performance.)

L. DU BOIS: *Edenie*

7 March. Antwerp

(Original French) text by C. Lemonnier (from his novel, *L'Ile Vierge*), produced in a Flemish translation by L. van Riel. Three acts.

The last opera of the Belgian composer.

PARKER: *Mona*

14 March. New York, M.

Text by B. Hooker. Three acts.

The opera was awarded the $10.000 prize of the Metropolitan Opera House.

"*Mona* remains the great American opera—the strongest, most significant, most rewarding" (P. Rosenfeld, 1936).

ZICHY: *Rodostó*

20 March. Budapest

Text by the composer. Prologue, 2 parts and epilogue.

The third part of Zichy's *Rákóczy* trilogy (see 1905 and 1909).

Also given at Breslau May 1916 and Prague June 1916 (in German, translated by J. Prüwer?).

DUPONT: *La Farce du Cuvier*

21 March. Brussels, M.

Text by M. Léna (founded on the French 15th-century play). Two acts.

Given at Lille December 1912; Paris, Th.S.B. 28 May 1915, etc.

Frequently revived in Belgium and France.

(BOURGAULT-DUCOUDRAY): *Myrdhin*

28 March. Nantes

Text by S. Arnaud. Four acts.

Bourgault-Ducoudray's last opera, produced two years after his death.

(12 February is wrongly given in the printed libretto as the date of the first performance.)

WEIS: *Útok na Mlýn*
(The Attack on the Mill)

29 March. Prague, Cz.

(Original German) text by R. Batka (founded on
E. Zola's *L'Attaque du Moulin*), Czech version by?
Three acts.

In German, Vienna, V.O. 13 March 1914.

PEROSI: *Pompeji*

6 April. Vienna, V.O.

Text by K. Schreder and R. and M. Prosl (founded
on Bulwer Lytton's novel). Four acts.

Perosi's only opera.

C. RADOUX: *Oudelette*

11 April. Brussels, M.

Text by R. Ledent. Three acts.

The most important opera of the Belgian composer.

BUSONI: *Die Brautwahl*

13 April. Hamburg

Text by the composer (founded on a story by E.
T. A. Hoffmann). Three acts and epilogue.

Busoni's first performed opera. Given in a revised version at Mannheim 24 May 1913. Revived
Berlin, D.O. 7 January 1926.

LACCETTI: *Hoffmann*

15 April. Naples, S.C.

Text by V. Bianchi and T. Spada (dealing with
the life of E. T. A. Hoffmann). Three acts.

Revived Naples, S.C. 30 January 1932.

MULÈ: *La Baronessa di Carini*

16 April. Palermo

Text by F. P. Mulè, the brother of the composer.
One act.

Mulè's first opera. Revived Naples March 1933;
Malta 6 January 1934; Cairo February 1939 (in
Italian).

DE LARA: *Naïl*

22 April. Paris, Gaîté

Text by J. Bois. Three acts.

In English (translated by E. Evans), London,
C.G. 18 July 1919.

HOLBROOKE: *The Children of Don*

15 June. London, L.O.H.

Text by T. E. Ellis (the first part of a trilogy, *The
Cauldron of Annwen*, founded on Welsh legends;
see 1914 and 1929). Prologue and 3 acts.

In German (translated by H. Schilling), Vienna,
V.O. 29 March 1923 (see for an account of the
peculiar circumstances of that Vienna production,
F. Weingartner's *Lebenserinnerungen*, Vol.II, 1929,
pp.371–74).

SCHREKER: *Der ferne Klang*

18 August. Frankfort

Text by the composer. Three acts.

Schreker's first opera (written 1903–09). Given
at:

PRAGUE 20 May 1920 (in German).
GRAZ Spring 1924 (in German).
LENINGRAD 9 May 1925 (in Russian).
BERLIN 11 May 1925 (in German).
STOCKHOLM 28 September 1927 (in Swedish).

LEONCAVALLO: *Zingari*

16 September. London, Hippodrome

(Italian) text by E. Cavacchioli and G. Emanuel
(after Pushkin). Two acts.

One of the operas the success of which was
interrupted by the war; given at:

MILAN, T.L. 30 November 1912 (in Italian).
CHICAGO 23 March 1913 (in Italian).
MAYENCE 6 March 1914 (in German, translated by
E. Thieben).
MALTA 1914 (in Italian).
BUENOS AIRES 7 August 1916 (in Italian).

R. STRAUSS: *Ariadne auf Naxos*

25 October. Stuttgart

Text by H. von Hofmannsthal.

In its original form a one-act opera to be given after Molière's *Le Bourgeois Gentilhomme* (for which Strauss wrote incidental music). In the second (1916) version, the reference to Molière was dropped altogether and a scenic prelude was added instead.

The first version was, in German, also produced at Zurich 5 December 1912; Prague 7 December 1912; Berlin 27 February 1913; Amsterdam 1914; in English (translated by S. Maugham), London, H.M.'s 27 May 1913.

The second version was first produced at Vienna 4 October 1916 and subsequently given at:

BERLIN 1 November 1916 (in German).

BUDAPEST 19 April 1919 (in Hungarian, translated by Z. Harsányi).

GRAZ 12 March 1920.

AMSTERDAM January 1924 (in German).

LONDON, C.G. 27 May 1924 (in German).

TURIN, T.D.T. 7 December 1925 (in Italian, translated by O. Schanzer).

STOCKHOLM 27 November 1926 (in Swedish).

PHILADELPHIA 1 November 1928 (in German).

BRUSSELS 17 March 1930 (in French, translated by P. Spaak).

HELSINKI 12 May 1931 (in Finnish, translated by A. af Enehjelm).

NEW YORK 5 December 1934 (at the Juilliard School, in English, translated by A. Kalisch).

ROME, T.R. 28 March 1935 (in German).

ANTWERP 28 September 1935 (in Flemish).

PARIS, CH.É. 10 September 1937 (in German).

G. OREFICE: *Radda*

25 October. Milan, T.L.

Text by C. Vallini (founded on a story by M. Gorky). One act.

Orefice's last opera.

RÓZYCKI: *Meduza*

26 October. Warsaw

Text by C. Jellenta. Three acts.

The second opera of the Polish composer (dealing with incidents in the life of Leonardo da Vinci).

CAMUSSI: *La Dubarry*

7 November. Milan, T.L.

Text by C. Antona Traversi and E. Golisciani. Three acts and epilogue.

Camussi's first opera. In Italian also given at London, C.G. 3 July 1913.

ENNA: *Nattergallen*
(The Nightingale)

10 November. Copenhagen

Text by K. Friis-Møller (from H. C. Andersen's tale). Three acts.

Written about the same time as Stravinsky's opera of the same subject (see 1914).

ZANDONAI: *Melenis*

13 November. Milan, T.d.V.

Text by M. Spiritini and C. Zangarini (founded on a French poem by L. Bouilhet). Three acts. Unsuccessful.

WIENIAWSKI: *Megae*

December. Warsaw

Text by the composer and M. Synnestvedt. Three scenes.

Wieniawski's first opera; successful in Poland, revived at Warsaw 1927; Lemberg 4 October 1930.

Also given in Russian, Petrograd March 1916 (as one of the extremely few Polish operas which were produced at the Imperial Theatre there) and at Moscow in 1920.

1913

AUBERT: *La Forêt bleue*

7 January. Geneva

Text by J. Chenevière (founded on Perrault's tale). Three acts.

Aubert's only opera.

In French also given at Boston 8 March 1913 and revived Paris, O.C. 10 June 1924.

Broadcast from London 17 December 1928 (English version by H. Klein).

PAHISSA: *Gala Placidia*

15 January. Barcelona, L.

Text from A. Guimerá's tragedy of the same title. Three acts.

One of the most important operas of the Catalan composer; successful in Spain; revived Barcelona February 1933.

DOHNANYI: *Tante Simona*

22 January. Dresden

Text by V. Heindl. One act.

Dohnanyi's first opera. In German also, Berlin, D.O. 9 April 1913, etc.

In Hungarian (translated by V. Lányi), Budapest 1913 (at the People's Opera) and revived there at the State Opera 6 December 1933.

FOURDRAIN: *Madame Roland*

12 February. Rouen

Text by A. Bernède and P. de Choudens. Three acts.

Paris, Gaîté 1 April 1914.

d'OLLONE: *Le Retour*

13 February. Angers

Text by the composer. Two acts.

d'Ollone's first opera. Revived Paris, O. 6 June 1919.

BUFFIN: *Kaatje*

22 February. Brussels, M.

Text by H. Cain (founded on P. Spaak's comedy of the same title). Three acts.

Buffin's first (and so far only) opera.

In French also given at Monte Carlo 14 March 1914 and revived at Brussels 4 November 1921 (in an enlarged 4-act version) and again 13 October 1936.

DAMROSCH: *Cyrano*

27 February. New York, M.

Text by W. J. Henderson (founded on the play by E. Rostand). Four acts.

GASCO: *La Leggenda delle sette Torri*

2 March. Rome, C.

Text by O. Schanzer (suggested by Dante Gabriel Rossetti water-colour, *The Tune of Seven Towers*, 1857). One act.

Gasco's only performed opera.

FAURÉ: *Pénélope*

4 March. Monte Carlo

Text by R. Fauchois. Three acts.

Fauré's most important opera. First given at Paris, Ch.É. 10 May 1913 and revived O.C. 20 January 1919 and 14 March 1931.

Given at Brussels 1 December 1913 (in French); Antwerp 15 March 1924 (in Flemish, translated by M. Sabbe).

SCHREKER: *Das Spielwerk und die Prinzessin*

15 March. Vienna, O. and Frankfort

Text by the composer. Three acts.

First produced at Vienna and Frankfort the same night. Revived in a reduced one-act version as *Das Spielwerk*, Munich 30 October 1920; Mayence 16 May 1929.

BRETÓN: *Tabaré*

26 March. Madrid, T.R.

Text by the composer (founded on a poem by the Uruguayan poet, J. Zorrilla de San Martín). Three acts.

Bretón's last greater success.

FALLA: *La Vie brève*

1 April. Nice

(Original Spanish) text by C. Fernández Shaw, French version by P. Milliet. Two acts.

Falla's first opera; it had been awarded the first
prize in a competition by the Real Academia de
Bellas Artes de San Fernando in 1905, but the
composer had to wait 8 years and go to another
country to have it performed.

Given at:

PARIS, O.C. 6 January 1914 (in French; revived 12
March 1928).

MADRID, Z. 14 November 1914 (for the first time
in the original Spanish).

BRUSSELS 12 April 1923 (in French).

BUENOS AIRES 26 July 1923 (in Spanish).

NEW YORK, M. 7 March 1926 (in Spanish).

GERA 13 November 1926 (in German, translated
by L. Andersen).

PRAGUE November 1928 (in German, translated
by L. Andersen).

MOSCOW 9 November 1928 (in Russian, translated
by K. A. Lipskerov).

BUDAPEST 19 November 1933 (in Hungarian,
translated by K. Nádasdy).

MILAN, SC. 30 January 1934 (in Italian, translated
by O. Andolfi).

BERLIN, HOCHSCHULE August 1936 (in German).

HELSINKI 23 March 1938 (in Finnish).

ZEHNTNER: *Dorval, der vierjährige Posten*

4 April. Basle

Text by the composer, founded on T. Körner's
libretto (first set by Schubert in 1815; see
1896). One act.

Revived at Basle 21 January 1935 (as *Amfeld der
Söldner*, in two acts).

MONTEMEZZI: *L'Amore dei tre Re*

10 April. Milan, Sc.

Text by S. Benelli (from his play of the same title
1910). Three acts.

Montemezzi's most important opera; successful
in Italy and abroad. Given at:

NEW YORK, M. 2 January 1914 (in Italian).

PARIS, CH.É. 25 April 1914 (in Italian).

LONDON, C.G. 27 May 1914 (in Italian).

BUENOS AIRES 11 July 1914 (in Italian).

MADRID 1915 (in Italian).

PRAGUE 16 April 1916 (in Czech).

RIO DE JANEIRO 12 September 1919 (in Italian).

BERLIN, D.O. 20 September 1919 (in German,
translated by A. Brüggemann).

LISBON February 1920 (in Italian).

MONTE CARLO 2 March 1920 (in Italian).

VIENNA, V.O. 16 February 1922 (in German).

ANTWERP February 1925 (in French).

HAGUE January 1927 (in Italian).

NICE March 1927 (in French).

GOTHENBURG March 1927 (in Swedish).

LJUBLJANA 30 January 1928 (in Slovenian, translated by N. Štritov).

LAUNIS: *Seitsemän Veljestä*
(Seven Brothers)

11 April. Helsinki

Text by the composer (founded on a novel by A.
Kivi). Four acts.

Launis's first opera; revived Helsinki 21 November 1923.

LATTÈS: *Il était une Bergère*

16 April. Paris, O.C.

Text by A. Rivoire (*conte mélodique*). One act.

Successful in France; revived Paris, O.C. 26
June 1919 and given there until 1925.

In German (translated by R. Presber), Mayence
6 March 1914.

(MASSENET): *Panurge*

25 April. Paris, Gaîté

Text by G. Spitzmüller and M. Boukay (after
Rabelais). *Haulte farce musicale*. Four acts.

The first of Massenet's posthumous operas,
produced the year after his death.

(MARCELLO): *Arianna*

27 April. Venice, Liceo

Text by V. Cassani (*intreccio scenico-musicale*). Two
acts.

The opera was written in 1727; it was not performed in Benedetto Marcello's lifetime. An un-

dated libretto was printed, probably at Venice. The music was discovered in the Milanese private collection of L. Arrigoni (see his letter to *Il Bibliofilo* in November 1884) and published in 1885 by O. Chilesotti in vocal score as Vol.IV of the *Biblioteca di Rarità Musicali*. Parts of the music were performed in concert form under Chilesotti at Turin 19 June 1886 and elsewhere. It was from the 1885 edition that, in 1913, the work was re-orchestrated (by Vittore Veneziani) and produced at the Liceo Benedetto Marcello, Venice, in concert form.

G. CHARPENTIER: *Julien* ou *La Vie du Poète*

4 June. Paris, O.C.
Text by the composer. Prologue and 4 acts.

A sequel to *Louise* (see 1900), but much less successful (20 performances).

Outside Paris, only given at New York, M. 27 January 1914 (in French) and Prague 20 May 1914 (in Czech). Never revived so far.

ALPAERTS: *Shylock*

22 November. Antwerp
(Flemish) text by H. Melis (after Shakespeare). Three acts.

The only opera of the Belgian composer.

WOLF-FERRARI: *Der Liebhaber als Arzt*

4 December. Dresden
(Original Italian) text by E. Golisciani (*L'Amore Medico*, from Molière's comedy), German version by R. Batka. Two acts.
PRAGUE 2 February 1914 (in Czech).
NEW YORK, M. 25 March 1914 (in the original Italian).
TURIN, T.R. 6 March 1929 (in Italian).
ROCHESTER, N.Y. July 1934 (in English, as *Dr. Cupid*, translated by C. Aveling).

MASCAGNI: *Parisina*

15 December. Milan, Sc.
Text by G. d'Annunzio. Four acts (reduced to 3 acts after the first performance).

Outside Italy only given at Buenos Aires 27 May 1914.

1914

SAMUEL-HOLEMAN: *La jeune Fille à la Fenêtre*

7 January. Paris, Th. des Arts
Text by C. Lemonnier. One-act monodrama. Written in 1904. Produced at Paris by the Société Française des Amis de la Musique. Revived Brussels 16 January 1926, by the Cercle artistique et littéraire.

WAGHALTER: *Mandragola*

23 January. Berlin, D.O.
Text by P. Eger (from Macchiavelli's comedy). Three acts.

Successful on German stages; revived at the same theatre 12 October 1919.

In English (translated by A. Kreymborg), New York 4 March 1925.

CASADESUS: *Cachaprès*

2 February. Brussels, M.
Text by H. Cain and C. Lemonnier (from Lemonnier's novel, *Un Mâle*). Three acts.
Casadesus's first opera.

USANDIZAGA: *Las Golondrinas* (The Swallows)

4 February. Madrid, T. Price
Text by G. Martínez Sierra. Three acts.

Usandizaga's most important opera and one of the outstanding works of modern Spanish music. Successful in Spain. Revived Barcelona 14 December 1929; Buenos Aires 21 November 1934; Madrid Summer 1935.

SMAREGLIA: *L'Abisso*

10 February. Milan, Sc.
Text by S. Benco. Three acts.

Smareglia's last opera. Revived Trieste 26 January 1926.

DUPUIS: *Het Lied van Heer Halewijn*

14 February. Antwerp

(Original French) text by L. Solvay, Flemish version by H. Melis. Three acts.

The opera is developed from the composer's Prix de Rome cantata (first performed at Brussels 25 November 1903).

ZANDONAI: *Francesca da Rimini*

19 February. Turin, T.R.

Text by T. Ricordi (from G. d'Annunzio's tragedy, first produced with musical intermezzi by Scontrino, Rome 9 December 1901). Four acts.

Zandonai's chief work; very successful in Italy where it is still given every season. Milan, Sc. 22 February 1916, etc. Also produced at:

LONDON, C.G. 16 July 1914 (in Italian).

BUENOS AIRES 18 May 1915 (in Italian).

RIO DE JANEIRO 6 September 1915 (in Italian).

NEW YORK, M. 22 December 1916 (in Italian).

CHICAGO 5 January 1917 (in Italian).

MALTA 1918 (in Italian).

TRIESTE 14 December 1919 (in Italian).

CAIRO November 1920 (in Italian).

BRUSSELS 9 November 1923 (in French, translated by M. Vaucaire).

LYONS 27 February 1924 (in French, translated by M. Vaucaire).

ALTENBURG 19 March 1925 (in German, translated by A. Brüggemann).

BARCELONA 13 November 1926 (in Italian).

BUDAPEST 3 May 1929 (in Hungarian, translated by V. Lányi).

HAGUE January 1930 (in Italian).

WARSAW March 1932 (in Polish).

LJUBLJANA 14 March 1935 (in Slovenian).

STOCKHOLM 23 October 1937 (in Swedish).

LISBON Spring 1938 (in Italian).

(MASSENET): *Cléopâtre*

23 February. Monte Carlo

Text by L. Payen. Four acts.

The second of Massenet's posthumous operas. In French also, Chicago 10 January 1916; New York 11 February 1919; Paris, Th.L. (Vaudeville) 27 October 1919; Liége January 1921.

(PONCHIELLI): *I Mori di Valenza*

17 March. Monte Carlo

Text by A. Ghislanzoni. Four acts.

Written in 1879 but not performed in Ponchielli's lifetime. The work was discovered in 1902 and orchestrated by A. Cadore. Subsequently given at Milan, Arena 19 July 1914 and revived Cairo Carnival 1931.

MESSAGER: *Béatrice*

21 March. Monte Carlo

Text by R. de Flers and G. A. de Caillavet. Four acts.

In French also, Buenos Aires 15 July 1916; Rio de Janeiro 20 September 1916; Paris, O.C. 23 November 1917 and revived there 25 October 1927.

F. SCHMIDT: *Notre Dame*

1 April. Vienna, O.

Text by the composer and L. Wilk (after Victor Hugo). Two acts.

Schmidt's first and best opera; also given at Budapest 14 December 1916 (in Hungarian, translated by V. Lányi); Berlin 8 May 1918 (in German); Ljubljana Autumn 1923 (in Slovenian). Revived at Vienna 14 December 1938.

ALFANO: *L'Ombra di Don Giovanni*

2 April. Milan, Sc.

Text by E. Moschino. Three acts.

Revived Florence May 1941 (in a new version, a *Don Giovanni di Manara*).

SINDING: *Der heilige Berg*

19 April. Dessau

(German) text by D. Duncker. Prologue and 2 acts.

The only opera of the well-known Norwegian composer. Given at Oslo 16 November 1931 in concert form.

KEUSSLER: *Gefängnisse*

22 April. Prague, G.

Text by the composer (*Sinfonisches Drama*). Three parts.

Keussler's first opera.

BACHELET: *Scemo*

6 May. Paris, O.

Text by C. Méré. Three acts.

Bachelet's first opera. Revived Paris, O.C. 20 May 1926.

RABAUD: *Mârouf, Savetier du Caire*

15 May. Paris, O.C.

Text by L. Népoty (from a story in the *Arabian Nights*, in J. C. Mardrus's French version). Five acts.

Rabaud's best and most successful work; given on many French stages and at:

STOCKHOLM 16 October 1915 (in Swedish, translated by S. Nyblom).

MILAN, SC. 24 March 1917; Rome, C. 29 December 1920, etc. (in Italian, translated by C. Clausetti).

BUENOS AIRES 24 July 1917 (in Italian).

RIO DE JANEIRO 5 September 1917 (in Italian).

NEW YORK, M. 19 December 1917 (in French) and 21 May 1937 (in English, translated by M. Marshall and G. Mead).

GENEVA 18 January 1918 (in French).

BRUSSELS 8 May 1919 (in French).

BARCELONA, TIVOLI 1919 and L. 15 April 1922 (in French); a Catalan version by J. Pena was published in 1922.

ZURICH May 1924 (in German, translated by O. Neitzel).

CAIRO Carnival 1926 (in Italian).

DESSAU 13 November 1926 (in German).

VIENNA 24 January 1929 (in German).

ZAGREB 23 March 1929 (in Croatian).

ANTWERP 20 February 1937 (in Flemish).

First given at the Paris Opéra 22 June 1928 (revived 10 January 1940); revived at the Scala, Milan 18 January 1939. Not yet produced in England.

WEINGARTNER: *Kain und Abel*

17 May. Darmstadt

Text by the composer. One act.

Also given at Vienna 4 December 1914; Prague 1915.

A Catalan translation by J. Pena was published in 1925.

SIEGEL: *Herr Dandolo*

23 May. Essen

Text by W. Vesper (founded on an Italian comedy by G. Giraud). Three acts.

Siegel's first opera; first produced at the Tonkünstlerfest of the Allgemeiner Deutscher Musikverein. Revived Munich 19 July 1919 and once more Lübeck April 1937.

BIANCHINI: *Radda*

25 May. Paris, Gaîté

(Original Italian) text by P. Bianchini (founded on a novel by M. Gorki), French version by J. de Marliave. Two acts.

Bianchini's first opera. Revived in the original Italian, Venice, F. 24 January 1924.

ANDREAE: *Ratcliff*

25 May. Duisburg

Text from H. Heine's tragedy. Four scenes.

The first opera of the Swiss composer; first produced at the Tonkünstlerfest of the Allgemeiner Deutscher Musikverein. Zurich 11 April 1916.

STRAVINSKY: *Rossignol*

26 May. Paris, O.

(Russian) text by the composer and S. N. Mitusov (from H. C. Andersen's tale). Three acts.

Stravinsky's first opera; the first act had been written in 1908–09, the second and third act in 1913–14. First produced at Paris by B. Sanine and revived there 2 February 1920, with choreography by L. Massine, as a symphonic ballet, called *Le Chant du Rossignol*. Outside Paris, given at:

LONDON, D.L. 18 June 1914 (in Russian) and C.G. 12 November 1919 (in English, translated by E. Agate).

LENINGRAD Autumn 1920 (in Russian).

MANNHEIM 5 May 1923 (in German).

NEW YORK, M. 7 March 1926 (in French, translated by M. D. Calvocoressi).

MILAN, SC. 14 May 1926 (in Italian, translated by R. Küfferle).

BUENOS AIRES 28 June 1927 (in Italian, translated by R. Küfferle).

PRAGUE May 1935 (in German).

VIVES: *Maruxa*

28 May. Madrid, T.R.

Text by L. P. Frutos. *Egloga lírica.* Two acts.

One of the most successful works of the Spanish composer. Given at Barcelona, Novedades 21 September 1914 and L. 18 November 1916.

In Spanish also, New York 19 April 1919.

In Italian (translated by A. Nessi), Palermo 23 April 1924.

Still very popular in Spain and South America.

MACKENZIE: *The Cricket on the Hearth*

6 June. London, R.A.M.

Text by J. R. Sturgis (after Dickens). Three acts.

Revived at the R.A.M. 12 July 1922 and 15 July 1936. Publicly produced Glasgow 13 August 1923. The opera had been published as early as 1901.

GRAENER: *Don Juans letztes Abenteuer*

11 June. Leipzig

Text by O. Anthes. Three acts.

Graener's first success.

In German also, Prague January 1920; Basle 12 May 1922; Berlin, D.O. 23 May 1924, etc. Revived in a new version, Hamburg 25 October 1935.

HOLBROOKE: *Dylan: Son of the Wave*

4 July. London, D.L.

Text by T. E. Ellis. Three acts.

The second part of his Welsh trilogy (see 1912 and 1929); this part had been published first (in 1910).

BOUGHTON: *The Immortal Hour*

26 August. Glastonbury

Text adapted from the plays and poems of "Fiona Macleod" (W. Sharp). Two acts.

First given at the Old Vic., London 31 May 1920 (by the Glastonbury players); Birmingham 23 June 1921, and (by the Birmingham players) London, Regent Th. 13 October 1922 (given for 216 nights). Further revivals: London, Kingsway 30 January 1926; New York 6 April 1926 (by the Opera Players, Grove Street); Stroud, Glos. 11 September 1934; London, R.A.M. 11 July 1939.

Few English operas have enjoyed such a lasting success.

TURINA: *Margot*

10 October. Madrid, Z.

Text by G. Martínez Sierra (*Comedia lírica*). Three acts.

Turina's first opera.

1915

FRANCHETTI: *Notte di Leggenda*

14 January. Milan, Sc.

Text by G. Forzano. One act.

Successful in Italy.

GIORDANO: *Madame Sans-Gêne*

25 January. New York, M.

Text by R. Simoni (from the French play by V. Sardou and E. Moreau). Three acts.

Produced in New York in Italian, and subsequently given at:

TURIN 28 February 1915; Milan, T.d.V. 18 September 1915, etc. (in Italian).

MONTE CARLO 19 March 1916 (in French, translated by P. Milliet).

PARIS, O.C. 10 June 1916 (in French, translated by P. Milliet).

MALTA 1917 (in Italian).

BUENOS AIRES 5 August 1919 (in Italian).

BRESLAU 4 March 1931 (in German, translated by A. Brüggemann).

Frequently revived in Italy.

LACCETTI: *Il Miracolo*

February. Naples, S.C.

Text by E. Moschino (founded on a Spanish story by J. Zorrilla). Three acts.

Successful in Italy.

PIZZETTI: *Fedra*

20 March. Milan, Sc.

Text by G. d'Annunzio (originally published as a tragedy in 1909). Three acts.

Pizzetti's first opera and one of his most important works. After the war revived at Parma 27 January 1920 and in Italian also given at Buenos Aires 11 August 1920; Montevideo August 1920; Rio de Janeiro 3 September 1920; Lisbon December 1926.

In French (translated by A. Doderet), Paris, O. 7 June 1923.

ROMANI: *Fedra*

3 April. Rome, C.

Text by A. Lenzoni (*rapsodia tragica*). One act.

Awarded the first prize in a competition instituted by the City of Rome. Revived London, C.G. 18 June 1931 (in Italian).

PARKER: *Fairyland*

1 July. Los Angeles

Text by B. Hooker. Three acts.

This opera was awarded the $10.000 prize of the National Federation of Women's Clubs.

SCHILLINGS: *Mona Lisa*

26 September. Stuttgart

Text by B. Dovsky. Prologue, 2 acts and epilogue.

Schillings's most successful work and one of the most popular German operas of the 20th century. After its success, the composer (who died in 1933) did not write another opera.

In German also given at Vienna 4 October 1915; Berlin 15 October 1915 (100th performance 8 June 1925); Prague 1 January 1916; Strasbourg 6 February 1916; Basle 3 December 1916; Amsterdam January 1918; Barcelona 27 January 1923; New York, M. 1 March 1923; Oslo May 1923.

In Lettish, Riga 16 May 1923.

In Finnish, Helsinki 22 April 1924.

In Swedish, Stockholm 28 October 1924.

In Russian, Leningrad 27 March 1926.

In Polish, Warsaw December 1926.

In French (translated by P. Spaak), Brussels 4 February 1928.

L. NIELSEN: *Isbella*

8 October. Copenhagen

Text by P. A. Rosenberg. One act.

The first opera of the Danish composer Ludolf Nielsen (no relation to C. A. Nielsen).

NOVÁK: *Zvíkovský Rarášek*
(The Imp of Zvikov)

10 October. Prague, Cz.

Text from a comedy by L. Stroupežnický. One act.

Novák's first opera. Revived Prague 1 December 1930.

OLENIN: *Kudeyar*
Кудеяр

26 November. Moscow

Text by the composer. Olenin's only opera.

LEROUX: *Les Cadeaux de Noël*

25 December. Paris, O.C.

Text by E. Fabre (*conte héroïque*). One act.

Subsequently given at Rome, C. 3 March 1917; Milan, Sc. 7 March 1917 (in French; first opera ever sung there in a language other than Italian) and 28 March 1917 (in Italian); Monte Carlo 8 April 1917 (in French).

1916

BARKWORTH: *Romeo and Juliet*

7 January. Middlesbrough

Text by the composer (arranged from Shakespeare). Four acts.

First given in London, Surrey 10 April 1920 and revived at the R.C.M. 30 November 1926.

STANFORD: *The Critic;* or, *An Opera Rehearsed*

14 January. London, Shaftesbury

Text by L. C. James (after Sheridan). Two acts.

The last of Stanford's operas which was produced in his lifetime.

SMYTH: *The Boatswain's Mate*

28 January. London, Shaftesbury

Text by the composer (founded on a story by W. W. Jacobs). One act.

Revived London, Old Vic 30 March 1922 and C.G. 11 June 1923.

GRANADOS: *Goyescas*

28 January. New York, M.

Text by F. Periquet y Zuaznabar. Three scenes.

Granados's last opera, the music made up chiefly from his piano suite of the same title (1912). First Spanish opera produced in New York. On his return to Europe the composer was drowned when the "Sussex" was torpedoed in the Channel 24 March 1916.

Revived Paris, O. 17 December 1919 (in French, translated by L. Laloy); Buenos Aires 8 August 1929 (in Spanish); Milan, Sc. 28 December 1937 (in Italian); Barcelona Summer 1940 (in Spanish).

WEINGARTNER: *Dame Kobold*

23 February. Darmstadt

Text by the composer (after Calderón). Three acts.

Berlin, D.O. 17 March 1916, etc. Revived Basle 20 November 1932.

d'ALBERT: *Die toten Augen*

5 March. Dresden

(Original French) text by M. Henry, German version by H. H. Ewers. Prologue and 1 act.

(The French original *Les Yeux morts* was first published in *La Revue de Hollande*, October 1916.)

One of d'Albert's greatest successes; the opera was given at:

BERLIN, D.O. 26 October 1916 (in German).
GRAZ November 1917 (in German).
BASLE 6 January 1918 (in German).
COPENHAGEN 17 March 1918 (in Danish, translated by L. C. Nielsen).
VIENNA, V.O. 19 February 1919 (in German).
PRAGUE January 1920 (in German).
STOCKHOLM 27 September 1920 (in Swedish).
WARSAW Autumn 1920 (in Polish).
BUDAPEST 12 November 1921 (in Hungarian, translated by A. Kern).
CHICAGO 1 November 1923 (in German).
NEW YORK 3 January 1924 (in German).
ANTWERP 27 September 1924 (in Flemish).
HAGUE January 1925 (in Dutch).
LJUBLJANA 1925 (in Slovenian).
RIGA 12 September 1925 (in Lettish).
ZAGREB 8 April 1933 (in Croatian).
SOFIA 11 April 1938 (in Bulgarian).

KORNGOLD: *Violanta* and *Der Ring des Polykrates*

28 March. Munich

Two one-act operas, produced on the same bill. Text of *Violanta* by H. Müller; text of *Der Ring des Polykrates* from a comedy by H. Teweles (1889).

The first operas of the then 19 year old composer. Successful in Germany. Both operas were subsequently given at Vienna 10 April 1916; Berlin 2 November 1917; Prague 1918; and, in Swedish, Stockholm 19 September 1918.

Violanta was also given at Budapest 27 February 1918 (in Hungarian, translated by K. Sebestyén) and New York 6 November 1926 (in German).

Der Ring des Polykrates was also given at Helsinki 14 March 1931 (in Finnish).

Revived at Vienna 14 March 1929 (in German).

J. BRANDTS-BUYS: *Die Schneider von Schönau*

1 April. Dresden

Text by B. Warden and I. M. Welleminsky. Three acts.

The most successful opera of the Dutch composer.

In German also, Vienna 20 February 1917; Berlin, D.O. 25 October 1917; Basle 15 March 1929. In Dutch, Amsterdam 1917.

H. HUBER: *Die schöne Bellinda*

2 April. Berne

Text by G. Bundi. Prologue and 3 acts.

Successful in Switzerland; produced both at Basle and Zurich 11 November 1917.

DUPUIS: *La Passion*

2 April. Monte Carlo.

Text by J. Méry and P. de Choudens. Four acts. Dupuis's chief work.

In French also, Liége 2 April 1920; Antwerp December 1925; Brussels 4 December 1934.

Revived Liége December 1938; Brussels 21 March 1940.

MONLEONE: *Suona la Ritirata*

23 May. Milan, T.L.

Text by G. Monleone, the brother of the composer (founded on a German play, *Zapfenstreich*, by F. A. Beyerlein). Three acts.

Revived in German, Cottbus 21 March 1926.

DE ROGATIS: *Huemac*

28 July. Buenos Aires

(Italian) text by E. Montagne (on an *Inca* subject). One act.

Also given at Rio de Janeiro 13 September 1916 and revived at Buenos Aires in 1932.

BIENSTOCK: *Sandro der Narr*

24 September. Stuttgart

Text by "H. H. Hinzelmann" (pseudonym of K. M. von Levetzow and L. Feld). Three acts.

Bienstock's last opera; revived Stuttgart May 1930.

BITTNER: *Das höllisch Gold*

15 October. Darmstadt

Text by the composer (from a play by Hans Sachs). One act.

Bittner's most successful opera; given at Vienna, V.O. 17 April 1917; Berlin, D.O. 13 December 1917; Prague 1918; Basle 5 January 1919, etc. Revived Vienna, O. 4 December 1925.

NOVÁK: *Karlštejn*

18 November. Prague, Cz.

Text by O. Fischer (founded on a comedy by J. Vrchlický). Three acts.

Revived Prague 4 December 1930 and 24 March 1936.

HOLST: *Sāvitri*

5 December. London, Wellington Hall

Text by the composer (*An Episode from the Mahābharata*). One act.

Holst's first performed opera; first produced by the London School of Opera; revived in London, Lyric 23 June 1921; C.G. 28 June 1923; R.C.M. 1926; Sadler's Wells 23 October 1935; Oxford 9 March 1937; Cincinnati Summer 1939.

KIENZL: *Das Testament*

6 December. Vienna, V.O.

Text by the composer (founded on a story by P. Rosegger). Two acts.

Berlin, D.O. 22 December 1916; Graz 27 January 1917, etc.

LENDVAI: *Elga*

6 December. Mannheim

Text by M. von Zobeltitz (from G. Hauptmann's play of the same title). *Ein Nocturnus.* Seven scenes.

Lendvai's only opera. Given in a new version, Leipzig 15 October 1918.

BRUNEAU: *Les quatre Journées*

25 December. Paris, O.C.

Text by the composer (after Zola). Four acts.

Performed 8 times in 1916–17. Not revived so far.

In 1916 was published (and produced?) one of the earliest of the very few original Greek operas:

Ho Protomastoras

(The Master Mason)

by M. Kalomoiris, text from P. Psiloreites's tragedy (1910) of the same title, 2 acts, with an intermezzo. The opera was revived in concert form at Athens in 1930 (to celebrate the centenary of Greek independence).

For an account of the work, see *Revue Musicale*, October 1930.

1917

OBERLEITHNER: *Der eiserne Heiland*

20 January. Vienna, V.O.

Text by B. Warden and I. M. Welleminsky. Three acts.

Oberleitner's most successful opera. Given at Berlin, D.O. 21 September 1918, etc.

In Hungarian, Budapest May 1918. Revived Vienna, O. 15 June 1930.

ZEMLINSKY: *Eine florentinische Tragödie*

30 January. Stuttgart

Text: Oscar Wilde's play in M. Meyerfeld's German version. One act.

In German also, Vienna 27 April 1917; Prague 1917. Revived Brünn 1929.

LAUNIS: *Kullervo*

28 February. Helsinki

Text by A. Kivi (from the *Kalevala*). Three acts.

Revived Helsinki 19 April 1934. The opera was broadcast in a French version by C. Boissard from

Nice 30 July 1938, and produced there on the stage in March 1940.

DE KOVEN: *The Canterbury Pilgrims*

8 March. New York, M.

Text by P. W. Mackaye. Four acts.

De Koven's first attempt at grand opera. Given at Philadelphia 20 March 1917.

RÓZYCKI: *Eros und Psyche*

10 March. Breslau

(Original Polish) text by J. Zulawski, German version by S. Goldenring and F. Leo. Five acts.

One of Rózycki's best works; awarded the grand prize of the Polish State in 1931. First given at Warsaw 2 September 1917 (in the original Polish).

In Slovenian, Osijek, Jugoslavia Spring 1923 and Ljubljana 30 March 1927.

In Swedish, Stockholm 23 February 1935.

PUCCINI: *La Rondine*

27 March. Monte Carlo

Text by G. Adami (translated from a German libretto by A. M. Willner and H. Reichert). Three acts.

(Originally, the work had been planned as an operetta for the Vienna Carl-Theater.) Produced at Monte Carlo in Italian; subsequently given at Bologna 5 June 1917; Milan 7 October 1917; Rome January 1918; Naples 26 February 1918, etc.

BUENOS AIRES 24 May 1917 (in Italian).

RIO DE JANEIRO 1 September 1917 (in Italian).

VIENNA, V.O. 9 October 1920 (in German, retranslated by R. S. Hoffmann).

MALTA 1921 (in Italian).

MONTE CARLO February 1926 (this time in French, translated by P. Milliet).

BUDAPEST April 1927 (in Hungarian, translated by Z. Harsányi).

KIEL 5 November 1927 (in German).

NEW YORK 10 March 1928 (in Italian); revived 17 January 1936.

DETROIT 7 May 1935 (in English, translated by K. de Jaffa).

The opera was broadcast from London 24 June 1929 (English version by D. M. Craig).

DE SABATA: *Il Macigno*
31 March. Milan, Sc.

Text by A. Colantuoni. Three acts.

De Sabata's first opera. Given at the Scala 3 times only.

ENNA: *Gloria Arsena*
15 April. Copenhagen

Text by the composer and O. Hansen (after A. Dumas). Four acts.

In German (translated by C. Wechselmann), Halle 28 April 1918.

MASCAGNI: *Lodoletta*
30 April. Rome, C.

Text by G. Forzano (founded on Ouida's *Two Little Wooden Shoes*). Three acts.

Successful in Italy.

In Italian also given at Buenos Aires 29 July 1917; Rio de Janeiro 17 September 1917; New York, M. 12 January 1918; Montevideo 1918; Malta 1919; Lisbon June 1939.

In German (translated by R. Batka), Vienna, V.O. 9 April 1920.

BUSONI: *Turandot* and *Arlecchino*
11 May. Zurich

Two short operas, produced on the same bill.

Turandot

Text by the composer (from Gozzi's comedy). Two acts.

Busoni's music was developed from incidental pieces written for Max Reinhardt's production of Gozzi's play (in K. Vollmöller's German version) at Berlin, Deutsches Th. 27 October 1911 (and New Haven 31 December 1912 and London, St. J.'s 18 January 1913 in an English version by J. Bithell).

Arlecchino

Ein theatralisches Capriccio. One act. Text by the composer.

Both operas were also given at Frankfort 21 October 1918 and Berlin 19 May 1921.

Arlecchino was revived at Vienna, V.O. 11 February 1926 and Prague June 1928 (in German). Broadcast from London 27 January 1939 (in English, translated by E. J. Dent). In Italian, Venice, F. 30 January 1940. *Turandot* was broadcast from Turin 29 November 1936 (in Italian).

PFITZNER: *Palestrina*
12 June. Munich

Text by the composer (*Musikalische Legende*). Three acts.

Pfitzner's most important work. Produced by the Munich company subsequently at Basle 20 November 1917; Berne 22 November 1917; and Zurich 24 November 1917.

First given at Vienna 1 March 1919; Berlin 11 October 1919; Frankfort 28 March 1920; Cologne 15 May 1920; Stuttgart 24 October 1920 and in many other German towns; also produced at Antwerp February 1939 (in German, by the Cologne opera company).

(It may be mentioned that there exists an earlier opera of the same title and on the same subject, a *Wort- und Tondichtung für die Schaubühne*, text and music by M. E. Sachs, which was produced at Regensburg 18 March 1886).

(MUSORGSKY): *Sorochinskaya Yarmarka*
Сорочинская Ярмарка
(The Fair of Sorochintsy)
26 October. Petrograd

Text by the composer (founded on an episode from Gogol's *Evenings on a Farm near Dikanka*). Three acts.

Musorgsky had begun to work at this opera as early as 1875; he left it unfinished, without the greater part of the last act and without orchestration. Several attempts were made to restore the opera. Prior to 1917, the work had been heard semi-publicly at St. Petersburg, Comedia Theatre 30 December 1911.

Another version, with orchestration by Y. S. Sakhnovsky, and with spoken dialogue supplied by K. A. Mardzhanov, was produced at the Free Theatre, Moscow 3 November 1913 and revived there on 10 January 1925.

In 1917, the opera was produced in a version by C. Kyui (who added music of his own) at the Musical Drama Theatre. His version has since been replaced by yet another one for which N. N. Cherepnin was responsible, and it was in the Cherepnin version that the opera made its way into many countries. It was first produced at Monte Carlo 17 March 1923 (in French, translated by L. Laloy) and subsequently given at:

BARCELONA 23 December 1924 (in Russian).

BRUSSELS 12 January 1925 (in French).

BRESLAU 6 May 1925 ('n German, translated by H. Möller).

ZAGREB 31 June 1925 (in Croatian).

REICHENBERG Autumn 1928 (in German).

BUENOS AIRES 26 September 1929 (in Russian).

VIENNA 5 January 1930 (in concert form) and 13 February 1935 (on the stage; in German).

NEW YORK, M. 29 November 1930 (in Italian).

RIGA 18 February 1932 (in Lettish).

LONDON, FORTUNE TH. 17 February 1934 (in Russian) and C.G. 24 November 1936 (in English, translated by E. Agate; revived Savoy 6 October 1941 and Adelphi 2 February 1942 (in Russian).

SOFIA 10 June 1936 (in Bulgarian).

STOCKHOLM 19 November · 1938 (in Swedish, translated by W. Sebaldin and H. Sandberg).

TRIESTE January 1940 (in Italian).

Yet another version, by V. Y. Shebalin and P. A. Lamm, was produced at Leningrad, Little Opera Theatre 21 December 1931 and Moscow 12 January 1932.

KAUN: *Sappho*

27 October. Leipzig

Text by the composer (from F. Grillparzer's play). Three acts.

Kaun's first performed opera.

SEKLES: *Scharazade*

2 November. Mannheim

Text by G. von Bassewitz. Three acts.

Sekles's first opera. Graz October 1919; Berlin 5 June 1920, etc.

COURVOISIER: *Lanzelot und Elaine*

3 November. Munich

Text by W. Bergh (after Tennyson). Four acts.

Courvoisier's first opera; also given at Basle 28 April 1918.

S. WAGNER: *An allem ist Hütchen schuld*

6 December. Stuttgart

Text by the composer. Three acts.

Revived Berlin, Hochschule für Musik 24 March 1934.

PFITZNER: *Christelflein*

11 December. Dresden

Text by I. von Stach. Two acts.

(Developed from incidental music to I. von Stach's Christmas play, first produced at Munich 11 December 1906.)

The operatic version was also given (in German) at Strasbourg 13 January 1918; Berlin 19 November 1921; Prague December 1921; Graz December 1923; Zurich 17 December 1924; Basle 17 December 1926; Vienna, V.O. 6 December 1938.

HADLEY: *Azora, Daughter of Montezuma*

26 December. Chicago

Text by D. Stevens. Three acts.

New York 26 January 1918, etc.

1918

NEVIN: *The Daughter of the Forest*

5 January. Chicago

Text by R. Hartley. One act.

Nevin's second and last opera.

LAZZARI: *Le Sauteriot*

19 January. Chicago

Text by H. P. Roché and M. Périer (founded on a German play by E. von Keyserling, *Ein Frühlingsopfer*). Three acts.

In French also given at New York 11 February 1918; Paris, O.C. 8 April 1920.

In Flemish, Antwerp 1927.

RADEGLIA: *Schaaban*

20 February. Vienna, V.O.

(Original Turkish) text by Djelal Essad Bey, German version by R. Batka. Three acts.

The last opera of Radeglia, who was the composer of the Turkish national anthem. Probably the first and only Turkish opera ever produced in Europe; there is no record that the original was performed at Constantinople at all.

CADMAN: *Shanewis*

23 March. New York, M.

Text by N. R. Eberhardt. Two acts.

Cadman's first performed opera. Revived Denver, Colorado 5 December 1924; Los Angeles 24 June 1926.

KLENAU: *Kjartan und Gudrun*

4 April. Mannheim

Text by the composer. Three acts.

Revived in a new version as *Gudrun auf Island*, Hagen, Westphalia 27 November 1924.

SCHREKER: *Die Gezeichneten*

25 April. Frankfort

Text by the composer. Three acts.

Given at Munich 15 February 1919; Vienna 27 February 1920; Berlin 5 January 1921 and on many other German stages.

BARTOK: *A Kékszakállú Herceg Vára*
(Duke Blue-Beard's Castle)

24 May. Budapest

Text by B. Balázs. One act.

Bartok's only opera.

In German (translated by W. Ziegler), Frankfort 13 May 1922; Berlin, D.O. 16 January 1929.

Revived Budapest Spring 1937; in Hungarian also given at Florence 5 May 1938 (by a Hungarian company at the Maggio Musicale Fiorentino).

GRAENER: *Theophano*

5 June. Munich

Text by O. Anthes. Three acts.

In German also, Brünn June 1919.

Revived in a new version (as *Byzanz*), Leipzig 22 April 1922.

MARINUZZI: *Jacquerie*

11 August. Buenos Aires

Text by A. Donaudy. Three acts.

Marinuzzi's most successful opera; in Italian also, given at Rio de Janeiro 30 September 1918; Rome 6 March 1919, etc.; Chicago 17 November 1920 (at the inauguration of the Auditorium); New York 4 February 1921.

(SCHUBERT): *Fernando*

18 August. Magdeburg

Text by A. Stadler. One act.

Written in 1815; produced only 103 years later (music revised by B. Engelke).

NOETZEL: *Meister Guido*

15 September. Carlsruhe

Text by the composer. Three acts.

Munich 20 February 1920, etc. In German also, Zurich February 1923. Revived Graz 7 May 1932.

STRAVINSKY: *Histoire du Soldat*

28 September. Lausanne

Text by C. F. Ramuz (*Histoire lue, jouée et dansée*). Two parts.

Certainly very far from being an opera in the traditional sense of the word, the work should nevertheless be recorded as an experimental attempt at simplifying and developing forms. See

Stravinsky's autobiography for details regarding the conception, composition, and production of the work. After the war, given at:

LONDON 20 July 1920 (in concert form, at Wigmore Hall; parts only) and 10 July 1927 (on the stage, by the Arts Theatre Club; English version by R. Newmarch).

BRUSSELS 17 January 1923 (in concert form).

FRANKFORT 20 June 1923 (in concert form) and 10 June 1924 (on the stage); German version by H. Reinhart.

BERLIN 13 January 1924 (stage; at the Volksbühne).

NEW YORK 23 March 1924 (concert).

PARIS, CH.É. 24 April 1924 (stage).

ROME 8 April 1925 (stage; at the T. Odescalchi).

BRNO 24 November 1925 (in Czech).

ATHENS 28 January 1926 (concert).

VIENNA, V.O. 11 February 1926 (concert).

AMSTERDAM 27 February 1926 (in Dutch, translated by M. Nijhoff).

BUENOS AIRES June 1926 (concert).

COPENHAGEN 27 May 1927 (in Danish, translated by G. Hetsch, concert).

WARSAW 8 December 1927 (in Polish, translated by J. Tuwim).

PRAGUE 10 December 1927 (in Czech) and December 1935 (in German).

CAMBRIDGE 7 November 1928 (stage performance).

LIVERPOOL 11 January 1929 (stage performance).

BUDAPEST Spring 1929 (stage performance).

BARCELONA Summer 1935 (in concert form).

TEL-AVIV November 1939 (in Hebrew, translated by A. Hammeiri).

MONTEMEZZI: *La Nave*

1 November. Milan, Sc.

Text by T. Ricordi (from G. d'Annunzio's tragedy which had been first produced with musical intermezzi by Pizzetti at Rome 11 January 1908). Prologue and 3 acts.

In Italian also, Chicago 18 November 1919. Revived Rome 14 December 1938.

S. WAGNER: *Schwarzschwanenreich*

5 November. Carlsruhe

Text by the composer. Three acts.

Given on many German stages and (in German) also at Antwerp 7 December 1937.

H. HUBER: *Frutta di Mare*

24 November. Basle

Text by F. Karmin. Three acts.

Huber's last opera.

WEHRLI: *Das heiss Eisen*

11 December. Berne

Text from a play by Hans Sachs. One act.

Zurich 30 May 1920.

PUCCINI: *Trittico*

14 December. New York, M.

Consists of three one-act operas; *Il Tabarro*, text by G. Adami (founded on D. Gold's *Houppelande*); *Suor Angelica*, text by G. Forzano; *Gianni Schicchi*, text by G. Forzano.

Performances of the whole triptych took place at:

ROME, C. 11 January 1919 (in Italian).

BUENOS AIRES 25 June 1919 (in Italian).

RIO DE JANEIRO 22 September 1919 (in Italian).

CHICAGO 6 December 1919 (in Italian).

LONDON, C.G. 18 June 1920 (in Italian) and Duke's Hall 13 July 1937 (in English; R.A.M. performance).

VIENNA 20 October 1920 (in German, translated by A. Brüggemann).

STOCKHOLM 20 November 1920 (in Swedish).

HAMBURG 2 February 1921 (in German, translated by A. Brüggemann).

PRAGUE 8 February 1921 (in German, translated by A. Brüggemann).

MONTE CARLO 24 March 1921 (in Italian).

LJUBLJANA 10 June 1922 (in Slovenian, translated by I. Šorli).

BUDAPEST 9 December 1922 (in Hungarian, translated by K. Nádasdy).

GHENT January 1923 (in French).

BERNE Autumn 1924 (in German).
ZAGREB 12 May 1927 (in Croatian).
BERLIN 28 March 1928 (in German).
KAUNAS 13 January 1933 (in Lithuanian).
SOFIA 20 January 1936 (in Bulgarian).

Besides (and in many cases before) the cyclic performances, productions of the single operas took place as follows:

Il Tabarro

BERLIN, D.O. 26 March 1924 (in German).
ANTWERP 1924 (in French, translated by D. Gold).
MALTA Carnival 1924 (in Italian).
OSLO February 1934 (in Norwegian).
LONDON, S.'S W. 23 October 1935 (in English, translated by H. Withers).

Suor Angelica

LYONS March 1929 (in French, translated by P. Ferrier).
LONDON, R.A.M. 21 July 1931 (in English, translated by H. Withers).

There was an audition of *Suor Angelica* at the convent of Vicopelago (near Lucca) where Puccini's eldest sister was a nun.

Gianni Schicchi

BRUSSELS 5 January 1922 (in French, translated by P. Ferrier).
PARIS, O.C. 6 November 1922 (in French, translated by P. Ferrier).
BERLIN 25 April 1923 (in German).
GLASGOW 7 November 1923 (in English, translated by P. Pitt).
LONDON, C.G. 15 January 1924 (in English, translated by P. Pitt).
COPENHAGEN 23 April 1924 (in Danish, translated by S. Levyson).
ZURICH 14 February 1926 (in German).
BUCHAREST April 1927 (in Rumanian).
AMSTERDAM December 1928 (in Italian).
MALTA 1929 (in Italian).
HELSINKI 14 March 1931 (in Finnish).
RIGA 3 September 1932 (in Lettish).
NEW YORK 23 February 1933 (in English, at the Juilliard School of Music) and 27 January 1936 (at the Metropolitan).
PRAGUE 13 January 1937 (in Czech).

J. B. FOERSTER: *Nepřemoženi* (The Invincibles)

19 December. Prague, Cz.

Text by the composer. Four acts.

Revived Prague 5 December 1929 and 17 September 1936.

1919

FÉVRIER: *Gismonda*

14 January. Chicago

Text by H. Cain and L. Payen (from V. Sardou's play). Four acts.

In French also, given at New York 27 January 1919; Paris, O.C. 15 October 1919; Ghent January 1921; Geneva 16 December 1921; Cairo January 1922.

SANTOLIQUIDO: *Ferhuda*

30 January. Tunis

Text by the composer. *Scene di Vita Araba.* Three acts.

This seems to be the first and only Italian opera originally produced at Tunis. Vocal score published.

(OFFENBACH): *Der Goldschmied von Toledo*

7 February. Mannheim

Text by K. G. Zwerenz (founded on E. T. A. Hoffmann's *Das Fräulein von Scuderi*). Three acts.

Said to be a posthumous work of Offenbach, but really a pasticcio from his less known works, especially from *Der schwarze Korsar* (Vienna 1872), arranged by J. Stern and A. Zamara.

In German also given at Vienna, V.O. 10 February 1920, etc; Brünn 1928.

In English (translated by C. Aveling), Edinburgh 16 March 1922; London, C.G. 4 May 1922.

In Polish, Lemberg 1922.

R. BOSSI: *Passa la Ronda!*

3 March. Milan, T.L.

Text by L. Orsini (from a play by R. Francheville). One act.

In German (translated by W. Weber), Bremen 3 October 1928.

HUGO: *The Temple Dancer*
BREIL: *The Legend*

12 March. New York, M.

Two one-act operas by American composers. Text of *The Temple Dancer* by J. Bell-Ranske; text of *The Legend* by J. Byrne. Unsuccessful.

BARRIOS and CAMPO: *El Avapiés*

8 March. Madrid, T.R.

Text by T. Borrás. Three acts.

(For an account of this Spanish opera, see J. B. Trend, *A Picture of Modern Spain*, p.179.)

MESSAGER: *Monsieur Beaucaire*

7 April. Birmingham

(Original French) text by A. Rivoire and P. Veber (founded on a story by N. B. Tarkington). English version by F. Lonsdale, lyrics by A. Ross. Prologue and 3 acts.

Messager's last great success.

In English subsequently given in London, Prince's 19 April 1919 (for 221 nights); New York 11 December 1919; Montreal 18 October 1920; revived London, Daly's 16 November 1931.

In the original French, Paris, Th. Marigny 21 November 1925; Monte Carlo November 1927. Revived Paris, Gaîté Lyrique 5 October 1929 and 31 August 1935; Buenos Aires 23 June 1938.

HAHN: *Nausicaa*
FAURÉ: *Masques et Bergamasques*

10 April. Monte Carlo

Two short operas, librettos by R. Fauchois. *Nausicaa* (2 acts) was also produced at Liége February 1922 and revived at the O.C., Paris 18 June 1923. *Masques et Bergamasques* (*divertissement lyrique*, 1 act) was first given at the O.C., Paris 4 March 1920 (revived 14 March 1931) and on many other French stages; in French also, Cairo Spring 1938.

SCHOECK: *Don Ranudo de Colibrados*

16 April. Zurich

Text by A. Rüeger (founded on Holberg's comedy of the same title). Four acts.

The first great success of the Swiss composer. Given at Stuttgart 26 November 1919; Basle 30 September 1920; Berne 7 November 1920, and revived in a reduced version Dresden 3 October 1930; Zurich 24 January 1931; Berne 30 October 1931 and September 1940.

SAVIN: *Ksenia*

29 May. Zurich

(Original Serbian) text by the composer, German version by W. Haeser.

The first opera of the Serbian composer.

VIVES: *Balada de Carnaval*

5 July. Madrid, Gran T.

Text by L. Fernández Ardavín and J. Montero. One act.

Barcelona 12 January 1920, etc.

ZANDONAI: *La Via della Finestra*

27 July. Pesaro

Text by G. Adami (founded on a comedy by Scribe). Three acts.

Successful in Italy; Rome 2 February 1920, etc. Also Malta 1 March 1920.

Revived in a reduced two-act version, Trieste 18 January 1923; Milan, Sc. 6 January 1930; Pesaro July 1937.

BERUTTI: *Gli Eroi*

23 August. Buenos Aires

(Original Spanish) text by the composer (founded on an episode in V. F. López's novel, *La Loca de la Guardia*), Italian version by E. Campana. Prologue and 3 acts.

The last opera of the Argentine composer.

GAITO: *Cayo Petronio*

2 September. Buenos Aires

(Italian) text by U. Romanelli. Three acts.

Gaito's most successful opera; revived at Buenos Aires 12 July 1938.

ATTERBERG: *Härvard Harpolekare*

29 September. Stockholm

Text by the composer. Two acts.

Atterberg's first opera. In German, Chemnitz March 1936.

R. STRAUSS: *Die Frau ohne Schatten*

10 October. Vienna, O.

Text by H. von Hofmannsthal (from his story of the same title). Three acts.

Not nearly as successful as his former works; given at Dresden 22 October 1919; Berlin 18 April 1920; and on other German stages.

In German also, Zurich November 1932; Venice, F. 16 September 1934 (by the Vienna O. company).

In Italian (translated by R. Küfferle), Rome, T.R. 20 April 1938; Milan, Sc. 5 January 1940.

RANGSTRÖM: *Die Kronbraut*

21 October. Stuttgart

Text from A. Strindberg's *Kronbruden*, in E. Schering's German version. Four acts.

The most important opera of the Swedish composer; first given in Swedish at Stockholm 30 November 1922 and revived there 25 November 1927 and 30 November 1936.

DELIUS: *Fennimore und Gerda*

21 October. Frankfort

(German) text by the composer. *Zwei Episoden aus dem Leben Niels Lyhnes nach dem Roman von J. P. Jacobsen.* Delius's last opera.

BÖRRESEN: *Den kongelige Gast*
(The Royal Guest)

15 November. Copenhagen

Text by S. Leopold (founded on a story by H. Pontoppidan). One act.

Börresen's first opera.

In Danish also given at Stockholm 7 May 1927 (by the Copenhagen company); revived Copenhagen 29 August 1929.

SAMUEL-ROUSSEAU: *Tarass Boulba*

22 November. Paris, Th.L.

Text by L. de Gramont (after Gogol). Five acts.

Lyons 25 March 1920, etc. Revived Paris, O.C. 10 March 1933.

A. WOLFF: *L'Oiseau bleu*

27 December. New York, M.

Text from M. Maeterlinck's play. Four acts.

In French also given at Brussels 21 April 1920.

1920

DE KOVEN: *Rip van Winkle*

2 January. Chicago

Text by P. W. Mackaye (after W. Irving). Three acts.

New York 30 January 1920, etc.

PEDROLLO: *La Veglia*

2 January. Milan, T.L.

Text by C. Linati (founded on J. M. Synge's *The Shadow of the Glen*). One act.

In Italian also given at New York 20 December 1924. Revived Vicenza 27 January 1932.

In German (as *Die Totenwache*), Lucerne 8 January 1933.

In English, London, Arts Theatre Club 12 May 1935.

LEVADÉ: *La Rôtisserie de la Reine Pédauque*

12 January. Paris, O.C.

Text by G. Docquois (from Anatole France's novel). Four acts.

Successful in France. Revived at the O.C. 1 March 1931 and 15 April 1937.

MACLEAN: *Quentin Durward*

13 January. Newcastle

Text by S. Ross (after W. Scott). Three acts.
London, Ly. 4 June 1920.
(The opera had been published as early as 1894).

SCHREKER: *Der Schatzgräber*

21 January. Frankfort

Text by the composer. Prologue, 4 acts, and epilogue.
Schreker's most successful opera.
In German also given at Zurich December 1920; Graz 5 March 1922; Berlin 3 April 1922; Vienna 18 October 1922; Basle 28 May 1923; Prague January 1924.

CASSADO: *Il Monaco nero*

24 January. Barcelona, L.

(Italian) text founded on a play by F. Soler.
Cassado's only opera.

REZNICEK: *Ritter Blaubart*

29 January. Darmstadt

Text by H. Eulenberg. Three acts.
In German also given at Berlin 31 October 1920; Zurich December 1921; Prague November 1922; Graz Spring 1923.

MERIKANTO: *Regina von Emmeritz*

30 January. Helsinki

Text by W. Sola (founded on the play by Z. Topelius). Five acts.
The last opera of the Finnish composer.

HADLEY: *Cleopatra's Night*

31 January. New York, M.

Text by A. L. Pollock (founded on T. Gautier's *Une Nuit de Cléopâtre*). Two acts.
The last opera of the American composer.

KAUN: *Der Fremde*

23 February. Dresden

Text by F. Rauch (founded on the tale *Gevatter Tod* by the brothers Grimm). Four scenes.

Revived in a new version at Altenburg 27 January 1924 and once more at Weimar 13 June 1935.

DAVICO: *La Dogaressa*

26 February. Monte Carlo

Text by G. M. Gatti. One act.
Davico's first opera.

PEDROLLO: *L'Uomo che ride*

6 March. Rome, C.

Text by A. Lega (from V. Hugo's *L'Homme qui rit*). Three acts.
Successful in Italy; Milan, T. Carcano 20 October 1921, etc.

FÉVRIER: *La Damnation de Blanchefleur*

13 March. Monte Carlo

Text by M. Léna. Two acts.
Bordeaux December 1920, etc.; in French also, Liége March 1921.

ALALEONA: *Mirra*

31 March. Rome, C.

Text by the composer (from V. Alfieri's tragedy). Two acts and an interlude.
Alaleona's only opera.

ENNA: *Komedianter*

8 April. Copenhagen

Text by the composer and O. Hansen (founded on V. Hugo's *L'Homme qui rit*, like Pedrello's Italian opera, produced one month earlier). Prologue and 3 acts.
Revived at Copenhagen 30 October 1929.

GATTY: *The Tempest*

17 April. London, Surrey

Text by R. Gatty (the brother of the composer), after Shakespeare. Three acts.
Revived at the Old Vic, London 24 April 1922; R.C.M. 1925.

JANÁČEK: *Výlety Páně Broučkovy*
(Mr. Brouček's Adventures)

23 April. Prague, Cz.

Text by V. Dyck and F. S. Procházka (after Svatopluk Čech). Consists of two parts dealing with Mr. Brouček's excursion to the moon, and to the 15th century, respectively. Revived Brno January 1939.

BROGI: *Isabella Orsini*

24 April. Florence, Politeama

Text by V. Soldani and E. Coselschi (founded on F. D. Guerrazzi's novel of the same title). Four acts.

Successful in Italy and South America; São Paulo Summer 1920, etc.

GRAENER: *Schirin und Gertraude*

28 April. Dresden

Text by E. Hardt (from his comedy of the same title). Four acts.

Revived Zurich 12 May 1926; Berlin 15 September 1936.

WEINGARTNER: *Die Dorfschule* and *Meister Andrea*

13 May. Vienna, O.

Text of both operas by the composer; *Die Dorfschule*, founded on a Japanese play *Terakoya*. One act. *Meister Andrea*, from E. Geibel's play. Two acts.

Die Dorfschule was subsequently given at:
BRÜNN 1920 (in German).
LJUBLJANA 1921 (in Slovenian).
BUENOS AIRES 6 July 1922 (in Italian).
RIO DE JANEIRO 5 October 1922 (in Italian).
BARCELONA 17 February 1925 (in Catalan, translated by J. Pena).
CREFELD 7 February 1928 (for the first time in Germany).
BASLE 28 October 1928 (in German).

Meister·Andrea was revived at Basle 28 October 1928, and Heidelberg 1928.

MORET: *Lorenzaccio*

19 May. Paris, O.C.

Text from A. de Musset's play (without much alteration). Four acts.

Successful in France; in French also given at Chicago 27 October 1930.

GURIDI: *Amaya*

22 May. Bilbao

(Basque) text by J. M. Arroita-Jáuregui (founded on *Amaya o Los Vascos en el Siglo VIII*, a story by Francisco Navarro Villoslada). Three acts and epilogue.

Very successful in Spain and South America. Revived at Bilbao September 1922; Madrid 1923, etc.; Buenos Aires 19 August 1930; Barcelona May 1934.

A. KALNIŅŠ: *Banuta*

29 May. Riga

Text by A. Krūmņiš. Four acts.

First Lettish opera produced at the newly-founded Latvijas Nacionāla Opera, Riga (inaugurated, with *Tannhäuser*, 2 December 1919). Revived there 7 October 1937. (Strictly speaking, *Banuta* was not the very first original Lettish opera, having been preceded by an amateurish work, *Spoku Stunda*, by J. Ozols, which was performed at Riga as early as 1890.)

d'INDY: *La Légende de Saint Christophe*

6 June. Paris, O.

Text by the composer. Three acts.

(STEPHAN): *Die ersten Menschen*

1 July. Frankfort

Text by O. Borngraeber. Two acts.

Stephan's only opera, produced five years after his death.

Revived at Bochum 13 March 1922 (in concert form); Crefeld 14 June 1927; Basle 27 March 1928.

(HACQUART): *De triomfeerende Min*
(Love's Triumph)

7 July. Arnhem

Text by D. Buijsero. One act.

The first Dutch opera, written and published as early as 1680 (see 1680 for details) was produced for the first time in 1920, under the direction of P. A. van Westhreene, who orchestrated the work and added an overture. Produced by the Dutch Singing Club, "J. S. Bach"; the libretto was reprinted on that occasion.

G. F. MALIPIERO: *Sept Chansons*

10 July. Paris, O.

(Original Italian) text (*Sette Canzoni*) by the composer; French version by H. Prunières.

The first of Malipiero's works for the stage which was produced. It consists of seven dramatic notturnos ("sette espressioni drammatiche"), called in the original: *I Vagabondi*; *A Vespro*; *Il Ritorno*; *L'Ubbriaco*; *La Serenata*; *Il Campanaro*; and *L'Alba delle Ceneri*. The whole forms the second part of a trilogy *L'Orfeide*; the first part or prologue is called *La Morte delle Maschere*, the third part *L'Orfeo ossia L'ottava Canzone* (1 act).

The whole trilogy was first produced at Düsseldorf 30 October 1925 (see 1925). The *Sette Canzoni*, after the first production in Paris, were also given at Aachen April 1924 (in German, translated by W. Aron and E. Orthmann); New York 29 March 1925 (in concert form); Turin 18 May 1926 (for the first time in Italy and in Italian); Rome 8 January 1929, etc.

For an account of the work see S. Goddard in *The Chesterian*, November 1930, and G. F. Malipiero, *ibid.*, December 1930.

PRATELLA: *L'Aviatore Dro*

4 September. Lugo

Text by the composer. Three acts.
Pratella's chief work.

FRANCKENSTEIN: *Des Kaisers Dichter*

2 November. Hamburg

Text by R. Lothar. Three acts.
(An opera dealing with the life of the Chinese poet, Li Tai Po.)
Successful on German stages; in German also, Brünn 1927; revived Graz 21 February 1931, etc.

BRUNEAU: *Le Roi Candaule*

1 December. Paris, O.C.

Text by M. Donnay. Five acts.
Given at the O.C. 18 times in 1920–21, but not revived so far.

BRAUNFELS: *Die Vögel*

4 December. Munich

Text by the composer (after Aristophanes). Two acts.
Braunfels's most successful opera; given at Berlin 20 December 1921; Graz 31 October 1923; Vienna, V.O. 21 January 1925, etc.

KORNGOLD: *Die tote Stadt*

4 December. Hamburg and Cologne

Text by P. Schott (founded on G. Rodenbach's play *Bruges-la-Morte*). Three acts.
Korngold's most successful opera; given at
VIENNA 10 January 1921 (in German).
NEW YORK, M. 19 November 1921 (in German).
PRAGUE February 1922 (in German).
ZURICH c. November 1922.
ANTWERP 6 January 1923 (in Flemish).
BERLIN 12 April 1924 (in German).
BUDAPEST Spring 1925 (in Hungarian).
LEMBERG March 1928 (in Polish).
AMSTERDAM Spring 1929 (in German).
Revived Vienna 6 May 1936 (in German).

SOMERVILLE: *David Garrick*

9 December. London, C.G.

Text by the composer (from T. W. Robertson's play). Three acts.
Revived in a new version London, Queen's 2 March 1922 and once more Duke of York's 9 June 1932.

(LEONCAVALLO): *Edipo Re*

13 December. Chicago

Text by the composer (after Sophocles). One act.

In Italian also given at New York 21 February 1921; apparently never produced in Italy (but broadcast from Turin 13 October 1939). Apart from several operettas which were also produced after his death, this was Leoncavallo's last work for the stage.

1921

PETRAUSKAS: *Birute*

16 February. Kaunas

Text by the composer.

The first Lithuanian opera, produced at the newly-founded Lithuanian National Theatre, "Lietuvos Valstybes Teatras".

DE BOECK: *La Route d'Émeraude*

25 February. Ghent

Text by M. Hautier (founded on a novel by E. Demolder). Five acts.

The most successful opera of the Belgian composer (not a ballet as stated in Riemann's *Musiklexikon*). Frequently revived in Belgium; Antwerp 3 November 1922; Brussels 12 November 1926 and 20 January 1939.

DE LARA: *Les trois Mousquetaires*

3 March. Cannes

Text by H. Cain and L. Payen (founded on the play by A. Dumas and A. Maquet). Six scenes.

In English (translated by A. Kalisch), Newcastle 2 May 1924; London, Scala 17 June 1924.

(DUPONT): *Antar*

11 March. Paris, O.

Text by C. Ganem. Four acts.

Dupont's last opera; successful in France; in French also given at Antwerp 2 January 1922; Ghent 23 January 1922; Brussels 10 November 1922; Geneva 2 February 1923, etc.

(The opera was written in 1913, but not produced until 7 years after the composer's death.)

BÖRRESEN: *Kaddara*

16 March. Copenhagen

Text by C. M. Norman-Hansen. Three acts.

Probably the first opera dealing with an Eskimo subject.

Also produced at Brussels 17 March 1924 (in French, translated by P. Spaak) and Königsberg 31 January 1925 (in German, translated by B. Dumont du Voitel).

MARSICK: *La Jane*

29 March. Liége

Text by the composer (?). One act.

Successful in Belgium; revived Liége February 1926 and Antwerp November 1926.

VITTADINI: *Anima allegra*

15 April. Rome, C.

Text by G. Adami and L. Motta (founded on a Spanish comedy by the brothers Álvarez Quintero). Three acts.

Vittadini's most successful work; given on many Italian stages and in Italian also, Barcelona April 1922; Palma, Mallorca May 1922; New York 14 February 1923; Buenos Aires Summer 1924; Rio de Janeiro 15 September 1924; S. Francisco 26 September 1925; Cairo January 1931.

In French (translated by J. Marcalti), Ghent 22 February 1922; Geneva 2 March 1926.

MASCAGNI: *Il Piccolo Marat*

2 May. Rome, C.

Text by G. Forzano and G. Targioni-Tozzetti. Three acts.

Very successful in Italy and also given at:

BUENOS AIRES 20 September 1921 (in Italian).

DRESDEN 11 March 1922 (in German, translated by K. Scheidemantel).

COPENHAGEN 10 May 1922 (in Danish, translated by J. Lehmann).

RIO DE JANEIRO 24 September 1922 (in Italian).

MALTA 1923 (in Italian).

SZEGED Summer 1924 (in Hungarian).

PARIS, G.L. 12 November 1928 (in Italian).

WELLESZ: *Die Prinzessin Girnara*

15 May. Hanover

Text by J. Wassermann (*Weltspiel und Legende*). Two acts.

Wellesz's first opera; revived in a new version Mannheim 2 September 1928.

GATTY: *Prince Ferelon;* or, *The Princess's Suitors*

21 May. London, Old Vic

Text by the composer (*A musical extravaganza*). One act.

The opera had been previously produced by the Florence Ettlinger Opera School on 27 November 1919. Revived London, R.C.M. 10 December 1930 and 1 June 1933.

MEDIŅŠ: *Uguns un Nakts* (Fire and Night)

26 May. Riga

Text by J. Rainis. Four acts.

Successful Lettish opera; a second part followed in December 1921.

HINDEMITH: *Mörder, Hoffnung der Frauen* and *Das Nusch-Nuschi*

4 June. Stuttgart

Two one-act operas. Text of *Mörder, Hoffnung der Frauen* by O. Kokoschka; text of *Das Nusch-Nuschi* by F. Blei.

Both operas were also given at Prague April 1923. *Das Nusch-Nuschi* was revived in a new version at Königsberg 22 January 1931, and also given at Antwerp 2 March 1933 (in Flemish).

HONEGGER: *Le Roi David*

11 June. Mézières

Text by R. Morax (*Psaume dramatique*). Two parts.

First produced on the stage of the Th. Jorat, Mézières, Switzerland.

In a revised concert version (3 parts) first given at Winterthur 2 December 1923 (in German, translated by H. Reinhart).

The concert version was subsequently heard at Brussels 16 December 1923; Paris, Salle Gaveau 19 March 1924; Hague 19 November 1924; Buenos Aires 28 August 1925; New York 26 October 1925; Rome 4 April 1926; Zurich 18 June 1926; Vienna 15 December 1926; London, Albert Hall 17 March 1927 (English version by E. Agate); Leningrad September 1927; Athens December 1931; Viipuri December 1933; Tunis 1938.

On the stage, this work, after its first production, was given only in Paris, Ch.É. 3 May 1924 (in French), and at Cambridge 10 May 1929 (in English, translated by D. Arundell).

FRANCHETTI and GIORDANO: *Giove a Pompei*

5 July. Rome, T. La Pariola

Text by L. Illica and E. Romagnoli. Three acts.

First produced at Rome in the open air; subsequently given at Venice, T. Malibran 17 July 1921, etc.

CAMPBELL: *Thais and Talmaae*

13 September. Manchester

Text by C. H. Bourne (founded on Anatole France's novel). One act.

Campbell's only opera; successful on English stages.

Given at London, C.G. 8 November 1921 and revived London, King's (Hammersmith) 18 September 1928 (and once more 15 January 1937, broadcast).

JANÁČEK: *Káta Kabanová*

23 October. Brno

Text by V. Červinka (founded on Ostrovsky's play, *Groza*). Three acts.

Apart from *Její Pastorkyňa* (see 1904), Janáček's best-known work.

First given at Prague 30 November 1922 (in Czech) and January 1928 (in German).

In German (translated by M. Brod), Cologne 9 November 1922; Berlin 31 May 1926, etc.

In Slovenian (translated by N. Štritov), Ljubljana 26 May 1934.

In Croatian, Zagreb 28 March 1936.

HÜE: *Dans l'Ombre de la Cathédrale*

7 December. Paris, O.C.

Text by M. Léna and H. Ferrare (from a novel by V. Blasco Ibáñez). Three acts.

Hüe's most successful work.

In French also given at Liége December 1923; Geneva 22 January 1926; Antwerp 25 December 1926; Algiers November 1928.

ALFANO: *La Leggenda di Sakuntala*

10 December. Bologna, T.C.

Text by the composer (founded on the Indian play by Kalidasa). Three acts.

Alfano's first great success and one of his chief works. Given on many Italian stages and in Italian also at Buenos Aires 5 August 1923, and subsequently at Montevideo.

In German (translated by A. Brüggemann), Düsseldorf 25 May 1924.

In Flemish, Antwerp 6 December 1924.

PROKOFIEV:
L'Amour des trois Oranges

30 December. Chicago

(Original Russian) text (*Lyubov k trem Apelsinam*) by the composer (from Gozzi's comedy), produced in a French version by V. Janacopulos. Four acts.

Prokofiev's first performed opera; an earlier work, *Igrok*, written before 1917, was not produced until 1929 (see there).

L'Amour des trois Oranges was subsequently given at:

NEW YORK 14 February 1922 (in French).

COLOGNE 14 March 1925 (in German, translated by V. Miller).

BERLIN 9 October 1926 (in German, translated by V. Miller).

LENINGRAD 18 February 1926 (in Russian).

MOSCOW 1927 (in Russian).

LJUBLJANA 30 October 1927 (in Slovenian, translated by N. Štritov).

1922

SILVER: *La Mégère apprivoisée*

30 January. Paris, O.

Text by H. Cain and E. Adenis (from Shakespeare's *Taming of the Shrew* in P. Delair's French version, 1891). Four acts.

Successful in France; in French also given at Antwerp March 1923 and Geneva 18 March 1924.

ROOTHAM: *The two Sisters*

14 February. Cambridge

Text by M. Fausset (founded on the ballad *The twa Sisters o'Binnorie*). Three acts.

Rootham's only opera.

ZANDONAI: *Giulietta e Romeo*

14 February. Rome, C.

Text by A. Rossato (after Shakespeare). Three acts.

One of the latest (and not the least successful) of the numerous operatic works on that subject (see 1776).

Given all over Italy and at:

BUENOS AIRES 30 July 1922 (in Italian).

RIO DE JANEIRO 27 September 1922 (in Italian).

GHENT January 1924 (in French, translated by P. Spaak).

MALTA Carnival 1925 (in Italian).

ALEXANDRIA March 1925 (in Italian).

MAYENCE 10 April 1927 (in German, translated by A. Brüggemann).

VREULS: *Olivier le Simple*

9 March. Brussels, M.

Text by J. Delacre. Three acts.

The first opera of the Belgian composer.

ZICH: *Vina*
(The Sin)

14 March. Prague, Cz.

Text by J. Hilbert (from his play of the same title, 1896). Three acts.

Revived Prague 11 April 1929.

LUALDI: *La Figlia del Re*

18 March. Turin, T.R.

Text by the composer. Three acts.

Lualdi's first greater work for the stage; awarded the Edith MacCormick prize in 1917. Successful in Italy. Revived Rome January 1939.

DOHNÁNYI: *A Vajda Tornya*
(The Tower of the Voyvod)

19 March. Budapest

Text by V. Lányi (translated from a German libretto by H. H. Ewers and M. Henry). Three acts. In German, Düsseldorf 2 March 1926.

HINDEMITH: *Sancta Susanna*

26 March. Frankfort

Text by A. Stramm. One act.

Performed on the same bill with a revival of his two other one-act operas (see 1921).

In German also given at Prague April 1923.

(MASSENET): *Amadis*

1 April. Monte Carlo

Text by J. Claretie. Prologue and 3 acts.

The last of Massenet's posthumous works; *Amadis* was written as early as 1902.

In French also given at Bordeaux 19 December 1922 and Geneva 9 January 1925.

FRANCHETTI: *Glauco*

8 April. Naples, S.C.

Text by G. Forzano (founded on a play by E. L. Morselli, 1919). Three acts.

Franchetti's last opera.

DONAUDY: *La Fiamminga*

25 April. Naples, S.C.

Text by A. Donaudy (the brother of the composer). One act.

Donaudy's last opera.

SCHOECK: *Venus*

10 May. Zurich

Text by A. Rüeger (from a story by P. Mérimée). Three acts.

Revived in a new version, Zurich 26 November 1933; Berne 22 April 1934.

ZILCHER: *Doktor Eisenbart*

21 May. Leipzig and Mannheim

Text by H. W. von Waltershausen (from a play by O. Falckenberg). Three acts.

Zilcher's only opera.

MEDIŅŠ: *Deevi un Cilveki*
(Gods and Men)

23 May. Riga

Text by L. Paegles. Four acts.

Lettish opera on an Egyptian subject.

ZEMLINSKY: *Der Zwerg*

28 May. Cologne

Text by G. C. Claren (founded on O. Wilde's *The Birthday of the Infanta*). One act.

In German also given at Vienna 24 November 1923; Prague Spring 1926; Berlin 22 November 1926.

STRAVINSKY: *Renard* and *Mavra*

2 June. Paris, O.
Renard

(Original Russian) text by the composer (founded on Russian folktales), produced in a French version by C. F. Ramuz; *Histoire burlesque chantée et jouée*. One act.

The work was written for Princess Edmond de Polignac's private theatre and had been performed there previously to its production at the Opéra. Also given at

NEW YORK 2 December 1923 (in French, in concert form).

BERLIN 7 June 1925 (in German).

AMSTERDAM December 1933 (in Dutch, translated by M. Nijhoff).

PRAGUE April 1935 (in German).

Broadcast from London 12 April 1935 (in English, translated by C. D. Freeman).

Mavra

(Original Russian) text by B. Kochno (founded on Pushkin's *The little House in Kolomna*), produced in a French version by J. Larmanjat. One act.

Previously to its production at the Opéra, the work had been performed privately at the Hôtel Continental, Paris. Also given at

KIEL 7 November 1925 (in German, translated by A. Eluchen).

PRAGUE 1927 (in Czech; at the State Conservatoire).

BERLIN 25 February 1928 (in German).

LENINGRAD Spring 1928 (in Russian).

LONDON 27 April 1934 (broadcast; in English).

PHILADELPHIA 28 December 1934 (in English, translated by E. R. Burness).

WILLIAMS: *The Shepherds of the delectable Mountains*

11 July. London, R.C.M.

Text from Bunyan's *The Pilgrim's Progress*. A *Pastoral Episode*. One act.

Vaughan Williams's first opera. Frequently revived on English stages, viz., Clifton 13 October 1924; R.C.M. again 1926; London, Court 12 June 1928; Edinburgh 29 April 1936; London, R.C.M. 7 July 1936.

BOUGHTON: *Alkestis*

26 August. Glastonbury

Text from Euripides's tragedy in G. Murray's English version. Two acts.

London, C.G. 11 January 1924.

BACHELET: *Quand la Cloche sonnera*

6 November. Paris, O.C.

Text by Y. d'Hansewick and P. de Wattyne. One act.

Bachelet's most successful work, frequently revived on French stages.

In French also, Basle 15 May 1923; Brussels 21 December 1923; Antwerp October 1924; Geneva 20 February 1925; Luxemburg November 1926.

LATTUADA: *La Tempesta*

23 November. Milan, T.d.V.

Text by A. Rossato (after Shakespeare). Prologue and 3 acts.

Lattuada's first performed opera; successful in Italy.

ROLAND-MANUEL: *Isabelle et Pantalon*

11 December. Paris, Tr.L.

Text by M. Jacob. Two acts.

Roland-Manuel's only opera.

In German (translated by A. Rebner), Kiel 7 November 1925.

PIZZETTI: *Debora e Jaele*

16 December. Milan, Sc.

Text by the composer. Three acts.

One of Pizzetti's chief works; awarded a prize by the Italian Academy in 1931. Revived at the Scala 30 December 1936. Outside Italy given at:

BUENOS AIRES 17 June 1923 (in Italian; revived there Summer 1933).

HAMBURG 27 September 1928 (in German, translated by A. Brüggemann).

BRUSSELS 23 March 1929 (in French, translated by P. Spaak).

CRAS: *Polyphème*

29 December. Paris, O.C.

Text by A. Samain. Four acts.

Cras's only opera; awarded the prize of the City of Paris in 1921.

1923

BIANCHINI: *Il Principe e Nuredha*

24 January. Venice, F.

Text by M. Star (*leggenda orientale*). One act.

In French (as *Le Prince enchaîné*), Monte Carlo 5 April 1923; Ghent February 1924.

BAUSSNERN: *Satyros*

31 January. Basle

Text by the composer (founded on Goethe's poem). Prologue and 2 acts.

In German also given at Weimar 24 November 1923.

MULÈ: *La Monacella della Fontana*

17 February. Trieste

Text by G. Adami. One act.

Along with Bianchini's *Il Principe e Nuredha* (see above), awarded the prize of the Italian Government for 1922. Successful and frequently revived in Italy.

In Italian also, Lisbon May 1938; Rio de Janeiro and São Paulo Summer 1938.

SAMUEL-ROUSSEAU: *Le Hulla*

9 March. Paris, O.C.

Text by A. Rivoire. Four acts.

Successful in France. In French also given at Geneva 12 March 1925.

B. SCHUSTER: *Der Dieb des Glückes*

10 March. Wiesbaden

Text by the composer. Three acts.

Successful in Germany; Berlin 12 June 1926.

BERR: *Der tote Gast*

23 March. Basle

Text by R. Lothar (founded on a story by H. Zschokke). Three acts.

Berr's only opera.

FALLA: *El Retablo de Maese Pedro*

23 March. Sevilla

Text adapted from a chapter in Cervantes's *Don Quixote*. One act.

First produced in concert form at the Teatro San Fernando, Seville, and subsequently given at:

PARIS 25 June 1923 (in French, translated by G. J. Aubry); produced at Princess Edmond de Polignac's private theatre; repeated 13 November 1923 at the Concerts Wiéner and revived at the O.C. 12 March 1928.

MADRID 28 March 1924 (in Spanish; in concert form).

CLIFTON (BRISTOL) 14 October 1924 (in English, translated by J. B. Trend).

BARCELONA 7 February 1925 (in Spanish).

NEW YORK 29 December 1925 (in Spanish).

ZURICH 23 January 1926 (in German, translated by H. Jelmoli).

BRUSSELS 8 February 1926 (in concert form).

AMSTERDAM 26 April 1926 (in concert form).

BUENOS AIRES June 1926 (in Spanish).

COLOGNE 13 January 1927 (in German).

BERLIN 2 March 1927 (in German).

LONDON, COURT TH. 12 June 1928 (in English).

VENICE, T. GOLDONI 10 September 1932 (in Italian); Florence, Palazzo Pitti 17 February 1934 (in concert form).

LISBON December 1936 (in concert form).

OXFORD 30 November 1937 (in English).

PRAGUE December 1938 (in Czech, by the Pritomnost Society).

PAHISSA: *Marianela*

31 March. Barcelona, L.

Text by J. and S. Álvarez Quintero (founded on a novel by B. Pérez Galdos). Three acts.

RICCITELLI: *I Compagnazzi*

10 April. Rome, C.

Text by G. Forzano. One act.

Very successful in Italy.

In Italian also produced at Buenos Aires 22 July 1923 and New York, M. 2 January 1924.

RESPIGHI: *Belfagor*

26 April. Milan, Sc.

Text by C. Guastalla (founded on a comedy by
E. L. Morselli). Prologue, 2 acts, and epilogue.

In German (translated by R. S. Hoffmann),
Hamburg 10 March 1925.

GÁL: *Die heilige Ente*

29 April. Düsseldorf

Text by K. M. von Levetzow and L. Feld. *Ein
Spiel mit Göttern und Menschen*, prologue and 3 acts.

Gál's most successful opera.

In German also given at Berlin, D.O. 19 September 1925; Prague 17 January 1926.

RÓŻYCKI: *Casanova*

3 May. Warsaw

Text by J. Krzewiński. Prologue, 3 parts, and
epilogue.

Successful in Poland. Revived Poznań February
1936.

Also given at Belgrade Spring 1932 (in Serbian)
and Antwerp 26 November 1932 (in Flemish).

NOVÁK: *Lucerna*

(The Lantern)

13 May. Prague, Cz.

Text by H. Jelinek (founded on a play by A.
Jirásek). Four acts.

In Czech also given at Vienna, Stadt Th. 5 May
1929 (by a company from Bratislava). Revived
Prague 28 September 1930.

In Slovenian (translated by N. Štritov), Ljubljana 8 October 1931.

HOLST: *The perfect Fool*

14 May. London, C.G.

Text by the composer. One act.

Successful in London; not revived so far.

ROUSSEL: *Padmavati*

1 June. Paris, O.

Text by L. Laloy. *Opéra-ballet.* Two acts.

Roussel's first opera.

SMYTH: *Fête galante*

4 June. Birmingham

Text by E. Shanks (founded on a story by M.
Baring). *A Dance-Dream.* One act.

Subsequently produced at C.G., London 11
June 1923 and at R.C.M. 1925.

PALMER: *Sruth Na Maoile*

(The Sea of Moyle)

25 July. Dublin

Text by T. O'Ceallaigh (T. O'Kelly), founded on
the Irish saga of *The Children of Lir.*

Successful Irish opera, revived at Dublin 13
August 1924.

VIVES: *Doña Francisquita*

17 October. Madrid, T. Apolo

Text by F. Romero and G. Fernández Shaw
(from Lope de Vega's comedy, *La discreta Ena-
morada*). Three acts.

Successful Spanish comic opera; Barcelona, Tivoli February 1924, etc. Revived in Spanish, Buenos Aires 2 November 1934.

In French (translated by A. de Badet and R.
Bergeret), Monte Carlo January 1934; Brussels 9
June 1934; Vichy Summer 1934.

REZNICEK: *Holofernes*

27 October. Berlin, D.O.

Text by the composer (founded on F. Hebbel's
Judith). Two acts.

One of the numerous modern *Judith* operas.

HUBAY: *Karenina Anna*

10 November. Budapest

Text by S. Góth (founded on Tolstoi's novel).
Three acts.

Successful at Budapest.

Also given at Duisburg 22 October 1932 and
Vienna 9 February 1936 (in German, translated
by H. Liebstöckl).

J. B. FOERSTER: *Srdce*
(The Heart)

15 November. Prague, Cz.

Text by the composer. Prologue, 2 acts and epilogue.
Revived Prague 1 February 1930.

PAUMGARTNER: *Die Höhle von Salamanca*

20 November. Dresden

Text by the composer (after Cervantes). One act.
Given on some German stages and also at Leningrad Spring 1928 (in Russian, by the Opera Studio of the Leningrad Conservatoire), and by the Russian singers also at Salzburg 6 August 1928.

BATH: *Bubbles*

26 November. Belfast

Text from Lady I. A. Gregory's play *Spreading the News.* One act.
In English also given at London, Scala 11 June 1924.
(The opera is stated to have been produced first at Milan 3 January 1920, in Italian, as *Bubbole*; I could not find a record of that production.)

MILHAUD: *La Brebis égarée*

10 December. Paris, O.C.

Text by F. Jammes (*Roman musical*). Three acts.
Milhaud's first opera. Revived in German (as *Die Rückkehr*, translated by E. Orthmann) Mannheim 2 December 1929.

1924

JONGEN: *Thomas L'Agnelet, Gentilhomme de Fortune*

14 February. Brussels, M.

Text by C. Farrère (*Roman musical*). Four acts.
The most important opera of the Belgian composer.

POLDINI: *Farsangi Lakodalom*
(Wedding in Carnival)

16 February. Budapest

Text by E. Vajda. Three acts.
Successful Hungarian comic opera. Also given at Dresden 24 October 1925 and Vienna 22 February 1926 (in German, translated by B. Diósy) and London, Gaiety 6 October 1926 (in English, as *Love Adrift*, translated by M. D. Calvocoressi).

LATTUADA: *Sandha*

21 February. Genoa, C.F.

Text by F. Fontana (*tragedia indiana*). One act.
Successful in Italy.

CARTER: *The white Bird*

6 March. Chicago

Text by B. Hooker. One act.
Successful American opera. In German (translated by F. Rémond), Osnabrück 15 November 1927. Revived (in English) New York 7 February 1937.

BARILLI: *Emiral*

11 March. Rome, C.

Text by the composer. One act.
Barilli's first performed opera. Awarded the State Prize of the Italian Government in 1923.

TOURNEMIRE: *Les Dieux sont morts*

19 March. Paris, O.

Text by E. Berteaux. Two acts.
The only opera of the French organist.

WELLESZ: *Alkestis*

20 March. Mannheim

Text by H. von Hofmannsthal (founded on Euripides's tragedy). One act.
Berlin, D.O. 1 June 1930.

SCHREKER: *Irrelohe*

27 March. Cologne

Text by the composer. Three acts.
Stuttgart 29 March 1924, etc.

RABAUD: *L'Appel de la Mer*

10 April. Paris, O.C.

Text by the composer (from Synge's *Riders to the Sea*). One act.

In French also given at Brussels 12 January 1925.

In German (translated by G. Brecher), Leipzig 6 May 1927.

MACKENZIE: *The Eve of St. John*

16 April. Liverpool

Text by E. Farjeon. One act.

Mackenzie's last opera. London, H.M.'s 26 June 1924.

MAURICE: *Andromeda*

23 April. Basle

(Original French) text by M. Maurice (the wife of the composer), German version by H. v. Gumppenberg. Three acts.

In German also, Zurich 4 February 1925; Weimar 10 March 1931.

BERNERS:
Le Carrosse du Saint-Sacrement

24 April. Paris, Ch.É.

Text from P. Mérimée's play (1825). One act.

Lord Berners's only opera.

(BOITO): *Nerone*

1 May. Milan, Sc.

Text by the composer. Four acts.

Bologna 12 October 1924, etc.; Rome 25 February 1928 (inauguration of the Teatro Reale dell' Opera). Open air performance: Udine 28 July 1928. Outside Italy given at:

STOCKHOLM 9 April 1926 (in Swedish, translated by H. Key).

BUENOS AIRES 22 May 1926 (in Italian).

RIO DE JANEIRO July 1926 (in Italian).

SANTIAGO, CHILE Summer 1926 (in Italian).

CAIRO February 1928 (in Italian).

STUTTGART 5 May 1928 (in German, translated by E. Lert).

Boito had been working on this, his second and last opera, for very many years. The project is mentioned in a letter as early as 1862. The text was first published in 1901 as a poetic drama (in 5 acts). At his death in 1918 the work was still unfinished. In 1924, the opera was produced in a version by V. Tommasini and A. Toscanini.

SOLTYS: *Panie Kochanku*

3 May. Lemberg

Text by H. Kopia (from a play by J. I. Kraszewski, 1867). Three acts.

The last opera of the Polish composer.

ROBBIANI: *Anna Karenina*

6 May. Rome, C.

(Original French) text by E. Guiraud (after Tolstoi), Italian version by the composer. Three acts.

Awarded the State Prize of the Italian Government.

SCHÖNBERG: *Erwartung*

6 June. Prague

Text by M. Pappenheim (*Mimodrama*). One act (4 scenes).

Written in 1909, published 1916. First produced at the second I.S.C.M. Festival; subsequently given at:

WIESBADEN 22 January 1928 (in German).

BERLIN 7 June 1930 (in German).

BRUSSELS 6 May 1936 (in French, translated by J. Weterings).

Broadcast from London 9 January 1931 (in German).

KŘENEK: *Der Sprung über den Schatten*

9 June. Frankfort

Text by the composer. Three acts.

Performed at the Tonkünstlerfest of the Allgemeiner Deutscher Musikverein.

In Russian (translated by S. Y. Levik), Leningrad 21 May 1927.

ANDREAE: *Abenteuer des Casanova*

17 *June.* Dresden

Text by F. Lion. Consists of 4 one-act operas.

Successful in Switzerland. Zurich 1925, etc. Revived Basle December 1938.

SACHS: *Les Burgraves*

18 *June.* Paris, Ch.É.

Text from V. Hugo's drama. Four acts.

Sachs's only opera.

In French also given at The Hague, November 1925 and Barcelona 5 February 1926.

LUALDI: *Le Furie d'Arlecchino*

19 *June.* Buenos Aires

Text by L. Orsini (*intermezzo giocoso*). One act.

In Italian also given at New York 20 December 1924; Venice, F. 30 April 1925, etc., Geneva 8 April 1929.

In German (translated by K. H. Gutheim), Hagen 26 May 1929.

Still popular in Italy. (Stated sometimes to have been produced at the T. Carcano, Milan, as early as 1915, a statement which I could not verify.)

A. PALMA: *Nazdah*

19 *June.* Buenos Aires

(Italian) text by G. de San Leo (founded on J. M. Eça de Queiroz's story *La Nodriza*). One act.

The first opera of the Argentine composer.

JACHINO: *Giocondo e il suo Re*

24 *June.* Milan, T.d.V.

Text by G. Forzano (founded on an episode in Ariosto's *Orlando furioso*). Three acts.

Jachino's first opera. Successful in Italy; Rome 6 April 1926, etc.

WILLIAMS: *Hugh the Drover;* or, *Love in the Stocks*

4 *July.* London, R.C.M.

Text by H. H. Child. Two acts.

Vaughan Williams's most successful work for the stage. Publicly performed 10 days later, Lon-

don, H.M.'s 14 July 1924. In English also, Toronto 1931.

Revived at the R.C.M. 16 June 1933 (in a revised version) and at Sadler's Wells 21 April 1937 (in the original version).

BOUGHTON: *The Queen of Cornwall*

21 *August.* Glastonbury

Text: T. Hardy's play (1923), with alterations. Two acts.

Revived Liverpool 13 January 1927.

(26 August is incorrectly indicated as date of first performance in the printed score.)

BANTOCK: *The Seal Woman*

27 *September.* Birmingham

Text by M. K. Fraser (*Celtic folk-opera*). Two acts.

Bantock's last opera. Not yet given in London.

MILES: *Markheim*

13 *October.* Clifton (near Bristol)

Text by the composer (from R. L. Stevenson's story). *Dramatic Sketch.* One act.

(The opera had previously been heard, with piano accompaniment, at Shirehampton in 1922 and in London, Metropolitan Th. 10 February 1923.)

Revived Liverpool 17 February 1928, etc.

SCHÖNBERG: *Die glückliche Hand*

14 *October.* Vienna, V.O.

Text by the composer (*Drama mit Musik*). One act (4 scenes).

In German also given at Breslau 24 March 1928; New York, M. 22 April 1930 (by the League of Composers); Berlin 7 June 1930.

The work had been published as early as 1913.

KŘENEK: *Zwingburg*

21 *October.* Berlin, O.

Text by F. Werfel, based on an anonymous scenario (*Szenische Kantate*). One act.

Křenek's first work for the stage, written before *Der Sprung über den Schatten* (see above).

MADETOJA: *Pohjalaisia*
(The East Bothnians)

25 October. Helsinki

Text by the composer (from a play by A. Järvi-luoma). Three acts.

The most successful Finnish opera so far written. Given at Helsinki 88 times until 1937.

Also produced at Kiel 4 November 1926 (in German, translated by G. Schneid); Stockholm 27 April 1927 (in Swedish); Copenhagen February 1939 (in Danish).

WIDOR: *Nerto*

27 October. Paris, O.

Text by M. Léna (from F. Mistral's poem). Four acts.

Widor's last opera.

R. STRAUSS: *Intermezzo*

4 November. Dresden

Text by the composer (*Bürgerliche Komödie mit sinfonischen Zwischenspielen*). Two acts.

In German also given Berlin at 28 March 1925; Graz 25 April 1925; Prague 1925; Vienna 15 January 1927; Berne 1929; Budapest 12 November 1929.

In Italian (translated by O. Schanzer), Barcelona 16 November 1925.

KAREL: *Ilseino Srdce*
(Ilse's Heart)

11 November. Prague, Cz.

Text by K. H. Hilar. Three acts.
Karel's first opera.

BRAUNFELS: *Don Gil von den grünen Hosen*

15 November. Munich

Text by the composer (from Tirso de Molina's comedy). Three acts.
Vienna 7 May 1925.

JANÁČEK: *Lišky Příhody Bystroušky*
(The sly little Fox)

16 November. Brno

Text by the composer (founded on a story by R. Těsnohlídek). Three acts.

In Czech also, Prague 18 May 1925 (revived 31 May 1937).

In German (translated by M. Brod), Mayence 13 February 1927.

SZÁNTÓ: *Taifun*

29 November. Mannheim

(Original Hungarian) text by M. Lengyel, German version by J. Mohacsy. Three acts.

Szántó's only opera.

Given also at Antwerp 7 November 1925 (in Flemish); Budapest 26 February 1926 (in Hungarian) Vienna, V.O. 21 February 1928 (in German).

HAMERIK: *Stepan*

30 November. Mayence

(Original Danish) text by F. Nygaard, German version by F. von der Stucken. Three acts.

In Flemish, Antwerp 21 March 1925; in Danish, Copenhagen 31 March 1926.

The first opera on a Soviet Russian theme.

MARQUEZ: *Sor Beatriz*

20 December. Barcelona, L.

(Spanish) text by V. Gassol, founded on Maeterlinck's play. Two acts.

Marquez's only opera.

GIORDANO: *La Cena delle Beffe*

20 December. Milan, Sc.

Text by S. Benelli (from his play of the same title, 1910). Four acts.

Successful in Italy; also given at:
BUENOS AIRES 28 August 1925 (in Italian).
BARCELONA 7 November 1925 (in Italian).
NEW YORK, M. 2 January 1926 (in Italian).
GABLONZ 16 January 1926 (in German, translated by E. Lert).

PRAGUE 1926 (in German, translated by E. Lert).
MALTA 1926 (in Italian).
CHICAGO 27 November 1926 (in Italian).
WARSAW November 1927 (in Polish).
NICE 24 April 1930 (in Italian).

d'OLLONE: *L'Arlequin*

24 December. Paris, O.

Text by J. Sarment. Five acts.
In French also, Antwerp November 1925.

1925

VOLLERTHUN: *Island-Saga*

17 January. Munich

Text by B. Thiersch. Three acts.
Given with alterations at Weimar 28 February 1926.
In German also, Hague 15 January 1929. Revived Rostock 5 January 1940.

ATTERBERG: *Bäckahästen*
(The River Horse)

23 January. Stockholm

Text by A. Österling. Four acts.
In German (as *Das Wogenross*), Dessau 27 November 1927.

ETTINGER: *Juana* and
Der eifersüchtige Trinker

7 February. Nuremberg

Two one-act operas, text by G. Kaiser and by F. Freksa respectively.
Ettinger's first works for the stage.

MORENO-TORROBA: *La Virgen de Mayo*

14 February. Madrid, T.R.

Text by P. Max. One act.
The best work of the Spanish composer.

WOLF-FERRARI: *Gli Amanti sposi*

19 February. Venice, F.

Text by G. Forzano (founded on Goldoni's comedy *Il Ventaglio*). Three acts.
In German (as *Das Liebesband der Marchesa*, translated by F. Rau), Dresden 2 April 1925; Zurich November 1926.

CAMUSSI: *Scàmpolo*

22 February. Trieste

Text by D. Niccodemi (from his comedy of the same title, 1916). Three acts.
Successful in Italy.
In German, Dortmund April 1939.

ZANDONAI: *I Cavalieri di Ekebù*

7 March. Milan, Sc.

Text by A. Rossato (founded on S. Lagerlöf's *Gösta Berling*). Four acts.
Successful in Italy; Rome 28 March 1925, etc.
Outside Italy, given at:
BUENOS AIRES 28 July 1925 (in Italian).
STOCKHOLM 20 November 1928 (in Swedish, translated by S. Lindström).
NUREMBERG 15 March 1930 (in German, translated by E. Lert).
RIGA 16 October 1935 (in Lettish).

OVERHOFF: *Mira*

18 March. Essen

Text by A. Hospelt. Two parts.
Overhoff's first opera. Revived Heidelberg May 1934.

RAVEL: *L'Enfant et les Sortilèges*

21 March. Monte Carlo

Text by Colette (*fantaisie lyrique*). Two parts.
Ravel's second and last opera.
In French also given at Paris, O.C. 1 February 1926; Brussels 11 February 1926; San Francisco 19 September 1930; Florence, P. 2 May 1939.
In Czech (translated by J. Fiala), Prague 17 February 1927.

In German (translated by E. Bloch), Leipzig 6 May 1927; Vienna 14 March 1929.

Transferred to the repertory of the Paris Opéra 17 May 1939.

HOLST: *At the Boar's Head*

3 April. Manchester

Text by the composer (from Shakespeare's *King Henry IV*). One act.

London, Golder's Green Hippodrome 20 April 1925; R.C.M. 1926. Revived New York, Mac Dowell Club 16 February 1935.

LUALDI: *Il Diavolo nel Campanile*

22 April. Milan, Sc.

Text by the composer (after E. A. Poe). One act. In German, Stuttgart 18 May 1938.

(STANFORD): *The Travelling Companion*

30 April. Liverpool

Text by H. Newbolt (from H. C. Andersen's fairy-tale). Four acts.

Stanford's last opera. Published in 1919, it was not performed until one year after the composer's death.

First produced by amateurs; on the professional stage, Bristol 25 October 1926.

Revived Falmouth 25 October 1934; London, Sadler's Wells 3 April 1935.

MARIOTTE: *Esther Princesse d'Israèl*

4 May. Paris, O.

Text from a play by André Dumas and S. C. Leconte. Three acts.

SATIE: *Socrate*

May. Prague

Text from Plato's dialogues in V. Cousin's French version. *Drame symphonique avec voix.* Three parts.

Published in 1919; first public audition Paris, Soc. Nationale de Musique, 14 February 1920; written for Princess de Polignac's private theatre

and produced there prior to 1925, when the work received its first public stage performance at the third I.S.C.M. Festival in a Czech version by?.

(BUSONI): *Doktor Faust*

21 May. Dresden

Text by the composer. Consists of 2 prologues, 1 scenic interlude, and 3 scenes.

Busoni's last opera, completed by P. Jarnach.

Also produced at Frankfort 29 June 1927; Berlin 27 October 1927; London, Queen's Hall 17 March 1937 (in concert form; English version by E. J. Dent).

SCOTT: *Der Alchimist*

28 May. Essen

(Original English) text by the composer, German version by H. Andreae. Three scenes.

Scott's first (and so far only) opera.

VITTADINI: *Nazareth*

28 May. Pavia

Text by G. Adami (from a story by S. Lagerlöf). *Visione lirica.* One act.

In Italian also given at Monte Carlo, March 1926.

WEISMANN: *Leonce und Lena*

21 June. Freiburg

Text by the composer (from G. Büchner's comedy of the same title and with additions from W. Calé). Three acts.

One of Weismann's best works.

ROUSSEL: *La Naissance de la Lyre*

1 July. Paris, O.

Text by T. Reinach (founded on Sophocles's *Ichneutai*). One act (3 scenes).

SCHIUMA: *Tabaré*

6 August. Buenos Aires

(Italian) text by G. C. Rovesi (founded on a poem by the Uruguayan poet, J. Zorrilla de San Martín). Three acts.

Schiuma's most successful work, frequently revived at Buenos Aires.

JOTEYKO: *Zygmunt August*

29 August. Warsaw

Text by the composer (from L. Rydel's trilogy, 1913). Five acts.

Successful in Poland: Lemberg 3 May 1926, etc.

LANDRÉ: *Beatrijs*

October. Hague

Text by F. Rutten. Four acts.

In Dutch also produced at Paris, O. 19 February 1926 (by the Hague company).

KAUN: *Menandra*

29 October. Brunswick, Kiel, Osnabrück
and Rostock

Text by the composer and F. Jansen (founded on the latter's poem *Hypatia*). Three acts.

First produced in four different towns the same night.

Revived with alterations Bremerhaven 1927; Hanover 15 September 1928.

G. F. MALIPIERO: *L'Orfeide*

30 October. Düsseldorf

(Original Italian) text by the composer, first produced in a German version by W. Aron and E. Orthmann. Three parts (see for details 10 July 1920).

In Russian given at Leningrad 24 November 1928; in the original Italian, Venice, F. 23 February 1936.

R. BOSSI: *Volpino il Calderaio*

13 November. Milan, T. Carcano

Text by L. Orsini (from Shakespeare's *The Taming of the Shrew*). One act.

In German, Lübeck 7 November 1937.

A. BERG: *Wozzeck*

14 December. Berlin, O.

Text from G. Büchner's drama (written 1836), reduced to 15 scenes (against 25 in the original). Three acts.

Berg's first opera and one of the chief works of modern dramatic music. Given at Berlin 21 times until 1932 and subsequently on 16 other German stages (Oldenburg 5 March 1929; then Essen, Aachen, Düsseldorf, Königsberg, Lübeck, Cologne, Gera, Brunswick, Darmstadt, Frankfort, Freiburg, Wuppertal, Leipzig, Chemnitz, Mannheim).

Outside Germany given at:

PRAGUE 11 November 1926 (in Czech).

LENINGRAD 13 June 1927 (in Russian).

VIENNA 30 March 1930 (in German).

AMSTERDAM and ROTTERDAM October 1930 (in German, by the Aachen company).

PHILADELPHIA 19 March 1931 (in German).

ZURICH 17 October 1931 (in German).

NEW YORK 24 November 1931 (in German).

BRUSSELS 29 February 1932 (in French, translated by P. Spaak).

BRÜNN 6 December 1932 (in German).

LONDON, QUEEN'S HALL 14 March 1934 (concert performance, in German).

JANÁČEK: *Šárka*

December. Brno

Text by J. Zeyer. Three acts.

This was Janáček's first opera, written as early as 1887. Third act orchestrated by Janáček's pupil, O. Chlubna.

VREULS: *Un Songe d'une Nuit d'été*

17 December. Brussels, M.

Text by P. Spaak (after Shakespeare). Three acts. Successful in Belgium.

Revived Ghent, February 1937 and in the same month also given at Luxemburg.

LAPARRA: *Le Joueur de Viole*

24 December. Paris, O.C.

Text by the composer. Four acts.

Successful in Paris. In French also, Antwerp January 1928.

1926

NOVÁK: *Děďův Odkaz*
(The Grandfather's Will)

16 January. Brno

Text by A. Klášterský (founded on a poem by A. Heyduk). Three acts.

In Czech also given at Prague 22 December 1926.

SHAW: *Mr. Pepys*

11 February. London, Everyman

Text by C. Bax. *Ballad-Opera*. Three acts.

Given at the Royalty, London 9 March of the same year.

HONEGGER: *Judith*

13 February. Monte Carlo

Text by R. Morax. Three acts.

Previously performed in a non-operatic version, as a play with incidental music, at Mézières, Switzerland 13 June 1925. The opera was also given at:

ROTTERDAM 1926 (in concert form).

COLOGNE 13 January 1927 (in German, translated by L. Melitz).

CHICAGO 27 January 1927 (in French).

BOSTON 11 February 1927 (in French).

BRUSSELS 8 March 1927 (in French).

ZURICH 1927 (in German).

ANTWERP 17 January 1931 (in Flemish).

NAPLES, S.C. 19 January 1937 (in Italian, translated by G. Savagnone).

MALIPIERO: *La Bottega da Caffè,*
Sior Todero Brontolon and
Le Baruffe Chiozzotte

24 March. Darmstadt

Tre Commedie Goldoniani, the original Italian text adapted from three of Goldoni's comedies, pro-

duced in a German version by W. Aron. One act each.

So far, the three operas have never been revived as a trilogy: *La Bottega da Caffè* was revived at Pola 27 March 1936 (in the original Italian).

Sior Todero Brontolon was also given at Monte Carlo March 1928 (in Italian) and at Antwerp 25 April 1929 (in Flemish).

WEILL: *Der Protagonist*

27 March. Dresden

Text by G. Kaiser. One act.

Weill's first opera. Also given at Berlin, D.O. 14 October 1928.

GURLITT: *Wozzeck*

22 April. Bremen

Text: a new setting of G. Büchner's drama, one year after A. Berg's opera of the same title. Eighteen scenes and epilogue.

(PUCCINI): *Turandot*

25 April. Milan, Sc.

Text by G. Adami and R. Simoni (after Gozzi). Three acts.

Puccini's last opera, completed, after his death in 1924, by F. Alfano who added the last duet and the final scene. So far the last world success in the history of opera. The first production (under Toscanini) was announced for 24 April but postponed to the day after. Subsequently, the opera was given at Rome 29 April 1926 and all over Italy and at:

BUENOS AIRES 26 June 1926 (in Italian).

RIO DE JANEIRO July 1926 (in Italian).

DRESDEN 4 July 1926 (in German, translated by A. Brüggemann).

VIENNA 14 October 1926 (in German, translated by A. Brüggemann).

BERLIN 6 November 1926 (in German, translated by A. Brüggemann).

NEW YORK 16 November 1926 (in Italian); Philadelphia 1 December 1926, etc.

BRUSSELS 17 December 1926 (in French, translated by P. Spaak).

CAIRO March 1927 (in Italian).

MONTE CARLO March 1927 (in Italian).

BERNE March 1927 (in German).

LONDON, C.G. 7 June 1927 (in Italian).

PRAGUE 10 June 1927 (in Czech, translated by J. Bole), and 14 March 1934 (in German).

BUDAPEST 14 November 1927 (in Hungarian, translated by V. Lányi).

STOCKHOLM 29 December 1927 (in Swedish).

BASLE 19 February 1928 (in German).

PARIS, O. 2 April 1928 (in French).

ZAGREB 26 May 1928 (in Croatian).

MALTA 1928 (in Italian).

MELBOURNE 1928 (in Italian).

HAGUE and AMSTERDAM October 1928 (in Italian).

BARCELONA December 1928 (in Italian).

HALIFAX 27 September 1929 (for the first time in English, translated by R. H. Elkin).

HELSINKI 13 November 1929 (in Finnish).

RIGA 15 February 1930 (in Lettish).

BELGRADE Summer 1930 (in Serbian).

SOFIA 10 October 1930 (in Bulgarian).

LJUBLJANA 23 April 1932 (in Slovenian, translated by M. Polič).

WARSAW December 1932 (in Polish).

CAGLIARI, SARDINIA April 1934 (in Italian).

CLUJ 23 February 1936 (in Rumanian).

CASTELNUOVO-TEDESCO: La Mandragola

4 May. Venice, F.

Text from Macchiavelli's comedy. Three acts.

Castelnuovo-Tedesco's first opera; awarded the prize of the Italian Government for 1925.

In German (translated by R. S. Hoffmann), Wiesbaden 26 February 1928.

MILHAUD: Les Malheurs d'Orphée

7 May. Brussels, M.

Text by A. Lunel. Three acts.

In French also given at Paris, Th. Femina 27 February 1927; Buenos Aires 10 October 1927; Amsterdam May 1928 (in concert form).

S. SALOMON: Leonora Christina

20 May. Copenhagen

Text by A. Barfoed. Four acts.

Salomon's first performed opera.

In Danish also produced at Stockholm 7 May 1927 (by the Copenhagen company).

CAETANI: Hypatia

23 May. Weimar

Text by the composer. Three acts.

Revived Basle 1 December 1937.

SZYMANOWSKI: Krol Roger

19 June. Warsaw

Text by J. Iwaszkiewicz. Three acts.

Szymanowski's most important opera.

Successful in Poland; also given at Duisburg 28 October 1928 (in German, translated by R. S. Hoffmann) and Prague 21 October 1932 (in Czech).

SCHJELDERUP: Sturmvögel

19 September. Schwerin

Text by the composer. Three acts.

Schjelderup's last opera.

In German also given at Oslo, Spring 1927 (by the Schwerin company).

BRYSON: The Leper's Flute

15 October. Glasgow

Text by J. Colvin. Four acts.

Bryson's only opera.

Subsequently given in London, Golder's Green Hippodrome 7 December 1927.

KODÁLY: Háry János

16 October. Budapest

Text by B. Paulini and Z. Harsányi (founded on a poem by J. Garay). Prologue, 5 parts, and epilogue.

Kodály's first opera (or rather ballad opera, founded upon popular Hungarian tunes). Successful in Hungary.

In German (translated by R. S. Hoffmann), Cologne 26 September 1931.

HINDEMITH: *Cardillac*

9 November. Dresden

Text by F. Lion (founded on E. T. A. Hoffmann's *Das Fräulein von Scuderi*). Three acts.

In German also given at Vienna 3 March 1927; Prague March 1927; Berlin 30 June 1928, etc. London, Queen's Hall 18 December 1936 (in concert form; English version by F. H. White).

d'ALBERT: *Der Golem*

14 November. Frankfort

Text by F. Lion. Three acts.

In German also given at Berne. November 1926; Brünn 1927.

In Polish, Lemberg January 1928.

PEDROLLO: *Delitto e Castigo*

16 November. Milan, Sc.

Text by G. Forzano (founded on Dostoevsky's novel). Three acts.

In German (translated by W. Dahms), Breslau 9 April 1930.

KŘENEK: *Orpheus und Eurydike*

27 November. Cassel

Text by O. Kokoschka. Three acts.

CADMAN: *A Witch of Salem*

8 December. Chicago

Text by N. R. Eberhardt. Two acts.

Given on many American stages.

JANÁČEK: *Več Makropulos*

(The Makropulos Case)

18 December. Brno

Text by the composer (founded on K. Čapek's play of the same title). Three acts.

First given at Prague 1 March 1928 (in Czech). In German (translated by M. Brod), Frankfort 14 February 1929; Vienna, W. Autumn 1937.

1927

SCHOECK: *Penthesilea*

8 January. Dresden

Text by the composer (from H. von Kleist's play of the same title). One act.

Schoeck's chief work; given at Zurich 15 May 1928; Basle 22 May 1930; Berne 10 May 1936. Revived Zurich 23 June 1939.

LA VIÑA: *La Espigadora*

(The Gleaner)

12 January. Barcelona, L.

Text by F. Pérez Dolz.

The most successful work of the Spanish composer; awarded the first prize in a competition arranged by the Liceo Theatre.

IBERT: *Angélique*

28 January. Paris, Th. Bériza

Text by Nino. One act.

Ibert's first opera. Successful in Paris; revived at the O.C. 2 June 1930. Also given at:

BERLIN 27 September 1929 (in German, translated by M. Pappenheim).

BRNO January 1936 (in Czech).

PRAGUE 13 January 1937 (in Czech).

VIENNA, STADT TH. 22 September 1937 (in French).

NEW YORK 8 November 1937 (in French).

MRACZEK: *Herrn Dürers Bild*

29 January. Hanover

Text by A. Ostermann (founded on a story by F. K. Ginzkey). Three acts.

In German also, Prague 13 November 1927.

RÓZYCKI: *Beatrice Cenci*

30 January. Warsaw

Text by the composer (founded on a play by J. Slowacki). Five acts.

Successful in Poland. Revived Poznań January 1936.

KŘENEK: *Jonny spielt auf*

10 February. Leipzig

Text by the composer. Two parts (11 scenes).

Křenek's best-known work; for a few years very successful, produced on most German stages and given in other countries as well. The first productions were at:

PRAGUE June 1927 (in German).
ZURICH 1927 (in German).
BERLIN 8 October 1927 (in German).
VIENNA 31 December 1927 (in German).
BUDAPEST 21 March 1928 (in Hungarian).
ZAGREB 1 April 1928 (in Croatian).
PARIS, CH.É. 21 June 1928 (in French, translated by N. Steinhoff and A. Mauprey).
LJUBLJANA 23 July 1928 (in Slovenian).
LENINGRAD 13 November 1928 and Moscow 15 May 1929 (in Russian, translated by M. Galperin and E. Gerken).
ANTWERP 22 November 1928 (in Flemish).
HELSINKI 16 December 1928 (in Finnish).
NEW YORK, M. 19 January 1929 (in German).
RIGA 20 December 1929 (in Lettish).
COPENHAGEN 9 October 1930 (in Danish, translated by M. Dam).
WARSAW Winter 1933 (in Polish).

GNECCHI: *La Rosiera*

12 February. Gera

(Original Italian) text by the composer and C. Zangarini (founded on A. de Musset's *On ne badine pas avec l'amour*), German version by R. Batka and H. Schilling-Ziemssen. Three acts.

In German also given at Vienna, V.O. 31 March 1928.

In Czech, Plzeň (Pilsen) 23 November 1927.

In the original Italian, Trieste 24 January 1931, etc.

GRAENER: *Hanneles Himmelfahrt*

17 February. Dresden and Breslau

Text by G. Graener (the brother of the composer), founded on the play by G. Hauptmann. Two acts.

Berlin, D.O. 3 June 1927, etc.

TAYLOR: *The King's Henchman*

17 February. New York, M.

Text by E. St. Vincent Millay. Three acts.

The first opera of the American composer.

DELANNOY: *Le Poirier de Misère*

21 February. Paris, O.C.

Text by J. Limozin and A. de la Tourrasse (*mystère*). Three acts.

Delannoy's first opera.

PETERSON-BERGER: *Adils och Elisiv*

27 February. Stockholm

Text by the composer. Three acts.

The last opera of the Swedish composer.

WEILL: *Royal Palace*

2 March. Berlin, Kroll's

Text by I. Goll. One act.

Weill's second opera; unsuccessful.

PICK-MANGIAGALLI: *Basi e Bote*

3 March. Rome, Arg.

Text by A. Boito (written 1881, originally intended for himself; first published in *La Lettura* in 1914). Three acts.

After several ballets this was Pick-Mangiagalli's first opera; also given at Hamburg 31 January 1931 (in German, translated by W. Wolff).

GAUBERT: *Naïla*

7 April. Paris, O.

Text by M. Léna (*conte oriental*). Three acts.

The first of Gaubert's operas which was produced at the Paris Opéra (where the composer had been chief conductor since 1920).

WEINBERGER: *Švanda Dudák*
(Shvanda the Bagpiper)

27 April. Prague, Cz.

Text by M. Kareš (cf. note on Hřimalý's opera of the same title, 1896). Two acts.

Weinberger's first opera; one of the most successful works ever written by a Czech composer, in fact, after Smetana's *Prodaná Nevésta* (see 1866) about the only Czech opera the success of which was not, more or less, limited to its country and language.

Very successful in Czechoslovakia; also given at

BRESLAU 16 December 1928 (in German, translated by M. Brod).

PRAGUE May 1929 (for the first time in German there).

BASLE 25 September 1929 (in German).

LJUBLJANA 5 October 1929 (in Slovenian).

BERLIN 29 November 1929 (in German).

BUDAPEST April 1930 (in Hungarian).

ZAGREB 26 April 1930 (in Croatian).

VIENNA 16 October 1930 (in German).

HELSINKI 21 November 1930 (in Finnish).

RIGA 6 December 1930 (in Lettish).

SOFIA 6 November 1931 (in Bulgarian).

NEW YORK, M. 7 November 1931 (in German).

ANTWERP February 1932 (in French).

COPENHAGEN 21 March 1933 (in Danish).

WARSAW 1933 (in Polish).

LONDON, C.G. 11 May 1934 (in German).

STRASBOURG 1934 (in French).

BUENOS AIRES 18 July 1935 (in German).

LYONS January 1936 (in French).

Italian version by C. Castelfranchi published Trieste 1938.

ALFANO: *Madonna Imperia*

5 May. Turin, T. di T.

Text by A. Rossato (founded on one of H. de Balzac's *Contes drôlatiques*). One act.

Successful in Italy. In Italian also given at New York, M. 8 February 1928.

In German (translated by W. Klein), Vienna 23 February 1928; Wiesbaden 26 February 1928.

GUI: *La Fata Malerba*

15 May. Turin, T. di T.

Text by F. Salvatori. Three acts.

Gui's first opera.

STRAVINSKY: *Oedipus Rex*

30 May. Paris, Th. S.B.

(Original French) text by J. Cocteau (after Sophocles), translated into Latin by J. Danielou. *Opéra Oratorio.* Two acts.

In Paris produced as an oratorio, in concert form, as in most countries. There were, however, some productions on the stage, in Austria, Germany, and America.

Given (everywhere in Latin) at:

VIENNA 23 February 1928 (first stage production).

BOSTON 24 February 1928 (in concert form).

BERLIN, KROLL'S 25 February 1928 (stage).

NEW YORK 8 March 1928 (concert) and 21 April 1931 (stage).

AMSTERDAM 24 April 1928 (concert).

LENINGRAD May 1928 (stage).

LJUBLJANA 9 November 1928 (stage).

BUDAPEST 14 December 1928 (stage).

PHILADELPHIA 10 April 1931 (stage).

BUENOS AIRES 11 August 1931 (stage).

ZURICH 1933 (stage).

BARCELONA January 1934 (stage).

LONDON, QUEEN'S HALL 12 February 1936 (concert).

FLORENCE 22 May 1937 (concert).

MILHAUD: *Die Entführung der Europa*
TOCH: *Die Prinzessin auf der Erbse*
HINDEMITH: *Hin und Zurück*

17 July. Baden-Baden

Three short operas, produced at the Chamber Music Festival, Baden-Baden. The fourth work on the bill was K. Weill's *Mahagonny*, a *Songspiel* which was afterwards transformed into an opera (see 1930).

Die Entführung der Europa

(Original French) text by H. Hoppenot (*L'Enlèvement d'Europe*), produced in a German version by R. S. Hoffmann. Eight scenes. Belongs to a series of *opéra-minutes* which was given in its entirety one year later at Wiesbaden (see 1928).

Die Prinzessin auf der Erbse

Text by B. Elkan (after H. C. Andersen). One act. In German also, Basle 9 May 1928; Prague

December 1929. In English (translated by M. J. Farquhar), New York 9 June 1936 Biltmore Th.

Hin und zurück

Text by M. Schiffer. *Sketch mit Musik*. One act. In German also, Basle 9 May 1928; Prague December 1929; Zurich 1930; Berlin 29 November 1930. In Hungarian (translated by M. László), Budapest 13 January 1929.

KORNGOLD: *Das Wunder der Heliane*

7 October. Hamburg

Text by H. Müller (founded on a play by H. Kaltneker). Three acts.

In German also, Vienna 29 October 1927; Berlin 5 April 1928, etc.

RESPIGHI: *Die versunkene Glocke*

18 November. Hamburg

(Original Italian) text by C. Guastalla *La Campana sommersa* (founded on G. Hauptmann's play), German version by W. Wolff. Four acts.

In German, revived at Zurich 17 November 1934.

In the original Italian first given at New York, M. 24 November 1928; Milan, Sc. 4 April 1929, etc. Buenos Aires 2 August 1929.

In Flemish, Antwerp 31 March 1931.

SAMUEL-ROUSSEAU: *Le bon Roi Dagobert*

5 December. Paris, O.C.

Text by A. Rivoire (founded on his comedy of the same title). Four acts.

Very successful in France.

In French also given at Algiers December 1928; Antwerp January 1929; Brussels 28 November 1932.

Revived Paris, O.C. 5 May 1938; Brussels 12 January 1940.

MILHAUD: *Le pauvre Matelot*

16 December. Paris, O.C.

Text by J. Cocteau (*Complainte en trois actes*).

Milhaud's most successful work for the stage. Given at:

BRUSSELS 28 December 1927 (in French).

BERLIN 27 September 1929 (in German, translated by M. Pappenheim).

Revived in a new version (with reduced orchestration), at:

GENEVA 15 November 1934 (in French).

TURIN, T. DI TORINO December 1934 (in French).

PRAGUE April 1935 (in German).

PHILADELPHIA 1 April 1937 (in English, translated by L. N. Finley).

NEW YORK, NEW AMSTERDAM TH. 11 April 1937 (in English) and 44th Street Th. 10 November 1937 (in French).

VIENNA, STADT TH. 22 September 1937 (in French).

PARIS, O.C. 3 February 1938 (in French).

ANTWERP 8 March 1940 (in French).

HONEGGER: *Antigone*

28 December. Brussels, M.

Text by J. Cocteau (after Sophocles). Three acts.

In German (translated by L. Melitz), Essen 11 January 1928, etc.

In English translated by F. Ferguson), New York, American Laboratory Th. 24 April 1930.

Revived Zurich 8 June 1934.

WOLF-FERRARI: *Sly*

29 December. Milan, Sc.

Text by G. Forzano (founded on the prologue to Shakespeare's *The Taming of the Shrew*). Three acts.

The subtitle reads *La Leggenda del Dormiente risvegliato*.

Successful in Italy and other countries. Given at:

DRESDEN 15 October 1928, GRAZ 1 March 1929, BERLIN 11 May 1929 and BASLE 24 May 1929 (in German, translated by W. Dahms).

ANTWERP January 1930 (in Flemish).

BUDAPEST 31 January 1931 (in Hungarian, translated by V. Lányi).

RIGA 17 November 1932 (in Lettish).

VIENNA, V.O. 26 September 1934 (in German).

1928

LAZZARI: *La Tour de Feu*

16 January. Paris, O.

Text by the composer. Three acts.

Revived Paris, O. 17 April 1939.

Film effects for the first time in opera occur in the third act of *La Tour de Feu*.

BRUNEAU: *Angelo, Tyran de Padoue*

16 January. Paris, O.C.

Text by C. Méré (founded on V. Hugo's drama). Five acts.

Given at the O.C. 19 times until 1929.

K. H. DAVID: *Traumwandel*

29 January. Zurich

Text by the composer (founded on a story by Turgenev). Two acts.

The most important work of the Swiss composer.

CHEREPNIN: *Ol-Ol*

31 January. Weimar

(Original Russian) text from L. Andreev's play *The Days of our Life* (*Dni nashei zhizni*), German version by R. S. Hoffmann. Three acts.

Cherepnin's first opera. Revived at:

LJUBLJANA 16 October 1933 (in Slovenian).

NEW YORK 9 February 1934 (in Russian).

VIENNA 2 March 1934 (in German, by the Österreichisches Studio).

ZANDONAI: *Giuliano*

4 February. Naples, S.C.

Text by A. Rossato (founded on G. Flaubert's *St. Julien l'Hospitalier*). Prologue, 2 acts, and epilogue.

In Italian also given at Rio de Janeiro 15 September 1928.

WEILL: *Der Zar lässt sich photographieren*

18 February. Leipzig

Text by G. Kaiser. One act.

In German also given at Berlin, D.O. 14 October 1928; Prague November 1928.

In Slovenian (translated by N. Štritov), Ljubljana 15 October 1931.

G. F. MALIPIERO: *Der falsche Harlekin*

8 March. Mayence

(Original Italian) text (*Il finto Arlecchino*) by the composer, German version by R. S. Hoffmann. Two parts.

(This short opera which was produced at Mayence on a triple-bill with revivals of Toch's *Prinzessin auf der Erbse* und Hindemith's *Hin und zurück*, see 1927, forms part of a trilogy *Misteri di Venezia*, see 1932.) Revived Budapest 28 February 1932 (in Hungarian, translated by K. Nádasdy); Stuttgart 18 May 1938 (in German). In the original Italian given at San Remo 5 March 1933; Venice 18 January 1934, etc.; Amsterdam February 1935; revived Rome 7 February 1939.

MULÈ: *Dafni*

14 March. Rome, T.R.

Text by E. Romagnoli (*Poema pastorale*). Three acts.

The first new opera produced at the "Teatro Reale dell' Opera", late T. Costanzi, Rome, inaugurated with Boito's *Nerone*, 28 February 1928. Successful in Italy. Also given at Malta January 1933 (in Italian); Düsseldorf December 1938 (in German, translated by J. Popelka).

FERROUD: *Chirurgie*

20 March. Monte Carlo

Text by D. Roche and A. G. Block (founded on a story by A. P. Chekhov). One act.

Ferroud's first and only opera. In French also given at Strasbourg 1928; Paris, Ch.É. 19 June 1929.

LILIEN: *Beatrix*

24 March. Antwerp

(Flemish) text by H. Teirlinck (from his novel *Ik dien*). Three acts.

Subsequently given at:

BRUSSELS 31 March 1928 (in French, translated by the librettist himself).

HANOVER 14 April 1928 (in German, translated by W. Klein).

PRAGUE 1 April 1931 (in Czech, translated by M. Harlassová-Schrödlová).

BRÜNN 1931 (in German).

ZÁDOR: *A Holtak Szigete*
(The Island of the Dead)

29 March. Budapest

Text by V. Lányi (translated from a German libretto by G. K. Zwerenz). Two acts.

Given in the original German at Carlsruhe 6 December 1928.

G. F. MALIPIERO: *Filomela und ihr Narr*

31 March. Prague, G.

(Original Italian) text by the composer (*Filomela e l'Infatuato*), produced in a German version by R. S. Hoffmann. Three parts.

Apparently never given in Italy or elsewhere, but in the original Italian broadcast from London 21 February 1936.

ETTINGER: *Frühlings Erwachen*

14 April. Leipzig

Text from F. Wedekind's play of the same title. Three acts.

MILHAUD: *Der befreite Theseus* and *Die verlassene Ariadne*

20 April. Wiesbaden

(Original French) text by H. Hoppenot, produced in a German version by R. S. Hoffmann. Two one-act operas of the same series of "opéras-minutes" of which the first, *Die Entführung der Europa*, had been produced at Baden-Baden the year before (see 1927).

All three operas were revived at Budapest 28 February 1932 (in Hungarian, translated by K. Nádasdy).

KŘENEK: *Schwergewicht, Der Diktator* and *Das geheime Königreich*

6 May. Wiesbaden

Three one-act operas; text by the composer.

Also produced at Berlin 2 December 1928. *Schwergewicht* (sub-title *Die Ehre der Nation*) was also given at Prague December 1929 (in German); Lemberg 1933 (in Polish); Amsterdam June 1934 (by the Dutch Chamber Opera).

(SCHUBERT): *Die Freunde von Salamanca*

6 May. Halle

Original text by J. Mayrhofer. Two acts.

Written in 1815; not performed in Schubert's lifetime. Of the original libretto only the lyrics are extant; for the Halle 1928 production new dialogue was supplied by G. Ziegler.

Revived in another version (new libretto by H. Moericke and J. Raimer; prologue and 3 acts) at Basle 10 May 1934.

TOFFT: *Anathema*

10 May. Copenhagen

Text by the composer (founded on a story by P. Mérimée). Prologue and 3 acts.

After *Vifandaka*, produced at Copenhagen 30 years' earlier, this was Tofft's second and last opera.

DRAGOI: *Napasta*

May. Bucharest

Text from J. L. Caragiale's play of the same title. Three acts.

The most successful opera of the Rumanian composer.

PIZZETTI: *Fra Gherardo*

16 May. Milan, Sc.

Text by the composer. Three acts.

In Italian also, Buenos Aires 27 July 1928; Rome 5 February 1929, etc. New York, M. 21 March 1929.

In German (translated by A. Brüggemann), Hamburg 4 June 1931.

R. STRAUSS: *Die ägyptische Helena*

6 June. Dresden

Text by H. von Hofmannsthal. Two acts. Produced at:

VIENNA 11 June 1928 (in German).
BERLIN 7 October 1928 (in German).
NEW YORK, M. 6 November 1928 (in German).
GENEVA 20 September 1929 (in German).
MONTE CARLO 15 February 1930 (in French, translated by R. Gunsbourg).
HAGUE 26 April 1930 (in German).
ANTWERP 14 October 1930 (in Flemish).
BUDAPEST 31 October 1932 (in Hungarian, translated by V. Lányi).
STRASBOURG 5 December 1932 (in German).

Given with some alterations at Salzburg 14 August 1933.

REUTTER: *Saul*

15 July. Baden-Baden

Text: by A. Lernet-Holenia. One act.

Reutter's first opera. Revived Prague April 1935 (in German).

WEILL: *Die Dreigroschenoper*

31 August. Berlin, Th. am Schiffbauerdamm

Text: a modern version of John Gay's *The Beggar's Opera* (see 1728), founded on a German translation by E. Hauptmann, lyrics by B. Brecht (who also used ballads by F. Villon and R. Kipling). Prologue and 8 scenes.

Very successful in Germany; also produced at:

PRAGUE 31 December 1928 (in German).
VIENNA, RAIMUND TH. 9 March 1929 (in German).
WARSAW 4 May 1929 (in Polish, translated by O. Winbrun and W. Broniewski).
BASLE 31 May 1929 (in German).
AMSTERDAM October 1929 (in Dutch).
COPENHAGEN, NY TH. 15 January 1930 (in Danish, translated by M. Dam); revived Riddersalen 17 September 1937.

MOSCOW, KAMERNY TH. 1930 (in Russian).
BUDAPEST 1 September 1930 (in Hungarian, translated by J. Heltai).
PARIS, TH. MONTPARNASSE 14 October 1930 (in French, translated by N. Steinhoff and A. Mauprey); revived Th. de l'Étoile 28 September 1937.
NEW YORK, EMPIRE 13 April 1933 (in English, as *The Threepenny Opera*, translated by C. Cochran and J. Krimsky).
LONDON, QUEENS' HALL 8 February 1935 (in concert form; English version by C. D. Freeman).

JEREMIÁŠ: *Bratři Karamazovi*

8 October. Prague, Cz.

Text by J. Maria (after Dostoevsky). Three acts. Jeremiáš's first opera. Brno 17 October 1929. In German (translated by P. Eisner), Augsburg 28 March 1931; Berne 4 January 1932.

Revived in Czech, Prague 17 April 1935.

LOTHAR: *Tyll*

4 October. Weimar

Text by H. F. Koenigsgarten (*Eine Ulenspiegel-Oper*). Three acts.

Lothar's first opera.

In German also given at Berlin, D.O. 1 September 1929; Basle 28 April 1930.

In Russian (translated by P. G. Antokolsky), Moscow, Arts Th. 26 February 1931.

KROHN: *Tuhotulva*
(Deluge)

25 October. Helsinki

Text by H. Haahti. Three acts.

The only opera of the well-known Finnish composer and musicologist.

TOLDRÁ: *El Giravolt de Maig*
(May-Dance)

27 October. Barcelona

Successful Catalan comic one-act opera.

WETZLER: *Die baskische Venus*

18 November. Leipzig

Text by L. Wetzler (the wife of the composer), founded on a story by P. Mérimée. Two acts.

Wetzler's first opera. Also given at Basle 6 November 1933.

d'ALBERT: *Die schwarze Orchidee*

1 December. Leipzig

Text by K. M. von Levetzow (*Opera grotesca*). Three acts.

The last opera of d'Albert which was produced in his lifetime. Being of the *Jonny spielt auf* school it was a transitory success on German stages. Berlin, D.O. 9 June 1929, etc.

HØFFDING: *Kejserens nye Klaeder*
(The Emperor's New Clothes)

19 December. Copenhagen

Text by the composer (founded on the tale by H. C. Andersen). Three scenes.

Høffding's first opera.

1929

HOLST: *The golden Goose*

11 January. Liverpool

Text by J. M. Joseph (*Choral Ballet*), founded on a tale by the brothers Grimm. One act.

First produced in the open air Warwick Castle 4 July 1929.

Revived London Hyde Park July 1935.

GIORDANO: *Il Re*

12 January. Milan, Sc.

Text by G. Forzano. One act (3 scenes).

In Italian also given at Buenos Aires 5 July 1929, etc.

In German (translated by W. Dahms), Berlin 5 November 1929; Prague 13 April 1930.

In Hungarian (translated by Károly Kristóf), Budapest April 1930.

HOLBROOKE: *Bronwen*

1 February. Huddersfield

Text by T. E. Ellis. Three acts.

The last part of the trilogy *The Cauldron of Annwen* (see 1912 and 1914). This part had been published in 1922.

DOHNÁNYI: *A Tenor*

9 February. Budapest

(Original German) text by E. Góth (founded on C. Sternheim's comedy *Bürger Schippel*), Hungarian version by Z. Harsányi. Three acts.

Successful in Hungary.

In German given at Nuremberg 24 February 1929; Berlin, D.O. 18 December 1929; Prague 1930.

LATTUADA: *Le Preziose ridicole*

9 February. Milan, Sc.

Text by A. Rossato (founded on Molière's comedy). One act.

Successful in Italy. Also given at:

BUENOS AIRES 17 August 1929 (in Italian).

PRAGUE 13 April 1930 (in German, translated by W. Dahms).

BERLIN 27 October 1930 (in German, translated by W. Dahms).

NEW YORK, M. 10 December 1930 (in Italian).

BRUSSELS 4 January 1932 (in French, translated by P. Spaak).

MALTA January 1935 (in Italian).

CAIRO March 1935 (in Italian).

CLUJ, RUMANIA 29 March 1936 (in Italian).

HAGUE December 1937 (in Italian).

LAPARRA: *Las Toreras*

February. Lille

Text by the composer (founded on a comedy by Tirso de Molina). One act.

Successful on French stages; Bordeaux 14 February 1930, etc.

WILLIAMS: *Sir John in Love*

21 March. London, R.C.M.

Text from Shakespeare's *The Merry Wives of Windsor*. Four acts.

Revived at the R.C.M. 3 July 1939.

FÉVRIER: *La Femme nue*

23 March. Monte Carlo

Text by L. Payen (founded on the play by H. Bataille). Four acts.

Successful on French stages. Paris, O.C. 25 April 1932; Algiers January 1933; Tournai November 1933.

CANTELOUBE: *Le Mas*

3 April. Paris, O.

Text by the composer. Three acts.

Canteloube's first opera; it had been awarded the Prix Heugel in 1925.

BRAND: *Maschinist Hopkins*

13 April. Duisburg

Text by the composer. Prologue and 3 acts.

Also given at:

ZURICH January 1930 (in German).

BERLIN, D.O. 22 March 1930 (in German).

PRAGUE 7 October 1930 (in Czech).

STOCKHOLM 5 March 1931 (in Swedish).

KHARKOV 1931 (in Ukrainian).

TOVEY: *The Bride of Dionysus*

23 April. Edinburgh

Text by R. C. Trevelyan. Three acts.

Tovey's only opera. Revived Edinburgh 25 April 1932.

LEVADÉ: *La Peau de Chagrin*

24 April. Paris, O.C.

Text by P. Decourcelle and M. Carré fils (from H. de Balzac's novel). Four acts.

Very successful on French stages.

In French also given at Antwerp December 1929.

KAMINSKI: *Jürg Jenatsch*

27 April. Dresden

Text by the composer (founded on C. F. Meyer's novel). Six scenes.

Kaminski's first opera.

Revived in an enlarged version, Nuremberg 1937.

PROKOFIEV: *Le Joueur*

29 April. Brussels, M.

(Original Russian) text (*Igrok*, founded on Dostoevsky's novel) by the composer, French version by P. Spaak. Four acts.

The opera was to be produced at the Maryinski Theatre, Petrograd, in 1917 (under the direction of Albert Coates); because of the revolution the performance did not take place.

CASAVOLO: *Il Gobbo del Califfo*

4 May. Rome, T.R.

Text by A. Rossato. One act.

Successful in Italy. Also given at:

STUTTGART 29 October 1931 (in German, translated by A. Brüggemann).

BUENOS AIRES 20 September 1932 (in Italian).

STOCKHOLM 29 December 1938 (in Swedish).

KOGOJ: *Črne Maske*
(Black Masks)

7 May. Ljubljana

Text by J. Vidmar (founded on L. Andreev's play of the same title). Two acts.

Kogoj's first opera. Important work of the modern Slovenian school.

IBERT: *Persée et Andromède* ou *Le plus Heureux des Trois*

15 May. Paris, O.

Text by Nino (after one of J. Laforgue's *Moralités légendaires*). Two acts.

LATTUADA: *Don Giovanni*

18 May. Naples, S.C.

Text by A. Rossato (founded on the Spanish drama by J. Zorrilla). Four acts.

HINDEMITH: *Neues vom Tage*

8 June. Berlin, Kroll's

Text by M. Schiffer. Three parts.

The last of Hindemith's operas which was produced in Germany.

GOOSSENS: *Judith*

25 June. London, C.G.

Text by A. Bennett. One act.

Goossens's first opera.

In English also given at Philadelphia 26 December 1929.

Revived 21 October 1938 (broadcast from London).

BOERO: *El Matrero*
(The Rogue)

12 July. Buenos Aires

Text by Y. Rodriguez (*Leyenda dramática*). Three acts.

Successful Spanish opera. (The librettist is a native of Uruguay).

Revived at Buenos Aires 30 August 1934 and 25 July 1936.

N. BERG: *Engelbrekt*

21 September. Stockholm

Text by the composer. Four acts.

In German (translated by F. Tutenberg), Brunswick 8 December 1933.

RYTEL: *Ijola*

October. Warsaw

Text from a play by J. Zulawski (1905). Four acts.

The first opera of the Polish composer.

KŘIČKA: *Bily Pán*
(The white Gentleman)

27 November. Brno

Text by J. Löwenbach-Budín (founded on O. Wilde's *Canterville Ghost*). Eleven scenes.

In German (translated by P. Eisner, reduced to 6 scenes), Breslau 14 November 1931; Vienna

31 December 1932. Given at Prague, May 1932 (in German) and 10 October 1933 (in Czech).

COATES: *Samuel Pepys*

21 December. Munich

(Original English) text by W. P. Drury and R. Pryce, produced in a German version by M. Meyerfeld. One act.

Coates's first performed opera.

1930

IBERT: *Le Roi d'Yvetot*

15 January. Paris, O.C.

Text by J. Limozin and A. de la Tourrasse. Four acts.

In German (translated by O. Springer and W. Ullmann), Düsseldorf 20 February 1936; Graz 28 November 1936; Prague December 1937.

KŘENEK: *Leben des Orest*

19 January. Leipzig

Text by the composer. Five acts.

Berlin 4 March 1930, etc. The last of Křenek's operas which was produced in Germany.

BRAUNFELS: *Galatea*

26 January. Cologne

Text by S. Baltus (*Ein griechisches Märchen*). One act.

Berlin, D.O. 25 February 1931.

SCHÖNBERG: *Von heute auf morgen*

1 February. Frankfort

Text by "Max Blonda" (pseudonym). One act.

After *Erwartung* and *Die glückliche Hand* (see 1924), Schönberg's third work for the stage; unsuccessful.

WEILL: *Aufstieg und Fall der Stadt Mahagonny*

9 March. Leipzig

Text by B. Brecht (originally a *Songspiel*, first performed at the Chamber Music Festival, Baden-Baden 1927). Three acts.

Also given at Prague May 1930; Berlin, Th. am Kurfürstendamm 21 December 1931;Vienna, Raimund Th. 26 April 1932.

In concert form also given at Paris 11 December 1932 (by the "La Sérénade" society) and at Rome 29 December 1933.

LETOREY: *Le Sicilien* ou *L'Amour Peintre*

19 March. Paris, O.C.

Text by A. Dumas (after Molière). Two acts.
Revived Paris, O.C. 7 May 1935.

(JANÁČEK): *Z Mrtvého Domu* (From the House of the Dead)

12 April. Brno

Text by the composer (from Dostoevsky's novel). Three acts.

Janáček's last opera; after the composer's death completed by O. Zitek (text) and B. Bakala (music). First given at Prague 21 February 1931 (in Czech).

In German (translated by M. Brod), Mannheim 14 December 1930; Berlin 29 May 1931.

ALFANO: *L'ultimo Lord*

19 April. Naples, S.C.

Text by U. Falena. Three acts.

Monte Carlo April 1932 (in French, translated by H. Cain).

PIZZETTI: *Lo Straniero*

29 April. Rome, T.R.

Text by the composer. Two acts.

Successful in Italy; Milan, Sc. 7 January 1931, etc.

In Italian also given at Buenos Aires 4 July 1930.

MILHAUD: *Christoph Columbus*

5 May. Berlin, O.

(Original French) text by P. Claudel, produced in a German version by R. S. Hoffmann. Two parts (27 scenes).

First given at Paris, Salle Pleyel 6 December 1936 (in concert form); broadcast from London 16 January 1937 (English version by A. Perry); from Antwerp 17 January 1940 (Flemish version by A. Van de Velde).

ANTHEIL: *Transatlantic*

25 May. Frankfort

(Original English) text (*The People's Choice*) by the composer, produced in a German version by R. S. Hoffmann. Three acts.

Antheil's first opera.

DELANNOY: *Le Fou de la Dame*
ROSENTHAL: *Rayons de Soieries*

2 June. Paris, O.C.

Le Fou de la Dame

Text by J. Limozin and A. de la Tourrasse (*chanson de geste*). One act.

Previously, the work had been performed in concert form at the seventh I.S.C.M. festival, Geneva 6 April 1929.

Also given at Ljubljana 15 October 1931 (in Slovenian, translated by N. Štritov).

Rayons de Soieries

Text by Nino. One act.

In French also given at Brussels 4 January 1932.

TOCH: *Der Fächer*

8 June. Königsberg

Text by F. Lion. Three acts.

First produced at the festival of the Allgemeiner Deutscher Musikverein.

SCHOECK: *Vom Fischer un syner Fru*

3 October. Dresden

Text by the composer from P. O. Runge's low-German version of Grimm's fairy-tale. Seven scenes.

Zurich 24 January 1931; Berne 30 October 1931, etc. In German also, Strasbourg, October 1933.

GURLITT: *Soldaten*

9 November. Düsseldorf

Text by the composer (from a play by J. M. R. Lenz, 1776). Three acts.

In German also, Prague 17 January 1931; Berlin, D.O. 13 November 1931.

REZNICEK: *Spiel oder Ernst?*
LOTHAR: *Lord Spleen*

11 November. Dresden

Spiel oder Ernst?

Text by P. Knudsen. One act.

In German also, Berlin 31 December 1930, etc. Prague June 1931.

In Swedish, Stockholm 27 September 1934. In English (as *Fact and Fiction*, translated by H. Pleasants), Philadelphia 1941.

Lord Spleen

Text by H.F. Koenigsgarten (from Ben Jonson's *Epicoene*). Two acts.

In German also, Berlin, D.O. 25 February 1931; Prague June 1931; Graz Autumn 1931, etc.

GOTOVAC: *Morana*

29 November. Brno

(Original Croatian) text by A. Muradbegović, Czech version by? Three acts.

Successful Croat opera; subsequently given at Zagreb 3 October 1931; Belgrade January 1932; in Slovenian, Ljubljana 5 February 1933.

RATHAUS: *Fremde Erde*

10 December. Berlin, O.

Text by K. Palffy-Wanieck. Five acts. Rathaus's first opera.

FOREST: *Camille*

10 December. Chicago

Text by the composer (like Verdi's *Traviata* founded on Dumas's *La Dame aux Camélias*). Prologue and 3 acts.

First new opera produced at the Civic Opera House, Chicago, inaugurated (with *Aïda*), 4 November 1929.

HONEGGER: *Les Aventures du Roi Pausole*

12 December. Paris, B.P.

Text by A. Willemetz (from a novel by P. Louÿs). Three acts.

Honegger's first attempt as a composer of operettas. Successful on French stages. In French also, Geneva July 1932.

1931

BRUNEAU: *Virginie*

7 January. Paris, O.

Text by H. Duvernois. Three acts.

The last opera of the then 74 years old composer.

POUEIGH: *Perkin*

16 January. Bordeaux

Text by P. B. Gheusi (after P. Harispe). *Légende basque*, 3 acts.

Paris, O. 26 January 1934.

MONTEMEZZI: *La Notte di Zoraima*

31 January. Milan, Sc.

Text by M. Ghisalberti. One act.

Successful in Italy. In Italian also, New York, M. 2 December 1931.

In Swedish, Stockholm 16 October 1931.

TAYLOR: *Peter Ibbetson*

7 February. New York, M.

Text by the composer and C. Collier (from the novel by G. Du Maurier). Three acts.

Successful on American stages.

ROGER-DUCASSE: *Cantegril*

9 February. Paris, O.C.

Text by R. Escholier. Four acts.

Apart from a mimodrame *Orphée* (St. Petersburg 1914, Paris 1926, Hanover 1929), Roger-Ducasse's only work for the stage. Given at the O.C. 18 times until 1932.

PERSICO: *La Bisbetica domata*

12 February. Rome, T.R.

Text by A. Rossato (from Shakespeare's *Taming of the Shrew*). Four acts.

Persico's first opera. Successful in Italy. Naples S.C. 5 February 1935.

LAPARRA: *L'illustre Fregona*

16 February. Paris, O.

Text by the composer (*zarzuela*, founded on a story by Cervantes). Three acts.

Successful in France; Nice 20 February 1932, etc. Revived Paris, O. 21 February 1940.

Also given at Stockholm 16 January 1932 (in Swedish); Buenos Aires 30 July 1937 (in French).

HUBAY: *Az Álarc*

(The Mask)

26 February. Budapest

Text by F. Martos and S. Góth (founded on a German play by R. Lothar). Three acts.

In German, Carlsruhe 12 November 1931.

WEINBERGER: *Die geliebte Stimme*

28 February. Munich

(Original Czech) text (*Milovaný Hlas*) by the composer (from a German novel by R. Michel), produced in a German version by R. Michel. Three acts.

YSAYE: *Piér li Houïeu*

(Peter the Collier)

4 March. Liége

(Walloon) text by the composer. One act.

The only operatic attempt of the famous Belgian violinist, produced two months before his death. Given at Brussels 25 April 1931.

(Since Hamal's 18th century comic operas, see 1757, this seems to be about the only modern work written in the language of the Liége country.)

WOLF-FERRARI: *La Vedova scaltra*

5 March. Rome, T.R.

Text by M.Ghisalberti (from Goldoni's comedy). Three acts.

Successful in Italy. In Italian also given at Zurich 31 May 1931; Malta 19 February 1934; Cairo 1936.

In German (translated by W. Dahms), Berlin and Cologne 21 October 1931.

Lettish translation by R. Egle published 1935.

KONJOVIĆ: *Koštana*

16 April. Zagreb

Text founded on B. Stanković's play of the same title. Five scenes.

Successful Croatian folk-opera. Also given at Ljubljana 7 November 1931 (in Slovenian, translated by N. Štritov); Brno September 1932 and Prague 14 December 1935 (in Czech, translated by Z. Knitl).

(MAGNARD): *Guercoeur*

24 April. Paris, O.

Text by the composer. Three acts.

The work had been written as early as 1900. The greater part of the score was burnt in the war (when the composer was killed in the village of Baron, Oise, 3 September 1914). The opera was restored, from the manuscript of the second act and from the vocal score of the rest, by G. Ropartz.

G. F. MALIPIERO: *Komödie des Todes*

15 May. Munich

(Original Italian) text (*Torneo Notturno*) by the composer, produced in a German version by H. F. Redlich.

The work consists of seven nocturnes, called in the original: *Le Serenate*; *La Tormenta*; *La Foresta*; *La Taverna del Buon Tempo*; *Il Foculare spento*; *Il Castello della Noia*; and *La Prigione*. Not yet produced in Italy.

HABA: *Die Mutter*

17 May. Munich

Text by the composer. Ten scenes.

The first opera written (or, at any rate, produced) in quarter tones. Awarded the Czechoslovakian State prize in 1931.

WELLESZ: *Die Bakchantinnen*

20 June. Vienna, O.

Text by the composer (from Euripides's tragedy). Two acts.

HONEGGER: *Amphion*

23 June. Paris, O.

Text by P. Valéry (*mélodrame*). One act.

In German (translated by W. Klein), Zurich 14 June 1933.

LEMBA: *Armastus ja Surm*

(Love and Death)

October. Tallinn

Text by J. Oengo (founded on his poem *Aegna*). Five acts.

One of the earliest original Estonian operas.

VOLLERTHUN: *Der Freikorporal*

10 November. Hanover

Text by R. Lothar (founded on *Die Geschwister*, a story by G. Freytag). Three acts.

Vollerthun's most successful opera; given at Berlin, D.O. 10 June 1933, etc.

PFITZNER: *Das Herz*

12 November. Berlin, O. and Munich

Text by H. Mahner-Mons. Three acts.

Successful in Germany. In German also given at Brünn 24 November 1931; Prague 28 November 1931; Graz 16 January 1932; Vienna 28 January 1932; Zurich 31 January 1932; Strasbourg 27 February 1932. In Swedish, Stockholm 14 April 1932.

GRAENER: *Friedemann Bach*

13 November. Schwerin

Text by R. Lothar. Three acts.

Successful in Germany; Berlin, D.O. 23 January 1932, etc.

GRUENBERG: *Jack and the Beanstalk*

19 November. New York, Juilliard School

Text by J. Erskine (*A Fairy opera for the Childlike*). Three acts.

Successful in the U.S.A. Publicly performed at 44th Street Th., New York 21 December 1931. Revived Chicago 14 November 1936.

1932

MILHAUD: *Maximilien*

4 January. Paris, O.

Text by A. Lunel (translated from a German libretto by R. S. Hoffmann, founded on F. Werfel's play *Juarez und Maximilian*). Three acts.

SCHULHOFF: *Plameny*

(Flames)

27 January. Brno

Text by K. J. Beneš. Two acts.

Schulhoff's first performed opera.

GOLDSCHMIDT:

Der gewaltige Hahnrei

14 February. Mannheim

Text by the composer (from F. Crommelynck's drama *Le Cocu magnifique*). Three acts. Goldschmidt's first opera.

HAGEMAN: *Tragödie in Arezzo*

18 February. Freiburg

(Original English) text by A. F. Goodrich (from R. Browning's *The Ring and the Book*), produced in a German version by W. Wolff and J. Kapp. Prologue and 3 acts.

In German also given at Vienna, V.O. 19 March 1935 (as *Caponsacchi*).

In the original English, New York, M. 4 February 1937.

WEILL: *Die Bürgschaft*

10 March. Berlin, D.O.

Text by C. Neher (founded on a parable by J. G. Herder). Prologue and 3 acts.

The last of Weill's operas which was produced in Germany.

RESPIGHI: *Maria Egiziaca*

16 March. New York, Carnegie Hall

Text by C. Guastalla (*Mistero. Trittico per Concerto*). Three episodes.

Originally performed in concert form; later on also produced in operatic form. Given at:
ROME, AUGUSTEO 24 April 1932 (in Italian).
BUENOS AIRES 23 July 1933 (in Italian).
PRAGUE October 1933 (in German).
HELSINKI 25 October 1933 (in Finnish).
MALTA Carnival 1934 (in Italian).
TUNIS April 1934 (in Italian).
PARIS, O.C. 1 June 1934 (in French, translated by J. Chantavoine).
AMSTERDAM February 1935 (in Italian).
LONDON 11 April 1937 (in concert form, at the Hyde Park Hotel).

CASELLA: *La Donna Serpente*

17 March. Rome, T.R.

Text by C. Lodovici (from Gozzi's comedy). Prologue and 3 acts.

In German (translated by H.F. Redlich), Mannheim 4 March 1934.

MASCAGNI: *Pinotta*

23 March. San Remo

Text by G. Targioni-Tozzetti. Two acts.

This was Mascagni's first opera; written as early as 1880. The score had been lost for 50 years and was recovered by chance. The composer himself conducted *Pinotta* at its first production, on the same bill with a performance of *Cavalleria Rusticana*, which was stated to have been the 13,000th representation of that work.

MARINUZZI: *Palla de' Mozzi*

5 April. Milan, Sc.

Text by G. Forzano. Three acts.

In Italian also given at Buenos Aires 11 July 1933.

In German (translated by V. Medicus), Berlin, D.O. April 1940.

HEGER: *Der Bettler Namenlos*

8 April. Munich

Text by the composer (an *Odysseus* opera). Three acts.

Vienna 10 November 1932, etc.

KODÁLY: *Székely Fonó*
(The Spinning Room of the Szekelys)

24 April. Budapest

Text by B. Szabolcsi. One act.

Developed from a short play with songs, produced at a Budapest cabaret about 1925. Very successful Hungarian ballad opera.

Also given at Milan 14 January 1933 (in Italian, as *La Filanda Magiara*, translated by R. Küfferle; the first Hungarian opera which was ever produced in Italy).

In German, Brunswick 9 February 1938.

The opera was broadcast from London on 26 May 1933 (English version by M. D. Calvocoressi).

BARANOVIĆ: *Striženo-Košeno*
(Shorn-Mown)

4 May. Zagreb

Text by G. Krklec. Three acts.

Successful Serbo-Croatian folk-opera.

CASELLA: *La Favola d'Orfeo*

6 September. Venice, T. Goldoni

A new setting of the favola by Angelo Ambrogini, detto Poliziano, which was first produced with incidental music by one Germi at the Ducal court of Mantua, 18 July 1472. (First printed, Bologna 1494). One act.

In Italian also given at Amsterdam February 1935.

In German (translated by H. F. Redlich), Stuttgart 18 May 1938.

Produced at Venice on the same bill with Malipiero's one-act symphonic drama *Panthea* (hardly to be called an opera as it contains no words).

LUALDI: *La Grançeola*

10 September. Venice, T. Goldoni

Text by the composer (after a story by R. Bacchelli). One act.

In Italian also, Malta January 1935.

In German (translated by R. Franz), Leipzig March 1938.

(d'ALBERT): *Mister Wu*

29 September. Dresden

Text by "M. Karlev" (pseudonym of K. M. von Levetzow), founded on the English play by H. M. Vernon and H. Owen. Three acts.

d'Albert's last opera; completed after his death by L. Blech.

Also given at Vienna, V.O. 3 November 1932.

SCHREKER: *Der Schmied von Gent*

29 October. Berlin, D.O.

Text by the composer (*Grosse Zauberoper*), founded on C. de Coster's *Smetse Smee*. Three acts.

Schreker's last opera.

WEINBERGER: *Lidé z Pokerflatu*

19 November. Brno

Text by M. Kareš (from Bret Harte's *The Outcasts of Poker Flat*). Five acts.

G. F. MALIPIERO: *Mysterium Venedigs*

15 December. Coburg

(Original Italian) text by the composer, produced in a German version by R. S. Hoffmann.

A trilogy, consisting of three parts, viz. *Le Aquile di Aquileia* (3 scenes); *Il finto Arlecchino* (see 1928); and *I Corvi di San Marco* (a one-act *dramma musicale* without words).

1933

GRUENBERG: *Emperor Jones*

7 January. New York, M.

Text by K. de Jaffa (from E. G. O'Neill's drama). Seven scenes.

Successful in U.S.A. Also given at Amsterdam March 1934 (in Dutch).

ROBBIANI: *Romanticismo*

10 January. Venice, F.

Text by A. Rossato (founded on a comedy by G. Rovetta, 1903). Three acts.

(The opera had previously been broadcast from Turin 27 September 1932.)

KAREL: *Smrt Kmotřička*
(Godmother Death)

3 February. Brno

Text by S. Lom. Three acts.

Karel's most successful opera.

In Czech also, Prague 31 March 1933; Bratislava March 1935.

In Slovenian (translated by M. Polič), Ljubljana 7 November 1936.

KARNAVIČIUS: *Gražina*

16 February. Kaunas

Text by K. Inčiura (founded on a poem by A. Mickiewicz). Five acts.

Written for the 15th anniversary of the independence of the Lithuanian State.

ZANDONAI: *La Farsa amorosa*

22 February. Rome, T.R.

Text by A. Rossato (founded on P. A. de Alarcón's *El Sombrero de tres Picos*). Three acts and 2 scenic intermezzi.

Successful in Italy.

In French (translated by P. Spaak), Brussels 27 November 1933.

In Czech, Brno June 1936.

PIJPER: *Halewijn*

13 June. Amsterdam

Text by E. von Lokhorst (founded on one of C. de Coster's Flemish Tales).

Produced at the eleventh I.S.C.M. festival. The composer had treated the same subject in a choral work (first performed Amsterdam 27 March 1922).

CANTELOUBE: *Vercingétorix*

26 June. Paris, O.

Text by E. Clémentel and J. H. Louwyck. Four acts.

R. STRAUSS: *Arabella*

1 July. Dresden

Text by H. von Hofmannsthal from his story *Lucidor*. Three acts.

Of Strauss's later operas, the most successful one. Given at:

BERLIN 12 October 1933 (in German).
VIENNA 21 October 1933 (in German).
OLOMOUC 1933 (in Czech, translated by O. F. Babler).
STOCKHOLM 30 December 1933 (in Swedish).
BASLE 25 February 1934 (in German).
MONTE CARLO 9 March 1934 (in French, translated by R. Gunsbourg).
LONDON, C.G. 17 May 1934 (in German).
BUENOS AIRES 16 August 1934 (in German).
AMSTERDAM 29 November 1934 (in German).
BUDAPEST 28 December 1934 (in Hungarian, translated by V. Lányi).
GENOA 27 February 1936 (in Italian, translated by O. Schanzer).
PRAGUE December 1937 (in German).

A. KALNIŅŠ: *Dzimtenes Atmoda*
(The Country's Awakening)

9 September. Riga

Text by A. Krumņis. Four acts.
Successful Lettish historical opera.

ZEMLINSKY: *Der Kreidekreis*

14 October. Zurich

Text from the homonymous play by "Klabund" (A. Henschke). Three acts.

In German also given at Stettin 16 January 1934; Berlin 23 January 1934; Prague 9 December 1934.

In Czech, Bratislava December 1934.

(HOFFMANN): *Aurora*

5 November. Bamberg

Text by F. I. von Holbein. Three acts.

The opera was written for the Bamberg theatre (where E. T. A. Hoffmann was conductor from 1808–12), *c.*1811, but the production did not take place then. (The text was later set to music by Gläser whose setting was produced at Berlin, Kgst. 29 March 1836.) Hoffmann's score was recovered by M. Voigt at Würzburg in 1905 and was, in 1933, produced in a revised version by L. Böttcher. A duet from the opera was published by E. Kroll in *Zeitschrift für Musikwissenschaft*, Vol.IV (1921–22).

1934

FERRARI-TRECATE: *Le Astuzie di Bertoldo*

10 January. Genoa, C.F.

Text by C. Zangarini (founded on a comedy by O. Lucarini). Three acts.
Successful in Italy.

G. F. MALIPIERO: *Die Legende vom vertauschten Sohn*

13 January. Brunswick

(Original Italian) text (*La Favola del Figlio cambiato*) by L. Pirandello, produced in a German version by H. F. Redlich. Three acts.

In Italian, first given at Rome 24 March 1934 (after a few nights banned by the Fascist authorities).

HAUG: *Madrisa*

15 January. Basle

Text by J. Jegerlehner. Three acts.
Successful Swiss folk-opera.

SHOSTAKOVICH: *Lady Macbeth Mtsenskago Uyezda*
Леди Макбетъ Мценскаго Уѣзда
(Lady Macbeth of Mtsensk District)

22 January. Leningrad

Text by the composer and A. Preis (founded on a novel by N. S. Lyeskov). Four acts.

So far the most successful opera by a Soviet Russian composer; first given at Moscow two days later, 24 January 1934. A production of the opera took place at the first Leningrad Theatre Festival, 27 May 1934, when the work became known to Western and American critics. Outside Russia given at:

CLEVELAND 31 January 1935 (in Russian).

NEW YORK, M. 5 February 1935 (in Russian).

PHILADELPHIA 5 April 1935 (in Russian).

STOCKHOLM 16 November 1935 (in Swedish).

PRAGUE 29 January 1936 (in German).

LJUBLJANA 12 February 1936 (in Slovenian, translated by N. Štritov).

LONDON, QUEEN'S HALL 18 March 1936 (concert performance, in English, translated by M. D. Calvocoressi).

ZURICH 1936 (in German).

COPENHAGEN 10 October 1936 (in Danish, translated by P. Ostroumoff).

ZAGREB 16 June 1937 (in Croatian).

BRATISLAVA 25 November 1938 (in Slovakian).

RESPIGHI: *La Fiamma*

23 January. Rome, T.R.

Text by C. Guastalla (founded on a Danish play by H. Wiers-Jenssen). Three acts.

Very successful in Italy; also given at:

BUENOS AIRES 6 July 1934 (in Italian).

MONTEVIDEO July 1934 (in Italian).

BUDAPEST 16 April 1935 (in Hungarian, translated by K. Nádasdy); in Hungarian also, Milan, Sc. 12 January 1940 (by the Budapest company).

CHICAGO 2 December 1935 (in Italian).

BERLIN 7 June 1936 (in German, translated by J. Kapp).

MORAVSKÁ OSTRAVA 3 March 1937 (in Czech, translated by K. Kügler).

LJUBLJANA 21 April 1937 (in Slovenian, translated by N. Štritov).

VIENNA 8 June 1937 (in German).

ATTERBERG: *Fanal*

27 January. Stockholm

(Original German) text by O. Ritter and I. M.

Welleminsky (founded on H. Heine's ballad *Der Schelm von Bergen*), Swedish version by the composer. Three acts.

In German (as *Flammendes Land*), Brunswick 17 February 1934.

In Norwegian, Oslo 1934.

V. THOMSON: *Four Saints in three Acts*

7 February. Hartford, Conn.

Text by G. Stein (*An Opera to be sung*). In spite of the title, the opera has, in true surrealistic spirit, 4 acts (and there are at least 15 Saints).

A concert performance had been given at Ann Arbor, Mich. 20 May 1933. In 1934 the work was produced by the Society of Friends and Enemies of Modern Music at the opening of the Avery Memorial Theatre, Hartford, in a stage version by F. Ashton. The opera was sung by negroes. First given at New York, 44th Street Th. 20 February 1934.

HANSON: *Merry Mount*

10 February. New York, M.

Text by R. L. Stokes (founded on a story by N. Hawthorne). Three acts.

The first opera of the American composer. Previously heard in concert form at Ann Arbor, Mich. 20 May 1933.

REFICE: *Cecilia*

15 February. Rome, T.R.

Text by E. Mucci (*azione sacra*). Three episodes.

Very successful in Italy; in Italian also given at Buenos Aires 4 October 1934; Montevideo October 1934; Malta 2 February 1935; Rio de Janeiro and São Paulo July 1935; Santiago, Chile September 1936.

ANTHEIL: *Helen retires*

28 February. New York, Juilliard School

Text by J. Erskine. Three acts.

The first opera of Antheil's which was produced in America.

LEMBA: *Elga*

March. Tallinn

(Estonian) text by J. Oengo (from the play by G. Hauptmann).

ROCCA: *Il Dibuc*

24 March. Milan, Sc.

Text by R. Simoni (from the Yiddish play by S. Anski). Prologue and 3 acts.

Successful in Italy; Rome 28 December 1935, etc. Also given at:

WARSAW 22 May 1935 (in Polish).

DETROIT, MASONIC TEMPLE 6 May 1936 (in English, translated by A. Coates).

NEW YORK, CARNEGIE HALL 14 May 1936 (in English, translated by A. Coates).

ZAGREB 13 June 1936 (in Croatian).

BRATISLAVA 14 April 1937 (in Slovakian).

WITKOWSKY: *La Princesse lointaine*

26 March. Paris, O.

Text by the composer (founded on the play by E. Rostand). Four acts.

Apart from a one-act opéra-comique produced at Nantes as early as 1891, Witkowsky's only work for the stage.

COLLINGWOOD: *Macbeth*

12 April. London, S.'s Wells

Text by the composer (from Shakespeare). Three acts.

Excerpts from the opera had previously been given in concert form at Queen's Hall, London 10 November 1927 (with piano accompaniment).

STRAVINSKY: *Perséphone*

30 April. Paris, O.

Text by A. Gide. Melodrama, 3 parts; mostly given in concert form.

LONDON, QUEEN'S HALL 28 November 1934 (concert performance).

BOSTON, SYMPHONY HALL 15 March 1935 (concert performance).

NEW YORK, CARNEGIE HALL 4 February 1936 (concert performance).

MONTE CARLO February 1936 (concert performance).

BUENOS AIRES 17 May 1936 (concert performance).

RIO DE JANEIRO Summer 1936 (concert performance).

BRUNSWICK 5 June 1937 (in German, translated by F. Schröder).

FLORENCE 21 May 1939 (concert performance).

GLIÈRE: *Shakh-Senem*

4 May. Baku

Text by M. Galperin. Four acts.

An opera the music of which is founded on Azerbaidzhan tunes. Date of first performance according to N. Slonimsky; according to Riemann's *Musiklexikon* the work had been produced at Baku already in 1927. For an account of the opera see *Le Ménestrel*, July 6, 1934.

First given at Moscow 1938.

HORTON: *Kykunkor, the Witch*

7 May. New York, Unity Theatre Studio

A dance opera the music of which is founded upon African tunes; produced by negroes.

(The composer, Asadata Dafora Horton, is a native of Sierra Leone.)

OSTRČIL: *Honzovo Království* (John's Kingdom)

May. Brno

Text by J. Maránek (founded on a story by Tolstoi). Seven scenes.

Ostrčil's last opera.

Given at Prague 3 April 1935 (in Czech) and January 1938 (in German).

RABAUD: *Rolande et le mauvais Garçon*

28 May. Paris, O.

Text by L. Népoty. Five acts.

In French also given at Buenos Aires 29 July 1938.

BOUGHTON: *The Lily Maid*

10 September. Stroud, Glos.

Text by the composer. Two acts.
London, Winter Garden 12 January 1937.

(BLODEK): *Zítek*

3 October. Prague, Cz.

Text by K. Sabina. Originally in 3 acts.
Blodek's second and last opera, written as early as 1868. The first act was produced 60 years after the composer's death, on the same bill with a revival of his *V Studni* (see 1867).

LLOYD: *Iernin*

6 November. Penzance

Text by W. Lloyd. *A Celtic saga-opera.* Three acts.
London, Ly. 19 June 1935.

HOLENIA: *Viola*

17 November. Graz

Text by O. Widowitz (from Shakespeare's *Twelfth Night*). Prologue and 3 acts.
In German also given at Munich November 1935.

(MOSONYI): *Álmos*

6 December. Budapest

Text by the composer (from a play by E. Szigligeti). Two acts.
The opera was written as early as 1862; first produced 64 years after the composer's death; after *Szép Ilonka* (see 1861) his second and last opera.

1935

MASGAGNI: *Nerone*

16 January. Milan, Sc.

Text by G. Targioni-Tozzetti (from a comedy by P. Cossa, 1872). Three acts.
Given on many Italian stages. In Italian also, Zurich 16 June 1937.

SEYMOUR: *In the Pasha's Garden*

24 January. New York, M.

Text by H. C. Tracy (from a story by H. G. Dwight). One act.
Seymour's first opera.

MULÉ: *Liolà*

2 February. Naples, S.C.

Text by A. Rossato (from a comedy by L. Pirandello, 1917). Three acts.
Successful in Italy.

MARIOTTE: *Gargantua*

17 February. Paris, O.C.

Text by Armory (*Scènes Rabelaisiennes*). Four (produced in 3) acts.
Revived Paris, O.C. 1 December 1938.

MADETOJA: *Juha*

17 February. Helsinki

Text by the composer (from a novel by J. Aho). Important modern Finnish opera.

WAGNER-RÉGENY: *Der Günstling*

20 February. Dresden

Text by C. Neher (founded on G. Büchner's German version of Victor Hugo's *Marie Tudor*). Three acts.
The full title reads: *Der Günstling oder Die letzten Tage des grossen Herrn Fabiano.*
Successful in Germany. In German also, Graz 16 November 1935.
In Slovenian (translated by M. Polič), Ljubljana 29 January 1936.
In French (translated by P. Spaak), Brussels 14 February 1936.

GUERRINI: *La Vigna*

7 March. Rome, T.R.

Text by the composer and A. Testoni (founded on a 16th century story by A. F. Grazzini). Three acts.

HAHN: *Le Marchand de Venise*

25 March. Paris, O.

Text by M. Zamaçois (after Shakespeare). Three acts.

Revived Paris, O. 2 May 1938.

BENNETT: *Maria Malibran*

8 April. New York, Juilliard School

Text by R. A. Simon. Three acts.

The first opera of the American composer.

PIZZETTI: *Orsèolo*

4 May. Florence, T.C.

Text by the composer. Three acts.

Successful in Italy: Milan 15 January 1936, Rome 10 March 1936, etc.

In Italian also, Buenos Aires 26 July 1938.

R. STRAUSS: *Die schweigsame Frau*

24 June. Dresden

Text by S. Zweig (founded on Ben Jonson's *Epicoene*). Three acts

In German also, Zurich 16 May 1936; Prague 3 June 1937.

In Italian (translated by O. Schanzer), Milan, Sc. 11 March 1936.

GERSHWIN: *Porgy and Bess*

30 September. Boston

Text by Du Bose Heyward and Ira Gershwin (adapted from a play by Dⁿ Bose and Dorothy Heyward). Three acts.

Successful in U.S.A. First given in New York, Alvin Th. 10 October 1935.

DZERZHINSKY: *Tikhy Don*

Тихий Дон

(The quiet Don)

22 October. Leningrad

Text from M. Sholokhov's novel of the same title. Four acts.

Very successful in Russian; Moscow 8 January 1936, etc.

In Ukrainian Dnyepropetrovsk January 1937; in Azerbaidzhan Baku March 1937.

In Czech (translated by I. Urban) Brno 31 January 1937.

In Latvian Riga 20 December 1940.

GOTOVAC: *Ero s Onoga svijeta*

(A Rogue falls from Heaven)

2 November. Zagreb

Text by M. Begović. Three acts.

Successful Croatian comic opera.

In Slovenian (translated by R. Petelinova), Ljubljana 15 February 1938.

In German (translated by R. Dvörnik-Cobenzl), Carlsruhe 3 April 1938, etc. Berlin March 1940.

In Croatian also given at Frankfort 15 June 1939 (by the Belgrade company).

In Bulgarian, Sofia 1940.

Italian translation by R. Nikolic published Trieste 1938.

1936

ALFANO: *Cyrano di Bergerac*

22 January. Rome, T.R.

(Original French) text by H. Cain (from the play by E. Rostand), Italian version by C. Meano and F. Brusa. Four acts.

In Italian also given at Buenos Aires 21 May 1937.

In the original French, Paris, O.C. 29 May 1936.

G. F. MALIPIERO: *Giulio Cesare*

8 February. Genoa, C.F.

Text by the composer (after Shakespeare). Three acts (7 scenes).

In Italian also given at Buenos Aires 28 May 1936; Rio de Janeiro August 1936, etc.; New York, Carnegie Hall 13 January 1937 (in concert form, in an abridged version).

In German (translated by G. C. Winkler), Gera December 1938.

WOLF-FERRARI: *Il Campiello*

12 February. Milan, Sc.

Text by M. Ghisalberti (from a comedy by C. Goldoni). Three acts.

In German (translated by F. X. Friedl and the composer), Munich 27 December 1936; Berlin 20 May 1937.

J. KALNIŅŠ: *Hamlets*

17 February. Riga

Text by the composer (founded on the Lettish version, by J. Rozes, of Shakespeare's tragedy). Three acts.

N. BERG: *Judith*

22 February. Stockholm

Text by the composer (founded on the German play by F. Hebbel). Five acts.

Produced at the opening of the International Music Festival, Stockholm.

ENESCO: *Oedipe*

10 March. Paris, O.

Text by E. Fleg. Four acts.

The first opera of the Rumanian composer (written as early as 1921).

USPENSKY: *Farkhad i Shirin*

25 March. Tashkent

An opera produced at the national opera-house of Tashkent, capital of the Uzbek Soviet Republic in Central Asia (founded 1 November 1928). Presumably written in the Uzbek language (entry according to N. Slonimsky, *Music since 1900*).

Also given at Moscow May 1937.

PAUMGARTNER: *Rossini in Neapel*

27 March. Zurich

Text by H. Adler. Three acts.

Successful on German stages; given at Vienna 3 January 1937; Prague February 1937; Dresden 10 April 1937, etc.

In Swedish, Stockholm 26 November 1936.

In French (translated by G. Dalman), Brussels 14 December 1936.

(Parts of the music are adapted from Rossini's own minor works.)

VLADIGEROV: *Tsar Kaloyan*

Царь Калоянъ

20 April. Sofia

Text by F. Popova-Mutafova. Four acts.

The first opera of the well-known Bulgarian composer and violinist.

Also given at Ljubljana 15 May 1937 (in Slovenian, translated by D. Švara).

WILLIAMS: *The poisoned Kiss*, or *The Empress and the Necromancer*

12 May. Cambridge

Text by E. Sharp (*A romantic extravaganza*). Three acts.

London, Sadler's Wells 18 May 1936; New York, Juilliard School 21 April 1937.

PEDROLLO: *L'Amante in Trappola*

22 September. Vicenza

Text by G. Franceschini. One act.

Successful in Italy.

In German, Dortmund April 1939.

ROCCA: *In Terra di Leggenda*

1 October. Bergamo

Text by C. Meano. Three acts.

(The opera had been previously given in concert form at the Palazzo dell'Arte, Milan, on 28 September 1933.)

ROUSSEL: *Testament Tetý Karoliny* (Aunt Carolina's Will)

14 November. Olomouc

(Original French) text (*Le Testament de la Tante Caroline*) by Nino, first produced in a Czech version by J. Reisserova. Three acts.

In the original French, Paris, O.C. 11 March 1937.

In German, Prague 18 April 1937.

Roussel's last opera, produced the year before his death.

COATES: *Pickwick*

20 November. London, C.G.

Text by the composer (after Dickens). Three acts.

The first opera of Coates which was produced in London.

1937

KLENAU: *Rembrandt van Rijn*

23 January. Berlin, O.

Text by the composer. Four acts.

Successful in Germany.

(RESPIGHI): *Lucrezia*

24 February. Milan, Sc.

Text by C. Guastalla. One act (*3 momenti*).

Respighi's last opera, completed by his wife, Elsa Olivieri Respighi.

In Italian also given at Buenos Aires 13 August 1937 and Rio de Janeiro Summer 1937.

In Czech, Olomouc September 1937.

(The work forms a trilogy with *Maria Egiziaca*, see 1932, and the ballet *Gli Uccelli*; they are now usually given on the same bill.)

SCHOECK: *Massimilla Doni*

2 March. Dresden

Text by A. Rüeger (from H. de Balzac's novel). Three acts.

Zurich 13 March 1937, etc.

HONEGGER and IBERT: *L'Aiglon*

11 March. Monte Carlo

Text by H. Cain (from the play by E. Rostand). Five acts.

Successful on French stages; Paris, O. 1 September 1937; Brussels 10 November 1938.

(The opera was to be produced at Naples on 28 February 1939; for political reasons the performance was cancelled at short notice.)

MENOTTI: *Amelia goes to the Ball*

1 April. Philadelphia

(Original Italian) text (*Amelia al Ballo*) by the composer, first produced in an English version by G. Mead. One act.

In English also, New York 11 April 1937 at the New Amsterdam Th.; 3 March 1938 at the Metropolitan Opera-House.

In the original Italian first given at S. Remo 4 April 1938.

In Swedish, Stockholm 30 December 1939.

ROCCA: *La Morte di Frine*

24 April. Milan, Sc.

Text by C. Meano (*Leggenda tragica*). One act.

Rio de Janeiro Summer 1937, etc.

(The work had previously been broadcast from Turin 31 May 1936.)

GHISLANZONI: *Re Lear*

24 April. Rome, T.R.

Text by the composer (after Shakespeare). Three acts.

Successful in Italy.

CASELLA: *Il Deserto tentato*

6 May. Florence, T.C.

Text by C. Pavolini (*Mistero*). One act.

First produced at the Maggio Musicale Fiorentino. An opera glorifying the Abyssinian war.

DAMROSCH: *The Man without a Country*

12 May. New York, M.

Text by A. Guiterman (founded on a story by E. E. Hale), scenario by the composer. Two acts.

(A. BERG): *Lulu*

2 June. Zurich

Text by the composer (adapted from F. Wedekind's plays *Erdgeist* and *Die Büchse der Pandora*). Three acts.

Berg's second and last opera; the work was not quite finished at his death. Two acts and fragments of the third act were produced at Zurich. (An orchestra suite from the opera had been heard in many countries in 1934–35).

GOOSSENS: *Don Juan de Mañara*

24 June. London, C.G.

Text by A. Bennett. Four acts.

See *The Chesterian*, nos.97 (1931), and 123 (1935).

WEINBERGER: *Wallenstein*

18 November. Vienna, O.

(Original Czech) text by M. Kareš (from Schiller's tragedy), produced in a German version by M. Brod. Six scenes.

WILLIAMS: *Riders to the Sea*

1 December. London, R.C.M.

Text by J. M. Synge. One act.

Publicly performed Cambridge 22 February 1938.

1938

MILHAUD: *Esther de Carpentras*

3 February. Paris, O.C.

Text by A. Lunel. Two acts.

(The libretto had been published as early as 1928).

HOLST: *The wandering Scholar*

21 February. London, Toynbee Hall

Text by C. Bax. Produced by Toynbee Hall Opera Club.

VEREMANS: *Anna-Marie*

22 February. Antwerp

Text by F. Timmermans. Four acts.

In Flemish also given at Cologne May 1938 (by the Antwerp company).

LATTUADA: *La Caverna di Salamanca*

1 March. Genoa, C.F.

Text by V. Piccoli (after Cervantes). One act.

COELHO: *Belkiss*

March. Lisbon, Coliseu

Text from E. de Castro's drama, *Belkiss, Rainha de Sabá* (1894). Three acts.

The most important of the very few original Portuguese operas of recent years. Awarded a prize in a Spanish opera competition.

R. BIANCHI: *Proserpina*

23 March. Milan, Sc.

Text by S. Benelli. Three acts.

G. F. MALIPIERO: *Antonio e Cleopatra*

4 May. Florence, T.C.

Text by the composer (after Shakespeare). Three acts.

In German (translated by G. C. Winkler), Bremen 29 January 1939

HONEGGER: *Jeanne d'Arc au Bûcher*

12 May. Basle

Text by P. Claudel (*Oratorio dramatique*). Eleven scenes.

Also given at Orléans 6 May 1939; Paris, Palais de Chaillot 13 June 1939; Brussels 25 February 1940.

HINDEMITH: *Mathis der Maler*

28 May. Zurich

Text by the composer. Seven scenes.

In German also given at Amsterdam 9 March 1939 (by the Zurich company).

In English (translated by D. M. Craig), London, Queen's Hall 15 March 1939 (in concert form).

KŘENEK: *Karl V*

15 June. Prague, G.

Text by the composer (*Bühnenwerk mit Musik*). Two parts.

The opera was published in 1933; originally it had been written for the Vienna State Opera. Fragments were performed at the I.S.C.M. Festival, Barcelona 18 April 1936.

DUPÉRIER: *Zadig*

17 June. Paris, O.C.

Text by A. F. Hérold (from Voltaire's novel). Four acts.

R. STRAUSS: *Friedenstag*

24 July. Munich

Text by J. Gregor. One act.

In German also given at Zurich 4 February 1939; Berlin 8 March 1939; Graz May 1939; Vienna 10 June 1939, etc.

In Italian (translated by R. Küfferle), Venice, F. 30 January 1940.

English vocal score (translated by R. Capell) published 1938.

WEILL: *Knickerbocker Holiday*

26 September. Hartford, Conn.

Text by M. Anderson. Two acts.

The first opera of Weill's written and produced in America.

R. STRAUSS: *Daphne*

15 October. Dresden

Text by J. Gregor (*Bukolische Tragödie*). One act.

First produced on the same bill with a revival of *Friedenstag* (see above).

In German also, Berlin 8 March 1939; Graz May 1939, etc.

In Flemish, Antwerp 7 October 1939.

LLOYD: *The Serf*

20 October. London, C.G.

Text by W. Lloyd (the father of the composer). Three acts.

1939

WOLF-FERRARI: *La Dama boba*

1 February. Milan, Sc.

Text by M. Ghisalberti (from a comedy by Lope da Vega). Three acts.

In German (translated by the composer and F. Rau), Mayence 18 June 1939; Berlin 22 June 1939.

SAUGUET: *La Chartreuse de Parme*

16 March. Paris, O.

Text by A. Lunel (founded on Stendhal's novel). Four acts.

PANIZZA: *Bisanzio*

25 July. Buenos Aires

Text by G. Macchi. Three acts.

The opera had been written about 1925.

MILHAUD: *Medee*

7 October. Antwerp

(Original French) text by M. Milhaud, the wife of the composer (after Euripides), produced in a Flemish version by A. L. Baeyens. One act (3 scenes).

The opera had been commissioned by the French Government in 1938. First given in the original French at the Opéra, Paris 8 May 1940.

PRATELLA: *Fabiano*

9 December. Bologna, T.C.

Text by A. Beltramelli. Prologue, 2 acts, and epilogue.

ROCCA: *Monte Ivnor*

23 December. Rome, T.R.

Text by C. Meano. Three acts.

1940

FERRARI-TRECATE: *Ghirlino*

4 February. Milan, Sc.

Text by E. Anceschi. Three acts.

ZANELLA: *Il Revisore*

20 February. Trieste

Text by A. Lega (founded upon Gogol's comedy). Three acts.

VILLA-LOBOS: *Izaht*

6 April. Rio de Janeiro

Text by F. Azevedo and E. Villalba. Four acts.

Concert performance. Written 1912–14, revised 1932.

I. INDEX OF OPERAS

with names of composers and years of first performance under which they will be found. Titles are, occasionally, shortened, and arranged in alphabetical order, disregarding the articles (in all languages). Modified letters, like Ä, Ö, Ø, Š, Ü, are treated as A, O, S, U. In order to keep the index within reasonable bounds, no alternative or translated titles are listed as a rule. There are, however, cross-references where the original title of a well-known opera is unfamiliar, as in the case of Mozart's *Don Giovanni* (*Il Dissoluto punito*) or Smetana's *Bartered Bride* (*Prodaná Nevěsta*).

Amphion (Naumann), 1778
Amphion (Honegger), 1931
Amy Robsart (Lara), 1893
An allem ist Hütchen schuld (S. Wagner), 1917
Anacréon (Cherubini), 1803
Anacréon chez Polycrate (Grétry), 1797
Anathema (Tofft), 1928
Ancêtre (Saint-Saëns), 1906
Andrea Chenier (Giordano), 1896
Andrea Crini (Trneček), 1900
Andromaque (Grétry), 1780
Andromeda (Giacobbi), 1610
Andromeda (Manelli), 1637
Andromeda (Reichardt), 1788
Andromeda (Maurice), 1924
Andromeda, see also Persée
Andromède (Dassoucy), 1650
Angélique (Ibert), 1927
Angelo (Kyui), 1876
Angelo (Bruneau), 1928
Angelus (Naylor), 1909
Angenehme Betrug (Keiser and Graupner), 1707
Angiolina (Salieri), 1800
Anima allegra (Vittadini), 1921
Anna Bolena (Donizetti), 1830
Anna Karenina (Robbiani), 1924
Anna Karenina, see also Karenina Anna
Anna-Marie (Veremans), 1938
Annette et Lubin (Blaise), 1762
Anno e un Giorno (Benedict), 1836
Antar (Dupont), 1921
Antichambre (Dalayrac, 1802
Antigona (Orlandini), 1718
Antigona delusa da Alceste (P. A. Ziani), 1660
Antigone (Zingarelli), 1790
Antigone (Honegger), 1927
Antigono (Hasse), 1743
Antigono (Gluck), 1756
Antigono (Durán), 1760
Antioco (Hasse), 1721
Antiope (C. Pallavicino), 1689
Anton (Galeotti), 1900
Antonio e Cleopatra (G. F. Malipiero), 1938
Apajune (Millöcker), 1880
Aphrodite (C. Erlanger), 1906.
Apollo deluso (Sances), 1669
Apollo et Hyacinthus (Mozart), 1767
Apollo's Wettgesang (Sutor), 1808
Apotheke (Neefe), 1771
Appel de la Mer (Rabaud), 1924
Arabella (R. Strauss), 1933
Arabi nelle Gallie (Pacini), 1827
Arbore di Diana (Martin y Soler), 1787
Arbre enchanté (Gluck), 1759

Arcadia in Brenta (Galuppi), 1749
Archers (Carr), 1796
Arden Énok (Raimann), 1894
Aretusa (Vitali), 1620
Argia (Cesti), 1655
Ariadne (Kusser), 1692
Ariadne, see also Verlassene Ariadne
Ariadne auf Naxos (G. Benda), 1775
Ariadne auf Naxos (R. Strauss), 1912
Ariadne in Crete (Handel), 1734
Ariane (Cambert), 1674
Ariane (Massenet), 1906
Ariane dans l'Isle de Naxos (Edelmann), 1782
Ariane et Barbe-bleue (Dukas), 1907
Arianna (Monteverdi), 1608
Arianna (Marcello), 1913
Arianna e Teseo (Porpora), 1714
Ariarate (Tarchi), 1786
Ariodant (Méhul), 1799
Ariodante (Pollarolo), 1716
Ariodante (Handel), 1735
Aristippe (R. Kreutzer), 1808
Aristomene Messenio (Sances), 1670
Arlecchino (Busoni), 1917
Arlecchino, see also Furie d'Arlecchino
Arlequin (d'Ollone), 1924
Arlesiana (Cilea), 1897
Armaillis (Doret), 1906
Armastus ja Surm (Lemba), 1931
Arme Heinrich (Pfitzner), 1895
Arme Jonathan (Millöcker), 1890
Armida (B. Ferrari), 1639
Armida (Traetta), 1761
Armida (Salieri), 1771
Armida (Sacchini), 1772
Armida (Naumann), 1773
Armida (Mysliveczek), 1779
Armida (Haydn), 1784
Armida (Rossini), 1817
Armida (Dvořák), 1904
Armida, see also Gerusalemme liberata, Renaud,
Rinaldo, Selva incantata.
Armida abbandonata (Jommelli), 1770
Armide (Lully), 1686
Armide (Gluck), 1777
Arminio (Steffani), 1707
Arminio (Handel), 1737
Arminio (Hasse), 1745
Arminius, see also Chi la dura la vince, Thusnelde
Armor (Lazzari), 1898
Armourer of Nantes (Balfe), 1863
Arnjlot (Peterson-Berger), 1910
Aroldo (Verdi), see Stiffelio
Arsene (Seydelmann), 1779

Margarita la Tornera (Chapi), 1909
Margherita (Brüggemann), 1910
Margherita d'Anjou (Meyerbeer), 1820
Margherita d'Orleans (Restano), 1897
Margot (Turina), 1914
Mari de Circonstances (Plantade), 1813
María del Carmen (Granados), 1898
Maria di Rohan (Donizetti), 1843
Maria di Rudenz (Donizetti), 1838
Maria Dulcis (Bustini), 1902
Maria Egiziaca (Respighi), 1932
Maria Malibran (Bennett), 1935
Maria Padilla (Donizetti), 1841
Maria Tudor (Kashperov), 1859
Mariage aux Lanternes (Offenbach), 1857
Mariage de Télémaque (Terrasse), 1910
Mariage extravagant (Gautier), 1857
Mariages Samnites (Grétry), 1776
Marianela (Pahissa), 1923
Marianne (Dalayrac), 1796
Marie (Hérold), 1826
Marie-Magdeleine (Massenet), 1903
Marie Stuart (Niedermeyer), 1844
Marie von Montalban (Winter), 1800
Marina (Arrieta), 1871
Marino Faliero (Donizetti), 1835
Mario Wetter (Machado), 1898
Marioara (Kosmovici and Schmeidler), 1904
Marion Delorme (Ponchielli), 1885
Mariotta (Gade), 1850
Maris Garçons (Berton), 1806
Marisagnet (Haarklou), 1910
Maritana (Wallace), 1845
Marito e l'Amante (F. Ricci), 1852
Marito Giogatore (Orlandini), 1718
Markheim (Miles), 1924
Mârouf (Rabaud), 1914
Marqueza (Miró), 1848
Marquise de Brinvilliers (Auber, etc.), 1831
Martha (Flotow), 1847
Martire (Samara), 1894
Martyrs (Donizetti), 1840
Maruxa (Vives), 1914
Maruzza (Floridia), 1894
Marya (Melcer), 1904
Marya (Statkowski), 1906
Mas (Canteloube), 1929
Masagniello (Keiser), 1706
Masaniello (Carafa), 1827
Masaniello, see also Muette de Portici
Maschera (Kastner), 1841
Maschere (Mascagni), 1901
Maschinist Hopkins (Brand), 1929
Mascotte (Audran), 1880

Maskarade (C. A. Nielsen), 1906
Masnadieri (Verdi), 1847
Masques et Bergamasques (Fauré), 1919
Massimillo Doni (Schoeck), 1937
Massimo Puppieno (C. Pallavicino), 1684
Mataswintha (Scharwenka), 1896
Matelda (Abbate), 1902
Mathilde von Guise (J. N. Hummel), 1810
Mathis der Maler (Hindemith), 1938
Matilda of Hungary (Wallace), 1847
Matilde di Shabran (Rossini), 1821
Matrimoni in Maschera (Rutini), 1763
Matrimonio per Concorso (Jommelli), 1766
Matrimonio segreto (Cimarosa), 1792
Máti Míla (Bendl), 1895
Matrero (Boero), 1929
Matrosen (Flotow), 1845
Matti per Amore (Cocchi), 1754
Mauritio (Gabrieli), 1686
Mavra (Stravinsky), 1922
Maximilien (Milhaud), 1932
Mazeppa (Chaikovsky), 1884
Mazeppa (Minhejmer), 1900
Measure for Measure, see Liebesverbot
Medea (G. Benda), 1775
Medea (Pacini), 1843
Medea, see also Jason
Medea in Atene (Gianettini), 1675
Medea in Corinto (Mayr), 1813
Médecin malgré lui (Gounod), 1858
Médecin Turc (Isouard), 1803
Médée (M. A. Charpentier), 1693
Médée (Cherubini), 1797
Medee (Milhaud), 1939
Médée et Jason (Salomon), 1713
Medici (Leoncavallo), 1893
Medio Evo Latino (Panizza), 1900
Medonte, Rè di Epiro (Sarti), 1777
Medoro (Gagliano), 1619
Medoro (Luzzo), 1658
Meduza (Rózycki), 1912
Meergeuse (Škroup), 1851
Mefistofele (Boito), 1868
Megae (Wieniawski), 1912
Mégère apprivoisée (Silver), 1922
Meister Andrea (Weingartner), 1920
Meister Guido (Noetzel), 1918
Meister Martin (Weissheimer), 1879
Meister Martin (Lacombe), 1897
Meistersinger (R. Wagner), 1868
Meleagro (M. A. Ziani), 1706
Melenis (Zandonai), 1912
Melnik, Koldun, Obmanshchik i Svat (Fomin),
   1779

Rattenfänger von Hameln (Nessler), 1879
Ratto della Sposa (P. Guglielmi), 1765
Ratto delle Sabine (Agostini), 1680
Ratto di Proserpina (Winter), 1804
Räuberbraut (Ries), 1828
Rauchfangkehrer (Salieri), 1781
Ravnen (J. P. E. Hartmann), 1832
Raymond (A. Thomas), 1851
Rayons de Soieries (Rosenthal), 1930
Re (Giordano), 1929
Re Enzo (Respighi), 1905
Re Lear (Ghislanzoni), 1937
Re Pastore (Uttini), 1755
Re Pastore (Gluck), 1756
Re Pastore (Mozart), 1775
Re Pastore, see also Royal Shepherd
Re Teodoro in Venezia (Paisiello), 1784
Regenbrüder (I. Lachner), 1839
Regina (Lortzing), 1899
Regina di Cipro (Pacini), 1846
Regina di Golconda (Donizetti), 1828
Regina von Emmeritz (Merikanto), 1920
Régine (Adam), 1839
Reginella (Braga), 1871
Reine de Chypre (Halévy), 1841
Reine de Saba (Gounod), 1862
Reine d'un Jour (Adam), 1839
Reine Fiammette (Leroux), 1903
Reine Topaze (Massé), 1856
Rektor a General (Skuherský), 1873
Rembrandt van Rijn (Klenau), 1937
Renard (Stravinsky), 1922
Renaud (Häffner), 1801
Renaud d'Ast (Dalayrac), 1787
Rencontre imprévue (Gluck), 1764
Rencontre imprévue (Mandl), 1889
Rendez-vous bourgeois (Isouard), 1807
Retablo de Maese Pedro (Falla), 1923
Retour (d'Ollone), 1913
Rêve (Bruneau), 1891
Rêve d'Amour (Auber), 1869
Revisore (Zanella), 1940
Revoltosa (Chapi), 1897
Rhea (Samara), 1908
Rheingold (R. Wagner), 1869
Rhéna (Eeden), 1912
Riccardo I (Handel), 1727
Riccardo III (Salvayre), 1883
Ricciardo e Zoraide (Rossini), 1818
Richard Cœur-de-Lion (Grétry), 1784
Ricimero (Jommelli), 1740
Ricimero (Majo), 1758
Riders to Sea (Williams), 1937
Rien de trop (Boieldieu), 1811

Rienzi (R. Wagner), see Cola Rienzi
Rigoletto (Verdi), 1851
Rigueurs du Cloître (Berton), 1790
Rinaldo (Handel), 1711
Rinaldo, see also Renaud
Rinaldo und Alcina (Paradis), 1797
Ring des Polykrates (Korngold), 1916
Rip van Winkle (Bristow), 1855
Rip van Winkle (Planquette), 1882
Rip van Winkle (Koven), 1920
Risa di Democrito (Pistocchi), 1700
Risurrezione (Alfano), 1904
Rita (Donizetti), 1860
Riti d'Efeso (Farinelli), 1803
Ritornata di Londra (Fischietti), 1756
Ritorno di Pulcinella (Vin. Fioravanti), 1837
Ritorno d'Ulisse (Monteverdi), 1641
Ritter Blaubart (Reznicek), 1920
Ritter Pázmán (J. Strauss), 1892
Rivale di se stesso (Weigl), 1808
Rivali concordi (Steffani), 1692
Robert (Gyrowetz), 1813
Robert-le-Diable (Meyerbeer), 1831
Roberto d'Evereux (Donizetti), 1837
Robin Hood (Shield), 1784
Robin Hood (Macfarren), 1860
Robin Hood (Koven), 1890
Robin Hood, see also Maid Marian
Robin's Ende (Künnecke), 1909
Robinson (Jensen), 1834
Robinson Crusoé (Offenbach), 1867
Rodelinda (Handel), 1725
Rodelinda (Graun), 1741
Rodostó (Zichy), 1912
Rodrigo und Zimene (Aiblinger), 1821
Rognyeda (Serov), 1865
Roi Arthus (Chausson), 1903
Roi Candaule (Bruneau), 1920
Roi David (Honegger), 1921
Roi de Lahore (Massenet), 1877
Roi d'Ys (Lalo), 1888
Roi d'Yvetot (Adam), 1842
Roi d'Yvetot (Ibert), 1930
Roi et le Fermier (Monsigny), 1762
Roi l'a dit (Delibes), 1873
Roi malgré lui (Chabrier), 1887
Roland (Lully), 1685
Roland (Piccinni), 1778
Roland, see also Orlando
Roland à Roncevaux (Mermet), 1864
Roland Mester (Zichy), 1899
Roland von Berlin (Leoncavallo), 1904
Rolande et le mauvais Garçon (Rabaud), 1934
Rolands Knappen (Lortzing), 1849

Ulisse all' Isola di Circe (Zamponi), 1650
Ultimo Abenzerraggio (Pedrell), 1874
Ultimo Giorno di Pompei (Pacini), 1825
Ultimo Lord (Alfano), 1930
Ulysses (Keiser), 1722
Ulysses, see also Bettler Namenlos, Calypso, Circe, Kirke, Nausicaa, Odysseus, Penelope, Ritorno d'Ulisse, Ulisse
Undina (Lvov), 1848
Undine (Hoffmann), 1816
Undine (Girschner), 1837
Undine (Lortzing), 1845
Ungdom og Galskab (Dupuy), 1806
Ungleiche Heyrath (Telemann), 1725
Uniform (Weigl), 1805
Unmöglichste von allem (Urspruch), 1897
Unsichtbare (Eule), 1809
Unter Räubern (Rubinstein), 1883
Unterbrochene Opferfest (Winter), 1796
Uomo che ride (Pedrollo), 1920
Urvasi (Dluski), 1902
Uthal (Méhul), 1806
Útok na Mlýn (Weis), 1912
Utopia (Sullivan), 1893

V Studni (Blodek), 1867
Vaisseau-Fantôme (Dietsch), 1842
Vajda Tornya (Dohnányi), 1922
Vakula Kuznyets (Chaikovsky), 1876
Val d'Andorre (Halévy), 1848
Valentine de Milan (Méhul), 1822
Valet de Chambre (Carafa), 1823
Valle de Andorra (Gaztambide), 1852
Vampyr (Marschner), 1828
Vampyr (Lindpaintner), 1828
Vanda (Dvořák), 1876
Vasall von Szigeth (Smareglia), 1889
Več Makropulos (Janáček), 1926
Vecchio geloso (Alessandri), 1781
Vedova scaltra (Wolf-Ferrari), 1931
Veggente (E. M. Bossi), 1890
Veglia (Pedrollo), 1920
Velleda (Lenepveu), 1882
Vendemmia (Gazzaniga), 1778
Vendetta (Pizzi), 1906
Vendetta di Nino (Bianchi), 1790
Veneno es de Amor la Embidia (Durón), 1697
Ventaglio (Raimondi), 1831
Venus (Schoeck), 1922
Venus and Adonis (Blow), 1684
Vénus et Adonis (Desmarets), 1697
Vêpres Siciliennes (Verdi), 1855
Vera Costanza (Anfossi), 1776
Vera Costanza (Haydn), 1779

Verbena de la Paloma (Bretón), 1894
Verbum nobile (Moniuszko), 1861
Vercingétorix (Canteloupe), 1933
Verdammte Staat-Sucht (Keiser), 1703
Verde Gaio (Rente), 1876
Verful cu Dor (Skibinski), 1879
Vergine del Sole (Cimarosa), 1789
Verlassene Ariadne (Milhaud), 1928
Vernarrte Prinzess (Chelius), 1905
Véronique (Messager), 1898
Verschleierte Profet (Stanford), 1881
Verschworenen (Schubert), 1861
Versiegelt (Blech), 1908
Versunkene Glocke (Zöllner), 1899
Versunkene Glocke (Respighi), 1927
Vert-Vert (Offenbach), 1869
Verwandelten Weiber (J. A. Hiller), 1766
Vespasiano (C. Pallavicino), 1678
Vespasiano, see also Tito Vespasiano
Vestale (Spontini), 1807
Vestale (Pucitta), 1810
Vestale (Mercadante), 1840
Vestalin (Guhr), 1814
Vestas Feuer (Weigl), 1805
Veuve Grapin (Flotow), 1859
Via della Finestra (Zandonai), 1919
Viaggiatori felici (Anfossi), 1780
Viaggio a Reims (Rossini), 1825
Vice-Admiral (Millöcker), 1886
Vicende d'Amore (P. Guglielmi), 1784
Vicende della Sorte (Piccinni), 1761
Victorine (Mellon), 1859
Vie brève (Falla), 1913
Vie Parisienne (Offenbach), 1866
Vieil Aigle (Gunsbourg), 1909
Vieille (Fétis), 1826
Viejecita (Caballero), 1897
Vier Grobiane (Wolf-Ferrari), 1906
Vierjährige Posten (Schubert), 1896
Vierjährige Posten, see also Dorval
Vifandaka (Tofft), 1898
Vigna (Guerrini), 1835
Vikingeblod (Lange-Müller), 1900
Village Coquettes (Hullah), 1836
Villanella ingentilita (P. Guglielmi), 1779
Villanella rapita (Bianchi), 1783
Villi (Puccini), 1884
Vina (Zich), 1922
Vingança da Cigana (Leal Moreira), 1794
Viola (Weis), 1892
Viola (Holenia), 1934
Violanta (Korngold), 1916
Virgen de Mayo (Moreno-Torroba), 1925
Virginia (Mercadante), 1866

II. INDEX OF COMPOSERS

Operas of which the librettos were written, or partly written, by the composer, are marked with an *

Le Duc d'Olonne, 1842
La Part du Diable, 1843
La Sirène, 1844
La Barcarolle, 1845
Haydée, 1847
L'Enfant prodigue, 1850
Zerline, 1851
Marco Spada, 1852
Manon Lescaut, 1856
La Circassienne, 1861
Le premier Jour de Bonheur, 1868
Rêve d'Amour, 1869
    see also col. 117, 330, 409, 453, 632, 710, 900,
       1051, 1271
Aubert, Louis François Marie (1877–)
La Forêt bleue, 1913
Audinot, Nicolas Médard (1730–1801)
*Le Tonnelier, 1761
Audran, Edmond (1842–1901)
Le Grand Mogol, 1877
Les Noces d'Olivette, 1879
La Mascotte, 1880
Gillette de Narbonne, 1882
La Cigale et la Fourmi, 1886
Miss Hélyett, 1890
L'Enlèvement de la Toledad, 1894
La Poupée, 1896
Auletta, Pietro (1698–1771)
Orazio, 1737
    see also col. 138, 139, 169, 197, 213, 228, 323
d'Auvergne, Antoine, see Dauvergne
d'Avossa, Giuseppe (1716–1796)
La Pupilla, 1763
Azzali, Augusto (18..–)
Lhidiac, 1893

Bach, Johann Christian (1735–1782)
Alessandro nell' Indie, 1762
Orione, 1763
Lucio Silla, 1774
La Clemenza di Scipione, 1778
Amadis de Gaule, 1779
    see also col. 75, 220, 261
Bach, Leonhard Emil (1849–1902)
The Lady of Longford, 1894
Bachelet, Alfred (1864–1944)
Scemo, 1914
Quand la Cloche sonnera, 1922
    see also col. 191
Badia, Carlo Agostino (1672–1738)
La Psiche, 1703
Balfe, Michael William (1808–1870)
The Siege of Rochelle, 1835
The Maid of Artois, 1836

Diadeste, 1838
Falstaff, 1838
Keolanthe, 1841
Le Puits d'Amour, 1843
The Bohemian Girl, 1843
Les quatre Fils Aymon, 1844
The Daughter of St. Mark, 1844
The Enchantress, 1845
L'Étoile de Séville, 1845
The Bondman, 1846
The Maid of Honour, 1847
The Devil's in it, 1852
Pittore e Duca, 1854
The Rose of Castille, 1857
Satanella, 1858
The Puritan's Daughter, 1861
The Armourer of Nantes, 1863
Il Talismano, 1874
    see also col. 167, 480, 591, 760, 800, 817
Bantock, Granville (1868–1946)
*Caedmar, 1892
The Seal Woman, 1924
Baranović, Krešimir (1894–)
Striženo-Košeno, 1932
    see also col. 1211
Barbieri, Carlo Emanuele di (1822–1867)
Perdita, 1865
    see also col. 723
Barbieri, Francisco Asenjo (1823–1894)
Gloria y Peluca, 1850
Tramoya, 1850
Jugar con Fuego, 1851
Los Diamantes de la Corona, 1854
Pan y Toros, 1864
El Barberillo de Lavapiés, 1874
    see also col. 867, 873
Barilli, Bruno (1880–1952)
*Emiral, 1924
Barkworth, John Edmund (1858–1929)
*Romeo and Juliet, 1916
    see also col. 353
Barnett, John (1802–1890)
The Mountain Sylph, 1834
Fair Rosamond, 1837
Farinelli, 1839
Barrios, Angel (1886–)
El Avapiés (with Campo), 1919
Bartay, András (1798–1856)
Csel, 1839
Barthélemon, François Hippolyte (1741–1808)
Pelopida, 1766
    see also col. 222, 250
Bartók, Bela (1881–1945)
A Kékszakállú Herceg Vára, 1918

Bernabei, Giuseppe Antonio (1649–1732)
  L'Ascanio, 1686
    see also col. 40
Bernardini, Marcello, called Marcello di Capua
    (c.1740–18..)
  *Il Conte di bell' Umore, 1783
    see also col. 545
Bernasconi, Andrea (1706–1784)
  Temistocle, 1740
Berners, Gerald Hugh Tyrwhitt-Wilson, Lord
    (1883–1950)
  Le Carrosse du Saint-Sacrement, 1924
Berr, José (1874–)
  Der tote Gast, 1923
Bertali, Antonio (1605–1669)
  Theti, 1652
  L'Inganno d'Amore, 1653
    see also col. 45
Bertin, Louise Angélique (1805–1877)
  *Fausto, 1831
  La Esméralda, 1836
Bertin de la Doué, T. (c.1680–1745)
  Ajax, 1716
Berton, Henri Montan (1767–1844)
  Les Promesses de Mariage, 1787
  Les Rigueurs du Cloître, 1790
  *Ponce de Léon, 1797
  Montano et Stéphanie, 1799
  Le Délire, 1799
  Le grand Deuil, 1801
  Le Concert interrompu, 1802
  Aline, Reine de Golconde, 1803
  Les Maris Garçons, 1806
  Virginie, 1823
    see also col. 230, 242, 288, 292, 375, 459, 478,
      489, 550, 736
Bertoni, Ferdinando Giuseppe (1725–1813)
  Le Pescatrici, 1751
  Orfeo, ed Euridice, 1776
  Quinto Fabio, 1778
    see also col. 349, 367, 392
Berutti, Arturo (1862–1938)
  Tarass Bulba, 1895
  Pampa, 1897
  Yupanky, 1899
  *Gli Eroi, 1919
Berwald, Franz Adolf (1796–1868)
  Estrella de Soria, 1862
    see also col. 606
Bianchi, Francesco (1752–1810)
  La Villanella rapita, 1783
  La Vendetta di Nino, 1790
    see also col. 506, 992
Bianchi, Renzo (1887–)

Proserpina, 1938
Bianchini, Guido (1885–)
  Radda, 1914
  Il Principe e Nuredha, 1923
Biber, Heinrich Ignaz Franz von (1644–1704)
  Chi la dura la vince, 1687
Bienstock, Heinrich (1894–1918)
  Sandro der Narr, 1916
Bierey, Gottlob Benedikt (1772–1840)
  Rosette, das Schweizer Hirtenmädchen, 1806
  Wladimir, Fürst von Novgorod, 1807
    see also col. 536, 667
Bishop, Henry Rowley (1786–1855)
  The Circassian Bride, 1809
  The Maniac, 1810
  Maid Marian, 1822
  Clari, 1823
  Aladdin, 1826
    see also col. 89, 162, 257, 280, 291, 322, 383,
      391, 427, 455, 456, 463, 613, 626, 654,678,
      719, 720, 727, 729, 734, 736
Bittner, Julius (1874–1939)
  *Die rote Gret, 1907
  *Der Musikant, 1910
  *Der Bergsee, 1911
  *Das höllisch Gold, 1916
Bizet, Georges (1838–1875)
  Les Pêcheurs de Perles, 1863
  La jolie Fille de Perth, 1867
  Djamileh, 1872
  Carmen, 1875
  Don Procopio, 1906
    see also col. 1027, 1117
Blaise, Benoît (17..–1772)
  Annette et Lubin, 1762
  Isabelle et Gertrude, 1765
    see also col. 75, 117, 130, 179, 313
Blamont, François Colin de (1690–1760)
  Les Festes Grecques et Romaines, 1723
Blangini, Felice (1781–1841)
  Nephtali, 1806
  Le Sacrifice d'Abraham, 1810
    see also col. 427, 736
Blaramberg, Pavel Ivanovich (1841–1907)
  Tushintsi, 1895
Blavet, Michel (1700–1768)
  Le Jaloux corrigé, 1752
Blech, Leo (1871–)
  Das war ich, 1902
  Alpenkönig und Menschenfeind, 1903
  Versiegelt, 1908
    see also col. 1421
Bloch, Ernest (1880–)
  Macbeth, 1910

The Immortal Hour, 1914
Alkestis, 1922
The Queen of Cornwall, 1924
*The Lily Maid, 1934
Boulanger, Ernest Henri Alexandre (1815–1900)
Les Sabots de la Marquise, 1854
see also col. 653, 922
Bourgault-Ducoudray, Louis Albert (1840–1910)
Thamara, 1891
Myrdhin, 1912
see also col. 601
Bovy-Lysberg, Charles Samuel (1821–1873)
La Fille du Carillonneur, 1854
Boxberg, Christian Ludwig (1670–1729)
*Sardanapalus, 1698
see also col. 93
Boyce, William (1710–1779)
The Chaplet, 1749
Braga, Gaetano (1829–1907)
Reginella, 1871
Brand, Max (1896–)
*Maschinist Hopkins, 1929
Brandts-Buys, Henry (1850–1905)
Albrecht Beiling, 1891
Brandts-Buys, Jan (1868–1933)
Die Schneider von Schönau, 1916
Braunfels, Walter (1882–)
*Prinzessin Brambilla, 1909
*Die Vögel, 1920
*Don Gil von den grünen Hosen, 1924
Galatea, 1930
Bredal, Ivar Frederik (1800–1864)
Bruden fra Lammermoor, 1832
Bree, Jean Bernard van (1801–1857)
Saffo, 1834
Breil, Joseph Carl (1870–1926)
The Legend, 1919
Bretón, Tómas (1850–1923)
*Gli Amanti di Teruel, 1889
Garin, 1892
La Verbena de la Paloma, 1894
*La Dolores, 1895
*Raquel, 1900
*Tabaré, 1913
Bréville, Pierre de (1861–1949)
Eros vainqueur, 1910
Bristow, George Frederick (1825–1898)
Rip van Winkle, 1855
Brogi, Renato (1873–1924)
Isabella Orsini, 1920
Bronner, Georg (1666–1724)
Echo und Narcissus, 1693
Broschi, Riccardo (c.1701–1756)
Merope, 1732

see also col. 165
Bruch, Max (1838–1920)
Scherz, List und Rache, 1858
Die Loreley, 1863
Hermione, 1872
see also col. 1129
Brucken-Fock, Emile van (1857–)
Seleneia, 1895
Brüggemann, Alfred (1873–)
*Margherita, 1910
see also col. 1201, 1240, 1256, 1261, 1303,
1322, 1325, 1331, 1346, 1363, 1364, 1368,
1388,1404, 1408.
Brüll, Ignaz (1846–1907)
Das goldene Kreuz, 1875
Der Landfriede, 1877
Gringoire, 1892
Bruneau, Alfred (1857–1934)
Le Rêve, 1891
L'Attaque du Moulin, 1893
Messidor, 1897
L'Ouragan, 1901
L'Enfant Roi, 1905
*Naïs Micoulin, 1907
*Les quatre Journées, 1916
Le Roi Candaule, 1920
Angelo, Tyran de Padoue, 1928
Virginie, 1931
Bruni, Antonio Bartolommeo (1751–1821)
Toberne, 1795
Le Major Palmer, 1797
Brusa, Giovanni Francesco (d. after 1768)
Le Statue, 1756
see also col. 232
Bryson, Ernest (1867–1942)
The Leper's Flute, 1926
Buck, Dudley (1839–1909)
Deseret, 1880
see also col. 844
Buffin, Victor (1867–)
Kaatje, 1913
Buini, Giuseppe Maria (c.1695–1739)
*Malmocor, 1728
see also col. 138, 159
Bulant, Jean (18th ct.)
Zbitenshchik, 1787
Bungert, August (1845–1915)
*Odysseus' Heimkehr, 1896
*Kirke, 1898
*Nausikaa, 1901
*Odysseus' Tod, 1903
Bunning, Herbert (1863–1937)
Princesse Osra, 1902
Buongiorno, Crescenzo (1864–1903)

Das Mädchenherz, 1901
Busoni, Ferruccio (1866–1924)
★Die Brautwahl, 1912
★Turandot, 1917
★Arlecchino, 1917
★Doktor Faust, 1925
Bustini, Alessandro (1876–)
Maria Dulcis, 1902
Buzzi, Antonio (1815–1891)
Saul, 1843

Caballero, Manuel Fernandez (1835–1906)
El Salto del Pasiego, 1878
La Viejecita, 1897
Gigantes y Cabezudos, 1898
Caccini, Francesca (1588–16..)
La Liberazione di Ruggiero, 1625
Caccini, Giulio (c.1545–1618)
Il Rapimento di Cefalo, 1600
L'Euridice, 1602
see also col. 1, 2, 3, 4, 9, 11
Cadman, Charles Wakefield (1881–1946)
Shanewis, 1918
A Witch of Salem, 1926
Caetani, Roffredo (1871–)
★Hypatia, 1926
Cafaro, Pasquale (c.1715–1787)
La Disfatta di Dario, 1756
see also col. 463
Cagnoni, Antonio (1828–1896)
Don Bucefalo, 1847
Papà Martin, 1871
Caldara, Antonio (1670–1736)
Ifigenia in Aulide, 1718
Lucio Papirio, 1719
Gianguir, 1724
Don Chisciotte, 1727
La Pazienza di Socrate con due Moglie (with
J. G. Reutter), 1731
Il Demetrio, 1731
Sancio Panza, 1733
Achille in Sciro, 1736
see also col. 141, 151, 154, 168, 171, 172, 179,
183, 184, 185, 191, 192, 196–203, 208, 210,
214, 215, 219, 225, 233, 238, 251, 271, 294,
365, 410, 512
Cambert, Robert (c.1628–1677)
Pastorale, 1659
Pomone, 1671
Les Peines et les Plaisirs de l'Amour, 1672
Ariane, 1674
see also col. 33, 51, 55
Campana, Fabio (1819–1882)

Esmeralda, 1869
see also col. 783
Campbell, Colin Macleod (1890–1953)
Thais and Talmaae, 1921
Campo (y Zabaleta), Conrado del (1879–1953)
El Avapiés (with Barrios), 1919
Campra, André (1660–1744)
L'Europe galante, 1697
Hésione, 1700
Tancrède, 1702
Iphigénie en Tauride (with Demarets), 1704
Les Festes Vénitiennes, 1710
Idoménée, 1712
Camille, Reine des Volsques, 1717
see also col. 84, 154
Camussi, Ezio (1883–)
La Dubarry, 1912
Scàmpolo, 1925
Candeille, Pierre Joseph (1744–1827)
Castor et Pollux, 1791
see also col. 191
Cannabich, Carl (1771–1806)
Palmer und Amalia, 1803
Canobbio, Carlo (1741–1822)
Nachalnoye Upravlenie Olega (with Pash-
keevich and Sarti), 1790
Canteloube, Joseph (1879–)
★Le Mas, 1929
Vercingétorix, 1933
Caproli, Carlo (c.1650)
Le Nozze di Peléo e di Theti, 1654
see also col. 41
Capua, Marcello di, see Bernardini
Capua, Rinaldo di, see Rinaldo
Carafa, Michele (1787–1872)
Gabriella di Vergy, 1816
Le Solitaire, 1822
Le Valet de Chambre, 1823
Masaniello, 1827
La Prison d'Édimbourg, 1833
see also col. 664, 687, 736, 803
Cardoso, Domingo Cyriaco de (1846–1900)
O Burro do Senhor Alcaide, 1891
Carey, Henry (c.1687–1743)
★The Contrivances, 1729
see also col. 159, 163
Carnicer, Ramón (1789–1855)
Adele di Lusignano, 1819
Il Dissoluto punito, 1822
Colombo, 1831
Ismalia, 1838
Carr, Benjamin (1768–1831)
The Archers, 1796
see also col. 163. 510

Julie, 1772
L'Erreur d'un Moment, 1773
Les trois Fermiers, 1777
Blaise et Babet, 1783
Alexis et Justine, 1785
Diaz (de la Peña), Eugenio (1837–1901)
La Coupe du Roi de Thulé, 1873
Dibbern, Karl (1855–)
*Odja, 1901
Dibdin, Charles (1745–1814)
Lionel and Clarissa, 1768
The Padlock, 1768
The Ephesian Matron, 1769
*The Waterman, 1774
*The Seraglio, 1776
  see also col. 175, 222, 226, 241, 258, 277, 283,
  305, 315
Dieter, Christian Ludwig (1757–1822)
Belmont und Constanze, 1784
  see also col. 381, 394
Dietsch, Pierre Louis Philippe (1808–1865)
Le Vaisseau-Fantôme, 1842
  see also col. 827
Dittersdorf, Karl Ditters von (1739–1799)
Betrug durch Aberglauben, 1786
Doctor und Apotheker, 1786
Democrito corretto, 1787
Die Liebe im Narrenhaus, 1787
*Hironimus Knicker, 1789
*Das rothe Kaeppchen, 1790
Der Gutsherr, 1791
  see also col. 422, 469, 542
Dluski, Erasmus (1857–1923)
*Urvasi, 1902
Dobrzyński, Ignaz Felix (1807–1867)
Monbar, 1863
Dohnányi, Ernö (1877–)
Tante Simona, 1913
A Vajda Tornya, 1922
A Tenor, 1929
Donaudy, Stefano (1879–)
La Fiamminga, 1922
Donizetti, Gaetano (1797–1848)
Zoraida di Granata, 1822
L'Ajo nell' Imbarazzo, 1824
Olivo e Pasquale, 1827
Gli Esiliati in Siberia, 1827
Il Borgomastro di Saardam, 1827
L'Esule di Roma, 1828
La Regina di Golconda, 1828
Anna Bolena, 1830
*Fausta, 1832
L'Elisir d'Amore, 1832
Il Furioso nell' Isola di San Domingo, 1833

Parisina, 1833
Torquato Tasso, 1833
Lucrezia Borgia, 1833
Gemma di Vergy, 1834
Marino Faliero, 1835
Lucia di Lammermoor, 1835
Belisario, 1836
*Il Campanello di Notte, 1836
*Betly, 1836
Roberto d'Evereux, Comte d'Essex, 1837
Maria di Rudenz, 1838
La Fille du Régiment, 1840
Les Martyrs, 1840
La Favorite, 1840
Adelia, 1841
Maria Padilla, 1841
Linda di Chamounix, 1842
*Don Pasquale, 1843
Maria di Rohan, 1843
Don Sébastien, Roi de Portugal, 1843
Rita, 1860
Il Duca d'Alba, 1882
  see also col. 288, 315, 618, 712, 734, 742, 762,
  764.
Dopper, Cornelis (1870–1939)
Het Eerekruis, 1903
William Ratcliff, 1909
Doppler, Albert Franz (1821–1883)
Grof Benjowsky, 1847
Ilka, 1849
Wanda, 1856
Judith, 1870
Doret, Gustave (1866–1943)
Les Armaillis, 1906
  see also col. 265
Dorn, Heinrich (1804–1892)
Der Schöffe von Paris, 1838
Die Nibelungen, 1854
  see also col. 702, 825
Doss, Adolf von (1825–1886)
Percifal, 1883
Draeseke, Felix (1835–1913)
*Herrat, 1892
Draghi, Antonio (1635–1700)
Achille in Sciro, 1663
Leonida in Tegea, 1670
La Lanterna di Diogene, 1674
La Patienza di Socrate, 1680
La Chimera, 1682
  see also col. 104, 120, 166, 172, and Index of
  Librettits
Dragoi, Sabin (1894–)
Napasta, 1928
Drieberg, Friedrich von (1780–1856)

Ernst II, Duke of Saxe-Coburg-Gotha (1818–
    1893)
    Casilda, 1851
    Santa Chiara, 1854
    Diana von Solange, 1858
    see also col. 1168
Eslava, Miguel Hilarión (1807–1878)
    Il Solitario del Monte Selvaggio, 1841
Espín y Guillén, Joaquín (1812–1881)
    Padilla, 1845
Esposito, Eugenio (18..–)
    Il Borghese Gentiluomo, 1905
Esser, Heinrich (1818–1872)
    Die zwei Prinzen, 1845
Esteve, Pablo (18th ct.)
    *Los Jardineros de Aranjuez, 1768.
    see also col. 220, 244, 298
Ettinger, Max (1874–1951)
    Juana, 1925
    Der eifersüchtige Trinker, 1925
    Frühlings Erwachen, 1928
Eugen, Duke of Wurttemberg (1788–1857)
    *Die Geisterbraut, 1842
Eule, Carl David (1776–1827)
    Der Unsichtbare, 1809

Fabrizi, Vincenzo (c.1765–?)
    Li due Castellani burlati, 1785
    see also col. 358, 441
Faccio, Franco (1840–1891)
    Amleto, 1865
    see also col. 677, 733, 885, 986
Falchi, Stanislao (1851–1922)
    Il Trillo del Diavolo, 1899
Fall, Leo (1873–1925)
    Die Dollarprinzessin, 1907
Falla, Manuel de (1876–1946)
    La Vie brève, 1913
    El Retablo de Maese Pedro, 1923
Farinelli, Giuseppe (1769–1836)
    Teresa e Claudio, 1801
    I Riti d'Efeso, 1803
Fasch, Johann Friedrich (1688–1758)
    Lucius Verus, 1711
Fauré, Gabriel Urbain (1845–1924)
    Prométhée, 1900
    Pénélope, 1913
    Masques et Bergamasques, 1919
Fedeli, Ruggiero (c.1655–1722)
    Almira, 1703
Federici, Francesco (17..–18..)
    Zaira, 1803
Feo, Francesco (1691–1761)
    L'Amor tirannico, 1713

Siface, 1723
Ferrandini, Giovanni (c.1715–1793).
    Catone in Utica, 1753
    see also col. 36
Ferrari, Benedetto (1597–1681)
    *L'Armida, 1639
    *Il Pastor regio, 1640
    see also Index of Librettists
Ferrari, Gabriella (1860–1921)
    Le Cobzar, 1909
Ferrari, Serafino Amadeo de (1824–1885)
    Pipelè, 1855
Ferrari-Trecate, Luigi (1884–)
    Le Astuzie di Bertoldo, 1934
    Ghirlino, 1940
Ferroni, Vincenzo (1858–1934)
    Rudello, 1890
Ferroud, Pierre Octave (1900–1936)
    Chirurgie, 1928
Fesca, Alexander Ernst (1820–1849)
    Der Troubadour, 1847
Fesca, Friedrich Ernst (1789–1826)
    Cantemire, 1820
    see also col. 863
Fétis, François Joseph (1784–1871)
    La Vieille, 1826
    see also col. 14, 77, 518, 656, 971
Février, Henri (1875–)
    Monna Vanna, 1909
    Gismonda, 1919
    La Damnation de Blanchefleur, 1920
    La Femme nue, 1929
Fibich, Zdenko (1850–1900)
    Bukovín, 1874
    Blaník, 1881
    Nevěsta Messinská, 1884
    Námluvy Pelopovy, 1890
    Smír Tantalův, 1891
    Smrt Hippodamie, 1891
    Bouřc, 1895
    Hedy, 1896
    Šárka, 1897
    Pád Arkuna, 1900
    see also col. 1261
Filiasi, Lorenzo (1878–)
    Manuel Menendez, 1904
Fino, Giocondo (1867–)
    Il Battista, 1906
Fioravanti, Valentino (1764–1837)
    *Il Furbo contro al Furbo, 1796
    Le Cantatrici villane, 1799
    La Capricciosa pentita, 1802
    I Virtuosi ambulanti, 1807
    see also col. 402

La Vendemmia, 1778
La Moglie capricciosa, 1785
Don Giovanni Tenorio, 1787
see also col. 358, 489, 545
Genée, Richard (1823–1895)
Der Seekadett, 1876
Nanon, 1877
see also Index of Librettists
Generali, Pietro (1783–1832)
Pamela nubile, 1804
Le Lagrime di una Vedova, 1808
Adelina, 1810
I Baccanti di Roma, 1816
Genovés (y Lapetra), Tomás (1806–1861)
El Rapto, 1832
see also col. 860
Georges, Alexandre (1850–1938)
Miarka, 1905
Gerlach, Theodor (1861–)
*Liebeswogen, 1903
German, Edward (1862–1936)
Merrie England, 1902
Gershwin, George (1898–1937)
Porgy and Bess, 1935
Gervais, Charles Hubert (1671–1744)
Hypermnestre, 1716
Gevaert, François Auguste (1828–1908)
Quentin Durward, 1858
see also col. 177, 276, 592
Ghislanzoni, Alberto (1897–)
*Re Lear, 1937
Giacobbi, Girolamo (1567–1629)
Andromeda, 1610
Giacomelli, Geminiano (c.1692–1740)
Cesare in Egitto, 1735
see also col. 137
Giannetti, Giovanni (1869–1934)
Cristo alla Festa di Purim, 1904
Giannettini, Antonio (1648–1721)
Medea in Atene, 1675
see also col. 85
Gilson, Paul (1865–1942)
Prinses Zonneschijn, 1903
Zeevolk, 1904
Giordani, Tommaso (c.1730–1806)
La Disfatta di Dario, 1789
see also col. 160, 230, 250, 262, 280, 433
Giordano, Umberto (1867–1948)
Mala Vita, 1892
Andrea Chenier, 1896
Fedora, 1898
Siberia, 1903
Marcella, 1907
Mese Mariano, 1910

Madame Sans-Gêne, 1915
Giove a Pompei (with Franchetti), 1921
La Cena delle Beffe, 1924
Il Re, 1929
Giosa, Nicola de (1820–1885)
Don Checco, 1850
Napoli di Carnovale, 1876
Girschner, Karl Friedrich (1794–1860)
Undine, 1837
Gläser, Franz (1798–1861)
Des Adlers Horst, 1832
Bryllupet vet Como-Søen, 1849
see also col. 702, 796, 1424
Gleason, Frederick Grant (1848–1903)
*Otho Visconti, 1907
Glière, Reinhold Moritsovich (1875–1950)
Shakh-Senem, 1934
Glinka, Mikhail Ivanovich (1804–1857)
Zhizn za Tsarya, 1836
*Ruslan i Lyudmila, 1842
see also col. 179, 641, 714, 773, 836, 1082
Glover, William Howard (1819–1875)
*Ruy Blas, 1861
Gluck, Christoph Willibald (1714–1787)
Artaserse, 1741
Demetrio, 1742
Demofoonte, 1742
Il Tigrane, 1743
La Sofonisba, 1744
Ipermestra, 1744
La Caduta de' Giganti, 1746
Artamene, 1746
Le Nozze d'Ercole e d'Ebe, 1747
Semiramide riconosciuta, 1748
La Contesa dei Numi, 1749
Ezio, 1750
La Clemenza di Tito, 1752
Le Cinesi, 1754
L'Innocenza giustificata, 1755
Antigono, 1756
Il Re Pastore, 1756
L'Isle de Merlin, 1758
La Cythère assiégée, 1759
L'Arbre enchanté, 1759
L'Yvrogne corrigé, 1760
Le Cadi dupé, 1761
Orfeo, ed Euridice, 1762
Il Trionfo di Clelia, 1763
La Rencontre imprévue, 1764
Il Telemaco, 1765
Alceste, 1767
Paride e Elena, 1770
Iphigénie en Aulide, 1774
Armide, 1777

Iphigénie en Tauride, 1779
Écho et Narcisse, 1779
  see also col. 8, 79, 80, 185, 205, 225, 233, 247,
    250, 272, 273, 274, 282, 351, 365, 377, 385,
    410, 431
Gnecchi, Vittorio (1876–)
  Cassandra, 1905
  *La Rosiera, 1927
Gnecco, Francesco (1769–1810)
  *Filandro e Carolina, 1804
  *La Prova d'una Opera seria, 1805
  see also col. 475
Gobatti, Stefano (1852–1913)
  I Goti, 1873
Godard, Benjamin (1849–1895)
  Pédro de Zalaméa, 1884
  Jocelyn, 1888
  La Vivandière, 1895
Goetz, Hermann (1840–1876)
  Der Widerspänstigen Zähmung, 1874
  *Francesca da Rimini, 1877
Goetzl, Anselm (1876–1923)
  Zierpuppen, 1905
Goldmark, Karl (1830–1915)
  Die Königin von Saba, 1875
  Merlin, 1886
  Das Heimchen am Herd, 1896
  Die Kriegsgefangene, 1899
  Berlichingen Götz, 1902
  Ein Wintermärchen, 1908
  see also col. 1219
Goldschmidt, Adalbert von (1848–1906)
  *Heliantus, 1884
Goldschmidt, Berthold (1903–)
  *Der gewaltige Hahnrei, 1932
Gomes, Antonio Carlos (1836–1896)
  Noite do Castello, 1861
  Il Guarany, 1870
  Fosca, 1873
  Salvator Rosa, 1874
  Lo Schiavo, 1889
Gomis, José Melchor (1791–1836)
  Le Portefaix, 1835
Goossens, Eugène (1893–)
  Judith, 1929
  Don Juan de Mañara, 1937
Gordigiani, Giovanni Battista (1795–1871)
  *Consuelo, 1846
Gossec, François Joseph (1734–1829)
  Les Pêcheurs, 1766
  Toinon et Toinette, 1767
  Sabinus, 1773
  see also col. 57, 158, 254, 255, 296
Gotovac, Jacov (1895–)

Morana, 1930
Ero s Onoga svijeta, 1935
Goula, Juan (1843–1917)
  A la Voreta del Mar, 1881
Gounod, Charles François (1818–1893)
  Sapho, 1851
  La Nonne sanglante, 1854
  *Le Médecin malgré lui, 1858
  Faust, 1859
  Philémon et Baucis, 1860
  La Colombe, 1860
  La Reine de Saba, 1862
  Mireille, 1864
  Roméo et Juliette, 1867
  Cinq Mars, 1877
  Polyeucte, 1878
  Le Tribut de Zamora, 1881
  see also col. 353
Grabu, Lewis (*d. after* 1694)
  Albion and Albanius, 1685
  see also col. 48, 54, 55
Graener, Paul, (1872–1944)
  Don Juans letztes Abenteuer, 1914
  Theophano, 1918
  Schirin und Gertraude, 1920
  Hanneles Himmelfahrt, 1927
  Friedemann Bach, 1931
Grammann, Karl (1842–1897)
  *Melusine, 1875
Granados (y Campina), Enrique (1867–1916)
  Maria del Carmen, 1898
  Goyescas, 1916
Grandjean, Axel (1847–1932)
  Colomba, 1882
Graun, Karl Heinrich (1704–1759)
  Sinilde, 1727
  Rodelinda, Regina de' Longobardi, 1741
  Cleopatra e Cesare, 1742
  Artaserse, 1743
  Demofoonte, Re di Tracia, 1746
  Ifigenia in Aulide, 1748
  Silla, 1753
  Montezuma, 1755
  Merope, 1756
  see also col. 136, 154
Graupner, Christoph (1683–1760)
  Der angenehme Betrug (with Keiser), 1707
  Dido, Koenigin von Carthago, 1707
Grazioli, Filippo (1773–1840)
  La Festa della Riconoscenza, 1821
Greber, Jakob (16..–17..)
  The Loves of Ergasto, 1705
  see also col. 123
Grechaninov, Aleksandr Tikhonovich (1864–)

Haan, Willem de (1849–1930)
  Die Kaiserstochter, 1885
Haarklou, Johannes (1847–1925)
  Fra gamle Dage, 1894
  Marisagnet, 1910
Haba, Alois (1893–)
  *Die Mutter, 1931
Hackländer, Friedrich Wilhelm (1816–1877)
  *Soldatenleben, 1848
Hacquart, Carolus (c.1649–c.1730)
  De triomfeerende Min, 1680 and 1920
Hadley, Henry Kimball (1871–1937)
  Safié, 1909
  Azora, Daughter of Montezuma, 1917
  Cleopatra's Night, 1920
Haeser, Georg (1865–)
  *Hadlaub, 1903
Häffner, Johann Christian Friedrich (1759–1833)
  Electra 1787
  Renaud, 1801
    see also col. 491
Hageman, Richard (1882–)
  Tragödie in Arezzo, 1932
    see also col. 1102
Hahn, Reynaldo (1875–1947)
  La Carmélite, 1902
  Nausicaa, 1919
  Le Marchand de Venise, 1935
Haibel, Jakob (1761–1826)
  Der Tiroler Wastel, 1796
Halévy, Jacques Fromental Élie (1799–1862)
  La Dilettante d'Avignon, 1829
  La Juive, 1835
  L'Éclair, 1835
  Guido et Ginèvra, 1838
  Le Shérif, 1839
  Le Guitarréro, 1841
  La Reine de Chypre, 1841
  Charles VI, 1843
  Les Mousquetaires de la Reine, 1846
  Le Val d'Andorre, 1848
  La Fée aux Roses, 1849
  La Tempesta, 1850
  Jaguarita l'Indienne, 1855
  La Magicienne, 1858
  Noah, 1885
    see also col. 751, 817, 916, 1051, 1210
Hallén, Andreas (1846–1925)
  Harald der Wiking, 1881
  Häxfällan, 1896
  Waldmarsskatten, 1899
Hallström, Ivar (1826–1901)
  Den Bergtagna, 1874
  Neaga, 1885

Halvorsen, Johan (1864–1935)
  Mot Nordpolen, 1911
Hamal, Jean Noël (1709–1778)
  Voëgge di Chôfontaine, 1757
    see also col. 1415
Hamerik, Ebbe (1898–1951)
  Stepan, 1924
Handel, Georg Friedrich (1685–1759)
  Almira, 1705
  Agrippina, 1709
  Rinaldo, 1711
  Il Pastor fido, 1712
  Teseo, 1713
  Amadigi di Gaula, 1715
  Il Radamisto, 1720
  Il Muzio Scevola (with G. Bononcini and
    Mattei), 1721
  Il Floridante, 1721
  Ottone, Re di Germania, 1723
  Flavio, Re de' Longobardi, 1723
  Giulio Cesare in Egitto, 1724
  Tamerlano, 1724
  Rodelinda, 1725
  Scipione, 1726
  Alessandro, 1726
  Admeto, Re di Tessaglia, 1727
  Riccardo I, Re d'Inghilterra, 1727
  Siroe, Re di Persia, 1728
  Tolomeo, Re di Egitto, 1728
  Lotario, 1729
  Partenope, 1730
  Poro, Re dell' Indie, 1731
  Ezio, 1732
  Sosarme, Re di Media, 1732
  Acis and Galatea, 1732
  Orlando, 1733
  Ariadne in Crete, 1734
  Ariodante, 1735
  Alcina, 1735
  Atalanta, 1736
  Arminio, 1737
  Giustino, 1737
  Berenice, 1737
  Faramondo, 1738
  Serse, 1738
  Deidamia, 1741
    see also col. 111, 116, 125, 127, 128, 142, 143,
      159, 168, 181, 189, 198, 204, 261, 658
Hanson, Howard (1896–)
  Merry Mount, 1934
d'Harcourt, Eugène (1859–1918)
  Le Tasse, 1903
    see also col. 690, 883

Kaiser, Alfred (1872–1917)
 *Stella Maris, 1910
   see also Index of Librettists
Kalliwoda, Johann Wenceslaus (1801–1866)
 Blanda, 1847
Kalniņš, Alfreds (1879–)
 Banuta, 1920
 Dzimtenes Atmoda, 1933
Kalniņš, Janis (1904–)
 *Hamlets, 1936
Kalomoiris, Manolis (1883–)
 Ho Protomastoras, 1916
Kamieński, Maciej (1734–1821)
 Nedza Uszczesliwiona, 1778
 Zoška, 1781
Kaminski, Heinrich (1886–1946)
 *Jürg Jenatsch, 1929
Karel, Rudolf (1880–1945)
 Ilseino Srdce, 1924
 Smrt Kmotřička, 1933
Karnavičius, Jurgio (1885–)
 Gražina, 1933
Kashperov, Vladimir Nikitich (1827–1894)
 Maria Tudor, 1859
 Groza, 1867
Kastner, Johann Georg (1810–1867)
 La Maschera, 1841
Kauer, Ferdinand (1751–1831)
 Das Donauweibchen, 1798
Kaun, Hugo (1863–1932)
 *Sappho, 1917
 Der Fremde, 1920
 *Menandra, 1925
Keil, Alfredo (1850–1907)
 Donna Bianca, 1888
 Irene, 1893
 Serrana, 1899
Keiser, Reinhard (1674–1739)
 Basilius, 1694
 Circe, 1696
 Penelope, 1696
 Der geliebte Adonis, 1697
 Augustus, 1698
 Orpheus, 1698
 La Forza della Virtù, 1700
 Stoertebecker und Joedge Michaels, 1701
 Die verdammte Staat-Sucht, 1703
 Nebucadnezar, 1704
 Octavia, 1705
 Masagniello furioso, 1706
 Der angenehme Betrug (with Graupner), 1707
 Desiderius, Koenig der Longobarden, 1709
 Croesus, 1711
 Fredegunda, 1715

 Die grossmüthige Tomyris, 1717
 Ulysses, 1722
 Der laecherliche Printz Jodelet, 1726
 Circe, 1734
   see also col. 92, 96, 112, 124, 125, 132, 166
Kelley, Edgar Stillman (1857–1944)
 Puritania, 1892
Kerll, Johann Kaspar (1627–1693)
 L'Oronte, 1657
 L'Erinto, 1661
Keussler, Gerhard von (1874–1949)
 *Gefängnisse, 1914
Kienlen, Johann Christoph (1784–*c*.1830)
 Claudine von Villa Bella, 1810
Kienzl, Wilhelm (1857–1941)
 *Der Evangelimann, 1895
 *Don Quixote, 1898
 Der Kuhreigen, 1911
 *Das Testament, 1916
Kistler, Cyrill (1848–1907)
 Kunihild, 1884
Kittl, Johann Friedrich (1806–1868)
 Bianca und Giuseppe, 1848
Klein, Bernhard (1793–1832)
 Dido, 1823
Klein, Bruno Oskar (1858–1911)
 Kenilworth, 1895
Kleinheinz, Franz Xaver (1772–1832)
 Harald, 1814
Klenau, Paul von (1883–1946)
 *Kjartan und Gudrun, 1918
 *Rembrandt van Rijn, 1937
Klose, Friedrich (1862–1942)
 Ilsebill, 1903
Klughardt, August (1847–1902)
 Die Hochzeit des Mönchs, 1886
Kodály, Zoltán (1882–)
 Háry János, 1926
 Székely Fonó, 1932
Kogoj, Marij (1895–)
 Črne Maske, 1929
Kohout, Joseph (*c*.1736–1793)
 Le Serrurier, 1764
Konjović, Petar (1882–)
 Koštana, 1931
Korngold, Erich Wolfgang (1897–)
 Violanta, 1916
 Der Ring des Polykrates, 1916
 Die tote Stadt, 1920
 Das Wunder der Heliane, 1927
   see also 970, 1106
Kosmovici, Georg (18..–?)
 Marioara (with Schmeidler), 1904
Kospoth, Otto Carl Erdmann von (1753–1817)

Il Governatore, 1747
Giunio Bruto, 1748
see also col. 195
Löhner, Johann (1645–1705)
*Theseus, 1688
Lohse, Otto (1858–1925)
Der Prinz wider Willen, 1890
Lorenzani, Paolo (c.1640–1713)
Nicandro e Fileno, 1681
Orontée, 1688
see also col. 20, 41, 107
Lortzing, Gustav Albert (1801–1851)
*Die beiden Schützen, 1837
*Czaar und Zimmermann, 1837
*Hans Sachs, 1840
*Casanova, 1841
*Der Wildschütz, 1842
*Undine, 1845
*Der Waffenschmied, 1846
*Zum Grossadmiral, 1847
*Rolands Knappen, 1849
*Die vornehmen Dilettanten, 1851
*Regina, 1899
see also col. 309, 647, 708, 1001
Lothav, Mark (1902–)
Tyll, 1928
Lord Spleen, 1930
see also col. 358
Lotti, Antonio (c.1667–1740)
Alessandro Severo, 1716
Giove in Argo, 1717
Teofane, 1719
see also col. 41, 146
Løvenskjold, Hermann Severin (1815–1870)
Turandot, 1854
Lualdi, Adriano (1887–)
*La Figlia del Re, 1922
Le Furie d'Arlecchino, 1924
*Il Diavolo nel Campanile, 1925
*La Grançeola, 1932
see also col. 369
Luccio, Francesco (17th ct.)
Il Medoro, 1658
Lully, Jean Baptiste (1632–1687)
Les Festes de l'Amour et de Bacchus, 1672
Cadmus et Hermione, 1673
Alceste, 1674
Thésée, 1675
Atys, 1676
Isis, 1677
Psyché, 1678
Bellérophon, 1679
Proserpine, 1680
Persée, 1682

Phaéton, 1683
Amadis, 1684
Roland, 1685
Armide, 1686
Acis et Galatée, 1686
see also col. 30, 41, 53, 54, 56, 57, 59, 61, 65, 71, 77, 83, 84, 94, 100, 107, 174, 359, 362, 377, 573
Lux, Friedrich (1820–1895)
Das Käthchen von Heilbronn, 1846
Der Schmied von Ruhla, 1882
Lvov, Aleksei Fedorovich (1798–1870)
Bianca und Gualtiero, 1844
Undina, 1848

MacAlpin, Colin (1870–)
The Cross and the Crescent, 1903
MacCunn, Hamish (1868–1916)
Jeanie Deans, 1894
Diarmid, 1897
Macfarren, George Alexander (1813–1887)
The Devil's Opera, 1838
An Adventure of Don Quixote, 1846
King Charles II, 1849
Robin Hood, 1860
Jessy Lea, 1863
Helvellyn, 1864
see also col. 86, 761
Machado, Augusto (1845–1924)
Lauriane, 1883
Mario Wetter, 1898
Mackenzie, Alexander Campbell (1847–1935)
Colomba, 1883
The Cricket on the Hearth, 1914
The Eve of St. John, 1924
Maclean, Alick (1872–1936)
Quentin Durward, 1920
Madetoja, Leevi (1887–1947)
*Pohjalaisia, 1924
*Juha, 1935
Magnard, Albéric (1865–1914)
*Bérénice, 1911
*Guercœur, 1931
Maillart, Louis Aimé (1817–1871)
Gastibelza, 1847
Les Dragons de Villars, 1856
Les Pêcheurs de Catane, 1860
Lara, 1864
Majo, Francesco di (1732–1770)
Ricimero, Rè dei Goti, 1758
Ifigenia in Tauride, 1764
see also col. 236, 317
Major, Gyula (1858–1925)
Erzsike, 1901

Maldere, Pierre van (1724–1768)
 La Bagarre, 1763
  see also col. 185
Malipiero, Francesco (1824–1887)
 Alberigo da Romano, 1846
Malipiero, Gian Francesco (1882–)
 *Sept Chansons, 1920
 *L'Orfeide, 1925
 La Bottega da Caffè, 1926
 Sior Todero Brontolon, 1926
 Le Baruffe Chiozzotte, 1926
 *Der falsche Harlekin, 1928
 *Filomela und ihr Narr, 1928
 *Komödie des Todes, 1931
 *Mysterium Venedigs, 1932
 Die Legende vom vertauschten Sohn, 1934
 *Giulio Cesare, 1936
 *Antonio e Cleopatra, 1938
  see also col. 5, 6, 18, 859, 1420
Mancinelli, Luigi (1848–1921)
 Isora di Provenza, 1884
 Ero e Leandro, 1897
 Paolo e Francesca, 1907
  see also col. 885, 1075
Mancini, Francesco (1679–1739)
 Gli Amanti generosi, 1705
 L'Engelbertha (with A. Orefice), 1709
  see also col. 122
Mandl, Richard (1859–1918)
 La Rencontre imprévue, 1889
Manelli, Francesco (1595–c.1667)
 L'Andromeda, 1637
 La Maga fulminata, 1638
  see also col. 15, 17, 18
Manén, Joan (1883–)
 *Acté, 1903
Mangold, Karl (1813–1889)
 Tanhäuser, 1846
Marais, Marin (1656–1728)
 Alcione, 1706
Marazzoli, Marco (c.1619–1662)
 Chi soffre, speri (with V. Mazzocchi), 1639
 Dal Male il Bene (with Abbatini), 1653
 La Vita umana, 1656
  see also col. 20
Marcello, Benedetto (1686–1739)
 Arianna, 1913
Marchetti, Filippo (1831–1902)
 Romeo e Giulietta, 1865
 Ruy Blas, 1869
  see also col. 353
Maréchal, Henri (1842–1924)
 Les Amoureux de Catherine, 1876
Maria, P. A. D. della, see Della Maria

Maria Antonia Walpurgis, Electress of Saxony
 ("E.T.P.A.") (1724–1780)
 *Il Trionfo della Fedeltà, 1754
 *Talestri, Regina delle Amazoni, 1760
  see also col. 207
Mariani, Giovanni Battista (17th ct.)
 Amore vuol Gioventù, 1659
Marinuzzi, Gino (1882–1945)
 Jacquerie, 1918
 Palla de' Mozzi, 1932
  see also col. 1098
Mariotte, Antoine (1875–1944)
 Salomé, 1908
 Esther Princesse d'Israèl, 1925
 Gargantua, 1935
Marliani, Marco Aurelio (1805–1849)
 Il Bravo, 1834
 La Xacarilla, 1839
  see also col. 834
Marquez (Puig), Antonio (1897–)
 Sor Beatriz, 1924
Marschner, Heinrich August (1795–1861)
 Der Holzdieb, 1825
 Der Vampyr, 1828
 Der Templer und die Jüdin, 1829
 Des Falkners Braut, 1832
 Hans Heiling, 1833
 Das Schloss am Ätna, 1836
 Der Bäbu, 1838
 Kaiser Adolph von Nassau, 1845
 Sangeskönig Hiarne, 1863
  see also col. 682, 716, 731, 801
Marsick, Armand (1878–)
 La Jane, 1921
Martin y Soler, Vicente (1754–1806)
 Il Burbero di buon Cuore, 1786
 Una Cosa rara, 1786
 L'Arbore di Diana, 1787
 Gore Bogatyr Kosometovich, 1789
 Fedul s Detmi (with Pashkeevich), 1791
 La Scola de Maritati, 1795
 L'Isola del Piacere, 1795
  see also col. 180, 385, 397, 458, 485
Martinez de la Roca, Joaquín (16..–17..)
 Los Desagravios de Troya, 1712
Martini, Jean Paul Egide (1741–1816)
 L'Amoureux de quinze Ans, 1771
 Henri IV, 1774
 Le Droit du Seigneur, 1783
  see also col. 259
Marty, Georges Eugène (1860–1908)
 Daria, 1905
Mascagni, Pietro (1863–1945)
 Cavalleria rusticana, 1890

Une Folie, 1802
Joanna, 1802
Le Trésor supposé, 1802
Héléna, 1803
Les deux Aveugles de Tolède, 1806
Uthal, 1806
Gabrielle d'Estrées, 1806
Joseph, 1807
Le Prince Troubadour, 1813
La Journée aux Aventures, 1816
Valentine de Milan, 1822
 see also col. 605
Melani, Jacopo (1623–1676)
 Il Potesta di Colognole, 1656
 Ercole in Tebe, 1661
 Girello, 1670
 see also col. 20
Melartin, Erkki Gustaf (1875–1937)
 Aino, 1909
Melcer, Henryk (1869–1928)
 Marya, 1904
Mellon, Alfred (1820–1867)
 Victorine, 1859
Mendelssohn, Felix (1809–1847)
 Die Hochzeit des Gamacho, 1827
 Die Heimkehr aus der Fremde, 1851
 see also col. 610, 882, 962, 963, 1129
Menotti, Gian Carlo (1911–)
 *Amelia goes to the Ball, 1937
Mercadante, Saverio (1795–1870)
 Elisa e Claudio, 1821
 Caritea, Regina di Spagna, 1826
 Gabriella di Vergy, 1828
 I Normanni a Parigi, 1832
 I Briganti, 1836
 Il Giuramento, 1837
 Elena da Feltre, 1838
 Il Bravo, 1839
 La Vestale, 1840
 Leonora, 1844
 Gli Orazi ed i Curiazi, 1846
 Virginia, 1866
 see also col. 506, 670, 795, 797, 801, 971
Merikanto, Oscar (1868–1924)
 Pohjan Neito, 1908
 Elinan Surma, 1910
 Regina von Emmeritz, 1920
Mermet, Auguste (1810–1889)
 *Roland à Roncevaux, 1864
 *Jeanne d'Arc, 1876
 see also col. 480
Mertens, Joseph (1834–1901)
 Liederik, de Rentmeester, 1875
 De zwarte Kapitein, 1877

Messager, André (1853–1929)
 La Béarnaise, 1885
 La Basoche, 1890
 Madame Chrysanthème, 1893
 Les p'tites Michu, 1897
 Véronique, 1898
 Fortunio, 1907
 Béatrice, 1914
 Monsieur Beaucaire, 1919
Meyer von Schauensee, Franz Joseph Leonti
 (1720–1789)
 *Hans Hüttenstock, 1769
Meyerbeer, Giacomo (1791–1864)
 Jephta's Gelübde, 1812
 Wirth und Gast, 1813
 Romilda e Costanza, 1817
 Emma di Resburgo, 1819
 Margherita d'Anjou, 1820
 Il Crociato in Egitto, 1824
 Robert-le-Diable, 1831
 Les Huguenots, 1836
 Ein Feldlager in Schlesien, 1844
 Le Prophète, 1849
 L'Étoile du Nord, 1854
 Le Pardon de Ploërmel, 1859
 L'Africaine, 1865
 see also col. 199, 747, 784, 797, 916, 994,
 1051, 1130
Migoni, Francisco Xavier (1811–1861)
 Sampiero, 1853
Mihalovich, Ödön (1842–1929)
 Hagbarth und Signe, 1882
 Toldi Szerelme, 1893
 Eliána, 1908
Miles, Philip Napier (1865–1935)
 *Markheim, 1924
Milhaud, Darius (1892–)
 La Brebis égarée, 1923
 Les Malheurs d'Orphée, 1926
 Die Entführung der Europa, 1927
 Le pauvre Matelot, 1927
 Der befreite Theseus, 1928
 Die verlassene Ariadne, 1928
 Christoph Columbus, 1930
 Maximilien, 1932
 Esther de Carpentras, 1938
 Medee, 1939
 see also col. 1079
Milligen, Simon van (1849–1929)
 Brinio, 1889
Millöcker, Karl (1842–1899)
 Apajune der Wassermann, 1880
 Der Bettelstudent, 1882
 Gasparone, 1884

Noronha, Francisco de Sá (1820–1881)
  Beatrice do Portogallo, 1863
Noskowski, Zygmund (1846–1909)
  Livia Quintilla, 1898
Nouguès, Jean (1875–1932)
  Quo vadis, 1909
  L'Auberge rouge, 1910
  L'Aigle, 1912
  see also col. 1282
Novák, Vitězslav (1870–1949)
  Zvíkovský Rarášek, 1915
  Karlštejn, 1916
  Lucerna, 1923
  Dědův Odkaz, 1926

Oberleithner, Max von (1868–1935)
  Der eiserne Heiland, 1917
O'Dwyer, Robert (1860–)
  Eithne, 1910
Offenbach, Jacques (1819–1880)
  L'Alcôve, 1847
  Pepito, 1853
  Les deux Aveugles, 1855
  Le Mariage aux Lanternes, 1857
  Mesdames de la Halle, 1858
  Orphée aux Enfers, 1858
  Geneviève de Brabant, 1859
  Daphnis et Chloé, 1860
  Barkouf, 1860
  La Chanson de Fortunio, 1861
  Le Pont des Soupirs, 1861
  Monsieur et Madame Denis, 1862
  Bavard et Bavarde, 1862
  Lischen et Fritzchen, 1863
  La belle Hélène, 1864
  Barbe-Bleue, 1866
  La Vie parisienne, 1866
  La Grande-Duchesse de Gérolstein, 1867
  Robinson Crusoé, 1867
  L'Ile de Tulipatan, 1868
  La Périchole, 1868
  Vert-Vert, 1869
  Les Brigands, 1869
  La Princesse de Trébizonde, 1869
  Fantasio, 1872
  La jolie Parfumeuse, 1873
  Madame l'Archiduc, 1874
  La Créole, 1875
  Madame Favart, 1878
  La Fille du Tambour-Major, 1879
  Les Contes d'Hoffmann, 1881
  Der Goldschmied von Toledo, 1919
  see also col. 629, 958, 979, 995, 1025
Olenin, Aleksandr Aleksyeevich (1865–)

*Kudeyar, 1915
d'Ollone, Max (1875–)
  *Le Retour, 1913
  L'Arlequin, 1924
Onslow, Georges (1784–1852)
  Le Colporteur, 1827
Oosterzee, Cornelie van (1863–)
  Das Gelöbnis, 1910
Orefice, Antonio (c.1690–c.1733)
  L'Engelberta (with Mancini), 1709
  Patrò Calienno de la Costa, 1709
Orefice, Giacomo (1865–1922)
  Chopin, 1901
  Radda, 1912
  see also col. 5, 6, 7
Orlandi, Fernando (1777–1848)
  Il Podestà di Chioggia, 1801
  La Dama Soldato, 1808
Orlandini, Giuseppe Maria (1688–c.1750)
  Amore e Maestà, 1715
  Antigona, 1718
  Il Marito Giogatore, 1718
  Nerone, 1721
  see also col. 41, 110, 144, 159
Ostrčil, Otakar (1879–1935)
  Vlasty Skon, 1904
  Kunálovy Oči, 1908
  Poupě, 1911
  Honzovo Království, 1934
Otremba, Gustav (18..–?)
  Olenca (with Caudella), 1880
Ottoboni, Pietro (1667–1740)
  *Il Colombo, 1690
  see also Index of Librettists
Oudrid (y Segura), Cristóbal (1825–1877)
  Buenas Noches, Señor Don Simón, 1852
  El Postillón de la Rioja, 1856
  see also col. 873
Overhoff, Kurt (1902–)
  Mira, 1925

Pacchierotti, Ubaldo (1877–1916)
  Eidelberga mia, 1908
Pacheco, Fabián Garcia (c.1725–c.1808)
  En Casa de Nadie no se meta Nadie, 1770
Pacini, Giovanni (1796–1867)
  Adelaide e Comingio, 1817
  Il Barone di Dolsheim, 1818
  La Schiava in Bagdad, 1820
  La Gioventù di Enrico V, 1820
  L'ultimo Giorno di Pompei, 1825
  Gli Arabi nelle Gallie, 1827
  Saffo, 1840

La Fidanzata Corsa, 1842
Medea, 1843
Lorenzino de' Medici, 1845
Bondelmonte, 1845
La Regina di Cipro, 1846
Il Saltimbanco, 1858
*Niccolo dei Lapi, 1873
    see also col. 705, 1093
Pacius, Friedrich (1809–1891)
Kung Carls Jakt, 1852
Lorelei, 1887
Paderewski, Ignacy Jan (1860–1941)
Manru, 1901
Paer, Ferdinando (1771–1839)
Il Tempo fa Giustizia a tutti, 1792
L'Intrigo amoroso, 1795
Il Principe di Taranto, 1797
La Virtù al Cimento, 1798.
Camilla, 1799
Poche, ma buone, 1800
Achille, 1801
I Fuorusciti di Firenze, 1802
Sargino, 1803
Leonora, 1804
Sofonisba, 1805
Agnese di Fitz-Henry, 1809
Le Maître de Chapelle, 1821
Un Caprice de Femme, 1834
    see also col. 167, 291, 426, 474, 540, 573, 585,
    590, 736
Pagliardi, Giovanni Maria (17th ct.)
Caligula delirante, 1672
Lisimaco, 1673
    see also col. 140
Pahissa, Jaime (1880–)
La Presó de Lleida, 1906
Gala Placidia, 1913
Marianela, 1923
Paisiello, Giovanni (1740–1816)
Le finte Contesse, 1766
L'Idolo Cinese, 1767
Il Duello, 1774
Il Credulo deluso, 1774
La Frascatana, 1774
La Discordia fortunata, 1775
Socrate immaginario, 1775
Le due Contesse, 1776
Gli Astrologi immaginari, 1779
La finta Amante, 1780
La Serva Padrona, 1781
Il Barbiere di Siviglia, 1782
Il Re Teodoro in Venezia, 1784
Le Gare generose, 1786
Pirro, 1787

La Modista Raggiratrice, 1787
L'Amor contrastato, 1788
Nina, 1789
I Zingari in Fiera, 1789
La Locanda, 1791
I Giuochi d'Agrigento, 1792
L'Elfrida, 1792
Proserpine, 1803
    see also col. 16, 41, 69, 139, 176, 177, 178, 180,
    213, 234, 262, 368, 426, 430, 438, 440, 466,
    473
Paladilhe, Emile (1844–1926)
Le Passant, 1872
Patrie, 1886
Pallavicino, Carlo (c.1630–1688)
Galieno, 1675
Il Vespasiano, 1678
Le Amazoni nell'Isole fortunate, 1679
Massimo Puppieno, 1684
Penelope la Casta, 1685
L'Amazone Corsara, 1686
La Gierusalemme liberata, 1687
L'Antiope, 1689
    see also col. 16, 17
Pallavicino, Vincenzo (18th ct.)
Lo Speziale (with Fischietti), 1755
    see also col. 302
Palma, Athos (1891–)
Nazdah, 1924
Palma, Silvestro (1762–1834)
La Pietra simpatica, 1795
Palmer, Geoffrey Molyneux (1882–)
Sruth na Maoile, 1923
Palmgren, Selim (1878–1951)
*Daniel Hjort, 1910
Paneck, Johann Baptist (18th ct.)
Die christliche Judenbraut, 1789
Panizza, Ettore (1875–)
Il Fidanzato del Mare, 1897
Medio Evo Latino, 1900
Aurora, 1908
Bisanzio, 1939
Paradis, Maria Theresia von (1759–1824)
Rinaldo und Alcina, 1797
Parelli, Attilio (1874–1945)
I dispettosi Amanti, 1912
Parker, Horatio William (1863–1919)
Mona, 1912
Fairyland, 1915
Parry, Joseph (1841–1903)
Blodwen, 1878
Sylvia, 1895
Pashkeevich, Vasily Aleksyeevich (18th ct.)
Fevey, 1786

Nachalnoye Upravlenie Olega (with Sarti and Canobbio), 1790

Fedul s Detmi (with Martin y Soler), 1791

Pasquini, Bernardo (1637–1710)
La Donna ancora è fedele, 1676
Dov'è Amore è Pietà, 1679

Paulli, Holger Simon (1810–1891)
Lodsen, 1851

Paumgartner, Bernhard (1887–)
*Die Höhle von Salamanca, 1923
Rossini in Neapel, 1936

Pavesi, Stefano (1779–1850)
Un Avvertimento ai Gelosi, 1803
Ser Marcantonio, 1810
see also col. 663

Pedrell, Felipe (1841–1922)
*L'ultimo Abenzerraggio, 1874
I Pirenei, 1902
see also col. 120, 300, 1270

Pedrollo, Arrigo (1878–)
La Veglia, 1920
L'Uomo che ride, 1920
Delitto e Castigo, 1926
L'Amante in Trappola, 1936
see also col. 1354

Pedrotti, Carlo (1817–1893)
Fiorina, 1851
Tutti in Maschera, 1856
Guerra in quattro, 1861
see also col. 885

Peellaert, August Philipp de (1793–1876)
Agnes Sorel, 1824
Teniers, 1826

Pelissier, Victor (17..–18..)
Edwin and Angelina, 1796
see also col. 414, 473

Pentenrieder, Franz Xaver (1813–1867)
Die Nacht zu Paluzzi, 1840

Pepusch, John Christopher (1667–1752)
Thomyris, Queen of Scythia, 1707
The Beggar's Opera, 1728
Polly (adapted by Arnold), 1777
see also col. 159

Peranda, Marco Giuseppe (c.1600–1675)
Dafne (with Bontempi), 1671

Pereira, Miguel Angelo (1843–1901)
Eurico, 1870

Pérez, Davide (1711–1778)
Siroe, 1740
Demetrio, 1741
Alessandro nell'Indie, 1745
Solimano, 1757
see also col. 228

Perfall, Karl von (1824–1907)

Raimondin, 1881
Junker Heinz, 1886

Pergolesi, Giovanni Battista (1710–1736)
Lo Frate 'nnamorato, 1732
La Serva Padrona, 1733
La Contadina astuta, 1734
Olimpiade, 1735
Il Flaminio, 1735
see also col. 32, 81, 105, 184, 187, 188, 211, 222, 223, 225, 389, 390, 500

Peri, Achille (1812–1880)
Vittore Pisani, 1857
Giuditta, 1860

Peri, Jacopo (1561–1633)
La Dafne, 1597
L'Euridice, 1600
La Flora (with Gagliano), 1628
see also col. 3, 4, 9, 10

Perosi, Marziano (1875–)
Pompeji, 1912

Persiani, Giuseppe (1799–1869)
Inez de Castro, 1835
see also col. 816

Persico, Mario (1892–)
La Bisbetica domata, 1931

Persuis, Louis Lue Loiseau de (1769–1819)
Le Triomphe de Trajan (with Lesueur), 1807
Jérusalem délivrée, 1812

Perti, Jacopo Antonio (1661–1756)
Il Furio Camillo, 1692
see also col. 77, 133, 151, 183, 190

Pescetti, Giovanni Battista (c.1704–1766)
Demetrio, 1732
see also col. 154, 171, 183

Pessard, Emile (1843–1917)
Les Folies amoureuses, 1891

Peterson-Berger, Olof Wilhelm (1867–1942)
*Ran, 1933
*Arnjlot, 1910
*Adils och Elisiv, 1927
see also col. 976

Petrauskas, Miskas (18..–)
*Birute, 1921

Petrella, Errico (1813–1877)
Le Precauzioni, 1851
Marco Visconti, 1854
Elnava, 1856
Jone, 1858
La Contessa d'Amalfi, 1864
I Promessi Sposi, 1869

Pfeiffer, Georges Jean (1835–1908)
Le Légataire universel, 1901

Pfitzner, Hans (1869–1949)
Der arme Heinrich, 1895

Die Rose vom Liebesgarten, 1901
*Palestrina, 1917
Christelflein, 1917
Das Herz, 1931
   see also col. 647, 713, 722
Philidor, François André Danican (1726–1795)
Le Diable à quatre, 1756,
Blaise le Savetier, 1759
Le Soldat Magicien, 1760
Le Jardinier et son Seigneur, 1761
Le Maréchal ferrant, 1761
Sancho Pança dans son Isle, 1762
Le Bûcheron, 1763
Le Sorcier, 1764
Tom Jones, 1765
Ernelinde Princesse de Norvège, 1767
La belle Esclave, 1787
   see also col. 73, 167, 254, 259, 305, 313, 361
Philpot, Stephen Rowland (1870–1950)
Dante and Beatrice, 1889
Piccinni, Nicola (1728–1800)
La buona Figliuola, 1760
Le Vicende della Sorte, 1761
La buona Figliuola maritata, 1761
Il Cavaliere per Amore, 1762
Le Contadine bizarre, 1763
Gli Stravaganti, 1764
Il Barone di Torreforte, 1765
La Pescatrice, 1766
Le finte Gemelle, 1771
Alessandro nell'Indie, 1774
Roland, 1778
Atys, 1780
Iphigénie en Tauride, 1781
Didon, 1783
Le faux Lord, 1783
Pénélope, 1785
   see also col. 59, 77, 176, 213, 225, 245, 286, 293,
     298, 327, 377, 385, 426
Pick-Mangiagalli, Riccardo (1882–1949)
Basi e Bote, 1927
Pierné, Gabriel (1863–1937)
La Coupe enchantée, 1895
La Fille de Tabarin, 1901
On ne badine pas avec l'Amour, 1910
Pierson, Henry Hugh (1816–1873)
Leila, 1848
Contarini, 1872
Pijper, Willem (1894–1947)
Halewijn, 1933
Pinsuti, Ciro (1829–1888)
Il Mercante di Venezia, 1873
Pistocchi, Francesco Antonio (1659–1726)
Il Narciso, 1697

Le Risa di Democrito, 1700
   see also col. 47, 69, 364
Pixis, Johann Peter (1788–1874)
Almazinde, 1820
Bibiana, 1829
Pizzetti, Ildebrando (1880–)
Fedra, 1915
*Debora e Jaele, 1922
*Fra Gherardo, 1928
*Lo Straniero, 1930
*Orsèolo, 1935
   see also col. 1345
Pizzi, Emilio (1861–1931)
William Ratcliff, 1889
Gabriella, 1893
La Rosalba, 1899
Vendetta, 1906
Planquette, Robert (1848–1903)
Les Cloches de Corneville, 1877
Rip van Winkle, 1882
Plantade, Charles Henri (1764–1839)
Le Mari de Circonstances, 1813
Platania, Pietro (1828–1907)
Spartaco, 1891
Poise, Ferdinand (1828–1892)
Bonsoir, Voisin, 1853
La Surprise de l'Amour, 1877
L'Amour Médecin, 1880
Jolli Gilles, 1884
   see also col. 275
Poissl, Johann Nepomuk von (1783–1865)
Athalia, 1814
*Der Wettkampf zu Olympia, 1815
*Nittetis, 1817
   see also col. 431, 523, 660
Poldini, Ede (1869–)
A Csavargó és Királylány, 1903
Farsangi Lakodalom, 1924
Pollarolo, Carlo Francesco (1653–1722)
Ottone, 1694
Gl'Inganni felici, 1695
Faramondo, 1699
Le Pazzie degli Amanti, 1701
Ariodante, 1716
   see also col. 32, 104, 126, 139, 143, 147, 148,
     149, 163, 169, 192, 215, 277
Ponchielli, Amilcare (1834–1886)
I Promessi Sposi, 1856
I Lituani, 1874
Gioconda, 1876
Il Figliuol prodigo, 1880
Marion Delorme, 1885
I Mori di Valenza, 1914
   see also col. 885

Villa-Lobos, Hector (1887–)
    Izaht, 1940
Villanueva, Felipe (1863–1893)
    Keofar, 1893
Vinci, Leonardo (1690–1730)
    Li Zite 'n Galera, 1722
    Silla Dittatore, 1723
    Astianatte, 1725
    Siroe, Re di Persia, 1726
    La Caduta dei Decemviri, 1727
    Artaserse, 1730
        see also col. 139, 161, 165, 166, 172, 181, 192,
            193, 196, 198, 201, 203, 208, 224, 229, 256,
            270, 334, 1318
Vitali, Filippo (15..–16..)
    L'Aretusa, 1620
Vittadini, Franco (1884–1948)
    Anima allegra, 1921
    Nazareth, 1925
Vittori, Loreto (1604–1670)
    *La Galatea, 1639
Vivaldi, Antonio (c.1675–1741)
    Arsilda, Regina di Ponto, 1716
    L'Olimpiade, 1734
        see also col. 110
Vives, Amadeo (1871–1932)
    Don Lucas del Cigarral, 1899
    Euda d'Uriach, 1900
    Maruxa, 1914
    Balada de Carnaval, 1919
    Dona Francisquita, 1923
Vivier, Albert Joseph (1816–1903)
    Spadillo le Tavernier, 1857
Vladigerov, Panchu (1899–)
    Tsar Kaloyan, 1936
Vogel, Charles Louis Adolphe (1802–1892)
    Le Siège de Leyde, 1847
Vogel, Johann Christoph (1756–1788)
    La Toison d'Or, 1786
    Démophon, 1789
Vogl, Heinrich (1845–1900)
    Der Fremdling, 1899
Vogler, Georg Joseph (1749–1814)
    Castore e Polluce, 1787
    Samori, 1804
        see also col. 333, 344
Vollerthun, Georg (1876–)
    Island-Saga, 1925
    Der Freikorporal, 1931
Vreuls, Victor (1876–1944)
    Olivier le Simple, 1922
    Un Songe d'une Nuit d'Été, 1925

Waelput, Hendrik (1845–1885)
    Stella, 1881
Waghalter, Ignaz (1882–1949)
    Mandragola, 1914
Wagner, Richard (1813–1883)
    *Das Liebesverbot, 1836
    *Cola Rienzi, 1842
    *Der fliegende Holländer, 1843
    *Tannhäuser, 1845
    *Lohengrin, 1850
    *Tristan und Isolde, 1865
    *Die Meistersinger von Nürnberg, 1868
    *Das Rheingold, 1869
    *Die Walküre, 1870
    *Siegfried, 1876
    *Götterdämmerung, 1876
    *Parsifal, 1882
    *Die Feen, 1888
        see also col. 231, 336, 359, 362, 455, 591, 595,
            752, 759, 811, 817, 845, 857, 889, 895, 914,
            946, 954, 1031, 1103, 1110, 1184, 1217
Wagner, Siegfried (1869–1930)
    *Der Bärenhäuter, 1899
    *Der Kobold, 1904
    *Banadietrich, 1910
    *An allem ist Hütchen schuld, 1917
    *Schwarzschwanenreich, 1918
Wagner-Régeny, Rudolf (1903–)
    Der Günstling, 1935
Wallace, William Vincent (1812–1865)
    Maritana, 1845
    Matilda of Hungary, 1847
    Lurline, 1860
    The Amber Witch, 1861
    The Desert Flower, 1863
        see also col. 761, 957
Walter, Ignaz (1759–1822)
    Der Spiegelritter, 1791
    Doktor Faust, 1797
        see also col. 472
Walter, Thomas Christian (1749–1788)
    Den provede Troskab, 1774
        see also col. 332
Waltershausen, Hermann Wolfgang von (1882–)
    *Oberst Chabert, 1912
        see also Index of Librettists
Webber, Amherst (1867–1946)
    Fiorella, 1905
        see also col. 1030
Weber, Bernhard Anselm (1766–1821)
    Mudarra, 1800
    Die Wette, 1805
        see also col. 360, 405, 414, 470, 499, 531, 543,
            585

III. INDEX OF LIBRETTISTS

including authors from whose works opera librettos were taken; names of such authors, and dates of first productions of such operas in italics. Dates in brackets refer to wrong or doubtful attribution of authorship. For composers who were their own librettists *see* Index II; for translators, *see* also Index IV.

A'Beckett, Gilbert Arthur, 1884, 84, 93
   see also col. 764, 782, 786, 832, 840, 1015, 1105
Ablesimov, Aleksandr Onesimovich, 1779
About, Edmond, 1860
Abrányi, Emil, 1893, 98, 1907, 08
   see also col. 255, 264, 621, 693, 825, 890, 963, 964, 976, 1024, 1094, 1111, 1171, 1177, 1179, 1192
Acciaiuoli, Filippo, 1670, 80
"Accursi, Michele", *see* Ruffini, G.
Adami, Giuseppe, 1917, 18, 19, 21, 23, 25, 26
Addison, Joseph, 1707, 33, 49
   see also col. 115, 410
Adenis, Édouard, 1922
Adenis, Jules, 1867, 67, 86, 98, 1901, 07
   see also col. 272, 275
Aderer, Adolphe, 1905
Adler, B., 1892
Adler, Hans, 1936
Adlerbeth, Gudmund Göran, 1778, 82
   see also col. 407
Adlerstein, *see* Janotyckh von Adlerstein
Aeschylus, 1895, 1902
Aho, Juhani, 1935
Aignan, Étienne, 1798, 1806
Aksakov, Konstantin Sergyeevich, 1828
Alarcón, Pedro Antonio de, 1892, 96, 1933
d'Albaret, 1746
Alboize du Pujol, Jules Édouard, 1849
Alcaini, Giorgio Giacomo, 1657
Alencar, José de, 1870
Alexandre, André, 1893
Alexis, Willibald, 1904
Alfieri, Vittorio, 1866, 1920
d'Allainval, *see* Soulas d'Allainval
Allfeld, Philipp, 1880
Almeida Garrett, João Baptista de, 1863, 88, 91
Altés y Alabert, Juan Bautista, 1874
Álvarez Quintero, Serafin and Joaquin, *1921, 23*
Amalteo, Aurelio, 1650, 1705
d'Ambreville, *see* Desessarts d'Ambreville
Ambrogini, Angelo, see *Poliziani*
Ancelot, François, 1835, 37, 41, 87
Ancelot, Jacques Arsène Polycarpe François, 1851

Anceschi, Elio, 1940
Anczyc, Wladyslaw Ludwik, 1873
   see also col. 958, 962
Andersen, Hans Christian, 1832, 32, 46, 49, 97, *1900, 01, 03, 12, 14, 25, 27, 28*
Andersen, Vilhelm, 1906
Anderson, Maxwell, 1938
Andreae, Helmut, 1925
Andreev, Leonid Nikolaevich, 1928, 29
Andrei, Antonio, 1778
   see also col. 261, 287, 383, 393
Andreotti, Domenico, 1836
Anelli, Angelo, 1784, 98, 1801, 02, 10, 13, *43*
d'Angelantonio, Francesco, 1905
Anile, Antonio, 1904
Anne, Théodore, 1844
d'Annunzio, Gabriele, *1906, 13, 14, 15, 18*
Anseaume, Louis, 1757, 58, 59, 59, 60, 60, 60, 60, 61, 62, 63, 66, 68, 69
   see also col. 130, 210, 223
Anski, Salomon, 1934
Anthes, Otto, 1914, 18
Anton Ulrich, Duke of Brunswick, 1657, 59
Antona Traversi, Camillo, 1912
Apel, Johann August, 1821
Apolloni, Apollonio, 1655, 61
Arago, Étienne, 1841, 51
Arany, János, 1892, 93
Arapov, Pimen Nikolaevich, 1822
   see also col. 521
Arceri, Luigi, 1853
Ardavin, L. F., *see* Fernández Ardavin
Argyll, Duke of, *see* Campbell
d'Arienzo, Marco, 1844, 51, 74, 76
Ariosti, Attilio, 1702
Ariosto, Lodovico, 1619, 25, 58, 1735, 35, 72, 82, 97, 99, 1801, 1924
Aristophanes, 1861, 1920
Arlberg, Fritz, 1856
   see also col. 558, 757, 822, 826, 910, 918, 1040, 1108
d'Arlincourt, Charles Victor Prévôt, *1822, 27, 29*
Armory, —, *1935*
Arnao, Antonio, 1876
   see also col. 791

Constant, M., 1895
Contini, Domenico Filippo, 1676, 79
Cooper, James Fennimore, 1834, 56
Coppée, François, 1872, *94, 96, 97, 1903*
Corder, Frederick, 1893
  see also col. 687, 966, 976, 1014, 1055, 1097
"Cordier, Jules" (i.e. Eléonore Tenaille de Vaulabelle), 1860
Corghi, Carlo, 1856
Cormon, Eugène, 1847, 55, 56, 57, 58, 59, 60, 60, 63, 64, 65, 67, 67, 68, 69, 75
Corneille, Pierre, 1650, *75, 78, 1723, 35, 42, 1821, 40, 46, 85*
Corneille, Thomas, 1678, 79, 93, *1789*
Corradi, Giulio Cesare, 1676, 78, 86, 87, *95*
Corsini, Ottaviano, 1620
Cortesi, Lodovico, 1659
Corvo, Nicolò, 1709
Coselschi, Eugenio, 1920
Cossa, Pietro, 1935
Costenoble, Karl Ludwig, 1809
  see also col. 398, 524
Coster, Charles de, 1932, 33
Cottin, Sophie, 1827, 37
Cournol, Hippolyte, 1822
Cousin, Victor, 1925
Cousin —, 1790
Coutts, Francis Burdett, Baron Latymer, *see* Money-Coutts
Cramer, C. G., see Kramer
Cramer, Karl, 1858
"Cratisto, Jamejo," *see* Colloredo
Crémieux, Hector, 1858, *59,* 60, 61, 61, 67, 69, 73
  see also col. 993
Crescini, Jacopo, 1836, 60
Creuzé de Lesser, Augustin François, 1805, 06, 09, 11, 11, 13
  see also col. 230
Croffut, William Augustus, 1880
"Croisset, Francis de" (i.e. Francis Wiener), 1905
Croizette, Armand, *1811*
Crommelynck, Fernand, 1932
Cruz, Ramon de la, 1768, 68, 69, 70, 72
  see also col. 215, 220, 225, 240, 269, 279, 284, 298, 308
Csery, Péter, 1822
Cziglányi, Béla, 1903
Csiky, Gergely, 1893
  see also col. 1014
Cuinet Dorbeil, *1782*
  see also col. 343
Cuno, Heinrich, 1829
Cuno, Mauritz, 1707
Czanyuga, József, 1862

Dahn, Felix, *1885, 96,* 99
Dambeck, Johann, 1811
Danchet, Antoine, 1700, 02, 04, 10, 12, 17, *81*
Dancourt, L. H., 1759, 64, 75
Daniélou, J., 1927
Da Ponte, Lorenzo, *see* Ponte
Dasent Sir George Webbe, 1906
Daspuro, Nicolo ("P. Suardon"), *1891, 92*
Daudet, Alphonse, 1897, 97
D'Avenant, Sir William, 1656
Davesne, Bertin, 1765
David, Domenico, *1700, 23, 25*
  see also col. 149.
Davidson, John, 1903
Davis, Gustav, 1894, 95
Decker, H., 1906
Decomberousse, Alexis Barbe Benoît, 1851
Decourcelle, Pierre, 1897, 1929
Decrept, Étienne, 1909
De Forges, P. A. A., *see* Pittaud de Forges
Defranceschi, Carlo Prospero, 1799, 1800, 00
Deinhardstein, Johann Ludwig Ferdinand, 1840
Dejaure, Jean Élie Bédéno, 1791, 99, 1801
"Delacour, Alfred" (i.e. Alfred Charlemagne Lartigue), 1865, 76, 77
  see also col. 851, 1037, 1050
Delacre, Jules, 1922
Delair, P., 1922
Delaporte, Michel, 1862
Delavigne, Casimir, 1843, *69*
Delavigne, Germain, 1823, 25, 26, 28, 31, 43, 54
Delestre-Poirson, Charles Gaspard, 1828
Delmar, Axel, 1893, 95
"Delormeil", *see* Lénéka.
Delrieu, Étienne Joseph Bernard, 1802
Demeter, Dimitrije, 1846, 97
  see also col. 739, 957, 977
Demolder, Eugène, 1921
Demoustier, Charles Albert, 1792
Dennery, A. P., *see* d'Ennery
Dercy, P.,[1] 1793, 1804, 06
Desaugiers, Auguste Félix, 1823
  see also col. 410, 443
Desaugiers, Marc Antoine Madeleine, *1857*
  see also col. 410, 582
Des Boulmiers, Jean Auguste Julien, 1767
  see also col. 252
Deschamps, Émile, 1826, 36
  see also col. 453

[1] Alphonse François Dercy (stated to have written these librettos in the Author List of *Washington Catalogue*, p.1234) is a 19th ct. author. P. Dercy died before 1804, acc. to the preface in the *Ossian* libretto; acc. to Montglond his real name was Palat.

Eguílaz, Luis de, 1878
Einsiedel, Friedrich Hildebrand von, 1798, 98
  see also col. 330, 471, 473
Elizabeth, Queen of Rumania ("Carmen Sylva"),
  1879, 85, *1904*
Elkan, Benno, 1927
Ellis, Thomas Evelyn (Baron Howard de
  Walden), 1912, 14, 29
Emanuel, Guglielmo, 1912
Eminescu, Mihail, 1879
Empis, Adolphe Joseph Simonis, 1822
Engel, Johann Jacob, 1771
Engelen, Henri, 1903
d'Ennery, Adolphe Philippe, *1845*, 47, 52, *57*, 68,
  69, 72, 81, *85*, 85
Envallsson, Carl, 1784
  see also col. 138, 177, 221, 233, 235, 241, 245,
    251, 252, 253, 254, 266, 267, 275, 278, 282,
    285, 287, 289, 294, 308, 344, 351, 356, 366,
    369, 372, 385, 391, 414, 431, 445, 459, 462,
    481, 488, 501, 540
Ephraïm, Armand, 1905
Erckmann, Emile, 1876, 82, 91, 92, 1900, 01
"Erckmann-Chatrian," see Erckmann, E., and
  Chatrian, P. A.
Erler, Hermann, 1904
Erskine, John, 1931, 34
Escholier, Raymond, 1931
Escuder, Juan Francisco, 1712
Esménard, Joseph Alphonse, 1807, 09
Estcourt, Richard, 1708
Étienne, Charles Guillaume, 1801, 04, *05*, 05, 08,
  10, 10, 14, 14, 16, 16, *17*, *18*, 22
Étienne de Jouy, Victor Joseph, 1804, 07, 09, 10,
  10, 12, 13, *14*, 29.
  see also col. 657
Eulenberg, Herbert, 1920
Euripides, 1922, 24, 31, 39
Evald, Johan, 1778, 80
Ewers, Hanns Heinz, 1916, 22

F.B.A.F., *Abate*, 1775
Faassen, Rosier, 1877
Fabbrichesi, Salvatore, 1850
Faber, William, 1883
  see also col. 985
Fabre, Émile, 1915
Fabre, Ferdinand, 1895
Fabry, Jacques Joseph, 1757
Falbaire, C. G. F. de, *see* Fenouillot de Falbaire
Falckenberg, Otto, 1922
"Falconer, Edmund" (i.e. Edmund O'Rourke),
  1857, 58, 59

Falena, Ugo, 1930
Fallström, Daniel, 1889
Falsen, Enevold de, 1797, 1800
  see also col. 499, 504
"Falzari, Felix" (i.e. Hans Hoffmann), 1896
  see also col. 1000, 1183, 1273
Farjeon, Eleanor, 1924
Farnie, Henry Brougham, 1864, 82
  see also col. 919, 944, 948, 951, 955, 985, 991,
    993, 1008, 1040, 1048, 1058, 1062, 1064,
    1075, 1076, 1080, 1085, 1087
"Farrère, Claude" (i.e. Frédéric Charles Bargone),
  1924
Fattorini, Tebaldo, 1675
  see also col. 42
Fauchois, René, 1913, 19
Fausset, Marjorie, 1922
Faustini, Giovanni, 1643, 51
Favart, Charles Simon, 1741, 53, 55, *59, 62, 65,
  65, 66, 67*, 68, *68, 68, 70, 70*, 73, *79, 82, 82, 83,
  89, 99*
  see also, col. 53, 57, 69, 81, 84, 105, 123, 130,
    138, 156, 179, 185, 194, 195, 196, 202, 210,
    218, 219, 221, 222, 223, 255, 259, 292, 372
Favart, Marie Justine Benoîte, 1762
  see also col. 130, 218
Favières, Edmond Guillaume François de, 1791,
  97, 1802, 03, 13
Feddersen, Benjamin, 1888
Federici, Camillo, 1810
Federico, Gennaro Antonio, 1732, 33, 35, 39, 54
  81, 87, *1857*
Feind, Barthold, 1705, 06, 09
  see also col. 112, 124, 126
Fekete, Mihály, 1861
"Feld, Leo" (i.e. Leo Hirschfeld), 1910, 16, 23
"Fels, Roderich" (i.e. S. Rosenfeld), 1878
  see also col. 1036
Feliú y Codina, José, *1895*, 98
Fenouillot de Falbère, Charles George, 1770
Fercal, Cesare, 1888, 92, 93, 99
  see also col. 1102
Fernald, Chester Bailey, 1905
Fernandes dos Reis, Antonio José, 1861
Fernández Ardavín, Luis, 1919
Fernández Shaw, Carlos, 1897, 99, 1909, 13
Fernández Shaw, Guillermo, 1923
Ferrare, Henry, 1921
Ferrari, Benedetto, 1637, 38, 53,
Ferretti, Jacopo, 1811, 17, 20, 21, 21, 24, 27, 32,
  33, 33, 34, 34, 34, 35, 36,
  see also col. 549, 682
Ferrier, Jeanne, 1910
Ferrier, Paul, 1880, 92, 1901, 04, 07, 07, 10

Gandonnière, Almire, 1893
Gane, Nikolae, 1900
Ganem, Chekri, 1921
Gans zu Putlitz, Gustav Heinrich, 1853, 85
see also col. 835
Garal, Pierre de, 1888
Garay, János, 1926
García Gutiérrez, Antonio, *1853, 53, 57*
Garnir, George, 1903, 04
see also col. 1147
Garrick, David (1755), 67, *92*
see also col. 89, 228, 283
Garrido, Eduardo, 1887
see also col. 1050, 1076
Gassol, Ventura, 1924
Gatti, Guido Maria, 1920
Gatty, (David) Ivor (Vaughan), 1909
Gatty, Reginald (Arthur Allix), 1906, 20
see also col. 502
Gaugiran-Nanteuil, Charles, 1806, 12
Gautier, Théophile, 1885, 1920
Gay, John, 1728, 32, 77, *1928*
Gay, Sophie, 1821
Gazzoletti, Antonio, 1867
Gedeonov, M. A., 1842
Gedeonov, Stepan Aleksandrovich, 1892
Gehe, Eduard Heinrich, 1823, 26, 32
Geibel, Emanuel, 1863, 87, *1920*
Geiger, J. J. (pseud.?), 1893
Genée, Richard, 1873, 74, 75, 76, 79, 80, 80, 80, 81, 82, 83, 84, 86
see also col. 983, 1004, 1008, 1015, 1020, 1081, 1115, 1133, 1136, 1141, 1143
Genlis, Comtesse de (Stéphanie Félicité Brulart de Sillery), 1791, 1831, 35
Gerber, E., 1854
Gerhäuser, Emil, 1906
see also col. 1145
Gerstenberg, Heinrich Wilhelm von, 1775
German, Ludomir, 1896, 98, 1900
see also col. 999, 1078, 1153, 1189, 1223, 1225
Gershwin, Ira, 1935
Gessner, Salomon, 1770, 94
see also col. 530
Gherardini, Giovanni, 1817
Gheusi, Pierre Barthélemy, 1898, 1900, 01, 02, 05, 10, 31
Ghigi, Stefano, *1723, 29*
Ghisalberti, Mario, 1931, 31, 36, 39,
Ghislanzoni, Antonio, 1859, 69, 71, 71, 71, 73, 74 74, 86, 91, 91, 91, 1914
see also col. 959
Giacometti, Paolo, 1863
Giacomo, Salvatore di, 1910

Giacosa, Giuseppe, 1896, 1900, 04
Giannone, Pietro, 1850
see also col. 767
Gide, André, 1934
Gieseke, Karl Ludwig, 1789, (90), 91
see also col. 242, 243, 379, 382, 426, 445, 459, 476, 480, 482, 490, 500, 508
Gigli, Girolamo, 1701
Gilardoni, Domenico, 1826, 27, 27, 28, 31, 32
Gilbert, Gabriel, 1672
Gilbert, Sir William Schwenck, 1871, 75, 77, 78, 79, 81, 82, 84, 85, 87, 88, 89, 93, 96
see also col. 977, 991, 1011
Gille, Philippe, 1880, 82, 83, 84, 93
see also col. 1030
Ginzkey, Franz Karl, 1927
Giovannini, Pietro, 1781
Giraud, Giovanni, 1824, 34, 40, 1914
Giraud, Pierre François, 1808
Girzik, Franz Xaver, 1789
see also col. 371, 382, 383, 390, 396, 405, 409, 417, 423, 437, 444, 447, 450, 511, 512
Gisberti, Domenico, 1672
Giuliani, Camillo, 1843
Godard d'Aucour de Saint-Just, Claude, 1797, 98, 1800, 06, 12, *13, 18*
Godet, Philippe, 1894
Godio, Guglielmo, 1895
Goethe, Johann Wolfgang von, 1780, *87, 89, 97, 1800,* 01, 10, 31, *58, 59, 66,* 68, *87, 92, 93, 99, 1902, 10, 23*
see also col. 328, 433, 494, 672
Gogol, Nikolai Vasilevich, 1876, 80, 95, 1909, 17, 19, 40
Gold, Didier, 1918
Goldenring, Stefanja, 1917
Goldoni, Carlo, 1743, 48, *48,* 49, *49, 49,* 50, *50,* 51, *52, 52,* 54, *54,* 55, *55, 55, 55,* 56, 57, *57, 58, 58,* 59, 60, *60, 60, 61, 61,* 63, (66), (67), *67, 67,* 68, 68, *69, 70, 71, 72, 73,* 74, *76, 77, 78, 79,* 82, *86, 88, 92, 96, 1831, 56, 79, 1903, 06, 25, 26, 26, 26, 31, 36*
see also col. 206, 210, 342
Goldsmith, Oliver, 1796
Golisciani, Enrico, 1878, 85, 92, *92,* 96, 1909, 11, 12, 13
see also col. 515, 906, 1011, 1028, 1037, 1040, 1182
Goll, Iwan, 1927
Gollmick, Karl, 1866
see also col. 796, 805, 815, 829, 833, 852, 870, 878, 881, 892, 939
Gondinet, Edmond, 1873, 80, 83
Gonella, Francesco, 1794, 96

Hofmann, Friedrich, 1879
Hofmann, Georg Ernst von, 1820, 20, 20, 23
  see also col. 749, 766
Hofmannsthal, Hugo von, 1909, 11, 12, 19, 24, 28, 33
Holbein, Franz Ignaz von, 1807, (11), 28, 1933
Holberg, Ludvig af, 1906, 19
Holst, Hans Peter, 1882
  see also col. 423, 889, 904, 923, 933, 999, 1029, 1045
Holtei, Karl von, 1832
  see also col. 477, 638, 651
Hood, Basil, 1899, 1901, 02
  see also col. 1281
Hooker, Brian, 1912, 15, 24
Hope, Anthony, 1902
Hopfen, Hans, 1896
Hopffer, Emil, 1872
Hoppenot, Henri, 1927, 28, 28
Hornicke, Demetrius, 1890
Hospelt, Arthur, 1925
Hostinský, Otakar, 1884, 85
Hotter, —, 1701
Houdar de La Motte, Antoine, 1697, 97, 99, 1700, 06, 53
Howard de Walden, Baron, see Ellis, T. E.
Huber, Franz Xaver[1], 1796, 99, 1804, 13
  see also col. 392, 406
Hueffer, Francis, 1883
  see also col. 1127
Hughes, John, 1712
Hugo, Victor, 1833, 36, 37, 38, 44, 47, 51, 51, 61, 63, 64, 69, 69, 76, 76, 83, 84, 85, 1904, 14, 20, 20, 24, 28, 35
Huhn, Eugenie von, 1910
Hull, Thomas, 1765
Humperdinck, Hedwig, 1905
Hunold ("Menantes"), Christian Friedrich, 1704
Hutt, Johann, 1902
Hvasser, Daniel, 1858

Ibsen, Henrik, 1899, 1905
Ihlee, Johann Jakob, 1793, 1819
  see also col. 492, 520, 538, 539, 543, 548, 555, 566, 567, 574
Illica, Luigi, 1889, 92, 92, 93, 93, 94, 95, 96, 96, 98, 99, 1900, 00, 00, 01, 01, 01, 02, 03, 03, 04, 05, 06, 08, 09, 09, 09, 11, 21
Immermann, Karl, 1887
Inčiura, K., 1933
Interdonato, Stefano, 1873

[1] Acc. to Wurzbach, there are two authors of the same name, F.X.H. from Bohemia, 17.. -c.1809, author of Soliman, and F.X.H. from Munderfing, Upper Austria, 1760-18.., author of Opferfest.

Ipsen, Alfred, 1892
Irving, Washington, 1830, 55, 1920
  see also col. 679
Ivanovich, Cristoforo, 1669, 73
  see also col. 70
Iwaszkiewicz, Jaroslaw, 1926

Jacob, Max, 1922
Jacobi, Johann Georg, 1770
Jacobs, William Wymark, 1916
Jacobsen, Jens Peter, 1919
Jacobson, Leopold, 1907, 08
Jacoby, Wilhelm, 1885
  see also col. 818
Jaffa, Kathleen de, 1933
  see also col. 1339
"Jaime, Adolphe" (the Younger; real name Gem), 1859, 62, 69, 72
  see also col. 1016
Jakab, István, 1839
  see also col. 751, 755, 763, 766, 769, 788, 790
"Jamejo Crastisto," see Colloredo, G. B.
James, Lewis Cairns, 1916
Jammes, Francis, 1923
Janacopulos, Vera, 1921
Janotyckh von Adlerstein, János, 1849
Jansen, Ferdinand, 1925
Jars, Antoine Gabriel, 1803, 05
Järviluoma, Artturi, 1924
Jaubert, Ernest François, 1898
Jegerlehner, Johannes, 1934
Jelinek, Hanuš, 1923
Jellenta, Cezary, 1912
Jessop, George H., 1896
Jester, Friedrich Ernst, 1791, 96
  see also col. 615
Jevon, Thomas, 1731
  see also col. 52
Jirásek, Alois, 1898, 1923
Jókai, Mor, 1885
Jolin, Johan Christofer, 1858
Jones, Paul, 1910
Jonson, Benjamin, 1800, 1930, 35
Joseph, Joseph Maron, 1929
Jouffroy, Achille de, 1828, 28
Jünger, Johann Friedrich, 1791

Kaiser, Alfred, 1906
Kaiser, Georg, 1925, 26, 28
Kalashnikov, Piotr I., 1869, 71
  see also col. 645, 659, 779, 831, 874, 892, 908, 940, 983
Kalbeck, Max, 1889, 92, 94, 1909
  see also col. 237, 238, 301, 342, 983, 1000, 1072,

Lafortelle, A. M., 1827

Lafrique, Armand, 1887
see also col. 1119

Lagerlöf, Selma, 1925, 25

Lagomaggiore, A. G., 1897

"Lalli, Domenico" (i.e. Sebastiano Biancardi), 1711, 13, 14, 15, 16, *17*

Laloy, Louis, 1923
see also col. 387, 1033, 1226, 1229, 1333, 1341

La Marre, Abbé de, 1753

La Martelière, Jean Henri Ferdinand, 1816

Lamartine, Marie Louis Alphonse de, 1888

La Motte, A. H., *see* Houdar de La Motte

La Motte Fouqué, Friedrich de, 1816, 37, *45*

Lambrecht, Matthias Georg, 1788
see also col. 538, 571, 573, 600

Landoy, Eugène, 1892

Langlé, Ferdinand, 1853, 56, *58*

Lányi, Viktor, 1922, 28
see also col. 178, 479, 781, 829, 878, 960, 989, 1051, 1099, 1151, 1163, 1272, 1308, 1312, 1319, 1325, 1326, 1389, 1398, 1403, 1423

Lapointe, Armand, 1858

La Ribadière, de, 1759

Larmanjat, Jacques, 1922

La Roque, Antoine de, 1713

Larra (y Sanchez de Castro), Mariano José de, 1832, 63, 74

Larrañaga, Gonzalo, 1893

Larrañaga, G. R., *see* Romero Larrañaga

Larreta, E. R., *see* Rodríguez Larreta

L'Arronge, Adolf, 1899

Larsonneur, A., 1889

La Salle d'Offémont, Adrien Nicolas de, 1766
see also col. 210

Lassus, L. A. de, *see* Augé de Lassus

La Serre, Jean Louis Ignace de, 1720, 26

Lathrop, George Parsons, 1896

Laujon, Pierre, 1747, 71
see also col. 57, 80, 130, 202

"*Laun, Friedrich*" (*i.e. Friedrich August Schulze*), *1821*
see also col. 556

"Laurencin, M." (i.e. Paul Aimé Chapelle), 1862
see also col. 827

Lauzières (de Thémines), Achille de, 1884
see also col. 836, 865, 940, 988, 993, 998, 1015, 1044, 1060, 1063, 1074, 1080, 1103, 1113

Laval, —, 1783

Law, Arthur, 1893

Lax, Louis,[1] 1893

Lazheshnikov, Ivan Ivanovich, 1874

[1] Acc. to Goedeke, Vol. III[1], p. 912, pseud. of Georg Ernst Adam Wahlert.

Lebland du Roullet, François Louis Gaud, 1774, 84
see also col. 295

Lebœuf, Jean Joseph, *1801*
see also col. 324

Lebrun-Tossa, Jean Antoine, 1796

Leclerc, Michel, 1688

Leclerc de la Bruère, Charles Antoine, 1739, 84
see also col. 72

Leclercq, Michel Théodore, 1808

Leconte, Sébastien Charles, 1925

Ledent, Richard, 1912

Le Fanu, Joseph Sheridan, 1896

Lefèvre de Marcouville, Pierre Augustin, 1760
see also col. 105

Lega, Antonio, 1920, 40
see also col. 360, 702, 1143, 1275, 1304

Le Goffic, Charles, 1912

Legouvé, Ernest, 1902

Lehmann, Julius, 1896
see also col. 264, 936, 964, 1010, 1034, 1056, 1099, 1153, 1251, 1268, 1276, 1295, 1306, 1360

Leitner, Gottfried von, 1835

"Leloir, Louis" (i.e. Louis Sallot), 1910

Le Lorrain, Jacques, 1910

Lemaire, Ferdinand, 1877

Lemaître, Jules, 1910

Lemer, Gaetano, 1721

Le Métel d'Ouville, Antoine, 1760

Lemierre, Antoine Marin, 1800, 05, 23

Lemoine, Gustave, 1886

Lemonnier, Camille, 1912, 14, 14

Lemonnier, Pierre René,[1] 1761, 61

Léna, Maurice, 1902, 08, 12, 20, 21, 24, 27
see also col. 976

Lénéka, André ("Delormeil"), 1891, 1905

Lengyel, Menyhért, 1924

Lennep, Jacob van, 1834, *89*

Lensky, Dmitry Timofeevich, 1857
see also col. 719, 733

Lenz, Jacob Michael Reinhold, 1930

Lenzoni, Alfredo, 1915

Leo, Felicitas, 1917

"Léon, Victor" (i.e. Victor Hirschfeld), 1887, 92, 97, 98, 1901, 05
see also col. 1133, 1178, 1194

Leoncavallo, Ruggiero, 1898
see also col. 1141

Leonhardt-Lyser, Caroline, 1848

Leopold, Carl Gustaf af, 1787
see also col. 308, 359

[1] Not Guillaume Antoine as stated in the Author List of *Washington Catalogue*, p. 1305.

Leopold, Svend, 1919
"Lereno Secinuntino," *see* Caldas Barbosa
Lermontov, Mikhail Yurevich, 1875, 80
Lernet-Holenia, Alexander, 1928
Lersner, Friedrich Maximilian, 1722
Lesage, Alain René 1752, 58, 64, 93, 1858
see also col. 69, 84
Lesguillon, Jean Pierre François, 1834
see also col. 630
Leterrier, Eugène, 1874, 75, 77, 79, 85
see also col. 1083
Leuven, Adolphe de (i.e. Adolphe de Ribbing),
1836, 36, 38, 39, 42, 43, 44, 47, 47, 50, 50, 51,
52, 53, 53, 53, 54, 55, 56, 56, 58, 63, 88
see also col. 690, 708, 766
Levetzow, Karl Michael von, 1916, 23, 28, 32
Levin, Poul, 1898
Lewald, August, 1833
see also col. 501, 711, 754
Lewis, Matthew Gregory, 1854
Lhérie, Victor, 1836
Lichtenstein, Carl August Ludwig von, 1827
see also col. 663, 695, 699, 710, 711, 717, 720,
727, 734, 746, 749, 759, 764, 766, 769, 786,
791, 794, 796, 798, 799, 803, 808
Liebstöckl, Hans, 1911
see also col. 1287, 1289, 1372
Lima, Pedro de, 1870
Limozin, Jean, 1927, 30, 30
Linati, Carlo, 1920
Lindau, M. E. (pseud.?), 1872
Linley, George, 1838
see also col. 897, 925
Lion, Ferdinand, 1924, 26, 26, 30
"Liorat, Armand" (i.e. Georges Degas), 1897
Lipiner, Siegfried, 1886
Livigni, Filippo, 1774, 80, 81, 81, 83, 85, 85, 85,
86, 90, 97
Lloyd, William, 1934, 38
Lobato, Gervasio, 1891
Lockroy, Joseph Philippe, 1851, 52, 55, 56, 56, 75
see also col. 833
Locle, C. du, *see* Du Locle
Lodovici, Cesare, 1932
"Logau, Gotthold" (i.e. Henrik Glogau), 1851
Loghem, Martinus Gesinus Lambertus van, 1889
Lohmann, Peter, 1881
Lokhorst, Emmy van, 1933
"Lom, Stanislav" (i.e. Stanislav Mojžíš), 1933
Long, John Luther, 1904
Longchamps, Charles de, 1803
Longus, 1759
Lonsdale, Frederick, 1919
Lopes de Mendonça, Henrique, 1899

López, Vicente Fedel, 1919
López Silva, José, 1897
Lorenzi, Giovanni Battista, 1767, 74, 75, 79, 80,
87, 89, 91, 95, *1835*
see also col. 358
Lorin, Jules, 1854
Lorne, Marquis of, *see* Campbell
"Lorrain, Jean" (i.e. Paul Alexandre Martin
Duval), 1900, 10
"Lothar, Rudolf" (i.e. Rudolf Spitzer), 1903,
09, 20, 23, 31, 31, 31
"Loti, Pierre" (i.e. Louis Marie Julien Viaud), 1893
Louis XVI, King of France, 1783
see also col. 73, 489
Louis XVIII, King of France, *see* Provence
Lourdet de Santerre, Jean Baptiste, 1759, 62, 82
see also col. 130
Louwyck, J. H., 1933
Louÿs, Pierre, 1906, 11, 30
Löwenbach-Budín, Jan, 1929
Luca, Pasquale de, 1905
Lucarini, Ostilio, 1934
Lucas, Hippolyte, 1845, 47, 62
see also col. 777, 782, 817, 820
Lucchini, Antonio Maria, 1717, 31, 65
Luceño (y Becerra), Tomás, 1899
Lucini, Giovanni Battista, 1690
Lunel, Armand, 1926, 32, 38, 39
Lurieu, J. J. G. de, *see* Gabriel de Lurieu
Lyeskov, Nikolai Semenovich, 1934
Lyser, Johann Peter Theodor, 1832, 44
see also col. 477, 834, 842
*Lytton, Edward Bulwer, Lord Lytton (1825), 42, 45,
55, 58, 68, 76, 1912*

Macchi, Gustavo, 1890, 99, 1905, 39
see also col. 690, 1027, 1116, 1172, 1299
Macchiavelli, Niccolò, 1914, 26
MacClintock, Walter, 1910
Macfarren, George, 1838, 46
see also col. 701, 759, 789
Mácha, Karel Hynek, 1900
Machaček, Simeon Karel, 1884
see also col. 464, 479, 552, 604, 605, 608, 610,
643, 648, 649
Mackaye, Percy Wallace, 1917, 20
MacLellan, Charles M. S., 1892
"Macleod, Fiona," *see* Sharp, W.
MacNally, Leonard, 1784
see also col. 414
Macy, John Albert, 1911
Maeterlinck, Maurice, *1902, 07, 07, 09, 19, 24*
Maffei, Andrea, 1847, *95*
Maggi, Giacomo, 1701

Rojas (Zorrilla), Francisco de, 1899
Rolli, Paolo Antonio, 1720, 20, 21, 21, 26, 26, 27,
27, 41, 41
see also col. 129, 131, 132, 140, 144, 183
Rolt, Richard, 1764, 64
Romagnoli, Ettore, 1921, 28
Romanelli, Luigi, 1801, 02, 06, 08, 11, 12, 21, 27
see also col. 555
Romanelli, Umberto, 1919
Romani, Felice, 1813, 13, 13, 14, 17, 18, 18, 18,
19, 19, 19, 19, 20, (20), (20), 25, 25, 27, 28, 28,
29, 30, 30, 31, 31, 31, 32, 32, 33, 33, 33, 33, 34,
35, 38, 38, 39, 40, 40, 41
see also col. 704
Romano, José Filippe Ovidio, 1850, 91
Romero, Federico, 1923
Romero Larrañaga, Gregorio, 1845
Roquette, Otto, 1881
Rosegger, Peter, 1916
Rosenberg, Peter Andreas, 1900, 15
see also col. 1221
Rosier, Joseph Bernard, 1850, 51
"Rosmer, Ernst" (i.e. Elsa Bernstein-Porges),
1910
Rosoy, B. F. de, see Rozoy
Rospigliosi, Giulio (Pope Clement IX), 1632, 33,
39, 42, 53, (56)
Rospigliosi, Jacopo, 1656
"Ross, Adrian" (i.e. Arthur Reed Ropes), 1919
see also col. 1067, 1269, 1278, 1281
Ross, Sheridan, 1920.
Rossato, Arturo, 1922, 22, 25, 27, 28, 29, 29, 29,
31, 33, 33, 35
see also col. 7
Rossetti, Dante Gabriel, 1913
Rossetti, Domenico, 1805
Rossi, Gaetano, 1798, 99, 1801, 02, 03, 04, 04, 10,
10, 12, 12, 13, 15, 16, 17, 17, 19, 22, 23, 24, 31,
37, 38, 39, 41, 41, 42, 52
Rossi, Giacomo, 1711, 12
Rost, Alexander, 1847
Rostand, Edmond, 1913, 34, 36, 37
Rothauser, M., 1903
Rouget de Lisle, Claude Joseph, 1827
Roullet, see Gand Lebland du Roullet
Rousseau, Jean Baptiste, 1697
Rousseau, Jean Jacques, 1752, 68, 70, 79, 90, 1809
Rovesi, Giorgio Carlo, 1925
Rovetta, Gerolamo, 1933
Rowlands, William, 1878
Roy, Pierre Charles, 1705, 12
see also col. 84
Royer, Alphonse, 1840
see also col. 650, 771, 828, 831, 844

Rozen (Rosen), Baron Georgy Fedorovich, 1836
Rozes, Jūlijs, 1936
Rozoy, Barnabé Farmian de, 1774, 76
see also col. 328
Rubino, Francesco, 1849
Rudall, H. A., 1893
Rüeger, Armin, 1919, 22, 37
Rüffer, Eduard, 1868
Ruffini, Giacomo, 1843
see also col. 833
Rullmann, Wilhelm, 1878
Runge, Philipp Otto, 1930
Rutten, Felix, 1925
Ryan, Michael Desmond, 1849, 52
see also col. 820
Rydel, Lucyan, 1925
Rytkönen, Antti, 1908

Sabina, Karel, 1865, 66, 66, 67, 1934
Sacchèro, Giacomo, 1841
Sacher-Masoch, L. von, 1893
Sachs, Hans, 1916, 18
Saddumene, Bernardo, 1722
Saint-Cyr, J. A., see Révéroni Sant-Cyr
Saint-Etienne, Sylvain, 1851
Saint-Foix, G. F. P. de, see Poullain de Saint-Foix
Saint-Georges, J. H., see Vernoy de Saint-
Georges
Saint-Hilaire, A., see Villain de Saint-Hilaire
Saint-Just, C., see Godard d'Aucourt de Saint-
Just
Saint-Marcel (A. H. P. Tardieu de Saint-
Marcel?), 1810
Saint-Marcellin, J. V., see Fontanes de Saint-
Marcellin
Saint-Pierre, Jacques Henri Bernardin de, 1791,
1817, 76
Saint-Victor, J. M. B., see Bins de Saint-Victor
Saintine, Xavier Boniface, 1835, 42
Salis (Seewis), Johann Gaudenz von, 1800
Salvadori, Andrea, 1619, 28
Salvatori, Fausto, 1927
Salvi, Antonio, 1715, 16, 18, 25, 25, 27, 29, 35, 37,
37, 41
see also col. 203, 215
Samain, Albert, 1922
San Leo, G. de, 1924
"Sand, George" (i.e. Baroness Amandine Aurore
Lucie Dudevant), 1846, 69, 83, 96, 1902
Santerre, J. B. L. de, see Lourdet de Santerre
Sanz Pérez, José, 1849
see also col. 879
Sapio, Giuseppe, 1852
Saracinelli, Ferdinando, 1625

IV. GENERAL INDEX

containing (*a*) all persons not mentioned in Indexes II and III; (*b*) a small selection of subjects, and (*c*) countries and towns; under the names of the latter only events of some significance are listed, as important first productions, openings of theatres, etc.

Faber, Johann Heinrich, 235, 241, 251, 253, 254, 266, 267, 270, 275, 277, 278, 281, 283, 294, 298, 304, 310, 314, 316, 320, 321, 326, 329, 331, 332
Faber, Peter Ditlev, 676
Fabre, Augustin, 77
Fagan, Christophe Barthelemy, 242
Faggioli, Michel Angelo, 122
Faixá, Manuel M., 301
Falk, Richard, 183, 400
Fallee, Bernardus Antonius, 470, 501, 569, 581, 623
Färber, Siegfried, 279
Farin de Hautemer, —, 210, 223
Farinelli, see Broschi, Carlo
Farmer, Henry George, 306
Farnese, Odoardo, Duke of Parma, 13
Farnese, Ranuccio II, Duke of Parma, 46
Farquhar, Marion Jones, 1397
Farrenc, Jacques Hippolyte Aristide, 591
Farrobo das Larangeiras, Conde, 840, 847
Fassini, Sesto, 142
Fatouville, Nolant de, 75
Favart, Charles Nicolas Justin, 259
Fawcett, John, 643
Fáy, J. Béla, 1081, 1195
Federici, Vincenzo, 442, 576
Fedorov, P. S., 870
Fehr, Max, 196, 265
Feilding, Basil, 2nd Earl of Denbigh, 16
Feleki, Miklós, 427, 928
Felix, Oscar, 911
Fellinger, Robert, 472
Ferdinand II, Roman Emperor, 10
Ferdinand III, Roman Emperor, 29
Ferdinand (IV), King of the Romans, 29
Ferdinand IV (III of Sicily, I of the two Sicilies), King of Naples, 257, 295, 347, 704
Ferdinand VI, King of Spain, 234
Ferdinand, Archduke of Austria, 319, 347
Ferdinand, Prince of Parma, 261
Ferdinand Charles, Archduke of Austria, 29, 35
"Féré, Octave" (i.e. Charles Octave Mogeta), 925
Ferenczi, Zoltan, 263
Ferguson, Francis, 1398
Ferguson, Robert, 257
"Ferguut, Jan" (i.e. Jan van Droogenbroeck), 846
Fermin del Rey, 328
Fernández Grájal, Tomás, 815
Fernández y Gonzales, Rogelio, 1100
Ferradini, Antonio, 195
Ferrara, 625, 832
Ferrarese, Adriana, 425
Ferrari, G. G., 398, 420

Ferro, A. H., 1304
Feszteticz, Albert, 657
Fiala, Jaromír, 387, 1382
Fiedler, Friedrich, 1270
Fiedler, Gottlieb, 82, 84, 87, 89, 92, 95, 97, 103
Filípek, Václav, 528
Finale, 439
Findeizen, Nikolai Fedorovich, 177, 256, 357, 441, 451, 496
Finley, Lorraine Noel, 1398
Finnish Operas, (898), (1129), (1198), 1295, 1300, 1322, 1337, 1353, 1379, 1404, 1430
Finzi, Aldo, 202
Fiocco, Pierre Antoine, 38, 56, 67, 75, 81, 101
Fiore, Stefano Andrea, 122
Fischer, A., 414
Fischer, Anton Joseph, 314, 462, 464
Fischer, Ernst, 1020
Fischer, Georg, 356
Fisher, John Abraham, 353
Fitz-Gerald, Shafto Justin Adair, 1063
Fiume, 947
Flavigny, —, 321, 329, 331
Fleischmann, Friedrich, 542
Flemish Operas (see also Dutch Operas), 987, 1047, 1090, 1197, 1217, 1238, 1245, 1249, 1260, 1283, 1314, 1323, 1400, 1437
Flemmich, Heinrich, 1065
Fleurigny, Henri de, 235
Flintberg, Carl Henrik, 222
Floncel, Albert François, 49, 150
Flood, William Henry Grattan, 55, 85, 159
Florence, 1–4, 9, 10, and passim
Florence, Maggio Musicale Fiorentino, 191, 687, 721, 756, 765, 820, 1344, 1436
Florence, Teatro della Pergola, 35
Florimo, Francesco, 65, 98, 139, 163, 239, 351, 576
Florio, Caryl, 1060
Foà, Mauro, 62, 134, 179
Fokine, Mikhail, 1293
Fokke Simonsz, Arend, 494, 537, 555, 580
Foman, Josef, 1269
Font, Auguste, 259
Fontainebleau, 71, 100, 105, 217, 224, and passim
Fontana, Uranio, 708
Forkel, Johann Nikolaus, 239
Forman, Alfred, 976
Formenti, Lorenzo, 458
Forster, Karol, 724
Fortis, Leone, 874
Förtsch, Johann Philipp, 94, 124
Fortun, Tomás, 970
Fourcaud, Louis de, 976
Fox, George, 160

[1] These translations are attributed to F.L.W. Meyer by Sonneck und others; as Meyer was born in 1755 he cannot have been the author.

IMPRIME EN SUISSE